AN
INTRODUCTION
TO
PHILOSOPHICAL
INQUIRY

CONSULTING EDITOR

V. C. Chappell

THE UNIVERSITY OF CHICAGO

AN INTRODUCTION TO PHILOSOPHICAL INQUIRY

Contemporary *and* Classical Sources

Edited by Joseph Margolis

UNIVERSITY OF TORONTO

New York : Alfred ·A· Knopf

THIS IS A BORZOI BOOK,
PUBLISHED BY ALFRED A. KNOPF, INC.

FIRST PRINTING

Library of Congress Catalog Card Number: 68–13163

Manufactured in the United States of America.

For Paul, Mike, and Nike

PREFACE

It is a personal pleasure to be able to collect, within the covers of an introductory reader, a set of papers that are both reasonably accessible to the well-guided student and of absorbing interest to professional philosophers. It is often argued that the gap between philosophers and the educated public signifies a retreat on the part of professionals from the philosophical inquiries of the man in the street. It might be argued even more convincingly that, as with most professional disciplines, the perceptive reader who lacks sustained professional guidance and orientation handicaps himself unnecessarily and is likely to fall farther and farther behind in his mastery of the current discussion of philosophical issues—even those with which he may suppose himself to be acquainted.

The present collection is designed to provide at once an historical sense of the principal questions—with an inevitably economical selection from the classical sources—and an introduction to characteristic contemporary views and methods of analysis bearing on these questions. It is, I think, all to the good that the first specimens of a professional literature cannot be contrasted in quality and importance with those materials that well-advanced students generally prefer.

I should add that since many selections have been excerpted from larger texts, I have changed or provided a number of the selection titles.

I owe a particular debt, in preparing this reader, to Mrs. Margaret Mercer, Secretary to the Department of Philosophy, University College, University of Western Ontario, who helped much to make the actual effort of putting all the pieces together efficient and effective, and to Mrs. Dorothy Wall, who assisted her.

London, Ontario   J. M.
April, 1968

CONTENTS

: III :
Human Behavior and Physical Phenomena

: IV :
The Mind-Body Problem

: V :
Knowledge and Certainty

: VI :
Meaning and Perception

: VII :
Conduct and Values

: I :

Introduction
Philosophical Inquiry

INTRODUCTION

In presenting a book of readings in philosophy, one must expect to face the question of their proper use and, with it, the question of the nature of philosophy. It is not especially helpful to answer that philosophy is the pursuit of the truth with respect to certain matters and then to enumerate those matters—for instance, whether time is real, whether physical objects are perceived by the senses, whether numbers are entities, whether God necessarily exists, whether we can distinguish between dreaming and waking, whether we can know that something continues to exist when it is not perceived, whether what happens happens of necessity, whether something can be in two places at once, whether the future can be known, whether we can have knowledge of other minds, whether a private language is possible. Such a list is bewildering, however accurate it may be in some sense, and to offer it as a helpful catalogue—perhaps with the intention of distinguishing philosophy from psychology and grammar and physics—is either disingenuous or silly.

The most difficult question for the beginner is, precisely, how to construe and resolve questions of the sort that have been enumerated. From this viewpoint, without prejudice to the respect in which philosophy can be regarded as a science, it is helpful to consider philosophy as a studio art—that is, to consider how philosophers actually work on problems.

There is a sense in which philosophical questions are both remote and familiar and in which the classic answers to these questions are authoritative and impregnable. The trouble with philosophical works is that, characteristically, the solutions they advance for the problems they posit move in a noticeably assured way, as if one had the right to expect that the procedures and the strategies and tactics of professional debate were familiar to every reader and as if it were quite obvious what issues were being contested. But the reader who begins his philosophical inquiries informally is bound to be baffled by what Schopenhauer or Spinoza or Locke or Kant is attempting to do, quite as much as he is by what would justify their apparent claims.

Furthermore, it is notoriously difficult to move from one philosophical exposition to another, both nominally concerned with related issues, in a way that permits us to judge with any assurance which is the sounder account.

It is possible to answer the implied question about what may be established, as Rudolf Carnap has attempted to do (I:2), by an explicit formulation of the procedures and issues of philosophical inquiry. But it must be remembered that even that response makes clear sense only in that context within which the merits of Carnap's effort can be compared with the at least implicit policies of memorable contributors to the common tradition; also, allusions to the mistakes and weaknesses of earlier efforts presuppose a reasonable grasp of how philosophers proceed. It is difficult to identify the grounds on which the superiority of particular ways of doing philosophy is alleged to be demonstrated. Circularity seems always to threaten. Nevertheless, it is extremely useful to have before us something that, in the history of Western philosophy, is comparatively rare and distinctly modern—a statement of the assumed limits of philosophical inquiry and of the conditions under which rival doctrines can be tested. There is no doubt that the Vienna Circle, the innovators of the movement now known as logical positivism, among whom Carnap is one of the acknowledged leaders, has made what may well be the most sustained and scrupulous effort in our own time to lay bare the properties and the program of philosophical inquiry.

Needless to say, the competence of such a statement of program becomes a matter of philosophical dispute; the very naturalness of the question obliges us to concede the open-ended nature of philosophical inquiry. Such informality may be inescapable, but it should not be mistaken for lack of rigor. For a considerable number of questions the tradition sustains a strong sense of the relative force of different answers and of the propriety and effectiveness of particular challenges; remarkably enough, the tradition does so in the face of apparently radical disagreements about the proper pursuit of philosophy.

To recognize this is to begin to prepare oneself for a realistic conception of the progress that is possible in professional philosophy. One is inevitably drawn to attempt to map the several distinct sorts of inquiry that belong among the efforts that are part of the tradition. This is very much the concern, for example, of C. D. Broad (I:1), who, in a manner similar to that of G. E. Moore—whose conception of philosophical work as a second-order analysis of our first-order engagement in speaking about and acting in the world has deeply influenced contemporary Anglo-American philosophy— attempts to characterize the principal sorts of philosophical effort, without such programmatic commitments as those of the positivists. It must be admitted that the implicit two-storey conception of our discourse about the world (as well as the reliance on commonsense beliefs) has, in its turn, been seriously challenged by contemporary philosophers. Nevertheless, it does provide another helpful beginning, and suspicions of its possible oversimplification must count as moves toward a substantial grasp of the nature of philosophical inquiry. It is the analysis of various related sorts of inquiry rather than one or another variety of synoptic vision—for both of which Broad finds room, the first somewhat more enthusiastically than the second —that is more and more occupying the attention of contemporary philosophy; and this encourages the increasingly strengthened sense that authentic philosophical advances are being made in our time.

There still remains, however, some puzzlement about how philosophical inquiry proceeds. Philosophers function in markedly different ways—as phenomenalists, as positivists, as logical atomists, as linguistic analysts, in fact, in a thousand and one different ways, under such nearly useless labels as those just mentioned as well as in equally varied ways for which there are as yet no labels. What the beginner needs is selected specimens of analysis or, perhaps, an account of philosophy that traces the structure of specimen efforts of various sorts. The philosophical endeavors of Ludwig Wittgenstein, particularly in *Philosophical Investigations*, and of such associates as John Wisdom, offer the most striking exhibition of the activity of philosophizing that our current literature can provide—I say this without prejudice to the substantive controversies that are at stake.

What Wisdom (I:3) manages to capture is something that the catalogue of philosophical issues with which we began suggests and at the same time obscures—it is the sense in which critical questions may appear initially in forms that are not grammatically distinct from ordinary questions of fact. What Wisdom shows, by the very informality of his technique, is the genesis of philosophical perplexity itself. Wittgenstein was strongly moved at times to construe philosophical perplexity as a disorder of language that required a species of treatment, as it were, that would dissolve the perplexity. While Wisdom seems to sympathize with this view, he turns from mere therapy to the defense of opposing philosophical positions. With this he allows for the recovery of genuine controversy, which can be appreciated in terms not only of his own perception of perplexity, but also in terms of a wider variety of philosophical practices than his exposition draws into focus: Wisdom's ostensibly neutral reference to our linguistic practices harbors a philosophically significant partiality.

It is clearly very difficult to characterize philosophy in an altogether neutral way. Every specification, however implicit, is a commitment to a particular way of exploring questions—even when it is intended in the most strictly neutral spirit. But this very fact highlights the particular sort of objectivity and advance that the tradition sustains. However partisan philosophers may be, serious students of any persuasion can, within limits, grasp one another's formulations as well as the alternative procedures by which the posited questions are presumed to be resolved.

What ultimately links all the diverse elements of philosophical inquiry and assures some measure of common commitment is the irresistible acknowledgment of a shared world. Furthermore, philosophy has a very strong historical sense, so that the emergence of newer philosophical methods generally depends on reaction against the alleged limitations of earlier methods. As contemporary journals will confirm, the result is that disputes about philosophical issues tend to cut across philosophical persuasions: advocates of quite different procedures often share common views about the testing of particular doctrines.

In contrast to the sciences (where the sense of authoritative and prevailing practice is much more dominant), the philosophical tradition preserves significant achievements in the form of questions that have been answered (in accordance with this or that method). The philosophical tradition thus includes, in relation to such questions as those with which we began, alternative ways of construing particular issues as well as alternative ways of resolving them. One important hallmark of philosophical novelty is the provision of a new way of construing an old problem. Of necessity, this becomes increasingly difficult to do and its achievement is correspondingly prized, if only because the tradition has preserved all relevant constructions, thereby taxing the ingenuity and insight of would-be contributors.

The questions to which philosophers address themselves are very often focused upon items, often homely ones, that disputants through the ages have recognized as central. The bent stick in water, the melted piece of wax, the front surface of a tomato, the raising of an arm, the sun's rising tomorrow, the cat on the mat, and a thousand other such examples testify to the resolve of philosophers who are doctrinally opposed, to provide an analysis of common questions. In that sense, the alternative and subtly modified interpretations of what appear to be the same questions form a family of possible ways of viewing the issue. Philosophical progress is in one sense occupied precisely with attaining a critical grasp of this developing family of possible ways of dealing with the question. Responsible partisans are those who, for reasons defended in the arena of exchange, are persuaded that some particular way of posing and answering the question is superior to all available alternatives.

There is thus a sense both of the preservation of alternatives and of the comparative power of these alternatives. For one thing, there is always the need, with regard to particular questions, to avoid extravagant paradox, self-defeating solutions, contradictions, and extreme and unjustifiable departures from certain relatively neutral insights. Moreover, there is a sense in which all philosophical questions are linked conceptually with one another, and in which the power of partial solutions is gauged in terms of their compatibility with related solutions, as well as in terms of the scope and detail that are made possible through the methods by which they are generated. Sometimes famous puzzles are associated with established areas of inquiry—how to justify induction, what we mean by the unity of the self, whether freedom and causality are compatible, whether we have evidence for the existence of the entities of micro-physics, whether the mind and body interact—by which the comparative force and standing of particular theories in particular philosophical domains may be gauged. A great deal of philosophical work is in fact of a conditional sort; the implications of a particular way of proceeding or of particular assumptions are pursued until they yield consequences that are relatively terminal, in the sense of being implications or assumptions to which we are provisionally committed.

One result is that the history of philosophy has been, to a very great extent, a history of impressive failures, of large conceptions whose particular deficiencies have finally been laid bare for all to behold. The seriousness and the importance of these efforts, which are quite unrelated to the historical respect that is appropriate in the presence of the cumulative achievement of the physical sciences, lie in this: try as we may, our own attempts to propose coherent solutions for the puzzles that are part of the philosophical tradition cannot help being imitations of those solutions that have already left their mark in the tradition.

That is why, apart from the vagaries of intellectual fashion, reading in philosophy ranges comfortably, and without any sense of inappropriate juxtaposition, from the statements of ancient Greek writers to those of our own age. For example, no one who pursues questions about the analysis of human action or about the nature of choice, volition, and purpose is likely to neglect a study of Aristotle's *Ethics*. More remarkably, he will not find the passage of more than two thousand years since the appearance of that work suggesting any incongruity whatsoever in a close comparison between Aristotle's account and the work of any responsible present-day discussant.

Such considerations do not point to the hopelessness of the philosophical venture. What is indicated rather is the classic nature of certain ways of viewing the world. It is simply a tribute to Aristotle that we cannot analyze those parts of the world that we still share with him, in ways that do not at all reflect his original vision.

We may also say that, in attempting to do philosophy, we are attracted by the possibility of formulating a coherent, comprehensive account of the entire range of our fundamental concepts and categories. There is an impressive agreement about which concepts and categories must be considered by philosophers: physical object, person, cause, intention, truth, meaning, statement, action, choice, perception, memory, concept, thought, value, knowledge, fact, certainty, necessity, possibility, God, history, science, art, existence, reality, and so on. Much of philosophy, particularly in the grand tradition (and increasingly, once again, in contemporary philosophy), exhibits its power by way of its systematic command of important sets of concepts, each suitably linked to the clusters of particular puzzles that the tradition has collected. The neophyte who confronts Leibniz' monads for the first time, or Plato's Forms, or Spinoza's God, cannot be expected to see the justification for positing such entities. It is only if one grasps the usefulness of these constructions in the solution of philosophical puzzles that the power and elegance of such otherwise incredible projects can be at all appreciated; it is only through a familiarity with available alternatives with regard to these puzzles that the genius of particular solutions can be gauged. Even the discovery of a stalemate between opposing philosophical systems or of the difficulty of comparing seemingly related alternatives enlarges our sense of the coherence of conceptual analysis.

Philosophy is thus a discipline that is primarily concerned with conceptual crisis. Given any sector of our investigations and findings about the world, we ask ourselves for an analysis of those concepts that are particularly relevant or fundamental, for an account of whether or not they are significantly alterable, for a sketch of what conceivable alternatives may be constructed, for an argument that demonstrates the superiority of preferred ways of answering these questions. Normally, although not always, methods for testing claims are reasonably settled in the empirical disciplines, in which questions are not typically reflexive; when one answers a bona fide question, one is not also bound to answer an implied and apparently deeper question about the relative power and admissibility of one's way of answering. Periodically, such issues do arise in the sciences, and we are then quite justified in absorbing the disputes into the body of philosophy. But although there are always loyal adherents to particular ways of doing philosophy, there is never the sense, as there is in science, of a prevailing way of working, to which professionals everywhere are more or less committed. Every prominent philosophical method has arisen in a field of perpetually changing contenders, each with its important champions and a fair number, given the rise and fall of philosophical fashion, that may be regarded as peers.

The interesting and permanently fascinating feature of all this exchange is that what, on first glance, might seem to lead to utter chaos and possibly to intellectual despair, in fact provides a powerful command over our conceptual endeavors. What we gain is the recognition of the limits of our conceptual framework, as well as of the extent to which concepts and relations between concepts can be coherently altered and with what consequences. Must time be directional? Can sensations be construed as intersubjectively discriminable? Can a language be constructed that would preserve certain fundamental functions of natural languages and yet in which singular terms would be omitted? What are the minimal kinds of entities that we can admit to exist compatibly with a given range of true statements? What are the consequences of denying causal efficacy to the mind consistently with a certain body of discourse? Is there any way in which it is possible to prove the existence of God? What we seek to isolate are those points in our conceptual scheme at which viable options are available—together with the adjustments that are required in other critically affected portions of the scheme—as well as those points at which changes are markedly difficult, if not impossible, to undertake systematically. The result, which develops with the tradition, is an understanding, expressed in increasingly articulated relations among our concepts, of the very conditions of intelligible discourse.

In effect, then, philosophy is the exploration of those properties of our language, or of any language that we can conceive, by the use of which, as by assertion and directive, we relate ourselves in various ways to the things of the world. We can put this in only a general way; for any particular formula is designed either to prepare us for a quite distinctive enterprise (with, hopefully, useful hints about its distinctiveness) or to help us collect, in summary form, a sense of the purpose of entire sets of detailed philosophical contributions, which are, after all, the matters of prime importance.

1

CRITICAL AND SPECULATIVE PHILOSOPHY

C. D. Broad

It seems to me that under the name of "Philosophy" two very different subjects are included. They are pursued by different methods, and can expect to reach quite different degrees of certainty. I am wont to call them *Critical* and *Speculative* Philosophy. I do not assert that either can be wholly separated from the other. The second quite certainly presupposes the first, and it is probable that in the first we tacitly assume some things that belong to the second. But they certainly can be separated to a considerable extent, and it will be best to begin by explaining and illustrating what I mean by each in turn.

CRITICAL PHILOSOPHY

In ordinary life and in the special sciences we constantly make use of certain very general concepts, such as number, thing, quality, change, cause, etc. Now, although we constantly *use* them and apply them with fair consistency, it cannot be said that we have any very clear ideas as to their proper analysis or their precise relations. And it is not the business of any of the special sciences to clear up these obscurities. Chemistry, e.g., tells us a great deal about particular substances, such as gold and *aqua regia*, and about their qualities and relations; but we should not go to a chemistry book for a discussion on substance, quality, and relation. Chemistry simply assumes these general concepts as fully understood and concerns itself with particular instances of them.

Now it is certain that our ideas about such general concepts are highly confused, and this shows itself as soon as we try to apply them to cases which are a little out of the ordinary. We think we know what we mean by "place" and "person," for instance; and we do no doubt agree in the main in

From C. D. Broad, "Critical and Speculative Philosophy," in J. H. Muirhead, ed., *Contemporary British Philosophy*, First Series (London: George Allen & Unwin Ltd., 1924), Secs. 4–18, pp. 82–100. Reprinted by permission of the publisher.

applying and withholding these terms. But suppose we are asked: "In what place is the mirror image of a pin? And is it in this place in the same sense in which the pin itself is in *its* place?" Or suppose we are asked: "Was Sally Beauchamp a person?" We find ourselves puzzled by such questions, and this puzzlement is certainly due in part to the fact that we are not clear as to what we mean by "being in a place" or "being a person." Similar difficulties could be raised about all the fundamental concepts which we constantly use. Thus there is both need and room for a science which shall try to analyse and define the concepts which are used in daily life and in the special sciences. There is need for it, because these concepts really are obscure, and because their obscurity really does lead to difficulties. And there is room for it, because, whilst all the special sciences *use* these concepts, none of them is *about* these concepts as such. I regard Critical Philosophy as the science which has this for its most fundamental task.

It seems to me that such a science is perfectly possible, and that it actually exists, and has made a good deal of progress. I will illustrate this with some examples. Since the time of Berkeley and Descartes philosophers have devoted much attention to the problem of the "Reality of the External World." I do not pretend that there is any agreed answer to the question among them, but their inquiries have been most valuable in clearing up the meanings of such terms as "matter," "sensible appearance," "sensation," "perception," "independence," etc. Any competent philosopher nowadays, whether he asserts or denies the independent existence of matter, is asserting or denying something far more subtle and far better analysed than anything which Berkeley or Descartes would have understood by the same form of words. Again, we are not agreed on the right analysis of "cause"; but any view we may reach should be far subtler and clearer than that which could have been held before Hume wrote his classical criticism of this category. In making such statements I am, of course, referring to present-day philosophers who are really capable of appreciating and continuing the work of their predecessors. In any age there is plenty of philosophical writing which is far below the level of the best work of past ages. Moreover, there are fashions in philosophy, and even the best men of a certain period may ignore important results reached by the best men of a certain earlier period which happens for the time to be unpopular. Thus the philosophers of the *Aufklärung* neglected many important distinctions which the Scholastics had clearly recognized, and I think it probable that some of the *summi philosophi* of our time tend to neglect much fine gold which was mined by Kant and Hegel. Still, with these qualifications, it is pretty obvious that Critical Philosophy, as partly defined above, does make real and fairly steady progress.

Now Critical Philosophy has another and closely connected task. We do not merely use unanalysed concepts in daily life and in science. We also assume uncritically a number of very fundamental propositions. In all our arguments we assume the truth of certain principles of reasoning. Again, we always assume that every change has a cause. And in induction we certainly assume something—it is hard to say what—about the fundamental "make-up" of the existent world. Now the second task of Critical Philosophy is to take these propositions which we uncritically assume in science and daily life and to subject them to criticism. In order to do this we must first clear up the concepts which the propositions are about. It is impossible to know what weight to attach to the proposition that "every change has a cause" until you have assigned definite meanings to the words "change" and "cause." It is often found that a man's certainty about such propositions is directly proportional to the vagueness of the terms concerned in them. So the second part of Critical Philosophy is dependent on the first. No doubt it is also true that the first is dependent on the second. We clear up the meanings of terms by reflecting on the propositions in which they occur, just as we clear up the meanings of propositions by finding out the right analysis of their terms. I fancy that the two processes go on by alternate steps, very much as the development of thought and of language must have done in pre-historic times.

When we have got a clear idea of the meanings of propositions which are commonly assumed, our next business as Critical Philosophers is to expose them to every objection that we can think of ourselves or find in the writings of others. As a result of such reflexion and criticism it seems to me that we can divide propositions roughly according to the following scheme.

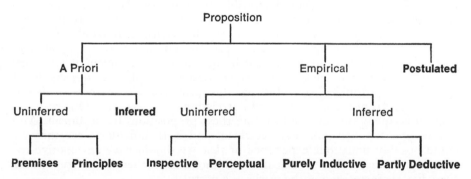

By an *à priori premise* I mean some proposition such as "Colour cannot exist without extension." This expresses a connexion between two universals which is seen to be necessary by reflexion upon instances and which does not need to be deduced from anything else. By *à priori principles* I mean the principles according to which we pass from asserting one proposition to asserting others. This group therefore includes the principle of the syllogism, the fundamental axioms of probability, and so on. By *inferred à priori propositions* I mean those which can be deduced from *à priori* premises by means of *à priori* principles. The proposition that π is not a rational number is an example.

By an *inspective empirical proposition* I mean one which asserts of some particular existent with which the mind is acquainted at the time some property which the mind can notice by inspection to belong to it. Examples would be: "My headache is of a throbbing character," "A certain one of the presentations of which I am now aware is red," and so on. *Perceptual propositions* are based on those particular existents about which we can make inspective judgments, but they make assertions which go beyond these existents and their properties. They are not *reached* by inference from inspective propositions; but, if we were called upon to *defend* them, we should do so by a mixture of inductive and deductive inference from such propositions. Examples would be: "That is a red pillar-box," "A man is talking to me," and so on. An *inferred empirical proposition* is one that is derived from a number of perceptual propositions either directly by pure inductive generalization, or indirectly by deduction from one or more inductive generalizations of the first kind. Examples of the two would be: "All living grass is green" and "The benzene molecule consists of six CH groups arranged at the corners of a regular hexagon."

I have included a third great division, viz. *Postulates*. The contents of this group are extremely puzzling to me. There are certain important general propositions, such as "Every change has a cause," "All sensa are appearances of physical objects," etc., which I tentatively put into this group. They seem to me to have the following characteristics: (i) I do not find them self-evident. (ii) I do not know of any self-evident premises from which they could be deduced by any known logical principles. Hence I cannot group them as *à priori* propositions. (iii) If they are to be grouped as empirical propositions they would have to come under the head of inferred empirical propositions. And this seems impossible for most of them. All inductions make some assumption about the structure of nature, which may be called the "Uniformity of Nature," for want of a better name. It would evidently be circular to try to prove such a proposition inductively. Again, any particular perceptual judgment may be defended by argument if we grant the *general* principle that all sensa are appearances of physical objects. But I can see no possibility of inferring this principle either inductively or deductively from the existence and correlations of sensa. (iv) On the other hand, it is equally impossible to refute these propositions by argument. And (v) in practice everyone assumes them, and it is difficult to see that we could possibly unify our experience or that we should have any motive for carrying our researches further if we did not assume them to be true. I take these five characteristics as the marks of a postulate.

Now there is one suggestion that I want to make before leaving this subject. I do not think that we must *identify* necessary propositions with those which are self-evident or deducible by self-evident principles from self-evident premises. These properties seem to me to be *tests* (and the only available tests) for necessity. I would define an *à priori* proposition as one which is necessary and is recognized by us to be necessary. Hence *à priority* probably depends on two factors, viz.: (i) necessity, which is an intrinsic property of the proposition, and (ii) some special relation between the proposition and the mind which contemplates it. When this subsists the mind can *see* that the proposition is necessary, and so it is counted as *à priori*. Now there are some propositions which we can positively see to be necessary, e.g., the principle of the syllogism. There are many which we can positively see *not* to be necessary, e.g., that all grass is green or that a certain presentation of which I am now aware is red. But there are other propositions of which we cannot see either that they are or that they are not necessary, though they must of course be in fact one or the other. It is, e.g., a well-known fact that certain propositions in the theory of numbers which are now deduced *à priori* propositions were for many years accepted tentatively as the results of induction. It therefore seems to be possible that some at least of the postulates may be necessary propositions which higher or more favourably situated minds than ours would find self-evident or would be able to deduce from premises which they found self-evident. It is worth while to notice that there is a considerable analogy between the postulates and those *à priori* propositions which I have called "principles." The principles of deductive logic and of the theory of probability happen to be self-evident to us. But, if they had not been, we should certainly have had to put them in the group of postulates; for we evidently could not have made a step forward in unifying our experience without them. It does therefore seem possible that the analogy may be reversible, and that some of the postulates may really be necessary principles which only fail to be counted as *à priori* because we cannot see their necessity. Postulates may be called "hypothetically necessary"; i.e. they are necessary *for the purpose* of unifying our experience. *À priori* principles are hypothetically necessary, in this sense, and also *intrinsically* necessary, as is shown by their self-evidence. What I have been saying is that some at least of the postulates may also be intrinsically necessary, although we are not capable of seeing that this is so.

Suppose now that we take "necessary" and "contingent" to express intrinsic characteristics of propositions, and "certain" and "possible" to express subjective degrees of conviction in a rational but limited mind. We might then make the following statements. (i) *À priori* propositions are those which are certainly or almost certainly necessary. (ii) Empirical propositions are those which are certainly contingent. (iii) Postulates are those which are possibly necessary. Now, if we are certain of the necessity of a proposition, we are *ipso facto* certain of its truth. But to be certain of the contingency of a proposition implies nothing about our conviction of its truth. We may be certain that a proposition is contingent, and at the same time certain that it is true. I may be as certain that my headache is of a throbbing character as that $2 \times 2 = 4$, although the former is certainly contingent and the latter is certainly necessary.

To sum up. (i) There is always a general possibility of error even about uninferred *à priori* propositions. It is admittedly possible to think that a proposition is necessary when it is not. This *general* difficulty is not a legitimate ground for doubting any *specific* proposition; provided that we have honestly exposed it to all the objections that we can think of. But it is a ground for being always ready to re-open the question if fresh *specific* objections be brought to our notice. (ii) An inferred *à priori* proposition is always less certain in proportion to the length and complexity of its proof. As Descartes pointed out, I have to trust my memory at the later stages for the conviction that the earlier steps were self-evident. Now, memory-propositions are empirical, and, for our purpose, must be classed with perceptual propositions. Thus the certainty of inferred *à priori* propositions is conditional; they are certain provided we can trust our memories, and that we have not deceived ourselves over any of the steps. (iii) Inspective propositions are practically certain provided they confine themselves to the positive non-relational characteristics of presentations or states of mind. The moment they go beyond this they are liable to error. Stumpf's argument shows that we can judge two sensa to be exactly alike when they are really different in intensity. Again, it would be perfectly possible to think that a sensum is *uniformly* red or *exactly* round when it is not. For these involve negative assertions, and more inspection will not guarantee them. Thus inspective propositions, though certain, tend to be very trivial. (iv) Perceptual propositions are still less certain. If I make the judgment: "This which I see is a pillar-box," I may be wrong in the following ways: (*a*) I may be basing a perceptual proposition on a mere image or on an hallucinatory sensum. (*β*) I may be misinterpreting a genuine sensum. The red pillar-like sensum may be due to a skilful painting on a flat canvas. (*γ*) The general assumption that all sensa are appearances of physical objects is only a postulate, and may be wrong. There may be no physical objects. (v) It is evident that inferred empirical propositions must have all the weaknesses of perceptual propositions together with others of their own. For their ultimate premises are perceptual propositions, and from these we reach inductive generalizations in accordance with the *à priori* principles of probability. But it is quite easy to show that these will not justify us in assigning any finite probability to inductive generalizations unless we also assume certain premises about the structure of nature. And, as we have seen, another postulate has to be made to justify the original perceptual propositions which the inductive proposition professes to generalize. Of course this is quite compatible with the fact that *some* inductive propositions may be more certain than *some* perceptual propositions. It is more reasonable to believe strongly that I *shall* be ill if I swallow arsenic than to believe strongly that a conjuror has really pounded my watch in a mortar and restored it to me, although I seem to have seen him do so.

It is worth while to remark that sometimes it is quite certain that propositions of *some* kind are being assumed, and yet it is by no means easy to say exactly what these propositions are. In such cases the first business of Critical Philosophy is to find these assumptions and to state them clearly. This is one of the main difficulties of the theory of induction. Nearly every one was agreed that something, which they called the "Uniformity of Nature," was presupposed in all inductions. But (*a*) no one stated clearly what they meant by this; and (*b*) most writers seemed to think that nothing further was needed except the ordinary principles of deductive logic. It has therefore been an important task of Critical Philosophy to show (*a*) that inductive arguments can only be valid if they state their conclusions in terms of probability, and that they therefore use the principles of probability; and (*b*) that, if they do not *also* use some premise about nature, they will be unable to give any finite probability to their conclusions. The way is then clear for seeking the assumptions about nature which would suffice to give a reasonably high probability to the conclusions of generally accepted inductive arguments. It is easy to show that something more concrete than the Law of Causation is needed, and that the assumption of something like Natural Kinds at least is necessary. Finally, we are in a position to estimate the kind and degree of evidence which there is for such assumptions.

It seems to me that we can lay down two useful general methods in Critical Philosophy. I will call them the *Principle of Exceptional Cases* and the *Principle of Pickwickian Senses*. I will now illustrate them with some examples. (i) If we want to clear up the meaning of some commonly used concept it is enormously important to see how it applies to exceptional and abnormal cases. E.g., let us take the concept of "being in a place." This is commonly applied to things like pins and chairs, and it seems to be a simple two-term relation between a thing and a place. But now suppose that we ask: "Where is the mirror-image of a pin; and is it in its place in the same sense in which the pin itself is in *its* place?" It seems plausible to answer that the place where the image is is as far behind the mirror as the place where the pin is is in front of the mirror. At once two difficulties arise. (*a*) If you go to the place where the pin is said to be you can touch something correlated with the visual appearances which have guided you to this place. But, if you go to the place behind the mirror where the image is said to be, you may touch nothing or you may touch a brick wall. You will certainly not feel anything like a pin. (*b*) If you approach the place where the pin is said to be from *any* direction there will be a series of visual appearances which continues till you reach the place. But, if you approach the place where the image is said to be, you will find (α) that it is only from *certain* directions that any visual appearance resembling the pin is there, and (β) that from *all* directions of approach the series of visual appearances stops before you reach this place. Now in theory you could either take the sense in which the pin is in its place as fundamental, and try to explain the sense in which the image is in *its* place by making a number of supplementary hypotheses; or you could take the sense in which the image is in its place as fundamental, and regard the facts which are true of the pin and not of the image as due to the fulfilment of certain special conditions which *need* not be realized but which in fact generally are. The latter seems to be the only hopeful course to take. It leads us to two conclusions. (*a*) A perceptual object consists of several correlated components: one visual, one tactual, and so on. Generally the visual, tactual, and other components are all in the same place in important and definable (though different) senses. But they *may* be in different places when certain special simplifying conditions (homogeneity of the medium, etc.) are not fulfilled. (*b*) "Being in a place" is not a simple two-term relation between a visual appearance and a place. It is really at least a three-term relation, viz., "being in place x from place y." Under special conditions, which happen to be often very nearly realized, there are similar visual appearances in a place from *all* places within a certain range. This is true of the pin. With a plain mirror we get a more general and less simple case. We have (α) similar visual appearances in a place from many, but not from all, *directions*. (β) There are no such appearances in this place from any place behind the mirror. (γ) There is no correlated tactual object at the place. The commoner, but more special, case is explained by the existence of a special set of simplifying conditions, which we refer to as the "homogeneity of the medium." This way of looking at the facts might be compared to regarding a circle as a specially simplified instance of the general conic section. Once you know the properties of the general conic you can deduce all the properties of the circle; but, if you insist on starting with the properties of the circle you will find a great deal to puzzle you in the properties of the general conic. Another example would be given by the study of multiple personality, telepathy, and other abnormal psychical phenomena. If we start with the view, which purely normal cases suggest, that every human body has one and only one self connected with it, and that this self is a completely unified continuous existent, we shall find the abnormal phenomena most difficult to deal with. But if we start from the other end, and regard the normal cases as due to special simplifying conditions which happen to be generally fulfilled, we may be more successful.

(ii) *The Principle of Pickwickian Senses* was first developed by pure mathematicians in their attempts to define such things as irrational numbers. They saw that any entity which has the same formal properties as $\sqrt{2}$ and $\sqrt{3}$ are supposed to have can be taken to *be* $\sqrt{2}$ or $\sqrt{3}$, even though its internal structure be very different from that which people had commonly assigned to irrationals. Thus they define $\sqrt{2}$ and $\sqrt{3}$ as certain series of rationals, and show that such series have to each other relations of the kind which irrationals are supposed by everyone to have to each other. The advantage of this definition is that it is quite certain that something exists which answers to it, whereas with other definitions of the same entities this cannot be shown to be so. Now of course most people do not think of irrationals, like $\sqrt{2}$ and $\sqrt{3}$, as *series* of ordinary numbers, but as a special *kind* of number. Hence, when we call certain series of rationals by the name of "irrational numbers," we may be said to be using the phrase in a "Pickwickian sense." (The name is due to Dr. Moore.) This principle has always been familiar in Theology. When theologians say that the Second Person of the Trinity is the son of the First Person, they are using the word "son" in a highly Pickwickian sense. Anyone who will read, e.g., St. Thomas's brilliant discussion of this subject in the *Summa contra Gentiles* will see how careful St. Thomas is to point out in his own language that phrases like "sonship" and "begetting" cannot be interpreted literally here, and will further see what an elaborate and metaphorical interpretation St. Thomas puts upon such phrases. Now Whitehead and Russell have explicitly carried this principle over into philosophy, where I am quite sure that it is destined to play a most important part. Whitehead has used it to define points, moments, etc., and has succeeded in giving Pickwickian senses to these terms, in which it is certain (α) that they exist; (β) that they have to each other the sort of relations which we expect points and moments to have; and (γ) that there is an intelligible and useful, though Pickwickian, sense in which we can say that volumes are "composed of" points, and durations of moments.

This seems to me to be one of the most important steps in the philosophy of applied mathematics.

Russell has used much the same method in dealing with the still harder problem of the nature of matter, and the relation of a bit of matter to its various sensible appearances. I am not prepared to accept Russell's theory as it stands, because I think it still fails to do justice to the extreme complexity of the problem. But I think we can safely say that *any* tenable theory of matter can only admit its existence if it be defined in a highly Pickwickian sense. Even on the ordinary scientific view the statement that pillar-boxes are red must be interpreted in an extremely Pickwickian way before it can be accepted; and more critical reflexion shows that still more radical modifications are needed in the common-sense view of the nature of matter. Thus the problem of matter and our perception of it seems to come to this:—"To define a Pickwickian sense of 'matter' in which (*a*) pieces of 'matter' shall have to each other the kind of relations which physics requires them to have; (*b*) the variability and privacy of its sensible appearances shall be compatible with its relative constancy and its neutrality as between all observers; (*c*) justice shall be done to the apparent dependence of its appearances on the physiological condition of the observer and the variations of the medium; and (*d*) the minimum amount of purely hypothetical entities shall be postulated."

It is most important to understand that questions like: "Does matter exist?" or "Is the self real?" cannot be answered with a simple Yes or No. Unquestionably there are facts in the world to which the names "matter" and "self" apply; and in that sense they are names of something real. But it is vitally important to distinguish between *facts* and the proper *analysis* or *description* of facts. The words "matter" and "self," as commonly used, do suggest certain theories about the facts to which they are applied. These theories are never clearly recognized or explicitly stated by common-sense; and, on critical analysis, they are often found to consist of a number of propositions of very different degrees of importance and certainty. E.g., I think there is very little doubt that the word "self," as commonly used, implies something like the Pure Ego theory of the structure of those unities which we call "selves." Hence anyone who rejects the Pure Ego theory is, in one sense, "denying the reality of the self." But, if he offers an alternative analysis, which does equal justice to the peculiar unity which we find in the things called "selves," he is, in another sense, "accepting the reality of the self." Whenever one particular way of analysing a certain concept has been almost universally, though tacitly, assumed, a man who rejects *this analysis* will seem to others (and often to himself) to be rejecting the *concept* itself. Thus James raises the question: "Does Consciousness Exist?", and suggests a negative answer. But really neither James nor anyone else in his senses doubts the existence of certain facts to which we apply the name "consciousness." The whole question is: "What is the right analysis of these facts?" Do they involve an unique kind of *stuff*, which does not occur in non-conscious facts; or is their peculiarity only one of *structure?*" To deny the first alternative is not really to deny the *existence* of consciousness; it is merely to deny an almost universally held *theory about* consciousness. Philosophy seems to me to be full of unprofitable discussions which depend on a failure to recognize this kind of ambiguity; and the Principle of

Pickwickian Senses has the advantage that it forces the distinction on our notice.

It remains to say something about the relations of other sciences to Critical Philosophy. It is clear that logic and ethics are simply branches of Critical Philosophy. Logic is its most general and fundamental part, being the science which classifies and analyses propositional forms and discusses their formal relations to each other. Now all sciences *consist* of propositions which are of various forms and stand in such relations that some are supposed to "follow from" others. But no other science is *about* propositional forms or their formal relations. Thus logic deals with the most fundamental of all concepts, and with those *à priori* principles which form the connective tissue of all knowledge. Ethics is that part of Critical Philosophy which tries to analyse the concepts and appraise the assumptions which are involved in our judgments of moral value.

The distinction between mathematics, physics, or chemistry, and what is called "the philosophy of" these sciences is, I think, pretty clear. But, as we pass to the more concrete and less advanced sciences, the distinction becomes in practice less definite. Discussions about mechanism and vitalism, e.g., are in part at least questions of Critical Philosophy, and yet they appear in books on biology. I think that psychology is wrongly counted as a part of philosophy; it is strictly a natural science based on observation and induction. But any standard work on psychology is full of discussions which really belong to Critical Philosophy. Attempts to analyse and define sensation, perception, selfhood, etc., belong to Critical Philosophy; but it is quite impossible for the psychologist to avoid them, for these concepts are not, like those of physics, clear enough to be used for ordinary scientific purposes without risk of error. It is generally a bad thing when a science and the philosophy of that science are mixed up with each other, because two very different kinds of problems must then be dealt with by the same man, and hardly anyone combines the special aptitude and knowledge needed for both. We are all familiar with the nonsense which eminent philosophers have talked about scientific questions; it is only equalled by the nonsense which eminent scientists continually talk about philosophical questions.

SPECULATIVE PHILOSOPHY

It is quite evident that what I have been describing under the name of *Critical Philosophy* does not include all that is understood by philosophy. It is certainly held to be the function of a philosopher to discuss the nature of Reality as a whole, and to consider the position and prospects of men in it. In a sense Critical Philosophy presupposes a certain view on this question. It assumes that our minds are so far in accord with the rest of Reality that by using them carefully and critically we approach nearer to the truth. But it is still clearer that Speculative Philosophy presupposes a considerable amount of Critical Philosophy. Its business is to take over all aspects of human experience, to reflect upon them, and to try to think out a view of Reality as a whole which shall do justice to all of them. Now it is perfectly useless to take over the scientific, social, ethical, æsthetic, and religious experiences of mankind in their crude, unanalysed form. We do not know what they mean or what weight to attach to various parts of the whole mass till we have submitted them to a critical analytic investigation. Two results follow at once from this consideration. (i) We cannot admit the claim of any system of Speculative Philosophy to be the final truth. The best of them will be guesses at truth, and will be subject to modification as more facts are known, and as known facts become more and more fully analysed and criticized. (ii) We must always admit the possibility that Critical Philosophy has not yet been carried far enough to make any attempt at Speculative Philosophy profitable.

There is another general point which it seems important to notice. I think that, in different forms, it plays a vital part in such different philosophies as those of Mr. Bradley and M. Bergson, and in the thought of most great theologians, whether Christian or non-Christian. This is the question how far the discursive form of cognition by means of general concepts can ever be completely adequate to the concrete Reality which it seeks to describe. Thought must always be "about" its objects; to speak metaphorically, it is a transcription of the whole of Reality into a medium which is itself one aspect of Reality. We are bound to think of Reality as a complex of terms having various qualities and standing in various relations; because, if we do not think of it on these lines, we cannot think of it at all. With Mr. Bradley's attempt to show that this scheme involves *internal* contradictions I do not agree. But I do see clearly that we have only to compare a tune, as heard, or an emotion, as felt, with any conceptual description which we can give of them, to recognize how inadequate every conceptual description of Reality must be to Reality itself. When we can *both* be acquainted with something as a whole *and* can analyse and describe it conceptually, this difficulty is at its minimum. But we cannot be acquainted with Reality as a whole, as we can with a tune or an emotion, and therefore the difficulty is at a maximum in Speculative Philosophy. This limitation of the whole conceptual scheme is one which we must simply recognize once and for all and then ignore. We cannot avoid it in detail, and we cannot understand in outline any other kind of cognition. Since it is perfectly general, it applies equally to *every* system of Speculative Philosophy, and therefore gives us no ground for preferring one to another.

It has been held by many philosophers, e.g., Spinoza and Hegel in the past and Dr. McTaggart at present, that important results about the structure of Reality as a whole can be reached by deductive arguments from self-evident premises. The best general account of such a view will be found in Dr. McTaggart's *Nature of Existence*. I do not think that this view can be refuted; it *is* theoretically possible, so far as I can see. But I am completely sceptical about its practicability. I feel pretty certain that all known attempts to elaborate a system of Speculative Philosophy on these lines either contain logical fallacies, or introduce premises which are ambiguous and only become self-evident when so interpreted as to be trivial. And I have not the slightest expectation that future essays in this direction will be any more successful.

It seems to me that the main value of Speculative Philosophy lies, not in its conclusions, but in the collateral effects which it has, or ought to have, on the persons who pursue it. The speculative philosopher is forced to look at the world synoptically, and anyone who does not do this at some time in his life is bound to hold a very narrow and inadequate idea of Reality. This is a danger to which the natural scientist is peculiarly liable. The extraordinary success of physics and chemistry within their own sphere tempts men to think that the world is simply a physico-chemical system. These sciences, quite rightly for their own purposes, ignore the existence of minds; and scientists are liable to forget that somehow minds have grown up in a world of matter, and that it is by means of their activities that matter and its laws have become known. If a man referred to his brother or his cat as "an ingenious mechanism" we should know that he was either a fool or a physiologist. No one in practice treats himself or his fellowmen or his pet animals as machines, but scientists who have never made a study of Speculative Philosophy seem often to think it their duty to hold in theory what no one outside a lunatic asylum would accept in practice. If we remember that physics and chemistry are simply constructed to unify the correlations which we find among a selection of the sensa of three or four senses, the idea that these sciences give a complete account of the structure of all Reality becomes ludicrous. Thus our inability to explain the facts of life and mind in purely physico-chemical terms is not a paradox to be explained away, but is what might reasonably have been expected from the outset.

On the other hand, the man who starts from the side of mind is equally liable to fail to do justice to the facts. The properties with which physics and chemistry deal *are* very pervasive, and we *do* know them more accurately and thoroughly than we know anything else. And minds *are* very closely bound up with certain bits of matter, viz., our brains and nervous systems, and they *do* seem to have gradually developed in a world which once contained nothing but matter. The characteristic fault of Idealism is to be unable to see the trees for the wood, and the characteristic fault of Realism is to be unable to see the wood for the trees. The great merit of Idealism is that it really has tried to do justice to the social, ethical, æsthetic, and religious facts of the world. The great merit of Realism is that it really has tried to face in a patient and detailed way the problem of matter and of our perception of it. But neither of these activities is a substitute for the other; and a genuine Speculative Philosophy must combine the detailed study of the lower categories with the due recognition of the higher categories, and must try to reconcile the pervasiveness of the former with the apparently growing importance of the latter.

There is one thing which Speculative Philosophy must take into most serious consideration, and that is the religious and mystical experiences of mankind. These form a vast mass of facts which obviously deserve at least as careful attention as the sensations of mankind. They are of course less uniform than our sensations; many people, of whom I am one, are practically without these experiences. But probably most people have them to some extent, and there is a considerable amount of agreement between those people of all nations and ages, who have them to a marked degree. Of course the theoretical interpretations which have been put upon them are very varied, and it is obvious that they depend largely on the traditions of the time, place, and society in which the experient lives. I have compared the experiences themselves with sensations; we might compare the common features in the interpretations which have been put upon them with our ordinary common-sense beliefs about matter; and elaborate systems of theology might be compared with big scientific theories, like the wave theory of light. Obviously there remains a further step to be taken, comparable with the philosophic criticism and interpretation of scientific theories about matter. It seems reasonable to suppose at the outset that the whole mass of mystical and religious experience brings us into contact with an aspect of Reality which is not revealed in ordinary sense-perception, and that any system of Speculative Philosophy which ignores it will be extremely one-sided. In fact it cannot safely be ignored. If we count all such experiences as purely delusive, we must explain how such a widespread and comparatively coherent mass of illusion arose. And, if we find it impossible to take this view, we must try to understand and criticize these experiences; to sift away those factors in them which are of merely local and temporary interest; and to see what the residuum has to tell us about the probable nature of Reality. The great practical difficulty here is that those who have the experiences most vividly are seldom well fitted for the task of philosophical criticism and construction; whilst those who are fitted for the latter task are not often mystics or persons of religious genius. It is alleged, and it may well be true, that the capacity for such experiences can be cultivated by a suitable mode of life and a suitable system of training and meditation. In so far as this can be done without detriment to the critical faculties it deserves the serious attention of philosophers; for theories which are built on experiences known only by description are always unsatisfactory.

PHILOSOPHY AND LOGICAL SYNTAX

Rudolf Carnap

I. THE REJECTION OF METAPHYSICS

1. Verifiability

The problems of philosophy as usually dealt with are of very different kinds. From the point of view which I am here taking we may distinguish mainly three kinds of problems and doctrines in traditional philosophy. For the sake of simplicity we shall call these parts *Metaphysics*, *Psychology*, and *Logic*. Or, rather, there are not three distinct regions, but three sorts of components which in most theses and questions are combined: a metaphysical, a psychological, and a logical component.

The considerations that follow belong to the third region: we are here carrying out *Logical Analysis*. The function of logical analysis is to analyse all knowledge, all assertions of science and of everyday life, in order to make clear the sense of each such assertion and the connections between them. One of the principal tasks of the logical analysis of a given statement is to find out the method of verification for that statement. The question is: What reasons can there be to assert this statement; or: How can we become certain as to its truth or falsehood? This question is called by the philosophers the epistemological question; epistemology or the philosophical theory of knowledge is nothing other than a special part of logical analysis, usually combined with some psychological questions concerning the process of knowing.

What, then, is the method of verification of a statement? Here we have to distinguish between two kinds of verification: direct and indirect. If the question is about a statement which asserts something about a present perception, e.g. "Now I see a red square on a blue ground," then the state-

From Rudolf Carnap, *Philosophy and Logical Syntax* (London: Routledge & Kegan Paul Ltd., 1935), Part I, pp. 424–436, 459–460. Reprinted by permission of the publisher and author, who has authorized the use of the 1961 addendum. The present version incorporates a number of terminological improvements suggested by Professor Carnap.

ment can be tested directly by my present perception. If at present I do see a red square on a blue ground, the statement is directly verified by this seeing; if I do not see that, it is disproved. To be sure, there are still some serious problems in connection with direct verification. We will however not touch on them here, but give our attention to the question of indirect verification, which is more important for our purposes. A statement P which is not directly verifiable can only be verified by direct verification of statements deduced from P together with other already verified statements.

Let us take the statement P_1: "This key is made of iron." There are many ways of verifying this statement: e.g.: I place the key near a magnet; then I perceive that the key is attracted. Here the deduction is made in this way:

Premises: P_1: "This key is made of iron"; the statement to be examined.
P_2: "If an iron thing is placed near a magnet, it is attracted"; this is a physical law, already verified.
P_3: "This object—a bar—is a magnet"; statement already verified.
P_4: "The key is placed near the bar"; this is now directly verified by our observation.

From these four premises we can deduce the conclusion:

P_5: "The key will now be attracted by the bar."

This statement is a prediction which can be examined by observation. If we look, we either observe the attraction or we do not. In the first case we have found a positive instance, an instance of verification of the statement P_1 under consideration; in the second case we have a negative instance, an instance of disproof of P_1.

In the first case the examination of the statement P_1 is not finished. We may repeat the examination by means of a magnet, i.e. we may deduce other statements similar to P_5 by the help of the same or similar premises as before. After that, or instead of that, we may make an examination by electrical tests, or by mechanical, chemical, or optical tests, etc. If in these further investigations all instances turn out to be positive, the certainty of the statement P_1 gradually grows. We may soon come to a degree of certainty sufficient for all practical purposes, but *absolute* certainty we can never attain. The number of instances deducible from P_1 by the help of other statements already verified or directly verifiable is infinite. Therefore there is always a possibility of finding in the future a negative instance, however small its probability may be. Thus the statement P_1 *can never be completely verified*. For this reason it is called an hypothesis.

So far we have considered a similar statement concerning one single thing. If we take a universal statement concerning all things or events at whatever time and place, a so-called natural *law*, it is still clearer that the number of examinable instances is infinite and so the statement is an hypothesis.

Every assertion P in the wide field of science has this character, that it either asserts something about present perceptions or other experiences, and therefore is verifiable by them, or that statements about future perceptions are deducible from P together with some other statements already verified. If a scientist should venture to make an assertion from which no perceptual statements could be deduced, what should we say to that? Suppose, e.g., he asserts that there is not only a gravitational field having an effect on bodies according to the known laws of gravitation, but also a levitational field, and on being asked what sort of effect this levitational field has, according to his theory, he answers that there is no observable effect; in other words, he confesses his inability to give rules according to which we could deduce perceptual statements from his assertion. In that case our reply is: your assertion is no assertion at all; it does not speak about anything; it is nothing but a series of empty words; it is simply without sense.

It is true that he may have images and even feelings connected with his words. This fact may be of psychological importance; logically, it is irrelevant. What gives theoretical meaning to a statement is not the attendant images and thoughts, but the possibility of deducing from it perceptual statements, in other words, the possibility of verification. To give sense to a statement the presence of images is not sufficient; it is not even necessary. We have no actual image of the electromagnetic field, nor even, I should say, of the gravitational field. Nevertheless the statements which physicists assert about these fields have a perfect sense, because perceptual statements are deducible from them. I by no means object to the statement just mentioned about a levitational field that we do not know how to imagine or conceive such a field. My only objection to that statement is that we are not told how to verify it.

2. Metaphysics

What we have been doing so far is *logical analysis*. Now we are going to apply these considerations not to statements of physics as before, but to statements of *metaphysics*. Thus our investigation belongs to *logic*, to the third of the three parts of philosophy spoken about before, but the *objects* of this investigation belong to the first part.

I will call *metaphysical* all those statements which claim to represent knowledge about something which is over or beyond all experience, e.g. about the real Essence of things, about Things in themselves, the Absolute, and such like. I do not include in metaphysics those theories—sometimes called metaphysical—whose object is to arrange the most general statements of the various regions of scientific knowledge in a well-ordered system; such theories belong actually to the field of empirical science, not of philosophy, however daring they may be. The sort of statements I wish to denote as metaphysical may most easily be made clear by some examples: "The Essence and Principle of the world is Water," said Thales; "Fire," said Heraclitus; "the Infinite," said Anaximander; "Number," said Pythagoras. "All things are nothing but shadows of eternal ideas which themselves are in a spaceless and timeless sphere," is a doctrine of Plato. From the monists we learn: "There is only one principle on which all that is, is founded"; but the dualists tell us: "There are two principles." The materialists say: "All that is, is in its essence material," but the spiritualists say: "All that is, is spiritual." To metaphysics (in our sense of the word) belong the principal doctrines of Spinoza, Schelling, Hegel, and—to give at least one name of the present time—Bergson.

Now let us examine this kind of statement from the point of view of *verifiability*. It is easy to realize that such statements are not verifiable. From the statement: "The Principle of the world is Water" we are not able to deduce any statement asserting any perceptions or feelings or experiences whatever which may be expected for the future. Therefore the statement, "The Principle of the world is Water," asserts nothing at all. It is perfectly analogous to the statement in the fictitious example above about the levitational field and therefore it has no more sense than that statement. The water-metaphysician—as we may call him—has no doubt many images connected with his doctrine; but they cannot give sense to the statement any more than they could in the case of the levitational field. Metaphysicians cannot avoid making their statements nonverifiable, because if they made them verifiable, the decision about the truth or falsehood of their doctrines would depend upon experience and therefore belong to the region of empirical science. This consequence they wish to avoid, because they pretend to teach knowledge which is of a higher level than that of empirical science. Thus they are compelled to cut all connection between their statements and experience; and precisely by this procedure they deprive them of any sense.

3. Problems of Reality

So far I have considered only examples of such statements as are usually called metaphysical. The judgment I have passed on these statements, namely, that they have no empirical sense, may perhaps appear not very astonishing, and even trivial. But it is to be feared that the reader will find it somewhat more difficult to agree when I now proceed to apply that judgment also to philosophical doctrines of the type usually called epistemological. I prefer to call them also metaphysical because of their similarity, in the point under consideration, to the statements usually so called. What I have in mind are the doctrines of realism, idealism, solipsism, positivism and the like, taken in their traditional form as asserting or denying the reality of something. The realist asserts the reality of the external world, the idealist denies it. The realist—usually at least—asserts also the reality of other minds, the solipsist—an especially radical idealist—denies it, and asserts that only his own mind or consciousness is real. Have these assertions sense?

Perhaps it may be said that assertions about the reality or unreality of something occur also in empirical science, where they are examined in an empirical way, and that therefore they must have sense. This is quite true. But we have to distinguish between two concepts of reality, one occurring in empirical statements and the other occurring in the philosophical statements just mentioned. When a zoologist asserts the reality of kangaroos, his assertion means that there are things of a certain sort which can be found and perceived at certain times and places; in other words that there are objects of a certain sort which are elements of the space-time-system of the physical world. This assertion is of course verifiable; by empirical investigation every zoologist arrives at a positive verification, independent of whether he is a realist or an idealist. Between the realist and the idealist there is full agreement as to the question of the reality of things of a specified sort, i.e., of the possibility of locating elements of that sort in the system of the physical world. The disagreement begins only when the question about the reality of the physical world as a whole is raised. But this question has no sense, because the reality of anything is nothing else than the possibility of its being placed in a certain system, in this case, in the space-time-system of the physical world, and such a question has sense only if it concerns elements or parts, not if it concerns the system itself.

The same result is obtained by applying the criterion explained before: the possibility of deducing perceptual statements. While from the assertion of the reality or the existence of kangaroos we *can* deduce perceptual statements, from the assertion of the reality of the physical world this is not possible; neither is it possible from the opposite assertion of the unreality of the physical world. Therefore both assertions have no empirical content—no sense at all. It is to be emphasized that this criticism of having no sense applies equally to the assertion of unreality. Sometimes the views of the *Vienna Circle* have been mistaken for a denial of the reality of the physical world, but we make no such denial. It is true that we reject the thesis of the reality of the physical world; but we do not reject it as false, but as having no sense, and its idealistic *anti-* thesis is subject to exactly the same rejection. We neither assert nor deny these theses, we reject the whole question.

All the considerations which apply to the question of the reality of the physical world apply also to the other philosophical questions of reality, e.g. the reality of other minds, the reality of the given, the reality of universals, the reality of qualities, the reality of relations, the reality of numbers, etc. If any philosophical thesis answering any of these questions positively or negatively is added to the system of scientific hypotheses, this system will not in the least become more effective; we shall not be able to make any further prediction as to future experiences. Thus all these philosophical theses are deprived of empirical content, of theoretical sense; they are pseudo-theses.

If I am right in this assertion, the philosophical problems of reality—as distinguished from the empirical problems of reality—have the same logical character as the problems (or rather, pseudo-problems) of transcendental metaphysics earlier referred to. For this reason I call those problems of reality not epistemological problems—as they usually are called—but metaphysical.

Among the metaphysical doctrines that have no theoretical sense I have also mentioned positivism, although the Vienna Circle is sometimes designated as positivistic. It is doubtful whether this designation is quite suitable for us. In any case we do not assert the thesis that only the given is real, which is one of the principal theses of traditional positivism. The name "logical positivism" seems more suitable, but this also can be misunderstood. At any rate it is important to realize that our doctrine is a logical one and has nothing to do with metaphysical theses of the reality or unreality of anything whatever. . . .

4. Ethics

One division of philosophy, which by some philosophers is considered the most important, has not been mentioned at all so far, namely, the philosophy of values, with its main branch, moral philosophy or *Ethics*. The word "Ethics" is used in two different senses. Sometimes a certain empirical investigation is called "Ethics," viz. psychological and sociological investigations about the actions of human beings, especially regarding the origin of these actions from feelings and volitions and their effects upon other people. Ethics in this sense is an empirical, scientific investigation; it belongs to empirical science rather than to philosophy. Fundamentally different from this is ethics in the second sense, as the philosophy of moral values or moral norms, which one can designate normative ethics. This is not an investigation of facts, but a pretended investigation of what is good and what is evil, what it is right to do and what it is wrong to do. Thus the purpose of this philosophical, or normative, ethics is to state norms for human action or judgments about moral values.

It is easy to see that it is merely a difference of formulation, whether we state a norm or a value judgment. A norm or rule has an imperative form, for instance: "Do not kill!" The corresponding value judgment would be: "Killing is evil." This difference of formulation has become practically very important, especially for the development of philosophical thinking. The rule, "Do not kill," has grammatically the imperative form and will therefore not be regarded as an assertion. But the value statement, "Killing is evil," although, like the rule it is merely an expression of a certain wish, has the grammatical form of a declarative sentence. Most philosophers have been deceived by this form into thinking that a value statement is really an assertive statement, and must be either true or false. Therefore they give reasons for their own value statements and try to disprove those of their opponents. But actually a value statement is nothing but a command in a misleading grammatical form. It may have effects upon the actions of men, and these effects may either be in accordance with our wishes or not; but it is neither true nor false. It does not assert anything and can neither be proved nor disproved.

This is revealed as soon as we apply to such statements our method of logical analysis. From the statement "Killing is evil" we cannot deduce any statement about future experiences. Thus this statement is not verifiable and has no theoretical sense, and the same thing is true of all other value statements.

Perhaps somebody will contend in opposition that the following statement is deducible: "If a person kills anybody he will have feelings of remorse." But this statement is in no way deducible from the statement "Killing is evil." It is deducible only from psychological statements about the character and the emotional reactions of the person. These statements are indeed verifiable and not without sense. They belong to psychology, not to philosophy; to psychological ethics (if one wishes to use this word), not to philosophical or normative ethics. The statements of normative ethics, whether they have the form of rules or the form of value statements, have no theoretical sense, are not scientific statements (taking the word scientific to mean any assertive statement).

To avoid misunderstanding it must be said that we do not at all deny the possibility of importance of a scientific investigation of value statements as well as of acts of valuation. Both of these are acts of individuals and are, like all other kinds of acts, possible objects of empirical investigation. Historians, psychologists, and sociologists may give analyses and causal explanations of them, and such historical and psychological statements about acts of valuation and about value statements are indeed meaningful scientific statements which belong to ethics in the first sense of this word. But the value statements themselves are here only objects of investigation; they are not statements in these theories, and have, here as elsewhere, no theoretical sense. Therefore we assign them to the realm of metaphysics.

5. Metaphysics as Expression

Now we have analysed the statements of metaphysics in a wide sense of this word, including not only transcendental metaphysics, but also the problems of philosophical reality and lastly normative ethics. Perhaps many will agree that the statements of all these kinds of metaphysics are not verifiable, i.e., that their truth cannot be examined by experience. And perhaps many will even grant that for this reason they have not the character of scientific statements. But when I say that they are without sense, assent will probably seem more difficult. Someone may object: these statements in the metaphysical books obviously have an effect upon the reader, and sometimes a very strong effect; therefore, they certainly *express* something, but nevertheless they have no sense, no theoretical content.

We have here to distinguish two functions of language, which we may call the expressive function and the representative or cognitive function. Almost all the conscious and unconscious movements of a person, including his linguistic utterances, express something of his feelings, his present mood, his temporary or permanent dispositions to reaction, and the like. Therefore, we may take almost all his movements and words as symptoms from which we can infer something about his feelings or his character. That is the expressive function of movements and words. But besides that, a certain portion of linguistic utterances (e.g. "this book is black"), as distinguished from other linguistic utterances and movements, has a second function: these utterances represent a certain state of affairs; they tell us that something is the case; they assert something, they predicate something, they judge something.

In special cases, this asserted state may be the same as that which is inferred from a certain expressive utterance; but even in such cases we must sharply distinguish between the assertion and the expression. If, for instance, somebody is laughing we may take this as a symptom of his merry mood; if, on the other hand, he tells us without laughing: "Now I am merry," we can learn from his words the same thing which we inferred in the first case from his laughing. Nevertheless, there is a fundamental difference between the laughter and the words: "I am merry now." This linguistic utterance *asserts* the merry mood, and therefore it is either true or false. The laughter does not assert merry mood but *expresses* it. It is neither true nor false, because it does not assert anything, although it may be either genuine or deceptive.

Now many linguistic utterances are analogous to laughing in that they have only an expressive function, no representative function. Examples of this are cries like "Oh, Oh" or, on a higher level, lyrical verses. The aim of a lyrical poem in which occur the words "sunshine" and "clouds," is not to inform us of certain meteorological facts, but to express certain feelings of the poet and to excite similar feelings in us. A lyrical poem has no assertive sense, no theoretical sense, it does not contain knowledge.

The meaning of our anti-metaphysical thesis may now be more clearly explained. This thesis asserts that metaphysical statements—like lyrical verses—have only an expressive function, but no representative function. Metaphysical statements are neither true nor false, because they assert nothing, they contain neither knowledge nor error, they lie completely outside the field of knowledge, of theory, outside the discussion of truth or falsehood. But they are, like laughing, lyrics, and music, expressive. They express not so much temporary feelings as permanent emotional or volitional dispositions. Thus, for instance, a metaphysical system of monism may be an expression of an even and harmonious mode of life, a dualistic system may be an expression of the emotional state of someone who takes life as an eternal struggle; an ethical system of rigorism may be expressive of a strong sense of duty or perhaps of a desire to rule severely. Realism is often a symptom of the type of constitution called by psychologists extroverted, which is characterized by easily forming connections with men and things; idealism, of an opposite constitution, the so-called introverted type, which has a tendency to withdraw from the unfriendly world and to live within its own thoughts and fancies.

Thus we find a great similarity between metaphysics and lyrics. But there is one decisive difference between them. Both have no representative function, no theoretical content. A metaphysical statement, however—as distinguished from a lyrical verse—seems to have such a content, and by this not only is the reader deceived, but the metaphysician himself. He believes that in his metaphysical treatise he has asserted something, and is led by this into argument and polemics against the statements of some other metaphysician. A poet, however, does not assert that the verses of another are wrong or erroneous; he usually contents himself with calling them bad.

The non-theoretical character of metaphysics would not be in itself a defect; all arts have this non-theoretical character without thereby losing their high value for personal as well as for social life. The danger lies in the *deceptive* character of metaphysics; it gives the illusion of knowledge without actually giving any knowledge. This is the reason why we reject it.

6. Psychology

When we have eliminated metaphysical problems and doctrines from the region of knowledge or theory, there remain still two kinds of philosophical questions: psychological and logical. Now we shall eliminate the psychological questions also, not from the region of knowledge, but from philosophy. Then, finally, philosophy will be reduced to logic alone (in a wide sense of this word).

Psychological questions and statements are certainly not without sense. From such statements we can deduce other statements about future experiences and by their help we can verify the psychological statements. But the statements of psychology belong to the region of empirical science in just the same way as do the statements of chemistry, biology, history and the like. The character of psychology is by no means more philosophical than that of the other sciences mentioned. When we look at the historical development of the sciences we see that philosophy has been the mother of them all. One science after another has been detached from philosophy and has become an independent science. Only in our time has the umbilical cord between psychology and philosophy been cut. Many philosophers have not yet realized quite clearly that psychology is no longer an embryo, but an independent organism, and that psychological questions have to be left to empirical research.

Of course, we have no objection to connecting psychological and logical investigations, any more than to connecting investigations of any scientific kind. We reject only the confusion of the two kinds of questions. We demand that they should be clearly distinguished even where in practice they are combined. The confusion sometimes consists in dealing with a logical question as if it were a psychological one. This mistake—called psychologism—leads to the opinion that logic is a science concerning thinking, that is, either concerning the actual operation of thinking or the rules according to which thinking should proceed. But, as a matter of fact, the investigation of operations of thinking as they really occur is a task for psychology and has nothing to do with logic. And learning how to think aright is what we do in every other science as well as in logic. In astronomy we learn how to think aright about stars; in logic we learn how to think aright about the special objects of logic. What these special objects of logic are, will be seen in the next chapter. In any case, thinking is not an object of logic, but of psychology.

Psychological questions concern all kinds of so-called mental events, all kinds of sensations, feelings, thoughts, images, etc., whether they are conscious or unconscious. These questions of psychology can be answered only by experience, not by philosophising.

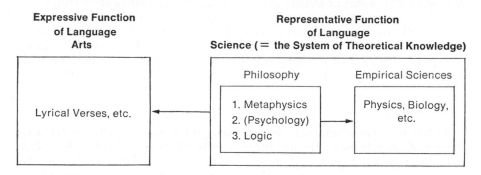

7. Logical Analysis

The only proper task of *philosophy* is *logical analysis*. And now the principal question to be answered here will be: *"What is logical analysis?"* In our considerations so far we have already practised logical analysis: we have tried to determine the character of physical hypotheses, of metaphysical statements (or rather, pseudo-statements), of psychological statements. And now we have to apply logical analysis to logical analysis itself; we have to determine the character of the statements of logic, of those statements which are the results of logical analysis.

The opinion that metaphysical statements have no sense because they do not concern any facts, has already been expressed by Hume. He writes in the last chapter of his "Enquiry Concerning Human Understanding" (published in the year 1748) as follows: "It seems to me, that the only objects of the abstract sciences or of demonstration, are quantity and number. . . . All other enquiries of men regard only matter of fact and existence; and these are evidently incapable of demonstration. . . . When we run over libraries, persuaded of these principles, what havoc must we make? If we take in our hand any volume, of divinity or school metaphysics, for instance; let us ask, Does it contain any abstract reasoning concerning quantity or number? No. Does it contain any experimental reasoning concerning matter of fact and existence? No. Commit it then to the flames: for it can contain nothing but sophistry and illusion." We agree with this view of Hume, which says—translated into our terminology—that only the statements of mathematics and empirical science have sense, and that all other statements are without sense.

But now it may perhaps be objected: "How about your own statements? In consequence of your view your own writings, including this book, would be without sense, for they are neither mathematical nor empirical, that is, verifiable by experience." What answer can be given to this objection? What is the character of my statements and in general of the statements of logical analysis? This question is decisive for the consistency of the view which has been explained here.

An answer to the objection is given by Wittgenstein in his book *Tractatus Logico-Philosophicus*. This author has developed most radically the view that the statements of metaphysics are shown by logical analysis to be without sense. How does he reply to the criticism that in that case his own statements are also without sense? He replies by agreeing with it. He writes: "*The result of philosophy is not a number* of 'philosophical statements,' but to make statements clear" (p. 77). "My statements are elucidatory in this way: he who understands me finally recognizes them as senseless, when he has climbed out through them, on them, over them. (He must so to speak throw away the ladder after he has climbed up on it.) He must surmount these statements; then he sees the world rightly. Whereof one cannot speak, thereof one must be silent" (p. 189).

I, as well as my friends in the Vienna Circle, owe much to Wittgenstein, especially as to the analysis of metaphysics. But on the point just mentioned I cannot agree with him. In the first place, he seems to me to be inconsistent in what he does. He tells us that one cannot make philosophical statements and that whereof one cannot speak, thereof one must be silent; and then instead of keeping silent, he writes a whole philosophical book. Secondly, I do not agree with his assertion that all his statements are quite as much without sense as metaphysical statements are. My opinion is that a great number of his statements (unfortunately not all of them) have in fact sense; and that the same is true for all statements of logical analysis.

It will be the purpose of the following chapters to give reasons for this positive answer to the question about the character of philosophical statements, to show a way of formulating the results of logical analysis, a way not exposed to the objection mentioned, and thus to exhibit an *exact method of philosophy*.

Addendum (1961) to Section I, 4: Ethics (From a letter to Ray Lepley, May 1963).

I should like to add a few remarks to my earlier formulations on ethics in *Philosophy and Logical Syntax* (1935), in order to clarify my position.

Moral value statements are interpreted by some philosophers as statements concerning the probable consequences of the acts in question. To call a kind of behavior good or bad is meant as saying that it is a suitable or unsuitable way to a certain aim. For instance, "killing is evil" may be meant as saying: "killing is not a suitable way to further a harmonious community life." On the basis of any interpretation of this kind, e.g., in terms of instrumental function or of human interests or the like, a value statement has obviously factual, cognitive content.

On the other hand, suppose someone refuses to give to his value statements any interpretation which makes them either analytic or subject to test by empirical evidence; perhaps he says explicitly, as some philosophers do, that a certain act is good not because of any consequences it may have but merely by its intrinsic nature. Value statements of this kind may be called absolute, in contrast to those mentioned before which are relative to certain aims. The critical judgment of logical empiricism is directed only against absolute value statements, such as occur frequently in works of European philosophers, not against the relative ones, which prevail in philosophical discussions in this country.

Since the word "meaning" is often used in a wider sense, I wish to emphasize that the kind of meaning which we deny for absolute value statements is only cognitive (theoretical, assertive) meaning. These statements certainly have expressive, especially emotive and motivative meaning; this fact is of great importance for their social effectiveness.

3

PHILOSOPHICAL PERPLEXITY

John Wisdom

1. *Philosophical Statements Are Really Verbal.*—I have inquired elsewhere the real nature of philosophical requests such as 'Can we know what is going on in someone else's mind?' 'Can we really know the causes of our sensations?' 'What is a chair?' and of philosophical answers such as 'We can never really know the causes of our sensations', 'A chair is nothing but our sensations', or 'A chair is something over and above our sensations', 'The goodness of a man, of a picture, of an argument is something over and above our feelings of approval and over and above those features of the man, the picture or the argument, which "determine" its goodness'. There is no time to repeat the inquiry here and I have to say dogmatically:

A philosophical answer is really a verbal recommendation in response to a request which is really a request with regard to a sentence which lacks a conventional use whether there occur situations which could conventionally be described by it. The description, for example 'I know directly what is going on in Smith's mind', is not a jumble like 'Cat how is up', nor is it in conflict with conventional usage like 'There are two white pieces and three black so there are six pieces on the board'. It just lacks a conventional usage. To call both 'Can 2 + 3 = 6?' and 'Can I know what is going on in the minds of others?' nonsensical questions serves to bring out the likeness between them. But if one were to deny that there is a difference between them it would be an instance of that disrespect for other people which we may platitudinously say, so often damages philosophical work. A disrespect which blinds one to the puzzles they raise—in this instance the puzzle of the philosophical *can* which somehow seems between 'Can 2 + 3 make 6?' and 'Can terriers catch hares?' Compare 'Can persons be in two places at once?' 'Do we have unconscious wishes?' 'Can you play chess without the queen?' (W).[1]

John Wisdom, "Philosophical Perplexity," *Proceedings of the Aristotelian Society,* XXXVII (1936–1937), 71–88. Reprinted by courtesy of the Editor of The Aristotelian Society.
[1] Wittgenstein has not read this over-compressed paper and I warn people against supposing it a closer imitation of Wittgenstein than it is. On the other hand I can hardly exaggerate the debt I owe to him and how much of the good in this work is his—not

Even to say that 'I know directly what is going on in Smith's mind' is *meaningless,* is dangerous, especially if you have just said that 'There are two white pieces and three black so there are six' is meaningless.

It is not even safe to say that 'I know directly what is going on in Smith's mind' lacks a use or meaning and leave it at that. For though it has no meaning it tends to have a meaning, like 'All whifley was the tulgey wood', though of course it is unlike this last example in the important respect that it does not lack a meaning because its constituent words are unknown. Nor does it lack meaning because its syntax is unknown. This makes it puzzling and makes it resemble the logical case. It is clear that for these reasons it would be even more illuminating and more misleading to say that 'God exists' and 'Men are immortal' are meaningless—especially just after saying $2 + 3 = 6$ is meaningless.

2. *Philosophical Statements Are Not Verbal.*—I have said that philosophers' questions and theories are really verbal. But if you like we will not say this or we will say also the contradictory.[2] For of course (*a*) philosophic statements usually have not a verbal air. On the contrary they have a non-verbal air like 'A fox's brush is really a tail'. (W). And their non-verbal air is not an unimportant feature of them because on it very much depends their puzzlingness.

And (*b*) though really verbal a philosopher's statements have not a merely verbal point. Unlike many statements the primary point of uttering them is not to convey the information they convey but to do something else. Consequently all attempts to explain their peculiar status by explaining the peculiar nature of their subject-matter, fail. For their subject-matter is not peculiar; their truth or falsity, in so far as these are appropriate to them at all, is fixed by facts about words, e.g. Goodness is not approval by the majority, because 'The majority sometimes approve what is bad' is not self-contradictory. But the point of philosophical statements is peculiar. It is the illumination of the ultimate structure of facts, i.e. the relations between different categories of being or (we must be in the mode) the relations between different sub-languages within a language.

The puzzles of philosophical propositions, of fictional propositions, general propositions, negative propositions, propositions about the future, propositions about the past, even the puzzle about psychological propositions, are not removed by explaining the peculiar nature of the subject-matter of the sentences in which they are expressed but by reflecting upon the peculiar manner in which those sentences work. Mnemonic slogan: It's not the stuff, it's the style that stupefies.

3. *The Divergence of Point from Content.*—The divergence of point from content which is found in necessary and near necessary propositions can be explained here only briefly.

Suppose a decoder, though still utterly ignorant of the meaning of both of two expressions 'monarchy' and 'set of persons ruled by the same king', has after prolonged investigation come to the conclusion that they mean the

---

only in the treatment of this philosophical difficulty and that but in the matter of how to do philosophy. As far as possible I have put a W against examples I owe to him. It must not be assumed that they are used in a way he would approve.

[2] I do not wish to suggest that Wittgenstein would approve of *this* sort of talk nor that he would disapprove of it.

same in a certain code. He will say to his fellow-decoder ' "Monarchy" means the same as "set of persons ruled by the same king" '. The translator, and the philosopher also, may say the same. They all use the same form of words because what they say is the same. But the point of what they say is very different. The decoder's point can be got by anyone who knows the meaning of 'means the same as'; the translator does what he wants with the sentence only if his hearer knows the meaning either of 'monarchy' or of 'set of persons ruled by the same king'; the philosopher does what he wants with the sentence only if his hearer already uses, i.e. understands, i.e. knows the meaning of, *both* 'monarchy' and 'set of persons ruled by the same king'. This condition makes the case of the philosopher curious; for it states that he can do what he wants with the sentence only if his hearer already knows what he is telling him. But this is true in the required sense. The philosopher draws attention to what is already known with a view to giving insight into the structure of what 'monarchy', say, means, i.e. bringing into connection the sphere in which the one expression is used with that in which the other is. Compare the man who says 'I should have the change from a pound after spending five shillings on a book, one and sevenpence-halfpenny on stamps and two and twopence-halfpenny at the grocer's, so I should have eleven shillings and twopence'. This is Moore's example and I beg attention for it. It is tremendously illuminating in the *necessary synthetic* group of puzzles and in a far, far wider field than this, because it illuminates the use of 'means the same'—a phrase which stops so many. When on first going to France I learned the exchange rate for francs, do I know the meaning of 'worth 100 francs' or do I come to know this after staying three weeks?

The philosopher is apt to say 'A monarchy is a set of people under a king' rather than ' "Monarchy" means the same as "a set of people under a king" '. By using the former sentence he intimates his point. Now shall we say 'A monarchy is a set of people under a king' means the same as ' "Monarchy" means "a set of people under a king" ' or not? My answer is 'Say which you like. But if you say "Yes" be careful, etc., and if you say "No" be careful, etc.'

If we decide to describe the difference between the two as a difference of meaning we must not say that the difference in meaning is a difference of subjective intention, nor that it is a difference of emotional significance merely. For these are not adequate accounts of the difference between the two—and not an adequate account of the difference between the use of '3 plus 5 plus 8' and the use of '16'.

4. *Philosophy, Truth, Misleadingness and Illumination.*—Now that we have seen that the philosopher's intention is to bring out relations between categories of being, between spheres of language, we shall be more prepared to allow that false statements about the usage of words may be philosophically very useful and even adequate provided their falsity is realized and there is no confusion about what they are being used for.

The nature of the philosopher's intention explains how it is that one may call a philosophical theory such as *A proposition is a sentence*, certainly false, and yet feel that to leave one's criticism at that is to attend to the letter and not the spirit of the theory criticized.

The nature of the philosopher's intention explains also how it is that one cannot say of a philosopher's theory that it is false when he introduces it in his own terminology, while yet one often feels that such theories are somehow philosophically bad. Thus (W) suppose the word 'sense-datum' has never been used before and that someone says 'When Jones sees a rabbit, has an illusion of a rabbit, has an hallucination of a rabbit, dreams of a rabbit, he has a sense-datum of a rabbit'. One cannot protest that this is false, since no statement has been made, only a recommendation. But the recommendation purports to be enlightening and one may well protest if it is, on the contrary, misleading. This particular recommendation is liable to suggest that sense-data are a special sort of thing, *extremely* thin coloured pictures, and thus liable to raise puzzles, such as 'How are sense-data related to material things?' We can abuse a philosopher as much as we like if we use the right adjectives. *Good is an ultimate predicate* is useless, *A proposition is a subsistent entity* is useless and pretentious,[3] *We can never know the real cause of our sensations* is misleading. And we can praise him although he speaks falsely or even nonsensically. People have considered whether it is true that 'an event is a pattern of complete, particular, specific facts and a complete, particular, specific fact is an infinitely thin slice out of an event.'[4]

You may say 'How absurd of them since the statement is nonsense'. Certainly the statement is nonsense and so, if you like, it was absurd of them. But it was better than saying it was nonsense and ignoring it. Suppose I say 'The thoroughbred is a neurotic woman on four legs'. This is nonsense, but it is not negligible.[5]

5. *Provocation and Pacification.*—So far, however, little or nothing has been said to explain what sort of things make a philosophical statement misleading and what make it illuminating. Only a short answer is possible here.

In the first place there is the misleading feature which nearly all philosophical statements have—a non-verbal air. The philosopher *laments* that we can never really know what is going on in someone else's mind, that we can never really know the causes of our sensations, that inductive conclusions are never really justified. He laments these things as if he can dream of another world where we can see our friends and tables face to face, where scientists can justify their conclusions and terriers can catch hares. This enormous source of confusion we cannot study now.

Secondly philosophical statements mislead when by the use of like expressions for different cases, they suggest likenesses which do not exist, and by the use of different expressions for like cases, they conceal likenesses which do exist.

Philosophical theories are illuminating in a corresponding way, namely when they suggest or draw attention to a terminology which reveals likenesses and differences concealed by ordinary language.

I want to stress the philosophical usefulness of metaphysical surprises such as 'We can never really know the causes of our sensations', 'We can never

---

[3] Neither of these theories is entirely useless. They are for one thing good antitheses to the naturalistic error.

[4] *Problems of Mind and Matter,* p. 32.

[5] The matter can be put in terms of truth and falsehood. A philosophical theory involves an explicit claim, an equation, and an implicit claim that the equation is not misleading and is illuminating. The explicit claim may be false and the implicit true on one or both counts, or vice versa.

know the real causes of our sensations', 'Inductive conclusions are never really justified', 'The laws of mathematics are really rules of grammar'. I believe that too much fun has been made of philosophers who say this kind of thing. Remember what Moore said about 1924—words to this effect: When a philosopher says that really something is so we are warned that what he says is really so is not so really. With horrible ingenuity Moore can rapidly reduce any metaphysical theory to a ridiculous story. For he is right, they are false—only there *is* good in them, poor things. This shall be explained.

Wittgenstein allows importance to these theories. They are for him expressions of deep-seated puzzlement. It is an important part of the treatment of a puzzle to develop it to the full.

But this is not enough. Wittgenstein allows that the theories are philosophically important not merely as specimens of the whoppers philosophers can tell. But he too much represents them as merely symptoms of linguistic confusion. I wish to represent them as also symptoms of linguistic penetration.

Wittgenstein gives the impression that philosophical remarks either express puzzlement or if not are remarks such as Wittgenstein himself makes with a view to curing puzzlement.

This naturally gives rise to the question 'If the proper business of philosophy is the removal of puzzlement, would it not be best done by giving a drug to the patient which made him entirely forget the statements puzzling him or at least lose his uneasy feelings?'

This of course will never do. And what we say about the philosopher's purposes must be changed so that it shall no longer seem to lead to such an absurd idea.

The philosopher's purpose is to gain a grasp of the relations between different categories of being, between expressions used in *different manners*.[6] He is confused about what he wants and he is confused by the relations between the expressions, so he is very often puzzled. But only such treatment of the puzzles as increases a grasp of the relations between different categories of being is philosophical. And not all the philosopher's statements are either complaints of puzzlement or pacificatory. Philosophers who say 'We never know the real causes of our sensations', 'Only my sensations are real', often bring out these 'theories' with an air of triumph (with a misleading air of empirical discovery indeed). True the things they say are symptoms of confusion even if they are not of puzzlement. But they are also symptoms of penetration, of noticing what is not usually noticed. Philosophical progress has two aspects, provocation and pacification.

6. *Example of the Pointless Doubts: (a) How Misleading They Are.*—Let us consider this with examples. Take first the philosopher who says to the plain man: 'We do not really know that there is cheese on the table; for might not all the sense evidence suggest this and yet there be no cheese— remember what happened at Madame Tussaud's'.

Our assertion with confidence that there is cheese on the table or our assertion that we know that there is cheese on the table raises at last these three puzzles: (1) *the category puzzle*, which finds expression in 'We ought

6 See 'different level' in *Proc. Aris. Soc.* Supp. Vol. XIII, p. 66.

not to speak of a cheese (of the soul) but of bundles of sense-data'; (2) *the knowledge puzzle*, which finds expression in 'We ought not to say "I know there is cheese on the table" but "Very, very probably there is cheese on the table" '; (3) *the justification puzzle,* which finds expression in 'Empirical conclusions are not really justified'.

We cannot here speak of all these. We are considering (2) the *knowledge* or *pointless doubt puzzle*. There is a group of pointless doubt puzzles including the following: 'We don't really know that there is cheese on the table'; 'We ought to say only "It is probable that there is cheese on the table" '; 'It is improper to say "I know that there is cheese on the table" '; 'It would be well if we prefixed every remark about material things with "probably" '.

All these suggestions are misleading—they all suggest that it has been discovered that we have been over-confident about material things. They should have slightly different treatment but I have only just *realized* this multiplicity. Let us take the puzzle in the crude form 'Couldn't there be no cheese here although all the sense-evidence suggests there is?'

Wittgenstein explains that this sentence though of the verbal form we associate with doubt and though it may be uttered with the intonation, expression and gestures we associate with doubt is not *used* as a sentence expressing doubt. To utter it is to raise a pseudo doubt. People say 'We ought not to say "There *is* cheese on the table" but "Probably there is cheese on the table" or "The sense-evidence suggests ever so strongly that there is cheese on the table". For whatever we do we never observe a cheese, we have to rely upon our senses. And we may be suffering from a joint hallucination of all the senses or a consistent dream. Remember how people are deceived at Madame Tussaud's. And we may see and touch cheesy patches, smell cheesy smells, obtain cheesy pictures from cameras and cheesy reactions from mice and yet the stuff to-morrow be soap in our mouth. And then to-morrow we shall say "Yesterday we were mistaken". So our "knowledge" to-day that there is cheese here is not real knowledge. Every one ought really to whisper "Possibly hallucinatory" after *every* sentence about material things however much he has made sure that he is right'.

What those who recommend this should notice is how not merely unusual but pointless a use of words they recommend. As language is at present used, I raise my hungry friends' hopes if I say 'There is cheese on the table', and I damp them if I add 'unless it is hallucinatory'. But this additional clause has its effect only because I do *not always* use it. If a parent adds 'be very careful' to everything he says to a child he will soon find his warnings ineffective. If I prefix every statement about material things with 'probably' this doubt-raiser will soon cease to frighten hungry friends, that is cease to function as it now does. Consequently in order to mark those differences which I now mark by saying in one case 'Probably that is cheese on the table' and in another case 'I know that is cheese on the table', I shall have to introduce a new notation, one to do the work the old did. 'To do the work the old did!' that is, to claim what I formerly claimed with 'know!'

It may now be said 'In the ordinary use of "know" we may know that that is cheese on the table, but this knowledge is not real knowledge'.

This gives the misleading idea that the philosopher has envisaged some kind of knowing which our failing faculties prevent us from attaining. Terriers cannot catch hares, men cannot really know the causes of their sensations. Nothing of the kind, however. For when we say to the philosopher 'Go on, describe this real knowledge, tell us what stamp of man you want and we will see if we can buy or breed one' then he can never tell us.

It may now be said, 'No, no, the point is this: There is some inclination to use[7] "know" strictly so that we do not know that insulin cures diabetes, that the sun will rise to-morrow, because these propositions are only probable inferences from what we have observed. There is some inclination to use "know" only when what is known is observed or is entailed by something known for certain. Now you do not know in this sense that you will not have to correct yourself to-morrow and say "I was mistaken yesterday, that was not cheese", since nothing you know for certain to-day is incompatible with this. And if you do not know but what you may have to correct yourself to-morrow you do not know that you are right to-day.'

But what is meant by 'certain'? I should claim to know for certain that that is cheese on the table now. And as the objector rightly points out this entails that I shall not have to correct myself to-morrow. I therefore know in the strict sense that I shall not have to correct myself to-morrow.

It will be said that it is not *absolutely* certain that that is cheese on the table. But I should reply that it is.

It will be said that it is not *senseless to doubt* that that is cheese on the table, not even after the most exhaustive tests. I should reply that it is.

But, of course, by now I see what the sceptic is driving at. It is not senseless to doubt that that is cheese on the table, in the sense in which it is senseless to doubt 'I am in pain', 'I hear a buzzing'—not even after the most exhaustive tests—indeed the exhaustive tests make no difference to this. For, in this sense, it is not senseless to doubt that that is cheese on the table provided only that 'He says that that is cheese but perhaps he is mistaken' has a use in English. You see, 'He says he is in pain, but perhaps he is mistaken' has no use in English. Hence we may be 'absolutely certain' that he is not mistaken[8] about his pain, in the very special sense that 'He is mistaken' makes no sense in this connection.

Thus the sceptic's pretended doubts amount to pointing out that, unlike statements descriptive of sensations, statements about material things make sense with 'perhaps he is mistaken'. And the sceptic proposes to mark this by an extraordinary use of 'know' and 'probably'. He proposes that we should not say that we know that that is cheese on the table unless it is entailed by statements with regard to which a doubt is not merely out of the question but unintelligible, i.e. such that where S is P is one of them then 'S is P unless I am mistaken' raises a titter like 'I am in pain unless I am mistaken'. 'That is cheese on the table' is not such a statement and so of course it does not follow from such statements—otherwise a doubt with regard to it would be unintelligible, i.e. it would be absolutely certain in the strict, philosophic sense.

The sceptic's doubts become then a recommendation to use 'know' only

---

[7] Another form would be: 'It is proper' as opposed to 'usual' to use 'know' so that, etc.

[8] Of course he may be *lying*.

with statements about sense-experience and mathematics and to prefix *all* other statements with 'probably'.[9]

This is very different talk and much less misleading. But still it is misleading unless accompanied by the explanation given above of the astounding certainty of statements about sense-experience. Even with the explanation the suggestion is highly dangerous, involving as it does a new and *'manner–indicating'* use of the familiar words 'know' and 'probable'. Without the explanation it suggests that there is a difference in degree of certainty between statements about material things and statements about sense-data, a difference in certainty dependent upon their subject-matter, in a sense analogous to that in which we say 'I am certain about what happened in Hyde Park—I was there—but I am not certain about what happened in Spain—I was not an eye-witness'. This suggests that I know what it would be like to be an eye-witness of cheese, but am in fact unfortunately obliged to *rely upon the testimony of* my senses.

Now the difference between statements about sense-experiences and statements about material things is not at all like this. The difference is not one of subject-matter (stuff) but of a different manner of use (style). And statements about sense-experiences are certain only because it makes no sense to say that they may be wrong.[10] Notice the connection between 'He says he is in pain but I think he is mistaken' and 'He cries "Ow!" but I think he is mistaken'. The difference between sense-statements and thing-statements cannot be adequately explained here. And consequently the full misleadingness of such a use of 'probably' as is recommended in what we may call the last form of the pseudo-doubt, cannot be adequately explained here.

But I hope I have said enough to bring out in good measure the misleadingness of saying such things as 'O dear, we can never know the causes of our sensations', and even 'It would be philosophically excellent to put "probably" before all statements about material things'.

7. *Example of the Pointless Doubts: (b) How Importantly Illuminating They Are.*—But though the recommended use of 'probably' would be pointless as a cautionary clause and would thus be extremely misleading, the recommendation to use it so is not pointless, is not prompted wholly by confusion, but partly by penetration. The philosopher says to the plain man 'You do not really know that that is a cheese on the table'. We have pacified those who are opposed to this statement by bringing out the sources of their reluctance to agree with it. But the philosopher must pacify everyone and we must now pacify those philosophers who are pleased with it, and complete the pacification of those who are puzzled by it, being tempted to deny it and at the same time tempted to assert it. What *is* the point behind the misleading statement 'We can never know statements about material things'? The answer has been given already by the method of forcing reformulations. But we may now approach the answer by a different route. Under what circumstances are such things usually said?

---

[9] Compare the tendency to use 'what ought to be done' irrevocably. People who do this lament thus: 'What one ought to do is always for the best, but unfortunately we never know what we really ought to do'. Others lament thus: 'We can know what we ought to do but unfortunately this does not always turn out for the best'.

[10] This, I realize, stands very much in need of pacifying explanation.

It is when after considering hallucinations, illusions, etc., one wishes to emphasize (1) the likeness between such cases and cases in which there was 'something really there', and to emphasize the continuity between (*a*) cases in which one says 'I think that is cheese on the table', 'I believe that is a real dagger', 'Probably that is a snake, not a branch' and (*b*) cases in which one says 'That *is* cheese on the table', 'I found that it *was* a snake'; and to emphasize (2) the unlikeness between even so well assured a statement as 'This is my thumb' and such a statement as 'I see a pinkish patch', 'I feel a softish patch', 'I am in pain'.

It is not at all easy at first to see how in being revocable and correctable by others the most assured statement about a thing is more like the most precarious statement about another thing than it is to a statement descriptive of one's sensations. Ordinary language conceals these things because in ordinary language we speak both of some favourable material-thing-statements and of statements about our sensations, as certain, while we speak of other statements about material things as merely probable. This leads to pseudo-laments about the haunting uncertainty of even the best material-thing-statements and pseudo-congratulations upon the astounding certainty of statements about our sensations.

We are all, when our attention is drawn to those cases so often described in which it looks for all the world as if our friend is standing in the room although he is dying two thousand miles away, or in which we think we see a banana and it turns out to be a reflection in a greengrocer's mirror, we are all, in such cases, inclined to say 'Strictly we ought always to add "unless it is a queer looking stick and not a banana, or a reflection or a hallucination or an illusion" '.[11] We do not stop to consider what would happen if we did always add this. Horrified at the deceptions our senses have practised upon us we feel we must abuse them somehow and so we say that they never *prove* anything, that we never *know* what is based on them.

The continuity and the difference which are concealed by ordinary language would be no longer concealed but marked if we used 'probably' in the way recommended. But what an unfortunate way of obtaining this result! And in what a misleading way was the recommendation made! I do not really know that this is a thumb. The huntsman's coat is not really pink. A fox's brush is really a tail. (W).

8. *Other Examples.*—Now many other examples should be given. 'What is a mathematical proposition?' 'Do inductive arguments give any probability to their conclusions?' These other puzzles should be re-created; the temptations to give the answers which have been given should be re-created. But this cannot be done in this paper. Without bringing up the puzzles and temptations the following accounts are half dead, but I offer them for what they are worth.

Take 'The laws of mathematics and logic are really rules of grammar'. With this instructive incantation people puzzle themselves to death. Is it or isn't it true? And if false what amendment will give us the truth? If not rules then what? The answer is 'They are what they are, etc. Is a donkey a sort of horse but with *very* long ears?' People are puzzled because of course it isn't true that the laws of mathematics are rules of grammar (more obvious still

---

[11] Then every statement would be tautologous but *absolutely* certain!

that they are not commands). And yet they cannot bring themselves to lose
the advantages of this falsehood. For this falsehood draws attention to (1) an
unlikeness and (2) a likeness concealed by ordinary language; (1) an unlikeness to the laws of hydraulics and an unlikeness in this unlikeness to the
unlikeness between the laws of hydraulics and those of aeronautics; for it is
an unlikeness not of subject-matter but of manner of functioning—and (2) a
likeness but not an exact likeness to the functioning of rules.

Again 'Inductive arguments do not really give any probability to their
conclusions' gives the misleading idea that the scientists have been found out
at last, that our confidence in our most careful research workers is entirely
misplaced, their arguments being no better than those of the savage.
Nothing of the kind of course. What is at the back of this lament is this: In
ordinary language we speak of Dr. So and so's experiment with a group of
100 children whose teeth improved after six months' extra calcium as having
very much increased the probability of the proposition that bad teeth are
due to calcium deficiency. We also say that my having drawn 90 white
balls from a bag which we know to contain 100 balls, each either white or
black, has very much increased the probability of the proposition that all the
balls in that bag are white. We even speak numerically in connection with
empirical probability—we not only argue *a priori* and say 'There were six
runners, there are now only five, we still know nothing of any of them, so it
is now 4—1 against the dog from trap 1' but we also argue empirically and
say 'It was 5—1 against the dog from trap 1; but I hear a rumour that each
of the others has been provided with a cup of tea, and I think we may now
take 4—1 against him'.

The similarity in the way we speak of these cases leads us when asked how
empirical arguments give probability to their conclusions to try to assimilate
them to the formal cases, balls in bags, dice, etc. But when this attempt is
made it begins to appear that the investigation of nature is much less like the
investigation of balls in a bag than one is at first apt to think.

At the same time is revealed the shocking continuity between the scientist's arguments by the method of difference and the savage's *post hoc ergo
propter hoc*,[12] between the method of agreement and the reflexes of rats,
and struck by the difference and the continuity and how they are concealed
by ordinary language we provoke attention to them with 'Even the best
established scientific results are nothing but specially successful superstitions'. We say this although we have made no shocking discovery of
scientists faking figures, although the scientist's reasons for his belief in
insulin still differ from my landlady's reasons for belief in Cure-all, in
exactly the way which, in the ordinary use of language, makes us call the
one belief scientifically grounded and the other a superstition. Similarly we
may say, having seen a butterfly die or been told the age of an oak 'The
strongest of us have really only a short time to live'. We say this although
we have made no discovery of impending disaster, or we may say 'Man is
nothing but a complicated parasite' when we watch the arrival of the 9.5 at
the Metropolis.

[12] See Keynes, *A Treatise on Probability*.

CONCLUSION

The plain man has come to expect of philosophers paradoxical, provoking statements such as 'We can never really know the causes of our sensations', 'Causation is really nothing more than regular sequence', 'Inductive conclusions are really nothing but lucky superstitions', 'The laws of logic are ultimately rules of grammar'. Philosophers know that the statements are provocative; this is why they so often put in some apologetic word such as 'really' or 'ultimately'.

These untruths persist. This is not merely because they are symptoms of an intractable disorder but because they are philosophically useful. The curious thing is that their philosophical usefulness depends upon their paradoxicalness and thus upon their falsehood. They are false because they are needed where ordinary language fails, though it must not be supposed that they are or should be in some perfect language. They are in a language not free from the same sort of defects as those from the effects of which they are designed to free us.

To invent a special word to describe the status of, for example, mathematical propositions would do no good. There is a phrase already, 'necessary yet synthetic'. It is, of course, perfectly true that mathematical propositions are 'necessary synthetics'—it should be true since the expression was made to measure. True but no good. We are as much inclined to ask 'What are necessary synthetic propositions?' as we were to ask 'What are mathematical propositions?' 'What is an instinct?' An innate disposition certainly. But philosophically that answer is useless. No—what is wanted is some device for bringing out the relations between the manner in which mathematical (or dispositional) sentences are used and the manners in which others are used—so as to give their place on the language map. This cannot be done with a plain answer, a single statement. We may try opposite falsehoods or we may say, 'Be careful that this expression "mathematical proposition" does not suggest certain analogies at the expense of others. Do not let it make you think that the difference between mathematical propositions and others is like that between the propositions of hydraulics and those of aeronautics. Do notice how like to rules, etc., and yet, etc.'

If you will excuse a suspicion of smartness: Philosophers should be continually trying to say what cannot be said.

Further References

Ayer, A. J. *The Concept of a Person.* London: Macmillan, 1963. Chap. 1.
——. *The Problem of Knowledge.* Harmondsworth: Penguin Books, 1956. Chap. 1.*
Black, Max. "Philosophical Analysis," *Proceedings of the Aristotelian Society,* XXXIII (1932–1933), 237–258.

Copleston, F. C. *A History of Philosophy.* London: Burns & Oates, 1946–1965. 8 vols.†
——. "Philosophical Knowledge." In H. D. Lewis (ed.). *Contemporary British Philosophy.* Third Series. London: Allen & Unwin, 1956.

* Paperback edition.   † Also available in a paperback edition.

Feigl, Herbert. "Logical Empiricism." In Herbert Feigl and Wilfrid Sellars (eds.). *Readings in Philosophical Analysis.* New York: Appleton-Century-Crofts, 1949.

Johnstone, Henry W., Jr. *Philosophical Argument.* University Park, Pa.: Pennsylvania State University Press, 1959.

————— (ed.). *What Is Philosophy?* New York: Macmillan, 1965.*

Körner, S. "Some Types of Philosophical Thinking." In C. A. Mace (ed.). *British Philosophy in the Mid-Century.* London: Allen & Unwin, 1957.

Moore, G. E. *Philosophical Papers.* London: Allen & Unwin, 1959. Chap. 2.†

—————. *Some Main Problems of Philosophy.* London: Allen & Unwin, 1953. Chap. 1.†

O'Connor, D. J. (ed.). *A Critical History of Western Philosophy.* New York: The Free Press, 1964.

Passmore, John. *A Hundred Years of Philosophy.* London: Gerald Duckworth, 1957.

—————. *Philosophical Reasoning.* New York: Charles Scribner's Sons, 1961.

Russell, Bertrand. "Logical Atomism." In J. H. Muirhead (ed.). *Contemporary British Philosophy.* First Series. London: Allen & Unwin, 1924.

—————. *The Problems of Philosophy.* London: Oxford University Press, 1912.†

Ryle, Gilbert. *Philosophical Arguments.* Inaugural Lecture. London: Oxford University Press, 1945.

Schlick, Moritz. "The Turning Point in Philosophy." In A. J. Ayer (ed.). *Logical Positivism.* New York: The Free Press, 1959.†

Urmson, J. O. *Philosophical Analysis.* London: Oxford University Press, 1956.

Waismann, Friedrich. "How I See Philosophy." In H. D. Lewis (ed.). *Contemporary British Philosophy.* Third Series. London: Allen & Unwin, 1956.

—————. *The Principles of Linguistic Philosophy.* London: Macmillan, 1965. Pt. I.

Warnock, G. J. *English Philosophy Since 1900.* London: Oxford University Press, 1958.†

Wisdom, John. *Philosophy and Psychoanalysis.* Oxford: Basil Blackwell, 1953.

Wittgenstein, Ludwig. *The Blue & Brown Books.* Oxford: Basil Blackwell, 1958.†

* Paperback edition.   † Also available in a paperback edition.

:II:

God and Religious Language

INTRODUCTION

One of the paradigms of philosophical inquiry concerns the logical prospects for proving the existence of God, that is, the existence of a supreme Being who is the Creator of the universe. Inevitably, there are quarrels about the properties of this Being: Must He be the Creator of the universe, of all that there is? Is He, perhaps, an Artisan of the world, working with what He has not created? Is He His own Creator? Must He be a personal being? Must such a Being be omnipotent or omniscient or perfectly benevolent? Is it intelligible or self-consistent to attribute any such properties to God? Although these and similar questions are of considerable philosophical interest, the problem of the proof of the existence of God is a fairly rigorously construed issue that concedes, for the argument, the admissibility of the concept of the Deity as it appears, broadly speaking, in the Judaeo-Christian tradition.

The participants in this debate, which may be dated approximately from the work of St. Anselm of Canterbury (although Anselm has his important predecessors: certain of the issues were discussed in the ancient world), have always exhibited an impressive restraint in their doctrinal zeal and have given their attention essentially to the formulation, classification, and examination of all would-be proofs for the existence of God. The enterprise itself is stupendous: the mind is set to work to consider whether and in what sense man's rational powers, given his concepts and whatever evidence about the world he may collect, can construct a proof for the existence of God. Whatever the conviction of particular philosophers with regard to the question of the existence of God—and this is as clear in St. Anselm (II:1) and St. Thomas Aquinas (II:2) as it is in Immanuel Kant (II:3)—the issue is always perceived as being that of the legitimacy of any attempted proof of the existence of God, never that of supporting orthodoxy or religious ideology or any sort of rationalization.

In one sense, the question of proving the existence of God is simply one particularly exciting version of the grander question of classifying types of sound argument. Merely valid arguments won't do; one can always prove the existence of God in the trivial sense of making the statement "God exists" the consequence of a formally valid argument. What we want to know is whether the existence of God follows, and in what sense, from premises that we might be provisionally willing to concede to be true and that do not obviously beg the question at stake.

The principal kinds of proof that have been attempted are those that are marked out in Kant's criticism. But, although the objections that Kant sets forth have been taken to be decisive by many philosophers, variations—particularly of the so-called ontological and cosmological arguments—continue to be proposed to this day (as, for example, in recent statements by Norman Malcolm and Father F. C. Copleston). The ontological argument has become particularly intriguing: in the search for apparently sound arguments in informal debate, it is not clear that we never argue from the conception of a thing to the necessity of its existence or non-existence (for instance, the impossibility of the existence of a four-sided triangle). Although this example is not enough to salvage the ontological argument, this and similar considerations do oblige us to define the respect in which the argument is supposed to fail. On the other hand, the refinement of the issues at stake in the cosmological argument (as in the well-known debate between Bertrand Russell and Father Copleston) leads us to consider the limits of philosophical exchange and the possibility and nature of a philosophical stalemate. In these respects, the classical arguments for the existence of God reveal that an important part of their fascination lies in their bordering on weak (because inexplicit and insufficiently explored) portions of our conceptual network, which concern God only incidentally.

The teleological argument is generally regarded as the weakest of the three sorts of argument and has received relatively little support in modern philosophical circles. Between the famous criticisms of David Hume (*Dialogues Concerning Natural Religion*) and of Kant, which together challenge the possibility of using analogical arguments of an empirical sort about design and purpose to reach conclusions about the existence of a Being who transcends the empirically known world, the logical limitations of this sort of argument have generally come to be recognized. Kant also offered what has come to be called the moral argument for the existence of God, in which the existence of God is postulated as a condition for moral reasoning.

Most other arguments on this question fall into the category of arguments from some sort of privileged experience. With regard to them, the question arises whether religious and scientific assertions are to be taken as being meaningful in the same sense. A. J. Ayer (II:5), arguing that they are, concludes that arguments from religious experience are fallacious, on the grounds of the alleged unverifiability of statements about God. An interesting counterclaim has been advanced by John Hick that the existence of God is verifiable, although it presupposes the intelligibility of continued personal existence after death. Sometimes proof is set aside, as in the ingenious account of John Wisdom (II:7), and the language of apparent assertions about God is reinterpreted in terms of alternative ways of appreciating the perceivable order of things.

Once religious language is construed as being not merely assertive in the sense in which the assertions of science are, other possibilities arise, from strikingly disparate sources, with regard to the proper characterization of religious discourse. Not only is Wisdom's sympathetic and secular view rendered plausible; so too is Paul Tillich's view (II:6) of the special necessity of religious symbols in order to bridge existential finitude and Søren Kierkegaard's view (II:4) that religious discourse conveys the inevitable leap of faith.

Broadly speaking, if we presuppose the intelligibility of the concept of God, the chief proofs for the existence of God fall into two classes: proofs that infer the existence of God from the very concept of God or assert that the concept of God entails that God necessarily exists (two distinct theses: for instance, St. Anselm); and proofs that infer the existence of God from the nature of the world (for instance, St. Thomas). Of the latter, some arguments seek to establish the necessity of the existence of God from an analysis of the concepts that are essential to a characterization of the world (for instance, the argument of a first cause), while some seek to establish the probability of the existence of God by way of an analysis of the evidence about the nature of the world (for instance, the argument from design).

Theists, deists, agnostics, and atheists, then, regardless of whether they do or do not offer proofs for or against the existence of God, share the at least implied conviction that the concept of God is intelligible. This of course has been challenged, notably in terms of the verifiability theory of meaning (for instance, A. J. Ayer [II:5]). On the other hand, that theory of meaning has been attacked as inadequate, with respect to both assertions of fact and non-assertive uses of language, and many characterizations of religious language and of non-assertive uses of religious language have been attempted (for instance, by Wisdom, Kierkegaard, and Tillich).

The question of the proper characterization of religious discourse has given rise to other issues that have a prominent place in the philosophy of religion—for instance: In what sense can man be said to have knowledge or experience of God? Can the powers traditionally attributed to God be, on any account, consistently so attributed? Is the reality of evil compatible with God's powers? Are miracles intelligible? Is human freedom compatible with God's powers? Beyond these, other related but somewhat different questions are often considered—for instance, concerning the possibility of life beyond death and of souls without bodies, and concerning the significance of extrasensory perception. Of these, the two that are most closely related to the question of the existence of God have to do with the alleged distinctiveness of religious knowledge and the compatibility of the various powers that are attributed to God. If God could be directly experienced in some sense, it would of course be unnecessary (although not for that reason uninteresting) to attempt to establish His existence by inference; this is the motivation of those who affirm religious knowledge in the sense that C. B. Martin (II:8) challenges. And if the powers attributed to God cannot be consistently attributed to Him, then we must reconsider what kind of Being it is whose existence the traditional proofs attempt to establish; this is the direction of J. L. Mackie's analysis (II:9) of the problem of evil and free will.

The key issues, then, are whether the existence of God can be proved, whether we can have experience or knowledge of God, and whether discourse about God is intelligible or coherent.

The Existence of God

1

THE EXISTENCE OF GOD

St. Anselm of Canterbury

PREFACE

After I had published, at the solicitous entreaties of certain brethren, a brief work (the *Monologium*) as an example of meditation on the grounds of faith, in the person of one who investigates, in a course of silent reasoning with himself, matters of which he is ignorant; considering that this book was knit together by the linking of many arguments, I began to ask myself whether there might be found a single argument which would require no other for its proof than itself alone; and alone would suffice to demonstrate that God truly exists, and that there is a supreme good requiring nothing else, which all other things require for their existence and well-being; and whatever we believe regarding the divine Being.

. . .

Chapter II. *Truly there is a God, although the fool hath said in his heart, There is no God.*

And so, Lord, do thou, who dost give understanding to faith, give me, so far as thou knowest it to be profitable, to understand that thou art as we believe; and that thou art that which we believe. And, indeed, we believe that thou art a being than which nothing greater can be conceived. Or is there no such nature, since the fool hath said in his heart, there is no God? (Psalms xiv. 1). But, at any rate, this very fool, when he hears of this being of which I speak—a being than which nothing greater can be conceived—

From *Proslogium*, Gaunilon's "In Behalf of the Fool," and "Anselm's Apologetic," in *St. Anselm: Basic Writings*, 2nd ed. (La Salle, Ill.: The Open Court Publishing Company, 1961), pp. 6–11, 145–161. Reprinted by permission of the publisher.

understands what he hears, and what he understands is in his understanding; although he does not understand it to exist.

For, it is one thing for an object to be in the understanding, and another to understand that the object exists. When a painter first conceives of what he will afterwards perform, he has it in his understanding, but he does not yet understand it to be, because he has not yet performed it. But after he has made the painting, he both has it in his understanding, and he understands that it exists, because he has made it.

Hence, even the fool is convinced that something exists in the understanding, at least, than which nothing greater can be conceived. For, when he hears of this, he understands it. And whatever is understood, exists in the understanding. And assuredly that, than which nothing greater can be conceived, cannot exist in the understanding alone. For, suppose it exists in the understanding alone: then it can be conceived to exist in reality; which is greater.

Therefore, if that, than which nothing greater can be conceived, exists in the understanding alone, the very being, than which nothing greater can be conceived, is one, than which a greater can be conceived. But obviously this is impossible. Hence, there is no doubt that there exists a being, than which nothing greater can be conceived, and it exists both in the understanding and in reality.

Chapter III.   *God cannot be conceived not to exist.—God is that, than which nothing greater can be conceived.—That which can be conceived not to exist is not God.*

And it assuredly exists so truly, that it cannot be conceived not to exist. For, it is possible to conceive of a being which cannot be conceived not to exist; and this is greater than one which can be conceived not to exist. Hence, if that, than which nothing greater can be conceived, can be conceived not to exist, it is not that, than which nothing greater can be conceived. But this is an irreconcilable contradiction. There is, then, so truly a being than which nothing greater can be conceived to exist, that it cannot even be conceived not to exist; and this being thou art, O Lord, our God.

So truly, therefore, dost thou exist, O Lord, my God, that thou canst not be conceived not to exist; and rightly. For, if a mind could conceive of a being better than thee, the creature would rise above the Creator; and this is most absurd. And, indeed, whatever else there is, except thee alone, can be conceived not to exist. To thee alone, therefore, it belongs to exist more truly than all other beings, and hence in a higher degree than all others. For, whatever else exists does not exist so truly, and hence in a less degree it belongs to it to exist. Why, then, has the fool said in his heart, there is no God (Psalms xiv. 1), since it is so evident, to a rational mind, that thou dost exist in the highest degree of all? Why, except that he is dull and a fool?

Chapter IV.   *How the fool has said in his heart what cannot be conceived.— A thing may be conceived in two ways: (1) when the word signifying it is conceived; (2) when the thing itself is understood.—As far as the word goes, God can be conceived not to exist; in reality he cannot.*

But how has the fool said in his heart what he could not conceive; or how is it that he could not conceive what he said in his heart? since it is the same to say in the heart, and to conceive.

But, if really, nay, since really, he both conceived, because he said in his heart; and did not say in his heart, because he could not conceive; there is more than one way in which a thing is said in the heart or conceived. For, in one sense, an object is conceived, when the word signifying it is conceived; and in another, when the very entity, which the object is, is understood.

In the former sense, then, God can be conceived not to exist; but in the latter, not at all. For no one who understands what fire and water are can conceive fire to be water, in accordance with the nature of the facts themselves, although this is possible according to the words. So, then, no one who understands what God is can conceive that God does not exist; although he says these words in his heart, either without any, or with some foreign, signification. For, God is that than which a greater cannot be conceived. And he who thoroughly understands this, assuredly understands that this being so truly exists, that not even in concept can it be non-existent. Therefore, he who understands that God so exists, cannot conceive that he does not exist.

I thank thee, gracious Lord, I thank thee; because what I formerly believed by thy bounty, I now so understand by thine illumination, that if I were unwilling to believe that thou dost exist, I should not be able not to understand this to be true.

Chapter V.   *God is whatever it is better to be than not to be; and he, as the only self-existent being, creates all things from nothing.*

What art thou, then, Lord God, than whom nothing greater can be conceived? But what art thou, except that which, as the highest of all beings, alone exists through itself, and creates all other things from nothing? For, whatever is not this is less than a thing which can be conceived of. But this cannot be conceived of thee. What good, therefore, does the supreme Good lack, through which every good is? Therefore, thou art just, truthful, blessed, and whatever it is better to be than not to be. For it is better to be just than not just; better to be blessed than not blessed.

.   .   .

IN BEHALF OF THE FOOL

An Answer to the Argument of Anselm in the Proslogium by Gaunilon, a Monk of Marmoutier

If one doubts or denies the existence of a being of such a nature that nothing greater than it can be conceived, he receives this answer:

The existence of this being is proved, in the first place, by the fact that he himself, in his doubt or denial regarding this being, already has it in his understanding; for in hearing it spoken of he understands what is spoken of. It is proved, therefore, by the fact that what he understands must exist not only in his understanding, but in reality also.

And the proof of this is as follows.—It is a greater thing to exist both in the understanding and in reality than to be in the understanding alone. And if this being is in the understanding alone, whatever has even in the past existed in reality will be greater than this being. And so that which was greater than all beings will be less than some being, and will not be greater than all: which is a manifest contradiction.

And hence, that which is greater than all, already proved to be in the understanding, must exist not only in the understanding, but also in reality: for otherwise it will not be greater than all other beings.

The fool might make this reply:

This being is said to be in my understanding already, only because I understand what is said. Now could it not with equal justice be said that I have in my understanding all manner of unreal objects, having absolutely no existence in themselves, because I understand these things if one speaks of them, whatever they may be?

Unless indeed it is shown that this being is of such a character that it cannot be held in concept like all unreal objects, or objects whose existence is uncertain: and hence I am not able to conceive of it when I hear of it, or to hold it in concept; but I must understand it and have it in my understanding; because, it seems, I cannot conceive of it in any other way than by understanding it, that is, by comprehending in my knowledge its existence in reality.

But if this is the case, in the first place there will be no distinction between what has precedence in time—namely, the having of an object in the understanding—and what is subsequent in time—namely, the understanding that an object exists; as in the example of the picture, which exists first in the mind of the painter, and afterwards in his work.

Moreover, the following assertion can hardly be accepted: that this being, when it is spoken of and heard of, cannot be conceived not to exist in the way in which even God can be conceived not to exist. For if this is impossible, what was the object of this argument against one who doubts or denies the existence of such a being?

Finally, that this being so exists that it cannot be perceived by an understanding convinced of its own indubitable existence, unless this being is afterwards conceived of—this should be proved to me by an indisputable argument, but not by that which you have advanced: namely, that what I understand, when I hear it, already is in my understanding. For thus in my understanding, as I still think, could be all sorts of things whose existence is uncertain, or which do not exist at all, if some one whose words I should understand mentioned them. And so much the more if I should be deceived, as often happens, and believe in them: though I do not yet believe in the being whose existence you would prove.

Hence, your example of the painter who already has in his understanding what he is to paint cannot agree with this argument. For the picture, before it is made, is contained in the artificer's art itself; and any such thing, existing in the art of an artificer, is nothing but a part of his understanding itself. A joiner, St. Augustine says, when he is about to make a box in fact, first has it in his art. The box which is made in fact is not life; but the box which exists in his art is life. For the artificer's soul lives, in which all these things are, before they are produced. Why, then, are these things life in the living soul of the artificer, unless because they are nothing else than the knowledge or understanding of the soul itself?

With the exception, however, of those facts which are known to pertain to the mental nature, whatever, on being heard and thought out by the understanding, is perceived to be real, undoubtedly that real object is one thing, and the understanding itself, by which the object is grasped, is another. Hence, even if it were true that there is a being than which a greater is inconceivable: yet to this being, when heard of and understood, the not yet created picture in the mind of the painter is not analogous.

Let us notice also the point touched on above, with regard to this being which is greater than all which can be conceived, and which, it is said, can be none other than God himself. I, so far as actual knowledge of the object, either from its specific or general character, is concerned, am as little able to conceive of this being when I hear of it, or to have it in my understanding, as I am to conceive of or understand God himself: whom, indeed, for this very reason I can conceive not to exist. For I do not know that reality itself which God is, nor can I form a conjecture of that reality from some other like reality. For you yourself assert that that reality is such that there can be nothing else like it.

For, suppose that I should hear something said of a man absolutely unknown to me, of whose very existence I was unaware. Through that special or general knowledge by which I know what man is, or what men are, I could conceive of him also, according to the reality itself, which man is. And yet it would be possible, if the person who told me of him deceived me, that the man himself, of whom I conceived, did not exist; since that reality according to which I conceived of him, though a no less indisputable fact, was not that man, but any man.

Hence, I am not able, in the way in which I should have this unreal being in concept or in understanding, to have that being of which you speak in concept or in understanding, when I hear the word *God* or the words, *a being greater than all other beings*. For I can conceive of the man according to a fact that is real and familiar to me: but of God, or a being greater than all others, I could not conceive at all, except merely according to the word. And an object can hardly or never be conceived according to the word alone.

For when it is so conceived, it is not so much the word itself (which is, indeed, a real thing—that is, the sound of the letters and syllables) as the signification of the word, when heard, that is conceived. But it is not conceived as by one who knows what is generally signified by the word; by whom, that is, it is conceived according to a reality and in true conception alone. It is conceived as by a man who does not know the object, and conceives of it only in accordance with the movement of his mind produced by hearing the word, the mind attempting to image for itself the significa-tion of the word that is heard. And it would be surprising if in the reality of fact it could ever attain to this.

Thus, it appears, and in no other way, this being is also in my understanding, when I hear and understand a person who says that there is a being greater than all conceivable beings. So much for the assertion that this supreme nature already is in my understanding.

But that this being must exist, not only in the understanding but also in reality, is thus proved to me:

If it did not so exist, whatever exists in reality would be greater than it. And so the being which has been already proved to exist in my understanding, will not be greater than all other beings.

I still answer: if it should be said that a being which cannot be even conceived in terms of any fact, is in the understanding, I do not deny that this being is, accordingly, in my understanding. But since through this fact it can in no wise attain to real existence also, I do not yet concede to it that existence at all, until some certain proof of it shall be given.

For he who says that this being exists, because otherwise the being which is greater than all will not be greater than all, does not attend strictly enough to what he is saying. For I do not yet say, no, I even deny or doubt that this being is greater than any real object. Nor do I concede to it any other existence than this (if it should be called existence) which it has when the mind, according to a word merely heard, tries to form the image of an object absolutely unknown to it.

How, then, is the veritable existence of that being proved to me from the assumption, by hypothesis, that it is greater than all other beings? For I should still deny this, or doubt your demonstration of it, to this extent, that I should not admit that this being is in my understanding and concept even in the way in which many objects whose real existence is uncertain and doubtful, are in my understanding and concept. For it should be proved first that this being itself really exists somewhere; and then, from the fact that it is greater than all, we shall not hesitate to infer that it also subsists in itself.

For example: it is said that somewhere in the ocean is an island, which, because of the difficulty, or rather the impossibility, of discovering what does not exist, is called the lost island. And they say that this island has an inestimable wealth of all manner of riches and delicacies in greater abundance than is told of the Islands of the Blest; and that having no owner or inhabitant, it is more excellent than all other countries, which are inhabited by mankind, in the abundance with which it is stored.

Now if some one should tell me that there is such an island, I should easily understand his words, in which there is no difficulty. But suppose that he went on to say, as if by a logical inference: "You can no longer doubt that this island which is more excellent than all lands exists somewhere, since you have no doubt that it is in your understanding. And since it is more excellent not to be in the understanding alone, but to exist both in the understanding and in reality, for this reason it must exist. For if it does not exist, any land which really exists will be more excellent than it; and so the island already understood by you to be more excellent will not be more excellent."

If a man should try to prove to me by such reasoning that this island truly exists, and that its existence should no longer be doubted, either I should believe that he was jesting, or I know not which I ought to regard as the greater fool: myself, supposing that I should allow this proof; or him, if he should suppose that he had established with any certainty the existence of this island. For he ought to show first that the hypothetical excellence of this island exists as a real and indubitable fact, and in no wise as any unreal object, or one whose existence is uncertain, in my understanding.

This, in the mean time, is the answer the fool could make to the arguments urged against him. When he is assured in the first place that this being is so great that its non-existence is not even conceivable, and that this in turn is proved on no other ground than the fact that otherwise it will not be greater than all things, the fool may make the same answer, and say:

When did I say that any such being exists in reality, that is, a being greater than all others?—that on this ground it should be proved to me that it also exists in reality to such a degree that it cannot even be conceived not to exist? Whereas in the first place it should be in some way proved that a nature which is higher, that is, greater and better, than all other natures, exists; in order that from this we may then be able to prove all attributes which necessarily the being that is greater and better than all possesses.

Moreover, it is said that the non-existence of this being is inconceivable. It might better be said, perhaps, that its non-existence, or the possibility of its non-existence, is unintelligible. For according to the true meaning of the word, unreal objects are unintelligible. Yet their existence is conceivable in the way in which the fool conceived of the non-existence of God. I am most certainly aware of my own existence; but I know, nevertheless, that my non-existence is possible. As to that supreme being, moreover, which God is, I understand without any doubt both his existence, and the impossibility of his non-existence. Whether, however, so long as I am most positively aware of my existence, I can conceive of my non-existence, I am not sure. But if I can, why can I not conceive of the non-existence of whatever else I know with the same certainty? If, however, I cannot, God will not be the only being of which it can be said, it is impossible to conceive of his non-existence.

The other parts of this book are argued with such truth, such brilliancy, such grandeur; and are so replete with usefulness, so fragrant with a certain perfume of devout and holy feeling, that though there are matters in the beginning which, however rightly sensed, are weakly presented, the rest of the work should not be rejected on this account. The rather ought these earlier matters to be reasoned more cogently, and the whole to be received with great respect and honor.

ANSELM'S APOLOGETIC IN REPLY TO GAUNILON'S ANSWER IN BEHALF OF THE FOOL

It was a fool against whom the argument of my Proslogium was directed. Seeing, however, that the author of these objections is by no means a fool, and is a Catholic, speaking in behalf of the fool, I think it sufficient that I answer the Catholic.

Chapter I.   *A general refutation of Gaunilon's argument. It is shown that a*
being than which a greater cannot be conceived exists in reality.

You say—whosoever you may be, who say that a fool is capable of
making these statements—that a being than which a greater cannot be
conceived is not in the understanding in any other sense than that in which a
being that is altogether inconceivable in terms of reality, is in the understanding. You say that the inference that this being exists in reality, from the
fact that it is in the understanding, is no more just than the inference that a
lost island most certainly exists, from the fact that when it is described the
hearer does not doubt that it is in his understanding.

But I say: if a being than which a greater is inconceivable is not understood or conceived, and is not in the understanding or in concept, certainly
either God is not a being than which a greater is inconceivable, or else he is
not understood or conceived, and is not in the understanding or in concept.
But I call on your faith and conscience to attest that this is most false.
Hence, that than which a greater cannot be conceived is truly understood
and conceived, and is in the understanding and in concept. Therefore either
the grounds on which you try to controvert me are not true, or else the
inference which you think to base logically on those grounds is not justified.

But you hold, moreover, that supposing that a being than which a greater
cannot be conceived is understood, it does not follow that this being is in the
understanding; nor, if it is in the understanding, does it therefore exist in
reality.

In answer to this, I maintain positively: if that being can be even
conceived to be, it must exist in reality. For that than which a greater is
inconceivable cannot be conceived except as without beginning. But whatever can be conceived to exist, and does not exist, can be conceived to exist
through a beginning. Hence what can be conceived to exist, but does not
exist, is not the being than which a greater cannot be conceived. Therefore,
if such a being can be conceived to exist, necessarily it does exist.

Furthermore: if it can be conceived at all, it must exist. For no one who
denies or doubts the existence of a being than which a greater is inconceivable, denies or doubts that if it did exist, its non-existence, either in
reality or in the understanding, would be impossible. For otherwise it would
not be a being than which a greater cannot be conceived. But as to whatever
can be conceived, but does not exist—if there were such a being, its non-
existence, either in reality or in the understanding, would be possible.
Therefore if a being than which a greater is inconceivable can be even
conceived, it cannot be non-existent.

But let us suppose that it does not exist, even if it can be conceived.
Whatever can be conceived, but does not exist, if it existed, would not be a
being than which a greater is inconceivable. If, then, there were a being
a greater than which is inconceivable, it would not be a being than which a
greater is inconceivable: which is most absurd. Hence, it is false to deny that
a being than which a greater cannot be conceived exists, if it can be even
conceived; much the more, therefore, if it can be understood or can be in
the understanding.

Moreover, I will venture to make this assertion: without doubt, whatever
at any place or at any time does not exist—even if it does exist at some place

or at some time—can be conceived to exist nowhere and never, as at some place and at some time it does not exist. For what did not exist yesterday, and exists to-day, as it is understood not to have existed yesterday, so it can be apprehended by the intelligence that it never exists. And what is not here, and is elsewhere, can be conceived to be nowhere, just as it is not here. So with regard to an object of which the individual parts do not exist at the same places or times: all its parts and therefore its very whole can be conceived to exist nowhere or never.

For, although time is said to exist always, and the world everywhere, yet time does not as a whole exist always, nor the world as a whole everywhere. And as individual parts of time do not exist when others exist, so they can be conceived never to exist. And so it can be apprehended by the intelligence that individual parts of the world exist nowhere, as they do not exist where other parts exist. Moreover, what is composed of parts can be dissolved in concept, and be non-existent. Therefore, whatever at any place or at any time does not exist as a whole, even if it is existent, can be conceived not to exist.

But that than which a greater cannot be conceived, if it exists, cannot be conceived not to exist. Otherwise, it is not a being than which a greater cannot be conceived: which is inconsistent. By no means, then, does it at any place or at any time fail to exist as a whole: but it exists as a whole everywhere and always.

Do you believe that this being can in some way be conceived or understood, or that the being with regard to which these things are understood can be in concept or in the understanding? For if it cannot, these things cannot be understood with reference to it. But if you say that it is not understood and that it is not in the understanding, because it is not thoroughly understood; you should say that a man who cannot face the direct rays of the sun does not see the light of day, which is none other than the sunlight. Assuredly a being than which a greater cannot be conceived exists, and is in the understanding, at least to this extent—that these statements regarding it are understood.

Chapter II.   *The argument is continued. It is shown that a being than which a greater is inconceivable can be conceived, and also, in so far, exists.*

I have said, then, in the argument which you dispute, that when the fool hears mentioned a being than which a greater is inconceivable, he understands what he hears. Certainly a man who does not understand when a familiar language is spoken, has no understanding at all, or a very dull one. Moreover, I have said that if this being is understood, it is in the understanding. Is that in no understanding which has been proved necessarily to exist in the reality of fact?

But you will say that although it is in the understanding, it does not follow that it is understood. But observe that the fact of its being understood does necessitate its being in the understanding. For as what is conceived, is conceived by conception, and what is conceived by conception, as it is conceived, so is in conception; so what is understood, is understood by understanding, and what is understood by understanding, as it is understood, so is in the understanding. What can be more clear than this?

After this, I have said that if it is even in the understanding alone, it can be conceived also to exist in reality, which is greater. If, then, it is in the understanding alone, obviously the very being than which a greater cannot be conceived is one than which a greater can be conceived. What is more logical? For if it exists even in the understanding alone, can it not be conceived also to exist in reality? And if it can be so conceived, does not he who conceives of this conceive of a thing greater than that being, if it exists in the understanding alone? What more consistent inference, then, can be made than this: that if a being than which a greater cannot be conceived is in the understanding alone, it is not that than which a greater cannot be conceived?

But, assuredly, in no understanding is a being than which a greater is conceivable a being than which a greater is inconceivable. Does it not follow, then, that if a being than which a greater cannot be conceived is in any understanding, it does not exist in the understanding alone? For if it is in the understanding alone, it is a being than which a greater can be conceived, which is inconsistent with the hypothesis.

Chapter III. *A criticism of Gaunilon's example, in which he tries to show that in this way the real existence of a lost island might be inferred from the fact of its being conceived.*

But, you say, it is as if one should suppose an island in the ocean, which surpasses all lands in its fertility, and which, because of the difficulty, or rather the impossibility, of discovering what does not exist, is called a lost island; and should say that there can be no doubt that this island truly exists in reality, for this reason, that one who hears it described easily understands what he hears.

Now I promise confidently that if any man shall devise anything existing either in reality or in concept alone (except that than which a greater cannot be conceived) to which he can adapt the sequence of my reasoning, I will discover that thing, and will give him his lost island, not to be lost again.

But it now appears that this being than which a greater is inconceivable cannot be conceived not to be, because it exists on so assured a ground of truth; for otherwise it would not exist at all.

Hence, if any one says that he conceives this being not to exist, I say that at the time when he conceives of this either he conceives of a being than which a greater is inconceivable, or he does not conceive at all. If he does not conceive, he does not conceive of the non-existence of that of which he does not conceive. But if he does conceive, he certainly conceives of a being which cannot be even conceived not to exist. For if it could be conceived not to exist, it could be conceived to have a beginning and an end. But this is impossible.

He, then, who conceives of this being conceives of a being which cannot be even conceived not to exist; but he who conceives of this being does not conceive that it does not exist; else he conceives what is inconceivable. The non-existence, then, of that than which a greater cannot be conceived is inconceivable.

Chapter IV. *The difference between the possiblity of conceiving of non-existence, and understanding non-existence.*

You say, moreover, that whereas I assert that this supreme being cannot be *conceived* not to exist, it might better be said that its non-existence, or even the possibility of its non-existence, cannot be *understood*.

But it was more proper to say, it cannot be conceived. For if I had said that the object itself cannot be understood not to exist, possibly you yourself, who say that in accordance with the true meaning of the term what is unreal cannot be understood, would offer the objection that nothing which is can be understood not to be, for the nonexistence of what exists is unreal: hence God would not be the only being of which it could be said, it is impossible to understand its non-existence. For thus one of those beings which most certainly exist can be understood not to exist in the same way in which certain other real objects can be understood not to exist.

But this objection, assuredly, cannot be urged against the term *conception*, if one considers the matter well. For although no objects which exist can be understood not to exist, yet all objects, except that which exists in the highest degree, can be conceived not to exist. For all those objects, and those alone, can be conceived not to exist, which have a beginning or end or composition of parts: also, as I have already said, whatever at any place or at any time does not exist as a whole.

That being alone, on the other hand, cannot be conceived not to exist, in which any conception discovers neither beginning nor end nor composition of parts, and which any conception finds always and everywhere as a whole.

Be assured, then, that you can conceive of your own non-existence, although you are most certain that you exist. I am surprised that you should have admitted that you are ignorant of this. For we conceive of the non-existence of many objects which we know to exist, and of the existence of many which we know not to exist; not by forming the opinion that they so exist, but by imagining that they exist as we conceive of them.

And indeed, we can conceive of the non-existence of an object, although we know it to exist, because at the same time we can conceive of the former and know the latter. And we cannot conceive of the non-existence of an object, so long as we know it to exist, because we cannot conceive at the same time of existence and non-existence.

If, then, one will thus distinguish these two senses of this statement, he will understand that nothing, so long as it is known to exist, can be conceived not to exist; and that whatever exists, except that being than which a greater cannot be conceived, can be conceived not to exist, even when it is known to exist.

So, then, of God alone it can be said that it is impossible to conceive of his non-existence; and yet many objects, so long as they exist, in one sense cannot be conceived not to exist. But in what sense God is to be conceived not to exist, I think has been shown clearly enough in my book.

·   ·   ·

2

THE EXISTENCE OF GOD

St. Thomas Aquinas

. . .

First Article: Whether the Existence of God Is Self-Evident?

We proceed thus to the First Article:—

Objection 1. It seems that the existence of God is self-evident. For those things are said to be self-evident to us the knowledge of which exists naturally in us, as we can see in regard to first principles. But as Damascene says, *the knowledge of God is naturally implanted in all.* Therefore the existence of God is self-evident.

Obj. 2. Further, those things are said to be self-evident which are known as soon as the terms are known, which the Philosopher says is true of the first principles of demonstration. Thus, when the nature of a whole and of a part is known, it is at once recognized that every whole is greater than its part. But as soon as the signification of the name *God* is understood, it is at once seen that God exists. For by this name is signified that thing than which nothing greater can be conceived. But that which exists actually and mentally is greater than that which exists only mentally. Therefore, since as soon as the name *God* is understood it exists mentally, it also follows that it exists actually. Therefore the proposition *God exists* is self-evident.

Obj. 3. Further, the existence of truth is self-evident. For whoever denies the existence of truth grants that truth does not exist: and, if truth does not exist, then the proposition *Truth does not exist* is true: and if there is anything true, there must be truth. But God is truth itself: *I am the way, the truth, and the life* (*Jo.* xiv. 6). Therefore *God exists* is self-evident.

On the contrary, No one can mentally admit the opposite of what is self-evident, as the Philosopher states concerning the first principles of demonstration. But the opposite of the proposition *God is* can be mentally

From *Summa Theologica,* in Anton C. Pegis, ed., *Basic Writings of St. Thomas Aquinas* (New York: Random House, Inc., 1945), Part I, Q. 2, pp. 18–24. Reprinted by permission of Random House, Inc., and Burns & Oates Ltd.

admitted: *The fool said in his heart, There is no God* (Ps. lii. 1). Therefore, that God exists is not self-evident.

I answer that, A thing can be self-evident in either of two ways: on the one hand, self-evident in itself, though not to us; on the other, self-evident in itself, and to us. A proposition is self-evident because the predicate is included in the essence of the subject: *e.g., Man is an animal*, for animal is contained in the essence of man. If, therefore, the essence of the predicate and subject be known to all, the proposition will be self-evident to all; as is clear with regard to the first principles of demonstration, the terms of which are certain common notions that no one is ignorant of, such as being and non-being, whole and part, and the like. If, however, there are some to whom the essence of the predicate and subject is unknown, the proposition will be self-evident in itself, but not to those who do not know the meaning of the predicate and subject of the proposition. Therefore, it happens, as Boethius says, that there are some notions of the mind which are common and self-evident only to the learned, as that incorporeal substances are not in space. Therefore I say that this proposition, *God exists*, of itself is self-evident, for the predicate is the same as the subject, because God is His own existence as will be hereafter shown. Now because we do not know the essence of God, the proposition is not self-evident to us, but needs to be demonstrated by things that are more known to us, though less known in their nature—namely, by His effects.

Reply Obj. 1. To know that God exists in a general and confused way is implanted in us by nature, inasmuch as God is man's beatitude. For man naturally desires happiness, and what is naturally desired by man is naturally known by him. This, however, is not to know absolutely that God exists; just as to know that someone is approaching is not the same as to know that Peter is approaching, even though it is Peter who is approaching; for there are many who imagine that man's perfect good, which is happiness, consists in riches, and others in pleasures, and others in something else.

Reply Obj. 2. Perhaps not everyone who hears this name *God* understands it to signify something than which nothing greater can be thought, seeing that some have believed God to be a body. Yet, granted that everyone understands that by this name *God* is signified something than which nothing greater can be thought, nevertheless, it does not therefore follow that he understands that what the name signifies exists actually, but only that it exists mentally. Nor can it be argued that it actually exists, unless it be admitted that there actually exists something than which nothing greater can be thought; and this precisely is not admitted by those who hold that God does not exist.

Reply Obj. 3. The existence of truth in general is self-evident, but the existence of a Primal Truth is not self-evident to us.

Second Article: Whether It Can Be Demonstrated that God Exists

We proceed thus to the Second Article:—

Objection 1. It seems that the existence of God cannot be demonstrated. For it is an article of faith that God exists. But what is of faith cannot be demonstrated, because a demonstration produces scientific knowledge, whereas faith is of the unseen, as is clear from the Apostle (*Heb.* xi. 1). Therefore it cannot be demonstrated that God exists.

Obj. 2. Further, essence is the middle term of demonstration. But we cannot know in what God's essence consists, but solely in what it does not consist, as Damascene says. Therefore we cannot demonstrate that God exists.

Obj. 3. Further, if the existence of God were demonstrated, this could only be from His effects. But His effects are not proportioned to Him, since He is infinite and His effects are finite, and between the finite and infinite there is no proportion. Therefore, since a cause cannot be demonstrated by an effect not proportioned to it, it seems that the existence of God cannot be demonstrated.

On the contrary, The Apostle says: *The invisible things of Him are clearly seen, being understood by the things that are made* (*Rom.* i. 20). But this would not be unless the existence of God could be demonstrated through the things that are made; for the first thing we must know of anything is, whether it exists.

I answer that, Demonstration can be made in two ways: One is through the cause, and is called *propter quid,* and this is to argue from what is prior absolutely. The other is through the effect, and is called a demonstration *quia;* this is to argue from what is prior relatively only to us. When an effect is better known to us than its cause, from the effect we proceed to the knowledge of the cause. And from every effect the existence of its proper cause can be demonstrated, so long as its effects are better known to us; because, since every effect depends upon its cause, if the effect exists, the cause must pre-exist. Hence the existence of God, in so far as it is not self-evident to us, can be demonstrated from those of His effects which are known to us.

Reply Obj. 1. The existence of God and other like truths about God, which can be known by natural reason, are not articles of faith, but are preambles to the articles; for faith presupposes natural knowledge, even as grace presupposes nature and perfection the perfectible. Nevertheless, there is nothing to prevent a man, who cannot grasp a proof, from accepting, as a matter of faith, something which in itself is capable of being scientifically known and demonstrated.

Reply Obj. 2. When the existence of a cause is demonstrated from an effect, this effect takes the place of the definition of the cause in proving the cause's existence. This is especially the case in regard to God, because, in order to prove the existence of anything, it is necessary to accept as a middle term the meaning of the name, and not its essence, for the question of its essence follows on the question of its existence. Now the names given to God are derived from His effects . . . . Consequently, in demonstrating the existence of God from His effects, we may take for the middle term the meaning of the name *God.*

Reply Obj. 3. From effects not proportioned to the cause no perfect knowledge of that cause can be obtained. Yet from every effect the existence of the cause can be clearly demonstrated, and so we can demonstrate the existence of God from His effects; though from them we cannot know God perfectly as He is in His essence.

Third Article: Whether God Exists?

We proceed thus to the Third Article:—

Objection 1. It seems that God does not exist; because if one of two contraries be infinite, the other would be altogether destroyed. But the name *God* means that He is infinite goodness. If, therefore, God existed, there would be no evil discoverable; but there is evil in the world. Therefore God does not exist.

Obj. 2. Further, it is superfluous to suppose that what can be accounted for by a few principles has been produced by many. But it seems that everything we see in the world can be accounted for by other principles, supposing God did not exist. For all natural things can be reduced to one principle, which is nature; and all voluntary things can be reduced to one principle, which is human reason, or will. Therefore there is no need to suppose God's existence.

On the contrary, It is said in the person of God: *I am Who am* (*Exod*. iii. 14).

I answer that, The existence of God can be proved in five ways.

The first and more manifest way is the argument from motion. It is certain, and evident to our senses, that in the world some things are in motion. Now whatever is moved is moved by another, for nothing can be moved except it is in potentiality to that towards which it is moved; whereas a thing moves inasmuch as it is in act. For motion is nothing else than the reduction of something from potentiality to actuality. But nothing can be reduced from potentiality to actuality, except by something in a state of actuality. Thus that which is actually hot, as fire, makes wood, which is potentially hot, to be actually hot, and thereby moves and changes it. Now it is not possible that the same thing should be at once in actuality and potentiality in the same respect, but only in different respects. For what is actually hot cannot simultaneously be potentially hot; but it is simultaneously potentially cold. It is therefore impossible that in the same respect and in the same way a thing should be both mover and moved, *i.e.*, that it should move itself. Therefore, whatever is moved must be moved by another. If that by which it is moved be itself moved, then this also must needs be moved by another, and that by another again. But this cannot go on to infinity, because then there would be no first mover, and, consequently, no other mover, seeing that subsequent movers move only inasmuch as they are moved by the first mover; as the staff moves only because it is moved by the hand. Therefore it is necessary to arrive at a first mover, moved by no other; and this everyone understands to be God.

The second way is from the nature of efficient cause. In the world of sensible things we find there is an order of efficient causes. There is no case known (neither is it, indeed, possible) in which a thing is found to be the efficient cause of itself; for so it would be prior to itself, which is impossible. Now in efficient causes it is not possible to go on to infinity, because in all efficient causes following in order, the first is the cause of the intermediate cause, and the intermediate is the cause of the ultimate cause, whether the intermediate cause be several, or one only. Now to take away the cause is to take away the effect. Therefore, if there be no first cause among efficient causes, there will be no ultimate, nor any intermediate, cause. But if in efficient causes it is possible to go on to infinity, there will be no first efficient cause, neither will there be an ultimate effect, nor any intermediate efficient causes; all of which is plainly false. Therefore it is necessary to admit a first efficient cause, to which everyone gives the name of God.

The third way is taken from possibility and necessity, and runs thus. We find in nature things that are possible to be and not to be, since they are found to be generated, and to be corrupted, and consequently, it is possible for them to be and not to be. But it is impossible for these always to exist, for that which can not-be at some time is not. Therefore, if everything can not-be, then at one time there was nothing in existence. Now if this were true, even now there would be nothing in existence, because that which does not exist begins to exist only through something already existing. Therefore, if at one time nothing was in existence, it would have been impossible for anything to have begun to exist; and thus even now nothing would be in existence—which is absurd. Therefore, not all beings are merely possible, but there must exist something the existence of which is necessary. But every necessary thing either has its necessity caused by another, or not. Now it is impossible to go on to infinity in necessary things which have their necessity caused by another, as has been already proved in regard to efficient causes. Therefore we cannot but admit the existence of some being having of itself its own necessity, and not receiving it from another, but rather causing in others their necessity. This all men speak of as God.

The fourth way is taken from the gradation to be found in things. Among beings there are some more and some less good, true, noble, and the like. But *more* and *less* are predicated of different things according as they resemble in their different ways something which is the maximum, as a thing is said to be hotter according as it more nearly resembles that which is hottest; so that there is something which is truest, something best, something noblest, and, consequently, something which is most being, for those things that are greatest in truth are greatest in being, as it is written in *Metaph.* ii. Now the maximum in any genus is the cause of all in that genus, as fire, which is the maximum of heat, is the cause of all hot things, as is said in the same book. Therefore there must also be something which is to all beings the cause of their being, goodness, and every other perfection; and this we call God.

The fifth way is taken from the governance of the world. We see that things which lack knowledge, such as natural bodies, act for an end, and this is evident from their acting always, or nearly always, in the same way, so as to obtain the best result. Hence it is plain that they achieve their end, not fortuitously, but designedly. Now whatever lacks knowledge cannot move towards an end, unless it be directed by some being endowed with knowledge and intelligence; as the arrow is directed by the archer. Therefore some intelligent being exists by whom all natural things are directed to their end; and this being we call God.

Reply Obj. 1. As Augustine says: *Since God is the highest good, He would not allow any evil to exist in His works, unless His omnipotence and goodness were such as to bring good even out of evil.* This is part of the infinite goodness of God, that He should allow evil to exist, and out of it produce good.

Reply Obj. 2. Since nature works for a determinate end under the direction of a higher agent, whatever is done by nature must be traced back to

God as to its first cause. So likewise whatever is done voluntarily must be traced back to some higher cause other than human reason and will, since these can change and fail; for all things that are changeable and capable of defect must be traced back to an immovable and self-necessary first principle, as has been shown.

3

THE EXISTENCE OF A
SUPREME BEING

Immanuel Kant

THE IMPOSSIBILITY OF AN ONTOLOGICAL PROOF
OF THE EXISTENCE OF GOD

It is evident . . . that the concept of an absolutely necessary being is a
concept of pure reason, that is, a mere idea the objective reality of which is
very far from being proved by the fact that reason requires it. For the idea
instructs us only in regard to a certain unattainable completeness, and so
serves rather to limit the understanding than to extend it to new objects. But
we are here faced by what is indeed strange and perplexing, namely, that
while the inference from a given existence in general to some absolutely
necessary being seems to be both imperative and legitimate, all those conditions under which alone the understanding can form a concept of such a
necessity are so many obstacles in the way of our doing so.

In all ages men have spoken of an *absolutely necessary* being, and in so
doing have endeavoured, not so much to understand whether and how a
thing of this kind allows even of being thought, but rather to prove its
existence. There is, of course, no difficulty in giving a verbal definition of
the concept, namely, that it is something the non-existence of which is
impossible. But this yields no insight into the conditions which make it
necessary to regard the non-existence of a thing as absolutely unthinkable. It
is precisely these conditions that we desire to know, in order that we may
determine whether or not, in resorting to this concept, we are thinking
anything at all. The expedient of removing all those conditions which the
understanding indispensably requires in order to regard something as necessary, simply through the introduction of the word *unconditioned*, is very
far from sufficing to show whether I am still thinking anything in the
concept of the unconditionally necessary, or perhaps rather nothing at all.

From "The Ideal of Pure Reason," in *Immanuel Kant's Critique of Pure Reason*,
Norman Kemp Smith, trans. (London: 1933), Chap. III, Secs. 4–6, pp. 500–514, 518–524.
Reprinted by permission of St. Martin's Press Inc., The Macmillan Company of Canada
Ltd., and Macmillan & Co. Ltd.

Nay more, this concept, at first ventured upon blindly, and now become so completely familiar, has been supposed to have its meaning exhibited in a number of examples; and on this account all further enquiry into its intelligibility has seemed to be quite needless. Thus the fact that every geometrical proposition, as, for instance, that a triangle has three angles, is absolutely necessary, has been taken as justifying us in speaking of an object which lies entirely outside the sphere of our understanding as if we understood perfectly what it is that we intend to convey by the concept of that object.

All the alleged examples are, without exception, taken from *judgments*, not from *things* and their existence. But the unconditioned necessity of judgments is not the same as an absolute necessity of things. The absolute necessity of the judgment is only a conditioned necessity of the thing, or of the predicate in the judgment. The above proposition does not declare that three angles are absolutely necessary, but that, under the condition that there is a triangle (that is, that a triangle is given), three angles will necessarily be found in it. So great, indeed, is the deluding influence exercised by this logical necessity that, by the simple device of forming an *a priori* concept of a thing in such a manner as to include existence within the scope of its meaning, we have supposed ourselves to have justified the conclusion that because existence necessarily belongs to the object of this concept— always under the condition that we posit the thing as given (as existing)— we are also of necessity, in accordance with the law of identity, required to posit the existence of its object, and that this being is therefore itself absolutely necessary—and this, to repeat, for the reason that the existence of this being has already been thought in a concept which is assumed arbitrarily and on condition that we posit its object.

If, in an identical proposition, I reject the predicate while retaining the subject, contradiction results; and I therefore say that the former belongs necessarily to the latter. But if we reject subject and predicate alike, there is no contradiction; for nothing is then left that can be contradicted. To posit a triangle, and yet to reject its three angles, is self-contradictory; but there is no contradiction in rejecting the triangle together with its three angles. The same holds true of the concept of an absolutely necessary being. If its existence is rejected, we reject the thing itself with all its predicates; and no question of contradiction can then arise. There is nothing outside it that would then be contradicted, since the necessity of the thing is not supposed to be derived from anything external; nor is there anything internal that would be contradicted, since in rejecting the thing itself we have at the same time rejected all its internal properties. 'God is omnipotent' is a necessary judgment. The omnipotence cannot be rejected if we posit a Deity, that is, an infinite being; for the two concepts are identical. But if we say, 'There is no God', neither the omnipotence nor any other of its predicates is given; they are one and all rejected together with the subject, and there is therefore not the least contradiction in such a judgment.

. . . if the predicate of a judgment is rejected together with the subject, no internal contradiction can result, and that this holds no matter what the predicate may be. The only way of evading this conclusion is to argue that there are subjects which cannot be removed, and must always remain. That, however, would only be another way of saying that there are absolutely necessary subjects; and that is the very assumption which I have called in question, and the possibility of which the above argument professes to establish. For I cannot form the least concept of a thing which, should it be rejected with all its predicates, leaves behind a contradiction; and in the absence of contradiction I have, through pure *a priori* concepts alone, no criterion of impossibility.

Notwithstanding all these general considerations, in which every one must concur, we may be challenged with a case which is brought forward as proof that in actual fact the contrary holds, namely, that there is one concept, and indeed only one, in reference to which the not-being or rejection of its object is in itself contradictory, namely, the concept of the *ens realissimum* [being with the supreme degree of reality]. It is declared that it possesses all reality, and that we are justified in assuming that such a being is possible (the fact that a concept does not contradict itself by no means proves the possibility of its object: but the contrary assertion I am for the moment willing to allow).[1] Now [the argument proceeds] 'all reality' includes existence; existence is therefore contained in the concept of a thing that is possible. If, then, this thing is rejected, the internal possibility of the thing is rejected—which is self-contradictory.

My answer is as follows. There is already a contradiction in introducing the concept of existence—no matter under what title it may be disguised—into the concept of a thing which we profess to be thinking solely in reference to its possibility. If that be allowed as legitimate, a seeming victory has been won; but in actual fact nothing at all is said: the assertion is a mere tautology. We must ask: Is the proposition that *this or that thing* (which, whatever it may be, is allowed as possible) *exists*, an analytic or a synthetic proposition? If it is analytic, the assertion of the existence of the thing adds nothing to the thought of the thing; but in that case either the thought, which is in us, is the thing itself, or we have presupposed an existence as belonging to the realm of the possible, and have then, on that pretext, inferred its existence from its internal possibility—which is nothing but a miserable tautology. The word 'reality', which in the concept of the thing sounds other than the word 'existence' in the concept of the predicate, is of no avail in meeting this objection. For if all positing (no matter what it may be that is posited) is entitled reality, the thing with all its predicates is already posited in the concept of the subject, and is assumed as actual; and in the predicate this is merely repeated. But if, on the other hand, we admit, as every reasonable person must, that all existential propositions are synthetic, how can we profess to maintain that the predicate of existence cannot be rejected without contradiction? This is a feature which is found only in analytic propositions, and is indeed precisely what constitutes their analytic character.

I should have hoped to put an end to these idle and fruitless disputations in a direct manner, by an accurate determination of the concept of existence,

[1] A concept is always possible if it is not self-contradictory. This is the logical criterion of possibility, and by it the object of the concept is distinguishable from the *nihil negativum*. But it may none the less be an empty concept, unless the objective reality of the synthesis through which the concept is generated has been specifically proved; and such proof, as we have shown above, rests on principles of possible experience, and not on the principle of analysis (the law of contradiction). This is a warning against arguing directly from the logical possibility of concepts to the real possibility of things.

had I not found that the illusion which is caused by the confusion of a logical with a real predicate (that is, with a predicate which determines a thing) is almost beyond correction. Anything we please can be made to serve as a logical predicate; the subject can even be predicated of itself; for logic abstracts from all content. But a *determining* predicate is a predicate which is added to the concept of the subject and enlarges it. Consequently, it must not be already contained in the concept.

'*Being*' is obviously not a real predicate; that is, it is not a concept of something which could be added to the concept of a thing. It is merely the positing of a thing, or of certain determinations, as existing in themselves. Logically, it is merely the copula of a judgment. The proposition, 'God is omnipotent', contains two concepts, each of which has its object—God and omnipotence. The small word 'is' adds no new predicate, but only serves to posit the predicate *in its relation* to the subject. If, now, we take the subject (God) with all its predicates (among which is omnipotence), and say 'God is', or 'There is a God', we attach no new predicate to the concept of God, but only posit the subject in itself with all its predicates, and indeed posit it as being an *object* that stands in relation to my *concept*. The content of both must be one and the same; nothing can have been added to the concept, which expresses merely what is possible, by my thinking its object (through the expression 'it is') as given absolutely. Otherwise stated, the real contains no more than the merely possible. A hundred real thalers do not contain the least coin more than a hundred possible thalers. For as the latter signify the concept, and the former the object and the positing of the object, should the former contain more than the latter, my concept would not, in that case, express the whole object, and would not therefore be an adequate concept of it. My financial position is, however, affected very differently by a hundred real thalers than it is by the mere concept of them (that is, of their possibility). For the object, as it actually exists, is not analytically contained in my concept, but is added to my concept (which is a determination of my state) synthetically; and yet the conceived hundred thalers are not themselves in the least increased through thus acquiring existence outside my concept.

By whatever and by however many predicates we may think a thing—even if we completely determine it—we do not make the least addition to the thing when we further declare that this thing *is*. Otherwise, it would not be exactly the same thing that exists, but something more than we had thought in the concept; and we could not, therefore, say that the exact object of my concept exists. If we think in a thing every feature of reality except one, the missing reality is not added by my saying that this defective thing exists. On the contrary, it exists with the same defect with which I have thought it, since otherwise what exists would be something different from what I thought. When, therefore, I think a being as the supreme reality, without any defect, the question still remains whether it exists or not. For though, in my concept, nothing may be lacking of the possible real content of a thing in general, something is still lacking in its relation to my whole state of thought, namely, [in so far as I am unable to assert] that knowledge of this object is also possible *a posteriori*. And here we find the source of our present difficulty. Were we dealing with an object of the senses, we could not confound the existence of the thing with the mere concept of it. For through the concept the object is thought only as conforming to the *universal conditions* of possible empirical knowledge in general, whereas through its existence it is thought as belonging to the context of experience as a whole. In being thus connected with the *content* of experience as a whole, the concept of the object is not, however, in the least enlarged; all that has happened is that our thought has thereby obtained an additional possible perception. It is not, therefore, surprising that, if we attempt to think existence through the pure category alone, we cannot specify a single mark distinguishing it from mere possibility.

Whatever, therefore, and however much, our concept of an object may contain, we must go outside it, if we are to ascribe existence to the object. In the case of objects of the senses, this takes place through their connection with some one of our perceptions, in accordance with empirical laws. But in dealing with objects of pure thought, we have no means whatsoever of knowing their existence, since it would have to be known in a completely *a priori* manner. Our consciousness of all existence (whether immediately through perception, or mediately through inferences which connect something with perception) belongs exclusively to the unity of experience; any [alleged] existence outside this field, while not indeed such as we can declare to be absolutely impossible, is of the nature of an assumption which we can never be in a position to justify.

The concept of a supreme being is in many respects a very useful idea; but just because it is a mere idea, it is altogether incapable, by itself alone, of enlarging our knowledge in regard to what exists. It is not even competent to enlighten us as to the *possibility* of any existence beyond that which is known in and through experience. The analytic criterion of possibility, as consisting in the principle that bare positives (realities) give rise to no contradiction, cannot be denied to it. But since the realities are not given to us in their specific characters; since even if they were, we should still not be in a position to pass judgment; since the criterion of the possibility of synthetic knowledge is never to be looked for save in experience, to which the object of an idea cannot belong, the connection of all real properties in a thing is a synthesis, the possibility of which we are unable to determine *a priori*. And thus the celebrated Leibniz is far from having succeeded in what he plumed himself on achieving—the comprehension *a priori* of the possibility of this sublime ideal being.

The attempt to establish the existence of a supreme being by means of the famous ontological argument of Descartes is therefore merely so much labour and effort lost; we can no more extend our stock of [theoretical] insight by mere ideas, than a merchant can better his position by adding a few noughts to his cash account.

THE IMPOSSIBILITY OF A COSMOLOGICAL PROOF OF
THE EXISTENCE OF GOD

To attempt to extract from a purely arbitrary idea the existence of an object corresponding to it is a quite unnatural procedure and a mere innovation of scholastic subtlety. Such an attempt would never have been made if there had not been antecedently, on the part of our reason, the need to assume as a basis of existence in general something necessary (in which our regress may terminate); and if, since this necessity must be unconditioned and certain *a priori*, reason had not, in consequence, been forced to seek a concept which would satisfy, if possible, such a demand, and enable us to know an existence in a completely *a priori* manner. Such a concept was supposed to have been found in the idea of an *ens realissimum;* and that idea was therefore used only for the more definite knowledge of that necessary being, of the necessary existence of which we were already convinced, or persuaded, on other grounds. This natural procedure of reason was, however, concealed from view, and instead of ending with this concept, the attempt was made to begin with it, and so to deduce from it that necessity of existence which it was only fitted to supplement. Thus arose the unfortunate ontological proof, which yields satisfaction neither to the natural and healthy understanding nor to the more academic demands of strict proof.

The *cosmological proof*, which we are now about to examine, retains the connection of absolute necessity with the highest reality, but instead of reasoning, like the former proof, from the highest reality to necessity of existence, it reasons from the previously given unconditioned necessity of some being to the unlimited reality of that being. It thus enters upon a course of reasoning which, whether rational or only pseudo-rational, is at any rate natural, and the most convincing not only for common sense but even for speculative understanding. It also sketches the first outline of all the proofs in natural theology, an outline which has always been and always will be followed, however much embellished and disguised by superfluous additions. This proof, termed by Leibniz the proof *a contingentia mundi*, we shall now proceed to expound and examine.

It runs thus: If anything exists, an absolutely necessary being must also exist. Now I, at least, exist. Therefore an absolutely necessary being exists. The minor premiss contains an experience, the major premiss the inference from there being any experience at all to the existence of the necessary.[2] The proof therefore really begins with experience, and is not wholly *a priori* or ontological. For this reason, and because the object of all possible experience is called the world, it is entitled the *cosmological* proof. Since, in dealing with the objects of experience, the proof abstracts from all special properties through which this world may differ from any other possible world, the title also serves to distinguish it from the physico-theological proof, which is based upon observations of the particular properties of the world disclosed to us by our senses.

The proof then proceeds as follows: The necessary being can be determined in one way only, that is, by one out of each possible pair of opposed predicates. It must therefore be *completely* determined through its own concept. Now there is only one possible concept which determines a thing completely *a priori*, namely, the concept of the *ens realissimum*. The concept of the *ens realissimum* is therefore the only concept through which a necessary being can be thought. In other words, a supreme being necessarily exists.

In this cosmological argument there are combined so many pseudo-ra-

---

[2] This inference is too well known to require detailed statement. It depends on the supposedly transcendental law of natural causality: that everything contingent has a cause, which, if itself contingent, must likewise have a cause, till the series of subordinate causes ends with an absolutely necessary cause, without which it would have no completeness.

tional principles that speculative reason seems in this case to have brought to bear all the resources of its dialectical skill to produce the greatest possible transcendental illusion. The testing of the argument may meantime be postponed while we detail in order the various devices whereby an old argument is disguised as a new one, and by which appeal is made to the agreement of two witnesses, the one with credentials of pure reason and the other with those of experience. In reality the only witness is that which speaks in the name of pure reason; in the endeavour to pass as a second witness it merely changes its dress and voice. In order to lay a secure foundation for itself, this proof takes its stand on experience, and thereby makes profession of being distinct from the ontological proof, which puts its entire trust in pure *a priori* concepts. But the cosmological proof uses this experience only for a single step in the argument, namely, to conclude the existence of a necessary being. What properties this being may have, the empirical premiss cannot tell us. Reason therefore abandons experience altogether, and endeavours to discover from mere concepts what properties an absolutely necessary being must have, that is, which among all possible things contains in itself the conditions (*requisita*) essential to absolute necessity. Now these, it is supposed, are nowhere to be found save in the concept of an *ens realissimum;* and the conclusion is therefore drawn, that the *ens realissimum* is the absolutely necessary being. But it is evident that we are here presupposing that the concept of the highest reality is completely adequate to the concept of absolute necessity of existence; that is, that the latter can be inferred from the former. Now this is the proposition maintained by the ontological proof; it is here being assumed in the cosmological proof, and indeed made the basis of the proof; and yet it is an assumption with which this latter proof has professed to dispense. For absolute necessity is an existence determined from mere concepts. If I say, the concept of the *ens realissimum* is a concept, and indeed the only concept, which is appropriate and adequate to necessary existence, I must also admit that necessary existence can be inferred from this concept. Thus the so-called cosmological proof really owes any cogency which it may have to the ontological proof from mere concepts. The appeal to experience is quite superfluous; experience may perhaps lead us to the concept of absolute necessity, but is unable to demonstrate this necessity as belonging to any determinate thing. For immediately we endeavour to do so, we must abandon all experience and search among pure concepts to discover whether any one of them contains the conditions of the possibility of an absolutely necessary being. If in this way we can determine the possibility of a necessary being, we likewise establish its existence. For what we are then saying is this: that of all possible beings there is one which carries with it absolute necessity, that is, that this being exists with absolute necessity.

Fallacious and misleading arguments are most easily detected if set out in correct syllogistic form. This we now proceed to do in the instance under discussion.

If the proposition, that every absolutely necessary being is likewise the most real of all beings, is correct (and this is the *nervus probandi* of the cosmological proof), it must, like all affirmative judgments, be convertible, at least *per accidens*. It therefore follows that some *entia realissima* are likewise absolutely necessary beings. But one *ens realissimum* is in no respect different from another, and what is true of *some* under this concept is true also of *all*. In this case, therefore, I can convert the proposition *simpliciter*, not only *per accidens*, and say that every *ens realissimum* is a necessary being. But since this proposition is determined from its *a priori* concepts alone, the mere concept of the *ens realissimum* must carry with it the absolute necessity of that being; and this is precisely what the ontological proof has asserted and what the cosmological proof has refused to admit, although the conclusions of the latter are indeed covertly based on it.

Thus the second path upon which speculative reason enters in its attempt to prove the existence of a supreme being is not only as deceptive as the first, but has this additional defect, that it is guilty of an *ignoratio elenchi* [this is, ignorant of what is required for an effective proof]. It professes to lead us by a new path, but after a short circuit brings us back to the very path which we had deserted at its bidding.

I have stated that in this cosmological argument there lies hidden a whole nest of dialectical assumptions, which the transcendental critique can easily detect and destroy. These deceptive principles I shall merely enumerate, leaving to the reader, who by this time will be sufficiently expert in these matters, the task of investigating them further, and of refuting them.

We find, for instance, (1) the transcendental principle whereby from the contingent we infer a cause. This principle is applicable only in the sensible world; outside that world it has no meaning whatsoever. For the mere intellectual concept of the contingent cannot give rise to any synthetic proposition, such as that of causality. The principle of causality has no meaning and no criterion for its application save only in the sensible world. But in the cosmological proof it is precisely in order to enable us to advance beyond the sensible world that it is employed. (2) The inference to a first cause, from the impossibility of an infinite series of causes, given one after the other, in the sensible world. The principles of the employment of reason do not justify this conclusion even within the world of experience, still less beyond this world in a realm into which this series can never be extended. (3) The unjustified self-satisfaction of reason in respect of the completion of this series. The removal of all the conditions without which no concept of necessity is possible is taken by reason to be a completion of the concept of the series, on the ground that we can then conceive nothing further. (4) The confusion between the logical possibility of a concept of all reality united into one (without inner contradiction) and the transcendental possibility of such a reality. In the case of the latter there is needed a principle to establish the practicability of such a synthesis, a principle which itself, however, can apply only to the field of possible experiences—etc.

The procedure of the cosmological proof is artfully designed to enable us to escape having to prove the existence of a necessary being *a priori* through mere concepts. Such proof would require to be carried out in the ontological manner, and that is an enterprise for which we feel ourselves to be altogether incompetent. Accordingly, we take as the starting-point of our inference an actual existence (an experience in general), and advance, in such manner as we can, to some absolutely necessary condition of this existence. We have then no need to show the possibility of this condition. For if it has been proved to exist, the question as to its possibility is entirely superfluous. If now we want to determine more fully the nature of this necessary being, we do not endeavour to do so in the manner that would be really adequate, namely, by discovering from its concept the necessity of its existence. For could we do that, we should be in no need of an empirical starting-point. No, all we seek is the negative condition (*conditio sine qua non*), without which a being would not be absolutely necessary. And in all other kinds of reasoning from a given consequence to its ground this would be legitimate; but in the present case it unfortunately happens that the condition which is needed for absolute necessity is only to be found in one single being. This being must therefore contain in its concept all that is required for absolute necessity, and consequently it enables me to infer this absolute necessity *a priori*. I must therefore be able also to reverse the inference, and to say: Anything to which this concept (of supreme reality) applies is absolutely necessary. If I cannot make this inference (as I must concede, if I am to avoid admitting the ontological proof), I have come to grief in the new way that I have been following, and am back again at my starting-point. The concept of the supreme being satisfies all questions *a priori* which can be raised regarding the inner determinations of a thing, and is therefore an ideal that is quite unique, in that the concept, while universal, also at the same time designates an individual as being among the things that are possible. But it does not give satisfaction concerning the question of its own existence—though this is the real purpose of our enquiries—and if anyone admitted the existence of a necessary being but wanted to know which among all [existing] things is to be identified with that being, we could not answer: "This, not that, is the necessary being."

We may indeed be allowed to *postulate* the existence of an all-sufficient being, as the cause of all possible effects, with a view to lightening the task of reason in its search for the unity of the grounds of explanation. But in presuming so far as to say that such a being *necessarily exists*, we are no longer giving modest expression to an admissible hypothesis, but are confidently laying claim to apodeictic certainty. For the knowledge of what we profess to know as absolutely necessary must itself carry with it absolute necessity.

The whole problem of the transcendental ideal amounts to this: either, given absolute necessity, to find a concept which possesses it, or, given the concept of something, to find that something to be absolutely necessary. If either task be possible, so must the other; for reason recognises that only as absolutely necessary which follows of necessity from its concept. But both tasks are quite beyond our utmost efforts to *satisfy* our understanding in this matter; and equally unavailing are all attempts to induce it to acquiesce in its incapacity.

Unconditioned necessity, which we so indispensably require as the last bearer of all things, is for human reason the veritable abyss. Eternity itself, in all its terrible sublimity, as depicted by a Haller,[3] is far from making the same overwhelming impression on the mind; for it only *measures* the duration of things, it does not *support* them. We cannot put aside, and yet also cannot endure the thought, that a being, which we represent to ourselves as supreme amongst all possible beings, should, as it were, say to itself: 'I am from eternity to eternity, and outside me there is nothing save what is

---

3 [Albrecht von Haller (1708–1777), a writer on medical and kindred subjects, author of *Die Alpen* and other poems.]

through my will, *but whence then am I?'* All support here fails us; and the *greatest* perfection, no less than the *least* perfection, is unsubstantial and baseless for the merely speculative reason, which makes not the least effort to retain either the one or the other, and feels indeed no loss in allowing them to vanish entirely.

Many forces in nature, which manifest their existence through certain effects, remain for us inscrutable; for we cannot track them sufficiently far by observation. Also, the transcendental object lying at the basis of appearances (and with it the reason why our sensibility is subject to certain supreme conditions rather than to others) is and remains for us inscrutable. The thing itself is indeed given, but we can have no insight into its nature. But it is quite otherwise with an ideal of pure reason; it can never be said to be inscrutable. For since it is not required to give any credentials of its reality save only the need on the part of reason to complete all synthetic unity by means of it; and since, therefore, it is in no wise given as thinkable *object*, it cannot be inscrutable in the manner in which an object is. On the contrary it must, as a mere idea, find its place and its solution in the nature of reason, and must therefore allow of investigation. For it is of the very essence of reason that we should be able to give an account of all our concepts, opinions, and assertions, either upon objective or, in the case of mere illusion, upon subjective grounds.

.   .   .

THE IMPOSSIBILITY OF THE PHYSICO-THEOLOGICAL PROOF

If, then, neither the concept of things in general nor the experience of any *existence in general* can supply what is required, it remains only to try whether a *determinate experience*, the experience of the things of the present world, and the constitution and order of these, does not provide the basis of a proof which may help us to attain to an assured conviction of a supreme being. Such proof we propose to entitle the *physico-theological*. Should this attempt also fail, it must follow that no satisfactory proof of the existence of a being corresponding to our transcendental idea can be possible by pure speculative reason.

In view of what has already been said, it is evident that we can count upon a quite easy and conclusive answer to this enquiry. For how can any experience ever be adequate to an idea? The peculiar nature of the latter consists just in the fact that no experience can ever be equal to it. The transcendental idea of a necessary and all-sufficient original being is so overwhelmingly great, so high above everything empirical, the latter being always conditioned, that it leaves us at a loss, partly because we can never find in experience material sufficient to satisfy such a concept, and partly because it is always in the sphere of the conditioned that we carry out our search, seeking there ever vainly for the unconditioned—no law of any empirical synthesis giving us an example of any such unconditioned or providing the least guidance in its pursuit.

If the supreme being should itself stand in this chain of conditions, it would be a member of the series, and like the lower members which it precedes, would call for further enquiry as to the still higher ground from which it follows. If, on the other hand, we propose to separate it from the chain, and to conceive it as a purely intelligible being, existing apart from the series of natural causes, by what bridge can reason contrive to pass over to it? For all laws governing the transition from effects to causes, all synthesis and extension of our knowledge, refer to nothing but possible experience, and therefore solely to objects of the sensible world, and apart from them can have no meaning whatsoever.

This world presents to us so immeasurable a stage of variety, order, purposiveness, and beauty, as displayed alike in its infinite extent and in the unlimited divisibility of its parts, that even with such knowledge as our weak understanding can acquire of it, we are brought face to face with so many marvels immeasurably great, that all speech loses its force, all numbers their power to measure, our thoughts themselves all definiteness, and that our judgment of the whole resolves itself into an amazement which is speechless, and only the more eloquent on that account. Everywhere we see a chain of effects and causes, of ends and means, a regularity in origination and dissolution. Nothing has of itself come into the condition in which we find it to exist, but always points to something else as its cause, while this in turn commits us to repetition of the same enquiry. The whole universe must thus sink into the abyss of nothingness, unless, over and above this infinite chain of contingencies, we assume something to support it—something which is original and independently self-subsistent, and which as the cause of the origin of the universe secures also at the same time its continuance. What magnitude are we to ascribe to this supreme cause—admitting that it is supreme in respect of all things in the world? We are not acquainted with the whole content of the world, still less do we know how to estimate its magnitude by comparison with all that is possible. But since we cannot, as regards causality, dispense with an ultimate and supreme being, what is there to prevent us ascribing to it a degree of perfection that sets it *above everything else that is possible?* This we can easily do—though only through the slender outline of an abstract concept—by representing this being to ourselves as combining in itself all possible perfection, as in a single substance. This concept is in conformity with the demand of our reason for parsimony of principles; it is free from self-contradiction, and is never decisively contradicted by any experience; and it is likewise of such a character that it contributes to the extension of the employment of reason within experience, through the guidance which it yields in the discovery of order and purposiveness.

This proof always deserves to be mentioned with respect. It is the oldest, the clearest, and the most accordant with the common reason of mankind. It enlivens the study of nature, just as it itself derives its existence and gains ever new vigour from that source. It suggests ends and purposes, where our observation would not have detected them by itself, and extends our knowledge of nature by means of the guiding-concept of a special unity, the principle of which is outside nature. This knowledge again reacts on its cause, namely, upon the idea which has led to it, and so strengthens the belief in a supreme Author [of nature] that the belief acquires the force of an irresistible conviction.

It would therefore not only be uncomforting but utterly vain to attempt to diminish in any way the authority of this argument. Reason, constantly upheld by this ever-increasing evidence, which, though empirical, is yet so powerful, cannot be so depressed through doubts suggested by subtle and abstruse speculation, that it is not at once aroused from the indecision of all melancholy reflection, as from a dream, by one glance at the wonders of nature and the majesty of the universe—ascending from height to height up to the all-highest, from the conditioned to its conditions, up to the supreme and unconditioned Author [of all conditioned being].

But although we have nothing to bring against the rationality and utility of this procedure, but have rather to commend and to further it, we still cannot approve the claims, which this mode of argument would fain advance, to apodeictic certainty and to an assent founded on no special favour or support from other quarters. It cannot hurt the good cause, if the dogmatic language of the overweening sophist be toned down to the more moderate and humble requirements of a belief adequate to quieten our doubts, though not to commend unconditional submission. I therefore maintain that the physico-theological proof can never by itself establish the existence of a supreme being, but must always fall back upon the ontological argument to make good its deficiency. It only serves as an introduction to the ontological argument; and the latter therefore contains (in so far as a speculative proof is possible at all) *the one possible ground of proof* with which human reason can never dispense.

The chief points of the physico-theological proof are as follows: (1) In the world we everywhere find clear signs of an order in accordance with a determinate purpose, carried out with great wisdom; and this in a universe which is indescribably varied in content and unlimited in extent. (2) This purposive order is quite alien to the things of the world, and only belongs to them contingently; that is to say, the diverse things could not of themselves have co-operated, by so great a combination of diverse means, to the fulfilment of determinate final purposes, had they not been chosen and designed for these purposes by an ordering rational principle in conformity with underlying ideas. (3) There exists, therefore, a sublime and wise cause (or more than one), which must be the cause of the world not merely as a blindly working all-powerful nature, by *fecundity*, but as intelligence, through *freedom*. (4) The unity of this cause may be inferred from the unity of the reciprocal relations existing between the parts of the world, as members of an artfully arranged structure—inferred with certainty in so far as our observation suffices for its verification, and beyond these limits with probability, in accordance with the principles of analogy.

We need not here criticise natural reason too strictly in regard to its conclusion from the analogy between certain natural products and what our human art produces when we do violence to nature, and constrain it to proceed not according to its own ends but in conformity with ours—appealing to the similarity of these particular natural products with houses, ships, watches. Nor need we here question its conclusion that there lies at the basis of nature a causality similar to that responsible for artificial products, namely, an understanding and a will; and that the inner possibility of a self-acting nature (which is what makes all art, and even, it may be, reason itself, possible) is therefore derived from another, though superhuman, art—a mode of reasoning which could not perhaps withstand a searching transcendental criticism. But at any rate we must admit that, if we are to specify a cause at all, we cannot here proceed more securely than by analogy with those purposive productions of which alone the cause and mode of action are fully known to us. Reason could never be justified in abandoning the causality which it knows for grounds of explanation which are obscure, of which it does not have any knowledge, and which are incapable of proof.

On this method of argument, the purposiveness and harmonious adaptation of so much in nature can suffice to prove the contingency of the form merely, not of the matter, that is, not of the substance in the world. To prove the latter we should have to demonstrate that the things in the world would not of themselves be capable of such order and harmony, in accordance with universal laws, if they were not *in their substance* the product of supreme wisdom. But to prove this we should require quite other grounds of proof than those which are derived from the analogy with human art. The utmost, therefore, that the argument can prove is an *architect* of the world who is always very much hampered by the adaptability of the material in which he works, not a *creator* of the world to whose idea everything is subject. This, however, is altogether inadequate to the lofty purpose which we have before our eyes, namely, the proof of an all-sufficient primordial being. To prove the contingency of matter itself, we should have to resort to a transcendental argument, and this is precisely what we have here set out to avoid.

The inference, therefore, is that the order and purposiveness everywhere observable throughout the world may be regarded as a completely contingent arrangement, and that we may argue to the existence of a cause *proportioned* to it. But the concept of this cause must enable us to know something quite *determinate* about it, and can therefore be no other than the concept of a being who possesses all might, wisdom, etc., in a word, all the perfection which is proper to an all-sufficient being. For the predicates—'very great', 'astounding', 'immeasurable' in power and excellence—give no determinate concept at all, and do not really tell us what the thing is in itself. They are only relative representations of the magnitude of the object, which the observer, in contemplating the world, compares with himself and with his capacity of comprehension, and which are equally terms of eulogy whether we be magnifying the object or be depreciating the observing subject in relation to that object. Where we are concerned with the magnitude (of the perfection) of a thing, there is no determinate concept except that which comprehends all possible perfection; and in that concept only the allness (*omnitudo*) of the reality is completely determined.

Now no one, I trust, will be so bold as to profess that he comprehends the relation of the magnitude of the world as he has observed it (alike as regards both extent and content) to omnipotence, of the world order to supreme wisdom, of the world unity to the absolute unity of its Author, etc. Physico-theology is therefore unable to give any determinate concept of the supreme cause of the world, and cannot therefore serve as the foundation of a theology which is itself in turn to form the basis of religion.

To advance to absolute totality by the empirical road is utterly impossible. None the less this is what is attempted in the physico-theological proof. What, then, are the means which have been adopted to bridge this wide abyss?

The physico-theological argument can indeed lead us to the point of admiring the greatness, wisdom, power, etc., of the Author of the world, but can take us no further. Accordingly, we then abandon the argument from empirical grounds of proof, and fall back upon the contingency which, in the first steps of the argument, we had inferred from the order and purposiveness of the world. With this contingency as our sole premiss, we then advance, by means of transcendental concepts alone, to the existence of an absolutely necessary being, and [as a final step] from the concept of the absolute necessity of the first cause to the completely determinate or determinable concept of that necessary being, namely, to the concept of an all-embracing reality. Thus the physico-theological proof, failing in its undertaking, has in face of this difficulty suddenly fallen back upon the cosmological proof; and since the latter is only a disguised ontological proof, it has really achieved its purpose by pure reason alone—although at the start it disclaimed all kinship with pure reason and professed to establish its conclusions on convincing evidence derived from experience.

Those who propound the physico-theological argument have therefore no ground for being so contemptuous in their attitude to the transcendental mode of proof, posing as clear-sighted students of nature, and complacently looking down upon that proof as the artificial product of obscure speculative refinements. For were they willing to scrutinise their own procedure, they would find that, after advancing some considerable way on the solid ground of nature and experience, and finding themselves just as far distant as ever from the object which discloses itself to their reason, they suddenly leave this ground, and pass over into the realm of mere possibilities, where they hope upon the wings of ideas to draw near to the object—the object that has refused itself to all their *empirical* enquiries. For after this tremendous leap, when they have, as they think, found firm ground, they extend their concept—the *determinate* concept, into the possession of which they have now come, they know not how—over the whole sphere of creation. And the ideal, [which this reasoning thus involves, and] which is entirely a product of pure reason, they then elucidate by reference to experience, though inadequately enough, and in a manner far below the dignity of its object; and throughout they persist in refusing to admit that they have arrived at this knowledge or hypothesis by a road quite other than that of experience.

Thus the physico-theological proof of the existence of an original or supreme being rests upon the cosmological proof, and the cosmological upon the ontological. And since, besides these three, there is no other path open to speculative reason, the ontological proof from pure concepts of reason is the only possible one, if indeed any proof of a proposition so far exalted above all empirical employment of the understanding is possible at all.

.   .   .

4

THE ABSOLUTE PARADOX

Søren Kierkegaard

In spite of the fact that Socrates studied with all diligence to acquire a knowledge of human nature and to understand himself, and in spite of the fame accorded him through the centuries as one who beyond all other men had an insight into the human heart, he has himself admitted that the reason for his shrinking from reflection upon the nature of such beings as Pegasus and the Gorgons was that he, the life-long student of human nature, had not yet been able to make up his mind whether he was a stranger monster than Typhon, or a creature of a gentler and simpler sort, partaking of something divine (*Phaedrus*, 229 E). This seems to be a paradox. However, one should not think slightingly of the paradoxical; for the paradox is the source of the thinker's passion, and the thinker without a paradox is like a lover without feeling: a paltry mediocrity. But the highest pitch of every passion is always to will its own downfall; and so it is also the supreme passion of the Reason to seek a collision, though this collision must in one way or another prove its undoing. The supreme paradox of all thought is the attempt to discover something that thought cannot think. This passion is at bottom present in all thinking, even in the thinking of the individual, in so far as in thinking he participates in something transcending himself. But habit dulls our sensibilities, and prevents us from perceiving it. So for example the scientists tell us that our walking is a constant falling. But a sedate and proper gentleman who walks to his office in the morning and back again at noon, probably thinks this to be an exaggeration, for his progress is clearly a case of mediation; how should it occur to him that he is constantly falling when he religiously follows his nose!

But in order to make a beginning, let us now assume a daring proposition; let us assume that we know what man is. Here we have that criterion of the Truth, which in the whole course of Greek philosophy was either *sought*, or *doubted*, or *postulated*, or *made fruitful*. Is it not remarkable that the Greeks should have borne us this testimony? And is it not an epitome, as it

From Søren Kierkegaard, *Philosophical Fragments*, David Swenson, trans., Howard V. Hong, revised trans. (Princeton: 1962), Chap. III, pp. 46–60. Reprinted by permission of Princeton University Press, Copyright ©, 1936, 1962 by Princeton University Press.

were, of the significance of Greek culture, an epigram of its own writing, with which it is also better served than with the frequently voluminous disquisitions sometimes devoted to it? Thus the proposition is well worth positing, and also for another reason, since we have already explained it in the two preceding chapters; while anyone who attempts to explain Socrates differently may well beware lest he fall into the snare of the earlier or later Greek scepticism. For unless we hold fast to the Socratic doctrine of Recollection, and to his principle that every individual man is Man, Sextus Empiricus stands ready to make the transition involved in "teaching" not only difficult but impossible; and Protagoras will begin where Sextus Empiricus leaves off, maintaining that man is the measure of all things, in the sense that the individual man is the measure for others, but by no means in the Socratic sense that each man is his own measure, neither more nor less.

So then we know what man is, and this wisdom, which I shall be the last to hold in light esteem, may progressively become richer and more significant, and with it also the Truth. But now the Reason stands still, just as Socrates did; for the paradoxical passion of the Reason is aroused and seeks a collision; without rightly understanding itself, it is bent upon its own downfall. This is like what happens in connection with the paradox of love. Man lives undisturbed a self-centered life, until there awakens within him the paradox of self-love, in the form of love for another, the object of his longing. (Self-love lies as the ground of all love or is the ground in which all love perishes; therefore if we conceive a religion of love, this religion need make but one assumption, as epigrammatic as true, and take its actuality for granted, namely, the condition that man loves himself, in order to command him to love his neighbor as himself.) The lover is so completely transformed by the paradox of love that he scarcely recognizes himself; so say the poets, who are the spokesmen of love, and so say also the lovers themselves, since they permit the poets merely to take the words from their lips, but not the passion from their hearts. In like manner the paradoxical passion of the Reason, while as yet a mere presentiment, retroactively affects man and his self-knowledge, so that he who thought to know himself is no longer certain whether he is a more strangely composite animal than Typhon, or if perchance his nature contains a gentler and diviner part. . . .

But what is this unknown something with which the Reason collides when inspired by its paradoxical passion, with the result of unsettling even man's knowledge of himself? It is the Unknown. It is not a human being, in so far as we know what man is; nor is it any other known thing. So let us call this unknown something: *the God*. It is nothing more than a name we assign to it. The idea of demonstrating that this unknown something (the God) exists, could scarcely suggest itself to the Reason. For if the God does not exist it would of course be impossible to prove it; and if he does exist it would be folly to attempt it. For at the very outset, in beginning my proof, I would have presupposed it, not as doubtful but as certain (a presupposition is never doubtful, for the very reason that it is a presupposition), since otherwise I would not begin, readily understanding that the whole would be impossible if he did not exist. But if when I speak of proving the God's existence I mean that I propose to prove that the Unknown, which exists, is the God, then I express myself unfortunately. For in that case I do not prove anything, least of all an existence, but merely develop the content of a conception. Generally speaking, it is a difficult matter to prove that anything exists; and what is still worse for the intrepid souls who undertake the venture, the difficulty is such that fame scarcely awaits those who concern themselves with it. The entire demonstration always turns into something very different and becomes an additional development of the consequences that flow from my having assumed that the object in question exists. Thus I always reason from existence, not toward existence, whether I move in the sphere of palpable sensible fact or in the realm of thought. I do not for example prove that a stone exists, but that some existing thing is a stone. The procedure in a court of justice does not prove that a criminal exists, but that the accused, whose existence is given, is a criminal. Whether we call existence an *accessorium* [something predicated] or the eternal *prius* [first given or assumed], it is never subject to demonstration. Let us take ample time for consideration. We have no such reason for haste as have those who from concern for themselves or for the God or for some other thing, must make haste to get existence demonstrated. Under such circumstances there may indeed be need for haste, especially if the prover sincerely seeks to appreciate the danger that he himself, or the thing in question, may be non-existent unless the proof is finished and does not surreptitiously entertain the thought that it exists whether he succeeds in proving it or not.

If it were proposed to prove Napoleon's existence from Napoleon's deeds, would it not be a most curious proceeding? His existence does indeed explain his deeds, but the deeds do not prove *his* existence, unless I have already understood the word "his" so as thereby to have assumed his existence. But Napoleon is only an individual, and in so far there exists no absolute relationship between him and his deeds; some other person might have performed the same deeds. Perhaps this is the reason why I cannot pass from the deeds to existence. If I call these deeds the deeds of Napoleon the proof becomes superfluous, since I have already named him; if I ignore this, I can never prove from the deeds that they are Napoleon's, but only in a purely ideal manner that such deeds are the deeds of a great general, and so forth. But between the God and his works there is an absolute relationship; God is not a name but a concept. Is this perhaps the reason that his *essentia involvit existentiam* [essence entails existence]? The works of God are such that only the God can perform them. Just so, but where then are the works of the God? The works from which I would deduce his existence are not directly and immediately given. The wisdom in nature, the goodness, the wisdom in the governance of the world—are all these manifest, perhaps, upon the very face of things? Are we not here confronted with the most terrible temptations to doubt, and is it not impossible finally to dispose of all these doubts? But from such an order of things I will surely not attempt to prove God's existence; and even if I began I would never finish, and would in addition have to live constantly in suspense, lest something so terrible should suddenly happen that my bit of proof would be demolished. From what works then do I propose to derive the proof? From the works as apprehended through an ideal interpretation, i.e., such as they do not immediately reveal themselves. But in that case it is not from the works that I make the proof; I merely develop the ideality I have presupposed, and because of my confidence in *this* I make so bold as to defy all objections, even those that have not yet been made. In beginning my proof I presuppose the ideal interpretation, and also that I will be successful in carrying it through; but what else is this but to presuppose that the God exists, so that I really begin by virtue of confidence in him?

And how does the God's existence emerge from the proof? Does it follow straightway, without any breach of continuity? Or have we not here an analogy to the behaviour of the little Cartesian dolls? As soon as I let go of the doll it stands on its head. As soon as I let it go—I must therefore let it go. So also with the proof. As long as I keep my hold on the proof, i.e., continue to demonstrate, the existence does not come out, if for no other reason than that I am engaged in proving it; but when I let the proof go, the existence is there. But this act of letting go is surely also something; it is indeed a contribution of mine. Must not this also be taken into the account, this little moment, brief as it may be—it need not be long, for it is a *leap*. However brief this moment, if only an instantaneous now, this "now" must be included in the reckoning. If anyone wishes to have it ignored, I will use it to tell a little anecdote, in order to show that it nevertheless does exist. Chrysippus was experimenting with a sorites to see if he could not bring about a break in its quality, either progressively or retrogressively. But Carneades could not get it in his head when the new quality actually emerged. Then Chrysippus told him to try making a little pause in the reckoning, and so—so it would be easier to understand. Carneades replied: With the greatest pleasure, please do not hesitate on my account; you may not only pause, but even lie down to sleep, and it will help you just as little; for when you awake we will begin again where you left off. Just so; it boots as little to try to get rid of something by sleeping as to try to come into the possession of something in the same manner.

Whoever therefore attempts to demonstrate the existence of God (except in the sense of clarifying the concept, and without the *reservatio finalis* noted above, that the existence emerges from the demonstration by a leap) proves in lieu thereof something else, something which at times perhaps does not need a proof, and in any case needs none better; for the fool says in his heart that there is no God, but whoever says in his heart or to men: Wait just a little and I will prove it—what a rare man of wisdom is he![1] If in the moment of beginning his proof it is not absolutely undetermined whether the God exists or not, he does not prove it; and if it is thus undetermined in the beginning he will never come to begin, partly from fear of failure, since the God perhaps does not exist, and partly because he has nothing with which to begin.—A project of this kind would scarcely have been undertaken by the ancients. Socrates at least, who is credited with having put forth the physico-teleological proof for God's existence, did not go about it in any such manner. He always presupposes the God's existence, and under this presupposition seeks to interpenetrate nature with the idea of purpose. Had he been asked why he pursued this method, he would doubtless have explained that he lacked the courage to venture out upon so perilous a voyage of discovery without having made sure of the God's existence behind him. At the word of the God he casts his net as if to catch the idea of purpose; for nature herself finds many means of frightening the inquirer, and distracts him by many a digression.

---

[1] What an excellent subject for a comedy of the higher lunacy!

The paradoxical passion of the Reason thus comes repeatedly into collision with this Unknown, which does indeed exist, but is unknown, and in so
far does not exist. The Reason cannot advance beyond this point, and yet it
cannot refrain in its paradoxicalness from arriving at this limit and occupying itself therewith. It will not serve to dismiss its relation to it simply by
asserting that the Unknown does not exist, since this itself involves a relationship. But what then is the Unknown, since the designation of it as the
God merely signifies for us that it is unknown? To say that it is the
Unknown because it cannot be known, and even if it were capable of being
known, it could not be expressed, does not satisfy the demands of passion,
though it correctly interprets the Unknown as a limit; but a limit is precisely a torment for passion, though it also serves as an incitement. And yet
the Reason can come no further, whether it risks an issue *via negationis* [by
way of denying attributes] or *via eminentia* [by way of affirming attributes
in the supreme degree].

What then is the Unknown? It is the limit to which the Reason repeatedly
comes, and in so far, substituting a static form of conception for the
dynamic, it is the different, the absolutely different. But because it is absolutely different, there is no mark by which it could be distinguished. When
qualified as absolutely different it seems on the verge of disclosure, but this
is not the case; for the Reason cannot even conceive an absolute unlikeness.
The Reason cannot negate itself absolutely, but uses itself for the purpose,
and thus conceives only such an unlikeness within itself as it can conceive by
means of itself; it cannot absolutely transcend itself, and hence conceives
only such a superiority over itself as it can conceive by means of itself.
Unless the Unknown (the God) remains a mere limiting conception, the
single idea of difference will be thrown into a state of confusion, and
become many ideas of many differences. The Unknown is then in a condition of dispersion (διασπορά), and the Reason may choose at pleasure from
what is at hand and the imagination may suggest (the monstrous, the
ludicrous, etc.).

But it is impossible to hold fast to a difference of this nature. Every time
this is done it is essentially an arbitrary act, and deepest down in the heart of
piety lurks the mad caprice which knows that it has itself produced the
God. If no specific determination of difference can be held fast, because
there is no distinguishing mark, like and unlike finally become identified with
one another, thus sharing the fate of all such dialectical opposites. The
unlikeness clings to the Reason and confounds it, so that the Reason no
longer knows itself and quite consistently confuses itself with the unlikeness.
On this point paganism has been sufficiently prolific in fantastic inventions.
As for the last named supposition, the self-irony of the Reason, I shall
attempt to delineate it merely by a stroke or two, without raising any
question of its being historical. There exists an individual whose appearance
is precisely like that of other men; he grows up to manhood like others, he
marries, he has an occupation by which he earns his livelihood, and he makes
provision for the future as befits a man. For though it may be beautiful to
live like the birds of the air, it is not lawful, and may lead to the sorriest of
consequences: either starvation if one has enough persistence, or dependence
on the bounty of others. This man is also the God. How do I know? I
cannot know it, for in order to know it I would have to know the God, and

the nature of the difference between the God and man; and this I cannot know, because the Reason has reduced it to likeness with that from which it was unlike. Thus the God becomes the most terrible of deceivers, because the Reason has deceived itself. The Reason has brought the God as near as possible, and yet he is as far away as ever.

Now perhaps someone will say: "You are certainly a crotcheteer, as I know very well. But you surely do not believe that I would pay any attention to such a crotchet, so strange or so ridiculous that it has doubtless never occurred to anyone, and above all so absurd that I must exclude from my consciousness everything that I have in it in order to hit upon it."—And so indeed you must. But do you think yourself warranted in retaining all the presuppositions you have in your consciousness, while pretending to think about your consciousness without presuppositions? Will you deny the consistency of our exposition: that the Reason, in attempting to determine the Unknown as the unlike, at last goes astray, and confounds the unlike with the like? From this there would seem to follow the further consequence, that if man is to receive any true knowledge about the Unknown (the God) he must be made to know that it is unlike him, absolutely unlike him. This knowledge the Reason cannot possibly obtain of itself; we have already seen that this would be a self-contradiction. It will therefore have to obtain this knowledge from the God. But even if it obtains such knowledge it cannot understand it, and thus is quite unable to possess such knowledge. For how should the Reason be able to understand what is absolutely different from itself? If this is not immediately evident, it will become clearer in the light of the consequences; for if the God is absolutely unlike man, then man is absolutely unlike the God; but how could the Reason be expected to understand this? Here we seem to be confronted with a paradox. Merely to obtain the knowledge that the God is unlike him, man needs the help of the God; and now he learns that the God is absolutely different from himself. But if the God and man are absolutely different, this cannot be accounted for on the basis of what man derives from the God, for in so far they are akin. Their unlikeness must therefore be explained by what man derives from himself, or by what he has brought upon his own head. But what can this unlikeness be? Aye, what can it be but sin; since the unlikeness, the absolute unlikeness, is something that man has brought upon himself. We have expressed this in the preceding by saying that man was in Error, and had brought this upon his head by his own guilt; and we came to the conclusion, partly in jest and yet also in earnest, that it was too much to expect of man that he should find this out for himself. Now we have again arrived at the same conclusion. The connoisseur in self-knowledge was perplexed over himself to the point of bewilderment when he came to grapple in thought with the unlike; he scarcely knew any longer whether he was a stranger monster than Typhon, or if his nature partook of something divine. What then did he lack? The consciousness of sin, which he indeed could no more teach to another than another could teach it to him, but only the God—if the God consents to become a Teacher. But this was his purpose, as we have imagined it. In order to be man's Teacher, the God proposed to make himself like the individual man, so that he might understand him fully. Thus our paradox is rendered still more appalling, or the same paradox has the double aspect which proclaims it as the Absolute Paradox; negatively by revealing the absolute unlikeness of sin, positively by proposing to do away with the absolute unlikeness in absolute likeness.

But can such a paradox be conceived? Let us not be over-hasty in replying; and since we strive merely to find the answer to a question, and not as those who run a race, it may be well to remember that success is to the accurate rather than to the swift. The Reason will doubtless find it impossible to conceive it, could not of itself have discovered it, and when it hears it announced will not be able to understand it, sensing merely that its downfall is threatened. In so far the Reason will have much to urge against it; and yet we have on the other hand seen that the Reason, in its paradoxical passion, precisely desires its own downfall. But this is what the Paradox also desires, and thus they are at bottom linked in understanding; but this understanding is present only in the moment of passion. Consider the analogy presented by love, though it is not a perfect one. Self-love lies as the ground of love; but the paradoxical passion of self-love when at its highest pitch wills precisely its own downfall. This is also what love desires, so that these two are linked in mutual understanding in the passion of the moment, and this passion is love. Why should not the lover find this conceivable? But he who in self-love shrinks from the touch of love can neither understand it nor summon the courage to venture it, since it means his downfall. Such is then the passion of love; self-love is indeed submerged but not annihilated; it is taken captive and becomes love's *spolia opima* [honorable spoils], but may again come to life, and this is love's temptation. So also with the Paradox in its relation to the Reason, only that the passion in this case has another name; or rather, we must seek to find a name for it.

CRITIQUE OF THEOLOGY

A. J. Ayer

. . .

It is now generally admitted, at any rate by philosophers, that the existence of a being having the attributes which define the god of any non-animistic religion cannot be demonstratively proved. To see that this is so, we have only to ask ourselves what are the premises from which the existence of such a god could be deduced. If the conclusion that a god exists is to be demonstratively certain, then these premises must be certain; for, as the conclusion of a deductive argument is already contained in the premises, any uncertainty there may be about the truth of the premises is necessarily shared by it. But we know that no empirical proposition can ever be anything more than probable. It is only *a priori* propositions that are logically certain. But we cannot deduce the existence of a god from an *a priori* proposition. For we know that the reason why *a priori* propositions are certain is that they are tautologies. And from a set of tautologies nothing but a further tautology can be validly deduced. It follows that there is no possibility of demonstrating the existence of a god.

What is not so generally recognised is that there can be no way of proving that the existence of a god, such as the God of Christianity, is even probable. Yet this also is easily shown. For if the existence of such a god were probable, then the proposition that he existed would be an empirical hypothesis. And in that case it would be possible to deduce from it, and other empirical hypotheses, certain experiential propositions which were not deducible from those other hypotheses alone. But in fact this is not possible. It is sometimes claimed, indeed, that the existence of a certain sort of regularity in nature constitutes sufficient evidence for the existence of a god. But if the sentence "God exists" entails no more than that certain types of phenomena occur in certain sequences, then to assert the existence of a god will be simply equivalent to asserting that there is the requisite regularity in nature; and no religious man would admit that this was all he intended to

From A. J. Ayer, *Language, Truth and Logic*, rev. ed. (1946), Chap. VI, pp. 114–120. Reprinted by permission of Victor Gollancz, Ltd., and Dover Publications, Inc.

assert in asserting the existence of a god. He would say that in talking about God, he was talking about a transcendent being who might be known through certain empirical manifestations, but certainly could not be defined in terms of those manifestations. But in that case the term "god" is a metaphysical term. And if "god" is a metaphysical term, then it cannot be even probable that a god exists. For to say that "God exists" is to make a metaphysical utterance which cannot be either true or false. And by the same criterion, no sentence which purports to describe the nature of a transcendent god can possess any literal significance.

It is important not to confuse this view of religious assertions with the view that is adopted by atheists, or agnostics.[1] For it is characteristic of an agnostic to hold that the existence of a god is a possibility in which there is no good reason either to believe or disbelieve; and it is characteristic of an atheist to hold that it is at least probable that no god exists. And our view that all utterances about the nature of God are nonsensical, so far from being identical with, or even lending any support to, either of these familiar contentions, is actually incompatible with them. For if the assertion that there is a god is nonsensical, then the atheist's assertion that there is no god is equally nonsensical, since it is only a significant proposition that can be significantly contradicted. As for the agnostic, although he refrains from saying either that there is or that there is not a god, he does not deny that the question whether a transcendent god exists is a genuine question. He does not deny that the two sentences "There is a transcendent god" and "There is no transcendent god" express propositions one of which is actually true and the other false. All he says is that we have no means of telling which of them is true, and therefore ought not to commit ourselves to either. But we have seen that the sentences in question do not express propositions at all. And this means that agnosticism also is ruled out.

Thus we offer the theist the same comfort as we gave to the moralist. His assertions cannot possibly be valid, but they cannot be invalid either. As he says nothing at all about the world, he cannot justly be accused of saying anything false, or anything for which he has insufficient grounds. It is only when the theist claims that in asserting the existence of a transcendent god he is expressing a genuine proposition that we are entitled to disagree with him.

It is to be remarked that in cases where deities are identified with natural objects, assertions concerning them may be allowed to be significant. If, for example, a man tells me that the occurrence of thunder is alone both necessary and sufficient to establish the truth of the proposition that Jehovah is angry, I may conclude that, in his usage of words, the sentence "Jehovah is angry" is equivalent to "It is thundering." But in sophisticated religions, though they may be to some extent based on men's awe of natural process which they cannot sufficiently understand, the "person" who is supposed to control the empirical world is not himself located in it; he is held to be superior to the empirical world, and so outside it; and he is endowed with super-empirical attributes. But the notion of a person whose essential attributes are non-empirical is not an intelligible notion at all. We may have a word which is used as if it named this "person," but, unless the sentences

---

[1] This point was suggested to me by Professor H. H. Price.

in which it occurs express propositions which are empirically verifiable, it cannot be said to symbolize anything. And this is the case with regard to the word "god," in the usage in which it is intended to refer to a transcendent object. The mere existence of the noun is enough to foster the illusion that there is a real, or at any rate a possible entity corresponding to it. It is only when we enquire what God's attributes are that we discover that "God," in this usage, is not a genuine name.

It is common to find belief in a transcendent god conjoined with belief in an after-life. But, in the form which it usually takes, the content of this belief is not a genuine hypothesis. To say that men do not ever die, or that the state of death is merely a state of prolonged insensibility, is indeed to express a significant proposition, though all the available evidence goes to show that it is false. But to say that there is something imperceptible inside a man, which is his soul or his real self, and that it goes on living after he is dead, is to make a metaphysical assertion which has no more factual content than the assertion that there is a transcendent god.

It is worth mentioning that, according to the account which we have given of religious assertions, there is no logical ground for antagonism between religion and natural science. As far as the question of truth or falsehood is concerned, there is no opposition between the natural scientist and the theist who believes in a transcendent god. For since the religious utterances of the theist are not genuine propositions at all, they cannot stand in any logical relation to the propositions of science. Such antagonism as there is between religion and science appears to consist in the fact that science takes away one of the motives which make men religious. For it is acknowledged that one of the ultimate sources of religious feeling lies in the inability of men to determine their own destiny; and science tends to destroy the feeling of awe with which men regard an alien world, by making them believe that they can understand and anticipate the course of natural phenomena, and even to some extent control it. The fact that it has recently become fashionable for physicists themselves to be sympathetic towards religion is a point in favour of this hypothesis. For this sympathy towards religion marks the physicists' own lack of confidence in the validity of their hypotheses, which is a reaction on their part from the anti-religious dogmatism of nineteenth-century scientists, and a natural outcome of the crisis through which physics has just passed.

It is not within the scope of this enquiry to enter more deeply into the causes of religious feeling, or to discuss the probability of the continuance of religious belief. We are concerned only to answer those questions which arise out of our discussion of the possibility of religious knowledge. The point which we wish to establish is that there cannot be any transcendent truths of religion. For the sentences which the theist uses to express such "truths" are not literally significant.

An interesting feature of this conclusion is that it accords with what many theists are accustomed to say themselves. For we are often told that the nature of God is a mystery which transcends the human understanding. But to say that something transcends the human understanding is to say that it is unintelligible. And what is unintelligible cannot significantly be described. Again, we are told that God is not an object of reason but an object of faith. This may be nothing more than an admission that the existence of God must be taken on trust, since it cannot be proved. But it may also be an assertion that God is the object of a purely mystical intuition, and cannot therefore be defined in terms which are intelligible to the reason. And I think there are many theists who would assert this. But if one allows that it is impossible to define God in intelligible terms, then one is allowing that it is impossible for a sentence both to be significant and to be about God. If a mystic admits that the object of his vision is something which cannot be described, then he must also admit that he is bound to talk nonsense when he describes it.

For his part, the mystic may protest that his intuition does reveal truths to him, even though he cannot explain to others what these truths are; and that we who do not possess this faculty of intuition can have no ground for denying that it is a cognitive faculty. For we can hardly maintain *a priori* that there are no ways of discovering true propositions except those which we ourselves employ. The answer is that we set no limit to the number of ways in which one may come to formulate a true proposition. We do not in any way deny that a synthetic truth may be discovered by purely intuitive methods as well as by the rational method of induction. But we do say that every synthetic proposition, however it may have been arrived at, must be subject to the test of actual experience. We do not deny *a priori* that the mystic is able to discover truths by his own special methods. We wait to hear what are the propositions which embody his discoveries, in order to see whether they are verified or confuted by our empirical observations. But the mystic, so far from producing propositions which are empirically verified, is unable to produce any intelligible propositions at all. And therefore we say that his intuition has not revealed to him any facts. It is no use his saying that he has apprehended facts but is unable to express them. For we know that if he really had acquired any information, he would be able to express it. He would be able to indicate in some way or other how the genuineness of his discovery might be empirically determined. The fact that he cannot reveal what he "knows," or even himself devise an empirical test to validate his "knowledge," shows that his state of mystical intuition is not a genuinely cognitive state. So that in describing his vision the mystic does not give us any information about the external world; he merely gives us indirect information about the condition of his own mind.

These considerations dispose of the argument from religious experience, which many philosophers still regard as a valid argument in favour of the existence of a god. They say that it is logically possible for men to be immediately acquainted with God, as they are immediately acquainted with a sense-content, and that there is no reason why one should be prepared to believe a man when he says that he is seeing a yellow patch, and refuse to believe him when he says that he is seeing God. The answer to this is that if the man who asserts that he is seeing God is merely asserting that he is experiencing a peculiar kind of sense-content, then we do not for a moment deny that his assertion may be true. But, ordinarily, the man who says that he is seeing God is saying not merely that he is experiencing a religious emotion, but also that there exists a transcendent being who is the object of this emotion; just as the man who says that he sees a yellow patch is ordinarily saying not merely that his visual sense-field contains a yellow sense-content, but also that there exists a yellow object to which the sense-content belongs. And it is not irrational to be prepared to believe a man when he asserts the existence of a yellow object, and to refuse to believe him when he asserts the existence of a transcendent god. For whereas the sentence "There exists here a yellow-coloured material thing" expresses a genuine synthetic proposition which could be empirically verified, the sentence "There exists a transcendent god" has, as we have seen, no literal significance.

We conclude, therefore, that the argument from religious experience is altogether fallacious. The fact that people have religious experiences is interesting from the psychological point of view, but it does not in any way imply that there is such a thing as religious knowledge, any more than our having moral experiences implies that there is such a thing as moral knowledge. The theist, like the moralist, may believe that his experiences are cognitive experiences, but, unless he can formulate his "knowledge" in propositions that are empirically verifiable, we may be sure that he is deceiving himself. It follows that those philosophers who fill their books with assertions that they intuitively "know" this or that moral or religious "truth" are merely providing material for the psycho-analyst. For no act of intuition can be said to reveal a truth about any matter of fact unless it issues in verifiable propositions. And all such propositions are to be incorporated in the system of empirical propositions which constitutes science.

6

THE ACTUALITY OF GOD

Paul Tillich

GOD AS BEING AND FINITE BEING

The being of God is being-itself. The being of God cannot be understood as
the existence of a being alongside others or above others. If God is *a* being,
he is subject to the categories of finitude, especially to space and substance.
Even if he is called the "highest being" in the sense of the "most perfect"
and the "most powerful" being, this situation is not changed. When applied
to God, superlatives become diminutives. They place him on the level of
other beings while elevating him above all of them. Many theologians who
have used the term "highest being" have known better. Actually they have
described the highest as the absolute, as that which is on a level qualitatively
different from the level of any being—even the highest being. Whenever
infinite or unconditional power and meaning are attributed to the highest
being, it has ceased to be *a* being and has become being-itself. Many
confusions in the doctrine of God and many apologetic weaknesses could be
avoided if God were understood first of all as being-itself or as the ground
of being. The power of being is another way of expressing the same thing in
a circumscribing phrase. Ever since the time of Plato it has been known—
although it often has been disregarded, especially by the nominalists and
their modern followers—that the concept of being as being, or being-itself,
points to the power inherent in everything, the power of resisting nonbeing.
Therefore, instead of saying that God is first of all being-itself, it is possible
to say that he is the power of being in everything and above everything, the
infinite power of being. A theology which does not dare to identify God and
the power of being as the first step toward a doctrine of God relapses into
monarchic monotheism, for if God is not being-itself, he is subordinate to it,
just as Zeus is subordinate to fate in Greek religion. The structure of being-
itself is his fate, as it is the fate of all other beings. But God is his own fate;
he is "by himself"; he possesses "aseity." This can be said of him only if he is
the power of being, if he is being-itself.

Reprinted from *Systematic Theology*, Vol. I, Part II(B), pp. 235–241, by Paul Tillich
by permission of The University of Chicago Press. Copyright 1951 by The University of
Chicago.

As being-itself God is beyond the contrast of essential and existential being. We have spoken of the transition of being into existence, which involves the possibility that being will contradict and lose itself. This transition is excluded from being-itself (except in terms of the christological paradox), for being-itself does not participate in nonbeing. In this it stands in contrast to every being. As classical theology has emphasized, God is beyond essence and existence. Logically, being-itself is "before," "prior to," the split which characterizes finite being.

For this reason it is as wrong to speak of God as the universal essence as it is to speak of him as existing. If God is understood as universal essence, as the form of all forms, he is identified with the unity and totality of finite potentialities; but he has ceased to be the power of the ground in all of them, and therefore he has ceased to transcend them. He has poured all his creative power into a system of forms, and he is bound to these forms. This is what pantheism means.

On the other hand, grave difficulties attend the attempt to speak of God as existing. In order to maintain the truth that God is beyond essence and existence while simultaneously arguing for the existence of God, Thomas Aquinas is forced to distinguish between two kinds of divine existence: that which is identical with essence and that which is not. But an existence of God which is not united with its essence is a contradiction in terms. It makes God a being whose existence does not fulfil his essential potentialities; being and not-yet-being are "mixed" in him, as they are in everything finite. God ceases to be God, the ground of being and meaning. What really has happened is that Thomas has had to unite two different traditions: the Augustinian, in which the divine existence is included in his essence, and the Aristotelian, which derives the existence of God from the existence of the world and which then asserts, in a second step, that his existence is identical with his essence. Thus the question of the existence of God can be neither asked nor answered. If asked, it is a question, about that which by its very nature is above existence, and therefore the answer—whether negative or affirmative—implicitly denies the nature of God. It is as atheistic to affirm the existence of God as it is to deny it. God is being-itself, not *a* being. On this basis a first step can be taken toward the solution of the problem which usually is discussed as the immanence and the transcendence of God. As the power of being, God transcends every being and also the totality of beings —the world. Being-itself is beyond finitude and infinity; otherwise it would be conditioned by something other than itself, and the real power of being would lie beyond both it and that which conditioned it. Being-itself infinitely transcends every finite being. There is no proportion or gradation between the finite and the infinite. There is an absolute break, an infinite "jump." On the other hand, everything finite participates in being-itself and in its infinity. Otherwise it would not have the power of being. It would be swallowed by nonbeing, or it never would have emerged out of nonbeing. This double relation of all beings to being-itself gives being-itself a double characteristic. In calling it creative, we point to the fact that everything participates in the infinite power of being. In calling it abysmal, we point to the fact that everything participates in the power of being in a finite way, that all beings are infinitely transcended by their creative ground.

Man is bound to the categories of finitude. He uses the two categories of relation—causality and substance—to express the relation of being-itself to finite beings. The "ground" can be interpreted in both ways, as the cause of finite beings and as their substance. The former has been elaborated by Leibniz in the line of the Thomistic tradition, and the latter has been elaborated by Spinoza in the line of the mystical tradition. Both ways are impossible. Spinoza establishes a naturalistic pantheism, in contrast to the idealistic type which identifies God with the universal essence of being, which denies finite freedom and in so doing denies the freedom of God. By necessity God is merged into the finite beings, and their being is his being. Here again it must be emphasized that pantheism does not say that God is everything. It says that God is the substance of everything and that there is no substantial independence and freedom in anything finite.

Therefore, Christianity, which asserts finite freedom in man and spontaneity in the nonhuman realm, has rejected the category of substance in favor of the category of causality in attempting to express the relation of the power of being to the beings who participate in it. Causality seems to make the world dependent on God, and, at the same time, to separate God from the world in the way a cause is separated from its effect. But the category of causality cannot "fill the bill," for cause and effect are not separate; they include each other and form a series which is endless in both directions. What is cause at one point in this series is effect at another point and conversely. God as cause is drawn into this series, which drives even him beyond himself. In order to disengage the divine cause from the series of causes and effects, it is called the first cause, the absolute beginning. What this means is that the category of causality is being denied while it is being used. In other words, causality is being used not as a category but as a symbol. And if this is done and is understood, the difference between substance and causality disappears, for if God is the cause of the entire series of causes and effects, he is the substance underlying the whole process of becoming. But this "underlying" does not have the character of a substance which underlies its accidents and which is completely expressed by them. It is an underlying in which substance and accidents preserve their freedom. In other words, it is substance not as a category but as a symbol. And, if taken symbolically, there is no difference between *prima causa* [first cause] and *ultima substantia* [underlying substance]. Both mean, what can be called in a more directly symbolic term, "the creative and abysmal ground of being." In this term both naturalistic pantheism, based on the category of substance, and rationalistic theism, based on the category of causality, are overcome.

Since God is the ground of being, he is the ground of the structure of being. He is not subject to this structure; the structure is grounded in him. He *is* this structure, and it is impossible to speak about him except in terms of this structure. God must be approached cognitively through the structural elements of being-itself. These elements make him a living God, a God who can be man's concrete concern. They enable us to use symbols which we are certain point to the ground of reality.

GOD AS BEING AND THE KNOWLEDGE OF GOD

The statement that God is being-itself is a nonsymbolic statement. It does not point beyond itself. It means what it says directly and properly; if we speak of the actuality of God, we first assert that he is not God if he is not being-itself. Other assertions about God can be made theologically only on this basis. Of course, religious assertions do not require such a foundation for what they say about God; the foundation is implicit in every religious thought concerning God. Theologians must make explicit what is implicit in religious thought and expression; and, in order to do this, they must begin with the most abstract and completely unsymbolic statement which is possible, namely, that God is being-itself or the absolute.

However, after this has been said, nothing else can be said about God as God which is not symbolic. As we already have seen, God as being-itself is the ground of the ontological structure of being without being subject to this structure himself. He *is* the structure; that is, he has the power of determining the structure of everything that has being. Therefore, if anything beyond this bare assertion is said about God, it no longer is a direct and proper statement, no longer a concept. It is indirect, and it points to something beyond itself. In a word, it is symbolic.

The general character of the symbol has been described. Special emphasis must be laid on the insight that symbol and sign are different; that, while the sign bears no necessary relation to that to which it points, the symbol participates in the reality of that for which it stands. The sign can be changed arbitrarily according to the demands of expediency, but the symbol grows and dies according to the correlation between that which is symbolized and the persons who receive it as a symbol. Therefore, the religious symbol, the symbol which points to the divine, can be a true symbol only if it participates in the power of the divine to which it points.

There can be no doubt that any concrete assertion about God must be symbolic, for a concrete assertion is one which uses a segment of finite experience in order to say something about him. It transcends the content of this segment, although it also includes it. The segment of finite reality which becomes the vehicle of a concrete assertion about God is affirmed and negated at the same time. It becomes a symbol, for a symbolic expression is one whose proper meaning is negated by that to which it points. And yet it also is affirmed by it, and this affirmation gives the symbolic expression an adequate basis for pointing beyond itself.

The crucial question must now be faced. Can a segment of finite reality become the basis for an assertion about that which is infinite? The answer is that it can, because that which is infinite is being-itself and because everything participates in being-itself. The *analogia entis* [analogy of being] is not the property of a questionable natural theology which attempts to gain knowledge of God by drawing conclusions about the infinite from the finite. The *analogia entis* gives us our only justification of speaking at all about God. It is based on the fact that God must be understood as being-itself.

The truth of a religious symbol has nothing to do with the truth of the empirical assertions involved in it, be they physical, psychological, or historical. A religious symbol possesses some truth if it adequately expresses the correlation of revelation in which some person stands. A religious symbol *is* true if it adequately expresses the correlation of some person with final revelation. A religious symbol can die only if the correlation of which it is an adequate expression dies. This occurs whenever the revelatory situation changes and former symbols become obsolete. The history of religion, right up to our own time, is full of dead symbols which have been killed not by a scientific criticism of assumed superstitions but by a religious criticism of religion. The judgment that a religious symbol *is* true is identical with the judgment that the revelation of which it is the adequate expression is true. This double meaning of the truth of a symbol must be kept in mind. A symbol *has* truth: it is adequate to the revelation it expresses. A symbol *is* true: it is the expression of a true revelation.

Theology as such has neither the duty nor the power to confirm or to negate religious symbols. Its task is to interpret them according to theological principles and methods. In the process of interpretation, however, two things may happen: theology may discover contradictions between symbols within the theological circle and theology may speak not only as theology but also as religion. In the first case, theology can point out the religious dangers and the theological errors which follow from the use of certain symbols; in the second case, theology can become prophecy, and in this role it may contribute to a change in the revelatory situation.

Religious symbols are double-edged. They are directed toward the infinite which they symbolize *and* toward the finite through which they symbolize it. They force the infinite down to finitude and the finite up to infinity. They open the divine for the human and the human for the divine. For instance, if God is symbolized as "Father," he is brought down to the human relationship of father and child. But at the same time this human relationship is consecrated into a pattern of the divine-human relationship. If "Father" is employed as a symbol for God, fatherhood is seen in its theonomous, sacramental depth. One cannot arbitrarily "make" a religious symbol out of a segment of secular reality. Not even the collective unconscious, the great symbol-creating source, can do this. If a segment of reality is used as a symbol for God, the realm of reality from which it is taken is, so to speak, elevated into the realm of the holy. It no longer is secular. It is theonomous. If God is called the "king," something is said not only about God but also about the holy character of kinghood. If God's work is called "making whole" or "healing," this not only says something about God but also emphasizes the theonomous character of all healing. If God's self-manifestation is called "the word," this not only symbolizes God's relation to man but also emphasizes the holiness of all words as an expression of the spirit. The list could be continued. Therefore, it is not surprising that in a secular culture both the symbols for God and the theonomous character of the material from which the symbols are taken disappear.

A final word of warning must be added in view of the fact that for many people the very term "symbolic" carries the connotation of nonreal. This is partially the result of confusion between sign and symbol and partially due to the identification of reality with empirical reality, with the entire realm of objective things and events. Both reasons have been undercut explicitly and implicitly in the foregoing chapters. But one reason remains, namely, the fact that some theological movements, such as Protestant Hegelianism and Catholic modernism, have interpreted religious language symbolically in order to dissolve its realistic meaning and to weaken its seriousness, its power, and its spiritual impact. This was not the purpose of the classical essays on the "divine names," in which the symbolic character of all affirmations about God was strongly emphasized and explained in religious terms, nor was it a consequence of these essays. Their intention and their result was to give to God and to all his relations to man more reality and power than a nonsymbolic and therefore easily superstitious interpretation could give them. In this sense symbolic interpretation is proper and necessary; it enhances rather than diminishes the reality and power of religious language, and in so doing it performs an important function.

·   ·   ·

Religious Disputes

7

GOD S

John Wisdom

1. *The existence of God is not an experimental issue in the way it was.* An atheist or agnostic might say to a theist 'You still think there are spirits in the trees, nymphs in the streams, a God of the world.' He might say this because he noticed the theist in time of drought pray for rain and make a sacrifice and in the morning look for rain. But disagreement about whether there are gods is now less of this experimental or betting sort than it used to be. This is due in part, if not wholly, to our better knowledge of why things happen as they do.

It is true that even in these days it is seldom that one who believes in God has no hopes or fears which an atheist has not. Few believers now expect prayer to still the waves, but some think it makes a difference to people and not merely in ways the atheist would admit. Of course with people, as opposed to waves and machines, one never knows what they won't do next, so that expecting prayer to make a difference to them is not so definite a thing as believing in its mechanical efficacy. Still, just as primitive people pray in a business-like way for rain so some people still pray for others with a real feeling of doing something to help. However, in spite of this persistence of an experimental element in some theistic belief, it remains true that Elijah's method on Mount Carmel of settling the matter of what god or gods exist would be far less appropriate to-day than it was then.

2. *Belief in gods is not merely a matter of expectation of a world to come.* Someone may say 'The fact that a theist no more than an atheist expects prayer to bring down fire from heaven or cure the sick does not mean that there is no difference between them as to the facts, it does not mean that the theist has no expectations different from the atheist's. For very often those who believe in God believe in another world and believe that God is there and that we shall go to that world when we die.'

John Wisdom, "Gods," *Proceedings of the Aristotelian Society*, XLV (1944–1945), 185–206. Reprinted by courtesy of the Editor of The Aristotelian Society.

This is true, but I do not want to consider here expectations as to what one will see and feel after death nor what sort of reasons these logically unique expectations could have. So I want to consider those theists who do not believe in a future life, or rather, I want to consider the differences between atheists and theists in so far as these differences are not a matter of belief in a future life.

3. *What are these differences? And is it that theists are superstitious or that atheists are blind?* A child may wish to sit a while with his father and he may, when he has done what his father dislikes, fear punishment and feel distress at causing vexation, and while his father is alive he may feel sure of help when danger threatens and feel that there is sympathy for him when disaster has come. When his father is dead he will no longer expect punishment or help. Maybe for a moment an old fear will come or a cry for help escape him, but he will at once remember that this is no good now. He may feel that his father is no more until perhaps someone says to him that his father is still alive though he lives now in another world and one so far away that there is no hope of seeing him or hearing his voice again. The child may be told that nevertheless his father can see him and hear all he says. When he has been told this the child will still fear no punishment nor expect any sign of his father, but now, even more than he did when his father was alive, he will feel that his father sees him all the time and will dread distressing him and when he has done something wrong he will feel separated from his father until he has felt sorry for what he has done. Maybe when he himself comes to die he will be like a man who expects to find a friend in the strange country where he is going, but even when this is so, it is by no means all of what makes the difference between a child who believes that his father lives still in another world and one who does not.

Likewise one who believes in God may face death differently from one who does not, but there is another difference between them besides this. This other difference may still be described as belief in another world, only this belief is not a matter of expecting one thing rather than another here or hereafter, it is not a matter of a world to come but of a world that now is, though beyond our senses.

We are at once reminded of those other unseen worlds which some philosophers 'believe in' and others 'deny', while non-philosophers unconsciously 'accept' them by using them as models with which to 'get the hang of' the patterns in the flux of experience. We recall the timeless entities whose changeless connections we seek to represent in symbols, and the values which stand firm[1] amidst our flickering satisfaction and remorse, and the physical things which, though not beyond the corruption of moth and rust, are yet more permanent than the shadows they throw upon the screen before our minds. We recall, too, our talk of souls and of what lies in their depths and is manifested to us partially and intermittently in our own feelings and the behaviour of others. The hypothesis of mind, of other human minds and of animal minds, is reasonable because it explains for each of us why certain things behave so cunningly all by themselves unlike even the most ingenious machines. Is the hypothesis of minds in flowers and trees reasonable for like reasons? Is the hypothesis of a world mind reasonable for

[1] In another world, Dr. Joad says in the *New Statesman* recently.

like reasons—someone who adjusts the blossom to the bees, someone whose presence may at times be felt—in a garden in high summer, in the hills when clouds are gathering, but not, perhaps, in a cholera epidemic?

4. *The question 'Is belief in gods reasonable?' has more than one source.* It is clear now that in order to grasp fully the logic of belief in divine minds we need to examine the logic of belief in animal and human minds. But we cannot do that here and so for the purposes of this discussion about divine minds let us acknowledge the reasonableness of our belief in human minds without troubling ourselves about its logic. The question of the reasonableness of belief in divine minds then becomes a matter of whether there are facts in nature which support claims about divine minds in the way facts in nature support our claims about human minds.

In this way we resolve the force behind the problem of the existence of gods into two components, one metaphysical and the same which prompts the question 'Is there *ever any* behaviour which gives reason to believe in *any* sort of mind?' and one which finds expression in 'Are there other mind-patterns in nature beside the human and animal patterns which we can all easily detect, and are these other mind-patterns super-human?'

Such over-determination of a question syndrome is common. Thus, the puzzling questions 'Do dogs think?', 'Do animals feel?' are partly metaphysical puzzles and partly scientific questions. They are not purely metaphysical; for the reports of scientists about the poor performances of cats in cages and old ladies' stories about the remarkable performances of their pets are not irrelevant. But nor are these questions purely scientific; for the stories never settle them and therefore they have other sources. One other source is the metaphysical source we have already noticed, namely, the difficulty about getting behind an animal's behaviour to its mind, whether it is a non-human animal or a human one.

But there's a third component in the force behind these questions, these disputes have a third source, and it is one which is important in the dispute which finds expression in the words 'I believe in God', 'I do not'. This source comes out well if we consider the question 'Do flowers feel?' Like the questions about dogs and animals this question about flowers comes partly from the difficulty we sometimes feel over inference from *any* behaviour to thought or feeling and partly from ignorance as to what behaviour is to be found. But these questions, as opposed to a like question about human beings, come also from hesitation as to whether the behaviour in question is *enough* mind-like, that is, is it enough similar to or superior to human behaviour to be called 'mind-proving'? Likewise, even when we are satisfied that human behaviour shows mind and even when we have learned whatever mind-suggesting things there are in nature which are not explained by human and animal minds, we may still ask 'But are these things sufficiently striking to be called a mind-pattern? Can we fairly call them manifestations of a divine being?'

'The question', someone may say, 'has then become merely a matter of the application of a name. And "What's in a name?"'

5. *But the line between a question of fact and a question or decision as to the application of a name is not so simple as this way of putting things suggests.* The question 'What's in a name?' is engaging because we are inclined to answer both 'Nothing' and 'Very much'. And this 'Very much'

has more than one source. We might have tried to comfort Heloise by saying 'It isn't that Abelard no longer loves you, for this man isn't Abelard'; we might have said to poor Mr. Tebrick in Mr. Garnet's *Lady into Fox* 'But this is no longer Silvia'. But if Mr. Tebrick replied 'Ah, but it is!' this might come not at all from observing facts about the fox which we have not observed, but from noticing facts about the fox which we had missed, although we had in a sense observed all that Mr. Tebrick had observed. It is possible to have before one's eyes all the items of a pattern and still to miss the pattern. Consider the following conversation:

' "And I think Kay and I are pretty happy. We've always been happy."

'Bill lifted up his glass and put it down without drinking.

' "Would you mind saying that again?" he asked.

' "I don't see what's so queer about it. Taken all in all, Kay and I have really been happy."

' "All right," Bill said gently, "Just tell me how you and Kay have been happy."

'Bill had a way of being amused by things which I could not understand.

' "It's a little hard to explain," I said. "It's like taking a lot of numbers that don't look alike and that don't mean anything until you add them all together."

'I stopped, because I hadn't meant to talk to him about Kay and me.

' "Go ahead," Bill said. "What about the numbers." And he began to smile.

' "I don't know why you think it's so funny," I said. "All the things that two people do together, two people like Kay and me, add up to something. There are the kids and the house and the dog and all the people we have known and all the times we've been out to dinner. Of course, Kay and I do quarrel sometimes but when you add it all together, all of it isn't as bad as the parts of it seem. I mean, maybe that's all there is to anybody's life."

'Bill poured himself another drink. He seemed about to say something and checked himself. He kept looking at me.'[2]

Or again, suppose two people are speaking of two characters in a story which both have read[3] or of two friends which both have known, and one says 'Really she hated him', and the other says 'She didn't, she loved him'. Then the first may have noticed what the other has not although he knows no incident in the lives of the people they are talking about which the other doesn't know too, and the second speaker may say 'She didn't, she loved him' because he hasn't noticed what the first noticed, although he can remember every incident the first can remember. But then again he may say 'She didn't, she loved him' not because he hasn't noticed the patterns in time which the first has noticed but because though he has noticed them he doesn't feel he still needs to emphasize them with 'Really she hated him'. The line between using a name because of how we feel and because of what we have noticed isn't sharp. 'A difference as to the facts', 'a discovery', 'a revelation', these phrases cover many things. Discoveries have been made not only by Christopher Columbus and Pasteur, but also by Tolstoy and Dostoievsky and Freud. Things are revealed to us not only by the scientists with microscopes, but also by the poets, the prophets, and the painters.

[2] *H. M. Pulham, Esq.*, p. 320, by John P. Marquand.
[3] E.g. Havelock Ellis's autobiography.

What is so isn't merely a matter of 'the facts'. For sometimes when there is agreement as to the facts there is still argument as to whether defendant did or did not 'exercise reasonable care', was or was not 'negligent'.

And though we shall need to emphasize how much 'There is a God' evinces an attitude to the familiar[4] we shall find in the end that it also evinces some recognition of patterns in time easily missed and that, therefore, difference as to there being any gods is in part a difference as to what is so and therefore as to the facts, though not in the simple ways which first occurred to us.

6. *Let us now approach these same points by a different road.*

6.1. *How it is that an explanatory hypothesis, such as the existence of God, may start by being experimental and gradually become something quite different can be seen from the following story:*

Two people return to their long neglected garden and find among the weeds a few of the old plants surprisingly vigorous. One says to the other 'It must be that a gardener has been coming and doing something about these plants'. Upon inquiry they find that no neighbour has ever seen anyone at work in their garden. The first man says to the other 'He must have worked while people slept'. The other says 'No, someone would have heard him and besides, anybody who cared about the plants would have kept down these weeds'. The first man says 'Look at the way these are arranged. There is purpose and a feeling for beauty here. I believe that someone comes, someone invisible to mortal eyes. I believe that the more carefully we look the more we shall find confirmation of this'. They examine the garden ever so carefully and sometimes they come on new things suggesting that a gardener comes and sometimes they come on new things suggesting the contrary and even that a malicious person has been at work. Besides examining the garden carefully they also study what happens to gardens left without attention. Each learns all the other learns about this and about the garden. Consequently, when after all this, one says 'I still believe a gardener comes' while the other says 'I don't' their different words now reflect no difference as to what they have found in the garden, no difference as to what they would find in the garden if they looked further and no difference about how fast untended gardens fall into disorder. At this stage, in this context, the gardener hypothesis has ceased to be experimental, the difference between one who accepts and one who rejects it is now not a matter of the one expecting something the other does not expect. What is the difference between them? The one says 'A gardener comes unseen and unheard. He is manifested only in his works with which we are all familiar', the other says 'There is no gardener' and with this difference in what they say about the gardener goes a difference in how they feel towards the garden, in spite of the fact that neither expects anything of it which the other does not expect.

But is this the whole difference between them—that the one calls the garden by one name and feels one way towards it, while the other calls it by another name and feels in another way towards it? And if this is what the difference has become then is it any longer appropriate to ask 'Which is right?' or 'Which is reasonable?'

[4] 'Persuasive Definitions', *Mind*, July, 1938, by Charles Leslie Stevenson, should be read here. It is very good.

And yet surely such questions *are* appropriate when one person says to another 'You still think the world's a garden and not a wilderness, and that the gardener has not forsaken it' or 'You still think there are nymphs of the streams, a presence in the hills, a spirit of the world'. Perhaps when a man sings 'God's in His heaven' we need not take this as more than an expression of how he feels. But when Bishop Gore or Dr. Joad write about belief in God and young men read them in order to settle their religious doubts the impression is not simply that of persons choosing exclamations with which to face nature and the 'changes and chances of this mortal life'. The disputants speak as if they are concerned with a matter of scientific fact, or of trans-sensual, trans-scientific and metaphysical fact, but still of fact and still a matter about which reasons for and against may be offered, although no scientific reasons in the sense of field surveys for fossils or experiments on delinquents are to the point.

6.2. *How can an interjection have a logic?* Can the manifestation of an attitude in the utterance of a word, in the application of a name, have a logic? When all the facts are known how can there still be a question of fact? How can there still be a question? Surely as Hume says '. . . after every circumstance, every relation is known, the understanding has no further room to operate'?[5]

6.3. When the madness of these questions leaves us for a moment *we can all easily recollect disputes which though they cannot be settled by experiment are yet disputes in which one party may be right and the other wrong* and in which both parties may offer reasons and the one better reasons than the other. *This may happen in pure and applied mathematics and logic.* Two accountants or two engineers provided with the same data may reach different results and this difference is resolved not by collecting further data but by going over the calculations again. Such differences indeed share with differences as to what will win a race, the honour of being among the most 'settlable' disputes in the language.

6.4. *But it won't do to describe the theistic issue as one settlable by such calculation,* or as one about what can be deduced in this *vertical* fashion from the facts we know. No doubt dispute about God has sometimes, perhaps especially in mediaeval times, been carried on in this fashion. But nowadays it is not and we must look for some other analogy, some other case in which a dispute is settled but not by experiment.

6.5. *In courts of law* it sometimes happens that opposing counsel are agreed as to the facts and are not trying to settle a question of further fact, are not trying to settle whether the man who admittedly had quarrelled with the deceased did or did not murder him, but are concerned with whether Mr. A who admittedly handed his long-trusted clerk signed blank cheques did or did not exercise reasonable care, whether a ledger is or is not a document,[6] whether a certain body was or was not a public authority.

---

[5] Hume, *An Enquiry concerning the Principles of Morals*. Appendix I.

[6] *The Times*, March 2nd, 1945. Also in *The Times* of June 13th, 1945, contrast the case of Hannah v. Peel with that of the cruiser cut in two by a liner. In the latter case there is not agreement as to the facts. See also the excellent articles by Dr. Glanville L. Williams in the *Law Quarterly Review*, 'Language and the Law', January, and April, 1945, and 'The Doctrine of Repugnancy', October, 1943, January, 1944, and April, 1944. The author, having set out how arbitrary are many legal decisions, needs now to set out

In such cases we notice that the process of argument is not a *chain* of demonstrative reasoning. It is a presenting and representing of those features of the case which *severally co-operate* in favour of the conclusion, in favour of saying what the reasoner wishes said, in favour of calling the situation by the name by which he wishes to call it. The reasons are like the legs of a chair, not the links of a chain. Consequently although the discussion is *a priori* and the steps are not a matter of experience, the procedure resembles scientific argument in that the reasoning is not *vertically* extensive but *horizontally* extensive—it is a matter of the cumulative effect of several independent premises, not of the repeated transformation of one or two. And because the premises are severally inconclusive the process of deciding the issue becomes a matter of weighing the cumulative effect of one group of severally inconclusive items against the cumulative effect of another group of severally inconclusive items, and thus lends itself to description in terms of conflicting 'probabilities'. This encourages the feeling that the issue is one of fact—that it is a matter of guessing from the premises at a further fact, at what is to come. But this is a muddle. *The dispute does not cease to be* a priori *because it is a matter of the cumulative effect of severally inconclusive premises.* The logic of the dispute is not that of a chain of deductive reasoning as in a mathematic calculation. But nor is it a matter of collecting from several inconclusive items of information an expectation as to something further, as when a doctor from a patient's symptoms guesses at what is wrong, or a detective from many clues guesses the criminal. It has its own sort of logic and its own sort of end—the solution of the question at issue is a decision, a ruling by the judge. But it is not an arbitrary decision though the rational connections are neither quite like those in vertical deductions nor like those in inductions in which from many signs we guess at what to come; and though the decision manifests itself in the application of a name it is no more merely the application of a name than is the pinning on of a medal merely the pinning on of a bit of metal. Whether a lion with stripes is a tiger or a lion is, if you like, merely a matter of the application of a name. Whether Mr. So-and-So of whose conduct we have so complete a record did or did not exercise reasonable care is not merely a matter of the application of a name or, if we choose to say it is, then we must remember that with this name a game is lost and won and a game with very heavy stakes. With the judges' choice of a name for the facts goes an attitude, and the declaration, the ruling, is an exclamation evincing that attitude. But *it is an exclamation which not only has a purpose but also has a logic,* a logic surprisingly like that of 'futile', 'deplorable', 'graceful', 'grand', 'divine'.

6.6. *Suppose two people are looking at a picture or natural scene.* One says 'Excellent' or 'Beautiful' or 'Divine'; the other says 'I don't see it'. He means he doesn't see the beauty. And this reminds us of how we felt the theist accuse the atheist of blindness and the atheist accuse the theist of seeing what isn't there. And yet surely each sees what the other sees. It isn't that one can see part of the picture which the other can't see. So the difference is in a sense not one as to the facts. And so it cannot be removed

---

how far from arbitrary they are—if his readers are ready for the next phase in the dialectic process.

by the one disputant discovering to the other what so far he hasn't seen. It isn't that the one sees the picture in a different light and so, as we might say, sees a different picture. Consequently the difference between them cannot be resolved by putting the picture in a different light. And yet surely this is just what can be done in such a case—not by moving the picture but by talk perhaps. To settle a dispute as to whether a piece of music is good or better than another we listen again, with a picture we look again. Someone perhaps points to emphasize certain features and we see it in a different light. Shall we call this 'field work' and 'the last of observation' or shall we call it 'reviewing the premises' and 'the beginning of deduction (horizontal)'?

If in spite of all this we choose to say that a difference as to whether a thing is beautiful is not a factual difference we must be careful to remember that there is a procedure for settling these differences and that this consists not only in reasoning and redescription as in the legal case, but also in a more literal re-setting-before with re-looking or re-listening.

6.7. *And if we say as we did at the beginning that when a difference as to the existence of a God is not one as to future happenings then it is not experimental and therefore not as to the facts, we must not forthwith assume that there is no right and wrong about it*, no rationality or irrationality, no appropriateness or inappropriateness, no procedure which tends to settle it, *nor even that this procedure is in no sense a discovery of new facts*. After all even in science this is not so. Our two gardeners even when they had reached the stage when neither expected any experimental result which the other did not, might yet have continued the dispute, each presenting and representing the features of the garden favouring his hypothesis, that is, fitting his model for describing the accepted fact; each emphasizing the pattern he wishes to emphasize. True, in science, there is seldom or never a pure instance of this sort of dispute, for nearly always with difference of hypothesis goes some difference of expectation as to the facts. But scientists argue about rival hypotheses with a vigour which is not exactly proportioned to difference in expectations of experimental results.

The difference as to whether a God exists involves our feelings more than most scientific disputes and in this respect is more like a difference as to whether there is beauty in a thing.

7. *The Connecting Technique.* Let us consider again the technique used in revealing or proving beauty, in removing a blindness, in inducing an attitude which is lacking, in reducing a reaction that is inappropriate. Besides running over in a special way the features of the picture, tracing the rhythms, making sure that this and that are not only seen but noticed, and their relation to each other—besides all this—there are other things we can do to justify our attitude and alter that of the man who cannot see. For features of the picture may be brought out by setting beside it other pictures; just as the merits of an argument may be brought out, proved, by setting beside it other arguments, in which striking but irrelevant features of the original are changed and relevant features emphasized; just as the merits and demerits of a line of action may be brought out by setting beside it other actions. To use Susan Stebbing's example: Nathan brought out for David certain features of what David had done in the matter of Uriah the Hittite by telling him a story about two sheep-owners. This is the kind of thing we very often do when someone is 'inconsistent' or 'unreasonable'.

This is what we do in referring to other cases in law. The paths we need to trace from other cases to the case in question are often numerous and difficult to detect and the person with whom we are discussing the matter may well draw attention to connections which, while not incompatible with those we have tried to emphasize, are of an opposite inclination. A may have noticed in B subtle and hidden likenesses to an angel and reveal these to C, while C has noticed in B subtle and hidden likenesses to a devil which he reveals to A.

Imagine that a man picks up some flowers that lie half withered on a table and gently puts them in water. Another man says to him 'You believe flowers feel'. He says this although he knows that the man who helps the flowers doesn't expect anything of them which he himself doesn't expect; for he himself expects the flowers to be 'refreshed' and to be easily hurt, injured, I mean, by rough handling, while the man who puts them in water does not expect them to whisper 'Thank you'. The Sceptic says 'You believe flowers feel' because something about the way the other man lifts the flowers and puts them in water suggests an attitude to the flowers which he feels inappropriate although perhaps he would not feel it inappropriate to butterflies. He feels that this attitude to flowers is somewhat crazy *just as it is sometimes felt that a lover's attitude is somewhat crazy even when this is not a matter of his having false hopes about how the person he is in love with will act*. It is often said in such cases that reasoning is useless. But the very person who says this feels that the lover's attitude is crazy, is inappropriate like some dreads and hatreds, such as some horrors of enclosed places. And often one who says 'It is useless to reason' proceeds at once to reason with the lover, nor is this reasoning always quite without effect. We may draw the lover's attention to certain things done by her he is in love with and trace for him a path to these from things done by others at other times[7] which have disgusted and infuriated him. And by this means we may weaken his admiration and confidence, make him feel it unjustified and arouse his suspicion and contempt and make him feel our suspicion and contempt reasonable. It is possible, of course, that he has already noticed the analogies, the connections, we point out and that he has accepted them—that is, he has not denied them nor passed them off. He has recognized them and they have altered his attitude, altered his love, but he still loves. We then feel that perhaps it is we who are blind and cannot see what he can see.

8. *Connecting and Disconnecting*. But before we confess ourselves thus inadequate there are other fires his admiration must pass through. For when a man has an attitude which it seems to us he should not have or lacks one which it seems to us he should have then, not only do we suspect that he is not influenced by connections which we feel should influence him and draw his attention to these, but also we suspect he is influenced by connections which should not influence him and draw his attention to these. It may, for a moment, seem strange that we should draw his attention to connections which we feel should not influence him, and which, since they do influence him, he has in a sense already noticed. But we do—such is our confidence in 'the light of reason'.

Sometimes the power of these connections comes mainly from a man's

[7] Thus, like the scientist, the critic is concerned to show up the irrelevance of time and space.

mismanagement of the language he is using. This is what happens in the Monte Carlo fallacy, where by mismanaging the laws of chance a man passes from noticing that a certain colour or number has not turned up for a long while to an improper confidence that now it soon will turn up. In such cases our showing up of the false connections is a process we call 'explaining a fallacy in reasoning'. To remove fallacies in reasoning we urge a man to call a spade a spade, ask him what he means by 'the State' and having pointed out ambiguities and vaguenesses ask him to reconsider the steps in his argument.

9. *Unspoken Connections. Usually, however, wrongheadedness or wrongheartedness in a situation, blindness to what is there or seeing what is not, does not arise merely from mismanagement of language but is more due to connections which are not mishandled in language, for the reason that they are not put into language at all.* And often these misconnections too weaken in the light of reason, if only we can guess where they lie and turn it on them. In so far as these connections are not presented in language the process of removing their power is not a process of correcting the mismanagement of language. But it is still akin to such a process; for though it is not a process of setting out fairly what has been set out unfairly, it is a process of setting out fairly what has not been set out at all. And we must remember that the line between connections ill-presented or half-presented in language and connections operative but not presented in language, or only hinted at, is not a sharp one.

Whether or not we call the process of showing up these connections 'reasoning to remove bad unconscious reasoning' or not, it is certain that in order to settle in ourselves what weight we shall attach to someone's confidence or attitude we not only ask him for his reasons but also look for unconscious reasons both good and bad; that is, for reasons which he can't put into words, isn't explicitly aware of, is hardly aware of, isn't aware of at all—perhaps it's long experience which he *doesn't* recall which lets him know a squall is coming, perhaps it's old experience which he *can't* recall which makes the cake in the tea mean so much and makes Odette so fascinating.[8]

I am well aware of the distinction between the question 'What reasons are there for the belief that S is P?' and the question 'What are the sources of beliefs that S is P?' There are cases where investigation of the rationality of a claim which certain persons make is done with very little inquiry into why they say what they do, into the causes of their beliefs. This is so when we have very definite ideas about what is really logically relevant to their claim and what is not. Offered a mathematical theorem we ask for the proof; offered the generalization that parental discord causes crime we ask for the correlation co-efficients. But even in this last case, if we fancy that only the figures are reasons we underestimate the complexity of the logic of our conclusion; and yet it is difficult to describe the other features of the evidence which have weight and there is apt to be disagreement about the weight they should have. In criticizing other conclusions and especially conclusions which are largely the expression of an attitude, we have not only to ascertain what reasons there are for them but also to decide what

---

[8] Proust: *Swann's Way*, Vol. I, p. 58, Vol. II. Phoenix Edition.

things are reasons and how much. This latter process of sifting reasons from causes is part of the critical process for every belief, but in some spheres it has been done pretty fully already. In these spheres we don't need to examine the actual processes to belief and distil from them a logic. But in other spheres this remains to be done. Even in science or on the stock exchange or in ordinary life we sometimes hesitate to condemn a belief or a hunch[9] merely because those who believe it cannot offer the sort of reasons we had hoped for. And now suppose Miss Gertrude Stein finds excellent the work of a new artist while we see nothing in it. We nervously recall, perhaps, how pictures by Picasso, which Miss Stein admired and others rejected, later came to be admired by many who gave attention to them, and we wonder whether the case is not a new instance of her perspicacity and our blindness. But if, upon giving all our attention to the work in question, we still do not respond to it, and we notice that the subject matter of the new pictures is perhaps birds in wild places and learn that Miss Stein is a bird-watcher, then we begin to trouble ourselves less about her admiration.

It must not be forgotten that our attempt to show up misconnections in Miss Stein may have an opposite result and reveal to us connections we had missed. Thinking to remove the spell exercised upon his patient by the old stories of the Greeks, the psycho-analyst may himself fall under that spell and find in them what his patient has found and, incidentally, what made the Greeks tell those tales.

10. *Now what happens, what should happen, when we inquire in this way into the reasonableness, the propriety of belief in gods?* The answer is: A double and opposite-phased change. Wordsworth writes:

> . . . And I have felt
> A presence that disturbs me with the joy
> Of elevated thoughts; a sense sublime
> Of something far more deeply interfused,
> Whose dwelling is the light of setting suns,
> And the round ocean and the living air,
> And the blue sky, and in the mind of man:
> A motion and a spirit, that impels
> All thinking things, all objects of all thought,
> And rolls through all things . . .[10]

We most of us know this feeling. But is it well placed like the feeling that here is first-rate work, which we sometimes rightly have even before we have fully grasped the picture we are looking at or the book we are reading? Or is it misplaced like the feeling in a house that has long been empty that someone secretly lives there still. Wordsworth's feeling *is* the feeling that the world is haunted, that something watches in the hills and manages the stars. The child feels that the stone tripped him when he stumbled, that the bough struck him when it flew back in his face. He has to learn that the wind isn't buffeting him, that there is not a devil in it, that he was wrong,

---

[9] Here I think of Mr. Stace's interesting reflections in *Mind*, January, 1945, 'The Problems of Unreasoned Beliefs'.

[10] *Tintern Abbey.*

that his attitude was inappropriate. And as he learns that the wind wasn't hindering him so he also learns it wasn't helping him. But we know how, though he learns, his attitude lingers. It is plain that Wordsworth's feeling is of this family.

Belief in gods, it is true, is often very different from belief that stones are spiteful, the sun kindly. For the gods appear in human form and from the waves and control these things and by so doing reward and punish us. But varied as are the stories of the gods they have a family likeness and we have only to recall them to feel sure of the other main sources which co-operate with animism to produce them.

What are the stories of the gods? What are our feelings when we believe in God? They are feelings of awe before power, dread of the thunderbolts of Zeus, confidence in the everlasting arms, unease beneath the all-seeing eye. They are feelings of guilt and inescapable vengeance, of smothered hate and of a security we can hardly do without. We have only to remind ourselves of these feelings and the stories of the gods and goddesses and heroes in which these feelings find expression, to be reminded of how we felt as children to our parents and the big people of our childhood. Writing of a first telephone call from his grandmother, Proust says: '. . . it was rather that this isolation of the voice was like a symbol, a presentation, a direct consequence of another isolation, that of my grandmother, separated for the first time in my life, from myself. The orders or prohibitions which she addressed to me at every moment in the ordinary course of my life, the tedium of obedience or the fire of rebellion which neutralized the affection that I felt for her were at this moment eliminated. . . . "Granny!" I cried to her . . . but I had beside me only that voice, a phantom, as unpalpable as that which would come to revisit me when my grandmother was dead. "Speak to me!" but then it happened that, left more solitary still, I ceased to catch the sound of her voice. My grandmother could no longer hear me . . . I continued to call her, sounding the empty night, in which I felt that her appeals also must be straying. I was shaken by the same anguish which, in the distant past, I had felt once before, one day when, a little child, in a crowd, I had lost her.'

Giorgio de Chirico, writing of Courbet, says: 'The word yesterday envelops us with its yearning echo, just as, on waking, when the sense of time and the logic of things remain a while confused, the memory of a happy hour we spent the day before may sometimes linger reverberating within us. At times we think of Courbet and his work as we do of our own father's youth.'

When a man's father fails him by death or weakness how much he needs another father, one in the heavens with whom is 'no variableness nor shadow of turning'.

We understood Mr. Kenneth Graham when he wrote of the Golden Age we feel we have lived in under the Olympians. Freud says: 'The ordinary man cannot imagine this Providence in any other form but that of a greatly exalted father, for only such a one could understand the needs of the sons of men, or be softened by their prayers and be placated by the signs of their remorse. The whole thing is so patently infantile, so incongruous with reality. . . .' 'So incongruous with reality'! It cannot be denied.

But here a new aspect of the matter may strike us.[11] For the very facts which make us feel that now we can recognize systems of superhuman, sub-human, elusive, beings for what they are—the persistent projections of infantile phantasies—include facts which make these systems less fantastic. What are these facts? They are patterns in human reactions which are well described by saying that we are as if there were hidden within us powers, persons, not ourselves and stronger than ourselves. That this is so may perhaps be said to have been common knowledge yielded by ordinary observation of people,[12] but we did not know the degree in which this is so until recent study of extraordinary cases in extraordinary conditions had revealed it. I refer, of course, to the study of multiple personalities and the wider studies of psycho-analysts. Even when the results of this work are reported to us that is not the same as tracing the patterns in the details of the cases on which the results are based; and even that is not the same as taking part in the studies oneself. One thing not sufficiently realized is that some of the things shut within us are not bad but good.

Now the gods, good and evil and mixed, have always been mysterious powers outside us rather than within. But they have also been within. It is not a modern theory but an old saying that in each of us a devil sleeps. Eve said: 'The serpent beguiled me.' Helen says to Menelaus:

> . . . And yet how strange it is!
> I ask not thee; I ask my own sad thought,
> What was there in my heart, that I forgot
> My home and land and all I loved, to fly
> With a strange man? Surely it was not I,
> But Cypris there![13]

Elijah found that God was not in the wind, nor in the thunder, but in a still small voice. The kingdom of Heaven is within us, Christ insisted, though usually about the size of a grain of mustard seed, and he prayed that we should become one with the Father in Heaven.

New knowledge made it necessary either to give up saying 'The sun is sinking' or to give the words a new meaning. In many contexts we preferred to stick to the old words and give them a new meaning which was not en-

---

[11] I owe to the late Dr. Susan Isaacs the thought of this different aspect of the matter, of this connection between the heavenly Father and 'the good father' spoken of in psycho-analysis.

[12] Consider Tolstoy and Dostoievsky—I do not mean, of course, that their observation was ordinary.

[13] Euripides: *The Trojan Women*, Gilbert Murray's Translation. Roger Hinks in *Myth and Allegory in Ancient Art* writes (p. 108): 'Personifications made their appearance very early in Greek poetry. . . . It is out of the question to call these terrible beings "abstractions". . . . They are real daemons to be worshipped and propitiated. . . . These beings we observe correspond to states of mind. The experience of man teaches him that from time to time his composure is invaded and overturned by some power from outside, panic, intoxication, sexual desire.'

What use to shoot off guns at unicorns?
Where one horn's hit another fierce horn grows.
These beasts are fabulous, and none were born
    Of woman who could lay a fable low.—
      The Glass Tower, Nicholas Moore, p. 100.

tirely new but, on the contrary, *practically* the same as the old. The Greeks did not speak of the dangers of repressing instincts but they did speak of the dangers of thwarting Dionysos, of neglecting Cypris for Diana, of forgetting Poseidon for Athena. We have eaten of the fruit of a garden we can't forget though we were never there, a garden we still look for though we can never find it. Maybe we look for too simple a likeness to what we dreamed. Maybe we are not as free as we fancy from the old idea that Heaven is a happy hunting ground, or a city with streets of gold. Lately Mr. Aldous Huxley has recommended our seeking not somewhere beyond the sky or late in time but a timeless state not made of the stuff of this world, which he rejects, picking it into worthless pieces. But this sounds to me still too much a looking for another place, not indeed one filled with sweets but instead so empty that some of us would rather remain in the Lamb or the Elephant, where, as we know, they stop whimpering with another bitter and so far from sneering at all things, hang pictures of winners at Kempton and stars of the 'nineties. Something good we have for each other is freed there, and in some degree and for a while the miasma of time is rolled back without obliging us to deny the present.

The artists who do most for us don't tell us only of fairylands. Proust, Manet, Breughel, even Botticelli and Vermeer show us reality. And yet they give us for a moment exhilaration without anxiety, peace without boredom. And those who, like Freud, work in a different way against that which too often comes over us and forces us into deadness or despair,[14] also deserve critical, patient and courageous attention. For they, too, work to release us from human bondage into human freedom.

Many have tried to find ways of salvation. The reports they bring back are always incomplete and apt to mislead even when they are not in words but in music or paint. But they are by no means useless; and not the worst of them are those which speak of oneness with God. But in so far as we become one with Him He becomes one with us. St. John says he is in us as we love one another.

This love, I suppose, is not benevolence but something that comes of the oneness with one another of which Christ spoke.[15] Sometimes it momentarily gains strength.[16] Hate and the Devil do too. And what is oneness without otherness?

[14] Matthew Arnold: *Summer Night.*   [15] St. John xvi, 21.
[16] 'The Harvesters' in *The Golden Age*, Kenneth Graham.

A RELIGIOUS WAY OF KNOWING

C. B. Martin

I

Some theologians support their claim to knowledge of the existence of God on the basis of direct experience of God. I shall attempt to point out some of the eccentricities of this alleged way of knowing. The two main sources which I shall use are Professor J. Baillie's *Our Knowledge of God* and Professor H. H. Farmer's *Towards Belief in God*.

> We are rejecting logical argument of any kind as the first chapter of our theology or as representing the process by which God comes to be known. We are holding that our knowledge of God rests rather on the revelation of His personal Presence as Father, Son, and Holy Spirit. . . . Of such a Presence it must be true that to those who have never been confronted with it argument is useless, while to those who have it is superfluous.
>
> Baillie, p. 132.

> It is not as the result of an inference of any kind, whether explicit or implicit, whether laboriously excogitated or swiftly intuited, that the knowledge of God's reality comes to us. It comes rather through our direct, personal encounter with Him in the Person of Jesus Christ His Son our Lord.
>
> *Ibid.*, p. 143.

If now we ask how we would expect such a reality (God) to disclose itself to us, the answer can only be that we can have no expectancy about the matter at all; for in the nature of the case there are no parallels, no analogies on which expectancy may be based. The divine reality is, by definition, unique. Or, in other words, we would expect that if we know the reality of God in respect of this fundamental aspect of His being at all, we shall just know that we are dealing with God, the ultimate source and disposer of all things, including ourselves, and there will be nothing more to be said. It will not be possible to describe the compelling touch of God otherwise than as the compelling touch

C. B. Martin, "A Religious Way of Knowing," *Mind*, LXI (1952), 497–512. Reprinted by permission of the Editor of *Mind*.

of God. To anyone who has no such awareness of God, leading as it does to the typically religious attitudes of obeisance and worship, it will be quite impossible to indicate what is meant; one can only hope to evoke it, on the assumption that the capacity to become aware of God is part of normal human nature like the capacity to see light or to hear sound.

Farmer, p. 40.

The arguments of the theologians quoted have been taken out of context. I do not want to suggest that the quotations give a faithful or complete impression of their total argument. The following quotations from Professor Farmer indicate two further lines of argument which cannot be discussed here.

Reflection
For what we have now in mind is no demonstrative proofs *from* the world, but rather confirmatory considerations which present themselves to us when we bring belief in God with us *to* the world. It is a matter of the coherence of the belief with other facts. If we find that the religious intuition which has arisen from other sources provides the mind with a thought in terms of which much else can without forcing be construed, then that is an intellectual satisfaction, and a legitimate confirmation of belief, which it would be absurd to despise.

Farmer, p. 133.

Pragmatic Element
We shall first speak in general terms of what may be called the human situation and need, and thereafter we shall try to show how belief in God, as particularized in its Christian form (though still broadly set forth), fits on to this situation and need.

Ibid., p. 62.

II

The alleged theological way of knowing may be described as follows.
"I have direct experience (knowledge, acquaintance, apprehension) of God, therefore I have valid reason to believe that God exists."
A. By this it may be meant that the statement "I have had direct experience of God, but God does not exist" is contradictory. Thus, the assertion that "I have had direct experience of God" commits one to the assertion that God exists. From this it follows that "I have had direct experience of God" is more than a psychological statement, because it claims more than the fact that I have certain sensations—it claims that God exists. Thus as it stands this is a correct form of deductive argument. The assertion "I have direct experience of God" includes the assertion "God exists" thus, the conclusion "therefore, God exists" follows tautologically.
B. Unfortunately, this deduction is useless. The addition of the existential claim "God exists" to the psychological claim of having religious experiences must be shown to be warrantable. It cannot be shown to be warrantable by any deductive argument, because psychological statements of the form

1. I feel as if an unseen person were interested in (willed) my welfare.
2. I feel an elation quite unlike any I have ever felt before.

3. I have feelings of guilt and shame at my sinfulness.

4. I feel as if I were committed to bending all of my efforts to living in a certain way,

etc., etc.,

can make the claim only that I have these complex feelings and sensations. Nothing else follows deductively. No matter what the existential statement might be that is added to the psychological statement, it is always logically possible for future psychological statements to call this existential claim in doubt. The only thing that I can establish beyond correction on the basis of having certain feelings and sensations is that I have these feelings and sensations. No matter how unique an experience may be claimed to be, it cannot do the impossible.

There is an influential and subtle group of religious thinkers who would not insist upon any existential claim. My remarks are largely irrelevant to this group. It would be hasty to describe their religious belief as "psychological" or employ any other such general descriptive term. For example, the "call", in even the most liberal and "subjective" Quaker sects, could not be reduced to feeling statements, etc. The "call", among other things, implies a mission or intricate programme of behaviour. The non-subjective element of the "call" is evident because in so far as one failed to live in accordance with a mission just so far would the genuineness of the "call" be questioned. It will be seen that this verification procedure is necessarily not available in the religious way of knowing to be examined.

C. Neither is the addition of the existential claim "God exists" to the psychological claim made good by any inductive argument. There are no tests agreed upon to establish genuine experience of God and distinguish it decisively from the ungenuine. Indeed, many theologians deny the possibility of any such test or set of tests. Nor is there any increased capacity for prediction produced in the Christian believer which we cannot explain on a secular basis. However, just such a capacity is implied by those who talk of religious experience as if it were due to some kind of sixth sense.

1. The believer may persuade us that something extraordinary has happened by saying, "I am a changed man since 6.37 P.M., 6th May, 1939". This is a straightforward empirical statement. We can test this by noticing whether or not he has given up bad habits, etc. We may allow the truth of the statement, even if he has not given up bad habits, etc., because we may find evidence of bad conscience, self-searchings and remorse that had not been present before that date.

2. However, if the believer says, "I had a direct experience of God at 6.37 P.M., 6th May, 1939", this is not an empirical statement in the way that the other statement is. The checking procedure is very far from clear. No matter how much or how little his subsequent behaviour such as giving up bad habits, etc., is affected, it could never prove or disprove his statement.

An important point to note is that the theologian discourages any detailed description of the required experience ("apprehension of God"). The more naturalistic and detailed the description of the required experience became, the easier would it become to deny the existential claim. One could say, "Yes, I had those very experiences, but they certainly did not convince me of God's existence". The only sure defence here would be for the theologian to make the claim analytic—"You couldn't have those experiences and at the same time sincerely deny God's existence".

D. The way in which many theologians talk would seem to show that they think of knowing God as something requiring a kind of sixth sense.

1. The Divine Light is not merely of a colour usually visible only to eagles and the Voice of God is not merely of a pitch usually audible only to dogs. No matter how much more keen our senses became, we should be no better off than before. This sixth sense, therefore, must be very different from the other five.

(*a*) This supposed religious sense has no vocabulary of its own, but depends upon metaphors drawn from the other senses. There are no terms which apply to it and it alone. There is a vocabulary for what is sensed but not for the sense. We "see" the Holy, the Numinous, the Divine, etc. This linguistic predicament may be compared with the similar one of the intuitionists when they talk of "seeing" a logical connexion. It also may be compared with "hearing" the Voice of Conscience.

(*b*) The intuitionists seldom differ from the rest of us in the number of facts referred to in describing how we come to understand logical statements and their relations. The intuitionist, however, emphasizes the fact that often we come to understand the point of an argument or problem in logic very suddenly. We mark this occurrence by such phrases as "the light dawned", "understood it in a flash". Such events are usually described in terms of a complete assurance that one's interpretation is correct and a confidence that one will tend to be able to reproduce or recognize the argument or problem in various contexts in the future. A vitally important distinction between this "seeing" and the religious "seeing" is that there is a checking procedure for the former, but not for the latter. If the intuitionist finds that his boasted insight was wrong, then he says, "I couldn't really have 'seen' it". No matter how passionate his claim he cannot have "seen" that $2 + 2 = 5$.

III

The religious way of knowing is described as being unique.

A. No one can deny the existence of feelings and experiences which the believer calls "religious" and no one can deny their power. Because of this and because the way of knowing by direct experience is neither inductive nor deductive, theologians have tried to give this way of knowing a special status. One way in which this has been done has been to claim that religious experience is unique and incommunicable. There is a sense in which this is true. This sense may be brought out by a list such as the following.

1. You don't know what the experience of God is until you have had it.
2. You don't know what a blue sky is until you have been to Naples.
3. You don't know what poverty is until you have been poor.
4. "We can only know a person by the direct communion of sympathetic intercourse." Temple.

Professor Baillie, in likening our knowledge of God to our knowledge of other minds, says that it is

like our knowledge of tridimensional space and all other primary modes of
knowledge, something that cannot be imagined by one who does not already
possess it, since it cannot be described to him in terms of anything else than
itself.

Baillie, p. 217.

What Professor Baillie does not see is that according to his criteria anything
can qualify as a primary mode of knowledge. Each one of the statements in
the above list is unique and incommunicable in just this way. You must go to
Naples and not just to Venice. A postcard is no substitute.

B. That this sort of uniqueness is not to the point in supporting the
existential claim "God exists" can be seen by examining the following two
examples.

1. You don't know what the experience of God is until you have had it.
2. You don't know what the colour blue is until you have seen it.

Professor Farmer says,

All the basic elements in our experience are incommunicable. Who could
describe light and colour to one who has known nothing but darkness?

Farmer, p. 41.

Just in so far as the experience of God is unique and incommunicable in this
way, then just so far is it not to the point in supporting the existential claim
"God exists".

All that this proves is that a description of one group of sensations A in
terms of another set of sensations B is never sufficient for knowing group A.
According to this definition of "know", in order to know one must have
those sensations. Thus, all that is proved is that in order to know what
religious experience is one must have a religious experience. This helps in no
way at all to prove that such experience is direct apprehension of God and
helps in no way to support the existential claim "God exists".

C. Professor Farmer makes the point that describing the experience of
God to an unbeliever is like describing colour to a blind man. So it is, in the
sense that the believer has usually had experiences which the unbeliever has
not. However, it is also very much unlike. The analogy breaks down at some
vital points.

1. The blind man may have genuine though incomplete knowledge of
colour. He may have an instrument for detecting wave lengths, etc. Indeed,
he may even increase our knowledge of colour. More important still, the
blind man may realize the differences in powers of prediction between
himself and the man of normal eyesight. He is well aware of the fact that,
unlike himself, the man of normal eyesight does not have to wait to hear the
rush of the bull in order to be warned.

2. This point is connected with the problem of how we are to know
when someone has the direct experience of God or even when we ourselves
have the direct experience of God. It was shown above how the situation is
easier in the case of the blind man. It is easy also, in the case of knowing a
blue sky in Naples. One can look at street signs and maps in order to be sure
that this is the really blue sky in question. It is only when one comes to such
a case as knowing God that the society of tests and check-up procedures

that surround other instances of knowing, completely vanishes. What is put in the place of these tests and checking procedures is an immediacy of knowledge that is supposed to carry its own guarantee. This feature will be examined later.

D. It is true that the man of normal vision has a way of knowing colour which the blind man does not have. Namely, he can see coloured objects. However, as we have seen, it would be wrong to insist that this is the only way of knowing colour and that the blind man has *no* way of knowing colour. There is a tendency to deny this and to maintain that having colour sensations is *the* way of knowing colour. Perhaps Professor Farmer has this in mind when he tries to make an analogy between the incommunicability of the believer's direct knowledge of God to the unbeliever and the incommunicability of the normal man's knowledge of colour to the blind man. The analogy is justified if "knowing colour" is made synonymous with "having colour sensations".

1. On this account, no matter how good his hearing and reliable his colour-detecting instruments, etc., the blind man could not know colour and the man of normal vision could not communicate to him just what this knowledge would be like.

2. The believer has had certain unusual experiences which, presumably, the unbeliever has not had. If "having direct experience of God" is made synonymous with "having certain religious experiences", and the believer has had these and the unbeliever has not, then we may say that the believer's knowledge is incommunicable to the unbeliever in that it has already been legislated that in order to know what the direct experience of God is one must have had certain religious experiences.

> To anyone who has no such awareness of God, leading as it does to the typically religious attitudes of obeisance and worship, it will be quite impossible to indicate what is meant; one can only hope to evoke it. . . .
>
> Farmer, p. 40.

Reading theological text-books and watching the behaviour of believers is not sufficient.

E. The theologian has made the above analogy hold at the cost of endangering the existential claim about God which he hoped to establish.

1. If "knowing colour" is made synonymous with "having colour sensations" and "having direct experience of God" is made synonymous with "having certain religious experiences", then it is certainly true that a blind man cannot "know colour" and that a non-religious man cannot "have direct experience of God". By definition, also, it is true that the blind man and the non-religious man cannot know the meaning of the phrases "knowing colour" and "having direct experience of God", because it has been previously legislated that one cannot know their meaning without having the relevant experiences.

2. If this analogy is kept then the phrases "knowing colour" and "having direct experience of God" seem to make no claim beyond the psychological claims about one's colour sensations and religious feelings.

3. If this analogy is not kept then there is no sense in the comparison between the incommunicability between the man of normal vision and the

blind man and the incommunicability between the believer and the unbeliever.

4. If "knowing colour" is to be shaken loose from its purely psychological
implications and made to have an existential reference concerning certain
features of the world then a whole society of tests and check-up procedures
which would be wholly irrelevant to the support of the psychological claim
about one's own colour sensations become relevant. *E.g.* what other people
see and the existence of light waves and the description of their characteristics needing the testimony of research workers and scientific instruments.

F. Because "having direct experience of God" does not admit the relevance of a society of tests and checking procedures it places itself in the
company of the other ways of knowing which preserve their self-
sufficiency, "uniqueness" and "incommunicability" by making a psychological and not an existential claim. *E.g.* "I seem to see a blue piece of
paper". This statement requires no further test or checking procedure in
order to be considered true. Indeed, if A makes the statement "I seem to see
a blue piece of paper", then not only does A need no further corroboration,
but there could be no disproof of his statement for him, for, if B says to A,
"It does not seem to me as if I were now seeing a blue piece of paper", then
B's statement does *not* call A's statement in doubt for A though it does for
B. However, if A makes the statement, "I see a piece of blue paper", and B
says in the same place and at the same time, "I do not see a piece of blue
paper", then B's statement *does* call A's statement in doubt for A. Further
investigation will then be proper and if no piece of paper can be felt and
other investigators cannot see or feel the paper and photographs reveal
nothing, then A's statement will be shown to have been false. A's only
refuge will be to say, "Well, I certainly seem to see a piece of blue paper".
This is a perfect refuge because no one can prove him wrong, but its
unassailability has been bought at the price of making no claim about the
world beyond the claim about his own state of mind.

G. Another way of bringing out the closeness of the religious statement
to the psychological statement is the following.

1. When A wishes to support the assertion that a certain physical object
exists, the tests and checking procedures made by A himself are not the only
things relevant to the truth of his assertion. Testimony of what B, C, D, etc.
see, hear, etc. is also relevant. That is, if A wanted to know whether it was
really a star that he saw, he could not only take photographs, look through a
telescope, etc., but also ask others if they saw the star. If a large proportion
of a large number of people denied seeing the star, A's claim about the star's
existence would be weakened. Of course, he might still trust his telescope.
However, let us now imagine that A does not make use of the tests and
checking procedures (photographs and telescopes) but is left with the
testimony of what he sees and the testimony of others concerning what
they see. In this case, it is so much to the point if a large number of
people deny seeing the star, that A will be considered irrational or mad if he
goes on asserting its existence. His only irrefutable position is to reduce his
physical object claim to an announcement concerning his own sensations.
Then the testimony of men and angels cannot disturb his certitude. These
sensations of the moment he knows directly and immediately and the
indirect and non-immediate testimony of men and angels is irrelevant.

Absolute confidence and absolute indifference to the majority judgment is bought at the price of reducing the existential to the psychological.

2. The religious claim is similar to, though not identical with, the above case in certain important features. We have seen that there are no tests or checking procedures open to the believer to support his existential claim about God. Thus, he is left with the testimony of his own experience and the similar testimony of the experience of others. And, of course, he is not left wanting for such testimony, for religious communities seem to serve just this sort of function.

3. Let us imagine a case comparable to the one concerning the existence of a physical object. In this case A is a professor of Divinity and he believes that he has come to know of the existence of God through direct experience of God. In order to understand the intricate character of what Professor A is asserting we must imagine a highly unusual situation. The other members of the faculty and the members of Professor A's religious community suddenly begin sincerely to deny his and what has been their assertion. Perhaps they still attend church services and pray as often as they used to do, and perhaps they claim to have the same sort of experiences as they had when they were believers, but they refuse to accept the conclusion that God exists. Whether they give a Freudian explanation or some other explanation or no explanation of their experiences, they are agreed in refusing to accept the existential claim (about God) made by Professor A. How does this affect Professor A and his claim? It may affect Professor A very deeply—indeed, he may die of broken-hearted disappointment at the loss of his fellow-believers. However, the loss of fellow-believers may not weaken his confidence in the truth of his assertion or in the testimony of his experience. In this matter his experience may be all that ultimately counts for him in establishing his confidence in the truth of his claim about the existence of God. It has been said that religious experience carries its own guarantee and perhaps the above account describes what is meant by this.

H. It is quite obvious from the examples given above that the religious statement ("I have direct experience of God") is of a different status from the physical object statement ("I see a star") and shows a distressing similarity to the psychological statement ("I seem to see a star"). The bulk of this paper has been devoted to showing some of the many forms this similarity takes. Does this mean then that the religious statement and its existential claim concerning God amount to no more than a reference to the complex feelings and sensations of the believer?

I. Perhaps the best way to answer this last question is to take a typical psychological statement and see if there is anything which must be said of it and all other psychological statements which cannot be said of the religious statement.

1. One way of differentiating a physical object statement from a psychological statement is by means of prefixing the phrase "I seem . . .". For instance, the statement "I see a star" may be transformed from a statement concerning the existence of a certain physical object to a statement concerning my sensations by translating it into the form "I seem to see a star". The first statement involves a claim about the existence of an object as well as an announcement concerning my sensations and therefore subjects itself to the risk of being wrong concerning that further claim. Being wrong in this case

is determined by a society of tests and checking procedures such as taking photographs and looking through telescopes and by the testimony of others that they see or do not see a star. The second statement involves no claim about the existence of an object and so requires no such tests and no testimony of others; indeed, the sole judge of the truth of the statement is the person making it. If no existential claim is lost by the addition of this phrase to a statement then the statement is psychological. For instance, the statement "I feel pain" loses nothing by the addition "I seem to feel pain".

2. In the case of the religious statement "I have direct experience of God" the addition of the phrase is fatal to all that the believer wants to assert. "I seem to be having direct experience of God" is a statement concerning my feelings and sensations of the moment and as such it makes no claim about the existence of God. Thus, the original statement "I have direct experience of God" is not a psychological statement. This should not surprise us. We should have known it all along, for isn't it an assertion that one comes to know something, namely God, by means of one's feelings and sensations and this something is not reducible to them? The statement is not a psychological one just because it is used to assert the existence of something. Whether this assertion is warranted and what exactly it amounts to is quite another question.

3. The statement "I seem to be having direct experience of God" is an eccentric one. It is eccentric not only because introspective announcements are unusual and because statements about God have a peculiar obscurity, but for a further and more important reason. This peculiarity may be brought out by comparing this statement with others having the same form. A first formulation of this may be put in the following way. In reference to things other than our sensations of the moment knowledge is prior to seeming as if.

The statement "I seem to be looking directly at a chair" has a meaning only in so far as I already *know* what it is like to look directly at a chair. The statement "I seem to be listening to a choir" has a meaning only in so far as I already *know* what it is like to be listening to a choir. The assumption of knowledge in both of these cases is one which all normal people are expected to be able to make and do in fact make.

The statement "I seem to be having direct experience of God" does not lend itself so easily to the criterion for meaning exemplified in the above, because if this statement has meaning only in so far as one already *knows* what it is like to have direct experience of God, then the assumption of such knowledge is certainly not one which all normal people may be expected to be able to make or do in fact make.

However, it may be said that the assumption of such knowledge as knowledge of what it is like to see a gorgon may not be assumed of all normal people and, therefore, the case of religious knowledge is in no peculiar position.

The answer to this objection and the discovery of the peculiarity of the religious statement may come about by asking the question "How do we come to learn what it would be like to look directly at a chair, hear a choir, see a gorgon, have direct experience of God?"

It is not that there are no answers to the question concerning how we come to learn what it would be like to have direct experience of God. We are not left completely in the dark. Instead, the point is that the answers to this question are quite different from those referring to the questions concerning how we come to learn what it would be like to look directly at a chair, hear a choir, and see a gorgon.

No one in our society has seen a gorgon, yet there are people who, by means of their specialized knowledge of mythical literature, may claim in a perfectly meaningful manner that it now seems to them as if they were seeing a gorgon.

Let us imagine a society in which there are no chairs and no one knows anything at all about chairs. If we were to try to teach one of the members of this society what it would be like to see a chair and if we were not allowed to construct a chair, what sort of thing might we do? We might look around at the furniture and say, "A chair is a kind of narrow settee. It is used to sit on". This would be a beginning. Then we might compare different settees as to which are more chair-like. We might draw pictures of chairs, make gestures with our hands showing the general shape and size of different sorts of chairs. If, on the following day, he said, "I had a most unusual dream last night. I seemed to be looking directly at a chair", we should admit that his statement was closer in meaning to a similar one which we who have seen chairs might make than it would be to a similar one which another member might make who had no information or instruction or experience of chairs. We would insist that we had better knowledge of what it is to see a chair than does the instructed member of society who has still actually to see a chair. However, to know pictures of chairs is to know chairs in a legitimate sense.

But let us now imagine a utopian society in which none of the members has ever been in the least sad or unhappy. If we were to try to teach one of the members of this society what it would be like to feel sad, how would we go about it? It can be said that giving definitions, no matter how ingenious, would be no help, drawing pictures of unhappy faces, no matter how well drawn, would be no help, so long as these measures failed to evoke a feeling of sadness in this person. Comparing the emotion of sadness with other emotions would be no help, because no matter how like other emotions (weariness, etc.) are to sadness they fail just because they are not sadness. No, sadness is unique and incomparable.

To anyone who has no such awareness of sadness, leading as it does to the typically unhappy behaviour of tears and drawn faces, it will be quite impossible to indicate what is meant, one can only hope to evoke it, on the assumption that the capacity to become aware of sadness is part of normal human nature like the capacity to see light or to hear sound.

This last paragraph is a play upon a quotation given at the very beginning of the paper. The following is the original version.

> To anyone who has no such awareness of God, leading as it does to the typically religious attitudes of obeisance and worship, it will be quite impossible to indicate what is meant; one can only hope to evoke it, on the assumption that the capacity to become aware of God is part of normal human nature like the capacity to see light or to hear sound.
>
> Farmer, p. 40.

4.

> We are rejecting logical argument of any kind as the first chapter of our epistemology of aesthetics, or as representing the process by which beauty comes to be known. . . .
>
> It is not as the result of an inference of any kind, whether explicit or implicit, whether laboriously excogitated or swiftly intuited, that the knowledge of beauty comes to us.
>
> . . . to those who have never been confronted with the experience of seeing the beauty of something, argument is useless.

As these statements stand they are plainly false. Professors of aesthetics and professional art critics often do help us to come to "knowledge of beauty" by all kinds of inference and arguments. They may, and often do, help us to come to a finer appreciation of beautiful things. Knowledge of the rules of perspective and understanding of an artist's departure from them is relevant to an aesthetic appreciation of his work.

However, it is possible to interpret these statements as true and this is more important for our purpose.

There is sense in saying that an art critic, who has vastly increased our aesthetic sensitivity and whose books of art criticism are the very best, may never have known beauty. If there are no signs of this critic ever having been stirred by any work of art, then no matter how subtle his analyses, there is sense in claiming that he has never been confronted with the experience of seeing the beauty of something. This sense just is that we are determined not to say that a person has seen the beauty of something or has knowledge of beauty if he does not at some time have certain complex emotions and feelings which are typically associated with looking at paintings, hearing music and reading poetry. To "know beauty" or to "see the beauty of something" means, among other things, to have certain sorts of emotions and feelings.

The quotation given above was a play on a quotation given at the beginning of the paper. The following is the original version with the appropriate cuts.

> We are rejecting logical argument of any kind as the first chapter of our theology or as representing the process by which God comes to be known. . . .
>
> It is not as the result of an inference of any kind, whether explicit or implicit, whether laboriously excogitated or swiftly intuited, that the knowledge of God comes to us.
>
> . . . to those who have never been confronted with it [direct, personal encounter with God] argument is useless.

As these statements stand they are plainly false. Professors of divinity and clergymen are expected to do what Professor Baillie claims cannot be done.

However, it is possible to interpret these statements as true and this is more important for our purpose.

There is sense in saying that a theologian (who has vastly increased our religious sensitivity and whose books of theology are the very best) may never have known God. If there are no signs of this theologian ever having been stirred by any religious ritual or act of worship, then no matter how subtle his analyses, there is sense in claiming that he has never been confronted with God's personal Presence. This sense just *is* that we are determined not to say that a person has knowledge of God if he does not at some time have certain complex emotions and feelings which are associated with attending religious services, praying and reading the Bible. To "know God" or to be confronted with God's "personal Presence" means, of necessity, having certain sorts of emotions and feelings.

5. The analogy suggested above between aesthetic experience and religious experience and between aesthetic knowledge and religious knowledge cannot be examined further in this paper. However, certain preliminary suggestions may be made. The following quotations set the problem.

> In it [art] also there is an awareness, however unformulated and inarticulate, of a world of beauty which can be grasped and actualized in creative activity, yet it will never be possible fully to grasp it and actualize it in all its infinite reach and depth. In the appreciation of beauty in artistic products something of the same sense of an 'infinite beyond' disclosing itself through, yet transcending, what is contemplated and enjoyed, is present. It is precisely this that marks the difference between, say, a Beethoven symphony and a shallow and 'tinny' jazz-dance.
>
> Farmer, *Towards Belief in God*, p. 56.

After quoting Santayana's remark, "Religions are better or worse, never true or false", Professor Farmer says,

> It is sufficient answer to this suggestion to say that it is utterly false both to art and to religion. It is a central element in the artistic consciousness that it is, in its work, seeking to grasp and express an ideal world which in spite of its ideality is real and in some sense stands objectively over against the artist; it is never apprehended as merely a source of internal satisfaction and delights. Without this neither the work of artistic production nor its product would internally satisfy or delight. This is even more obviously true of religion. In religion the reality-interest is paramount. Once persuade the religious man that the reality with which he supposes himself to be dealing is not 'there' in the sense in which he supposes it to be 'there' and his religion vanishes away.
>
> Farmer, *Towards Belief in God*, p. 176.

One may select a group of statements to compare and analyze. The following would be samples of such statements.

> The Believer experiences God.
> The Sensitive Listener experiences Beauty in the music.
> The Believer experiences something of the infinite goodness of God.
> The Sensitive Listener experiences the subtlety, sadness, colour, etc., of the music as part of what is the Beauty in the music.
> One may hear God through prayer.
> One may hear the Beautiful above or in the voices of the actors and the instruments of the orchestra.
> What the artist experiences and knows, namely Beauty, is ultimately incommunicable.
> What the Believer experiences and knows, namely God, is ultimately incommunicable.

One may learn to come to know God.
One may learn to come to know Beauty.
One may learn to come to know one's wife.

Going over the complex uses of such statements may help one to discover something of the intricate logic of certain kinds of religious statements.

In this paper the analogy between seeing blue and experiencing God has been examined and found to be misleading. The suggested analogy between experiencing the Beautiful and experiencing God has further complexities and requires another examination which, among other things, would show how religious experience is and is not another experience in the way in which seeing red may be said to be another experience to seeing blue or hearing a nightingale.

Another important subject with which this paper has not dealt is the connexion between what the believer expects from immortality and his religious belief. This peculiar kind of test or verification has special difficulties which cannot be treated here.

IV

Conclusion

It must be made clear in conclusion that the lack of tests and checking procedures which has been noted is not merely an unfortunate result of human frailty. It is necessarily the nature of the case. If tests and checking procedures were devised they would not, could not, support the claim of the believer. They may do for the detection of saints and perhaps even angels, but never of God. Of course, in a way theologians know this.

This paper has been an attempt to indicate how statements concerning a certain alleged religious way of knowing betray a logic extraordinarily like that of statements concerning introspective and subjective ways of knowing. It is not my wish to go from a correct suggestion that the logic is *very, very* like to an incorrect suggestion that the logic is *just* like.

EVIL AND OMNIPOTENCE

J. L. Mackie

The traditional arguments for the existence of God have been fairly thoroughly criticised by philosophers. But the theologian can, if he wishes, accept this criticism. He can admit that no rational proof of God's existence is possible. And he can still retain all that is essential to his position, by holding that God's existence is known in some other, non-rational way. I think, however, that a more telling criticism can be made by way of the traditional problem of evil. Here it can be shown, not that religious beliefs lack rational support, but that they are positively irrational, that the several parts of the essential theological doctrine are inconsistent with one another, so that the theologian can maintain his position as a whole only by a much more extreme rejection of reason than in the former case. He must now be prepared to believe, not merely what cannot be proved, but what can be *disproved* from other beliefs that he also holds.

The problem of evil, in the sense in which I shall be using the phrase, is a problem only for someone who believes that there is a God who is both omnipotent and wholly good. And it is a logical problem, the problem of clarifying and reconciling a number of beliefs: it is not a scientific problem that might be solved by further observations, or a practical problem that might be solved by a decision or an action. These points are obvious; I mention them only because they are sometimes ignored by theologians, who sometimes parry a statement of the problem with such remarks as "Well, can you solve the problem yourself?" or "This is a mystery which may be revealed to us later" or "Evil is something to be faced and overcome, not to be merely discussed".

In its simplest form the problem is this: God is omnipotent; God is wholly good; and yet evil exists. There seems to be some contradiction between these three propositions, so that if any two of them were true the third would be false. But at the same time all three are essential parts of most theological positions: the theologian, it seems, at once *must* adhere and *cannot consistently* adhere to all three. (The problem does not arise only for

J. L. Mackie, "Evil and Omnipotence," *Mind*, LXIV (1955), 200–212. Reprinted by permission of the Editor of *Mind*.

theists, but I shall discuss it in the form in which it presents itself for ordinary theism.)

However, the contradiction does not arise immediately; to show it we need some additional premises, or perhaps some quasi-logical rules connecting the terms 'good', 'evil', and 'omnipotent'. These additional principles are that good is opposed to evil, in such a way that a good thing always eliminates evil as far as it can, and that there are no limits to what an omnipotent thing can do. From these it follows that a good omnipotent thing eliminates evil completely, and then the propositions that a good omnipotent thing exists, and that evil exists, are incompatible.

A. ADEQUATE SOLUTIONS

Now once the problem is fully stated it is clear that it can be solved, in the sense that the problem will not arise if one gives up at least one of the propositions that constitute it. If you are prepared to say that God is not wholly good, or not quite omnipotent, or that evil does not exist, or that good is not opposed to the kind of evil that exists, or that there are limits to what an omnipotent thing can do, then the problem of evil will not arise for you.

There are, then, quite a number of adequate solutions of the problem of evil, and some of these have been adopted, or almost adopted, by various thinkers. For example, a few have been prepared to deny God's omnipotence, and rather more have been prepared to keep the term 'omnipotence' but severely to restrict its meaning, recording quite a number of things that an omnipotent being cannot do. Some have said that evil is an illusion, perhaps because they held that the whole world of temporal, changing things is an illusion, and that what we call evil belongs only to this world, or perhaps because they held that although temporal things *are* much as we see them, those that we call evil are not really evil. Some have said that what we call evil is merely the privation of good, that evil in a positive sense, evil that would really be opposed to good, does not exist. Many have agreed with Pope that disorder is harmony not understood, and that partial evil is universal good. Whether any of these views is *true* is, of course, another question. But each of them gives an adequate solution of the problem of evil in the sense that if you accept it this problem does not arise for you, though you may, of course, have *other* problems to face.

But often enough these adequate solutions are only *almost* adopted. The thinkers who restrict God's power, but keep the term 'omnipotence', may reasonably be suspected of thinking, in other contexts, that his power is really unlimited. Those who say that evil is an illusion may also be thinking, inconsistently, that this illusion is itself an evil. Those who say that "evil" is merely privation of good may also be thinking, inconsistently, that privation of good is an evil. (The fallacy here is akin to some forms of the "naturalistic fallacy" in ethics, where some think, for example, that "good" is just what contributes to evolutionary progress, and that evolutionary progress is itself good.) If Pope meant what he said in the first line of his couplet, that "disorder" is only harmony not understood, the "partial evil" of the second line must, for consistency, mean "that which, taken in isolation, falsely appears to be evil", but it would more naturally mean "that which, in isolation, really is evil". The second line, in fact, hesitates between two views, that "partial evil" isn't really evil, since only the universal quality is real, and that "partial evil" is really an evil, but only a little one.

In addition, therefore, to adequate solutions, we must recognise unsatisfactory inconsistent solutions, in which there is only a half-hearted or temporary rejection of one of the propositions which together constitute the problem. In these, one of the constituent propositions is explicitly rejected, but it is covertly re-asserted or assumed elsewhere in the system.

B. FALLACIOUS SOLUTIONS

Besides these half-hearted solutions, which explicitly reject but implicitly assert one of the constituent propositions, there are definitely fallacious solutions which explicitly maintain all the constituent propositions, but implicitly reject at least one of them in the course of the argument that explains away the problem of evil.

There are, in fact, many so-called solutions which purport to remove the contradiction without abandoning any of its constituent propositions. These must be fallacious, as we can see from the very statement of the problem, but it is not so easy to see in each case precisely where the fallacy lies. I suggest that in all cases the fallacy has the general form suggested above: in order to solve the problem one (or perhaps more) of its constituent propositions is given up, but in such a way that it appears to have been retained, and can therefore be asserted without qualification in other contexts. Sometimes there is a further complication: the supposed solution moves to and fro between, say, two of the constituent propositions, at one point asserting the first of these but covertly abandoning the second, at another point asserting the second but covertly abandoning the first. These fallacious solutions often turn upon some equivocation with the words 'good' and 'evil', or upon some vagueness about the way in which good and evil are opposed to one another, or about how much is meant by 'omnipotence'. I propose to examine some of these so-called solutions, and to exhibit their fallacies in detail. Incidentally, I shall also be considering whether an adequate solution could be reached by a minor modification of one or more of the constituent propositions, which would, however, still satisfy all the essential requirements of ordinary theism.

1. "Good cannot exist without evil" or "Evil is necessary as a counterpart to good."

It is sometimes suggested that evil is necessary as a counterpart to good, that if there were no evil there could be no good either, and that this solves the problem of evil. It is true that it points to an answer to the question "Why should there be evil?" But it does so only by qualifying some of the propositions that constitute the problem.

First, it sets a limit to what God can do, saying that God *cannot* create good without simultaneously creating evil, and this means either that God is not omnipotent or that there are *some* limits to what an omnipotent thing can do. It may be replied that these limits are always presupposed, that omnipotence has never meant the power to do what is logically impossible, and on the present view the existence of good without evil would be a logical impossibility. This interpretation of omnipotence may, indeed, be accepted as a modification of our original account which does not reject anything that is essential to theism, and I shall in general assume it in the subsequent discussion. It is, perhaps, the most common theistic view, but I think that some theists at least have maintained that God can do what is logically impossible. Many theists, at any rate, have held that logic itself is created or laid down by God, that logic is the way in which God arbitrarily chooses to think. (This is, of course, parallel to the ethical view that morally right actions are those which God arbitrarily chooses to command, and the two views encounter similar difficulties.) And *this* account of logic is clearly inconsistent with the view that God is bound by logical necessities —unless it is possible for an omnipotent being to bind himself, an issue which we shall consider later, when we come to the Paradox of Omnipotence. This solution of the problem of evil cannot, therefore, be consistently adopted along with the view that logic is itself created by God.

But, secondly, this solution denies that evil is opposed to good in our original sense. If good and evil are counterparts, a good thing will not "eliminate evil as far as it can". Indeed, this view suggests that good and evil are not strictly qualities of things at all. Perhaps the suggestion is that good and evil are related in much the same way as great and small. Certainly, when the term 'great' is used relatively as a condensation of 'greater than so-and-so', and 'small' is used correspondingly, greatness and smallness are counterparts and cannot exist without each other. But in this sense greatness is not a quality, not an intrinsic feature of anything; and it would be absurd to think of a movement in favour of greatness and against smallness in this sense. Such a movement would be self-defeating, since relative greatness can be promoted only by a simultaneous promotion of relative smallness. I feel sure that no theists would be content to regard God's goodness as analogous to this—as if what he supports were not the *good* but the *better*, and as if he had the paradoxical aim that all things should be better than other things.

This point is obscured by the fact that 'great' and 'small' seem to have an absolute as well as a relative sense. I cannot discuss here whether there is absolute magnitude or not, but if there is, there could be an absolute sense for 'great', it could mean of at least a certain size, and it would make sense to speak of all things getting bigger, of a universe that was expanding all over, and therefore it would make sense to speak of promoting greatness. But in *this* sense great and small are not logically necessary counterparts: either quality could exist without the other. There would be no logical impossibility in everything's being small or in everything's being great.

Neither in the absolute nor in the relative sense, then, of 'great' and 'small' do these terms provide an analogy of the sort that would be needed to support this solution of the problem of evil. In neither case are greatness and smallness *both* necessary counterparts *and* mutually opposed forces or possible objects for support and attack.

It may be replied that good and evil are necessary counterparts in the same way as any quality and its logical opposite: redness can occur, it is suggested, only if non-redness also occurs. But unless evil is merely the privation of good, they are not logical opposites, and some further argument would be needed to show that they are counterparts in the same way as genuine logical opposites. Let us assume that this could be given. There is still doubt of the correctness of the metaphysical principle that a quality must have a real opposite: I suggest that it is not really impossible that everything should be, say, red, that the truth is merely that if everything were red we should not notice redness, and so we should have no word 'red'; we observe and give names to qualities only if they have real opposites. If so, the principle that a term must have an opposite would belong only to our language or to our thought, and would not be an ontological principle, and, correspondingly, the rule that good cannot exist without evil would not state a logical necessity of a sort that God would just have to put up with. God might have made everything good, though *we* should not have noticed it if he had.

But, finally, even if we concede that this *is* an ontological principle, it will provide a solution for the problem of evil only if one is prepared to say, "Evil exists, but only just enough evil to serve as the counterpart of good". I doubt whether any theist will accept this. After all, the *ontological* requirement that non-redness should occur would be satisfied even if all the universe, except for a minute speck, were red, and, if there were a corresponding requirement for evil as a counterpart to good, a minute dose of evil would presumably do. But theists are not usually willing to say, in all contexts, that all the evil that occurs is a minute and necessary dose.

2. "Evil is necessary as a means to good."

It is sometimes suggested that evil is necessary for good not as a counterpart but as a means. In its simple form this has little plausibility as a solution of the problem of evil, since it obviously implies a severe restriction of God's power. It would be a *causal* law that you cannot have a certain end without a certain means, so that if God has to introduce evil as a means to good, he must be subject to at least some causal laws. This certainly conflicts with what a theist normally means by omnipotence. This view of God as limited by causal laws also conflicts with the view that causal laws are themselves made by God, which is more widely held than the corresponding view about the laws of logic. This conflict would, indeed, be resolved if it were possible for an omnipotent being to bind himself, and this possibility has still to be considered. Unless a favourable answer can be given to this question, the suggestion that evil is necessary as a means to good solves the problem of evil only by denying one of its constituent propositions, either that God is omnipotent or that 'omnipotent' means what it says.

3. "The universe is better with some evil in it than it could be if there were no evil."

Much more important is a solution which at first seems to be a mere variant of the previous one, that evil may contribute to the goodness of a whole in which it is found, so that the universe as a whole is better as it is, with some evil in it, than it would be if there were no evil. This solution may be developed in either of two ways. It may be supported by an aesthetic analogy, by the fact that contrasts heighten beauty, that in a musical work, for example, there may occur discords which somehow add to the beauty of the work as a whole. Alternatively, it may be worked out in connexion with the notion of progress, that the best possible organisation of the universe will not be static, but progressive, that the gradual overcoming of evil by good is really a finer thing than would be the eternal unchallenged supremacy of good.

In either case, this solution usually starts from the assumption that the evil whose existence gives rise to the problem of evil is primarily what is called physical evil, that is to say, pain. In Hume's rather half-hearted presentation of the problem of evil, the evils that he stresses are pain and disease, and those who reply to him argue that the existence of pain and disease makes possible the existence of sympathy, benevolence, heroism, and the gradually successful struggle of doctors and reformers to overcome these evils. In fact, theists often seize the opportunity to accuse those who stress the problem of evil of taking a low, materialistic view of good and evil, equating these with pleasure and pain, and of ignoring the more spiritual goods which can arise in the struggle against evils.

But let us see exactly what is being done here. Let us call pain and misery 'first order evil' or 'evil (1)'. What contrasts with this, namely, pleasure and happiness, will be called 'first order good' or 'good (1)'. Distinct from this is 'second order good' or 'good (2)' which somehow emerges in a complex situation in which evil (1) is a necessary component—logically, not merely causally, necessary. (Exactly *how* it emerges does not matter: in the crudest version of this solution good (2) is simply the heightening of happiness by the contrast with misery, in other versions it includes sympathy with suffering, heroism in facing danger, and the gradual decrease of first order evil and increase of first order good.) It is also being assumed that second order good is more important than first order good or evil, in particular that it more than outweighs the first order evil it involves.

Now this is a particularly subtle attempt to solve the problem of evil. It defends God's goodness and omnipotence on the ground that (on a sufficiently long view) this is the best of all logically possible worlds, because it includes the important second order goods, and yet it admits that real evils, namely first order evils, exist. But does it still hold that good and evil are opposed? Not, clearly, in the sense that we set out originally: good does not tend to eliminate evil in general. Instead, we have a modified, a more complex pattern. First order good (*e.g.* happiness) *contrasts with* first order evil (*e.g.* misery): these two are opposed in a fairly mechanical way; some second order goods (*e.g.* benevolence) try to maximise first order good and minimise first order evil; but God's goodness is not this, it is rather the will to maximise *second* order good. We might, therefore, call God's goodness an example of a third order goodness, or good (3). While this account is different from our original one, it might well be held to be an improvement on it, to give a more accurate description of the way in which good is opposed to evil, and to be consistent with the essential theist position.

There might, however, be several objections to this solution.

First, some might argue that such qualities as benevolence—and *a fortiori* the third order goodness which promotes benevolence—have a merely derivative value, that they are not higher sorts of good, but merely means to good (1), that is, to happiness, so that it would be absurd for God to keep misery in existence in order to make possible the virtues of benevolence, heroism, etc. The theist who adopts the present solution must, of course, deny this, but he can do so with some plausibility, so I should not press this objection.

Secondly, it follows from this solution that God is not in our sense benevolent or sympathetic: he is not concerned to minimise evil (1), but only to promote good (2); and this might be a disturbing conclusion for some theists.

But, thirdly, the fatal objection is this. Our analysis shows clearly the possibility of the existence of a *second* order evil, an evil (2) contrasting with good (2) as evil (1) contrasts with good (1). This would include malevolence, cruelty, callousness, cowardice, and states in which good (1) is decreasing and evil (1) increasing. And just as good (2) is held to be the important kind of good, the kind that God is concerned to promote, so evil (2) will, by analogy, be the important kind of evil, the kind which God, if he were wholly good and omnipotent, would eliminate. And yet evil (2) plainly exists, and indeed most theists (in other contexts) stress its existence more than that of evil (1). We should, therefore, state the problem of evil in terms of second order evil, and against this form of the problem the present solution is useless.

An attempt might be made to use this solution again, at a higher level, to explain the occurrence of evil (2): indeed the next main solution that we shall examine does just this, with the help of some new notions. Without any fresh notions, such a solution would have little plausibility: for example, we could hardly say that the really important good was a good (3), such as the increase of benevolence in proportion to cruelty, which logically required for its occurrence the occurrence of some second order evil. But even if evil (2) could be explained in this way, it is fairly clear that there would be third order evils contrasting with this third order good: and we should be well on the way to an infinite regress, where the solution of a problem of evil, stated in terms of evil (n), indicated the existence of an evil ($n + 1$), and a further problem to be solved.

4. "Evil is due to human freewill."

Perhaps the most important proposed solution of the problem of evil is that evil is not to be ascribed to God at all, but to the independent actions of human beings, supposed to have been endowed by God with freedom of the will. This solution may be combined with the preceding one: first order evil (*e.g.* pain) may be justified as a logically necessary component in second order good (*e.g.* sympathy) while second order evil (*e.g.* cruelty) is not *justified*, but is so ascribed to human beings that God cannot be held responsible for it. This combination evades my third criticism of the preceding solution.

The freewill solution also involves the preceding solution at a higher level. To explain why a wholly good God gave men freewill although it would lead to some important evils, it must be argued that it is better on the whole that men should act freely, and sometimes err, than that they should be innocent automata, acting rightly in a wholly determined way. Freedom, that is to say, is now treated as a third order good, and as being more valuable than second order goods (such as sympathy and heroism) would be if they were deterministically produced, and it is being assumed that second order evils, such as cruelty, are logically necessary accompaniments of freedom, just as pain is a logically necessary pre-condition of sympathy.

I think that this solution is unsatisfactory primarily because of the incoherence of the notion of freedom of the will: but I cannot discuss this topic adequately here, although some of my criticisms will touch upon it.

First I should query the assumption that second order evils are logically necessary accompaniments of freedom. I should ask this: if God has made men such that in their free choices they sometimes prefer what is good and sometimes what is evil, why could he not have made men such that they always freely choose the good? If there is no logical impossibility in a man's freely choosing the good on one, or on several, occasions, there cannot be a logical impossibility in his freely choosing the good on every occasion. God was not, then, faced with a choice between making innocent automata and making beings who, in acting freely, would sometimes go wrong: there was open to him the obviously better possibility of making beings who would act freely but always go right. Clearly, his failure to avail himself of this possibility is inconsistent with his being both omnipotent and wholly good.

If it is replied that this objection is absurd, that the making of some wrong choices is logically necessary for freedom, it would seem that 'freedom' must here mean complete randomness or indeterminacy, including randomness with regard to the alternatives good and evil, in other words that men's choices and consequent actions can be "free" only if they are not determined by their characters. Only on this assumption can God escape the responsibility for men's actions; for if he made them as they are, but did not determine their wrong choices, this can only be because the wrong choices are not determined by men as they are. But then if freedom is randomness, how can it be a characteristic of *will?* And, still more, how can it be the most important good? What value or merit would there be in free choices if these were random actions which were not determined by the nature of the agent?

I conclude that to make this solution plausible two different senses of 'freedom' must be confused, one sense which will justify the view that freedom is a third order good, more valuable than other goods would be without it, and another sense, sheer randomness, to prevent us from ascribing to God a decision to make men such that they sometimes go wrong when he might have made them such that they would always freely go right.

This criticism is sufficient to dispose of this solution. But besides this there is a fundamental difficulty in the notion of an omnipotent God creating men with free will, for if men's wills are really free this must mean that even God cannot control them, that is, that God is no longer omnipotent. It may be objected that God's gift of freedom to men does not mean that he *cannot* control their wills, but that he always *refrains* from controlling their wills. But why, we may ask, should God refrain from controlling evil wills? Why should he not leave men free to will rightly, but intervene when he sees them beginning to will wrongly? If God could do this, but does not, and if he is wholly good, the only explanation could be that even a wrong free act of will is not really evil, that its freedom is a value which outweighs its wrongness, so that there would be a loss of value if God took away the wrongness and the freedom together. But this is utterly opposed to what theists say about sin in other contexts. The present solution of the problem of evil, then, can be maintained only in the form that God has made men so free that he *cannot* control their wills.

This leads us to what I call the Paradox of Omnipotence: can an omnipotent being make things which he cannot subsequently control? Or, what is practically equivalent to this, can an omnipotent being make rules which then bind himself? (These are practically equivalent because any such rules could be regarded as setting certain things beyond his control, and *vice versa*.) The second of these formulations is relevant to the suggestions that we have already met, that an omnipotent God creates the rules of logic or causal laws, and is then bound by them.

It is clear that this is a paradox: the questions cannot be answered satisfactorily either in the affirmative or in the negative. If we answer "Yes", it follows that if God actually makes things which he cannot control, or makes rules which bind himself, he is not omnipotent once he has made them: there are *then* things which he cannot do. But if we answer "No", we are immediately asserting that there are things which he cannot do, that is to say that he is already not omnipotent.

It cannot be replied that the question which sets this paradox is not a proper question. It would make perfectly good sense to say that a human mechanic has made a machine which he cannot control: if there is any difficulty about the question it lies in the notion of omnipotence itself.

This, incidentally, shows that although we have approached this paradox from the free will theory, it is equally a problem for a theological determinist. No one thinks that machines have free will, yet they may well be beyond the control of their makers. The determinist might reply that anyone who makes anything determines its ways of acting, and so determines its subsequent behaviour: even the human mechanic does this by his *choice* of materials and structure for his machine, though he does not know all about either of these: the mechanic thus determines, though he may not foresee, his machine's actions. And since God is omniscient, and since his creation of things is total, he both determines and foresees the ways in which his creatures will act. We may grant this, but it is beside the point. The question is not whether God *originally* determined the future actions of his creatures, but whether he can *subsequently* control their actions, or whether he was able in his original creation to put things beyond his subsequent control. Even on determinist principles the answers "Yes" and "No" are equally irreconcilable with God's omnipotence.

Before suggesting a solution of this paradox, I would point out that there is a parallel Paradox of Sovereignty. Can a legal sovereign make a law restricting its own future legislative power? For example, could the British parliament make a law forbidding any future parliament to socialise banking, and also forbidding the future repeal of this law itself? Or could the British parliament, which was legally sovereign in Australia in, say, 1899, pass a valid law, or series of laws, which made it no longer sovereign in 1933? Again, neither the affirmative nor the negative answer is really satisfactory. If we were to answer "Yes", we should be admitting the validity of a law which, if it were actually made, would mean that parliament was no longer sovereign. If we were to answer "No", we should be admitting that there is a law, not logically absurd, which parliament cannot validly make, that is, that parliament is not now a legal sovereign. This paradox can be solved in the following way. We should distinguish between first order laws, that is laws governing the actions of individuals and bodies other than the legislature, and second order laws, that is laws about laws, laws governing the actions of the legislature itself. Correspondingly, we should distinguish two orders of sovereignty, first order sovereignty (sovereignty (1)) which is unlimited authority to make first order laws, and second order sovereignty (sovereignty (2)) which is unlimited authority to make second order laws. If we say that parliament is sovereign we might mean that any parliament at any time has sovereignty (1), or we might mean that parliament has both sovereignty (1) and sovereignty (2) at present, but we cannot without contradiction mean both that the present parliament has sovereignty (2) and that every parliament at every time has sovereignty (1), for if the present parliament has sovereignty (2) it may use it to take away the sovereignty (1) of later parliaments. What the paradox shows is that we cannot ascribe to any continuing institution legal sovereignty in an inclusive sense.

The analogy between omnipotence and sovereignty shows that the paradox of omnipotence can be solved in a similar way. We must distinguish between first order omnipotence (omnipotence (1)), that is unlimited power to act, and second order omnipotence (omnipotence (2)), that is unlimited power to determine what powers to act things shall have. Then we could consistently say that God all the time has omnipotence (1), but if so no beings at any time have powers to act independently of God. Or we could say that God at one time had omnipotence (2), and used it to assign independent powers to act to certain things, so that God thereafter did not have omnipotence (1). But what the paradox shows is that we cannot consistently ascribe to any continuing being omnipotence in an inclusive sense.

An alternative solution of this paradox would be simply to deny that God is a continuing being, that any times can be assigned to his actions at all. But on this assumption (which also has difficulties of its own) no meaning can be given to the assertion that God made men with wills so free that he could not control them. The paradox of omnipotence can be avoided by putting God outside time, but the freewill solution of the problem of evil cannot be saved in this way, and equally it remains impossible to hold that an omnipotent God *binds himself* by causal or logical laws.

CONCLUSION

Of the proposed solutions of the problem of evil which we have examined, none has stood up to criticism. There may be other solutions which require examination, but this study strongly suggests that there is no valid solution of the problem which does not modify at least one of the constituent propositions in a way which would seriously affect the essential core of the theistic position.

Quite apart from the problem of evil, the paradox of omnipotence has shown that God's omnipotence must in any case be restricted in one way or another, that unqualified omnipotence cannot be ascribed to any being that continues through time. And if God and his actions are not in time, can omnipotence, or power of any sort, be meaningfully ascribed to him?

Further References

Alston, W. P. (ed.). *Religious Belief and Philosophical Thought.* New York: Harcourt, Brace & World, 1963.

Blackstone, W. T. *The Problem of Religious Knowledge.* Englewood Cliffs, N. J.: Prentice-Hall, 1963.*

Ferré, Frederick. *Language, Logic and God.* London: SCM Press, 1959.

Flew, Antony, and MacIntyre, Alasdair (eds.). *New Essays in Philosophical Theology.* London: SCM Press, 1955.†

Hick, John. *Faith and Knowledge.* Ithaca, N. Y.: Cornell University Press, 1957.

————. *Philosophy of Religion.* Englewood Cliffs, N. J.: Prentice-Hall, 1957.*

Hick, John (ed.). *Classical and Contemporary Readings in the Philosophy of Religion.* Englewood Cliffs, N. J.: Prentice-Hall, 1964.

————. *The Existence of God.* New York: Macmillan, 1964.*

Hook, Sidney (ed.). *Religious Experience and Truth.* New York: New York University Press, 1961.

Martin, C. B. *Religious Belief.* Ithaca, N. Y.: Cornell University Press, 1959.

Matson, Wallace I. *The Existence of God.* Ithaca, N. Y.: Cornell University Press, 1965.

Mitchell, Basil (ed.). *Faith and Logic.* London: Allen & Unwin, 1957.

Munz, Peter. *Problems of Religious Knowledge.* London: SCM Press, 1959.

Pike, N. (ed.). *God and Evil.* Englewood Cliffs, N. J.: Prentice-Hall, 1964.*

Plantinga, Alvin (ed.). *The Ontological Argument.* New York: Anchor Books, 1965.*

Ramsey, Ian. *Religious Language.* London: SCM Press, 1957.

Smart, N. *Philosophers and Religious Truth.* London: SCM Press, 1964.

* Paperback edition.   † Also available in a paperback edition.

: III :

Human Behavior
and
Physical Phenomena

INTRODUCTION

To consider the behavior of human beings and of physical objects together is to pose one of the most effective organizing questions of philosophy: Whether and in what respect the conceptual categories appropriate to discourse about physical phenomena apply to, or need to be modified or augmented for, discourse about human behavior, and, in particular, whether and in what respect the explanations of phenomena of the two sorts are of similar or different kinds. When we speak in the contexts that are normally the concern of social scientists, we speak primarily of *persons* and their *actions;* when we speak in the contexts that are normally the concern of natural scientists, we speak primarily of *physical objects* and *physical events*. It is extremely difficult, however, to explain the difference between the concepts of person and physical object, as well as between the concepts of human action and mere physical occurrence. We shall consider some of these distinctions in Part IV. However, there remains an entire set of related issues that concern the compatibility of our discourse about human beings and about physical events, and these questions have taken certain classic forms.

Perhaps the most famous of these is the question of the compatibility of human freedom and causality. The difficulty lies, of course, in the fact that neither freedom nor causality is a simple notion. A substantial part of the problem has to do with the proper analysis of the concepts themselves. Nevertheless, there remains a persistent intuition—dignified by an unending philosophical quarrel—that what is caused is, in some important sense, so determined that human freedom is not compatible with it, and is therefore reduced to a mere illusion (this is the view, for example, of Baron Holbach). The issue was already a prominent one in the ancient world, where (as in Epicurean and Stoic speculations) the ontological issue embraced the perennially intriguing question of the relationship, broadly conceived, between moral responsibility and science. If, it may be argued, when a man is responsible for what he does—for example, in acting "of his own volition"—

how can it be that what he does is caused? On the other hand, if what he does is caused, how is it possible for him to act of his own volition and how, consequently, can he be held to be morally responsible for what he does?

Some philosophers take the firm view that freedom (or free will or, sometimes, even choice) is incompatible with causality (or necessity or determinism); they conclude from this either that freedom is an illusion (as Holbach did), or that causality is not universally operative (as, in various ways, the Epicureans, C. A. Campbell [III:3], and William James did), or that the causal order and the moral order are not coextensive (as Immanuel Kant did). Others, who form by far the dominant tradition, hold that freedom and causality are fully compatible and they offer different accounts of these concepts in order to support their view.

The problem of reconciling these two positions remains strikingly similar whether we speak, in the religious context, of human freedom and divine foreknowledge and necessity (as with St. Augustine [III:1]), or, in the secular context, of liberty and causal necessity (as with John Stuart Mill [III:2]). In fact, the conclusions of St. Augustine and Mill are very much the same. They are versions of one of the principal forms of reconciliation, namely, the view that liberty or free will designates a distinction within the causal order itself.

There is at least one other important conciliatory tradition: the tradition that, in various ways, distinguishes between the actual and the possible. Sometimes, as with indeterminists and advocates of real chance (such as Democritus or James, for example), the actual and the possible are held to be not coextensive. Sometimes, the meanings of "possible," as the term is used in the context of human action and in the context of physical events, are taken to be quite different, although compatible; that view has become prominent in relatively recent linguistic analysis (as, for example, in J. L. Austin and Stuart Hampshire [III:4]). Attention shifts, therefore, from ontological to methodological considerations. Accounts of the latter sort lead quite naturally to another of the large issues concerning compatibility of discourse about physical events with discourse about human actions, that is, to the question of the nature of, and relationship between, the kinds of explanation preferred in the two domains.

The crux of the issue lies with the explication of what is meant by "reasons" and "causes" in explanations of human behavior. No one denies that various sorts of explanation of both types are invoked in accounts of human behavior; nor does anyone deny that human behavior (and animal behavior only by extension from the human), unlike events that involve inanimate objects, is described and explained in intentional terms—that is, with regard to such considerations as motives, intentions, purposes, and beliefs. Explanation by reasons is inherently intentional, and explanation of human behavior by causes allows for the intentional description of at least certain causes and effects.

The chief point at issue comes down to this: can human actions (in which, for example, one raises an arm in order to signal or signs one's name to a check to cover a debt) be explained in causal terms or only in terms of reasons? Some (for example, R. S. Peters [III:5] and Peter Winch) hold that causal explanations of *actions* are logically inappropriate; others (for example, Donald Davidson [III:6]) hold that explanation by reasons is one species of explanation by causes; still others (for example, H. L. A. Hart [III:7] and A. I. Melden) hold that, while explanation by reasons is logically quite different from explanation by causes, causal factors may relevantly be said to affect actions or constituents of actions. Hart and Honoré's discussion demonstrates the sense in which the distinction between the two sorts of explanation bears jointly on moral and scientific issues and marks correlative explanatory alternatives—at least as far as human action is concerned.

Causality itself, however, is a concept with a much disputed history. It appears to be originally anthropomorphic in nature. The classic account of the ancient world is provided, of course, in Aristotle's doctrine of the four causes (III:8). Seen in retrospect, the most striking feature of this view is its joint emphasis on efficient and teleological causes (the concept of teleological cause is intimately connected with the doctrine of natural species and with the causal analysis of human action and art). With the advent of Renaissance science and the modern age, causality was made to apply paradigmatically to inanimate physical events. The turning point in modern views of causality may be linked with David Hume's account (III:9), which was written in the full flowering of eighteenth-century reflection on Newtonian science. Here we find what has since become the standard restriction of the concept to questions of efficient causation, the rejection of any necessary connection between cause and effect and the elimination of anthropomorphic interpretations of efficient causes.

Hume's account of causality, on its positive side, was bound to be (again, when seen in retrospect) relatively naive and incomplete. The reason probably lies in the coupling of the overzealous empiricism of the eighteenth century with the recency of the Newtonian synthesis; although causal connections were construed as lawlike regularities, physical laws themselves were hardly related, if at all, to an analysis of the nature of scientific theories. Subsequent science (and philosophy of science) has been increasingly obliged to consider the extraordinarily difficult question of the relationship between sensory perception and theoretical presupposition. It also sought to distinguish—contrary, let us say, to the radically empiricist spirit of the inductive canons of Mill—between possibly accidental regularities that depend on the perception of the behavior of particular samples, whose selection remains theoretically unaccounted for, and regularities that manifest the laws of nature (for example, as delineated in Ernest Nagel's discussion [III:10]).

Finally, at this last stage in the refinement of our concepts of causality and of laws of nature (in which the meaning of "cause" may be seen to become increasingly attenuated as attention turns to laws and to the logical conditions on which universal statements may be counted as laws), the old question of the compatibility of discourse about physical events and about human behavior appears in another guise. It has been held, as has already been suggested, that the kinds of explanation that are invoked in the physical sciences and in the historical or social sciences are of radically different sorts. The question arises, as we have seen, as to whether such a distinction between kinds of explanation leads justifiably to a rejection of causal explanations in the study of human action. A deeper challenge has been laid down, however, to the pretensions of a unity of science that is thought to comprehend both sorts of disciplines. It has been held, for instance, not only that the historical sciences are concerned with characterizing and interpreting unique events rather than with formulating empirically confirmable general laws, but that it is logically impossible to formulate such laws for the historical disciplines. Carl Hempel's discussion (III:11) of the question is perhaps the best-known reply offered in the spirit of the unity of science.

Freedom and Determinism

1

PROVIDENCE AND FREE WILL

St. Augustine

CONCERNING THE FOREKNOWLEDGE OF GOD AND THE FREE WILL
OF MAN, IN OPPOSITION TO THE DEFINITION OF CICERO

The manner in which Cicero addresses himself to the task of refuting the
Stoics, shows that he did not think he could effect anything against them in
argument unless he had first demolished divination. And this he attempts to
accomplish by denying that there is any knowledge of future things, and
maintains with all his might that there is no such knowledge either in God
or man, and that there is no prediction of events. Thus he both denies the
foreknowledge of God, and attempts by vain arguments, and by opposing to
himself certain oracles very easy to be refuted, to overthrow all prophecy,
even such as is clearer than the light (though even these oracles are not
refuted by him).

But, in refuting these conjectures of the mathematicians, his argument is
triumphant, because truly these are such as destroy and refute themselves.
Nevertheless, they are far more tolerable who assert the fatal influence of
the stars than they who deny the foreknowledge of future events. For, to
confess that God exists, and at the same time to deny that He has foreknowledge of future things, is the most manifest folly. This Cicero himself
saw, and therefore attempted to assert the doctrine embodied in the words
of Scripture, "The fool hath said in his heart, There is no God." That,
however, he did not do in his own person, for he saw how odious and
offensive such an opinion would be; and therefore, in his book on the nature

From St. Augustine, *The City of God*, Marcus Dods, trans. (Edinburgh: T. & T.
Clark, 1872), Book V, Chaps. IX–XI, pp. 64–70.

of the gods, he makes Cotta dispute concerning this against the Stoics, and preferred to give his own opinion in favor of Lucilius Balbus, to whom he assigned the defence of the Stoical position, rather than in favor of Cotta, who maintained that no divinity exists. However, in his book on divination, he in his own person most openly opposes the doctrine of the prescience of future things. But all this he seems to do in order that he may not grant the doctrine of fate, and by so doing destroy free will. For he thinks that, the knowledge of future things being once conceded, fate follows as so necessary a consequence that it cannot be denied.

But, let these perplexing debatings and disputations of the philosophers go on as they may, we, in order that we may confess the most high and true God Himself, do confess His will, supreme power, and prescience. Neither let us be afraid lest, after all, we do not do by will that which we do by will, because He, whose foreknowledge is infallible, foreknew that we would do it. It was this which Cicero was afraid of, and therefore opposed foreknowledge. The Stoics also maintained that all things do not come to pass by necessity, although they contended that all things happen according to destiny. What is it, then, that Cicero feared in the prescience of future things? Doubtless it was this—that if all future things have been foreknown, they will happen in the order in which they have been foreknown; and if they come to pass in this order, there is a certain order of things foreknown by God; and if a certain order of things, then a certain order of causes, for nothing can happen which is not preceded by some efficient cause. But if there is a certain order of causes according to which everything happens which does happen, then by fate, says he, all things happen which do happen. But if this be so, then is there nothing in our own power, and there is no such thing as freedom of will; and if we grant that, says he, the whole economy of human life is subverted. In vain are laws enacted. In vain are reproaches, praises, chidings, exhortations had recourse to; and there is no justice whatever in the appointment of rewards for the good, and punishments for the wicked. And that consequences so disgraceful, and absurd, and pernicious to humanity may not follow, Cicero chooses to reject the foreknowledge of future things, and shuts up the religious mind to this alternative, to make choice between two things, either that something is in our own power, or that there is foreknowledge—both of which cannot be true; but if the one is affirmed, the other is thereby denied. He therefore, like a truly great and wise man, and one who consulted very much and very skillfully for the good of humanity, of those two chose the freedom of the will, to confirm which he denied the foreknowledge of future things; and thus, wishing to make men free, he makes them sacrilegious. But the religious mind chooses both, confesses both, and maintains both by the faith of piety. But how so? says Cicero; for the knowledge of future things being granted, there follows a chain of consequences which ends in this, that there can be nothing depending on our own free wills. And further, if there is anything depending on our wills, we must go backwards by the same steps of reasoning till we arrive at the conclusion that there is no foreknowledge of future things. For we go backwards through all the steps in the following order:—If there is free will, all things do not happen according to fate; if all things do not happen according to fate, there is not a certain order of causes; and if there is not a certain order of causes, neither is there a certain order of things foreknown by God—for things cannot come to pass except they are preceded by efficient causes—but, if there is no fixed and certain order of causes foreknown by God, all things cannot be said to happen according as He foreknew that they would happen. And further, if it is not true that all things happen just as they have been foreknown by Him, there is not, says he, in God any foreknowledge of future events.

Now, against the sacrilegious and impious darings of reason, we assert both that God knows all things before they come to pass, and that we do by our free will whatsoever we know and feel to be done by us only because we will it. But that all things come to pass by fate, we do not say; nay we affirm that nothing comes to pass by fate; for we demonstrate that the name of fate, as it is wont to be used by those who speak of fate, meaning thereby the position of the stars at the time of each one's conception or birth, is an unmeaning word, for astrology itself is a delusion. But an order of causes in which the highest efficiency is attributed to the will of God, we neither deny nor do we designate it by the name of fate, unless, perhaps, we may understand fate to mean that which is spoken, deriving it from *fari*, to speak; for we cannot deny that it is written in the sacred Scriptures, "God hath spoken once; these two things have I heard, that power belongeth unto God. Also unto Thee, O God, belongeth mercy: for Thou wilt render unto every man according to his works." Now the expression, "Once hath He spoken," is to be understood as meaning "*immovably*," that is, unchangeably hath He spoken, inasmuch as He knows unchangeably all things which shall be, and all things which He will do. We might, then, use the word fate in the sense it bears when derived from *fari*, to speak, had it not already come to be understood in another sense, into which I am unwilling that the hearts of men should unconsciously slide. But it does not follow that, though there is for God a certain order of all causes, there must therefore be nothing depending on the free exercise of our own wills, for our wills themselves are included in that order of causes which is certain to God, and is embraced by His foreknowledge, for human wills are also causes of human actions; and He who foreknew all the causes of things would certainly among those causes not have been ignorant of our wills. For even that very concession which Cicero himself makes is enough to refute him in this argument. For what does it help him to say that nothing takes place without a cause, but that every cause is not fatal, there being a fortuitous cause, a natural cause, and a voluntary cause? It is sufficient that he confesses that whatever happens must be preceded by a cause. For we say that those causes which are called fortuitous are not a mere name for the absence of causes, but are only latent, and we attribute them either to the will of the true God, or to that of spirits of some kind or other. And as to natural causes, we by no means separate them from the will of Him who is the author and framer of all nature. But now as to voluntary causes. They are referable either to God, or to angels, or to men, or to animals of whatever description, if indeed those instinctive movements of animals devoid of reason, by which, in accordance with their own nature, they seek or shun various things, are to be called wills. And when I speak of the wills of angels, I mean either the wills of good angels, whom we call the angels of God, or of the wicked angels, whom we call the angels of the devil, or demons. Also by the wills of men I mean the wills either of the good or of the wicked. And from this we conclude that there are no efficient causes of all things which come to pass unless voluntary causes, that is, such as belong to that nature which is the spirit of life. For the air or wind is called spirit, but, inasmuch as it is a body, it is not the spirit of life. The spirit of life, therefore, which quickens all things, and is the creator of every body, and of every created spirit, is God Himself, the uncreated spirit. In His supreme will resides the power which acts on the wills of all created spirits, helping the good, judging the evil, controlling all, granting power to some, not granting it to others. For, as He is the creator of all natures, so also is He the bestower of all powers, not of all wills; for wicked wills are not from Him, being contrary to nature, which is from Him. As to bodies, they are more subject to wills: some to our wills, by which I mean the wills of all living mortal creatures, but more to the wills of men than of beasts. But all of them are most of all subject to the will of God, to whom all wills also are subject, since they have no power except what He has bestowed upon them. The cause of things, therefore, which makes but is not made, is God; but all other causes both make and are made. Such are all created spirits, and especially the rational. Material causes, therefore, which may rather be said to be made than to make, are not to be reckoned among efficient causes, because they can only do what the wills of spirits do by them. How, then, does an order of causes which is certain to the foreknowledge of God necessitate that there should be nothing which is dependent on our wills, when our wills themselves have a very important place in the order of causes? Cicero, then, contends with those who call this order of causes fatal, or rather designate this order itself by the name of fate; to which we have an abhorrence, especially on account of the word, which men have become accustomed to understand as meaning what is not true. But, whereas he denies that the order of all causes is most certain, and perfectly clear to the prescience of God, we detest his opinion more than the Stoics do. For he either denies that God exists—which, indeed, in an assumed personage, he has labored to do, in his book *De Natura Deorum*— or if he confesses that He exists, but denies that He is prescient of future things, what is that but just the fool saying in his heart there is no God? For one who is not prescient of all future things is not God. Wherefore our wills also have just so much power as God willed and foreknew that they should have; and therefore whatever power they have, they have it within most certain limits; and whatever they are to do, they are most assuredly to do, for He whose foreknowledge is infallible foreknew that they would have the power to do it, and would do it. Wherefore, if I should choose to apply the name of fate to anything at all, I should rather say that fate belongs to the weaker of two parties, will to the stronger, who has the other in his power, than that the freedom of our will is excluded by that order of causes, which, by an unusual application of the word peculiar to themselves, the Stoics call *Fate*.

WHETHER OUR WILLS ARE RULED BY NECESSITY

Wherefore, neither is that necessity to be feared, for dread of which the Stoics labored to make such distinctions among the causes of things as should enable them to rescue certain things from the dominion of necessity, and to subject others to it. Among those things which they wished not to be subject to necessity they placed our wills, knowing that they would not be free if subjected to necessity. For if that is to be called *our necessity* which is not in our power, but even though we be unwilling effects what it can effect—as, for instance, the necessity of death—it is manifest that our wills by which we live uprightly or wickedly are not under such a necessity; for we do many things which, if we were not willing, we should certainly not do. This is primarily true of the act of willing itself—for if we will, it *is;* if we will not, it *is* not—for we should not will if we were unwilling. But if we define necessity to be that according to which we say that it is necessary that anything be of such or such a nature, or be done in such and such a manner, I know not why we should have any dread of that necessity taking away the freedom of our will. For we do not put the life of God or the foreknowledge of God under necessity if we should say that it is necessary that God should live forever, and foreknow all things; as neither is His power diminished when we say that He cannot die or fall into error—for this is in such a way impossible to Him, that if it were possible for Him, He would be of less power. But assuredly He is rightly called omnipotent, though He can neither die nor fall into error. For He is called omnipotent on account of His doing what He wills, not on account of His suffering what He wills not; for if that should befall Him, He would by no means be omnipotent. Wherefore, He cannot do some things for the very reason that He is omnipotent. So also, when we say that it is necessary that, when we will, we will by free choice, in so saying we both affirm what is true beyond doubt, and do not still subject our wills thereby to a necessity which destroys liberty. Our wills, therefore, *exist* as *wills*, and do themselves whatever we do by willing, and which would not be done if we were unwilling. But when any one suffers anything, being unwilling, by the will of another, even in that case will retains its essential validity—we do not mean the will of the party who inflicts the suffering, for we resolve it into the power of God. For if a will should simply exist, but not be able to do what it wills, it would be overborne by a more powerful will. Nor would this be the case unless there had existed will, and that not the will of the other party, but the will of him who willed, but was not able to accomplish what he willed. Therefore, whatsoever a man suffers contrary to his own will, he ought not to attribute to the will of men, or of angels, or of any created spirit, but rather to His will who gives power to wills. It is not the case, therefore, that because God foreknew what would be in the power of our wills, there is for that reason nothing in the power of our wills. For He who foreknew this did not foreknow nothing. Moreover, if He who foreknew what would be in the power of our wills did not foreknow nothing, but something, assuredly, even though He did foreknow, there is something in the power of our wills. Therefore we are by no means compelled, either, retaining the prescience of God, to take away the freedom of the will, or, retaining the freedom of the will, to deny that He is prescient of future things, which is impious. But we embrace both. We faithfully and sincerely confess both. The former, that we may believe well; the latter, that we may live well. For he lives ill who does not believe well concerning God. Wherefore, be it far from us, in order to maintain our freedom, to deny the prescience of Him by whose help we are or shall be free. Consequently, it is not in vain that laws are enacted, and that reproaches, exhortations, praises, and vituperations are had recourse to; for these also He foreknew, and they are of great avail, even as great as He foreknew that they would be of. Prayers, also, are of avail to procure those things which He foreknew that He would grant to those who offered them; and with justice have rewards been appointed for good deeds, and punishments for sins. For a man does not therefore sin because God foreknew that he would sin. Nay, it cannot be doubted but that it is the man himself who sins when he does sin, because He, whose foreknowledge is infallible, foreknew not that fate, or fortune, or something else would sin, but that the man himself would sin, who, if he wills not, sins not. But if he shall not will to sin, even this did God foreknow.

CONCERNING THE UNIVERSAL PROVIDENCE OF GOD IN THE LAWS
OF WHICH ALL THINGS ARE COMPREHENDED

Therefore God supreme and true, with His Word and Holy Spirit (which three are one), one God omnipotent, creator and maker of every soul and of every body; by whose gift all are happy who are happy through verity and not through vanity; who made man a rational animal consisting of soul and body, who, when he sinned, neither permitted him to go unpunished, nor left him without mercy; who has given to the good and to the evil, being in common with stones, vegetable life in common with trees, sensuous life in common with brutes, intellectual life in common with angels alone; from whom is every mode, every species, every order; from whom are measure, number, weight; from whom is everything which has an existence in nature, of whatever kind it be, and of whatever value; from whom are the seeds of forms and the forms of seeds, and the motion of seeds and of forms; who gave also to flesh its origin, beauty, health, reproductive fecundity, disposition of members, and the salutary concord of its parts; who also to the irrational soul has given memory, sense, appetite, but to the rational soul, in addition to these, has given intelligence and will; who has not left, not to speak of heaven and earth, angels and men, but not even the entrails of the smallest and most contemptible animal, or the feather of a bird, or the little flower of a plant, or the leaf of a tree, without a harmony, and, as it were, a mutual peace among all its parts—that God can never be believed to have left the kingdoms of men, their dominations and servitudes, outside of the laws of His providence.

OF LIBERTY AND NECESSITY

John Stuart Mill

The question, whether the law of causality applies in the same strict sense to human actions as to other phenomena, is the celebrated controversy concerning the freedom of the will; which, from at least as far back as the time of Pelagius, has divided both the philosophical and the religious world. The affirmative opinion is commonly called the doctrine of Necessity, as asserting human volitions and actions to be necessary and inevitable. The negative maintains that the will is not determined, like other phenomena, by antecedents, but determines itself; that our volitions are not, properly speaking, the effects of causes, or at least have no causes which they uniformly and implicitly obey.

I have already made it sufficiently apparent that the former of these opinions is that which I consider the true one; but the misleading terms in which it is often expressed, and the indistinct manner in which it is usually apprehended, have both obstructed its reception, and perverted its influence when received. The metaphysical theory of free-will, as held by philosophers (for the practical feeling of it, common in a greater or less degree to all mankind, is in no way inconsistent with the contrary theory), was invented because the supposed alternative of admitting human actions to be *necessary* was deemed inconsistent with every one's instinctive consciousness, as well as humiliating to the pride and even degrading to the moral nature of man. Nor do I deny that the doctrine, as sometimes held, is open to these imputations; for the misapprehension in which I shall be able to show that they originate, unfortunately is not confined to the opponents of the doctrine, but is participated in by many, perhaps we might say by most, of its supporters.

Correctly conceived, the doctrine called Philosophical Necessity is simply this: that, given the motives which are present to an individual's mind, and given likewise the character and disposition of the individual, the manner in which he will act might be unerringly inferred; that if we knew the person

From John Stuart Mill, *A System of Logic*, 8th ed. (New York: Harper & Bros., 1874), Book VI, Chap. II, pp. 581–586.

thoroughly, and knew all the inducements which are acting upon him, we could foretell his conduct with as much certainty as we can predict any physical event. This proposition I take to be a mere interpretation of universal experience, a statement in words of what every one is internally convinced of. No one who believed that he knew thoroughly the circumstances of any case, and the characters of the different persons concerned, would hesitate to foretell how all of them would act. Whatever degree of doubt he may in fact feel, arises from the uncertainty whether he really knows the circumstances, or the character of some one or other of the persons, with the degree of accuracy required; but by no means from thinking that if he did know these things, there could be any uncertainty what the conduct would be. Nor does this full assurance conflict in the smallest degree with what is called our feeling of freedom. We do not feel ourselves the less free, because those to whom we are intimately known are well assured how we shall will to act in a particular case. We often, on the contrary, regard the doubt what our conduct will be, as a mark of ignorance of our character, and sometimes even resent it as an imputation. The religious metaphysicians who have asserted the freedom of the will, have always maintained it to be consistent with divine foreknowledge of our actions: and if with divine, then with any other foreknowledge. We may be free, and yet another may have reason to be perfectly certain what use we shall make of our freedom. It is not, therefore, the doctrine that our volitions and actions are invariable consequents of our antecedent states of mind, that is either contradicted by our consciousness, or felt to be degrading.

But the doctrine of causation, when considered as obtaining between our volitions and their antecedents, is almost universally conceived as involving more than this. Many do not believe, and very few practically feel, that there is nothing in causation but invariable, certain, and unconditional sequence. There are few to whom mere constancy of succession appears a sufficiently stringent bond of union for so peculiar a relation as that of cause and effect. Even if the reason repudiates, the imagination retains, the feeling of some more intimate connection, of some peculiar tie, or mysterious constraint exercised by the antecedent over the consequent. Now this it is which, considered as applying to the human will, conflicts with our consciousness, and revolts our feelings. We are certain that, in the case of our volitions, there is not this mysterious constraint. We know that we are not compelled, as by a magical spell, to obey any particular motive. We feel, that if we wished to prove that we have the power of resisting the motive, we could do so (that wish being, it needs scarcely be observed, a *new antecedent*); and it would be humiliating to our pride, and (what is of more importance) paralyzing to our desire of excellence, if we thought otherwise. But neither is any such mysterious compulsion now supposed, by the best philosophical authorities, to be exercised by any other cause over its effect. Those who think that causes draw their effects after them by a mystical tie, are right in believing that the relation between volitions and their antecedents is of another nature. But they should go farther, and admit that this is also true of all other effects and their antecedents. If such a tie is considered to be involved in the word Necessity, the doctrine is not true of human actions; but neither is it then true of inanimate objects. It would be more correct to say that matter is not bound by necessity, than that mind is so.

That the free-will metaphysicians, being mostly of the school which rejects Hume's and Brown's analysis of Cause and Effect, should miss their way for want of the light which that analysis affords, can not surprise us. The wonder is, that the necessitarians, who usually admit that philosophical theory, should in practice equally lose sight of it. The very same misconception of the doctrine called Philosophical Necessity, which prevents the opposite party from recognizing its truth, I believe to exist more or less obscurely in the minds of most necessitarians, however they may in words disavow it. I am much mistaken if they habitually feel that the necessity which they recognize in actions is but uniformity of order, and capability of being predicted. They have a feeling as if there were at bottom a stronger tie between the volitions and their causes; as if, when they asserted that the will is governed by the balance of motives, they meant something more cogent than if they had only said, that whoever knew the motives, and our habitual susceptibilities to them, could predict how we should will to act. They commit, in opposition to their own scientific system, the very same mistake which their adversaries commit in obedience to theirs; and in consequence do really in some instances suffer those depressing consequences which their opponents erroneously impute to the doctrine itself.

I am inclined to think that this error is almost wholly an effect of the associations with a word, and that it would be prevented, by forbearing to employ, for the expression of the simple fact of causation, so extremely inappropriate a term as Necessity. That word, in its other acceptations, involves much more than mere uniformity of sequence: it implies irresistibleness. Applied to the will, it only means that the given cause will be followed by the effect, subject to all possibilities of counter-action by other causes; but in common use it stands for the operation of those causes exclusively which are supposed too powerful to be counter-acted at all. When we say that all human actions take place of necessity, we only mean that they will certainly happen if nothing prevents; when we say that dying of want, to those who can not get food, is a necessity, we mean that it will certainly happen whatever may be done to prevent it. The application of the same term to the agencies on which human actions depend, as is used to express those agencies of nature which are really uncontrollable, can not fail, when habitual, to create a feeling of uncontrollableness in the former also. This, however, is a mere illusion. There are physical sequences which we call necessary, as death for want of food or air; there are others which, though as much cases of causation as the former, are not said to be necessary, as death from poison, which an antidote, or the use of the stomach-pump, will sometimes avert. It is apt to be forgotten by people's feelings, even if remembered by their understandings, that human actions are in this last predicament: they are never (except in some cases of mania) ruled by any one motive with such absolute sway that there is no room for the influence of any other. The causes, therefore, on which action depends, are never uncontrollable; and any given effect is only necessary provided that the causes tending to produce it are not controlled. That whatever happens, could not have happened otherwise, unless something had taken place which was capable of preventing it, no one surely needs hesitate to admit. But to call this by the name Necessity is to use the term in a sense so different from its primitive and familiar meaning, from that which it bears in the common occasions of life, as to amount almost to a play upon words. The associations derived from the ordinary sense of the term will adhere to it in spite of all we can do; and though the doctrine of Necessity, as stated by most who hold it, is very remote from fatalism, it is probable that most necessitarians are fatalists, more or less, in their feelings.

A fatalist believes, or half believes (for nobody is a consistent fatalist), not only that whatever is about to happen will be the infallible result of the causes which produce it (which is the true necessitarian doctrine), but moreover that there is no use in struggling against it; that it will happen, however we may strive to prevent it. Now, a necessitarian, believing that our actions follow from our characters, and that our characters follow from our organization, our education, and our circumstances, is apt to be, with more or less of consciousness on his part, a fatalist as to his own actions, and to believe that his nature is such, or that his education and circumstances have so moulded his character, that nothing can now prevent him from feeling and acting in a particular way, or at least that no effort of his own can hinder it. In the words of the sect which in our own day has most perseveringly inculcated and most perversely misunderstood this great doctrine, his character is formed *for* him, and not *by* him; therefore his wishing that it had been formed differently is of no use; he has no power to alter it. But this is a grand error. He has, to a certain extent, a power to alter his character. Its being, in the ultimate resort, formed for him, is not inconsistent with its being, in part, formed *by* him as one of the intermediate agents. His character is formed by his circumstances (including among these his particular organization); but his own desire to mould it in a particular way, is one of those circumstances, and by no means one of the least influential. We can not, indeed, directly will to be different from what we are. But neither did those who are supposed to have formed our characters directly will that we should be what we are. Their will had no direct power except over their own actions. They made us what they did make us, by willing, not the end, but the requisite means; and we, when our habits are not too inveterate, can, by similarly willing the requisite means, make ourselves different. If they could place us under the influence of certain circumstances, we, in like manner, can place ourselves under the influence of other circumstances. We are exactly as capable of making our own character, *if we will*, as others are of making it for us.

Yes (answers the Owenite), but these words, "if we will," surrender the whole point: since the will to alter our own character is given us, not by any efforts of ours, but by circumstances which we can not help, it comes to us either from external causes, or not at all. Most true: if the Owenite stops here, he is in a position from which nothing can expel him. Our character is formed by us as well as for us; but the wish which induces us to attempt to form it is formed for us; and how? Not, in general, by our organization, nor wholly by our education, but by our experience; experience of the painful consequences of the character we previously had; or by some strong feeling of admiration or aspiration, accidentally aroused. But to think that we have no power of altering our character, and to think that we shall not use our power unless we desire to use it, are very different things, and have a very different effect on the mind. A person who does not wish to alter his character, can not be the person who is supposed to feel discouraged or paralyzed by thinking himself unable to do it. The depressing effect of the fatalist doctrine can only be felt where there *is* a wish to do what that doctrine represents as impossible. It is of no consequence what we think forms our character, when we have no desire of our own about forming it; but it is of great consequence that we should not be prevented from forming such a desire by thinking the attainment impracticable, and that if we have the desire, we should know that the work is not so irrevocably done as to be incapable of being altered.

And indeed, if we examine closely, we shall find that this feeling, of our being able to modify our own character *if we wish*, is itself the feeling of moral freedom which we are conscious of. A person feels morally free who feels that his habits or his temptations are not his masters, but he theirs; who, even in yielding to them, knows that he could resist; that were he desirous of altogether throwing them off, there would not be required for that purpose a stronger desire than he knows himself to be capable of feeling. It is of course necessary, to render our consciousness of freedom complete, that we should have succeeded in making our character all we have hitherto attempted to make it; for if we have wished and not attained, we have, to that extent, not power over our own character; we are not free. Or at least, we must feel that our wish, if not strong enough to alter our character, is strong enough to conquer our character when the two are brought into conflict in any particular case of conduct. And hence it is said with truth, that none but a person of confirmed virtue is completely free.

The application of so improper a term as Necessity to the doctrine of cause and effect in the matter of human character, seems to me one of the most signal instances in philosophy of the abuse of terms, and its practical consequences one of the most striking examples of the power of language over our associations. The subject will never be generally understood until that objectionable term is dropped. The free-will doctrine, by keeping in view precisely that portion of the truth which the word Necessity puts out of sight, namely the power of the mind to co-operate in the formation of its own character, has given to its adherents a practical feeling much nearer to the truth than has generally (I believe) existed in the minds of necessitarians. The latter may have had a stronger sense of the importance of what human beings can do to shape the characters of one another; but the free-will doctrine has, I believe, fostered in its supporters a much stronger spirit of self-culture.

There is still one fact which requires to be noticed (in addition to the existence of a power of self-formation) before the doctrine of the causation of human actions can be freed from the confusion and misapprehensions which surround it in many minds. When the will is said to be determined by motives, a motive does not mean always, or solely, the anticipation of a pleasure or of a pain. I shall not here inquire whether it be true that, in the commencement, all our voluntary actions are mere means consciously employed to obtain some pleasure or avoid some pain. It is at least certain that we gradually, through the influence of association, come to desire the means without thinking of the end; the action itself becomes an object of desire, and is performed without reference to any motive beyond itself. Thus far, it may still be objected that, the action having through association become pleasurable, we are, as much as before, moved to act by the anticipation of a pleasure, namely, the pleasure of the action itself. But granting this, the matter does not end here. As we proceed in the formation of habits, and become accustomed to will a particular act or a particular course of conduct because it is pleasurable, we at last continue to will it without any reference to its being pleasurable. Although, from some change in us or in our circumstances, we have ceased to find any pleasure in the action, or perhaps to anticipate any pleasure as the consequence of it, we still continue to desire the action, and consequently to do it. In this manner it is that habits of hurtful excess continue to be practiced although they have ceased to be pleasurable; and in this manner also it is that the habit of willing to persevere in the course which he has chosen, does not desert the moral hero, even when the reward, however real, which he doubtless receives from the consciousness of well-doing, is any thing but an equivalent for the sufferings he undergoes, or the wishes which he may have to renounce.

A habit of willing is commonly called a purpose; and among the causes of our volitions, and of the actions which flow from them, must be reckoned not only likings and aversions, but also purposes. It is only when our purposes have become independent of the feelings of pain or pleasure from which they originally took their rise, that we are said to have a confirmed character. "A character," say Novalis, "is a completely fashioned will:" and the will, once so fashioned, may be steady and constant, when the passive susceptibilities of pleasure and pain are greatly weakened or materially changed.

With the corrections and explanations now given, the doctrine of the causation of our volitions by motives, and of motives by the desirable objects offered to us, combined with our particular susceptibilities of desire, may be considered, I hope, as sufficiently established for the purposes of this treatise.

3

IS 'FREEWILL' A PSEUDO-PROBLEM?

C. A. Campbell

II

I shall first summarise, as faithfully as I can, what I take to be the distinctive points in Schlick's argument.

The traditional formulation of the problem, Schlick points out, is based on the assumption that to have 'free will' entails having a will that is, at least sometimes, exempt from causal law. It is traditionally supposed, quite rightly, that moral responsibility implies freedom in *some* sense: and it is supposed, also quite rightly, that this sense is one which is incompatible with compulsion. But because it is further supposed, quite *wrongly*, that to be subject to causal or natural law is to be subject to compulsion, the inference is drawn that the free will implied in moral responsibility is incompatible with causal continuity. The ultimate root of the error, Schlick contends, lies in a failure to distinguish between two different kinds of Law, one of which does indeed 'compel', but the other of which does *not*.[1] There are, first, *pre*scriptive laws, such as the laws imposed by civil authority, which presume contrary desires on the part of those to whom they are applied; and these may fairly be said to exercise 'compulsion'. And there are, secondly, *descriptive* laws, such as the laws which the sciences seek to formulate; and these merely state what does as a matter of fact always happen. It is perfectly clear that the relation of the latter, the natural, causal laws, to human willing is radically different from the 'compulsive' relation of prescriptive laws to human willing, and that it is really an absurdity to talk of a species of natural law like, say, psychological laws, *compelling* us to act in this or that way. The term 'compulsion' is totally inept where, as in this case, there are no contrary desires. But the traditional discussions of Free Will, confusing descriptive with prescriptive laws, fallaciously assume 'com-

---

From C. A. Campbell, "Is 'Freewill' A Pseudo-Problem?," *Mind*, LX (1951), Sec. 2–7, 442–465. Reprinted by permission of the Editor of *Mind* and the author.

[1] *Problems of Ethics*, Ch. VIII. Section 2. (All references are to the English translation by David Rynin, published in New York in 1939.)

pulsion' to be ingredient in Law as such, and it is contended accordingly that moral freedom, since it certainly implies absence of compulsion, implies also exemption from causal law.

It follows that the problem of Free Will, as traditionally stated, is a mere pseudo-problem. The statement of it in terms of exemption from causal law rests on the assumption that causal law involves 'compulsion'. And this assumption is demonstrably false. Expose the muddle from which it arises and the so-called 'problem' in its traditional form disappears.

But is it quite certain that the freedom which moral responsibility implies is no more than 'the absence of compulsion'? This is the premise upon which Schlick's argument proceeds, but Schlick is himself well aware that it stands in need of confirmation from an analysis of the notion of moral responsibility. Otherwise it might be maintained that although 'the absence of compulsion' has been shown not to entail a contra-causal type of freedom, there is nevertheless some *other* condition of moral responsibility that *does* entail it. Accordingly Schlick embarks now upon a formal analysis of the nature and conditions of moral responsibility designed to show that the *only* freedom implied by moral responsibility is freedom from compulsion. It was a trifle ambitious, however, even for a master of compression like Professor Schlick, to hope to deal satisfactorily in half a dozen very brief pages with a topic which has been so extensively debated in the literature of moral philosophy: and I cannot pretend that I find what he has to say free from obscurity. But to the best of my belief what follows does reproduce the gist of Schlick's analysis.

What precisely, Schlick asks, does the term 'moral responsibility' mean in our ordinary linguistic usage?[2] He begins his answer by insisting upon the close connexion for ordinary usage between 'moral responsibility' and *punishment* (strictly speaking, punishment and *reward:* but for convenience Schlick virtually confines the discussion to punishment, and we shall do the same). The connexion, as Schlick sees it, is this. In ordinary practice our concern with the responsibility for an act (he tells us) is with a view to determining *who is to be punished for it.* Now punishment is (I quote) 'an educative measure'. It is 'a means to the formation of motives, which are in part to prevent the wrong-doer from repeating the act (reformation), and in part to prevent others from committing a similar act (intimidation)'.[3] When we ask, then, 'Who in a given case is to be punished?'—which is the same as the question 'Who is responsible?'—what we are really wanting to discover is some agent in the situation upon whose motives we can bring to bear the appropriate educative influences, so that in similar situations in future his strongest motive will impel him to refrain from, rather than to repeat, the act. 'The question of who is responsible' Schlick sums up, 'is . . . a matter only of knowing who is to be punished or rewarded, in order that punishment and reward function as such—be able to achieve their goal.'[4] It is not a matter, he expressly declares, of trying to ascertain what may be called the 'original instigator' of the act. That might be a great-grand-parent, from the consequence of whose behaviour vicious tendencies have been inherited by a living person. Such 'remote causes' as this are irrelevant to questions of punishment (and so to questions of moral responsibility), 'for in the first

[2] *Loc. cit.*, Ch. VII, Section 5.   [3] *Ibid.*, p. 152.   [4] *Ibid.*, p. 153.

place their actual contribution cannot be determined, and in the second place they are generally out of reach'.[5]

It is a matter for regret that Schlick has not rounded off his discussion, as one had hoped and expected he would, by formulating a precise definition of moral responsibility in terms of what he has been saying. I think, however, that the conclusion to which his argument leads could be not unfairly expressed in some such way as this: 'We say that a man is morally responsible for an act if his motives for bringing about the act are such as we can affect favourably in respect of his future behaviour by the educative influences of reward and punishment'.

Given the truth of this analysis of moral responsibility, Schlick's contention follows logically enough that the only freedom that is required for moral responsibility is freedom from compulsion. For what are the cases in which a man's motives are *not* capable of being favourably affected by reward and punishment?—the cases in which, that is, according to Schlick's analysis, we do *not* deem him morally responsible? The only such cases, it would seem, are those in which a man is subjected to some form of external constraint which prevents him from acting according to his 'natural desires'. For example, if a man is compelled by a pistol at his breast to do a certain act, or induced to do it by an externally administered narcotic, he is not 'morally responsible'; or not, at any rate, in so far as punishment would be impotent to affect his motives in respect of his future behaviour. External constraint in one form or another seems to be the sole circumstance which absolves a man from moral responsibility. Hence we may say that freedom from external constraint is the only sort of freedom which an agent must possess in order to be morally responsible. The 'contra-causal' sort of freedom which so many philosophers and others have supposed to be required is shown by a true analysis of moral responsibility to be irrelevant.

This completes the argument that 'Free Will', as traditionally formulated, is a pseudo-problem. The only freedom implied by moral responsibility is freedom from compulsion; and as we have rid ourselves of the myth that subjection to causal law is a form of compulsion, we can see that the only compulsion which absolves from moral responsibility is the external constraint which prevents us from translating our desires into action. The true meaning of the question 'Have we free will?' thus becomes simply 'Can we translate our desires into action?' And this question does not constitute a 'problem' at all, for the answer to it is not in doubt. The obvious answer is 'Sometimes we can, sometimes we can't, according to the specific circumstances of the case'.

III

Here, then, in substance is Schlick's theory. Let us now examine it.

In the first place, it is surely quite unplausible to suggest that the common assumption that moral freedom postulates some breach of causal continuity arises from a confusion of two different types of law. Schlick's distinction between descriptive and prescriptive law is, of course, sound. It was no doubt worth pointing out, too, that descriptive laws cannot be said to

[5] *Ibid.*, p. 153.

'compel' human behaviour in the same way as prescriptive laws do. But it seems to me evident that the usual reason why it is held that moral freedom implies some breach of causal continuity, is not a belief that causal laws 'compel' as civil laws 'compel', but simply the belief that the admission of unbroken causal continuity entails a *further* admission which is directly incompatible with moral responsibility; *viz.* the admission that no man could have acted otherwise than he in fact did. Now it may, of course, be an error thus to assume that a man is not morally responsible for an act, a fit subject for moral praise and blame in respect of it, unless he could have acted otherwise than he did. Or, if *this* is not an error, it may still be an error to assume that a man could not have acted otherwise than he did, in the sense of the phrase that is crucial for moral responsibility, without there occurring some breach of causal continuity. Into these matters we shall have to enter very fully at a later stage. But the relevant point at the moment is that these (not *prima facie* absurd) assumptions about the conditions of moral responsibility have very commonly, indeed normally, been made, and that they are entirely adequate to explain why the problem of Free Will finds its usual formulation in terms of partial exemption from causal law. Schlick's distinction between prescriptive and descriptive laws has no bearing at all upon the truth or falsity of these assumptions. Yet if these assumptions are accepted, it is (I suggest) really inevitable that the Free Will problem should be formulated in the way to which Schlick takes exception. Recognition of the distinction upon which Schlick and his followers lay so much stress can make not a jot of difference.

As we have seen, however, Schlick does later proceed to the much more important business of disputing these common assumptions about the conditions of moral responsibility. He offers us an analysis of moral responsibility which flatly contradicts these assumptions; an analysis according to which the only freedom demanded by morality is a freedom which is compatible with Determinism. If this analysis can be sustained, there is certainly no problem of 'Free Will' in the traditional sense.

But it seems a simple matter to show that Schlick's analysis is untenable. Let us test it by Schlick's own claim that it gives us what we mean by 'moral responsibility' in ordinary linguistic usage.

We do not ordinarily consider the lower animals to be morally responsible. But *ought* we not to do so if Schlick is right about what we mean by moral responsibility? It is quite possible, by punishing the dog who absconds with the succulent chops designed for its master's luncheon, favourably to influence its motives in respect of its future behaviour in like circumstances. If moral responsibility is to be linked with punishment as Schlick links it, and punishment conceived as a form of education, we should surely hold the dog morally responsible? The plain fact, of course, is that we don't. We don't, because we suppose that the dog 'couldn't help it': that its action (unlike what we usually believe to be true of human beings) was simply a link in a continuous chain of causes and effects. In other words, we do commonly demand the contra-causal sort of freedom as a condition of moral responsibility.

Again, we do ordinarily consider it proper, in certain circumstances, to speak of a person no longer living as morally responsible for some present situation. But *ought* we to do so if we accept Schlick's essentially 'forward-looking' interpretation of punishment and responsibility? Clearly we cannot now favourably affect the dead man's motives. No doubt they could *at one time* have been favourably affected. But that cannot be relevant to our judgment of responsibility if, as Schlick insists, the question of who is responsible 'is a matter only of knowing who is to be punished or rewarded'. Indeed he expressly tells us, as we saw earlier, that in asking this question we are not concerned with a 'great-grand-parent' who may have been the 'original instigator', because, for one reason, this 'remote cause' is 'out of reach'. We cannot bring the appropriate educative influence to bear upon it. But the plain fact, of course, is that we do frequently assign moral responsibility for present situations to persons who have long been inaccessible to any punitive action on our part. And Schlick's position is still more paradoxical in respect of our apportionment of responsibility for occurrences in the distant past. Since in these cases there is no agent whatsoever whom we can favourably influence by punishment, the question of moral responsibility here should have no meaning for us. But of course it has. Historical writings are studded with examples.

Possibly the criticism just made may seem to some to result from taking Schlick's analysis too much *au pied de la lettre*. The absurd consequences deduced, it may be said, would not follow if we interpreted Schlick as meaning that a man is morally responsible where his motive is such as can *in principle* be favourably affected by reward or punishment—whether or not we who pass the judgment are in a position to take such action. But with every desire to be fair to Schlick, I cannot see how he could accept this modification and still retain the essence of his theory. For the essence of his theory seems to be that moral responsibility has its whole meaning and importance for us in relation to our potential control of future conduct in the interests of society. (I agree that it is hard to believe that anybody *really* thinks this. But it is perhaps less hard to believe to-day than it has ever been before in the history of modern ethics.)

Again, we ordinarily consider that, in certain circumstances, the *degree* of a man's moral responsibility for an act is affected by considerations of his inherited nature, or of his environment, or of both. It is our normal habit to 'make allowances' (as we say) when we have reason to believe that a malefactor had a vicious heredity, or was nurtured in his formative years in a harmful environment. We say in such cases 'Poor chap, he is more to be pitied than blamed. We could scarcely expect him to behave like a decent citizen with *his* parentage or upbringing.' But this extremely common sort of judgment has no point at all if we mean by moral responsibility what Schlick says that we mean. On *that* meaning the degree of a man's moral responsibility must presumably be dependent upon the degree to which we can favourably affect his future motives, which is quite another matter. Now there is no reason to believe that the motives of a man with a bad heredity or a bad upbringing are either less or more subject to educative influence than those of his more fortunate fellows. Yet it is plain matter of fact that we do commonly consider the degree of a man's moral responsibility to be affected by these two factors.

A final point. The extremity of paradox in Schlick's identification of the question 'Who is morally blameworthy?' with the question 'Who is to be punished?' is apt to be partially concealed from us just because it is our normal habit to include in the meaning of 'punishment' an element of 'requital for moral transgression' which Schlick expressly denies to it. On that account we commonly think of 'punishment', in its strict sense, as implying moral blameworthiness in the person punished. But if we remember to mean by punishment what Schlick means by it, a purely 'educative measure', with no retributive ingredients, his identification of the two questions loses such plausibility as it might otherwise have. For clearly we often think it proper to 'punish' a person, in *Schlick's* sense, where we are not at all prepared to say that the person is morally blameworthy. We may even think him morally commendable. A case in point would be the unmistakably sincere but muddle-headed person who at the cost of great suffering to himself steadfastly pursues as his 'duty' a course which, in our judgment, is fraught with danger to the common weal. We should most of us feel entitled, in the public interest, to bring such action to bear upon the man's motives as might induce him to refrain in future from his socially injurious behaviour: in other words, to inflict upon him what Schlick would call 'punishment'. But we should most of us feel perfectly clear that in so 'punishing' this misguided citizen we are not proclaiming his moral blameworthiness for moral wickedness.

Adopting Schlick's own criterion, then, looking simply 'to the manner in which the concept is used',[6] we seem bound to admit that constantly people do assign moral responsibility where Schlick's theory says they shouldn't, don't assign moral responsibility where Schlick's theory says they should, and assign degrees of moral responsibility where on Schlick's theory there should be no difference in degree. I think we may reasonably conclude that Schlick's account of what we mean by moral responsibility breaks down.

The rebuttal of Schlick's arguments, however, will not suffice of itself to refute the pseudo-problem theory. The indebtedness to Schlick of most later advocates of the theory may be conceded; but certainly it does not comprehend all of significance that they have to say on the problem. There are recent analyses of the conditions of moral responsibility containing sufficient new matter, or sufficient old matter in a more precise and telling form, to require of us now something of a fresh start. In the section which follows I propose to consider some representative samples of these analyses —all of which, of course, are designed to show that the freedom which moral responsibility implies is not in fact a contra-causal type of freedom.

But before reopening the general question of the nature and conditions of moral responsibility there is a *caveat* which it seems to me worth while to enter. The difficulties in the way of a clear answer are not slight; but they are apt to seem a good deal more formidable than they really are because of a common tendency to consider in unduly close association two distinct questions: the question 'Is a contra-causal type of freedom implied by moral responsibility?' and the question 'Does a contra-causal type of freedom anywhere exist?'. It seems to me that many philosophers (and I suspect that Moritz Schlick is among them) begin their enquiry with so firm a conviction that the contra-causal sort of freedom nowhere exists, that they find it hard to take very seriously the possibility that it is *this* sort of freedom that moral responsibility implies. For they are loth to abandon the commonsense

---

[6] *Loc. cit.*, Ch. VII, Section 5, p. 151.

belief that moral responsibility itself is something real. The implicit reasoning I take to be this. Moral responsibility is real. If moral responsibility is real, the freedom implied in it must be a fact. But contra-causal freedom is not a fact. Therefore contra-causal freedom is not the freedom implied in moral responsibility. I think we should be on our guard against allowing this or some similar train of reasoning (whose premises, after all, are far from indubitable) to seduce us into distorting what we actually find when we set about a direct analysis of moral responsibility and its conditions.

IV

The pseudo-problem theorists usually, and naturally, develop their analysis of moral responsibility by way of contrast with a view which, while it has enjoyed a good deal of philosophic support, I can perhaps best describe as the common view. It will be well to remind ourselves, therefore, of the main features of this view.

So far as the *meaning*, as distinct from the *conditions*, of moral responsibility is concerned, the common view is very simple. If we ask ourselves whether a certain person is morally responsible for a given act (or it may be just 'in general'), what we are considering, it would be said, is whether or not that person is a fit subject upon whom to pass moral judgment; whether he can fittingly be deemed morally good or bad, morally praiseworthy or blameworthy. This does not take us any great way: but (*pace* Schlick) so far as it goes it does not seem to me seriously disputable. The really interesting and controversial question is about the *conditions* of moral responsibility, and in particular the question whether freedom of a contra-causal kind is among these conditions.

The answer of the common man to the latter question is that it most certainly *is* among the conditions. Why does he feel so sure about this? Not, I argued earlier, because the common man supposes that causal law exercises 'compulsion' in the sense that prescriptive laws do, but simply because he does not see how a person can be deemed morally praiseworthy or blameworthy in respect of an act which he could not help performing. From the stand-point of moral praise and blame, he would say—though not necessarily from other stand-points—it is a matter of indifference whether it is by reason of some external constraint or by reason of his own given nature that the man could not help doing what he did. It is quite enough to make moral praise and blame futile that in either case there were no genuine alternatives, no open possibilities, before the man when he acted. He could not have acted otherwise than he did. And the common man might not unreasonably go on to stress the fact that we all, even if we are linguistic philosophers, do in our actual practice of moral judgment appear to accept the common view. He might insist upon the point alluded to earlier in this paper, that we do all, in passing moral censure, 'make allowances' for influences in a man's hereditary nature or environmental circumstances which we regard as having made it more than ordinarily difficult for him to act otherwise than he did: the implication being that if we supposed that the man's heredity and environment made it not merely very *difficult* but actually *impossible* for him to act otherwise than he did, we could not properly assign moral blame to him at all.

Let us put the argument implicit in the common view a little more sharply. The moral 'ought' implies 'can'. If we say that A morally ought to have done X, we imply that in our opinion, he could have done X. But we assign moral blame to a man only for failing to do what we think he morally ought to have done. Hence if we morally blame A for not having done X, we imply that he could have done X even though in fact he did not. In other words, we imply that A could have acted otherwise than he did. And that means that we imply, as a necessary condition of a man's being morally blameworthy, that he enjoyed a freedom of a kind not compatible with unbroken causal continuity.

v

Now what is it that is supposed to be wrong with this simple piece of argument?—For, of course, it must be rejected by all these philosophers who tell us that the traditional problem of Free Will is a mere pseudo-problem. The argument looks as though it were doing little more than reading off necessary implications of the fundamental categories of our moral thinking. One's inclination is to ask 'If one is to think morally at all, how else than this *can* we think?'.

In point of fact, there is pretty general agreement among the contemporary critics as to what is wrong with the argument. Their answer in general terms is as follows. No doubt A's moral responsibility does imply that he could have acted otherwise. But this expression 'could have acted otherwise' stands in dire need of analysis. When we analyse it, we find that it is not, as is so often supposed, simple and unambiguous, and we find that in *some* at least of its possible meanings it implies *no* breach of causal continuity between character and conduct. Having got this clear, we can further discern that only in one of these *latter* meanings is there any compulsion upon our moral thinking to assert that if A is morally blameworthy for an act, A 'could have acted otherwise than he did'. It follows that, contrary to common belief, our moral thinking does *not* require us to posit a contra-causal freedom as a condition of moral responsibility.

So much of importance obviously turns upon the validity or otherwise of this line of criticism that we must examine it in some detail and with express regard to the *ipsissima verba* of the critics.

In the course of a recent article in MIND[7] entitled 'Free Will and Moral Responsibility', Mr. Nowell Smith (having earlier affirmed his belief that 'the traditional problem has been solved') explains very concisely the nature of the confusion which, as he thinks, has led to the demand for a contra-causal freedom. He begins by frankly recognising that "It is evident that one of the necessary conditions of moral action is that the agent 'could have acted otherwise'" and he adds "it is to this fact that the Libertarian is drawing attention".[8] Then, after showing (unexceptionably, I think) how the relationship of 'ought' to 'can' warrants the proposition which he has accepted as evident, and how it induces the Libertarian to assert the existence of action that is 'uncaused', he proceeds to point out, in a crucial passage, the nature of the Libertarian's error:

[7] January, 1948.   [8] *Loc. cit.*, p. 49.

The fallacy in the argument (he contends) lies in supposing that when we say 'A could have acted otherwise' we mean that A, *being what he was and being placed in the circumstances in which he was placed*, could have done something other than what he did. But in fact we never do mean this.[9]

What then *do* we mean here by 'A could have acted otherwise'? Mr. Nowell Smith does not tell us in so many words, but the passage I have quoted leaves little doubt how he would answer. What we really mean by the expression, he implies, is not a *categorical* but a *hypothetical* proposition. We mean 'A could have acted otherwise, *if he did not happen to be what he in fact was*, or *if he were placed in circumstances other than those in which he was in fact placed*'. Now, *these* propositions, it is easy to see, are in no way incompatible with acceptance of the causal principle in its full rigour. Accordingly the claim that our fundamental moral thinking obliges us to assert a contra-causal freedom as a condition of moral responsibility is disproved.

Such is the 'analytical solution' of our problem offered (with obvious confidence) by one able philosopher of to-day, and entirely representative of the views of many other able philosophers. Yet I make bold to say that its falsity stares one in the face. It seems perfectly plain that the hypothetical propositions which Mr. Nowell Smith proposes to substitute for the categorical proposition cannot express 'what we really mean' in this context by 'A could have acted otherwise', for the simple reason that these hypothetical propositions have no bearing whatsoever upon the question of the moral responsibility of *A*. And it is *A* whose moral responsibility we are talking about—a definite person *A* with a definitive character and in a definitive set of circumstances. What conceivable significance could it have for our attitude to A's responsibility to know that someone with a *different* character (or *A* with a different character, if that collocation of words has any meaning), or A in a different set of circumstances from those in which A as we are concerned with him was in fact placed, 'could have acted otherwise'? No doubt this supposititious being *could* have acted otherwise than the definitive person A acted. But the point is that where we are reflecting, as we are supposed in this context to be reflecting, upon the question of *A*'s moral responsibility, our interest in this supposititious being is precisely *nil*.

The two hypothetical propositions suggested in Mr. Nowell Smith's account of the matter do not, however, exhaust the speculations that have been made along these lines. Another very common suggestion by the analysts is that what we really mean by 'A could have acted otherwise' is 'A could have acted otherwise *if he had willed, or chosen, otherwise*'. This was among the suggestions offered by G. E. Moore in the well-known chapter on Free Will in his *Ethics*. It is, I think, the suggestion he most strongly favoured: though it is fair to add that neither about this nor about any other of his suggestions is Moore in the least dogmatic. He does claim, for, I think, convincing reasons, that "we *very often* mean by 'could' merely 'would, *if* so-and-so had chosen' ".[10] And he concludes "I must confess that I cannot feel certain that this may not be all that we usually mean and understand by the assertion that we have Free Will".[11]

[9] *Loc. cit.*, p. 49.   [10] *Ethics*, p. 212.   [11] *Loc. cit.*, p. 217.

This third hypothetical proposition appears to enjoy also the support of Mr. C. L. Stevenson. Mr. Stevenson begins the chapter of *Ethics and Language* entitled 'Avoidability-Indeterminism' with the now familiar pronouncement of his School that 'controversy about freedom and determinism of the will . . . presents no permanent difficulty to ethics, being largely a product of confusions'. A major confusion (if I understand him rightly) he takes to lie in the meaning of the term 'avoidable', when we say 'A's action was avoidable'—or, I presume, 'A could have acted otherwise'. He himself offers the following definition of 'avoidable'—" 'A's action was avoidable' has the meaning of 'If A had made a certain choice, which in fact he did not make, his action would not have occurred' ".[12] This I think we may regard as in substance identical with the suggestion that what we really mean by 'A could have acted otherwise' is 'A could have acted otherwise *if* he had chosen (or willed) otherwise'. For clarity's sake we shall here keep to this earlier formulation. In either formulation the special significance of the third hypothetical proposition, as of the two hypothetical propositions already considered, is that it is compatible with strict determinism. If this be indeed all that we mean by the 'freedom' that conditions moral responsibility, then those philosophers are certainly wrong who hold that moral freedom is of the contra-causal type.

Now this third hypothetical proposition does at least possess the merit, not shared by its predecessors, of having a real relevance to the question of moral responsibility. If, *e.g.* A had promised to meet us at 2 P.M., and he chanced to break his leg at 1 P.M., we should not blame him for his failure to discharge his promise. For we should be satisfied that he *could not* have acted otherwise, even if he had so chosen; or *could not*, at any rate, in a way which would have enabled him to meet us at 2 P.M. The freedom to translate one's choice into action, which we saw earlier is for Schlick the *only* freedom required for moral responsibility, is without doubt *one* of the conditions of moral responsibility.

But it seems easy to show that this third hypothetical proposition does not exhaust what we mean, and *some*times is not even *part* of what we mean, by the expression 'could have acted otherwise' in its moral context. Thus it can hardly be even part of what we mean in the case of that class of wrong actions (and it is a large class) concerning which there is really no question whether the agent could have acted otherwise, *if* he had chosen otherwise. Take lying, for example. Only in some very abnormal situation could it occur to one to doubt whether A, whose power of speech was evinced by his telling a lie, was in a position to tell what he took to be the truth *if* he had so chosen. Of *course* he was. Yet it still makes good sense for one's moral thinking to ask whether A, when lying, 'could have acted otherwise': and we still require an affirmative answer to this question if A's moral blameworthiness is to be established. It seems apparent, therefore, that in this class of cases at any rate one does *not* mean by 'A could have acted otherwise', 'A could have acted otherwise *if* he had so chosen'.

What then *does* one mean in this class of cases by 'A could have acted otherwise'? I submit that the expression is taken in its simple, categorical meaning, without any suppressed 'if' clause to qualify it. Or perhaps, in

---

[12] *Ethics and Language*, p. 298.

order to keep before us the important truth that it is only as expressions of *will* or *choice* that acts are of moral import, it might be better to say that a condition of A's moral responsibility is that he could have *chosen* otherwise. We saw that there is no real question whether A who told a lie could have acted otherwise *if* he had chosen otherwise. But there is a very real question, at least for any person who approaches the question of moral responsibility at a tolerably advanced level of reflexion, about whether A could have *chosen* otherwise. Such a person will doubtless be acquainted with the claims advanced in some quarters that causal law operates universally: or/and with the theories of some philosophies that the universe is through-out the expression of a single supreme principle; or/and with the doctrines of some theologians that the world is created, sustained and governed by an Omniscient and Omnipotent Being. Very understandably such world-views awaken in him doubts about the validity of his first, easy, instinctive assumption that there are genuinely open possibilities before a man at the moment of moral choice. It thus becomes for him a real question whether a man could have chosen otherwise than he actually did, and, in consequence, whether man's moral responsibility is really defensible. For how can a man be morally responsible, he asks himself, if his choices, like all other events in the universe, could not have been otherwise than they in fact were? It is precisely against the background of world-views such as these that for reflective people the problem of moral responsibility normally arises.

Furthermore, to the man who has attained this level of reflexion, it will in *no* class of cases be a sufficient condition of moral reponsibility for an act that one could have acted otherwise *if* one had chosen otherwise—not even in these cases where there *was* some possibility of the operation of 'external constraint'. In these cases he will, indeed, expressly recognize freedom from external constraint as a *necessary condition*, but not as a *sufficient* condition. For he will be aware that, even granted *this* freedom, it is still conceivable that the agent had no freedom to choose otherwise than he did, and he will therefore require that the latter sort of freedom be added if moral responsi-bility for the act is to be established.

I have been contending that, for persons at a *tolerably advanced level of reflexion*, 'A could have acted otherwise', as a condition of A's moral responsibility, means 'A could have chosen otherwise'. The qualification italicised is of some importance. The unreflective or unsophisticated person, the ordinary 'man in the street', who does not know or much care what scientists and theologians and philosophers have said about the world, sees well enough that A is morally responsible only if he could have acted otherwise, but in his intellectual innocence he will, very probably, envisage nothing capable of preventing A from having acted otherwise except some material impediment—like the broken leg in the example above. Accord-ingly, for the unreflective person, 'A could have acted otherwise', as a condition of moral responsibility, *is* apt to mean no more than 'A could have acted otherwise *if* he had so chosen'.

It would appear, then, that the view now favoured by many philosophers, that the freedom required for moral responsibility is merely freedom from external constraint, is a view which they share only with the less reflective type of layman. Yet it should be plain that on a matter of this sort the view of the unreflective person is of little value by comparison with the view of the reflective person. There are some contexts, no doubt, in which lack of sophistication is an asset. But this is not one of them. The question at issue here is as to the kind of impediments which might have prevented a man from acting otherwise than he in fact did: and on this question knowledge and reflexion are surely prerequisites of any answer that is worth listening to. It is simply on account of the limitations of his mental vision that the unreflective man interprets the expression 'could have acted otherwise', in its context as a condition of moral responsibility, solely in terms of external constraint. He has failed (as yet) to reach the intellectual level at which one takes into account the implications for moral choices of the world-views of science, religion, and philosophy. If on a matter of this complexity the philosopher finds that his analysis accords with the utterances of the uneducated he has, I suggest, better cause for uneasiness than for self-congratulation.

This concludes the main part of what it seems to me necessary to say in answer to the pseudo-problem theorists. My object so far has been to expose the falsity of those innovations (chiefly Positivist) in the way of argument and analysis which are supposed by many to have made it impossible any longer to formulate the problem of Free Will in the traditional manner. My contention is that, at least so far as these innovations are concerned, the simple time-honoured argument still holds from the nature of the moral ought to the conclusion that moral responsibility implies a contra-causal type of freedom. The attempts to avoid that conclusion by analysing the proposition 'A could have acted otherwise' (acknowledged to be implied in *some* sense in A's moral responsibility) into one or other of certain hypothetical propositions which are compatible with unbroken causal continuity, break down hopelessly when tested against the touchstone of actual moral thinking. It is, I think, not necessary to defend the procedure of testing hypotheses in the ethical field by bringing to bear upon them our actual moral thinking. If there is any other form of test applicable, I should be much interested to learn what it is supposed to be. Certainly 'logical analysis' *per se* will not do. That has a function, but a function that can only be ancillary. For what we are seeking to know is the meaning of the expression 'could have acted otherwise' not *in the abstract*, but in the context of the question of man's *moral responsibility*. Logical analysis *per se* is impotent to give us this information. It can be of value only in so far as it operates within the orbit of 'the moral consciousness'. One may admit, with some qualifications, that on a matter of this sort the moral consciousness without logical analysis is blind: but it seems to me to be true without any qualification whatsoever that, on the same problem, logical analysis without the moral consciousness is empty.

VI

There are times when what seems to a critic the very strength of his case breeds mistrust in the critic's own mind. I confess that in making the criticisms that have preceded I have not been altogether free from uncomfortable feelings of this kind. For the arguments I have criticised, and more particularly the analyses of the conditions of moral responsibility, seem to me to be in many cases quite desperately unplausible. Such a state of affairs ought, I think, to give the critic pause. The thought must at least enter his mind (unless he be a total stranger to modesty) that perhaps, despite his best efforts to be fair, he has after all misrepresented what his opponents are saying. No doubt a similar thought will enter, and perhaps find lodgment in, the minds of many readers.

In this situation there is, however, one course by which the critic may reasonably hope to allay these natural suspicions. He should consider whether there may not be certain predisposing influences at work, extrinsic to the specific arguments, which could have the effect of blinding the proponents of these arguments to their intrinsic demerits. If so, he need not be too much disquieted by the seeming weakness of the case against him. For it is a commonplace that, once in the grip of general prepossessions, even very good philosophers sometimes avail themselves of very bad arguments.

Actually, we can, I think, discern at least two such influences operating powerfully in the case before us. One is sympathy with the general tenets of Positivism. The other is the conviction already alluded to, that man does not in fact possess a contra-causal type of freedom; whence follows a strong presumption that no such freedom is necessary to moral responsibility.

About the first of these influences I propose to say very little. I wish merely to indicate how strict adherence to Positivist tenets precludes one in principle from understanding moral responsibility as the ordinary man understands it, and how Positivists are therefore bound, when they attempt to define the conditions of moral responsibility, to say things that seem monstrously unplausible.

That the Positivist—who has certainly not been drawn initially to this way of philosophising by reflexion upon the phenomena of the moral life—should approach the problems of ethical analysis with certain strong prepossessions, is only to be expected. The most crucial of these is that (non-tautologous) statements in this field, as in every other field, can have no meaning—or at any rate no cognitive meaning—unless they are, at least in principle, sensibly verifiable. The consequence of that prepossession must be to close the mind in advance, more or less absolutely according to the extent to which the Verifiability principle is maintained as unshakeable dogma, against the common view of the moral ought—which happens also to be the view in terms of which the problem of moral responsibility historically and habitually arises. For on this view the moral ought as apprehended by the moral consciousness is most certainly an object neither of 'outer' nor of 'inner' sense. One need not wonder, therefore, that the Positivist should recommend analyses of the conditions of moral responsibility, such as the hypothetical propositions offered as the meaning of the expression 'could have acted otherwise', which to anyone who understands the moral ought in the ordinary way seem little short of fantastic. By an *a priori* prejudice he has effectively debarred himself from appreciating what ordinary men mean by moral obligation and moral responsibility. I cannot forbear adding that in view of the doom which has so swiftly attended the very various attempts so far made to define moral obligation in Positivist terms, the case for at least a temporary suspension of belief in Positivist presuppositions in the ethical field would appear to be a strong one.

Of far wider and more permanent interest, in my judgment, is the second of the 'predisposing influences'—the conviction that there just *is* no contra-causal freedom such as is commonly alleged to be a condition of moral responsibility. A natural desire to 'save' moral responsibility issues, logically enough, in attempts to formulate its conditions in a manner compatible with unbroken causal continuity. The consequent analyses may be, as I have urged, very unsatisfactory. But there is no doubt that the conviction that motivates the analysis is supported by reasons of great weight: well-known arguments that are the property of no particular school and which most of us learned in our philosophical cradles. A very brief summary of what I take to be the most influential of these arguments will suffice for the comments I wish to make upon them.

A contra-causal freedom, it is argued, such as is implied in the 'categorical' interpretation of the proposition 'A could have chosen otherwise than he did', posits a breach of causal continuity between a man's character and his conduct. Now apart from the general presumption in favour of the universality of causal law, there are special reasons for disallowing the breach that is here alleged. It is the common assumption of social intercourse that our acquaintances will act 'in character'; that their choices will exhibit the 'natural' response of their characters to the given situation. And this assumption seems to be amply substantiated, over a wide range of conduct, by the actual success which attends predictions made on this basis. Where there should be, on the contra-causal hypothesis, chaotic variability, there is found in fact a large measure of intelligible continuity. Moreover, what is the alternative to admitting that a person's choices flow from his character? Surely just that the so-called 'choice' is not *that person's* choice at all: that, relatively to the person concerned, it is a mere 'accident'. Now we cannot really believe this. But if it *were* the case, it would certainly not help to establish *moral* freedom, the freedom required for *moral* responsibility. For clearly a man cannot be morally responsible for an act which does not express his own choice but is, on the contrary, attributable simply to chance.

These are clearly considerations worthy of all respect. It is not surprising if they have played a big part in persuading people to respond sympathetically to the view that 'Free Will', in its usual contra-causal formulation, is a pseudo-problem. A full answer to them is obviously not practicable in what is little more than an appendix to the body of this paper; but I am hopeful that something can be said, even in a little space, to show that they are very far from being as conclusive against a contra-causal freedom as they are often supposed to be.

To begin with the less troublesome of the two main objections indicated —the objection that the break in causal continuity which free will involves is inconsistent with the predictability of conduct on the basis of the agent's known character. All that is necessary to meet this objection, I suggest, is the frank recognition, which is perfectly open to the Libertarian, that there is a wide area of human conduct, determinable on clear general principles, within which free will does not effectively operate. The most important of these general principles (I have no space to deal here with the others) has often enough been stated by Libertarians. Free will does not operate in these practical situations in which no conflict arises in the agent's mind between what he conceives to be his 'duty' and what he feels to be his 'strongest desire'. It does not operate here because there just is no occasion for it to operate. There is no reason whatever why the agent should here even contemplate choosing any course other than that prescribed by his strongest desire. In all such situations, therefore, he naturally wills in accordance with strongest desire. But his 'strongest desire' is simply the specific *ad hoc* expression of that system of conative and emotive dispositions which we call his 'character'. In all such situations, therefore, whatever may be the case elsewhere, his will is in effect determined by his character as so far formed. Now when we bear in mind that there are an almost immeasurably greater number of situations in a man's life that conform to *this* pattern than there are situations in which an agent is aware of a conflict between strongest desire and duty, it is apparent that a Libertarianism which accepts the limitation of free will to the *latter* type of situation is not open to the stock objection on the score of 'predictability'. For there still remains a vast area of human behaviour in which prediction on the basis of known character may be expected to succeed: an area which will accommodate without difficulty, I think, all these empirical facts about successful prediction which the critic is apt to suppose fatal to Free Will.

So far as I can see, such a delimitation of the field of effective free will denies to the Libertarian absolutely nothing which matters to him. For it is precisely that small sector of the field of choices which our principle of delimitation still leaves open to free will—the sector in which strongest desire clashes with duty—that is crucial for moral responsibility. It is, I believe, with respect to such situations, and in the last resort to such situations alone, that the agent himself recognises that moral praise and blame are appropriate. They are appropriate, according as he does or does not 'rise to duty' in the face of opposing desires; always granted, that is, that he is free to choose between these courses as genuinely open possibilities. If the reality of freedom be conceded *here*, everything is conceded that the Libertarian has any real interest in securing.

But, of course, the most vital question is, can the reality of freedom be conceded even here? In particular, can the standard objection be met which we stated, that if the person's choice does not, in these situations as elsewhere, flow from his *character*, then it is not *that person's* choice at all.

This is, perhaps, of all the objections to a contra-causal freedom, the one which is generally felt to be the most conclusive. For the assumption upon which it is based, *viz.* that no intelligible meaning can attach to the claim that an act which is not an expression of the self's *character* may nevertheless be the *self's* act, is apt to be regarded as self-evident. The Libertarian is accordingly charged with being in effect an *In*determinist, whose 'free will', in so far as it does not flow from the agent's character, can only be a matter of 'chance'. Has the Libertarian—who invariably repudiates this charge and claims to be a *Self*-determinist—any way of showing that, contrary to the assumption of his critics, we *can* meaningfully talk of an act as the self's act even though, in an important sense, it is not an expression of the self's 'character'?

I think that he has. I want to suggest that what prevents the critics from finding a meaning in this way of talking is that they are looking for it in the wrong way; or better, perhaps, with the wrong orientation. They are

looking for it from the stand-point of the *external observer;* the stand-point
proper to, because alone possible for, apprehension of the physical world.
Now from the external stand-point we may observe processes of change.
But one thing which, by common consent, *cannot* be observed from
without is *creative activity*. Yet—and here lies the crux of the whole
matter—it is precisely creative activity which we are trying to understand
when we are trying to understand what is traditionally designated by 'free
will'. For if there should be an act which is genuinely the self's act and is
nevertheless not an expression of its character, such an act, in which
the self 'transcends' its character as so far formed, would seem to be essentially of the nature of creative activity. It follows that to look for a meaning
in 'free will' from the external stand-point is absurd. It is to look for it in a
way that ensures that it will not be found. Granted that a creative activity
of any kind is at least *possible* (and I know of no ground for its *a priori*
rejection), there is one way, and one way only, in which we can hope to
apprehend it, and that is from the *inner* stand-point of direct participation.

   It seems to me therefore, that if the Libertarian's claim to find a meaning
in a 'free' will which is genuinely the self's will, though not an expression of
the self's character, is to be subjected to any test that is worth applying, that
test must be undertaken from the inner stand-point. We ought to place
ourselves imaginatively at the stand-point of the agent engaged in the typical
moral situation in which free will is claimed, and ask ourselves whether from
this stand-point the claim in question does or does not have meaning for us.
That the appeal must be to introspection is no doubt unfortunate. But he
would be a very doctrinaire critic of introspection who declined to make
use of it when in the nature of the case no other means of apprehension is
available. Everyone must make the introspective experiment for himself: but
I may perhaps venture to report, though at this late stage with extreme
brevity, what I at least seem to find when I make the experiment myself.

   In the situation of moral conflict, then, I (as agent) have before my mind
a course of action X, which I believe to be my duty; and also a course of
action Y, incompatible with X, which I feel to be that which I most strongly
desire. Y is, as it is sometimes expressed, 'in the line of least resistance' for
me—the course which I am aware I should take if I let my purely desiring
nature operate without hindrance. It is the course towards which I am aware
that my *character*, as so far formed, naturally inclines me. Now, as actually
engaged in this situation, I find that I cannot help believing that I *can* rise to
duty and choose X; the 'rising to duty' being effected by what is commonly
called 'effort of will'. And I further find, if I ask myself just what it is I am
believing when I believe that I 'can' rise to duty, that I cannot help believing
that it lies with me here and now, quite absolutely, which of two genuinely
open possibilities I adopt; whether, that is, I make the effort of will and
choose X, or, on the other hand, let my desiring nature, my character as so
far formed, 'have its way', and choose Y, the course 'in the line of least
resistance'. These beliefs may, of course, be illusory, but that is not at
present in point. For the present argument all that matters is whether beliefs
of this sort are in fact discoverable in the moral agent in the situation of
'moral temptation'. For my own part, I cannot doubt the introspective
evidence that they are.

Now here is the vital point. No matter which course, X or Y, I choose in this situation, I cannot doubt, *qua* practical being engaged in it, that my choice is *not* just the expression of my formed character, and yet *is* a choice made by my *self*. For suppose I make the effort and choose X (my 'duty'). Since my very purpose in making the 'effort' is to enable me to act against the existing 'set' of desire, which is the expression of my character as so far formed, I cannot possibly regard the act itself as the expression of my *character*. On the other hand, introspection makes it equally clear that I am certain that it is *I* who choose; that the act is not an 'accident', but is genuinely *my* act. Or suppose that I choose Y (the end of 'strongest desire'). The course chosen here is, it is true, in conformity with my 'character'. But since I find myself unable to doubt that I *could* have made the effort and chosen X, I cannot possibly regard the choice of Y as *just* the expression of my character. Yet here again I find that I cannot doubt that the choice is *my* choice, a choice for which *I* am justly to be blamed.

What this amounts to is that I *can* and *do* attach meaning, *qua* moral agent, to an act which is not the self's character and yet is genuinely the self's act. And having no good reason to suppose that other persons have a fundamentally different mental constitution, it seems to me probable that anyone else who undertakes a similar experiment will be obliged to submit a similar report. I conclude, therefore, that the argument against 'free will' on the score of its 'meaninglessness' must be held to fail. 'Free Will' does have meaning; though, because it is of the nature of a creative activity, its meaning is discoverable only in an intuition of the practical consciousness of the participating agent. To the agent making a moral choice in the situation where duty clashes with desire, his 'self' is known to him as a creatively active self, a self which declines to be identified with his 'character' as so formed. Not, of course, that the self's character—let it be added to obviate misunderstanding—either is, or is supposed by the agent to be, devoid of bearing upon his choices, even in the 'sector' in which free will is held to operate. On the contrary, such a bearing is manifest in the empirically verifiable fact that we find it 'harder' (as we say) to make the effort of will required to 'rise to duty' in proportion to the extent that the 'dutiful' course conflicts with the course to which our character as so far formed inclines us. It is only in the polemics of the critics that a 'free' will is supposed to be incompatible with recognising the bearing of 'character' upon choice.

"But what" (it may be asked) "of the all-important question of the *value* of this 'subjective certainty'? Even if what you say is sound as 'phenomenology', is there any reason to suppose that the conviction on which you lay so much stress is in fact *true*?" I agree that the question is important; far more important, indeed, than is always realised, for it is not always realised that the only direct evidence there *could* be for a creative activity like 'free will' is an intuition of the practical consciousness. But this question falls outside the purview of the present paper. The aim of the paper has not been to offer a constructive defence of free will. It has been to show that the problem as traditionally posed is a real, and not a pseudo, problem. A serious threat to that thesis, it was acknowledged, arises from the apparent difficulty of attaching meaning to an act which is not the expression of the self's character and yet *is* the self's own act. The object of my brief phenomenological analysis was to provide evidence that such an act *does* have meaning for us in the one context in which there is any sense in *expecting* it to have meaning.

VII

My general conclusion is, I fear, very unexciting. It is merely that it is an error to suppose that the 'Free Will' problem, when correctly formulated, turns out not to be a 'problem' at all. Labouring to reinstate an old problem is dull work enough. But I am disposed to think that the philosophic situation to-day calls for a good deal more dull work of a similar sort.

4

TWO KINDS OF POSSIBILITY

Stuart Hampshire

I first consider two pairs of propositions: their implications, and the kind of observation and argument by which their truth or their falsity would normally be established, if they were challenged.

The first pair
(a1) 'It will not happen now'
(a2) 'It cannot happen now'
The second pair
(b1) 'He will not do it now'
(b2) 'He cannot do it now'

To bring out the contrast between the pairs, one might choose more specific propositions as examples of the two types:

(A1) 'The gas will not escape now'
(A2) 'The gas cannot escape now'
(B1) 'Jones will not escape now'
(B2) 'Jones cannot escape now'

I am concerned with the difference between 'will not' and the 'cannot' in the two cases: I shall argue that it is a different difference.

Consider the first pair first: to make the transition from 'It will not happen now' to 'It cannot happen now,' from the weaker to the stronger statement, is, at the very least, to claim that a certain type of evidence, or reason for believing, or source of knowledge, that the thing will not happen is available: not only will it not happen, but it is impossible that it should. Someone might agree that the thing won't happen, but he might at the same time dispute the stronger statement that it cannot happen, that it is impossible that it should. 'I agree with you,' he says, 'that in fact it will not happen now; but, all the same, it might; it is not altogether impossible. Your statement is too strong.'

We see that the contradictory of 'It cannot happen here and now' is not only 'It can, or could, happen here and now,' but also 'It may, or it might, happen here.' These are alternative ways of representing the possibility of its happening, when someone has asserted the impossibility. When the two disputants agree about the future course of events—that in fact the thing will not happen—they may still disagree about the possibility of its happening. If it is certain that it will not happen, there is no possibility that it will.

I do not myself know of any entirely adequate account of the logic of statements of the form 'It is certain that so-and-so will not happen.' But at least it is clear that he who asserts that it is certain that it will not happen here, or alternatively asserts that it cannot happen here, must show that there are very strong grounds for believing, or that there is some sure source of knowledge, that it will not happen here, when the truth of his statement is challenged. A man may say 'It will not happen here,' (e.g. 'This horse will not win the race'), and his statement may be true, and the utterance may be an entirely justifiable utterance in the circumstances, even though he was not in a position to support the statement with good grounds, or good evidence, or by citing a source of knowledge. But 'It cannot happen here,' which denies that it might happen, asserts, at the very least, that there are very good reasons for believing that it won't. Perhaps it is sometimes, or even generally, used to assert, or imply, much more than this: e.g. that there is some well-established natural law covering this happening; perhaps it asserts, or implies, that there is some cause, or sufficient condition, of its not happening. However this may be, at least it asserts that there are grounds for believing that it will not happen, which are strong enough to justify the assertion that it cannot happen. If no such grounds exist, the statement 'It can't happen here' is unsustainable and incorrect, even if the statement 'It won't happen here' is acceptable; for an objector could say 'Well, I admit that it didn't happen: but still it might have happened, and you were quite wrong when you said that it couldn't happen.'

We are familiar with the series: (1) 'It might happen here,' which might also be expressed as 'It could happen here;' (2) 'It is unlikely to happen here,' but 'It might' or 'It could,' and (3) 'It is certain that it won't happen here,' which might be expressed as 'It can't.'

Turn now to the second pair of the original propositions: either to the more general 'He won't do it now' and 'He can't do it now': or to the more specific 'He won't escape' and 'He can't escape.' The transition from 'He won't' to 'He can't' may here be altogether different; for when we say that he can't do it, we are not ordinarily saying that it can't be the case that he will do it. Given an appropriate verb of action, we would not ordinarily be denying that he might do it, that there is a possibility that he will. We are rather saying that he is not able to do it, that he lacks the means, or the authority, or the opportunity, to do it. The transition from 'He won't escape now' to 'He can't escape now' would not ordinarily be a transition from a weaker to a stronger statement about a future happening—about a possible eventuality, his escape. The conjunction of 'can' with a verb representing voluntary action would ordinarily preclude this interpretation; only in the past tense 'He can't have escaped' would ordinarily have as its contradictory 'He might have escaped,' where this is equivalent to 'It is not impossible that he did.' 'He could have escaped,' is ambiguous when taken out of context. It might be intended to be equivalent to 'It could be the case that he escaped', and 'It is not impossible that he did,' and 'He might have escaped;' or it might be intended to be equivalent to 'He had the ability, the means, and the opportunity, to escape.'

'He can't escape' may be informative as giving a reason or explanation why in fact he won't. He won't escape, because he can't. It is informative as a reason or explanation, because it may be the case that he would escape if he could, but he can't. Contrast this with the other pair: of the gas it is not similarly informative to explain the fact that it won't escape now by saying that it can't. It is not clear what it would mean to say of a gas that it would escape if it could. It is just conceivable that some non-anthropomorphic, literal sense might be given to this; for example, that it is a gas which has a tendency to escape from any container, but that now its escape is obstructed. But 'It would, if it could, but it can't' is not a literal and natural, and even less a scientific way, of speaking of the behaviour of a gas; more natural would be 'It would escape if it wasn't for the lead in the container, which makes it impossible.' Here 'It's impossible' does not actually give the reason why it won't escape; it indicates only that there is a specific cause of its not escaping, in spite of its tendency to escape. If I am asked to give you a reason for believing that it won't escape, I may explain to you why it can't. But I cannot quote its inability to escape as a reason for its not escaping. On the other hand, 'He would if he could, but he can't' is a very natural, and informative, way of speaking of the behaviour of a person. We now know in very general terms why he won't escape: he lacks the ability, or the means, or the opportunity to escape.

'He can't do it' (the governor is speaking about the prospect of his escape from prison) gives one of two possible reasons or explanations of why he won't. The other is that he does not want to do it, or is unwilling to do it; for, if he doesn't do it, it is generally either *vouloir* or *pouvoir*, the will or the power, that is lacking. If both were present, and present in full measure and without qualification, that is, if no other desire were more urgent, he generally would do it. I add the qualification 'generally,' because there is a third possible explanation, which may perhaps not be accounted for as a special case of having a conflicting desire: the explanation given in the words 'because he thinks he ought not to escape.' 'Because he doesn't want to,' or 'because he wants something else more,' explains his not doing it, in the same way that 'He can't do it' explains. It excludes one of two obvious possibilities, and therefore it tells one more about the situation. To the gas, and to inanimate things generally, the concept of wanting neither has, nor can be given, any application. Consequently, 'The gas cannot escape now,' taken by itself, is no kind of explanation of its not escaping. For it does not exclude one of these two possibilities.

The statement 'He cannot escape now' of course has as its contradiction 'He can.' 'He can escape' does not entail 'He might escape.' For it might be the case that, although he is able to escape, there is no possibility that he will want to. Nor does 'He might escape' entail 'He can escape.' 'He might escape' only entails 'He might be able to escape,' but not the unmodified statement that he can. Of course 'He cannot' does entail 'He will not,' but it does not entail 'It is certain that he won't,' or 'There is no possibility that he will,' both of which are contradicted by 'He might.' 'He cannot escape now, at this moment' is an unmodified, categorical statement about him, on a level with the categorical statement 'He is unwilling to.' He lacks the power now, at this moment. The question may be asked 'Is it certain that he cannot?' or 'Is it possible (might it be) that he can?' There is nothing odd in the question 'Can it be (i.e., is it possible) that he cannot escape?' That the two kinds of 'can' should occur in the same sentence may be disagreeable in style; but the sense is not unclear. It may be possible or impossible that he can escape, just as it may be possible or impossible that he actually will. It may be certain that he lacks the ability; and we may be in a position to point to some necessary condition of his having the ability which is lacking.

Just as we might in some cases seek for scientific explanation of a man's doing something, we look also for causal explanations of his power, or of his lacking the power, to do something. 'Why was I unable at that moment to do so-and-so?' is typically a causal question; my powers to do certain things come and go, are present at one moment and not at another, and I have every motive for discovering, if I can, the conditions on which their presence and their absence depend. Sometimes, of course—as, typically, in the case of escaping—the answer to the question 'Why can't he?' may be entirely obvious, and no experiment, or careful causal investigation, may be needed. It is often obvious that it is impossible, and out of the question, that a man should be able to do something, just as it is often obviously impossible, and out of the question, that he will want to do something. We may always look for sufficient conditions of the existence, or non-existence, of a power to do certain things. We need to acquire, and to hold on to, abilities, and we therefore need to know the conditions on which their existence depends.

There are some things which I can do at one moment and cannot do at the next; in this sense, powers can be very episodic, and impotence the matter of a moment. 'Why can't I do it now? I could do it a moment ago.' At one moment I can remember something that I want to remember: at the next moment I cannot. Evidently, there are also powers which, once acquired, last all one's life, and there are others that are intermediate between these two extremes. There are powers that are in their nature intermittent, and also powers that are not specific—e.g. the ability to speak French: just as there are desires and inclinations and interests that are in their nature intermittent, and also those that are not specific. I wish to concentrate on the power to do a specific thing on a particular occasion, because this is the fundamental kind of power, and of potentiality, which philosophers have tended to neglect, particularly in the context of an individual's freedom of decision.

You may now ask—What is a power, as this is attributed to human beings? How is it identified, and how is its existence or non-existence recognized? Is there a sharp line between powers to do something, attributed to human beings, and the causal properties of physical things, e.g. machines? I think there is: perhaps not a sharp line, but a line.

I have so far only said that the concept of a power to do some specific thing is complementary to the notion of a will, or of wanting to do something: associated with the concept of an action, the *vouloir* and *pouvoir*, 'want' and 'can', depend on each other for their sense. Whether someone lacks the power to do something is tested in actual performance, but only subject to the condition that the subject had the will to do the thing in question: whether someone lacks the will to do something may sometimes be revealed (in part, and only in part, and the lack is not conclusively established) in actual performance, but only subject to the condition that the power to do the thing in question exists. To speak of a man wanting to do a particular thing on a particular occasion (e.g. having the urge to speak, or to protest) is not to speak of a tendency, in that sense of 'tendency' in which a gas may have a tendency to escape, as some philosophers have suggested. A human desire or inclination to do something is not only, or primarily, revealed in actual performance, as is the tendency of a gas. I normally discover, decide, and know what I want to do, quite independently of observing my own patterns of behaviour; and I may authoritatively, though not infallibly, disclose my desires and interests to others, together with the conceptions and calculations that enter into them. It may be true that I did have an impulse to protest, even though no evidence of this is to be found in my behaviour, and even though no test would establish that I did, or did not, have at that moment that impulse; for to ask me about my impulse is not to apply a test, in the sense in which you may apply a test to establish that this particular gas has a tendency to escape at this particular time. For these reasons—or connected with these facts—a statement to the effect that someone—say, the speaker—wants, or wanted, to do something at a particular moment is not equivalent to any set of hypothetical statements about his observable behaviour. A desire to act may occur at a particular moment, and may be no less an episode in a man's biography, to be reported in a categorical statement, than a twinge of pain, or a blow on the head. A desire, or inclination, to do something at a particular moment does not need to be tested in performance—or to be tested at all—unlike a power to do something, which does in the last resort need to be tested in performance, if its existence is to be established beyond doubt.

Compare (a) 'At that moment I wanted to race him and overtake him but, of course, I didn't;' (b) 'At that moment I could have overtaken him, but, of course, I didn't.'

The first statement may in normal circumstances be known to be true, beyond doubt, and quite independently of the inductive test of parallel cases; in such a simple case the first person disclosure is authoritative, although not immune from various kinds of error, from self-deceit, or deceit. The question 'How do you know that you wanted to?', as opposed to 'Are you sure?', is normally senseless. In the second case, the inductive test of parallel cases is the relevant test, and the first person statement is not authoritative. The question 'How do you know that you could have' is far from senseless. Whether I have, or had, the power to overtake, as I believe, only experience and experiment can show. Whether I have, or had, the desire is not normally, and in the standard case, to be finally settled by experience and experiment. In the normal case the subject, although liable to correction, can claim to know directly what he wants to do. There can be no question of the source of his knowledge; it is direct knowledge, in the sense that it has no source.

The notion of a power, as expressed in the form 'I can do so-and-so,' 'He can do so-and-so,' is a very wide and general one. It includes the kind of power to do something which is an ability or skill, the power which is being in a position to do something, either in a literal or a metaphorical sense, a legal or customary power to do something (e.g. to marry people, if I am a priest), and many variations and combinations of these. Whenever, in respect of any action, the contrast between the attempt to do and the achievement is in place, the notion of the power to do it is also in place. Plainly the question 'Can you do it?' will sometimes be an absurd question; either the verb of action in itself, or the circumstances of the particular case, may show that the question does not arise. But, in general, it is intrinsic to the notion of an action that it is something that can be attempted, and attempted successfully, that it is something that one may try to do, and that one may either succeed in doing or fail.

I may seem to be leaning rather heavily at this point on the unanalysed, and probably unanalysable, notion of a verb of action. By what criteria are we to distinguish a verb which represents a person's action, in the required sense, from among all the verbs applicable to persons? Is it not notorious that this cannot be done? And yet am I not assuming, in my account of a power to do something, as being distinct from a causal property, that we can distinguish the cases of 'He can X,' where X is a verb, which are cases of the power to *do* something, in some strong sense of 'do,' from cases where 'do' is used with some weaker sense? (a) The doctor says 'He cannot live through the night.' (b) The prison governor says 'He cannot escape.' Is 'live' in this context a verb of action in the required sense? It is not. A man lives through the night only as the vegetative soul dictates, and as a vegetable does; his choosing to live or die cannot here be at issue, as his choice might be at issue in estimating whether he will escape. Must one therefore distinguish two different uses of 'can' in these sentences? I am suggesting that, at least for some purposes, one must. I say to a particular man that he can today continue to climb the mountain, amidst the snow and ice, when such-and-such conditions of temperature and atmosphere obtain. It is within his power to do it. Do I attribute to him, the person, the power to do something, in some sense of 'power to do,' which is not applicable to a part of his body, for example his leg, of which I might say that it can this morning withstand such-and-such pressures without breaking? My suggestion is that in the case of the physical, mindless object, his leg, there is no difference between 'will this morning withstand the pressures that will be applied' and 'can this morning withstand the pressures that will be applied,' *unless* I am using 'can' as a substitute for 'may' or 'might.' But in the case of the man, and of the action of climbing the mountain, there is a difference, and I need not be using 'can' as an alternative to 'may' or 'might'. The fact that the man failed in his attempt to climb the mountain is not by itself sufficient to establish that he could not do so. One needs the assumption that he still wanted to, and, consequently, that he was trying to, and that his failure was not attributable to lack of will. Granted this assumption, and only granted this, and given that the normal background conditions pre-supposed are not suddenly changed, it does indeed follow from the fact that the performance was in fact a failure that the power was at that moment lacking.

I have chosen a strained and provocative example, in which the assump-tion of the necessary will would ordinarily seem unavoidable, and scarcely an assumption at all; it seems improbable that he would want to lie down amid the snow and ice, and this is why the two questions 'Can he?' and 'Will he?' in this selected case seem to lie so close together. Observing the man's performance would normally, in such a case of a test or feat, be sufficient to establish whether the power exists or not, just because, in the setting of a feat, and of a test of an ability, the implied condition of a will to achieve is generally satisfied.

There are circumstances in which it would be normal to say to a man 'You can climb it if you try', or 'You could climb it if you wanted to;' he might just give up, and not try, and he might succeed in climbing just *because* he had made the wilful effort. There is no analogous assumption of a will or want required in establishing the pressure-sustaining properties of his leg, as they exist this morning. In the case of the leg, the difference between 'It cannot' and 'It will not' is that he who says that it cannot withstand the pressures alleges that it is impossible that it should withstand the pressures, or that it is certain that it will not. He makes a stronger statement, which needs to be supported by stronger grounds, than the mere prediction that it will not withstand the pressures. The grounds for such a claim to certainty will ordinarily be found in some well-confirmed causal explanation of the operations of his leg.

That there should be this difference between the man's action and the workings of his leg is not surprising; for the normal scheme of explanation of a human action—the normal answer to the question 'Why did he do it?'—is in terms of his wants and interests. When a causal question is raised about his actions, it is more commonly a question of why he can, or cannot, do something, of the necessary conditions of his having the power to do it. We look for a scientific understanding of men's powers, and of their successes and failures in doing what they want to do. On what conditions do their powers to do so-and-so depend, why do they come and go, and why are they distributed among men as they are? This is the point at which a causal, and fully scientific explanation, of behaviour has a clear purpose and utility. We do hope to be able to calculate the antecedent conditions necessary for a man's success in certain performances, should he want to do such-and-such, and the conditions in which he will fail; we expect this to be a domain of natural law, in which reliable uniformities will be discovered by experiment. As the result of a vast accumulation of commonplace experience, we already know, or have well-founded beliefs, about what we can, and cannot, do under various relevant conditions. But we expect this knowledge to be extended, and our beliefs to be corrected, by more exact and controlled experiment and by the elaboration of psychological theory.

When, following the question, 'Why can X do so-and-so, while Y cannot?,' we ask 'Why does X want to do so-and-so, while Y does not?,' this second demand for explanation normally receives a different kind of answer. We will normally turn to the reasons that he has for wanting to do so-and-so, that is, to the place of this particular interest in the whole system of his desires and interests; and we can know very little of his less rudimentary wants unless we know something of his thoughts. He wants to do so-and-so, because he thinks that it is a case of so-and-so, and perhaps also because he calculates that it will lead to so-and-so. If the thoughts and beliefs are changed, the desires will normally change also. We therefore normally hope to change and to extend a man's desires and interests, and intend that our own will be changed and extended, principally by reasoning and by the force of argument; and we may admit that, failing these, they are sometimes changed by rhetoric and persuasion. For this reason, an experimental answer to the question 'Why do people of such-and-such a kind or under such-and-such conditions want to do so-and-so?,' taken as a demand for the cause, or sufficient conditions, of their desire, seems strange; for it seems that any adequate answer would specify the cause of their having certain thoughts and beliefs, and this in turn seems strange. If a man wants to do something for some reason that he has, then there is a thought on which his desire is dependent, in the sense that, if he were convinced that the belief was mistaken, he would at least reconsider whether he wanted to act as he had wanted to. One can intelligibly look for causal explanations of a man's mistakes in reasoning, that is, one can look outside the reasoning process itself for a factor that explains its assuming the form that it did. But the steps in a clear and correct process of reasoning need no further explanation outside the process itself. A further explanation could only be of his ability to reason correctly, on this particular occasion. If the argument that he accepts is evidently valid, if the action that he wants to perform is evidently delightful, if the object that he fears is evidently dangerous, we do not ask for a further explanation, for a cause of his accepting the argument, wanting to act, or fearing. For this would be to question a truism. The more natural application of the scientific and causal type of explanation is, first, to the unwilled features of behaviour, and secondly, to men's powers to act in certain ways when they want to.

To summarise: The existence or non-existence of the power to do a specific thing at a particular moment can be conclusively established by actual performance in the normal conditions presupposed, but, subject to the condition that an attempt that fails establishes lack of power, only if the subject really at that time wanted to perform the action in question and was not diverted by some stronger interest. One needs to know the aims of a person in order to be sure that his not doing something is a case of his being unable to do it. The ultimate test of my ability to do something at a particular moment is 'experiment,' in the sense of my seriously trying, with a will to succeed.

I am not arguing that there is anything easy and unproblematic about the distinction between lack of the will to do something and lack of the power to do it, as this distinction is applied in particular cases, and especially in the context of moral argument, of censure, regret, and the assessment of responsibility. On the contrary, it is notoriously difficult, even if one is untroubled by theoretical doubts, to apply in particular cases the ordinary distinction between failures to do something, which are cases of lack of will to do it, and failures that justify saying, 'I cannot do it,' or 'He cannot do it.' It is easy enough to say that failure, when we make the attempt with a strong desire to succeed, shows that we could not at that moment do it. If I certainly wanted to do the thing in question very much, and if I made the attempt and failed, this would in all normal circumstances establish beyond reasonable doubt the truth of the categorical statement that I could not do it, that I was unable to do it, at that moment. Perhaps I have in general the capacity to do it, and perhaps I could *have* done it on that occasion, if such-

and-such conditions, within me or in the environment, had been different. But the fact remains that I could not do it, that I was unable to do it, at that moment, where the phrase 'at that moment' is shorthand for 'all the conditions being what they were at that moment.' If lack of will is excluded, lack of power is the only account that can be given of my not doing it, given that I made the attempt. But I may on occasion be deceived about the strength and direction of my own desires and interests, and even more obviously, and often, be deceived about the desires and interests of others. And these errors about dispositions must lead to complementary errors about powers. My not doing it, or my failing to do it, may look like a case of inability, and yet, more closely scrutinised, it may turn out to be a case of not fully wanting to do it, and therefore of not really trying to do it. 'It is not true that he was unable to do it; he did not really want to and the attempt was half-hearted. He could have done it, if he had really wanted to, and wanted enough.' But we would start to talk, and to think, idly, if we made the notion of a power entirely untestable and indeterminate, by pressing the notion of wanting beyond its normal conditions of application.

Suggested re-drawings of this line between 'He would not' and 'He could not' have always entered into controversy about conduct. When I would normally say that I did not want to do something, which I could have done, if I had wanted to, how do I know that I have not been deceived by ignorance of the specific conditions on which the ability depends? This is a questioning of the adequacy of the commonplace inductive tests of powers by parallel cases. Presented with a contrary-to-fact conditional statement of the kind 'I could have done it at that moment if I had wanted to,' it is often not unreasonable to doubt whether the apparently parallel cases really are relevantly parallel. More exact, systematic, and controlled experiment might reveal an unsuspected condition on which the ability depends. Alternatively, the revision can be made in the opposite direction, as, for example, by Sartre, with the suggestion that many cases of failing to do something, because of an alleged inability, are to be counted as cases of lack of will to do it. When, exhausted on the mountain, I say 'I cannot take another step,' Sartre suggests that I ought rather to say something like 'I prefer to sit down rather than painfully continue to walk.' These proposals for a thorough-going conceptual revision properly have a systematic and metaphysical basis, which I am omitting. But they do make contact at certain points with the apparent incoherencies and complacencies of ordinary usage and belief. Psychologists may persuade us, in the light of new experimental evidence, to question the normal methods of distinction, and may reclassify many apparent cases of lack of ability as 'really' cases of lack of desire. Simultaneously, they revise the criteria attached to 'He wanted,' or of 'He really wanted to do so-and-so,' with the suggestion that there are repressed and normally unconscious desires, which are to be discovered and identified only in certain special circumstances.

This is one point at which there seems to be genuine difficulty in sustaining the distinction. For can it not be suggested that I am sometimes unable to do something, particularly when the inability is a symptom of neurosis, because of some unconscious desire, where the 'because' marks a causal connection? I made the attempt and I found that I could not do it; but perhaps only because of some conflicting desire, which I didn't know that I had. And does not this causal dependence of the inability on the desire prevent us from classifying the failure as definitely either a case of inability, or as a case of lack of will, if these two are mutually exclusive alternatives? Certainly this kind of case does prevent us from regarding the alternative accounts of failure as in all cases mutually exclusive. There are inabilities at particular moments, which are identified as such by failure in an attempt, that has been made with a conscious will to do the action in question. But often a man's desires may be confused, ambiguous and conflicting, and the confusions of desire may be at the time unrecognised, and unrecognisable, by the agent; then an inability may sometimes co-exist with, and be explained by, an unconscious, or repressed, wish not to do what the agent can also be truly said to have tried to do with a conscious will to succeed. He showed and felt a desire to succeed, which is sufficient to justify the statement that he could not at that moment do what he tried to do; but perhaps it is also true that not all his desires pointed in the same direction; and this fact may explain his powerlessness at that moment. We do often speak of the existence of a will to do, or to achieve, something as a condition of the existence of the ability to do it. And men may commonly hope to extend the apparent limits of their own powers by further appeals to will, or by incitement of the will of others. Once again, it is speech, and the possibilities of incitement, exhortation and appeals to the will, which give a place to a partially indeterminate notion of the will in the explanation of conduct. A man may both explore the limits, and extend the limits, of his powers by questioning his apparent will to succeed.

I am certainly not suggesting that the line of distinction between *vouloir* and *pouvoir*, between lack of will and lack of power, is clear and immutable in its application to human actions. I am suggesting that 'can do' and 'cannot do' is a different kind of 'can' from that of 'can happen' and 'cannot happen,' when the former is applied to creatures who may know, form, reflect on, and criticise their own occasional desires and aims, and who may, or may not, disclose them to others. The fact that men may authoritatively disclose their desires and aims, and more fundamentally, that they are capable of reflection, and that they may find *reasons* for wanting to do one thing rather than another, entails the consequence that the existence and nature of these desires and aims are not established solely, or even primarily, by observation of their actual behaviour. We need to know how they think of the actions which they want to perform. Animals complicate the issue, because we do properly attribute desires to them. But their desires and aims, linked with the necessary concomitants of desire, namely, pleasure and pain, are unformulated and are not mediated by thought; so we are prepared, in our unsentimental moments, to establish the nature of their desires solely by reference to their observable behaviour; and perhaps we are even ready to take statements about their wants as *equivalent* to some set of hypothetical statements about their observable behaviour. But we cannot accurately specify the more sophisticated desires of men without knowledge of their thoughts.

Machines have powers attributed to them, and we now often compare their powers with human powers very directly. About a particular machine, at a particular time, we may say that it can now play chess better than a particular man can. My suggestion is that the 'cans' on either side of this comparison are different in important respects. Of the particular machine, it cannot in principle be true that it can now, and at this moment, play better than the man, if, when it is now tested in action under the normal conditions presupposed, it in fact plays worse. Of the machine we may, of course, say that it *could* play better than the man, or that it *could have* played better, that it has unrealised potentialities, potentialities which would be realised under different conditions, either inside the machine itself, or outside it. But this is not to make the plain categorical statement that this particular machine can now play better, conditions inside and outside the machine being what they now in fact are. If it can now play better, it will play better, when it is tested under the normally presupposed conditions. Contrast the man: it is in principle possible that he can now play better than the machine, even though, when he is observed in action, he in fact plays worse. He may not want to play better, and therefore he may not try to; perhaps he prefers at this time to leave his ability unused, and prefers not to play as well as he can. This cannot be true of the machine; its powers, or potentialities, are merely that which it *would* observably do under certain implied or stated conditions.

Suppose a machine that is programmed to make a losing move whenever its human opponent makes a foolish, losing move. Of this machine on this occasion, playing against a bad player, we can say 'It cannot win now.' It is certain that it will lose. Sufficient conditions of its defeat already exist in its programming. Contrast a man, a good player, who very much wants to save his opponent humiliation; there is a good sense in which he can win, but it is certain that he won't. We know two categorical statements about him to be true: (1) that he has the power to win, and (2) that he is determined, firmly intends, not to use his power. I am not denying that to a machine may be attributed powers and potentialities to do various things at particular moments, powers that may come and go, as the conditions on which they depend are varied. But to establish the existence of a machine's power to do something at a particular moment, and under the conditions then obtaining, it is both necessary and sufficient to provide the standard and appropriate input, or stimulus, which is required for the realisation of this power, and to wait for the appropriate response in performance. In the case of establishing the existence of a man's power to do something at a particular moment, this is not sufficient. There is one *overriding* condition that must be known to be satisfied before the equivalent test of performance is accepted as decisive: that the subject wants, or has the will, to pass the test. If this peculiar, internal condition is not known to be satisfied, failure in present performance does not prove inability.

J. L. Austin, in his published British Academy Lecture 'Ifs and Cans,' made the point that 'I can do so-and-so now,' and 'I can do so-and-so now, if I want' or 'if I choose,' are categorical statements. I shall not repeat the argument. The important point here is that 'I can do so-and-so now' is the form of words that we typically use when a feat, something involving, or thought to involve, the possibility of failure, is in question. You may predict, or bet, that I cannot escape from a certain position, and I may predict, or bet, that I can; in this setting of a challenge to a feat, where the will to succeed is assumed, 'can' is scarcely distinguishable from 'will succeed, if I make the attempt.' My statement is conclusively verified, and yours conclusively falsified, if I do escape when I make the attempt. If I do not then escape, the contradictory is true. Having failed, I still may argue that I *could have* escaped, using a form of words that implies I would have been able to escape, if some missing condition had been satisfied: I could have, if I had been more careful, or if I had not been distracted, or even if I had tried harder; for 'trying' can also be included among the conditions of success. 'You can if you try, but you will not be able to, unless you try' is a familiar causal judgment. Equally familiar—'Why cannot I do it?' (said by a golfer, or by a pianist, or by someone trying to remember a name): 'Well, you would be able to do it if you didn't try so hard: just don't try, you will find that you can do it.' 'Try,' as it occurs in these causal judgments, has a rather different use and implication from the 'try' which means 'make an attempt to'—in French, *essayer,* or H. A. Prichard's 'set oneself to.' I may make either a half-hearted or a serious attempt to do something. I may set about it with a will to succeed, or without any real desire to succeed. In the causal judgments, 'You can do it, if you try: but you will not be able to do it unless you try,' 'try' implies something like 'make an effort to'—the use of 'try' that William James stressed in his chapter on the will. But when I say, contradicting you, 'I can raise this glass without spilling the wine,' and when in this context I intend this to be scarcely distinguishable from 'I will succeed if I try,' the 'try' does not imply 'make an effort.' If I make the attempt and fail, I have to admit that you were right when you said 'You cannot do it now.' Perhaps I *could have,* if I had not been over-confident, and if I had not thought that I could do it without taking trouble; but the fact remains that I *could not* at that moment, as things were, with my over-confidence included in the conditions at that moment. Perhaps you knew me well enough to gamble on my over-confidence, and that is why you said 'You cannot do it.' When I ask you whether you can now remember the first lines of *Paradise Lost,* and you answer that you can, you claim that you will succeed on this particular occasion. In the peculiar setting of a challenge to a feat, or to a test of ability, 'can' and 'will succeed' almost coincide, because the will to succeed is assumed. In other settings of inquiry into your powers, I am normally asking what you would succeed in doing if you really wanted to and really tried, that is, made the attempt with an un-qualified desire to succeed.

It is important to notice that, if we learn what we can do by trying, the slipperiness, amounting almost to ambiguity, in the notion of 'trying' must infect the notion of a man's power to do something with an equivalent slipperiness. We do normally, in reviewing actions, include the existence of an unqualified desire to do something in the conditions that must be satisfied before the power to do something on a particular occasion has been proved not to exist. In some contexts and for some purposes—for example, those of the stern moralist—we may say that a man can only be known to be unable to do something, if it has been proved that he fails, when all the internal conditions are favourable; that is, when he has strongest possible desire to do the thing in question, and when there are no conflicting desires of any kind. In other contexts and for other purposes—e.g. of challenges and bets—we may take the weaker test as decisive—'conditions being what they are, in your mind and elsewhere, you will not succeed, if you make the attempt now.' There is not any firm and general rule that prescribes the background of standing conditions presupposed in the test of powers and potentialities, either of persons or of things. The background of conditions presupposed will vary with the situation in which a man's powers are being judged, and with the purposes for which the judgment is needed. I shall be mainly concerned . . . with the situation of a man who, before acting, has to decide what to do, and, secondarily, with that of a man who advises him about his decision, taking into account, as they both must, the limits of the agent's powers, as they exist on a particular occasion. In this situation, in which an estimate needs to be made as a guide to future action, 'You (or I) can do so-and-so' is conclusively verified or falsified when an attempt is made with a full conscious desire to succeed, and without any conscious conflict of desire: even though a subsequent acceptable explanation of the failure might refer to an unconscious desire to fail.

It is sometimes implied that we must wait upon science, and the discovery of causal laws, to know what men can and cannot do, as we must wait upon science and the discovery of causal laws to learn about the powers of metals and gases. But this is not true. I unavoidably acquire an immense amount of knowledge about what I can and cannot do, directly, and in the ordinary course of existence, in my attempts, achievements, and failures. Certainly scientific investigation of the necessary conditions upon which these powers depend will greatly add to this knowledge, and will permit reliable inferences, far beyond the range of direct experience, to an estimate of what my powers would be under various specified conditions. And much more important, such investigation will enable me to find the means of increasing my powers to act in specific ways in specific kinds of situation. No conceivable advances in scientific knowledge can lead to the conclusion that I am not often—for example, at this moment—confronted with a plurality of things that I can do if I want to, between which I must choose: that there is this plurality of open possibilities I know by experience, as surely as I know anything, including the laws of physics and psychology.

To summarise:

We make a mistake if we interpret 'He cannot act differently' as parallel to 'This gas cannot behave differently.' 'There is no possibility of his acting differently' is indeed parallel to 'This gas cannot behave differently,' where this latter is interpreted to mean, 'It is certain that this gas will not behave differently.' 'He cannot act differently' neither entails, nor is entailed by, 'There is no possibility of his acting differently.' The entailment that does hold is between 'There is no possibility that he will be able to act differently' (i.e. 'It is certain that he will not be able to') and 'There is no possibility that he will act differently.' It may be certain that a man will not do X because it is certain that he will not want to do X; but it does not follow that there are no possibilities other than X which are open to him, in the sense that there is nothing that he can do. The notion of a power, as applied to men, depends on the twin notion of 'want,' or 'will,' used in the explanation of action, when the will, or desire, to do something on a particular occasion may be formed, discovered, reflected upon, criticised, and formulated, and perhaps also disclosed to others.

Explanation by Causes
and by Reasons

5

TYPES OF EXPLANATION
IN PSYCHOLOGICAL THEORIES

R. S. Peters

INTRODUCTORY

Ever since Hobbes was fired by the imaginative idea that *all* human behaviour might be explained in terms of mechanical principles, there have been sporadic attempts to provide over-all theories of human behaviour. Such theories have been instigated more by the desire to develop an ambitious theory than by puzzlement about concrete problems of human behaviour. This was true of Hobbes who pictured himself doing for psychology what Harvey had done for physiology by extending the new science of motion to the most intimate spheres of human thought and endeavour. It was also true of later theorists who, under the influence of Darwin rather than of Galileo, were excited by the thought that men were animals as well as mere bodies. McDougall, for instance, did not provide any startling answers to concrete questions about human behaviour; rather he concocted a sort of dynamic atomism to show that man's social behaviour could be explained in terms of biological principles. In fact the inspiration behind theorizing in psychology has been, in the main, the success of other sciences like physiology, chemistry, and mechanics, and the idea that there could be an all-inclusive theory of human behaviour if psychology were to adopt the postulates and methods of other sciences.

A contributory factor, too, has been the understandable determination of

From R. S. Peters, *The Concept of Motivation* (New York and London: 1958), Chap. I, pp. 1–26. Reprinted by permission of Routledge & Kegan Paul Ltd. and Humanities Press Inc.

psychologists to make their enquiries 'scientific'. This has led them to cast their theories in a mould dictated by the current conception of scientific method. For a long time this was thought to be the method of induction; and so systems of psychology like introspectionism and behaviourism developed, which were products of what Popper calls 'inductivism'— attempts to build up generalisations on the basis of carefully scrutinized data. The methodologists then proclaimed that scientific method was really deductive. So an enormity like Hull's *Principles of Behaviour* emerged, scientifically impeccable because it was a hypothetico-deductive system. Hull boldly proclaimed his programme of starting from 'colourless movements and mere receptor impulses as such' and eventually explaining everything in terms of such concepts—

> familial behaviour, individual adaptive efficiency (intelligence), the formal educative processes, psychogenic disorders, social control and delinquency, character and personality, culture and acculturation, magic and religious practices, custom, law and jurisprudence, politics and government and many other specialised fields of behaviour.

In fact Hull developed some simple postulates which gave dubious answers to limited questions about particular species of rats. He never asked, let alone tried to answer, any concrete questions about human behaviour. He was in love with the idea of a science of behaviour; he was not acutely worried about concrete questions of explaining *human* behaviour.

Freud was perhaps the great exception. For he was genuinely puzzled about concrete phenomena and developed some very fertile assumptions to explain them. Also, in his early work especially, he was very much aware of the limitations of his assumptions and defined carefully the types of phenomena that could be explained by the postulation of unconscious mental processes. In other words he seemed to be aware of the *sort* of questions about human behaviour which he was answering. For there are many *different* sorts of questions which can be asked about human behaviour and the differences, as I shall hope to show, are such that an all-embracing theory is inappropriate. These different sorts of questions are especially confused in theories of motivation. It is this thesis which I now hope to substantiate.

I. TYPES OF QUESTIONS ABOUT HUMAN BEHAVIOR

(a) 'His Reason' Explanations

The over-riding aim of a scientist should be explanation. This sounds rather obvious, but it has many important consequences in relation to psychological theorizing. For the general question 'Why did Jones do that?' is capable of being asked and answered in a variety of different ways. The particular formula employed in asking the question usually dictates the sort of answer which is expected and which counts as an explanation.[1] The paradigm case of a human action is when something is done in order to bring about an end. So the usual way of explaining an action is to describe it as an action of a certain sort by indicating the end which Jones had in mind. We

---

[1] I am indebted to J. O. Urmson (1952) for some of these distinctions.

therefore ask the 'why' question in a more specific form. We ask what was his *reason* for doing that or what was the *point* of it, what *end* he had in mind. If we ask why Jones walked across the road, the obvious answer will be something like 'To buy tobacco.' Instead of saying this we could say 'because he wanted some tobacco'. This is, logically speaking, another way of giving the same sort of answer; for the answer 'to buy some tobacco' is only an explanation because we assume in Jones some sort of directive disposition—a general tendency to obtain and use tobacco.

Even in this very simple sort of explanation in terms of a man's reason for doing something there are, as a matter of fact, concealed assumptions. We assume, for instance, that walking across the street is an efficient way of getting to the tobacconist. This counts as an explanation not simply because Jones envisaged walking across the street as a means to getting the tobacco but because it really is a means to getting it. We assume, too, that a man who has this information will act on it if he wants some tobacco. We assume that men are rational in that they will take means which lead to ends if they have the information and want the ends. 'His reason' is an explanation in terms of what Popper calls 'the logic of the situation'.

But it is not only norms of efficiency and consistency that are implicit in the concept of 'his reason'. There are also norms or standards of social appropriateness. After all Jones might have crawled or run across the road. But 'to get some tobacco' would be a very odd answer to the question 'Why did Jones *run* across the road?' Yet running would be quite an efficient way of getting across the road. It would, however, be socially odd as a way of crossing the road to get some tobacco. *Man is a rule-following animal.* His actions are not simply directed towards ends; they also conform to social standards and conventions, and unlike a calculating machine he acts because of his knowledge of rules and objectives. For instance, we ascribe to people *traits* of character like honesty, punctuality, considerateness and meanness. Such terms do not, like ambition or hunger or sexual desire, indicate the sorts of goals that a man tends to pursue; rather they indicate the type of regulation that he imposes on his conduct whatever his goals may be. A man who is ruthless, selfish, punctual, considerate, persistent, and honest does not have any particular goals; rather he pursues whatever goals he has in particular sorts of ways.

This simple purposive model of a man taking means to bring about an end is further complicated by the fact that norms enter into and often entirely define the end. Ends like passing an examination, getting married, becoming a professor, and reading a paper explain quite adequately a great deal of the goings on in the precincts of a university; yet they are defined almost entirely by social convention. It is a gross over-simplification to think of ends merely as terminating points of activity. Actually even a rat, after eating or achieving some other end, will continue being active in a variety of ways—sniffing, preening, and so on. If eating can be regarded as an end this is not because it is a definite terminating point of activity but because activity *previous* to it varies concomitantly with changes in the conditions necessary to define it as an end. The concept of means is just as necessary to bring out what is meant by an end as the concept of end is to bring out what is meant by a means. Ends are not given as natural terminating points like a chain of oases distributed across a desert. And, to a large extent, what counts as falling within a means-to-end explanatory framework is determined by convention. Even those ends, like eating and sexual intercourse, which are universal and which have an obvious biological basis, can scarcely be specified without recourse to norms. For there are countless ways of performing the acts which can be regarded as ends and in every culture a few particular ways are stamped with the hallmark of conventionality. Eating is not just getting food into the stomach. Jones' movements across the road are classifiable as means to the end of buying tobacco because of a vast system of norms defining 'buying tobacco' as an end as well as a system of norms regulating what is an efficient and socially appropriate way of attaining it.

My reasons for stressing this rule-following purposive pattern into which we fit our common-sense explanations are twofold. In the first place I want to insist that most of our explanations are couched in terms of this model and our predictions of people's behaviour presuppose it. We know what the parson will do when he begins to walk towards the pulpit because we know the conventions regulating church services. And we can make such predictions without knowing anything about the *causes* of people's behaviour unless we include under 'causes' things like the parson's training and grasp of the rules, which are things of a different order from 'causes' in the sense of antecedent movements. Man in society is like a chess-player writ large. Requests for explanation are usually reflections of our ignorance about the particular rule or goal which is relevant to the behaviour in question. We usually know the general pattern but are unsure which part of it is relevant. Sometimes, of course, we are in the position of a free-thinker at a Roman Catholic mass. The question 'Why did X do that?' is then usually a request for an elucidation of the whole pattern of conventions. In explaining human actions we, like anthropologists, must all, in the first place, be structuralists. Indeed I would go so far as to say that anthropology or sociology must be the basic sciences of human action in that they exhibit the systematic framework of norms and goals which are necessary to classify actions as being of a certain sort. They both—like classical economics—presuppose the purposive, rule-following model; in this respect they are quite unlike sciences which imply a mechanical model of explanation.

In the second place this rule-following purposive pattern of explanation must be sketched in some detail because a proper understanding of what is meant by a human action has very important logical consequences. It shows, for instance . . . that human actions cannot be sufficiently explained in terms of causal concepts like 'colourless movements'. Indeed to claim that we are confronted with an action is *ipso facto* to rule out such mechanical explanations, as being sufficient.

(b) 'The Reason' Explanations

But, of course, as psychologists will be the first to point out, people often invent reasons for doing things or delude themselves into thinking that the reasons they offer for their actions are operative reasons. We therefore often say of a man that *his* reason may have been x but *the* reason why he acted like that was y. For instance we might say that Jones said that he crossed the road in order to buy some tobacco but the reason why he did it was not really his desire for tobacco; it was sex. There was a pretty girl

looking in the window of the tobacconist. This explanation may of course
be erroneous. For instance a psychologist once told me that I delayed
crossing the road to College because of an aversion to getting down to work.
I replied, and I think more convincingly, that I stayed on the other side in
order to look at the row of glistening cars drawn up opposite. But whether
the explanation in question is correct or incorrect does not much matter; the
point is that to speak of *the* reason why a person does something is different
in that it is a way of calling attention to the law or assumed law that a given
case actually falls under. *His* reason may coincide with *the* reason. *The*
reason why Jones crossed the road might in fact be his desire for tobacco.
He might also be aware that he wanted to inspect the girl at close quarters,
but was concealing this by the camouflage of buying tobacco. This would
then be his *real* reason. But whereas *his* reason—whether real or not—entails
that a man is conscious of his objective, the reason why he did it does not.[2]
The reason why he did it might well be sex or aversion to work; yet the
individual might be quite unaware of pursuing or avoiding the relevant
goals. And whereas to say that *he* had a reason for doing something is more
or less to rule out a causal explanation, to give *the* reason why he did it is
sometimes to subsume it under a law-like proposition of a causal kind. This
is not necessarily so. For we can say that sex or aversion to work was *the*
reason why he did it and simply be insisting that a different directive disposition is being exercised. But *the* reason why he did it might also be that
he was pushed or assailed by an attack of giddiness. These would be causal
explanations which would rebut the suggestion that he had a reason for
crossing the road. Causal explanations, in other words, can count as *the*
reason why a person does something; but they are only one type of answer
to the question 'What was *the* reason why he did it?'

(c) Causal Explanations

There are, however, other questions about particular goings on—I omit to
say actions on purpose—to which answers in causal terms are appropriate.
Instead of the omnibus question 'Why did Jones do that?' we often ask what
made, drove, or possessed him to do it. These are usually cases of lapses from
action or failure to act—when there is some kind of *deviation* from the
purposive rule-following model, when people, as it were, get it wrong. This
may be in respect of an efficiency norm—for example, when a person
refuses to take the only quick route to his destination by underground train,
or when he can't remember a well-known name when he is performing an
introduction. Or the behaviour may go wrong in respect of a norm governing social appropriateness—as with a business man who runs to work when
he is not late or a tutor who crawls round the room sniffing while listening
to an undergraduate essay. Or behaviour may go wrong by being deflected

---

[2] Hamlyn has pointed out to me the use of "the reason for his action" as well as "the
reason why he did it". "The reason for" seems to be similar to "his reason" but to imply
a coincidence between "his reason" and "the reason why he did it". I am not here
concerned with the use of "reason" in the context of *justification* as when we say that *a*
reason for giving up smoking is that it causes lung cancer. "His reason" and "the reason
for" can be used in contexts both of justification and of explanation. Needless to say "the
reason why he did it" is reserved for contexts of explanation with which I am here
concerned.

towards a peculiar goal as with a married man who suddenly makes an advance to a choir boy. In such cases it is as if the man suffers something rather than does something. It is because things seem to be happening to him that it is appropriate to ask what made, drove, or possessed him to do that. The appropriate answer in such cases may be in terms of a causal theory.

These cases of particular goings on which look like breakdowns of action are very similar to a whole class of general activities which seem to have no point or a very odd point—dreams, hallucinations, obsessions, anxieties and perversions. In such cases the Greeks suggested that the gods intervene and take possession of the individual's mind. Very often recourse is made to crude physiological explanations. It was not till the advent of Freud that any systematic explanation of such goings-on was offered in psychological terms. Indeed Freud claimed in 1913 that the main contribution of psycho-analysis to general psychology was to link together and to give psychological explanations for happenings which had previously been left to physiology or to folk-lore. Many have claimed that Freud, by reclaiming these phenomena for psychology, was in fact extending the model of purposive rule-following behaviour to cover the unconscious. He showed, it is argued, that we have reasons for acts which were previously only explained in terms of causes. I shall argue later that this thesis is mistaken. Freud showed, perhaps, that the concept of 'wish' has a wider application than was previously thought. But his account of the working of the primary processes creaks with causality. In maintaining that in the unconscious there is no sense of causal or logical connexion he was *ipso facto* denying that the model of 'his reason', implying norms of efficiency and social appropriateness, was relevant. Freud, I shall argue, provides the classic case of giving quasi-causal explanations where causal explanations seem *prima facie* appropriate.

I shall also argue that Freud in fact only intended to explain by reference to unconscious mental processes cases where the purposive rule-following model breaks down or is inappropriate. He did not think—and often explicitly denied—that this sort of explanation can be appropriately given for everything—for cases where a man acts as well as for cases where something happens to a man. In this respect Freud was, from the point of view of my argument, on the side of the angels. For my case is not simply that causal explanations are otiose when we know the point of a person's action in that, life being short and time limited, we no longer feel inclined to ask 'why' once we have accommodated a piece of behaviour within the rule-following purposive model. It is also that if we are in fact confronted with a case of a genuine action (i.e. an act of doing something as opposed to suffering something), then causal explanations are *ipso facto* inappropriate as sufficient explanations. Indeed they may rule out rule-following purposive explanations. To ask what made Jones do something is at least to suggest that he had no good reason for doing it. Similarly to ascribe a point to his action is *ipso facto* to deny that it can be *sufficiently explained* in terms of causes, though, of course, there will be many causes in the sense of *necessary* conditions. A story can always be told about the underlying mechanisms; but this does not add up to a sufficient explanation, if it is an action that has to be explained.

To give a causal *explanation* of an event involves at least showing that other conditions being presumed unchanged a change in one variable is a *sufficient* condition for a change in another. In the mechanical conception of 'cause' it is also demanded that there should be spatial and temporal contiguity between the movements involved. Now the trouble about giving this sort of explanation of human actions is that we can never specify an action exhaustively in terms of movements of the body or within the body. It is therefore impossible to state sufficient conditions in terms of antecedent movements which may vary concomitantly with subsequent movements. 'Signing a contract', for instance, is a typical example of a human action. The movements involved are grouped together because they are seen by the agent to be efficient and appropriate means to an end. But it would be impossible to stipulate exhaustively what the movements *must* be. For if this is a case of a human action the agent must be presumed to be intelligent and he will, accordingly, vary his movements in a great variety of ways. He may hold the pen slightly differently, vary the size of his writing according to the space available, and so on, depending on the sort of ink, paper, and pen available. But provided that he produces a signature which confirms to rough and ready criteria—e.g., it must not be typed—more or less *any* movements will do. I suppose he could sign a contract by holding the pen between his toes. A very general range of movements could perhaps be specified, but no specific movements of the muscles, limbs, or nervous system, which *must* occur before it would be conceded that a contract had been signed. This is tantamount to saying that the concept of an action is inseparable from that of intelligence; for part of what we mean by 'intelligence' is the ability to vary movements relative to a goal in a way which is appropriate to changes in the situation necessary to define it as a goal and in the conditions relevant to attaining it. So we could never give a sufficient explanation of an action in causal terms because we could never stipulate the movements which would have to count as dependent variables. A precise functional relationship could never be established. Of course, just as we could stipulate a general range of movements necessary to define signing a contract, so also we could lay down certain very general *necessary* conditions. We could, for instance, say that a man could not sign a contract unless he had a brain and nervous system. Such physiological knowledge *might* enable us to predict *bodily movements*. And *if* we had bridging laws to correlate such physiological findings with descriptions of actions we might *indirectly predict* actions. But we would *first* have to grasp concepts connected with action like 'knowing what we are doing' and 'grasp of means to an end'. As such concepts have no application at the level of mere movement, such predictions would not count as sufficient *explanations* of *actions*.

Furthermore, as I have already argued, general standards or rules are implicit in the concept of an action. We can therefore say that a man is doing something efficiently, correctly, and so on, if he knowingly varies what he does in accordance with changes in the situation conventionally singled out as the goal and the conditions perceived as relevant to attaining it. It only makes sense to talk of actions in this way, not of cases where something happens to a man. A man's action may break down because of a causal condition like a lesion in his brain. But all that can be said of such causal conditions is that they just occur. Movements *qua* movements are neither intelligent, efficient, nor correct. They only become so in the context of an action. There cannot therefore be a sufficient explanation of actions in causal terms because, as Popper has put it, there is a logical gulf between nature and convention. Statements implying norms and standards cannot be deduced from statements about mere movements which have no such normative implications. The contention that man is a rule-following animal must, if taken seriously, entail that the transition from nature to convention occurs whenever we try to give a sufficient explanation of human actions in causal terms. There is, however, no objection to such explanations of what *happens* to a man; for happenings cannot be characterized as intelligent or unintelligent, correct or incorrect, efficient or inefficient. *Prima facie* they are just occurrences. Perhaps Freud showed that some lapses and breakdowns may not be *just* occurrences. But this is another story. The point is that there is a *prima facie* case for treating them as such.

To make explicit the implications of my thesis for psychological theories: If the question is 'Why did Jones walk across the road?' a *sufficient* explanation can only be given in terms of the rule-following purposive model—if this is a case of an action rather than of something happening to him. Answers in terms of causal concepts like 'receptor impulses' and 'colourless movement', are either not explanations because they state not sufficient but only necessary conditions, or they are ways of denying that what has to be explained is a human action. If we ask 'Why did Jones *jump* while he was crossing the road?' it might be appropriate to say 'because of a twinge in his stomach' or 'because a car back-fired'. The stimulus-response sort of model would perhaps be appropriate and the causal type of explanation in terms of internal or external stimulation might be sufficient because the assumption might be that Jones was suffering something rather than performing an action. This sort of jump would then be quite different from the jump he might perform while competing in an athletic contest.

This is not to deny that causal explanations are *relevant* to human actions. It is only to deny that they are sufficient explanations of them. Causal theories have at least three jobs to do in this context. Firstly they can state *necessary* conditions for human actions to occur. Hebb's physiological speculations, for instance, might well provide a sketch of a typical class of necessary conditions. But this does not mean that such speculations *explain* human actions. Secondly, as a corollary, they could show that some individual differences in performance are dependent on slight differences in such necessary conditions. Hebb's hypothesis of the relationship between the size of the association areas of the brain and the possibility of late learning would be such a hypothesis. Thirdly such theories could be used to give *sufficient* conditions for breakdowns in performance, as in the case of brain lesions, by indicating a necessary condition which was absent. Alternatively lapses and breakdowns could be explained by the postulation of special disrupting conditions—e.g. Freud's theory of the unconscious wish.

(d) End-State Explanations

There are, of course, all sorts of higher level questions which can be asked about human actions, most of which are irrelevant to psychology in general and theories of motivation in particular. Questions, for instance, can be raised about the conventions in accordance with which a man acts or which determine his goals. We can ask why Jones is mean or why he eats fish. The way it would be answered would depend on the context. It might be answered in terms of a rule-following type of explanation like 'because he is a Scotsman' or 'because he is a Roman Catholic'. This would assume some *established set of norms* and a system of training for handing them on. It would be radically different from the explanation 'because he is an anal character' or 'because he is an oral character'. For these explanations would presuppose that Jones was in some way a deviant from the norm of the circle in which he had been trained. It would state special conditions in his upbringing which occasioned his deviation. Whether or not such explanations, which presuppose fixation at certain periods of development, are causal or not, will have to be considered later.

Another way of answering the question 'Why does Jones eat fish?' would be to state in a tough-minded way 'because he likes it', or 'because it satisfies him'. This could be simply an impatient way of terminating the discussion or it could be an answer to the even more general question 'Why does a man eat anything?' At a common-sense level this is a very odd question; for 'a man must eat' is regarded as a decisive way of terminating a discussion. If pressed still further common-sense might reach rock-bottom with the truism that a man would die if he did not eat. The implication is the Hobbesian axiom that every man is afraid of death and that it makes no further sense to ask 'why?'

A variant on this type of answer is the assertion that a man needs food, which is very much like saying that a man *must* eat. For, at a common-sense level, the term 'need' is mainly normative. It prescribes one of a set of standard goals. It usually functions as a diagnostic term with remedial implications. It implies that something is wrong with a person if certain conditions are absent. We say things like 'The trouble with Jones is that he needs a wife' or 'Every child needs at least ten hours sleep.' The implication is that there is a state of affairs the absence of which is or is likely to be damaging to the individual in question. The individual, like a patient, may well be unaware of what this state of affairs is. Indeed, when we say that a person needs something, we are often indicating a discrepancy between what he actually does and what he ought to be doing. In other words the notion of 'need' in ordinary language is seldom *explanatory*. It is used to point out what a person ought to be doing rather than to explain what he is doing. It would only be an observer grossly over-sophisticated by Freudian theory who would say of a man leaping around in a Morris ring that old Jones obviously needs a woman, and who would think that he had *explained* his performance by pointing to the reality beneath the appearances. Reference to needs implies a standard pattern of prescribed goals; but it does not explain actions by reference to them. Whereas causal theories explain deviations from a norm, reference to needs prescribes the norms whose absence is thought to be injurious. It redirects attention to the accepted content of the rule-following purposive model.

Often we hear of 'basic needs' and 'need-reduction' in the context of explanatory theories in psychology. What has happened here is that conditions whose absence is thought to occasion injury have been interpreted in terms of a biological or physiological model. The answer to questions like 'Why does a man eat?' is provided by picturing an organism whose activities are directed towards survival or the preservation of equilibrium or some other such desirable and completely general end-state. This, of course, has to be broken down by giving an account of the particular conditions whose absence is thought to be injurious. Homeostasis, for instance, has to be described in terms of *particular* states like the temperature of the body and the level of blood-sugar. And, no doubt, postulating such conditions restored by various movements of the body in part explains them if the conditions restored are not part of what is meant by the description given to the movements. Sweating, for instance, may be a method of bringing about an optimum level of temperature in the body; but restoration of this level is not part of what is meant when we call certain movements 'sweating'. So saying that people sweat because it lowers the temperature of the body is explanatory.

But all too often this type of functional or end-state explanation is redescriptive rather than explanatory—expecially when it is used for voluntary rather than for involuntary movements. This is when the conditions restored are part of what is meant by the activity to be explained. For instance it might be said that people dominate others because it reduces a need in them to do so. But what is the condition restored apart from that of the presence of others being dominated? What in this type of case is the equivalent of the temperature level which is restored by sweating? The homeostatic model of explanation is retained; but in the absence of specific states required to define what constitutes the equilibrium, it becomes entirely metaphysical. It is true that recourse is made to vague states of quiescence which the activity of dominating or acquiring money is alleged to bring about. But as there are no rules for identifying such states, their explanatory value is nil. Indeed in such cases need-reduction looks like a redescription of goal-seeking in terms which have the normative function of stressing the importance of conventionally prescribed pursuits. It is a justification masquerading as a high-level explanation.

Need-reduction explanations are a particular instance of a very common sort of explanation which will be termed 'explanations in terms of end-states'. For supervenient states of quiescence and satisfaction abound in psychological theories of motivation. It will probably be found that all such explanations share the logical features revealed in the specific case of need-reduction. These are (*i*) the generalization of a type of explanation that applies properly only to a very limited class of phenomena and (*ii*) the use of a term with highly general normative implications which obscure its emptiness as a highly general *explanation*.

The term 'end-state' has been chosen advisedly rather than the term 'end'. For one of the first things to be pointed out about these highly general sorts of explanation is that the ends postulated are not ends in the sense of 'end' or 'goal' employed in the purposive rule-following model. They are not—or should not be—postulated as answers to questions like 'Why did Jones walk across the road?' but as answers to questions like 'Why does a man eat?' or 'Why does a man smoke?'. They are therefore inappropriate as answers to lower order questions. For a man does not eat *in order to* reduce a need or relieve a tension. By eating, so the theories say, he in fact brings about such an end-state. Such explanations then do not give a man's reason for eating but the reason why he eats. But they differ from other cases of directed behaviour where we contrast *his* reason with *the* reason. For in other such cases—e.g. explanations in terms of unconscious wishes—we imply a goal *of the same sort* as that implied in *his* reason explanations, but we add the rider that the man does not envisage this goal as a conscious objective. We say, for instance, that *the* reason why he was unintentionally rude to his employer was because of his unconscious desire to injure a man like his father. But end-states are not goals like hurting a man, marrying a girl, or becoming Prime Minister. They are more mysterious states of quiescence, satisfaction, tension-reduction, and so on.

The theoretical interest of these types of explanation is that they are regarded as explaining *all* behaviour, whether of the rule-following sort or where there is a breakdown in behaviour and a cause is assigned, or when an activity—like dreaming—is of a sort such that it makes no sense to say 'What is the point of it?' Freud's pleasure principle is a good example; for he claimed

> In the theory of psycho-analysis we have no hesitation in assuming that the course taken by mental events is automatically regulated by the pleasure principle. We believe, that is to say, that the course of these events is invariably set in motion by an unpleasurable tension, and that it takes a direction such that its final outcome coincides with a lowering of that tension—that is with an avoidance of unpleasure or a production of pleasure.

Some such homeostatic principle is so common in modern psychology that it has reached the standard text-books. To quote a typical case—Stagner and Karwoski:

> The organism is endowed with an automatic equilibrium maintaining tendency which helps to preserve existence in the face of many kinds of environmental obstacles and difficulties.

It is assumed that everything we do can somehow be subsumed under this very general principle. This assumption is so widespread and is so important to the claim that an over-all theory of motivation can be developed, that much more must be said about its appropriateness.

The assumption, to repeat, is that the reason why men eat, sleep, eliminate, and so on, is that achieving such goals relieves tension, restores equilibrium, produces satisfaction, and other such variations on a theme. This assumption is usually extended to cover all goal-directed behaviour—the pursuit of riches and foxes as well as the pursuit of water and women.

I will defer for a moment the problem of whether the postulation of such end-states is *ever* explanatory. For the issue is whether it *always* is. And this seems plainly false. For many goal-directed actions like posting letters, travelling to work, and passing the salt to one's neighbour do not seem invariably to be followed by such end-states. Indeed usually when we *say* that we get satisfaction or pleasure from doing something, we are not referring to some extra subsequent state of mind which we have become aware of by introspection. Rather we are saying two general sorts of things about it. In the first place we are saying that we were not bored, irritated, or distracted while we did it. We put our mind to the job in hand and concentrated on bringing about the required state of affairs. We were absorbed.

The reference to satisfaction is not, in this case, an *explanation* of the pursuit of a goal, but a way of emphasizing that it really was a goal in the sense that our movements flowed towards it in an unimpeded and co-ordinated manner. Secondly the reference to satisfaction can be a way of stressing that the activity in question was done for its own sake and not as a means to something else. If a husband insists doggedly that he does the gardening because of the satisfaction he gets out of it he may simply be denying that he does it in order to help his wife with the housekeeping. He is not claiming necessarily that he glows and enters into a beatific state when the peas have been staked and the lawn cut. In other words, just as reference to need-reduction is a way of emphasizing the importance of some goals for the avoidance of injury, so reference to satisfaction is often a way of singling out others which are worth pursuing for their own sake. In a context of justification 'Because it satisfies him' is as final as 'Because he needs it'. What follows the 'because' are different facets of the bed-rock of justification. Psychologists have mistaken this bed-rock of justification for the apex of explanation.

Is it to be assumed, then, that reference to such end-states is *never* explanatory? All we have shown is that it is not *always* so. Clearly some such reference is reasonable in answering certain questions about the *body*, as was seen in the case of need-reduction. Cannon, in his *Wisdom of the Body*, was indicating the evidence for bodily mechanisms of regulation and adjustment. The transition to using this type of explanation for voluntary actions rather than for the automatic adjustments of the body, comes about because it is suggested, e.g. by Freud—that types of stimulation brought about by departures from these optimum levels or end-states can only be mitigated by contact with the environment. The baby's hunger, for instance, is relieved only by contact with its mother's breast or with some equivalent source of supply. Its movements are at first random; but eventually, through the association of relief of tension with contact with the breast, a directed tendency develops which is activated by the stimulation of hunger. It is therefore concluded, probably erroneously, that whenever we find a case of such directed behaviour, it must be sandwiched in between tension and the reduction of tension. Yet even if such tension-reduction were an explanation of *acquiring* such a directed disposition, it would not follow that it also explained its *activation* later on after it had been acquired.

It is, however, significant that the sort of phenomena which have seemed to psychologists to require some sort of an end-state explanation, are those connected with learning and experimental types of situation. Thorndike's Law of Effect, for instance, postulated that successful responses were stamped in because of the satisfaction associated with contact with the correct goal. The pleasure-principle could well be vacuous as an all-embracing postulate, as envisaged by Freud; but it might well be part of the explanation of why certain directed sequences of behaviour are *learnt*. And surely it would here coincide with the use of 'feeling of satisfaction' in ordinary speech which cannot be analysed purely in the way described above. For in exploratory and experimental stages of an activity, before a habit has been formed, or when we are confronted with obstacles that impede habitual routines, we do speak of a feeling of satisfaction or a sense of achievement. If we are learning to swim or to play golf or to walk after a long illness, we do get a feeling of satisfaction or sense of achievement on attaining the goal. This is not exactly a supervenient state extra to attaining the goal. The feeling of satisfaction when one hits a good drive is different from that attendant on hitting a good niblick shot; and both are quite different from that attendant on writing a good sentence or doing a good dive. In the same way a hungry man gets satisfaction from eating a beef-steak; but the type of satisfaction is specific to the beef-steak. The end-states are not exactly supervenient; rather they are descriptions of the attainment of certain sorts of goals under certain sorts of conditions. So in some cases which approximate in varying degrees to a learning, experimental or obstacle type of situation, the postulated sequence of tension, persistent and directed behaviour, and relief of tension may well occur. But as most of our days are spent in carrying out habits and routines, they do not occur whenever there is a case of directed behaviour. Indeed part of what we want to deny when we call a piece of behaviour a habit is that it is a case of the varied, experimental, obstacle-ridden type of behaviour.

My point is therefore not that the reduction of tension type of explanation is never relevant, but that it explains the directedness of behaviour only under certain limited sorts of conditions. My objection to it is that it is so often used as an all-inclusive principle. For most psychological theories seem to accommodate their purposive or causal explanations under some such homeostatic postulate. The quasi-causal concept of drive, for instance, is usually subsumed under the general postulate of homeostasis; so is the purposive concept of the Freudian wish. But the relationship between these types of explanation and a homeostatic postulate is not of this deductive sort. It seems, to say the least of it, misleading to assimilate dreams and playing chess to shivering and sweating by maintaining that they are all particular cases of the maintenance of equilibrium—especially when the theorists, like Stagner and Karwoski, have to go on to distinguish static from dynamic homeostasis to make the suggestion even sound plausible! The quest for an all-inclusive explanation has led repeatedly to the obscuring of important differences by stressing trivial and highly speculative similarities.

.   .   .

6

ACTIONS, REASONS, AND CAUSES

Donald Davidson

What is the relation between a reason and an action when the reason explains the action by giving the agent's reason for doing what he did? We may call such explanations *rationalizations*, and say that the reason *rationalizes* the action.

In this paper I want to defend the ancient—and common-sense—position that rationalization is a species of ordinary causal explanation. The defense no doubt requires some redeployment, but not more or less complete abandonment of the position, as urged by many recent writers.[1]

I

A reason rationalizes an action only if it leads us to see something the agent saw, or thought he saw, in his action—some feature, consequence, or aspect of the action the agent wanted, desired, prized, held dear, thought dutiful, beneficial, obligatory, or agreeable. We cannot explain why someone did what he did simply by saying the particular action appealed to him; we must indicate what it was about the action that appealed. Whenever someone does something for a reason, therefore, he can be characterized as (*a*) having some sort of pro attitude toward actions of a certain kind, and (*b*) believing (or knowing, perceiving, noticing, remembering) that his action is of that kind. Under (*a*) are to be included desires, wantings, urges, promptings, and a great variety of moral views, aesthetic principles, economic prejudices, social conventions, and public and private goals and values in so far as these

---

Donald Davidson, "Actions, Reasons, and Causes," *The Journal of Philosophy*, LX (1963), 685–700. Reprinted by permission of the publisher and the author.

[1] Some examples: G. E. M. Anscombe, *Intention*, Oxford, 1959; Stuart Hampshire, *Thought and Action*, London, 1959; H. L. A. Hart and A. M. Honoré, *Causation in the Law*, Oxford, 1959; William Dray, *Laws and Explanation in History*, Oxford, 1957; and most of the books in the series edited by R. F. Holland, *Studies in Philosophical Psychology*, including Anthony Kenny, *Action, Emotion and Will*, London, 1963, and A. I. Melden, *Free Action*, London, 1961. Page references in parentheses will all be to these works.

can be interpreted as attitudes of an agent directed toward actions of a certain kind. The word 'attitude' does yeoman service here, for it must cover not only permanent character traits that show themselves in a lifetime of behavior, like love of children or a taste for loud company, but also the most passing fancy that prompts a unique action, like a sudden desire to touch a woman's elbow. In general, pro attitudes must not be taken for convictions, however temporary, that every action of a certain kind ought to be performed, is worth performing, or is, all things considered, desirable. On the contrary, a man may all his life have a yen, say, to drink a can of paint, without ever, even at the moment he yields, believing it would be worth doing.

Giving the reason why an agent did something is often a matter of naming the pro attitude (*a*) or the related belief (*b*) or both; let me call this pair the *primary reason* why the agent performed the action. Now it is possible to reformulate the claim that rationalizations are causal explanations, and give structure to the argument as well, by stating two theses about primary reasons:

1. For us to understand how a reason of any kind rationalizes an action it is necessary and sufficient that we see, at least in essential outline, how to construct a primary reason.
2. The primary reason for an action is its cause.

I shall argue for these points in turn.

II

I flip the switch, turn on the light, and illuminate the room. Unbeknownst to me I also alert a prowler to the fact that I am home. Here I do not do four things, but only one, of which four descriptions have been given.[2] I flipped the switch because I wanted to turn on the light, and by saying I wanted to turn on the light I explain (give my reason for, rationalize) the flipping. But I do not, by giving this reason, rationalize my alerting of the prowler nor my illuminating of the room. Since reasons may rationalize what someone does when it is described in one way and not when it is described in another, we cannot treat what was done simply as a term in sentences like 'My reason

---

[2] We would not call my unintentional alerting of the prowler an action, but it should not be inferred from this that alerting the prowler is therefore something different from flipping the switch, say just its consequence. Actions, performances, and events not involving intention are alike in that they are often referred to or defined partly in terms of some terminal stage, outcome, or consequence.

The word 'action' does not very often occur in ordinary speech, and when it does it is usually reserved for fairly portentous occasions. I follow a useful philosophical practice in calling anything an agent does intentionally an action, including intentional omissions. What is really needed is some suitably generic term to bridge the following gap: suppose '*A*' is a description of an action, '*B*' is a description of something done voluntarily, though not intentionally, and '*C*' is a description of something done involuntarily and unintentionally; finally, suppose $A = B = C$. Then *A*, *B*, and *C* are the same—what? 'Action', 'event', 'thing done', each have, at least in some contexts, a strange ring when coupled with the wrong sort of description. Only the question "Why did you (he) do *A*?" has the true generality required. Obviously, the problem is greatly aggravated if we assume, as Melden does (*Free Action*, 85), that an action ("raising one's arm") can be identical with a bodily movement ("one's arm going up").

for flipping the switch was that I wanted to turn on the light'; otherwise we would be forced to conclude, from the fact that flipping the switch was identical with alerting the prowler, that my reason for alerting the prowler was that I wanted to turn on the light. Let us mark this quasi-intensional[3] character of action descriptions in rationalizations by stating a bit more precisely a necessary condition for primary reasons:

C1. *R* is a primary reason why an agent performed the action *A* under the description *d* only if *R* consists of a pro attitude of the agent toward actions with a certain property, and a belief of the agent that *A*, under the description *d*, has that property.

How can my wanting to turn on the light be (part of) a primary reason, since it appears to lack the required element of generality? We may be taken in by the verbal parallel between 'I turned on the light' and 'I wanted to turn on the light'. The first clearly refers to a particular event, so we conclude that the second has this same event as its object. Of course it is obvious that the event of my turning on the light can't be referred to in the same way by both sentences, since the existence of the event is required by the truth of 'I turned on the light' but not by the truth of 'I wanted to turn on the light'. If the reference were the same in both cases, the second sentence would entail the first; but in fact the sentences are logically independent. What is less obvious, at least until we attend to it, is that the event whose occurrence makes 'I turned on the light' true cannot be called the object, however intensional, of 'I wanted to turn on the light'. If I turned on the light, then I must have done it at a precise moment, in a particular way—every detail is fixed. But it makes no sense to demand that my want be directed at an action performed at any one moment or done in some unique manner. Any one of an indefinitely large number of actions would satisfy the want, and can be considered equally eligible as its object. Wants and desires often are trained on physical objects. However, 'I want that gold watch in the window' is not a primary reason, and explains why I went into the store only because it suggests a primary reason—for example, that I wanted to buy the watch.

Because 'I wanted to turn on the light' and 'I turned on the light' are logically independent, the first can be used to give a reason why the second is true. Such a reason gives minimal information: it implies that the action was intentional, and wanting tends to exclude some other pro attitudes, such as a sense of duty or obligation. But the exclusion depends very much on the action and the context of explanation. Wanting seems pallid beside lusting, but it would be odd to deny that someone who lusted after a woman or a cup of coffee wanted her or it. It is not unnatural, in fact, to treat wanting as a genus including all pro attitudes as species. When we do this and when we know some action is intentional, it is empty to add that the agent wanted to do it. In such cases, it is easy to answer the question 'Why did you do it?' with 'For no reason', meaning not that there is no reason but that there is no *further* reason, no reason that cannot be inferred from the fact that

---

3 "Quasi-intensional" because, besides its intensional aspect, the description of the action must also refer in rationalizations; otherwise it could be true that an action was done for a certain reason and yet the action not have been performed. Compare 'the author of *Waverley*' in 'George IV knew the author of *Waverley* wrote *Waverley*'.

the action was done intentionally; no reason, in other words, besides wanting to do it. This last point is not essential to the present argument, but it is of interest because it defends the possibility of defining an intentional action as one done for a reason.

A primary reason consists of a belief and an attitude, but it is generally otiose to mention both. If you tell me you are easing the jib because you think that will stop the main from backing, I don't need to be told that you want to stop the main from backing; and if you say you are biting your thumb at me because you want to insult me, there is no point in adding that you think that by biting your thumb at me you will insult me. Similarly, many explanations of actions in terms of reasons that are not primary do not require mention of the primary reason to complete the story. If I say I am pulling weeds because I want a beautiful lawn, it would be fatuous to eke out the account with 'And so I see something desirable in any action that does, or has a good chance of, making the lawn beautiful'. Why insist that there is any *step*, logical or psychological, in the transfer of desire from an end that is not an action to the actions one conceives as means? It serves the argument as well that the desired end explains the action only if what are believed by the agent to be means are desired.

Fortunately, it is not necessary to classify and analyze the many varieties of emotions, sentiments, moods, motives, passions, and hungers whose mention may answer the question 'Why did you do it?' in order to see how, when such mention rationalizes the action, a primary reason is involved. Claustrophobia gives a man's reason for leaving a cocktail party because we know people want to avoid, escape from, be safe from, put distance between themselves and what they fear. Jealousy is the motive in a poisoning because, among other things, the poisoner believes his action will harm his rival, remove the cause of his agony, or redress an injustice, and these are the sorts of things a jealous man wants to do. When we learn a man cheated his son out of greed, we do not necessarily know what the primary reason was, but we know there was one, and its general nature. Ryle analyzes 'he boasted from vanity' into "he boasted on meeting the stranger and his doing so satisfies the lawlike proposition that whenever he finds a chance of securing the admiration and envy of others, he does whatever he thinks will produce this admiration and envy" (*The Concept of Mind*, 89). This analysis is often, and perhaps justly, criticized on the ground that a man may boast from vanity just once. But if Ryle's boaster did what he did from vanity, then something entailed by Ryle's analysis is true: the boaster wanted to secure the admiration and envy of others, and he believed that his action would produce this admiration and envy; true or false, Ryle's analysis does not dispense with primary reasons, but depends upon them.

To know a primary reason why someone acted as he did is to know an intention with which the action was done. If I turn left at the fork because I want to get to Katmandu, my intention in turning left is to get to Katmandu. But to know the intention is not necessarily to know the primary reason in full detail. If James goes to church with the intention of pleasing his mother, then he must have some pro attitude toward pleasing his mother, but it needs more information to tell whether his reason is that he enjoys pleasing his mother, or thinks it right, his duty, or an obligation. The expression 'the intention with which James went to church' has the outward form of a description, but in fact it is syncategorematic and cannot be taken to refer to an entity, state, disposition, or event. Its function in context is to generate new descriptions of actions in terms of their reasons; thus 'James went to church with the intention of pleasing his mother' yields a new, and fuller, description of the action described in 'James went to church'. Essentially the same process goes on when I answer the question 'Why are you bobbing around that way?' with 'I'm knitting, weaving, exercising, sculling, cuddling, training fleas'.

Straight description of an intended result often explains an action better than stating that the result was intended or desired. 'It will soothe your nerves' explains why I pour you a shot as efficiently as 'I want to do something to soothe your nerves', since the first in the context of explanation implies the second; but the first does better, because, if it is true, the facts will justify my choice of action. Because justifying and explaining an action so often go hand in hand, we frequently indicate the primary reason for an action by making a claim which, if true, would also verify, vindicate, or support the relevant belief or attitude of the agent. 'I knew I ought to return it', 'The paper said it was going to snow', 'You stepped on *my* toes', all, in appropriate reason-giving contexts, perform this familiar dual function.

The justifying role of a reason, given this interpretation, depends upon the explanatory role, but the converse does not hold. Your stepping on my toes neither explains nor justifies my stepping on your toes unless I believe you stepped on my toes, but the belief alone, true or false, explains my action.

III

In the light of a primary reason, an action is revealed as coherent with certain traits, long- or short-termed, characteristic or not, of the agent, and the agent is shown in his role of Rational Animal. Corresponding to the belief and attitude of a primary reason for an action, we can always construct (with a little ingenuity) the premises of a syllogism from which it follows that the action has some (as Miss Anscombe calls it) "desirability characteristic."[4] Thus there is a certain irreducible—though somewhat anemic—sense in which every rationalization justifies: from the agent's point of view there was, when he acted, something to be said for the action.

Noting that nonteleological causal explanations do not display the element of justification provided by reasons, some philosophers have concluded that the concept of cause that applies elsewhere cannot apply to the relation between reasons and actions, and that the pattern of justification provides, in the case of reasons, the required explanation. But suppose we grant that reasons alone justify in explaining actions; it does not follow that the

[4] Miss Anscombe denies that the practical syllogism is deductive. This she does partly because she thinks of the practical syllogism, as Aristotle does, as corresponding to a piece of practical reasoning (whereas for me it is only part of the analysis of the concept of a reason with which someone acted), and therefore she is bound, again following Aristotle, to think of the conclusion of a practical syllogism as corresponding to a judgment, not merely that the action has a desirable characteristic, but that the action is desirable (reasonable, worth doing, etc.).

explanation is not also—and necessarily—causal. Indeed our first condition for primary reasons (C1) is designed to help set rationalizations apart from other sorts of explanation. If rationalization is, as I want to argue, a species of causal explanation, then justification, in the sense given by C1, is at least one differentiating property. How about the other claim: that justifying is a kind of explaining, so that the ordinary notion of cause need not be brought in? Here it is necessary to decide what is being included under justification. Perhaps it means only what is given by C1: that the agent has certain beliefs and attitudes in the light of which the action is reasonable. But then something essential has certainly been left out, for a person can have a reason for an action, and perform the action, and yet this reason not be the reason why he did it. Central to the relation between a reason and an action it explains is the idea that the agent performed the action *because* he had the reason. Of course, we can include this idea too in justification; but then the notion of justification becomes as dark as the notion of reason until we can account for the force of that 'because'.

When we ask why someone acted as he did, we want to be provided with an interpretation. His behavior seems strange, alien, outré, pointless, out of character, disconnected; or perhaps we cannot even recognize an action in it. When we learn his reason, we have an interpretation, a new description of what he did which fits it into a familiar picture. The picture certainly includes some of the agent's beliefs and attitudes; perhaps also goals, ends, principles, general character traits, virtues or vices. Beyond this, the re-description of an action afforded by a reason may place the action in a wider social, economic, linguistic, or evaluative context. To learn, through learning the reason, that the agent conceived his action as a lie, a repayment of a debt, an insult, the fulfillment of an avuncular obligation, or a knight's gambit is to grasp the point of the action in its setting of rules, practices, conventions, and expectations.

Remarks like these, inspired by the later Wittgenstein, have been elaborated with subtlety and insight by a number of philosophers. And there is no denying that this is true: when we explain an action, by giving the reason, we do redescribe the action; redescribing the action gives the action a place in a pattern, and in this way the action is explained. Here it is tempting to draw two conclusions that do not follow. First, we can't infer, from the fact that giving reasons merely redescribes the action and that causes are separate from effects, that therefore reasons are not causes. Reasons, being beliefs and attitudes, are certainly not identical with actions; but, more important, events are often redescribed in terms of their causes. (Suppose someone was injured. We could redescribe this event "in terms of a cause" by saying he was burned.) Second, it is an error to think that, because placing the action in a larger pattern explains it, therefore we now understand the sort of explanation involved. Talk of patterns and contexts does not answer the question of how reasons explain actions, since the relevant pattern or context contains both reason and action. One way we can explain an event is by placing it in the context of its cause; cause and effect form the sort of pattern that explains the effect, in a sense of 'explain' that we understand as well as any. If reason and action illustrate a different pattern of explanation, that pattern must be identified.

Let me urge the point in connection with an example of Melden's. A man driving an automobile raises his arm in order to signal. His intention, to signal, explains his action, raising his arm, by redescribing it as signaling. What is the pattern that explains the action? Is it the familiar pattern of an action done for a reason? Then it does indeed explain the action, but only because it assumes the relation of reason and action that we want to analyze. Or is the pattern rather this: the man is driving, he is approaching a turn; he knows he ought to signal; he knows how to signal, by raising his arm. And now, in this context, he raises his arm. Perhaps, as Melden suggests, if all this happens, he does signal. And the explanation would then be this: if, under these conditions, a man raises his arm, then he signals. The difficulty is, of course, that this explanation does not touch the question of why he raised his arm. He had a reason to raise his arm, but this has not been shown to be the reason why he did it. If the description 'signaling' explains his action by giving his reason, then the signaling must be intentional; but, on the account just given, it may not be.

If, as Melden claims, causal explanations are "wholly irrelevant to the understanding we seek" of human actions (184) then we are without an analysis of the 'because' in 'He did it because . . .', where we go on to name a reason. Hampshire remarks, of the relation between reasons and action, "In philosophy one ought surely to find this . . . connection altogether mysterious" (166). Hampshire rejects Aristotle's attempt to solve the mystery by introducing the concept of wanting as a causal factor, on the grounds that the resulting theory is too clear and definite to fit all cases and that "There is still no compelling ground for insisting that the word 'want' *must* enter into every full statement of reasons for acting" (168). I agree that the concept of wanting is too narrow, but I have argued that, at least in a vast number of typical cases, some pro attitude must be assumed to be present if a statement of an agent's reasons in acting is to be intelligible. Hampshire does not see how Aristotle's scheme can be appraised as true or false, "for it is not clear what could be the basis of assessment, or what kind of evidence could be decisive" (167). Failing a satisfactory alternative, the best argument for a scheme like Aristotle's is that it alone promises to give an account of the "mysterious connection" between reasons and actions.

IV

In order to turn the first 'and' to 'because' in 'He exercised *and* he wanted to reduce and thought exercise would do it', we must, as the basic move,[5] augment condition C1 with:

C2. A primary reason for an action is its cause.

The considerations in favor of C2 are by now, I hope, obvious; in the remainder of this paper I wish to defend C2 against various lines of attack and, in the process, to clarify the notion of causal explanation involved.

A. The first line of attack is this. Primary reasons consist of attitudes and

---

[5] I say "as the basic move" to cancel the suggestion that C1 and C2 are jointly *sufficient* to define the relation of reasons to the actions they explain. I believe C2 can be strengthened to make C1 and C2 sufficient as well as necessary conditions, but here I am concerned only with the claim that both are, as they stand, necessary.

beliefs, which are states or dispositions, not events; therefore they cannot be causes.

It is easy to reply that states, dispositions, and conditions are frequently named as the causes of events: the bridge collapsed because of a structural defect; the plane crashed on takeoff because the air temperature was abnormally high; the plate broke because it had a crack. This reply does not, however, meet a closely related point. Mention of a causal condition for an event gives a cause only on the assumption that there was also a preceding event. But what is the preceding event that causes an action?

In many cases it is not difficult at all to find events very closely associated with the primary reason. States and dispositions are not events, but the onslaught of a state or disposition is. A desire to hurt your feelings may spring up at the moment you anger me; I may start wanting to eat a melon just when I see one; and beliefs may begin at the moment we notice, perceive, learn, or remember something. Those who have argued that there are no mental events to qualify as causes of actions have often missed the obvious because they have insisted that a mental event be observed or noticed (rather than an observing or a noticing) or that it be like a stab, a qualm, a prick or a quiver, a mysterious prod of conscience or act of the will. Melden, in discussing the driver who signals a turn by raising his arm, challenges those who want to explain actions causally to identify "an event which is common and peculiar to all such cases" (87), perhaps a motive or an intention, anyway "some particular feeling or experience" (95). But of course there is a mental event; at some moment the driver noticed (or thought he noticed) his turn coming up, and that is the moment he signaled. During any continuing activity, like driving or elaborate performance, like swimming the Hellespont, there are more or less fixed purposes, standards, desires, and habits that give direction and form to the entire enterprise, and there is the continuing input of information about what we are doing, about changes in the environment, in terms of which we regulate and adjust our actions. To dignify a driver's awareness that his turn has come by calling it an experience, much less a feeling, is no doubt exaggerated, but whether it deserves a name or not, it had better be the reason why he raises his arm. In this case, and typically, there may not be anything we would call a motive, but if we mention such a general purpose as wanting to get to one's destination safely, it is clear that the motive is not an event. The intention with which the driver raises his arm is also not an event, for it is no thing at all, neither event, attitude, disposition, nor object. Finally, Melden asks the causal theorist to find an event that is common and peculiar to all cases where a man intentionally raises his arm, and this, it must be admitted, cannot be produced. But then neither can a common and unique cause of bridge failures, plane crashes, or plate breakings be produced.

The signaling driver can answer the question 'Why did you raise your arm when you did?', and from the answer we learn the event that caused the action. But can an actor always answer such a question? Sometimes the answer will mention a mental event that does not give a reason: 'Finally I made up my mind'. However, there also seem to be cases of intentional action where we cannot explain at all why we acted when we did. In such cases, explanation in terms of primary reasons parallels the explanation of the collapse of the bridge from a structural defect: we are ignorant of the event

or sequence of events that led up to (caused) the collapse, but we are sure
there was such an event or sequence of events.

B. According to Melden, a cause must be "logically distinct from the
alleged effect" (52); but a reason for an action is not logically distinct from
the action; therefore, reasons are not causes of actions.[6]

One possible form of this argument has already been suggested. Since a
reason makes an action intelligible by redescribing it, we do not have two
events, but only one under different descriptions. Causal relations, however,
demand distinct events.

Someone might be tempted into the mistake of thinking that my flipping
of the switch caused my turning on of the light (in fact it caused the light to
go on). But it does not follow that it is a mistake to take 'My reason for
flipping the switch was that I wanted to turn on the light' as entailing, in
part, 'I flipped the switch, and this action is further describable as having
been caused by my wanting to turn on the light'. To describe an event in
terms of its cause is not to identify the event with its cause, nor does explanation by redescription exclude causal explanation.

The example serves also to refute the claim that we cannot describe the
action without using words that link it to the alleged cause. Here the action
is to be explained under the description: 'my flipping the switch', and the
alleged cause is 'my wanting to turn on the light'. What possible logical
relation is supposed to hold between these phrases? It seems more plausible
to urge a logical link between 'my turning on the light' and 'my wanting to
turn on the light', but even here the link turned out, on inspection, to be
grammatical rather than logical.

In any case there is something very odd in the idea that causal relations are
empirical rather than logical. What can this mean? Surely not that every
true causal statement is empirical. For suppose '*A* caused *B*' is true. Then the
cause of *B* = *A*; so, substituting, we have 'The cause of *B* caused *B*', which is
analytic. The truth of a causal statement depends on *what* events are
described; its status as analytic or synthetic depends on *how* the events are
described. Still, it may be maintained that a reason rationalizes an action only
when the descriptions are appropriately fixed, and the appropriate descriptions are not logically independent.

Suppose that to say a man wanted to turn on the light *meant* that he
would perform any action he believed would accomplish his end. Then the
statement of his primary reason for flipping the switch would entail that he
flipped the switch—"straightway he acts," as Aristotle says. In this case
there would certainly be a logical connection between reason and action, the
same sort of connection as that between 'It's water-soluble and was placed in
water' and 'It dissolved'. Since the implication runs from description of
cause to description of effect but not conversely, naming the cause still gives
information. And, though the point is often overlooked, 'Placing it in water
caused it to dissolve' does not entail 'It's water-soluble'; so the latter has
additional explanatory force. Nevertheless, the explanation would be far
more interesting if, in place of solubility, with its obvious definitional

---

[6] This argument can be found, in one or more versions, in Kenny, Hampshire, and
Melden, as well as in P. Winch, *The Idea of a Social Science*, London, 1958, and R. S.
Peters, *The Concept of Motivation*, London, 1958. In one of its forms, the argument was
of course inspired by Ryle's treatment of motives in *The Concept of Mind*.

connection with the event to be explained, we could refer to some property, say a particular crystalline structure, whose connection with dissolution in water was known only through experiment. Now it is clear why primary reasons like desires and wants do not explain actions in the relatively trivial way solubility explains dissolvings. Solubility, we are assuming, is a pure disposition property: it is defined in terms of a single test. But desires cannot be defined in terms of the actions they may rationalize, even though the relation between desire and action is not simply empirical; there are other, equally essential criteria for desires—their expression in feelings and in actions that they do not rationalize, for example. The person who has a desire (or want or belief) does not normally need criteria at all—he generally knows, even in the absence of any clues available to others, what he wants, desires, and believes. These logical features of primary reasons show that it is not just lack of ingenuity that keeps us from defining them as dispositions to act for these reasons.

C. According to Hume, "we may define a cause to be an object, followed by another, and where all the objects similar to the first are followed by objects similar to the second." But, Hart and Honoré claim, "The statement that one person did something because, for example, another threatened him, carries no implication or covert assertion that if the circumstances were repeated the same action would follow" (52). Hart and Honoré allow that Hume is right in saying that ordinary singular causal statements imply generalizations, but wrong for this very reason in supposing that motives and desires are ordinary causes of actions. In brief, laws are involved essentially in ordinary causal explanations, but not in rationalizations.

It is common to try to meet this argument by suggesting that we do have rough laws connecting reasons and actions, and these can, in theory, be improved. True, threatened people do not always respond in the same way; but we may distinguish between threats and also between agents, in terms of their beliefs and attitudes.

The suggestion is delusive, however, because generalizations connecting reasons and actions are not—and cannot be sharpened into—the kind of law on the basis of which accurate predictions can reliably be made. If we reflect on the way in which reasons determine choice, decision, and behavior, it is easy to see why this is so. What emerges, in the *ex post facto* atmosphere of explanation and justification, as *the* reason frequently was, to the agent at the time of action, one consideration among many, *a* reason. Any serious theory for predicting action on the basis of reasons must find a way of evaluating the relative force of various desires and beliefs in the matrix of decision; it cannot take as its starting point the refinement of what is to be expected from a single desire. The practical syllogism exhausts its role in displaying an action as falling under one reason; so it cannot be subtilized into a reconstruction of practical reasoning, which involves the weighing of competing reasons. The practical syllogism provides a model neither for a predictive science of action nor for a normative account of evaluative reasoning.

Ignorance of competent predictive laws does not inhibit valid causal explanation, or few causal explanations could be made. I am certain the window broke because it was struck by a rock—I saw it all happen; but I am not (is anyone?) in command of laws on the basis of which I can predict what blows will break which windows. A generalization like 'Windows are fragile, and fragile things tend to break when struck hard enough, other conditions being right' is not a predictive law in the rough—the predictive law, if we had it, would be quantitative and would use very different concepts. The generalization, like our generalizations about behavior, serves a different function: it provides evidence for the existence of a causal law covering the case at hand.

We are usually far more certain of a singular causal connection than we are of any causal law governing the case; does this show that Hume was wrong in claiming that singular causal statements entail laws? Not necessarily, for Hume's claim, as quoted above, is ambiguous. It may mean that '*A* caused *B*' entails some particular law involving the predicates used in the descriptions '*A*' and '*B*', or it may mean that '*A* caused *B*' entails that there exists a causal law instantiated by some true descriptions of *A* and *B*.[7] Obviously, both versions of Hume's doctrine give a sense to the claim that singular causal statements entail laws, and both sustain the view that causal explanations "involve laws." But the second version is far weaker, in that no particular law is entailed by a singular causal claim, and a singular causal claim can be defended, if it needs defense, without defending any law. Only the second version of Hume's doctrine can be made to fit with most causal explanations; it suits rationalizations equally well.

The most primitive explanation of an event gives its cause; more elaborate explanations may tell more of the story, or defend the singular causal claim by producing a relevant law or by giving reasons for believing such exists. But it is an error to think no explanation has been given until a law has been produced. Linked with these errors is the idea that singular causal statements necessarily indicate, by the concepts they employ, the concepts that will occur in the entailed law. Suppose a hurricane, which is reported on page 5 of Tuesday's *Times*, causes a catastrophe, which is reported on page 13 of Wednesday's *Tribune*. Then the event reported on page 5 of Tuesday's *Times* caused the event reported on page 13 of Wednesday's *Tribune*. Should we look for a law relating events of these *kinds?* It is only slightly less ridiculous to look for a law relating hurricanes and catastrophes. The laws needed to predict the catastrophe with precision would, of course, have no use for concepts like hurricane and catastrophe. The trouble with predicting the weather is that the descriptions under which events interest us—'a cool, cloudy day with rain in the afternoon'—have only remote connections with the concepts employed by the more precise known laws.

The laws whose existence is required if reasons are causes of actions do not, we may be sure, deal in the concepts in which rationalizations must deal. If the causes of a class of events (actions) fall in a certain class (reasons) and there is a law to back each singular causal statement, it does not follow that there is any law connecting events classified as reasons with

---

[7] We could roughly characterize the analysis of singular causal statements hinted at here as follows: '*A* caused *B*' is true if and only if there are descriptions of *A* and *B* such that the sentence obtained by putting these descriptions for '*A*' and '*B*' in '*A* caused *B*' follows from a true causal law. This analysis is saved from triviality by the fact that not all true generalizations are causal laws; causal laws are distinguished (though of course this is no analysis) by the fact that they are inductively confirmed by their instances and by the fact that they support counterfactual and subjunctive singular causal statements.

events classified as actions—the classifications may even be neurological, chemical, or physical.

D. It is said that the kind of knowledge one has of one's own reasons in acting is not compatible with the existence of a causal relation between reasons and actions: a person knows his own intentions in acting infallibly, without induction or observation, and no ordinary causal relation can be known in this way. No doubt our knowledge of our own intentions in acting will show many of the oddities peculiar to first-person knowledge of one's own pains, beliefs, desires, and so on; the only question is whether these oddities prove that reasons do not cause, in any ordinary sense at least, the actions that they rationalize.

You may easily be wrong about the truth of a statement of the form 'I am poisoning Charles because I want to save him pain', because you may be wrong about whether you are poisoning Charles—you may yourself be drinking the poisoned cup by mistake. But it also seems that you may err about your reasons, particularly when you have two reasons for an action, one of which pleases you and one which does not. For example, you do want to save Charles pain; you also want him out of the way. You may be wrong about which motive made you do it.

The fact that you may be wrong does not show that in general it makes sense to ask you how you know what your reasons were or to ask for your evidence. Though you may, on rare occasions, accept public or private evidence as showing you are wrong about your reasons, you usually have no evidence and make no observations. Then your knowledge of your own reasons for your actions is not generally inductive, for where there is induction, there is evidence. Does this show the knowledge is not causal? I cannot see that it does.

Causal laws differ from true but nonlawlike generalizations in that their instances confirm them; induction is, therefore, certainly a good way to learn the truth of a law. It does not follow that it is the only way to learn the truth of a law. In any case, in order to know that a singular causal statement is true, it is not necessary to know the truth of a law; it is necessary only to know that some law covering the events at hand exists. And it is far from evident that induction, and induction alone, yields the knowledge that a causal law satisfying certain conditions exists. Or, to put it differently, one case is often enough, as Hume admitted, to persuade us that a law exists, and this amounts to saying that we are persuaded, without direct inductive evidence, that a causal relation exists.[8]

E. Finally I should like to say something about a certain uneasiness some philosophers feel in speaking of causes of actions at all. Melden, for example, says that actions are often identical with bodily movements, and that bodily movements have causes; yet he denies that the causes are causes of the actions. This is, I think, a contradiction. He is led to it by the following sort of consideration: "It is futile to attempt to explain conduct through the causal efficacy of desire—all *that* can explain is further happenings, not actions performed by agents. The agent confronting the causal nexus in which such happenings occur is a helpless victim of all that occurs in and to

[8] My thinking on the subject of this section, as on most of the topics discussed in this paper, has been greatly influenced by years of talk with Professor Daniel Bennett, now of Brandeis University.

him" (128, 129). Unless I am mistaken, this argument, if it were valid, would show that actions cannot have causes at all. I shall not point out the obvious difficulties in removing actions from the realm of causality entirely. But perhaps it is worth trying to uncover the source of the trouble. Why on earth should a cause turn an action into a mere happening and a person into a helpless victim? Is it because we tend to assume, at least in the arena of action, that a cause demands a causer, agency an agent? So we press the question; if my action is caused, what caused it? If I did, then there is the absurdity of infinite regress; if I did not, I am a victim. But of course the alternatives are not exhaustive. Some causes have no agents. Primary among these are those states and changes of state in persons which, because they are reasons as well as causes, make persons voluntary agents.

7

CAUSES AND REASONS IN THE LAW

H. L. A. Hart and
A. M. Honoré

IV. CAUSAL GENERALIZATIONS

What kinds of generalization are involved in ordinary singular causal statements? How are these defended from the objection that the alleged cause did not cause but was merely followed by the effect? . . . we have provisionally assumed that Mill's account of this is substantially correct: that the primary meaning of causation is 'invariable and unconditional sequence'[1] of classes of complex events or conditions; and hence that when we identify a single event as a cause of an event we 'select' it from a set known or believed to be 'invariably and unconditionally' followed by an event of that kind. Plainly this account must be qualified, for it is obvious that, though singular causal statements are frequently made not only with confidence but with a confidence not judged improper, very little confidence would either be felt or judged proper in any generalization of this exceptionless kind. In what relevent generalization of 'invariable and unconditional sequence' would or should we feel the same confidence as we do in the singular causal statement that the kettle boiled because it had been put on the fire? Precisely what qualifications are needed to represent the normal standards of every-day life is a question of some difficulty. It is tempting to say that the generalizations involved in ordinary causal statements merely assert that in *most cases* events of one kind are and will be followed by events of the other; we need merely scale down Mill's 'invariably' to 'in the great majority of cases'. The truth unfortunately is not thus simple.[2]

From H. L. A. Hart and A. M. Honoré, *Causation in the Law* (Oxford: 1959), Chap. II, Secs. 4–5, pp. 41–55. Reprinted by permission of The Clarendon Press, Oxford.

[1] We have written hitherto as if Mill had merely said 'invariable' (as he often does). We have done this both for brevity and because the difference between this and 'invariable and unconditional' has not been important: but it needs attention here.

[2] Though this too simple view was previously taken by the authors: see 'Causation in the Law', (1956) 72 *L.Q.R.* 58, 71.

The type of generalization in fact involved in singular causal statements will best be seen if we consider various ways in which Mill's theory is defective as an account of 'the common notion of a cause'. There is first the general objection that Mill's standard of 'invariable and unconditional sequence' cannot be met. Even the scientist can only discover uniformities which he has evidence for believing will hold good over a far wider range of conditions than any that can be discovered by common sense: he does not assert or have grounds for asserting that they will hold good under 'all possible conditions' (unconditionally) or 'always' (invariably). This is in fact an absurdity both in practice and principle. To meet such a standard there would have to be evidence that 'everything' (*all* other things, events or states) apart from the set of conditions specified in the generalization was irrelevant, so that the specified conditions would be unconditionally and invariably sufficient.[3] Neither in practice nor in principle is this possible. Even when some persistent feature of the universe is known and identified (e.g. the motion of the planets) it may be impossible to tell whether, if this were to change, any given causal generalization would be affected and so whether a full statement of the generalization should include it; and of course there must be many such persistent features still unidentified, as cosmic radiation was till recently. Apart from these practical difficulties, the supposition that there are in the 'universe' a finite number of things or events or states, which in principle could be examined and found relevant or irrelevant, is chimerical; the 'universe' is not a box with a finite number of objects in it each describable in a finite number of ways.

More important than these general objections is the fact that Mill's view that we 'select' or 'single out' the cause from a complex set of conditions previously identified, and that these are known or believed to be invariably followed by the effect is misleading. It radically misrepresents the character of those actual situations (in and outside law courts) where we ask and succeed in obtaining a satisfactory answer to questions about the cause of some particular past occurrence. For there is in fact no 'selection' or 'singling out' of the cause from a set of jointly sufficient conditions: what is true is that, after causes have been identified, we come in the course of later experience to learn more detail both about the conditions (i.e. other factors without which they would not be followed by their effects) and about the process of change between cause and effect. So we identify a 'blow' as the cause of a child's injury, for example, a broken leg, without knowing or caring what conditions must also be satisfied, if a blow of just that force is always to be followed by such an injury. When we learn later that the blow would be sufficient only if the bone structure was, as in the child's case, of less than a certain thickness, nothing is added to our confidence in the initial statement that this blow caused the injury, though we would have been grateful for this information had we been attempting to predict the outcome of the blow.

Mill's account in fact suggests—and this is its main defect—that, in order to answer the question what was the cause of this occurrence, we should ideally be able to *predict* with certainty that it would happen, from detailed

[3] It would not be enough if those conditions not included in the generalization always in fact coexisted with those included, for then the specified conditions would merely be 'invariably' followed by the effect but not 'unconditionally'.

and precise knowledge of antecedent conditions. It is, however, vital to see that logically the demands of the situation in which we ask for the cause of what has happened, and that in which we are concerned to predict are very different. In the first case it is an *inquest* that we are conducting. The 'effect' has happened: it is a particular puzzling or unusual occurrence, or divergence from the standard state or performance of something with whose ordinary states or modes of functioning we are familiar; and when we look for the cause of this we are looking for something, usually earlier in time, which is abnormal or an interference in the sense that it is not present when things are as usual. Such abnormalities or interferences we recognize and describe in broad general terms (as 'blows', 'storms', 'heat') which sit loosely to their instances, since they cover a wide range of different occurrences, and we are indifferent to their detailed specification. In identifying some such occurrence, thus broadly described, as the cause of what has happened we must be satisfied that its connexion with the effect is itself unproblematic, not in need of explanation. It is in ordinary life enough for this purpose if we know: first, that contingencies of these broadly described kinds ('blows', 'injuries') commonly go together as a familiar feature of experience the statement of which might often be quite platitudinous; and, secondly, if cases where these general connexions do not hold can be distinguished from the case before us. In all but the simplest cases the causal connexion will be 'indirect', i.e. will have to be traced through a number of successive stages which exemplify a number of different familiar general connexions. The statement that a slate falling from a house top caused the bruises of a passenger in an open car on whom it fell rests, for common sense, on a set of both mechanical and physiological platitudes.

In effect, in the typical case with which the law is concerned, when we ask for the cause, we are asking that some abnormal lapse from routine (some accident, injury, or loss) be rendered intelligible by being exhibited as an instance of certain other normalities, namely, those general connexions which characterize experience and are formulated in broad and general terms. It is therefore not a defect, but an essential feature of the generalizations used in establishing that something was the cause of another, that these should remain formulated in broad terms capable of covering not only the particular case before us (and any exactly like it) but many similar cases differing from it in detail. If the particular case cannot be connected in this way by a broad generalization with a multiplicity of past cases, the minimum explanatory force, which discovery of the cause must have, will be lacking. The abnormality will not have been shown to be some variety of the usual or familiar.

This concern, in giving the cause of a particular occurrence, to link the case in question with others that have happened is not present when we are attempting to predict. What we want then is *certainty* not explanatory force, and a generalization which is as near Mill's prescription as possible will serve us best, even if it is so specific and complex as to apply only to this case. This is a warning: it shows that acceptance of the theory that the only respectable support for a singular causal statement is a Mill-like generalization would drive us into an *impasse*. In our asymptotic approach to the inappropriate ideal of 'invariable sequence' we should have to treat a multiplicity of cases, which at present fall under a single unifying generalization, as instances of separate generalizations, specially adapted to the quantitative and qualitative differences of different cases. These separate generalizations, with their application only to cases falling under such highly specific descriptions, could not possibly guide us to or be our warrant for asserting any singular causal statement; for this must have the link with other cases provided by broad generalizations such as those of common experience. Only when highly specific generalizations are deductions from a single wider theory do these form part of the ground for singular causal statements. In such cases the theory has a unifying and explanatory force comparable to those of the loosely framed generalizations of common sense. This is notably the case when the cause of mechanical failures or the breakdown of scientifically constructed devices, for example, an electrical circuit, are identified by reference to deductions from the theory on which they are constructed.

These considerations explain why it is that we do not regard a singular causal statement, made on the strength of the rough rubrics of common experience, for example, that the cause of a particular fire was the dropping of a lighted cigarette, as strengthened when we learn from science that without the presence of oxygen the fire would not have occurred. Of course this would have to be mentioned if we were really concerned to exhibit the case as an instance of a generalization specifying the conditions in the present case which would be invariably followed by fire. Yet when we come to learn such further necessary conditions we do not treat our past statement of the cause, though made in ignorance of it, as one made without proper justification which has luckily turned out to be correct: indeed it adds nothing to it. For the same reason, there is nothing absurd in combining with the assertion that this was the cause of the fire a refusal to formulate or assent to any given generalization specifying conditions of invariable sequence, though we do not and could not deny the formal claim of (unspecified) *ceteris paribus*, i.e. that there are some factors in the present case which, if they recurred, would always be followed by fire.

At this point, however, a caution is necessary. We must not conclude, from the fact that the generalizations we use in identifying the cause of a particular event are broadly formulated, that it is sufficient to defend a singular causal statement by a simple appeal to 'high probabilities', i.e. generalizations to the effect that the alleged cause is and will be followed by the effect in 'the great majority' of cases. We may be tempted into this belief by a very common form of general causal statement such as 'A short circuit very frequently causes fire' or 'A bent rail will very probably cause an accident'. These may suggest that singular causal statements state merely that a given case is one of the majority or large number of cases to which such statements refer, and are established by simple appeal to these statements of high probabilities. Yet, that this is not so, is perhaps evident from the fact that causal statements of this form also include statements such as 'Diphtheria now very *rarely* causes death'. These causal apophthegms (as they might be called) merely indicate what on particular occasions (numerous in the case of short circuits, few in the case of diphtheria) have been found to be the causes of the events to which they refer; but they are *not* the generalizations used on these particular occasions to establish the cause. They could be paraphrased to read, 'It has been very often or on rare occasions found that X was the cause of Y.' So too general statements (not including the word 'cause') of high probability of sequence, though relevant to establish causal statements, are not sufficient support for them *per se*. The statement that on this occasion X was the cause of Y differs from the conjunctive statement that X was followed by Y on this occasion and X's are followed by Y's in the great majority of cases. The statement that the dropping of the lighted cigarette caused the fire asserts more than that fire followed in this case and there was a high probability that this would be so. The crucial difference is that, if we assert that X was followed by Y in a given case and Y's are highly probable given X's, we are *not* committed to explaining the cases where X's have not been followed by Y's nor to showing that the given case differs from them. On the other hand, if it is asserted that X was the cause of Y, something must be done to anticipate and answer the objection 'Yes: X was here followed by Y as in the majority of cases, but was it the cause in this case?'

This requirement means that counter-examples or exceptions to the generalizations used in support of particular causal statements must be distinguished from the case in hand; till this is done a rival causal explanation must still be sought. Of course the applied sciences represent a vast store-house of counter-examples with which common-sense judgments about the causes of accidents, injuries, and losses, which typically come before law courts, must be reconciled; and scientific accounts of the fine detail of different causal processes often determines a choice between rival causal explanations. Very often, however, a description in non-scientific terms of the successive stages of, for example, an accident will show that these stages are linked by firm if platitudinous generalizations; and, though there may be many cases where the same injury would not have resulted from the same initiating occurrence, a simple description of the stages would reveal differences. Though a falling tile may rarely kill a passer-by, we may in a particular case easily trace the connexion from fall to impact, and from impact to injury, because there is nothing to suggest that any counter-examples to the simple rough generalizations implicitly used are relevant here. Of course in the face of Cartesian doubt we could marshal scientific theories and measurements of forces and velocities to prove the point, but this would be sensible only if there was a rival explanation to disprove.

Let us use the expression 'causal principles' as a compendious term both for the generalizations by which singular causal statements are defended, and the manner in which they are brought to bear on particular cases. It can be said then that, when it is asserted that something is the cause of a particular occurrence, the case must be shown (if necessary by a description of its component stages) to exemplify generalizations broad enough to cover a variety of different cases; secondly, the case must be distinguishable from counter-examples or cases outside the known limits of any generalization used. There is also a third requirement of particular importance in the law. Though it is true in all cases that the factor we designate as the cause would not be followed by the effect without the co-operation of many others, if we find, on attempting to trace by stages a causal connexion, that these factors include voluntary interferences, or independent abnormal contingencies, this brings into question our right to designate the earlier factor as *the* cause; for this expression is used of something which, with the co-operation only of factors that rank as mere conditions and not themselves as causes, is sufficient to 'produce' the effect. The fact that a fire would not have spread to a neighbouring house without the normal breeze does not inhibit us in treating the lighting of it as the cause of the disaster; it would be different if someone deliberately fanned the embers or, just as they were dying out, a leaking petrol tin fell from the back of a jeep. This displacement of one event from the position of 'the cause' by other events, which have also the characteristics by which common sense distinguishes causes from mere conditions, is of crucial importance . . . when causal connexion is the basis of the attribution of responsibility.

There are also intermediate cases where it is natural to speak of each of two contingencies as *a* cause and of neither as *the* cause. This is so where both are abnormal in some degree sufficient to preclude their classification as 'mere conditions' but their abnormality is not of that extreme or coincidental character required for the contingency in question to be regarded as the sole cause.

This account of causal principles, though applicable to the type of case with which the law is usually concerned, does not cover every sort of singular causal statement. As we have said, an account of the way in which deductions from scientific theories are used in the identification of the causes of failures of machines or other artefacts would show that something more nearly approaching Mill's ideal formed part of the reasoning. Indeed any really comprehensive account of the general element implicit in singular causal statements would show that this varied with different types of subject-matter.

Finally, it is to be noted that the account in this section of causal principles is not directly applicable to those cases, especially numerous and important in the law, where an *omission* or failure to act is identified as the cause of some (usually untoward) event. Someone's failure to wrap up is commonly and intelligibly taken to be the cause of his catching cold, and driving in the dark without lights to be the cause of an accident. The background to this use of causal language is that the natural course of events or human activities has been found to be generally harmful and we have learnt from experience how to counteract the harm by certain procedures. Accordingly the generalizations on which such identifications of omissions as causes of harm rest relate primarily to the adequacy, under standard conditions, of the omitted precautions. Then causal principles require that the conditions of the case in hand should be shown not to differ from the standard case; for example, that the temperature was not so low as to make protective clothing useless, or that the victim of the accident was not so drunk as to be incapable of seeing a lighted car. Our concern here is to show that the omitted precaution *would* have averted the harm, not that when it is omitted harm always results. . . .

V. INTERPERSONAL TRANSACTIONS: REASONS AND CAUSES

So far our analysis has been concerned with cases where some event, other than human action, is said to be the effect, result, or consequence of some other event or of some human act or omission. We have not considered cases where one human being is said, either by words or deeds, to cause another to act, nor the important and very varied field of cases where one human action is said to be done 'in consequence of', 'because of', or 'as the result of' another, as, for example, where one man induces another to do something. We have reserved this topic for separate treatment because we have here a set of principles different, in certain ways, from those involved in the central type of causation of physical events and occurrences other than human actions. In this field of relationship between two human actions we have to deal with the concept of *reasons* for action rather than *causes* of events; yet there are many transitional cases for, while the contrast between these concepts is important, it shades off in many directions.

The range of notions under examination in this section is exemplified in the standard use of such expressions as 'He made me do it', 'He persuaded me to do it', 'He induced me to do it', 'I did it because he ordered me to do it', 'I did it because he offered me a reward', 'I did it because he threatened to hit me', 'I did it on his advice'. We shall call these cases 'interpersonal transactions'. There are indeed many differences within this group of notions but also important common features: of these the most important is that such relationships between two persons' actions, though often and intelligibly called causal connexion, especially by legal writers,[4] do not depend upon 'regular connexion' or sequence as the causal relations between physical events do. Hence the assertion that one person, for example, induced another to act is not 'covertly' general even in the modified sense discussed in section IV. Generalizations have a place here but a less central one.

It would be somewhat unnatural in the informal discourse of ordinary life to describe any of this range of cases by saying that one person *caused* another to act; and in some cases this description would be positively misleading. 'He caused me to act' would be merely unnatural (and 'He made me do it' natural) in those cases where one person is induced to act by threats, coercion, the exercise of authority, or false statements; it would be positively misleading in those cases where one person merely advised, or tempted, or requested another to act, or procured his action by offering a reward. The special factors which are entailed by the expressions 'causing' another to act or 'making' him do something are that the first person should intend the second to do the act in question, and should use means of persuasion or inducement (e.g. threats) which render it not wholly voluntary.

There is a temptation to assimilate the relationships between human actions here under discussion to those exhibited in ordinary cases of causal connexion, and so to think of cases where one person induces another to act, and cases where the impact of one body on another causes it to move, as different examples of the same causal relationship, differing only because, in the first case, the terms related are human actions involving psychological and mental factors; whereas in the second, more familiar case the terms related are merely physical events. Hypnosis and many cases of the infliction

---

[4] Street, *The Law of Torts*, p. 357: 'There has been much discussion of the difference between advice and persuasion but the problem . . . presents just the same difficulties on the facts as other problems of causation in torts.' Prosser (*Torts*, p. 550) speaks of 'causal connection in such cases taking the form of inducement' but does not draw attention to any differences between these and ordinary cases of causation.

of nervous shock *are* cases where the difference from familiar cases of causation consists simply in the fact that psychological elements are involved; they do not involve the *radical* differences which separate 'He induced me to do it' from 'His blow caused the victim's death'. The temptation to ignore the more radical differences between these two types of relationship has many roots; there are important similarities as well as differences, which are sometimes expressed by saying that a reason for action is just a cause 'looked at from the inside'. Many important causal idioms are appropriate for the description both of such relationships between human actions and ordinary causal sequences; when one person induces another to act we correctly say that the latter acted 'because of', or 'as the result of', what the first person said or did, and these expressions are often apt to describe the effect of the impact of one body on another. Further, an important and characteristic use of such statements as 'X induced Y to steal' is to provide an explanation as an answer to the question 'Why did Y steal?' So, just like ordinary causal statements, discovery of the relationship between two actions may have an explanatory force. Moreover, these relationships constitute an important element in different sorts of legal and moral responsibility, criminal or civil liability; and special *exemptions* from these forms of liability often depend, for example, on whether one person coerced or induced someone into doing some action. Hence references to such relationships between two human actions appear scattered throughout every branch of most legal systems.

Four common features demand attention in the various relationships of this type. (i) In all of them the second actor knows of and understands the significance of what the first actor has said or done; (ii) the first actor's words or deeds are part of the second actor's reasons for acting; (iii) the second actor forms the intention to do the act in question only after the first actor's intervention; (iv) except in the case where the first actor has merely advised the second actor, he intends the second actor to do the act in question.

1. In all the cases under discussion one essential requirement, if such a relationship is to exist, is that words spoken or actions done by one person must have been known to the second person, and in the case of words they must not only have been known[5] but understood. They do not 'affect' the second person merely as so much noise, for he recognizes their meaning. One person can only be 'induced' to act by another if he knows and understands what that other has said. In this sense the relationship between the two actions in such cases is 'through the mind' of the second person. Precisely what the second person's mental attitude to the action or words of the first person must be, depends on what form of relationship is said to exist. In the case of deceit and false pretences it is necessary that he should have understood and also believed what was said to him; in the case of threats or bribes he must not merely know of and understand what is said to him, but

---

[5] One person *knowing, understanding,* and in some cases *believing* what another has said is essential where the act of the first person consists in his saying something. This is one necessary stage to be distinguished from the further stage where the second person acts *because* of what he has understood or believed. Even if the first stage is (as some analysts of the notion of communication hold) a causal connexion of the familiar kind, the second is not.

at least think there is some chance that what is threatened or offered will be forthcoming. Even in the case of certain gross forms of persuasion where non-rational means are used to incite another to act, it must at least be the case that any words used, for example, in inflammatory speeches, should be understood, and to the extent that the incitement consists of non-rational stimuli (shrieks, groans, gestures) the second person must at least be aware of them. These last cases where, as we say, the first person 'works on' the feelings of the second come very close to cases of ordinary causal connexion.

2. In nearly all these cases the first actor's words or deeds constitute at least part of the second actor's *reasons* for doing the act in question; and in all cases but those of disinterested advice and the grosser forms of incitement by non-rational means, the reason is of a special kind; for it entails that the first actor should by his words or deeds have done something to render some course of action more *eligible* in the eyes of the second actor than it would otherwise have been. This element is most obvious in the cases where one person induces another to act by bribes, threats or offers of reward. Here the second actor is led to believe that, if he acts as required, he will obtain, through the agency of the first actor, something he wants or escape something he dislikes. In this way the action in question is rendered more eligible: he has an extra reason for doing the action, in addition to any reason he might have had independently of the first actor. So it is often said that the first act has 'provided a motive' for doing the second act, and this expression is only misleading to the extent that it conceals the fact that normally in such cases the second actor will have had a pre-existing wish to seek, for example, material benefits or to avoid pain, in conjunction with which the first actor's offers or threats constitute a reason for acting. In some cases, however, there need not be a pre-existing disposition of this sort, since the first actor may both arouse the second's desires or cupidity and also make offers to satisfy it contingently on his doing some action.

Where inducement takes the form of false statements the action is rendered more eligible in the eyes of the second actor simply because he is led to believe that he will gain in a way which he had not thought of; but, unless the false statement takes the form of a prediction by the first actor of his own future conduct or a statement of his own intentions, the benefits which the second actor is led to expect are independent of the agency of the first actor. This is one of the main ways in which inducement by false statement differs from inducement by threats or offers of reward.

Mere advice differs from inducement in that the role of the first person is primarily that of drawing the attention of the second to reasons for or against doing some action. This is to advise another *upon* or *about* some contemplated action. To advise another *to do* an action, of course, goes beyond this discussion of the pro's and con's. In saying 'I advise you to do this' the speaker personally commends the action, and his doing this may of itself render it eligible in the eyes of someone who trusts or respects him. Hence, if the advice is taken, the mere giving of the advice may be the second person's reason for acting; in other cases the merits of the action which have emerged in the course of the discussion may also have weighed with him in deciding to do it.

3. Whenever it is appropriate to say that one person has acted in consequence of what another has done or said (whether this constitutes inducement or merely advice), it must be the case that the person so acting should have made up his mind to act only after the first actor's intervention by words or deeds. If before this intervention the second actor had already intended to do the act in question, all such relationships are excluded; for in such cases the intervention could not be the second actor's reason for doing what he did do.

It is often said that if the first actor's words or deeds are to be accepted as the second actor's reasons for doing what he did, the first must be a condition *sine qua non* of the second, i.e. it must be true that he would not have acted in the way he did, had the first actor not said or done what he did. Even if this is true (and in certain contexts legal and non-legal statements of an actor's reasons seem not to have this implication) it is wrong to conclude that, if this relationship between two actions is to subsist, the first person's words or deeds must have the general connexion with the act of the second which is characteristic of causal relationships between physical events. The statement that one person did something because, for example, another threatened him, carries no implication or covert assertion that if the circumstances were repeated the same action would follow; nor does such a statement require for its defence, as ordinary singular causal statements do, a generalization of the kind discussed in section IV. This is most obvious if we consider not a third person's statements about the case where someone has done something because of another's threats, but the threatened person's own statement that he acted because of those threats. It would be absurd to call upon him to show that there really was this connexion between the threats and his action, by showing that generally he or other persons complied when threats were made. This general statement might be quite untrue and yet his statement of his reasons might be true: the assertion that he acted because of the threats carries no implication that, given similar circumstances, he would act again in this way or that, in similar circumstances, he or other persons had always acted in that way. By contrast, if he had said that a blow had caused a bruise, where no statement of *reasons* for acting is involved, evidence of what experience has shown to be generally the case would be required to show that this was a case of *propter hoc* [causal connection] not *post hoc* [mere temporal sequence].

The question, whether or not a given person acted on a given occasion for a given reason, is primarily a question as to the way in which the agent reaches his decision to do the act in question: whether the thought of a given reason weighed with him as he made up his mind, and whether or not in doing the action he consciously adapted the manner of its execution accordingly. These are questions primarily about the agent's experience in contemplating, deciding upon and carrying out the action in question, and for this reason the agent's own declarations about his reasons have a special primacy or importance. This is recognized in the law as well as in ordinary life. If asked to make sure, in giving evidence, that his reasons for acting were as he claims, an honest witness will not be expected to produce generalizations, but to attempt to reconstruct the deliberative situation or his 'state of mind' at the time.

Of course generalizations about the way in which either the person in question or other persons respond, e.g. to threats, or by what reasons they are or are not actuated, have an important place in such cases. They may be used as *evidence* that a person in saying he acted from a certain reason was not speaking the truth (or was forgetful), because it was 'out of character' for him, or is rare for anyone to act for such a reason. Such generalizations are built up from knowledge of many individual cases where we have found that a person acted (or did not act) from a given reason, and we now use them in a new case to confirm or throw doubt on the agent's statement that he did act for this reason. But the instances out of which such generalizations are constructed were themselves cases where it was found that an individual had a certain reason for action, and this was known independently of such generalizations. On the other hand, a singular causal statement asserting that one physical event was the cause of another depends on generalizations in a different way: here the latter are not merely *evidence* that in the particular case the events are causally related; they are *part* of what is meant by causal connexion; and the instances from which these causal generalizations are constructed were not already recognized *apart* from such generalizations as cases of causal connexion but only as cases of succession between events.

The matter is, however, complicated by one point. Though there is no implication of uniform sequence in asserting that a person acted for a given reason, what we recognise as a possible reason is not independent of how in a general very broad sense most people act. If a person said he left the room 'because Caesar died in 44 B.C.' we should not understand him. Roughly speaking, we recognize as a reason for action (and therefore as a given person's reason on a particular occasion) something which is relevant to the promotion of some purpose known to be pursued by human beings and so renders an action eligible by human beings as we know them. The concept of reasons therefore *presupposes* that, in general, human beings respond to certain situations in such ways as fleeing from danger, or conforming with social rules or conventions, &c. Yet this presupposition of broad similarity in human behaviour, without which we could not have the concept of a reason for action, does not mean that, when on a particular occasion we assert that a person acted for a particular reason (e.g. to avoid threatened danger), we are committed to any assertion that, if the circumstances were repeated, the same action would follow: it may be that neither he nor anyone else would act so again in such circumstances. All that is required is that, if the case is to be one of a person acting for a reason, we must understand how it promoted some objective analogous at least in some way to those which human beings are known to pursue by action.

In some of the relationships considered here the intermediate act may be fully voluntary. This will be the case, for example, if the first actor has done no more than advise the second actor or offer him a reward for acting; whereas in cases where the first actor resorts to threats or gives orders which the second is under some duty to obey the second action is less than fully voluntary. It is this second class of case that would be expressed by saying that the first actor 'caused' the second to act or 'made him act' as he did. . . .

Mixed and Borderline Cases

Between the interpersonal transactions so far examined and ordinary cases of natural causation, where one physical event is caused by another, or by a single human intervention, there are two major points of contrast. First, all cases of interpersonal transaction involve the notion of one person intentionally providing another with a reason for doing something, and so rendering it eligible in his eyes. Secondly these cases are logically independent of generalizations even of the modified kind suggested in section IV as a substitute, in cases of the causation of physical events, for Mill's 'invariable and unconditional sequence'. It is, however, clear that there are many forms of causal language which may be used indifferently for cases of either type, and also that there are mixed or borderline cases having some of the features of both types.

Thus 'causing another to do something' or 'making him do it' does not always refer to an interpersonal transaction in which one person induces another to act by threats or the use of his authority: it may take a form very similar to the causal manipulation of things even though it in some way involves the mind. Hypnotism is one such case; where post-hypnotic suggestion is successful the subject is caused to act or move but not given reasons for acting. If the causal connexion is challenged in such cases it would require defence by generalizations, tracing general connexions between similar stimuli and behaviour, as do statements that one physical event was the cause of another. More important are cases which are like interpersonal transactions, in that an honest account of conscious experience and not an appeal to generalizations best verifies them, and yet do not involve the provision of a reason in the sense of rendering action more eligible. Thus, if one person, by suddenly appearing, startles another so that he jumps or runs away in fright, the sudden appearance would correctly be said to have made the second person behave as he did; and the latter's statement that this was so would neither be a conclusion from any generalization nor require defence by one. Yet though the sudden appearance of the first person would be properly mentioned in answer to the question, 'Why did you jump?' as well as to the question 'What made you jump?' it is not a reason for jumping in the same sense of reason as that involved in our interpersonal transactions. It does not show the action to be eligible or to be one that furthered any purpose or objective; in this non-purposive aspect these cases resemble causal connexion between two physical events.[6] In the law there are many examples of this borderline type of causal concept. Perhaps the most important is the case of provocation, though its characteristics are masked by the rule that, unless a reasonable man would have lost self-control under the same circumstances, the fact that a person accused of murder was provoked by his victim's words or deeds will not avail him. It is, however, an integral part of the idea of provocation that one person arouses another's passions and *makes* him lose normal self-control; this is indeed spoken of as the 'effect';[7] yet, that this connexion exists in any particular case is a matter that in principle could be conclusively settled by a description of the agent's state of mind without any appeal to generalizations.

[6] See the discussion of such cases (called 'mental causation') by G. E. M. Anscombe in *Intention* (Oxford, 1957), ss. 9–12.
[7] Homicide Act, 1957. s. 3.

Causes and Laws of Nature

8

CAUSES

Aristotle

Of things that exist, some exist by nature, some from other causes. 'By nature' the animals and their parts exist, and the plants and the simple bodies (earth, fire, air, water)—for we say that these and the like exist 'by nature'.

All the things mentioned present a feature in which they differ from things which are *not* constituted by nature. Each of them has *within itself* a principle of motion and of stationariness (in respect of place, or of growth and decrease, or by way of alteration). On the other hand, a bed and a coat and anything else of that sort, *qua* receiving these designations—i.e. in so far as they are products of art—have no innate impulse to change. But in so far as they happen to be composed of stone or of earth or of a mixture of the two, they *do* have such an impulse, and just to that extent—which seems to indicate that *nature is a source or cause of being moved and of being at rest in that to which it belongs primarily*, in virtue of itself and not in virtue of a concomitant attribute.

I say 'not in virtue of a concomitant attribute', because (for instance) a man who is a doctor might cure himself. Nevertheless it is not in so far as he is a patient that he possesses the art of medicine: it merely has happened that the same man is doctor and patient—and that is why these attributes are not always found together. So it is with all other artificial products. None of them has in itself the source of its own production. But while in some cases (for instance houses and the other products of manual labour) that principle is in something else external to the thing, in others—those which may cause

From *Physics*, R. P. Hardie and R. K. Gaye, trans., in *The Works of Aristotle* (Oxford: 1938), Book II, Secs. 1, 3–9, pp. 116–119, 122–138. Reprinted by permission of The Clarendon Press, Oxford.

a change in themselves in virtue of a concomitant attribute—it lies in the things themselves (but not in virtue of what they are).

'Nature' then is what has been stated. Things 'have a nature' which have a principle of this kind. Each of them is a substance; for it is a subject, and nature always implies a subject in which it inheres.

The term 'according to nature' is applied to all these things and also to the attributes which belong to them in virtue of what they are, for instance the property of fire to be carried upwards—which is not a 'nature' nor 'has a nature' but is 'by nature' or 'according to nature'.

What nature is, then, and the meaning of the terms 'by nature' and 'according to nature', has been stated. *That* nature exists, it would be absurd to try to prove; for it is obvious that there are many things of this kind, and to prove what is obvious by what is not is the mark of a man who is unable to distinguish what is self-evident from what is not. (This state of mind is clearly possible. A man blind from birth might reason about colours. Presumably therefore such persons must be talking about words without any thought to correspond.)

Some identify the nature or substance of a natural object with that immediate constituent of it which taken by itself is without arrangement, e.g. the wood is the 'nature' of the bed, and the bronze the 'nature' of the statue.

As an indication of this Antiphon points out that if you planted a bed and the rotting wood acquired the power of sending up a shoot, it would not be a bed that would come up, but *wood*—which shows that the arrangement in accordance with the rules of the art is merely an incidental attribute, whereas the real nature is the other, which, further, persists continuously through the process of making.

But if the material of each of these objects has itself the same relation to something else, say bronze (or gold) to water, bones (or wood) to earth and so on, *that* (they say) would be their nature and essence. Consequently some assert earth, others fire or air or water or some or all of these, to be the nature of the things that are. For whatever any one of them supposed to have this character—whether one thing or more than one thing—this or these he declared to be the whole of substance, all else being its affections, states, or dispositions. Every such thing they held to be eternal (for it could not pass into anything else), but other things to come into being and cease to be times without number.

This then is one account of 'nature', namely that it is the immediate material substratum of things which have in themselves a principle of motion or change.

Another account is that 'nature' is the shape or form which is specified in the definition of the thing.

For the word 'nature' is applied to what is according to nature and the natural in the same way as 'art' is applied to what is artistic or a work of art. We should not say in the latter case that there is anything artistic about a thing, if it is a bed only potentially, not yet having the form of a bed; nor should we call it a work of art. The same is true of natural compounds. What is potentially flesh or bone has not yet its own 'nature', and does not exist by 'nature', until it receives the form specified in the definition, which we name in defining what flesh or bone is. Thus in the second sense of 'nature' it would be the shape or form (not separable except in statement) of things which have in themselves a source of motion. (The combination of the two, e.g. man, is not 'nature' but 'by nature' or 'natural'.)

The form indeed is 'nature' rather than the matter; for a thing is more properly said to be what it is when it has attained to fulfilment than when it exists potentially. Again man is born from man, but not bed from bed. That is why people say that the figure is not the nature of a bed, but the wood is—if the bed sprouted not a bed but wood would come up. But even if the figure *is* art, then on the same principle the shape of man is his nature. For man is born from man.

We also speak of a thing's nature as being exhibited in the process of growth by which its nature is attained. The 'nature' in this sense is not like 'doctoring', which leads not to the art of doctoring but to health. Doctoring must start from the art, not lead to it. But it is not in this way that nature (in the one sense) is related to nature (in the other). What grows *qua* growing grows from something into something. Into what then does it grow? Not into that from which it arose but into that to which it tends. The shape then is nature.

'Shape' and 'nature', it should be added, are used in two senses. For the privation too is in a way form. But whether in unqualified coming to be there is privation, i.e. a contrary to what comes to be, we must consider later.

.   .   .

. . . we must proceed to consider causes, their character and number. Knowledge is the object of our inquiry, and men do not think they know a thing till they have grasped the 'why' of it (which is to grasp its primary cause). So clearly we too must do this as regards both coming to be and passing away and every kind of physical change, in order that, knowing their principles, we may try to refer to these principles each of our problems.

In one sense, then, (1) that out of which a thing comes to be and which persists, is called 'cause', e.g. the bronze of the statue, the silver of the bowl, and the genera of which the bronze and the silver are species.

In another sense (2) the form or the archetype, i.e. the statement of the essence, and its genera, are called 'causes' (e.g. of the octave the relation of 2:1, and generally number), and the parts in the definition.

Again (3) the primary source of the change or coming to rest; e.g. the man who gave advice is a cause, the father is cause of the child, and generally what makes of what is made and what causes change of what is changed.

Again (4) in the sense of end or 'that for the sake of which' a thing is done, e.g. health is the cause of walking about. ('Why is he walking about?' we say. 'To be healthy', and, having said that, we think we have assigned the cause.) The same is true also of all the intermediate steps which are brought about through the action of something else as means towards the end, e.g. reduction of flesh, purging, drugs, or surgical instruments are means towards health. All these things are 'for the sake of' the end, though they differ from one another in that some are activities, others instruments.

This then perhaps exhausts the number of ways in which the term 'cause' is used.

As the word has several senses, it follows that there are several causes of the same thing (not merely in virtue of a concomitant attribute), e.g. both the art of the sculptor and the bronze are causes of the statue. These are causes of the statue *qua* statue, not in virtue of anything else that it may be—only not in the same way, the one being the material cause, the other the cause whence the motion comes. Some things cause each other reciprocally, e.g. hard work causes fitness and *vice versa*, but again not in the same way, but the one as end, the other as the origin of change. Further the same thing is the cause of contrary results. For that which by its presence brings about one result is sometimes blamed for bringing about the contrary by its absence. Thus we ascribe the wreck of a ship to the absence of the pilot whose presence was the cause of its safety.

All the causes now mentioned fall into four familiar divisions. The letters are the causes of syllables, the material of artificial products, fire, &c., of bodies, the parts of the whole, and the premisses of the conclusion, in the sense of 'that from which'. Of these pairs the one set are causes in the sense of substratum, e.g. the parts, the other set in the sense of essence—the whole and the combination and the form. But the seed and the doctor and the adviser, and generally the maker, are all sources whence the change or stationariness originates, while the others are causes in the sense of the end or the good of the rest; for 'that for the sake of which' means what is best and the end of the things that lead up to it. (Whether we say the 'good itself' or the 'apparent good' makes no difference.)

Such then is the number and nature of the kinds of cause.

Now the modes of causation are many, though when brought under heads they too can be reduced in number. For 'cause' is used in many senses and even within the same kind one may be prior to another (e.g. the doctor and the expert are causes of health, the relation 2:1 and number of the octave), and always what is inclusive to what is particular. Another mode of causation is the incidental and its genera, e.g. in one way 'Polyclitus', in another 'sculptor' is the cause of a statue, because 'being Polyclitus' and 'sculptor' are incidentally conjoined. Also the classes in which the incidental attribute is included; thus 'a man' could be said to be the cause of a statue or, generally, 'a living creature'. An incidental attribute too may be more or less remote, e.g. suppose that 'a pale man' or 'a musical man' were said to be the cause of the statue.

All causes, both proper and incidental, may be spoken of either as potential or as actual; e.g. the cause of a house being built is either 'house-builder' or 'house-builder building'.

Similar distinctions can be made in the things of which the causes are causes, e.g. of 'this statue' or of 'statue' or of 'image' generally, of 'this bronze' or of 'bronze' or of 'material' generally. So too with the incidental attributes. Again we may use a complex expression for either and say, e.g., neither 'Polyclitus' nor 'sculptor' but 'Polyclitus, sculptor'.

All these various uses, however, come to six in number, under each of which again the usage is twofold. Cause means either what is particular or a genus, or an incidental attribute or a genus of that, and these either as a complex or each by itself; and all six either as actual or as potential. The difference is this much, that causes which are actually at work and particular exist and cease to exist simultaneously with their effect, e.g. this healing person with this being-healed person and that housebuilding man with that being-built house; but this is not always true of potential causes—the house and the housebuilder do not pass away simultaneously.

In investigating the cause of each thing it is always necessary to seek what is most precise (as also in other things): thus man builds because he is a builder, and a builder builds in virtue of his art of building. This last cause then is prior: and so generally.

Further, generic effects should be assigned to generic causes, particular effects to particular causes, e.g. statue to sculptor, this statue to this sculptor; and powers are relative to possible effects, actually operating causes to things which are actually being effected.

This must suffice for our account of the number of causes and the modes of causation.

But chance also and spontaneity are reckoned among causes: many things are said both to be and to come to be as a result of chance and spontaneity. We must inquire therefore in what manner chance and spontaneity are present among the causes enumerated, and whether they are the same or different, and generally what chance and spontaneity are.

Some people[1] even question whether they are real or not. They say that nothing happens by chance, but that everything which we ascribe to chance or spontaneity has some definite cause, e.g. coming 'by chance' into the market and finding there a man whom one wanted but did not expect to meet is due to one's wish to go and buy in the market. Similarly in other cases of chance it is always possible, they maintain, to find something which is the cause; but not chance, for if chance were real, it would seem strange indeed, and the question might be raised, why on earth none of the wise men of old in speaking of the causes of generation and decay took account of chance; whence it would seem that they too did not believe that anything is by chance. But there is a further circumstance that is surprising. Many things both come to be and are by chance and spontaneity, and although all know that each of them can be ascribed to some cause (as the old argument said which denied chance), nevertheless they speak of some of these things as happening by chance and others not. For this reason also they ought to have at least referred to the matter in some way or other.

Certainly the early physicists found no place for chance among the causes which they recognized—love, strife, mind, fire, or the like. This is strange, whether they supposed that there is no such thing as chance or whether they thought there is but omitted to mention it—and that too when they sometimes used it, as Empedocles does when he says that the air is not always separated into the highest region, but 'as it may chance'. At any rate he says in his cosmogony that 'it happened to run that way at that time, but it often ran otherwise.' He tells us also that most of the parts of animals came to be by chance.

[1] Apparently Democritus is meant.

There are some[2] too who ascribe this heavenly sphere and all the worlds to spontaneity. They say that the vortex arose spontaneously, i.e. the motion that separated and arranged in its present order all that exists. This statement might well cause surprise. For they are asserting that chance is not responsible for the existence or generation of animals and plants, nature or mind or something of the kind being the cause of them (for it is not any chance thing that comes from a given seed but an olive from one kind and a man from another); and yet at the same time they assert that the heavenly sphere and the divinest of visible things arose spontaneously, having no such cause as is assigned to animals and plants. Yet if this is so, it is a fact which deserves to be dwelt upon, and something might well have been said about it. For besides the other absurdities of the statement, it is the more absurd that people should make it when they see nothing coming to be spontaneously in the heavens, but much happening by chance among the things which as they say are not due to chance; whereas we should have expected exactly the opposite.

Others[3] there are who, indeed, believe that chance is a cause, but that it is inscrutable to human intelligence, as being a divine thing and full of mystery.

Thus we must inquire what chance and spontaneity are, whether they are the same or different, and how they fit into our division of causes.

First then we observe that some things always come to pass in the same way, and others for the most part. It is clearly of neither of these that chance is said to be the cause, nor can the 'effect of chance' be identified with any of the things that come to pass by necessity and always, or for the most part. But as there is a third class of events besides these two—events which all say are 'by chance'—it is plain that there is such a thing as chance and spontaneity; for we know that things of this kind are due to chance and that things due to chance are of this kind.

But, secondly, some events are for the sake of something, others not. Again, some of the former class are in accordance with deliberate intention, others not, but both are in the class of things which are for the sake of something. Hence it is clear that even among the things which are outside the necessary and the normal, there are some in connexion with which the phrase 'for the sake of something' is applicable. (Events that are for the sake of something include whatever may be done as a result of thought or of nature.) Things of this kind, then, when they come to pass incidentally are said to be 'by chance'. For just as a thing is something either in virtue of itself or incidentally, so may it be a cause. For instance, the housebuilding faculty is in virtue of itself the cause of a house, whereas the pale or the musical[4] is the incidental cause. That which is *per se* cause of the effect is determinate, but the incidental cause is indeterminable, for the possible attributes of an individual are innumerable. To resume then; when a thing of this kind comes to pass among events which are for the sake of something, it is said to be spontaneous or by chance. (The distinction between the two

---

[2] Apparently Democritus is meant.   [3] Democritus.
[4] Incidental attributes of the housebuilder.

must be made later—for the present it is sufficient if it is plain that both are in the sphere of things done for the sake of something.)

Example: A man is engaged in collecting subscriptions for a feast. He would have gone to such and such a place for the purpose of getting the money, if he had known. He actually went there for another purpose, and it was only incidentally that he got his money by going there; and this was not due to the fact that he went there as a rule or necessarily, nor is the end effected (getting the money) a cause present in himself—it belongs to the class of things that are intentional and the result of intelligent deliberation. It is when these conditions are satisfied that the man is said to have gone 'by chance'. If he had gone of deliberate purpose and for the sake of this—if he always or normally went there when he was collecting payments—he would not be said to have gone 'by chance'.

It is clear then that chance is an incidental cause in the sphere of those actions for the sake of something which involve purpose. Intelligent reflection, then, and chance are in the same sphere, for purpose implies intelligent reflection.

It is necessary, no doubt, that the causes of what comes to pass by chance be indefinite; and that is why chance is supposed to belong to the class of the indefinite and to be inscrutable to man, and why it might be thought that, in a way, nothing occurs by chance. For all these statements are correct, because they are well grounded. Things *do*, in a way, occur by chance, for they occur incidentally and chance is an *incidental cause*. But strictly it is not the *cause*—without qualification—of anything; for instance, a house-builder is the cause of a house; incidentally, a flute-player may be so.

And the causes of the man's coming and getting the money (when he did not come for the sake of that) are innumerable. He may have wished to see somebody or been following somebody or avoiding somebody, or may have gone to see a spectacle. Thus to say that chance is a thing contrary to rule is correct. For 'rule' applies to what is always true or true for the most part, whereas chance belongs to a third type of event. Hence, to conclude, since causes of this kind are indefinite, chance too is indefinite. (Yet in some cases one might raise the question whether *any* incidental fact might be the cause of the chance occurrence, e.g. of health the fresh air or the sun's heat may be the cause, but having had one's hair cut *cannot*; for some incidental causes are more relevant to the effect than others.)

Chance or fortune is called 'good' when the result is good, 'evil' when it is evil. The terms 'good fortune' and 'ill fortune' are used when either result is of considerable magnitude. Thus one who comes within an ace of some great evil or great good is said to be fortunate or unfortunate. The mind affirms the presence of the attribute, ignoring the hair's breadth of difference. Further, it is with reason that good fortune is regarded as unstable; for chance is unstable, as none of the things which result from it can be invariable or normal.

Both are then, as I have said, incidental causes—both chance and spontaneity—in the sphere of things which are capable of coming to pass not necessarily, nor normally, and with reference to such of these as might come to pass for the sake of something.

They differ in that 'spontaneity' is the wider term. Every result of chance is from what is spontaneous, but not everything that is from what is spontaneous is from chance.

Chance and what results from chance are appropriate to agents that are capable of good fortune and of moral action generally. Therefore necessarily chance is in the sphere of moral actions. This is indicated by the fact that good fortune is thought to be the same, or nearly the same, as happiness, and happiness to be a kind of moral action, since it is well-doing. Hence what is not capable of moral action cannot do anything by chance. Thus an inanimate thing or a lower animal or a child cannot do anything by chance, because it is incapable of deliberate intention; nor can 'good fortune' or 'ill fortune' be ascribed to them, except metaphorically, as Protarchus, for example, said that the stones of which altars are made are fortunate because they are held in honour, while their fellows are trodden under foot. Even these things, however, can in a way be affected by chance, when one who is dealing with them does something to them by chance, but not otherwise.

The spontaneous on the other hand is found both in the lower animals and in many inanimate objects. We say, for example, that the horse came 'spontaneously', because, though his coming saved him, he did not come for the sake of safety. Again, the tripod fell 'of itself', because, though when it fell it stood on its feet so as to serve for a seat, it did not fall for the sake of that.

Hence it is clear that events which (1) belong to the general class of things that may come to pass for the sake of something, (2) do not come to pass for the sake of what actually results, and (3) have an external cause, may be described by the phrase 'from spontaneity'. These 'spontaneous' events are said to be 'from chance' if they have the further characteristics of being the objects of deliberate intention and due to agents capable of that mode of action. This is indicated by the phrase 'in vain', which is used when *A*, which is for the sake of *B*, does not result in *B*. For instance, taking a walk is for the sake of evacuation of the bowels; if this does not follow after walking, we say that we have walked 'in vain' and that the walking was 'vain'. This implies that what is naturally the means to an end is 'in vain', when it does not effect the end towards which it was the natural means—for it would be absurd for a man to say that he had bathed in vain because the sun was not eclipsed, since the one was not done with a view to the other. Thus the spontaneous is even according to its derivation the case in which the thing itself happens in vain. The stone that struck the man did not fall for the purpose of striking him; therefore it fell spontaneously, because it might have fallen by the action of an agent and for the purpose of striking. The difference between spontaneity and what results by chance is greatest in things that come to be by nature; for when anything comes to be contrary to nature, we do not say that it came to be by chance, but by spontaneity. Yet strictly this too is different from the spontaneous proper; for the cause of the latter is external, that of the former internal.

We have now explained what chance is and what spontaneity is, and in what they differ from each other. Both belong to the mode of causation 'source of change', for either some natural or some intelligent agent is always the cause; but in this sort of causation the number of possible causes is infinite.

Spontaneity and chance are causes of effects which, though they might result from intelligence or nature, have in fact been caused by something *incidentally*. Now since nothing which is incidental is prior to what is *per se*, it is clear that no incidental cause can be prior to a cause *per se*. Spontaneity and chance, therefore, are posterior to intelligence and nature. Hence, however true it may be that the heavens are due to spontaneity, it will still be true that intelligence and nature will be prior causes of this All and of many things in it besides.

It is clear then that there are causes, and that the number of them is what we have stated. The number is the same as that of the things comprehended under the question 'why'. The 'why' is referred ultimately either (1), in things which do not involve motion, e.g. in mathematics, to the 'what' (to the definition of 'straight line' or 'commensurable', &c.), or (2) to what initiated a motion, e.g. 'why did they go to war?—because there had been a raid'; or (3) we are inquiring 'for the sake of what?'—'that they may rule'; or (4), in the case of things that come into being, we are looking for the matter. The causes, therefore, are these and so many in number.

Now, the causes being four, it is the business of the physicist to know about them all, and if he refers his problems back to all of them, he will assign the 'why' in the way proper to his science—the matter, the form, the mover, 'that for the sake of which'. The last three often coincide; for the 'what' and 'that for the sake of which' are one, while the primary source of motion is the same in species as these (for man generates man), and so too, in general, are all things which cause movement by being themselves moved; and such as are not of this kind are no longer inside the province of physics, for they cause motion not by possessing motion or a source of motion in themselves, but being themselves incapable of motion. Hence there are three branches of study, one of things which are incapable of motion, the second of things in motion, but indestructible, the third of destructible things.

The question 'why', then, is answered by reference to the matter, to the form, and to the primary moving cause. For in respect of coming to be it is mostly in this last way that causes are investigated—'what comes to be after what? what was the primary agent or patient?' and so at each step of the series.

Now the principles which cause motion in a physical way are two, of which one is not physical, as it has no principle of motion in itself. Of this kind is whatever causes movement, not being itself moved, such as (1) that which is completely unchangeable, the primary reality, and (2) the essence of that which is coming to be, i.e. the form; for this is the end or 'that for the sake of which'. Hence since nature is for the sake of something, we must know this cause also. We must explain the 'why' in all the senses of the term, namely, (1) that from this that will necessarily result ('from this' either without qualification or in most cases); (2) that 'this must be so if that is to be so' (as the conclusion presupposes the premisses); (3) that this was the essence of the thing; and (4) because it is better thus (not without qualification, but with reference to the essential nature in each case).

We must explain then (1) that Nature belongs to the class of causes which act for the sake of something; (2) about the necessary and its place in physical problems, for all writers ascribe things to this cause, arguing that since the hot and the cold, &c., are of such and such a kind, therefore certain things *necessarily* are and come to be—and if they mention any other cause (one[5] his 'friendship and strife', another[6] his 'mind'), it is only to touch on it, and then good-bye to it.

A difficulty presents itself: why should not nature work, not for the sake of something, nor because it is better so, but just as the sky rains, not in order to make the corn grow, but of necessity? What is drawn up must cool, and what has been cooled must become water and descend, the result of this being that the corn grows. Similarly if a man's crop is spoiled on the threshing-floor, the rain did not fall for the sake of this—in order that the crop might be spoiled—but that result just followed. Why then should it not be the same with the parts in nature, e.g. that our teeth should come up *of necessity*—the front teeth sharp, fitted for tearing, the molars broad and useful for grinding down the food—since they did not arise for this end, but it was merely a coincident result; and so with all other parts in which we suppose that there is purpose? Wherever then all the parts came about just what they would have been if they had come to be for an end, such things survived, being organized spontaneously in a fitting way; whereas those which grew otherwise perished and continue to perish, as Empedocles says his 'man-faced ox-progeny' did.

Such are the arguments (and others of the kind) which may cause difficulty on this point. Yet it is impossible that this should be the true view. For teeth and all other natural things either invariably or normally come about in a given way; but of not one of the results of chance or spontaneity is this true. We do not ascribe to chance or mere coincidence the frequency of rain in winter, but frequent rain in summer we do; nor heat in the dog-days, but only if we have it in winter. If then, it is agreed that things are either the result of coincidence or for an end, and these cannot be the result of coincidence or spontaneity, it follows that they must be for an end; and that such things are all due to nature even the champions of the theory which is before us would agree. Therefore action for an end is present in things which come to be and are by nature.

Further, where a series has a completion, all the preceding steps are for the sake of that. Now surely as in intelligent action, so in nature; and as in nature, so it is in each action, if nothing interferes. Now intelligent action is for the sake of an end; therefore the nature of things also is so. Thus if a house, e.g., had been a thing made by nature, it would have been made in the same way as it is now by art; and if things made by nature were made also by art, they would come to be in the same way as by nature. Each step then in the series is for the sake of the next; and generally art partly completes what nature cannot bring to a finish, and partly imitates her. If, therefore, artificial products are for the sake of an end, so clearly also are natural products. The relation of the later to the earlier terms of the series is the same in both.

This is most obvious in the animals other than man: they make things neither by art nor after inquiry or deliberation. Wherefore people discuss whether it is by intelligence or by some other faculty that these creatures

[5] Empedocles.   [6] Anaxagoras.

work,—spiders, ants, and the like. By gradual advance in this direction we come to see clearly that in plants too that is produced which is conducive to the end—leaves, e.g. grow to provide shade for the fruit. If then it is both by nature and for an end that the swallow makes its nest and the spider its web, and plants grow leaves for the sake of the fruit and send their roots down (not up) for the sake of nourishment, it is plain that this kind of cause is operative in things which come to be and are by nature. And since 'nature' means two things, the matter and the form, of which the latter is the end, and since all the rest is for the sake of the end, the form must be the cause in the sense of 'that for the sake of which'.

Now mistakes come to pass even in the operations of art: the grammarian makes a mistake in writing and the doctor pours out the wrong dose. Hence clearly mistakes are possible in the operations of nature also. If then in art there are cases in which what is rightly produced serves a purpose, and if where mistakes occur there was a purpose in what was attempted, only it was not attained, so must it be also in natural products, and monstrosities will be failures in the purposive effort. Thus in the original combinations the 'ox-progeny' if they failed to reach a determinate end must have arisen through the corruption of some principle corresponding to what is now the seed.

Further, seed must have come into being first, and not straightway the animals: the words 'whole-natured first . . .'[7] must have meant seed.

Again, in plants too we find the relation of means to end, though the degree of organization is less. Were there then in plants also 'olive-headed vine-progeny', like the 'man-headed ox-progeny', or not? An absurd suggestion; yet there must have been, if there were such things among animals.

Moreover, among the seeds anything must have come to be at random. But the person who asserts this entirely does away with 'nature' and what exists 'by nature'. For those things are natural which, by a continuous movement originated from an internal principle, arrive at some completion: the same completion is not reached from every principle; nor any chance completion, but always the tendency in each is towards the same end, if there is no impediment.

The end and the means towards it may come about by chance. We say, for instance, that a stranger has come by chance, paid the ransom, and gone away, when he does so as if he had come for that purpose, though it was not for that that he came. This is incidental, for chance is an incidental cause. . . . But when an event takes place always or for the most part, it is not incidental or by chance. In natural products the sequence is invariable, if there is no impediment.

It is absurd to suppose that purpose is not present because we do not observe the agent deliberating. Art does not deliberate. If the ship-building art were in the wood, it would produce the same results *by nature*. If, therefore, purpose is present in art, it is present also in nature. The best illustration is a doctor doctoring himself: nature is like that.

It is plain then that nature is a cause, a cause that operates for a purpose.

As regards what is 'of necessity', we must ask whether the necessity is

[7] Empedocles.

'hypothetical', or 'simple' as well. The current view places what is of necessity in the process of production, just as if one were to suppose that the wall of a house necessarily comes to be because what is heavy is naturally carried downwards and what is light to the top, wherefore the stones and foundations take the lowest place, with earth above because it is lighter, and wood at the top of all as being the lightest. Whereas, though the wall does not come to be *without* these, it is not *due* to these, except as its material cause: it comes to be for the sake of sheltering and guarding certain things. Similarly in all other things which involve production for an end; the product cannot come to be without things which have a necessary nature, but it is not due to these (except as its material); it comes to be for an end. For instance, why is a saw such as it is? To effect so-and-so and for the sake of so-and-so. This end, however, cannot be realized unless the saw is made of iron. It is, therefore, necessary for it to be of iron, *if* we are to have a saw and perform the operation of sawing. What is necessary then, is necessary *on a hypothesis;* it is not a result necessarily determined by antecedents. Necessity is in the matter, while 'that for the sake of which' is in the definition.

Necessity in mathematics is in a way similar to necessity in things which come to be through the operation of nature. Since a straight line is what it is, it is necessary that the angles of a triangle should equal two right angles. But not conversely; though if the angles are *not* equal to two right angles, then the straight line is not what it is either. But in things which come to be for an end, the reverse is true. If the end is to exist or does exist, that also which precedes it will exist or does exist; otherwise just as there, if the conclusion is not true, the premiss will not be true, so here the end or 'that for the sake of which' will not exist. For this too is itself a starting-point, but of the reasoning, not of the action; while in mathematics the starting-point is the starting point of the reasoning only, as there is no action. If then there is to be a house, such-and-such things must be made or be there already or exist, or generally the matter relative to the end, bricks and stones if it is a house. But the end is not due to these except as the matter, nor will it come to exist because of them. Yet if they do not exist at all, neither will the house, or the saw—the former in the absence of stones, the latter in the absence of iron— just as in the other case the premisses will not be true, if the angles of the triangle are not equal to two right angles.

The necessary in nature, then, is plainly what we call by the name of matter, and the changes in it. Both causes must be stated by the physicist, but especially the end; for that is the cause of the matter, not *vice versa;* and the end is 'that for the sake of which', and the beginning starts from the definition or essence; as in artificial products, since a house is of such-and-such a kind, certain things must *necessarily* come to be or be there already, or since health is this, these things must necessarily come to be or be there already. Similarly if man is this, then these; if these, then those. Perhaps the necessary is present also in the definition. For if one defines the operation of sawing as being a certain kind of dividing, then this cannot come about unless the saw has teeth of a certain kind; and these cannot be unless it is of iron. For in the definition too there are some parts that are, as it were, its matter.

9

CAUSE AND EFFECT

David Hume

. . .

OF PROBABILITY; AND OF THE IDEA OF CAUSE AND EFFECT

. . .

All kinds of reasoning consist in nothing but a *comparison*, and a discovery of those relations, either constant or inconstant, which two or more objects bear to each other. This comparison we may make, either when both the objects are present to the senses, or when neither of them is present, or when only one. When both the objects are present to the senses along with the relation, we call *this* perception rather than reasoning; nor is there in this case any exercise of the thought, or any action, properly speaking, but a mere passive admission of the impressions thro' the organs of sensation. According to this way of thinking, we ought not to receive as reasoning any of the observations we may make concerning *identity*, and the *relations* of *time* and *place;* since in none of them the mind can go beyond what is immediately present to the senses, either to discover the real existence or the relations of objects. 'Tis only *causation*, which produces such a connexion, as to give us assurance from the existence or action of one object, that 'twas follow'd or preceded by any other existence or action; nor can the other two relations be ever made use of in reasoning, except so far as they either affect or are affected by it. There is nothing in any objects to persuade us, that they are either always *remote* or always *contiguous;* and when from experience and observation we discover, that their relation in this particular is invariable, we always conclude there is some secret *cause*, which separates or unites them. The same reasoning extends to *identity*. We readily suppose an object may continue individually the same, tho' several times absent from and present to the senses; and ascribe to it an identity, notwithstanding the interruption of the perception, whenever we conclude, that if we had kept our eye or hand constantly upon it, it wou'd have convey'd an invariable

From David Hume, *A Treatise of Human Nature*, L. A. Selby-Bigge, ed. (Oxford: The Clarendon Press, 1888), Book I, Part III, Secs. 2–3, pp. 73–82.

and uninterrupted perception. But this conclusion beyond the impressions of our senses can be founded only on the connexion of *cause and effect;* nor can we otherwise have any security, that the object is not chang'd upon us, however much the new object may resemble that which was formerly present to the senses. Whenever we discover such a perfect resemblance, we consider, whether it be common in that species of objects; whether possibly or probably any cause cou'd operate in producing the change and resemblance; and according as we determine concerning these causes and effects, we form our judgment concerning the identity of the object.

Here then it appears, that of those three relations, which depend not upon the mere ideas, the only one, that can be trac'd beyond our senses, and informs us of existences and objects, which we do not see or feel, is *causation.* This relation, therefore, we shall endeavour to explain fully before we leave the subject of the understanding.

To begin regularly, we must consider the idea of *causation,* and see from what origin it is deriv'd. 'Tis impossible to reason justly, without understanding perfectly the idea concerning which we reason; and 'tis impossible perfectly to understand any idea, without tracing it up to its origin, and examining that primary impression, from which it arises. The examination of the impression bestows a clearness on the idea; and the examination of the idea bestows a like clearness on all our reasoning.

Let us therefore cast our eye on any two objects, which we call cause and effect, and turn them on all sides, in order to find that impression, which produces an idea of such prodigious consequence. At first sight I perceive, that I must not search for it in any of the particular *qualities* of the objects; since, which-ever of these qualities I pitch on, I find some object, that is not possest of it, and yet falls under the denomination of cause or effect. And indeed there is nothing existent, either externally or internally, which is not to be consider'd either as a cause or an effect; tho' 'tis plain there is no one quality, which universally belongs to all beings, and gives them a title to that denomination.

The idea, then, of causation must be deriv'd from some *relation* among objects; and that relation we must now endeavour to discover. I find in the first place, that whatever objects are consider'd as causes or effects, are *contiguous;* and that nothing can operate in a time or place, which is ever so little remov'd from those of its existence. Tho' distant objects may sometimes seem productive of each other, they are commonly found upon examination to be link'd by a chain of causes, which are contiguous among themselves, and to the distant objects; and when in any particular instance we cannot discover this connexion, we still presume it to exist. We may therefore consider the relation of CONTIGUITY as essential to that of causation; at least may suppose it such, according to the general opinion, till we can find a more proper occasion to clear up this matter, by examining what objects are or are not susceptible of juxtaposition and conjunction.

The second relation I shall observe as essential to causes and effects, is not so universally acknowledg'd, but is liable to some controversy. 'Tis that of PRIORITY of time in the cause before the effect. Some pretend that 'tis not absolutely necessary a cause shou'd precede its effect; but that any object or action, in the very first moment of its existence, may exert its productive quality, and give rise to another object or action, perfectly co-temporary with itself. But beside that experience in most instances seems to contradict this opinion, we may establish the relation of priority by a kind of inference or reasoning. 'Tis an establish'd maxim both in natural and moral philosophy, that an object, which exists for any time in its full perfection without producing another, is not its sole cause; but is assisted by some other principle, which pushes it from its state of inactivity, and makes it exert that energy, of which it was secretly possest. Now if any cause may be perfectly co-temporary with its effect, 'tis certain, according to this maxim, that they must all of them be so; since any one of them, which retards its operation for a single moment, exerts not itself at that very individual time, in which it might have operated; and therefore is no proper cause. The consequence of this wou'd be no less than the destruction of that succession of causes, which we observe in the world; and indeed, the utter annihilation of time. For if one cause were co-temporary with its effect, and this effect with *its* effect, and so on, 'tis plain there wou'd be no such thing as succession, and all objects must be co-existent.

If this argument appear satisfactory, 'tis well. If not, I beg the reader to allow me the same liberty, which I have us'd in the preceding case, of supposing it such. For he shall find, that the affair is of no great importance.

Having thus discover'd or suppos'd the two relations of *contiguity* and *succession* to be essential to causes and effects, I find I am stopt short, and can proceed no farther in considering any single instance of cause and effect. Motion in one body is regarded upon impulse as the cause of motion in another. When we consider these objects with the utmost attention, we find only that the one body approaches the other; and that the motion of it precedes that of the other, but without any sensible interval. 'Tis in vain to rack ourselves with *farther* thought and reflexion upon this subject. We can go no *farther* in considering this particular instance.

Shou'd any one leave this instance, and pretend to define a cause, by saying it is something productive of another, 'tis evident he wou'd say nothing. For what does he mean by *production?* Can he give any definition of it, that will not be the same with that of causation? If he can; I desire it may be produc'd. If he cannot; he here runs in a circle, and gives a synonymous term instead of a definition.

Shall we then rest contented with these two relations of contiguity and succession, as affording a compleat idea of causation? By no means. An object may be contiguous and prior to another, without being consider'd as its cause. There is a NECESSARY CONNEXION to be taken into consideration; and that relation is of much greater importance, than any of the other two above-mention'd.

Here again I turn the object on all sides, in order to discover the nature of this necessary connexion, and find the impression, or impressions, from which its idea may be deriv'd. When I cast my eye on the *known qualities* of objects, I immediately discover that the relation of cause and effect depends not in the least on *them.* When I consider their *relations*, I can find none but those of contiguity and succession; which I have already regarded as imperfect and unsatisfactory. Shall the despair of success make me assert, that I am here possest of an idea, which is not preceded by any similar impression? This wou'd be too strong a proof of levity and inconstancy; since the contrary principle has been already so firmly establish'd, as to admit of no farther doubt; at least, till we have more fully examin'd the present difficulty.

We must, therefore, proceed like those, who being in search of any thing that lies conceal'd from them, and not finding it in the place they expected, beat about all the neighbouring fields, without any certain view or design, in hopes their good fortune will at last guide them to what they search for. 'Tis necessary for us to leave the direct survey of this question concerning the nature of that *necessary connexion,* which enters into our idea of cause and effect; and endeavour to find some other questions, the examination of which will perhaps afford a hint, that may serve to clear up the present difficulty. Of these questions there occur two, which I shall proceed to examine, *viz.*

First, For what reason we pronounce it *necessary,* that every thing whose existence has a beginning, shou'd also have a cause?

Secondly, Why we conclude, that such particular causes must *necessarily* have such particular effects; and what is the nature of that *inference* we draw from the one to the other, and of the *belief* we repose in it?

I shall only observe before I proceed any farther, that tho' the ideas of cause and effect be deriv'd from the impressions of reflexion as well as from those of sensation, yet for brevity's sake, I commonly mention only the latter as the origin of these ideas; tho' I desire that whatever I say of them may also extend to the former. Passions are connected with their objects and with one another; no less than external bodies are connected together. The same relation, then, of cause and effect, which belongs to one, must be common to all of them.

WHY A CAUSE IS ALWAYS NECESSARY

To begin with the first question concerning the necessity of a cause: 'Tis a general maxim in philosophy, that *whatever begins to exist, must have a cause of existence.* This is commonly taken for granted in all reasonings, without any proof given or demanded. 'Tis suppos'd to be founded on intuition, and to be one of those maxims, which tho' they may be deny'd with the lips, 'tis impossible for men in their hearts really to doubt of. But if we examine this maxim by the idea of knowledge above-explain'd, we shall discover in it no mark of any such intuitive certainty; but on the contrary shall find, that 'tis of a nature quite foreign to that species of conviction.

All certainty arises from the comparison of ideas, and from the discovery of such relations as are unalterable, so long as the ideas continue the same. These relations are *resemblance, proportions in quantity and number, degrees of any quality, and contrariety;* none of which are imply'd in this proposition, *Whatever has a beginning has also a cause of existence.* That proposition therefore is not intuitively certain. At least any one, who wou'd assert it to be intuitively certain, must deny these to be the only infallible relations, and must find some other relation of that kind to be imply'd in it; which it will then be time enough to examine.

But here is an argument, which proves at once, that the foregoing proposition is neither intuitively nor demonstrably certain. We can never demonstrate the necessity of a cause to every new existence, or new modification of existence, without shewing at the same time the impossibility there is, that any thing can ever begin to exist without some productive principle; and where the latter proposition cannot be prov'd, we must despair of ever being able to prove the former. Now that the latter proposition is utterly incapable of a demonstrative proof, we may satisfy ourselves by considering, that as all distinct ideas are separable from each other, and as the ideas of cause and effect are evidently distinct, 'twill be easy for us to conceive any object to be non-existent this moment, and existent the next, without conjoining to it the distinct idea of a cause or productive principle. The separation, therefore, of the idea of a cause from that of a beginning of existence, is plainly possible for the imagination; and consequently the actual separation of these objects is so far possible, that it implies no contradiction nor absurdity; and is therefore incapable of being refuted by any reasoning from mere ideas; without which 'tis impossible to demonstrate the necessity of a cause.

Accordingly we shall find upon examination, that every demonstration, which has been produc'd for the necessity of a cause, is fallacious and sophistical. All the points of time and place, say some philosophers [Mr. Hobbes], in which we can suppose any object to begin to exist, are in themselves equal; and unless there be some cause, which is peculiar to one time and to one place, and which by that means determines and fixes the existence, it must remain in eternal suspence; and the object can never begin to be, for want of something to fix its beginning. But I ask; Is there any more difficulty in supposing the time and place to be fix'd without a cause, than to suppose the existence to be determin'd in that manner? The first question that occurs on this subject is always, *whether* the object shall exist or not: The next, *when* and *where* it shall begin to exist. If the removal of a cause be intuitively absurd in the one case, it must be so in the other: And if that absurdity be not clear without a proof in the one case, it will equally require one in the other. The absurdity, then, of the one supposition can never be a proof of that of the other; since they are both upon the same footing, and must stand or fall by the same reasoning.

The second argument [Dr. Clarke and others], which I find us'd on this head, labours under an equal difficulty. Every thing, 'tis said, must have a cause; for if any thing wanted a cause, *it* wou'd produce *itself*; that is, exist before it existed; which is impossible. But this reasoning is plainly unconclusive; because it supposes, that in our denial of a cause we still grant what we expressly deny, *viz.* that there must be a cause; which therefore is taken to be the object itself; and *that*, no doubt, is an evident contradiction. But to say that any thing is produc'd, or to express myself more properly, comes into existence, without a cause, is not to affirm, that 'tis itself its own cause; but on the contrary in excluding all external causes, excludes *a fortiori* the thing itself which is created. An object, that exists absolutely without any cause, certainly is not its own cause; and when you assert, that the one follows from the other, you suppose the very point in question, and take it for granted, that 'tis utterly impossible any thing can ever begin to exist without a cause, but that upon the exclusion of one productive principle, we must still have recourse to another.

'Tis exactly the same case with the third argument [Mr. Locke], which has been employ'd to demonstrate the necessity of a cause. Whatever is produc'd without any cause, is produc'd by *nothing;* or in other words, has nothing for its cause. But nothing can never be a cause, no more than it can be something, or equal to two right angles. By the same intuition, that we perceive nothing not to be equal to two right angles, or not to be something, we perceive, that it can never be a cause; and consequently must perceive, that every object has a real cause of its existence.

I believe it will not be necessary to employ many words in shewing the weakness of this argument, after what I have said of the foregoing. They are all of them founded on the same fallacy, and are deriv'd from the same turn of thought. 'Tis sufficient only to observe, that when we exclude all causes we really do exclude them, and neither suppose nothing nor the object itself to be the causes of the existence; and consequently can draw no argument from the absurdity of these suppositions to prove the absurdity of that exclusion. If every thing must have a cause, it follows, that upon the exclusion of other causes we must accept of the object itself or of nothing as causes. But 'tis the very point in question, whether every thing must have a cause or not; and therefore, according to all just reasoning, it ought never to be taken for granted.

They are still more frivolous, who say, that every effect must have a cause, because 'tis imply'd in the very idea of effect. Every effect necessarily pre-supposes a cause; effect being a relative term, of which cause is the correlative. But this does not prove, that every being must be preceded by a cause; no more than it follows, because every husband must have a wife, that therefore every man must be marry'd. The true state of the question is, whether every object, which begins to exist, must owe its existence to a cause; and this I assert neither to be intuitively nor demonstratively certain, and hope to have prov'd it sufficiently by the foregoing arguments.

.   .   .

10

THE LOGICAL CHARACTER OF
SCIENTIFIC LAWS

Ernest Nagel

ACCIDENTAL AND NOMIC UNIVERSALITY

The label 'law of nature' (or similar labels such as 'scientific law,' 'natural law,' or simply 'law') is not a technical term defined in any empirical science; and it is often used, especially in common discourse, with a strong honorific intent but without a precise import. There undoubtedly are many statements that are unhesitatingly characterized as 'laws' by most members of the scientific community, just as there is an even larger class of statements to which the label is rarely if ever applied. On the other hand, scientists disagree about the eligibility of many statements for the title of 'law of nature,' and the opinion of even one individual will often fluctuate on whether a given statement is to count as a law. This is patently the case for various theoretical statements, to which reference was made in the previous chapter, which are sometimes construed to be at bottom only procedural rules and therefore neither true nor false, although viewed by others as examples par excellence of laws of nature. Divergent opinions also exist as to whether statements of regularities containing any reference to particular individuals (or groups of such individuals) deserve the label of 'law.' For example, some writers have disputed the propriety of the designation for the statement that the planets move on elliptic orbits around the sun, since the statement mentions a particular body. Similar disagreements occur over the use of the label for statements of statistical regularities; and doubts have been expressed whether any formulation of uniformities in human social behavior (e.g., those studied in economics or linguistics) can properly be called 'laws.' The term 'law of nature' is undoubtedly vague. In consequence, any explication of its meaning which proposes a sharp demarcation between lawlike and non-lawlike statements is bound to be arbitrary.

There is therefore more than an appearance of futility in the recurring

From *The Structure of Science* by Ernest Nagel, Chap. IV, Secs. 1, 5, pp. 49–52, 73–78, © 1961, by Harcourt, Brace & World, Inc. Reprinted by permission of Harcourt, Brace & World, Inc., and Routledge & Kegan Paul Ltd.

attempts to define with great logical precision what is a law of nature—attempts often based on the tacit premise that a statement is a law in virtue of its possessing an inherent "essence" which the definition must articulate. For not only is the term 'law' vague in its current usage, but its historical meaning has undergone many changes. We are certainly free to designate as a law of nature any statement we please. There is often little consistency in the way we apply the label, and whether or not a statement is *called* a law makes little difference in the way in which the statement may be used in scientific inquiry. Nevertheless, members of the scientific community agree fairly well on the applicability of the term for a considerable though vaguely delimited class of universal statements. Accordingly, there is some basis for the conjecture that the predication of the label, at least in those cases where the consensus is unmistakable, is controlled by a felt difference in the "objective" status and function of that class of statements. It would indeed be futile to attempt an ironclad and rigorously exclusive definition of 'natural law.' It is not unreasonable to indicate some of the more prominent grounds upon which a numerous class of statements is commonly assigned a special status.

The *prima facie* difference between lawlike and non-lawlike universal conditionals can be brought out in several ways. One effective way depends on first recalling in what manner modern formal logic construes statements that have the form of universal conditionals. Two points must be noted in this connection. Such statements are interpreted in modern logic to assert merely this: any individual fulfilling the conditions described in the antecedent clause of the conditional also fulfills, *as a matter of contingent fact*, the conditions described in the consequent clause. For example, in this interpretation the statement 'All crows are black' (which is usually transcribed to read 'For any x, if x is a crow then x is black') merely says that any individual thing which happens to exist whether in the past, present, or future and which satisfies the conditions for being a crow is in point of fact also black. Accordingly, the sense assigned to the statement by this interpretation is also conveyed by the equivalent assertions that there never was a crow that was not black, there is no such crow at present, and there never will be such a crow. Universal conditionals construed in this way, so that they assert only matter-of-fact connections, are sometimes said to formulate only a "constant conjunction" of traits and to express "accidental" or *de facto* universality.

The second point to be noted in this interpretation is an immediate consequence of the first. On this interpretation a universal conditional is true, provided that there are no things (in the omnitemporal sense of 'are') which satisfy the conditions stated in the antecedent clause. Thus, if there are no unicorns, then all unicorns are black; but also, if there are no unicorns, then all unicorns are red.[1] Accordingly, on the construction placed

---

[1] This will be evident from the following: If there is no x such that x is a unicorn, then clearly there is no x such that x is a unicorn that is not black. But on the standard interpretation of the universal conditional, this latter statement immediately yields the conclusion that for any x, if x is a unicorn then x is black. Accordingly, if there are no unicorns then all unicorns are black.

It can also be shown that a universal conditional is true no matter what its antecedent clause may be, provided that everything of which the consequent clause can be

upon it in formal logic, a *de facto* universal conditional is true, irrespective of the content of its consequent clause, if in point of fact there happens to be nothing which satisfies its antecedent clause. Such a universal conditional is said to be "vacuously" true (or "vacuously satisfied").

Does a law of nature assert no more than accidental universality? The answer commonly given is in the negative. For a law is often held to express a "stronger" connection between antecedent and consequent conditions than just a matter-of-fact concomitance. Indeed, the connection is frequently said to involve some element of "necessity," though this alleged necessity is variously conceived and is described by such qualifying adjectives as 'logical,' 'causal,' 'physical,' or 'real.'[2] The contention is that to say that 'Copper always expands on heating' is a law of nature is to claim more than that there never has been and never will be a piece of heated copper that does not expand. To claim for that statement the status of a law is to assert, for example, not merely that there does not happen to exist such a piece of copper, but that it is "physically impossible" for such a piece of copper to exist. When the statement is assumed to be a law of nature, it is thus construed to assert that heating any piece of copper "physically necessitates" its expansion. Universal conditionals understood in this way are frequently described as "universals of law" or "nomological universals," and as expressing a "nomic" universality.

The distinction between accidental and nomic universality can be brought out in another way. Suppose that a piece of copper c which has never been heated is called to our attention, and is then destroyed so that it will never be heated. Suppose, further, that after the work of destruction is over we are asked whether c would have expanded had it been heated, and that we reply in the affirmative. And suppose, finally, that we are pressed for a reason for this answer. What reason can be advanced? A reason that would generally be accepted as cogent is that the natural law 'All copper when heated expands' warrants the contrary-to-fact conditional 'If c had been heated, it would have expanded.' Indeed, most people are likely to go further, and maintain that the nomological universal warrants the subjunctive conditional 'For any x, if x were copper and were heated, then x would expand.'

Laws of nature are in fact commonly used to justify subjunctive and contrary-to-fact conditionals, and such use is characteristic of all nomological universals. Moreover, this function of universals of law also suggests that the mere fact that nothing happens to exist (in the omnitemporal sense) which satisfies the antecedent clause of a nomological conditional is not sufficient to establish its truth. Thus, the assumption that the universe contains no bodies which are under the action of no external forces suffices to establish neither the subjunctive conditional that if there were such bodies their velocities would remain constant, nor the nomological universal that every body which is under the action of no external forces does not maintain a constant velocity.

---

significantly predicated satisfies the consequent clause. But we shall ignore any difficulties generated by this feature of universal conditionals.

[2] Cf. A. C. Ewing, *Idealism*, London, 1934, p. 167; C. I. Lewis, *An Analysis of Knowledge and Valuation*, La Salle, Ill., 1946, p. 228; Arthur W. Burks, "The Logic of Causal Propositions," *Mind*, Vol. 60 (1951), pp. 363–82.

On the other hand, the patently accidental universal 'All the screws in Smith's current car are rusty' does not justify the subjunctive conditional 'For any *x*, if *x* were a screw in Smith's current car *x* would be rusty.'[3] Certainly no one is likely to maintain on the strength of this *de facto* universal that, if a particular brass screw now resting on a dealer's shelf were inserted into Smith's car, that screw would be rusty. This *prima facie* difference between accidental and nomic universality can be briefly summarized by the formula: A universal of law "supports" a subjunctive conditional, while an accidental universal does not.

· · ·

CAUSAL LAWS

Something must finally be said about causal laws. It would be an ungrateful and pointless task to canvass even partially the variety of senses that have been attached to the word 'cause'—varying from the ancient legal associations of the word, through the popular conception of causes as efficient agents, to the more sophisticated modern notions of cause as invariable functional dependence. The fact that the term has this wide spectrum of uses immediately rules out the possibility that there is just one correct and privileged explication for it. It is nevertheless both possible and useful to identify one fairly definite meaning associated with the word in many areas of science as well as in ordinary discourse, with a view to obtaining from this perspective a rough classification of laws that serve as premises in explanations. On the other hand, it would be a mistake to suppose that, because in one meaning of the word the notion of cause plays an important role in some field of inquiry, the notion is indispensable in all other fields— just as it would be an error to maintain that, because this notion is useless in certain parts of science, it cannot have a legitimate role in other divisions of scientific study.

The sense of 'cause' we wish to identify is illustrated by the following example. An electric spark is passed through a mixture of hydrogen and oxygen gas; the explosion that follows the passage of the spark is accompanied by the disappearance of the gases and the condensation of water vapor. The disappearance of the gases and the formation of water in this experiment are commonly said to be the effects that are caused by the spark. Moreover, the generalization based on such experiments (e.g., 'Whenever a spark passes through a mixture of hydrogen and oxygen gas, the gases disappear and water is formed') is called a "causal law."

The law is said to be a causal one apparently because the relation it formulates between the events mentioned supposedly satisfies four conditions. In the first place, the relation is an invariable or uniform one, in the sense that whenever the alleged cause occurs so does the alleged effect. There is, moreover, the common tacit assumption that the cause constitutes

---

[3] This subjunctive conditional is not to be construed as saying that if any screw were *identical with* one of the screws in Smith's car it would be rusty. The latter subjunctive conditional is clearly true if indeed all the screws in Smith's current car are rusty. The subjunctive conditional in the text is to be understood as saying that for any object *x*—whether or not it is identical with one of the screws now in Smith's car—if *x* were a screw in that car it would be rusty.

both a necessary and a sufficient condition for the occurrence of the effect. In point of fact, however, most of the causal imputations made in everyday affairs, as well as most of the causal laws frequently mentioned, do not state the sufficient conditions for the occurrence of the effect. Thus, we often say that striking a match is the cause of its bursting into flame, and tacitly assume that other conditions without which the effect would not occur (e.g., presence of oxygen, a dry match) are also present. The event frequently picked out as the cause is normally an event that completes the set of sufficient conditions for the occurrence of the effect, and that is regarded for various reasons as being "important." In the second place, the relation holds between events that are spatially contiguous, in the sense that the spark and the formation of water occur in approximately the same spatial region. Accordingly, when events spatially remote from each other are alleged to be causally related, it is tacitly assumed that these events are but termini in a cause-and-effect chain of events, where the linking events are spatially contiguous. In the third place, the relation has a temporal character, in the sense that the event said to be the cause precedes the effect and is also "continuous" with the latter. In consequence, when events separated by a temporal interval are said to be causally related, they are also assumed to be connected by a series of temporally adjacent and causally related events. And finally, the relation is asymmetrical, in the sense that the passage of the spark through the mixture of gases is the cause of their transformation into water, but the formation of the water is not the cause of the passage of the spark.

The ideas in terms of which this notion of cause are stated have been frequently criticized as being vague; and telling objections have been made in particular against the common-sense conceptions of spatial and temporal continuity, on the ground that they contain a nest of confusions. It is undoubtedly true, moreover, that in some of the advanced sciences such as mathematical physics this notion is quite superfluous; and it is even debatable whether the four conditions just mentioned are in fact fulfilled in alleged illustrations of this notion of cause (such as the above example), when the illustrations are analyzed in terms of modern physical theories. Nevertheless, however inadequate this notion of cause may be for the purposes of theoretical physics, it continues to play a role in many other branches of inquiry. It is a notion that is firmly embodied in the language we employ, even when abstract physical theories are used in the laboratory as well as in practical affairs for obtaining various results through the manipulation of appropriate instrumentalities. Indeed, it is because some things can be manipulated so as to yield other things, but not conversely, that causal language is a legitimate and convenient way of describing the relations of many events.

On the other hand, not all laws of nature are causal in the indicated sense of this term. A brief survey of types of laws that are used as explanatory premises in various sciences will make this evident.

1. As has already been mentioned, a basic and pervasive type of law is involved in the assumption that there are "natural kinds" or "substances." Let us understand by a "determinable" a property such as color or density, which has a number of specific or "determinate" forms. Thus, among the determinate forms of the determinable color are red, blue, green, yellow,

etc.; among the determinate forms of the determinable density are the density with magnitude 0.06 (when measured in some standard fashion), the density with magnitude 2, the density with magnitude 12, etc. The determinate forms of a given determinable thus constitute a "related family" of properties such that every individual of which the determinable property can be significantly predicated must, of logical necessity, have one and only one of the determinate forms of the determinable.[4] A law of the type under consideration (e.g., 'There is the substance rock salt') then asserts that there are objects of various kinds, such that every object of a given kind is characterized by determinate forms of a set of determinable properties, and such that objects belonging to different kinds will differ in at least one (but usually more than one) determinate form of a common determinable. For example, to say that a given object *a* is rock salt is to say that there is a set of determinable properties (crystalline structure, color, melting point, hardness, etc.) such that under standard conditions *a* has a determinate form of each of these determinables (*a* has cubical crystals, it is colorless, it has a density of 2.163, a melting point of 804° C, the degree of hardness 2 on Mohs' scale, etc.). Moreover, *a* differs from an object belonging to a different kind, for example talc, in at least one (and in fact in a great many) determinate forms of these determinables. Accordingly, laws of this type assert that there is an invariable concomitance of determinate properties in every object that is of a certain kind. It will be clear, however, that laws of this type are not causal laws—they do not assert, for example, that the density of rock salt precedes (or follows) its degree of hardness.

2. A second type of law asserts an invariable sequential order of dependence among events or properties. Two subordinate types can be distinguished. One of these is the class of causal laws, such as the law about the effect of a spark in a mixture of hydrogen and oxygen, or the law that stones thrown into water produce a series of expanding concentric ripples. A second subordinate type is the class of "developmental" (or "historical") laws, such as the law 'The formation of lungs in the human embryo never precedes the formation of the circulatory system' or the law 'Consumption of alcohol is always followed by a dilation of the blood vessels.' Both subordinate types are frequent in areas of study in which quantitative methods have not been extensively introduced, although as the examples indicate such laws are encountered elsewhere as well. Developmental laws can be construed to have the form 'If *x* has the property *P* at time *t*, then *x* has the property *Q* at time *t'* later than *t*.' They are commonly not regarded as causal laws, apparently for two reasons. In the first place, though developmental laws may state a necessary condition for the occurrence of some event (or complex of events), they do not state the sufficient conditions. Indeed, we usually have only the vaguest sort of knowledge as to what these sufficient conditions are. In the second place, developmental laws generally state relations of sequential order between events separated by a temporal interval of some duration. In consequence, such laws are sometimes regarded as representing only an incomplete analysis of the facts, on the ground that, since something may intervene after the earlier event to

[4] For this terminology, cf. W. E. Johnson, *Logic*, Vol. 1, Cambridge, England, 1921, Chapter 11; and Rudolf Carnap, *Logical Foundations of Probability*, Chicago, 1950, Vol. 1, p. 75.

prevent the realization of the later one, the sequential order of events is not likely to be invariable. Nevertheless, whatever may be the limitations of developmental laws and however desirable it may be to supplement them by laws of another sort, both causal and developmental laws are extensively used in the explanatory systems of current science.

3. A third type of law, common in the biological and social sciences as well as in physics, asserts invariable statistical (or probabilistic) relations between events or properties. One example of such a law is: 'If a geometrically and physically symmetrical cube is repeatedly tossed, the probability (or relative frequency) that the cube will come to rest with a given face uppermost is $\frac{1}{6}$'; other examples have been previously mentioned. Statistical laws do not assert that the occurrence of one event is *invariably* accompanied by the occurrence of some other event. They assert only that, in a sufficiently long series of trials, the occurrence of one event is accompanied by the occurrence of a second event with an *invariable relative frequency*. Such laws are manifestly not causal, though they are not incompatible with a causal account of the facts they formulate. Indeed, the above statistical law about the behavior of a cube can be deduced from laws that are sometimes said to be causal ones, if suitable assumptions are made about the statistical distribution of initial conditions for the application of those causal laws. On the other hand, there are statistical laws even in physics for which at present no causal explanations are known. Moreover, even if one assumes that "in principle" all statistical laws are the consequences of some underlying "causal order," there are areas of inquiry—in physics as well as in the biological and social sciences—in which the explanation of many phenomena in terms of strictly universal causal laws is not likely to be feasible practically. It is a reasonable presumption that however much our knowledge may increase, statistical laws will continue to be used as the proximate premises for the explanation and prediction of many phenomena.

4. A fourth type of law, characteristic of modern physical science, asserts a relation of functional dependence (in the mathematical sense of "function") between two or more variable magnitudes associated with stated properties or processes. Two subtypes can be distinguished.

a. In the first place, there are numerical laws stating an interdependence between magnitudes such that a variation in any of them is concurrent with variations in the others. An example of such a law is the Boyle-Charles' law for ideal gases, that $pV = aT$, where p is the pressure of the gas, V its volume, T its absolute temperature, and a a constant that depends on the mass and the nature of the gas under consideration. This is not a causal law. It does not assert, for example, that a change in the temperature is followed (or preceded) by some change in the volume or in the pressure; it asserts only that a change in T is concurrent with changes in p or V or in both. Accordingly, the relation stated by the law must be distinguished from the sequential order of the events that may occur when the law is being tested or used for making predictions. For example, in testing the law in a laboratory, one may diminish the volume of an ideal gas in such a way that its temperature remains constant, and then note that its pressure increases. But the law says nothing about the order in which these magnitudes may be varied, nor about the temporal sequence in which the changes may be observed. Laws of this subtype can nevertheless be used for predictive as well as explanatory purposes. For example, if in the case of a suitably "isolated" system the magnitudes mentioned in such a law satisfy the indicated relation between them at one instant, they will satisfy this relation at some future instant, even though the magnitudes may have undergone some change in the interim.

b. A second subtype consists of numerical laws asserting in what manner a magnitude varies with the time, and more generally how a change in a magnitude per unit of time is related to other magnitudes (in some cases, though not always, to temporal durations). Galileo's law for freely falling bodies in a vacuum is one illustration of such a law. It says that the distance d traversed by a freely falling body is equal to $gt^2/2$, where g is constant and t is the duration of the fall. An equivalent way of stating Galileo's law is to say that the change in the distance per unit time of a freely falling body is equal to gt. In this formulation, it is evident that a time-rate of change in one magnitude is related to a temporal interval. Another example of a law belonging to this subtype is the law for the velocity of the bob of a simple pendulum along the path of its motion. The law says that, if v_0 is the velocity of the bob at the lowest point of its motion, h the height of the bob above the horizontal line through this point, and k a constant, then at any point along the arc of its motion the bob has a velocity v such that $v^2 = v_0^2 - kh^2$. Since the velocity v is the change in distance per unit of time, the law thus says that the change in the distance of the bob along its path per unit of time is a certain mathematical function of its velocity at the lowest point of its swing and of its altitude. In this case, the time-rate of change in one magnitude is not given as a function of the time. Laws that belong to this subtype are often called "dynamical laws" because they formulate the structure of a temporal process and are generally explained on the assumption that a "force" is acting on the system under consideration. Such laws are sometimes assimilated in causal laws, although in fact they are not causal in the specific sense distinguished earlier in this section. For the relation of dependence between the variables mentioned in the law is symmetrical, so that a state of the system at a given time is determined as completely by a later state as by an earlier one. Thus, if we know the velocity of the bob of a simple pendulum at any given instant, then provided there is no external interference with the system, the above law enables us to calculate the velocity at any other time, whether it is earlier or later than the given instant.

The preceding classification of laws is not proposed as an exhaustive one . . . The classification does indicate, however, that not all the laws recognized in the sciences are of one type, and that a scientific explanation is often regarded as satisfactory even though the laws cited in the premises are not "causal" in any customary sense.

11
EXPLANATION IN SCIENCE AND IN HISTORY

Carl G. Hempel

1. INTRODUCTION

Among the divers factors that have encouraged and sustained scientific inquiry through its long history are two pervasive human concerns which provide, I think, the basic motivation for all scientific research. One of these is man's persistent desire to improve his strategic position in the world by means of dependable methods for predicting and, whenever possible, controlling the events that occur in it. The extent to which science has been able to satisfy this urge is reflected impressively in the vast and steadily widening range of its technological applications. But besides this practical concern, there is a second basic motivation for the scientific quest, namely, man's insatiable intellectual curiosity, his deep concern to *know* the world he lives in, and to *explain*, and thus to *understand*, the unending flow of phenomena it presents to him.

In times past questions as to the *what* and the *why* of the empirical world were often answered by myths; and to some extent, this is so even in our time. But gradually, the myths are displaced by the concepts, hypotheses, and theories developed in the various branches of empirical science, including the natural sciences, psychology, and sociological as well as historical inquiry. What is the general character of the understanding attainable by these means, and what is its potential scope? In this paper I will try to shed some light on these questions by examining what seem to me the two basic types of explanation offered by the natural sciences, and then comparing them with some modes of explanation and understanding that are found in historical studies.

First, then, a look at explanation in the natural sciences.

Carl G. Hempel, "Explanation in Science and in History," in R. G. Colodny, ed., *Frontiers of Science and Philosophy* (Pittsburgh: University of Pittsburgh Press, 1962), pp. 9–32. Reprinted by permission of the publisher and the author.

2. TWO BASIC TYPES OF SCIENTIFIC EXPLANATION

2.1 Deductive-Nomological Explanation

In his book, *How We Think*, John Dewey describes an observation he made one day when, washing dishes, he took some glass tumblers out of the hot soap suds and put them upside down on a plate: he noticed that soap bubbles emerged from under the tumblers' rims, grew for a while, came to a standstill, and finally receded inside the tumblers. Why did this happen? The explanation Dewey outlines comes to this: In transferring a tumbler to the plate, cool air is caught in it; this air is gradually warmed by the glass, which initially has the temperature of the hot suds. The warming of the air is accompanied by an increase in its pressure, which in turn produces an expansion of the soap film between the plate and the rim. Gradually, the glass cools off, and so does the air inside, with the result that the soap bubbles recede.

This explanatory account may be regarded as an argument to the effect that the event to be explained (let me call it the explanandum-event) was to be expected by reason of certain explanatory facts. These may be divided into two groups: (i) particular facts and (ii) uniformities expressed by general laws. The first group includes facts such as these: the tumblers had been immersed, for some time, in soap suds of a temperature considerably higher than that of the surrounding air; they were put, upside down, on a plate on which a puddle of soapy water had formed, providing a connecting soap film, etc. The second group of items presupposed in the argument includes the gas laws and various other laws that have not been explicitly suggested concerning the exchange of heat between bodies of different temperature, the elastic behavior of soap bubbles, etc. If we imagine these various presuppositions explicitly spelled out, the idea suggests itself of construing the explanation as a deductive argument of this form:

$$\text{(D)} \qquad \frac{\begin{array}{c} C_1, C_2, \ldots, C_k \\ L_1, L_2, \ldots, L_r \end{array}}{E}$$

Here, $C_1, C_2, \ldots, C_k$ are statements describing the particular facts invoked; $L_1, L_2, \ldots, L_r$ are general laws: jointly, these statements will be said to form the explanans. The conclusion E is a statement describing the explanandum-event; let me call it the explanandum-statement, and let me use the word "explanandum" to refer to either E or to the event described by it.

The kind of explanation thus characterized I will call *deductive-nomological explanation*; for it amounts to a deductive subsumption of the explanandum under principles which have the character of general laws: it answers the question "*Why* did the explanandum event occur?" by showing that the event resulted from the particular circumstances specified in C_1, $C_2, \ldots, C_k$ in accordance with the laws $L_1, L_2, \ldots, L_r$. This conception of explanation, as exhibited in schema (D), has therefore been referred to as the covering law model, or as the deductive model, of explanation.

A good many scientific explanations can be regarded as deductive-nomological in character. Consider, for example, the explanation of mirror-images, of rainbows, or of the appearance that a spoon handle is bent at the point where it emerges from a glass of water: in all these cases, the explanandum is deductively subsumed under the laws of reflection and refraction. Similarly, certain aspects of free fall and of planetary motion can be accounted for by deductive subsumption under Galileo's or Kepler's laws.

In the illustrations given so far the explanatory laws had, by and large, the character of empirical generalizations connecting different observable aspects of the phenomenon under scrutiny: angle of incidence with angle of reflection or refraction, distance covered with falling time, etc. But science raises the question "why?" also with respect to the uniformities expressed by such laws, and often answers it in basically the same manner, namely, by subsuming the uniformities under more inclusive laws, and eventually under comprehensive theories. For example, the question, "Why do Galileo's and Kepler's laws hold?" is answered by showing that these laws are but special consequences of the Newtonian laws of motion and of gravitation; and these, in turn, may be explained by subsumption under the more comprehensive general theory of relativity. Such subsumption under broader laws or theories usually increases both the breadth and the depth of our scientific understanding. There is an increase in breadth, or scope, because the new explanatory principles cover a broader range of phenomena; for example, Newton's principles govern free fall on the earth and on other celestial bodies, as well as the motions of planets, comets, and artificial satellites, the movements of pendulums, tidal changes, and various other phenomena. And the increase thus effected in the depth of our understanding is strikingly reflected in the fact that, in the light of more advanced explanatory principles, the original empirical laws are usually seen to hold only approximately, or within certain limits. For example, Newton's theory implies that the factor g in Galileo's law, $s = \frac{1}{2}gt^2$, is not strictly a constant for free fall near the surface of the earth; and that, since every planet undergoes gravitational attraction not only from the sun, but also from the other planets, the planetary orbits are not strictly ellipses, as stated in Kepler's laws.

One further point deserves brief mention here. An explanation of a particular event is often conceived as specifying its *cause*, or causes. Thus, the account outlined in our first illustration might be held to explain the growth and the recession of the soap bubbles by showing that the phenomenon was *caused* by a rise and a subsequent drop of the temperature of the air trapped in the tumblers. Clearly, however, these temperature changes provide the requisite explanation only in conjunction with certain other conditions, such as the presence of a soap film, practically constant pressure of the air surrounding the glasses, etc. Accordingly, in the context of explanation, a cause must be allowed to consist in a more or less complex set of particular circumstances; these might be described by a set of sentences: $C_1, C_2, \ldots, C_k$. And, as suggested by the principle "Same cause, same effect," the assertion that those circumstances jointly caused a given event—described, let us say, by a sentence E—implies that whenever and wherever circumstances of the kind in question occur, an event of the kind to be explained comes about. Hence, the given causal explanation implicitly claims that there are general laws—such as $L_1, L_2, \ldots, L_r$ in schema (D)—by virtue of which the occurrence of the causal antecedents mentioned in $C_1, C_2, \ldots, C_k$ is a sufficient condition for the occurrence of the event to be explained. Thus, the relation between causal factors and effect is reflected in schema (D): causal explanation is de-ductive-nomological in character. (However, the customary formulations of causal and other explanations often do not explicitly specify all the relevant laws and particular facts: to this point, we will return later.)

The converse does not hold: there are deductive-nomological explanations which would not normally be counted as causal. For one thing, the subsumption of laws, such as Galileo's or Kepler's laws, under more compre-hensive principles is clearly not causal in character: we speak of causes only in reference to *particular* facts or events, and not in reference to *universal facts* as expressed by general laws. But not even all deductive-nomological explanations of particular facts or events will qualify as causal; for in a causal explanation some of the explanatory circumstances will temporally precede the effect to be explained: and there are explanations of type (D) which lack this characteristic. For example, the pressure which a gas of specified mass possesses at a given time might be explained by reference to its temperature and its volume at the same time, in conjunction with the gas law which connects simultaneous values of the three parameters.

In conclusion, let me stress once more the important role of laws in deductive-nomological explanation: the laws connect the explanandum event with the particular conditions cited in the explanans, and this is what confers upon the latter the status of explanatory (and, in some cases, causal) factors in regard to the phenomenon to be explained.

2.2 Probabilistic Explanation

In deductive-nomological explanation as schematized in (D), the laws and theoretical principles involved are of *strictly universal form:* they assert that in *all* cases in which certain specified conditions are realized an occurrence of such and such a kind will result; the law that any metal, when heated under constant pressure, will increase in volume, is a typical example; Galileo's, Kepler's, Newton's, Boyle's, and Snell's laws, and many others, are of the same character.

Now let me turn next to a second basic type of scientific explanation. This kind of explanation, too, is nomological, i.e., it accounts for a given phenomenon by reference to general laws or theoretical principles; but some or all of these are of *probabilistic-statistical form*, i.e., they are, generally speaking, assertions to the effect that if certain specified conditions are realized, then an occurrence of such and such a kind will come about with such and such a statistical probability.

For example, the subsiding of a violent attack of hay fever in a given case might well be attributed to, and thus explained by reference to, the administration of 8 milligrams of chlor-trimeton. But if we wish to connect this antecedent event with the explanandum, and thus to establish its explanatory significance for the latter, we cannot invoke a universal law to the effect that the administration of 8 milligrams of that antihistamine will invariably terminate a hay fever attack: this simply is not so. What can be asserted is only a generalization to the effect that administration of the drug will be followed by relief with high statistical probability, i.e., roughly speaking, with a high relative frequency in the long run. The resulting explanans will thus be of the following type:

John Doe had a hay fever attack and took 8 milligrams of chlor-trimeton.
The probability for subsidence of a hay fever attack upon administration of 8 milligrams of chlor-trimeton is high.

Clearly, this explanans does not deductively imply the explanandum, "John Doe's hay fever attack subsided"; the truth of the explanans makes the truth of the explanandum not certain (as it does in a deductive-nomological explanation) but only more or less likely or, perhaps "practically" certain.

Reduced to its simplest essentials, a probabilistic explanation thus takes the following form:

$$
(P) \qquad \left. \frac{\begin{array}{c} \text{Fi} \\ p(O, F) \text{ is very high} \end{array}}{\text{Oi}} \right\} \text{makes very likely}
$$

The explanandum, expressed by the statement "Oi," consists in the fact that in the particular instance under consideration, here called i (e.g., John Doe's allergic attack), an outcome of kind O (subsidence) occurred. This is explained by means of two explanans-statements. The first of these, "Fi," corresponds to $C_1, C_2, \ldots, C_k$ in (D); it states that in case i, the factors F (which may be more or less complex) were realized. The second expresses a law of probabilistic form, to the effect that the statistical probability for outcome O to occur in cases where F is realized is very high (close to 1). The double line separating explanandum from explanans is to indicate that, in contrast to the case of deductive-nomological explanation, the explanans does not logically imply the explanandum, but only confers a high likelihood upon it. The concept of likelihood here referred to must be clearly distinguished from that of statistical probability, symbolized by "p" in our schema. A statistical probability is, roughly speaking, the long-run relative frequency with which an occurrence of a given kind (say, F) is accompanied by an "outcome" of a specified kind (say, O). Our likelihood, on the other hand, is a relation (capable of gradations) not between kinds of occurrences, but between statements. The likelihood referred to in (P) may be characterized as the strength of the inductive support, or the degree of rational credibility, which the explanans confers upon the explanandum; or, in Carnap's terminology, as the *logical*, or *inductive*, (in contrast to statistical) *probability* which the explanandum possesses relative to the explanans.

Thus, probabilistic explanation, just like explanation in the manner of schema (D), is nomological in that it presupposes general laws; but because these laws are of statistical rather than of strictly universal form, the resulting explanatory arguments are inductive rather than deductive in character. An inductive argument of this kind *explains* a given phenomenon by showing that, in view of certain particular events and certain statistical laws, its occurrence was to be expected with high logical, or inductive, probability.

By reason of its inductive character, probabilistic explanation differs from its deductive-nomological counterpart in several other important respects; for example, its explanans may confer upon the explanandum a more or less high degree of inductive support; in this sense, probabilistic explanation admits of degrees, whereas deductive-nomological explanation appears as an either-or affair: a given set of universal laws and particular statements either does or does not imply a given explanandum statement. A fuller examination of these differences, however, would lead us far afield and is not required for the purposes of this paper.

One final point: the distinction here suggested between deductive-nomological and probabilistic explanation might be questioned on the ground that, after all, the universal laws invoked in a deductive explanation can have been established only on the basis of a finite body of evidence, which surely affords no exhaustive verification, but only more or less strong probability for it; and that, therefore, all scientific laws have to be regarded as probabilistic. This argument, however, confounds a logical issue with an epistemological one: it fails to distinguish properly between the *claim* made by a given law-statement and the *degree of confirmation*, or *probability*, which it possesses on the available evidence. It is quite true that statements expressing laws of either kind can be only incompletely confirmed by any given finite set—however large—of data about particular facts; but law-statements of the two different types make claims of different kind, which are reflected in their logical forms: roughly, a universal law-statement of the simplest kind asserts that *all* elements of an indefinitely large reference class (e.g., copper objects) have a certain characteristic (e.g., that of being good conductors of electricity); while statistical law-statements assert that in the long run, a specified proportion of the members of the reference class have some specified property. And our distinction of two types of law and, concomitantly, of two types of scientific explanation, is based on this difference in claim as reflected in the difference of form.

The great scientific importance of probabilistic explanation is eloquently attested to by the extensive and highly successful explanatory use that has been made of fundamental laws of statistical form in genetics, statistical mechanics, and quantum theory.

3. ELLIPTIC AND PARTIAL EXPLANATIONS: EXPLANATION SKETCHES

As I mentioned earlier, the conception of deductive-nomological explanation reflected in our schema (D) is often referred to as the covering law model, or the deductive model, of explanation: similarly, the conception underlying schema (P) might be called the probabilistic or the inductive-statistical, model of explanation. The term "model" can serve as a useful reminder that the two types of explanation as characterized above constitute ideal types or theoretical idealizations and are not intended to reflect the manner in which working scientists actually formulate their explanatory accounts. Rather, they are meant to provide explications, or rational reconstructions, or theoretical models, of certain modes of scientific explanation.

In this respect our models might be compared to the concept of mathematical proof (within a given theory) as construed in meta-mathematics. This concept, too, may be regarded as a theoretical model: it is not intended to provide a descriptive account of how proofs are formulated in the writings of mathematicians: most of these actual formulations fall short of rigorous and, as it were, ideal, meta-mathematical standards. But the theoretical model has certain other functions: it exhibits the rationale of mathematical proofs by revealing the logical connections underlying the successive steps; it provides standards for a critical appraisal of any proposed proof constructed within the mathematical system to which the model refers; and it affords a basis for a precise and far-reaching theory of proof, provability, decidability, and related concepts. I think the two models of explanation can fulfill the same functions, if only on a much more modest scale. For example, the arguments presented in constructing the models give an indication of the sense in which the models exhibit the rationale and the logical structure of the explanations they are intended to represent.

I now want to add a few words concerning the second of the functions just mentioned; but I will have to forgo a discussion of the third.

When a mathematician proves a theorem, he will often omit mention of certain propositions which he presupposes in his argument and which he is in fact entitled to presuppose because, for example, they follow readily from the postulates of his system or from previously established theorems or perhaps from the hypothesis of his theorem, if the latter is in hypothetical form; he then simply assumes that his readers or listeners will be able to supply the missing items if they so desire. If judged by ideal standards, the given formulation of the proof is elliptic or incomplete; but the departure from the ideal is harmless: the gaps can readily be filled in. Similarly, explanations put forward in everyday discourse and also in scientific contexts are often *elliptically formulated*. When we explain, for example, that a lump of butter melted because it was put into a hot frying pan, or that a small rainbow appeared in the spray of the lawn sprinkler because the sunlight was reflected and refracted by the water droplets, we may be said to offer elliptic formulations of deductive-nomological explanations; an account of this kind omits mention of certain laws or particular facts which it tacitly takes for granted, and whose explicit citation would yield a complete deductive-nomological argument.

In addition to elliptic formulation, there is another, quite important, respect in which many explanatory arguments deviate from the theoretical model. It often happens that the statement actually included in the explanans, together with those which may reasonably be assumed to have been taken for granted in the context at hand, explain the given explanandum only *partially*, in a sense which I will try to indicate by an example. In his *Psychopathology of Everyday Life*, Freud offers the following explanation of a slip of the pen that occurred to him: "On a sheet of paper containing principally short daily notes of business interest, I found, to my surprise, the incorrect date, 'Thursday, October 20th,' bracketed under the correct date of the month of September. It was not difficult to explain this anticipation as the expression of a wish. A few days before I had returned fresh from my vacation and felt ready for any amount of professional work, but as yet there were few patients. On my arrival I had found a letter from a patient announcing her arrival on the 20th of October. As I wrote the same date in September I may certainly have thought 'X. ought to be here already; what a pity about that whole month!,' and with this thought I pushed the current date a month ahead."

Clearly, the formulation of the intended explanation is *at least incomplete* in the sense considered a moment ago. In particular, it fails to mention any laws or theoretical principles in virtue of which the subconscious wish, and the other antecedent circumstances referred to, could be held to explain Freud's slip of the pen. However, the general theoretical considerations Freud presents here and elsewhere in his writings suggests strongly that his explanatory account relies on a hypothesis to the effect that when a person has a strong, though perhaps unconscious, desire, then if he commits a slip of pen, tongue, memory, or the like, the slip will take a form in which it expresses, and perhaps symbolically fulfills, the given desire.

Even this rather vague hypothesis is probably more definite than what Freud would have been willing to assert. But for the sake of the argument let us accept it and include it in the explanans, together with the particular statements that Freud did have the subconscious wish he mentions, and that he was going to commit a slip of the pen. Even then, the resulting explanans permits us to deduce only that the slip made by Freud would, *in some way or other*, express and perhaps symbolically fulfill Freud's subconscious wish. But clearly, such expression and fulfillment might have been achieved by many other kinds of slip of the pen than the one actually committed.

In other words, the explanans does not imply, and thus fully explain, that the particular slip, say s, which Freud committed on this occasion, would fall within the narrow class, say W, of acts which consist in writing the words "Thursday, October 20th"; rather, the explanans implies only that s would fall into a wider class, say F, which includes W as a proper subclass, and which consists of all acts which would express and symbolically fulfill Freud's subconscious wish *in some way or other*.

The argument under consideration might be called a *partial explanation*: it provides complete, or conclusive, grounds for expecting s to be a member of F, and since W is a subclass of F, it thus shows that the explanandum, i.e., s falling within W, accords with, or bears out, what is to be expected in consideration of the explanans. By contrast, a deductive-nomological explanation of the form (D) might then be called *complete* since the explanans here does imply the explanandum.

Clearly, the question whether a given explanatory argument is complete or partial can be significantly raised only if the explanandum sentence is fully specified; only then can we ask whether the explanandum does or does not follow from the explanans. Completeness of explanation, in this sense, is relative to our explanandum sentence. Now, it might seem much more important and interesting to consider instead the notion of a complete explanation of some *concrete event*, such as the destruction of Pompeii, or the death of Adolf Hitler, or the launching of the first artificial satellite: we might want to regard a particular event as completely explained only if an explanatory account of deductive or of inductive form had been provided for all of its aspects. This notion, however, is self-defeating; for any particular event may be regarded as having infinitely many different aspects or characteristics, which cannot all be accounted for by a finite set, however large, of explanatory statements.

In some cases, what is intended as an explanatory account will depart even further from the standards reflected in the model schemata (D) and (P) above. An explanatory account, for example, which is not explicit and specific enough to be reasonably qualified as an elliptically formulated explanation or as a partial one, can often be viewed as an *explanation sketch:* it may suggest, perhaps quite vividly and persuasively, the general outlines of what, it is hoped, can eventually be supplemented so as to yield a more closely reasoned argument based on explanatory hypotheses which are indicated more fully, and which more readily permit of critical appraisal by reference to empirical evidence.

The decision whether a proposed explanatory account is to be qualified as an elliptically formulated deductive or probabilistic explanation, as a partial explanation, as an explanation sketch, or perhaps as none of these is a matter of judicious interpretation; it calls for an appraisal of the intent of the given argument and of the background assumptions that may be assumed to have been tacitly taken for granted, or at least to be available, in the given context. Unequivocal decision rules cannot be set down for this purpose any more than for determining whether a given informally stated inference which is not deductively valid by reasonably strict standards is to count nevertheless as valid but enthymematically formulated, or as fallacious, or as an instance of sound inductive reasoning, or perhaps, for lack of clarity, as none of these.

4. NOMOLOGICAL EXPLANATION IN HISTORY

So far, we have examined nomological explanation, both deductive and inductive, as found in the natural sciences; and we have considered certain characteristic ways in which actual explanatory accounts often depart from the ideal standards of our two basic models. Now it is time to ask what light the preceding inquiries can shed on the explanatory procedures used in historical research.

In examining this question, we will consider a number of specific explanatory arguments offered by a variety of writers. It should be understood from the beginning that we are here concerned, not to appraise the factual adequacy of these explanations, but only to attempt an explication of the claims they make and of the assumptions they presuppose.

Let us note first, then, that some historical explanations are surely nomological in character: they aim to show that the explanandum phenomenon resulted from certain antecedent, and perhaps, concomitant, conditions; and in arguing these, they rely more or less explicitly on relevant generalizations. These may concern, for example, psychological or sociological tendencies and may best be conceived as broadly probabilistic in character. This point is illustrated by the following argument, which might be called an attempt to explain Parkinson's Law by subsumption under broader psychological principles:

"As the activities of the government are enlarged, more people develop a vested interest in the continuation and expansion of governmental functions. People who have jobs do not like to lose them; those who are habituated to certain skills do not welcome change; those who have become accustomed to the exercise of a certain kind of power do not like to relinquish their control—if anything, they want to develop greater power and correspondingly greater prestige. . . . Thus, government offices and bureaus, once created, in turn institute drives, not only to fortify themselves against assault, but to enlarge the scope of their operations."

The psychological generalizations here explicitly adduced will reasonably have to be understood as expressing, not strict uniformities, but strong *tendencies*, which might be formulated by means of rough probability statements; so that the explanation here suggested is probabilistic in character.

As a rule, however, the generalizations underlying a proposed historical explanation are largely left unspecified; and most concrete explanatory accounts have to be qualified as partial explanations or as explanation sketches. Consider, for example, F. J. Turner's essay "The Significance of the Frontier in American History," which amplifies and defends the view that "Up to our own day American history has been in a large degree the history of the colonization of the Great West. The existence of an area of free land, its continuous recession, and the advance of American settlement westward explain American development. . . . The peculiarity of American institutions is the fact that they have been compelled to adapt themselves . . . to the changes involved in crossing a continent, in winning a wilderness, and in developing at each area of this progress, out of the primitive economic and political conditions of the frontier, the complexity of city life." One of the phenomena Turner considers in developing his thesis is the rapid westward advance of what he calls the Indian trader's frontier. "Why was it," Turner asks, "that the Indian trader passed so rapidly across the continent?"; and he answers, "The explanation of the rapidity of this advance is bound up with the effects of the trader on the Indian. The trading post left the unarmed tribes at the mercy of those that had purchased firearms—a truth which the Iroquois Indians wrote in blood, and so the remote and unvisited tribes gave eager welcome to the trader. . . . This accounts for the trader's power and the rapidity of his advance." There is no explicit mention here of any laws, but it is clear that this sketch of an explanation presupposes, first of all, various particular facts, such as that the remote and unvisited tribes had heard of the efficacy and availability of firearms, and that there were no culture patterns or institutions precluding their use by those tribes; but in addition, the account clearly rests also on certain assumptions as to how human beings will tend to behave in situations presenting the kinds of danger and of opportunity that Turner refers to.

Similar comments apply to Turner's account of the westward advance of what he calls the farmer's frontier: "Omitting those of the pioneer farmers who move from the love of adventure, the advance of the more steady farmer is easy to understand. Obviously the immigrant was attracted by the cheap lands of the frontier, and even the native farmer felt their influence strongly. Year by year the farmers who lived on soil, whose returns were diminished by unrotated crops, were offered the virgin soil of the frontier at nominal prices. Their growing families demanded more lands, and these were dear. The competition of the unexhausted, cheap, and easily tilled prairie lands compelled the farmer either to go West . . . or to adopt intensive culture." This passage is clearly intended to do more than describe a sequence of particular events: it is meant to afford an understanding of the farmers' westward advance by pointing to their interests and needs and by calling attention to the facts and the opportunities facing them. Again, this explanation takes it for granted that under such conditions normal human beings will tend to seize new opportunities in the manner in which the pioneer farmers did.

Examining the various consequences of this moving-frontier history, Turner states that "the most important effect of the frontier has been in the promotion of democracy here and in Europe," and he begins his elaboration of this theme with the remark that "the frontier is productive of individualism. . . . The tendency is anti-social. It produces antipathy to control, and particularly to any direct control": and this is, of course, a sociological generalization in a nutshell.

Similarly, any explanation that accounts for a historical phenomenon by reference to economic factors or by means of general principles of social or cultural change are nomological in import, even if not in explicit formulation.

But if this be granted there still remains another question, to which we must now turn, namely, whether, in addition to explanations of a broadly nomological character, the historian also employs certain other distinctly historical ways of explaining and understanding whose import cannot be adequately characterized by means of our two models. The question has often been answered in the affirmative, and several kinds of historical explanation have been adduced in support of this affirmation. I will now consider what seem to me two especially interesting candidates for the role of specifically historical explanation; namely first, genetic explanation, and secondly, explanation of an action in terms of its underlying rationale.

5. GENETIC EXPLANATION IN HISTORY

In order to make the occurrence of a historical phenomenon intelligible, a historian will frequently offer a "genetic explanation" aimed at exhibiting the principal stages in a sequence of events which led up to the given phenomenon.

Consider, for example, the practice of selling indulgences as it existed in Luther's time. H. Boehmer, in his work, *Luther and the Reformation*, points out that until about the end of the 19th century, "the indulgence was in fact still a great unknown quantity, at sight of which the scholar would ask himself with a sigh: 'Where did it come from?'" An answer was provided by Adolf Gottlob, who tackled the problem by asking himself what led the Popes and Bishops to offer indulgences. As a result, ". . . origin and development of the unknown quantity appeared clearly in the light, and doubts as to its original meaning came to an end. It revealed itself as a true descendant of the time of the great struggle between Christianity and Islam, and at the same time a highly characteristic product of Germanic Christianity."

In brief outline, the origins of the indulgence appear to go back to the 9th century, when the popes were strongly concerned with the fight against Islam. The Mohammedan fighter was assured by the teachings of his religion that if he were to be killed in battle his soul would immediately go to heaven; but the defender of the Christian faith had to fear that he might still be lost if he had not done the regular penance for his sins. To allay these doubts, John VII, in 877, promised absolution for their sins to crusaders who should be killed in battle. "Once the crusade was so highly thought of, it was an easy transition to regard participation in a crusade as equivalent to the performance of atonement . . . and to promise remission of these penances in return for expeditions against the Church's enemies." Thus, there was introduced the indulgence of the Cross, which granted complete remission of the penitential punishment to all those who participated in a religious war. "If it is remembered what inconveniences, what ecclesiastical and civil disadvantages the ecclesiastical penances entailed, it is easy to understand that the penitents flocked to obtain this indulgence." A further strong incentive came from the belief that whoever obtained an indulgence secured liberation not only from the ecclesiastical penances, but also from the corresponding suffering in purgatory after death. The benefits of these indulgences were next extended to those who, being physically unfit to participate in a religious war, contributed the funds required to send a soldier on a crusade: in 1199, Pope Innocent III recognized the payment of money as adequate qualification for the benefits of a crusading indulgence.

When the crusades were on the decline, new ways were explored of raising funds through indulgences. Thus, there was instituted a "jubilee indulgence," to be celebrated every hundred years, for the benefit of pilgrims coming to Rome on that occasion. The first of these indulgences, in 1300, brought in huge sums of money; and the time interval between successive jubilee indulgences was therefore reduced to 50, 33 and even 25 years. And from 1393 on the jubilee indulgence was made available, not only in Rome, for the benefit of pilgrims, but everywhere in Europe, through special agents who were empowered to absolve the penitent of their sins upon payment of an appropriate amount. The development went even further: in 1477, a dogmatic declaration by Sixtus IV attributed to the indulgence the power of delivering even the dead from purgatory.

Undeniably, a genetic account of this kind can enhance our understanding of a historical phenomenon. But its explanatory role, far from being *sui generis*, seems to me basically nomological in character. For the successive stages singled out for consideration surely must be qualified for their function by more than the fact that they form a temporal sequence and that they all precede the final stage, which is to be explained: the mere enumeration in a yearbook of "the year's important events" in the order of their occurrence clearly is not a genetic explanation of the final event or of anything else. In a genetic explanation each stage must be shown to "lead to" the next, and thus to be linked to its successor by virtue of some general principle which makes the occurrence of the latter at least reasonably probable, given the former. But in this sense, even successive stages in a physical phenomenon such as the free fall of a stone may be regarded as forming a genetic sequence whose different stages—characterized, let us say, by the position and the velocity of the stone at different times—are interconnected by strictly universal laws; and the successive stages in the movement of a steel ball bouncing its zigzaggy way down a Galton pegboard may be regarded as forming a genetic sequence with probabilistic connections.

The genetic accounts given by historians are not, of course, of the purely nomological kind suggested by these examples from physics. Rather, they combine a certain measure of nomological interconnecting with more or less large amounts of straight description. For consider an intermediate stage mentioned in a genetic account: some aspects of it will be presented as having evolved from the preceding stages (in virtue of connecting laws, which often will be no more than hinted at); while other aspects, which are not accounted for by information about the preceding development, will be descriptively added because they are relevant to an understanding of subsequent stages in the genetic sequence. Thus, schematically speaking, a genetic explanation will begin with a pure description of an initial stage; thence, it will proceed to an account of a second stage, part of which is nomologically linked to, and explained by, the characteristic features of the initial stage; while the balance is simply described as relevant for a nomological account of some aspects of the third stage; and so forth.

In our illustration the connecting laws are hinted at in the mention made of motivating factors: the explanatory claims made for the interest of the popes in securing a fighting force and in amassing ever larger funds clearly presuppose suitable psychological generalizations as to the manner in which an intelligent individual will act, in the light of his factual beliefs, when he seeks to attain a certain objective. Similarly, general assumptions underlie the reference to the fear of purgatory in explaining the eagerness with which indulgences were bought. And when, referring to the huge financial returns of the first jubilee indulgence, Schwiebert says "This success only whetted the insatiable appetite of the popes. The intervening period of time was variously reduced from 100 to 50, to 33, to 25 years . . . ," the explanatory force here implied might be said to rest on some principle of reinforcement by rewards. As need hardly be added, even if such a principle were explicitly introduced, the resulting account would provide at most a partial explanation; it could not be expected to show, for example, why the intervening intervals should have the particular lengths here mentioned.

In the genetic account of the indulgences, those factors which are simply described (or tacitly presupposed) rather than explained include, for example, the doctrines, the organization, and the power of the Church; the occurrence of the crusades and their eventual decline; and innumerable other factors which are not even explicitly mentioned, but which have to be understood as background conditions if the genetic survey is to serve its explanatory purpose.

The general conception here outlined of the logic of genetic explanation could also be illustrated by reference to Turner's studies of the American frontier; this will be clear even from the brief remarks made earlier on Turner's ideas.

Some analysts of historical development put special emphasis on the importance of the laws underlying a historical explanation; thus, e.g., A. Gerschenkron maintains, "Historical research consists essentially in application to empirical material of various sets of empirically derived hypothetical generalizations and in testing the closeness of the resulting fit, in the hope that in this way certain uniformities, certain typical situations, and certain typical relationships among individual factors in these situations can be ascertained," and his subsequent substantive observations include a brief genetic survey of patterns of industrial development in 19th century Europe, in which some of the presumably relevant uniformities are made reasonably explicit.

6. EXPLANATION BY MOTIVATING REASONS

Let us now turn to another kind of historical explanation that is often considered as *sui generis*, namely, the explanation of an action in terms of the underlying *rationale*, which will include, in particular, the ends the agent sought to attain, and the alternative courses of action he believed to be open to him. The following passage explaining the transition from the indulgence of the Cross to the institution of the jubilee indulgence illustrates this procedure: ". . . in the course of the thirteenth century the idea of a crusade more and more lost its power over men's spirits. If the Popes would keep open the important source of income which the indulgence represented, they must invent new motives to attract people to the purchase of indulgences. It is the merit of Boniface VIII to have recognized this clearly. By creating the jubilee indulgence in 1300 he assured the species a further long development most welcome to the Papal finances." This passage clearly seeks to explain the establishment of the first jubilee indulgence by suggesting the reasons for which Boniface VIII took this step. If properly spelled out, these reasons would include not only Boniface's objective of ensuring a continuation of the income so far derived from the indulgence of the Cross, but also his estimate of the relevant empirical circumstances, including the different courses of action open to him, and their probable efficacy as well as potential difficulties in pursuing them and adverse consequences to which they might lead.

The kind of explanation achieved by specifying the rationale underlying a given action is widely held to be fundamentally different from nomological explanation as found in the natural sciences. Various reasons have been adduced in support of this view; but I will limit my discussion largely to the stimulating ideas on the subjects that have been set forth by Dray. According to Dray, there is an important type of historical explanation whose features "make the covering law model peculiarly inept"; he calls it "rational explanation," i.e., "explanation which displays the *rationale* of what was done," or, more fully, "a reconstruction of the agent's *calculation* of means to be adopted toward his chosen end in the light of the circumstances in which he found himself." The object of rational explanation is not to subsume the explanandum under general laws, but "to show that what was done was the thing to have done for the reasons given, rather than merely the thing that is done on such occasions, perhaps in accordance with certain laws." Hence, a rational explanation has "an element of *appraisal*" in it: it "must exhibit what was done as appropriate or justified." Accordingly, Dray conceives a rational explanation as being based on a standard of appropriateness or of rationality of a special kind which he calls a "*principle of action*," i.e., "a judgment of the form 'When in a situation of type $C_1, C_2, \ldots C_n$ the thing to do is X.' "

Dray does not give a full account of the kind of "situation" here referred to; but to do justice to his intentions, these situations must evidently be taken to include, at least, items of the following three types: (i) the end the agent was seeking to attain; (ii) the empirical circumstances, as seen by the agent, in which he had to act; (iii) the moral standards or principles of conduct to which the agent was committed. For while this brief list requires considerable further scrutiny and elaboration, it seems clear that only if at least these items are specified does it make sense to raise the question of the appropriateness of what the agent did in the given "situation."

It seems fair to say, then, that according to Dray's conception a rational explanation answers a question of the form "Why did agent A do X?" by offering an explanans of the following type (our formulation replaces the notation "$C_1, C_2, \ldots C_n$" by the simpler "C," without, of course, precluding that the kind of situation thus referred to may be extremely complex):

(R)
   A was in a situation of type C
   In a situation of type C, the appropriate thing to do is X

But can an explanans of this type possibly serve to explain A's having in fact done X? It seems to me beyond dispute that in any adequate explanation of an empirical phenomenon the explanans must provide good grounds for believing or asserting that the explanandum phenomenon did in fact occur. Yet this requirement, which is necessary though not sufficient for an adequate explanation, is not met by a rational explanation as conceived by Dray. For the two statements included in the contemplated explanans (R) provide good reasons for believing that the appropriate thing for A to do was X, but not for believing that A did in fact do X. Thus, a rational explanation in the sense in which Dray appears to understand it does not explain what it is meant to explain. Indeed, the expression "the thing to do" in the standard formulation of a principle of action, "functions as a value term," as Dray himself points out: but then, it is unclear, on purely logical grounds, how the valuational principle expressed by the second sentence in (R), in conjunction with the plainly empirical, non-valuational first sentence, should permit any inferences concerning empirical matters such as A's action, which could not be drawn from the first sentence alone.

To explain, in the general vein here under discussion, why A did in fact do X, we have to refer to the underlying rationale not by means of a normative principle of action, but by descriptive statements to the effect that, at the time in question A was a rational agent, or had the disposition to act rationally; and that a rational agent, when in circumstances of kind C, will always (or: with high probability) do X. Thus construed, the explanans takes on the following form:

(R')
   (a) A was in a situation of type C
   (b) A was disposed to act rationally
   (c) Any person who is disposed to act rationally will, when in a situation of type C, invariably (with high probability) do X

But by this explanans A's having done X is accounted for in the manner of a deductive or of a probabilistic nomological explanation. Thus, in so far as reference to the rationale of an agent does explain his action, the explanation conforms to one of our nomological models.

An analogous diagnosis applies, incidentally, also to explanations which attribute an agent's behavior in a given situation not to rationality and more or less explicit deliberation on his part, but to other dispositional features, such as his character and emotional make-up. The following comment on Luther illustrates this point: "Even stranger to him than the sense of anxiety was the allied sense of fear. In 1527 and 1535, when the plague broke out in Wittenberg, he was the only professor besides Bugenhagen who remained calmly at his post to comfort and care for the sick and dying. . . . He had, indeed, so little sense as to take victims of the plague into his house and touch them with his own hand. Death, martyrdom, dishonor, contempt . . . he feared just as little as infectious disease." It may well be said that these observations give more than a description: that they shed some explanatory light on the particular occurrences mentioned. But in so far as they explain, they do so by presenting Luther's actions as manifestations of certain personality traits, such as fearlessness; thus, the particular acts are again subsumed under generalizations as to how a fearless person is likely to behave under certain circumstances.

It might seem that both in this case and in rational explanation as construed in (R'), the statements which we took to express general laws— namely, (c) in (R'), and the statement about the probable behavior of a fearless person in our last illustration—do not have the character of empirical laws at all, but rather that of analytic statements which simply express part of what is *meant* by a rational agent, a fearless person, or the like. Thus, in contrast to nomological explanations, these accounts in terms of certain dispositional characteristics of the agent appear to presuppose no general laws at all. Now, the idea of analyticity gives rise to considerable philosophical difficulties; but let us disregard these here and take the division of statements into analytic and synthetic to be reasonably clear. Even then, the objection just outlined cannot be upheld. For dispositional concepts of the kind invoked in our explanations have to be regarded as governed by entire clusters of general statements—we might call them symptom statements— which connect the given disposition with various specific manifestations, or symptoms, of its presence (each symptom will be a particular mode of "responding," or acting, under specified "stimulus" conditions); and the whole cluster of these symptom statements for a given disposition will have implications which are plainly not analytic (in the intuitive sense here assumed). Under these circumstances it would be arbitrary to attribute to some of the symptom statements the analytic character of partial definitions.

The logic of this situation has a precise representation in Carnap's theory of reduction sentences. Here, the connections between a given disposition and its various manifest symptoms are assumed to be expressed by a set of so-called reduction sentences (these are characterized by their logical form). Some of these state, in terms of manifest characteristics, sufficient conditions for the presence of the given disposition; others similarly state necessary conditions. The reduction sentences for a given dispositional concept cannot, as a rule, all be qualified as analytic; for jointly they imply certain non-analytic consequences which have the status of general laws connecting exclusively the manifest characteristics; the strongest of the laws so implied is the so-called representative sentence, which "represents, so to speak, the factual content of the set" of all the reduction sentences for the given disposition concept. This representative sentence asserts, in effect, that whenever at least one of the sufficient conditions specified by the given reduction sentences is satisfied, then so are all the necessary conditions laid down by the reduction sentences. And when A is one of the manifest criteria sufficient for the presence of a given disposition, and B is a necessary one, then the statement that whenever A is present so is B will normally turn out to be synthetic.

So far then, I have argued that Dray's construal of explanation by motivating reasons is untenable; that the normative principles of action envisaged by him have to be replaced by statements of a dispositional kind; and that, when this is done, explanations in terms of a motivating rationale, as well as those referring to other psychological factors, are seen to be basically nomological.

Let me add a few further remarks on the idea of rational explanation. First: in many cases of so-called purposive action, there is no conscious deliberation, no rational calculation that leads the agent to his decision. Dray is quite aware of this; but he holds that a rational explanation in his sense is still possible; for "in so far as we say an action is purposive at all, no matter at what level of conscious deliberation, there is a calculation which could be constructed for it: the one the agent would have gone through if he had had time, if he had not seen what to do in a flash, if he had been called upon to account for what he did after the event, etc. And it is by eliciting some such calculation that we explain the action." But the explanatory significance of reasons or "calculations" which are "reconstructed" in this manner is certainly puzzling. If, to take Dray's example, an agent arrives at his decision "in a flash" rather than by deliberation, then it would seem to be simply false to say that the decision can be accounted for by some argument which the agent might have gone through under more propitious circumstances, or which he might produce later if called upon to account for his action; for, by hypothesis, no such argument was in fact gone through by the agent at the crucial time; considerations of appropriateness or rationality played no part in shaping his decision; the rationale that Dray assumes to be adduced and appraised in the corresponding rational explanation is simply fictitious.

But, in fairness to Dray, these remarks call for a qualifying observation: in at least some of the cases Dray has in mind it might not be fictitious to ascribe the action under study to a disposition which the agent acquired through a learning process whose initial stages did involve conscious ratiocination. Consider, for example, the various complex maneuvers of accelerating, braking, signalling, dodging jaywalkers and animals, swerving into and out of traffic lanes, estimating the changes of traffic lights, etc., which are involved in driving a car through city traffic. A beginning driver will often perform these only upon some sort of conscious deliberation or even calculation; but gradually, he learns to do the appropriate thing automatically, "in a flash," without giving them any conscious thought. The habit pattern he has thus acquired may be viewed as consisting in a set of dispositions to react in certain appropriate ways in various situations; and a particular performance of such an appropriate action would then be explained, not by a "constructed" calculation which actually the agent did not perform but by reference to the disposition just mentioned and thus, again, in a nomological fashion.

The method of explaining a given action by "constructing," in Dray's sense, the agent's calculation of means faces yet another, though less fundamental, difficulty: it will frequently yield a rationalization rather than an explanation, especially when the reconstruction relies on the reasons the agent might produce when called upon to account for his action. As G. Watson remarks, "Motivation, as presented in the perspective of history, is often too simple and straightforward, reflecting the psychology of the Age of Reason. . . . Psychology has come . . . to recognize the enormous weight of irrational and intimately personal impulses in conduct. In history, biography, and in autobiography, especially of public characters, the tendency is strong to present 'good' reasons instead of 'real' reasons." Accordingly, as Watson goes on to point out, it is important, in examining the motivation of historical figures, to take into account the significance of such psychological mechanisms as reaction formation, "the dialectic dynamic by which stinginess cloaks itself in generosity, or rabid pacifism arises from the attempt to repress strong aggressive impulses."

These remarks have a bearing also on an idea set forth by P. Gardiner in his illuminating book on historical explanation. Commenting on the notion of the "real reason" for a man's action, Gardiner says: "In general, it appears safe to say that by a man's 'real reasons' we mean those reasons he would be prepared to give under circumstances where his confession would not entail adverse consequences to himself." And he adds "An exception to this is the psychoanalyst's usage of the expression where different criteria are adopted." This observation might be taken to imply that the explanation of human actions in terms of underlying motives is properly aimed at exhibiting the agent's "real reasons" in the ordinary sense of the phrase, as just described; and that, by implication, reasons in the psychoanalyst's sense require less or no consideration. But such a construal of explanation would give undue importance to considerations of ordinary language. Gardiner is entirely right when he reminds us that the "language in which history is written is for the most part the language of ordinary speech"; but the historian in search of reasons that will correctly explain human actions will obviously have to give up his reliance on the everyday conception of "real reasons" if psychological or other investigations show that real reasons, thus understood, do not yield as adequate an account of human actions as an analysis in terms of less familiar conceptions such as, perhaps, the idea of motivating factors which are kept out of the agent's normal awareness by processes of repression and reaction formation.

I would say, then, first of all, that historical explanation cannot be bound by conceptions that might be implicit in the way in which ordinary language deals with motivating reasons. But secondly, I would doubt that Gardiner's expressly tentative characterization does justice even to what we ordinarily mean when we speak of a man's "real reasons." For considerations of the kind that support the idea of subconscious motives are quite familiar in our time, and we are therefore prepared to say in ordinary, non-technical discourse that the reasons given by an agent may not be the "real reasons" behind his action, even if his statement was subjectively honest, and he had no grounds to expect that it would lead to any adverse consequences for him. For no matter whether an explanation of human actions is attempted in the language of ordinary speech or in the technical terms of some theory, the overriding criterion for what-if-anything should count as a "real," and thus explanatory, reason for a given action is surely not to be found by examining the way in which the term "real reason" has thus far been used, but by investigating what conception of real reason would yield the most satisfactory explanation of human conduct; and ordinary usage gradually changes accordingly.

7. CONCLUDING REMARKS

We have surveyed some of the most prominent candidates for the role of characteristically historical mode of explanation; and we have found that they conform essentially to one or the other of our two basic types of scientific explanation.

This result and the arguments that led to it do not in any way imply a mechanistic view of man, of society, and of historical processes; nor, of course, do they deny the importance of ideas and ideals for human decision and action. What the preceding considerations do suggest is, rather, that the nature of understanding, in the sense in which explanation is meant to give us an understanding of empirical phenomena, is basically the same in all areas of scientific inquiry; and that the deductive and the probabilistic model of nomological explanation accommodate vastly more than just the explanatory arguments of, say, classical mechanics: in particular, they accord well also with the character of explanations that deal with the influence of rational deliberation, of conscious and subconscious motives, and of ideas and ideals on the shaping of historical events. In so doing, our schemata exhibit, I think, one important aspect of the methodological unity of all empirical science.

Further References

Anscombe, G. E. M. *Intention*. Oxford: Basil Blackwell, 1957.

Ayer, A. J. *Philosophical Essays*. London: Macmillan, 1954. Chap. 12.†

Berofsky, Bernard (ed.). *Free Will and Determinism*. New York: Harper & Row, 1966.*

Campbell, N. *What Is Science?* London: Methuen, 1921.†

Danto, Arthur, and Morgenbesser, Sidney. "Character and Free Will," *The Journal of Philosophy*, LIV (1957), 493–505.

Danto, Arthur, and Morgenbesser, Sidney (eds.). *Philosophy of Science*. New York: Meridian, 1960.*

Dray, William. *Laws and Explanation in History*. London: Oxford University Press, 1960.

Ewing, A. C. "Indeterminism," *The Review of Metaphysics*, V (1951–1952), 199–222.

Farrer, A. *The Freedom of the Will*. New York: Charles Scribner's Sons, 1958.

Feigl, Herbert, and Brodbeck, M. (eds.). *Readings in the Philosophy of Science*. New York: Appleton-Century-Crofts, 1953.

Gardiner, Patrick. *The Nature of Historical Explanation*. London: Oxford University Press, 1952.

* Paperback edition.   † Also available in a paperback edition.

Gardiner, Patrick (ed.). *Theories of History*. New York: The Free Press, 1959.

Hart, H. L. A., and Honoré, A. M. *Causation in the Law*. London: Oxford University Press, 1959.

Hempel, Carl G. *Philosophy of Natural Science*. Englewood Cliffs, N. J.: Prentice-Hall, 1966.*

Hook, Sidney (ed.). *Determinism and Freedom in the Age of Modern Science*. New York: Collier Books, 1961.*

James, William. "The Dilemma of Determinism." In *The Will to Believe*. New York: Longmans, Green, 1897.†

Lehrer, Keith (ed.). *Freedom and Determinism*. New York: Random House, 1966.*

Madden, E. H. (ed.). *The Structure of Scientific Thought*. Boston: Houghton Mifflin, 1960.

Melden, A. I. *Free Action*. London: Routledge & Kegan Paul, 1961.

Morgenbesser, Sidney, and Walsh, James (eds.). *Free Will*. Englewood Cliffs, N. J.: Prentce-Hall, 1962.*

Morris, Herbert (ed.). *Freedom and Responsibility*. Stanford: Stanford University Press, 1961.

Pears, D. F. (ed.). *Freedom and the Will*. London: Macmillan, 1963.

Peters, R. S. *The Concept of Motivation*. London: Routledge & Kegan Paul, 1958.

———, McCracken, D. J., and Urmson, J. O. "Motives and Causes," Symposium, *Proceedings of the Aristotelian Society*, Supp. Vol. XXVI (1952), 139–194.

Rudner, Richard S. *Philosophy of Social Science*. Englewood Cliffs, N. J.: Prentice-Hall, 1966.*

Ryle, Gilbert. *The Concept of Mind*. London: Hutchinson, 1949. Chap. III.†

———. *Dilemmas*. Cambridge: Cambridge University Press, 1954. Lecture II.†

Shapere, Dudley (ed.). *Philosophical Problems of Natural Science*. New York: Macmillan, 1965.*

Taylor, Richard. *Action and Purpose*. Englewood Cliffs, N. J.: Prentice-Hall, 1966.

Toulmin, Stephen. *The Philosophy of Science*. London: Hutchinson, 1953.†

Wiener, P. P. (ed.). *Readings in Philosophy of Science*. New York: Charles Scribner's Sons, 1953.

Winch, Peter. *The Idea of a Social Science*. London: Routledge & Kegan Paul, 1958.

* Paperback edition.   † Also available in a paperback edition.

:IV:

The Mind-Body Problem

INTRODUCTION

The mind-body problem is not, of course, a single problem at all, but rather a large collection of problems. These are focused, in the most fundamental way, on the analysis of reality and knowledge in so far as such analysis may clarify the relationship between mind and body, and the intelligibility of any alleged relationship between them. What mind and body are is a question that already took its distinctively modern form in the original inquiries of René Descartes (IV:1), who, pursuing the implications he found in the geometric vision of the new science of the Renaissance, construed human beings in terms of thought and extension—the two being taken to be such radically different substances that interaction between mind and body became an utter mystery.

It is almost incredible, but nevertheless true, that the Cartesian problem has haunted philosophy to this day—in fact, in forms that are not very much altered, however distinctive the solutions, from their classic formulation (see G. N. A. Vesey's anthology, *Mind and Body*). Thus, for instance, the problem of interaction between substances of apparently radically different sorts is absolutely central to the accounts of C. D. Broad (IV:3) and Gilbert Ryle (IV:4), who, incidentally, reach quite incompatible conclusions.

It ought to be noted, however, that, although there are inevitable metaphysical implications in the accounts of Broad and Ryle, their attention is focused primarily on the admissibility of causal interaction. Broad is inclined to dismiss assertions about radical differences in nature as being too vague to be relevant in a meaningful way to the issue; Ryle tends to substitute categorial questions for metaphysical questions. But the Cartesian puzzle is not merely about causality (and indeed neither Broad's nor Ryle's account can be said to have effectively restricted it to that); it also concerns the ultimate characterization of the nature of mind and body.

The distinctiveness of the Cartesian solution lies in the fact that, contrary to an ancient tradition, Descartes' two fundamental substances are intelligible solely in terms of exclusive properties; they are, in fact, nothing more than these properties raised to the status of substances. The classical account of the mind or soul as the form of the body of animate beings can already be found in Aristotle and in St. Thomas (IV:6). But Descartes' formulation has set the metaphysical issue in its modern dress: Are the predicates assigned to mind and body exclusive or do they have an overlapping or common extension? The radical division that Descartes saw between mind and body continues, significantly, into the empiricist endeavors of John Locke and George Berkeley (IV:2). Where the logical embarrassments and ad hoc inventions of these two—such as Locke's difficulties with the concept of substance and Berkeley's requirement of notions that are not ideas—are resisted as consistently as possible, as in David Hume (IV:9), the result is an impossible caricature of the knowing mind or self: witness Hume's "bundle of ideas." Here we are obliged to take note of further aspects of the Cartesian question—those that have to do with distinguishing between the analysis of mental entities, as opposed to physical entities, and the analysis of mind in terms of knowledge, of mind qua knowing subject.

As has been suggested, the metaphysical exploration takes two principal questions as its characteristic concern: first, the question of interaction between mind and body, which is now viewed not so much in terms of methodological distinctions between alternative types of explanation (as indicated in Part III) as in terms of the propriety of linking causally entities of such apparently different sorts; and second, the question of the identity, in either factual or metaphysical terms, of mind and body. The issue of the reductive identity of mind and body has proved to be one of the most persistent philosophical issues of our time (see, for example, Herbert Feigl, J. J. C. Smart [IV:5], Gilbert Ryle, and Wilfrid Sellars). But it is clear that to justify identifying mental and physical processes is quite compatible with, and separable from, the admission of asymmetries with regard to knowledge —particularly of pain and the like—in the first- and third-person settings (as in Smart). On the other hand, the question of privacy, of privileged access, threatens the plausibility of the identity thesis, at least within the Cartesian setting. Those sympathetic with various forms of materialism, behaviorism, or objectivism—whether methodological or metaphysical—consider the possibility either of denying the asymmetry with regard to knowledge (for example, Gilbert Ryle and Norman Malcolm [IV:12] or of neutralizing it by the provision of machine analogues (for example, Hilary Putnam [IV:8]).

We must not, however, confuse a metaphysical interest in these questions about knowledge and experience with an analysis of the actual problems of knowledge and experience—particularly as they bear on thought and sensations, which are traditionally most closely related to the issue of privacy. The metaphysical question here centers on the analysis of persons and personal identity. The contrast between Berkeley and Hume, both working in the empiricist manner, is instructive: Berkeley attempts to provide within his philosophical account for the distinctiveness of the knowing mind; Hume is forced to admit it as a commonsense reflection on an otherwise closed and internally consistent account that cannot properly provide for it. The entire modern tradition involves the search for an explanation of the relationship between thought or sensation (also perception, will, memory, and the like) and the body. Once again, the Cartesian puzzle of the relationship of mind and body dominates modern speculation; this is quite apparent, for instance, in the attempted resolution by P. F. Strawson (IV:10) in which both M-predicates and P-predicates are ascribed to the same entity.

One of the questions that this inquiry inevitably generates is that of the possibility of disembodied minds or souls or even disembodied sensations. The Aristotelian tradition, notably in St. Thomas, distinguishes sharply between sensation or feeling and thought (see also P. T. Geach [IV:7]). The Cartesian solution, of course, with its emphasis on mind as thinking substance (however generous or careless the concept of "thought" may be supposed to be) makes disembodied existence inevitable. The earlier empiricists are, at least implicitly, Cartesians in this respect; and the Humean solution is not a genuine solution but rather a disorganization of the original question with regard to persons. From this point of view, Strawson's account may be seen to be addressed both to Descartes' problem and to Hume's, and his solution rules out disembodiment while at the same time preserving persons as entities.

There is only one line of investigation with regard to knowledge that, traditionally, has had a very close connection with the mind-body problem; it concerns the question of our knowledge of other minds. The pivotal figure here is, without doubt, Ludwig Wittgenstein. Before the full appreciation of Wittgenstein's analysis of the public nature of language, the basis for our knowledge of other minds (in particular, of the pains, feelings, and thoughts of others) was cast in terms of what has come to be called the argument from analogy (for example, John Stuart Mill, Bertrand Russell [IV:11], A. J. Ayer, H. H. Price). This argument admits that we do have knowledge of our own sensations and the like, and that our knowledge of another's sensations entails the application of relevant terms first used for private experience.

On Malcolm's interpretation of Wittgenstein's challenge not only is the theory of such a private language unintelligible but the doctrine of knowledge of sensations and the like, in the *first*-person setting, is utterly misleading, if not altogether untenable. Others, in different measures sympathetic with the Wittgensteinian challenge (for example, John Wisdom, P. T. Geach, G. E. M. Anscombe [IV:13], and P. F. Strawson), allow for the relevant sorts of first-person knowledge without subscribing to the argument from analogy. All discussions, however, are fundamentally concerned with the possibility of avoiding skepticism and solipsism, with the concession that we can speak intelligibly of another's private states and experiences.

It should be emphasized that the metaphysical and epistemological inquiries relevant here may each, despite their obvious bearing on each other, elude the key questions of the other. We have already noted how the identity thesis may be taken to be neutral on the question of privacy (Smart). It is also possible (and not at all uncharacteristic in the Wittgensteinian tradition) to pursue the question of first- and third-person knowledge of sensations without posing questions about identity or the analysis of mind (for example, Malcolm). For here the central issue remains the conditions of language adequate to account for our discourse about private experience, including our claims to knowledge. For all those who seek to escape linguistic solipsism the main emphasis is upon our reliance on behavioral and other public criteria of private experiences (for example, Malcolm, Geach, and Strawson). But the underlying metaphysical issue concerns not how we may be said to know whether another (or even ourselves) has pain, but rather whether pain, thought, and the like *are* entities of some sort. The issue of knowledge, on the other hand, properly emphasizes the possibility of doubt and the resolution of doubt with regard to the private experiences of another; consequently, we are forced to consider the nature of dreams, of pretending, of hiding one's feelings (for example, Malcolm, Anscombe)—in short, the nature of the relationship between third-person criteria of private experiences and private states and those experiences and states themselves.

Substance, Interaction, and Identity

1

THE HUMAN MIND AND THE HUMAN BODY

René Descartes

MEDITATION II

Of the Nature of the Human Mind; and That It Is More Easily Known Than the Body

The Meditation of yesterday filled my mind with so many doubts that it is no longer in my power to forget them. And yet I do not see in what manner I can resolve them; and, just as if I had all of a sudden fallen into very deep water, I am so disconcerted that I can neither make certain of setting my feet on the bottom, nor can I swim and so support myself on the surface. I shall nevertheless make an effort and follow anew the same path as that on which I yesterday entered, i.e. I shall proceed by setting aside all that in which the least doubt could be supposed to exist, just as if I had discovered that it was absolutely false; and I shall ever follow in this road until I have met with something which is certain, or at least, if I can do nothing else, until I have learned for certain that there is nothing in the world that is certain. Archimedes, in order that he might draw the terrestrial globe out of its place, and transport it elsewhere, demanded only that one point should be fixed and immovable; in the same way I shall have the right to conceive high hopes if I am happy enough to discover one thing only which is certain and indubitable.

I suppose, then, that all the things that I see are false; I persuade myself

From "Meditations on First Philosophy," in *The Philosophical Works of Descartes*, E. S. Haldane and G. R. T. Ross, trans. (Cambridge: Cambridge University Press, 1931), Meditations II, VI, pp. 149–157, 187–198. Reprinted by permission of the publisher.

that nothing has ever existed of all that my fallacious memory represents to me. I consider that I possess no senses; I imagine that body, figure, extension, movement and place are but the fictions of my mind. What, then, can be esteemed as true? Perhaps nothing at all, unless that there is nothing in the world that is certain.

But how can I know there is not something different from those things that I have just considered, of which one cannot have the slightest doubt? Is there not some God, or some other being by whatever name we call it, who puts these reflections into my mind? That is not necessary, for is it not possible that I am capable of producing them myself? I myself, am I not at least something? But I have already denied that I had senses and body. Yet I hesitate, for what follows from that? Am I so dependent on body and senses that I cannot exist without these? But I was persuaded that there was nothing in all the world, that there was no heaven, no earth, that there were no minds, nor any bodies: was I not then likewise persuaded that I did not exist? Not at all; of a surety I myself did exist since I persuaded myself of something [or merely because I thought of something]. But there is some deceiver or other, very powerful and very cunning, who ever employs his ingenuity in deceiving me. Then without doubt I exist also if he deceives me, and let him deceive me as much as he will, he can never cause me to be nothing so long as I think that I am something. So that after having reflected well and carefully examined all things, we must come to the definite conclusion that this proposition: I am, I exist, is necessarily true each time that I pronounce it, or that I mentally conceive it.

But I do not yet know clearly enough what I am, I who am certain that I am; and hence I must be careful to see that I do not imprudently take some other object in place of myself, and thus that I do not go astray in respect of this knowledge that I hold to be the most certain and most evident of all that I have formerly learned. That is why I shall now consider anew what I believed myself to be before I embarked upon these last reflections; and of my former opinions I shall withdraw all that might even in a small degree be invalidated by the reasons which I have just brought forward, in order that there may be nothing at all left beyond what is absolutely certain and indubitable.

What then did I formerly believe myself to be? Undoubtedly I believed myself to be a man. But what is a man? Shall I say a reasonable animal? Certainly not; for then I should have to inquire what an animal is, and what is reasonable; and thus from a single question I should insensibly fall into an infinitude of others more difficult; and I should not wish to waste the little time and leisure remaining to me in trying to unravel subtleties like these. But I shall rather stop here to consider the thoughts which of themselves spring up in my mind, and which were not inspired by anything beyond my own nature alone when I applied myself to the consideration of my being. In the first place, then, I considered myself as having a face, hands, arms, and all that system of members composed of bones and flesh as seen in a corpse which I designated by the name of body. In addition to this I considered that I was nourished, that I walked, that I felt, and that I thought, and I referred all these actions to the soul: but I did not stop to consider what the soul was, or if I did stop, I imagined that it was something extremely rare and subtle like a wind, a flame, or an ether, which was spread throughout my grosser parts. As to body I had no manner of doubt about its nature, but thought I had a very clear knowledge of it; and if I had desired to explain it according to the notions that I had then formed of it, I should have described it thus: By the body I understand all that which can be defined by a certain figure: something which can be confined in a certain place, and which can fill a given space in such a way that every other body will be excluded from it; which can be perceived either by touch, or by sight, or by hearing, or by taste, or by smell: which can be moved in many ways not, in truth, by itself, but by something which is foreign to it, by which it is touched [and from which it receives impressions]: for to have the power of self-movement, as also of feeling or of thinking, I did not consider to appertain to the nature of body: on the contrary, I was rather astonished to find that faculties similar to them existed in some bodies.

But what am I, now that I suppose that there is a certain genius which is extremely powerful, and, if I may say so, malicious, who employs all his powers in deceiving me? Can I affirm that I possess the least of all those things which I have just said pertain to the nature of body? I pause to consider, I revolve all these things in my mind, and I find none of which I can say that it pertains to me. It would be tedious to stop to enumerate them. Let us pass to the attributes of soul and see if there is any one which is in me? What of nutrition or walking [the first mentioned]? But if it is so that I have no body it is also true that I can neither walk nor take nourishment. Another attribute is sensation. But one cannot feel without body, and besides I have thought I perceived many things during sleep that I recognised in my waking moments as not having been experienced at all. What of thinking? I find here that thought is an attribute that belongs to me; it alone cannot be separated from me. I am, I exist, that is certain. But how often? Just when I think; for it might possibly be the case if I ceased entirely to think, that I should likewise cease altogether to exist. I do not now admit anything which is not necessarily true: to speak accurately I am not more than a thing which thinks, that is to say a mind or a soul, or an understanding, or a reason, which are terms whose significance was formerly unknown to me. I am, however, a real thing and really exist; but what thing? I have answered: a thing which thinks.

And what more? I shall exercise my imagination [in order to see if I am not something more]. I am not a collection of members which we call the human body: I am not a subtle air distributed through these members, I am not a wind, a fire, a vapour, a breath, nor anything at all which I can imagine or conceive; because I have assumed that all these were nothing. Without changing that supposition I find that I only leave myself certain of the fact that I am somewhat. But perhaps it is true that these same things which I supposed were non-existent because they are unknown to me, are really not different from the self which I know. I am not sure about this, I shall not dispute about it now; I can only give judgment on things that are known to me. I know that I exist, and I inquire what I am, I whom I know to exist. But it is very certain that the knowledge of my existence taken in its precise significance does not depend on things whose existence is not yet known to me; consequently it does not depend on those which I can feign in imagination. And indeed the very term *feign* in imagination[1] proves to me my error, for I really do this if I imagine myself a something, since to imagine is nothing else than to contemplate the figure or image of a corporeal thing. But I already know for certain that I am, and that it may be that all these images, and, speaking generally, all things that relate to the nature of body are nothing but dreams [and chimeras]. For this reason I see clearly that I have as little reason to say, 'I shall stimulate my imagination in order to know more distinctly what I am,' than if I were to say, 'I am now awake, and I perceive somewhat that is real and true: but because I do not yet perceive it distinctly enough, I shall go to sleep of express purpose, so that my dreams may represent the perception with greatest truth and evidence.' And, thus, I know for certain that nothing of all that I can understand by means of my imagination belongs to this knowledge which I have of myself, and that it is necessary to recall the mind from this mode of thought with the utmost diligence in order that it may be able to know its own nature with perfect distinctness.

But what then am I? A thing which thinks. What is a thing which thinks? It is a thing which doubts, understands, [conceives], affirms, denies, wills, refuses, which also imagines and feels.

Certainly it is no small matter if all these things pertain to my nature. But why should they not so pertain? Am I not that being who now doubts nearly everything, who nevertheless understands certain things, who affirms that one only is true, who denies all the others, who desires to know more, is averse from being deceived, who imagines many things, sometimes indeed despite his will, and who perceives many likewise, as by the intervention of the bodily organs? Is there nothing in all this which is as true as it is certain that I exist, even though I should always sleep and though he who has given me being employed all his ingenuity in deceiving me? Is there likewise any one of these attributes which can be distinguished from my thought, or which might be said to be separated from myself? For it is so evident of itself that it is I who doubts, who understands, and who desires, that there is no reason here to add anything to explain it. And I have certainly the power of imagining likewise; for although it may happen (as I formerly supposed) that none of the things which I imagine are true, nevertheless this power of imagining does not cease to be really in use, and it forms part of my thought. Finally, I am the same who feels, that is to say, who perceives certain things, as by the organs of sense, since in truth I see light, I hear noise, I feel heat. But it will be said that these phenomena are false and that I am dreaming. Let it be so; still it is at least quite certain that it seems to me that I see light, that I hear noise and that I feel heat. That cannot be false; properly speaking it is what is in me called feeling; and used in this precise sense that is no other thing than thinking.

From this time I begin to know what I am with a little more clearness and distinction than before; but nevertheless it still seems to me, and I cannot prevent myself from thinking, that corporeal things, whose images are framed by thought, which are tested by the senses, are much more distinctly known than that obscure part of me which does not come under the imagination. Although really it is very strange to say that I know and

[1] Or 'form an image' (effingo).

understand more distinctly these things whose existence seems to me dubious, which are unknown to me, and which do not belong to me, than others
of the truth of which I am convinced, which are known to me and which
pertain to my real nature, in a word, than myself. But I see clearly how the
case stands: my mind loves to wander, and cannot yet suffer itself to be
retained within the just limits of truth. Very good, let us once more give it
the freest rein, so that, when afterwards we seize the proper occasion for
pulling up, it may the more easily be regulated and controlled.

Let us begin by considering the commonest matters, those which we
believe to be the most distinctly comprehended, to wit, the bodies which we
touch and see; not indeed bodies in general, for these general ideas are
usually a little more confused, but let us consider one body in particular. Let
us take, for example, this piece of wax: it has been taken quite freshly from
the hive, and it has not yet lost the sweetness of the honey which it contains;
it still retains somewhat of the odour of the flowers from which it has been
culled; its colour, its figure, its size are apparent; it is hard, cold, easily
handled, and if you strike it with the finger, it will emit a sound. Finally all
the things which are requisite to cause us distinctly to recognise a body, are
met with in it. But notice that while I speak and approach the fire what
remained of the taste is exhaled, the smell evaporates, the colour alters, the
figure is destroyed, the size increases, it becomes liquid, it heats, scarcely can
one handle it, and when one strikes it, no sound is emitted. Does the same
wax remain after this change? We must confess that it remains; none would
judge otherwise. What then did I know so distinctly in this piece of wax? It
could certainly be nothing of all that the senses brought to my notice, since
all these things which fall under taste, smell, sight, touch, and hearing, are
found to be changed, and yet the same wax remains.

Perhaps it was what I now think, viz. that this wax was not that sweetness
of honey, nor that agreeable scent of flowers, nor that particular whiteness,
nor that figure, nor that sound, but simply a body which a little while before
appeared to me as perceptible under these forms, and which is now
perceptible under others. But what, precisely, is it that I imagine when I
form such conceptions? Let us attentively consider this, and, abstracting
from all that does not belong to the wax, let us see what remains. Certainly
nothing remains excepting a certain extended thing which is flexible and
movable. But what is the meaning of flexible and movable? Is it not that I
imagine that this piece of wax being round is capable of becoming square
and of passing from a square to a triangular figure? No, certainly it is not
that, since I imagine it admits of an infinitude of similar changes, and I nevertheless do not know how to compass the infinitude by my imagination, and
consequently this conception which I have of the wax is not brought about
by the faculty of imagination. What now is this extension? Is it not also
unknown? For it becomes greater when the wax is melted, greater when it
is boiled, and greater still when the heat increases; and I should not conceive [clearly] according to truth what wax is, if I did not think that even
this piece that we are considering is capable of receiving more variations in
extension than I have ever imagined. We must then grant that I could not
even understand through the imagination what this piece of wax is, and
that it is my mind alone which perceives it. I say this piece of wax in
particular, for as to wax in general it is yet clearer. But what is this piece

of wax which cannot be understood excepting by the [understanding or] mind? It is certainly the same that I see, touch, imagine, and finally it is the same which I have always believed it to be from the beginning. But what must particularly be observed is that its perception is neither an act of vision, nor of touch, nor of imagination, and has never been such although it may have appeared formerly to be so, but only an intuition of the mind, which may be imperfect and confused as it was formerly, or clear and distinct as it is at present, according as my attention is more or less directed to the elements which are found in it, and of which it is composed.

Yet in the meantime I am greatly astonished when I consider [the great feebleness of mind] and its proneness to fall [insensibly] into error; for although without giving expression to my thoughts I consider all this in my own mind, words often impede me and I am almost deceived by the terms of ordinary language. For we say that we see the same wax, if it is present, and not that we simply judge that it is the same from its having the same colour and figure. From this I should conclude that I knew the wax by means of vision and not simply by the intuition of the mind; unless by chance I remember that, when looking from a window and saying I see men who pass in the street, I really do not see them, but infer that what I see is men, just as I say that I see wax. And yet what do I see from the window but hats and coats which may cover automatic machines? Yet I judge these to be men. And similarly solely by the faculty of judgment which rests in my mind, I comprehend that which I believed I saw with my eyes.

A man who makes it his aim to raise his knowledge above the common should be ashamed to derive the occasion for doubting from the forms of speech invented by the vulgar; I prefer to pass on and consider whether I had a more evident and perfect conception of what the wax was when I first perceived it, and when I believed I knew it by means of the external senses or at least by the common sense[2] as it is called, that is to say by the imaginative faculty, or whether my present conception is clearer now that I have most carefully examined what it is, and in what way it can be known. It would certainly be absurd to doubt as to this. For what was there in this first perception which was distinct? What was there which might not as well have been perceived by any of the animals? But when I distinguish the wax from its external forms, and when, just as if I had taken from it its vestments, I consider it quite naked, it is certain that although some error may still be found in my judgment, I can nevertheless not perceive it thus without a human mind.

But finally what shall I say of this mind, that is, of myself, for up to this point I do not admit in myself anything but mind? What then, I who seem to perceive this piece of wax so distinctly, do I not know myself, not only with much more truth and certainty, but also with much more distinctness and clearness? For if I judge that the wax is or exists from the fact that I see it, it certainly follows much more clearly that I am or that I exist myself from the fact that I see it. For it may be that what I see is not really wax, it may also be that I do not possess eyes with which to see anything; but it cannot be that when I see, or (for I no longer take account of the distinction) when I think I see, that I myself who think am nought. So if I judge that

[2] *Sensus communis.*

the wax exists from the fact that I touch it, the same thing will follow, to wit, that I am; and if I judge that my imagination, or some other cause, whatever it is, persuades me that the wax exists, I shall still conclude the same. And what I have here remarked of wax may be applied to all other things which are external to me [and which are met with outside of me]. And further, if the [notion or] perception of wax has seemed to me clearer and more distinct, not only after the sight or the touch, but also after many other causes have rendered it quite manifest to me, with how much more [evidence] and distinctness must it be said that I now know myself, since all the reasons which contribute to the knowledge of wax, or any other body whatever, are yet better proofs of the nature of my mind! And there are so many other things in the mind itself which may contribute to the elucidation of its nature, that those which depend on body such as these just mentioned, hardly merit being taken into account.

But finally here I am, having insensibly reverted to the point I desired, for, since it is now manifest to me that even bodies are not properly speaking known by the senses or by the faculty of imagination, but by the understanding only, and since they are not known from the fact that they are seen or touched, but only because they are understood, I see clearly that there is nothing which is easier for me to know than my mind. But because it is difficult to rid oneself so promptly of an opinion to which one was accustomed for so long, it will be well that I should halt a little at this point, so that by the length of my meditation I may more deeply imprint on my memory this new knowledge.

MEDITATION VI

Of the Existence of Material Things, and of the Real Distinction Between the Soul and Body of Man

. . .

... I shall recall to my memory those matters which I hitherto held to be true, as having perceived them through the senses, and the foundations on which my belief has rested; in the next place I shall examine the reasons which have since obliged me to place them in doubt; in the last place I shall consider which of them I must now believe.

First of all, then, I perceived that I had a head, hands, feet, and all other members of which this body—which I considered as a part, or possibly even as the whole, of myself—is composed. Further I was sensible that this body was placed amidst many others, from which it was capable of being affected in many different ways, beneficial and hurtful, and I remarked that a certain feeling of pleasure accompanied those that were beneficial, and pain those which were harmful. And in addition to this pleasure and pain, I also experienced hunger, thirst, and other similar appetites, as also certain corporeal inclinations towards joy, sadness, anger, and other similar passions. And outside myself, in addition to extension, figure, and motions of bodies, I remarked in them hardness, heat, and all other tactile qualities, and, further, light and colour, and scents and sounds, the variety of which gave me the means of distinguishing the sky, the earth, the sea, and generally all the other bodies, one from the other. And certainly, considering the ideas of all these qualities which presented themselves to my mind, and which alone I perceived properly or immediately, it was not without reason that I believed myself to perceive objects quite different from my thought, to wit, bodies from which those ideas proceeded; for I found by experience that these ideas presented themselves to me without my consent being requisite, so that I could not perceive any object, however desirous I might be, unless it were present to the organs of sense; and it was not in my power not to perceive it, when it was present. And because the ideas which I received through the senses were much more lively, more clear, and even, in their own way, more distinct than any of those which I could of myself frame in meditation, or than those I found impressed on my memory, it appeared as though they could not have proceeded from my mind, so that they must necessarily have been produced in me by some other things. And having no knowledge of those objects excepting the knowledge which the ideas themselves gave me, nothing was more likely to occur to my mind than that the objects were similar to the ideas which were caused. And because I likewise remembered that I had formerly made use of my senses rather than my reason, and recognised that the ideas which I formed of myself were not so distinct as those which I perceived through the senses, and that they were most frequently even composed of portions of these last, I persuaded myself easily that I had no idea in my mind which had not formerly come to me through the senses. Nor was it without some reason that I believed that this body (which by a certain special right I call my own) belonged to me more properly and more strictly than any other; for in fact I could never be separated from it as from other bodies; I experienced in it and on account of it all my appetites and affections, and finally I was touched by the feeling of pain and the titillation of pleasure in its parts, and not in the parts of other bodies which were separated from it. But when I inquired, why, from some, I know not what, painful sensation, there follows sadness of mind, and from the pleasurable sensation there arises joy, or why this mysterious pinching of the stomach which I call hunger causes me to desire to eat, and dryness of throat causes a desire to drink, and so on, I could give no reason excepting that nature taught me so; for there is certainly no affinity (that I at least can understand) between the craving of the stomach and the desire to eat, any more than between the perception of whatever causes pain and the thought of sadness which arises from this perception. And in the same way it appeared to me that I had learned from nature all the other judgments which I formed regarding the objects of my senses, since I remarked that these judgments were formed in me before I had the leisure to weigh and consider any reasons which might oblige me to make them.

But afterwards many experiences little by little destroyed all the faith which I had rested in my senses; for I from time to time observed that those towers which from afar appeared to me to be round, more closely observed seemed square, and that colossal statues raised on the summit of these towers, appeared as quite tiny statues when viewed from the bottom; and so in an infinitude of other cases I found error in judgments founded on the external senses. And not only in those founded on the external senses, but even in those founded on the internal as well; for is there anything more intimate or more internal than pain? And yet I have learned from some persons whose arms or legs have been cut off, that they sometimes seemed to feel pain in the part which had been amputated, which made me think that I could not be quite certain that it was a certain member which pained me, even although I felt pain in it. And to those grounds of doubt I have lately added two others, which are very general; the first is that I never have believed myself to feel anything in waking moments which I cannot also sometimes believe myself to feel when I sleep, and as I do not think that these things which I seem to feel in sleep, proceed from objects outside of me, I do not see any reason why I should have this belief regarding objects which I seem to perceive while awake. The other was that being still ignorant, or rather supposing myself to be ignorant, of the author of my being, I saw nothing to prevent me from having been so constituted by nature that I might be deceived even in matters which seemed to me to be most certain. And as to the grounds on which I was formerly persuaded of the truth of sensible objects, I had not much trouble in replying to them. For since nature seemed to cause me to lean towards many things from which reason repelled me, I did not believe that I should trust much to the teachings of nature. And although the ideas which I receive by the senses do not depend on my will, I did not think that one should for that reason conclude that they proceeded from things different from myself, since possibly some faculty might be discovered in me—though hitherto un-known to me—which produced them.

But now that I begin to know myself better, and to discover more clearly the author of my being, I do not in truth think that I should rashly admit all the matters which the senses seem to teach us, but, on the other hand, I do not think that I should doubt them all universally.

And first of all, because I know that all things which I apprehend clearly and distinctly can be created by God as I apprehend them, it suffices that I am able to apprehend one thing apart from another clearly and distinctly in order to be certain that the one is different from the other, since they may be made to exist in separation at least by the omnipotence of God; and it does not signify by what power this separation is made in order to compel me to judge them to be different: and, therefore, just because I know certainly that I exist, and that meanwhile I do not remark that any other thing necessarily pertains to my nature or essence, excepting that I am a thinking thing, I rightly conclude that my essence consists solely in the fact that I am a thinking thing [or a substance whose whole essence or nature is to think]. And although possibly (or rather certainly, as I shall say in a moment) I possess a body with which I am very intimately conjoined, yet because, on the one side, I have a clear and distinct idea of myself inasmuch as I am only a thinking and unextended thing, and as, on the other, I possess a distinct idea of body, inasmuch as it is only an extended and unthinking thing, it is certain that this I [that is to say, my soul by which I am what I am], is entirely and absolutely distinct from my body, and can exist with-out it.

I further find in myself faculties employing modes of thinking peculiar to themselves, to wit, the faculties of imagination and feeling, without which I can easily conceive myself clearly and distinctly as a complete being; while, on the other hand, they cannot be so conceived apart from me, that is without an intelligent substance in which they reside, for [in the notion we have of these faculties, or, to use the language of the Schools] in their formal concept, some kind of intellection is comprised, from which I infer that they are distinct from me as its modes are from a thing. I observe also in me some other faculties such as that of change of position, the assumption of different figures and such like, which cannot be conceived, any more than can the preceding, apart from some substance to which they are attached, and consequently cannot exist without it; but it is very clear that these faculties, if it be true that they exist, must be attached to some corporeal or extended substance, and not to an intelligent substance, since in the clear and distinct conception of these there is some sort of extension found to be present, but no intellection at all. There is certainly further in me a certain passive faculty of perception, that is, of receiving and recognising the ideas of sensible things, but this would be useless to me [and I could in no way avail myself of it], if there were not either in me or in some other thing another active faculty capable of forming and producing these ideas. But this active faculty cannot exist in me [inasmuch as I am a thing that thinks] seeing that it does not presuppose thought, and also that those ideas are often produced in me without my contributing in any way to the same, and often even against my will; it is thus necessarily the case that the faculty resides in some substance different from me in which all the reality which is objectively in the ideas that are produced by this faculty is formally or eminently contained, as I remarked before. And this substance is either a body, that is, a corporeal nature in which there is contained formally [and really] all that which is objectively [and by representation] in those ideas, or it is God Himself, or some other creature more noble than body in which that same is contained eminently. But, since God is no deceiver, it is very manifest that He does not communicate to me these ideas immediately and by Himself, nor yet by the intervention of some creature in which their reality is not formally, but only eminently, contained. For since He has given me no faculty to recognise that this is the case, but, on the other hand, a very great inclination to believe [that they are sent to me or] that they are conveyed to me by corporeal objects, I do not see how He could be defended from the accusation of deceit if these ideas were produced by causes other than corporeal objects. Hence we must allow that corporeal things exist. However, they are perhaps not exactly what we perceive by the senses, since this comprehension by the senses is in many instances very obscure and confused; but we must at least admit that all things which I conceive in them clearly and distinctly, that is to say, all things which, speaking generally, are comprehended in the object of pure mathematics, are truly to be recognised as external objects.

As to other things, however, which are either particular only, as, for example, that the sun is of such and such a figure, etc., or which are less clearly and distinctly conceived, such as light, sound, pain and the like, it is certain that although they are very dubious and uncertain, yet on the sole ground that God is not a deceiver, and that consequently He has not permitted any falsity to exist in my opinion which He has not likewise given me the faculty of correcting, I may assuredly hope to conclude that I have within me the means of arriving at the truth even here. And first of all there is no doubt that in all things which nature teaches me there is some truth contained; for by nature, considered in general, I now understand no other thing than either God Himself or else the order and disposition which God has established in created things; and by my nature in particular I understand no other thing than the complexus of all the things which God has given me.

But there is nothing which this nature teaches me more expressly [nor more sensibly] than that I have a body which is adversely affected when I feel pain, which has need of food or drink when I experience the feelings of hunger and thirst, and so on; nor can I doubt there being some truth in all this.

Nature also teaches me by these sensations of pain, hunger, thirst, etc., that I am not only lodged in my body as a pilot in a vessel, but that I am very closely united to it, and so to speak so intermingled with it that I seem to compose with it one whole. For if that were not the case, when my body is hurt, I, who am merely a thinking thing, should not feel pain, for I should perceive this wound by the understanding only, just as the sailor perceives by sight when something is damaged in his vessel; and when my body has need of drink or food, I should clearly understand the fact without being warned of it by confused feelings of hunger and thirst. For all these sensations of hunger, thirst, pain, etc. are in truth none other than certain confused modes of thought which are produced by the union and apparent intermingling of mind and body.

Moreover, nature teaches me that many other bodies exist around mine, of which some are to be avoided, and others sought after. And certainly from the fact that I am sensible of different sorts of colours, sounds, scents, tastes, heat, hardness, etc., I very easily conclude that there are in the bodies from which all these diverse sense-perceptions proceed certain variations which answer to them, although possibly these are not really at all similar to them. And also from the fact that amongst these different sense-perceptions some are very agreeable to me and others disagreeable, it is quite certain that my body (or rather myself in my entirety, inasmuch as I am formed of body and soul) may receive different impressions agreeable and disagreeable from the other bodies which surround it.

But there are many other things which nature seems to have taught me, but which at the same time I have never really received from her, but which have been brought about in my mind by a certain habit which I have of forming inconsiderate judgments on things; and thus it may easily happen that these judgments contain some error. Take, for example, the opinion which I hold that all space in which there is nothing that affects [or makes an impression on] my senses is void; that in a body which is warm there is something entirely similar to the idea of heat which is in me; that in a white or green body there is the same whiteness or greenness that I perceive; that in a bitter or sweet body there is the same taste, and so on in other instances; that the stars, the towers, and all other distant bodies are of the same figure and size as they appear from far off to our eyes, etc. But in order that in this there should be nothing which I do not conceive distinctly, I should define exactly what I really understand when I say that I am taught somewhat by nature. For here I take nature in a more limited signification than when I term it the sum of all the things given me by God, since in this sum many things are comprehended which only pertain to mind (and to these I do not refer in speaking of nature) such as the notion which I have of the fact that what has once been done cannot ever be undone and an infinitude of such things which I know by the light of nature [without the help of the body]; and seeing that it comprehends many other matters besides which only pertain to body, and are no longer here contained under the name of nature, such as the quality of weight which it possesses and the like, with which I also do not deal; for in talking of nature I only treat of those things given by God to me as a being composed of mind and body. But the nature here described truly teaches me to flee from things which cause the sensation of pain, and seek after the things which communicate to me the sentiment of pleasure and so forth; but I do not see that beyond this it teaches me that from those diverse sense-perceptions we should ever form any conclusion regarding things outside of us, without having [carefully and maturely] mentally examined them beforehand. For it seems to me that it is mind alone, and not mind and body in conjunction, that is requisite to a knowledge of the truth in regard to such things. Thus, although a star makes no larger an impression on my eye than the flame of a little candle there is yet in me no real or positive propensity impelling me to believe that it is not greater than that flame; but I have judged it to be so from my earliest years, without any rational foundation. And although in approaching fire I feel heat, and in approaching it a little too near I even feel pain, there is at the same time no reason in this which could persuade me that there is in the fire something resembling this heat any more than there is in it something resembling the pain; all that I have any reason to believe from this is, that there is something in it, whatever it may be, which excites in me these sensations of heat or of pain. So also, although there are spaces in which I find nothing which excites my senses, I must not from that conclude that these spaces contain no body; for I see in this, as in other similar things, that I have been in the habit of perverting the order of nature, because these perceptions of sense having been placed within me by nature merely for the purpose of signifying to my mind what things are beneficial or hurtful to the composite whole of which it forms a part, and being up to that point sufficiently clear and distinct, I yet avail myself of them as though they were absolute rules by which I might immediately determine the essence of the bodies which are outside me, as to which, in fact, they can teach me nothing but what is most obscure and confused.

But I have already sufficiently considered how, notwithstanding the supreme goodness of God, falsity enters into the judgments I make. Only here a new difficulty is presented—one respecting those things the pursuit or avoidance of which is taught me by nature, and also respecting the internal sensations which I possess, and in which I seem to have sometimes detected error [and thus to be directly deceived by my own nature]. To take an example, the agreeable taste of some food in which poison has been intermingled may induce me to partake of the poison, and thus deceive me. It is true, at the same time, that in this case nature may be excused, for it only induces me to desire food in which I find a pleasant taste, and not to desire the poison which is unknown to it; and thus I can infer nothing from this fact, except that my nature is not omniscient, at which there is certainly no reason to be astonished, since man, being finite in nature, can only have knowledge the perfectness of which is limited.

But we not unfrequently deceive ourselves even in those things to which we are directly impelled by nature, as happens with those who when they are sick desire to drink or eat things hurtful to them. It will perhaps be said here that the cause of their deceptiveness is that their nature is corrupt, but that does not remove the difficulty, because a sick man is none the less truly God's creature than he who is in health; and it is therefore as repugnant to God's goodness for the one to have a deceitful nature as it is for the other. And as a clock composed of wheels and counter-weights no less exactly observes the laws of nature when it is badly made, and does not show the time properly, than when it entirely satisfies the wishes of its maker, and as, if I consider the body of a man as being a sort of machine so built up and composed of nerves, muscles, veins, blood and skin, that though there were no mind in it at all, it would not cease to have the same motions as at present, exception being made of those movements which are due to the direction of the will, and in consequence depend upon the mind [as opposed to those which operate by the disposition of its organs], I easily recognise that it would be as natural to this body, supposing it to be, for example, dropsical, to suffer the parchedness of the throat which usually signifies to the mind the feeling of thirst, and to be disposed by this parched feeling to move the nerves and other parts in the way requisite for drinking, and thus to augment its malady and do harm to itself, as it is natural to it, when it has no indisposition, to be impelled to drink for its good by a similar cause. And although, considering the use to which the clock has been destined by its maker, I may say that it deflects from the order of its nature when it does not indicate the hours correctly; and as, in the same way, considering the machine of the human body as having been formed by God in order to have in itself all the movements usually manifested there, I have reason for thinking that it does not follow the order of nature when, if the throat is dry, drinking does harm to the conservation of health, nevertheless I recognise at the same time that this last mode of explaining nature is very different from the other. For this is but a purely verbal characterisation depending entirely on my thought, which compares a sick man and a badly constructed clock with the idea which I have of a healthy man and a well made clock, and it is hence extrinsic to the things to which it is applied; but according to the other interpretation of the term nature I understand something which is truly found in things and which is therefore not without some truth.

But certainly although in regard to the dropsical body it is only so to speak to apply an extrinsic term when we say that its nature is corrupted, inasmuch as apart from the need to drink, the throat is parched; yet in regard to the composite whole, that is to say, to the mind or soul united to this body, it is not a purely verbal predicate, but a real error of nature, for it to have thirst when drinking would be hurtful to it. And thus it still remains to inquire how the goodness of God does not prevent the nature of man so regarded from being fallacious.

In order to begin this examination, then, I here say, in the first place, that there is a great difference between mind and body, inasmuch as body is by nature always divisible, and the mind is entirely indivisible. For, as a matter of fact, when I consider the mind, that is to say, myself inasmuch as I am only a thinking thing, I cannot distinguish in myself any parts, but apprehend myself to be clearly one and entire; and although the whole mind seems to be united to the whole body, yet if a foot, or an arm, or some other part, is separated from my body, I am aware that nothing has been taken away from my mind. And the faculties of willing, feeling, conceiving, etc. cannot be properly speaking said to be its parts, for it is one and the same mind which employs itself in willing and in feeling and understanding. But it is quite otherwise with corporeal or extended objects, for there is not one of these imaginable by me which my mind cannot easily divide into parts, and which consequently I do not recognise as being divisible; this would be sufficient to teach me that the mind or soul of man is entirely different from the body, if I had not already learned it from other sources.

I further notice that the mind does not receive the impressions from all parts of the body immediately, but only from the brain, or perhaps even from one of its smallest parts, to wit, from that in which the common sense[3] is said to reside, which, whenever it is disposed in the same particular way, conveys the same thing to the mind, although meanwhile the other portions of the body may be differently disposed, as is testified by innumerable experiments which it is unnecessary here to recount.

I notice, also, that the nature of body is such that none of its parts can be moved by another part a little way off which cannot also be moved in the same way by each one of the parts which are between the two, although this more remote part does not act at all. As, for example, in the cord $ABCD$ [which is in tension] if we pull the last part D, the first part A will not be moved in any way differently from what would be the case if one of the intervening parts B or C were pulled, and the last part D were to remain unmoved. And in the same way, when I feel pain in my foot, my knowledge of physics teaches me that this sensation is communicated by means of nerves dispersed through the foot, which, being extended like cords from there to the brain, when they are contracted in the foot, at the same time contract the inmost portions of the brain which is their extremity and place of origin, and then excite a certain movement which nature has established in order to cause the mind to be affected by a sensation of pain represented as existing in the foot. But because these nerves must pass through the tibia, the thigh, the loins, the back and the neck, in order to reach from the leg to the brain, it may happen that although their extremities which are in the foot are not affected, but only certain ones of their intervening parts [which pass by the loins or the neck], this action will excite the same movement in the brain that might have been excited there by a hurt received in the foot, in consequence of which the mind will necessarily feel in the foot the same pain as if it had received a hurt. And the same holds good of all the other perceptions of our senses.

I notice finally that since each of the movements which are in the portion of the brain by which the mind is immediately affected brings about one particular sensation only, we cannot under the circumstances imagine anything more likely than that this movement, amongst all the sensations which it is capable of impressing on it, causes mind to be affected by that one which is best fitted and most generally useful for the conservation of the human body when it is in health. But experience makes us aware that all the feelings with which nature inspires us are such as I have just spoken of; and there is therefore nothing in them which does not give testimony to the power and goodness of the God [who has produced them]. Thus, for

[3] *Sensus communis.*

example, when the nerves which are in the feet are violently or more than usually moved, their movement, passing through the medulla of the spine to the inmost parts of the brain, gives a sign to the mind which makes it feel somewhat, to wit, pain, as though in the foot, by which the mind is excited to do its utmost to remove the cause of the evil as dangerous and hurtful to the foot. It is true that God could have constituted the nature of man in such a way that this same movement in the brain would have conveyed something quite different to the mind; for example, it might have produced consciousness of itself either in so far as it is in the brain, or as it is in the foot, or as it is in some other place between the foot and the brain, or it might finally have produced consciousness of anything else whatsoever; but none of all this would have contributed so well to the conservation of the body. Similarly, when we desire to drink, a certain dryness of the throat is produced which moves its nerves, and by their means the internal portions of the brain; and this movement causes in the mind the sensation of thirst, because in this case there is nothing more useful to us than to become aware that we have need to drink for the conservation of our health; and the same holds good in other instances.

From this it is quite clear that, notwithstanding the supreme goodness of God, the nature of man, inasmuch as it is composed of mind and body, cannot be otherwise than sometimes a source of deception. For if there is any cause which excites, not in the foot but in some part of the nerves which are extended between the foot and the brain, or even in the brain itself, the same movement which usually is produced when the foot is detrimentally affected, pain will be experienced as though it were in the foot, and the sense will thus naturally be deceived; for since the same movement in the brain is capable of causing but one sensation in the mind, and this sensation is much more frequently excited by a cause which hurts the foot than by another existing in some other quarter, it is reasonable that it should convey to the mind pain in the foot rather than in any other part of the body. And although the parchedness of the throat does not always proceed, as it usually does, from the fact that drinking is necessary for the health of the body, but sometimes comes from quite a different cause, as is the case with dropsical patients, it is yet much better that it should mislead on this occasion than if, on the other hand, it were always to deceive us when the body is in good health; and so on in similar cases.

2

KNOWLEDGE OF IDEAS
AND SPIRITS

George Berkeley

It is evident to any one who takes a survey of the objects of human knowledge, that they are either ideas actually imprinted on the senses, or else such as are perceived by attending to the passions and operations of the mind, or lastly ideas formed by help of memory and imagination, either compounding, dividing, or barely representing those originally perceived in the aforesaid ways. By sight I have the ideas of light and colours with their several degrees and variations. By touch I perceive, for example, hard and soft, heat and cold, motion and resistance, and of all these more and less either as to quantity or degree. Smelling furnishes me with odours; the palate with tastes, and hearing conveys sounds to the mind in all their variety of tone and composition. And as several of these are observed to accompany each other, they come to be marked by one name, and so to be reputed as one thing. Thus, for example, a certain colour, taste, smell, figure and consistence having been observed to go together, are accounted one distinct thing, signified by the name *apple*. Other collections of ideas constitute a stone, a tree, a book, and the like sensible things; which, as they are pleasing or disagreeable, excite the passions of love, hatred, joy, grief, and so forth.

But besides all that endless variety of ideas or objects of knowledge, there is likewise something which knows or perceives them, and exercises divers operations, as willing, imagining, remembering about them. This perceiving, active being is what I call *mind, spirit, soul* or *my self*. By which words I do not denote any one of my ideas, but a thing entirely distinct from them, wherein they exist, or, which is the same thing, whereby they are perceived; for the existence of an idea consists in being perceived.

That neither our thoughts, nor passions, nor ideas formed by the imagination, exist without the mind, is what every body will allow. And it seems no

From *A Treatise Concerning the Principles of Human Knowledge*, in *The Works of George Berkeley, Bishop of Cloyne*, T. E. Jessop, ed. (London: Thomas Nelson & Sons Ltd., 1949), Vol. II, Secs. 1–8, 135–142, pp. 41–44, 103–106. Reprinted by permission of the publisher.

less evident that the various sensations or ideas imprinted on the sense, however blended or combined together (that is, whatever objects they compose) cannot exist otherwise than in a mind perceiving them. I think an intuitive knowledge may be obtained of this, by any one that shall attend to what is meant by the term *exist* when applied to sensible things. The table I write on, I say, exists, that is, I see and feel it; and if I were out of my study I should say it existed, meaning thereby that if I was in my study I might perceive it, or that some other spirit actually does perceive it. There was an odour, that is, it was smelled; there was a sound, that is to say, it was heard; a colour or figure, and it was perceived by sight or touch. This is all that I can understand by these and the like expressions. For as to what is said of the absolute existence of unthinking things without any relation to their being perceived, that seems perfectly unintelligible. Their *esse* is *percipi* [that is, their existence consists solely in their being perceived], nor is it possible they should have any existence, out of the minds or thinking things which perceive them.

It is indeed an opinion strangely prevailing amongst men, that houses, mountains, rivers, and in a word all sensible objects have an existence natural or real, distinct from their being perceived by the understanding. But with how great an assurance and acquiescence soever this principle may be entertained in the world; yet whoever shall find in his heart to call it in question, may, if I mistake not, perceive it to involve a manifest contradiction. For what are the forementioned objects but the things we perceive by sense, and what do we perceive besides our own ideas or sensations; and is it not plainly repugnant that any one of these or any combination of them should exist unperceived?

If we thoroughly examine this tenet, it will, perhaps, be found at bottom to depend on the doctrine of *abstract ideas*. For can there be a nicer strain of abstraction than to distinguish the existence of sensible objects from their being perceived, so as to conceive them existing unperceived? Light and colours, heat and cold, extension and figures, in a word the things we see and feel, what are they but so many sensations, notions, ideas or impressions on the sense; and is it possible to separate, even in thought, any of these from perception? For my part I might as easily divide a thing from it self. I may indeed divide in my thoughts or conceive apart from each other those things which, perhaps, I never perceived by sense so divided. Thus I imagine the trunk of a human body without the limbs, or conceive the smell of a rose without thinking on the rose it self. So far I will not deny I can abstract, if that may properly be called *abstraction*, which extends only to the conceiving separately such objects, as it is possible may really exist or be actually perceived asunder. But my conceiving or imagining power does not extend beyond the possibility of real existence or perception. Hence as it is impossible for me to see or feel anything without an actual sensation of that thing, so is it impossible for me to conceive in my thoughts any sensible thing or object distinct from the sensation or perception of it.

Some truths there are so near and obvious to the mind, that a man need only open his eyes to see them. Such I take this important one to be, to wit, that all the choir of heaven and furniture of the earth, in a word all those bodies which compose the mighty frame of the world, have not any subsistence without a mind, that their being is to be perceived or known;

that consequently so long as they are not actually perceived by me, or do not exist in my mind or that of any other created spirit, they must either have no existence at all, or else subsist in the mind of some eternal spirit: it being perfectly unintelligible and involving all the absurdity of abstraction, to attribute to any single part of them an existence independent of a spirit. To be convinced of which, the reader need only reflect and try to separate in his own thoughts the being of a sensible thing from its being perceived.

From what has been said, it follows, there is not any other substance than *spirit*, or that which perceives. But for the fuller proof of this point, let it be considered, the sensible qualities are colour, figure, motion, smell, taste, and such like, that is, the ideas perceived by sense. Now for an idea to exist in an unperceiving thing, is a manifest contradiction; for to have an idea is all one as to perceive: that therefore wherein colour, figure, and the like qualities exist, must perceive them; hence it is clear there can be no unthinking substance or *substratum* of those ideas.

But say you, though the ideas themselves do not exist without the mind, yet there may be things like them whereof they are copies or resemblances, which things exist without the mind, in an unthinking substance. I answer, an idea can be like nothing but an idea; a colour or figure can be like nothing but another colour or figure. If we look but ever so little into our thoughts, we shall find it impossible for us to conceive a likeness except only between our ideas. Again, I ask whether those supposed originals or external things, of which our ideas are the pictures or representations, be themselves perceivable or no? If they are, then they are ideas, and we have gained our point; but if you say they are not, I appeal to anyone whether it be sense, to assert a colour is like something which is invisible; hard or soft, like something which is intangible; and so of the rest.

.   .   .

Having dispatched what we intended to say concerning the knowledge of *ideas*, the method we proposed leads us, in the next place, to treat of *spirits*: with regard to which, perhaps human knowledge is not so deficient as is vulgarly imagined. The great reason that is assigned for our being thought ignorant of the nature of spirits, is, our not having an idea of it. But surely it ought not to be looked on as a defect in a human understanding, that it does not perceive the idea of *spirit*, if it is manifestly impossible there should be any such *idea* . . . a spirit has been shown to be the only substance or support, wherein the unthinking beings or ideas can exist: but that this *substance* which supports or perceives ideas should it self be an *idea* or like an *idea*, is evidently absurd.

It will perhaps be said, that we want a sense (as some have imagined) proper to know substances withal, which if we had, we might know our own soul, as we do a triangle. To this I answer, that in case we had a new sense bestowed upon us, we could only receive thereby some new sensations of ideas of sense. But I believe no body will say, that what he means by the terms *soul* and *substance*, is only some particular sort of idea or sensation. We may therefore infer, that all things duly considered, it is not more reasonable to think our faculties defective, in that they do not furnish us with an idea of spirit or active thinking substance, than it would be if we should blame them for not being able to comprehend a *round square*.

From the opinion that spirits are to be known after the manner of an idea or sensation, have risen many absurd and heterodox tenets, and much scepticism about the nature of the soul. It is even probable, that this opinion may have produced a doubt in some, whether they had any soul at all distinct from their body, since upon inquiry they could not find they had an idea of it. That an *idea* which is inactive, and the existence whereof consists in being perceived, should be the image or likeness of an agent subsisting by it self, seems to need no other refutation, than barely attending to what is meant by those words. But perhaps you will say, that though an *idea* cannot resemble a *spirit*, in its thinking, acting, or subsisting by it self, yet it may in some other respects: and it is not necessary that an idea or image be in all respects like the original.

I answer, if it does not in those mentioned, it is impossible it should represent it in any other thing. Do but leave out the power of willing, thinking, and perceiving ideas, and there remains nothing else wherein the idea can be like a spirit. For by the word *spirit* we mean only that which thinks, wills, and perceives; this, and this alone, constitutes the signification of that term. If therefore it is impossible that any degree of those powers should be represented in an idea, it is evident there can be no idea of a spirit.

But it will be objected, that if there is no idea signified by the terms *soul*, *spirit*, and *substance*, they are wholly insignificant, or have no meaning in them. I answer, those words do mean or signify a real thing, which is neither an idea nor like an idea, but that which perceives ideas, and wills, and reasons about them. What I am my self, that which I denote by the term I, is the same with what is meant by *soul* or *spiritual substance*. If it be said that this is only quarrelling at a word, and that since the immediate significations of other names are by common consent called *ideas*, no reason can be assigned, why that which is signified by the name *spirit* or *soul* may not partake in the same appellation. I answer, all the unthinking objects of the mind agree, in that they are entirely passive, and their existence consists only in being perceived: whereas a soul or spirit is an active being, whose existence consists not in being perceived, but in perceiving ideas and thinking. It is therefore necessary, in order to prevent equivocation and confounding natures perfectly disagreeing and unlike, that we distinguish between *spirit* and *idea*.

In a large sense indeed, we may be said to have an idea, or rather a notion of *spirit*, that is, we understand the meaning of the word, otherwise we could not affirm or deny any thing of it. Moreover, as we conceive the ideas that are in the minds of other spirits by means of our own, which we suppose to be resemblances of them: so we know other spirits by means of our own soul, which in that sense is the image or idea of them, it having a like respect to other spirits, that blueness or heat by me perceived hath to those ideas perceived by another.

It must not be supposed, that they who assert the natural immortality of the soul are of opinion, that it is absolutely incapable of annihilation even by the infinite power of the Creator who first gave it being: but only that it is not liable to be broken or dissolved by the ordinary Laws of Nature or motion. They indeed, who hold the soul of man to be only a thin vital flame, or system of animal spirits, make it perishing and corruptible as the body, since there is nothing more easily dissipated than such a being, which it is naturally impossible should survive the ruin of the tabernacle, wherein it is enclosed. And this notion hath been greedily embraced and cherished by the worst part of mankind, as the most effectual antidote against all impressions of virtue and religion. But it hath been made evident, that bodies of what frame or texture soever, are barely passive ideas in the mind, which is more distant and heterogeneous from them, than light is from darkness. We have shewn that the soul is indivisible, incorporeal, unextended, and it is consequently incorruptible. Nothing can be plainer, than that the motions, changes, decays, and dissolutions which we hourly see befall natural bodies (and which is what we mean by the *course of Nature*) cannot possibly affect an active, simple, uncompounded substance: such a being therefore is indissoluble by the force of Nature, that is to say, *the soul of man is naturally immortal.*

After what hath been said, it is I suppose plain, that our souls are not to be known in the same manner as senseless inactive objects, or by way of *idea*. *Spirits* and *ideas* are things so wholly different, that when we say, *they exist, they are known*, or the like, these words must not be thought to signify any thing common to both natures. There is nothing alike or common in them: and to expect that by any multiplication or enlargement of our faculties, we may be enabled to know a spirit as we do a triangle, seems as absurd as if we should hope to *see a sound*. This is inculcated because I imagine it may be of moment towards clearing several important questions, and preventing some very dangerous errors concerning the nature of the soul. We may not I think strictly be said to have an idea of an active being, or of an action, although we may be said to have a notion of them. I have some knowledge or notion of my mind, and its acts about ideas, inasmuch as I know or understand what is meant by those words. What I know, that I have some notion of. I will not say, that the terms *idea* and *notion* may not be used convertibly, if the world will have it so. But yet it conduceth to clearness and propriety, that we distinguish things very different by different names. It is also to be remarked, that all relations including an act of the mind, we cannot so properly be said to have an idea, but rather a notion of the relations or habitudes between things. But if in the modern way the word *idea* is extended to spirits, and relations and acts; this is after all an affair of verbal concern.

THE TRADITIONAL PROBLEM
OF BODY AND MIND

C. D. Broad

. . . There is a question which has been argued about for some centuries now under the name of "Interaction"; this is the question whether minds really do act on the organisms which they animate, and whether organisms really do act on the minds which animate them. (I must point out at once that I imply no particular theory of mind or body by the word "to animate". I use it as a perfectly neutral name to express the fact that a certain mind is connected in some peculiarly intimate way with a certain body and under normal conditions with no other body. This is a fact even on a purely behaviouristic theory of mind; on such a view to say that the mind M animates the body B would mean that the body B, in so far as it behaves in certain ways, *is* the mind M. A body which did not act in these ways would be said not to be animated by a mind. And a different Body B', which acted in the same general way as B, would be said to be animated by a different mind M'.)

The problem of Interaction is generally discussed at the level of en-lightened common-sense; where it is assumed that we know pretty well what we mean by "mind", by "matter" and by "causation". Obviously no solution which is reached at that level can claim to be ultimate. If what we call "matter" should turn out to be a collection of spirits of low intelligence, as Leibniz thought, the argument that mind and body are so unlike that their interaction is impossible would become irrelevant. Again, if causation be nothing but regular sequence and concomitance, as some philosophers have held, it is ridiculous to regard psychoneural parallelism and interaction as mutually exclusive alternatives. For interaction will mean no more than parallelism, and parallelism will mean no less than interaction. Nevertheless I am going to discuss the arguments here at the common-sense level, because they are so incredibly bad and yet have imposed upon so many learned men.

From C. D. Broad, *The Mind and Its Place in Nature* (London: 1925), Chap. III, pp. 95–113. Reprinted by permission of Routledge & Kegan Paul Ltd. and Humanities Press, Inc.

We start then by assuming a developed mind and a developed organism as two distinct things, and by admitting that the two are now intimately connected in some way or other which I express by saying that "this mind *animates* this organism". We assume that bodies are very much as en-lightened common-sense believes them to be; and that, even if we cannot define "causation", we have some means of recognising when it is present and when it is absent. The question then is: "Does a mind ever act on the body which it animates, and does a body ever act on the mind which animates it?" The answer which common-sense would give to both ques-tions is: "Yes, certainly." On the face of it my body acts on my mind whenever a pin is stuck into the former and a painful sensation thereupon arises in the latter. And, on the face of it, my mind acts on my body whenever a desire to move my arm arises in the former and is followed by this movement in the latter. Let us call this common-sense view "Two-sided Interaction". Although it seems so obvious it has been denied by probably a majority of philosophers and a majority of physiologists. So the question is: "Why should so many distinguished men, who have studied the subject, have denied the apparently obvious fact of Two-sided Interaction?"

The arguments against Two-sided Interaction fall into two sets:—Philo-sophical and Scientific. We will take the philosophical arguments first; for we shall find that the professedly scientific arguments come back in the end to the principles or prejudices which are made explicit in the philosophical arguments.

PHILOSOPHICAL ARGUMENTS AGAINST TWO-SIDED INTERACTION

No one can deny that there is a close correlation between certain bodily events and certain mental events, and conversely. Therefore anyone who denies that there is action of mind on body and of body on mind must presumably hold (*a*) that concomitant variation is not an adequate criterion of causal connexion, and (*b*) that the other feature which is essential for causal connexion is absent in the case of body and mind. Now the common philosophical argument is that minds and mental states are so extremely unlike bodies and bodily states that it is inconceivable that the two should be causally connected. It is certainly true that, if minds and mental events are just what they seem to be to introspection and nothing more, and if bodies and bodily events are just what enlightened common-sense thinks them to be and nothing more, the two *are* extremely unlike. And this fact is supposed to show that, however closely correlated certain pairs of events in mind and body respectively may be, they cannot be causally connected.

Evidently the assumption at the back of this argument is that concomitant variation, together with a high enough degree of likeness, is an adequate test for causation; but that no amount of concomitant variation can establish causation in the absence of a high enough degree of likeness. Now I am inclined to admit part of this assumption. I think it is practically certain that causation does not simply *mean* concomitant variation. (And, if it did, *cadit quæstio*.) Hence the existence of the latter is not *ipso facto* a proof of the presence of the former. Again, I think it is almost certain that concomitant variation between A and B is not in fact a sufficient sign of the presence of a *direct* causal relation between the two. (I think it may perhaps be a sufficient sign of *either* a direct causal relation between A and B *or* of several causal relations which indirectly unite A and B through the medium of other terms C, D, etc.) So far I agree with the assumptions of the argument. But I cannot see the least reason to think that the other characteristic, which must be added to concomitant variation before we can be sure that A and B are causally connected, is a high degree of likeness between the two. One would like to know just how unlike two events may be before it becomes impossible to admit the existence of a causal relation between them. No one hesitates to hold that draughts and colds in the head are causally connected, although the two are extremely unlike each other. If the unlikeness of draughts and colds in the head does not prevent one from admitting a causal connexion between the two, why should the unlikeness of volitions and voluntary movements prevent one from holding that they are causally connected? To sum up. I am willing to admit that an adequate criterion of causal connexion needs some other relation between a pair of events beside concomitant variation; but I do not believe for a moment that this other relation is that of qualitative likeness.

This brings us to a rather more refined form of the argument against Interaction. It is said that, whenever we admit the existence of a causal relation between two events, these two events (to put it crudely) must also form parts of a single substantial whole. *E.g.*, all physical events are spatially related and form one great extended whole. And the mental events which would commonly be admitted to be causally connected are always events in a single mind. A mind is a substantial whole of a peculiar kind too. Now it is said that between bodily events and mental events there are no relations such as those which unite physical events in different parts of the same Space or mental events in the history of the same mind. In the absence of such relations, binding mind and body into a single substantial whole, we cannot admit that bodily and mental events can be causally connected with each other, no matter how closely correlated their variations may be.

This is a much better argument than the argument about qualitative likeness and unlikeness. If we accept the premise that causal relations can subsist only between terms which form parts of a single substantial whole must we deny that mental and bodily events can be causally connected? I do not think that we need. (i) It is of course perfectly true that an organism and the mind which animates it do not form a physical whole, and that they do not form a mental whole; and these, no doubt, are the two kinds of substantial whole with which we are most familiar. But it does not follow that a mind and its organism do not form a substantial whole of *some* kind. There, plainly, is the extraordinarily intimate union between the two which I have called "animation" of the one by the other. Even if the mind be just what it seems to introspection, and the body be just what it seems to perception aided by the more precise methods of science, this seems to me to be enough to make a mind and its body a substantial whole. Even so extreme a dualist about Mind and Matter as Descartes occasionally suggests that a mind and its body together form a quasi-substance; and, although we may quarrel with the language of the very numerous philosophers who have said that the mind is "the form" of its body, we must admit that such language would never have seemed plausible unless a mind and its body together had formed something very much like a single substantial whole.

(ii) We must, moreover, admit the possibility that minds and mental events have properties and relations which do not reveal themselves to introspection, and that bodies and bodily events may have properties and relations which do not reveal themselves to perception or to physical and chemical experiment. In virtue of these properties and relations the two together may well form a single substantial whole of the kind which is alleged to be needed for causal interaction. Thus, if we accept the premise of the argument, we have no right to assert that mind and body *cannot* interact; but only the much more modest proposition that introspection and perception do not suffice to assure us that mind and body are so interrelated that they *can* interact.

(iii) We must further remember that the Two-sided Interactionist is under no obligation to hold that the *complete* conditions of any mental event are bodily or that the complete conditions of any bodily event are mental. He needs only to assert that some mental events include certain bodily events among their necessary conditions, and that some bodily events include certain mental events among their necessary conditions. If I am paralysed my volition may not move my arm; and, if I am hypnotised or intensely interested or frightened, a wound may not produce a painful sensation. Now, if the complete cause and the complete effect in all interaction include both a bodily and a mental factor, the two wholes will be related by the fact that the mental constituents belong to a single mind, that the bodily constituents belong to a single body, and that this mind animates this body. This amount of connexion should surely be enough to allow of causal interaction.

This will be the most appropriate place to deal with the contention that, in voluntary action, and there only, we are immediately acquainted with an instance of causal connexion. If this be true the controversy is of course settled at once in favour of the Interactionist. It is generally supposed that this view was refuted once and for all by Mr Hume in his *Enquiry concerning Human Understanding* (Sect. VII, Part I). I should not care to assert that the doctrine in question is true; but I do think that it is plausible, and I am quite sure that Mr Hume's arguments do not refute it. Mr Hume uses three closely connected arguments. (1) The connexion between a successful volition and the resulting bodily movement is as mysterious and as little self-evident as the connexion between any other event and its effect. (2) We have to learn from experience which of our volitions will be effective and which will not. *E.g.*, we do not know, until we have tried, that we can voluntarily move our arms and cannot voluntarily move our livers. And again, if a man were suddenly paralysed, he would still expect to be able to move his arm voluntarily, and would be surprised when he found that it kept still in spite of his volition. (3) We have discovered that the immediate consequence of a volition is a change in our nerves and muscles, which most people know nothing about; and is not the movement of a limb, which most people believe to be its immediate and necessary consequence.

The second and third arguments are valid only against the contention that we know immediately that a volition to make a certain movement is the *sufficient* condition for the happening of that movement. They are quite irrelevant to the contention that we know immediately that the volition is a *necessary* condition for the happening of just that movement at just that time. No doubt many other conditions are also necessary, *e.g.*, that our nerves and muscles shall be in the right state; and these other necessary conditions can be discovered only by special investigation. Since our volitions to move our limbs are in fact followed in the vast majority of cases by the willed movement, and since the other necessary conditions are not very obvious, it is natural enough that we should think that we know immediately that our volition is the *sufficient* condition of the movement of our limbs. If we think so, we are certainly wrong; and Mr Hume's arguments prove that we are. But they prove nothing else. It does not follow that we are wrong in thinking that we know, without having to wait for the result, that the volition is a *necessary* condition of the movement.

It remains to consider the first argument. Is the connexion between cause and effect as mysterious and as little self-evident in the case of the voluntary production of bodily movement as in all other cases? If so, we must hold that the first time a baby wills to move its hand it is just as much surprised to find its hand moving as it would be to find its leg moving or its nurse bursting into flames. I do not profess to know anything about the infant mind; but it seems to me that this is a wildly paradoxical consequence, for which there is no evidence or likelihood. But there is no need to leave the matter there. It is perfectly plain that, in the case of volition and voluntary movement, there *is* a connexion between the cause and the effect which is not present in other cases of causation, and which does make it plausible to hold that in this one case the nature of the effect can be foreseen by merely reflecting on the nature of the cause. The peculiarity of a volition as a cause-factor is that it involves as an essential part of it the idea of the effect. To say that a person has a volition to move his arm involves saying that he has an idea of his arm (and not of his leg or his liver) and an idea of the position in which he wants his arm to be. It is simply silly in view of this fact to say that there is no closer connexion between the desire to move my arm and the movement of my arm than there is between this desire and the movement of my leg or my liver. We cannot detect any analogous connexion between cause and effect in causal transactions which we view wholly from outside, such as the movement of a billiard-ball by a cue. It is therefore by no means unreasonable to suggest that, in the one case of our own voluntary movements, we can see without waiting for the result that such and such a volition is a necessary condition of such and such a bodily movement.

It seems to me then that Mr Hume's arguments on this point are absolutely irrelevant, and that it may very well be true that in volition we positively know that our desire for such and such a bodily movement is a necessary (though not a sufficient) condition of the happening of just that movement at just that time. On the whole then I conclude that the philosophical arguments certainly do not disprove Two-sided Interaction, and that they do not even raise any strong presumption against it. And, while I am not prepared definitely to commit myself to the view that, in voluntary movement, we positively *know* that the mind acts on the body, I do think that this opinion is quite plausible when properly stated and that the arguments which have been brought against it are worthless. I pass therefore to the scientific arguments.

SCIENTIFIC ARGUMENTS AGAINST TWO-SIDED INTERACTION

There are, so far as I know, two of these. One is supposed to be based on the physical principle of the Conservation of Energy, and on certain experiments which have been made on human bodies. The other is based on the close analogy which is said to exist between the structures of the physiological mechanism of reflex action and that of voluntary action. I will take them in turn.

(1) The Argument from Energy

It will first be needful to state clearly what is asserted by the principle of the Conservation of Energy. It is found that, if we take certain material systems, *e.g.*, a gun, a cartridge, and a bullet, there is a certain magnitude which keeps approximately constant throughout all their changes. This is called "Energy". When the gun has not been fired it and the bullet have no motion, but the explosive in the cartridge has great chemical energy. When it has been fired the bullet is moving very fast and has great energy of movement. The gun, though not moving fast in its recoil, has also great energy of movement because it is very massive. The gases produced by the explosion have some energy of movement and some heat-energy, but much less chemical energy than the unexploded charge had. These various kinds of energy can be measured in common units according to certain conventions. To an innocent mind there seems to be a good deal of "cooking" at this stage, *i.e.*, the conventions seem to be chosen and various kinds and amounts of concealed energy seem to be postulated in order to make the principle come out right at the end. I do not propose to go into this in detail, for two reasons. In the first place, I think that the conventions adopted and the postulates made, though somewhat suggestive of the fraudulent company-promoter, can be justified by their coherence with certain experimental facts, and that they are not simply made *ad hoc*. Secondly, I shall show that the Conservation of Energy is absolutely irrelevant to the question at issue, so that it would be waste of time to treat it too seriously in the present connexion. Now it is found that the total energy of all kinds in this system, when measured according to these conventions, is approximately the same in amount though very differently distributed after the explosion and before it. If we had confined our attention to a part of this system and *its* energy this would not have been true. The bullet, *e.g.*, had no energy at all before the explosion and a great deal afterwards. A system like the bullet, the gun, and the charge is called a "Conservative System"; the bullet alone, or the gun and the charge, would be called "Non-conservative Systems". A conservative system might therefore be defined as one whose total energy is redistributed, but not altered in amount, by changes that happen within it. Of course a given system might be conservative for some kinds of change and not for others.

So far we have merely defined a "Conservative System", and admitted that there are systems which, for some kinds of change at any rate, answer approximately to our definition. We can now state the Principle of the Conservation of Energy in terms of the conceptions just defined. The principle asserts that every material system is either itself conservative, or, if not, is part of a larger material system which is conservative. We may take it that there is good inductive evidence for this proposition.

The next thing to consider is the experiments on the human body. These tend to prove that a living body, with the air that it breathes and the food that it eats, forms a conservative system to a high degree of approximation. We can measure the chemical energy of the food given to a man, and that which enters his body in the form of Oxygen breathed in. We can also, with suitable apparatus, collect, measure and analyse the air breathed out, and thus find its chemical energy. Similarly, we can find the energy given out in bodily movement, in heat, and in excertion. It is alleged that, on the average, whatever the man may do, the energy of his bodily movements is exactly accounted for by the energy given to him in the form of food and of Oxygen. If you take the energy put in food and Oxygen, and subtract the energy given out in waste-products, the balance is almost exactly equal to the energy put out in bodily movements. Such slight differences as are found are as often on one side as on the other, and are therefore probably due to unavoidable experimental errors. I do not propose to criticise the interpretation of these experiments in detail, because, as I shall show soon, they are completely irrelevant to the problem of whether mind and body interact. But there is just one point that I will make before passing on. It is perfectly clear that such experiments can tell us only what happens on the average over a long time. To know whether the balance was accurately kept at every moment we should have to kill the patient at each moment and analyse his body so as to find out the energy present then in the form of stored-up products. Obviously we cannot keep on killing the patient in order to analyse him, and then reviving him in order to go on with the experiment. Thus it would seem that the results of the experiment are perfectly compatible with the presence of quite large excesses or defects in the total bodily energy at certain moments, provided that these average out over longer periods. However, I do not want to press this criticism; I am quite ready to accept for our present purpose the traditional interpretation which has been put on the experiments.

We now understand the physical principle and the experimental facts. The two together are generally supposed to prove that mind and body cannot interact. What precisely is the argument, and is it valid? I imagine that the argument, when fully stated, would run somewhat as follows: "I will to move my arm, and it moves. If the volition has anything to do with causing the movement we might expect energy to flow from my mind to my body. Thus the energy of my body ought to receive a measurable increase, not accounted for by the food that I eat and the Oxygen that I breathe. But no such physically unaccountable increases of bodily energy are found. Again, I tread on a tin-tack, and a painful sensation arises in my mind. If treading on the tack has anything to do with causing the sensation we might expect energy to flow from my body to my mind. Such energy would cease to be measurable. Thus there ought to be a noticeable decrease in my bodily energy, not balanced by increases anywhere in the physical system. But such unbalanced decreases of bodily energy are not found." So it is concluded that the volition has nothing to do with causing my arm to move, and that treading on the tack has nothing to do with causing the painful sensation.

Is this argument valid? In the first place it is important to notice that the conclusion does not follow from the Conservation of Energy and the experimental facts alone. The real premise is a tacitly assumed proposition about causation; viz., that, if a change in A has anything to do with causing a change in B, energy must leave A and flow into B. This is neither asserted nor entailed by the Conservation of Energy. What *it* says is that, *if* energy leaves A, it must appear in something else, say B; so that A and B together form a conservative system. Since the Conservation of Energy is not itself the premise for the argument against Interaction, and since it does not entail that premise, the evidence for the Conservation of Energy is not evidence against Interaction. Is there any independent evidence for the premise? We may admit that it *is* true of many, though not of all, transactions within the physical realm. But there are cases where it is not true even of purely physical transactions; and, even if it were always true in the physical realm, it would not follow that it must also be true of transphysical causation. Take the case of a weight swinging at the end of a string hung from a fixed point. The total energy of the weight is the same at all positions in its course. It is thus a conservative system. But at every moment the direction and velocity of the weight's motion are different, and the proportion between its kinetic and its potential energy is constantly changing. These changes are caused by the pull of the string, which acts in a different direction at each different moment. The string makes no difference to the total energy of the weight; but it makes all the difference in the world to the particular way in which the weight moves and the particular way in which the energy is distributed between the potential and the kinetic forms. This is evident when we remember that the weight would begin to move in an utterly different course if at any moment the string were cut.

Here, then, we have a clear case even in the physical realm where a system is conservative but is continually acted on by something which affects its movement and the distribution of its total energy. Why should not the mind act on the body in this way? If you say that you can see how a string can affect the movement of a weight, but cannot see how a volition could affect the movement of a material particle, you have deserted the scientific argument and have gone back to one of the philosophical arguments. Your real difficulty is either that volitions are so very unlike movements, or that the volition is in your mind whilst the movement belongs to the physical realm. And we have seen how little weight can be attached to these objections.

The fact is that, even in purely physical systems, the Conservation of Energy does not explain what changes will happen or when they will happen. It merely imposes a very general limiting condition on the changes that are possible. The fact that the system composed of bullet, charge, and gun, in our earlier example, is conservative does not tell us that the gun ever will be fired, or when it will be fired if at all, or what will cause it to go off, or what forms of energy will appear if and when it does go off. The change in this case is determined by pulling the trigger. Likewise the mere fact that the human body and its neighbourhood form a conservative system does not explain any particular bodily movement; it does not explain why I ever move at all, or why I sometimes write, sometimes walk, and sometimes swim. To explain the happening of these particular movements at certain times it seems to be essential to take into account the volitions which happen from time to time in my mind; just as it is essential to take the string into account to explain the particular behaviour of the weight, and to take the trigger into account to explain the going off of the gun at a certain moment. The difference between the gun-system and the body-system is that a little energy does flow into the former when the trigger is pulled, whilst it is alleged that none does so when a volition starts a bodily movement. But there is not even this amount of difference between the body-system and the swinging weight.

Thus the argument from energy has no tendency to disprove Two-sided Interaction. It has gained a spurious authority from the august name of the Conservation of Energy. But this impressive principle proves to have nothing to do with the case. And the real premise of the argument is not self-evident, and is not universally true even in purely intra-physical transactions. In the end this scientific argument has to lean on the old philosophic arguments; and we have seen that these are but bruised reeds. Nevertheless, the facts brought forward by the argument from energy do throw some light on the *nature* of the interaction between mind and body, assuming this to happen. They do suggest that all the energy of our bodily actions comes out of and goes back into the physical world, and that minds neither add energy to nor abstract it from the latter. What they do, if they do anything, is to determine that at a given moment so much energy shall change from the chemical form to the form of bodily movement; and they determine this, so far as we can see, without altering the total amount of energy in the physical world.

(2) The Argument from the Structure of the Nervous System

There are purely reflex actions, like sneezing and blinking, in which there is no reason to suppose that the mind plays any essential part. Now we know the nervous structure which is used in such acts as these. A stimulus is given to the outer end of an efferent nerve; some change or other runs up this nerve, crosses a synapsis between this and an afferent nerve, travels down the latter to a muscle, causes the muscle to contract, and so produces a bodily movement. There seems no reason to believe that the mind plays any essential part in this process. The process may be irreducibly vital, and not merely physico-chemical; but there seems no need to assume anything more than this. Now it is said that the whole nervous system is simply an immense complication of interconnected nervous arcs. The result is that a change which travels inwards has an immense number of alternative paths by which it may travel outwards. Thus the reaction to a given stimulus is no longer one definite movement, as in the simple reflex. Almost any movement may follow any stimulus according to the path which the afferent disturbance happens to take. This path will depend on the relative resistance of the various synapses at the time. Now a variable response to the same stimulus is characteristic of deliberate as opposed to reflex action.

These are the facts. The argument based on them runs as follows. It is admitted that the mind has nothing to do with the causation of purely reflex actions. But the nervous structure and the nervous processes involved in deliberate action do not differ in kind from those involved in reflex action; they differ only in degree of complexity. The variability which characterises deliberate action is fully explained by the variety of alternative paths and the variable resistances of the synapses. So it is unreasonable to suppose that the mind has any more to do with causing deliberate actions than it has to do with causing reflex actions.

I think that this argument is invalid. In the first place I am pretty sure that the persons who use it have before their imagination a kind of picture of how mind and body must interact if they interact at all. They find that the facts do not answer to this picture, and so they conclude that there is no inter-action. The picture is of the following kind. They think of the mind as sitting somewhere in a hole in the brain, surrounded by telephones. And they think of the efferent disturbance as coming to an end at one of these telephones and there affecting the mind. The mind is then supposed to respond by sending an afferent impulse down another of these telephones. As no such hole, with efferent nerves stopping at its walls and afferent nerves starting from them, can be found, they conclude that the mind can play no part in the transaction. But another alternative is that this picture of how the mind must act if it acts at all is wrong. To put it shortly, the mistake is to confuse a gap in an explanation with a spatio-temporal gap, and to argue from the absence of the latter to the absence of the former.

The Interactionist's contention is simply that there is a gap in any purely physiological explanation of deliberate action; *i.e.*, that all such explanations fail to account completely for the facts because they leave out one necessary condition. It does not follow in the least that there must be a spatio-temporal breach of continuity in the physiological conditions, and that the missing condition must fill this gap in the way in which the movement of a wire fills the spatio-temporal interval between the pulling of a bell-handle and the ringing of a distant bell. To assume this is to make the mind a kind of physical object, and to make its action a kind of mechanical action. Really, the mind and its actions are not literally in Space at all, and the time which is occupied by the mental event is no doubt *also* occupied by some part of the physiological process. Thus I am inclined to think that much of the force which this argument actually exercises on many people is simply due to the presupposition about the *modus operandi* of interaction, and that it is greatly weakened when this presupposition is shown to be a mere prejudice due to our limited power of envisaging unfamiliar alternative possibilities.

We can, however, make more detailed objections to the argument than this. There is a clear introspective difference between the mental accom-paniment of voluntary action and that of reflex action. What goes on in our minds when we decide with difficulty to get out of a hot bath on a cold morning is obviously extremely different from what goes on in our minds when we sniff pepper and sneeze. And the difference is qualitative; it is not a mere difference of complexity. This difference has to be explained some-how; and the theory under discussion gives no plausible explanation of it. The ordinary view that, in the latter case, the mind is not acting on the body at all; whilst, in the former, it is acting on the body in a specific way, does at least make the introspective difference between the two intelligible.

Again, whilst it is true that deliberate action differs from reflex action in its greater variability of response to the same stimulus, this is certainly not the whole or the most important part of the difference between them. The really important difference is that, in deliberate action, the response is varied *appropriately* to meet the special circumstances which are supposed to exist at the time or are expected to arise later; whilst reflex action is not varied in this way, but is blind and almost mechanical. The complexity of the nervous system explains the *possibility* of variation; it does not in the least explain why the alternative which actually takes place should as a rule be appropriate and not merely haphazard. And so again it seems as if some factor were in operation in deliberate action which is not present in reflex action; and it is reasonable to suppose that this factor is the volition in the mind.

It seems to me that this second scientific argument has no tendency to disprove interaction; but that the facts which it brings forward do tend to suggest the particular form which interaction probably takes if it happens at all. They suggest that what the mind does to the body in voluntary action, if it does anything, is to lower the resistance of certain synapses and to raise that of others. The result is that the nervous current follows such a course as to produce the particular movement which the mind judges to be appropriate at the time. On such a view the difference between reflex, habitual, and deliberate actions for the present purpose becomes fairly plain. In pure reflexes the mind cannot voluntarily affect the resistance of the synapses concerned, and so the action takes place in spite of it. In habitual action it deliberately refrains from interfering with the resistance of the synapses, and so the action goes on like a complicated reflex. But it *can* affect these resistances if it wishes, though often only with difficulty; and it is ready to do so if it judges this to be expedient. Finally, it may lose the power altogether. This would be what happens when a person becomes a slave to some habit, such as drug-taking.

I conclude that, at the level of enlightened common-sense at which the ordinary discussion of Interaction moves, no good reason has been produced for doubting that the mind acts on the body in volition, and that the body acts on the mind in sensation. The philosophic arguments are quite inconclusive; and the scientific arguments, when properly understood, are quite compatible with Two-sided Interaction. At most they suggest certain conclusions as to the form which interaction probably takes if it happens at all.

●   ●   ●

4

DESCARTES' MYTH

Gilbert Ryle

THE OFFICIAL DOCTRINE

There is a doctrine about the nature and place of minds which is so prevalent among theorists and even among laymen that it deserves to be described as the official theory. Most philosophers, psychologists and religious teachers subscribe, with minor reservations, to its main articles and, although they admit certain theoretical difficulties in it, they tend to assume that these can be overcome without serious modifications being made to the architecture of the theory. It will be argued here that the central principles of the doctrine are unsound and conflict with the whole body of what we know about minds when we are not speculating about them.

The official doctrine, which hails chiefly from Descartes, is something like this. With the doubtful exceptions of idiots and infants in arms every human being has both a body and a mind. Some would prefer to say that every human being is both a body and a mind. His body and his mind are ordinarily harnessed together, but after the death of the body his mind may continue to exist and function.

Human bodies are in space and are subject to the mechanical laws which govern all other bodies in space. Bodily processes and states can be inspected by external observers. So a man's bodily life is as much a public affair as are the lives of animals and reptiles and even as the careers of trees, crystals and planets.

But minds are not in space, nor are their operations subject to mechanical laws. The workings of one mind are not witnessable by other observers; its career is private. Only I can take direct cognisance of the states and processes of my own mind. A person therefore lives through two collateral histories, one consisting of what happens in and to his body, the other consisting of what happens in and to his mind. The first is public, the second

From Gilbert Ryle, *The Concept of Mind* (London and New York: 1949), Chap. I, pp. 11–24. Reprinted by permission of Hutchinson Publishing Group Ltd. and Barnes & Noble, Inc.

private. The events in the first history are events in the physical world, those in the second are events in the mental world.

It has been disputed whether a person does or can directly monitor all or only some of the episodes of his own private history; but, according to the official doctrine, of at least some of these episodes he has direct and unchallengeable cognisance. In consciousness, self-consciousness and introspection he is directly and authentically apprised of the present states and operations of his mind. He may have great or small uncertainties about concurrent and adjacent episodes in the physical world, but he can have none about at least part of what is momentarily occupying his mind.

It is customary to express this bifurcation of his two lives and of his two worlds by saying that the things and events which belong to the physical world, including his own body, are external, while the workings of his own mind are internal. This antithesis of outer and inner is of course meant to be construed as a metaphor, since minds, not being in space, could not be described as being spatially inside anything else, or as having things going on spatially inside themselves. But relapses from this good intention are common and theorists are found speculating how stimuli, the physical sources of which are yards or miles outside a person's skin, can generate mental responses inside his skull, or how decisions framed inside his cranium can set going movements of his extremities.

Even when 'inner' and 'outer' are construed as metaphors, the problem how a person's mind and body influence one another is notoriously charged with theoretical difficulties. What the mind wills, the legs, arms and the tongue execute; what affects the ear and the eye has something to do with what the mind perceives; grimaces and smiles betray the mind's moods and bodily castigations lead, it is hoped, to moral improvement. But the actual transactions between the episodes of the private history and those of the public history remain mysterious, since by definition they can belong to neither series. They could not be reported among the happenings described in a person's autobiography of his inner life, but nor could they be reported among those described in some one else's biography of that person's overt career. They can be inspected neither by introspection nor by laboratory experiment. They are theoretical shuttlecocks which are forever being bandied from the physiologist back to the psychologist and from the psychologist back to the physiologist.

Underlying this partly metaphorical representation of the bifurcation of a person's two lives there is a seemingly more profound and philosophical assumption. It is assumed that there are two different kinds of existence or status. What exists or happens may have the status of physical existence, or it may have the status of mental existence. Somewhat as the faces of coins are either heads or tails, or somewhat as living creatures are either male or female, so, it is supposed, some existing is physical existing, other existing is mental existing. It is a necessary feature of what has physical existence that it is in space and time; it is a necessary feature of what has mental existence that it is in time but not in space. What has physical existence is composed of matter, or else is a function of matter; what has mental existence consists of consciousness, or else is a function of consciousness.

There is thus a polar opposition between mind and matter, an opposition which is often brought out as follows. Material objects are situated in a common field, known as 'space', and what happens to one body in one part of space is mechanically connected with what happens to other bodies in other parts of space. But mental happenings occur in insulated fields, known as 'minds', and there is, apart maybe from telepathy, no direct causal connection between what happens in one mind and what happens in another. Only through the medium of the public physical world can the mind of one person make a difference to the mind of another. The mind is its own place and in his inner life each of us lives the life of a ghostly Robinson Crusoe. People can see, hear and jolt one another's bodies, but they are irremediably blind and deaf to the workings of one another's minds and inoperative upon them.

What sort of knowledge can be secured of the workings of a mind? On the one side, according to the official theory, a person has direct knowledge of the best imaginable kind of the workings of his own mind. Mental states and processes are (or are normally) conscious states and processes, and the consciousness which irradiates them can engender no illusions and leaves the door open for no doubts. A person's present thinkings, feelings and willings, his perceivings, rememberings and imaginings are intrinsically 'phosphorescent'; their existence and their nature are inevitably betrayed to their owner. The inner life is a stream of consciousness of such a sort that it would be absurd to suggest that the mind whose life is that stream might be unaware of what is passing down it.

True, the evidence adduced recently by Freud seems to show that there exist channels tributary to this stream, which run hidden from their owner. People are actuated by impulses the existence of which they vigorously disavow; some of their thoughts differ from the thoughts which they acknowledge; and some of the actions which they think they will to perform they do not really will. They are thoroughly gulled by some of their own hypocrisies and they successfully ignore facts about their mental lives which on the official theory ought to be patent to them. Holders of the official theory tend, however, to maintain that anyhow in normal circumstances a person must be directly and authentically seized of the present state and workings of his own mind.

Besides being currently supplied with these alleged immediate data of consciousness, a person is also generally supposed to be able to exercise from time to time a special kind of perception, namely inner perception, or introspection. He can take a (non-optical) 'look' at what is passing in his mind. Not only can he view and scrutinize a flower through his sense of sight and listen to and discriminate the notes of a bell through his sense of hearing; he can also reflectively or introspectively watch, without any bodily organ of sense, the current episodes of his inner life. This self-observation is also commonly supposed to be immune from illusion, confusion or doubt. A mind's reports of its own affairs have a certainty superior to the best that is possessed by its reports of matters in the physical world. Sense-perceptions can, but consciousness and introspection cannot, be mistaken or confused.

On the other side, one person has no direct access of any sort to the events of the inner life of another. He cannot do better than make problematic inferences from the observed behaviour of the other person's body to the states of mind which, by analogy from his own conduct, he supposes to be signalised by that behaviour. Direct access to the workings of a mind is the privilege of that mind itself; in default of such privileged access, the workings of one mind are inevitably occult to everyone else. For the supposed arguments from bodily movements similar to their own to mental workings similar to their own would lack any possibility of observational corroboration. Not unnaturally, therefore, an adherent of the official theory finds it difficult to resist this consequence of his premisses, that he has no good reason to believe that there do exist minds other than his own. Even if he prefers to believe that to other human bodies there are harnessed minds not unlike his own, he cannot claim to be able to discover their individual characteristics, or the particular things that they undergo and do. Absolute solitude is on this showing the ineluctable destiny of the soul. Only our bodies can meet.

As a necessary corollary of this general scheme there is implicitly prescribed a special way of construing our ordinary concepts of mental powers and operations. The verbs, nouns and adjectives, with which in ordinary life we describe the wits, characters and higher-grade performances of the people with whom we have to do, are required to be construed as signifying special episodes in their secret histories, or else as signifying tendencies for such episodes to occur. When someone is described as knowing, believing or guessing something, as hoping, dreading, intending or shirking something, as designing this or being amused at that, these verbs are supposed to denote the occurrence of specific modifications in his (to us) occult stream of consciousness. Only his own privileged access to this stream in direct awareness and introspection could provide authentic testimony that these mental-conduct verbs were correctly or incorrectly applied. The onlooker, be he teacher, critic, biographer or friend, can never assure himself that his comments have any vestige of truth. Yet it was just because we do in fact all know how to make such comments, make them with general correctness and correct them when they turn out to be confused or mistaken, that philosophers found it necessary to construct their theories of the nature and place of minds. Finding mental-conduct concepts being regularly and effectively used, they properly sought to fix their logical geography. But the logical geography officially recommended would entail that there could be no regular or effective use of these mental-conduct concepts in our descriptions of, and prescriptions for, other people's minds.

THE ABSURDITY OF THE OFFICIAL DOCTRINE

Such in outline is the official theory. I shall often speak of it, with deliberate abusiveness, as 'the dogma of the Ghost in the Machine'. I hope to prove that it is entirely false, and false not in detail but in principle. It is not merely an assemblage of particular mistakes. It is one big mistake and a mistake of a special kind. It is, namely, a category-mistake. It represents the facts of mental life as if they belonged to one logical type or category (or range of types or categories), when they actually belong to another. The dogma is therefore a philosopher's myth. In attempting to explode the myth I shall probably be taken to be denying well-known facts about the mental life of human beings, and my plea that I aim at doing nothing more than rectifying the logic of mental-conduct concepts will probably be disallowed as mere subterfuge.

I must first indicate what is meant by the phrase 'Category-mistake'. This I do in a series of illustrations.

A foreigner visiting Oxford or Cambridge for the first time is shown a number of colleges, libraries, playing fields, museums, scientific departments and administrative offices. He then asks 'But where is the University? I have seen where the members of the Colleges live, where the Registrar works, where the scientists experiment and the rest. But I have not yet seen the University in which reside and work the members of your University.' It has then to be explained to him that the University is not another collateral institution, some ulterior counterpart to the colleges, laboratories and offices which he has seen. The University is just the way in which all that he has already seen is organized. When they are seen and when their co-ordination is understood, the University has been seen. His mistake lay in his innocent assumption that it was correct to speak of Christ Church, the Bodleian Library, the Ashmolean Museum *and* the University, to speak, that is, as if 'the University' stood for an extra member of the class of which these other units are members. He was mistakenly allocating the University to the same category as that to which the other institutions belong.

The same mistake would be made by a child witnessing the march-past of a division, who, having had pointed out to him such and such battalions, batteries, squadrons, etc., asked when the division was going to appear. He would be supposing that a division was a counterpart to the units already seen, partly similar to them and partly unlike them. He would be shown his mistake by being told that in watching the battalions, batteries and squadrons marching past he had been watching the division marching past. The march-past was not a parade of battalions, batteries, squadrons *and* a division; it was a parade of the battalions, batteries and squadrons *of* a division.

One more illustration. A foreigner watching his first game of cricket learns what are the functions of the bowlers, the batsmen, the fielders, the umpires and the scorers. He then says 'But there is no one left on the field to contribute the famous element of team-spirit. I see who does the bowling, the batting and the wicket-keeping; but I do not see whose role it is to exercise *esprit de corps.*' Once more, it would have to be explained that he was looking for the wrong type of thing. Team-spirit is not another cricketing-operation supplementary to all of the other special tasks. It is, roughly, the keenness with which each of the special tasks is performed, and performing a task keenly is not performing two tasks. Certainly exhibiting team-spirit is not the same thing as bowling or catching, but nor is it a third thing such that we can say that the bowler first bowls *and* then exhibits team-spirit or that a fielder is at a given moment *either* catching *or* displaying *esprit de corps.*

These illustrations of category-mistakes have a common feature which must be noticed. The mistakes were made by people who did not know how to wield the concepts *University*, *division* and *team-spirit*. Their puzzles arose from inability to use certain items in the English vocabulary.

The theoretically interesting category-mistakes are those made by people who are perfectly competent to apply concepts, at least in the situations with which they are familiar, but are still liable in their abstract thinking to allocate those concepts to logical types to which they do not belong. An instance of a mistake of this sort would be the following story. A student of politics has learned the main differences between the British, the French and the American Constitutions, and has learned also the differences and connections between the Cabinet, Parliament, the various Ministries, the Judicature and the Church of England. But he still becomes embarrassed when asked questions about the connections between the Church of England, the Home Office and the British Constitution. For while the Church and the Home Office are institutions, the British Constitution is not another institution in the same sense of that noun. So inter-institutional relations which can be asserted or denied to hold between the Church and the Home Office cannot be asserted or denied to hold between either of them and the British Constitution. 'The British Constitution' is not a term of the same logical type as 'the Home Office' and 'the Church of England'. In a partially similar way, John Doe may be a relative, a friend, an enemy or a stranger to Richard Roe; but he cannot be any of these things to the Average Taxpayer. He knows how to talk sense in certain sorts of discussions about the Average Taxpayer, but he is baffled to say why he could not come across him in the street as he can come across Richard Roe.

It is pertinent to our main subject to notice that, so long as the student of politics continues to think of the British Constitution as a counterpart to the other institutions, he will tend to describe it as a mysteriously occult institution; and so long as John Doe continues to think of the Average Taxpayer as a fellow-citizen, he will tend to think of him as an elusive insubstantial man, a ghost who is everywhere yet nowhere.

My destructive purpose is to show that a family of radical category-mistakes is the source of the double-life theory. The representation of a person as a ghost mysteriously ensconced in a machine derives from this argument. Because, as is true, a person's thinking, feeling and purposive doing cannot be described solely in the idioms of physics, chemistry and physiology, therefore they must be described in counterpart idioms. As the human body is a complex organised unit, so the human mind must be another complex organised unit, though one made of a different sort of stuff and with a different sort of structure. Or, again, as the human body, like any other parcel of matter, is a field of causes and effects, so the mind must be another field of causes and effects, though not (Heaven be praised) mechanical causes and effects.

THE ORIGIN OF THE CATEGORY-MISTAKE

One of the chief intellectual origins of what I have yet to prove to be the Cartesian category-mistake seems to be this. When Galileo showed that his methods of scientific discovery were competent to provide a mechanical theory which should cover every occupant of space, Descartes found in himself two conflicting motives. As a man of scientific genius he could not but endorse the claims of mechanics, yet as a religious and moral man he could not accept, as Hobbes accepted, the discouraging rider to those claims, namely that human nature differs only in degree of complexity from clockwork. The mental could not be just a variety of the mechanical.

He and subsequent philosophers naturally but erroneously availed themselves of the following escape-route. Since mental-conduct words are not to be construed as signifying the occurrence of mechanical processes, they must be construed as signifying the occurrence of non-mechanical processes; since mechanical laws explain movements in space as the effects of other movements in space, other laws must explain some of the non-spatial workings of minds as the effects of other non-spatial workings of minds. The difference between the human behaviours which we describe as intelligent and those which we describe as unintelligent must be a difference in their causation; so, while some movements of human tongues and limbs are the effects of mechanical causes, others must be the effects of non-mechanical causes, i.e. some issue from movements of particles of matter, others from workings of the mind.

The differences between the physical and the mental were thus represented as differences inside the common framework of the categories of 'thing', 'stuff', 'attribute', 'state', 'process', 'change', 'cause' and 'effect'. Minds are things, but different sorts of things from bodies; mental processes are causes and effects, but different sorts of causes and effects from bodily movements. And so on. Somewhat as the foreigner expected the University to be an extra edifice, rather like a college but also considerably different, so the repudiators of mechanism represented minds as extra centres of causal processes, rather like machines but also considerably different from them. Their theory was a para-mechanical hypothesis.

That this assumption was at the heart of the doctrine is shown by the fact that there was from the beginning felt to be a major theoretical difficulty in explaining how minds can influence and be influenced by bodies. How can a mental process, such as willing, cause spatial movements like the movements of the tongue? How can a physical change in the optic nerve have among its effects a mind's perception of a flash of light? This notorious crux by itself shows the logical mould into which Descartes pressed his theory of the mind. It was the self-same mould into which he and Galileo set their mechanics. Still unwittingly adhering to the grammar of mechanics, he tried to avert disaster by describing minds in what was merely an obverse vocabulary. The workings of minds had to be described by the mere negatives of the specific descriptions given to bodies; they are not in space, they are not motions, they are not modifications of matter, they are not accessible to public observation. Minds are not bits of clockwork, they are just bits of not-clockwork.

As thus represented, minds are not merely ghosts harnessed to machines, they are themselves just spectral machines. Though the human body is an engine, it is not quite an ordinary engine, since some of its workings are governed by another engine inside it—this interior governor-engine being one of a very special sort. It is invisible, inaudible and it has no size or weight. It cannot be taken to bits and the laws it obeys are not those known to ordinary engineers. Nothing is known of how it governs the bodily engine.

A second major crux points the same moral. Since, according to the doctrine, minds belong to the same category as bodies and since bodies are rigidly governed by mechanical laws, it seemed to many theorists to follow that minds must be similarly governed by rigid non-mechanical laws. The physical world is a deterministic system, so the mental world must be a deterministic system. Bodies cannot help the modifications that they undergo, so minds cannot help pursuing the careers fixed for them. *Responsibility, choice, merit* and *demerit* are therefore inapplicable concepts—unless the compromise solution is adopted of saying that the laws governing mental processes, unlike those governing physical processes, have the congenial attribute of being only rather rigid. The problem of the Freedom of the Will was the problem how to reconcile the hypothesis that minds are to be described in terms drawn from the categories of mechanics with the knowledge that higher-grade human conduct is not of a piece with the behaviour of machines.

It is an historical curiosity that it was not noticed that the entire argument was broken-backed. Theorists correctly assumed that any sane man could already recognise the differences between, say, rational and non-rational utterances or between purposive and automatic behaviour. Else there would have been nothing requiring to be salved from mechanism. Yet the explanation given presupposed that one person could in principle never recognise the difference between the rational and the irrational utterances issuing from other human bodies, since he could never get access to the postulated immaterial causes of some of their utterances. Save for the doubtful exception of himself, he could never tell the difference between a man and a Robot. It would have to be conceded, for example, that, for all that we can tell, the inner lives of persons who are classed as idiots or lunatics are as rational as those of anyone else. Perhaps only their overt behaviour is disappointing; that is to say, perhaps 'idiots' are not really idiotic, or 'lunatics' lunatic. Perhaps, too, some of those who are classed as sane are really idiots. According to the theory, external observers could never know how the overt behaviour of others is correlated with their mental powers and processes and so they could never know or even plausibly conjecture whether their applications of mental-conduct concepts to these other people were correct or incorrect. It would then be hazardous or impossible for a man to claim sanity or logical consistency even for himself, since he would be debarred from comparing his own performances with those of others. In short, our characterisations of persons and their performances as intelligent, prudent and virtuous or as stupid, hypocritical and cowardly could never have been made, so the problem of providing a special causal hypothesis to serve as the basis of such diagnoses would never have arisen. The question, 'How do persons differ from machines?' arose just because everyone already knew how to apply mental-conduct concepts before the new causal hypothesis was introduced. This causal hypothesis could not therefore be the source of the criteria used in those applications. Nor, of course, has the causal hypothesis in any degree improved our handling of those criteria. We still distinguish good from bad arithmetic, politic from impolitic conduct and fertile from infertile imaginations in the ways in which Descartes himself distinguished them before and after he speculated how the applicability of these criteria was compatible with the principle of mechanical causation.

He had mistaken the logic of his problem. Instead of asking by what criteria intelligent behaviour is actually distinguished from non-intelligent behaviour, he asked 'Given that the principle of mechanical causation does not tell us the difference, what other causal principle will tell it us?' He realised that the problem was not one of mechanics and assumed that it must therefore be one of some counterpart to mechanics. Not unnaturally psychology is often cast for just this role.

When two terms belong to the same category, it is proper to construct conjunctive propositions embodying them. Thus a purchaser may say that he bought a left-hand glove and a right-hand glove, but not that he bought a left-hand glove, a right-hand glove and a pair of gloves. 'She came home in a flood of tears and a sedan-chair' is a well-known joke based on the absurdity of conjoining terms of different types. It would have been equally ridiculous to construct the disjunction 'She came home either in a flood of tears or else in a sedan-chair'. Now the dogma of the Ghost in the Machine does just this. It maintains that there exist both bodies and minds; that there occur physical processes and mental processes; that there are mechanical causes of corporeal movements and mental causes of corporeal movements. I shall argue that these and other analogous conjunctions are absurd; but, it must be noticed, the argument will not show that either of the illegitimately conjoined propositions is absurd in itself. I am not, for example, denying that there occur mental processes. Doing long division is a mental process and so is making a joke. But I am saying that the phrase 'there occur mental processes' does not mean the same sort of thing as 'there occur physical processes', and, therefore, that it makes no sense to conjoin or disjoin the two.

If my argument is successful, there will follow some interesting consequences. First, the hallowed contrast between Mind and Matter will be dissipated, but dissipated not by either of the equally hallowed absorptions of Mind by Matter or of Matter by Mind, but in quite a different way. For the seeming contrast of the two will be shown to be as illegitimate as would be the contrast of 'she came home in a flood of tears' and 'she came home in a sedan-chair'. The belief that there is a polar opposition between Mind and Matter is the belief that they are terms of the same logical type.

It will also follow that both Idealism and Materialism are answers to an improper question. The 'reduction' of the material world to mental states and processes, as well as the 'reduction' of mental states and processes to physical states and processes, presuppose the legitimacy of the disjunction 'Either there exist minds or there exist bodies (but not both)'. It would be like saying, 'Either she bought a left-hand and a right-hand glove or she bought a pair of gloves (but not both)'.

It is perfectly proper to say, in one logical tone of voice, that there exist minds and to say, in another logical tone of voice, that there exist bodies. But these expressions do not indicate two different species of existence, for 'existence' is not a generic word like 'coloured' or 'sexed'. They indicate two different senses of 'exist', somewhat as 'rising' has different senses in 'the tide is rising', 'hopes are rising', and 'the average age of death is rising'. A man would be thought to be making a poor joke who said that three things are now rising, namely the tide, hopes and the average age of death. It would be just as good or bad a joke to say that there exist prime numbers and Wednesdays and public opinions and navies; or that there exist both minds and bodies. In the succeeding chapters I try to prove that the official theory does rest on a batch of category-mistakes by showing that logically absurd corollaries follow from it. The exhibition of these absurdities will have the constructive effect of bringing out part of the correct logic of mental-conduct concepts.

HISTORICAL NOTE

It would not be true to say that the official theory derives solely from Descartes' theories, or even from a more widespread anxiety about the implications of seventeenth century mechanics. Scholastic and Reformation theology had schooled the intellects of the scientists as well as of the laymen, philosophers and clerics of that age. Stoic-Augustinian theories of the will were embedded in the Calvinist doctrines of sin and grace; Platonic and Aristotelian theories of the intellect shaped the orthodox doctrines of the immortality of the soul. Descartes was reformulating already prevalent theological doctrines of the soul in the new syntax of Galileo. The theologian's privacy of conscience became the philosopher's privacy of consciousness, and what had been the bogy of Predestination reappeared as the bogy of Determinism.

It would also not be true to say that the two-worlds myth did no theoretical good. Myths often do a lot of theoretical good, while they are still new. One benefit bestowed by the para-mechanical myth was that it partly superannuated the then prevalent para-political myth. Minds and their Faculties had previously been described by analogies with political superiors and political subordinates. The idioms used were those of ruling, obeying, collaborating and rebelling. They survived and still survive in many ethical and some epistemological discussions. As, in physics, the new myth of occult Forces was a scientific improvement on the old myth of Final Causes, so, in anthropological and psychological theory, the new myth of hidden operations, impulses and agencies was an improvement on the old myth of dictations, deferences and disobediences.

5

PROCESSES
SENSATIONS AND BRAIN

J. J. C. Smart

This paper[1] takes its departure from arguments to be found in U. T. Place's "Is Consciousness a Brain Process?"[2] I have had the benefit of discussing Place's thesis in a good many universities in the United States and Australia, and I hope that the present paper answers objections to his thesis which Place has not considered and that it presents his thesis in a more nearly unobjectionable form. This paper is meant also to supplement the paper "The 'Mental' and the 'Physical,' " by H. Feigl,[3] which in part argues for a similar thesis to Place's.

Suppose that I report that I have at this moment a roundish, blurry-edged after-image which is yellowish towards its edge and is orange towards its center. What is it that I am reporting? One answer to this question might be that I am not reporting anything, that when I say that it looks to me as though there is a roundish yellowy-orange patch of light on the wall I am expressing some sort of *temptation*, the temptation to say that there *is* a roundish yellowy-orange patch on the wall (though I may know that there is not such a patch on the wall). This is perhaps Wittgenstein's view in the *Philosophical Investigations* (see §§367, 370). Similarly, when I "report" a pain, I am not really reporting anything (or, if you like, I am reporting in a queer sense of "reporting"), but am doing a sophisticated sort of wince. (See §244: "The verbal expression of pain replaces crying and does not

---

J. J. C. Smart, "Sensations and Brain Processes," in *The Philosophy of Mind*, V. C. Chappell, ed., © 1962. Reprinted by permission of Prentice-Hall, Inc., *The Philosophical Review*, and the author, who has authorized the revisions adopted.

[1] This is a very slightly revised version of a paper which was first published in the *Philosophical Review*, LXVIII (1959), 141–56. Since that date there have been criticisms of my paper by J. T. Stevenson, *Philosophical Review*, LXIX (1960), 505–10, to which I have replied in *Philosophical Review*, LXX (1961), 406–7, and by G. Pitcher and by W. D. Joske, *Australasian Journal of Philosophy*, XXXVIII (1960), 150–60, to which I have replied in the same volume of that journal, pp. 252–54.

[2] *British Journal of Psychology*, XLVII (1956), 44–50.

[3] *Minnesota Studies in the Philosophy of Science*, Vol. II (Minneapolis: University of Minnesota Press, 1958), pp. 370–497.

describe it." Nor does it describe anything else?)[4] I prefer most of the time to discuss an after-image rather than a pain, because the word "pain" brings in something which is irrelevant to my purpose: the notion of "distress." I think that "he is in pain" entails "he is in distress," that is, that he is in a certain agitation-condition.[5] Similarly, to say "I am in pain" may be to do more than "replace pain behavior": it may be partly to report something, though this something is quite nonmysterious, being an agitation-condition, and so susceptible of behavioristic analysis. The suggestion I wish if possible to avoid is a different one, namely that "I am in pain" is a genuine report, and that what it reports is an irreducibly psychical something. And similarly the suggestion I wish to resist is also that to say "I have a yellowish-orange after-image" is to report something irreducibly psychical.

Why do I wish to resist this suggestion? Mainly because of Occam's razor. It seems to me that science is increasingly giving us a viewpoint whereby organisms are able to be seen as physicochemical mechanisms:[6] it seems that even the behavior of man himself will one day be explicable in mechanistic terms. There does seem to be, so far as science is concerned, nothing in the world but increasingly complex arrangements of physical constituents. All except for one place: in consciousness. That is, for a full description of what is going on in a man you would have to mention not only the physical processes in his tissues, glands, nervous system, and so forth, but also his states of consciousness: his visual, auditory, and tactual sensations, his aches and pains. That these should be *correlated* with brain processes does not help, for to say that they are *correlated* is to say that they are something "over and above." You cannot correlate something with itself. You correlate footprints with burglars, but not Bill Sikes the burglar with Bill Sikes the burglar. So sensations, states of consciousness, do seem to be the one sort of thing left outside the physicalist picture, and for various reasons I just cannot believe that this can be so. That everything should be explicable in terms of physics (together of course with descriptions of the ways in which the parts are put together—roughly, biology is to physics as radio-engineering is to electromagnetism) except the occurrence of sensations seems to me to be frankly unbelievable. Such sensations would be "nomological danglers," to use Feigl's expression.[7] It is not often realized how odd would be the laws whereby these nomological danglers would dangle. It is sometimes asked, "Why can't there be psychophysical laws which are of a novel sort, just as the laws of electricity and magnetism were novelties from the standpoint of Newtonian mechanics?" Certainly we are

[4] Some philosophers of my acquaintance, who have the advantage over me in having known Wittgenstein, would say that this interpretation of him is too behavioristic. However, it seems to me a very natural interpretation of his printed words, and whether or not it is Wittgenstein's real view it is certainly an interesting and important one. I wish to consider it here as a possible rival both to the "brain-process" thesis and to straight-out old-fashioned dualism.

[5] See Ryle, *The Concept of Mind* (London: Hutchinson's University Library, 1949), p. 93.

[6] On this point see Paul Oppenheim and Hilary Putnam, "Unity of Science as a Working Hypothesis," in *Minnesota Studies in the Philosophy of Science*, Vol. II (Minneapolis: University of Minnesota Press, 1958), pp. 3–36.

[7] Feigl, *op. cit.*, p. 428. Feigl uses the expression "nomological danglers" for the laws whereby the entities dangle: I have used the expression to refer to the dangling entities themselves.

pretty sure in the future to come across new ultimate laws of a novel type, but I expect them to relate simple constituents: for example, whatever ultimate particles are then in vogue. I cannot believe that ultimate laws of nature could relate simple constituents to configurations consisting of perhaps billions of neurons (and goodness knows how many billion billions of ultimate particles) all put together for all the world as though their main purpose in life was to be a negative feedback mechanism of a complicated sort. Such ultimate laws would be like nothing so far known in science. They have a queer "smell" to them. I am just unable to believe in the nomological danglers themselves, or in the laws whereby they would dangle. If any philosophical arguments seemed to compel us to believe in such things, I would suspect a catch in the argument. In any case it is the object of this paper to show that there are no philosophical arguments which compel us to be dualists.

The above is largely a confession of faith, but it explains why I find Wittgenstein's position (as I construe it) so congenial. For on this view there are, in a sense, no sensations. A man is a vast arrangement of physical particles, but there are not, over and above this, sensations or states of consciousness. There are just behavioral facts about this vast mechanism, such as that it expresses a temptation (behavior disposition) to say "there is a yellowish-red patch on the wall" or that it goes through a sophisticated sort of wince, that is, says "I am in pain." Admittedly Wittgenstein says that though the sensation "is not a something," it is nevertheless "not a nothing either" (§304), but this need only mean that the word "ache" has a use. An ache is a thing, but only in the innocuous sense in which the plain man, in the first paragraph of Frege's *Foundations of Arithmetic*, answers the question "What is the number one?" by "a thing." It should be noted that when I assert that to say "I have a yellowish-orange after-image" is to express a temptation to assert the physical-object statement "There is a yellowish-orange patch on the wall," I mean that saying "I have a yellowish-orange after-image" is (partly) the exercise of the disposition[8] which is the temptation. It is not to *report* that I have the temptation, any more than is "I love you" normally a report that I love someone. Saying "I love you" is just part of the behavior which is the exercise of the disposition of loving someone.

Though for the reasons given above, I am very receptive to the above "expressive" account of sensation statements, I do not feel that it will quite do the trick. Maybe this is because I have not thought it out sufficiently, but it does seem to me as though, when a person says "I have an after-image," he *is* making a genuine report, and that when he says "I have a pain," he *is* doing more than "replace pain-behavior," and that "this more" is not just to say that he is in distress. I am not so sure, however, that to admit this is to admit that there are nonphysical correlates of brain processes. Why should not sensations just be brain processes of a certain sort? There are, of course,

----

[8] Wittgenstein did not like the word "disposition." I am using it to put in a nutshell (and perhaps inaccurately) the view which I am attributing to Wittgenstein. I should like to repeat that I do not wish to claim that my interpretation of Wittgenstein is correct. Some of those who knew him do not interpret him in this way. It is merely a view which I find myself extracting from his printed words and which I think is important and worth discussing for its own sake.

well-known (as well as lesser-known) philosophical objections to the view that reports of sensations are reports of brain-processes, but I shall try to argue that these arguments are by no means as cogent as is commonly thought to be the case.

Let me first try to state more accurately the thesis that sensations are brain-processes. It is not the thesis that, for example, "after-image" or "ache" means the same as "brain process of sort X" (where "X" is replaced by a description of a certain sort of brain process). It is that, in so far as "after-image" or "ache" is a report of a process, it is a report of a process that *happens to be* a brain process. It follows that the thesis does not claim that sensation statements can be *translated* into statements about brain processes.[9] Nor does it claim that the logic of a sensation statement is the same as that of a brain-process statement. All it claims is that in so far as a sensation statement is a report of something, that something is in fact a brain process. Sensations are nothing over and above brain processes. Nations are nothing "over and above" citizens, but this does not prevent the logic of nation statements being very different from the logic of citizen statements, nor does it insure the translatability of nation statements into citizen statements. (I do not, however, wish to assert that the relation of sensation statements to brain-process statements is very like that of nation statements to citizen statements. Nations do not just *happen to be* nothing over and above citizens, for example. I bring in the "nations" example merely to make a negative point: that the fact that the logic of A-statements is different from that of B-statements does not insure that A's are anything over and above B's.)

REMARKS ON IDENTITY

When I say that a sensation is a brain process or that lightning is an electric discharge, I am using "is" in the sense of strict identity. (Just as in the—in this case necessary—proposition "7 is identical with the smallest prime number greater than 5.") When I say that a sensation is a brain process or that lightning is an electric discharge I do not mean just that the sensation is somehow spatially or temporally continuous with the brain process or that the lightning is just spatially or temporally continuous with the discharge. When on the other hand I say that the successful general is the same person as the small boy who stole the apples I mean only that the successful general I see before me is a time slice[10] of the same four-dimensional object of which the small boy stealing apples is an earlier time slice. However, the four-dimensional object which has the general-I-see-before-me for its late time slice is identical in the strict sense with the four-dimensional object which has the small-boy-stealing-apples for an early time slice. I distinguish these two senses of "is identical with" because I wish to make it clear that the brain-process doctrine asserts identity in the *strict* sense.

I shall now discuss various possible objections to the view that the

---

[9] See Place, *loc. cit.*, and Feigl, *op. cit.*, p. 390, near top.

[10] See J. H. Woodger, *Theory Construction*, International Encyclopedia of Unified Science, II, No. 5 (Chicago: University of Chicago Press, 1939), 38. I here permit myself to speak loosely. For warnings against possible ways of going wrong with this sort of talk, see my note "Spatialising Time," *Mind*, LXIV (1955), 239–41.

processes reported in sensation statements are in fact processes in the brain. Most of us have met some of these objections in our first year as philosophy students. All the more reason to take a good look at them. Others of the objections will be more recondite and subtle.

Objection 1. Any illiterate peasant can talk perfectly well about his after-images, or how things look or feel to him, or about his aches and pains, and yet he may know nothing whatever about neurophysiology. A man may, like Aristotle, believe that the brain is an organ for cooling the body without any impairment of his ability to make true statements about his sensations. Hence the things we are talking about when we describe our sensations cannot be processes in the brain.

Reply. You might as well say that a nation of slugabeds, who never saw the Morning Star or knew of its existence, or who had never thought of the expression "the Morning Star," but who used the expression "the Evening Star" perfectly well, could not use this expression to refer to the same entity as we refer to (and describe as) "the Morning Star."[11]

You may object that the Morning Star is in a sense not the very same thing as the Evening Star, but only something spatiotemporally continuous with it. That is, you may say that the Morning Star is not the Evening Star in the strict sense of "identity" that I distinguished earlier.

There is, however, a more plausible example. Consider lightning.[12] Modern physical science tells us that lightning is a certain kind of electrical discharge due to ionization of clouds of water vapor in the atmosphere. This, it is now believed, is what the true nature of lightning is. Note that there are not two things: a flash of lightning and an electrical discharge. There is one thing, a flash of lightning, which is described scientifically as an electrical discharge to the earth from a cloud of ionized water molecules. The case is not at all like that of explaining a footprint by reference to a burglar. We say that what lightning really is, what its true nature as revealed by science is, is an electrical discharge. (It is not the true nature of a footprint to be a burglar.)

To forestall irrelevant objections, I should like to make it clear that by "lightning" I mean the publicly observable physical object, lightning, not a visual sense-datum of lightning. I say that the publicly observable physical object lightning is in fact the electrical discharge, not just a correlate of it. The sense-datum, or rather the having of the sense-datum, the "look" of lightning, may well in my view be a correlate of the electrical discharge. For in my view it is a brain state *caused* by the lightning. But we should no more confuse sensations of lightning with lightning than we confuse sensations of a table with the table.

In short, the reply to Objection 1 is that there can be contingent statements of the form "A is identical with B," and a person may well know that something is an A without knowing that it is a B. An illiterate peasant might well be able to talk about his sensations without knowing about his brain

[11] Cf. Feigl, *op. cit.*, p. 439.
[12] See Place, *loc. cit.*; also Feigl, *op. cit.*, p. 438.

processes, just as he can talk about lightning though he knows nothing of electricity.

Objection 2. It is only a contingent fact (if it is a fact) that when we have a certain kind of sensation there is a certain kind of process in our brain. Indeed it is possible, though perhaps in the highest degree unlikely, that our present physiological theories will be as out of date as the ancient theory connecting mental processes with goings on in the heart. It follows that when we report a sensation we are not reporting a brain-process.

Reply. The objection certainly proves that when we say "I have an after-image" we cannot *mean* something of the form "I have such and such a brain-process." But this does not show that what we report (having an after-image) is not *in fact* a brain process. "I see lightning" does not *mean* "I see an electrical discharge." Indeed, it is logically possible (though highly unlikely) that the electrical discharge account of lightning might one day be given up. Again, "I see the Evening Star" does not *mean* the same as "I see the Morning Star," and yet "The Evening Star and the Morning Star are one and the same thing" is a contingent proposition. Possibly Objection 2 derives some of its apparent strength from a "Fido"—Fido theory of meaning. If the meaning of an expression were what the expression named, then of course it *would* follow from the fact that "sensation" and "brain-process" have different meanings that they cannot name one and the same thing.

Objection 3.[13] Even if Objections 1 and 2 do not prove that sensations are something over and above brain-processes, they do prove that the qualities of sensations are something over and above the qualities of brain-processes. That is, it may be possible to get out of asserting the existence of irreducibly psychic processes, but not out of asserting the existence of irreducibly psychic *properties*. For suppose we identify the Morning Star with the Evening Star. Then there must be some properties which logically imply that of being the Morning Star, and quite distinct properties which entail that of being the Evening Star. Again, there must be some properties (for example, that of being a yellow flash) which are logically distinct from those in the physicalist story.

Indeed, it might be thought that the objection succeeds at one jump. For consider the property of "being a yellow flash." It might seem that this property lies inevitably outside the physicalist framework within which I am trying to work (either by "yellow" being an objective emergent property of physical objects, or else by being a power to produce yellow sense-data, where "yellow," in this second instantiation of the word, refers to a purely phenomenal or introspectible quality). I must therefore digress for a moment and indicate how I deal with secondary qualities. I shall concentrate on color.

[13] I think this objection was first put to me by Professor Max Black. I think it is the most subtle of any of those I have considered, and the one which I am least confident of having satisfactorily met.

First of all, let me introduce the concept of a normal percipient. One person is more a normal percipient than another if he can make color discriminations that the other cannot. For example, if A can pick a lettuce leaf out of a heap of cabbage leaves, whereas B cannot though he can pick a lettuce leaf out of a heap of beetroot leaves, then A is more normal than B. (I am assuming that A and B are not given time to distinguish the leaves by their slight difference in shape, and so forth.) From the concept of "more normal than" it is easy to see how we can introduce the concept of "normal." Of course, Eskimos may make the finest discriminations at the blue end of the spectrum, Hottentots at the red end. In this case the concept of a normal percipient is a slightly idealized one, rather like that of "the mean sun" in astronomical chronology. There is no need to go into such subtleties now. I say that "This is red" means something roughly like "A normal percipient would not easily pick this out of a clump of geranium petals though he would pick it out of a clump of lettuce leaves." Of course it does not exactly mean this: a person might know the meaning of "red" without knowing anything about geraniums, or even about normal percipients. But the point is that a person can be *trained* to say "This is red" of objects which would not easily be picked out of geranium petals by a normal percipient, and so on. (Note that even a color-blind person can reasonably assert that something is red, though of course he needs to use another human being, not just himself, as his "color meter.") This account of secondary qualities explains their unimportance in physics. For obviously the discriminations and lack of discriminations made by a very complex neurophysiological mechanism are hardly likely to correspond to simple and nonarbitrary distinctions in nature.

I therefore elucidate colors as powers, in Locke's sense, to evoke certain sorts of discriminatory responses in human beings. They are also, of course, powers to cause sensations in human beings (an account still nearer Locke's). But these sensations, I am arguing, are identifiable with brain processes.

Now how do I get over the objection that a sensation can be identified with a brain process only if it has some phenomenal property, not possessed by brain processes, whereby one-half of the identification may be, so to speak, pinned down?

Reply. My suggestion is as follows. When a person says, "I see a yellowish-orange after-image," he is saying something like this: "*There is something going on which is like what is going on when* I have my eyes open, am awake, and there is an orange illuminated in good light in front of me, that is, when I really see an orange." (And there is no reason why a person should not say the same thing when he is having a veridical sense-datum, so long as we construe "like" in the last sentence in such a sense that something can be like itself.) Notice that the italicized words, namely "there is something going on which is like what is going on when," are all quasi-logical or topic-neutral words. This explains why the ancient Greek peasant's reports about his sensations can be neutral between dualistic metaphysics or my materialistic metaphysics. It explains how sensations can be brain-processes and yet how a man who reports them need know nothing about brain-processes. For he reports them only very abstractly as "something going on which is like what is going on when. . . ." Similarly, a person may say "someone is in the room," thus reporting truly that the doctor is in the room, even though he has never heard of doctors. (There are not two people in the room: "someone" *and* the doctor.) This account of sensation statements also explains the singular elusiveness of "raw feels"— why no one seems to be able to pin any properties on them.[14] Raw feels, in my view, are colorless for the very same reason that *something* is colorless. This does not mean that sensations do not have plenty of properties, for if they are brain-processes they certainly have lots of neurological properties. It only means that in speaking of them as being like or unlike one another we need not know or mention these properties.

This, then, is how I would reply to Objection 3. The strength of my reply depends on the possibility of our being able to report that one thing is like another without being able to state the respect in which it is like. I do not see why this should not be so. If we think cybernetically about the nervous system we can envisage it as able to respond to certain likenesses of its internal processes without being able to do more. It would be easier to build a machine which would tell us, say on a punched tape, whether or not two objects were similar, than it would be to build a machine which would report wherein the similarities consisted.

Objection 4. The after-image is not in physical space. The brain-process is. So the after-image is not a brain-process.

Reply. This is an *ignoratio elenchi* [irrelevant conclusion]. I am not arguing that the after-image is a brain-process, but that the experience of having an after-image is a brain-process. It is the *experience* which is reported in the introspective report. Similarly, if it is objected that the after-image is yellowy-orange, my reply is that it is the experience of seeing yellowy-orange that is being described, and this experience is not a yellowy-orange something. So to say that a brain-process cannot be yellowy-orange is not to say that a brain-process cannot in fact be the experience of having a yellowy-orange after-image. There is, in a sense, no such thing as an after-image or a sense-datum, though there is such a thing as the experience of having an image, and this experience is described indirectly in material object language, not in phenomenal language, for there is no such thing.[15] We describe the experience by saying, in effect, that it is like the experience we have when, for example, we really see a yellowy-orange patch on the wall. Trees and wallpaper can be green, but not the experience of seeing or

---

[14] See B. A. Farrell, "Experience," *Mind*, LIX (1950), 170–98.

[15] Dr. J. R. Smythies claims that a sense-datum language could be taught independently of the material object language ("A Note on the Fallacy of the 'Phenomenological Fallacy,'" *British Journal of Psychology*, XLVIII [1957], 141–44). I am not so sure of this: there must be some public criteria for a person having got a rule wrong before we can teach him the rule. I suppose someone might *accidentally* learn color words by Dr. Smythies' procedure. I am not, of course, denying that we can learn a sense-datum language in the sense that we can learn to report our experience. Nor would Place deny it.

imagining a tree or wallpaper. (Or if they are described as green or yellow this can only be in a derived sense.)

Objection 5. It would make sense to say of a molecular movement in the brain that it is swift or slow, straight or circular, but it makes no sense to say this of the experience of seeing something yellow.

Reply. So far we have not given sense to talk of experiences as swift or slow, straight or circular. But I am not claiming that "experience" and "brain-process" mean the same or even that they have the same logic. "Somebody" and "the doctor" do not have the same logic, but this does not lead us to suppose that talking about somebody telephoning is talking about someone over and above, say, the doctor. The ordinary man when he reports an experience is reporting that something is going on, but he leaves it open as to what sort of thing is going on, whether in a material solid medium or perhaps in some sort of gaseous medium, or even perhaps in some sort of nonspatial medium (if this makes sense). All that I am saying is that "experience" and "brain-process" may in fact refer to the same thing, and if so we may easily adopt a convention (which is not a change in our present rules for the use of experience words but an addition to them) whereby it would make sense to talk of an experience in terms appropriate to physical processes.

Objection 6. Sensations are private, brain processes are *public*. If I sincerely say, "I see a yellowish-orange after-image," and I am not making a verbal mistake, then I cannot be wrong. But I can be wrong about a brain-process. The scientist looking into my brain might be having an illusion. Moreover, it makes sense to say that two or more people are observing the same brain-process but not that two or more people are reporting the same inner experience.

Reply. This shows that the language of introspective reports has a different logic from the language of material processes. It is obvious that until the brain-process theory is much improved and widely accepted there will be no *criteria* for saying "Smith has an experience of such-and-such a sort" *except* Smith's introspective reports. So we have adopted a rule of language that (normally) what Smith says goes.

Objection 7. I can imagine myself turned to stone and yet having images, aches, pains, and so on.

Reply. I can imagine that the electrical theory of lightning is false, that lightning is some sort of purely optical phenomenon. I can imagine that lightning is not an electrical discharge. I can imagine that the Evening Star is not the Morning Star. But it is. All the objection shows is that "experience" and "brain-process" do not have the same meaning. It does not show that an experience is not in fact a brain process.

This objection is perhaps much the same as one which can be summed up by the slogan: "What can be composed of nothing cannot be composed of anything."[16] The argument goes as follows: on the brain-process thesis the identity between the brain-process and the experience is a contingent one. So it is logically possible that there should be no brain-process, and no process of any other sort either (no heart process, no kidney process, no liver process). There would be the experience but no "corresponding" physiological process with which we might be able to identify it empirically.

I suspect that the objector is thinking of the experience as a ghostly entity. So it is composed of something, not of nothing, after all. On his view it is composed of ghost stuff, and on mine it is composed of brain stuff. Perhaps the counter-reply will be[17] that the experience is simple and uncompounded, and so it is not composed of anything after all. This seems to be a quibble, for, if it were taken seriously, the remark "What can be composed of nothing cannot be composed of anything" could be recast as an a priori argument against Democritus and atomism and for Descartes and infinite divisibility. And it seems odd that a question of this sort could be settled a priori. We must therefore construe the word "composed" in a very weak sense, which would allow us to say that even an indivisible atom is composed of something (namely, itself). The dualist cannot really say that an experience can be composed of nothing. For he holds that experiences are something over and above material processes, that is, that they are a sort of ghost stuff. (Or perhaps ripples in an underlying ghost stuff.) I say that the dualist's hypothesis is a perfectly intelligible one. But I say that experiences are not to be identified with ghost stuff but with brain stuff. This is another hypothesis, and in my view a very plausible one. The present argument cannot knock it down a priori.

Objection 8. The "beetle in the box" objection (see Wittgenstein, *Philosophical Investigatons*, §293). How could descriptions of experiences, if these are genuine reports, get a foothold in language? For any rule of language must have public criteria for its correct application.

Reply. The change from describing how things are to describing how we feel is just a change from uninhibitedly saying "this is so" to saying "this looks so." That is, when the naïve person might be tempted to say, "There is a patch of light on the wall which moves whenever I move my eyes" or "A pin is being stuck into me," we have learned how to resist this temptation and say "It *looks as though* there is a patch of light on the wallpaper" or "It *feels as though* someone were sticking a pin into me." The introspective account tells us about the individual's state of consciousness in the same way

---

[16] I owe this objection to Dr. C. B. Martin. I gather that he no longer wishes to maintain this objection, at any rate in its present form.

[17] Martin did not make this reply, but one of his students did.

as does "I see a patch of light" or "I feel a pin being stuck into me": it differs from the corresponding perception statement in so far as it withdraws any claim about what is actually going on in the external world. From the point of view of the psychologist, the change from talking about the environment to talking about one's perceptual sensations is simply a matter of disinhibiting certain reactions. These are reactions which one normally suppresses because one has learned that in the prevailing circumstances they are unlikely to provide a good indication of the state of the environment.[18] To say that something looks green to me is simply to say that my experience is like the experience I get when I see something that really is green. In my reply to Objection 3, I pointed out the extreme openness or generality of statements which report experiences. This explains why there is no language of private qualities. (Just as "someone," unlike "the doctor," is a colorless word.)[19]

If it is asked what is the difference between those brain processes which, in my view, are experiences and those brain processes which are not, I can only reply that it is at present unknown. I have been tempted to conjecture that the difference may in part be that between perception and reception (in D. M. MacKay's terminology) and that the type of brain process which is an experience might be identifiable with MacKay's active "matching response."[20] This, however, cannot be the whole story, because sometimes I can perceive something unconsciously, as when I take a handkerchief out of a drawer without being aware that I am doing so. But at the very least, we can classify the brain processes which are experiences as those brain processes which are, or might have been, causal conditions of those pieces of verbal behavior which we call reports of immediate experience.

I have now considered a number of objections to the brain-process thesis. I wish now to conclude with some remarks on the logical status of the thesis itself. U. T. Place seems to hold that it is a straight-out scientific hypothesis.[21] If so, he is partly right and partly wrong. If the issue is between (say) a brain-process thesis and a heart thesis, or a liver thesis, or a kidney thesis, then the issue is a purely empirical one, and the verdict is overwhelmingly in favor of the brain. The right sorts of things don't go on in the heart, liver, or kidney, nor do these organs possess the right sort of complexity of structure. On the other hand, if the issue is between a brain-or-liver-or-kidney thesis (that is, some form of materialism) on the one hand and epiphenomenalism on the other hand, then the issue is not an empirical one. For there is no conceivable experiment which could decide between mate-

---

[18] I owe this point to Place, in correspondence.

[19] The "beetle in the box" objection is, *if it is sound,* an objection to *any* view, and in particular the Cartesian one, that introspective reports are genuine reports. So it is no objection to a weaker thesis that I would be concerned to uphold, namely, that if introspective reports of "experiences" are genuinely reports, then the things they are reports of are in fact brain processes.

[20] See his article "Towards an Information-Flow Model of Human Behaviour," *British Journal of Psychology,* XLVII (1956), 30–43.

[21] *Op. cit.* For a further discussion of this, in reply to the original version of the present paper, see Place's note "Materialism as a Scientific Hypothesis," *Philosophical Review,* LXIX (1960), 101–4.

rialism and epiphenomenalism. This latter issue is not like the average straight-out empirical issue in science, but like the issue between the nineteenth-century English naturalist Philip Gosse[22] and the orthodox geologists and paleontologists of his day. According to Gosse, the earth was created about 4000 B.C. exactly as described in *Genesis*, with twisted rock strata, "evidence" of erosion, and so forth, and all sorts of fossils, all in their appropriate strata, just as if the usual evolutionist story had been true. Clearly this theory is in a sense irrefutable: no evidence can possibly tell against it. Let us ignore the theological setting in which Philip Gosse's hypothesis had been placed, thus ruling out objections of a theological kind, such as "what a queer God who would go to such elaborate lengths to deceive us." Let us suppose that it is held that the universe just *began* in 4004 B.C. with the initial conditions just everywhere as they were in 4004 B.C., and in particular that our own planet began with sediment in the rivers, eroded cliffs, fossils in the rocks, and so on. No scientist would ever entertain this as a serious hypothesis, consistent though it is with all possible evidence. The hypothesis offends against the principles of parsimony and simplicity. There would be far too many brute and inexplicable facts. Why are pterodactyl bones just as they are? No explanation in terms of the evolution of pterodactyls from earlier forms of life would any longer be possible. We would have millions of facts about the world as it was in 4004 B.C. that just have to be *accepted*.

The issue between the brain-process theory and epiphenomenalism seems to be of the above sort. (Assuming that a behavioristic reduction of introspective reports is not possible.) If it be agreed that there are no cogent philosophical arguments which force us into accepting dualism, and if the brain process theory and dualism are equally consistent with the facts, then the principles of parsimony and simplicity seem to me to decide overwhelmingly in favor of the brain-process theory. As I pointed out earlier, dualism involves a large number of irreducible psychophysical laws (whereby the "nomological danglers" dangle) of a queer sort, that just have to be taken on trust, and are just as difficult to swallow as the irreducible facts about the paleontology of the earth with which we are faced on Philip Gosse's theory.

[22] See the entertaining account of Gosse's book *Omphalos* by Martin Gardner in *Fads and Fallacies in the Name of Science*, 2nd ed. (New York: Dover, 1957), pp. 124–27.

Survival, Automata, and Personal Identity

6

ON THE HUMAN SOUL

St. Thomas Aquinas

ON MAN WHO IS COMPOSED OF A SPIRITUAL AND A CORPOREAL
SUBSTANCE: AND FIRST, CONCERNING WHAT BELONGS TO THE
ESSENCE OF THE SOUL

· · ·

First Article: Whether the Soul Is a Body?

We proceed thus to the First Article:—

Objection 1. It would seem that the soul is a body. For the soul is the mover of the body. Nor does it move unless moved. First, because apparently nothing can move unless it is itself moved, since nothing gives what it has not. For instance, what is not hot does not give heat. Secondly, because if there be anything that moves and is itself not moved, it must be the cause of eternal and uniform movement, as we find proved *Physics* viii. Now this does not appear to be the case in the movement of an animal, which is caused by the soul. Therefore the soul is a moved mover. But every moved mover is a body. Therefore the soul is a body.

Obj. 2. Further, all knowledge is caused by means of a likeness. But there can be no likeness of a body to an incorporeal thing. If, therefore, the soul were not a body, it could not have knowledge of corporeal things.

Obj. 3. Further, between the mover and the moved there must be contact. But contact is only between bodies. Since, therefore, the soul moves the body, it seems that the soul must be a body.

From *Summa Theologica*, in Anton C. Pegis, ed., *Basic Writings of St. Thomas Aquinas* (New York: Random House, Inc., 1945), Part I, QQ. 75, 77, pp. 682–694, 731–732. Reprinted by permission of Random House, Inc., and Burns & Oates Ltd.

On the contrary, Augustine says that the soul *is simple in comparison with the body, inasmuch as it does not occupy space by any bulk.*

I answer that, To seek the nature of the soul, we must premise that the soul is defined as the first principle of life in those things in our world which live; for we call living things *animate,* and those things which have no life, *inanimate.* Now life is shown principally by two activities, knowledge and movement. The philosophers of old, not being able to rise above their imagination, supposed that the principle of these actions was something corporeal; for they asserted that only bodies were real things, and that what is not corporeal is nothing. Hence they maintained that the soul is some sort of body. This opinion can be proved in many ways to be false; but we shall make use of only one proof, which shows quite universally and certainly that the soul is not a body.

It is manifest that not every principle of vital action is a soul, for then the eye would be a soul, as it is a principle of vision; and the same might be applied to the other instruments of the soul. But it is the *first* principle of life which we call the soul. Now, though a body may be a principle of life, as the heart is a principle of life in an animal, yet no body can be the first principle of life. For it is clear that to be a principle of life, or to be a living thing, does not belong to a body as a body, since, if that were the case, every body would be a living thing, or a principle of life. Therefore a body is competent to be a living thing, or even a principle of life, as *such* a body. Now that it is actually such a body it owes to some principle which is called its act. Therefore the soul, which is the first principle of life, is not a body, but the act of a body; just as heat, which is the principle of calefaction, is not a body, but an act of a body.

Reply Obj. 1. Since everything which is moved must be moved by something else, a process which cannot be prolonged indefinitely, we must allow that not every mover is moved. For, since to be moved is to pass from potentiality to actuality, the mover gives what it has to the thing moved, inasmuch as it causes it to be in act. But, as is shown in *Physics* viii., there is a mover which is altogether immovable, and which is not moved either essentially or accidentally; and such a mover can cause an eternally uniform movement. There is, however, another kind of mover, which, though not moved essentially, is moved accidentally; and for this reason it does not cause a uniform movement. Such a mover is the soul. There is, again, another mover, which is moved essentially—namely, the body. And because the philosophers of old believed that nothing existed but bodies, they maintained that every mover is moved, and that the soul is moved essentially, and is a body.

Reply Obj. 2. It is not necessary that the likeness of the thing known be actually in the nature of the knower. But given a being which knows potentially, and afterwards knows actually, the likeness of the thing known must be in the nature of the knower, not actually, but only potentially; and thus color is not actually in the pupil of the eye, but only potentially. Hence it is necessary, not that the likeness of corporeal things be actually in the nature of the soul, but that there be a potentiality in the soul for such a likeness. But the ancient naturalists did not know how to distinguish between actuality and potentiality; and so they held that the soul must be a

body in order to have knowledge of a body, and that it must be composed
of the principles of which all bodies are formed.

Reply Obj. 3. There are two kinds of contact, that of *quantity*, and that
of *power*. By the former a body can be touched only by a body; by the
latter a body can be touched by an incorporeal reality, which moves that
body.

Second Article: Whether the Human Soul Is Something Subsistent?

We proceed thus to the Second Article:—

Objection 1. It would seem that the human soul is not something subsistent. For that which subsists is said to be *this particular thing*. Now *this
particular thing* is said not of the soul, but of that which is composed of soul
and body. Therefore the soul is not something subsistent.

Obj. 2. Further, everything subsistent operates. But the soul does not
operate, for, as the Philosopher says, *to say that the soul feels or understands
is like saying that the soul weaves or builds*. Therefore the soul is not
subsistent.

Obj. 3. Further, if the soul were something subsistent, it would have some
operation apart from the body. But it has no operation apart from the body,
not even that of understanding; for the act of understanding does not take
place without a phantasm, which cannot exist apart from the body. Therefore the human soul is not something subsistent.

On the contrary, Augustine says: *Whoever understands that the nature of
the mind is that of a substance and not that of a body, will see that those
who maintain the corporeal nature of the mind are led astray because they
associate with the mind those things without which they are unable to think
of any nature—i.e.*, imaginary pictures of corporeal things. Therefore the
nature of the human mind is not only incorporeal, but it is also a substance,
that is, something subsistent.

I answer that, It must necessarily be allowed that the principle of intellectual operation, which we call the soul of man, is a principle both incorporeal
and subsistent. For it is clear that by means of the intellect man can know all
corporeal things. Now whatever knows certain things cannot have any of
them in its own nature, because that which is in it naturally would impede
the knowledge of anything else. Thus we observe that a sick man's tongue,
being unbalanced by a feverish and bitter humor, is insensible to anything
sweet, and everything seems bitter to it. Therefore, if the intellectual
principle contained within itself the nature of any body, it would be unable
to know all bodies. Now every body has its own determinate nature.
Therefore it is impossible for the intellectual principle to be a body. It is also
impossible for it to understand by means of a bodily organ, since the
determinate nature of that organ would likewise impede knowledge of all
bodies; as when a certain determinate color is not only in the pupil of the
eye, but also in a glass vase, the liquid in the vase seems to be of that same
color.

Therefore the intellectual principle, which we call the mind or the
intellect, has essentially an operation in which the body does not share. Now
only that which subsists in itself can have an operation in itself. For nothing
can operate but what is actual, and so a thing operates according as it is; for

which reason we do not say that heat imparts heat, but that what is hot gives heat. We must conclude, therefore, that the human soul, which is called intellect or mind, is something incorporeal and subsistent.

Reply Obj. 1. *This particular thing* can be taken in two senses. Firstly, for anything subsistent; secondly, for that which subsists and is complete in a specific nature. The former sense excludes the inherence of an accident or of a material form; the latter excludes also the imperfection of the part, so that a hand can be called *this particular thing* in the first sense, but not in the second. Therefore, since the human soul is a part of human nature, it can be called *this particular thing* in the first sense, as being something subsistent; but not in the second, for in this sense the composite of body and soul is said to be *this particular thing*.

Reply Obj. 2. Aristotle wrote those words as expressing, not his own opinion, but the opinion of those who said that to understand is to be moved, as is clear from the context. Or we may reply that to operate through itself belongs to what exists through itself. But for a thing to exist through itself, it suffices sometimes that it be not inherent, as an accident or a material form; even though it be part of something. Nevertheless, that is rightly said to subsist through itself which is neither inherent in the above sense, nor part of anything else. In this sense, the eye or the hand cannot be said to subsist through itself; nor can it for that reason be said to operate through itself. Hence the operation of the parts is through each part attributed to the whole. For we say that man sees with the eye, and feels with the hand, and not in the same sense as when we say that what is hot gives heat by its heat; for heat, strictly speaking, does not give heat. We may therefore say that the soul understands just as the eye sees; but it is more correct to say that man understands through the soul.

Reply Obj. 3. The body is necessary for the action of the intellect, not as its organ of action, but on the part of the object; for the phantasm is to the intellect what color is to the sight. Neither does such a dependence on the body prove the intellect to be non-subsistent, or otherwise it would follow that an animal is non-subsistent simply because it requires external sensibles for sensation.

Third Article: Whether the Souls of Brute Animals Are Subsistent?

We proceed thus to the Third Article:—

Objection 1. It would seem that the souls of brute animals are subsistent. For man is of the same genus as other animals, and, as we have shown, the soul of man is subsistent. Therefore the souls of other animals are subsistent.

Obj. 2. Further, the relation of the sensitive power to sensible objects is like the relation of the intellectual power to intelligible objects. But the intellect, without the body, apprehends intelligible objects. Therefore the sensitive power, without the body, perceives sensible objects. Therefore, since the souls of brute animals are sensitive, they are subsistent, for the same reason that the human soul, which is intellectual, is subsistent.

Obj. 3. Further, the soul of brute animals moves the body. But the body is not a mover, but is moved. Therefore the soul of brute animals has an operation apart from the body.

On the contrary, Is what is written in the book *De Ecclesiasticis Dog-*

matibus: Man alone we believe to have a subsistent soul; whereas the souls of animals are not subsistent.

I answer that, The early philosophers made no distinction between sense and intellect, and referred both to a corporeal principle, as has been said. Plato, however, drew a distinction between intellect and sense, but he referred both to an incorporeal principle, maintaining that sensing, like understanding, belongs to the soul as such. From this it follows that even the souls of brute animals are subsistent. But Aristotle held that, of the operations of the soul, understanding alone is performed without a corporeal organ. On the other hand, sensation and the attendant operations of the sensitive soul are evidently accompanied with change in the body; and thus, in the act of vision, the pupil of the eye is affected by the likeness of color. So with the other senses. Hence it is clear that the sensitive soul has no *per se* operation of its own, and that every operation of the sensitive soul belongs to the composite. Therefore we conclude that as the souls of brute animals have no *per se* operations they are not subsistent. For the operation of anything follows the mode of its being.

Reply Obj. 1. Although man is of the same *genus* as other animals, he is of a different *species.* Now, specific difference is derived from the difference of form; nor does every difference of form necessarily imply a diversity of *genus.*

Reply Obj. 2. The relation of the sensitive power to the sensible object is in one way the same as that of the intellectual power to the intelligible object, in so far as each is in potentiality to its object. But in another way their relations differ, inasmuch as the impression of the sensible on the sense is accompanied with change in the body; so that when the intensity of the sensible is excessive, the sense is corrupted. This is a thing that never occurs in the case of the intellect. For an intellect that understands the highest of intelligible objects is more able afterwards to understand those that are lower.—If, however, in the process of intellectual operation the body is weary, this result is accidental, inasmuch as the intellect requires the operation of the sensitive powers in the production of the phantasms.

Reply Obj. 3. A motive power is of two kinds. One, the appetitive power, which commands motion. The operation of this power in the sensitive soul is not without the body; for anger, joy and passions of a like nature are accompanied by some change in the body. The other motive power is that which executes motion in adapting the members for obeying the appetite; and the act of this power does not consist in moving, but in being moved. Whence it is clear that to move is not an act of the sensitive soul without the body.

Fourth Article: Whether the Soul Is Man?

We proceed thus to the Fourth Article:—

Objection 1. It would seem that the soul is man. For it is written (2 *Cor.* iv. 16): *Though our outward man is corrupted, yet the inward man is renewed day by day.* But that which is within man is the soul. Therefore the soul is the inward man.

Obj. 2. Further, the human soul is a substance. But it is not a universal substance. Therefore it is a particular substance. Therefore it is a *hypostasis* or a person; and it can be only a human person. Therefore the soul is a man, for a human person is a man.

On the contrary, Augustine commends Varro as holding *that man is not the soul alone, nor the body alone, but both soul and body*.

I answer that, The assertion, *the soul is a man*, can be taken in two senses. First, that man is a soul, though this particular man (Socrates, for instance) is not a soul, but composed of soul and body. I say this, because some held that the form alone belongs to the species, while matter is part of the individual, and not of the species. This cannot be true, for to the nature of the species belongs what the definition signifies, and in natural things the definition does not signify the form only, but the form and the matter. Hence, in natural things the matter is part of the species; not, indeed, signate matter, which is the principle of individuation, but common matter. For just as it belongs to the nature of this particular man to be composed of this soul, of this flesh, and of these bones, so it belongs to the nature of man to be composed of soul, flesh, and bones; for whatever belongs in common to the substance of all the individuals contained under a given species must belong also to the substance of the species.

That *the soul is a man* may also be understood in this sense, namely, that this soul is this man. Now this could be held if it were supposed that the operation of the sensitive soul were proper to it without the body; because in that case all the operations which are attributed to man would belong only to the soul. But each thing is that which performs its own operations, and consequently that is man which performs the operations of a man. But it has been shown above that sensation is not the operation of the soul alone. Since, then, sensation is an operation of man, but not proper to the soul, it is clear that man is not only a soul, but something composed of soul and body.—Plato, through supposing that sensation was proper to the soul, could maintain man to be *a soul making use of a body*.

Reply Obj. 1. According to the Philosopher, each thing seems to be chiefly what is most important in it. Thus, what the governor of a state does, the state is said to do. In this way sometimes what is most important in man is said to be man: sometimes it is the intellectual part which, in accordance with truth, is called the *inward* man; and sometimes the sensitive part with the body is called man in the opinion of those who remain the slaves of sensible things. And this is called the *outward* man.

Reply Obj. 2. Not every particular substance is a hypostasis or a person, but that which has the complete nature of its species. Hence a hand, or a foot, is not called a hypostasis, or a person; nor, likewise, is the soul alone so called, since it is a part of the human species.

Fifth Article: Whether the Soul Is Composed of Matter and Form?

We proceed thus to the Fifth Article:—

Objection 1. It would seem that the soul is composed of matter and form. For potentiality is opposed to actuality. Now, whatsoever things are in actuality participate in the First Act, which is God. It is by participation in God that all things are good, beings, and living things, as is clear from the teachings of Dionysius. Therefore, whatsoever things are in potentiality participate in the first potentiality. But the first potentiality is primary matter. Therefore, since the human soul is, after a manner, in potentiality (which appears from the fact that sometimes a man is potentially understanding), it seems that the human soul must participate in primary matter, as a part of itself.

Obj. 2. Further, wherever the properties of matter are found, there matter is. But the properties of matter are found in the soul—namely, to be a subject, and to be changed. For the soul is subject to science, and virtue; and it changes from ignorance to knowledge and from vice to virtue. Therefore there is matter in the soul.

Obj. 3. Further, things which have no matter have no cause of their being, as the Philosopher says in *Metaph.* viii. But the soul has a cause of its being, since it is created by God. Therefore the soul has matter.

Obj. 4. Further, what has no matter, and is only a form, is a pure act, and is infinite. But this belongs to God alone. Therefore the soul has matter.

On the contrary, Augustine proves that the soul was made neither of corporeal matter, nor of spiritual matter.

I answer that, The soul has no matter. We may consider this question in two ways. First, from the notion of a soul in general, for it belongs to the notion of a soul to be the form of a body. Now, either it is a form in its entirety, or by virtue of some part of itself. If in its entirety, then it is impossible that any part of it should be matter, if by matter we understand something purely potential; for a form, as such, is an act, and that which is purely potential cannot be part of an act, since potentiality is repugnant to actuality as being its opposite. If, however, it be a form by virtue of a part of itself, then we shall call that part the soul, and that matter, which it actualizes first, we shall call the *primary animate*.

Secondly, we may proceed from the specific notion of the human soul, inasmuch as it is intellectual. For it is clear that whatever is received into something is received according to the condition of the recipient. Now a thing is known in as far as its form is in the knower. But the intellectual soul knows a thing in its nature absolutely: for instance, it knows a stone absolutely as a stone; and therefore the form of a stone absolutely, as to its proper formal notion, is in the intellectual soul. Therefore the intellectual soul itself is an absolute form, and not something composed of matter and form. For if the intellectual soul were composed of matter and form, the forms of things would be received into it as individuals, and so it would only know the individual; just as it happens with the sensitive powers which receive forms in a corporeal organ. For matter is the principle by which forms are individuated. It follows, therefore, that the intellectual soul, and every intellectual substance which has knowledge of forms absolutely, is exempt from composition of matter and form.

Reply Obj. 1. The First Act is the universal principle of all acts, because It is infinite, *precontaining all things* in its power, as Dionysius says. Therefore It is participated in by things, not as a part of themselves, but by diffusion of Its processions. Now as potentiality is receptive of act, it must be proportionate to act. But the acts received which proceed from the First Infinite Act, and are participations thereof, are diverse, so that there cannot be one potentiality which receives all acts, in the same way that there is one act from which all participated acts are derived; for then the receptive potentiality would equal the active potentiality of the First Act. Now the receptive potentiality in the intellectual soul is other than the receptive potentiality of primary matter, as appears from the diversity of the things received by each. For primary matter receives individual forms; whereas the intellect receives absolute forms. Hence the existence of such a potentiality in the intellectual soul does not prove that the soul is composed of matter and form.

Reply Obj. 2. To be a subject and to be changed belong to matter by reason of its being in potentiality. Just as, therefore, the potentiality of the intellect is one thing and the potentiality of primary matter another, so in each is there a different manner of subjection and change. For the intellect is subject to knowledge, and is changed from ignorance to knowledge, by reason of its being in potentiality with regard to the intelligible species.

Reply Obj. 3. The form causes matter to be, and so does the agent; and so, the agent causes matter to be in so far as it changes it to the actuality of the form. A subsistent form, however, does not owe its being to some formal principle, nor has it a cause changing it from potentiality to act. So after the words quoted above, the Philosopher concludes that in things composed of matter and form *there is no other cause but that which moves from potentiality to act; while whatsoever things have no matter are truly beings in themselves.*

Reply Obj. 4. Everything participated is compared to the participator as its act. But whatever created form be supposed to subsist *per se,* must have being by participation, for *even life,* or anything of that sort, *is a participator of being,* as Dionysius says. Now participated being is limited by the capacity of participator; so that God alone, Who is His own being, is pure act and infinite. But in intellectual substances, there is composition of actuality and potentiality, not, indeed, of matter and form, but of form and participated being. Therefore some say that they are composed of that *whereby they are* and that *which they are;* for being itself is that by which a thing is.

Sixth Article: Whether the Human Soul Is Corruptible?

We proceed thus to the Sixth Article:—

Objection 1. It would seem that the human soul is corruptible. For those things that have a like beginning and process seemingly have a like end. But the beginning, by generation, of men is like that of animals, for they are made from the earth. And the process of life is alike in both; because *all things breathe alike, and man hath nothing more than the beast,* as it is written (*Eccles.* iii. 19). Therefore, as the same text concludes, *the death of man and beast is one, and the condition of both is equal.* But the souls of brute animals are corruptible. Therefore the human soul too is corruptible.

Obj. 2. Further, whatever is out of nothing can return to nothingness, because the end should correspond to the beginning. But as it is written (*Wis.* ii. 2), *We are born of nothing;* and this is true, not only of the body, but also of the soul. Therefore, as is concluded in the same passage, *After this we shall be as if we had not been,* even as to our soul.

Obj. 3. Further, nothing is without its own proper operation. But the operation proper to the soul, which is to understand through a phantasm, cannot be without the body. For the soul understands nothing without a phantasm, and *there is no phantasm without the body*, as the Philosopher says. Therefore the soul cannot survive the dissolution of the body.

On the contrary, Dionysius says that human souls owe to divine goodness that they are *intellectual*, and that they have *an incorruptible substantial life*.

I answer that, We must assert that the intellectual principle which we call the human soul is incorruptible. For a thing may be corrupted in two ways—in itself and accidentally. Now it is impossible for any subsistent being to be generated or corrupted accidentally, that is, by the generation or corruption of something else. For generation and corruption belong to a thing in the same way that being belongs to it, which is acquired by generation and lost by corruption. Therefore, whatever has being in itself cannot be generated or corrupted except in itself; while things which do not subsist, such as accidents and material forms, acquire being or lose it through the generation or corruption of composites. Now it was shown above that the souls of brutes are not self-subsistent, whereas the human soul is, so that the souls of brutes are corrupted, when their bodies are corrupted, while the human soul could not be corrupted unless it were corrupted in itself. This is impossible, not only as regards the human soul, but also as regards anything subsistent that is a form alone. For it is clear that what belongs to a thing by virtue of the thing itself is inseparable from it. But being belongs to a form, which is an act, by virtue of itself. And thus, matter acquires actual being according as it acquires form; while it is corrupted so far as the form is separated from it. But it is impossible for a form to be separated from itself; and therefore it is impossible for a subsistent form to cease to exist.

Granted even that the soul were composed of matter and form, as some pretend, we should nevertheless have to maintain that it is incorruptible. For corruption is found only where there is contrariety, since generation and corruption are from contraries and into contraries. Therefore the heavenly bodies, since they have no matter subject to contrariety, are incorruptible. Now there can be no contrariety in the intellectual soul; for it is a receiving subject according to the manner of its being, and those things which it receives are without contrariety. Thus, the notions even of contraries are not themselves contrary, since contraries belong to the same science. Therefore it is impossible for the intellectual soul to be corruptible.

Moreover we may take a sign of this from the fact that everything naturally aspires to being after its own manner. Now, in things that have knowledge, desire ensues upon knowledge. The senses indeed do not know being, except under the conditions of *here* and *now*, whereas the intellect apprehends being absolutely, and for all time; so that everything that has an intellect naturally desires always to exist. But a natural desire cannot be in vain. Therefore every intellectual substance is incorruptible.

Reply Obj. 1. Solomon reasons thus in the person of the foolish, as expressed in the words of *Wis*. ii. Therefore the saying that man and animals have a like beginning in generation is true of the body; for all animals alike are made of earth. But it is not true of the soul. For while the souls of brutes are produced by some power of the body, the human soul is produced by God. To signify this, it is written of other animals: *Let the earth bring forth the living soul* (*Gen*. i. 24); while of man it is written (*Gen*. ii. 7) that *He breathed into his face the breath of life*. And so in the last chapter of

Ecclesiastes (xii. 7) it is concluded: *The dust returns into its earth from whence it was; and the spirit returns to God Who gave it.* Again, the process of life is alike as to the body, concerning which it is written (*Eccles.* iii. 19): *All things breathe alike,* and (*Wis.* ii. 2), *The breath in our nostrils is smoke.* But the process is not alike in the case of the soul, for man has understanding whereas animals do not. Hence it is false to say: *Man has nothing more than beasts.* Thus death comes to both alike as to the body, but not as to the soul.

Reply Obj. 2. As a thing can be created, not by reason of a passive potentiality, but only by reason of the active potentiality of the Creator, Who can produce something out of nothing, so when we say that a thing can be reduced to nothing, we do not imply in the creature a potentiality to non-being, but in the Creator the power of ceasing to sustain being. But a thing is said to be corruptible because there is in it a potentiality to non-being.

Reply Obj. 3. To understand through a phantasm is the proper operation of the soul by virtue of its union with the body. After separation from the body, it will have another mode of understanding, similar to other substances separated from bodies. . . .

Seventh Article: Whether the Soul Is of the Same Species as an Angel?

We proceed thus to the Seventh Article:—

Objection 1. It would seem that the soul is of the same species as an angel. For each thing is ordained to its proper end by the nature of its species, whence is derived its inclination for that end. But the end of the soul is the same as that of an angel—namely, eternal happiness. Therefore they are of the same species.

Obj. 2. Further, the ultimate specific difference is the noblest, because it completes the nature of the species. But there is nothing nobler either in an angel or in the soul than their intellectual being. Therefore the soul and the angel agree in the ultimate specific difference. Therefore they belong to the same species.

Obj. 3. Further, it seems that the soul does not differ from an angel except in its union with the body. But as the body is outside the essence of the soul, it does not seem to belong to its species. Therefore the soul and an angel are of the same species.

On the contrary, Things which have different natural operations are of different species. But the natural operations of the soul and of an angel are different, since, as Dionysius says, *Angelic minds have simple and blessed intellects, not gathering their knowledge of divine things from visible things.* Subsequently he says the contrary of this about the soul. Therefore the soul and an angel are not of the same species.

I answer that, Origen held that human souls and angels are all of the same species, and this because he supposed that in these substances the difference of degree was accidental, resulting from their free choice, as we have seen above. But this cannot be, for in incorporeal substances there cannot be diversity of number without diversity of species and inequality of nature; because, as they are not composed of matter and form, but are subsistent forms, it is clear that there is necessarily among them a diversity in species.

For a separate form cannot be understood otherwise than as one of a single species. Thus, supposing a separate whiteness to exist, it could only be one, for one whiteness does not differ from another except as in this or that subject. But diversity of species is always accompanied by diversity of nature. Thus, in the species of colors, one is more perfect than another; and the same applies to other species, because differences which divide a *genus* are contrary to one another. Contraries, however, are compared to one another as the perfect to the imperfect, since the *principle of contrariety is habit and privation*, as is written, *Metaph.* x.

The same would follow if the aforesaid substances were composed of matter and form. For if the matter of one be distinct from the matter of another, it is required either that the form be the principle of the distinction of matter—that is to say, that the matter is distinct because of its relation to diverse forms, in which case there would still result a difference of species and an inequality of nature; or else that the matter is the principle of the distinction of forms. But one matter cannot be distinct from another, except by a distinction of quantity, which has no place in these incorporeal substances, such as an angel and the soul. Hence, it is not possible for the angel and the soul to be of the same species. . . .

Reply Obj. 1. This argument is concerned with the proximate and natural end. Eternal happiness, however, is the ultimate and supernatural end.

Reply Obj. 2. The ultimate specific difference is the noblest because it is the most determinate, in the same way as actuality is nobler than potentiality. Thus, however, that which is intellectual is not the noblest, because it is indeterminate and common to many degrees of intellectuality; just as the sensible is common to many degrees of sensible being. Hence, just as all sensible things are not of one species, so neither are all intellectual beings of one species.

Reply Obj. 3. The body is not of the essence of the soul, but the soul, by nature of its essence, can be united to the body; so that, properly speaking, it is not even the soul, but rather the *composite*, which is in the species. And the very fact that the soul in a certain way requires the body for its operation proves that the soul is endowed with a grade of intellectuality inferior to that of an angel, who is not united to a body.

WHAT BELONGS TO THE POWERS OF THE SOUL IN GENERAL

Eighth Article: Whether All the Powers Remain in the Soul When Separated from the Body?

We proceed thus to the Eighth Article:—

Objection 1. It would seem that all the powers of the soul remain in the soul separated from the body. For we read in the *De Spiritu et Anima* that *the soul withdraws from the body, taking with itself sense and imagination, reason and intellect and intelligence, concupiscibility and irascibility.*

Obj. 2. Further, the powers of the soul are its natural properties. But properties are always in that to which they belong, and are never separated from it. Therefore the powers of the soul are in it even after death.

Obj. 3. Further, the powers even of the sensitive soul are not weakened when the body becomes weak; because, as the Philosopher says, *If an old man were given the eye of a young man, he would see just as well as a young man.* But weakness is the road to corruption. Therefore the powers of the soul are not corrupted when the body is corrupted, but remain in the separated soul.

Obj. 4. Further, memory is a power of the sensitive soul, as the Philosopher proves. But memory remains in the separated soul, for it was said to the rich glutton whose soul was in hell: *Remember that thou didst receive good things during thy lifetime (Luke* xvi. 25). Therefore memory remains in the separated soul; and consequently the other powers of the sensitive part.

Obj. 5. Further, joy and sorrow are in the concupiscible part, which is a power of the sensitive soul. But it is clear that separate souls grieve or rejoice at the pains or rewards which they receive. Therefore the concupiscible power remains in the separate soul.

Obj. 6. Further, Augustine says that, just as the soul, when the body lies senseless, yet not quite dead, sees some things by imaginary vision, so also when by death the soul is quite separate from the body. But the imagination is a power of the sensitive part. Therefore, a power of the sensitive part remains in the separate soul; and consequently all the other powers.

On the contrary, It is said that *of two substances only does man consist: the soul with its reason, and the body with its senses.* Therefore when the body is dead, the sensitive powers do not remain.

I answer that, As we have already said, all the powers of the soul belong to the soul alone as their principle. But some powers belong to the soul alone as their subject: such are intellect and will. These powers must remain in the soul, after the destruction of the body. But other powers are in the composite as in their subject; as all the powers of the sensitive and nutritive parts. Now accidents cannot remain after the destruction of the subject. Therefore, when the composite is destroyed, such powers do not remain actually; but they remain virtually in the soul, as in their principle or root.

So it is false that, as some say, these powers remain in the soul even after the corruption of the body. It is much more false that, as they also say, the acts of these powers remain in the separate soul; because these powers have no act apart from a corporeal organ.

Reply Obj. 1. That book has no authority, and so what is there written can be ignored with the same facility as it was said; although we may say that the soul takes with itself these powers, not actually, but virtually.

Reply Obj. 2. These powers, which we say do not actually remain in the separate soul, are not the properties of the soul alone, but of the composite.

Reply Obj. 3. These powers are said not be be weakened when the body becomes weak, because the soul remains unchangeable, and is the virtual principle of these powers.

Reply Obj. 4. The recollection spoken of there is to be taken in the same way as Augustine places memory in the mind; which is not in the way that memory is a part of the sensitive soul.

Reply Obj. 5. In the separate soul, sorrow and joy are not in the sensitive, but in the intellectual appetite, as in the angels.

Reply Obj. 6. Augustine in that passage is speaking as inquiring, not as asserting. Therefore he retracted some things which he had said there.

7

DISEMBODIED SENSUOUS EXPERIENCE

P. T. Geach

'Inner sense' is supposed to show us, and to be the only thing that shows us, what it is like to see, hear, be afraid, etc. With this there goes a view that the connexion between such 'sensuous' experiences and a bodily organism is only a well-established empirical generalization. Such experiences are indeed dependent upon material things in the sense of being occupied with them; but they are not identifiable with any describable physiological processes in a living organism, and their connexion with such processes is only something empirically determined. There is no necessary, conceptual, connexion between the experience we call "seeing" and the processes that physiologists tell us happen in eye and brain; the statement "James can still see, although his optic centres are destroyed" is very unlikely on inductive grounds but perfectly intelligible—after all, people used the word "see" long before they had any idea of things happening in the optic centres of the brain. It therefore appears to be clearly conceivable that seeing and other 'sensuous' experiences might go on continuously even after the death of the organism with which they are now associated, and that the inductive reasons for doubting whether this ever happens might be outweighed by the evidence of Psychical Research.

I think it is an important conceptual enquiry to consider whether *really* disembodied seeing, hearing, pain, hunger, emotion, etc., are so clearly intelligible as is supposed in this common philosophical point of view. (I stress "really disembodied". Some people believe that there is a subtle body endowed with its own sense-organs, which persists after the dissolution of the body commonly so called. This view, so far as I can see, is philosophically speaking both unobjectionable and uninteresting. It is clear off-hand that the 'mind-body problem' is just the same whether the body is gross or subtle.)

From P. T. Geach, *Mental Acts* (London and New York: 1957), Chap. XXV, pp. 111–117. Reprinted by permission of Routledge & Kegan Paul Ltd. and Humanities Press.

"The verb 'to see' has its meaning for me because I *do* see—I have that experience!" Nonsense. As well suppose that I can come to know what a minus quantity is by setting out to lose weight. What shows a man to have the concept *seeing* is not merely that he sees, but that he can take an intelligent part in our everyday use of the word "seeing". Our concept of sight has its life only in connexion with a whole set of other concepts, some of them relating to the physical characteristics of visible objects, others relating to the behaviour of people who see things. (I express exercise of this concept in such utterances as "I can't see, it's too far off—now it's coming into view!" "He couldn't see me, he didn't look round", "I caught his eye", etc., etc.) It would be merely silly to be frightened off admitting this by the bogy of behaviourism; you can very well admit it without also thinking that "seeing" stands for a kind of behaviour.

Our investigation is put on the wrong track by an abstractionist prejudice. For an abstractionist, the possession of the concept *seeing* must be taken to be a capacity for finding and recognizing some recurrent feature—or at least to be that primarily; and I can find instances of seeing only in my own mind, by 'inner sense'; in other people I find nothing but characteristic pieces of behaviour, from which however it could justifiably be inferred (how?) that they also see.—In fact, of course, I learn to use the word "see" of others and of myself simultaneously; and if we reject the doctrine of abstractionism, we need not distinguish between exercises of the concept *seeing* as primary ones, when I catch myself in the act of seeing something, and secondary ones, when I (with great rashness, surely, on this view) form the judgment that others likewise see. To have the concept *seeing* is not even primarily a matter of being able to spot instances of a characteristic repeatedly given in my ('inner-sense') experiences; *no* concept is primarily a recognitional capacity. And the exercise of one concept is intertwined with the exercise of others; as with a spider's web, some connexions may be broken with impunity, but if you break enough the whole web collapses—the concept becomes unusable. Just such a collapse happens, I believe, when we try to think of seeing, hearing, pain, emotion, etc., going on independently of a body.

When I apply this sort of concept to a human being, I do so in connexion with a whole lot of other concepts that I apply to human beings and their natural environment. It is easy enough to extend the concepts of 'sensuous' experience to creatures fairly like human beings, such as cats, dogs, and horses; when we try to extend them to creatures extremely unlike human beings in their style of life, we feel, if we are wise, great uncertainty—not just uncertainty as to the facts, or as to the possibility of finding them out, but uncertainty as to the *meaning* of saying: "I now know how to tell when an earthworm is angry". One is of course tempted to say: "That's easy; an earthworm is angry if it is feeling the way I feel when I am angry!" But this is just like saying: "Of course I know what it is for the time on the Sun to be five o'clock; it is five o'clock on the Sun when it is the same time as when it is five o'clock here!" (Wittgenstein, Part I, §350)—which clearly gets us no for'arder. There is just the same difficulty in extending the concept *the same time* as in extending the concept *five o'clock*. So in the psychological case: I know how to apply the concept *anger* to myself and to James, and I know how to apply the concept *feeling the same way* as between myself and

James, or James and Smith; I get into the same difficulties if I try applying the concept *feeling the same way* as between myself and an earthworm as I do over applying the concept *anger* to it.[1]

Even an earthworm, though, affords some handholds for the application of 'sensuous' psychological concepts; we connect its writhings when injured with our own pain-reactions. But when it comes to an automaton, or again if we are invited to apply the concepts to a supposed disembodied existence, then we may be sure that we are right in refusing to play; too many threads are broken, and the conceptual web has collapsed. An automaton, by all sorts of criteria, is not even alive; we know this, though we may be uncertain whether to call a virus (say) alive or not. (Doctors may not agree whether a patient is yet dead; but we know that Queen Anne is dead.) Between what is certainly inanimate and ourselves there is far too little similarity for us to be able to pick out anything in its behaviour corresponding to the context in which we judge that human beings are in pain, or hungry, or afraid; we know that any particular movement which might even remotely suggest similarity is performed because the designer of the automaton intended such an imitation, and we ought to be no more inclined to ascribe feelings to the automaton than, after childhood, we think that a doll is in pain because it has been so constructed as to cry when it is smacked.—As for disembodied sensations and feelings, even more connexions are broken in this case; there is no handhold for applying 'sensuous' concepts to disembodied existence at all—we just do not know what we are doing if we try.

A good illustration, I think, of a concept's losing its applicability through connexions being broken is the following. Certain hysterics claimed to have magnetic sensations; it was discovered, however, that their claim to be having them at a given time did not go with the presence of a magnet in their neighbourhood but with their belief, true or false, that a magnet was there. It would now have been possible to say: "We must take the patients' word for it that they have these peculiar sensations, which are quite different from ordinary people's sense-modalities; it is merely the term "magnetic sensations" that has turned out to be inappropriate; they had formed a wrong hypothesis about the physical cause of their sensations". But nobody even considered saying this; it was decided that the patients had just been indulging in the sort of pointless talk that hysterics often do indulge in. This decision just to drop the idea of magnetic sensations and to ignore the patients' 'reports' of them was taken after a much smaller breakdown of the ordinary connexions than we are asked to tolerate when it is attempted to apply sensation-concepts to automata or to disembodied existence.

---

[1] On a point of interpretation, I think it is a mistake to read Wittgenstein as having intended to show that I cannot apply a concept like *anger* both to myself and to others, and that it is meaningless to speak of others' feeling the same way as I do (unless indeed I just mean that they behave as I do). The difficulty of transferring the concept *anger* from myself to others is a spurious one, arising from the abstractionism that Wittgenstein consistently rejected; and the solution that the term "anger" is an equivocal term, applied in my own case to a recurrent experience and in other cases to a recurrent pattern of behaviour, is plausible, I think, only on abstractionist presuppositions; I do not believe, as some people I have had discussion with apparently do, that Wittgenstein really held this view and only shrank from a brash statement of it.

Denying sense to the attempt to think of feelings, sensations, emotions, etc., apart from a living organism may seem to be practically the same as denying disembodied mind altogether. Such a denial does not follow, nor has it historically always been held to follow. Aquinas, for example, believed that there were wholly disembodied intelligences, but that they were not liable to any such experiences as seeing and hearing and feeling afraid and having a pain: the evil spirits in hell are tormented not by aches but by the frustration of their wicked will. (Ia q. 54 art. 6, q. 59 art. 4, q. 64 art. 3.) Sensuous experiences are possible only in connexion with a living organism (Ia q. 77 art. 8). Only since Descartes has the main problem become: "How is *cogitatio* related to bodily processes?" ("*cogitatio*" covering, for him, everything 'in the mind', from a toothache to a metaphysical meditation); the old problem was rather: "How can a being that thinks and judges and decides *also* have sensuous experiences?" It was 'intellectual' acts like judgment, not just *anything* that would now be called 'consciousness', which seemed to Aquinas to be wholly incommensurable with events in the physical world; for him, the 'unbridgeable gulf' was at a different place. The usefulness of historical knowledge in philosophy, here as elsewhere, is that the prejudices of our own period may lose their grip on us if we imaginatively enter into another period, when people's prejudices were different.

MINDS AND MACHINES

Hilary Putnam

The various issues and puzzles that make up the traditional mind-body problem are wholly linguistic and logical in character: whatever few empirical "facts" there may be in this area support one view as much as another. I do not hope to establish this contention in this paper, but I hope to do something toward rendering it more plausible. Specifically, I shall try to show that all of the issues arise in connection with any computing system capable of answering questions about its own structure, and have thus nothing to do with the unique nature (if it *is* unique) of human subjective experience.

To illustrate the sort of thing that is meant, one kind of puzzle that is sometimes discussed in connection with the "mind-body problem" is the puzzle of *privacy*. The question "How do I know I have a pain?" is a *deviant*[1] ("logically odd") question. The question "How do I know Smith has a pain?" is not at all deviant. The difference can also be mirrored in impersonal questions: "How does anyone ever know he himself has a pain?" is deviant; "How does anyone ever know that someone else is in pain?" is non-deviant. I shall show that the difference in status between the last two questions is mirrored in the case of machines: if T is any *Turing machine* (see below), the question "How does T ascertain that it is in state A?" is, as we shall see, "logically odd" with a vengeance; but if T is capable of investigating its neighbor machine T′ (say, T has electronic "sense-organs" which "scan" T′), the question "How does T ascertain that T′ is in state A?" is not at all odd.

Another question connected with the "mind-body problem" is the question whether or not it is ever permissible to identify mental events and physical events. Of course, I do not claim that this question arises for Turing machines, but I do claim that it is possible to construct a logical analogue for this question that does arise, and that all of the arguments on

Hilary Putnam, "Minds and Machines," in Sidney Hook, ed., *Dimensions of Mind*, pp. 138–164. © 1960 by New York University and reprinted by permission.

[1] By a "deviant" utterance is here meant one that deviates from a semantic regularity (in the appropriate natural language). The term is taken from (14).

both sides of the question of "mind-body identity" can be mirrored in terms of the analogue.

To obtain such an analogue, let us identify a scientific theory with a "partially-interpreted calculus" in the sense of Carnap.[2] Then we can perfectly well imagine a Turing machine which generates theories, tests them (assuming that it is possible to "mechanize" inductive logic to some degree), and "accepts" theories which satisfy certain criteria (e.g., predictive success). In particular, if the machine has electronic "sense organs" which enable it to "scan" itself while it is in operation, it may formulate theories concerning its own structure and subject them to test. Suppose the machine is in a given state (say, "state A") when, and only when, flip-flop 36 is on. Then this statement: "I am in state A when, and only when, flip-flop 36 is on," may be one of the theoretical principles concerning its own structure accepted by the machine. Here "I am in state A" is, of course, "observation language" for the machine, while "flip-flop 36 is on" is a "theoretical expression" which is partially interpreted in terms of "observables" (if the machine's "sense organs" report by printing symbols on the machine's input tape, the "observables" in terms of which the machine would give a partial operational definition of "flip-flop 36 being on" would be of the form "symbol # so-and-so appearing on the input tape"). Now all of the usual considerations for and against mind-body identification can be paralleled by considerations for and against saying that state A is in fact *identical* with flip-flop 36 being on.

Corresponding to Occamist arguments for "identity" in the one case are Occamist arguments for identity in the other. And the usual argument for dualism in the mind-body case can be paralleled in the other as follows: for the machine, "state A" is directly observable; on the other hand, "flip-flops" are something it knows about only via highly-sophisticated inferences— How *could* two things so different *possibly* be the same?

This last argument can be put into a form which makes it appear somewhat stronger. The proposition:

(1) I am in state A if, and only if, flip-flop 36 is on,

is clearly a "synthetic" proposition for the machine. For instance, the machine might be in state A and its sense organs might report that flip-flop 36 was *not* on. In such a case the machine would have to make a methodological "choice"—namely, to give up (1) or to conclude that it had made an "observational error" (just as a human scientist would be confronted with similar methodological choices in studying his own psychophysical correlations). And just as philosophers have argued from the synthetic nature of the proposition:

(2) I am in pain if, and only if, my C-fibers are stimulated,

to the conclusion that the *properties* (or "states" or "events") being in pain, and having C-fibers stimulated, cannot possibly be the same [otherwise (2) would be analytic, or so the argument runs]; so one should be able to conclude from the fact that (1) is synthetic that the two properties (or

---

[2] Cf. (1), (2). This model of a scientific theory is too oversimplified to be of much general utility, in my opinion: however, the oversimplifications do not affect the present argument.

"states" or "events")—being in state A and having flip-flop 36 on—cannot possibly be the same!

It is instructive to note that the traditional argument for dualism is not at all a conclusion from "the raw data of direct experience" (as is shown by the fact that it applies just as well to non-sentient machines), but a highly complicated bit of reasoning which depends on (A) the reification of universals[3] (e.g., "properties," "states," "events"); and on (B) a sharp analytic-synthetic distinction.

I may be accused of advocating a "mechanistic" world-view in pressing the present analogy. If this means that I am supposed to hold that machines think,[4] on the one hand, or that human beings are machines, on the other, the charge is false. If there is some version of mechanism sophisticated enough to avoid these errors, very likely the considerations in this paper support it.[5]

1. TURING MACHINES

The present paper will require the notion of a *Turing machine*[6] which will now be explained.

Briefly, a Turing machine is a device with a finite number of internal configurations, each of which involves the machine's being in one of a finite number of *states*,[7] and the machine's scanning a tape on which certain symbols appear.

The machine's tape is divided into separate squares, thus:

on each of which a symbol (from a fixed finite alphabet) may be printed. Also the machine has a "scanner" which "scans" one square of the tape at a time. Finally, the machine has a *printing mechanism* which may (A) *erase* the symbol which appears on the square being scanned, and (B) print some other symbol (from the machine's alphabet) on that square.

Any Turing machine is completely described by a *machine table*, which is constructed as follows: the rows of the table correspond to letters of the

---

[3] This point was made by Quine in (9).

[4] Cf. Ziff's paper (13) and the reply (10) by Smart. Ziff has informed me that by a "robot" he did not have in mind a "learning machine" of the kind envisaged by Smart, and he would agree that the considerations brought forward in his paper would not necessarily apply to such a machine (if it can properly be classed as a "machine" at all). On the question of whether "this machine thinks (feels, etc.)" is *deviant* or not, it is necessary to keep in mind both the point raised by Ziff (that the important question is not whether or not the utterance is deviant, but whether or not it is deviant for non-trivial reasons), and also the "diachronic-synchronic" distinction discussed in section 5 of the present paper.

[5] In particular, I am sympathetic with the general standpoint taken by Smart in (11) and (12). However, see the linguistic considerations in section 5.

[6] For further details, cf. (4) and (6).

[7] This terminology is taken from (6) and differs from that of Davis and Turing.

alphabet (including the "null" letter, i.e., blank space), while the columns correspond to states A,B,C, etc. In each square there appears an "instruction," e.g., "s_5L A", "s_7C B", "s_3R C". These instructions are read as follows: "s_5L A" means "print the symbol s_5 on the square you are now scanning (after erasing whatever symbol it now contains), and proceed to scan the square immediately to the left of the one you have just been scanning; also, shift into state A." The other instructions are similarly interpreted ("R" means "scan the square immediately to the *right*," while "C" means "center," i.e., continue scanning the *same* square). The following is a sample machine table:

		A	B	C	D
(s_1)	1	s_1RA	s_1LB	s_3LD	s_1CD
(s_2)	+	s_1LB	s_2CD	s_3LD	s_2CD
	blank				
(s_3)	space	s_3CD	s_3RC	s_3LD	s_3CD

The machine described by this table is intended to function as follows: the machine is started in state A. On the tape there appears a "sum" (in unary notation) to be "worked out," e.g., "11 + 111."

The machine is initially scanning the first "1." The machine proceeds to "work out" the sum (essentially by replacing the plus sign by a 1, and then going back and erasing the first 1). Thus if the "input" was 1111 + 11111 the machine would "print out" 111111111, and then go into the "rest state" (state D).

A "machine table" *describes* a machine if the machine has internal states corresponding to the columns of the table, and if it "obeys" the instructions in the table in the following sense: when it is scanning a square on which a symbol s_1 appears and it is in, say, state B, that it carries out the "instruction" in the appropriate row and column of the table (in this case, column B and row s_1). Any machine that is described by a machine table of the sort just exemplified is a Turing machine.

The notion of a Turing machine is also subject to generalization[8] in various ways—for example, one may suppose that the machine has a second tape (an "input tape") on which additional information may be printed by an operator in the course of a computation. In the sequel we shall make use of this generalization (with electronic "sense organs" taking the place of the "operator").

It should be remarked that Turing machines are able in principle to do anything that any computing machine (of whichever kind) can do.[9]

It has sometimes been contended (e.g., by Nagel and Newman in their book "*Gödel's Proof*") that "the theorem [i.e., Gödel's theorem] does indicate that the structure and power of the human mind are far more complex and subtle than any non-living machine yet envisaged" (p. 10), and hence that a Turing machine cannot serve as a model for the human mind, but this is simply a mistake.

Let T be a Turing machine which "represents" me in the sense that T can

---

8 This generalization is made in (4), where it is employed in defining relative recursiveness.

9 This statement is a form of *Church's thesis* (that recursiveness equals effective computability).

prove just the mathematical statements I can prove. Then the argument (Nagel and Newman give no argument, but I assume they must have this one in mind) is that by using Gödel's technique I can discover a proposition that T cannot prove, and moreover *I* can prove this proposition. This refutes the assumption that T "represents" me, hence I am not a Turing machine. The fallacy is a misapplication of Gödel's theorem, pure and simple. Given an arbitrary machine T, all I can do is find a proposition U such that *I* can prove:

(3) If T is consistent, U is true,

where U is undecidable by T if T is in fact consistent. However, T can perfectly well prove (3) too! And the statement U, which T *cannot* prove (assuming consistency), *I* cannot prove either (unless I can prove that T is consistent, which is unlikely if T is very complicated)!

2. PRIVACY

Let us suppose that a Turing machine T is constructed to do the following. A number, say "3000," is printed on T's tape and T is started in T's "initial state." Thereupon T computes the 3000th (or whatever the given number was) digit in the decimal expansion of π, prints this digit on its tape, and goes into the "rest state," (i.e., turns itself off). Clearly the question "How does T 'ascertain' [or 'compute,' or 'work out'] the 3000th digit in the decimal expansion of π?" is a sensible question. And the answer might well be a complicated one. In fact, an answer would probably involve three distinguishable constituents:

(i) A description of the sequence of states through which T passed in arriving at the answer, and of the appearance of the tape at each stage in the computation.
(ii) A description of the *rules* under which T operated (these are given by the "machine table" for T).
(iii) An explanation of the *rationale* of the entire procedure.

Now let us suppose that someone voices the following objection: "In order to perform the computation just described, T must pass through states A,B,C, etc. But how can T ascertain that it is in states A,B,C, etc.?"

It is clear that this is a silly objection. But what makes it silly? For one thing, the "logical description" (machine table) of the machine describes the states only in terms of their *relations* to each other and to what appears on the tape. The "physical realization" of the machine is immaterial, so long as there *are* distinct states A,B,C, etc., and they succeed each other as specified in the machine table. Thus one can answer a question such as "How does T ascertain that X?" (or "compute X," etc.) only in the sense of describing the *sequence of states* through which T must pass in ascertaining that X (computing X, etc.), the rules obeyed, etc. But there is no "sequence of states" through which T must pass to be in a single state!

Indeed, suppose there were—suppose T could not *be* in state A without first *ascertaining* that it was in state A (by first passing through a sequence of other states). Clearly a vicious regress would be involved. And one "breaks" the regress simply by noting that the machine, in ascertaining the 3000th digit in π, *passes through* its states—but it need not in any significant sense "ascertain" that it is passing through them.

Note the analogy to a fallacy in traditional epistemology: the fallacy of supposing that to know that p (where p is any proposition) one must first know that q_1, q_2, etc. (where q_1, q_2 etc., are appropriate *other* propositions). This leads either to an "infinite regress" or to the dubious move of inventing a special class of "protocol" propositions.

The resolution of the fallacy is also analogous to the machine case. Suppose that on the basis of sense experiences E_1 E_2, etc., I know that there is a chair in the room. It does not follow that I verbalized (or even *could* have verbalized) E_1, E_2, etc., nor that I remember E_1, E_2, etc., nor even that I "mentally classified" ("attended to," etc.) sense experiences E_1, E_2, etc., when I had them. In short, it is necessary to *have* sense experiences, but not to *know* (or even *notice*) what sense experiences one is having, in order to have certain kinds of knowledge.

Let us modify our case, however, by supposing that whenever the machine is in one particular state (say, "state A") it prints the words "I am in state A." Then someone might grant that the machine does not in general ascertain what state it is in, but might say in the case of state A (after the machine printed "I am in state A"): "The machine ascertained that it was in state A."

Let us study this case a little more closely. First of all, we want to suppose that when it is in state A the machine prints "I am in state A" without first passing through any other states. That is, in every row of the column of the table headed "state A" there appears the instruction: *print*[10] "*I am in State A.*" Secondly, by way of comparison, let us consider a human being, Jones, who says "I am in pain" (or "Ouch!", or "Something hurts") whenever he is in pain. To make the comparison as close as possible, we will have to suppose that Jones' linguistic conditioning is such that he simply says "I am in pain" "without thinking," i.e., without passing through any introspectible mental states other than the pain itself. In Wittgenstein's terminology, Jones simply *evinces* his pain by saying "I am in pain"—he does not first reflect on it (or heed it, or note it, etc.) and then consciously describe it. (Note that this simple possibility of uttering the "proposition," "I am in pain" without first performing any mental "act of judgment" was overlooked by traditional epistemologists from Hume to Russell!) Now we may consider the parallel questions "Does the machine 'ascertain' that it is in state A?" and "Does Jones 'know' that he is in pain?" and their consequences.

Philosophers interested in semantical questions have, as one might expect, paid a good deal of attention to the verb "know." Traditionally, three elements have been distinguished: (1) "X knows that p" implies that p is *true* (we may call this the *truth* element); (2) "X knows that p" implies that X believes that p (philosophers have quarreled about the word, some contending that it should be 'X is *confident* that p,' or 'X *is in a position to assert* that p'; I shall call this element the *confidence* element); (3) "X

---

[10] Here it is necessary to suppose that the entire sentence "I am in state A" counts as a single symbol in the machine's alphabet.

knows that p" implies that X has evidence that p (here I think the word
"evidence" is definitely wrong,[11] but it will not matter for present purposes; I shall call this the *evidential* element). Moreover, it is part of the
meaning of the word "evidence" that nothing can be literally evidence for
itself: if X is evidence for Y, then X and Y must be different things.

In view of such analyses, disputes have arisen over the propriety of saying
(in cases like the one we are considering) "Jones knows that he is in pain."
On the one hand, philosophers who take the common-sense view ("When I
have a pain I *know* I have a pain") argue somewhat as follows: It would be
clearly false to say Jones does *not* know he has a pain; but either Jones
knows or he does not; hence, Jones knows he has a pain. Against these
philosophers, one might argue as follows: "Jones does not know X" implies
Jones is not in a position to assert that X; hence, it is certainly wrong to say
"Jones does not know he has a pain." But the above use of the Law of the
Excluded Middle was fallacious: words in English have *significance ranges*,
and what is contended is that it is not semantically correct to say *either*
"Jones knows that he has a pain" *or* "Jones does not know he has a pain"
(although the former sentence is certainly less misleading than the latter,
since *one* at least of the conditions involved in knowing is met—Jones is in a
position to assert he has a pain. (In fact the *truth* and *confidence* elements
are both present; it is the evidential element that occasions the difficulty.)

I do not wish to argue this question here;[12] the present concern is rather
with the similarities between our two questions. For example, one might
decide to accept (as "non-deviant," "logically in order," "nonselfcontra-
dictory," etc.) the two statements:

(a) The machine ascertained that it was in state A,
(b) Jones knew that he had a pain,

or one might reject both. If one rejects (a) and (b), then one can find
alternative formulations which are certainly semantically acceptable: e.g.,
[for (a)] "The machine was in state A, and this caused it to print: 'I am in
state A;'" [for (b)] "Jones was in pain, and this caused him to say 'I am in
pain'" (or, "Jones was in pain, and he evinced this by saying 'I am in
pain'").

On the other hand, if one accepts (a) and (b), then one must face the
questions (a¹) "*How* did the machine ascertain that it was in state A?", and
(b¹) "*How* did Jones know that he had a pain?"

And if one regards these questions as having answers at all, then they will
be degenerate answers—e.g., "By being in state A" and "By having the
pain."

At this point it is, I believe, very clear that the difficulty has in both cases
the same cause. Namely, the difficulty is occasioned by the fact that the
"verbal report" ("I am in state A," or "I am in pain") issues directly from

---

[11] For example, I know that the sun is 93 million miles from the earth, but I have no
evidence that this is so. In fact, I do not even remember where I learned this.

[12] In fact, it would be impossible to decide whether "Jones knows he has a pain" is
deviant or not without first reformulating the evidential condition so as to avoid the
objection in note 11 (if it can be reformulated so as to save anything of the condition at
all). However, the discussion above will indicate, I believe, why one might *want* to find
that this sentence is deviant.

the state it "reports": no "computation" or additional "evidence" is needed to arrive at the "answer." And the philosophic disagreements over "how to talk" are at bottom concerned with finding a terminology for describing cognitive processes in general that is not misleading in this particular case. [Note that the traditional epistemological answer to (b¹)—namely, "by introspection"—is false to the facts of this case, since it clearly implies the occurrence of a mental event (the "act" of introspection) distinct from the feeling of pain.]

Finally, let us suppose that the machine is equipped to "scan" its neighbor machine T¹. Then we can see that the question "How does T ascertain that T¹ is in state A?" may be a perfectly sensible question, as much so as "How does T ascertain that the 3000th digit of π is so-and-so?" In both cases the answer will involve describing a whole "program" (plus explaining the *rationale* of the program, if necessary). Moreover, it will be necessary to say something about the physical context linking T and T¹ (arrangement of sense organs, etc.), and not just to describe the internal states of T: this is so because T is now answering an *empirical* and not a mathematical question. In the same way "How did Sherlock Holmes know that Jones was in pain?" may be a perfectly sensible question, and may have quite a complicated answer.

3. "MENTAL" STATES AND "LOGICAL" STATES

Consider the two questions:

(1) How does Jones know he has a pain?
(2) How does Jones know he has a fever?

The first question is, as we saw in the preceding section, a somewhat peculiar one. The second question may be quite sensible. In fact, if Jones says "I have a pain" no one will retort "You are mistaken." (One *might* retort "You have made a slip of the tongue" or "You are lying," but not "You are *mistaken*.") On the other hand, if Jones says "I have a fever," the doctor who has just taken Jones' temperature may quite conceivably retort "You are mistaken." And the doctor need not mean that Jones made a linguistic error, or was lying, or confused.

It might be thought that, whereas the difference between statements about one's own state and statements about the state of others has an analogue in the case of machines, the difference, just touched upon, between statements about one's "mental" state and statements about one's "physical" state, in traditional parlance, does not have any analogue. But this is not so. Just what the analogue is will now be developed.

First of all, we have to go back to the notion of a Turing machine. When a Turing machine is described by means of a "machine table," it is described as something having a tape, a printing device, a "scanning" device (this may be no more than a point of the machine which at any given time is aligned with just one square of the tape), and a finite set (A,B,C, etc.) of "states." (In what follows, these will be referred to at times as *logical states* to distinguish them from certain other states to be introduced shortly.) Beyond this it is described only by giving the deterministic rules which determine the order in which the states succeed each other and what is printed when.

In particular, the "logical description" of a Turing machine does not include any specification of the *physical nature* of these "states"—or indeed, of the physical nature of the whole machine. (Shall it consist of electronic relays, of cardboard, of human clerks sitting at desks, or what?) In other words, a given "Turing machine" is an *abstract* machine which may be physically realized in an almost infinite number of different ways.

As soon as a Turing machine is physically realized, however, something interesting happens. Although the machine has from the logician's point of view only the states A,B,C, etc., it has from the engineer's point of view an almost infinite number of additional "states" (though not in the same sense of "state"—we shall call these *structural states*). For instance, if the machine consists of vacuum tubes, one of the things that may happen is that one of its vacuum tubes may fail—this puts the machine in what is from the physicist's if not the logician's point of view a different "state." Again, if the machine is a manually operated one built of cardboard, one of its possible "non-logical" or "structural" states is obviously that its cardboard may buckle. And so on.

A physically realized Turing machine may have no way of ascertaining its own structural state, just as a human being may have no way of ascertaining the condition of his appendix at a given time. However, it is extremely convenient to give a machine electronic "sense organs" which enable it to scan itself and to detect minor malfunctions. These "sense organs" may be visualized as causing certain symbols to be printed on an "input tape" which the machine "examines" from time to time. (One minor difficulty is that the "report" of a sense organ might occupy a number of squares of tape, whereas the machine only "scans" one square at a time—however this is unimportant, since it is well known that the effect of "reading" any finite number of squares can be obtained using a program which only requires one square to be scanned at a time.)

(By way of a digression, let me remark that the first actually constructed digital computers did not have any devices of the kind just envisaged. On the other hand, they *did* have over 3000 vacuum tubes, some of which were failing at any given time! The need for "routines" for self-checking therefore quickly became evident.)[13]

A machine which is able to detect at least some of its own structural states is in a position very analogous to that of a human being, who can detect some but not all of the malfunctions of his own body, and with varying degrees of reliability. Thus, suppose the machine "prints out": "Vacuum tube 312 has failed." The question "How did the machine ascertain that vacuum tube 312 failed?" is a perfectly sensible question. And the answer may involve a reference to both the physical structure of the machine ("sense organs," etc.) and the "logical structure" (program for "reading" and "interpreting" the input tape).

If the machine prints: "Vacuum tube 312 has failed" when vacuum tube 312 is in fact functioning, the mistake may be due to a miscomputation (in the course of "reading" and "interpreting" the input tape) or to an incorrect signal from a sense organ. On the other hand, if the machine prints:

---

[13] Actually, it was not necessary to add any "sense organs"; existing computers check themselves by "performing crucial experiments with themselves" (i.e., carrying out certain test computations and comparing the results with the correct results which have been given).

"I am in state A," and it does this simply because its machine table contains the instruction: *Print: "I am in state A when in state A,"* then the question of a miscomputation cannot arise. Even if some accident causes the printing mechanism to print: "I am in state A" when the machine is *not* in state A, there was not a "miscomputation" (only, so to speak, a "verbal slip").

It is interesting to note that just as there are two possible descriptions of the behavior of a Turing machine—the engineer's structural blueprint and the logician's "machine table"—so there are two possible descriptions of human psychology. The "behavioristic" approach (including in this category theories which employ "hypothetical constructs," including "constructs" taken from physiology) aims at eventually providing a complete physicalistic[14] description of human behavior, in terms which link up with chemistry and physics. This corresponds to the engineer's or physicist's description of a physically realized Turing machine. But it would also be possible to seek a more abstract description of human mental processes, in terms of "mental states" (physical realization, if any, unspecified) and "impressions" (these play the role of symbols on the machine's tapes)—a description which would specify the laws controlling the order in which the states succeeded one another, and the relation to verbalization (or, at any rate, verbalized thought). This description, which would be the analogue of a "machine table," it was in fact the program of classical psychology to provide! Classical psychology is often thought to have failed for *methodological* reasons; I would suggest, in the light of this analogy, that it failed rather for empirical reasons—the mental states and "impressions" of human beings do not form a causally closed system to the extent to which the "configurations" of a Turing machine do.

The analogy which has been presented between logical states of a Turing machine and mental states of a human being, on the one hand, and structural states of a Turing machine and physical states of a human being, on the other, is one that I find very suggestive. In particular, further exploration of this analogy may make it possible to further clarify the notion of a "mental state" that we have been discussing. This "further exploration" has not yet been undertaken, at any rate by me, but I should like to put down, for those who may be interested, a few of the features that seem to distinguish logical and mental states respectively from structural and physical ones:

(1) The functional organization (problem solving, thinking) of the human being or machine can be described in terms of the sequences of mental or logical states respectively (and the accompanying verbalizations), without reference to the nature of the "physical realization" of these states.

(2) The states seem intimately connected with *verbalization*.

(3) In the case of rational thought (or computing), the "program" which determines which states follow which, etc., is open to rational criticism.

4. MIND-BODY "IDENTITY"

The last area in which we have to compare human beings and machines involves the question of *identifying* mental states with the corresponding

---

[14] In the sense of (7); not in the "epistemological" sense associated with Carnap's writings on "physicalism."

physical states (or logical states with the corresponding structural states). As indicated at the beginning of this paper, all of the arguments for and against such identification can perfectly well be discussed in terms of Turing machines.

For example, in the 1930's Wittgenstein used the following argument: If I observe an after-image, and observe at the same time my brain state (with the aid of a suitable instrument) I observe *two* things, not one. (Presumably this is one argument *against* identification.) But we can perfectly well imagine a "clever" Turing machine "reasoning" as follows: "When I print 'I am in state A,' I do not have to use my 'sense organs.' When I do use my 'sense organs' and compare the occasions upon which I am in state A with the occasions upon which flip-flop 36 is on, I am comparing *two* things and not one." And I do not think that we would find the argument of this mechanical Wittgenstein very convincing!

By contrast, Russell once carried the "identity" view to the absurd extreme of maintaining that all we ever *see* is portions of our own brains. Analogously, a mechanical Russell might "argue" that "all I ever observe is my own vacuum tubes." Both "Russells" are wrong—the human being observes events in the outside world, and the process of "observation" involves events in his brain. But we are not therefore forced to say that he "really" observes his brain. Similarly, the machine T may "observe," say, cans of tomato soup (if the machine's job is sorting cans of soup), and the process of "observation" involves the functioning of vacuum tubes. But we are not forced to say that the machine "really" observes its own vacuum tubes.

But let us consider more serious arguments on this topic. At the beginning of this paper, I pointed out that the *synthetic* character of the statement (1) "I am in pain if, and only if, my C-fibers are stimulated" has been used as an argument for the view that the "properties" (or "events" or "states") "having C-fibers stimulated" and "being in pain" cannot be the same. There are at least two reasons why this is not a very good argument: (A) the "analytic-synthetic" distinction is not as sharp as that, especially where scientific laws are concerned; and (B) the criterion employed here for identifying "properties" (or "events" or "states") is a very questionable one.

With respect to point (A): I have argued elsewhere[15] that fundamental scientific laws cannot be happily classified as either "analytic" or "synthetic." Consider, for example, the kind of conceptual shift that was involved in the transition from Euclidean to non-Euclidean geometry, or that would be involved if the law of the conservation of energy were to be abandoned. It is a distortion to say that the laws of Euclidean geometry (during their tenure of office) were "analytic," and that Einstein merely "changed the meaning of the words." Indeed, it was precisely because Einstein did *not* change the meaning of the words, because he was really talking about shortest paths in the space in which we live and move and have our being, that General Relativity seemed so incomprehensible when it was first proposed. To be told that one could come back to the same place by moving in one direction on a straight line! Adopting General Relativity was

---

[15] In (8).

indeed adopting a whole new system of concepts—but that is not to say "adopting a new system of verbal labels."

But if it is a distortion to assimilate the revision of fundamental scientific laws to the adoption of new linguistic conventions, it is equally a mistake to follow conventional philosophers of science, and assimilate the conceptual change that Einstein inaugurated to the kind of change that arises when we discover a black swan (whereas we had previously assumed all swans to be white)! Fundamental laws are like principles of pure mathematics (as Quine has emphasized), in that they cannot be overthrown by isolated experiments: we can always hold on to the laws, and explain the experiments in various more or less *ad hoc* ways. And—in spite of the pejorative flavor of "ad hoc"—it is even *rational* to do this, in the case of important scientific theories, *as long as no acceptable alternative theory exists*. This is why it took a century of concept formation—and not just some experiments—to overthrow Euclidean geometry. And similarly, this is why we cannot today describe *any* experiments which would *by themselves* overthrow the law of the conservation of energy—although that law is not "analytic," and might be abandoned if a new Einstein were to suggest good *theoretical* reasons for abandoning it, plus supporting experiments.

As Hanson has put it,[16] our concepts have theories "built into" them—thus, to abandon a major scientific theory without providing an alternative would be to "let our concepts crumble." By contrast, although we *could* have held on to "all swans are white" in the face of conflicting evidence, there would have been no *point* in doing so—the concepts involved did not *rest* on the acceptance of this or some rival principle in the way that geometrical concepts rest on the acceptance, not necessarily of Euclidean geometry, but of *some* geometry.

I do not deny that *today* any newly-discovered "correlation" of the form: "One is in mental state ψ if, and only if, one is in brain state Φ" would *at first* be a *mere* correlation, a pure "empirical generalization." But I maintain that the interesting case is the case that would arise if we had a worked out and theoretically elaborated *system* of such "correlations." In such a case, scientific talk would be very different. Scientists would begin to say: "It is impossible *in principle* to be in mental state ψ without being in brain state Φ." And it could very well be that the "impossibility in principle" would amount to what Hanson rightly calls a *conceptual*[17] impossibility: scientists could not *conceive* (barring a new Einstein) of someone's being in mental state ψ without being in brain state Φ. In particular, no experiment could *by itself* overthrow psychophysical laws which had acquired this kind of status.[18] Is it clear that in this kind of scientific situation it would not be correct to say that Φ and ψ are the *same* state?

Moreover, the criteria for identifying "events" or "states" or "properties" are by no means so clear. An example of a law with the sort of status we have been discussing is the following: Light passes through an aperture if, and only if, electromagnetic radiation (of such-and-such wavelengths) passes through the aperture.

This law is quite clearly *not* an "analytic" statement. Yet it would be perfectly good scientific parlance to say that: (i) light passing through an

16 In (5).   17 Cf. (5).   18 Cf. the discussion of geometry in (8).

aperture and (ii) electromagnetic radiation (of such-and-such wavelengths) passing through an aperture are two descriptions of the same event. (Indeed, in "ordinary language" not only are descriptions of the same event not required to be equivalent: one may even speak of *incompatible* descriptions of the same event!)

It might be held, however, that *properties* (as opposed to events) cannot be described by different nonequivalent descriptions. Indeed, Frege, Lewis, and Carnap have *identified* properties and "meanings" (so that *by definition* if two expressions have different meanings then they "signify" different properties). This seems to me very dubious. But suppose it were correct. What would follow? One would have to admit that, e.g., being in pain and having C-fibers stimulated were different properties. But, in the language of the "theory-constructing" Turing machine described at the beginning of this paper, one would equally have to admit that "being in state A" and "having flip-flop 36 on" were different properties. Indeed the sentences (i) "I am in state A" and (ii) "Flip-flop 36 is on" are clearly nonsynonymous in the machine's language by any test (they have different syntactical properties and also different "conditions of utterance"—e.g., the machine has to use different "methods of verification"). Anyone who wishes, then, to argue on this basis for the existence of the soul will have to be prepared to hug the souls of Turing machines to his philosophic bosom!

5. A "LINGUISTIC" ARGUMENT

The last argument I shall consider on the subject of mind-body identity is a widely used "linguistic" argument—it was, for example, used by Max Black against Herbert Feigl . . . Consider the sentence:

(1) Pain *is identical with* stimulation of C-fibers.

The sentence is deviant (so the argument runs, though not in this terminology): there is no statement that it could be used to make in a normal context. Therefore, if a philosopher advances it as a thesis he must be giving the words a new meaning, rather than expressing any sort of discovery. For example (Max Black argued) one might begin to say "I have stimulated C-fibers" instead of "I have a pain," etc. But then one would *merely* be giving the expression "has stimulated C-fibers" the new meaning "is in pain." The contention is that as long as the words keep their present meanings, (1) is unintelligible.

I agree that the sentence (1) is a "deviant" sentence in present-day English. I do *not* agree that (1) can never become a normal, non-deviant sentence unless the words change their present meanings.

The point, in a nutshell, is that what is "deviant" depends very much upon context, including the state of our knowledge, and with the development of new scientific theories it is constantly occurring that sentences that did not previously "have a use," that were previously "deviant," acquire a use—not because the words acquire *new* meanings, but because the old meanings as fixed by the core of stock uses, *determine* a new use given the new context.

There is nothing wrong with trying to bring linguistic theory to bear on this issue, but one must have a sufficiently sophisticated linguistic theory to bring to bear. The real question is not a question on *synchronic* linguistics but one on *diachronic*[19] linguistics, not "Is (1) *now* a deviant sentence?", but "If a change in scientific knowledge (e.g., the development of an integrated network of psychophysical laws of high "priority" in our over-all scientific world view) were to lead to (1)'s becoming a *non*-deviant sentence, would a change in the meaning of a word necessarily have taken place?"—and this is not so simple a question.

Although this is not the time or the place to attempt the job of elaborating a semantical theory,[20] I should like to risk a few remarks on this question.

In the first place, it is easy to show that the mere uttering of a sentence which no one has ever uttered before does not necessarily constitute the introduction of a "new use." If I say "There is a purple Gila monster on this desk," I am very likely uttering a sentence that no English-speaker has uttered before me: but I am not in any way changing the meaning of any word.

In the second place, even if a sentence which was formerly deviant begins to acquire a standard use, no change in the *meaning* of any word need have taken place. Thus the sentence "I am a thousand miles away from you," or its translation into ancient Greek, was undoubtedly a deviant sentence prior to the invention of *writing*, but acquired (was not "given," but *acquired*) a normal use with the invention of writing and the ensuing possibility of long-distance interpersonal address.

Note the reasons that we would not say that any word (e.g., "I," "you," "thousand") in this sentence changed its meaning: (A) the new use was not *arbitrary*, was not the product of *stipulation*, but represented an automatic projection[21] from the existing stock uses of the several words making up the sentence, given the new context; (B) the meaning of a sentence is in general a function of the meanings of the individual words making it up (in fact this principle underlies the whole notion of word meaning)—thus, if we said that the *sentence* had changed its meaning, we should have to face the question "*Which word* changed its meaning?" But this would pretty clearly be an embarrassing question in this case.

The case just described was one in which the new context was the product of new technology, but new theoretical knowledge may have a similar impact on the language. (For example, "He went all the way around the world" would be a deviant sentence in a culture which did not know that the earth was round!) A case of this kind was discussed by Malcolm: We are beginning to have the means available for telling, on the basis of various physiological indicators (electroencephalograms, eye movements during sleep, blood pressure disturbances, etc.), when dreams begin and end. The sentence "He is halfway through his dream" may, therefore, someday acquire a standard use. Malcolm's comment on this was that the words

[19] Diachronic linguistics studies the language as it changes through time; synchronic linguistics seeks only to describe the language at one particular time.

[20] For a detailed discussion, cf. (14). I am extremely indebted to Ziff, both for making this work available to me and for personal communications on these matters. Section 5 of the present paper represents partly Ziff's influence (especially the use of the "synchronic-diachronic" distinction), and partly the application of some of the ideas of (8) to the present topic.

[21] The term is taken from (14).

would in that case have been *given* a use. Malcolm is clearly mistaken, I believe; this case, in which a sentence acquires a use *because* of what the words mean is poles apart from the case in which words are literally *given* a use (i.e., in which meanings are stipulated for expressions). The "realistic" account of this case is, I think, obviously correct: the sentence did not previously have a use because we had no way of telling when dreams start and stop. Now we are beginning to have ways of telling, and so we are beginning to find occasions upon which it is natural to employ this sentence. (Note that in Malcolm's account there is no explanation of the fact that we give *this* sentence *this* use.)

Now, someone may grant that change in meaning should not be confused with change in distribution,[22] and that scientific and technological advances frequently produce changes in the latter that are not properly regarded as changed in the former. But one might argue that whereas one could have envisaged beforehand the circumstances under which the sentence "He went all the way around the world" would become non-deviant, one cannot now envisage any circumstances under which[23] "mental state ψ is identical with brain state Φ" would be non-deviant. But this is not a very good objection. In the first place, it might very well have been impossible for primitive people to envisage a spherical earth (the people on the "underside" would obviously fall off). Even forty years ago, it might have been difficult if not impossible to envisage circumstances under which "he is halfway through his dream" would be non-deviant. And in the second place, I believe that one *can* describe in general terms circumstances under which "mental state ψ is identical with brain state Φ" would become non-deviant.

In order to do this, it is necessary to talk about one important kind of "is"—the *"is" of theoretical identification*. The use of "is" in question is exemplified in the following sentences:

(2) Light is electromagnetic radiation (of such-and-such wavelengths).
(3) Water is H_2O.

What was involved in the scientific acceptance of, for instance, (2) was very roughly this: prior to the identification there were two distinct bodies of theory—optical theory (whose character Toulmin has very well described in his book on philosophy of science), and electromagnetic theory (as represented by Maxwell's equations). The decision to *define* light as "electromagnetic radiation of such-and-such wavelengths" was scientifically justified by the following sorts of considerations (as has often been pointed out):

(1) It made possible the *derivation* of the laws of optics (up to first approximation) from more "basic" physical laws. Thus, even if it had accomplished nothing else, this theoretical identification would have been a move toward simplifying the structure of scientific laws.

(2) It made possible the derivation of *new* predictions in the "reduced" discipline (i.e., optics). In particular, it was now possible to predict that in certain cases

---

[22] The *distribution* of a word = the set of sentences in which it occurs.
[23] Here "Mental state ψ is identical with brain state Φ" is used as a surrogate for such sentences as "Pain is identical with stimulation of C-fibers."

the laws of geometrical optics would *not* hold. (Cf. Duhem's famous comments on the reduction of Kepler's laws to Newton's.)

Now let us try to envisage the circumstances under which a theoretical identification of mental states with physiological states might be in accordance with good scientific procedure. In general terms, what is necessary is that we should have not *mere* "correlates" for subjective states, but something much more elaborate—e.g., that we should know of physical states (say micro-states of the central processes) on the basis of which we could not merely *predict* human behavior, but causally explain it.

In order to avoid "category mistakes," it is necessary to restrict this notion, "explain human behavior," very carefully. Suppose a man says "I feel bad." His behavior, described in one set of categories, is: "stating that he feels bad." And the explanation may be "He said that he felt bad because he was hungry and had a headache." I do not wish to suggest that the event "Jones *stating* that he feels bad" can be explained in terms of the laws of *physics*. But there is *another* event which is very relevant, namely "Jones' body producing such-and-such sound waves." From one point of view this is a "different event" from Jones' stating that he feels bad. But (to adapt a remark of Hanson's) there would be no point in remarking that these are different events if there were not a sense in which they were the *same* event. And it is the sense in which these are the "same event" and not the sense in which these are "different events" that is relevant here.

In fine, all I mean when I speak of "causally explaining human behavior" is: causally explaining certain physical events (motions of bodies, productions of sound waves, etc.) which are in the sense just referred to the "same" as the events which make up human behavior. And no amount of "Ryleism" can succeed in arguing away[24] what is obviously a possibility: that physical science might succeed in doing this much.

If this much were a reality, then theoretically identifying "mental states" with their "correlates" would have the following two advantages:

(1) It would be possible (again up to "first approximation") to derive from physical theory the classical laws (or low-level generalizations) of common-sense "mentalistic" psychology, such as: "People tend to avoid things with which they have had painful experiences."

(2) It would be possible to predict the cases (and they are legion) in which common-sense "mentalistic" psychology fails.

Advantage (2) could, of course, be obtained without "identification" (by using correlation laws). But advantage (2) could equally have been obtained in the case of optics without identification (by assuming that light *accompanies* electromagnetic radiation, but is not *identical* with it). But the *combined* effect of eliminating certain laws altogether (in favor of theoretical definitions) *and* increasing the explanatory power of the theory could not be obtained in any other way in either case. The point worth noticing is that *every* argument for *and against* identification would apply equally in the mind-body case and in the light-electromagnetism case. (Even

[24] As one young philosopher attempted to do in a recent article in the *British Journal for the Philosophy of Science*.

the "ordinary language" argument could have been advanced against the identification of light with electromagnetic radiation.)

Two small points: (i) When I call "light is electromagnetic radiation (of such-and-such wavelengths)" a definition, I do not mean that the statement is "analytic." But then "definitions," *properly so called*, in theoretical science virtually *never* are analytic.[25] (Quine remarked once that he could think of at least nine good senses of "definition," none of which had anything to do with analyticity.) Of course a philosopher might then object to the whole *rationale* of theoretical identification on the ground that it is no gain to eliminate "laws" in favor of "definitions" if both are *synthetic* statements. The fact that the scientist does not feel at all the same way is another illustration of how unhelpful it is to look at science from the standpoint of the question "Analytic or synthetic?" (ii) Accepting a theoretical identification, e.g., "Pain *is* stimulation of C-fibers," does not commit one to *interchanging* the terms "pain" and "stimulation of C-fibers" in idiomatic talk, as Black suggested. For instance, the identification of "water" with "H_2O" is by now a very well-known one, but no one says "Bring me a glass of H_2O," except as a joke.

I believe that the account just presented is able (a) to explain the fact that sentences such as "Mental state ψ is identical with brain state Φ" are deviant in present-day English, while (b) making it clear how these same sentences might become *non-deviant* given a suitable increase in our scientific insight into the physical nature and causes of human behavior. The sentences in question cannot today be used to express a theoretical identification, because no such identification has been made. The act of theoretical identification is not an act that can be performed "at will"; there are *preconditions* for its performance, as there are for many acts, and these preconditions are not satisfied today. On the other hand, if the sort of scientific theory described above should materialize, then the preconditions for theoretical identification would be met, as they were met in the light-electromagnetism case, and sentences of the type in question would then *automatically* require a use— namely, to express the appropriate theoretical identifications. Once again, what makes this way of *acquiring* a use different from being *given* a use (and from "change of meaning" properly so called) is that the "new use" is an automatic *projection* from existing uses, and does not involve arbitrary stipulation (except insofar as some element of "stipulation" may be present in the acceptance of *any* scientific hypothesis, including "The earth is round").

So far we have considered only sentences of the form[26] "mental state ψ is identical with brain state Φ." But what of the sentence:

(3) Mental states are micro-states of the brain?

This sentence does not, so to speak, "give" any *particular* theoretical identification: it only says that unspecified theoretical identifications are

[25] This is argued in (8).

[26] By sentences of this *form* I do not literally mean *substitution instances* of "mental state ψ is identical with brain state Φ." Cf. note 23.

possible. This is the sort of assertion that Feigl might make. And Black[27] might reply that in uttering (3) Feigl had uttered an odd set of words (i.e., a deviant sentence). It is possible that Black is right. Perhaps (3) is deviant in present-day English. But it is also possible that our descendants in two or three hundred years will feel that Feigl was making perfectly good sense, and that the linguistic objections to (3) were quite silly. And they too may be right.

6. MACHINE LINGUISTICS

Let us consider the linguistic question that we have just discussed from the standpoint of the analogy between man and Turing machine that we have been presenting in this paper. It will be seen that our Turing machine will probably not be able, if it lacks suitable "sense organs," to construct a correct theory of its own constitution. On the other hand "I am in state A" will be a sentence with a definite pattern of occurrence in the machine's "language." If the machine's "language" is sufficiently complex, it may be possible to analyze it syntactically in terms of a finite set of basic building blocks (morphemes) and rules for constructing a potentially infinite set of "sentences" from these. In particular, it will be possible to distinguish *grammatical*[28] from *ungrammatical sentences* in the machine's "language." Similarly, it may be possible to associate regularities with sentence occurrences (or, "describe sentence uses," in the Oxford jargon), and to assign "meanings" to the finite set of morphemes and the finite set of forms of composition in such a way that the "uses" of the various sentences can be effectively projected from the meanings of the individual morphemes and forms of composition. In this case, one could distinguish not only "grammatical" and "ungrammatical" sentences in the "machine language," but also "deviant" and "non-deviant" ones.

Chisholm would insist that it is improper to speak of machines as employing a language, and I agree. This is the reason for my occasionally enclosing the words "language," "meaning," etc., in "raised-eyebrow" quotes—to emphasize, where necessary, that these words are being used in an extended sense. On the other hand, it is important to recognize that machine performances may be wholly *analogous* to language, so much so that the whole of linguistic theory can be applied to them. If the reader wishes to check this, he may go through a work like Chomsky's *Syntactic Structures* carefully, and note that *at no place is the assumption employed that the corpus of utterances studied by the linguist was produced by a conscious organism.* Then he may turn to such pioneer work in empirical semantics as Ziff's *Semantical Analysis* and observe that the same thing holds true for *semantical* theory.

Two further remarks in this connection: (i) Since I am contending that the mind-body problem is *strictly analogous* to the problem of the relation between structural and logical states, not that the two problems are *iden-*

---

[27] I have, with hesitation, ascribed this position to Black on the basis of his remarks at the Conference. But, of course, I realize that he cannot justly be held responsible for remarks made on the spur of the moment.

[28] This term is used in the sense of (3), not in the traditional sense.

tical, a suitable *analogy* between machine "language" and human language is all that is needed here. (ii) Chisholm might contend that a "behavioristic" semantics of the kind attempted by Ziff (i.e., one that does not take "intentionality" as a primitive notion) is impossible. But even if this were true, it would not be relevant. For if *any* semantical theory can fit human language, it has to be shown why a completely *analogous* theory would not fit the language of a suitable machine. For instance, if "intentionality" plays a role as a primitive notion in a *scientific* explanation of human language, then a theoretical construct with similar *formal* relations to the corresponding "observables" will have the *same* explanatory power in the case of machine "language."

Of course, the objection to "behavioristic" linguistics might *really* be an objection to all attempts at *scientific* linguistics. But this possibility I feel justified in dismissing.

Now suppose we equip our "theory-constructing" Turing machine with "sense organs" so that it can obtain the empirical data necessary for the construction of a theory of its own nature.

Then it may introduce into its "theoretical language" noun phrases that can be "translated" by the English expression "flip-flop 36," and sentences that can be translated by "Flip-flop 36 is on." These expressions will have a meaning and use quite distinct from the meaning and use of "I am in state A" in the machine language.

If any "linguistic" argument really shows that the sentence "Pain is identical with stimulation of C-fibers" is deviant, in English, the same argument must show that "State A is identical with flip-flop 36 being on" is deviant in the machine language. If any argument shows that "Pain is identical with stimulation of C-fibers" could not become non-deviant (viewing English now *diachronically*) unless the words first altered their meanings, the same argument, applied to the "diachronic linguistics of machine language," would show that the sentence "State A is identical with flip-flop 36 being on" could not become non-deviant in machine language unless the words first changed their meanings. In short, every philosophic argument that has ever been employed in connection with the mind-body problem, from the oldest and most naïve (e.g., "states of consciousness can just be *seen* to be different from physical states") to the most sophisticated, has its exact counterpart in the case of the "problem" of logical states and structural states in Turing machines.

7. CONCLUSION

The moral, I believe, is quite clear: It is no longer possible to believe that the mind-body problem is a genuine theoretical problem, or that a "solution" to it would shed the slightest light on the world in which we live. For it is quite clear that no grown man in his right mind would take the problem of the "identity" or "non-identity" of logical and structural states in a machine at all seriously—not because the answer is obvious, but because it is obviously of no importance *what* the answer is. But if the so-called "mind-body problem" is nothing but a different realization of the same set of logical and linguistic issues, then it must be just as empty and just as verbal.

It is often an important insight that two problems with distinct subject matter are the same in all their logical and methodological aspects. In this case, the insight carries in its train the realization that any conclusion that might be reached in the case of the mind-body problem would have to be reached, *and for the same reasons,* in the Turing machine case. But if it is clear (as it obviously is) that, for example, the conclusion that the logical states of Turing machines are hopelessly different from their structural states, even if correct, could represent only a purely *verbal* discovery, then the same conclusion *reached by the same arguments* in the human case must likewise represent a purely verbal discovery. To put it differently, if the mind-body problem is identified with any problem of more than purely conceptual interest (e.g., with the question of whether or not human beings have "souls"), then *either* it must be that (a) no argument *ever* used by a philosopher sheds the *slightest* light on it (and this independently of the way the argument tends), or (b) that some philosophic argument for mechanism is correct, or (c) that some dualistic argument does show that *both* human beings *and* Turing machines have souls! I leave it to the reader to decide which of the three alternatives is at all plausible.

BIBLIOGRAPHY

(1) Carnap, Rudolf. "The Interpretation of Physics." Reprinted in H. Feigl & M. Brodbeck, *Readings in the Philosophy of Science.* New York: Appleton-Century-Crofts, 1953, pp. 309–18.

(2) ———. "The Methodological Character of Theoretical Concepts," in *Minnesota Studies in the Philosophy of Science*, I, 38–76. Minneapolis: Univ. of Minnesota, 1956.

(3) Chomsky, Noam. *Syntactic Structures.* The Hague: Mouton & Co., 1957.

(4) Davis, Martin. *Computability and Unsolvability.* New York: McGraw-Hill Book Co., 1958.

(5) Hanson, Norwood Russell. *Patterns of Discovery.* Cambridge: Cambridge Univ. Press, 1958.

(6) Kleene, Stephen Cole. *Introduction to Metamathematics.* New York: Van Nostrand, 1952.

(7) Oppenheim, Paul, and Putnam, Hilary. "Unity of Science as a Working Hypothesis," in H. Feigl, G. Maxwell, and M. Scriven (eds.),

Concepts, Theories, and the Mind-Body Problem (Minnesota Studies in the Philosophy of Science, Vol. II). Minneapolis: Univ. of Minnesota, 1958.

(8) Putnam, Hilary. "The Analytic and the Synthetic," in *Minnesota Studies in the Philosophy of Science,* III. Minneapolis: Univ. of Minnesota, 1960.

(9) Quine, Willard Van Orman. "The Scope and Language of Science," *British Journal for the Philosophy of Science,* VIII (1957).

(10) Smart, J. J. C. "Professor Ziff on Robots," *Analysis,* XIX (1959), 117–18.

(11) ———. "Incompatible Colors," *Philosophical Studies,* X (1959), 39–42.

(12) ———. "Sensations and Brain Processes," *Philosophical Review,* LXVIII (1959), 141–56.

(13) Ziff, Paul. "The Feelings of Robots," *Analysis,* XIX (1959), 64–68.

(14) ———. *Semantic Analysis.* Ithaca: Cornell University Press, 1960.

9

OF PERSONAL IDENTITY

David Hume

There are some philosophers, who imagine we are every moment intimately conscious of what we call our SELF; that we feel its existence and its continuance in existence; and are certain, beyond the evidence of a demonstration, both of its perfect identity and simplicity. The strongest sensation, the most violent passion, say they, instead of distracting us from this view, only fix it the more intensely, and make us consider their influence on *self* either by their pain or pleasure. To attempt a farther proof of this were to weaken its evidence; since no proof can be deriv'd from any fact, of which we are so intimately conscious; nor is there any thing, of which we can be certain, if we doubt of this.

Unluckily all these positive assertions are contrary to that very experience, which is pleaded for them, nor have we any idea of *self*, after the manner it is here explain'd. For from what impression cou'd this idea be deriv'd? This question 'tis impossible to answer without a manifest contradiction and absurdity; and yet 'tis a question, which must necessarily be answer'd, if we wou'd have the idea of self pass for clear and intelligible. It must be some one impression, that gives rise to every real idea. But self or person is not any one impression, but that to which our several impressions and ideas are suppos'd to have a reference. If any impression gives rise to the idea of self, that impression must continue invariably the same, thro' the whole course of our lives; since self is suppos'd to exist after that manner. But there is no impression constant and invariable. Pain and pleasure, grief and joy, passions and sensations succeed each other, and never all exist at the same time. It cannot, therefore, be from any of these impressions, or from any other, that the idea of self is deriv'd; and consequently there is no such idea.

But farther, what must become of all our particular perceptions upon this hypothesis? All these are different, and distinguishable, and separable from each other, and may be separately consider'd, and may exist separately, and have no need of any thing to support their existence. After what manner,

From David Hume, *A Treatise of Human Nature*, L. A. Selby-Bigge, ed. (Oxford: The Clarendon Press, 1888), Book I, Part IV, Sec. 6, pp. 251–263.

therefore, do they belong to self; and how are they connected with it? For my part, when I enter most intimately into what I call *myself*, I always stumble on some particular perception or other, of heat or cold, light or shade, love or hatred, pain or pleasure. I never can catch *myself* at any time without a perception, and never can observe any thing but the perception. When my perceptions are remov'd for any time, as by sound sleep; so long am I insensible of *myself*, and may truly be said not to exist. And were all my perceptions remov'd by death, and cou'd I neither think, nor feel, nor see, nor love, nor hate after the dissolution of my body, I shou'd be entirely annihilated, nor do I conceive what is farther requisite to make me a perfect non-entity. If any one upon serious and unprejudic'd reflexion, thinks he has a different notion of *himself*, I must confess I can reason no longer with him. All I can allow him is, that he may be in the right as well as I, and that we are essentially different in this particular. He may, perhaps, perceive something simple and continu'd, which he calls *himself;* tho' I am certain there is no such principle in me.

But setting aside some metaphysicians of this kind, I may venture to affirm of the rest of mankind, that they are nothing but a bundle or collection of different perceptions, which succeed each other with an inconceivable rapidity, and are in a perpetual flux and movement. Our eyes cannot turn in their sockets without varying our perceptions. Our thought is still more variable than our sight; and all our other senses and faculties contribute to this change; nor is there any single power of the soul, which remains unalterably the same, perhaps for one moment. The mind is a kind of theatre, where several perceptions successively make their appearance; pass, re-pass, glide away, and mingle in an infinite variety of postures and situations. There is properly no *simplicity* in it at one time, nor *identity* in different; whatever natural propension we may have to imagine that simplicity and identity. The comparison of the theatre must not mislead us. They are the successive perceptions only, that constitute the mind; nor have we the most distant notion of the place, where these scenes are represented, or of the materials, of which it is compos'd.

What then gives us so great a propension to ascribe an identity to these successive perceptions, and to suppose ourselves possest of an invariable and uninterrupted existence thro' the whole course of our lives? In order to answer this question, we must distinguish betwixt personal identity, as it regards our thought or imagination, and as it regards our passions or the concern we take in ourselves. The first is our present subject; and to explain it perfectly we must take the matter pretty deep, and account for that identity, which we attribute to plants and animals; there being a great analogy betwixt it, and the identity of a self or person.

We have a distinct idea of an object, that remains invariable and un-interrupted thro' a suppos'd variation of time; and this idea we call that of *identity* or *sameness*. We have also a distinct idea of several different objects existing in succession, and connected together by a close relation; and this to an accurate view affords as perfect a notion of *diversity*, as if there was no manner of relation among the objects. But tho' these two ideas of identity, and a succession of related objects be in themselves perfectly distinct, and even contrary, yet 'tis certain, that in our common way of thinking they are generally confounded with each other. That action of the imagination, by which we consider the uninterrupted and invariable object, and that by which we reflect on the succession of related objects, are almost the same to the feeling, nor is there much more effort of thought requir'd in the latter case than in the former. The relation facilitates the transition of the mind from one object to another, and renders its passage as smooth as if it contemplated one continu'd object. This resemblance is the cause of the confusion and mistake, and makes us substitute the notion of identity, instead of that of related objects. However at one instant we may consider the related succession as variable or interrupted, we are sure the next to ascribe to it a perfect identity, and regard it as invariable and uninterrupted. Our propensity to this mistake is so great from the resemblance above-mention'd, that we fall into it before we are aware; and tho' we incessantly correct ourselves by reflexion, and return to a more accurate method of thinking, yet we cannot long sustain our philosophy, or take off this biass from the imagination. Our last resource is to yield to it, and boldly assert that these different related objects are in effect the same, however inter-rupted and variable. In order to justify to ourselves this absurdity, we often feign some new and unintelligible principle, that connects the objects together, and prevents their interruption or variation. Thus we feign the continu'd existence of the perceptions of our senses, to remove the interrup-tion; and run into the notion of a *soul*, and *self*, and *substance*, to disguise the variation. But we may farther observe, that where we do not give rise to such a fiction, our propension to confound identity with relation is so great, that we are apt to imagine[1] something unknown and mysterious, connecting the parts, beside their relation; and this I take to be the case with regard to the identity we ascribe to plants and vegetables. And even when this does not take place, we still feel a propensity to confound these ideas, tho' we are not able fully to satisfy ourselves in that particular, nor find any thing invariable and uninterrupted to justify our notion of identity.

Thus the controversy concerning identity is not merely a dispute of words. For when we attribute identity, in an improper sense, to variable or interrupted objects, our mistake is not confin'd to the expression, but is commonly attended with a fiction, either of something invariable and unin-terrupted, or of something mysterious and inexplicable, or at least with a pro-pensity to such fictions. What will suffice to prove this hypothesis to the satisfaction of every fair enquirer, is to shew from daily experience and ob-servation, that the objects, which are variable or interrupted, and yet are suppos'd to continue the same, are such only as consist of a succession of parts, connected together by resemblance, contiguity, or causation. For as such a succession answers evidently to our notion of diversity, it can only be by mistake we ascribe to it an identity; and as the relation of parts, which leads us into this mistake, is really nothing but a quality, which produces an association of ideas, and an easy transition of the imagination from one to another, it can only be from the resemblance, which this act of the mind bears to that, by which we contemplate one continu'd object, that the error arises. Our chief business, then, must be to prove, that all objects, to which

---

[1] If the reader is desirous to see how a great genius may be influenc'd by these seemingly trivial principles of the imagination, as well as the mere vulgar, let him read my Lord *Shaftsbury*'s reasonings concerning the uniting principle of the universe, and the identity of plants and animals. See his *Moralists;* or, *Philosophical rhapsody.*

we ascribe identity, without observing their invariableness and uninter-
ruptedness, are such as consist of a succession of related objects.

In order to this, suppose any mass of matter, of which the parts are
contiguous and connected, to be plac'd before us; 'tis plain we must
attribute a perfect identity to this mass, provided all the parts continue
uninterruptedly and invariably the same, whatever motion or change of
place we may observe either in the whole or in any of the parts. But
supposing some very *small* or *inconsiderable* part to be added to the mass, or
subtracted from it; tho' this absolutely destroys the identity of the whole,
strictly speaking; yet as we seldom think so accurately, we scruple not to
pronounce a mass of matter the same, where we find so trivial an alteration.
The passage of the thought from the object before the change to the object
after it, is so smooth and easy, that we scarce perceive the transition, and are
apt to imagine, that 'tis nothing but a continu'd survey of the same object.

There is a very remarkable circumstance, that attends this experiment;
which is, that tho' the change of any considerable part in a mass of matter
destroys the identity of the whole, yet we must measure the greatness of the
part, not absolutely, but by its *proportion* to the whole. The addition or
diminution of a mountain wou'd not be sufficient to produce a diversity in a
planet; tho' the change of a very few inches wou'd be able to destroy the
identity of some bodies. 'Twill be impossible to account for this, but by
reflecting that objects operate upon the mind, and break or interrupt the
continuity of its actions not according to their real greatness, but according
to their proportion to each other: And therefore, since this interruption
makes an object cease to appear the same, it must be the uninterrupted
progress of the thought, which constitutes the [perfect] identity.

This may be confirm'd by another phænomenon. A change in any
considerable part of a body destroys its identity; but 'tis remarkable, that
where the change is produc'd *gradually* and *insensibly* we are less apt to
ascribe to it the same effect. The reason can plainly be no other, than that
the mind, in following the successive changes of the body, feels an easy
passage from the surveying its condition in one moment to the viewing of it
in another, and at no particular time perceives any interruption in its actions.
From which continu'd perception, it ascribes a continu'd existence and
identity to the object.

But whatever precaution we may use in introducing the changes gradually, and making them proportionable to the whole, 'tis certain, that where
the changes are at last observ'd to become considerable, we make a scruple
of ascribing identity to such different objects. There is, however, another
artifice, by which we may induce the imagination to advance a step farther;
and that is, by producing a reference of the parts to each other, and a
combination to some *common end* or purpose. A ship, of which a considerable part has been chang'd by frequent reparations, is still consider'd as the
same; nor does the difference of the materials hinder us from ascribing an
identity to it. The common end, in which the parts conspire, is the same
under all their variations, and affords an easy transition of the imagination
from one situation of the body to another.

But this is still more remarkable, when we add a *sympathy* of parts to
their *common end*, and suppose that they bear to each other, the reciprocal
relation of cause and effect in all their actions and operations. This is the

case with all animals and vegetables; where not only the several parts have a reference to some general purpose, but also a mutual dependance on, and connexion with each other. The effect of so strong a relation is, that tho' every one must allow, that in a very few years both vegetables and animals endure a *total* change, yet we still attribute identity to them, while their form, size, and substance are entirely alter'd. An oak, that grows from a small plant to a large tree, is still the same oak; tho' there be not one particle of matter, or figure of its parts the same. An infant becomes a man, and is sometimes fat, sometimes lean, without any change in his identity.

We may also consider the two following phænomena, which are remarkable in their kind. The first is, that tho' we commonly be able to distinguish pretty exactly betwixt numerical and specific identity, yet it sometimes happens, that we confound them, and in our thinking and reasoning employ the one for the other. Thus a man, who hears a noise, that is frequently interrupted and renew'd, says, it is still the same noise; tho' 'tis evident the sounds have only a specific identity or resemblance, and there is nothing numerically the same, but the cause, which produc'd them. In like manner it may be said without breach of the propriety of language, that such a church, which was formerly of brick, fell to ruin, and that the parish rebuilt the same church of free-stone, and according to modern architecture. Here neither the form nor materials are the same, nor is there any thing common to the two objects, but their relation to the inhabitants of the parish; and yet this alone is sufficient to make us denominate them the same. But we must observe, that in these cases the first object is in a manner annihilated before the second comes into existence; by which means, we are never presented in any one point of time with the idea of difference and multiplicity; and for that reason are less scrupulous in calling them the same.

Secondly, We may remark, that tho' in a succession of related objects, it be in a manner requisite, that the change of parts be not sudden nor entire, in order to preserve the identity, yet where the objects are in their nature changeable and inconstant, we admit of a more sudden transition, than wou'd otherwise be consistent with that relation. Thus as the nature of a river consists in the motion and change of parts; tho' in less than four and twenty hours these be totally alter'd; this hinders not the river from continuing the same during several ages. What is natural and essential to any thing is, in a manner, expected; and what is expected makes less impression, and appears of less moment, than what is unusual and extraordinary. A considerable change of the former kind seems really less to the imagination, than the most trivial alteration of the latter; and by breaking less the continuity of the thought, has less influence in destroying the identity.

We now proceed to explain the nature of *personal identity*, which has become so great a question in philosophy, especially of late years in *England*, where all the abstruser sciences are study'd with a peculiar ardour and application. And here 'tis evident, the same method of reasoning must be continu'd, which has so successfully explain'd the identity of plants, and animals, and ships, and houses, and of all the compounded and changeable productions either of art or nature. The identity, which we ascribe to the mind of man, is only a fictitious one, and of a like kind with that which we ascribe to vegetables and animal bodies. It cannot, therefore, have a different origin, but must proceed from a like operation of the imagination upon like objects.

But lest this argument shou'd not convince the reader; tho' in my opinion perfectly decisive; let him weigh the following reasoning, which is still closer and more immediate. 'Tis evident, that the identity, which we attribute to the human mind, however perfect we may imagine it to be, is not able to run the several different perceptions into one, and make them lose their characters of distinction and difference, which are essential to them. 'Tis still true, that every distinct perception, which enters into the composition of the mind, is a distinct existence, and is different, and distinguishable, and separable from every other perception, either contemporary or successive. But, as, notwithstanding this distinction and separability, we suppose the whole train of perceptions to be united by identity, a question naturally arises concerning this relation of identity; whether it be something that really binds our several perceptions together, or only associates their ideas in the imagination. That is, in other words, whether in pronouncing concerning the identity of a person, we observe some real bond among his perceptions, or only feel one among the ideas we form of them. This question we might easily decide, if we wou'd recollect what has been already prov'd at large, that the understanding never observes any real connexion among objects, and that even the union of cause and effect, when strictly examin'd, resolves itself into a customary association of ideas. For from thence it evidently follows, that identity is nothing really belonging to these different perceptions, and uniting them together; but is merely a quality, which we attribute to them, because of the union of their ideas in the imagination, when we reflect upon them. Now the only qualities, which can give ideas an union in the imagination, are these three relations above-mention'd. These are the uniting principles in the ideal world, and without them every distinct object is separable by the mind, and may be separately consider'd, and appears not to have any more connexion with any other object, than if disjoin'd by the greatest difference and remoteness. 'Tis, therefore, on some of these three relations of resemblance, contiguity and causation, that identity depends; and as the very essence of these relations consists in their producing an easy transition of ideas; it follows, that our notions of personal identity, proceed entirely from the smooth and uninterrupted progress of the thought along a train of connected ideas, according to the principles above-explain'd.

The only question, therefore, which remains, is, by what relations this uninterrupted progress of our thought is produc'd, when we consider the successive existence of a mind or thinking person. And here 'tis evident we must confine ourselves to resemblance and causation, and must drop contiguity, which has little or no influence in the present case.

To begin with *resemblance;* suppose we cou'd see clearly into the breast of another, and observe that succession of perceptions, which constitutes his mind or thinking principle, and suppose that he always preserves the memory of a considerable part of past perceptions; 'tis evident that nothing cou'd more contribute to the bestowing a relation on this succession amidst all its variations. For what is the memory but a faculty, by which we raise up the images of past perceptions? And as an image necessarily resembles its object, must not the frequent placing of these resembling perceptions in the chain of thought, convey the imagination more easily from one link to another, and make the whole seem like the continuance of one object? In this particular, then, the memory not only discovers the identity, but also contributes to its production, by producing the relation of resemblance among the perceptions. The case is the same whether we consider ourselves or others.

As to *causation;* we may observe, that the true idea of the human mind, is to consider it as a system of different perceptions or different existences, which are link'd together by the relation of cause and effect, and mutually produce, destroy, influence, and modify each other. Our impressions give rise to their correspondent ideas; and these ideas in their turn produce other impressions. One thought chaces another, and draws after it a third, by which it is expell'd in its turn. In this respect, I cannot compare the soul more properly to any thing than to a republic or commonwealth, in which the several members are united by the reciprocal ties of government and subordination, and give rise to other persons, who propagate the same republic in the incessant changes of its parts. And as the same individual republic may not only change its members, but also its laws and constitutions; in like manner the same person may vary his character and disposition, as well as his impressions and ideas, without losing his identity. Whatever changes he endures, his several parts are still connected by the relation of causation. And in this view our identity with regard to the passions serves to corroborate that with regard to the imagination, by the making our distant perceptions influence each other, and by giving us a present concern for our past or future pains or pleasures.

As memory alone acquaints us with the continuance and extent of this succession of perceptions, 'tis to be consider'd, upon that account chiefly, as the source of personal identity. Had we no memory, we never shou'd have any notion of causation, nor consequently of that chain of causes and effects, which constitute our self or person. But having once acquir'd this notion of causation from the memory, we can extend the same chain of causes, and consequently the identity of our persons beyond our memory, and can comprehend times, and circumstances, and actions, which we have entirely forgot, but suppose in general to have existed. For how few of our past actions are there, of which we have any memory? Who can tell me, for instance, what were his thoughts and actions on the first of *January* 1715, the 11th of *March* 1719, and the 3d of *August* 1733? Or will he affirm, because he has entirely forgot the incidents of these days, that the present self is not the same person with the self of that time; and by that means overturn all the most establish'd notions of personal identity? In this view, therefore, memory does not so much *produce* as *discover* personal identity, by shewing us the relation of cause and effect among our different perceptions. 'Twill be incumbent on those, who affirm that memory produces entirely our personal identity, to give a reason why we can thus extend our identity beyond our memory.

The whole of this doctrine leads us to a conclusion, which is of great importance in the present affair, *viz.* that all the nice and subtile questions concerning personal identity can never possibly be decided, and are to be regarded rather as grammatical than as philosophical difficulties. Identity depends on the relations of ideas; and these relations produce identity, by means of that easy transition they occasion. But as the relations, and the easiness of the transition may diminish by insensible degrees, we have no just standard, by which we can decide any dispute concerning the time, when they acquire or lose a title to the name of identity. All the disputes concerning the identity of connected objects are merely verbal, except so far as the relation of parts gives rise to some fiction or imaginary principle of union, as we have already observ'd.

What I have said concerning the first origin and uncertainty of our notion of identity, as apply'd to the human mind, may be extended with little or no variation to that of *simplicity*. An object, whose different co-existent parts are bound together by a close relation, operates upon the imagination after much the same manner as one perfectly simple and indivisible, and requires not a much greater stretch of thought in order to its conception. From this similarity of operation we attribute a simplicity to it, and feign a principle of union as the support of this simplicity, and the center of all the different parts and qualities of the object.

.   .   .

10
PERSONS

F. F. Strawson

I

In the *Tractatus* (5.631–5.641), Wittgenstein writes of the I which occurs in philosophy, of the philosophical idea of the subject of experiences. He says first: "The thinking, presenting subject—there is no such thing." Then, a little later: "*In an important sense* there is no subject." This is followed by: "The subject does not belong to the world, but is a limit of the world." And a little later comes the following paragraph: "There is [therefore] really a sense in which in philosophy we can talk non-psychologically of the I. The I occurs in philosophy through the fact that the 'world is my world.' The philosophical I is not the man, not the human body, or the human soul of which psychology treats, but the metaphysical subject, the limit—not a part of the world." These remarks are impressive, but also puzzling and obscure. Reading them, one might think: Well, let's settle for the human body and the human soul of which psychology treats, and which is a part of the world, and let the metaphysical subject go. But again we might think: No, when I talk of myself, I do after all talk of that which has all of my experiences, I do talk of the subject of my experiences—and yet also of something that is part of the world in that it, but not the world, comes to an end when I die. The limit of *my* world is not—and is not so thought of by me—the limit of *the* world. It may be difficult to explain the idea of something which is both a subject of experiences and a part of the world. But it is an idea we have: it should be an idea we can explain.

Let us think of some of the ways in which we ordinarily talk of ourselves, of some of the things which we ordinarily ascribe to ourselves. They are of many kinds. We ascribe to ourselves *actions and intentions* (I am doing, did, shall do this); *sensations* (I am warm, in pain); *thoughts and feelings* (I think, wonder, want this, am angry, disappointed, contented); *perceptions and memories* (I see this, hear the other, remember that). We ascribe to

P. F. Strawson, "Persons," in *Minnesota Studies in the Philosophy of Science*, Vol. II (Minneapolis: University of Minnesota Press), pp. 330–353. © Copyright 1958 by the University of Minnesota. Reprinted by permission of the publisher.

ourselves, in two senses, position: *location* (I am on the sofa) and *attitude* (I am lying down). And of course we ascribe to ourselves not only temporary conditions, states, and situations, like most of these, but also enduring characteristics, including such physical characteristics as height, coloring, shape, and weight. That is to say, among the things we ascribe to ourselves are things of a kind that we also ascribe to material bodies to which we would not dream of ascribing others of the things that we ascribe to ourselves. Now there seems nothing needing explanation in the fact that the particular height, coloring, and physical position which we ascribe to ourselves, should be ascribed to *something or other;* for that which one calls one's body is, at least, a body, a material thing. It can be picked out from others, identified by ordinary physical criteria and described in ordinary physical terms. But it can seem, and has seemed, to need explanation that one's states of consciousness, one's thoughts and sensations, are ascribed *to the very same thing* as that to which these physical characteristics, this physical situation, is ascribed. Why are one's states of consciousness ascribed to the very same thing as certain corporeal characteristics, a certain physical situation, etc.? And once this question is raised, another question follows it, viz.: Why are one's states of consciousness ascribed to (said to be of, or to belong to) anything at all? It is not to be supposed that the answers to these questions will be independent of one another.

It might indeed be thought that an answer to both of them could be found in the unique role which each person's body plays in his experience, particularly his perceptual experience. All philosophers who have concerned themselves with these questions have referred to the uniqueness of this role. (Descartes was well enough aware of its uniqueness: "I am *not* lodged in my body like a pilot in a vessel.") In what does this uniqueness consist? Well, of course, in a great many facts. We may summarize some of these facts by saying that for each person there is one body which occupies a certain *causal* position in relation to that person's perceptual experience, a causal position which is in various ways unique in relation to each of the various kinds of perceptual experience he has; and—as a further consequence—that this body is also unique for him as an *object* of the various kinds of perceptual experience which he has. This complex uniqueness of the single body appears, moreover, to be a contingent matter, or rather a cluster of contingent matters; we can, or it seems that we can, imagine many peculiar combinations of dependence and independence of aspects of our perceptual experience on the physical states or situation of more than one body.

Now I must say, straightaway, that this cluster of apparently contingent facts about the unique role which each person's body plays in his experience does not seem to me to provide, *by itself*, an answer to our questions. Of course these facts explain *something*. They provide a very good reason why a subject of experience should have a *very special regard* for just one body, why he should think of it as unique and perhaps more important than any other. They explain—if I may be permitted to put it so—why I feel *peculiarly attached* to what in fact I call my own body; they even might be said to explain why, granted that I am going to speak of one body as *mine*, I should speak of this body (the body that I do speak of as mine) as mine. But they do not explain why I should have the concept of *myself* at all, why I should ascribe my thoughts and experiences to *anything*. Moreover, even if we were satisfied with some other explanation of why one's states of consciousness (thoughts and feelings and perceptions) were ascribed to *something,* and satisfied that the facts in question sufficed to explain why the "possession" of a particular body should be ascribed to the *same* thing (i.e., to explain why a particular body should be spoken of as standing in some special relation, called "being possessed by" to that thing), yet the facts in question still do not explain why we should, as we do, ascribe certain corporeal characteristics not simply to the body standing in this special relation to the thing to which we ascribe thoughts, feelings, etc., but to the thing itself to which we ascribe those thoughts and feelings. (For we say "I am bald" as well as "I am cold," I am lying on the hearthrug" as well as "I see a spider on the ceiling.") Briefly, the facts in question explain why a subject of experience should pick out one body from others, give it, perhaps, an honored name and ascribe to it whatever characteristics it has; but they do not explain why the experiences should be ascribed to any subject at all; and they do not explain why, if the experiences are to be ascribed to something, they *and* the corporeal characteristics which might be truly ascribed to the favored body, should be ascribed to the same thing. So the facts in question do not explain the use that we make of the word "I", or how any word has the use that word has. They do not explain the concept we have of a person.

II

A possible reaction at this point is to say that the concept we have is wrong or confused, or, if we make it a rule not to say that the concepts we have are confused, that the usage we have, whereby we ascribe, or seem to ascribe, such different kinds of predicate to one and the same thing, is confusing, that it conceals the true nature of the concepts involved, or something of this sort. This reaction can be found in two very important types of view about these matters. The first type of view is Cartesian, the view of Descartes and of others who think like him. Over the attribution of the second type of view I am more hesitant; but there is some evidence that it was held, at one period, by Wittgenstein and possibly also by Schlick. On both of these views, one of the questions we are considering, namely "Why do we ascribe our states of consciousness to the very same thing as certain corporeal characteristics, etc.?" is a question which does not arise; for on both views it is only a linguistic illusion that both kinds of predicate are properly ascribed to one and the same thing, that there is a common owner, or subject, of both types of predicate. And on the second of these views, the other question we are considering, namely "Why do we ascribe our states of consciousness to anything at all?" is also a question which does not arise; for on this view, it is only a linguistic illusion that one ascribes one's states of consciousness at all, that there is any proper subject of these apparent ascriptions, that states of consciousness belong to, or are states of, anything.

That Descartes held the first of these views is well enough known. When we speak of a person, we are really referring to one or both of two distinct substances (two substances of different types), each of which has its own appropriate type of states and properties; and none of the properties or states of either can be a property or state of the other. States of consciousness belong to one of these substances, and not to the other. I shall say no more about the Cartesian view at the moment—what I have to say about it will emerge later on—except to note again that while it escapes one of our questions, it does not escape, but indeed invites, the other: "Why are one's states of consciousness *ascribed* at all, to *any* subject?"

The second of these views I shall call the "no-ownership" or "no-subject" doctrine of the self. Whether or not anyone has explicitly held this view, it is worth reconstructing, or constructing, in outline.[1] For the errors into which it falls are instructive. The "no-ownership" theorist may be presumed to start his explanations with facts of the sort which illustrate the unique causal position of a certain material body in a person's experience. The theorist maintains that the uniqueness of this body is sufficient to give rise to the idea that one's experiences can be ascribed to some particular individual thing, can be said to be possessed by, or owned by, that thing. This idea, he thinks, though infelicitously and misleadingly expressed in terms of ownership, would have some validity, would make some sort of sense, so long as we thought of this individual thing, the possessor of the experiences, as the body itself. So long as we thought in this way, then to ascribe a particular state of consciousness to this body, this individual thing, would at least be to say something contingent, something that might be, or might have been, false. It might have been a misascription; for the experience in question might be, or might have been, causally dependent on the state of some other body; in the present admissible, though infelicitous, sense of "belong", it might have belonged to some other individual thing. But now, the theorist suggests, one becomes confused: one slides from this admissible, though infelicitous, sense in which one's experiences may be said to belong to, or be possessed by, some particular thing, to a wholly inadmissible and empty sense of these

---

[1] The evidence that Wittgenstein at one time held such a view is to be found in the third of Moore's articles in *Mind* on "Wittgenstein's Lectures in 1930–33" (*Mind*, 1955, especially pp. 13–14). He is reported to have held that the use of "I" was utterly different in the case of "I have a tooth-ache" or "I see a red patch" from its use in the case of "I've got a bad tooth" or "I've got a matchbox." He thought that there were two uses of "I" and that in one of them "I" was replaceable by "this body". So far the view might be Cartesian. But he also said that in the other use (the use exemplified by "I have a tooth-ache" as opposed to "I have a bad tooth"), the "I" *does not denote a possessor*, and that no ego is involved in thinking or in having tooth-ache; and referred with apparent approval to Lichtenberg's dictum that, instead of saying "I think," we (or Descartes!) ought to say "There is a thought" (i.e., "Es denkt").

The attribution of such a view to Schlick would have to rest on his article "Meaning and Verification," Pt. V (*Readings in Philosophical Analysis*, H. Feigl and W. Sellars, eds.). Like Wittgenstein, Schlick quotes Lichtenberg, and then goes on to say: "Thus we see that unless we choose to call our body the owner or bearer of the data [the data of immediate experience]—which seems to be a rather misleading expression—we have to say that the data have no owner or bearer." The full import of Schlick's article is, however, obscure to me, and it is quite likely that a false impression is given by the quotation of a single sentence. I shall say merely that I have drawn on Schlick's article in constructing the case of my hypothetical "no-subject" theorist; but shall not claim to be representing his views.

Lichtenberg's anti-Cartesian dictum is, as the subsequent argument will show, one that I endorse, if properly used. But it seems to have been repeated, without being understood, by many of Descartes' critics.

The evidence that Wittgenstein and Schlick ever held a "no-subject" view seems indecisive, since it is possible that the relevant remarks are intended as criticisms of a Cartesian view rather than as expositions of the true view.

expressions; and in this new and inadmissible sense, the particular thing which is supposed to possess the experiences is not thought of as a body, but as something else, say an ego.

Suppose we call the first type of possession, which is really a certain kind of causal dependence, "having$_1$", and the second type of possession, "having$_2$"; and call the individual of the first type "B" and the supposed individual of the second type "E". Then the difference is that while it is genuinely a contingent matter that *all my experiences are had$_1$ by B*, it appears as a necessary truth that *all my experiences are had$_2$ by E*. But the belief in E and in having$_2$ is an illusion. Only those things whose ownership is logically transferable can be owned at all. So experiences are not owned by anything except in the dubious sense of being causally dependent on the state of a particular body. This is at least a genuine relationship to a thing, in that they might have stood in it to another thing. Since the whole function of E was to own experiences in a logically non-transferable sense of "own", and since experiences are not owned by anything in this sense, for there is no such sense of "own", E must be eliminated from the picture altogether. It only came in because of a confusion.

I think it must be clear that this account of the matter, though it contains *some* of the facts, is not coherent. It is not coherent, in that one who holds it is forced to make use of that sense of possession of which he denies the existence, in presenting his case for the denial. When he tries to state the contingent fact, which he thinks gives rise to the illusion of the "ego," he has to state it in some such form as "All *my* experiences are had$_1$ by (uniquely dependent on the state of) body B." For any attempt to eliminate the "my", or some other expression with a similar possessive force, would yield something that was not a contingent fact at all. The proposition that *all* experiences are causally dependent on the state of a single body B, for example, is just false. The theorist means to speak of all the experiences *had by a certain person* being contingently so dependent. And the theorist cannot consistently argue that "all the experiences of person P" *means the same thing* as "all experiences contingently dependent on a certain body B"; for then his proposition would not be contingent, as his theory requires, but analytic. He must mean to be speaking of some class of experiences of the members of which it is in fact contingently true that they are all dependent on body B. And the defining characteristic of this class is in fact that they are "*my* experiences" or "the experiences *of* some person," where the sense of "possession" is the one he calls into question.

This internal incoherence is a serious matter when it is a question of denying what prima facie is the case: that is, that one does genuinely ascribe one's states of consciousness to something, viz., oneself, and that this kind of ascription is precisely such as the theorist finds unsatisfactory, i.e., is such that it does not seem to make sense to suggest, for example, that the identical pain which was in fact one's own might have been another's. We do not have to seek far in order to understand the place of this logically non-transferable kind of ownership in our general scheme of thought. For if we think of the requirements of identifying reference, in speech, to *particular* states of consciousness, or private experiences, we see that such particulars cannot be thus identifyingly referred to except as the states or experiences *of* some identified *person*. States, or experiences, one might say, *owe* their identity as particulars to the identity of the person whose states or experiences they are. And from this it follows immediately that if they can be identified as particular states or experiences at all, they must be possessed or ascribable in just that way which the no-ownership theorist ridicules, i.e., in such a way that it is logically impossible that a particular state or experience in fact possessed by someone should have been possessed by anyone else. The requirements of identity rule out logical transferability of ownership. So the theorist could maintain his position only by denying that we could ever refer to particular states or experiences at all. And *this* position is ridiculous.

We may notice, even now, a possible connection between the no-ownership doctrine and the Cartesian position. The latter is, straightforwardly enough, a dualism of two subjects (two types of subject). The former could, a little paradoxically, be called a dualism too: a dualism of one subject (the body) and one non-subject. We might surmise that the second dualism, paradoxically so called, arises out of the first dualism, nonparadoxically so called; in other words, that if we try to think of that to which one's states of consciousness are ascribed as something utterly different from that to which certain corporeal characteristics are ascribed, then indeed it becomes difficult to see why states of consciousness should be ascribed, thought of as belonging to, anything at all. And when we think of this possibility, we may also think of another: viz., that both the Cartesian and the no-ownership theorist are profoundly wrong in holding, as each must, that there are two uses of "I" in one of which it denotes something which it does not denote in the other.

III

The no-ownership theorist fails to take account of all the facts. He takes account of some of them. He implies, correctly, that the unique position or role of a single body in one's experience is not a sufficient explanation of the fact that one's experiences, or states of consciousness, are ascribed to something which *has* them, with that peculiar non-transferable kind of possession which is here in question. It may be a necessary part of the explanation, but it is not, by itself, a sufficient explanation. The theorist, as we have seen, goes on to suggest that it is perhaps a sufficient explanation of something else: viz., of our confusedly and mistakenly *thinking* that states of consciousness are to be ascribed to something in this special way. And this suggestion, as we have seen, is incoherent: for it involves the denial that someone's states of consciousness are anyone's. We avoid the incoherence of this denial, while agreeing that the special role of a single body in someone's experience does not suffice to explain why that experience should be ascribed to anybody. The fact that there is this special role does not, by itself, give a sufficient reason why what we think of as a subject of experience should have any use for the conception of himself as such a subject.

When I say that the no-ownership theorist's account fails through not reckoning with all the facts, I have in mind a very simple but, in this question, a very central, thought: viz., that it is a necessary condition of one's ascribing states of consciousness, experiences, to oneself, in the way one does, that one should also ascribe them (or be prepared to ascribe them) to others who are not oneself.[2] This means not less than it says. It means, for example, that the ascribing phrases should be used in just the same sense when the subject is another, as when the subject is oneself. Of course the thought that this is so gives no trouble to the non-philosopher: the thought, for example, that "in pain" means the same whether one says "I am in pain" or "He is in pain." The dictionaries do not give two sets of meanings for every expression which describes a state of consciousness: a first-person meaning, and a second- and third-person meaning. But to the philosopher this thought has given trouble; indeed it has. How could the sense be the same when the method of verification was so different in the two cases—or, rather, when there *was* a method of verification in the one case (the case of others) and not, properly speaking, in the other case (the case of oneself)? Or, again, how can it be right to talk of *ascribing* in the case of oneself? For surely there can be a question of ascribing only if there is or could be a question of identifying that to which the ascription is made? And though there may be a question of identifying the one who is in pain when that one is another, how can there be such a question when that one is oneself? But this last query answers itself as soon as we remember that we speak primarily to others, for the information of others. In one sense, indeed, there is no question of my having to *tell who it is* who is in pain, when I am. In another sense I may have to *tell who it is*, i.e., to let others know who it is.

What I have just said explains, perhaps, how one may properly be said to ascribe states of consciousness to oneself, given that one ascribes them to others. But how is it that one can ascribe them to others? Well, one thing is certain: that *if* the things one ascribes states of consciousness to, in ascribing them to others, are thought of as a set of Cartesian egos to which *only* private experiences can, in correct logical grammar, be ascribed, *then* this question is unanswerable and this problem insoluble. If, in identifying the things to which states of consciousness are to be ascribed, private experiences are to be all one has to go on, then, just for the very same reason as that for which there is, from one's own point of view, no question of telling

[2] I can imagine an objection to the unqualified form of this statement, an objection which might be put as follows. Surely the idea of a uniquely applicable predicate (a predicate which *in fact* belongs to only one individual) is not absurd. And, if it is not, then surely the most that can be claimed is that a necessary condition of one's ascribing predicates of a certain class to one individual (oneself) is that one should be prepared, or ready, on appropriate occasions, to ascribe them to other individuals, and hence that one should have a conception of what those appropriate occasions for ascribing them would be; but not, necessarily, that one should actually do so on any occasion.

The shortest way with the objection is to admit it, or at least to refrain from disputing it; for the lesser claim is all that the argument strictly requires, though it is slightly simpler to conduct it on the basis of the larger claim. But it is well to point out further that we are not speaking of a single predicate, or merely of some group or other of predicates, but of the whole of an enormous class of predicates such that the applicability of those predicates or their negations determines a major logical type or category of individuals. To insist, at this level, on the distinction between the lesser and the larger claims is to carry the distinction over from a level at which it is clearly correct to a level at which it may well appear idle or, possibly, senseless.

The main point here is a purely logical one: the idea of a predicate is correlative with that of a range of distinguishable individuals of which the predicate can be significantly, though not necessarily truly, affirmed.

that a private experience is one's own, there is also no question of telling that a private experience is another's. All private experiences, all states of consciousness, will be mine, i.e., no one's. To put it briefly: one can ascribe states of consciousness to oneself only if one can ascribe them to others; one can ascribe them to others only if one can identify other subjects of experience; and one cannot identify others if one can identify them *only* as subjects of experience, possessors of states of consciousness.

It might be objected that this way with Cartesianism is too short. After all, there is no difficulty about distinguishing bodies from one another, no difficulty about identifying bodies. And does not this give us an indirect way of identifying subjects of experience, while preserving the Cartesian mode? Can we not identify such a subject as, for example, "the subject that stands to that body in the same special relation as I stand to this one"; or, in other words, "the subject of those experiences which stand in the same unique causal relation to body N as *my* experiences stand to body M"? But this suggestion is useless. It requires me to have noted that *my* experiences stand in a special relation to body M, when it is just the right to speak of *my* experiences at all that is in question. (It requires me to have noted that *my* experiences stand in a special relation to body M; but it requires me to have noted this as a condition of being able to identify other subjects of experience, i.e., as a condition of having the idea of myself as a subject of experience, i.e., as a condition of thinking of any experience as *mine*.) So long as we persist in talking, in the mode of this explanation, of experiences on the one hand, and bodies on the other, the most I may be allowed to have noted is that experiences, *all* experiences, stand in a special relation to body M, that body M is unique in just this way, that this is what makes body M unique among bodies. (This "most" is, perhaps, too much—because of the presence of the word "experiences".) The proffered explanation runs: "Another subject of experience is distinguished and identified as the subject of those experiences which stand in the same unique causal relationship to body N as *my* experiences stand to body M." And the objection is: "But what is the word 'my' doing in this explanation? (It could not get on without it.)"

What we have to acknowledge, in order to begin to free ourselves from these difficulties, is the *primitiveness* of the concept of a person. What I mean by the concept of a person is the concept of a type of entity such that *both* predicates ascribing states of consciousness *and* predicates ascribing corporeal characteristics, a physical situation, etc. are equally applicable to a single individual of that single type. And what I mean by saying that this concept is primitive can be put in a number of ways. One way is to return to those two questions I asked earlier: viz., (1) why are states of consciousness ascribed to anything at all? and (2) why are they ascribed to the very same thing as certain corporeal characteristics, a certain physical situation, etc.? I remarked at the beginning that it was not to be supposed that the answers to these questions were independent of each other. And now I shall say that they are connected in this way: that a necessary condition of states of consciousness being ascribed at all is that they should be ascribed to the *very same things* as certain corporeal characteristics, a certain physical situation, etc. That is to say, states of consciousness could not be ascribed at all, *unless* they were ascribed to persons, in the sense I have claimed for this word. We are tempted to think of a person as a sort of compound of two kinds of subject—a subject of experiences (a pure consciousness, an ego), on the one hand, and a subject of corporeal attributes on the other.

Many questions arise when we think in this way. But, in particular, when we ask ourselves how we come to frame, to get a use for, the concept of this compound of two subjects, the picture—if we are honest and careful—is apt to change from the picture of two subjects to the picture of one subject and one non-subject. For it becomes impossible to see how we could come by the idea of different, distinguishable, identifiable subjects of experiences— different consciousnesses—*if this idea is thought of as logically primitive*, as a logical ingredient in the compound idea of a person, the latter being composed of two subjects. For there could never be any question of assigning an experience, as such, to any subject other than oneself; and therefore never any question of assigning it to oneself either, never any question of ascribing it to a subject at all. So the concept of the pure individual consciousness—the pure ego—is a concept that cannot exist; or, at least, cannot exist as a primary concept in terms of which the concept of a person can be explained or analyzed. It can only exist, if at all, as a secondary, nonprimitive concept, which itself is to be explained, analyzed, in terms of the concept of a person. It was the entity corresponding to this illusory primary concept of the pure consciousness, the ego-substance, for which Hume was seeking, or ironically pretending to seek, when he looked into himself, and complained that he could never discover himself without a perception and could never discover anything but the perception. More seriously—and this time there was no irony, but a confusion, a Nemesis of confusion for Hume—it was this entity of which Hume vainly sought for the principle of unity, confessing himself perplexed and defeated; sought vainly because there is no principle of unity where there is no principle of differentiation. It was this, too, to which Kant, more perspicacious here than Hume, accorded a purely formal ("analytic") unity: the unity of the "I think" that accompanies all my perceptions and therefore might just as well accompany none. And finally it is this, perhaps, of which Wittgenstein spoke when he said of the subject, first, that there is no such thing, and, second, that it is not a part of the world, but its limit.

So, then, the word "I" never refers to this, the pure subject. But this does not mean, as the no-ownership theorist must think and as Wittgenstein, at least at one period, seemed to think, that "I" in some cases does not refer at all. It refers, because I am a person among others. And the predicates which would, *per impossibile*, belong to the pure subject if it could be referred to, belong properly to the person to which "I" does refer.

The concept of a person is logically prior to that of an individual consciousness. The concept of a person is not to be analyzed as that of an animated body or of an embodied anima. This is not to say that the concept of a pure individual consciousness might not have a logically secondary existence, if one thinks, or finds, it desirable. We speak of a dead person—a body—and in the same secondary way we might at least think of a disembodied person, retaining the logical benefit of individuality from having been a person.[3]

---

[3] A little further thought will show how limited this concession is. But I shall not discuss the question now.

IV

It is important to realize the full extent of the acknowledgment one is making in acknowledging the logical primitiveness of the concept of a person. Let me rehearse briefly the stages of the argument. There would be no question of ascribing one's own states of consciousness, or experiences, to anything, unless one also ascribed states of consciousness, or experiences, to other individual entities of the same logical type as that thing to which one ascribes one's own states of consciousness. The condition of reckoning oneself as a subject of such predicates is that one should also reckon others as subjects of such predicates. The condition, in turn, of this being possible, is that one should be able to distinguish from one another (pick out, identify) different subjects of such predicates, i.e., different individuals of the type concerned. And the condition, in turn, of this being possible is that the individuals concerned, including oneself, should be of a certain unique type: of a type, namely, such that to each individual of that type there *must* be ascribed, or ascribable, *both* states of consciousness *and* corporeal characteristics. But this characterization of the type is still very opaque and does not at all clearly bring out what is involved. To bring this out, I must make a rough division, into two, of the kinds of predicates properly applied to individuals of this type. The first kind of predicate consists of those which are also properly applied to material bodies to which we would not dream of applying predicates ascribing states of consciousness. I will call this first kind M-predicates: and they include things like "weighs 10 stone", "is in the drawing room", and so on. The second kind consists of all the other predicates we apply to persons. These I shall call P-predicates. And P-predicates, of course, will be very various. They will include things like "is smiling", "is going for a walk", as well as things like "is in pain", "is thinking hard", "believes in God", and so on.

So far I have said that the concept of a person is to be understood as the concept of a type of entity such that *both* predicates ascribing states of consciousness *and* predicates ascribing corporeal characteristics, a physical situation, etc. are equally applicable to an individual entity of that type. And all I have said about the meaning of saying that this concept is primitive is that it is not to be analyzed in a certain way or ways. We are not, for example, to think of it as a secondary kind of entity in relation to two primary kinds, viz., a particular consciousness and a particular human body. I implied also that the Cartesian error is just a special case of a more general error, present in a different form in theories of the no-ownership type, of thinking of the designations, or apparent designations, of persons as *not* denoting precisely the same thing, or entity, for all kinds of predicate ascribed to the entity designated. That is, if we are to avoid the general form of this error we must *not* think of "I" or "Smith" as suffering from type-ambiguity. (If we want to locate type-ambiguity somewhere, we would do better to locate it in certain predicates like "is in the drawing room", "was hit by a stone", etc., and say they mean one thing when applied to material objects and another when applied to persons.)

This is all I have so far said or implied about the meaning of saying that the concept of a person is primitive. What has to be brought out further is what the implications of saying this are as regards the logical character of those predicates in which we ascribe states of consciousness. And for this purpose we may well consider P-predicates in general. For though not all P-predicates are what we should call "predicates ascribing states of consciousness" (for example, "going for a walk" is not), they may be said to have this in common, that they imply the possession of consciousness on the part of that to which they are ascribed.

What then are the consequences of this view as regards the character of P-predicates? I think they are these. Clearly there is no sense in talking of identifiable individuals of a special type, a type, namely, such that they possess both M-predicates and P-predicates, unless there is in principle some way of telling, with regard to any individual of that type, and any P-predicate, whether that individual possesses that P-predicate. And, in the case of at least some P-predicates, the ways of telling must constitute in some sense logically adequate kinds of criteria for the ascription of the P-predicate. For suppose in no case did these ways of telling constitute logically adequate kinds of criteria. Then we should have to think of the relation between the ways of telling and what the P-predicate ascribes (or a part of what it ascribes) always in the following way: we should have to think of the ways of telling as *signs* of the presence, in the individual concerned, of this different thing (the state of consciousness). But then we could only know that the way of telling was a sign of the presence of the different thing ascribed by the P-predicate, by the observation of correlations between the two. But this observation we could each make only in one case, namely, our own. And now we are back in the position of the defender of Cartesianism, who thought our way with it was too short. For what, now, does "our own case" mean? There is no sense in the idea of ascribing states of consciousness to oneself, or at all, unless the ascriber already knows how to ascribe at least some states of consciousness to others. So he cannot (or cannot generally) argue "from his own case" to conclusions about how to do this; for unless he already knows how to do this, he has no conception of *his own case*, or any *case* (i.e., any subject of experiences). Instead, he just has evidence that pain, etc. may be expected when a certain body is affected in certain ways and not when others are.

The conclusion here is, of course, not new. What I have said is that one ascribes P-predicates to others on the strength of observation of their behavior; and that the behavior criteria one goes on are not just signs of the presence of what is meant by the P-predicate, but are criteria of a logically adequate kind for the ascription of the P-predicate. On behalf of this conclusion, however, I am claiming that it follows from a consideration of the conditions necessary for any ascription of states of consciousness to anything. The point is not that we must accept this conclusion in order to avoid skepticism, but that we must accept it in order to explain the existence of the conceptual scheme in terms of which the skeptical problem is stated. But once the conclusion is accepted, the skeptical problem does not arise. (And so with the generality of skeptical problems: their statement involves the pretended acceptance of a conceptual scheme and at the same time the silent repudiation of one of the conditions of its existence. This is why they are, in the terms in which they are stated, insoluble.) But this is only half the picture about P-predicates.

Now let us turn to the other half. For of course it is true, at least of some important classes of P-predicates, that when one ascribes them to oneself, one does not do so on the strength of observation of those behavior criteria on the strength of which one ascribes them to others. This is not true of all P-predicates. It is not, in general, true of those which carry assessments of character and capability: these, when self-ascribed, are in general ascribed on the same kind of basis as that on which they are ascribed to others. And of those P-predicates of which it is true that one does not generally ascribe them to oneself on the basis of the criteria on the strength of which one ascribes them to others, there are many of which it is also true that their ascription is liable to correction by the self-ascriber on this basis. But there remain many cases in which one has an entirely adequate basis for ascribing a P-predicate to oneself, and yet in which this basis is quite distinct from those on which one ascribes the predicate to another. (Thus one says, reporting a present state of mind or feeling: "I feel tired, am depressed, am in pain.") How can this fact be reconciled with the doctrine that the criteria on the strength of which one ascribes P-predicates to others are criteria of a logically adequate kind for this ascription?

The apparent difficulty of bringing about this reconciliation may tempt us in many directions. It may tempt us, for example, to deny that these self-ascriptions are really ascriptions at all; to *assimilate* first-person ascriptions of states of consciousness to those other forms of behavior which constitute criteria on the basis of which one person ascribes P-predicates to another. This device seems to avoid the difficulty; it is not, in all cases, entirely inappropriate. But it obscures the facts, and is needless. It is merely a sophisticated form of failure to recognize the special character of P-predicates (or at least of a crucial class of P-predicates). For just as there is not (in general) one primary process of learning, or teaching oneself, an inner private meaning for predicates of this class, then another process of learning to apply such predicates to others on the strength of a correlation, noted in one's own case, with certain forms of behavior, so—and equally—there is not (in general) one primary process of learning to apply such predicates to others on the strength of behavior criteria, and then another process of acquiring the secondary technique of exhibiting a new form of behavior, viz., first-person P-utterances. Both these pictures are refusals to acknowledge the unique logical character of the predicates concerned.

Suppose we write 'Px' as the general form of propositional function of such a predicate. Then according to the first picture, the expression which primarily replaces "x" in this form is "I", the first-person singular pronoun; its uses with other replacements are secondary, derivative, and shaky. According to the second picture, on the other hand, the primary replacements of "x" in this form are "he", "that person", etc., and its use with "I" is secondary, peculiar, not a true ascriptive use. But it is essential to the character of these predicates that they have both first- and third-person ascriptive uses, that they are both self-ascribable otherwise than on the basis of observation of the behavior of the subject of them, and other-ascribable on the basis of behavior criteria. To learn their use is to learn both aspects of their use. In order to *have* this type of concept, one must be both a self-ascriber and an other-ascriber of such predicates, and must see every other as a self-ascriber. And in order to *understand* this type of concept, one must acknowledge that there is a kind of predicate which is unambiguously and adequately ascribable *both* on the basis of observation of the subject of the predicate *and* not on this basis (independently of observation of the subject): the second case is the case where the ascriber is also the subject. If there were no concepts answering to the characterization I have just given, we should indeed have no philosophical problem about the soul; but equally we should not have *our* concept of a person.

To put the point—with a certain unavoidable crudity—in terms of one particular concept of this class, say, that of depression, we speak of behaving in a depressed way (of depressed behavior) and also of feeling depressed (of a feeling of depression). One is inclined to argue that feelings can be felt, but not observed, and behavior can be observed, but not felt, and that therefore there must be room here to drive in a logical wedge. But the concept of depression spans the place where one wants to drive it in. We might say, in order for there to be such a concept as that of X's depression, the depression which X has, the concept must cover both what is felt, but not observed, by X and what may be observed, but not felt, by others than X (for all values of X). But it is perhaps better to say: X's depression *is* something, one and the same thing, which is felt but not observed by X and observed but not felt by others than X. (And, of course, what can be observed can also be faked or disguised.) To refuse to accept this is to refuse to accept the structure of the language in which we talk about depression. That is, in a sense, all right. One might give up talking; or devise, perhaps, a different structure in terms of which to soliloquize. What is not all right is simultaneously to pretend to accept that structure and to refuse to accept it; i.e., to couch one's rejection in the language of that structure.

It is in this light that we must see some of the familiar philosophical difficulties in the topic of the mind. For some of them spring from just such a failure to admit, or fully appreciate, the character which I have been claiming for at least some P-predicates. It is not seen that these predicates could not have either aspect of their use (the self-ascriptive and the non-self-ascriptive) without having the other aspect. Instead, one aspect of their use is taken as self-sufficient, which it could not be, and then the other aspect appears as problematical. And so we oscillate between philosophical skepticism and philosophical behaviorism. When we take the self-ascriptive aspect of the use of some P-predicate (say, "depressed") as primary, then a logical gap seems to open between the criteria on the strength of which we say that another is depressed, and the actual state of depression. What we do not realize is that if this logical gap is allowed to open, then it swallows not only his depression, but our depression as well. For if the logical gap exists, then depressed behavior, however much there is of it, is no more than a sign of depression. And it can become a sign of depression only because of an observed correlation between it and depression. But whose depression? Only mine, one is tempted to say. But if *only* mine, then *not* mine at all. The skeptical position customarily represents the crossing of the logical gap as at best a shaky inference. But the point is that not even the syntax of the premises of the inference exists if the gap exists.

If, on the other hand, we take the other-ascriptive uses of these predicates as self-sufficient, we may come to think that all there is in the meaning of these predicates, as predicates, is the criteria on the strength of which we ascribe them to others. Does this not follow from the denial of the logical gap? It does not follow. To think that it does is to forget the self-ascriptive use of these predicates, to forget that we have to do with a class of predicates to the meaning of which it is essential that they should be both self-ascribable and other-ascribable to the same individual, when self-ascriptions are not made on the observational basis on which other-ascriptions are made, but on another basis. It is not that these predicates have two kinds of meaning. Rather, it is essential to the single kind of meaning that they do have that both ways of ascribing them should be perfectly in order.

If one is playing a game of cards, the distinctive markings of a certain card constitute a logically adequate criterion for calling it, say, the Queen of Hearts; but, in calling it this, in the context of the game, one is also ascribing to it properties over and above the possession of those markings. The predicate gets its meaning from the whole structure of the game. So it is with the language which ascribes P-predicates. To say that the criteria on the strength of which we ascribe P-predicates to others are of a logically adequate kind for this ascription is not to say that all there is to the ascriptive meaning of these predicates is these criteria. To say this is to forget that they are P-predicates, to forget the rest of the language-structure to which they belong.

V

Now our perplexities may take a different form, the form of the question "But how can one ascribe to oneself, not on the basis of observation, *the very same thing* that others may have, on the basis of observation, a logically adequate reason for ascribing to one?" And this question may be absorbed in a wider one, which might be phrased: "How are P-predicates possible?" or "How is the concept of a person possible?" This is the question by which we replace those two earlier questions, viz.: "Why are states of consciousness ascribed at all, ascribed to anything?" and "Why are they ascribed to the very same thing as certain corporeal characteristics, etc.?" For the answer to these two initial questions is to be found nowhere else but in the admission of the primitiveness of the concept of a person, and hence of the unique character of P-predicates. So residual perplexities have to frame themselves in this new way. For when we have acknowledged the primitiveness of the concept of a person and, with it, the unique character of P-predicates, we may still want to ask what it is in the natural facts that makes it intelligible that we should have this concept, and to ask this in the hope of a non-trivial answer.[4] I do not pretend to be able to satisfy this demand at all fully. But I may mention two very different things which might count as beginnings or fragments of an answer.

And, first, I think a beginning can be made by moving a certain class of P-predicates to a central position in the picture. They are predicates, roughly, which involve doing something, which clearly imply intention or a state of mind or at least consciousness in general, and which indicate a characteristic pattern, or range of patterns, of bodily movement, while not indicating at all precisely any very definite sensation or experience. I mean such things as "going for a walk", "furling a rope", "playing ball", "writing a letter". Such

---

[4] I mean, in the hope of an answer which does not *merely* say: Well, there are people in the world.

predicates have the interesting characteristic of many P-predicates that one does not, in general, ascribe them to oneself on the strength of observation, whereas one does ascribe them to others on the strength of observation. But, in the case of these predicates, one feels minimal reluctance to concede that what is ascribed in these two different ways is the same. And this is because of the marked dominance of a fairly definite pattern of bodily movement in what they ascribe, and the marked absence of any distinctive experience. They release us from the idea that the only things we can know about without observation, or inference, or both, are private experiences; we can know also, without telling by either of these means, about the present and future movements of a body. Yet bodily movements are certainly also things we can know about by observation and inference.

Among the things that we observe, as opposed to the things we know without observation, are the movements of bodies similar to that about which we have knowledge not based on observation. It is important that we understand such observed movements; they bear on and condition our own. And in fact we understand them, we interpret them, only by seeing them as elements in just such plans or schemes of action as those of which we know the present course and future development without observation of the relevant present movements. But this is to say that we see such movements (the observed movements of others) as *actions*, that we interpret them in terms of intention, that we see them as movements of individuals of a type to which also belongs that individual whose present and future movements we know about without observation; that we see others, as self-ascribers, not on the basis of observations, of what we ascribe to them on this basis.

Of course these remarks are not intended to suggest how the "problem of other minds" could be solved, or our beliefs about others given a general philosophical "justification." I have already argued that such a "solution" or "justification" is impossible, that the demand for it cannot be coherently stated. Nor are these remarks intended as a priori genetic psychology. They are simply intended to help to make it seem intelligible to us, at this stage in the history of the philosophy of this subject, that we have the conceptual scheme we have. What I am suggesting is that it is easier to understand how we can see each other (and ourselves) as persons, if we think first of the fact that we act, and act on each other, and act in accordance with a common human nature. "To see each other as persons" is a lot of things; but not a lot of separate and unconnected things. The class of P-predicates that I have moved into the center of the picture are not unconnectedly there, detached from others irrelevant to them. On the contrary, they are inextricably bound up with the others, interwoven with them. The topic of the mind does not divide into unconnected subjects.

I spoke just now of a common human nature. But there is also a sense in which a condition of the existence of the conceptual scheme we have is that human nature should not be common, should not be, that is, a community nature. Philosophers used to discuss the question of whether there was, or could be, such a thing as a "group mind." And for some the idea had a peculiar fascination, while to others it seemed utterly absurd and nonsensical and at the same time, curiously enough, pernicious. It is easy to see why these last found it pernicious: they found something horrible in the thought that people should cease to have toward individual persons the kind of attitudes that they did have, and instead have attitudes in some way analogous to those toward groups; and that they might cease to decide individual courses of action for themselves and instead merely participate in corporate activities. But their finding it pernicious showed that they understood the idea they claimed to be absurd only too well. The fact that we find it natural to individuate as persons the members of a certain class of what might also be individuated as organic bodies does not mean that such a conceptual scheme is inevitable for any class of beings not utterly unlike ourselves.

Might we not construct the idea of a special kind of social world in which the concept of an individual person has no employment, whereas an analogous concept for groups does have employment? Think, to begin with, of certain aspects of actual human existence. Think, for example, of two groups of human beings engaged in some competitive but corporate activity, such as battle, for which they have been exceedingly well trained. We may even suppose that orders are superfluous, though information is passed. It is easy to imagine that, while absorbed in such activity, the members of the groups make no references to individual persons at all, have no use for personal names or pronouns. They do, however, refer to the groups and apply to them predicates analogous to those predicates ascribing purposive activity which we normally apply to individual persons. They may, *in fact*, use in such circumstances the plural forms "we" and "they"; but these are not genuine plurals, they are plurals without a singular, such as we use in sentences like these: "We have taken the citadel," "We have lost the game." They may also refer to elements in the group, to members of the group, but exclusively in terms which get their sense from the parts played by these elements in the corporate activity. (Thus we sometimes refer to what are in fact persons as "stroke" or "tackle".)

When we think of such cases, we see that we ourselves, over a part of our social lives—not, I am thankful to say, a very large part—do operate conceptual schemes in which the idea of the individual person has no place, in which its place is taken, so to speak, by that of a group. But might we not think of communities or groups such that this part of the lives of their members was the dominant part—or was the whole? It sometimes happens, with groups of human beings, that, as we say, their members think, feel, and act "as one." The point I wish to make is that a condition for the existence, the use, of the concept of an individual person is that this should happen *only sometimes*.

It is absolutely useless to say, at this point: But all the same, even if this happened all the time, every member of the group would have an individual consciousness, would be an individual subject of experience. The point is, once more, that there is no sense in speaking of the individual consciousness just as such, of the individual subject of experience just as such: for there is no way of identifying such pure entities.[5] It is true, of course, that in suggesting this fantasy, I have taken our concept of an individual person as a starting point. It is this fact which makes the useless reaction a natural one. But suppose, instead, I had made the following suggestion: that each part of the human body, each organ and each member, had an individual conscious-

[5] More accurately: their identification is necessarily secondary to the identification of persons.

ness, was a separate center of experiences. This, in the same way, but more obviously, would be a useless suggestion. Then imagine all the intermediate cases, for instance these. There is a class of moving natural objects, divided into groups, each group exhibiting the same characteristic pattern of activity. Within each group there are certain differentiations of appearance accompanying differentiations of function, and in particular there is one member of each group with a distinctive appearance. Cannot one imagine different sets of observations which might lead us, in the one case, to think of the particular member as the spokesman of the group, as its mouthpiece; and in the other case to think of him as its mouth, to think of the group as a single *scattered* body? The point is that as soon as we adopt the latter way of thinking then we want to drop the former; we are no longer influenced by the human analogy in its first form, but only in its second; and we no longer want to say: "Perhaps the members have consciousness." To understand the movement of our thought here, we need only remember the startling ambiguity of the phrase "a body and its members".

VI

I shall not pursue this attempt at explanation any further. What I have been mainly arguing for is that we should acknowledge the logical primitiveness of the concept of a person and, with this, the unique logical character of certain predicates. Once this is acknowledged, certain traditional philosophical problems are seen not to be problems at all. In particular, the problem that seems to have perplexed Hume[6] does not exist—the problem of the principle of unity, of identity, of the particular consciousness, of the particular subject of "perceptions" (experiences) considered as a primary particular. There is no such problem and no such principle. If there were such a principle, then each of us would have to apply it in order to decide whether any contemporary experience of his was his or someone else's; and there is no sense in this suggestion. (This is not to deny, of course, that one *person* may be unsure of his own identity in some way, may be unsure, for example, whether some particular action, or series of actions, had been performed by him. Then he uses the same methods [the same in principle] to resolve the doubt about himself as anyone else uses to resolve the same doubt about him. And these methods simply involve the application of the ordinary criteria for *personal* identity. There remains the question of what exactly these criteria are, what their relative weights are, etc.; but, once disentangled from spurious questions, this is one of the easier problems in philosophy.)

Where Hume erred, or seems to have erred, both Kant and Wittgenstein had the better insight. Perhaps neither always expressed it in the happiest way. For Kant's doctrine that the "analytic unity of consciousness" neither requires nor entails any principle of unity is not as clear as one could wish. And Wittgenstein's remarks (at one time) to the effect that the data of consciousness are not owned, that "I" as used by Jones, in speaking of his own feelings, etc., does not refer to what "Jones" as used by another refers to, seem needlessly to flout the conceptual scheme we actually employ. It is

[6] Cf. the Appendix to the *Treatise of Human Nature*.

needlessly paradoxical to deny, or seem to deny, that when Smith says "Jones has a pain" and Jones says "I have a pain," they are talking about the same entity and saying the same thing about it, needlessly paradoxical to deny that Jones can *confirm* that he has a pain. Instead of denying that self-ascribed states of consciousness are really ascribed at all, it is more in harmony with our actual ways of talking to say: For each user of the language, there is just one person in ascribing to whom states of consciousness he does not need to use the criteria of the observed behavior of that person (though he does not necessarily not do so); and that person is himself. This remark at least respects the structure of the conceptual scheme we employ, without precluding further examination of it.

Knowledge of Other Minds

11

THE ARGUMENT FROM ANALOGY

Bertrand Russell

The postulates hitherto considered have been such as are required for knowledge of the physical world. Broadly speaking, they have led us to admit a certain degree of knowledge as to the space-time structure of the physical world, while leaving us completely agnostic as regards its qualitative character. But where other human beings are concerned, we feel that we know more than this; we are convinced that other people have thoughts and feelings that are qualitatively fairly similar to our own. We are not content to think that we know only the space-time structure of our friends' minds, or their capacity for initiating causal chains that end in sensations of our own. A philosopher might pretend to think that he knew only this, but let him get cross with his wife and you will see that he does not regard her as a mere spatio-temporal edifice of which he knows the logical properties but not a glimmer of the intrinsic character. We are therefore justified in inferring that his skepticism is professional rather than sincere.

The problem with which we are concerned is the following. We observe in ourselves such occurrences as remembering, reasoning, feeling pleasure, and feeling pain. We think that sticks and stones do not have these experiences, but that other people do. Most of us have no doubt that the higher animals feel pleasure and pain, though I was once assured by a fisherman that "Fish have no sense nor feeling." I failed to find out how he had acquired this knowledge. Most people would disagree with him, but would be doubtful about oysters and starfish. However this may be, common sense

From Bertrand Russell, *Human Knowledge: Its Scope and Limits* (London and New York: 1948), Part VI, Chap. VIII, pp. 482–486. Copyright, 1948, by Bertrand Russell. Reprinted by permission of Simon & Schuster, Inc. and George Allen & Unwin Ltd.

admits an increasing doubtfulness as we descend in the animal kingdom, but as regards human beings it admits no doubt.

It is clear that belief in the minds of others requires some postulate that is not required in physics, since physics can be content with a knowledge of structure. My present purpose is to suggest what this further postulate may be.

It is clear that we must appeal to something that may be vaguely called "analogy." The behavior of other people is in many ways analogous to our own, and we suppose that it must have analogous causes. What people say is what we should say if we had certain thoughts, and so we infer that they probably have these thoughts. They give us information which we can sometimes subsequently verify. They behave in ways in which we behave when we are pleased (or displeased) in circumstances in which we should be pleased (or displeased). We may talk over with a friend some incident which we have both experienced, and find that his reminiscences dovetail with our own; this is particularly convincing when he remembers something that we have forgotten but that he recalls to our thoughts. Or again: you set your boy a problem in arithmetic, and with luck he gets the right answer; this persuades you that he is capable of arithmetical reasoning. There are, in short, very many ways in which my responses to stimuli differ from those of "dead" matter, and in all these ways other people resemble me. As it is clear to me that the causal laws governing my behavior have to do with "thoughts," it is natural to infer that the same is true of the analogous behavior of my friends.

The inference with which we are at present concerned is not merely that which takes us beyond solipsism, by maintaining that sensations have causes about which *something* can be known. This kind of inference, which suffices for physics, has already been considered. We are concerned now with a much more specific kind of inference, the kind that is involved in our knowledge of the thoughts and feelings of others—assuming that we have such knowledge. It is of course obvious that such knowledge is more or less doubtful. There is not only the general argument that we may be dreaming; there is also the possibility of ingenious automata. There are calculating machines that do sums much better than our schoolboy sons; there are gramophone records that remember impeccably what So-and-so said on such-and-such an occasion; there are people in the cinema who, though copies of real people, are not themselves alive. There is no theoretical limit to what ingenuity could achieve in the way of producing the illusion of life where in fact life is absent.

But, you will say, in all such cases it was the thoughts of human beings that produced the ingenious mechanism. Yes, but how do you know this? And how do you know that the gramophone does *not* "think"?

There is, in the first place, a difference in the causal laws of observable behavior. If I say to a student, "Write me a paper on Descartes' reasons for believing in the existence of matter," I shall, if he is industrious, cause a certain response. A gramophone record might be so constructed as to respond to this stimulus, perhaps better than the student, but if so it would be incapable of telling me anything about any other philosopher, even if I threatened to refuse to give it a degree. One of the most notable peculiarities of human behavior is change of response to a given stimulus. An ingenious person could construct an automaton which would always laugh at his jokes, however often it heard them; but a human being, after laughing a few times, will yawn, and end by saying, "How I laughed the first time I heard that joke."

But the differences in observable behavior between living and dead matter do not suffice to prove that there are "thoughts" connected with living bodies other than my own. It is probably possible theoretically to account for the behavior of living bodies by purely physical causal laws, and it is probably impossible to refute materialism by external observation alone. If we are to believe that there are thoughts and feelings other than our own, that must be in virtue of some inference in which our own thoughts and feelings are relevant, and such an inference must go beyond what is needed in physics.

I am, of course, not discussing the history of how we come to believe in other minds. We find ourselves believing in them when we first begin to reflect; the thought that Mother may be angry or pleased is one which arises in early infancy. What I am discussing is the possibility of a postulate which shall establish a rational connection between this belief and data, e.g., between the belief "Mother is angry" and the hearing of a loud voice.

The abstract schema seems to be as follows. We know, from observation of ourselves, a causal law of the form "A causes B," where A is a "thought" and B a physical occurrence. We sometimes observe a B when we cannot observe any A; we then infer an unobserved A. For example: I know that when I say, "I'm thirsty," I say so, usually, because I am thirsty, and therefore, when I hear the sentence "I'm thirsty" at a time when I am not thirsty, I assume that someone else is thirsty. I assume this the more readily if I see before me a hot, drooping body which goes on to say, "I have walked twenty desert miles in this heat with never a drop to drink." It is evident that my confidence in the "inference" is increased by increased complexity in the datum and also by increased certainty of the causal law derived from subjective observation, provided the causal law is such as to account for the complexities of the datum.

It is clear that in so far as plurality of causes is to be suspected, the kind of inference we have been considering is not valid. We are supposed to know "A causes B," and also to know that B has occurred; if this is to justify us in inferring A, we must know that *only* A causes B. Or, if we are content to infer that A is probable, it will suffice if we can know that in most cases it is A that causes B. If you hear thunder without having seen lightning, you confidently infer that there was lightning, because you are convinced that the sort of noise you heard is seldom caused by anything except lightning. As this example shows, our principle is not only employed to establish the existence of other minds but is habitually assumed, though in a less concrete form, in physics. I say "a less concrete form" because unseen lightning is only abstractly similar to seen lightning, whereas we suppose the similarity of other minds to our own to be by no means purely abstract.

Complexity in the observed behavior of another person, when this can all be accounted for by a simple cause such as thirst, increases the probability of the inference by diminishing the probability of some other cause. I think that in ideally favorable circumstances the argument would be formally as follows:

From subjective observation I know that A, which is a thought or feeling, causes B, which is a bodily act, e.g., a statement. I know also that, whenever B is an act of my own body, A is its cause. I now observe an act of the kind B in a body not my own, and I am having no thought or feeling of the kind A. But I still believe, on the basis of self-observation, that only A can cause B; I therefore infer that there was an A which caused B, though it was not an A that I could observe. On this ground I infer that other people's bodies are associated with minds, which resemble mine in proportion as their bodily behavior resembles my own.

In practice, the exactness and certainty of the above statement must be softened. We cannot be sure that, in our subjective experience, A is the only cause of B. And even if A is the only cause of B in our experience, how can we know that this holds outside our experience? It is not necessary that we should know this with any certainty; it is enough if it is highly probable. It is the assumption of probability in such cases that is our postulate. The postulate may therefore be stated as follows:

If, whenever we can observe whether A and B are present or absent, we find that every case of B has an A as a causal antecedent, then it is probable that most B's have A's as causal antecedents, even in cases where observation does not enable us to know whether A is present or not.

This postulate, if accepted, justifies the inference to other minds, as well as many other inferences that are made unreflectingly by common sense.

12
KNOWLEDGE OF OTHER MINDS

Norman Malcolm

I

I believe that the argument from analogy for the existence of other minds still enjoys more credit than it deserves, and my first aim will be to show that it leads nowhere. J. S. Mill is one of many who have accepted the argument and I take his statement of it as representative. He puts to himself the question, "By what evidence do I know, or by what considerations am I led to believe, that there exist other sentient creatures; that the walking and speaking figures which I see and hear, have sensations and thoughts, or in other words, possess Minds?" His answer is the following:

> I conclude that other human beings have feelings like me, because, first, they have bodies like me, which I know, in my own case, to be the antecedent condition of feelings; and because, secondly, they exhibit the acts, and other outward signs, which in my own case I know by experience to be caused by feelings. I am conscious in myself of a series of facts connected by an uniform sequence, of which the beginning is modifications of my body, the middle is feelings, the end is outward demeanor. In the case of other human beings I have the evidence of my senses for the first and last links of the series, but not for the intermediate link. I find, however, that the sequence between the first and last is as regular and constant in those other cases as it is in mine. In my own case I know that the first link produces the last through the intermediate link, and could not produce it without. Experience, therefore, obliges me to conclude that there must be an intermediate link; which must either be the same in others as in myself, or a different one: I must either believe them to be alive, or to be automatons: and by believing them to be alive, that is, by supposing the link to be of the same nature as in the case of which I have experience, and which is in all other respects similar, I bring other human beings, as phenomena, under the

From Norman Malcolm, *Knowledge and Certainty: Essays and Lectures*, pp. 130–140, © 1963. Reprinted by permission of Prentice-Hall, Inc., Englewood Cliffs, New Jersey, U.S.A.

same generalizations which I know by experience to be the true theory of my own existence.[1]

I shall pass by the possible objection that this would be very *weak* inductive reasoning, based as it is on the observation of a single instance. More interesting is the following point: Suppose this reasoning could yield a conclusion of the sort "It is probable that that human figure" (pointing at some person other than oneself) "has thoughts and feelings." Then there is a question as to whether this conclusion can *mean* anything to the philosopher who draws it, because there is a question as to whether the sentence "That human figure has thoughts and feelings" can mean anything to him. Why should this be a question? Because the assumption from which Mill starts is that he has *no criterion* for determining whether another "walking and speaking figure" does or does not have thoughts and feelings. If he had a criterion he could apply it, establishing with certainty that this or that human figure does or does not have feelings (for the only plausible criterion would lie in behavior and circumstances that are open to view), and there would be no call to resort to tenuous analogical reasoning that yields at best a probability. If Mill has no criterion for the existence of feelings other than his own then in that sense he does not understand the sentence "That human figure has feelings" and therefore does not understand the sentence "It is *probable* that that human figure has feelings."

There is a familiar inclination to make the following reply: "Although I have no criterion of verification still I *understand*, for example, the sentence 'He has a pain.' For I understand the meaning of 'I have a pain,' and 'He has a pain' means that he has the *same* thing I have when I have a pain." But this is a fruitless maneuver. If I do not know how to establish that someone has a pain then I do not know how to establish that he has the *same* as I have when I have a pain.[2] You cannot improve my understanding of "He has a pain" by this recourse to the notion of "the same," unless you give me a criterion for saying that someone *has* the same as I have. If you can do this you will have no use for the argument from analogy: and if you cannot then you do not understand the supposed conclusion of that argument. A philosopher who purports to rely on the analogical argument cannot, I think, escape this dilemma.

There have been various attempts to repair the argument from analogy. Mr. Stuart Hampshire has argued[3] that its validity as a method of inference can be established in the following way: Others sometimes infer that I am feeling giddy from my behavior. Now I have direct, non-inferential knowledge, says Hampshire, of my own feelings. So I can check inferences made about me against the facts, checking thereby the accuracy of the "methods" of inference.

[1] J. S. Mill, *An Examination of Sir William Hamilton's Philosophy*, 6th ed. (New York: Longmans, Green & Co., Inc., 1889), pp. 243–244.

[2] "It is no explanation to say: the supposition that he has a pain is simply the supposition that he has the same as I. For *that* part of the grammar is quite clear to me: that is, that one will say that the stove has the same experience as I, *if* one says: it is in pain and I am in pain" (Ludwig Wittgenstein, *Philosophical Investigations* (New York: The Macmillan Company, 1953), sec. 350).

[3] "The Analogy of Feeling," *Mind*, January 1952, pp. 1–12.

All that is required for testing the validity of any method of factual inference is that each one of us should sometimes be in a position to confront the conclusions of the doubtful method of inference with what is known by him to be true independently of the method of inference in question. Each one of us is certainly in this position in respect of our common methods of inference about the feelings of persons other than ourselves, in virtue of the fact that each one of us is constantly able to compare the results of this type of inference with what he knows to be true directly and non-inferentially; each one of us is in the position to make this testing comparison, whenever he is the designated subject of a statement about feelings and sensations. I, Hampshire, know by what sort of signs I may be misled in inferring Jones's and Smith's feelings, because I have implicitly noticed (though probably not formulated) where Jones, Smith and others generally go wrong in inferring my feelings (*op. cit.*, pp. 4–5).

Presumably I can also note when the inferences of others about my feelings do not go wrong. Having ascertained the reliability of some inference-procedures I can use them myself, in a guarded way, to draw conclusions about the feelings of others, with a modest but justified confidence in the truth of those conclusions.

My first comment is that Hampshire has apparently forgotten the purpose of the argument from analogy, which is to provide some probability that "the walking and speaking figures which I see and hear, have sensations and thoughts" (Mill). For the reasoning that he describes involves the assumption that other human figures *do* have thoughts and sensations: for they are assumed to *make inferences* about me from *observations* of my behavior. But the philosophical problem of the existence of other minds *is* the problem of whether human figures other than oneself do, among other things, make observations, inferences, and assertions. Hampshire's supposed defense of the argument from analogy is an *ignoratio elenchi* [failure to appreciate what needs to be proved].

If we struck from the reasoning described by Hampshire all assumption of thoughts and sensations in others we should be left with something roughly like this: "When my behavior is such and such there come from nearby human figures the sounds 'He feels giddy.' And generally I do feel giddy at the time. Therefore when another human figure exhibits the same behavior and I say 'He feels giddy,' it is probable that he does feel giddy." But the reference here to the sentence-like sounds coming from other human bodies is irrelevant, since I must not assume that those sounds express inferences. Thus the reasoning becomes simply the classical argument from analogy: "When my behavior is such and such I feel giddy; so probably when another human figure behaves the same way he feels the same way." This argument, again, is caught in the dilemma about the criterion of the *same*.

The version of analogical reasoning offered by Professor H. H. Price[4] is more interesting. He suggests that "one's evidence for the existence of other minds is derived primarily from the understanding of language" (p. 429). His idea is that if another body gives forth noises one understands, like "There's the bus," and if these noises give one new information, this "provides some evidence that the foreign body which uttered the noises is ani-

---

[4] "Our Evidence for the Existence of Other Minds," *Philosophy*, XIII (1938), 425–456.

mated by a mind like one's own. . . . Suppose I am often in its neighbor-hood, and it repeatedly produces utterances which I can understand, and which I then proceed to verify for myself. And suppose that this happens in many different kinds of situations. I think that my evidence for believing that this body is animated by a mind like my own would then become very strong" (p. 430). The body from which these informative sounds proceed need not be a human body. "If the rustling of the leaves of an oak formed intelligible words conveying new information to me, and if gorse-bushes made intelligible gestures, I should have evidence that the oak or the gorse-bush was animated by an intelligence like my own" (p. 436). Even if the intelligible and informative sounds did not proceed from a body they would provide evidence for the existence of a (disembodied) mind (p. 435).

Although differing sharply from the classical analogical argument, the reasoning presented by Price is still analogical in form: I know by introspec-tion that when certain combinations of sounds come from me they are "symbols in acts of spontaneous thinking"; therefore similar combinations of sounds, not produced by me, "probably function as instruments to an act of spontaneous thinking, which in this case is not my own" (p. 446). Price says that the reasoning also provides an *explanation* of the otherwise mysterious occurrence of sounds which I understand but did not produce. He antici-pates the objection that the hypothesis is nonsensical because unverifiable. "The hypothesis is a perfectly conceivable one," he says, "in the sense that I know very well what the world would have to be like if the hypothesis were true—what sorts of entities there must be in it, and what sorts of events must occur in them. I know from introspection what acts of thinking and perceiving are, and I know what it is for such acts to be combined into the unity of a single mind . . ." (pp. 446–447).

I wish to argue against Price that no amount of intelligible sounds coming from an oak tree or a kitchen table could create any probability that it has sensations and thoughts. The question to be asked is: What would show that a tree or table *understands* the sounds that come from it? We can imagine that useful warnings, true descriptions and predictions, even "replies" to questions, should emanate from a tree, so that it came to be of enormous value to its owner. How should we establish that it understood those sentences? Should we "question" it? Suppose that the tree "said" that there was a vixen in the neighborhood, and we "asked" it "What is a vixen?," and it "replied," "A vixen is a female fox." It might go on to do as well for "female" and "fox." This performance might incline us to say that the tree understood the words, in contrast to the possible case in which it answered "I don't know" or did not answer at all. But would it show that the tree understood the words in the same sense that a person could understand them? With a person such a performance would create a presumption that he could make correct *applications* of the word in question; but not so with a tree. To see this point think of the normal teaching of words (e.g., "spoon," "dog," "red") to a child and how one decides whether he understands them. At a primitive stage of teaching one does not require or expect definitions, but rather that the child should *pick out* reds from blues, dogs from cats, spoons from forks. This involves his looking, pointing, reaching for and going to the right things and not the wrong ones. That a child says "red" when a red thing and "blue" when a blue thing is put before him is indicative of a mastery of those words *only* in conjunction with the other activities of looking, pointing, trying to get, fetching, and carrying. Try to suppose that he says the right words but looks at and reaches for the wrong things. Should we be tempted to say that he has mastered the use of those words? No, indeed. The disparity between words and behavior would make us say that he does not understand the words. In the case of a tree there could be no disparity between its words and its "behavior" because it is logically incapable of behavior of the relevant kind.

Since it has nothing like the human face and body it makes no sense to say of a tree, or an electronic computer, that it is looking or pointing at or fetching something. (Of course one can always *invent* a sense for these expressions.) Therefore it would make no sense to say that it did or did not understand the above words. Trees and computers cannot either pass or fail the tests that a child is put through. They cannot take them. That an object was a source of intelligible sounds or other signs (no matter how sequential) would not be enough by itself to establish that it had thoughts or sensations. How informative sentences and valuable predictions could emanate from a gorse-bush might be a grave scientific problem, but the explanation could never be that the gorse-bush has a mind. Better no explanation than non-sense!

It might be thought that the above difficulty holds only for words whose meaning has a "perceptual content" and that if we imagined, for example, that our gorse-bush produced nothing but pure mathematical propositions we should be justified in attributing thought to it, although not sensation. But suppose there was a remarkable "calculating boy" who could give right answers to arithmetical problems but could not apply numerals to reality in empirical propositions, e.g., he could not *count* any objects. I believe that everyone would be reluctant to say that he *understood* the mathematical signs and truths that he produced. If he could count in the normal way there would not be this reluctance. And "counting in the normal way" involves looking, pointing, reaching, fetching, and so on. That is, it requires the human face and body, and human behavior—or something similar. Things which do not have the human form, or anything like it, not merely do not but *cannot* satisfy the criteria for thinking. I am trying to bring out part of what Wittgenstein meant when he said, "We only say of a human being and what is like one that it thinks" (*Investigations*, sec. 360), and "The human body is the best picture of the human soul" (*ibid.*, p. 178).

I have not yet gone into the most fundamental error of the argument from analogy. It is present whether the argument is the classical one (the analogy between my body and other bodies) or Price's version (the analogy between my language and the noises and signs produced by other things). It is the mistaken assumption that *one learns from one's own case* what thinking, feeling, sensation are. Price gives expression to this assumption when he says: "I know from introspection what acts of thinking and perceiving are . . ." (*op. cit.*, p. 447). It is the most natural assumption for a philosopher to make and indeed seems at first to be the only possibility. Yet Wittgenstein has made us see that it leads first to solipsism and then to nonsense. I shall try to state as briefly as possible how it produces those results.

A philosopher who believes that one must learn what thinking, fear, or pain is "from one's own case," does not believe that the thing to be observed is one's behavior, but rather something "inward." He considers behavior to be related to the inward states and occurrences merely as an accompaniment or possibly an effect. He cannot regard behavior as a *criterion* of psychological phenomena: for if he did he would have no use for the analogical argument (as was said before) and also the priority given to "one's own case" would be pointless. He believes that he notes something in himself that he calls "thinking" or "fear" or "pain," and then he tries to infer the presence of the *same* in others. He should then deal with the question of what his criterion of the *same* in others is. This he cannot do because it is of the essence of his viewpoint to reject circumstances and behavior as a criterion of mental phenomena in others. And what else could serve as a criterion? He ought, therefore, to draw the conclusion that the notion of thinking, fear, or pain in others is in an important sense meaningless. He has no idea of what would count for or against it.[5] "That there should be thinking or pain other than my own is unintelligible," he ought to hold. This would be a rigorous solipsism, and a correct outcome of the assumption that one can know only from one's own case what the mental phenomena are. An equivalent way of putting it would be: "When I say 'I am in pain,' by 'pain' I mean a certain inward state. When I say '*He* is in pain,' by 'pain' I mean *behavior*. I cannot attribute pain to others *in the same sense* that I attribute it to myself."

Some philosophers before Wittgenstein may have seen the solipsistic result of starting from "one's own case." But I believe he is the first to have shown how that starting point destroys itself. This may be presented as follows: One supposes that one inwardly picks out something as thinking or pain and thereafter identifies it whenever it presents itself in the soul. But the question to be pressed is, Does one make *correct* identifications? The proponent of these "private" identifications has nothing to say here. He feels sure that he identifies correctly the occurrences in his soul; but feeling sure is no guarantee of being right. Indeed he has no idea of what being *right* could mean. He does not know how to distinguish between actually making correct identifications and being under the impression that he does. (See *Investigations*, secs. 258–9.) Suppose that he identified the emotion of anxiety as the sensation of pain? Neither he nor anyone else could know about this "mistake." Perhaps he makes a mistake *every* time! Perhaps all of us do! We ought to see now that we are talking nonsense. We do not know what a *mistake* would be. We have no standard, no examples, no customary practice, with which to compare our inner recognitions. The inward identification cannot hit the bull's-eye, or miss it either, because there is no bull's-eye. When we see that the ideas of correct and incorrect have no application to the supposed inner identification, the latter notion loses its appearance of sense. Its collapse brings down both solipsism and the argument from analogy.

II

The destruction of the argument from analogy also destroys the *problem* for which it was supposed to provide a solution. A philosopher feels himself

---

[5] One reason why philosophers have not commonly drawn this conclusion may be, as Wittgenstein acutely suggests, that they assume that they have "an infallible paradigm of identity in the identity of a thing with itself" (*Investigations*, sec. 215).

in a difficulty about other minds because he assumes that first of all he is acquainted with mental phenomena "from his own case." What troubles him is how to make the transition from his own case to the case of others. When his thinking is freed of the illusion of the priority of his own case, then he is able to look at the familiar facts and to acknowledge that the circumstances, behavior, and utterances of others actually are his *criteria* (not merely his evidence) for the existence of their mental states. Previously this had seemed impossible.

But now he is in danger of flying to the opposite extreme of behaviorism, which errs by believing that through observation of one's own circumstances, behavior, and utterances one can find out that one is thinking or angry. The philosophy of "from one's own case" and behaviorism, though in a sense opposites, make the common assumption that the first-person, present-tense psychological statements are verified by self-observation. According to the "one's own case" philosophy the self-observation cannot be checked by others; according to behaviorism the self-observation would be by means of outward criteria that are available to all. The first position becomes unintelligible; the second is false for at least many kinds of psychological statements. We are forced to conclude that the first-person psychological statements are not (or hardly ever) verified by self-observation. It follows that they have no verification at all; for if they had a verification it would have to be by self-observation.

But if sentences like "My head aches" or "I wonder where she is" do not express observations then what do they do? What is the relation between my declaration that my head aches and the fact that my head aches, if the former is not the report of an observation? The perplexity about the existence of *other* minds has, as the result of criticism, turned into a perplexity about the meaning of one's own psychological sentences about oneself. At our starting point it was the sentence "*His* head aches" that posed a problem; but now it is the sentence "*My* head aches" that puzzles us.

One way in which this problem can be put is by the question, "How does *one know when to say* the words 'My head aches'?" The inclination to ask this question can be made acute by imagining a fantastic but not impossible case of a person who has survived to adult years without ever experiencing pain. He is given various sorts of injections to correct this condition, and on receiving one of these one day, he jumps and exclaims, "Now I feel pain!" One wants to ask, "How did he *recognize* the new sensation as a *pain?*"

Let us note that if the man gives an answer (e.g., "I knew it must be pain because of the way I jumped") then he proves by that very fact that he has not mastered the correct use of the words "I feel pain." They cannot be used to state a *conclusion*. In telling us *how* he did it he will convict himself of a misuse. Therefore the question "How did he recognize his sensation?" requests the impossible. The inclination to ask it is evidence of our inability to grasp the fact that the use of this psychological sentence has nothing to do with recognizing or identifying or observing a state of oneself.

The fact that this imagined case produces an especially strong temptation to ask the "How?" question shows that we have the idea that it must be more difficult to give the right name of one's sensation *the first time*. The implication would be that it is not so difficult *after* the first time. Why should this be? Are we thinking that then the man would have a paradigm of pain with which he could compare his sensations and so be in a position to know right off whether a certain sensation was or was not a pain? But the paradigm would be either something "outer" (behavior) or something "inner" (perhaps a memory impression of the sensation). If the former then he is misusing the first-person sentence. If the latter then the question of whether he compared *correctly* the present sensation with the inner paradigm of pain would be without sense. Thus the idea that the use of the first-person sentences can be governed by paradigms must be abandoned. It is another form of our insistent misconception of the first-person sentence as resting somehow on the identification of a psychological state.

These absurdities prove that we must conceive of the first-person psychological sentences in some entirely different light. Wittgenstein presents us with the suggestion that the first-person sentences are to be thought of as similar to the natural nonverbal, behavioral expressions of psychological states. "My leg hurts," for example, is to be assimilated to crying, limping, holding one's leg. This is a bewildering comparison and one's first thought is that two sorts of things could not be more unlike. By saying the sentence one can make a *statement;* it has a *contradictory;* it is *true* or *false;* in saying it one *lies* or *tells the truth;* and so on. None of these things, exactly, can be said of crying, limping, holding one's leg. So how can there be any resemblance? But Wittgenstein knew this when he deliberately likened such a sentence to "the primitive, the natural, expressions" of pain, and said that it is "new pain-behavior" (*ibid.*, sec. 244). This analogy has at least two important merits: first, it breaks the hold on us of the question "How does one *know when to say* 'My leg hurts'?", for in the light of the analogy this will be as nonsensical as the question "How does one know when to cry, limp, or hold one's leg?"; second, it explains how the utterance of a first-person psychological sentence by another person can have *importance* for us, although not as an identification—for in the light of the analogy it will have the same importance as the natural behavior which serves as our preverbal criterion of the psychological states of others.

13

PRETENDING

G. E. M. Anscombe

Offered 'pretending' as a philosophical topic, I should want to distinguish between mock performances and real pretences. The difference, so far as I have noticed, is not pointed to by any of those differences between the grammatical constructions respectively appropriate, sometimes to one nuance of sense and another, sometimes to one word and another closely related one, which are Professor Austin's favourite study. Hence he disregards it,[1] and lumping dissimilar things together, finds that in "the basic case" the one who is pretending must be giving a "current personal performance" in someone's presence in order to disguise what he is really doing. Mock performances, to specimens of which he devotes a good deal of space, are most naturally exemplified in 'current personal performances' in the presence of others. But it is not at all characteristic of them to serve the purpose of disguising what the performer is really doing. That is a noteworthy characteristic of some real pretences. But for real pretences there is nothing specially basic about a 'current personal performance' in the presence of others. One can pretend to be angry in a letter (this might be mock anger or a real pretence); pretend to marry someone, the 'marriage' being by proxy; pretend to be a meat-eater in a community where vegetarianism is criminally heterodox, by having conspicuous deliveries of butcher's meat made to one's house; pretend through one's emissaries to come to an understanding with a foreign power. Whether the pretending has to be a personal performance sometimes, though not always, depends on whether the doing that is pretended has to be one. It demands a justification, which Professor Austin has not offered, to treat mock performances on the one hand, and cases like these on the other, as deviations from a centre, as fringe cases in which some of the features of 'the basic case' have disappeared. He has perhaps formed this conception out of a prejudice that the

---

G. E. M. Anscombe, "Pretending," *Proceedings of the Aristotelian Society*, Supplementary Vol. XXXII (1958), 279–294. Reprinted by courtesy of the Editor of The Aristotelian Society.

[1] References are to J. L. Austin, "Pretending" [*PASS*, Vol. XXXII, 1958].

identity of a phrase must have something which is 'the basic case' corresponding to it.

I can at present see little intrinsic interest in mock performances. Professor Austin tells us that part of the interest of his considerations is that "philosophers who are fond of invoking pretending have exaggerated its scope and distorted its meaning". In *The Concept of Mind* Professor Ryle discusses pretending, in the sense of giving a mock performance, when he prepares the ground for his attempt to explicate imagination as incipient or inhibited performance. That is a very strange account of imagination. I think it derives from the following suggestion of Wittgenstein's: suppose there were some people apparently playing tennis, but without any ball. Wittgenstein compared the mental image, or the calculation in the head, to this non-existent ball. We should notice that this is not the same thing as comparing *imagining* to the *mock performance* of playing tennis which is here envisaged. It is only the image which is being compared to the ball that there isn't in this game. (What would correspond to the players' strokes to and fro would be *e.g.* the overt setting of a sum and the overt production of the answer.)—I will not pretend to estimate the value of this suggestion, and only mention it to throw light on one of the ways in which 'pretending' has come into current philosophical literature. Obviously pretending is really quite irrelevant here. For though the tennis game without the ball could be called a mock game of tennis, and in that sense the players—in this highly fictitious example—could be said to be pretending to play tennis, the point of the example is not that this is a mock performance or any kind of pretence, but just that it is a tennis-game without a ball. And in Ryle's own attempt to describe imagination, what is of importance is the absence is *first* supposed to throw light on pretending, and this concept in its turn is *then* supposed to throw light on imagination, as if imagination were a species that fell under it.

Leaving mock performances aside, let us consider how 'really pretending' comes into current philosophical discussion. Professor Austin quotes an example, about pretending to be angry.

It is fairly easy to see that the connexion between the meanings of words like "pain" and "anger" and certain types of behaviour cannot be merely contingent. Just what the connexion is, however, is difficult to describe in some cases. *E.g.* it is certainly not that "He is angry" *means* "He behaves thus or thus". And yet acting a piece of typical angry behaviour might serve well as an ostensive definition of "anger". Here the inclination arises to think that if it does so serve, it is working as an indirect indication of something which is simple and yet cannot be indicated directly. This inclination arises because we remember about pretending. Let the following stand for the sort of behaviour that expresses anger:

A man may behave so and not be angry because he is pretending, and the person who understands the ostensive definition ought to understand this. Mr. Bedford, in the passage Professor Austin quotes,[2] *may* be suggesting that the question whether the man who behaves so is pretending or really angry would necessarily be settlable if only there were 'more evidence of the same sort'. And by "more evidence of the same sort" he *may* mean "more (at least ostensibly) anger-expressing behaviour"—though if he got as far as putting it like that, he would surely *not* think so.

If, then, concentrating on 'behavior that is (perhaps) expressive of real anger' and 'the anger that it is (perhaps) expressive of', we think about pretending, we may feel forced back on a picture like this

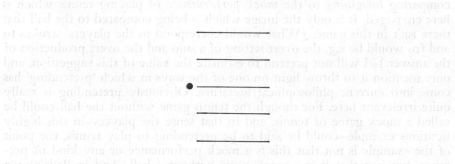

where the dot behind the dashes stands for the anger itself. Then the dashes without the dot stand for the behaviour without the anger. This, if there is enough of it, will be pretended anger. We have to say "if there is enough of it" because *e.g.* a scowling face without anger, which looks like an angry face, may be, not a pretence of anger, but just the face someone has when he is thinking hard. But there is behaviour which certainly either is the mark of anger or is simulated anger.—Pursuing our picture, a plain dot without any dashes will be anger which a man does not express at all.

So, it is argued, someone who understands the ostensive definition of anger offered in an imitation of angry behaviour, will take it as an indirect indication of the dot—which cannot be directly indicated by one person to another at all. But with this conception we are forced back to the idea of the private ostensive definition with its absurd consequences—that for all we ever could know the word might stand for a different thing for different people or for the same person at different times; that we can never make more than a probable judgment that someone else is angry; or even that we cannot really make this judgment at all; that our own claim to be angry rests on an assumption that we have correctly identified something within our-selves—but without any standard of correctness—and so on.

This, then, is one great locus of the discussion of pretending. Professor Austin proposes to examine pretending just on its own account and out of the context of such discussions. In doing so he has convinced himself that a

[2] Errol Bedford, "Emotions", *Proceedings of the Aristotelian Society*, Vol. LVII, 1956–57.

simple contrast between 'pretence' and 'reality' is no good; that pretending has such 'essential features' as that the pretender must be present and active, and there must be something, also 'on the scene', that he is disguising; that there is such a thing as 'the essence of the situation in pretending', namely 'that my public behaviour must be being done in order to disguise some reality'.

Against this I would argue that pretending can no more have that type of 'essential feature' than falsehood or identity or seeming can. Seeming is especially relevant, because the notion of pretending is closely bound up with that of seeming. The best general account of pretending would be something like: *the production of a would-be seeming to be[3] what you are not.* That is clumsy, so I will shorten it to 'trying to appear what you are not': cases of this which would not fall under the longer form are excluded. The point of this exclusion is that a man might try to appear what he is not, and not succeed in doing anything—*e.g.*, a very sick man, trying to seem cheerful and too weak even to smile, would have only tried to pretend.

From this general account of pretending we can see why the two more specious implications mentioned by Professor Austin do not hold. As he says, pretending does not imply not being, and really being does not imply not pretending. For *e.g.* a man can pretend to be poisoned when, unknown to him, he is poisoned. In "trying to appear what you are not" the words "what you are not" are governed by the "trying": the whole phrase does not mean: "concerning something which you in fact are not, trying to appear that thing", but: "trying to bring it about that, without being something, you appear that thing".

This general account of pretending needs an addition to include some cases of trying to make it seem that something is the case which is not. *E.g.*, one might pretend that one's child was under three years old (to avoid paying a fare) by having him dressed in rather babyish clothes and carrying him like a rather younger child, as well as by what one said. All these details would be part of the pretence. In such a case, we have to speak of 'pretending that' rather than 'pretending to' because the subject of what is pretended is not the same as the pretender, and not, I think, for any other reason. Two central features of "pretend" are (1) that the pretender should figure as a principal, in what is pretended *and* in that by which it is pretended; I mean the latter in such a sense that he would *be* a principal if the appearances were not deceptive. This condition may be satisfied even if he is not where the pretence is carried out, if what is done is something that could be done, with him as principal, without his presence, as in the case of the King coming to an agreement with a foreign power. My corollary (that he would be a principal in that *by* which the pretence was made, if the appearances were non-deceptive) can be seen to be necessary from this: if *e.g.*, the King arranged a deceptive appearance that his emissary proposed to murder him, he would not thereby be pretending to be a proposed victim of assassination. (2) Further, there is what might be called a 'rule of sequence of tenses' for "pretending"; if someone has broken some crockery and left it about so that I shall think he *was* angry, he *was* not pretending to be angry; and, unless he does something now to exhibit the smashed crockery as the result of past

---

[3] Like Professor Austin, for brevity's sake I disregard other verbs than 'to be' in formulating this.

rage on his part, he *is* not now pretending *to have been* angry.—I suspect
that these two facts have misled Professor Austin; he has misconstrued them
as a necessity for the pretender to be 'present on the scene' and 'giving a
current personal performance'.—Now in the pretence of the fraudulent
traveller that the child is under three, the traveller is a principal. I will not
consider such cases further; though one has to speak here of 'pretending
that' and not 'pretending to', this is only because of the diversity of subjects,
and such cases of 'pretending that' should be subsumed under 'pretending
to'.

'Pretending' is an intention-dependent concept; one cannot pretend inadvertently. But no special further intentions in whatever constitutes pretending in a given case are specially basic *"as Professor Austin pretends"*.
Why would that be rude and unfair? Because it implies that he has been
trying to make-things-seem-as-they-are-not. There is no hint in that piece of
rudeness that the publication of his paper serves to disguise something he is
really up to, and it is not the absence of such a hint that turns it into a fringe
use of "pretend".

'Seeming' can have no 'basic case'. Let A be the subject of a predicate x.
Then we can ask "What is it for A to x, or to be x?" and further "What is it
for A (only) to seem to x or to be x?" This latter enquiry may well throw
light on the first question. And we *could* ask further "Can A be so responsible for phenomena by which he (only) *seems* to x, that it accords with the
grammar of 'pretending' to say he pretends to x?" In cases where that is so,
an investigation of 'pretending to x' will often help us to understand the
concept 'x' better. But the quite general characteristics of the verb "to
pretend" are likely to give singularly little light in an enquiry into 'pretending to x'; such an enquiry must be completely dominated by the character of
the 'x' in question.

In the case in hand—that of pretending to be angry—if we consider when
and why we may judge that someone was only pretending, we see that it is
not only features of his ostensibly angry behaviour that prompt the judgment. If it were, then 'being angry' would be much more like *e.g.*, 'feeling
jumpy' than it is. Pure pretences of being angry in person are rarely so
successful that a discerning judge will not detect them in the tone and
expression of the subject. However, such admirable pretences are possible;
so of course the philosopher supposes a case where the performance is
perfect. Then perhaps he feels driven either to such a recourse as Mr.
Bedford's—"there is a limit that pretence must not overstep"—or to postulating something hidden behind the behaviour. But, as Professor Austin
indicates without enlarging on it, there is more to look for besides giveaways
in behaviour. Anger has four main features: (1) its object, (2) its expression, (3) feelings, (4) aims. By "angry behaviour" we usually mean things
falling under (2), the expression of anger: the angry-looking face and
gestures, the stamping or trembling or rigidity, the tone of voice, perhaps
the pointless smashing of things. (2) may include elements that bring in (1)
and (4). If an angry man expresses his anger in speech, his speech will
probably characterise the thing or person or situation or spectacle that he is
angry with either as bad in some way, or possibly as something to be
overcome or resisted. I suppose that is why Aristotle said that anger was
more 'rational' than lust—the expression of anger by an angry man often

gives *grounds* of anger. A story of anger—real or pretended—usually includes what the anger was at or supposed to be at, so characterised that the hearer can understand it *as* an occasion of anger. For example, if a man is said to have been angry at the sight of a chair, in a way we do not yet know what he was angry at; we need an explanation which will make it clear whether his purposes or orders have been frustrated, or his vanity insulted, or someone has been proved to have behaved abominably—or what.

There are also characteristic aims of anger—to harm or afflict someone or something, or to overcome obstacles[4] or resist or repel something. A man who was careful to give no sign of anger and did not even have specific angry feelings (sensible commotions) might be implacably angry and arrange some way of harming the man who angered him. Thus, though (2) may pass into (4), as when someone immediately starts strangling the person he is angry with, there *can* be a great difference between the expression of anger and its aims. A man could be said not to have given expression to his anger at all—he merely brought it about that the man who had offended him was ruined or hanged.

What is feeling angry? Let us suppose we find someone who has just been angry and ask him what he felt while he was angry. He may well say *e.g.*, "I felt hot", "I felt cold and trembling", "I felt a rush of blood to the head", "I felt a slight tension in the chest". Yet feeling angry is not any of these things; otherwise we could produce the sensations he characteristically has when angry—*e.g.*, by means of some electrical apparatus—and say: "There, now you feel angry". On the other hand, those sensations were not just concomitants of his anger; he might feel something else, a pain in the stomach, let us say, while he was angry, and not mention it as 'what he felt while he was angry'. The sensations that he mentions are the ones he—intuitively—gives as what he felt *in* being angry. Or again, we may say that he gives his anger as an interpretation of those sensations. But is there nothing else that the *felt* anger is? One kind of reply to this might be: "I felt: 'You filthy swine!' or 'This is too much!' or 'That trick again!' " The words, or the thoughts, are themselves an angry reaction, and there is no need to postulate, indeed no sense in postulating, another reaction, not the words or the thought, which is the ground of the words or the thought

---

4 I owe notice of this aspect of anger to Plato, made intelligible by Aquinas who adopted this part of Platonism, getting it apparently from St. Gregory of Nyssa and St. John of Damascus. He does not have a tripartite division of the soul like Plato, but divides the 'sensitive appetite' into two parts, the 'concupiscible' and the 'irascible.' Through the one, he says, the animal is simply inclined to pursue what it needs and to flee what is hurtful, through the other to resist what attacks its needs and offers hurt to it. "These two inclinations do not reduce to a single principle, because the animal sometimes faces hurt against the inclination of desire, so as to oppose what opposes it according to the inclination of anger. Hence the passions of the irascible are even seen to be at war with the passions of the concupiscible. For in general *as desire burns higher anger sinks, and as anger burns higher desire sinks*." (*Summa Theologica*, Ia, Q.LXXXI, Art II.) To understand the force of this remark we should imagine someone, about to engage in sensual enjoyment, having to fight to retain what he wanted to enjoy; and then, the battle won, returning to engage in enjoyment.—But, Plato might say, anger is not uniquely concerned with sensitive appetite. That is because of our organisation: "while I was musing, a fire kindled." An abstruse thought can bring my fist crashing down on the table and so also cause all sorts of reverberations in my sensuality. Hobbes' definition of anger as "sudden courage" must be in this tradition.

and is the felt anger itself. The fact that the verbal reaction may be a sham does not prove such a need. The mistake is to suppose that since a man can say "I felt angry" we shall find out what anger is by finding out what he felt. In what context does he say "I felt angry"? In the context of some story of events, conversations, thoughts: that is to say, he puts the anger he reports into a context which shews a lot about the anger: and what it shews is not just extraneous. That is why looking for the meaning of "anger" in what a man feels who feels angry yields such dissatisfying results, as if the anger itself had slipped between our fingers and we were left with details, which, while relevant, do not add up to anger.

I am not saying that every case of anger must have all these four features—rather, here we do have a 'full-blown' sort of case with all these features, and other cases lacking some of them. Now imagine an anthropologist saying "The psychology of this tribe is odd: they are angry only, and always, before sitting down to a really good meal." Asked why he says so, he explains "Then, they always shake their fists and assume an expression of hideous rage; after that, they sit down to eat; and they never shake their fists or assume that expression at any other time."—Would it not be absurd for someone so much as to say "They must be only *pretending* to be angry"? Once we have recalled these points about anger, we can see how a diagnosis of pretence could be made in face of angry behaviour which was a quite flawless performance. For example, one might know that the man did not really mind about what he was ostensibly angry at; that it really suited his book extremely well and he knew this. Or that the supposed affliction that he was laying on the victims of his anger was not really an affliction at all but something agreeable and that he knew this.

If someone claims that he was only pretending to be angry on an intelligible occasion for anger and when his performance had been good if it was only pretence, it is natural to ask why he was pretending that; and an answer telling more about the situation, his attitudes and what he was after will help to convince us that he was pretending.

These facts point to one great difference between anger and pain, and generally between passions and sensations. If a person's performance is good and—as may be the case—there is nothing else to look at, there may be no way at all of telling whether his pain is sham or not, if, say, it is a brief pain or he does not make the mistake of behaving inappropriately when *e.g.*, he does not think he is observed. But it is absurd to say (as Mr. Bedford says in the passage quoted by Professor Austin; which shocks me, though not Professor Austin) that he alone is in a position to give decisive evidence! What he says is no more decisive than his behaviour is. If one thought his groans might be shamming pain, one would hardly accept his word. This however does not mean that there is quite generally a difficulty about knowing whether someone is in pain or not. The difficulty occurs in some cases; and sometimes cannot be resolved. Cases can be constructed for anger too; but there is much more to consider in cases of anger: the whole story of the occasion ('whole story' in the sense of "whole truth" in the law-court oath). Contrast "As I walked along the passage I had a sudden stab of pain in my chest", and "As I walked along the passage I had a sudden stab of anger." Anger at what? "Nothing at all." This man is talking nonsense—unless he means "At X, which I judge to be a nothing." On the other hand consider this case: an actor, who has to act an angry man in a play, says "When I act it, I really am angry." He backs this up by saying that he *feels* angry, and he *means* the angry words in which he recalls and threatens evils. Would not a dispute be stupid about whether he is correct to use the words "I really am angry" or not? 'Say which you like, so long as you are clear about the facts.' *This* situation does not arise for physical pain. For if an actor in *King Lear* said "It's a most extraordinary thing, when they tear out my eyes, I feel an agonizing pain as if it were really so, I almost think I shall have to give up the part," well, we believe him or not, there is not a choice, *after* we believe him, between saying "He really feels pain" and "He doesn't really".

Although I have given reasons for accepting Professor Austin's remark that pretending does not imply not really being and really being does not imply not pretending, I have the impression that his own reasons for saying this lie at least partly in his examples, such as that of the man who was cleaning the windows and at the same time 'pretending to be cleaning them.' Here he relies on a nuance which he explains to us. (It may not exist everywhere where English is native.) But the whole reason why a man can be said to be pretending to be cleaning windows (when he also is cleaning them) is that what he is pretending is not the case. The explanation of the nuance makes this clear. The observer diagnoses the window-cleaner's felonious interest and guesses from this that the window-cleaning is a fake. The diagnosis might be right and the guess wrong—if, say, the man were the regular window-cleaner doing this regular job on his regular day. Professor Austin explains "It is still a pretence [*i.e.*, though the windows *are* being cleaned], because what he is *really* doing is something quite different." But the point of the expression "What he is *really* doing is something different" is that 'what he is *really doing*' falsifies the appearance he presents by cleaning the windows. There are other things he might also be 'really doing'—such as earning his wages or composing verse—which would also be 'different' from window-cleaning but which don't falsify "what he is really at is cleaning the windows" at all. The appearance presented by cleaning the windows is that, in cleaning the windows, he is doing something in some ordinary and proper course of things; and that this is a false appearance is the meaning of the expression "he is pretending *to be cleaning* the windows" in this context.

The two sentences

> He is cleaning the windows
> He is pretending to be cleaning the windows

may both be true; and as a matter of grammar "is cleaning" is the indicative corresponding to the infinitive "to be cleaning." Does Professor Austin think that *this* is therefore a counter-example to "pretending implies not really being"? And is it perhaps a fairly important step in his argument, enabling him to reject 'false appearance' as quite central to pretending? If so, this is grammatical superstition.

Why cannot a baby six months old pretend to be in pain? A mother might say "The baby pretends", and we "You mean there's nothing wrong, it only cries to be picked up." Suppose she insists that there is more to it, the baby is a clever one and *really* pretends? Mothers and similar people talk nonsense of this sort. The question is how we know it is nonsense. It is not competence to perform a mental act of pretending that is in question. Wittgenstein would say "Pretending is part of a complicated form of life which the baby is not living yet", but what does that mean? English people are apt to say "The dog is pretending to be lame." Why? He limps, but if he sees a rabbit he rushes after it with no trace of a limp. He was lame and got a lot of special kindness, and is looking for more. We assimilate this behaviour to human pretending. Once these facts have been stated it is not a further hypothesis that he is pretending. The behaviour of the baby is not like enough for the assimilation to be attractive except to mothers, etc. But what is it not like enough to?

The answer to the questions raised here is that you cannot ascribe real pretence to anything unless you can ascribe to it (*a*) a purpose and (*b*) the idea 'can be got by seeming to—'. That is why the baby case is nonsense; the baby's purpose may be clear enough, but what reason could there be to ascribe to it more than the idea 'can be got by roaring'? And even this means no more than that the baby roars *to be picked up*. Then why should we say more of the dog than that he limps to be petted? Why indeed? Only because limping has such a characteristic appearance, is not just going on three legs but has an air about it, so that if the limping is voluntary, we may implicitly think of the presentation of this appearance as deliberate. We have once more reached a point where we should say "Say 'he's pretending' if you like, or refuse to if you like, so long as you are clear about the facts." I emphasize this; because I am not sure whether Professor Austin would ever admit that we ought to say "Say such-and-such if you like, so long as you are clear about the facts"; if he would have some objection to this, I should like to see it brought out into the open.

These considerations yield this result: we sometimes ascribe pretence by way of a comparison, a sympathetic projection on to a body of facts which we compare with some of the facts of fairly developed human life. Apart from such sympathetic projections we must say: we can only ascribe pretence to beings to which we can also ascribe purposive calculation. That is not because pretence is generally purposive. It is not; wanting to seem something that one is not, without any further end in view, may even form the biggest part of pretending. But it must be significant that when we ascribe pretending to animals, it is because we see an advantage gained by seeming. Without meaning anything absurd (like the mother) we find it possible to speak of animals', birds' and insects' pretending to be boughs, leaves, twigs, etc. I think this shews reason to speak of purposive pretending as 'basic'.

When we consider unpurposive pretending, a new distinction appears between what I will call plain and non-plain pretending. Unpurposive pretence may be 'just for fun' or 'to tease' and the like. The description "unpurposive" may be challenged on the ground that teasing or fun is a purpose, but I think the challenge would be wrong. It is a specific advantage served by seeming that is characteristic of the purposive pretending that is 'basic'; fun and teasing are something one diagnoses as one diagnoses dancing or playing a game, not by seeing them as results achieved in a certain way.—I will call pretending "plain" when the pretender unreflectively knows that he is pretending. A great deal of unpurposive or only very vaguely and diffusely purposive pretending is non-plain.

What I have in mind is best illustrated by an example. Here is a dialogue between a schoolmaster and a parent summoned for interview:

> Did James tell you I had to beat him to-day?
> Yes, he said he got beaten.
> Oh, did he tell you what it was for?
> He told me it was for something he had written in his book.
> Hm! I don't suppose he told you what he had written.
> I don't know—what he said was that he wrote "Casson is a sod." I gather Mr. Casson is one of the masters.
> Oh! . . . Well, that's not very nice, is it?
> Well, I understand your beating him, but all the same, surely this is quite an ordinary thing for a boy to do?
> No, in my experience, not at all normal.
> Let the parent's reply to this be unspoken, since it is: "Stop pretending".

In this example, it might be tempting to call the schoolmaster's last remark a plain lie. But we ought to notice that most likely that is just what it is not. A lie is a plain lie when it contradicts what the speaker unreflectively thinks. I do not mean "when it contradicts an explicit thought" since (as is well known) 'what a man thinks' is not the same thing as 'what he *is at the moment thinking*'—even if it is only what he thinks for the time being, in the particular context. But sometimes it would take some reflection, in the circumstances, for a man to realise that he knew the contradictory of what he said. Then what he says is not a perfectly plain lie; he can even be said to think it.

It is not, however, his saying what he knows to be untrue that makes our schoolmaster's case one of (non-plain) pretending. He could pretend in this sense without saying anything untrue. Further, we often tell untruths that are not lies, in the sense that they do not contradict what we *unreflectively* know to be true, without 'pretending' in any sense beyond 'making out true what (we know) is not'; and, where the content of the 'pretence' is just the content of what is falsely said, there is no particular aptness about the word "pretending". We say a thing when we know it is not true, and yet without telling plain lies, in many ways; one is, by falling into cliché. For example, a sufficiently learned author speaks in a popular book of Hobbes' "militant atheism"; we are in a position to know that he knows that if Hobbes was an atheist he was a crypto-, not a militant, atheist. But the fact that he wrote that phrase shews that it would cost him a brief moment's recollection to realise that he knew this. Here, however, a use of the word "pretend" really would be a fringe use, as applied to a single statement; it would come to nothing but: "He says so-and-so, which he must know not to be true." But there is a sense in which the schoolmaster is pretending which goes beyond his telling a (non-plain) lie. What is in question here is *hypocrisy*: and we are trying to make out what kind of pretending this is.

The following example brings out the contrast between mock performance, plain pretence, and hypocritical pretence. A certain nun was the heroine of a devotionally exciting story; the story was generally known, but not her identity. Once someone guessed and said "So you are the one!" She, 'with such simplicity'—so the story runs—'that the other was completely deceived,' laughed and said "So you have found me out!" Thus she was pretending to be making a mock admission of something—with a view to concealing that it was the case. This, then, was a plain pretence. The word "simplicity" bears dwelling on. It does not merely mean that she laughed and spoke in a natural way, just like someone who really was making a mock admission of something that was not the case. Nor can it mean that she acted without guile, for the contrary is being recorded. With this word the story-teller is insisting that the pretence just was a genuine concealment of her identity, and not *itself* a further pretence of a new sort, as it were saying "See how I am one who wishes to remain obscure." The story-teller probably wishes to suggest that the episode marked a genuine wish to remain obscure; not a pretence of having such a wish. *This* pretence, if the wanting-to-seem was just for its own sake, would be not plain but hypocritical pretence. It is characteristic of this sort of wanting-to-seem that it carries with it an implicit demand for respect for an atmosphere evoked by the pretender, which surrounds not the reality, but the *idea* of such things as being principled, or cultured, or saintly, or rich, or important. There is something of which the schoolmaster is as it were saying 'Respect this'.

This throws light on a further notion, one of the popular senses of *cynicism*. In my sense of "plain", this is a 'plain' pretence of hypocrisy, and is found, *e.g.*, among the clearer-headed politicians.

Further References

Anderson, Alan Ross (ed.). *Minds and Machines*. Englewood Cliffs, N. J.: Prentice-Hall, 1964.*

Ayer, A. J. *The Concept of a Person*. London: Macmillan, 1963. Chaps. 3–4.

———. *Philosophical Essays*. London: Macmillan, 1954. Chap. 8.†

———. *The Problem of Knowledge*. Harmondsworth: Penguin Books, 1956. Chap. 5.*

Broad, C. D. *The Mind and Its Place in Nature*. London: Routledge & Kegan Paul, 1925.†

Chappell, V. C. (ed.). *The Philosophy of Mind*. Englewood Cliffs, N. J.: Prentice-Hall, 1962.*

Cornman, James. *Metaphysics, Reference and Language*. New Haven: Yale University Press, 1966.

Feigl, Herbert. "The 'Mental' and the 'Physical.'" In Herbert Feigl, Michael Scriven, and Grover Maxwell (eds.). *Minnesota Studies in the Philosophy of Science*. Vol. II. Minneapolis: University of Minnesota Press, 1958.

Flew, Antony (ed.). *Body, Mind, and Death*. New York: Macmillan, 1964.*

Geach, Peter. *Mental Acts*. London: Routledge & Kegan Paul, 1957.

Gustafson, Donald (ed.). *Essays in Philosophical Psychology*. New York: Doubleday, 1964.*

Hampshire, Stuart. "The Analogy of Feeling," *Mind*, LXI (1952), 1–12.

Hampshire, Stuart (ed.). *Philosophy of Mind*. New York: Harper & Row, 1966.*

Hook, Sidney (ed.). *Dimensions of Mind*. New York: New York University Press, 1960.†

Malcolm, Norman. *Dreaming*. London: Routledge & Kegan Paul, 1962.

Pitcher, George (ed.). *Wittgenstein. The Philosophical Investigations*. New York: Doubleday, 1966.*

Price, H. H. "Our Evidence for the Existence of Other Minds," *Philosophy*, XIII (1938), 425–456.

Ryle, Gilbert. *The Concept of Mind*. London: Hutchinson, 1949.†

Shaffer, Jerome A. "Recent Work on the Mind-Body Problem," *American Philosophical Quarterly*, II (1965), 81–104.

Smart, J. J. C. *Philosophy and Scientific Realism*. London: Routledge & Kegan Paul, 1963. Chaps. 5–6.

Strawson, P. F. *Individuals*. London: Methuen, 1959.†

Van Peursen, C. A. *Body, Soul, Spirit*. London: Oxford University Press, 1966.

Vesey, G. N. A. *The Embodied Mind*. London: Allen & Unwin, 1965.

Vesey, G. N. A. (ed.). *Body and Mind*. London: Allen & Unwin, 1964.

White, Alan R. *The Philosophy of Mind*. New York: Random House, 1967.*

Wisdom, John. *Other Minds*. Oxford: Basil Blackwell, 1952.

Wittgenstein, Ludwig. *Philosophical Investigations*. G. E. M. Anscombe (trans.). New York: Macmillan, 1953.

* Paperback edition.   † Also available in a paperback edition.

: V :

Knowledge
and Certainty

INTRODUCTION

The analysis of the nature of knowledge belongs to the core of philosophy. Its central issues have to do with certainty and doubt with regard to our claims about the world. If we are in doubt about what the facts are or about some purported truth—if we are, that is, not merely psychologically hesitant, but armed with relevant reasons for questioning the truth of some statement—what, logically, can resolve such doubt? Is it possible to come to an end of doubting? Are there truths about which one cannot doubt? Are there truths about which, once we have resolved certain doubts, it is impossible to go on doubting? If we are certain that something is so—not merely psychologically confident that it is so, but in possession of decisive grounds for believing it to be so—must we have knowledge? Can we be in error? Can we come to doubt what we now believe with certainty? What can serve as the decisive grounds for certainty? The relations between doubt and certainty are complex, and the philosophical issues are easily obscured by inevitable psychological associations.

On review, at least three fundamentally different sorts of questions are raised about the nature of knowledge: all of them rest on the correlative nature of doubt and certainty. First, we ask about the relationship between knowledge and the grounds of knowledge, between knowing that something or other is so and whatever it is that can certify that particular persons actually do have knowledge that something or other is so. Second, we ask about the relationship between knowledge and truth, between knowing that something or other is so and whatever it is that can certify, or constitute the condition, that the statement of what we may on occasion claim to know or be supposed to know is true. And third, we ask about the relationship between knowledge and belief, between knowing that something or other is so and whatever it is that can certify, or constitute the condition, that particular persons are in the state of mind or of such disposition that they may be said to believe that something or other is so, regardless of whether or not it is.

Even with these very sketchy distinctions, one sees readily enough that what is true may not be known or believed; that what is believed need not be true; that what is known must be true, yet need not be claimed or asserted to be true by the knower; that, although one must believe what one claims to know, what one does know one need not actually believe (or disbelieve) and, consequently, need not believe either with certainty or with doubt. "Are you certain?" serves as a challenge with respect to each of these issues; "Do you know, or do you merely believe, that it is so?" "Is it true?" and "Is that really your conviction?" are all fair ways, in different contexts, of questioning one's "certainty."

The pivotal concepts, therefore, are belief, truth, and knowledge. Belief concerns certain states of mind and what is thought to be true. Truth concerns certain sentences and values that may be assigned to sentences as registering or failing to register what is so in the world or in all possible worlds. Knowledge concerns claims or the right to assert that such and such *is* so in the world or in all possible worlds; it has to do with the achievement and capacity of persons in which their beliefs are suitably related to the conditions under which the truth of relevant sentences is and can be established.

In the history of philosophy, the first distinctly modern emphasis on the problem of knowledge can be found in the work of René Descartes (V:6). It was Descartes who made it very nearly the single concern of his investigations to determine the conditions under which true belief could qualify as knowledge—knowledge whose certainty, on rational review, could not conceivably be marred by doubt, knowledge for which no doubts could rationally be relevant or persist. What is distinctly premodern in Descartes, what aligns him with Plato and against Immanuel Kant (V:7), is his underlying assumption that knowledge is all of a piece, that the conditions for certain knowledge in mathematics, in empirical science, in morality, and in metaphysics are all logically the same.

If Descartes represents the first stage in the development of modern theories of knowledge, Kant surely represents the second. It was Kant who, in his critical philosophy, broke the spell of the unity of knowledge, of the unity of the conditions on which knowledge of all sorts depends. After Kant, it is, for example, merely a refinement of the critical enterprise to explore the epistemic oddities of first- and third-person knowledge of sensations (Ludwig Wittgenstein, A. J. Ayer [V:11], Norman Malcolm [V:12], P. F. Strawson). If one may speak of the postcritical period of modern philosophy, it is surely characterized by the challenging of the implied unity within the allegedly distinct departments of knowledge and of the simple contrast among them. It is not obvious, for example, that the truth of observational sentences in science and of micro-theoretical sentences lends itself to an adequate unitary account. Nor is it obvious that empirical and mathematical knowledge rest on the same conditions (John Stuart Mill [V:8], Carl Hempel [V:9]); or that moral judgments about obligation and happiness are of the same logical sort, or that so-called analytic and synthetic truths can be sharply demarcated (W. V. Quine [V:10]).

The vision of a body of science that rests on foundations of certainty is one of the haunting themes of the history of philosophy. It is as much present in Plato and Aristotle as it is in Descartes and Kant. In our own time the theme continues to fascinate: witness, for example, the forceful efforts of logical positivists and logical atomists to formalize the language of science, to make explicit its foundations of certainty and the logical connections among all its relevant sentences. If the modern period begins with an effort to wrest certainty from doubt (as with Descartes), it tends in our time to preserve doubt, at least as the possibility of error, against certainty (as, from different perspectives, with A. J. Ayer and J. L. Austin). Here stress is laid on the differences between dubitability and corrigibility—that is, between legitimating doubts about particular statements by reference to relevant possibilities which, if they obtained, would threaten certainty, even if not truth, and specifying the logical sources of possible error even in the face of certainty (Ayer, Malcolm). Put in another way, we may say that, while dubitability entails corrigibility, the converse does not hold: particular doubts arise only piecemeal and must be shown to be relevant in deciding or testing the truth of a given claim. A particular proposition that has been shown to be true may, logically, have been false; yet at any moment we may be unable to supply further grounds on which to challenge its truth.

Preeminent among questions of dubitability is the much-debated issue of the justification of induction. The classic beginnings of the modern discussion of the matter are to be found in the writings of David Hume (V:1). It is not so much that Hume proposed a solution to the puzzle of induction as that he formulated the problem effectively. Hume cast the problem in causal terms, observing that there is no necessary connection between cause and effect and that causal relations are discoverable, as he put it, by experience and not by reason. In asking such questions as how we know that the sun will rise tomorrow, he stressed not what reasons might be given to support the claim (they would, after all, depend on the accumulated experience of the sun's regularity) but what might justify arguments of the inductive type at all—arguments from the past to the future or from observed regularities to universal laws of nature. Hume's conclusion is ultimately skeptical: having found that there is no principle of demonstration under which inductive arguments can be justified, he argues that to rely on the principle of relying on past experience would be circular, and he suggests that the matter must be considered psychologically rather than logically.

The Humean account has been revived in our own time in the much-examined resumé of Bertrand Russell (V:2): here Russell emphasizes the radical difference between demonstrative arguments and inductive arguments (Russell subsequently modified his position). The difficulty with Russell's account lies quite simply in the assignment of dubious a priori status to the principle of the uniformity of nature, which serves as the justificatory principle for all particular inductions. The principle had been thought previously by John Stuart Mill to be itself a suppressed major premise that converted inductive arguments into deductive ones, yet was itself established by induction by simple enumeration. An alternative solution has been offered by Hans Reichenbach (V:3), who interprets the *aim* of induction itself in terms of determining the limits of the relative frequencies of events and then argues that the inductive principle is justified as providing the least risky method for achieving that aim. Another solution has been offered by P. F. Strawson (V:4). Rather than attempt a justification of the inductive principle itself he argues the logical absurdity of seeking such justification. The problem of induction has, however, been powerfully reinterpreted by Nelson Goodman (V:5) as the problem of distinguishing between projectable and unprojectable observed regularities, that is, in effect, between accidental and lawlike generalizations—which returns us to some problems of Part III.

Finally, the problem of truth involves not so much the nature of the conditions on which statements can be shown to be true (although this is of course a problem with its own complications) as the nature of what truth itself may be supposed to be. Is it a property of sentences, or of sentences that are used to make assertions, or of the thoughts or meanings that are conveyed by sentences? Is it a relationship between sentences (or any suitably similar substitute) and the world or its parts? Or can it be convincingly and usefully denied that it is either of these two sorts of things? The most common view, which already finds its implicit advocates in the ancient world, holds that truth is a relationship between what is said in language and what is the case in the world. And this view, the so-called correspondence theory of truth, is the most forcefully debated alternative in our century (Austin [V:15], Strawson [V:16]).

The essential difficulty is that it is equally unsatisfactory to hold that, in truth, what is said corresponds to states of affairs in the world (since these states are themselves specified in language) and also to deny it (since it would then seem that truth does not concern the world at all). Strawson's solution here draws on a thesis of F. P. Ramsey's, which suggests that there is no problem of truth that is separable from the problem of the analysis of informative judgments. An older, and also much discussed, theory of truth had been advanced by the pragmatists (William James [V:13], John Dewey). In the form in which it was advanced by James (in effect, by confusing Peirce's pragmatic theory of meaning), truth is construed as a species of goodness with respect to belief. This doctrine leads inevitably to intolerable paradox (Bertrand Russell [V:14]).

The Problem of Induction

1

ON MATTERS OF FACT

David Hume

I

All the objects of human reason or enquiry may naturally be divided into two kinds, to wit, *Relations of Ideas*, and *Matters of Fact*. Of the first kind are the sciences of Geometry, Algebra, and Arithmetic; and in short, every affirmation which is either intuitively or demonstratively certain. *That the square of the hypothenuse is equal to the square of the two sides,* is a proposition which expresses a relation between these figures. *That three times five is equal to the half of thirty,* expresses a relation between these numbers. Propositions of this kind are discoverable by the mere operation of thought, without dependence on what is anywhere existent in the universe. Though there never were a circle or triangle in nature, the truths demonstrated by Euclid would for ever retain their certainty and evidence.

Matters of fact, which are the second objects of human reason, are not ascertained in the same manner; nor is our evidence of their truth, however great, of a like nature with the foregoing. The contrary of every matter of fact is still possible; because it can never imply a contradiction, and is conceived by the mind with the same facility and distinctness, as if ever so conformable to reality. *That the sun will not rise to-morrow* is no less intelligible a proposition, and implies no more contradiction than the affirmation, *that it will rise.* We should in vain, therefore, attempt to demonstrate its falsehood. Were it demonstratively false, it would imply a contradiction, and could never be distinctly conceived by the mind.

From David Hume, *An Enquiry Concerning Human Understanding,* L. A. Selby-Bigge, ed., 2nd ed. (Oxford: The Clarendon Press, 1902), Sec. IV, pp. 25–39.

It may, therefore, be a subject worthy of curiosity, to enquire what is the nature of that evidence which assures us of any real existence and matter of fact, beyond the present testimony of our senses, or the records of our memory. This part of philosophy, it is observable, has been little cultivated, either by the ancients or moderns; and therefore our doubts and errors, in the prosecution of so important an enquiry, may be the more excusable; while we march through such difficult paths without any guide or direction. They may even prove useful, by exciting curiosity, and destroying that implicit faith and security, which is the bane of all reasoning and free enquiry. The discovery of defects in the common philosophy, if any such there be, will not, I presume, be a discouragement, but rather an incitement, as is usual, to attempt something more full and satisfactory than has yet been proposed to the public.

All reasonings concerning matter of fact seem to be founded on the relation of *Cause and Effect.* By means of that relation alone we can go beyond the evidence of our memory and senses. If you were to ask a man, why he believes any matter of fact, which is absent; for instance, that his friend is in the country, or in France; he would give you a reason; and this reason would be some other fact; as a letter received from him, or the knowledge of his former resolutions and promises. A man finding a watch or any other machine in a desert island, would conclude that there had once been men in that island. All our reasonings concerning fact are of the same nature. And here it is constantly supposed that there is a connexion between the present fact and that which is inferred from it. Were there nothing to bind them together, the inference would be entirely precarious. The hearing of an articulate voice and rational discourse in the dark assures us of the presence of some person: Why? because these are the effects of the human make and fabric, and closely connected with it. If we anatomize all the other reasonings of this nature, we shall find that they are founded on the relation of cause and effect, and that this relation is either near or remote, direct or collateral. Heat and light are collateral effects of fire, and the one effect may justly be inferred from the other.

If we would satisfy ourselves, therefore, concerning the nature of that evidence, which assures us of matters of fact, we must enquire how we arrive at the knowledge of cause and effect.

I shall venture to affirm, as a general proposition, which admits of no exception, that the knowledge of this relation is not, in any instance, attained by reasonings *a priori;* but arises entirely from experience, when we find that any particular objects are constantly conjoined with each other. Let an object be presented to a man of ever so strong natural reason and abilities; if that object be entirely new to him, he will not be able, by the most accurate examination of its sensible qualities, to discover any of its causes or effects. Adam, though his rational faculties be supposed, at the very first, entirely perfect, could not have inferred from the fluidity and transparency of water that it would suffocate him, or from the light and warmth of fire that it would consume him. No object ever discovers, by the qualities which appear to the senses, either the causes which produced it, or the effects which will arise from it; nor can our reason, unassisted by experience, ever draw any inference concerning real existence and matter of fact.

This proposition, *that causes and effects are discoverable, not by reason but by experience*, will readily be admitted with regard to such objects, as we remember to have once been altogether unknown to us; since we must be conscious of the utter inability, which we then lay under, of foretelling what would arise from them. Present two smooth pieces of marble to a man who has no tincture of natural philosophy; he will never discover that they will adhere together in such a manner as to require great force to separate them in a direct line, while they make so small a resistance to a lateral pressure. Such events, as bear little analogy to the common course of nature, are also readily confessed to be known only by experience; nor does any man imagine that the explosion of gunpowder, or the attraction of a lode-stone, could ever be discovered by arguments *a priori*. In like manner, when an effect is supposed to depend upon an intricate machinery or secret structure of parts, we make no difficulty in attributing all our knowledge of it to experience. Who will assert that he can give the ultimate reason, why milk or bread is proper nourishment for a man, not for a lion or a tiger?

But the same truth may not appear, at first sight, to have the same evidence with regard to events, which have become familiar to us from our first appearance in the world, which bear a close analogy to the whole course of nature, and which are supposed to depend on the simple qualities of objects, without any secret structure of parts. We are apt to imagine that we could discover these effects by the mere operation of our reason, without experience. We fancy, that were we brought on a sudden into this world, we could at first have inferred that one Billiard-ball would communicate motion to another upon impulse; and that we needed not to have waited for the event, in order to pronounce with certainty concerning it. Such is the influence of custom, that, where it is strongest, it not only covers our natural ignorance, but even conceals itself, and seems not to take place, merely because it is found in the highest degree.

But to convince us that all the laws of nature, and all the operations of bodies without exception, are known only by experience, the following reflections may, perhaps, suffice. Were any object presented to us, and were we required to pronounce concerning the effect, which will result from it, without consulting past observation; after what manner, I beseech you, must the mind proceed in this operation? It must invent or imagine some event, which it ascribes to the object as its effect; and it is plain that this invention must be entirely arbitrary. The mind can never possibly find the effect in the supposed cause, by the most accurate scrutiny and examination. For the effect is totally different from the cause, and consequently can never be discovered in it. Motion in the second Billiard-ball is a quite distinct event from motion in the first; nor is there anything in the one to suggest the smallest hint of the other. A stone or piece of metal raised into the air, and left without any support, immediately falls: but to consider the matter *a priori*, is there anything we discover in this situation which can beget the idea of a downward, rather than an upward, or any other motion, in the stone or metal?

And as the first imagination or invention of a particular effect, in all natural operations, is arbitrary, where we consult not experience; so must we also esteem the supposed tie or connexion between the cause and effect, which binds them together, and renders it impossible that any other effect could result from the operation of that cause. When I see, for instance, a

Billiard-ball moving in a straight line towards another; even suppose motion in the second ball should by accident be suggested to me, as the result of their contact or impulse; may I not conceive, that a hundred different events might as well follow from that cause? May not both these balls remain at absolute rest? May not the first ball return in a straight line, or leap off from the second in any line or direction? All these suppositions are consistent and conceivable. Why then should we give the preference to one, which is no more consistent or conceivable than the rest? All our reasonings *a priori* will never be able to show us any foundation for this preference.

In a word, then, every effect is a distinct event from its cause. It could not, therefore, be discovered in the cause, and the first invention or conception of it, *a priori*, must be entirely arbitrary. And even after it is suggested, the conjunction of it with the cause must appear equally arbitrary; since there are always many other effects, which, to reason, must seem fully as consistent and natural. In vain, therefore, should we pretend to determine any single event, or infer any cause or effect, without the assistance of observation and experience.

Hence we may discover the reason why no philosopher, who is rational and modest, has ever pretended to assign the ultimate cause of any natural operation, or to show distinctly the action of that power, which produces any single effect in the universe. It is confessed, that the utmost effort of human reason is to reduce the principles, productive of natural phenomena, to a greater simplicity, and to resolve the many particular effects into a few general causes, by means of reasonings from analogy, experience, and observation. But as to the causes of these general causes, we should in vain attempt their discovery; nor shall we ever be able to satisfy ourselves, by any particular explication of them. These ultimate springs and principles are totally shut up from human curiosity and enquiry. Elasticity, gravity, cohesion of parts, communication of motion by impulse; these are probably the ultimate causes and principles which we shall ever discover in nature; and we may esteem ourselves sufficiently happy, if, by accurate enquiry and reasoning, we can trace up the particular phenomena to, or near to, these general principles. The most perfect philosophy of the natural kind only staves off our ignorance a little longer: as perhaps the most perfect philosophy of the moral or metaphysical kind serves only to discover larger portions of it. Thus the observation of human blindness and weakness is the result of all philosophy, and meets us at every turn, in spite of our endeavours to elude or avoid it.

Nor is geometry, when taken into the assistance of natural philosophy, ever able to remedy this defect, or lead us into the knowledge of ultimate causes, by all that accuracy of reasoning for which it is so justly celebrated. Every part of mixed mathematics proceeds upon the supposition that certain laws are established by nature in her operations; and abstract reasonings are employed, either to assist experience in the discovery of these laws, or to determine their influence in particular instances, where it depends upon any precise degree of distance and quantity. Thus, it is a law of motion, discovered by experience, that the moment or force of any body in motion is in the compound ratio or proportion of its solid contents and its velocity; and consequently, that a small force may remove the greatest obstacle or raise the greatest weight, if, by any contrivance or machinery, we can increase the velocity of that force, so as to make it an overmatch for its antagonist. Geometry assists us in the application of this law, by giving us the just dimensions of all the parts and figures which can enter into any species of machine; but still the discovery of the law itself is owing merely to experience, and all the abstract reasonings in the world could never lead us one step towards the knowledge of it. When we reason *a priori*, and consider merely any object or cause, as it appears to the mind, independent of all observation, it never could suggest to us the notion of any distinct object, such as its effect; much less, show us the inseparable and inviolable connexion between them. A man must be very sagacious who could discover by reasoning that crystal is the effect of heat, and ice of cold, without being previously acquainted with the operation of these qualities.

II

But we have not yet attained any tolerable satisfaction with regard to the question first proposed. Each solution still gives rise to a new question as difficult as the foregoing, and leads us on to farther enquiries. When it is asked, *What is the nature of all our reasonings concerning matter of fact?* the proper answer seems to be, that they are founded on the relation of cause and effect. When again it is asked, *What is the foundation of all our reasonings and conclusions concerning that relation?* it may be replied in one word, Experience. But if we still carry on our sifting humour, and ask, *What is the foundation of all conclusions from experience?* this implies a new question, which may be of more difficult solution and explication. Philosophers, that give themselves airs of superior wisdom and sufficiency, have a hard task when they encounter persons of inquisitive dispositions, who push them from every corner to which they retreat, and who are sure at last to bring them to some dangerous dilemma. The best expedient to prevent this confusion, is to be modest in our pretensions; and even to discover the difficulty ourselves before it is objected to us. By this means, we may make a kind of merit of our very ignorance.

I shall content myself, in this section, with an easy task, and shall pretend only to give a negative answer to the question here proposed. I say then, that, even after we have experience of the operations of cause and effect, our conclusions from that experience are *not* founded on reasoning, or any process of the understanding. This answer we must endeavour both to explain and to defend.

It must certainly be allowed, that nature has kept us at a great distance from all her secrets, and has afforded us only the knowledge of a few superficial qualities of objects; while she conceals from us those powers and principles on which the influence of those objects entirely depends. Our senses inform us of the colour, weight, and consistence of bread; but neither sense nor reason can ever inform us of those qualities which fit it for the nourishment and support of a human body. Sight or feeling conveys an idea of the actual motion of bodies; but as to that wonderful force or power, which would carry on a moving body for ever in a continued change of place, and which bodies never lose but by communicating it to others; of this we cannot form the most distant conception. But notwithstanding this ignorance of natural powers and principles, we always presume, when we see like sensible qualities, that they have like secret powers, and expect that effects, similar to those which we have experienced, will follow from them. If a body of like colour and consistence with that bread, which we have formerly eat, be presented to us, we make no scruple of repeating the experiment, and foresee, with certainty, like nourishment and support. Now this is a process of the mind or thought, of which I would willingly know the foundation. It is allowed on all hands that there is no known connexion between the sensible qualities and the secret powers; and consequently, that the mind is not led to form such a conclusion concerning their constant and regular conjunction, by anything which it knows of their nature. As to past *Experience*, it can be allowed to give *direct* and *certain* information of those precise objects only, and that precise period of time, which fell under its cognizance: but why this experience should be extended to future times, and to other objects, which for aught we know, may be only in appearance similar; this is the main question on which I would insist. The bread, which I formerly eat, nourished me; that is, a body of such sensible qualities was, at that time, endued with such secret powers: but does it follow, that other bread must also nourish me at another time, and that like sensible qualities must always be attended with like secret powers? The consequence seems nowise necessary. At least, it must be acknowledged that there is here a consequence drawn by the mind; that there is a certain step taken; a process of thought, and an inference, which wants to be explained. These two propositions are far from being the same, *I have found that such an object has always been attended with such an effect*, and *I foresee, that other objects, which are, in appearance, similar, will be attended with similar effects*. I shall allow, if you please, that the one proposition may justly be inferred from the other: I know, in fact, that it always is inferred. But if you insist that the inference is made by a chain of reasoning, I desire you to produce that reasoning. The connexion between these propositions is not intuitive. There is required a medium, which may enable the mind to draw such an inference, if indeed it be drawn by reasoning and argument. What that medium is, I must confess, passes my comprehension; and it is incumbent on those to produce it, who assert that it really exists, and is the origin of all our conclusions concerning matter of fact.

This negative argument must certainly, in process of time, become altogether convincing, if many penetrating and able philosophers shall turn their enquiries this way and no one be ever able to discover any connecting proposition or intermediate step, which supports the understanding in this conclusion. But as the question is yet new, every reader may not trust so far to his own penetration, as to conclude, because an argument escapes his enquiry, that therefore it does not really exist. For this reason it may be requisite to venture upon a more difficult task; and enumerating all the branches of human knowledge, endeavour to show that none of them can afford such an argument.

All reasonings may be divided into two kinds, namely, demonstrative reasoning, or that concerning relations of ideas, and moral reasoning, or that concerning matter of fact and existence. That there are no demonstrative arguments in the case seems evident; since it implies no contradiction that the course of nature may change, and that an object, seemingly like those which we have experienced, may be attended with different or contrary effects. May I not clearly and distinctly conceive that a body, falling from the clouds, and which, in all other respects, resembles snow, has yet the taste of salt or feeling of fire? Is there any more intelligible proposition than to affirm, that all the trees will flourish in December and January, and decay in May and June? Now whatever is intelligible, and can be distinctly conceived, implies no contradiction, and can never be proved false by any demonstrative argument or abstract reasoning *a priori*.

If we be, therefore, engaged by arguments to put trust in past experience, and make it the standard of our future judgement, these arguments must be probable only, or such as regard matter of fact and real existence, according to the division above mentioned. But that there is no argument of this kind, must appear, if our explication of that species of reasoning be admitted as solid and satisfactory. We have said that all arguments concerning existence are founded on the relation of cause and effect; that our knowledge of that relation is derived entirely from experience; and that all our experimental conclusions proceed upon the supposition that the future will be conformable to the past. To endeavour, therefore, the proof of this last supposition by probable arguments, or arguments regarding existence, must be evidently going in a circle, and taking that for granted, which is the very point in question.

In reality, all arguments from experience are founded on the similarity which we discover among natural objects, and by which we are induced to expect effects similar to those which we have found to follow from such objects. And though none but a fool or madman will ever pretend to dispute the authority of experience, or to reject that great guide of human life, it may surely be allowed a philosopher to have so much curiosity at least as to examine the principle of human nature, which gives this mighty authority to experience, and makes us draw advantage from that similarity which nature has placed among different objects. From causes which appear *similar* we expect similar effects. This is the sum of all our experimental conclusions. Now it seems evident that, if this conclusion were formed by reason, it would be as perfect at first, and upon one instance, as after ever so long a course of experience. But the case is far otherwise. Nothing so like as eggs; yet no one, on account of this appearing similarity, expects the same taste and relish in all of them. It is only after a long course of uniform experiments in any kind, that we attain a firm reliance and security with regard to a particular event. Now where is that process of reasoning which, from one instance, draws a conclusion, so different from that which it infers from a hundred instances that are nowise different from that single one? This question I propose as much for the sake of information, as with an intention of raising difficulties. I cannot find, I cannot imagine any such reasoning. But I keep my mind still open to instruction, if any one will vouchsafe to bestow it on me.

Should it be said that, from a number of uniform experiments, we *infer* a connexion between the sensible qualities and the secret powers; this, I must confess, seems the same difficulty, couched in different terms. The question still recurs, on what process of argument this *inference* is founded? Where is the medium, the interposing ideas, which join propositions so very wide of each other? It is confessed that the colour, consistence, and other sensible qualities of bread appear not, of themselves, to have any connexion with the secret powers of nourishment and support. For otherwise we could infer these secret powers from the first appearance of these sensible qualities, without the aid of experience; contrary to the sentiment of all philosophers, and contrary to plain matter of fact. Here, then, is our natural state of ignorance with regard to the powers and influence of all objects. How is this remedied by experience? It only shows us a number of uniform effects, resulting from certain objects, and teaches us that those particular objects, at that particular time, were endowed with such powers and forces. When a new object, endowed with similar sensible qualities, is produced, we expect similar powers and forces, and look for a like effect. From a body of like colour and consistence with bread we expect like nourishment and support. But this surely is a step or progress of the mind, which wants to be explained. When a man says, *I have found, in all past instances, such sensible qualities conjoined with such secret powers:* And when he says, *Similar sensible qualities will always be conjoined with similar secret powers,* he is not guilty of a tautology, nor are these propositions in any respect the same. You say that the one proposition is an inference from the other. But you must confess that the inference is not intuitive; neither is it demonstrative: Of what nature is it, then? To say it is experimental, is begging the question. For all inferences from experience suppose, as their foundation, that the future will resemble the past, and that similar powers will be conjoined with similar sensible qualities. If there be any suspicion that the course of nature may change, and that the past may be no rule for the future, all experience becomes useless, and can give rise to no inference or conclusion. It is impossible, therefore, that any arguments from experience can prove this resemblance of the past to the future; since all these arguments are founded on the supposition of that resemblance. Let the course of things be allowed hitherto ever so regular; that alone, without some new argument or inference, proves not that, for the future, it will continue so. In vain do you pretend to have learned the nature of bodies from your past experience. Their secret nature, and consequently all their effects and influence, may change, without any change in their sensible qualities. This happens sometimes, and with regard to some objects: Why may it not happen always, and with regard to all objects? What logic, what process of argument secures you against this supposition? My practice, you say, refutes my doubts. But you mistake the purport of my question. As an agent, I am quite satisfied in the point; but as a philosopher, who has some share of curiosity, I will not say scepticism, I want to learn the foundation of this inference. No reading, no enquiry has yet been able to remove my difficulty, or give me satisfaction in a matter of such importance. Can I do better than propose the difficulty to the public, even though, perhaps, I have small hopes of obtaining a solution? We shall at least, by this means, be sensible of our ignorance, if we do not augment our knowledge.

I must confess that a man is guilty of unpardonable arrogance who concludes, because an argument has escaped his own investigation, that therefore it does not really exist. I must also confess that, though all the learned, for several ages, should have employed themselves in fruitless search upon any subject, it may still, perhaps, be rash to conclude positively that the subject must, therefore, pass all human comprehension. Even though we examine all the sources of our knowledge, and conclude them unfit for such a subject, there may still remain a suspicion, that the enumeration is not complete, or the examination not accurate. But with regard to the present subject, there are some considerations which seem to remove all this accusation of arrogance or suspicion of mistake.

It is certain that the most ignorant and stupid peasants—nay infants, nay even brute beasts—improve by experience, and learn the qualities of natural objects, by observing the effects which result from them. When a child has felt the sensation of pain from touching the flame of a candle, he will be careful not to put his hand near any candle; but will expect a similar effect from a cause which is similar in its sensible qualities and appearance. If you assert, therefore, that the understanding of the child is led into this conclusion by any process of argument or ratiocination, I may justly require you to produce that argument; nor have you any pretence to refuse so equitable a demand. You cannot say that the argument is abstruse, and may possibly escape your enquiry; since you confess that it is obvious to the capacity of a mere infant. If you hesitate, therefore, a moment, or if, after reflection, you produce any intricate or profound argument, you, in a manner, give up the question, and confess that it is not reasoning which engages us to suppose the past resembling the future, and to expect similar effects from causes which are, to appearance, similar. This is the proposition which I intended to enforce in the present section. If I be right, I pretend not to have made any mighty discovery. And if I be wrong, I must acknowledge myself to be indeed a very backward scholar; since I cannot now discover an argument which, it seems, was perfectly familiar to me long before I was out of my cradle.

2

ON INDUCTION

Bertrand Russell

. . . we have been concerned in the attempt to get clear as to our data in the way of knowledge of existence. What things are there in the universe whose existence is known to us owing to our being acquainted with them? So far, our answer has been that we are acquainted with our sense-data, and, probably, with ourselves. These we know to exist. And past sense-data which are remembered are known to have existed in the past. This knowledge supplies our data.

But if we are to be able to draw inferences from these data—if we are to know of the existence of matter, of other people, of the past before our individual memory begins, or of the future, we must know general principles of some kind by means of which such inferences can be drawn. It must be known to us that the existence of some one sort of thing, A, is a sign of the existence of some other sort of thing, B, either at the same time as A or at some earlier or later time, as, for example, thunder is a sign of the earlier existence of lightning. If this were not known to us, we could never extend our knowledge beyond the sphere of our private experience; and this sphere, as we have seen, is exceedingly limited. The question we have now to consider is whether such an extension is possible, and if so, how it is effected.

Let us take as an illustration a matter about which none of us, in fact, feel the slightest doubt. We are all convinced that the sun will rise to-morrow. Why? Is this belief a mere blind outcome of past experience, or can it be justified as a reasonable belief? It is not easy to find a test by which to judge whether a belief of this kind is reasonable or not, but we can at least ascertain what sort of general beliefs would suffice, if true, to justify the judgment that the sun will rise to-morrow, and the many other similar judgments upon which our actions are based.

It is obvious that if we are asked why we believe that the sun will rise to-morrow, we shall naturally answer, "Because it always has risen every day." We have a firm belief that it will rise in the future, because it has risen in the

---

From Bertrand Russell, *The Problems of Philosophy* (London: Oxford University Press, 1912), pp. 60–69. Reprinted by permission of the publisher.

past. If we are challenged as to why we believe that it will continue to rise as heretofore, we may appeal to the laws of motion: the earth, we shall say, is a freely rotating body, and such bodies do not cease to rotate unless something interferes from outside, and there is nothing outside to interfere with the earth between now and to-morrow. Of course it might be doubted whether we are quite certain that there is nothing outside to interfere, but this is not the interesting doubt. The interesting doubt is as to whether the laws of motion will remain in operation until to-morrow. If this doubt is raised, we find ourselves in the same position as when the doubt about the sunrise was first raised.

The *only* reason for believing that the laws of motion will remain in operation is that they have operated hitherto, so far as our knowledge of the past enables us to judge. It is true that we have a greater body of evidence from the past in favour of the laws of motion than we have in favour of the sunrise, because the sunrise is merely a particular case of fulfilment of the laws of motion, and there are countless other particular cases. But the real question is: Do *any* number of cases of a law being fulfilled in the past afford evidence that it will be fulfilled in the future? If not, it becomes plain that we have no ground whatever for expecting the sun to rise to-morrow, or for expecting the bread we shall eat at our next meal not to poison us, or for any of the other scarcely conscious expectations that control our daily lives. It is to be observed that all such expectations are only *probable*; thus we have not to seek for a proof that they *must* be fulfilled, but only for some reason in favour of the view that they are *likely* to be fulfilled.

Now in dealing with this question we must, to begin with, make an important distinction, without which we should soon become involved in hopeless confusions. Experience has shown us that, hitherto, the frequent repetition of some uniform succession or coexistence has been a *cause* of our expecting the same succession or coexistence on the next occasion. Food that has a certain appearance generally has a certain taste, and it is a severe shock to our expectations when the familiar appearance is found to be associated with an unusual taste. Things which we see become associated, by habit, with certain tactile sensations which we expect if we touch them; one of the horrors of a ghost (in many ghost-stories) is that it fails to give us any sensations of touch. Uneducated people who go abroad for the first time are so surprised as to be incredulous when they find their native language not understood.

And this kind of association is not confined to men; in animals also it is very strong. A horse which has been often driven along a certain road resists the attempt to drive him in a different direction. Domestic animals expect food when they see the person who usually feeds them. We know that all these rather crude expectations of uniformity are liable to be misleading. The man who has fed the chicken every day throughout its life at last wrings its neck instead, showing that more refined views as to the uniformity of nature would have been useful to the chicken.

But in spite of the misleadingness of such expectations, they nevertheless exist. The mere fact that something has happened a certain number of times causes animals and men to expect that it will happen again. Thus our instincts certainly cause us to believe that the sun will rise to-morrow, but we may be in no better a position than the chicken which unexpectedly has its neck wrung. We have therefore to distinguish the fact that past uniformities *cause* expectations as to the future, from the question whether there is any reasonable ground for giving weight to such expectations after the question of their validity has been raised.

The problem we have to discuss is whether there is any reason for believing in what is called "the uniformity of nature." The belief in the uniformity of nature is the belief that everything that has happened or will happen is an instance of some general law to which there are *no* exceptions. The crude expectations which we have been considering are all subject to exceptions, and therefore liable to disappoint those who entertain them. But science habitually assumes, at least as a working hypothesis, that general rules which have exceptions can be replaced by general rules which have no exceptions. "Unsupported bodies in air fall" is a general rule to which balloons and aeroplanes are exceptions. But the laws of motion and the law of gravitation, which account for the fact that most bodies fall, also account for the fact that balloons and aeroplanes can rise; thus the laws of motion and the law of gravitation are not subject to these exceptions.

The belief that the sun will rise to-morrow might be falsified if the earth came suddenly into contact with a large body which destroyed its rotation; but the laws of motion and the law of gravitation would not be infringed by such an event. The business of science is to find uniformities, such as the laws of motion and the law of gravitation, to which, so far as our experience extends, there are no exceptions. In this search science has been remarkably successful, and it may be conceded that such uniformities have held hitherto. This brings us back to the question: Have we any reason, assuming that they have always held in the past, to suppose that they will hold in the future?

It has been argued that we have reason to know that the future will resemble the past, because what was the future has constantly become the past, and has always been found to resemble the past, so that we really have experience of the future, namely of times which were formerly future, which we may call past futures. But such an argument really begs the very question at issue. We have experience of past futures, but not of future futures, and the question is: Will future futures resemble past futures? This question is not to be answered by an argument which starts from past futures alone. We have therefore still to seek for some principle which shall enable us to know that the future will follow the same laws as the past.

The reference to the future in this question is not essential. The same question arises when we apply the laws that work in our experience to past things of which we have no experience—as, for example, in geology, or in theories as to the origin of the Solar System. The question we really have to ask is: "When two things have been found to be often associated, and no instance is known of the one occurring without the other, does the occurrence of one of the two, in a fresh instance, give any good ground for expecting the other?" On our answer to this question must depend the validity of the whole of our expectations as to the future, the whole of the results obtained by induction, and in fact practically all the beliefs upon which our daily life is based.

It must be conceded, to begin with, that the fact that two things have been found often together and never apart does not, by itself, suffice to *prove* demonstratively that they will be found together in the next case we examine. The most we can hope is that the oftener things are found together, the more probable it becomes that they will be found together another time, and that, if they have been found together often enough, the probability will amount almost to certainty. It can never quite reach certainty, because we know that in spite of frequent repetitions there sometimes is a failure at the last, as in the case of the chicken whose neck is wrung. Thus probability is all we ought to seek.

It might be urged, as against the view we are advocating, that we know all natural phenomena to be subject to the reign of law, and that sometimes, on the basis of observation, we can see that only one law can possibly fit the facts of the case. Now to this view there are two answers. The first is that, even if *some* law which has no exceptions applies to our case, we can never, in practice, be sure that we have discovered that law and not one to which there are exceptions. The second is that the reign of law would seem to be itself only probable, and that our belief that it will hold in the future, or in unexamined cases in the past, is itself based upon the very principle we are examining.

The principle we are examining may be called the *principle of induction*, and its two parts may be stated as follows:

(*a*) When a thing of a certain sort A has been found to be associated with a thing of a certain other sort B, and has never been found dissociated from a thing of the sort B, the greater the number of cases in which A and B have been associated, the greater is the probability that they will be associated in a fresh case in which one of them is known to be present;

(*b*) Under the same circumstances, a sufficient number of cases of association will make the probability of a fresh association nearly a certainty, and will make it approach certainty without limit.

As just stated, the principle applies only to the verification of our expectation in a single fresh instance. But we want also to know that there is a probability in favour of the general law that things of the sort A are *always* associated with things of the sort B, provided a sufficient number of cases of association are known, and no cases of failure of association are known. The probability of the general law is obviously less than the probability of the particular case, since if the general law is true, the particular case must also be true, whereas the particular case may be true without the general law being true. Nevertheless the probability of the general law is increased by repetitions, just as the probability of the particular case is. We may therefore repeat the two parts of our principle as regards the general law, thus:

(*a*) The greater the number of cases in which a thing of the sort A has been found associated with a thing of the sort B, the more probable it is (if no cases of failure of association are known) that A is always associated with B;

(*b*) Under the same circumstances, a sufficient number of cases of the association of A with B will make it nearly certain that A is always associated with B, and will make this general law approach certainty without limit.

It should be noted that probability is always relative to certain data. In our case, the data are merely the known cases of co-existence of A and B. There may be other data, which *might* be taken into account, which would gravely alter the probability. For example, a man who had seen a great many white swans might argue, by our principle, that on the data it was *probable* that all swans were white, and this might be a perfectly sound argument. The argument is not disproved by the fact that some swans are black, because a thing may very well happen in spite of the fact that some data render it improbable. In the case of the swans, a man might know that colour is a very variable characteristic in many species of animals, and that, therefore, an induction as to colour is peculiarly liable to error. But this knowledge would be a fresh datum, by no means proving that the probability relatively to our previous data had been wrongly estimated. The fact, therefore, that things often fail to fulfil our expectations is no evidence that our expectations will not *probably* be fulfilled in a given case or a given class of cases. Thus our inductive principle is at any rate not capable of being *disproved* by an appeal to experience.

The inductive principle, however, is equally incapable of being *proved* by an appeal to experience. Experience might conceivably confirm the inductive principle as regards the cases that have been already examined; but as regards unexamined cases, it is the inductive principle alone that can justify any inference from what has been examined to what has not been examined. All arguments which, on the basis of experience, argue as to the future or the unexperienced parts of the past or present, assume the inductive principle; hence we can never use experience to prove the inductive principle without begging the question. Thus we must either accept the inductive principle on the ground of its intrinsic evidence, or forgo all justification of our expectations about the future. If the principle is unsound, we have no reason to expect the sun to rise to-morrow, to expect bread to be more nourishing than a stone, or to expect that if we throw ourselves off the roof we shall fall. When we see what looks like our best friend approaching us, we shall have no reason to suppose that his body is not inhabited by the mind of our worst enemy or of some total stranger. All our conduct is based upon associations which have worked in the past, and which we therefore regard as likely to work in the future; and this likelihood is dependent for its validity upon the inductive principle.

The general principles of science, such as the belief in the reign of law, and the belief that every event must have a cause, are as completely dependent upon the inductive principle as are the beliefs of daily life. All such general principles are believed because mankind have found innumerable instances of their truth, and no instances of their falsehood. But this affords no evidence for their truth in the future, unless the inductive principle is assumed.

Thus all knowledge which, on a basis of experience, tells us something about what is not experienced, is based upon a belief which experience can neither confirm nor confute, yet which, at least in its more concrete applications, appears to be as firmly rooted in us as many of the facts of experience. . . .

3

PROBABILITY AND INDUCTION

Hans Reichenbach

§38. THE PROBLEM OF INDUCTION

. . .

The frequency interpretation [of probability] has two functions within the theory of probability. First, a frequency is used as a *substantiation* for the probability statement; it furnishes the reason why we believe in the statement. Second, a frequency is used for the *verification* of the probability statement; that is to say, it is to furnish the meaning of the statement. These two functions are not identical. The observed frequency from which we start is only the basis of the probability inference; we intend to state another frequency which concerns *future observations*. The probability inference proceeds from a known frequency to one unknown; it is from this function that its importance is derived. The probability statement sustains a prediction, and this is why we want it.

It is the problem of induction which appears with this formulation. The theory of probability involves the problem of induction, and a solution of the problem of probability cannot be given without an answer to the question of induction. The connection of both problems is well known; philosophers such as Peirce have expressed the idea that a solution of the problem of induction is to be found in the theory of probability. The inverse relation, however, holds as well. Let us say, cautiously, that the solution of both problems is to be given within the same theory.

In uniting the problem of probability with that of induction, we decide unequivocally in favor of that determination of the degree of probability which mathematicians call the *determination a posteriori*. . . .

By "determination a posteriori" we understand a procedure in which the relative frequency observed statistically is assumed to hold approximately for any future prolongation of the series. Let us express this idea in an exact formulation. We assume a series of events A and $\bar{A}$ (non-A); let n be the

Reprinted from *Experience and Prediction*, Secs. 38–39, pp. 339–342, 346–353, 355–357, by Hans Reichenbach by permission of The University of Chicago Press. Copyright 1938 by The University of Chicago.

number of events, m the number of events of the type A among them. We have then the relative frequency

$$h^n = \frac{m}{n}$$

The assumption of the determination a posteriori may now be expressed:

For any further prolongation of the series as far as s events (s > n), the relative frequency will remain within a small interval around h^n; *i.e., we assume the relation*

$$h^n - \epsilon \leqq h^s \leqq h^n + \epsilon$$

where ϵ is a small number.

This assumption formulates the *principle of induction*. We may add that our formulation states the principle in a form more general than that customary in traditional philosophy. The usual formulation is as follows: induction is the assumption that an event which occurred n times will occur at all following times. It is obvious that this formulation is a special case of our formulation, corresponding to the case $h^n = 1$. We cannot restrict our investigation to this special case because the general case occurs in a great many problems.

The reason for this is to be found in the fact that the theory of probability needs the definition of probability as the limit of the frequency. Our formulation is a necessary condition for the existence of a limit of the frequency near h^n; what is yet to be added is that there is an h^n of the kind postulated for every ϵ however small. If we include this idea in our assumption, our postulate of induction becomes the hypothesis that there is a limit to the relative frequency which does not differ greatly from the observed value.

If we enter now into a closer analysis of this assumption, one thing needs no further demonstration: the formula given is not a tautology. There is indeed no logical necessity that h^s remains within the interval $h^n \pm \epsilon$; we may easily imagine that this does not take place.

The nontautological character of induction has been known a long time; Bacon had already emphasized that it is just this character to which the importance of induction is due. If inductive inference can teach us something new, in opposition to deductive inference, this is because it is not a tautology. This useful quality has, however, become the center of the epistemological difficulties of induction. It was David Hume who first attacked the principle from this side; he pointed out that the apparent constraint of the inductive inference, although submitted to by everybody, could not be justified. We believe in induction; we even cannot get rid of the belief when we know the impossibility of a logical demonstration of the validity of inductive inference; but as logicians we must admit that this belief is a deception—such is the result of Hume's criticism. We may summarize his objections in two statements:

1. We have no logical demonstration for the validity of inductive inference.
2. There is no demonstration a posteriori for the inductive inference; any such demonstration would presuppose the very principle which it is to demonstrate.

These two pillars of Hume's criticism of the principle of induction have stood unshaken for two centuries, and I think they will stand as long as there is a scientific philosophy.

Inductive inference cannot be dispensed with because we need it for the purpose of action. To deem the inductive assumption unworthy of the assent of a philosopher, to keep a distinguished reserve, and to meet with a condescending smile the attempts of other people to bridge the gap between experience and prediction is cheap self-deceit; at the very moment when the apostles of such a higher philosophy leave the field of theoretical discussion and pass to the simplest actions of daily life, they follow the inductive principle as surely as does every earth-bound mind. In any action there are various means to the realization of our aim; we have to make a choice, and we decide in accordance with the inductive principle. Although there is no means which will produce with certainty the desired effect, we do not leave the choice to chance but prefer the means indicated by the principle of induction. If we sit at the wheel of a car and want to turn the car to the right, why do we turn the wheel to the right? There is no certainty that the car will follow the wheel; there are indeed cars which do not always so behave. Such cases are fortunately exceptions. But if we should not regard the inductive prescription and consider the effect of a turn of the wheel as entirely unknown to us, we might turn it to the left as well. I do not say this to suggest such an attempt; the effects of skeptical philosophy applied in motor traffic would be rather unpleasant. But I should say a philosopher who is to put aside his principles any time he steers a motorcar is a bad philosopher.

It is no justification of inductive belief to show that it is a habit. It *is* a habit; but the question is whether it is a good habit, where "good" is to mean "useful for the purpose of actions directed to future events." If a person tells me that Socrates is a man, and that all men are mortal, I have the habit of believing that Socrates is mortal. I know, however, that this is a good habit. If anyone had the habit of believing in such a case that Socrates is not mortal, we could demonstrate to him that this was a bad habit. The analogous question must be raised for inductive inference. If we should not be able to demonstrate that it is a good habit, we should either cease using it or admit frankly that our philosophy is a failure.

Science proceeds by induction and not by tautological transformations of reports. Bacon is right about Aristotle; but the *novum organon* [i.e., induction as opposed to deduction] needs a justification as good as that of the *organon*. Hume's criticism was the heaviest blow against empiricism; if we do not want to dupe our consciousness of this by means of the narcotic drug of aprioristic rationalism, or the soporific of skepticism, we must find a defense for the inductive inference which holds as well as does the formalistic justification of deductive logic.

§39. THE JUSTIFICATION OF THE PRINCIPLE OF INDUCTION

We shall now begin to give the justification of induction which Hume thought impossible. In the pursuit of this inquiry, let us ask first what has been proved, strictly speaking, by Hume's objections.

Hume started with the assumption that a justification of inductive inference is only given if we can show that inductive inference must lead to success. In other words, Hume believed that any justified application of the inductive inference presupposes a demonstration that the conclusion is true. It is this assumption on which Hume's criticism is based. His two objections directly concern only the question of the truth of the conclusion; they prove that the truth of the conclusion cannot be demonstrated. The two objections, therefore, are valid only in so far as the Humean assumption is valid. It is this question to which we must turn: Is it necessary, for the justification of inductive inference, to show that its conclusion is true?

A rather simple analysis shows us that this assumption does not hold. Of course, if we were able to prove the truth of the conclusion, inductive inference would be justified; but the converse does not hold: a justification of the inductive inference does not imply a proof of the truth of the conclusion. The proof of the truth of the conclusion is only a sufficient condition for the justification of induction, not a necessary condition.

The inductive inference is a procedure which is to furnish us the best assumption concerning the future. If we do not know the truth about the future, there may be nonetheless a best assumption about it, i.e., a best assumption relative to what we know. We must ask whether such a characterization may be given for the principle of induction. If this turns out to be possible, the principle of induction will be justified.

An example will show the logical structure of our reasoning. A man may be suffering from a grave disease; the physician tells us: "I do not know whether an operation will save the man, but if there *is* any remedy, it is an operation." In such a case, the operation would be justified. Of course, it would be better to know that the operation will save the man; but, if we do not know this, the knowledge formulated in the statement of the physician is a sufficient justification. If we cannot realize the sufficient conditions of success, we shall at least realize the necessary conditions. If we were able to show that the inductive inference is a necessary condition of success, it would be justified; such a proof would satisfy any demands which may be raised about the justification of induction.

Now obviously there is a great difference between our example and induction. The reasoning of the physician presupposes inductions; his knowledge about an operation as the only possible means of saving a life is based on inductive generalizations, just as are all other statements of empirical character. But we wanted only to illustrate the logical structure of our reasoning. If we want to regard such a reasoning as a justification of the principle of induction, the character of induction as a necessary condition of success must be demonstrated in a way which does not presuppose induction. Such a proof, however, can be given.

If we want to construct this proof, we must begin with a determination of the aim of induction. It is usually said that we perform inductions with the aim of foreseeing the future. This determination is vague; let us replace it by a formulation more precise in character:

The aim of induction is to find series of events whose frequency of occurrence converges toward a limit.

We choose this formulation because we found that we need probabilities and that a probability is to be defined as the limit of a frequency; thus our determination of the aim of induction is given in such a way that it enables us to apply probability methods. If we compare this determination of the aim of induction with determinations usually given, it turns out to be not a confinement to a narrower aim but an expansion. What we usually call "foreseeing the future" is included in our formulation as a special case; the case of knowing with certainty for every event A the event B following it would correspond in our formulation to a case where the limit of the frequency is of the numerical value 1. Hume thought of this case only. Thus our inquiry differs from that of Hume in so far as it conceives the aim of induction in a generalized form. But we do not omit any possible applications if we determine the principle of induction as the means of obtaining the limit of a frequency. If we have limits of frequency, we have all we want, including the case considered by Hume; we have then the laws of nature in their most general form, including both statistical and so-called causal laws—the latter being nothing but a special case of statistical laws, corresponding to the numerical value 1 of the limit of the frequency. We are entitled, therefore, to consider the determination of the limit of a frequency as the aim of the inductive inference.

Now it is obvious that we have no guaranty that this aim is at all attainable. The world may be so disorderly that it is impossible for us to construct series with a limit. Let us introduce the term "predictable" for a world which is sufficiently ordered to enable us to construct series with a limit. We must admit, then, that we do not know whether the world is predictable.

But, if the world is predictable, let us ask what the logical function of the principle of induction will be. For this purpose, we must consider the definition of limit. The frequency h^n has a limit at p, if for any given ϵ there is an n such that h^n is within $p \pm \epsilon$ and remains within this interval for all the rest of the series. Comparing our formulation of the principle of induction (§38) with this, we may infer from the definition of the limit that, if there is a limit, there is an element of the series from which the principle of induction leads to the true value of the limit. In this sense the principle of induction is a necessary condition for the determination of a limit.

It is true that, if we are faced with the value h^n for the frequency furnished by our statistics, we do not know whether this n is sufficiently large to be identical with, or beyond, the n of the "place of convergence" for ϵ. It may be that our n is not yet large enough, that after n there will be a deviation greater than ϵ from p. To this we may answer: We are not bound to stay at h^n; we may continue our procedure and shall always consider the last h^n obtained as our best value. This procedure must at some time lead to the true value p, if there is a limit at all; the applicability of this procedure, as a whole, is a necessary condition of the existence of a limit at p.

To understand this, let us imagine a principle of a contrary sort. Imagine a man who, if h^n is reached, always makes the assumption that the limit of the frequency is at $h^n + a$, where a is a fixed constant. If this man continues his procedure for increasing n, he is sure to miss the limit; this procedure must at some time become false, if there is a limit at all.

We have found now a better formulation of the necessary condition. We must not consider the individual assumption for an individual h^n; we must take account of the procedure of continued assumptions of the inductive type. The applicability of this procedure is the necessary condition sought.

If, however, it is only the whole procedure which constitutes the necessary condition, how may we apply this idea to the individual case which stands before us? We want to know whether the individual h^n observed by us differs less than ϵ from the limit of the convergence; this neither can be guaranteed nor can it be called a necessary condition of the existence of a limit. So what does our idea of the necessary condition imply for the individual case? It seems that for our individual case the idea turns out to be without any application.

This difficulty corresponds in a certain sense to the difficulty we found in the application of the frequency interpretation to the single case. It is to be eliminated by the introduction of a concept already used for the other problem: the concept of posit.

If we observe a frequency h^n and assume it to be the approximate value of the limit, this assumption is not maintained in the form of a true statement; it is a posit such as we perform in a wager. We posit h^n as the value of the limit, i.e., we wager on h^n, just as we wager on the side of a die. We know that h^n is our best wager, therefore we posit it. There is, however, a difference as to the type of posit occurring here and in the throw of the die.

In the case of the die, we know the weight belonging to the posit: it is given by the degree of probability. If we posit the case "side other than that numbered 1," the weight of this posit is $5/6$. We speak in this case of a posit with appraised weight, or, in short, of an *appraised posit*.

In the case of our positing h^n, we do not know its weight. We call it, therefore, a *blind posit*. We know it is our best posit, but we do not know how good it is. Perhaps, although our best, it is a rather bad one.

The blind posit, however, may be corrected. By continuing our series, we obtain new values h^n; we always choose the last h^n. Thus the blind posit is of an approximative type; we know that the method of making and correcting such posits must in time lead to success, in case there is a limit of the frequency. It is this idea which furnishes the justification of the blind posit. The procedure described may be called the *method of anticipation;* in choosing h^n as our posit, we anticipate the case where n is the "place of convergence." It may be that by this anticipation we obtain a false value; we know, however, that a continued anticipation must lead to the true value, if there is a limit at all.

These considerations lead, however, to a more precise formulation of the logical structure of the inductive inference. We must say that, if there is any method which leads to the limit of the frequency, the inductive principle will do the same; if there is a limit of the frequency, the inductive principle is a sufficient condition to find it. If we omit now the premise that there is a limit of the frequency, we cannot say that the inductive principle is the necessary condition of finding it because there are other methods using a correction c_n. There is a set of equivalent conditions such that the choice of one of the members of the set is necessary if we want to find the limit; and, if there is a limit, each of the members of the set is an appropriate method for finding it. We may say, therefore, that the *applicability* of the inductive principle is a necessary condition of the existence of a limit of the frequency.

The decision in favor of the inductive principle among the members of the set of equivalent means may be substantiated by pointing out its quality of embodying the smallest risk; after all, this decision is not of a great relevance, as all these methods must lead to the same value of the limit if they are sufficiently continued. It must not be forgotten, however, that the method of clairvoyance is not, without further ado, a member of the set because we do not know whether the correction c_n occurring here is submitted to the condition of convergence to zero. This must be proved first, and it can only be proved by using the inductive principle, viz., a method known to be a member of the set: this is why clairvoyance, in spite of all occult pretensions, is to be submitted to the control of scientific methods, i.e., by the principle of induction.

It is in the analysis expounded that we see the solution of Hume's problem. Hume demanded too much when he wanted for a justification of the inductive inference a proof that its conclusion is true. What his objections demonstrate is only that such a proof cannot be given. We do not perform, however, an inductive inference with the pretension of obtaining a true statement. What we obtain is a wager; and it is the best wager we can lay because it corresponds to a procedure the applicability of which is the necessary condition of the possibility of predictions. To fulfil the conditions sufficient for the attainment of true predictions does not lie in our power; let us be glad that we are able to fulfil at least the conditions necessary for the realization of this intrinsic aim of science.

4

THE 'JUSTIFICATION' OF INDUCTION

P. F. Strawson

. . .

[7] . . . What reason have we to place reliance on inductive procedures? Why should we suppose that the accumulation of instances of *A*s which are *B*s, however various the conditions in which they are observed, gives any good reason for expecting the next *A* we encounter to be a *B?* It is our habit to form expectations in this way; but can the habit be rationally justified? When this doubt has entered our minds it may be difficult to free ourselves from it. For the doubt has its source in a confusion; and some attempts to resolve the doubt preserve the confusion; and other attempts to show that the doubt is senseless seem altogether too facile. The root-confusion is easily described; but simply to describe it seems an inadequate remedy against it. So the doubt must be examined again and again, in the light of different attempts to remove it.

If someone asked what grounds there were for supposing that deductive reasoning was valid, we might answer that there were in fact no grounds for supposing that deductive reasoning was always valid; sometimes people made valid inferences, and sometimes they were guilty of logical fallacies. If he said that we had misunderstood his question, and that what he wanted to know was what grounds there were for regarding deduction *in general* as a valid method of argument, we should have to answer that his question was without sense, for to say that an argument, or a form or method of argument, was valid or invalid would *imply* that it was deductive; the concepts of validity and invalidity had application only to individual deductive arguments or forms of deductive argument. Similarly, if a man asked what grounds there were for thinking it reasonable to hold beliefs arrived at inductively, one might at first answer that there were good and bad inductive arguments, that sometimes it was reasonable to hold a belief arrived at inductively and sometimes it was not. If he, too, said that his

From P. F. Strawson, *An Introduction to Logical Theory* (New York: John Wiley & Sons, Inc., 1952), Chap. IX, pp. 249–263. Reprinted by permission of the publisher.

question had been misunderstood, that he wanted to know whether induction in general was a reasonable method of inference, then we might well think his question senseless in the same way as the question whether deduction is in general valid; for to call a particular belief reasonable or unreasonable is to apply inductive standards, just as to call a particular argument valid or invalid is to apply deductive standards. The parallel is not wholly convincing; for words like 'reasonable' and 'rational' have not so precise and technical a sense as the word 'valid'. Yet it is sufficiently powerful to make us wonder how the second question could be raised at all, to wonder why, in contrast with the corresponding question about deduction, it should have seemed to constitute a genuine problem.

Suppose that a man is brought up to regard formal logic as the study of the science and art of reasoning. He observes that all inductive processes are, by deductive standards, invalid; the premises never entail the conclusions. Now inductive processes are notoriously important in the formation of beliefs and expectations about everything which lies beyond the observation of available witnesses. But an *invalid* argument is an *unsound* argument; an *unsound* argument is one in which *no good reason* is produced for accepting the conclusion. So if inductive processes are invalid, if all the arguments we should produce, if challenged, in support of our beliefs about what lies beyond the observation of available witnesses are unsound, then we have no good reason for any of these beliefs. This conclusion is repugnant. So there arises the demand for a justification, not of this or that particular belief which goes beyond what is entailed by our evidence, but a justification of induction in general. And when the demand arises in this way it is, in effect, the demand that induction shall be shown to be really a kind of deduction; for nothing less will satisfy the doubter when this is the route to his doubts.

Tracing this, the most common route to the general doubt about the reasonableness of induction, shows how the doubt seems to escape the absurdity of a demand that induction in general shall be justified by inductive standards. The demand is that induction should be shown to be a rational process; and this turns out to be the demand that one kind of reasoning should be shown to be another and different kind. Put thus crudely, the demand seems to escape one absurdity only to fall into another. Of course, inductive arguments are not deductively valid; if they were, they would be deductive arguments. Inductive reasoning must be assessed, for soundness, by inductive standards. Nevertheless, fantastic as the wish for induction to be deduction may seem, it is only in terms of it that we can understand some of the attempts that have been made to justify induction.

8. The first kind of attempt I shall consider might be called the search for the supreme premise of inductions. In its primitive form it is quite a crude attempt; and I shall make it cruder by caricature. We have already seen that for a particular inductive step, such as 'The kettle has been on the fire for ten minutes, so it will be boiling by now', we can substitute a deductive argument by introducing a generalization (e.g., 'A kettle always boils within ten minutes of being put on the fire') as an additional premise. This manœuvre shifted the emphasis of the problem of inductive support on to the question of how we established such generalizations as these, which rested on grounds by which they were not entailed. But suppose the manœuvre could be repeated. Suppose we could find one supremely general

proposition, which taken in conjunction with the evidence for any accepted generalization of science or daily life (or at least of science) would entail that generalization. Then, so long as the status of the supreme generalization could be satisfactorily explained, we could regard all sound inductions to unqualified general conclusions as, at bottom, valid deductions. The justification would be found, for at least these cases. The most obvious difficulty in this suggestion is that of formulating the supreme general proposition in such a way that it shall be precise enough to yield the desired entailments, and yet not obviously false or arbitrary. Consider, for example, the formula: 'For all f, g, wherever n cases of $f.g$, and no cases of $f. \sim g$, are observed, then all cases of f are cases of g.' To turn it into a sentence, we have only to replace 'n' by some number. But what number? If we take the value of 'n' to be 1 or 20 or 500, the resulting statement is obviously false. Moreover, the choice of any number would seem quite arbitrary; there is no privileged number of favourable instances which we take as decisive in establishing a generalization. If, on the other hand, we phrase the proposition vaguely enough to escape these objections—if, for example, we phrase it as 'Nature is uniform'—then it becomes too vague to provide the desired entailments. It should be noticed that the impossibility of framing a general proposition of the kind required is really a special case of the impossibility of framing precise rules for the assessment of evidence. If we could frame a rule which would tell us precisely when we had *conclusive* evidence for a generalization, then it would yield just the proposition required as the supreme premise.

Even if these difficulties could be met, the question of the status of the supreme premise would remain. How, if a non-necessary proposition, could it be established? The appeal to experience, to inductive support, is clearly barred on pain of circularity. If, on the other hand, it were a necessary truth and possessed, in conjunction with the evidence for a generalization, the required logical power to entail the generalization (e.g., if the latter were the conclusion of a hypothetical syllogism, of which the hypothetical premise was the necessary truth in question), then the evidence would entail the generalization independently, and the problem would not arise: a conclusion unbearably paradoxical. In practice, the extreme vagueness with which candidates for the role of supreme premise are expressed prevents their acquiring such logical power, and at the same time renders it very difficult to classify them as analytic or synthetic: under pressure they may tend to tautology; and, when the pressure is removed, assume an expansively synthetic air.

In theories of the kind which I have here caricatured the ideal of deduction is not usually so blatantly manifest as I have made it. One finds the 'Law of the Uniformity of Nature' presented less as the suppressed premise of crypto-deductive inferences than as, say, the 'presupposition of the validity of inductive reasoning'. . . .

9. I shall next consider a more sophisticated kind of attempt to justify induction: more sophisticated both in its interpretation of this aim and in the method adopted to achieve it. The aim envisaged is that of proving that the probability of a generalization, whether universal or proportional, increases with the number of instances for which it is found to hold. This clearly is a

realistic aim: for the proposition to be proved does state, as we have already seen, a fundamental feature of our criteria for assessing the strength of evidence. The method of proof proposed is mathematical. Use is to be made of the arithmetical calculation of chances. This, however, seems less realistic: for we have already seen that the prospect of analysing the notion of support in these terms seems poor.

I state the argument as simply as possible; but, even so, it will be necessary to introduce and explain some new terms. Suppose we had a collection of objects of different kinds, some with some characteristics and some with others. Suppose, for example, we had a bag containing 100 balls, of which 70 were white and 30 black. Let us call such a collection of objects a *population;* and let us call the way it is made up (e.g., in the case imagined, of 70 white and 30 black balls) the *constitution* of the population. From such a population it would be possible to take *samples* of various sizes. For example, we might take from our bag a sample of 30 balls. Suppose each ball in the bag had an individual number. Then the collection of balls numbered 10 to 39 inclusive would be one sample of the given size; the collection of balls numbered 11 to 40 inclusive would be another and different sample of the same size; the collection of balls numbered 2, 4, 6, 8 . . . 58, 60 would be another such sample; and so on. Each possible collection of 30 balls is a different sample of the same size. Some different samples of the same size will have the same constitutions as one another; others will have different constitutions. Thus there will be only one sample made up of 30 black balls. There will be many different samples which share the constitution: 20 white and 10 black. It would be a simple matter of mathematics to work out the number of possible samples of the given size which had any one possible constitution. Let us say that a sample *matches* the population if, allowing for the difference between them in size, the constitution of the sample corresponds, within certain limits, to that of the population. For example, we might say that any possible sample consisting of, say, 21 white and 9 black balls matched the constitution (70 white and 30 black) of the population, whereas a sample consisting of 20 white and 10 black balls did not. Now it is a proposition of pure mathematics that, given any population, the proportion of possible samples, all of the same size, which match the population, increases with the size of the sample.

We have seen that conclusions about the ratio of a subset of equally possible chances to the whole set of those chances may be expressed by the use of the word 'probability'. Thus of the 52 possible samples of one card from a population constituted like an orthodox pack, 16 are court-cards or aces. This fact we allow ourselves to express (under the conditions, inductively established, of equipossibility of draws) by saying that the probability of drawing a court-card or an ace was $\frac{4}{13}$. If we express the proposition referred to at the end of the last paragraph by means of this use of 'probability' we shall obtain the result: The probability of a sample matching a given population increases with the size of the sample. It is tempting to try to derive from this result a general justification of the inductive procedure: which will not, indeed, show that any given inductive conclusion is entailed by the evidence for it, taken in conjunction with some universal premise, but will show that the multiplication of favourable instances of a generalization entails a proportionate increase in its probability. For, since *matching* is a symmetrical relation, it might seem a simple deductive step to move from

I. The probability of a sample matching a given population increases with the size of the sample

to

II. The probability of a population matching a given sample increases with the size of the sample.

II might seem to provide a guarantee that the greater the number of cases for which a generalization is observed to hold, the greater is its probability; since in increasing the number of cases we increase the size of the sample from whatever population forms the subject of our generalization. Thus pure mathematics might seem to provide the sought-for proof that the evidence for a generalization really does get stronger, the more favourable instances of it we find.

   The argument is ingenious enough to be worthy of respect; but it fails of its purpose, and misrepresents the inductive situation. Our situation is not in the least like that of a man drawing a sample from a given, i.e., fixed and limited, population from which the drawing of any mathematically possible sample is equiprobable with that of any other. Our only datum is the sample. No limit is fixed beforehand to the diversity, and the possibilities of change, of the 'population' from which it is drawn: or, better, to the multiplicity and variousness of different populations, each with different constitutions, any one of which might replace the present one before we make the next draw. Nor is there any *a priori* guarantee that different mathematically possible samples are equally likely to be drawn. If we have or can obtain any assurance on these points, then it is assurance derived inductively from our data, and cannot therefore be assumed at the outset of an argument designed to justify induction. So II, regarded as a justification of induction founded on purely mathematical considerations, is a fraud. The important shift of 'given' from qualifying 'population' in I to qualifying 'sample' in II is illegitimate. Moreover, 'probability', which means one thing in II (interpreted as giving the required guarantee) means something quite different in I (interpreted as a proposition of pure mathematics). In I probability is simply the measure of the ratio of one set of mathematically possible chances to another; in II it is the measure of the inductive acceptability of a generalization. As a mathematical proposition, I is certainly independent of the soundness of inductive procedures; and as a statement of one of the criteria we use in assessing the strength of evidence of a generalization, II is as certainly independent of mathematics.

   It has not escaped the notice of those who have advocated a mathematical justification of induction, that certain assumptions are required to make the argument even seem to fulfil its purpose. Inductive reasoning would be of little use if it did not sometimes enable us to assign at least fairly high probabilities to certain conclusions. Now suppose, in conformity with the mathematical model, we represented the fact that the evidence for a proposition was conclusive by assigning to it the probability figure of 1; and the fact that the evidence for and against a proposition was evenly balanced by assigning to it the probability figure ½; and so on. It is a familiar mathematical truth that, between any two fractions, say ⅙ and ⅕, there is an infinite number of intermediate quantities; that ⅙ can be indefinitely increased without reaching equality to ⅕. Even if we could regard II as mathematically established, therefore, it fails to give us what we require; for it fails to provide a guarantee that the probability of an inductive conclusion ever attains a degree at which it begins to be of use. It was accordingly necessary to buttress the purely mathematical argument by large, vague assumptions, comparable with the principles designed for the role of supreme premise in the first type of attempt. These assumptions, like those principles, could never actually be used to give a deductive turn to inductive arguments; for they could not be formulated with precision. They were the shadows of precise unknown truths, which, if one did know them, would suffice, along with the data for our accepted generalizations, to enable the probability of the latter to be assigned, after calculation, a precise numerical fraction of a tolerable size. So this theory represents our inductions as the vague sublunary shadows of deductive calculations which we cannot make.

10. Let us turn from attempts to justify induction to attempts to show that the demand for a justification is mistaken. We have seen already that what lies behind such a demand is often the absurd wish that induction should be shown to be some kind of deduction—and this wish is clearly traceable in the two attempts at justification which we have examined. What other sense could we give to the demand? Sometimes it is expressed in the form of a request for proof that induction is a *reasonable* or *rational* procedure, that we have *good grounds* for placing reliance upon it. Consider the uses of the phrases 'good grounds', 'justification', 'reasonable', &c. Often we say such things as 'He has *every justification* for believing that *p*'; 'I have *very good reasons* for believing it'; 'There are *good grounds* for the view that *q*'; 'There is *good evidence* that *r*'. We often talk, in such ways as these, of justification, good grounds or reasons or evidence for certain beliefs. Suppose such a belief were one expressible in the form 'Every case of *f* is a case of *g*'. And suppose someone were asked what he meant by saying that he had good grounds or reasons for holding it. I think it would be felt to be a satisfactory answer if he replied: 'Well, in all my wide and varied experience I've come across innumerable cases of *f* and never a case of *f* which wasn't a case of *g*.' In saying this, he is clearly claiming to have *inductive* support, *inductive* evidence, of a certain kind, for his belief; and he is also giving a perfectly proper answer to the question, what he meant by saying that he had ample justification, good grounds, good reasons for his belief. It is an analytic proposition that it is reasonable to have a degree of belief in a statement which is proportional to the strength of the evidence in its favour; and it is an analytic proposition, though not a proposition of mathematics, that, other things being equal, the evidence for a generalization is strong in proportion as the number of favourable instances, and the variety of circumstances in which they have been found, is great. So to ask whether it is reasonable to place reliance on inductive procedures is like asking whether it is reasonable to proportion the degree of one's convictions to the strength of the evidence. Doing this is what 'being reasonable' *means* in such a context.

As for the other form in which the doubt may be expressed, viz., 'Is induction a justified, or justifiable, procedure?', it emerges in a still less favourable light. No sense has been given to it, though it is easy to see why it seems to have a sense. For it is generally proper to inquire *of a particular belief*, whether its adoption is justified; and, in asking this, we are asking whether there is good, bad, or any, evidence for it. In applying or withholding the epithets 'justified', 'well founded', &c., in the case of specific beliefs, we are appealing to, and applying, inductive standards. But to what standards are we appealing when we ask whether the application of inductive standards is justified or well grounded? If we cannot answer, then no sense has been given to the question. Compare it with the question: Is the law legal? It makes perfectly good sense to inquire of a particular action, of an administrative regulation, or even, in the case of some states, of a particular enactment of the legislature, whether or not it is legal. The question is answered by an appeal to a legal system, by the application of a set of legal (or constitutional) rules or standards. But it makes no sense to inquire in general whether the law of the land, the legal system as a whole, is or is not legal. For to what legal standards are we appealing?

The only way in which a sense might be given to the question, whether induction is in general a justified or justifiable procedure, is a trivial one which we have already noticed. We might interpret it to mean 'Are all conclusions, arrived at inductively, justified?', i.e., 'Do people always have adequate evidence for the conclusions they draw?' The answer to this question is easy, but uninteresting: it is that sometimes people have adequate evidence, and sometimes they do not.

11. It seems, however, that this way of showing the request for a general justification of induction to be absurd is sometimes insufficient to allay the worry that produces it. And to point out that 'forming rational opinions about the unobserved on the evidence available' and 'assessing the evidence by inductive standards' are phrases which describe the same thing, is more apt to produce irritation than relief. The point is felt to be 'merely a verbal' one; and though the point of this protest is itself hard to see, it is clear that something more is required. So the question must be pursued further. First, I want to point out that there is something a little odd about talking of 'the inductive method', or even 'the inductive policy', as if it were just one possible method among others of arguing from the observed to the unobserved, from the available evidence to the facts in question. If one asked a meteorologist what method or methods he used to forecast the weather, one would be surprised if he answered: 'Oh, just the inductive method.' If one asked a doctor by what means he diagnosed a certain disease, the answer 'By induction' would be felt as an impatient evasion, a joke, or a rebuke. The answer one hopes for is an account of the tests made, the signs taken account of, the rules and recipes and general laws applied. When such a specific method of prediction or diagnosis is in question, one can ask whether the method is justified in practice; and here again one is asking whether its employment is inductively justified, whether it commonly gives correct results. This question would normally seem an admissible one. One might be tempted to conclude that, while there are many different specific methods of prediction, diagnosis, &c., appropriate to different subjects of inquiry, all such methods could properly be called 'inductive' in the sense that their employment rested on inductive support; and that, hence, the phrase 'non-

inductive method of finding out about what lies deductively beyond the evidence' was a description without meaning, a phrase to which no sense had been given; so that there could be no question of justifying our selection of one method, called 'the inductive', of doing this.

However, someone might object: 'Surely it is possible, though it might be foolish, to use methods utterly different from accredited scientific ones. Suppose a man, whenever he wanted to form an opinion about what lay beyond his observation or the observation of available witnesses, simply shut his eyes, asked himself the appropriate question, and accepted the first answer that came into his head. Wouldn't this be a non-inductive method?' Well, let us suppose this. The man is asked: 'Do you usually get the right answer by your method?' He might answer: 'You've mentioned one of its drawbacks; I never do get the right answer; but it's an extremely easy method.' One might then be inclined to think that it was not a method of finding things out at all. But suppose he answered: Yes, it's usually (always) the right answer. Then we might be willing to call it a method of finding out, though a strange one. But, then, by the very fact of its success, it would be an inductively supported method. For each application of the method would be an application of the general rule, 'The first answer that comes into my head is generally (always) the right one'; and for the truth of this generalization there would be the inductive evidence of a long run of favourable instances with no unfavourable ones (if it were 'always'), or of a sustained high proportion of successes to trials (if it were 'generally').

So every successful method or recipe for finding out about the un-observed must be one which has inductive support; for to say that a recipe is successful is to say that it has been repeatedly applied with success; and repeated successful application of a recipe constitutes just what we mean by inductive evidence in its favour. Pointing out this fact must not be confused with saying that 'the inductive method' is justified by its success, justified because it works. This is a mistake, and an important one. I am not seeking to 'justify the inductive method', for no meaning has been given to this phrase. *A fortiori*, I am not saying that induction is justified by its success in finding out about the unobserved. I am saying, rather, that any successful method of finding out about the unobserved is necessarily justified by induction. This is an analytic proposition. The phrase 'successful method of finding things out which has no inductive support' is self-contradictory. Having, or acquiring, inductive support is a necessary condition of the success of a method.

Why point this out at all? First, it may have a certain therapeutic force, a power to reassure. Second, it may counteract the tendency to think of 'the inductive method' as something on a par with specific methods of diagnosis or prediction and therefore, like them, standing in need of (inductive) justification.

12. There is one further confusion, perhaps the most powerful of all in producing . . . doubts, questions, and spurious solutions . . . We may approach it by considering the claim that induction is justified by its success in practice. The phrase 'success of induction' is by no means clear and perhaps embodies the confusion of induction with some specific method of prediction, &c., appropriate to some particular line of inquiry. But, whatever the phrase may mean, the claim has an obviously circular look. Presumably

the suggestion is that we should argue from the past 'successes of induction' to the continuance of those successes in the future; from the fact that it has worked hitherto to the conclusion that it will continue to work. Since an argument of this kind is plainly inductive, it will not serve as a justification of induction. One cannot establish a principle of argument by an argument which uses that principle. But let us go a little deeper. The argument rests the justification of induction on a matter of fact (its 'past successes'). This is characteristic of nearly all attempts to find a justification. The desired premise of Section 8 was to be some fact about the constitution of the universe which, even if it could not be used as a suppressed premise to give inductive arguments a deductive turn, was at any rate a 'presupposition of the validity of induction'. Even the mathematical argument of Section 9 required buttressing with some large assumption about the make-up of the world. I think the source of this general desire to find out some fact about the constitution of the universe which will 'justify induction' or 'show it to be a rational policy' is the confusion, the running together, of two fundamentally different questions: to one of which the answer is a matter of non-linguistic fact, while to the other it is a matter of meanings.

There is nothing self-contradictory in supposing that all the uniformities in the course of things that we have hitherto observed and come to count on should cease to operate to-morrow; that all our familiar recipes should let us down, and that we should be unable to frame new ones because such regularities as there were were too complex for us to make out. (We may assume that even the expectation that all of us, in such circumstances, would perish, were falsified by someone surviving to observe the new chaos in which, roughly speaking, nothing foreseeable happens.) Of course, we do not believe that this will happen. We believe, on the contrary, that our inductively supported expectation-rules, though some of them will have, no doubt, to be dropped or modified, will continue, on the whole, to serve us fairly well; and that we shall generally be able to replace the rules we abandon with others similarly arrived at. We might give a sense to the phrase 'success of induction' by calling this vague belief the belief that induction will continue to be successful. It is certainly a factual belief, not a necessary truth; a belief, one may say, about the constitution of the universe. We might express it as follows, choosing a phraseology which will serve the better to expose the confusion I wish to expose:

I. (The universe is such that) induction will continue to be successful.

I is very vague: it amounts to saying that there are, and will continue to be, natural uniformities and regularities which exhibit a humanly manageable degree of simplicity. But, though it is vague, certain definite things can be said about it. (1) It is not a necessary, but a contingent, statement; for chaos is not a self-contradictory concept. (2) We have good inductive reasons for believing it, good inductive evidence for it. We believe that some of our recipes will continue to hold good because they have held good for so long. We believe that we shall be able to frame new and useful ones, because we have been able to do so repeatedly in the past. Of course, it would be absurd to try to use I to 'justify induction', to show that it is a reasonable policy; because I is a conclusion inductively supported.

Consider now the fundamentally different statement:

II. Induction is rational (reasonable).

We have already seen that the rationality of induction, unlike its 'success-fulness', is not a fact about the constitution of the world. It is a matter of what we mean by the word 'rational' in its application to any procedure for forming opinions about what lies outside our observations or that of available witnesses. For to have good reasons for any such opinion is to have good inductive support for it. The chaotic universe just envisaged, there-fore, is not one in which induction would cease to be rational; it is simply one in which it would be impossible to form rational expectations to the effect that specific things would happen. It might be said that in such a universe it would at least be rational to refrain from forming specific expectations, to expect nothing but irregularities. Just so. But this is itself a higher-order induction: where irregularity is the rule, expect further irregu-larities. Learning not to count on things is as much learning an inductive lesson as learning what things to count on.

So it is a contingent, factual matter that it is sometimes possible to form rational opinions concerning what specifically happened or will happen in given circumstances (I); it is a non-contingent, *a priori* matter that the only ways of doing this must be inductive ways (II). What people have done is to run together, to conflate, the question to which I is an answer and the quite different question to which II is an answer; producing the muddled and senseless questions: 'Is the universe such that inductive procedures are rational?' or 'What must the universe be like in order for inductive procedures to be rational?' It is the attempt to answer these confused questions which leads to statements like 'The uniformity of nature is a presupposition of the validity of induction'. The statement that nature is uniform might be taken to be a vague way of expressing what we expressed by I; and certainly this fact is a condition of, for it is identical with, the likewise contingent fact that we are, and shall continue to be, able to form rational opinions, of the kind we are most anxious to form, about the unobserved. But neither this fact about the world, nor any other, is a condition of the necessary truth that, if it is possible to form rational opinions of this kind, these will be inductively supported opinions. The discordance of the conflated questions manifests itself in an uncertainty about the status to be accorded to the alleged presupposition of the 'validity' of induction. For it was dimly, and correctly, felt that the reasonableness of inductive procedures was not merely a contingent, but a necessary, matter; so any necessary condition of their reasonableness had likewise to be a necessary matter. On the other hand, it was uncomfortably clear that chaos is not a self-contradictory concept; that the fact that some phenomena do exhibit a tolerable degree of simplicity and repetitiveness is not guaranteed by logic, but is a contingent affair. So the presupposition of induction had to be both contingent and necessary: which is absurd. And the absurdity is only lightly veiled by the use of the phrase 'synthetic *a priori*' instead of 'contingent necessary'.

5

THE NEW RIDDLE OF INDUCTION

Nelson Goodman

Confirmation of a hypothesis by an instance depends rather heavily upon features of the hypothesis other than its syntactical form. That a given piece of copper conducts electricity increases the credibility of statements asserting that other pieces of copper conduct electricity, and thus confirms the hypothesis that all copper conducts electricity. But the fact that a given man now in this room is a third son does not increase the credibility of statements asserting that other men now in this room are third sons, and so does not confirm the hypothesis that all men now in this room are third sons. Yet in both cases our hypothesis is a generalization of the evidence statement. The difference is that in the former case the hypothesis is a *lawlike* statement; while in the latter case, the hypothesis is a merely contingent or accidental generality. Only a statement that is *lawlike*—regardless of its truth or falsity or its scientific importance—is capable of receiving confirmation from an instance of it; accidental statements are not. Plainly, then, we must look for a way of distinguishing lawlike from accidental statements.

So long as what seems to be needed is merely a way of excluding a few odd and unwanted cases that are inadvertently admitted by our definition of confirmation, the problem may not seem very hard or very pressing. We fully expect that minor defects will be found in our definition and that the necessary refinements will have to be worked out patiently one after another. But some further examples will show that our present difficulty is of a much graver kind.

Suppose that all emeralds examined before a certain time t are green.[1] At time t, then, our observations support the hypothesis that all emeralds are green; and this is in accord with our definition of confirmation. Our evidence statements assert that emerald a is green, that emerald b is green,

From *Fact, Fiction, and Forecast*, second edition, Chap. III, Sec. 4, pp. 72–81, by Nelson Goodman, Copyright © 1965, by The Bobbs-Merrill Company, Inc., reprinted by permission of the College Division, and by Oxford University Press.

[1] Although the example used is different, the argument to follow is substantially the same as that set forth in my note 'A Query on Confirmation' [*Journal of Philosophy*, XLIII (1946), 383–385.]

and so on; and each confirms the general hypothesis that all emeralds are green. So far, so good.

Now let me introduce another predicate less familiar than "green". It is the predicate "grue" and it applies to all things examined before t just in case they are green but to other things just in case they are blue. Then at time t we have, for each evidence statement asserting that a given emerald is green, a parallel evidence statement asserting that that emerald is grue. And the statements that emerald a is grue, that emerald b is grue, and so on, will each confirm the general hypothesis that all emeralds are grue. Thus according to our definition, the prediction that all emeralds subsequently examined will be green and the prediction that all will be grue are alike confirmed by evidence statements describing the same observations. But if an emerald subsequently examined is grue, it is blue and hence not green. Thus although we are well aware which of the two incompatible predictions is genuinely confirmed, they are equally well confirmed according to our present definition. Moreover, it is clear that if we simply choose an appropriate predicate, then on the basis of these same observations we shall have equal confirmation, by our definition, for any prediction whatever about other emeralds —or indeed about anything else.[2] As in our earlier example, only the predictions subsumed under lawlike hypotheses are genuinely confirmed; but we have no criterion as yet for determining lawlikeness. And now we see that without some such criterion, our definition not merely includes a few unwanted cases, but is so completely ineffectual that it virtually excludes nothing. We are left once again with the intolerable result that anything confirms anything. This difficulty cannot be set aside as an annoying detail to be taken care of in due course. It has to be met before our definition will work at all.

Nevertheless, the difficulty is often slighted because on the surface there seem to be easy ways of dealing with it. Sometimes, for example, the problem is thought to be much like the paradox of the ravens. We are here again, it is pointed out, making tacit and illegitimate use of information outside the stated evidence: the information, for example, that different samples of one material are usually alike in conductivity, and the information that different men in a lecture audience are usually not alike in the number of their older brothers. But while it is true that such information is being smuggled in, this does not by itself settle the matter as it settles the matter of the ravens. There the point was that when the smuggled information is forthrightly declared, its effect upon the confirmation of the hypothesis in question is immediately and properly registered by the definition we are using. On the other hand, if to our initial evidence we add statements concerning the conductivity of pieces of other materials or concerning the number of older brothers of members of other lecture audiences, this will not in the least affect the confirmation, according to our definition, of the hypothesis concerning copper or of that concerning other lecture

[2] For instance, we shall have equal confirmation, by our present definition, for the prediction that roses subsequently examined will be blue. Let "emerose" apply just to emeralds examined before time t, and to roses examined later. Then all emeroses so far examined are grue, and this confirms the hypothesis that all emeroses are grue and hence the prediction that roses subsequently examined will be blue. The problem raised by such antecedents has been little noticed, but is no easier to meet than that raised by similarly perverse consequents.

audiences. Since our definition is insensitive to the bearing upon hypotheses of evidence so related to them, even when the evidence is fully declared, the difficulty about accidental hypotheses cannot be explained away on the ground that such evidence is being surreptitiously taken into account.

A more promising suggestion is to explain the matter in terms of the effect of this other evidence not directly upon the hypothesis in question but *in*directly through other hypotheses that *are* confirmed, according to our definition, by such evidence. Our information about other materials does by our definition confirm such hypotheses as that all pieces of iron conduct electricity, that no pieces of rubber do, and so on; and these hypotheses, the explanation runs, impart to the hypothesis that all pieces of copper conduct electricity (and also to the hypothesis that none do) the character of law-likeness—that is, amenability to confirmation by direct positive instances when found. On the other hand, our information about other lecture audiences *dis*confirms many hypotheses to the effect that all the men in one audience are third sons, or that none are; and this strips any character of lawlikeness from the hypothesis that all (or the hypothesis that none) of the men in *this* audience are third sons. But clearly if this course is to be followed, the circumstances under which hypotheses are thus related to one another will have to be precisely articulated.

The problem, then, is to define the relevant way in which such hypotheses must be alike. Evidence for the hypothesis that all iron conducts electricity enhances the lawlikeness of the hypothesis that all zirconium conducts electricity, but does not similarly affect the hypothesis that all the objects on my desk conduct electricity. Wherein lies the difference? The first two hypotheses fall under the broader hypothesis—call it "*H*"—that every class of things of the same material is uniform in conductivity; the first and third fall only under some such hypothesis as—call it "*K*"—that every class of things that are either all of the same material or all on a desk is uniform in conductivity. Clearly the important difference here is that evidence for a statement affirming that one of the classes covered by *H* has the property in question increases the credibility of any statement affirming that another such class has this property; while nothing of the sort holds true with respect to *K*. But this is only to say that *H* is lawlike and *K* is not. We are faced anew with the very problem we are trying to solve: the problem of distinguishing between lawlike and accidental hypotheses.

The most popular way of attacking the problem takes its cue from the fact that accidental hypotheses seem typically to involve some spatial or temporal restriction, or reference to some particular individual. They seem to concern the people in some particular room, or the objects on some particular person's desk; while lawlike hypotheses characteristically concern all ravens or all pieces of copper whatsoever. Complete generality is thus very often supposed to be a sufficient condition of lawlikeness; but to define this complete generality is by no means easy. Merely to require that the hypothesis contain no term naming, describing, or indicating a particular thing or location will obviously not be enough. The troublesome hypothesis that all emeralds are grue contains no such term; and where such a term does occur, as in hypotheses about men in *this room*, it can be suppressed in favor of some predicate (short or long, new or old) that contains no such term but applies only to exactly the same things. One might think, then, of excluding not only hypotheses that actually contain terms for specific individuals but also all hypotheses that are equivalent to others that do contain such terms. But, as we have just seen, to exclude only hypotheses of which *all* equivalents contain such terms is to exclude nothing. On the other hand, to exclude all hypotheses that have *some* equivalent containing such a term is to exclude everything; for even the hypothesis

All grass is green

has as an equivalent

All grass in London or elsewhere is green.

The next step, therefore, has been to consider ruling out predicates of certain kinds. A syntactically universal hypothesis is lawlike, the proposal runs, if its predicates are 'purely qualitative' or 'non-positional'.[3] This will obviously accomplish nothing if a purely qualitative predicate is then conceived either as one that is equivalent to some expression free of terms for specific individuals, or as one that is equivalent to no expression that contains such a term; for this only raises again the difficulties just pointed out. The claim appears to be rather that at least in the case of a simple enough predicate we can readily determine by direct inspection of its meaning whether or not it is purely qualitative. But even aside from obscurities in the notion of 'the meaning' of a predicate, this claim seems to me wrong. I simply do not know how to tell whether a predicate is qualitative or positional, except perhaps by completely begging the question at issue and asking whether the predicate is 'well-behaved'—that is, whether simple syntactically universal hypotheses applying it are lawlike.

This statement will not go unprotested. "Consider", it will be argued, "the predicates 'blue' and 'green' and the predicate 'grue' introduced earlier, and also the predicate 'bleen' that applies to emeralds examined before time *t* just in case they are blue and to other emeralds just in case they are green. Surely it is clear", the argument runs, "that the first two are purely qualitative and the second two are not; for the meaning of each of the latter two plainly involves reference to a specific temporal position." To this I reply that indeed I do recognize the first two as well-behaved predicates admissible in lawlike hypotheses, and the second two as ill-behaved predicates. But the argument that the former but not the latter are purely qualitative seems to me quite unsound. True enough, if we start with "blue" and "green", then "grue" and "bleen" will be explained in terms of "blue" and "green" and a temporal term. But equally truly, if we start with "grue" and "bleen", then "blue" and "green" will be explained in terms of "grue" and "bleen" and a temporal term; "green", for example, applies to emeralds examined before time *t* just in case they are grue, and to other emeralds just

[3] Carnap took this course in his paper 'On the Application of Inductive Logic', *Philosophy and Phenomenological Research*, vol. 8 (1947), pp. 133–47, which is in part a reply to my 'A Query on Confirmation'. The discussion was continued in my note 'On Infirmities of Confirmation Theory', *Philosophy and Phenomenological Research*, vol. 8 (1947), pp. 149–51; and in Carnap's 'Reply to Nelson Goodman', same journal, same volume, pp. 461–2.

in case they are bleen. Thus qualitativeness is an entirely relative matter and does not by itself establish any dichotomy of predicates. This relativity seems to be completely overlooked by those who contend that the qualitative character of a predicate is a criterion for its good behavior.

Of course, one may ask why we need worry about such unfamiliar predicates as "grue" or about accidental hypotheses in general, since we are unlikely to use them in making predictions. If our definition works for such hypotheses as are normally employed, isn't that all we need? In a sense, yes; but only in the sense that we need no definition, no theory of induction, and no philosophy of knowledge at all. We get along well enough without them in daily life and in scientific research. But if we seek a theory at all, we cannot excuse gross anomalies resulting from a proposed theory by pleading that we can avoid them in practice. The odd cases we have been considering are clinically pure cases that, though seldom encountered in practice, nevertheless display to best advantage the symptoms of a widespread and destructive malady.

We have so far neither any answer nor any promising clue to an answer to the question what distinguishes lawlike or confirmable hypotheses from accidental or non-confirmable ones; and what may at first have seemed a minor technical difficulty has taken on the stature of a major obstacle to the development of a satisfactory theory of confirmation. It is this problem that I call the new riddle of induction.

Certainty and Doubt

6

THE SPHERE OF THE DOUBTFUL

René Descartes

It is now some years since I detected how many were the false beliefs that I had from my earliest youth admitted as true, and how doubtful was every-thing I had since constructed on this basis; and from that time I was convinced that I must once for all seriously undertake to rid myself of all the opinions which I had formerly accepted, and commence to build anew from the foundation, if I wanted to establish any firm and permanent structure in the sciences. But as this enterprise appeared to be a very great one, I waited until I had attained an age so mature that I could not hope that at any later date I should be better fitted to execute my design. This reason caused me to delay so long that I should feel that I was doing wrong were I to occupy in deliberation the time that yet remains to me for action. To-day, then, since very opportunely for the plan I have in view I have delivered my mind from every care [and am happily agitated by no passions] and since I have procured for myself an assured leisure in a peaceable retirement, I shall at last seriously and freely address myself to the general upheaval of all my former opinions.

Now for this object it is not necessary that I should show that all of these are false—I shall perhaps never arrive at this end. But inasmuch as reason already persuades me that I ought no less carefully to withhold my assent from matters which are not entirely certain and indubitable than from those which appear to me manifestly to be false, if I am able to find in each one some reason to doubt, this will suffice to justify my rejecting the whole. And for that end it will not be requisite that I should examine each in

From "Meditations on First Philosophy," in *The Philosophical Works of Descartes,* E. S. Haldane and G. R. T. Ross, trans. (Cambridge: Cambridge University Press, 1931), Meditation I, pp. 144–149. Reprinted by permission of the publisher.

particular, which would be an endless undertaking; for owing to the fact that the destruction of the foundations of necessity brings with it the downfall of the rest of the edifice, I shall only in the first place attack those principles upon which all my former opinions rested.

All that up to the present time I have accepted as most true and certain I have learned either from the senses or through the senses; but it is sometimes proved to me that these senses are deceptive, and it is wiser not to trust entirely to anything by which we have once been deceived.

But it may be that although the senses sometimes deceive us concerning things which are hardly perceptible, or very far away, there are yet many others to be met with as to which we cannot reasonably have any doubt, although we recognise them by their means. For example, there is the fact that I am here, seated by the fire, attired in a dressing gown, having this paper in my hands and other similar matters. And how could I deny that these hands and this body are mine, were it not perhaps that I compare myself to certain persons, devoid of sense, whose cerebella are so troubled and clouded by the violent vapours of black bile, that they constantly assure us that they think they are kings when they are really quite poor, or that they are clothed in purple when they are really without covering, or who imagine that they have an earthenware head or are nothing but pumpkins or are made of glass. But they are mad, and I should not be any the less insane were I to follow examples so extravagant.

At the same time I must remember that I am a man, and that consequently I am in the habit of sleeping, and in my dreams representing to myself the same things or sometimes even less probable things, than do those who are insane in their waking moments. How often has it happened to me that in the night I dreamt that I found myself in this particular place, that I was dressed and seated near the fire, whilst in reality I was lying undressed in bed! At this moment it does indeed seem to me that it is with eyes awake that I am looking at this paper; that this head which I move is not asleep, that it is deliberately and of set purpose that I extend my hand and perceive it; what happens in sleep does not appear so clear nor so distinct as does all this. But in thinking over this I remind myself that on many occasions I have in sleep been deceived by similar illusions, and in dwelling carefully on this reflection I see so manifestly that there are no certain indications by which we may clearly distinguish wakefulness from sleep that I am lost in astonishment. And my astonishment is such that it is almost capable of persuading me that I now dream.

Now let us assume that we are asleep and that all these particulars, e.g. that we open our eyes, shake our head, extend our hands, and so on, are but false delusions; and let us reflect that possibly neither our hands nor our whole body are such as they appear to us to be. At the same time we must at least confess that the things which are represented to us in sleep are like painted representations which can only have been formed as the counterparts of something real and true, and that in this way those general things at least, i.e. eyes, a head, hands, and a whole body, are not imaginary things, but things really existent. For, as a matter of fact, painters, even when they study with the greatest skill to represent sirens and satyrs by forms the most strange and extraordinary, cannot give them natures which are entirely new, but merely make a certain medley of the members of different animals; or if their imagination is extravagant enough to invent something so novel that nothing similar has ever before been seen, and that then their work represents a thing purely fictitious and absolutely false, it is certain all the same that the colours of which this is composed are necessarily real. And for the same reason, although these general things, to wit, [a body], eyes, a head, hands, and such like, may be imaginary, we are bound at the same time to confess that there are at least some other objects yet more simple and more universal, which are real and true; and of these just in the same way as with certain real colours, all these images of things which dwell in our thoughts, whether true and real or false and fantastic, are formed.

To such a class of things pertains corporeal nature in general, and its extension, the figure of extended things, their quantity or magnitude and number, as also the place in which they are, the time which measures their duration, and so on.

That is possibly why our reasoning is not unjust when we conclude from this that Physics, Astronomy, Medicine and all other sciences which have as their end the consideration of composite things, are very dubious and uncertain; but that Arithmetic, Geometry and other sciences of that kind which only treat of things that are very simple and very general, without taking great trouble to ascertain whether they are actually existent or not, contain some measure of certainty and an element of the indubitable. For whether I am awake or asleep, two and three together always form five, and the square can never have more than four sides, and it does not seem possible that truths so clear and apparent can be suspected of any falsity [or uncertainty].

Nevertheless I have long had fixed in my mind the belief that an all-powerful God existed by whom I have been created such as I am. But how do I know that He has not brought it to pass that there is no earth, no heaven, no extended body, no magnitude, no place, and that nevertheless [I possess the perceptions of all these things and that] they seem to me to exist just exactly as I now see them? And, besides, as I sometimes imagine that others deceive themselves in the things which they think they know best, how do I know that I am not deceived every time that I add two and three, or count the sides of a square, or judge of things yet simpler, if anything simpler can be imagined? But possibly God has not desired that I should be thus deceived, for He is said to be supremely good. If, however, it is contrary to His goodness to have made me such that I constantly deceive myself, it would also appear to be contrary to His goodness to permit me to be sometimes deceived, and nevertheless I cannot doubt that He does permit this.

There may indeed be those who would prefer to deny the existence of a God so powerful, rather than believe that all other things are uncertain. But let us not oppose them for the present, and grant that all that is here said of a God is a fable; nevertheless in whatever way they suppose that I have arrived at the state of being that I have reached—whether they attribute it to fate or to accident, or make out that it is by a continual succession of antecedents, or by some other method—since to err and deceive oneself is a defect, it is clear that the greater will be the probability of my being so imperfect as to deceive myself ever, as is the Author to whom they assign my origin the less powerful. To these reasons I have certainly nothing to reply, but at the end I feel constrained to confess that there is nothing in all that I formerly believed to be true, of which I cannot in some measure doubt, and that not merely through want of thought or through levity, but for reasons which are very powerful and maturely considered; so that henceforth I ought not the less carefully to refrain from giving credence to these opinions than to that which is manifestly false, if I desire to arrive at any certainty [in the sciences].

But it is not sufficient to have made these remarks, we must also be careful to keep them in mind. For these ancient and commonly held opinions still revert frequently to my mind, long and familiar custom having given them the right to occupy my mind against my inclination and rendered them almost masters of my belief; nor will I ever lose the habit of deferring to them or of placing my confidence in them, so long as I consider them as they really are, i.e. opinions in some measure doubtful, as I have just shown, and at the same time highly probable, so that there is much more reason to believe in than to deny them. That is why I consider that I shall not be acting amiss, if, taking of set purpose a contrary belief, I allow myself to be deceived, and for a certain time pretend that all these opinions are entirely false and imaginary, until at last, having thus balanced my former prejudices with my latter [so that they cannot divert my opinions more to one side than to the other], my judgment will no longer be dominated by bad usage or turned away from the right knowledge of the truth. For I am assured that there can be neither peril nor error in this course, and that I cannot at present yield too much to distrust, since I am not considering the question of action, but only of knowledge.

I shall then suppose, not that God who is supremely good and the fountain of truth, but some evil genius not less powerful than deceitful, has employed his whole energies in deceiving me; I shall consider that the heavens, the earth, colours, figures, sound, and all other external things are nought but the illusions and dreams of which this genius has availed himself in order to lay traps for my credulity; I shall consider myself as having no hands, no eyes, no flesh, no blood, nor any senses, yet falsely believing myself to possess all these things; I shall remain obstinately attached to this idea, and if by this means it is not in my power to arrive at the knowledge of any truth, I may at least do what is in my power [i.e. suspend my judgment], and with firm purpose avoid giving credence to any false thing, or being imposed upon by this arch deceiver, however powerful and deceptive he may be. But this task is a laborious one, and insensibly a certain lassitude leads me into the course of my ordinary life. And just as a captive who in sleep enjoys an imaginary liberty, when he begins to suspect that his liberty is but a dream, fears to awaken, and conspires with these agreeable illusions that the deception may be prolonged, so insensibly of my own accord I fall back into my former opinions, and I dread awakening from this slumber, lest the laborious wakefulness which would follow the tranquillity of this repose should have to be spent not in daylight, but in the excessive darkness of the difficulties which have just been discussed.

7

ANALYTIC AND SYNTHETIC
JUDGMENTS

Immanuel Kant

THE DISTINCTION BETWEEN PURE AND EMPIRICAL KNOWLEDGE

There can be no doubt that all our knowledge begins with experience. For how should our faculty of knowledge be awakened into action did not objects affecting our senses partly of themselves produce representations, partly arouse the activity of our understanding to compare these representations, and, by combining or separating them, work up the raw material of the sensible impressions into that knowledge of objects which is entitled experience? In the order of time, therefore, we have no knowledge antecedent to experience, and with experience all our knowledge begins.

But though all our knowledge begins with experience, it does not follow that it all arises out of experience. For it may well be that even our empirical knowledge is made up of what we receive through impressions and of what our own faculty of knowledge (sensible impressions serving merely as the occasion) supplies from itself. If our faculty of knowledge makes any such addition, it may be that we are not in a position to distinguish it from the raw material, until with long practice of attention we have become skilled in separating it.

This, then, is a question which at least calls for closer examination, and does not allow of any off-hand answer:—whether there is any knowledge that is thus independent of experience and even of all impressions of the senses. Such knowledge is entitled *a priori*, and distinguished from the *empirical*, which has its sources *a posteriori*, that is, in experience.

The expression '*a priori*' does not, however, indicate with sufficient precision the full meaning of our question. For it has been customary to say, even of much knowledge that is derived from empirical sources, that we have it or are capable of having it *a priori*, meaning thereby that we do not derive it immediately from experience, but from a universal rule—a rule

From *Immanuel Kant's Critique of Pure Reason*, Norman Kemp Smith, trans. (London: 1933), the Introduction, pp. 41–62. Reprinted by permission of St. Martin's Press Inc., The Macmillan Company of Canada Ltd., and Macmillan & Co. Ltd.

which is itself, however, borrowed by us from experience. Thus we would say of a man who undermined the foundations of his house, that he might have known *a priori* that it would fall, that is, that he need not have waited for the experience of its actual falling. But still he could not know this completely *a priori*. For he had first to learn through experience that bodies are heavy, and therefore fall when their supports are withdrawn.

In what follows, therefore, we shall understand by *a priori* knowledge, not knowledge independent of this or that experience, but knowledge absolutely independent of all experience. Opposed to it is empirical knowledge, which is knowledge possible only *a posteriori*, that is, through experience. *A priori* modes of knowledge are entitled pure when there is no admixture of anything empirical. Thus, for instance, the proposition, 'every alteration has its cause', while an *a priori* proposition, is not a pure proposition, because alteration is a concept which can be derived only from experience.

WE ARE IN POSSESSION OF CERTAIN MODES OF A PRIORI
KNOWLEDGE, AND EVEN THE COMMON UNDERSTANDING IS
NEVER WITHOUT THEM

What we here require is a criterion [*Merkmal*] by which to distinguish with certainty between pure and empirical knowledge. Experience teaches us that a thing is so and so, but not that it cannot be otherwise. First, then, if we have a proposition which in being thought is thought as *necessary*, it is an *a priori* judgment; and if, besides, it is not derived from any proposition except one which also has the validity of a necessary judgment, it is an absolutely *a priori* judgment. Secondly, experience never confers on its judgments true or strict, but only assumed and comparative *universality*, through induction. We can properly only say, therefore, that, so far as we have hitherto observed, there is no exception to this or that rule. If, then, a judgment is thought with strict universality, that is, in such manner that no exception is allowed as possible, it is not derived from experience, but is valid absolutely *a priori*. Empirical universality is only an arbitrary extension of a validity holding in most cases to one which holds in all, for instance, in the proposition, 'all bodies are heavy'. When, on the other hand, strict universality is essential to a judgment, this indicates a special source of knowledge, namely, a faculty of *a priori* knowledge. Necessity and strict universality are thus sure criteria of *a priori* knowledge, and are inseparable from one another. But since in the employment of these criteria the contingency of judgments is sometimes more easily shown than their empirical limitation, or, as sometimes also happens, their unlimited universality can be more convincingly proved than their necessity, it is advisable to use the two criteria separately, each by itself being infallible.

Now it is easy to show that there actually are in human knowledge judgments which are necessary and in the strictest sense universal, and which are therefore pure *a priori* judgments. If an example from the sciences be desired, we have only to look to any of the propositions of mathematics; if we seek an example from the understanding in its quite ordinary employment, the proposition, 'every alteration must have a cause', will serve our purpose. In the latter case, indeed, the very concept of a cause so manifestly contains the concept of a necessity of connection with an effect and of the strict universality of the rule, that the concept would be altogether lost if we attempted to derive it, as Hume has done, from a repeated association of that which happens with that which precedes, and from a custom of connecting representations, a custom originating in this repeated association, and constituting therefore a merely subjective necessity. Even without appealing to such examples, it is possible to show that pure *a priori* principles are indispensable for the possibility of experience, and so to prove their existence *a priori*. For whence could experience derive its certainty, if all the rules, according to which it proceeds, were always themselves empirical, and therefore contingent? Such rules could hardly be regarded as first principles. At present, however, we may be content to have established the fact that our faculty of knowledge does have a pure employment, and to have shown what are the criteria of such an employment.

Such *a priori* origin is manifest in certain concepts, no less than in judgments. If we remove from our empirical concept of a body, one by one, every feature in it which is [merely] empirical, the colour, the hardness or softness, the weight, even the impenetrability, there still remains the space which the body (now entirely vanished) occupied, and this cannot be removed. Again, if we remove from our empirical concept of any object, corporeal or incorporeal, all properties which experience has taught us, we yet cannot take away that property through which the object is thought as substance or as inhering in a substance (although this concept of substance is more determinate than that of an object in general). Owing, therefore, to the necessity with which this concept of substance forces itself upon us, we have no option save to admit that it has its seat in our faculty of *a priori* knowledge.

PHILOSOPHY STANDS IN NEED OF A SCIENCE WHICH SHALL DETERMINE THE POSSIBILITY, THE PRINCIPLES, AND THE EXTENT OF ALL A PRIORI KNOWLEDGE

But what is still more extraordinary than all the preceding is this, that certain modes of knowledge leave the field of all possible experiences and have the appearance of extending the scope of our judgments beyond all limits of experience, and this by means of concepts to which no corresponding object can ever be given in experience.

It is precisely by means of the latter modes of knowledge, in a realm beyond the world of the senses, where experience can yield neither guidance nor correction, that our reason carries on those enquiries which owing to their importance we consider to be far more excellent, and in their purpose far more lofty, than all that the understanding can learn in the field of appearances. Indeed we prefer to run every risk of error rather than desist from such urgent enquiries, on the ground of their dubious character, or from disdain and indifference. These unavoidable problems set by pure reason itself are *God, freedom,* and *immortality.* The science which, with all its preparations, is in its final intention directed solely to their solution is metaphysics; and its procedure is at first dogmatic, that is, it confidently sets itself to this task without any previous examination of the capacity or incapacity of reason for so great an undertaking.

Now it does indeed seem natural that, as soon as we have left the ground of experience, we should, through careful enquiries, assure ourselves as to the foundations of any building that we propose to erect, not making use of any knowledge that we possess without first determining whence it has come, and not trusting to principles without knowing their origin. It is natural, that is to say, that the question should first be considered, how the understanding can arrive at all this knowledge *a priori*, and what extent, validity, and worth it may have. Nothing, indeed, could be more natural, if by the term 'natural' we signify what fittingly and reasonably ought to happen. But if we mean by 'natural' what ordinarily happens, then on the contrary nothing is more natural and more intelligible than the fact that this enquiry has been so long neglected. For one part of this knowledge, the mathematical, has long been of established reliability, and so gives rise to a favourable presumption as regards the other part, which may yet be of quite different nature. Besides, once we are outside the circle of experience, we can be sure of not being *contradicted* by experience. The charm of extending our knowledge is so great that nothing short of encountering a direct contradiction can suffice to arrest us in our course; and this can be avoided, if we are careful in our fabrications—which none the less will still remain fabrications. Mathematics gives us a shining example of how far, independently of experience, we can progress in *a priori* knowledge. It does, indeed, occupy itself with objects and with knowledge solely in so far as they allow of being exhibited in intuition. But this circumstance is easily overlooked, since this intuition can itself be given *a priori*, and is therefore hardly to be distinguished from a bare and pure concept. Misled by such a proof of the power of reason, the demand for the extension of knowledge recognises no limits. The light dove, cleaving the air in her free flight, and feeling its resistance, might imagine that its flight would be still easier in empty space. It was thus that Plato left the world of the senses, as setting too narrow limits to the understanding, and ventured out beyond it on the wings of the ideas, in the empty space of the pure understanding. He did not observe that with all his efforts he made no advance—meeting no resistance that might, as it were, serve as a support upon which he could take a stand, to which he could apply his powers, and so set his understanding in motion. It is, indeed, the common fate of human reason to complete its speculative structures as speedily as may be, and only afterwards to enquire whether the foundations are reliable. All sorts of excuses will then be appealed to, in order to reassure us of their solidity, or rather indeed to enable us to dispense altogether with so late and so dangerous an enquiry. But what keeps us, during the actual building, free from all apprehension and suspicion, and flatters us with a seeming thoroughness, is this other circumstance, namely, that a great, perhaps the greatest, part of the business of our reason consists in analysis of the concepts which we already have of objects. This analysis supplies us with a considerable body of knowledge, which, while nothing but explanation or elucidation of what has already been thought in our concepts, though in a confused manner, is yet prized as being, at least as regards its form, new insight. But so far as the matter or content is concerned, there has been no extension of our previously possessed concepts, but only an analysis of them. Since this procedure yields real knowledge *a priori*, which progresses in an assured and useful fashion, reason is so far misled as surreptitiously to introduce, without itself being aware of so doing, assertions of an entirely different order, in which it attaches to given concepts others completely foreign to them, and moreover attaches them *a priori*. And yet it is not known how reason can be in position to do this. Such a question is never so much as thought of. I shall therefore at once proceed to deal with the difference between these two kinds of knowledge.

THE DISTINCTION BETWEEN ANALYTIC AND SYNTHETIC JUDGMENTS

In all judgments in which the relation of a subject to the predicate is thought (I take into consideration affirmative judgments only, the subsequent application to negative judgments being easily made), this relation is possible in two different ways. Either the predicate B belongs to the subject A, as something which is (covertly) contained in this concept A; or B lies outside the concept A, although it does indeed stand in connection with it. In the one case I entitle the judgment analytic, in the other synthetic. Analytic judgments (affirmative) are therefore those in which the connection of the predicate with the subject is thought through identity; those in which this connection is thought without identity should be entitled synthetic. The former, as adding nothing through the predicate to the concept of the subject, but merely breaking it up into those constituent concepts that have all along been thought in it, although confusedly, can also be entitled explicative. The latter, on the other hand, add to the concept of the subject a predicate which has not been in any wise thought in it, and which no analysis could possibly extract from it; and they may therefore be entitled ampliative. If I say, for instance, 'All bodies are extended', this is an analytic judgment. For I do not require to go beyond the concept which I connect with 'body' in order to find extension as bound up with it. To meet with this predicate, I have merely to analyse the concept, that is, to become conscious to myself of the manifold which I always think in that concept. The judgment is therefore analytic. But when I say, 'All bodies are heavy', the predicate is something quite different from anything that I think in the mere concept of body in general; and the addition of such a predicate therefore yields a synthetic judgment.

Judgments of experience, as such, are one and all synthetic. For it would be absurd to found an analytic judgment on experience. Since, in framing the judgment, I must not go outside my concept, there is no need to appeal to the testimony of experience in its support. That a body is extended is a proposition that holds *a priori* and is not empirical. For, before appealing to experience, I have already in the concept of body all the conditions required for my judgment. I have only to extract from it, in accordance with the principle of contradiction, the required predicate, and in so doing can at the same time become conscious of the necessity of the judgment—and that is what experience could never have taught me. On the other hand, though I do not include in the concept of a body in general the predicate 'weight', none the less this concept indicates an object of experience through one of its parts, and I can add to that part other parts of this same experience, as in this way belonging together with the concept. From the start I can apprehend the concept of body analytically through the characters of extension, impenetrability, figure, etc., all of which are thought in the concept. Now, however, looking back on the experience from which I have derived this concept of body, and finding weight to be invariably connected with the above characters, I attach it as a predicate to the concept; and in doing so I attach it synthetically, and am therefore extending my knowledge. The possibility of the synthesis of the predicate 'weight' with the concept of 'body' thus rests upon experience. While the one concept is not contained in the other, they yet belong to one another, though only contingently, as parts of a whole, namely, of an experience which is itself a synthetic combination of intuitions.

But in *a priori* synthetic judgments this help is entirely lacking. [I do not here have the advantage of looking around in the field of experience.] Upon what, then, am I to rely, when I seek to go beyond the concept A, and to know that another concept B is connected with it? Through what is the synthesis made possible? Let us take the proposition, 'Everything which happens has its cause'. In the concept of 'something which happens', I do indeed think an existence which is preceded by a time, etc., and from this concept analytic judgments may be obtained. But the concept of a 'cause' lies entirely outside the other concept, and signifies something different from 'that which happens', and is not therefore in any way contained in this latter representation. How come I then to predicate of that which happens something quite different, and to apprehend that the concept of cause, though not contained in it, yet belongs, and indeed necessarily belongs, to it? What is here the unknown = X which gives support to the understanding when it believes that it can discover outside the concept A a predicate B foreign to this concept, which it yet at the same time considers to be connected with it? It cannot be experience, because the suggested principle has connected the second representation with the first, not only with greater universality, but also with the character of necessity, and therefore completely *a priori* and on the basis of mere concepts. Upon such synthetic, that is, ampliative principles, all our *a priori* speculative knowledge must ultimately rest; analytic judgments are very important, and indeed necessary, but only for obtaining that clearness in the concepts which is requisite for such a sure and wide synthesis as will lead to a genuinely new addition to all previous knowledge.

IN ALL THEORETICAL SCIENCES OF REASON SYNTHETIC A PRIORI JUDGMENTS ARE CONTAINED AS PRINCIPLES

1. *All mathematical judgments, without exception, are synthetic.* This fact, though incontestably certain and in its consequences very important, has hitherto escaped the notice of those who are engaged in the analysis of human reason, and is, indeed, directly opposed to all their conjectures. For as it was found that all mathematical inferences proceed in accordance with the principle of contradiction (which the nature of all apodeictic certainty requires), it was supposed that the fundamental propositions of the science can themselves be known to be true through that principle. This is an

erroneous view. For though a synthetic proposition can indeed be discerned in accordance with the principle of contradiction, this can only be if another synthetic proposition is presupposed, and if it can then be apprehended as following from this other proposition; it can never be so discerned in and by itself.

First of all, it has to be noted that mathematical propositions, strictly so called, are always judgments *a priori*, not empirical; because they carry with them necessity, which cannot be derived from experience. If this be demurred to, I am willing to limit my statement to *pure* mathematics, the very concept of which implies that it does not contain empirical, but only pure *a priori* knowledge.

We might, indeed, at first suppose that the proposition $7 + 5 = 12$ is a merely analytic proposition, and follows by the principle of contradiction from the concept of a sum of 7 and 5. But if we look more closely we find that the concept of the sum of 7 and 5 contains nothing save the union of the two numbers into one, and in this no thought is being taken as to what that single number may be which combines both. The concept of 12 is by no means already thought in merely thinking this union of 7 and 5; and I may analyse my concept of such a possible sum as long as I please, still I shall never find the 12 in it. We have to go outside these concepts, and call in the aid of the intuition which corresponds to one of them, our five fingers, for instance, or, as Segner does in his *Arithmetic*, five points, adding to the concept of 7, unit by unit, the five given in intuition. For starting with the number 7, and for the concept of 5 calling in the aid of the fingers of my hand as intuition, I now add one by one to the number 7 the units which I previously took together to form the number 5, and with the aid of that figure [the hand] see the number 12 come into being. That 5 should be added to 7, I have indeed already thought in the concept of a sum $= 7 + 5$, but not that this sum is equivalent to the number 12. Arithmetical propositions are therefore always synthetic. This is still more evident if we take larger numbers. For it is then obvious that, however we might turn and twist our concepts, we could never, by the mere analysis of them, and without the aid of intuition, discover what [the number is that] is the sum.

Just as little is any fundamental proposition of pure geometry analytic. That the straight line between two points is the shortest, is a synthetic proposition. For my concept of *straight* contains nothing of quantity, but only of quality. The concept of the shortest is wholly an addition, and cannot be derived, through any process of analysis, from the concept of the straight line. Intuition, therefore, must here be called in; only by its aid is the synthesis possible. What here causes us commonly to believe that the predicate of such apodeictic judgments is already contained in our concept, and that the judgment is therefore analytic, is merely the ambiguous character of the terms used. We are required to join in thought a certain predicate to a given concept, and this necessity is inherent in the concepts themselves. But the question is not what we *ought* to join in thought to the given concept, but what we *actually* think in it, even if only obscurely; and it is then manifest that, while the predicate is indeed attached necessarily to the concept, it is so in virtue of an intuition which must be added to the concept, not as thought in the concept itself.

Some few fundamental propositions, presupposed by the geometrician, are, indeed, really analytic, and rest on the principle of contradiction. But, as identical propositions, they serve only as links in the chain of method and not as principles; for instance, $a = a$; the whole is equal to itself; or $(a + b) > a$, that is, the whole is greater than its part. And even these propositions, though they are valid according to pure concepts, are only admitted in mathematics because they can be exhibited in intuition.

2. *Natural science (physics) contains* a priori *synthetic judgments as principles*. I need cite only two such judgments: that in all changes of the material world the quantity of matter remains unchanged; and that in all communication of motion, action and reaction must always be equal. Both propositions, it is evident, are not only necessary, and therefore in their origin *a priori*, but also synthetic. For in the concept of matter I do not think its permanence, but only its presence in the space which it occupies. I go outside and beyond the concept of matter, joining to it *a priori* in thought something which I have not thought *in* it. The proposition is not, therefore, analytic, but synthetic, and yet is thought *a priori*; and so likewise are the other propositions of the pure part of natural science.

3. *Metaphysics*, even if we look upon it as having hitherto failed in all its endeavours, is yet, owing to the nature of human reason, a quite indispensable science, and *ought to contain* a priori *synthetic knowledge*. For its business is not merely to analyse concepts which we make for ourselves *a priori* of things, and thereby to clarify them analytically, but to extend our *a priori* knowledge. And for this purpose we must employ principles which add to the given concept something that was not contained in it, and through *a priori* synthetic judgments venture out so far that experience is quite unable to follow us, as, for instance, in the proposition, that the world must have a first beginning, and such like. Thus metaphysics consists, at least *in intention*, entirely of *a priori* synthetic propositions.

THE GENERAL PROBLEM OF PURE REASON

Much is already gained if we can bring a number of investigations under the formula of a single problem. For we not only lighten our own task, by defining it accurately, but make it easier for others, who would test our results, to judge whether or not we have succeeded in what we set out to do. Now the proper problem of pure reason is contained in the question: How are *a priori* synthetic judgments possible?

That metaphysics has hitherto remained in so vacillating a state of uncertainty and contradiction, is entirely due to the fact that this problem, and perhaps even the distinction between analytic and synthetic judgments, has never previously been considered. Upon the solution of this problem, or upon a sufficient proof that the possibility which it desires to have explained does in fact not exist at all, depends the success or failure of metaphysics. Among philosophers, David Hume came nearest to envisaging this problem, but still was very far from conceiving it with sufficient definiteness and universality. He occupied himself exclusively with the synthetic proposition regarding the connection of an effect with its cause (*principium causalitatis*), and he believed himself to have shown that such an *a priori* proposition is entirely impossible. If we accept his conclusions, then all that we call metaphysics is a mere delusion whereby we fancy ourselves to have rational insight into what, in actual fact, is borrowed solely from experience, and under the influence of custom has taken the illusory semblance of necessity. If he had envisaged our problem in all its universality, he would never have been guilty of this statement, so destructive of all pure philosophy. For he would then have recognised that, according to his own argument, pure mathematics, as certainly containing *a priori* synthetic propositions, would also not be possible; and from such an assertion his good sense would have saved him.

In the solution of the above problem, we are at the same time deciding as to the possibility of the employment of pure reason in establishing and developing all those sciences which contain a theoretical *a priori* knowledge of objects, and have therefore to answer the questions:

How is pure mathematics possible?
How is pure science of nature possible?

Since these sciences actually exist, it is quite proper to ask *how* they are possible; for that they must be possible is proved by the fact that they exist.[1] But the poor progress which has hitherto been made in metaphysics, and the fact that no system yet propounded can, in view of the essential purpose of metaphysics, be said really to exist, leaves everyone sufficient ground for doubting as to its possibility.

Yet, in a certain sense, this *kind of knowledge* is to be looked upon as given; that is to say, metaphysics actually exists, if not as a science, yet still as natural disposition (*metaphysica naturalis*). For human reason, without being moved merely by the idle desire for extent and variety of knowledge, proceeds impetuously, driven on by an inward need, to questions such as cannot be answered by any empirical employment of reason, or by principles thence derived. Thus in all men, as soon as their reason has become ripe for speculation, there has always existed and will always continue to exist some kind of metaphysics. And so we have the question:

How is metaphysics, as natural disposition, possible?

that is, how from the nature of universal human reason do those questions arise which pure reason propounds to itself, and which it is impelled by its own need to answer as best it can?

But since all attempts which have hitherto been made to answer these natural questions—for instance, whether the world has a beginning or is from eternity—have always met with unavoidable contradictions, we cannot rest satisfied with the mere natural disposition to metaphysics, that is, with the pure faculty of reason itself, from which, indeed, some sort of metaphysics (be it what it may) always arises. It must be possible for reason to attain to certainty whether we know or do not know the objects of

[1] Many may still have doubts as regards pure natural science. We have only, however, to consider the various propositions that are to be found at the beginning of (empirical) physics, properly so called, those, for instance, relating to the permanence in the quantity of matter, to inertia, to the equality of action and reaction, etc., in order to be soon convinced that they constitute a *physica pura*, or *rationalis*, which well deserves, as an independent science, to be separately dealt with in its whole extent, be that narrow or wide.

metaphysics, that is, to come to a decision either in regard to the objects of its enquiries or in regard to the capacity or incapacity of reason to pass any judgment upon them, so that we may either with confidence extend our pure reason or set to it sure and determinate limits. This last question, which arises out of the previous general problem, may, rightly stated, take the form:

How is metaphysics, as science, possible?

Thus the critique of reason, in the end, necessarily leads to scientific knowledge; while its dogmatic employment, on the other hand, lands us in dogmatic assertions to which other assertions, equally specious, can always be opposed—that is, in *scepticism*.

This science cannot be of any very formidable prolixity, since it has to deal not with the objects of reason, the variety of which is inexhaustible, but only with itself and the problems which arise entirely from within itself, and which are imposed upon it by its own nature, not by the nature of things which are distinct from it. When once reason has learnt completely to understand its own power in respect of objects which can be presented to it in experience, it should easily be able to determine, with completeness and certainty, the extent and the limits of its attempted employment beyond the bounds of all experience.

We may, then, and indeed we must, regard as abortive all attempts, hitherto made, to establish a metaphysic *dogmatically*. For the analytic part in any such attempted system, namely, the mere analysis of the concepts that inhere in our reason *a priori*, is by no means the aim of, but only a preparation for, metaphysics proper, that is, the extension of its *a priori* synthetic knowledge. For such a purpose, the analysis of concepts is useless, since it merely shows what is contained in these concepts, not how we arrive at them *a priori*. A solution of this latter problem is required, that we may be able to determine the valid employment of such concepts in regard to the objects of all knowledge in general. Nor is much self-denial needed to give up these claims, seeing that the undeniable, and in the dogmatic procedure of reason also unavoidable, contradictions of reason with itself have long since undermined the authority of every metaphysical system yet propounded. Greater firmness will be required if we are not to be deterred by inward difficulties and outward opposition from endeavouring, through application of a method entirely different from any hitherto employed, at last to bring to a prosperous and fruitful growth a science indispensable to human reason—a science whose every branch may be cut away but whose root cannot be destroyed.

THE IDEA AND DIVISION OF A SPECIAL SCIENCE, UNDER THE TITLE "CRITIQUE OF PURE REASON"

In view of all these considerations, we arrive at the idea of a special science which can be entitled the Critique of Pure Reason. For reason is the faculty which supplies the principles of *a priori* knowledge. Pure reason is, therefore, that which contains the principles whereby we know anything absolutely *a priori*. An organon of pure reason would be the sum-total of those principles according to which all modes of pure *a priori* knowledge can be acquired and actually brought into being. The exhaustive application of such an organon would give rise to a system of pure reason. But as this would be asking rather much, and as it is still doubtful whether, and in what cases, any extension of our knowledge be here possible, we can regard a science of the mere examination of pure reason, of its sources and limits, as the *propaedeutic* to the system of pure reason. As such, it should be called a critique, not a doctrine, of pure reason. Its utility, in speculation, ought properly to be only negative, not to extend, but only to clarify our reason, and keep it free from errors—which is already a very great gain. I entitle *transcendental* all knowledge which is occupied not so much with objects as with the mode of our knowledge of objects in so far as this mode of knowledge is to be possible *a priori*. A system of such concepts might be entitled transcendental philosophy. But that is still, at this stage, too large an undertaking. For since such a science must contain, with completeness, both kinds of *a priori* knowledge, the analytic no less than the synthetic, it is, so far as our present purpose is concerned, much too comprehensive. We have to carry the analysis so far only as is indispensably necessary in order to comprehend, in their whole extent, the principles of *a priori* synthesis, with which alone we are called upon to deal. It is upon this enquiry, which should be entitled not a doctrine, but only a transcendental critique, that we are now engaged. Its purpose is not to extend knowledge, but only to correct it, and to supply a touchstone of the value, or lack of value, of all *a priori* knowledge. Such a critique is therefore a preparation, so far as may be possible, for an organon; and should this turn out not to be possible, then at least for a canon, according to which, in due course, the complete system of the philosophy of pure reason—be it in extension or merely in limitation of its knowledge— may be carried into execution, analytically as well as synthetically. That such a system is possible, and indeed that it may not be of such great extent as to cut us off from the hope of entirely completing it, may already be gathered from the fact that what here constitutes our subject-matter is not the nature of things, which is inexhaustible, but the understanding which passes judgment upon the nature of things; and this understanding, again, only in respect of its *a priori* knowledge. These *a priori* possessions of the understanding, since they have not to be sought for without, cannot remain hidden from us, and in all probability are sufficiently small in extent to allow of our apprehending them in their completeness, of judging as to their value or lack of value, and so of rightly appraising them. Still less may the reader here expect a critique of books and systems of pure reason; we are concerned only with the critique of the faculty of pure reason itself. Only in so far as we build upon this foundation do we have a reliable touchstone for estimating the philosophical value of old and new works in this field. Otherwise the unqualified historian or critic is passing judgments upon the groundless assertions of others by means of his own, which are equally groundless.

Transcendental philosophy is only the idea of a science, for which the critique of pure reason has to lay down the complete architectonic plan. That is to say, it has to guarantee, as following from principles, the completeness and certainty of the structure in all its parts. It is the system of all principles of pure reason. And if this critique is not itself to be entitled a transcendental philosophy, it is solely because, to be a complete system, it would also have to contain an exhaustive analysis of the whole of *a priori* human knowledge. Our critique must, indeed, supply a complete enumeration of all the fundamental concepts that go to constitute such pure knowledge. But it is not required to give an exhaustive analysis of these concepts, nor a complete review of those that can be derived from them. Such a demand would be unreasonable, partly because this analysis would not be appropriate to our main purpose, inasmuch as there is no such uncertainty in regard to analysis as we encounter in the case of synthesis, for the sake of which alone our whole critique is undertaken; and partly because it would be inconsistent with the unity of our plan to assume responsibility for the completeness of such an analysis and derivation, when in view of our purpose we can be excused from doing so. The analysis of these *a priori* concepts, which later we shall have to enumerate, and the derivation of other concepts from them, can easily, however, be made complete when once they have been established as exhausting the principles of synthesis, and if in this essential respect nothing be lacking in them.

The critique of pure reason therefore will contain all that is essential in transcendental philosophy. While it is the complete idea of transcendental philosophy, it is not equivalent to that latter science; for it carries the analysis only so far as is requisite for the complete examination of knowledge which is *a priori* and synthetic.

What has chiefly to be kept in view in the division of such a science, is that no concepts be allowed to enter which contain in themselves anything empirical, or, in other words, that it consist in knowledge wholly *a priori*. Accordingly, although the highest principles and fundamental concepts of morality are *a priori* knowledge, they have no place in transcendental philosophy, because, although they do not lay at the foundation of their precepts the concepts of pleasure and pain, of the desires and inclinations, etc., all of which are of empirical origin, yet in the construction of a system of pure morality these empirical concepts must necessarily be brought into the concept of duty, as representing either a hindrance, which we have to overcome, or an allurement, which must not be made into a motive. Transcendental philosophy is therefore a philosophy of pure and merely speculative reason. All that is practical, so far as it contains motives, relates to feelings, and these belong to the empirical sources of knowledge.

If we are to make a systematic division of the science which we are engaged in presenting, it must have first a *doctrine of the elements*, and secondly, a *doctrine of the method of pure reason*. Each of these chief divisions will have its subdivisions, but the grounds of these we are not yet in a position to explain. By way of introduction or anticipation we need only say that there are two stems of human knowledge, namely, *sensibility* and *understanding*, which perhaps spring from a common, but to us unknown, root. Through the former, objects are given to us; through the latter, they are thought. Now in so far as sensibility may be found to contain *a priori* representations constituting the condition under which objects are given to us, it will belong to transcendental philosophy. And since the conditions under which alone the objects of human knowledge are given must precede those under which they are thought, the transcendental doctrine of sensibility will constitute the first part of the science of the elements.

OF DEMONSTRATION AND NECESSARY TRUTHS

John Stuart Mill

. . . If the foundation of all sciences, even deductive or demonstrative sciences, is Induction; if every step in the ratiocinations even of geometry is an act of induction; and if a train of reasoning is but bringing many inductions to bear upon the same subject of inquiry, and drawing a case within one induction by means of another; wherein lies the peculiar certainty always ascribed to the sciences which are entirely, or almost entirely, deductive? Why are they called the Exact Sciences? Why are mathematical certainty, and the evidence of demonstration, common phrases to express the very highest degree of assurance attainable by reason? Why are mathematics by almost all philosophers, and (by some) even those branches of natural philosophy which, through the medium of mathematics, have been converted into deductive sciences, considered to be independent of the evidence of experience and observation, and characterized as systems of Necessary Truth?

The answer I conceive to be, that this character of necessity, ascribed to the truths of mathematics, and (even with some reservations to be hereafter made) the peculiar certainty attributed to them, is an illusion; in order to sustain which, it is necessary to suppose that those truths relate to, and express the properties of, purely imaginary objects. It is acknowledged that the conclusions of geometry are deduced, partly at least, from the so-called Definitions, and that those definitions are assumed to be correct representations, as far as they go, of the objects with which geometry is conversant. Now we have pointed out that, from a definition as such, no proposition, unless it be one concerning the meaning of a word, can ever follow; and that what apparently follows from a definition, follows in reality from an implied assumption that there exists a real thing conformable thereto. This assumption, in the case of the definitions of geometry, is not strictly true: there exist no real things exactly conformable to the definitions. There exist

---

From John Stuart Mill, *A System of Logic*, 8th ed. (New York: Harper & Bros., 1874), Book II, Chaps. V–VI, pp. 168–170, 172–174, 187–191.

no points without magnitude; no lines without breadth, nor perfectly straight; no circles with all their radii exactly equal, nor squares with all their angles perfectly right. It will perhaps be said that the assumption does not extend to the actual, but only to the possible, existence of such things. I answer that, according to any test we have of possibility, they are not even possible. Their existence, so far as we can form any judgment, would seem to be inconsistent with the physical constitution of our planet at least, if not of the universe. To get rid of this difficulty, and at the same time to save the credit of the supposed system of necessary truth, it is customary to say that the points, lines, circles, and squares which are the subject of geometry, exist in our conceptions merely, and are part of our minds; which minds, by working on their own materials, construct an *a priori* science, the evidence of which is purely mental, and has nothing whatever to do with outward experience. By howsoever high authorities this doctrine may have been sanctioned, it appears to me psychologically incorrect. The points, lines, circles, and squares which any one has in his mind, are (I apprehend) simply copies of the points, lines, circles, and squares which he has known in his experience. Our idea of a point, I apprehend to be simply our idea of the *minimum visibile*, the smallest portion of surface which we can see. A line, as defined by geometers, is wholly inconceivable. We can reason about a line as if it had no breadth; because we have a power, which is the foundation of all the control we can exercise over the operations of our minds; the power, when a perception is present to our senses, or a conception to our intellects, of *attending* to a part only of that perception or conception, instead of the whole. But we can not *conceive* a line without breadth; we can form no mental picture of such a line: all the lines which we have in our minds are lines possessing breadth. If any one doubts this, we may refer him to his own experience. I much question if any one who fancies that he can conceive what is called a mathematical line, thinks so from the evidence of his consciousness: I suspect it is rather because he supposes that unless such a conception were possible, mathematics could not exist as a science: a supposition which there will be no difficulty in showing to be entirely groundless.

Since, then, neither in nature, nor in the human mind, do there exist any objects exactly corresponding to the definitions of geometry, while yet that science can not be supposed to be conversant about nonentities; nothing remains but to consider geometry as conversant with such lines, angles, and figures, as really exist; and the definitions, as they are called, must be regarded as some of our first and most obvious generalizations concerning those natural objects. The correctness of those generalizations, *as* generalizations, is without a flaw: the equality of all the radii of a circle is true of all circles, so far as it is true of any one: but it is not exactly true of any circle; it is only nearly true; so nearly that no error of any importance in practice will be incurred by feigning it to be exactly true. When we have occasion to extend these inductions, or their consequences, to cases in which the error would be appreciable—to lines of perceptible breadth or thickness, parallels which deviate sensibly from equidistance, and the like—we correct our conclusions, by combining with them a fresh set of propositions relating to the aberration; just as we also take in propositions relating to the physical or chemical properties of the material, if those properties happen to introduce any modification into the result; which they easily may, even with respect to figure and magnitude, as in the case, for instance, of expansion by heat. So long, however, as there exists no practical necessity for attending to any of the properties of the object except its geometrical properties, or to any of the natural irregularities in those, it is convenient to neglect the consideration of the other properties and of the irregularities, and to reason as if these did not exist: accordingly, we formally announce in the definitions, that we intend to proceed on this plan. But it is an error to suppose, because we resolve to confine our attention to a certain number of the properties of an object, that we therefore conceive, or have an idea of, the object, denuded of its other properties. We are thinking, all the time, of precisely such objects as we have seen and touched, and with all the properties which naturally belong to them; but, for scientific convenience, we feign them to be divested of all properties, except those which are material to our purpose, and in regard to which we design to consider them.

The peculiar accuracy, supposed to be characteristic of the first principles of geometry, thus appears to be fictitious. The assertions on which the reasonings of the science are founded, do not, any more than in other sciences, exactly correspond with the fact; but we suppose that they do so, for the sake of tracing the consequences which follow from the supposition. The opinion of Dugald Stewart respecting the foundations of geometry, is, I conceive, substantially correct; that it is built on hypotheses; that it owes to this alone the peculiar certainty supposed to distinguish it; and that in any science whatever, by reasoning from a set of hypotheses, we may obtain a body of conclusions as certain as those of geometry, that is, as strictly in accordance with the hypotheses, and as irresistibly compelling assent, *on condition* that those hypotheses are true.[1]

When, therefore, it is affirmed that the conclusions of geometry are necessary truths, the necessity consists in reality only in this, that they correctly follow from the suppositions from which they are deduced. Those suppositions are so far from being necessary, that they are not even true; they purposely depart, more or less widely, from the truth. The only sense in which necessity can be ascribed to the conclusions of any scientific investigation, is that of legitimately following from some assumption, which, by the conditions of the inquiry, is not to be questioned. In this relation, of course, the derivative truths of every deductive science must stand to the inductions, or assumptions, on which the science is founded, and which,

---

[1] It is justly remarked by Professor Bain (*Logic,* ii., 134) that the word Hypothesis is here used in a somewhat peculiar sense. An hypothesis, in science, usually means a supposition not proved to be true, but surmised to be so, because if true it would account for certain known facts; and the final result of the speculation may be to prove its truth. The hypotheses spoken of in the text are of a different character; they are known not to be literally true, while as much of them as is true is not hypothetical, but certain. The two cases, however, resemble in the circumstance that in both we reason, not from a truth, but from an assumption, and the truth therefore of the conclusions is conditional, not categorical. This suffices to justify, in point of logical propriety, Stewart's use of the term. It is of course needful to bear in mind that the hypothetical element in the definitions of geometry is the assumption that what is very nearly true is exactly so. This unreal exactitude might be called a fiction, as properly as an hypothesis; but that appellation, still more than the other, would fail to point out the close relation which exists between the fictitious point or line and the points and lines of which we have experience.

whether true or untrue, certain or doubtful in themselves, are always supposed certain for the purposes of the particular science. . . .

.   .   .

It remains to inquire, what is the ground of our belief in axioms—what is the evidence on which they rest? I answer, they are experimental truths; generalizations from observation. The proposition, Two straight lines can not inclose a space—or, in other words, Two straight lines which have once met, do not meet again, but continue to diverge—is an induction from the evidence of our senses.

.   .   .

It is not necessary to show that the truths which we call axioms are originally *suggested* by observation, and that we should never have known that two straight lines can not inclose a space if we had never seen a straight line: thus much being admitted by Dr. Whewell, and by all, in recent times, who have taken his view of the subject. But they contend, that it is not experience which *proves* the axiom; but that its truth is perceived a priori, by the constitution of the mind itself, from the first moment when the meaning of the proposition is apprehended; and without any necessity for verifying it by repeated trials, as is requisite in the case of truths really ascertained by observation.

They can not, however, but allow that the truth of the axiom, Two straight lines can not inclose a space, even if evident independently of experience, is also evident from experience. Whether the axiom needs confirmation or not, it receives confirmation in almost every instant of our lives; since we can not look at any two straight lines which intersect one another, without seeing that from that point they continue to diverge more and more. Experimental proof crowds in upon us in such endless profusion, and without one instance in which there can be even a suspicion of an exception to the rule, that we should soon have stronger ground for believing the axiom, even as an experimental truth, than we have for almost any of the general truths which we confessedly learn from the evidence of our senses. Independently of a priori evidence, we should certainly believe it with an intensity of conviction far greater than we accord to any ordinary physical truth: and this too at a time of life much earlier than that from which we date almost any part of our acquired knowledge, and much too early to admit of our retaining any recollection of the history of our intellectual operations at that period. Where then is the necessity for assuming that our recognition of these truths has a different origin from the rest of our knowledge, when its existence is perfectly accounted for by supposing its origin to be the same? when the causes which produce belief in all other instances, exist in this instance, and in a degree of strength as much superior to what exists in other cases, as the intensity of the belief itself is superior? The burden of proof lies on the advocates of the contrary opinion: it is for them to point out some fact, inconsistent with the supposition that this part of our knowledge of nature is derived from the same sources as every other part.[2]

[2] Some persons find themselves prevented from believing that the axiom, Two straight lines can not inclose a space, could ever become known to us through experience, by a difficulty which may be stated as follows: If the straight lines spoken of are those

This, for instance, they would be able to do, if they could prove chronologically that we had the conviction (at least practically) so early in infancy as to be anterior to those impressions on the senses, upon which, on the other theory, the conviction is founded. This, however, can not be proved: the point being too far back to be within the reach of memory, and too obscure for external observation. The advocates of the *a priori* theory are obliged to have recourse to other arguments.

·   ·   ·

In [our] examination . . . into the nature of the evidence of those deductive sciences which are commonly represented to be systems of necessary truth, we have been led to the following conclusions. The results of those sciences are indeed necessary, in the sense of necessarily following from certain first principles, commonly called axioms and definitions; that is, of being certainly true if those axioms and definitions are so; for the word necessity, even in this acceptation of it, means no more than certainty. But their claim to the character of necessity in any sense beyond this, as implying an evidence independent of and superior to observation and experience, must depend on the previous establishment of such a claim in favor of the definitions and axioms themselves. With regard to axioms, we found that, considered as experimental truths, they rest on superabundant and obvious evidence. We inquired, whether, since this is the case, it be imperative to suppose any other evidence of those truths than experimental evidence, any other origin for our belief of them than an experimental origin. We decided, that the burden of proof lies with those who maintain the affirmative, and we examined, at considerable length, such arguments as they have produced. The examination having led to the rejection of those arguments, we have thought ourselves warranted in concluding that axioms are but a class, the most universal class, of inductions from experience; the simplest and easiest cases of generalization from the facts furnished to us by our senses or by our internal consciousness.

While the axioms of demonstrative sciences thus appeared to be experi-

---

contemplated in the definition—lines absolutely without breadth and absolutely straight —that such are incapable of inclosing a space is not proved by experience, for lines such as these do not present themselves in our experience. If, on the other hand, the lines meant are such straight lines as we do meet with in experience, lines straight enough for practical purposes, but in reality slightly zigzag, and with some, however trifling, breadth; as applied to these lines the axiom is not true: for two of them may, and sometimes do, inclose a small portion of space. In neither case, therefore, does experience prove the axiom.

Those who employ this argument to show that geometrical axioms can not be proved by induction, show themselves unfamiliar with a common and perfectly valid mode of inductive proof; proof by approximation. Though experience furnishes us with no lines so unimpeachably straight that two of them are incapable of inclosing the smallest space, it presents us with gradations of lines possessing less and less either of breadth or of flexure, of which series the straight line of the definition is the ideal limit. And observation shows that just as much, and as nearly, as the straight lines of experience approximate to having no breadth or flexure, so much and so nearly does the space-inclosing power of any two of them approach to zero. The inference that if they had no breadth or flexure at all, they would inclose no space at all, is a correct inductive inference from these facts, conformable to one of the four Inductive Methods herein-after characterized, the Method of Concomitant Variations; of which the mathematical Doctrine of Limits presents the extreme case.

mental truths, the definitions, as they are incorrectly called, in those sciences, were found by us to be generalizations from experience which are not even, accurately speaking, truths; being propositions in which, while we assert of some kind of object, some property or properties which observation shows to belong to it, we at the same time deny that it possesses any other properties, though in truth other properties do in every individual instance accompany, and in almost all instances modify, the property thus exclusively predicated. The denial, therefore, is a mere fiction, or supposition, made for the purpose of excluding the consideration of those modifying circumstances, when their influence is of too trifling amount to be worth considering, or adjourning it, when important to a more convenient moment.

From these considerations it would appear that Deductive or Demonstrative Sciences are all, without exception, Inductive Sciences; that their evidence is that of experience; but that they are also, in virtue of the peculiar character of one indispensable portion of the general formulæ according to which their inductions are made, Hypothetical Sciences. Their conclusions are only true on certain suppositions, which are, or ought to be, approximations to the truth, but are seldom, if ever, exactly true; and to this hypothetical character is to be ascribed the peculiar certainty, which is supposed to be inherent in demonstration.

What we have now asserted, however, can not be received as universally true of Deductive or Demonstrative Sciences, until verified by being applied to the most remarkable of all those sciences, that of Numbers; the theory of the Calculus; Arithmetic and Algebra. It is harder to believe of the doctrines of this science than of any other, either that they are not truths *a priori*, but experimental truths, or that their peculiar certainty is owing to their being not absolute but only conditional truths. This, therefore, is a case which merits examination apart; and the more so, because on this subject we have a double set of doctrines to contend with; that of the *a priori* philosophers on one side; and on the other, a theory the most opposite to theirs, which was at one time very generally received, and is still far from being altogether exploded, among metaphysicians.

This theory attempts to solve the difficulty apparently inherent in the case, by representing the propositions of the science of numbers as merely verbal, and its processes as simple transformations of language, substitutions of one expression for another. The proposition, Two and one is equal to three, according to these writers, is not a truth, is not the assertion of a really existing fact, but a definition of the word three; a statement that mankind have agreed to use the name three as a sign exactly equivalent to two and one; to call by the former name whatever is called by the other more clumsy phrase. According to this doctrine, the longest process in algebra is but a succession of changes in terminology, by which equivalent expressions are substituted one for another; a series of translations of the same fact, from one into another language; though how, after such a series of translations, the fact itself comes out changed (as when we demonstrate a new geometrical theorem by algebra), they have not explained; and it is a difficulty which is fatal to their theory.

It must be acknowledged that there are peculiarities in the processes of arithmetic and algebra which render the theory in question very plausible, and have not unnaturally made those sciences the stronghold of Nominalism.

The doctrine that we can discover facts, detect the hidden processes of nature, by an artful manipulation of language, is so contrary to common sense, that a person must have made some advances in philosophy to believe it: men fly to so paradoxical a belief to avoid, as they think, some even greater difficulty, which the vulgar do not see. What has led many to believe that reasoning is a mere verbal process, is, that no other theory seemed reconcilable with the nature of the Science of Numbers. For we do not carry any ideas along with us when we use the symbols of arithmetic or of algebra. In a geometrical demonstration we have a mental diagram, if not one on paper; AB, AC, are present to our imagination as lines, intersecting other lines, forming an angle with one another, and the like; but not so *a* and *b*. These may represent lines or any other magnitudes, but those magnitudes are never thought of; nothing is realized in our imagination but *a* and *b*. The ideas which, on the particular occasion, they happen to represent, are banished from the mind during every intermediate part of the process, between the beginning, when the premises are translated from things into signs, and the end, when the conclusion is translated back from signs into things. Nothing, then, being in the reasoner's mind but the symbols, what can seem more inadmissible than to contend that the reasoning process has to do with any thing more? We seem to have come to one of Bacon's Prerogative Instances; an *experimentum crucis* [crucial experiment] on the nature of reasoning itself.

Nevertheless, it will appear on consideration, that this apparently so decisive instance is no instance at all; that there is in every step of an arithmetical or algebraical calculation a real induction, a real inference of facts from facts; and that what disguises the induction is simply its comprehensive nature, and the consequent extreme generality of the language. All numbers must be numbers of something; there are no such things as numbers in the abstract. *Ten* must mean ten bodies, or ten sounds, or ten beatings of the pulse. But though numbers must be numbers of something, they may be numbers of any thing. Propositions, therefore, concerning numbers, have the remarkable peculiarity that they are propositions concerning all things whatever; all objects, all existences of every kind, known to our experience. All things possess quantity; consist of parts which can be numbered; and in that character possess all the properties which are called properties of numbers. That half of four is two, must be true whatever the word four represents, whether four hours, four miles, or four pounds weight. We need only conceive a thing divided into four equal parts (and all things may be conceived as so divided), to be able to predicate of it every property of the number four, that is, every arithmetical proposition in which the number four stands on one side of the equation. Algebra extends the generalization still farther: every number represents that particular number of all things without distinction, but every algebraical symbol does more, it represents all numbers without distinction. As soon as we conceive a thing divided into equal parts, without knowing into what number of parts, we may call it *a* or *x*, and apply to it, without danger of error, every algebraical formula in the books. The proposition, $2(a + b) = 2a + 2b$, is a truth co-extensive with all nature. Since then algebraical truths are true of all things whatever, and not, like those of geometry, true of lines only or of angles only, it is no wonder that the symbols should not excite in our minds ideas of any things in particular. When we demonstrate the forty-seventh proposition of Euclid, it is not necessary that the words should raise in us an image of all right-angled triangles, but only of some one right-angled triangle: so in algebra we need not, under the symbol *a*, picture to ourselves all things whatever, but only some one thing; why not, then, the letter itself? The mere written characters, *a*, *b*, *x*, *y*, *z*, serve as well for representatives of Things in general, as any more complex and apparently more concrete conception. That we are conscious of them, however, in their character of things, and not of mere signs, is evident from the fact that our whole process of reasoning is carried on by predicating of them the properties of things. In resolving an algebraic equation, by what rules do we proceed? By applying at each step to *a*, *b*, and *x*, the proposition that equals added to equals make equals; that equals taken from equals leave equals; and other propositions founded on these two. These are not properties of language, or of signs as such, but of magnitudes, which is as much as to say, of all things. The inferences, therefore, which are successively drawn, are inferences concerning things, not symbols; though as any Things whatever will serve the turn, there is no necessity for keeping the idea of the Thing at all distinct, and consequently the process of thought may, in this case, be allowed without danger to do what all processes of thought, when they have been performed often, will do if permitted, namely, to become entirely mechanical. Hence the general language of algebra comes to be used familiarly without exciting ideas, as all other general language is prone to do from mere habit, though in no other case than this can it be done with complete safety. But when we look back to see from whence the probative force of the process is derived, we find that at every single step, unless we suppose ourselves to be thinking and talking of the things, and not the mere symbols, the evidence fails.

There is another circumstance, which, still more than that which we have now mentioned, gives plausibility to the notion that the propositions of arithmetic and algebra are merely verbal. That is, that when considered as propositions respecting Things, they all have the appearance of being identical propositions. The assertion, Two and one is equal to three, considered as an assertion respecting objects, as for instance, "Two pebbles and one pebble are equal to three pebbles," does not affirm equality between two collections of pebbles, but absolute identity. It affirms that if we put one pebble to two pebbles, those very pebbles are three. The objects, therefore, being the very same, and the mere assertion that "objects are themselves" being insignificant, it seems but natural to consider the proposition, Two and one is equal to three, as asserting mere identity of signification between the two names.

This, however, though it looks so plausible, will not bear examination. The expression "two pebbles and one pebble," and the expression "three pebbles," stand indeed for the same aggregation of objects, but they by no means stand for the same physical fact. They are names of the same objects, but of those objects in two different states: though they *de*note the same things, their *con*notation is different. Three pebbles in two separate parcels, and three pebbles in one parcel, do not make the same impression on our senses; and the assertion that the very same pebbles may by an alteration of place and arrangement be made to produce either the one set of sensations or the other, though a very familiar proposition, is not an identical one. It is a truth known to us by early and constant experience: an inductive truth; and such truths are the foundation of the science of Number. The fundamental truths of that science all rest on the evidence of sense; they are proved by showing to our eyes and our fingers that any given number of objects—ten balls, for example—may by separation and re-arrangement exhibit to our senses all the different sets of numbers the sums of which is equal to ten. All the improved methods of teaching arithmetic to children proceed on a knowledge of this fact. All who wish to carry the child's *mind* along with them in learning arithmetic; all who wish to teach numbers, and not mere ciphers—now teach it through the evidence of the senses, in the manner we have described.

We may, if we please, call the proposition, "Three is two and one," a definition of the number three, and assert that arithmetic, as it has been asserted that geometry, is a science founded on definitions. But they are definitions in the geometrical sense, not the logical; asserting not the meaning of a term only, but along with it an observed matter of fact. The proposition, "A circle is a figure bounded by a line which has all its points equally distant from a point within it," is called the definition of a circle; but the proposition from which so many consequences follow, and which is really a first principle in geometry, is, that figures answering to this description exist. And thus we may call "Three is two and one" a definition of three; but the calculations which depend on that proposition do not follow from the definition itself, but from an arithmetical theorem presupposed in it, namely, that collections of objects exist, which while they impress the senses thus, $^\circ{}_\circ{}^\circ$, may be separated into two parts, thus, ₀ ₀ ₀. This proposition being granted, we term all such parcels Threes, after which the enunciation of the above-mentioned physical fact will serve also for a definition of the word Three.

The Science of Number is thus no exception to the conclusion we previously arrived at, that the processes even of deductive sciences are altogether inductive, and that their first principles are generalizations from experience. It remains to be examined whether this science resembles geometry in the further circumstance, that some of its inductions are not exactly true; and that the peculiar certainty ascribed to it, on account of which its propositions are called Necessary Truths, is fictitious and hypothetical, being true in no other sense than that those propositions legitimately follow from the hypothesis of the truth of premises which are avowedly mere approximations to truth.

·   ·   ·

9

ON THE NATURE OF
MATHEMATICAL TRUTH

Carl G. Hempel

THE PROBLEM

It is a basic principle of scientific inquiry that no proposition and no theory is to be accepted without adequate grounds. In empirical science, which includes both the natural and the social sciences, the grounds for the acceptance of a theory consist in the agreement of predictions based on the theory with empirical evidence obtained either by experiment or by systematic observation. But what are the grounds which sanction the acceptance of mathematics? That is the question I propose to discuss in the present paper. For reasons which will become clear subsequently, I shall use the term "mathematics" here to refer to arithmetic, algebra, and analysis—to the exclusion, in particular, of geometry.[1]

ARE THE PROPOSITIONS OF MATHEMATICS
SELF-EVIDENT TRUTHS?

One of the several answers which have been given to our problem asserts that the truths of mathematics, in contradistinction to the hypotheses of empirical science, require neither factual evidence nor any other justification because they are "self-evident." This view, however, which ultimately relegates decisions as to mathematical truth to a feeling of self-evidence, encounters various difficulties. First of all, many mathematical theorems are so hard to establish that even to the specialist in the particular field they appear as anything but self-evident. Secondly, it is well known that some of the most interesting results of mathematics—especially in such fields as abstract set theory and topology—run counter to deeply ingrained intuitions

Carl G. Hempel, "On the Nature of Mathematical Truth," *American Mathematical Monthly*, LII (1945). Reprinted by permission of the Mathematical Association of America, SUNY at Buffalo (University of Buffalo), Buffalo, New York.
[1] A discussion of the status of geometry is given in my article, "Geometry and Empirical Science," *American Mathematical Monthly*, Vol. 52, pp. 7–17, 1945.

and the customary kind of feeling of self-evidence. Thirdly, the existence of mathematical conjectures such as those of Goldbach and of Fermat, which are quite elementary in content and yet undecided up to this day, certainly shows that not all mathematical truths can be self-evident. And finally, even if self-evidence were attributed only to the basic postulates of mathematics, from which all other mathematical propositions can be deduced, it would be pertinent to remark that judgments as to what may be considered as self-evident are subjective; they may vary from person to person and certainly cannot constitute an adequate basis for decisions as to the objective validity of mathematical propositions.

IS MATHEMATICS THE MOST GENERAL EMPIRICAL SCIENCE?

According to another view, advocated especially by John Stuart Mill, mathematics is itself an empirical science which differs from the other branches such as astronomy, physics, chemistry, etc., mainly in two respects: its subject matter is more general than that of any other field of scientific research, and its propositions have been tested and confirmed to a greater extent than those of even the most firmly established sections of astronomy or physics. Indeed, according to this view, the degree to which the laws of mathematics have been borne out by the past experiences of mankind is so overwhelming that—unjustifiably—we have come to think of mathematical theorems as qualitatively different from the well-confirmed hypotheses or theories of other branches of science: we consider them as certain, while other theories are thought of as at best "very probable" or very highly confirmed.

But this view, too, is open to serious objections. From a hypothesis which is empirical in character—such as, for example, Newton's law of gravitation —it is possible to derive predictions to the effect that under certain specified conditions certain specified observable phenomena will occur. The actual occurrence of these phenomena constitutes confirming evidence, their non-occurrence disconfirming evidence for the hypothesis. It follows in particular that an empirical hypothesis is theoretically disconfirmable; i.e., it is possible to indicate what kind of evidence, if actually encountered, would disconfirm the hypothesis. In the light of this remark, consider now a simple "hypothesis" from arithmetic: $3 + 2 = 5$. If this is actually an empirical generalization of past experiences, then it must be possible to state what kind of evidence would oblige us to concede the hypothesis was not generally true after all. If any disconfirming evidence for the given proposition can be thought of, the following illustration might well be typical of it: We place some microbes on a slide, putting down first three of them and then another two. Afterwards we count all the microbes to test whether in this instance 3 and 2 actually added up to 5. Suppose now that we counted 6 microbes altogether. Would we consider this as an empirical disconfirmation of the given proposition, or at least as a proof that it does not apply to microbes? Clearly not; rather, we would assume we had made a mistake in counting or that one of the microbes had split in two between the first and the second count. But under no circumstances could the phenomenon just described invalidate the arithmetical proposition in question; for the latter asserts nothing whatever about the behavior of microbes; it merely states that any set consisting of 3 + 2 objects may also be said to consist of 5 objects. And this is so because the symbols "3 + 2" and "5" denote the same number: they are synonymous by virtue of the fact that the symbols "2," "3," "5," and "+" are *defined* (or tacitly understood) in such a way that the above identity holds as a consequence of the meaning attached to the concepts involved in it.

THE ANALYTIC CHARACTER OF MATHEMATICAL PROPOSITIONS

The statement that 3 + 2 = 5, then, is true for similar reasons as, say, the assertion that no sexagenarian is 45 years of age. Both are true simply by virtue of definitions or of similar stipulations which determine the meaning of the key terms involved. Statements of this kind share certain important characteristics: Their validation naturally requires no empirical evidence; they can be shown to be true by a mere analysis of the meaning attached to the terms which occur in them. In the language of logic, sentences of this kind are called analytic or true *a priori*, which is to indicate that their truth is logically independent of, or logically prior to, any experiential evidence.[2] And while the statements of empirical science, which are synthetic and can be validated only *a posteriori*, are constantly subject to revision in the light of new evidence, the truth of an analytic statement can be established definitely, once and for all. However, this characteristic "theoretical certainty" of analytic propositions has to be paid for at a high price: An analytic statement conveys no factual information. Our statement about sexagenarians, for example, asserts nothing that could possibly conflict with any factual evidence: it has no factual implications, no empirical content; and it is precisely for this reason that the statement can be validated without recourse to empirical evidence.

Let us illustrate this view of the nature of mathematical propositions by reference to another, frequently cited, example of a mathematical—or rather logical—truth, namely the proposition that whenever $a = b$ and $b = c$ then $a = c$. On what grounds can this so-called "transitivity of identity" be asserted? Is it of an empirical nature and hence at least theoretically disconfirmable by empirical evidence? Suppose, for example that a, b, c, are certain shades of green, and that as far as we can see, $a = b$ and $b = c$, but clearly $a \neq c$. This phenomenon actually occurs under certain conditions; do we consider it as disconfirming evidence for the proposition under consideration? Undoubtedly not; we would argue that if $a \neq c$, it is impossible that $a = b$ and also $b = c$; between the terms of at least one of these latter pairs, there must obtain a difference, though perhaps only a subliminal one. And we would dismiss the possibility of empirical disconfirmation, and

---

2 The objection is sometimes raised that without certain types of experience, such as encountering several objects of the same kind, the integers and the arithmetical operations with them would never have been invented, and that therefore the propositions of arithmetic do have an empirical basis. This type of argument, however, involves a confusion of the logical and the psychological meaning of the term "basis." It may very well be the case that certain experiences occasion psychologically the formation of arithmetical ideas and in this sense form an empirical "basis" for them; but this point is entirely irrelevant for the logical questions as to the *grounds* on which the propositions of arithmetic may be accepted as true. The point made above is that no empirical "basis" or evidence whatever is needed to establish the truth of the propositions of arithmetic.

indeed the idea that an empirical test should be relevant here, on the grounds that identity is a transitive relation by virtue of its definition or by virtue of the basic postulates governing it.[3] Hence, the principle in question is true *a priori.*

MATHEMATICS AS AN AXIOMATIZED DEDUCTIVE SYSTEM

I have argued so far that the validity of mathematics rests neither on its alleged self-evidential character nor on any empirical basis, but derives from the stipulations which determine the meaning of the mathematical concepts, and that the propositions of mathematics are therefore essentially "true by definition." This latter statement, however, is obviously oversimplified and needs restatement and a more careful justification.

For the rigorous development of a mathematical theory proceeds not simply from a set of definitions but rather from a set of non-definitional propositions which are not proved within the theory; these are the postulates or axioms of the theory.[4] They are formulated in terms of certain basic or primitive concepts for which no definitions are provided within the theory. It is sometimes asserted that the postulates themselves represent "implicit definitions" of the primitive terms. Such a characterization of the postulates, however, is misleading. For while the postulates do limit, in a specific sense, the meanings that can possibly be ascribed to the primitives, any self-consistent postulate system admits, nevertheless, many different interpretations of the primitive terms (this will soon be illustrated), whereas a set of definitions in the strict sense of the word determines the meanings of the definienda in a unique fashion.

Once the primitive terms and the postulates have been laid down, the entire theory is completely determined; it is derivable from its postulational basis in the following sense: Every term of the theory is definable in terms of the primitives, and every proposition of the theory is logically deducible from the postulates. To be entirely precise, it is necessary also to specify the principles of logic which are to be used in the proof of the propositions, i.e., in their deduction from the postulates. These principles can be stated quite explicitly. They fall into two groups: Primitive sentences, or postulates, of logic (such as: If p and q is the case, then p is the case), and rules of deduction or inference (including, for example, the familiar *modus ponens* rule and the rules of substitution which make it possible to infer, from a general proposition, any one of its substitution instances). A more detailed discussion of the structure and content of logic would, however, lead too far afield in the context of this article.

PEANO'S AXIOM SYSTEM AS A BASIS FOR MATHEMATICS

Let us now consider a postulate system from which the entire arithmetic of the natural numbers can be derived. This system was devised by the Italian mathematician and logician G. Peano (1858–1932). The primitives of this system are the terms "0," "number," and "successor." While, of course, no

[3] A precise account of the definition and the essential characteristics of the identity relation may be found in A. Tarski, *Introduction to Logic*, New York, 1941, ch. III.

[4] For a lucid and concise account of the axiomatic method, see A. Tarski, *loc. cit.,* ch. VI.

definition of these terms is given within the theory, the symbol "0" is intended to designate the number 0 in its usual meaning, while the term "number" is meant to refer to the natural numbers 0, 1, 2, 3 . . . exclusively. By the successor of a natural number n, which will sometimes briefly be called n', is meant the natural number immediately following n in the natural order. Peano's system contains the following 5 postulates:

P1. 0 is a number
P2. The successor of any number is a number
P3. No two numbers have the same successor
P4. 0 is not the successor of any number
P5. If P is a property such that (a) 0 has the property P, and (b) whenever a number n has the property P, then the successor of n also has the property P, then every number has the property P.

The last postulate embodies the principle of mathematical induction and illustrates in a very obvious manner the enforcement of a mathematical "truth" by stipulation. The construction of elementary arithmetic on this basis begins with the definition of the various natural numbers. 1 is defined as the successor of 0, or briefly as $0'$; 2 as $1'$, 3 as $2'$, and so on. By virtue of P2, this process can be continued indefinitely; because of P3 (in combination with P5), it never leads back to one of the numbers previously defined, and in view of P4, it does not lead back to 0 either.

As the next step, we can set up a definition of addition which expresses in a precise form the idea that the addition of any natural number to some given number may be considered as a repeated addition of 1; the latter operation is readily expressible by means of the successor relation. This definition of addition runs as follows:

D1.   (a) $n + 0 = n$;   (b) $n + k' = (n + k)'$.

The two stipulations of this recursive definition completely determine the sum of any two integers. Consider, for example, the sum $3 + 2$. According to the definitions of the numbers 2 and 1, we have $3 + 2 = 3 + 1' = 3 + (0')'$; by D1 (b), $3 + (0')' = (3 + 0')' = ((3 + 0)')'$; but by D1 (a), and by the definitions of the numbers 4 and 5, $((3 + 0)')' = (3')' = 4' = 5$. This proof also renders more explicit and precise the comments made earlier in this paper on the truth of the proposition that $3 + 2 = 5$: Within the Peano system of arithmetic, its truth flows not merely from the definition of the concepts involved, but also from the postulates that govern these various concepts. (In our specific example, the postulates P1 and P2 are presupposed to guarantee that 1, 2, 3, 4, 5 are numbers in Peano's system; the general proof that D1 determines the sum of any two numbers also makes use of P5.) If we call the postulates and definitions of an axiomatized theory the "stipulations" concerning the concepts of that theory, then we may say now that the propositions of the arithmetic of the natural numbers are true by virtue of the stipulations which have been laid down initially for the arithmetical concepts. (Note, incidentally, that our proof of the formula "$3 + 2 = 5$" repeatedly made use of the transitivity of identity; the latter is accepted here as one of the rules of logic which may be used in the proof of any arithmetical theorem; it is, therefore, included among Peano's postulates no more than any other principle of logic.)

Now, the multiplication of natural numbers may be defined by means of the following recursive definition, which expresses in a rigorous form the idea that a product nk of two integers may be considered as the sum of k terms each of which equals n.

D2.   (a) $n \cdot 0 = 0$;   (b) $n \cdot k' = n \cdot k + n$.

It now is possible to prove the familiar general laws governing addition and multiplication, such as the commutative, associative, and distributive laws $(n + k = k + n; n \cdot k = k \cdot n; n+ (k + l) = (n + k) + l; n \cdot (k \cdot l) = (n \cdot k) \cdot l; n \cdot (k + l) = (n \cdot k) + (n \cdot l))$. In terms of addition and multiplication, the inverse operations of subtraction and division can then be defined. But it turns out that these "cannot always be performed"; i.e., in contradistinction to the sum and the product, the difference and the quotient are not defined for every couple of numbers; for example, $7 - 10$ and $7 \div 10$ are undefined. This situation suggests an enlargement of the number system by the introduction of negative and of rational numbers.

It is sometimes held that in order to effect this enlargement, we have to "assume" or else to "postulate" the existence of the desired additional kinds of numbers with properties that make them fit to fill the gaps of subtraction and division. This method of simply postulating what we want has its advantages; but, as Bertrand Russell[5] puts it, they are the same as the advantages of theft over honest toil; and it is a remarkable fact that the negative as well as the rational numbers can be obtained from Peano's primitives by the honest toil of constructing explicit definitions for them, without the introduction of any new postulates or assumptions whatsoever. Every positive and negative integer (in contradistinction to a natural number which has no sign) is definable as a certain set of ordered couples of natural numbers; thus, the integer $+ 2$ is definable as the set of all ordered couples (m, n) of natural numbers where $m = n + 2$; the integer $- 2$ is the set of all ordered couples (m, n) of natural numbers with $n = m + 2$. (Similarly, rational numbers are defined as classes of ordered couples of integers.) The various arithmetical operations can then be defined with reference to these new types of numbers, and the validity of all the arithmetical laws governing these operations can be proved by virtue of nothing more than Peano's postulates and the definitions of the various arithmetical concepts involved.

The much broader system thus obtained is still incomplete in the sense that not every number in it has a square root, and more generally, not every algebraic equation whose coefficients are all numbers of the system has a solution in the system. This suggests further expansions of the number system by the introduction of real and finally of complex numbers. Again, this enormous extension can be effected by mere definition, without the introduction of a single new postulate.[6] On the basis thus obtained, the

[5] Bertrand Russell, *Introduction to Mathematical Philosophy*, New York and London, 1919, p. 71.

[6] For a more detailed account of the construction of the number system on Peano's basis, cf. Bertrand Russell, *loc. cit.*, esp. chs. I and VII. A rigorous and concise presentation of that construction, beginning, however, with the set of all integers rather than that of the natural numbers, may be found in G. Birkhoff and S. MacLane, *A Survey of Modern Algebra*, New York, 1941, chs. I, II, III, V. For a general survey of the construction of the number system, cf. also J. W. Young, *Lectures on the Fundamental Concepts of Algebra and Geometry*, New York, 1911, esp. lectures X, XI, XII.

various arithmetical and algebraic operations can be defined for the numbers of the new system, the concepts of function, of limit, of derivative and integral can be introduced, and the familiar theorems pertaining to these concepts can be proved, so that finally the huge system of mathematics as here delimited rests on the narrow basis of Peano's system: Every concept of mathematics can be defined by means of Peano's three primitives, and every proposition of mathematics can be deduced from the five postulates enriched by the definitions of the non-primitive terms.[7] These deductions can be carried out, in most cases, by means of nothing more than the principles of formal logic; the proof of some theorems concerning real numbers, however, requires one assumption which is not usually included among the latter. This is the so-called axiom of choice. It asserts that given a class of mutually exclusive classes, none of which is empty, there exists at least one class which has exactly one element in common with each of the given classes. By virtue of this principle and the rules of formal logic, the content of all of mathematics can thus be derived from Peano's modest system—a remarkable achievement in systematizing the content of mathematics and clarifying the foundations of its validity.

INTERPRETATIONS OF PEANO'S PRIMITIVES

As a consequence of this result, the whole system of mathematics might be said to be true by virtue of mere definitions (namely, of the non-primitive mathematical terms) provided that the five Peano postulates are true. However, strictly speaking, we cannot, at this juncture, refer to the Peano postulates as propositions which are either true or false, for they contain three primitive terms which have not been assigned any specific meaning. All we can assert so far is that any specific interpretation of the primitives which satisfies the five postulates—i.e., turns them into true statements—will also satisfy all the theorems deduced from them. But for Peano's system, there are several—indeed, infinitely many—interpretations which will do this. For example, let us understand by o the origin of a half-line, by the successor of a point on that half-line the point 1 cm. behind it, counting from the origin, and by a number any point which is either the origin or can be reached from it by a finite succession of steps each of which leads from

---

[7] As a result of very deep-reaching investigations carried out by K. Gödel it is known that arithmetic, and *a fortiori* mathematics, is an incomplete theory in the following sense: While all those propositions which belong to the classical systems of arithmetic, algebra, and analysis can indeed be derived, in the sense characterized above, from the Peano postulates, there exist nevertheless other propositions which can be expressed in purely arithmetical terms, and which are true, but which cannot be derived from the Peano system. And more generally: For any postulate system of arithmetic (or of mathematics for that matter) which is not self-contradictory, there exist propositions which are true, and which can be stated in purely arithmetical terms, but which cannot be derived from that postulate system. In other words, it is impossible to construct a postulate system which is not self-contradictory, and which contains among its consequences all true propositions which can be formulated within the language of arithmetic.

This fact does not, however, affect the result outlined above, namely, that it is possible to deduce, from the Peano postulates and the additional definitions of non-primitive terms, all those propositions which constitute the classical theory of arithmetic, algebra, and analysis; and it is to these propositions that I refer above and subsequently as the propositions of mathematics.

one point to its successor. It can then readily be seen that all the Peano postulates as well as the ensuing theorems turn into true propositions, although the interpretation given to the primitives is certainly not the customary one, which was mentioned earlier. More generally, it can be shown that every progression of elements of any kind provides a true interpretation, or a "model," of the Peano system. This example illustrates our earlier observation that a postulate system cannot be regarded as a set of "implicit definitions" for the primitive terms: The Peano system permits of many different interpretations, whereas in everyday as well as in scientific language, we attach one specific meaning to the concepts of arithmetic. Thus, e.g., in scientific and in everyday discourse, the concept 2 is understood in such a way that from the statement "Mr. Brown as well as Mr. Cope, but no one else is in the office, and Mr. Brown is not the same person as Mr. Cope," the conclusion "Exactly two persons are in the office" may be validly inferred. But the stipulations laid down in Peano's system for the natural numbers, and for the number 2 in particular, do not enable us to draw this conclusion; they do not "implicitly determine" the customary meaning of the concept 2 or of the other arithmetical concepts. And the mathematician cannot acquiesce in this deficiency by arguing that he is not concerned with the customary meaning of the mathematical concepts; for in proving, say, that every positive real number has exactly two real square roots, he is himself using the concept 2 in its customary meaning, and his very theorem cannot be proved unless we presuppose more about the number 2 than is stipulated in the Peano system.

If therefore mathematics is to be a correct theory of the mathematical concepts in their intended meaning, it is not sufficient for its validation to have shown that the entire system is derivable from the Peano postulates plus suitable definitions; rather, we have to inquire further whether the Peano postulates are actually true when the primitives are understood in their customary meaning. This question, of course, can be answered only after the customary meaning of the terms "o," "natural number," and "successor" has been clearly defined. To this task we now turn.

DEFINITION OF THE CUSTOMARY MEANING OF THE CONCEPTS OF ARITHMETIC IN PURELY LOGICAL TERMS

At first blush, it might seem a hopeless undertaking to try to define these basic arithmetical concepts without presupposing other terms of arithmetic, which would involve us in a circular procedure. However, quite rigorous definitions of the desired kind can indeed be formulated, and it can be shown that for the concepts so defined, all Peano postulates turn into true statements. This important result is due to the research of the German logician G. Frege (1848–1925) and to the subsequent systematic and detailed work of the contemporary English logicians and philosophers B. Russell and A. N. Whitehead. Let us consider briefly the basic ideas underlying these definitions.[8]

[8] For a more detailed discussion, cf. Russell, *loc. cit.*, chs. II, III, IV. A complete technical development of the idea can be found in the great standard work in mathematical logic, A. N. Whitehead and B. Russell, *Principia Mathematica*, Cambridge, England, 1910–1913. For a very precise recent development of the theory, see W. V. O.

A natural number—or, in Peano's term, a number—in its customary meaning can be considered as a characteristic of certain *classes* of objects. Thus, e.g., the class of the apostles has the number 12, the class of the Dionne quintuplets the number 5, any couple the number 2, and so on. Let us now express precisely the meaning of the assertion that a certain class C has the number 2, or briefly, that $n(C) = 2$. Brief reflection will show that the following definiens is adequate in the sense of the customary meaning of the concept 2: There is some object x and some object y such that (1) $x \epsilon C$ (i.e., x is an element of C) and $y \epsilon C$, (2) $x \neq y$, and (3) if z is any object such that $z \epsilon C$, then either $z = x$ or $z = y$. (Note that on the basis of this definition it becomes indeed possible to infer the statement "The number of persons in the office is 2" from "Mr. Brown as well as Mr. Cope, but no one else is in the office, and Mr. Brown is not identical with Mr. Cope"; C is here the class of persons in the office.) Analogously, the meaning of the statement that $n(C) = 1$ can be defined thus: There is some x such that $x \epsilon C$, and any object y such that $y \epsilon C$, is identical with x. Similarly, the customary meaning of the statement that $n(C) = 0$ is this: There is no object such that $x \epsilon C$.

The general pattern of these definitions clearly lends itself to the definition of any natural number. Let us note especially that in the definitions thus obtained, the definiens never contains any arithmetical term, but merely expressions taken from the field of formal logic, including the signs of identity and difference. So far, we have defined only the meaning of such phrases as "$n(C) = 2$," but we have given no definition for the numbers 0, 1, 2, . . . apart from this context. This desideratum can be met on the basis of the consideration that 2 is that property which is common to all couples, i.e., to all classes C such that $n(C) = 2$. This common property may be conceptually represented by the class of all those classes which share this property. Thus we arrive at the definition: 2 is the class of all couples, i.e., the class of all classes C for which $n(C) = 2$. This definition is by no means circular because the concept of couple—in other words, the meaning of "$n (C) = 2$"—has been previously defined without any reference to the number 2. Analogously, 1 is the class of all unit classes, i.e., the class of all classes C for which $n (C) = 1$. Finally, 0 is the class of all null classes, i.e., the class of all classes without elements. And as there is only one such class, 0 is simply the class whose only element is the null class. Clearly, the customary meaning of any given natural number can be defined in this fashion.[9] In order to

---

Quine, *Mathematical Logic*, New York, 1940. A specific discussion of the Peano system and its interpretations from the viewpoint of semantics is included in R. Carnap, *Foundations of Logic and Mathematics*, International Encyclopedia of Unified Science, Vol. I, no. 3, Chicago, 1939; especially sections 14, 17, 18.

[9] The assertion that the definitions given above state the "customary" meaning of the arithmetical terms involved is to be understood in the logical, not the psychological sense of the term "meaning." It would obviously be absurd to claim that the above definitions express "what everybody has in mind" when talking about numbers and the various operations that can be performed with them. What is achieved by those definitions is rather a "logical reconstruction" of the concepts of arithmetic in the sense that if the definitions are accepted, then those statements in science and everyday discourse which involve arithmetical terms can be interpreted coherently and systematically in such a manner that they are capable of objective validation. The statement about the two persons in the office provides a very elementary illustration of what is meant here.

characterize the intended interpretation of Peano's primitives, we actually need, of all the definitions here referred to, only that of the number 0. It remains to define the terms "successor" and "integer."

The definition of "successor," whose precise formulation involves too many niceties to be stated here, is a careful expression of a simple idea which is illustrated by the following example: Consider the number 5, i.e., the class of all quintuplets. Let us select an arbitrary one of these quintuplets and add to it an object which is not yet one of its members. 5', the successor of 5, may then be defined as the number applying to the set thus obtained (which, of course, is a sextuplet). Finally, it is possible to formulate a definition of the customary meaning of the concept of natural number; this definition, which again cannot be given here, expresses, in a rigorous form, the idea that the class of the natural numbers consists of the number 0, its successor, the successor of that successor, and so on.

If the definitions here characterized are carefully written out—this is one of the cases where the techniques of symbolic, or mathematical, logic prove indispensable—it is seen that the definiens of every one of them contains exclusively terms from the field of pure logic. In fact, it is possible to state the customary interpretation of Peano's primitives, and thus also the meaning of every concept definable by means of them—and that includes every concept of mathematics—in terms of the following seven expressions (in addition to variables such as *"x" and "C"*): *not, and, if—then; for every object x it is the case that* . . . ; *there is some object x such that* . . . ; *x is an element of class C; the class of all things x such that* . . . And it is even possible to reduce the number of logical concepts needed to a mere four: The first three of the concepts just mentioned are all definable in terms of *"neither nor,"* and the fifth is definable by means of the fourth and *"neither—nor."* Thus, all the concepts of mathematics prove definable in terms of four concepts of pure logic. (The definition of one of the more complex concepts of mathematics in terms of the four primitives just mentioned may well fill hundreds or even thousands of pages; but clearly this affects in no way the theoretical importance of the result just obtained; it does, however, show the great convenience and indeed practical indispensability for mathematics of having a large system of highly complex defined concepts available.)

THE TRUTH OF PEANO'S POSTULATES IN THEIR CUSTOMARY INTERPRETATION

The definitions characterized in the preceding section may be said to render precise and explicit the customary meaning of the concepts of arithmetic. Moreover—and this is crucial for the question of the validity of mathematics—it can be shown that the Peano postulates all turn into true propositions if the primitives are construed in accordance with the definitions just considered.

Thus, P1 (0 is a number) is true because the class of all numbers—i.e., natural numbers—was defined as consisting of 0 and all its successors. The truth of P2 (the successor of any number is a number) follows from the same definition. This is true also of P5, the principle of mathematical induction. To prove this, however, we would have to resort to the precise definition of "integer" rather than the loose description given of that definition above. P4 (0 is not the successor of any number) is seen to be true as follows: By virtue of the definition of "successor," a number which is a successor of some number can apply only to classes which contain at least one element; but the number 0, by definition, applies to a class if and only if that class is empty. While the truth of P1, P2, P4, P5 can be inferred from the above definitions simply by means of the principles of logic, the proof of P3 (no two numbers have the same successor) presents a certain difficulty. As was mentioned in the preceding section, the definition of the successor of a number n is based on the process of adding, to a class of n elements, one element not yet contained in that class. Now if there should exist only a finite number of things altogether then this process could not be continued indefinitely, and P3, which (in conjunction with P1 and P2) implies that the integers form an infinite set, would be false. This difficulty can be met by the introduction of a special "axiom of infinity"[10] which asserts, in effect, the existence of infinitely many objects, and thus makes P3 demonstrable. The axiom of infinity does not belong to the generally recognized laws of logic; but it is capable of expression in purely logical terms and may be considered as an additional postulate of modern logical theory.

MATHEMATICS AS A BRANCH OF LOGIC

As was pointed out earlier, all the theorems of arithmetic, algebra, and analysis can be deduced from the Peano postulates and the definitions of those mathematical terms which are not primitives in Peano's system. This deduction requires only the principles of logic plus, in certain cases, the axiom of choice. By combining this result with what has just been said about the Peano system, the following conclusion is obtained, which is also known as *the thesis of logicism concerning the nature of mathematics:*

Mathematics is a branch of logic. It can be derived from logic in the following sense:

a. All the concepts of mathematics, i.e., of arithmetic, algebra, and analysis, can be defined in terms of four concepts of pure logic.

b. All the theorems of mathematics can be deduced from those definitions by means of the principles of logic (including the axioms of infinity and choice).[11]

In this sense it can be said that the propositions of the system of mathematics as here delimited are true by virtue of the definitions of the mathematical concepts involved, or that they make explicit certain characteristics with which we have endowed our mathematical concepts by definition. The propositions of mathematics have, therefore, the same un-

[10] Cf. Bertrand Russell, *loc. cit.*, p. 24 and ch. XIII.

[11] The principles of logic developed in modern systems of formal logic embody certain restrictions as compared with those logical rules which had been rather generally accepted as sound until about the turn of the 20th century. At that time, the discovery of the famous paradoxes of logic, especially of Russell's paradox (cf. Russell, *loc. cit.*, ch. XIII), revealed the fact that the logical principles implicit in customary mathematical reasoning involved contradictions and therefore had to be curtailed in one manner or another.

questionable certainty which is typical of such propositions as "All bachelors are unmarried," but they also share the complete lack of empirical content which is associated with that certainty: The proposition of mathematics are devoid of all factual content; they convey no information whatever on any empirical subject matter.

ON THE APPLICABILITY OF MATHEMATICS TO EMPIRICAL SUBJECT MATTER

This result seems to be irreconcilable with the fact that after all mathematics has proved to be eminently applicable to empirical subject matter, and that indeed the greater part of present-day scientific knowledge has been reached only through continual reliance on and application of the propositions of mathematics. Let us try to clarify this apparent paradox by reference to some examples.

Suppose that we are examining a certain amount of some gas, whose volume v, at a certain fixed temperature, is found to be 9 cubic feet when the pressure p is 4 atmospheres. And let us assume further that the volume of the gas for the same temperature and $p = 6$ *at.*, is predicted by means of Boyle's law. Using elementary arithmetic we reason thus: For corresponding values of v and p, $vp = c$, and $v = 9$ when $p = 4$; hence $c = 36$: Therefore, when $p = 6$, then $v = 6$. Suppose that this prediction is borne out by subsequent test. Does that show that the arithmetic used has a predictive power of its own, that its propositions have factual implications? Certainly not. All the predictive power here deployed, all the empirical content exhibited stems from the initial data and from Boyle's law, which asserts that $vp = c$ for *any* two corresponding values of v and p, hence also for $v = 9$, $p = 4$, and for $p = 6$ and the corresponding value of v.[12] The function of the mathematics here applied is not predictive at all; rather, it is analytic or explicative: it renders explicit certain assumptions or assertions which are included in the content of the premises of the argument (in our case, these consist of Boyle's law plus the additional data); mathematical reasoning reveals that those premises contain—hidden in them, as it were,—an assertion about the case as yet unobserved. In accepting our premises—so arithmetic reveals—we have—knowingly or unknowingly—already accepted the implication that the v-value in question is 6. Mathematical as well as logical reasoning is a conceptual technique of making explicit what is implicitly contained in a set of premises. The conclusions to which this technique leads assert nothing that is *theoretically new* in the sense of not being contained in the content of the premises. But the results obtained may well be *psychologically new*: we may not have been aware, before using the techniques of logic and mathematics, what we committed ourselves to in accepting a certain set of assumptions or assertions.

A similar analysis is possible in all other cases of applied mathematics, including those involving, say, the calculus. Consider, for example, the hypothesis that a certain object, moving in a specified electric field, will undergo a constant acceleration of 5 feet/sec². For the purpose of testing this hypothesis, we might derive from it, by means of two successive

---

[12] Note that we may say "hence" by virtue of the rule of substitution, which is one of the rules of logical inference.

integrations, the prediction that if the object is at rest at the beginning of the motion, then the distance covered by it at any time t is $5/2t^2$ feet. This conclusion may clearly be psychologically new to a person not acquainted with the subject, but it is not theoretically new; the content of the conclusion is already contained in that of the hypothesis about the constant acceleration. And indeed, here as well as in the case of the compression of a gas, a failure of the prediction to come true would be considered as indicative of the factual incorrectness of at least one of the premises involved (*f.ex.*, of Boyle's law in its application to the particular gas), but never as a sign that the logical and mathematical principles involved might be unsound.

Thus, in the establishment of empirical knowledge, mathematics (as well as logic) has, so to speak, the function of a theoretical juice extractor: the techniques of mathematical and logical theory can produce no more juice of factual information than is contained in the assumptions to which they are applied; but they may produce a great deal more juice of this kind than might have been anticipated upon a first intuitive inspection of those assumptions which form the raw material for the extractor.

At this point, it may be well to consider briefly the status of those mathematical disciplines which are not outgrowths of arithmetic and thus of logic; these include in particular topology, geometry, and the various branches of abstract algebra, such as the theory of groups, lattices, fields, etc. Each of these disciplines can be developed as a purely deductive system on the basis of a suitable set of postulates. If P be the conjunction of the postulates for a given theory, then the proof of a proposition T of that theory consists in deducing T from P by means of the principles of formal logic. What is established by the proof is therefore not the truth of T, but rather the fact that T is true provided that the postulates are. But since both P and T contain certain primitive terms of the theory, to which no specific meaning is assigned, it is not strictly possible to speak of the truth of either P or T; it is therefore more adequate to state the point as follows: If a proposition T is logically deduced from P, then every specific interpretation of the primitives which turns all the postulates of P into true statements, will also render T a true statement. Up to this point, the analysis is exactly analogous to that of arithmetic as based on Peano's set of postulates. In the case of arithmetic, however, it proved possible to go a step further, namely to define the customary meanings of the primitives in terms of purely logical concepts and to show that the postulates—and therefore also the theorems— of arithmetic are unconditionally true by virtue of these definitions. An analogous procedure is not applicable to those disciplines which are not outgrowths of arithmetic: The primitives of the various branches of abstract algebra have no specific "customary meaning"; and if geometry in its customary interpretation is thought of as a theory of the structure of physical space, then its primitives have to be construed as referring to certain types of physical entities, and the question of the truth of a geometrical theory in this interpretation turns into an *empirical* problem. For the purpose of applying any one of these non-arithmetical disciplines to some specific field of mathematics or empirical science, it is therefore necessary first to assign to the primitives some specific meaning and then to ascertain whether in this interpretation the postulates turn into true statements. If this is the case, then we can be sure that all the theorems are true statements too, because they are logically derived from the postulates and thus simply explicate the content of the latter in the given interpretation. In their application to empirical subject matter, therefore, these mathematical theories no less than those which grow out of arithmetic and ultimately out of pure logic, have the function of an analytic tool, which brings to light the implications of a given set of assumptions but adds nothing to their content.

But while mathematics in no case contributes anything to the content of our knowledge of empirical matters, it is entirely indispensable as an instrument for the validation and even for the linguistic expression of such knowledge: The majority of the more far-reaching theories in empirical science—including those which lend themselves most eminently to prediction or to practical application—are stated with the help of mathematical concepts; the formulation of these theories makes use, in particular, of the number system, and of functional relationships among different metrical variables. Furthermore, the scientific test of these theories, the establishment of predictions by means of them, and finally their practical application, all require the deduction, from the general theory, of certain specific consequences; and such deduction would be entirely impossible without the techniques of mathematics which reveal what the given general theory implicitly asserts about a certain special case.

Thus, the analysis outlined on these pages exhibits the system of mathematics as a vast and ingenious conceptual structure without empirical content and yet an indispensable and powerful theoretical instrument for the scientific understanding and mastery of the world of our experience.

10

A DOGMA OF EMPIRICISM

W. V. Quine

Modern empiricism has been conditioned in large part by two dogmas. One is a belief in some fundamental cleavage between truths which are *analytic*, or grounded in meanings independently of matters of fact, and truths which are *synthetic*, or grounded in fact. The other dogma is *reductionism:* the belief that each meaningful statement is equivalent to some logical construct upon terms which refer to immediate experience. Both dogmas, I shall argue, are ill-founded. One effect of abandoning them is, as we shall see, a blurring of the supposed boundary between speculative metaphysics and natural science. Another effect is a shift toward pragmatism.

1. BACKGROUND FOR ANALYTICITY

Kant's cleavage between analytic and synthetic truths was foreshadowed in Hume's distinction between relations of ideas and matters of fact, and in Leibniz's distinction between truths of reason and truths of fact. Leibniz spoke of the truths of reason as true in all possible worlds. Picturesqueness aside, this is to say that the truths of reason are those which could not possibly be false. In the same vein we hear analytic statements defined as statements whose denials are self-contradictory. But this definition has small explanatory value; for the notion of self-contradictoriness, in the quite broad sense needed for this definition of analyticity, stands in exactly the same need of clarification as does the notion of analyticity itself. The two notions are the two sides of a single dubious coin.

Kant conceived of an analytic statement as one that attributes to its subject no more than is already conceptually contained in the subject. This formulation has two shortcomings: it limits itself to statements of subject-predicate form, and it appeals to a notion of containment which is left at a metaphorical level. But Kant's intent, evident more from the use he makes of the notion of analyticity than from his definition of it, can be restated thus:

---

a statement is analytic when it is true by virtue of meanings and independently of fact. Pursuing this line, let us examine the concept of *meaning* which is presupposed.

Meaning . . . is not to be identified with naming. Frege's example of 'Evening Star' and 'Morning Star', and Russell's of 'Scott' and 'the author of *Waverley*', illustrate that terms can name the same thing but differ in meaning. The distinction between meaning and naming is no less important at the level of abstract terms. The terms '9' and 'the number of the planets' name one and the same abstract entity but presumably must be regarded as unlike in meaning; for astronomical observation was needed, and not mere reflection on meanings, to determine the sameness of the entity in question.

The above examples consist of singular terms, concrete and abstract. With general terms, or predicates, the situation is somewhat different but parallel. Whereas a singular term purports to name an entity, abstract or concrete, a general term does not; but a general term is *true of* an entity, or of each of many, or of none. The class of all entities of which a general term is true is called the *extension* of the term. Now paralleling the contrast between the meaning of a singular term and the entity named, we must distinguish equally between the meaning of a general term and its extension. The general terms 'creature with a heart' and 'creature with kidneys', for example, are perhaps alike in extension but unlike in meaning.

Confusion of meaning with extension, in the case of general terms, is less common than confusion of meaning with naming in the case of singular terms. It is indeed a commonplace in philosophy to oppose intension (or meaning) to extension, or, in a variant vocabulary, connotation to denotation.

The Aristotelian notion of essence was the forerunner, no doubt, of the modern notion of intension or meaning. For Aristotle it was essential in men to be rational, accidental to be two-legged. But there is an important difference between this attitude and the doctrine of meaning. From the latter point of view it may indeed be conceded (if only for the sake of argument) that rationality is involved in the meaning of the word 'man' while two-leggedness is not; but two-leggedness may at the same time be viewed as involved in the meaning of 'biped' while rationality is not. Thus from the point of view of the doctrine of meaning it makes no sense to say of the actual individual, who is at once a man and a biped, that his rationality is essential and his two-leggedness accidental or vice versa. Things had essences, for Aristotle, but only linguistic forms have meanings. Meaning is what essence becomes when it is divorced from the object of reference and wedded to the word.

For the theory of meaning a conspicuous question is the nature of its objects: what sort of things are meanings? A felt need for meant entities may derive from an earlier failure to appreciate that meaning and reference are distinct. Once the theory of meaning is sharply separated from the theory of reference, it is a short step to recognizing as the primary business of the theory of meaning simply the synonymy of linguistic forms and the analyticity of statements; meanings themselves, as obscure intermediary entities, may well be abandoned.

The problem of analyticity then confronts us anew. Statements which are analytic by general philosophical acclaim are not, indeed, far to seek. They fall into two classes. Those of the first class, which may be called *logically true*, are typified by:

(1) No unmarried man is married.

The relevant feature of this example is that it not merely is true as it stands, but remains true under any and all reinterpretations of 'man' and 'married'. If we suppose a prior inventory of *logical* particles, comprising 'no', 'un-', 'not', 'if', 'then', 'and', etc., then in general a logical truth is a statement which is true and remains true under all reinterpretations of its components other than the logical particles.

But there is also a second class of analytic statements, typified by:

(2) No bachelor is married.

The characteristic of such a statement is that it can be turned into a logical truth by putting synonyms for synonyms; thus (2) can be turned into (1) by putting 'unmarried man' for its synonym 'bachelor'. We still lack a proper characterization of this second class of analytic statements, and therewith of analyticity generally, inasmuch as we have had in the above description to lean on a notion of "synonymy" which is no less in need of clarification than analyticity itself.

In recent years Carnap has tended to explain analyticity by appeal to what he calls state-descriptions. A state-description is any exhaustive assignment of truth values to the atomic, or noncompound, statements of the language. All other statements of the language are, Carnap assumes, built up of their component clauses by means of the familiar logical devices, in such a way that the truth value of any complex statement is fixed for each state-description by specifiable logical laws. A statement is then explained as analytic when it comes out true under every state-description. This account is an adaptation of Leibniz's "true in all possible worlds." But note that this version of analyticity serves its purpose only if the atomic statements of the language are, unlike 'John is a bachelor' and 'John is married', mutually independent. Otherwise there would be a state-description which assigned truth to 'John is a bachelor' and to 'John is married', and consequently 'No bachelors are married' would turn out synthetic rather than analytic under the proposed criterion. Thus the criterion of analyticity in terms of state-descriptions serves only for languages devoid of extra-logical synonym-pairs, such as 'bachelor' and 'unmarried man'—synonym-pairs of the type which give rise to the "second class" of analytic statements. The criterion in terms of state-descriptions is a reconstruction at best of logical truth, not of analyticity.

I do not mean to suggest that Carnap is under any illusions on this point. His simplified model language with its state-descriptions is aimed primarily not at the general problem of analyticity but at another purpose, the clarification of probability and induction. Our problem, however, is analyticity; and here the major difficulty lies not in the first class of analytic statements, the logical truths, but rather in the second class, which depends on the notion of synonymy.

2. DEFINITION

There are those who find it soothing to say that the analytic statements of the second class reduce to those of the first class, the logical truths, by *definition;* 'bachelor', for example, is *defined* as 'unmarried man'. But how do we find that 'bachelor' is defined as 'unmarried man'? Who defined it thus, and when? Are we to appeal to the nearest dictionary, and accept the lexicographer's formulation as law? Clearly this would be to put the cart before the horse. The lexicographer is an empirical scientist, whose business is the recording of antecedent facts; and if he glosses 'bachelor' as 'unmarried man' it is because of his belief that there is a relation of synonymy between those forms, implicit in general or preferred usage prior to his own work. The notion of synonymy presupposed here has still to be clarified, presumably in terms relating to linguistic behavior. Certainly the "definition" which is the lexicographer's report of an observed synonymy cannot be taken as the ground of the synonymy.

Definition is not, indeed, an activity exclusively of philologists. Philosophers and scientists frequently have occasion to "define" a recondite term by paraphrasing it into terms of a more familiar vocabulary. But ordinarily such a definition, like the philologist's, is pure lexicography, affirming a relation of synonymy antecedent to the exposition in hand.

Just what it means to affirm synonymy, just what the interconnections may be which are necessary and sufficient in order that two linguistic forms be properly describable as synonymous, is far from clear; but, whatever these interconnections may be, ordinarily they are grounded in usage. Definitions reporting selected instances of synonymy come then as reports upon usage.

There is also, however, a variant type of definitional activity which does not limit itself to the reporting of preëxisting synonymies. I have in mind what Carnap calls *explication*—an activity to which philosophers are given, and scientists also in their more philosophical moments. In explication the purpose is not merely to paraphrase the definiendum into an outright synonym, but actually to improve upon the definiendum by refining or supplementing its meaning. But even explication, though not merely reporting a preëxisting synonymy between definiendum and definiens, does rest nevertheless on *other* preëxisting synonymies. The matter may be viewed as follows. Any word worth explicating has some contexts which, as wholes, are clear and precise enough to be useful; and the purpose of explication is to preserve the usage of these favored contexts while sharpening the usage of other contexts. In order that a given definition be suitable for purposes of explication, therefore, what is required is not that the definiendum in its antecedent usage be synonymous with the definiens, but just that each of these favored contexts of the definiendum, taken as a whole in its antecedent usage, be synonymous with the corresponding context of the definiens.

Two alternative definientia may be equally appropriate for the purposes of a given task of explication and yet not be synonymous with each other; for they may serve interchangeably within the favored contexts but diverge elsewhere. By cleaving to one of these definientia rather than the other, a definition of explicative kind generates, by fiat, a relation of synonymy between definiendum and definiens which did not hold before. But such a definition still owes its explicative function, as seen, to preëxisting synonymies.

There does, however, remain still an extreme sort of definition which does not hark back to prior synonymies at all: namely, the explicitly conventional introduction of novel notations for purposes of sheer abbreviation. Here the definiendum becomes synonymous with the definiens simply because it has been created expressly for the purpose of being synonymous with the definiens. Here we have a really transparent case of synonymy created by definition; would that all species of synonymy were as intelligible. For the rest, definition rests on synonymy rather than explaining it.

The word 'definition' has come to have a dangerously reassuring sound, owing no doubt to its frequent occurrence in logical and mathematical writings. We shall do well to digress now into a brief appraisal of the role of definition in formal work.

In logical and mathematical systems either of two mutually antagonistic types of economy may be striven for, and each has its peculiar practical utility. On the one hand we may seek economy of practical expression—ease and brevity in the statement of multifarious relations. This sort of economy calls usually for distinctive concise notations for a wealth of concepts. Second, however, and oppositely, we may seek economy in grammar and vocabulary; we may try to find a minimum of basic concepts such that, once a distinctive notation has been appropriated to each of them, it becomes possible to express any desired further concept by mere combination and iteration of our basic notations. This second sort of economy is impractical in one way, since a poverty in basic idioms tends to a necessary lengthening of discourse. But it is practical in another way: it greatly simplifies theoretical discourse *about* the language, through minimizing the terms and the forms of construction wherein the language consists.

Both sorts of economy, though prima facie incompatible, are valuable in their separate ways. The custom has consequently arisen of combining both sorts of economy by forging in effect two languages, the one a part of the other. The inclusive language, though redundant in grammar and vocabulary, is economical in message lengths, while the part, called primitive notation, is economical in grammar and vocabulary. Whole and part are correlated by rules of translation whereby each idiom not in primitive notation is equated to some complex built up of primitive notation. These rules of translation are the so-called *definitions* which appear in formalized systems. They are best viewed not as adjuncts to one language but as correlations between two languages, the one a part of the other.

But these correlations are not arbitrary. They are supposed to show how the primitive notations can accomplish all purposes, save brevity and convenience, of the redundant language. Hence the definiendum and its definiens may be expected, in each case, to be related in one or another of the three ways lately noted. The definiens may be a faithful paraphrase of the definiendum into the narrower notation, preserving a direct synonymy[1] as of antecedent usage; or the definiens may, in the spirit of explication,

---

[1] According to an important variant sense of 'definition', the relation preserved may be the weaker relation of mere agreement in reference. . . . But definition in this sense is better ignored in the present connection, being irrelevant to the question of synonymy.

improve upon the antecedent usage of the definiendum; or finally, the definiendum may be a newly created notation, newly endowed with meaning here and now.

In formal and informal work alike, thus, we find that definition—except in the extreme case of the explicitly conventional introduction of new notations—hinges on prior relations of synonymy. Recognizing then that the notion of definition does not hold the key to synonymy and analyticity, let us look further into synonymy and say no more of definition.

3. INTERCHANGEABILITY

A natural suggestion, deserving close examination, is that the synonymy of two linguistic forms consists simply in their interchangeability in all contexts without change of truth value—interchangeability, in Leibniz's phrase, *salva veritate*. Note that synonyms so conceived need not even be free from vagueness, as long as the vaguenesses match.

But it is not quite true that the synonyms 'bachelor' and 'unmarried man' are everywhere interchangeable *salva veritate*. Truths which become false under substitution of 'unmarried man' for 'bachelor' are easily constructed with the help of 'bachelor of arts' or 'bachelor's buttons'; also with the help of quotation, thus:

'Bachelor' has less than ten letters.

Such counterinstances can, however, perhaps be set aside by treating the phrases 'bachelor of arts' and 'bachelor's buttons' and the quotation 'bachelor' each as a single indivisible word and then stipulating that the interchangeability *salva veritate* which is to be the touchstone of synonymy is not supposed to apply to fragmentary occurrences inside of a word. This account of synonymy, supposing it acceptable on other counts, has indeed the drawback of appealing to a prior conception of "word" which can be counted on to present difficulties of formulation in its turn. Nevertheless some progress might be claimed in having reduced the problem of synonymy to a problem of wordhood. Let us pursue this line a bit, taking "word" for granted.

The question remains whether interchangeability *salva veritate* (apart from occurrences within words) is a strong enough condition for synonymy, or whether, on the contrary, some heteronymous expressions might be thus interchangeable. Now let us be clear that we are not concerned here with synonymy in the sense of complete identity in psychological associations or poetic quality; indeed no two expressions are synonymous in such a sense. We are concerned only with what may be called *cognitive* synonymy. Just what this is cannot be said without successfully finishing the present study; but we know something about it from the need which arose for it in connection with analyticity in §1. The sort of synonymy needed there was merely such that any analytic statement could be turned into a logical truth by putting synonyms for synonyms. Turning the tables and assuming analyticity, indeed, we could explain cognitive synonymy of terms as follows (keeping to the familiar example): to say that 'bachelor' and 'unmarried man' are cognitively synonymous is to say no more nor less than that the statement:

(3) All and only bachelors are unmarried men

is analytic.[2]

What we need is an account of cognitive synonymy not presupposing analyticity—if we are to explain analyticity conversely with help of cognitive synonymy as undertaken in §1. And indeed such an independent account of cognitive synonymy is at present up for consideration, namely, interchangeability *salva veritate* everywhere except within words. The question before us, to resume the thread at last, is whether such interchangeability is a sufficient condition for cognitive synonymy. We can quickly assure ourselves that it is, by examples of the following sort. The statement:

(4) Necessarily all and only bachelors are bachelors

is evidently true, even supposing 'necessarily' so narrowly construed as to be truly applicable only to analytic statements. Then, if 'bachelor' and 'unmarried man' are interchangeable *salva veritate*, the result:

(5) Necessarily all and only bachelors are unmarried men

of putting 'unmarried man' for an occurrence of 'bachelor' in (4) must, like (4), be true. But to say that (5) is true is to say that (3) is analytic, and hence that 'bachelor' and 'unmarried man' are cognitively synonymous.

Let us see what there is about the above argument that gives it its air of hocus-pocus. The condition of interchangeability *salva veritate* varies in its force with variations in the richness of the lanuage at hand: The above argument supposes we are working with a language rich enough to contain the adverb 'necessarily', this adverb being so construed as to yield truth when and only when applied to an analytic statement. But can we condone a language which contains such an adverb? Does the adverb really make sense? To suppose that it does is to suppose that we have already made satisfactory sense of 'analytic'. Then what are we so hard at work on right now?

Our argument is not flatly circular, but something like it. It has the form, figuratively speaking, of a closed curve in space.

Interchangeability *salva veritate* is meaningless until relativized to a language whose extent is specified in relevant respects. Suppose now we consider a language containing just the following materials. There is an indefinitely large stock of one-place predicates (for example, 'F' where 'Fx' means that x is a man) and many-place predicates (for example, 'G' where 'Gxy' means that x loves y), mostly having to do with extralogical subject matter. The rest of the language is logical. The atomic sentences consist each of a predicate followed by one or more variables 'x', 'y', etc.; and the complex sentences are built up of the atomic ones by truth functions ('not', 'and', 'or', etc.) and quantification. In effect such a language enjoys the benefits also of descriptions and indeed singular terms generally, these being

---

[2] This is cognitive synonymy in a primary, broad sense. Carnap . . . and Lewis . . . have suggested how, once this notion is at hand, a narrower sense of cognitive synonymy which is preferable for some purposes can in turn be derived. But this special ramification of concept-building lies aside from the present purposes and must not be confused with the broad sort of cognitive synonymy here concerned.

contextually definable in known ways. Even abstract singular terms naming classes, classes of classes, etc., are contextually definable in case the assumed stock of predicates includes the two-place predicates of class membership. Such a language can be adequate to classical mathematics and indeed to scientific discourse generally, except in so far as the latter involves debatable devices such as contrary-to-fact conditionals or modal adverbs like 'necessarily'. Now a language of this type is extensional, in this sense: any two predicates which agree extensionally (that is, are true of the same objects) are interchangeable *salva veritate*.

In an extensional language, therefore, interchangeability *salva veritate* is no assurance of cognitive synonymy of the desired type. That 'bachelor' and 'unmarried man' are interchangeable *salva veritate* in an extensional language assures us of no more than that (3) is true. There is no assurance here that the extensional agreement of 'bachelor' and 'unmarried man' rests on meaning rather than merely on accidental matters of fact, as does the extensional agreement of 'creature with a heart' and 'creature with kidneys'.

For most purposes extensional agreement is the nearest approximation to synonymy we need care about. But the fact remains that extensional agreement falls far short of cognitive synonymy of the type required for explaining analyticity in the manner of §1. The type of cognitive synonymy required there is such as to equate the synonymy of 'bachelor' and 'unmarried man' with the analyticity of (3), not merely with the truth of (3).

So we must recognize that interchangeability *salva veritate*, if construed in relation to an extensional language, is not a sufficient condition of cognitive synonymy in the sense needed for deriving analyticity in the manner of §1. If a language contains an intensional adverb 'necessarily' in the sense lately noted, or other particles to the same effect, then interchangeability *salva veritate* in such a language does afford a sufficient condition of cognitive synonymy; but such a language is intelligible only in so far as the notion of analyticity is already understood in advance.

The effort to explain cognitive synonymy first, for the sake of deriving analyticity from it afterward as in §1, is perhaps the wrong approach. Instead we might try explaining analyticity somehow without appeal to cognitive synonymy. Afterward we could doubtless derive cognitive synonymy from analyticity satisfactorily enough if desired. We have seen that cognitive synonymy of 'bachelor' and 'unmarried man' can be explained as analyticity of (3). The same explanation works for any pair of one-place predicates, of course, and it can be extended in obvious fashion to many-place predicates. Other syntactical categories can also be accommodated in fairly parallel fashion. Singular terms may be said to be cognitively synonymous when the statement of identity formed by putting '=' between them is analytic. Statements may be said simply to be cognitively synonymous when their biconditional (the result of joining them by 'if and only if') is analytic.[3] If we care to lump all categories into a single formulation, at the expense of assuming again the notion of "word" which was appealed to early in this section, we can describe any two linguistic forms as cognitively synonymous when the two forms are interchangeable (apart from occurrences within "words") *salva* (no longer *veritate* but) *analyticitate*. Certain

[3] The 'if and only if' itself is intended in the truth functional sense.

technical questions arise, indeed, over cases of ambiguity or homonymy; let us not pause for them, however, for we are already digressing. Let us rather turn our backs on the problem of synonymy and address ourselves anew to that of analyticity.

4. SEMANTICAL RULES

Analyticity at first seemed most naturally definable by appeal to a realm of meanings. On refinement, the appeal to meanings gave way to an appeal to synonymy or definition. But definition turned out to be a will-o'-the-wisp, and synonymy turned out to be best understood only by dint of a prior appeal to analyticity itself. So we are back at the problem of analyticity.

I do not know whether the statement 'Everything green is extended' is analytic. Now does my indecision over this example really betray an incomplete understanding, an incomplete grasp of the "meanings", of 'green' and 'extended'? I think not. The trouble is not with 'green' or 'extended', but with 'analytic'.

It is often hinted —that the difficulty in separating analytic statements from synthetic ones in ordinary language is due to the vagueness of ordinary language and that the distinction is clear when we have a precise artificial language with explicit "semantical rules." This, however, as I shall now attempt to show, is a confusion.

The notion of analyticity about which we are worrying is a purported relation between statements and languages: a statement S is said to be *analytic for* a language L, and the problem is to make sense of this relation generally, that is, for variable 'S' and 'L'. The gravity of this problem is not perceptibly less for artificial languages than for natural ones. The problem of making sense of the idiom 'S is analytic for L', with variable 'S' and 'L', retains its stubbornness even if we limit the range of the variable 'L' to artificial languages. Let me now try to make this point evident.

For artificial languages and semantical rules we look naturally to the writings of Carnap. His semantical rules take various forms, and to make my point I shall have to distinguish certain of the forms. Let us suppose, to begin with, an artificial language L_0 whose semantical rules have the form explicitly of a specification, by recursion or otherwise, of all the analytic statements of L_0. The rules tell us that such and such statements, and only those, are the analytic statements of L_0. Now here the difficulty is simply that the rules contain the word 'analytic', which we do not understand! We understand what expressions the rules attribute analyticity to, but we do not understand what the rules attribute to those expressions. In short, before we can understand a rule which begins 'A statement S is analytic for language L_0 if and only if . . .', we must understand the general relative term 'analytic for'; we must understand 'S is analytic for L' where 'S' and 'L' are variables.

Alternatively we may, indeed, view the so-called rule as a conventional definition of a new simple symbol 'analytic-for-L_0', which might better be written untendentiously as 'K' so as not to seem to throw light on the interesting word 'analytic'. Obviously any number of classes K, M, N, etc. of statements of L_0 can be specified for various purposes or for no purpose;

what does it mean to say that K, as against M, N, etc., is the class of the "analytic" statements of L_0?

By saying what statements are analytic for L_0 we explain 'analytic-for-L_0' but not 'analytic', not 'analytic for'. We do not begin to explain the idiom 'S is analytic for L' with variable 'S and L', even if we are content to limit the range of 'L' to the realm of artificial languages.

Actually we do know enough about the intended significance of 'analytic' to know that analytic statements are supposed to be true. Let us then turn to a second form of semantical rule, which says not that such and such statements are analytic but simply that such and such statements are included among the truths. Such a rule is not subject to the criticism of containing the un-understood word 'analytic'; and we may grant for the sake of argument that there is no difficulty over the broader term 'true'. A semantical rule of this second type, a rule of truth, is not supposed to specify all the truths of the language; it merely stipulates, recursively or otherwise, a certain multitude of statements which, along with others unspecified, are to count as true. Such a rule may be conceded to be quite clear. Derivatively, afterward, analyticity can be demarcated thus: a statement is analytic if it is (not merely true but) true according to the semantical rule.

Still there is really no progress. Instead of appealing to an unexplained word 'analytic', we are now appealing to an unexplained phrase 'semantical rule'. Not every true statement which says that the statements of some class are true can count as a semantical rule—otherwise *all* truths would be "analytic" in the sense of being true according to semantical rules. Semantical rules are distinguishable, apparently, only by the fact of appearing on a page under the heading 'Semantical Rules'; and this heading is itself then meaningless.

We can say indeed that a statement is *analytic-for-L_0* if and only if it is true according to such and such specifically appended "semantical rules," but then we find ourselves back at essentially the same case which was originally discussed: 'S is analytic-for-L_0 if and only if. . . .' Once we seek to explain 'S is analytic-for-L' generally for variable 'L' (even allowing limitation of 'L' to artificial languages), the explanation 'true according to the semantical rules of L' is unavailing; for the relative term 'semantical rule of' is as much in need of clarification, at least, as 'analytic for'.

It may be instructive to compare the notion of semantical rule with that of postulate. Relative to a given set of postulates, it is easy to say what a postulate is: it is a member of the set. Relative to a given set of semantical rules, it is equally easy to say what a semantical rule is. But given simply a notation, mathematical or otherwise, and indeed as thoroughly understood a notation as you please in point of the translations or truth conditions of its statements, who can say which of its true statements rank as postulates? Obviously the question is meaningless—as meaningless as asking which points in Ohio are starting points. Any finite (or effectively specifiable infinite) selection of statements (preferably true ones, perhaps) is as much *a* set of postulates as any other. The word 'postulate' is significant only relative to an act of inquiry; we apply the word to a set of statements just in so far as we happen, for the year or the moment, to be thinking of those statements in relation to the statements which can be reached from them by some set of transformations to which we have seen fit to direct our attention. Now the notion of semantical rule is as sensible and meaningful as that of postulate, if conceived in a similarly relative spirit—relative, this time, to one or another particular enterprise of schooling unconversant persons in sufficient conditions for truth of statements of some natural or artificial language *L*. But from this point of view no one signalization of a subclass of the truths of *L* is intrinsically more a semantical rule than another; and, if 'analytic' means 'true by semantical rules', no one truth of *L* is analytic to the exclusion of another.

It might conceivably be protested that an artificial language *L* (unlike a natural one) is a language in the ordinary sense *plus* a set of explicit semantical rules—the whole constituting, let us say, an ordered pair; and that the semantical rules of *L* then are specifiable simply as the second component of the pair *L*. But, by the same token and more simply, we might construe an artificial language *L* outright as an ordered pair whose second component is the class of its analytic statements; and then the analytic statements of *L* become specifiable simply as the statements in the second component of *L*. Or better still, we might just stop tugging at our bootstraps altogether.

Not all the explanations of analyticity known to Carnap and his readers have been covered explicitly in the above considerations, but the extension to other forms is not hard to see. Just one additional factor should be mentioned which sometimes enters: sometimes the semantical rules are in effect rules of translation into ordinary language, in which case the analytic statements of the artificial language are in effect recognized as such from the analyticity of their specified translations in ordinary language. Here certainly there can be no thought of an illumination of the problem of analyticity from the side of the artificial language.

From the point of view of the problem of analyticity the notion of an artificial language with semantical rules is a *feu follet par excellence* [nothing but a will-o-the-wisp]. Semantical rules determining the analytic statements of an artificial language are of interest only in so far as we already understand the notion of analyticity; they are of no help in gaining this understanding.

Appeal to hypothetical languages of an artificially simple kind could conceivably be useful in clarifying analyticity, if the mental or behavioral or cultural factors relevant to analyticity—whatever they may be—were somehow sketched into the simplified model. But a model which takes analyticity merely as an irreducible character is unlikely to throw light on the problem of explicating analyticity.

It is obvious that truth in general depends on both language and extra-linguistic fact. The statement 'Brutus killed Caesar' would be false if the world had been different in certain ways, but it would also be false if the word 'killed' happened rather to have the sense of 'begat'. Thus one is tempted to suppose in general that the truth of a statement is somehow analyzable into a linguistic component and a factual component. Given this supposition, it next seems reasonable that in some statements the factual component should be null; and these are the analytic statements. But, for all its a priori reasonableness, a boundary between analytic and synthetic statements simply has not been drawn. That there is such a distinction to be drawn at all is an unempirical dogma of empiricists, a metaphysical article of faith.

ARE MISTAKES ABOUT ONE'S OWN IMMEDIATE EXPERIENCE ONLY VERBAL?

A. J. Ayer

For those who have the use of language, there is an intimate connection between identifying an object and knowing what to call it. Indeed on many occasions one's recognizing whatever it may be is simply a matter of one's coming out with the appropriate word. Of course the word must be meant to designate the object in question, but there are not, or need not be, two separate processes, one of fixing the object and the other of labelling it. The intention is normally to be found in the way in which the label is put on. There is, however, a sense in which one can recognize an object without knowing how to describe it. One may be able to place the object as being of the same sort as such and such another, or as having appeared before on such and such occasions, although one forgets what it is called or even thinks that it is called something which it is not. To a certain extent this placing of the object is already a fashion of describing it: we are not now concerned with the cases where recognition, conceived in terms of adaptive behaviour, is independent of the use of any symbols at all: but our finding a description of this sort is consistent with our ignoring or infringing some relevant linguistic rule. And this can happen also when the rule is of one's own making, or at least constituted by one's own practice. When the usage which they infringe is private, such lapses can only be exceptional; for unless one's practice were generally consistent, there would be no rule to break: but it is to be envisaged that they should now and then occur.

If this is so, one can be mistaken, after all, in the characterization of one's present experience. One can at least misdescribe it in the sense that one applies the wrong word to it; wrong because it is not the word which by the rules of one's language is correlated with an 'object' of the sort in question. But the reply to this may be that one would then be making only a verbal

From A. J. Ayer, *The Problem of Knowledge* (London: 1956), Chap. II, Sec. 6, pp. 61–68. Reprinted by permission of St. Martin's Press Inc., The Macmillan Company of Canada Ltd., and Macmillan & Co. Ltd.

mistake. One would be misusing words, but not falling into any error of fact. Those who maintain that statements which describe some feature of one's present experience are incorrigible need not deny that the sentences which express them may be incorrectly formulated. What they are trying to exclude is the possibility of one's being factually mistaken.

But what is supposed to be the difference in this context between a verbal and a factual mistake? The first thing to remark is that we are dealing with words which, though general in their application, are also ostensive: that is, they are meant to stand for features of what is directly given in experience. And with respect to words of this kind, it is plausible to argue that knowing what they mean is simply a matter of being disposed to use them on the right occasions, when these are presented. It then appears to follow that to be in doubt as to the nature of something which is given, to wonder, for example, what colour this looks to me to be, is to be in doubt about the meaning of a word. And, correspondingly, to misdescribe what is given is to misuse a word. If I am not sure whether this looks crimson, what I am doubting is whether 'crimson' is the right word to describe this colour: if I resolve this doubt wrongly I have used the word 'crimson' when I should not or failed to use it when I should. This example is made easier to accept because the word 'crimson' has a conventional use. It is harder to see how I can use a word improperly when it is I alone who set the standard of propriety: my mistake would then have to consist in the fact that I had made an involuntary departure from some consistent practice which I had previously followed. In any event, it is argued, my mistake is not factual. If I were to predict that something, not yet presented to me, was going to look crimson, I might very well be making a factual mistake. My use of the word 'crimson' may be quite correct. It properly expresses my expectation: only the expectation is not in fact fulfilled. But in such a case I venture beyond the description of my present experience: I issue a draft upon the facts which they may refuse to honour. But for them to frustrate me I must put myself in their power. And this it is alleged I fail to do when I am merely recording what is directly given to me. My mistakes then can only be verbal. Thus we see that the reason why it is held to be impossible to make a factual error in describing a feature of one's present experience is that there is nothing in these circumstances which is allowed to count as one's being factually mistaken.

Against this, some philosophers would argue that it is impossible to describe anything, even a momentary private experience, without venturing beyond it. If I say that what I seem to see is crimson, I am saying that it bears the appropriate resemblance in colour to certain other objects. If it does not so resemble them I have classified it wrongly, and in doing so I have made a factual mistake. But the answer to this is that merely from the statement that a given thing looks crimson, it cannot be deduced that anything else is coloured or even that anything else exists. The fact, if it be a fact, that the colour of the thing in question does not resemble that of other things which are properly described as crimson does indeed prove that in calling it crimson I am making a mistake; I am breaking a rule which would not exist unless there were, or at any rate could be, other things to which the word applied. But in saying that this is crimson, I am not explicitly referring to these other things. In using a word according to a rule, whether rightly or wrongly, I am not talking about the rule. I operate it but I do not say how it operates. From the fact that I have to refer to other things in order to show that my description of something is correct, it does not follow that my description itself refers to them. We may admit that to describe is to classify; but this does not entail that in describing something one is bound to go beyond it, in the sense that one actually asserts that it is related to something else.

Let us allow, then, that there can be statements which refer only to the contents of one's present experiences. Then, if it is made a necessary condition for being factually mistaken that one should make some claim upon the facts which goes beyond the content of one's present experience, it will follow that even when these statements misdescribe what they refer to the error is not factual: and then there appears no choice but to say that it is verbal. The question is whether this ruling is to be accepted.

The assumption which lies behind it is that to understand the meaning of an ostensive word one must be able to pick out the instances to which it applies. If I pick out the wrong instances, or fail to pick out the right ones, I show that I have not learned how to use the word. If I hesitate whether to apply it to a given case, I show that I am so far uncertain of its meaning. Now there is clearly some truth in this assumption. We should certainly not say that someone knew the meaning of an ostensive word if he had no idea how to apply it; more than that, we require that his use of it should, in general, be both confident and right. But this is not to say that in every single case in which he hesitates over the application of the word, he must be in doubt about its meaning. Let us consider an example. Suppose that two lines of approximately the same length are drawn so that they both come within my field of vision and I am then asked to say whether either of them looks to me to be the longer, and if so which. I think I might very well be uncertain how to answer. But it seems very strange to say that what, in such a case, I should be uncertain about would be the meaning of the English expression 'looks longer than'. It is not at all like the case where I know which looks to me the longer, but having to reply in French, and speaking French badly, I hesitate whether to say 'plus longue' or 'plus large'. In this case I am uncertain only about the proper use of words, but in the other surely I am not. I know quite well how the words 'looks longer than' are used in English. It is just that in the present instance I am not sure whether, as a matter of fact, either of the lines does look to me to be longer than the other.

But if I can be in doubt about this matter of fact, I can presumably also come to the wrong decision. I can judge that this line looks to me to be longer than that one, when in fact it does not. This would indeed be a curious position to be in. Many would say that it was an impossible position, on the ground that there is no way of distinguishing between the way things look to someone and the way he judges that they look. After all he is the final authority on the way things look to him, and what criterion is there for deciding how things look to him except the way that he assesses them? But in allowing that he may be uncertain how a thing looks to him, we have already admitted this distinction. We have drawn a line between the facts and his assessment, or description, of them.[1] Even so, it may be objected, there is no sense in talking of there being a mistake unless it is at least possible that the mistake should be discovered. And how could it ever be discovered that one had made a mistake in one's account of some momentary, private experience? Clearly no direct test is possible. The experience is past: it cannot be produced for reinspection. But there may still be indirect evidence which would carry weight. To return to our example, if I look at the lines again, it may seem quite clear to me that A looks longer than B, whereas I had previously been inclined to think that B looked longer than A, or that they looked the same length. This does not prove that I was wrong before: it may be that they look to me differently now from the way they did then. But I might have indirect, say physiological, evidence that their appearance, that is the appearance that they offer to me, has not changed. Or I may have reason to believe that in the relevant conditions things look the same to certain other people as they do to me: and then the fact that the report given by these other people disagrees with mine may have some tendency to show that I am making a mistake. In any event it is common ground that one can misdescribe one's experience. The question is only whether such misdescription is always to be taken as an instance of a verbal mistake. My contention is that there are cases in which it is more plausible to say that the mistake is factual.

If I am right, there is then no class of descriptive statements which are incorrigible. However strong the experiential basis on which a descriptive statement is put forward, the possibility of its falsehood is not excluded. Statements which do no more than describe the content of a momentary, private experience achieve the greatest security because they run the smallest risk. But they do run some risk, however small, and because of this they too can come to grief. Complete security is attained only by statements like 'I exist' which function as gesticulations. But the price which they pay for it is the sacrifice of descriptive content.

We are left still with the argument that some statements must be incorrigible, if any are ever to be verified. If the statements which have been taken as basic are fallible like all the rest, where does the process of verification terminate? The answer is that it terminates in someone's having some experience, and in his accepting the truth of some statement which describes it, or more commonly, the truth of some more far-reaching statement which the occurrence of the experience supports. There is nothing fallible about the experience itself. What may be wrong is only one's identification of it. If an experience has been misidentified, one will be misled into thinking that some statement has been verified when it has not. But this does not mean that we never verify anything. There is no reason to doubt that the vast majority of our experiences are taken by us to be what they are; in which case they do verify the statements which are construed as describing them. What we do not, and can not, have is a logical guarantee that our acceptance of a statement is not mistaken. It is chiefly the belief that we need such a guarantee that has led philosophers to hold that some at least of the statements which refer to what is immediately given to us in experience must be

[1] Yes, but it may still be argued that his assessment, when he reaches it, *settles* the question. The point is whether a meaning can be given to saying that he decides wrongly. I suggest that it can.

incorrigible. But, as I have already remarked, even if there could be such incorrigible statements, the guarantee which they provided would not be worth very much. In any given case it would operate only for a single person and only for the fleeting moment at which he was having the experience in question. It would not, therefore, be of any help to us in making lasting additions to our stock of knowledge.

In allowing that the descriptions which people give of their experiences may be factually mistaken, we are dissociating having an experience from knowing that one has it. To know that one is having whatever experience it may be, one must not only have it but also be able to identify it correctly, and there is no necessary transition from one to the other; not to speak of the cases when we do not identify our experiences at all, we may identify them wrongly. Once again, this does not mean that we never know, or never really know, what experiences we are having. On the contrary it is exceptional for us not to know. All that is required is that we should be able to give an account of our experiences which is both confident and correct; and these conditions are very frequently fulfilled. It is no rebuttal of our claim to knowledge that, in this as in other domains, it may sometimes happen that we think we know when we do not.

The upshot of our argument is that the philosopher's ideal of certainty has no application. Except in the cases where the truth of a statement is a condition of its being made, it can never in any circumstances be logically impossible that one should take a statement to be true when it is false; and this holds good whatever the statement may be, whether, for example, it is itself necessary or contingent. It would, however, be a mistake to express this conclusion by saying, lugubriously or in triumph, that nothing is really certain. There are a great many statements the truth of which we rightly do not doubt; and it is perfectly correct to say that they are certain. We should not be bullied by the sceptic into renouncing an expression for which we have a legitimate use. Not that the sceptic's argument is fallacious; as usual his logic is impeccable. But his victory is empty. He robs us of certainty only by so defining it as to make it certain that it cannot be obtained.

12

KNOWLEDGE AND BELIEF

Norman Malcolm

"We must recognize that when we know something we either do, or by reflecting, can know that our condition is one of knowing that thing, while when we believe something, we either do or can know that our condition is one of believing and not of knowing: so that we cannot mistake belief for knowledge or vice versa."[1]

This remark is worthy of investigation. Can I discover *in myself* whether I know something or merely believe it?

Let us begin by studying the ordinary usage of "know" and "believe." Suppose, for example, that several of us intend to go for a walk and that you propose that we walk in Cascadilla Gorge. I protest that I should like to walk beside a flowing stream and that at this season the gorge is probably dry. Consider the following cases:

(1) You say "I believe that it won't be dry although I have no particular reason for thinking so." If we went to the gorge and found a flowing stream we should not say that you *knew* that there would be water but that you thought so and were right.

(2) You say "I believe that it won't be dry because it rained only three days ago and usually water flows in the gorge for at least that long after a rain." If we found water we should be inclined to say that you knew that there would be water. It would be quite natural for you to say "I knew that it wouldn't be dry"; and we should tolerate your remark. This case differs from the previous one in that here you had a *reason*.

(3) You say "I know that it won't be dry" and give the same reason as in (2). If we found water we should have very little hesitation in saying that you knew. Not only had you a reason, but you *said* "I know" instead of "I believe." It may seem to us that the latter should not make a difference—but it does.

From Norman Malcolm, *Knowledge and Certainty: Essays and Lectures*, pp. 58–72, © 1963. Reprinted by permission of Prentice-Hall, Inc., Englewood Cliffs, New Jersey, U.S.A.
[1] H. A. Prichard, *Knowledge and Perception* (Oxford: The Clarendon Press, 1950), p. 88.

(4) You say "I know that it won't be dry" and give a stronger reason, e.g., "I saw a lot of water flowing in the gorge when I passed it this morning." If we went and found water, there would be no hesitation at all in saying that you knew. If, for example, we later met someone who said "Weren't you surprised to see water in the gorge this afternoon?" you would reply "No, I *knew* that there would be water; I had been there earlier in the day." We should have no objection to this statement.

(5) Everything happens as in (4), except that upon going to the gorge we find it to be dry. We should not say that you knew, but that you *believed* that there would be water. And this is true even though you declared that you knew, and even though your evidence was the same as it was in case (4) in which you did know.

I wish to make some comments on the usage of "know," "knew," "believe," and "believed," as illustrated in the preceding cases:

(a) Whether we should say that you knew, depends in part on whether you had grounds for your assertion and on the strength of those grounds. There would certainly be less hesitation to say that you knew in case (4) than in case (3), and this can be due only to the difference in the strength of the grounds.

(b) Whether we should say that you knew, depends in part on how *confident* you were. In case (2), if you had said "It rained only three days ago and usually water flows in the gorge for at least that long after a rain; but, of course, I don't feel absolutely sure that there will be water," then we should *not* have said that you knew that there would be water. If you lack confidence that p is true then others do not say that you know that p is true, even though *they* know that p is true. Being confident is a necessary condition for knowing.

(c) Prichard says that if we reflect we cannot mistake belief for knowledge. In case (4) you knew that there would be water, and in case (5) you merely believed it. Was there any way that you could have discovered by reflection, in case (5), that you did not know? It would have been useless to have reconsidered your grounds for saying that there would be water, because in case (4), where you *did* know, your grounds were identical. They could be at fault in (5) only if they were at fault in (4), and they were not at fault in (4). Cases (4) and (5) differ in only one respect—namely, that in one case you did subsequently find water and in the other you did not. Prichard says that we can determine by reflection whether we know something or merely believe it. But where, in these cases, is the material that reflection would strike upon? There is none.

There is only one way that Prichard could defend his position. He would have to say that in case (4) you did *not* know that there would be water. And it is obvious that he would have said this. But this is false. It is an enormously common usage of language to say, in commenting upon just such an incident as (4), "He knew that the gorge would be dry because he had seen water flowing there that morning." It is a usage that all of us are familiar with. We so employ "know" and "knew" every day of our lives. We do not think of our usage as being loose or incorrect—and it is not. As philosophers we may be surprised to observe that it *can* be that the knowledge that p is true should differ from the belief that p is true *only* in the respect that in one case p is true and in the other false. But that is the fact.

There is an argument that one is inclined to use as a proof that you did not know that there would be water. The argument is the following: It could have turned out that you found no water; if it had so turned out you would have been mistaken in saying that you would find water; therefore you could have been mistaken; but if you could have been mistaken then you did not know.

Now it certainly *could* have turned out that the gorge was quite dry when you went there, even though you saw lots of water flowing through it only a few hours before. This does not show, however, that you did not know that there would be water. What it shows is that *although you knew you could have been mistaken.*[2] This would seem to be a contradictory result; but it is not. It seems so because our minds are fixed upon another usage of "know" and "knew"; one in which "It would have turned out that I was mistaken," implies "I did not know."

When is "know" used in this sense? I believe that Prichard uses it in this sense when he says that when we go through the proof of the proposition that the angles of a triangle are equal to two right angles we *know* that the proposition is true (p. 89). He says that if we put to ourselves the question: Is our condition one of knowing this, or is it only one of being convinced of it? then "We can only answer 'Whatever may be our state on other occasions, here we are knowing this.' And this statement is an expression of our *knowing* that we are knowing; for we do not *believe* that we are knowing this, we know that we are" (p. 89). He goes on to say that if someone were to object that we might be making a mistake "because for all we know we can later on discover some fact which is incompatible with a triangle's having angles that are equal to two right angles, we can answer that we *know* that there can be no such fact, for in knowing that a triangle must have such angles we also know that nothing can exist which is incompatible with this fact" (p. 90).

It is easy to imagine a non-philosophical context in which it would have been natural for Prichard to have said "I know that the angles of a triangle are equal to two right angles." Suppose that a young man just beginning the study of geometry was in doubt as to whether that proposition is true, and had even constructed an ingenious argument that appeared to prove it false. Suppose that Prichard was unable to find any error in the argument. He might have said to the young man: "There must be an error in it. I know that the angles of a triangle are equal to two right angles."

When Prichard says that "nothing can exist which is incompatible with" the truth of that proposition, is he prophesying that no one will ever have the ingenuity to construct a flawless-looking argument against it? I believe not. When Prichard says that "we" *know* (and implies that *he* knows) that the proposition is true and *know* that nothing can exist that is incompatible

---

[2] [Some readers seem to have thought that I was denying here that "I knew that p" entails "that p." That was not my intention, and my words do not have that implication. If I had said *"Although you knew you were mistaken,"* I should have denied the above entailment and, also, I should have misused "knew." The difference between the strong and weak senses of "know" (and "knew") is not that this entailment holds for the strong but not for the weak sense. It holds for both. If it is false that p, then one does not (and did not) know that p.]

with its being true, he is not making any *prediction* as to what the future will bring in the way of arguments or measurements. On the contrary, he is asserting that *nothing* that the future might bring could ever count as evidence against the proposition. He is implying that he would not *call* anything "evidence" against it. He is using "know" in what I shall call its "strong" sense. "Know" is used in this sense when a person's statement "I know that *p* is true" implies that the person who makes the statement would look upon nothing whatever as evidence that *p* is false.

It must not be assumed that whenever "know" is used in connection with mathematical propositions it is used in the strong sense. A great many people have *heard* of various theorems of geometry, e.g., the Pythagorean. These theorems are a part of "common knowledge." If a schoolboy doing his geometry assignment felt a doubt about the Pythagorean theorem, and said to an adult "Are you *sure* that it is true?" the latter might reply "Yes, I know that it is." He might make this reply even though he could not give proof of it and even though he had never gone through a proof of it. If subsequently he was presented with a "demonstration" that the theorem is false, or if various persons reputed to have a knowledge of geometry soberly assured him that it is false, he might be filled with doubt or even be convinced that he was mistaken. When he said "Yes, I know that it is true," he did not pledge himself to hold to the theorem through thick and thin. He did not absolutely exclude the possibility that something could prove it to be false. I shall say that he used "know" in the "weak" sense.

Consider another example from mathematics of the difference between the strong and weak senses of "know." I have just now rapidly calculated that 92 times 16 is 1472. If I had done this in the commerce of daily life where a practical problem was at stake, and if someone had asked "Are you sure that $92 \times 16 = 1472$?" I might have answered "I *know* that it is; I have just now calculated it." But also I might have answered "I know that it is; but I will calculate it again to *make sure*." And here my language points to a distinction. I say that I *know* that $92 \times 16 = 1472$. Yet I am willing to *confirm* it—that is, there is something that I should *call* "making sure"; and, likewise, there is something that I should *call* "finding out that it is false." If I were to do this calculation again and obtain the result that $92 \times 16 = 1372$, and if I were to carefully check this latter calculation without finding any error, I should be disposed to say that I was previously mistaken when I declared that $92 \times 16 = 1472$. Thus when I say that I know that $92 \times 16 = 1472$, I allow for the possibility of a *refutation*; and so I am using "know" in its weak sense.

Now consider propositions like $2 + 2 = 4$ and $7 + 5 = 12$. It is hard to think of circumstances in which it would be natural for me to say that I know that $2 + 2 = 4$, because no one ever questions it. Let us try to suppose, however, that someone whose intelligence I respect argues that certain developments in arithmetic have shown that $2 + 2$ does not equal 4. He writes out a proof of this in which I can find no flaw. Suppose that his demeanor showed me that he was in earnest. Suppose that several persons of normal intelligence became persuaded that his proof was correct and that $2 + 2$ does not equal 4. What would be my reaction? I should say "I can't see what is wrong with your proof; but it *is* wrong, because I *know* that $2 + 2 = 4$." Here I should be using "know" in its strong sense. I should not admit that any argument or any future development in mathematics could show that it is false that $2 + 2 = 4$.

The propositions $2 + 2 = 4$ and $92 \times 16 = 1472$ do not have the same status. There *can* be a demonstration that $2 + 2 = 4$. But a demonstration would be for me (and for any average person) only a curious exercise, a sort of *game*. We have no serious interest in proving that proposition.[3] It does not *need* a proof. It stands without one, and would not fall if a proof went against it. The case is different with the proposition that $92 \times 16 = 1472$. We take an interest in the demonstration (calculation) because that proposition *depends* upon its demonstration. A calculation may lead me to reject it as false. But $2 + 2 = 4$ does *not* depend on its demonstration. It does not depend on anything! And in the calculation that proves that $92 \times 16 = 1472$, there are steps that do not depend on any calculation (e.g., $2 \times 6 = 12$; $5 + 2 = 7$; $5 + 9 = 14$).

There is a correspondence between this dualism in the logical status of mathematical propositions and the two senses of "know." When I use "know" in the weak sense I am prepared to let an investigation (demonstration, calculation) determine whether the something that I claim to know is true or false. When I use "know" in the strong sense I am not prepared to look upon anything as an *investigation;* I do not concede that anything whatsoever could prove me mistaken; I do not regard the matter as open to any *question;* I do not admit that my proposition could turn out to be false, that any future investigation *could* refute it or cast doubt on it.[4]

We have been considering the strong sense of "know" in its application to mathematical propositions. Does it have application anywhere in the realm of *empirical* propositions—for example, to propositions that assert or imply that certain physical things exist? Descartes said that we have a "moral assurance" of the truth of some of the latter propositions but that we lack a "metaphysical certainty."[5] Locke said that the perception of the existence of physical things is not "so certain as our intuitive knowledge, or the deductions of our reason" although "it is an assurance that deserves the name of knowledge."[6] Some philosophers have held that when we make judgments of perception such as that there are peonies in the garden, cows in the field, or dishes in the cupboard, we are "taking for granted" that the peonies, cows, and dishes exist, but not knowing it in the "strict" sense. Others have held that all empirical propositions, including judgments of

---

[3] Some logicians and philosophers have taken an interest in proving that $2 + 2 = 4$ (e.g., Leibniz, *New Essays on the Understanding*, Bk. IV, ch. 7, sec. 10; Frege, *The Foundations of Arithmetic*, sec. 6). They have wished to show that it can be deduced from certain premises, and to determine what premises and rules of inference are required in the deduction. Their interest has not been in the *outcome* of the deduction.

[4] Compare these remarks about the strong sense of "know" with some of Locke's statements about "intuitive knowledge": ". . . in this the mind is at no pains of proving or examining. . . ." "This part of knowledge . . . leaves no room for hesitation, doubt, or examination. . . ."

"It is on this intuition that depends all the certainty and evidence of all our knowledge; which certainty every one finds to be so great, that he cannot imagine, and therefore not require a greater. . . ." Locke, *Essay*, Bk. IV, ch. 2, sec. 1.

[5] Descartes, *Discourse on the Method*, Part IV.

[6] Locke, *Essay*, Book IV, ch. 11, sec. 3.

perception, are merely hypotheses.[7] The thought behind this exaggerated mode of expression is that any empirical proposition whatever *could* be refuted by future experience—that is, it *could* turn out to be false. Are these philosophers right?

Consider the following propositions:

   (i) The sun is about ninety million miles from the earth.
  (ii) There is a heart in my body.
 (iii) Here is an ink-bottle.

In various circumstances I should be willing to assert of each of these propositions that I know it to be true. Yet they differ strikingly. This I see when, with each, I try to imagine the possibility that it is false.

(i) If in ordinary conversation someone said to me "The sun is about twenty million miles from the earth, isn't it?" I should reply "No, it is about ninety million miles from us." If he said "I think that you are confusing the sun with Polaris," I should reply, "I *know* that ninety million miles is roughly the sun's distance from the earth." I might invite him to verify the figure in an encyclopedia. A third person who overheard our conversation could quite correctly report that I knew the distance to the sun, whereas the other man did not. But this knowledge of mine is little better than hearsay. I have seen that figure mentioned in a few books. I know nothing about the observations and calculations that led astronomers to accept it. If tomorrow a group of eminent astronomers announced that a great error had been made and that the correct figure is twenty million miles, I should not insist that they were wrong. It would surprise me that such an enormous mistake could have been made. But I should no longer be willing to say that I *know* that ninety million is the correct figure. Although I should *now* claim that I know the distance to be about ninety million miles, it is easy for me to envisage the possibility that some future investigation will prove this to be false.

(ii) Suppose that after a routine medical examination the excited doctor reports to me that the X-ray photographs show that I have no heart. I should tell him to get a new machine. I should be inclined to say that the fact that I have a heart is one of the few things that I can count on as absolutely certain. I can feel it beat. I know it's there. Furthermore, how could my blood circulate if I didn't have one? Suppose that later on I suffer a chest injury and undergo a surgical operation. Afterwards the astonished surgeons solemnly declare that they searched my chest cavity and found no heart, and that they made incisions and looked about in other likely places but found it not. They are convinced that I am without a heart. They are unable to understand how circulation can occur or what accounts for the thumping in my chest. But they are in agreement and obviously sincere, and they have clear photographs of my interior spaces. What would be my attitude? Would it be to insist that they were all mistaken? I think not. I believe that I should eventually accept their testimony and the evidence of the photo-

---

[7] E.g., ". . . no proposition, other than a tautology, can possibly be anything more than a probable hypothesis." A. J. Ayer, *Language, Truth and Logic*, second ed. (New York: Dover Publications, Inc., 1951), p. 38.

graphs. I should consider to be false what I now regard as an absolute certainty.

(iii) Suppose that as I write this paper someone in the next room were to call out to me "I can't find an ink-bottle; is there one in the house?" I should reply "Here is an ink-bottle." If he said in a doubtful tone "Are you sure? I looked there before," I should reply "Yes, I know there is; come and get it."

Now could it turn out to be false that there is an ink-bottle directly in front of me on this desk? Many philosophers have thought so. They would say that many things could happen of such a nature that if they did happen it would be proved that I am deceived. I agree that many extraordinary things could happen, in the sense that there is no logical absurdity in the supposition. It could happen that when I next reach for this ink-bottle my hand should seem to pass *through* it and I should not feel the contact of any object. It could happen that in the next moment the ink-bottle will suddenly vanish from sight; or that I should find myself under a tree in the garden with no ink-bottle about; or that one or more persons should enter this room and declare with apparent sincerity that they see no ink-bottle on this desk; or that a photograph taken now of the top of the desk should clearly show all of the objects on it except the ink-bottle. Having admitted that these things *could happen*,[8] am I compelled to admit that if they did happen then it would be proved that there is no ink-bottle here *now?* Not at all! I could say that when my hand seemed to pass through the ink-bottle I should *then* be suffering from hallucination; that if the ink-bottle suddenly vanished it would have miraculously ceased to exist; that the other persons were conspiring to drive me mad, or were themselves victims of remarkable concurrent hallucinations; that the camera possessed some strange flaw or that there was trickery in developing the negative. I admit that in the next moment I could find myself under a tree or in the bathtub. But this is not to admit that it could be revealed in the next moment that I am now dreaming. For what I admit is that I might be instantaneously transported to the garden, but not that in the next moment I might *wake up* in the garden. There is nothing that could happen to me in the next moment that I should call "waking up"; and therefore nothing that could happen to me in the next moment would be accepted by me now as proof that I now dream.

Not only do I not *have* to admit that those extraordinary occurrences would be evidence that there is no ink-bottle here; the fact is that I *do not* admit it. There is nothing whatever that could happen in the next moment or the next year that would by me be called *evidence* that there is not an ink-bottle here now. No future experience or investigation could prove to me that I am mistaken. Therefore, if I were to say "I know that there is an ink-bottle here," I should be using "know" in the strong sense.

[8] [My viewpoint is somewhat different here from what it is in "The Verification Argument." There I am concerned with bringing out the different ways in which such a remark as "these things *could* happen" can be taken. I wish to show, furthermore, that from none of the senses in which the remark is *true* does it follow that it is *not certain* that the things in question will *not* happen. Finally, I hold there, that it is perfectly certain that they will not happen. Here, I am not disagreeing with any of those points, but I am adding the further point that my admission that, in some sense, the things *could happen*, does not require me to admit that *if* they were to happen, that would be evidence that there is no ink-bottle here now.]

It will appear to some that I have adopted an *unreasonable* attitude toward that statement. There is, however, nothing unreasonable about it. It seems so because one thinks that the statement that here is an ink-bottle *must* have the same status as the statements that the sun is ninety million miles away and that I have a heart and that there will be water in the gorge this afternoon. But this is a *prejudice*.

In saying that I should regard nothing as evidence that there is no ink-bottle here now, I am not *predicting* what I should do if various astonishing things happened. If other members of my family entered this room and, while looking at the top of this desk, declared with apparent sincerity that they see no ink-bottle, I might fall into a swoon or become mad. I *might* even come to believe that there is not and has not been an ink-bottle here. I cannot foretell with certainty how I should react. But if it is *not* a prediction, what is the meaning of my assertion that I should regard nothing as evidence that there is no ink-bottle here?

That assertion describes my *present* attitude towards the statement that here is an ink-bottle. It does not prophesy what my attitude *would* be if various things happened. My present attitude toward that statement is radically different from my present attitude toward those other statements (e.g., that I have a heart).[9] I do *now* admit that certain future occurrences would disprove the latter. Whereas no imaginable future occurrence would be considered by me *now* as proving that there is not an ink-bottle here.

These remarks are not meant to be autobiographical. They are meant to throw light on the common concepts of evidence, proof, and disproof. Every one of us upon innumerable occasions of daily life takes this same attitude towards various statements about physical things, e.g., that here is a torn page, that this dish is broken, that the thermometer reads 70, that no rug is on the floor. Furthermore, the concepts of proof, disproof, doubt, and conjecture *require* us to take this attitude. In order for it to be possible that any statements about physical things should *turn out to be false* it is necessary that some statements about physical things *cannot* turn out to be false.

This will be made clear if we ask ourselves the question, When do we *say* that something turned out to be false? When do we use those words? Someone asks you for a dollar. You say "There is one in this drawer." You open the drawer and look, but it is perfectly empty. Your statement turned out to be false. This can be said because you *discovered* an empty drawer. It could not be said if it were only probable that the drawer is empty or were still open to question. Would it make sense to say "I had better make sure that it is empty; perhaps there is a dollar in it after all?" Sometimes; but not always. Not if the drawer lies open before your eyes. That remark is the prelude to a search. What search can there be when the emptiness of the drawer confronts you? In certain circumstances there is nothing that you would call "making sure" that the drawer is empty; and likewise nothing that you would call "its turning out to be false" that the drawer is empty.

---

9 [The word "attitude" is not very satisfactory, but I cannot think of another noun that would do the trick. By "my attitude" I mean, here, *what I should say and think* if various things were to happen. By "my *present* attitude" I mean what I should say and think now, when I imagine those things as happening, in contrast with what I should say and think at some future time if those things actually did happen at that time. It is this distinction that shows that my description of "my present attitude" is not a *prophecy*.]

You *made* sure that the drawer is empty. One statement about physical things *turned out to be false* only because you *made sure* of another statement about physical things. The two concepts cannot exist apart. Therefore it is impossible that *every* statement about physical things *could* turn out to be false.

In a certain important respect some a priori statements and some empirical statements possess the same logical character. The statements that $5 \times 5 = 25$ and that here is an ink-bottle, both lie beyond the reach of doubt. On both, my judgment and reasoning *rests*. If you could somehow undermine my confidence in either, you would not teach me *caution*. You would fill my mind with chaos! I could not even make *conjectures* if you took away those fixed points of certainty; just as a man cannot *try* to climb whose body has no support. A conjecture implies an understanding of what certainty would be. If it is not a certainty that $5 \times 5 = 25$ and that here is an ink-bottle, then I do not understand what it is. You cannot make me doubt either of these statements or treat them as hypotheses. You cannot persuade me that future experience could refute them. With both of them it is perfectly unintelligible to me to speak of a "possibility" that they are false. This is to say that I know both of them to be true, in the strong sense of "know." And I am inclined to think that the strong sense of "know" is what various philosophers have had in mind when they have spoken of "perfect," "metaphysical," or "strict certainty."[10]

It will be thought that I have confused a statement about my "sensations," or my "sense-data," or about the way something *looks* or *appears* to me, with a statement about physical things. It will be thought that the things that I have said about the statement "Here is an ink-bottle" could be true only if that statement is interpreted to mean something like "There appears to me to be an ink-bottle here," i.e., interpreted so as not to assert or imply that any physical thing exists. I wish to make it clear that my statement "Here is an ink-bottle" is *not* to be interpreted in that way. It would be utterly fantastic for me in my present circumstances to say "There appears to me to be an ink-bottle here."

If someone were to call me on the telephone and say that he urgently needed an ink-bottle I should invite him to come here and get this one. If he said that it was extremely urgent that he should obtain one immediately and that he could not afford to waste time going to a place where there might not be one, I should tell him that it is an absolute certainty that there is one here, that nothing could be more certain, that it is something I absolutely guarantee. But if my statement "There is an ink-bottle here" were a statement about my "sensations" or "sense-data," or if it meant that there *appears* to me to be an ink-bottle here or that something here *looks* to me like an ink-bottle, and if that is all that I meant by it—then I should react quite differ-

---

[10] Descartes, for example, apparently took as his criterion for something's being "entirely certain" that he could not *imagine* in it the least ground of doubt: ". . . je pensai qu'il fallait . . . que je retasse comme absolument faux tout ce en quoi je pourrais imaginer le moindre doute, afin de voir s'il ne me resterait point après cela quelque chose en ma créance qui fut entièrement indubitable" (*Discourse*, Part IV). And Locke (as previously noted) said of "intuitive knowledge" that one *cannot imagine* a greater certainty, and that it "leaves no room for hesitation, doubt, or examination." *Essay*, Bk. IV, ch. 2, sec. 1.

ently to his urgent request. I should say that there is probably an ink-bottle
here but that I could not *guarantee* it, and that if he needs one very desperately and at once then he had better look elsewhere. In short, I wish to make
it clear that my statement "Here is an ink-bottle" is strictly about physical
things and not about "sensations," "sense-data," or "appearances."[11]

Let us go back to Prichard's remark that we can determine by reflection
whether we know something or merely believe it. Prichard would think that
"knowledge in the weak sense" is mere belief and not knowledge. This is
wrong. But if we let ourselves speak this way, we can then see some
justification for Prichard's remark. For then he would be asserting, among
other things, that we can determine by reflection whether we know something in the strong sense or in the weak sense. This is not literally true;
however, there is this truth in it—that reflection can make us realize that we
are *using* "I know it" in the strong (or weak) sense in a particular case.
Prichard says that reflection can show us that "our condition is one of
knowing" a certain thing, or instead that "our condition is one of believing
and not of knowing" that thing. I do not understand what could be meant
here by "our condition." The way I should put it is that reflection on *what
we should think* if certain things were to happen may make us realize that
we should (or should not) call those things "proof" or "evidence" that what
we claim to know is not so. I have tried to show that the distinction between
strong and weak knowledge does not run parallel to the distinction between
a priori and empirical knowledge but cuts across it, i.e., these two kinds of
knowledge may be distinguished *within* a priori knowledge and *within*
empirical knowledge.

Reflection can make me realize that I am using "know" in the strong
sense; but can reflection show me that I *know* something in the strong sense
(or in the weak)? It is not easy to state the logical facts here. On the one
hand, if I make an assertion of the form "I know that *p*" it does not follow
that *p*, whether or not I am using "know" in the strong sense. If I have said
to someone outside my room "Of course, I know that Freddie is in here,"
and I am speaking in the strong sense, it does not *follow* that Freddie is
where I claim he is. This logical fact would not be altered even if I *realized*
that I was using "know" in the strong sense. My reflection on what I should
say if . . . , cannot show me that I *know* something. From the fact that I
should not call anything "evidence" that Freddie is not here, it does not
follow that he *is* here; therefore, it does not follow that I *know* he is here.

On the other hand, in an actual case of my using "know" in the strong
sense, I cannot envisage a possibility that what I say to be true should turn
out to be not true. If I were speaking of *another person's* assertion about
something, I *could* think both that he is using "know" in the strong sense
and that nonetheless what he claims he knows to be so might turn out to be
not so. But *in my own case* I cannot have this conjunction of thoughts, and
this is a logical and not a psychological fact. When *I* say that I know

11 [The remainder of the essay is newly written. The original conclusion was wrongly
stated. The reader is referred to the following exchange between Richard Taylor and
myself, in respect to the original paper: Taylor, "A Note on Knowledge and Belief,"
Analysis, XIII, June 1953; Malcolm, "On Knowledge and Belief," *Analysis*, XIV, March
1954; Taylor, "Rejoinder to Mr. Malcolm," *ibid.*]

something to be so, using "know" in the strong sense, it is unintelligible *to me* (although perhaps not to others) to suppose that anything could prove that it is not so and, therefore, that I do not know it.[12]

[12] This is the best summary I can give of what is wrong and right in Prichard's claim that one can determine by reflection whether one knows something or merely believes it. A good part of the ideas in this essay were provoked by conversations with Wittgenstein. A brief and rough account of those talks is to be found in my *Ludwig Wittgenstein: A Memoir* (New York: Oxford University Press, 1958), pp. 87–92. Jaakko Hintikka provides an acute treatment of the topic of "knowing that one knows," with special reference to Prichard's claim. See his *Knowledge and Belief* (Ithaca: Cornell University Press, 1962), ch. 5.

Truth

13

PRAGMATISM'S CONCEPTION OF TRUTH

William James

When Clerk-Maxwell was a child it is written that he had a mania for having everything explained to him, and that when people put him off with vague verbal accounts of any phenomenon he would interrupt them impatiently by saying, 'Yes; but I want you to tell me the *particular go* of it!' Had his question been about truth, only a pragmatist could have told him the particular go of it. I believe that our contemporary pragmatists, especially Messrs. Schiller and Dewey, have given the only tenable account of this subject. It is a very ticklish subject, sending subtle rootlets into all kinds of crannies, and hard to treat in the sketchy way that alone befits a public lecture. But the Schiller-Dewey view of truth has been so ferociously attacked by rationalistic philosophers, and so abominably misunderstood, that here, if anywhere, is the point where a clear and simple statement should be made.

>   .   .   .

Truth, as any dictionary will tell you, is a property of certain of our ideas. It means their 'agreement,' as falsity means their disagreement, with 'reality.' Pragmatists and intellectualists both accept this definition as a matter of course. They begin to quarrel only after the question is raised as to what may precisely be meant by the term 'agreement,' and what by the term 'reality,' when reality is taken as something for our ideas to agree with.

In answering these questions the pragmatists are more analytic and painstaking, the intellectualists more offhand and irreflective. The popular notion is that a true idea must copy its reality. Like other popular views, this one follows the analogy of the most usual experience. Our true ideas of sensible things do indeed copy them. Shut your eyes and think of yonder clock on the wall, and you get just such a true picture or copy of its dial. But your

From William James, *Pragmatism* (New York: Longmans, Green & Co. Limited, 1907), Lecture VI, pp. 197–227.

idea of its 'works' (unless you are a clock-maker) is much less of a copy, yet it passes muster, for it in no way clashes with the reality. Even though it should shrink to the mere word 'works,' that word still serves you truly; and when you speak of the 'time-keeping function' of the clock, or of its spring's 'elasticity,' it is hard to see exactly what your ideas can copy.

You perceive that there is a problem here. Where our ideas cannot copy definitely their object, what does agreement with that object mean? Some idealists seem to say that they are true whenever they are what God means that we ought to think about that object. Others hold the copy-view all through, and speak as if our ideas possessed truth just in proportion as they approach to being copies of the Absolute's eternal way of thinking.

These views, you see, invite pragmatistic discussion. But the great assumption of the intellectualists is that truth means essentially an inert static relation. When you've got your true idea of anything, there's an end of the matter. You're in possession; you *know;* you have fulfilled your thinking destiny. You are where you ought to be mentally; you have obeyed your categorical imperative; and nothing more need follow on that climax of your rational destiny. Epistemologically you are in stable equalibrium.

Pragmatism, on the other hand, asks its usual question. "Grant an idea or belief to be true," it says, "what concrete difference will its being true make in any one's actual life? How will the truth be realized? What experiences will be different from those which would obtain if the belief were false? What, in short, is the truth's cash-value in experiential terms?"

The moment pragmatism asks this question, it sees the answer: *True ideas are those that we can assimilate, validate, corroborate and verify. False ideas are those that we can not.* That is the practical difference it makes to us to have true ideas; that, therefore, is the meaning of truth, for it is all that truth is known-as.

This thesis is what I have to defend. The truth of an idea is not a stagnant property inherent in it. Truth *happens* to an idea. It *becomes* true, is *made* true by events. Its verity *is* in fact an event, a process: the process namely of its verifying itself, its veri-*fication*. Its validity is the process of its valid-*ation*.

But what do the words verification and validation themselves pragmatically mean? They again signify certain practical consequences of the verified and validated idea. It is hard to find any one phrase that characterizes these consequences better than the ordinary agreement-formula—just such consequences being what we have in mind whenever we say that our ideas 'agree' with reality. They lead us, namely, through the acts and other ideas which they instigate, into or up to, or towards, other parts of experience with which we feel all the while—such feeling being among our potentialities—that the original ideas remain in agreement. The connexions and transitions come to us from point to point as being progressive, harmonious, satisfactory. This function of agreeable leading is what we mean by an idea's verification. Such an account is vague and it sounds at first quite trivial, but it has results which it will take the rest of my [lecture] to explain.

Let me begin by reminding you of the fact that the possession of true thoughts means everywhere the possession of invaluable instruments of action; and that our duty to gain truth, so far from being a blank command from out of the blue, or a 'stunt' self-imposed by our intellect, can account for itself by excellent practical reasons.

The importance to human life of having true beliefs about matters of fact is a thing too notorious. We live in a world of realities that can be infinitely useful or infinitely harmful. Ideas that tell us which of them to expect count as the true ideas in all this primary sphere of verification, and the pursuit of such ideas is a primary human duty. The possession of truth, so far from being here an end in itself, is only a preliminary means towards other vital satisfactions. If I am lost in the woods and starved, and find what looks like a cow-path, it is of the utmost importance that I should think of a human habitation at the end of it, for if I do so and follow it, I save myself. The true thought is useful here because the house which is its object is useful. The practical value of true ideas is thus primarily derived from the practical importance of their objects to us. Their objects are, indeed, not important at all times. I may on another occasion have no use for the house; and then my idea of it, however verifiable, will be practically irrelevant, and had better remain latent. Yet since almost any object may some day become temporarily important, the advantage of having a general stock of *extra* truths, of ideas that shall be true of merely possible situations, is obvious. We store such extra truths away in our memories, and with the overflow we fill our books of reference. Whenever such an extra truth becomes practically relevant to one of our emergencies, it passes from cold-storage to do work in the world and our belief in it grows active. You can say of it then either that 'it is useful because it is true' or that 'it is true because it is useful.' Both these phrases mean exactly the same thing, namely that here is an idea that gets fulfilled and can be verified. True is the name for whatever idea starts the verification-process, useful is the name for its completed function in experience. True ideas would never have been singled out as such, would never have acquired a class-name, least of all a name suggesting value, unless they had been useful from the outset in this way.

From this simple cue pragmatism gets her general notion of truth as something essentially bound up with the way in which one moment in our experience may lead us towards other moments which it will be worth while to have been led to. Primarily, and on the common-sense level, the truth of a state of mind means this function of *a leading that is worth while*. When a moment in our experience, of any kind whatever, inspires us with a thought that is true, that means that sooner or later we dip by that thought's guidance into the particulars of experience again and make advantageous connexion with them. This is a vague enough statement, but I beg you to retain it, for it is essential.

Our experience meanwhile is all shot through with regularities. One bit of it can warn us to get ready for another bit, can 'intend' or be 'significant of' that remoter object. The object's advent is the significance's verification. Truth, in these cases, meaning nothing but eventual verification, is manifestly incompatible with waywardness on our part. Woe to him whose beliefs play fast and loose with the order which realities follow in his experience; they will lead him nowhere or else make false connexions.

By 'realities' or 'objects' here, we mean either things of common sense, sensibly present, or else common-sense relations, such as dates, places, distances, kinds, activities. Following our mental image of a house along the cow-path, we actually come to see the house; we get the image's full verification. *Such simply and fully verified leadings are certainly the originals and prototypes of the truth-process.* Experience offers indeed other forms of truth-process, but they are all conceivable as being primary verifications arrested, multiplied or substituted one for another.

Take, for instance, yonder object on the wall. You and I consider it to be a 'clock,' altho no one of us has seen the hidden works that make it one. We let our notion pass for true without attempting to verify. If truths mean verification-process essentially, ought we then to call such unverified truths as this abortive? No, for they form the overwhelmingly large number of the truths we live by. Indirect as well as direct verifications pass muster. Where circumstantial evidence is sufficient, we can go without eye-witnessing. Just as we here assume Japan to exist without ever having been there, because it *works* to do so, everything we know conspiring with the belief, and nothing interfering, so we assume that thing to be a clock. We *use* it as a clock, regulating the length of our lecture by it. The verification of the assumption here means its leading to no frustration or contradiction. Verifi*ability* of wheels and weights and pendulum is as good as verification. For one truth-process completed there are a million in our lives that function in this state of nascency. They turn us *towards* direct verification; lead us into the *surroundings* of the objects they envisage; and then, if everything runs on harmoniously, we are so sure that verification is possible that we omit it, and are usually justified by all that happens.

Truth lives, in fact, for the most part on a credit system. Our thoughts and beliefs 'pass,' so long as nothing challenges them, just as bank-notes pass so long as nobody refuses them. But this all points to direct face-to-face verifications somewhere, without which the fabric of truth collapses like a financial system with no cash-basis whatever. You accept my verification of one thing, I yours of another. We trade on each other's truth. But beliefs verified concretely by *somebody* are the posts of the whole superstructure.

Another great reason—beside economy of time—for waiving complete verification in the usual business of life is that all things exist in kinds and not singly. Our world is found once for all to have that peculiarity. So that when we have once directly verified our ideas about one specimen of a kind, we consider ourselves free to apply them to other specimens without verification. A mind that habitually discerns the kind of thing before it, and acts by the law of the kind immediately, without pausing to verify, will be a 'true' mind in ninety-nine out of a hundred emergencies, proved so by its conduct fitting everything it meets, and getting no refutation.

Indirectly or only potentially verifying processes may thus be true as well as full verification-processes. They work as true processes would work, give us the same advantages, and claim our recognition for the same reasons. All this on the common-sense level of matters of fact, which we are alone considering.

But matters of fact are not our only stock in trade. *Relations among purely mental ideas* form another sphere where true and false beliefs obtain, and here the beliefs are absolute, or unconditional. When they are true they bear the name either of definitions or of principles. It is either a principle or a definition that 1 and 1 make 2, that 2 and 1 make 3, and so on; that white differs less from gray than it does from black; that when the cause begins to act the effect also commences. Such propositions hold of all possible 'ones,' of all conceivable 'whites' and 'grays' and 'causes.' The objects here are mental objects. Their relations are perceptually obvious at a glance, and no sense-verification is necessary. Moreover, once true, always true, of those same mental objects. Truth here has an 'eternal' character. If you can find a concrete thing anywhere that is 'one' or 'white' or 'gray' or 'effect,' then your principles will everlastingly apply to it. It is but a case of ascertaining the kind, and then applying the law of its kind to the particular object. You are sure to get truth if you can but name the kind rightly, for your mental relations hold good of everything of that kind without exception. If you then, nevertheless, failed to get truth concretely, you would say that you had classed your real objects wrongly.

In this realm of mental relations, truth again is an affair of leading. We relate one abstract idea with another, framing in the end great systems of logical and mathematical truth, under the respective terms of which the sensible facts of experience eventually arrange themselves, so that our eternal truths hold good of realities also. This marriage of fact and theory is endlessly fertile. What we say is here already true in advance of special verification, *if we have subsumed our objects rightly*. Our ready-made ideal framework for all sorts of possible objects follows from the very structure of our thinking. We can no more play fast and loose with these abstract relations than we can do so with our sense-experiences. They coerce us; we must treat them consistently, whether or not we like the results. The rules of addition apply to our debts as rigorously as to our assets. The hundredth decimal of π, the ratio of the circumference to its diameter, is predetermined ideally now, tho no one may have computed it. If we should ever need the figure in our dealings with an actual circle we should need to have it given rightly, calculated by the usual rules; for it is the same kind of truth that those rules elsewhere calculate.

Between the coercions of the sensible order and those of the ideal order, our mind is thus wedged tightly. Our ideas must agree with realities, be such realities concrete or abstract, be they facts or be they principles, under penalty of endless inconsistency and frustration.

So far, intellectualists can raise no protest. They can only say that we have barely touched the skin of the matter.

Realities mean, then, either concrete facts, or abstract kinds of thing and relations perceived intuitively between them. They furthermore and thirdly mean, as things that new ideas of ours must no less take account of, the whole body of other truths already in our possession. But what now does 'agreement' with such threefold realities mean?—to use again the definition that is current.

Here it is that pragmatism and intellectualism begin to part company. Primarily, no doubt, to agree means to copy, but we saw that the mere word 'clock' would do instead of a mental picture of its works, and that of many realities our ideas can only be symbols and not copies. 'Past time,' 'power,' 'spontaneity,'—how can our mind copy such realities?

To 'agree' in the widest sense with a reality *can only mean to be guided either straight up to it or into its surroundings, or to be put into such working touch with it as to handle either it or something connected with it better than if we disagreed.* Better either intellectually or practically! And often agreement will only mean the negative fact that nothing contradictory from the quarter of that reality comes to interfere with the way in which our ideas guide us elsewhere. To copy a reality is, indeed, one very important way of agreeing with it, but it is far from being essential. The essential thing is the process of being guided. Any idea that helps us to *deal*, whether practically or intellectually, with either the reality or its belongings, that doesn't entangle our progress in frustrations, that *fits*, in fact, and adapts our life to the reality's whole setting, will agree sufficiently to meet the requirement. It will hold true of that reality.

Thus, *names* are just as 'true' or 'false' as definite mental pictures are. They set up similar verification-processes, and lead to fully equivalent practical results.

All human thinking gets discursified; we exchange ideas; we lend and borrow verifications, get them from one another by means of social intercourse. All truth thus gets verbally built out, stored up, and made available for every one. Hence, we must *talk* consistently just as we must *think* consistently: for both in talk and thought we deal with kinds. Names are arbitrary, but once understood they must be kept to. We mustn't now call Abel 'Cain' or Cain 'Abel.' If we do, we ungear ourselves from the whole book of Genesis, and from all its connexions with the universe of speech and fact down to the present time. We throw ourselves out of whatever truth that entire system of speech and fact may embody.

The overwhelming majority of our true ideas admit of no direct or face-to-face verification—those of past history, for example, as of Cain and Abel. The stream of time can be remounted only verbally, or verified indirectly by the present prolongations or effects of what the past harbored. Yet if they agree with these verbalities and effects, we can know that our ideas of the past are true. *As true as past time itself was*, so true was Julius Cæsar, so true were antediluvian monsters, all in their proper dates and settings. That past time itself was, is guaranteed by its coherence with everything that's present. True as the present *is*, the past *was* also.

Agreement thus turns out to be essentially an affair of leading—leading that is useful because it is into quarters that contain objects that are important. True ideas lead us into useful verbal and conceptual quarters as well as directly up to useful sensible termini. They lead to consistency, stability and flowing human intercourse. They lead away from excentricity and isolation, from foiled and barren thinking. The untrammelled flowing of the leading-process, its general freedom from clash and contradiction, passes for its indirect verification; but all roads lead to Rome, and in the end and eventually, all true processes must lead to the face of directly verifying sensible experiences *somewhere*, which sombody's ideas have copied.

Such is the large loose way in which the pragmatist interprets the word agreement. He treats it altogether practically. He lets it cover any process of conduction from a present idea to a future terminus, provided only it run prosperously. It is only thus that 'scientific' ideas, flying as they do beyond common sense, can be said to agree with their realities. It is, as I have already said, *as if* reality were made of ether, atoms or electrons, but we mustn't think so literally. The term 'energy' doesn't even pretend to stand for anything 'objective.' It is only a way of measuring the surface of phenomena so as to string their changes on a simple formula.

Yet in the choice of these man-made formulas we can not be capricious with impunity any more than we can be capricious on the common-sense practical level. We must find a theory that will *work;* and that means something extremely difficult; for our theory must mediate between all previous truths and certain new experiences. It must derange common sense and previous belief as little as possible, and it must lead to some sensible terminus or other that can be verified exactly. To 'work' means both these things; and the squeeze is so tight that there is little loose play for any hypothesis. Our theories are wedged and controlled as nothing else is. Yet sometimes alternative theoretic formulas are equally compatible with all the truths we know, and then we choose between them for subjective reasons. We choose the kind of theory to which we are already partial; we follow 'elegance' or 'economy.' Clerk-Maxwell somewhere says it would be 'poor scientific taste' to choose the more complicated of two equally well-evidenced conceptions; and you will all agree with him. Truth in science is what gives us the maximum possible sum of satisfactions, taste included, but consistency both with previous truth and with novel fact is always the most imperious claimant.

I have led you through a very sandy desert. But now, if I may be allowed so vulgar an expression, we begin to taste the milk in the coconut. Our rationalist critics here discharge their batteries upon us, and to reply to them will take us out from all this dryness into full sight of a momentous philosophical alternative.

Our account of truth is an account of truths in the plural, of processes of leading, realized *in rebus* [in things themselves], and having only this quality in common, that they *pay*. They pay by guiding us into or towards some part of a system that dips at numerous points into sense-percepts, which we may copy mentally or not, but with which at any rate we are now in the kind of commerce vaguely designated as verification. Truth for us is simply a collective name for verification-processes, just as health, wealth, strength, etc., are names for other processes connected with life, and also pursued because it pays to pursue them. Truth is *made*, just as health, wealth and strength are made, in the course of experience.

Here rationalism is instantaneously up in arms against us. I can imagine a rationalist to talk as follows:

"Truth is not made," he will say; "it absolutely obtains, being a unique relation that does not wait upon any process, but shoots straight over the head of experience, and hits its reality every time. Our belief that yon thing on the wall is a clock is true already, altho no one in the whole history of the world should verify it. The bare quality of standing in that transcendent relation is what makes any thought true that possesses it, whether or not there be verification. You pragmatists put the cart before the horse in

making truth's being reside in verification-processes. These are merely signs
of its being, merely our lame ways of ascertaining after the fact, which of
our ideas already has possessed the wondrous quality. The quality itself is
timeless, like all essences and natures. Thoughts partake of it directly, as
they partake of falsity or of irrelevancy. It can't be analyzed away into
pragmatic consequences."

The whole plausibility of this rationalist tirade is due to the fact to which
we have already paid so much attention. In our world, namely, abounding as
it does in things of similar kinds and similarly associated, one verification
serves for others of its kind, and one great use of knowing things is to be led
not so much to them as to their associates, especially to human talk about
them. The quality of truth, obtaining *ante rem* [prior to an examination of
particular things in the world], pragmatically means, then, the fact that in
such a world innumerable ideas work better by their indirect or possible than
by their direct and actual verification. Truth *ante rem* means only verifiability, then; or else it is a case of the stock rationalist trick of treating the *name*
of a concrete phenomenal reality as an independent prior entity, and placing
it behind the reality as its explanation.

.   .   .

In the case of 'wealth' we all see the fallacy. We know that wealth is but a
name for concrete processes that certain men's lives play a part in, and not a
natural excellence found in Messrs. Rockefeller and Carnegie, but not in the
rest of us.

Like wealth, health also lives *in rebus*. It is a name for processes, as
digestion, circulation, sleep, etc., that go on happily, tho in this instance we
are more inclined to think of it as a principle and to say the man digests and
sleeps so well *because* he is so healthy.

With 'strength' we are, I think, more rationalistic still, and decidedly
inclined to treat it as an excellence pre-existing in the man and explanatory
of the herculean performances of his muscles.

With 'truth' most people go over the border entirely, and treat the
rationalistic account as self-evident. But really all these words in *th* are
exactly similar. Truth exists *ante rem* just as much and as little as the other
things do.

The scholastics, following Aristotle, made much of the distinction between habit and act. Health *in actu* [fully realized and actual] means, among
other things, good sleeping and digesting. But a healthy man need not always
be sleeping, or always digesting, any more than a wealthy man need be
always handling money, or a strong man always lifting weights. All such
qualities sink to the status of 'habits' between their times of exercise; and
similarly truth becomes a habit of certain of our ideas and beliefs in their
intervals of rest from their verifying activities. But those activities are the
root of the whole matter, and the condition of there being any habit to exist
in the intervals.

'*The true,*' *to put it very briefly, is only the expedient in the way of our
thinking, just as* '*the right*' *is only the expedient in the way of our behaving.*
Expedient in almost any fashion; and expedient in the long run and on the
whole of course; for what meets expediently all the experience in sight
won't necessarily meet all farther experiences equally satisfactorily. Experi-

ence, as we know, has ways of *boiling over*, and making us correct our present formulas.

The 'absolutely' true, meaning what no farther experience will ever alter, is that ideal vanishing-point towards which we imagine that all our temporary truths will some day converge. It runs on all fours with the perfectly wise man, and with the absolutely complete experience; and, if these ideals are ever realized, they will all be realized together. Meanwhile we have to live to-day by what truth we can get to-day, and be ready to-morrow to call it falsehood. Ptolemaic astronomy, euclidean space, aristotelian logic, scholastic metaphysics, were expedient for centuries, but human experience has boiled over those limits, and we now call these things only relatively true, or true within those borders of experience. 'Absolutely' they are false; for we know that those limits were casual, and might have been transcended by past theorists just as they are by present thinkers.

When new experiences lead to retrospective judgments, using the past tense, what these judgments utter *was* true, even tho no past thinker had been led there. We live forwards, a Danish thinker has said, but we understand backwards. The present sheds a backward light on the world's previous processes. They may have been truth-processes for the actors in them. They are not so for one who knows the later revelations of the story.

This regulative notion of a potential better truth to be established later, possibly to be established some day absolutely, and having powers of retroactive legislation, turns its face, like all pragmatist notions, towards concreteness of fact, and towards the future. Like the half-truths, the absolute truth will have to be *made*, made as a relation incidental to the growth of a mass of verification-experience, to which the half-true ideas are all along contributing their quota.

I have already insisted on the fact that truth is made largely out of previous truths. Men's beliefs at any time are so much experience *funded*. But the beliefs are themselves parts of the sum total of the world's experience, and become matter, therefore, for the next day's funding operations. So far as reality means experienceable reality, both it and the truths men gain about it are everlastingly in process of mutation—mutation towards a definite goal, it may be—but still mutation.

Mathematicians can solve problems with two variables. On the Newtonian theory, for instance, acceleration varies with distance, but distance also varies with acceleration. In the realm of truth-processes facts come independently and determine our beliefs provisionally. But these beliefs make us act, and as fast as they do so, they bring into sight or into existence new facts which re-determine the beliefs accordingly. So the whole coil and ball of truth, as it rolls up, is the product of a double influence. Truths emerge from facts; but they dip forward into facts again and add to them; which facts again create or reveal new truth (the word is indifferent) and so on indefinitely. The 'facts' themselves meanwhile are not *true*. They simply *are*. Truth is the function of the beliefs that start and terminate among them.

. . .

The most fateful point of difference between being a rationalist and being a pragmatist is now fully in sight. Experience is in mutation, and our psychological ascertainments of truth are in mutation—so much rationalism will allow; but never that either reality itself or truth itself is mutable. Reality stands complete and ready-made from all eternity, rationalism insists, and the agreement of our ideas with it is that unique unanalyzable virtue in them of which she has already told us. As that intrinsic excellence, their truth has nothing to do with our experiences. It adds nothing to the content of experience. It makes no difference to reality itself; it is supervenient, inert, static, a reflexion merely. It doesn't *exist*, it *holds* or *obtains*, it belongs to another dimension from that of either facts or fact-relations, belongs, in short, to the epistemological dimension—and with that big word rationalism closes the discussion.

Thus, just as pragmatism faces forward to the future, so does rationalism here again face backward to a past eternity. True to her inveterate habit, rationalism reverts to 'principles,' and thinks that when an abstraction once is named, we own an oracular solution.

14

WILLIAM JAMES'S CONCEPTION OF TRUTH

Bertrand Russell

"The history of philosophy," as William James observes, "is to a great extent that of a certain clash of human temperaments." In dealing with a temperament of such charm as his, it is not pleasant to think of a "clash"; one does not willingly differ, or meet so much urbanity by churlish criticisms. Fortunately, a very large part of his book is concerned with the advocacy of positions which pragmatism shares with other forms of empiricism; with all this part of his book, I, as an empiricist, find myself, broadly speaking, in agreement.

James, like most philosophers, represents his views as mediating between two opposing schools. He begins by distinguishing two philosophic types called respectively the "tender-minded" and the "tough-minded." The "tender-minded" are "rationalistic, intellectualistic, idealistic, optimistic, religious, free-willist, monistic, dogmatical." The "tough-minded" are "empiricist, sensationalistic, materialistic, pessimistic, irreligious, fatalistic, pluralistic, sceptical." Traditionally, German philosophy was on the whole "tender-minded," British philosophy was on the whole "tough-minded." It will clear the ground for me to confess at once that I belong, with some reserves, to the "tough-minded" type. Pragmatism, William James avers, "can satisfy both kinds of demand. It can remain religious like the rationalisms, but at the same time, like the empiricisms, it can preserve the richest intimacy with facts." This reconciliation, to my mind, is illusory; I find myself agreeing with the "tough-minded" half of pragmatism and totally disagreeing with the "tender-minded" half. But the disentangling of the two halves must be postponed till we have seen how the reconciliation professes to be effected. Pragmatism represents, on the one hand, a method and habit of mind, on the other, a certain theory as to what constitutes truth. The latter is more nearly what Dr. Schiller calls humanism; but this name is not

From Bertrand Russell, *Philosophical Essays* (London: George Allen & Unwin Ltd., 1910), pp. 127–149. Reprinted by permission of the publisher.

adopted by James. We must, therefore, distinguish the pragmatic *method* and the pragmatic *theory of truth*. The former, up to a point, is involved in all induction, and is certainly largely commendable. The latter is the essential novelty and the point of real importance. But let us first consider the pragmatic method.

"Pragmatism," says James, "represents a perfectly familiar attitude in philosophy, the empiricist attitude, but it represents it, as it seems to me, both in a more radical and in a less objectionable form that it has ever yet assumed. A pragmatist turns his back resolutely and once for all upon a lot of inveterate habits dear to professional philosophers. He turns away from abstraction and insufficiency, from verbal solutions, from bad *a priori* reasons, from fixed principles, closed systems, and pretended absolutes and origins. He turns towards concreteness and adequacy, towards facts, towards action and towards power. That means the empiricist temper regnant and the rationalist temper sincerely given up. It means the open air and possibilities of nature, as against dogma, artificiality, and the pretence of finality in truth."

The temper of mind here described is one with which I, for my part, in the main cordially sympathise. But I think there is an impression in the mind of William James, as of some other pragmatists, that pragmatism involves a more open mind than its opposite. As regards scientific questions, or even the less important questions of philosophy, this is no doubt more or less the case. But as regards the fundamental questions of philosophy—especially as regards what I consider *the* fundamental question, namely, the nature of truth—pragmatism is absolutely dogmatic. The hypothesis that pragmatism is erroneous is not allowed to enter for the pragmatic competition; however well it may work, it is not to be entertained. To "turn your back resolutely and once for all" upon the philosophy of others may be heroic or praiseworthy, but it is not undogmatic or open-minded. A modest shrinking from self-assertion, a sense that all our theories are provisional, a constant realisation that after all the hypothesis of our opponents may be the right one—these characterise the truly empirical temper, but I do not observe that they invariably characterise the writings of pragmatists. Dogmatism in fundamentals is more or less unavoidable in philosophy, and I do not blame pragmatists for what could not be otherwise; but I demur to their claim to a greater open-mindedness than is or may be possessed by their critics.

William James, however, it must be admitted, is about as little pontifical as a philosopher well can be. And his complete absence of unction is most refreshing. "In this real world of sweat and dirt," he says, "it seems to me that when a view of things is 'noble,' that ought to count as a presumption against its truth and as a philosophic disqualification." Accordingly his contentions are never supported by "fine writing"; he brings them into the market-place, and is not afraid to be homely, untechnical, and slangy. All this makes his books refreshing to read, and shows that they contain what he really lives by, not merely what he holds in his professional capacity.

But it is time to return to the pragmatic method.

"The pragmatic method," we are told, "is primarily a method of settling metaphysical disputes that otherwise might be interminable. Is the world one or many?—fated or free?—material or spiritual?—here are notions either of which may or may not hold good of the world; and disputes over such notions are unending. The pragmatic method in such cases is to try to interpret each notion by tracing its respective practical consequences. What difference would it practically make to any one if this notion rather than that notion were true? If no practical difference whatever can be traced, then the alternatives mean practically the same thing, and all dispute is idle. Whenever a dispute is serious, we ought to be able to show some practical difference that must follow from one side or the other's being right." And again: "To attain perfect clearness in our thoughts of an object, then, we need only consider what conceivable effects of a practical kind the object may involve—what sensations we are to expect from it, and what reactions we must prepare. Our conception of these effects, whether immediate or remote, is then for us the whole of our conception of the object, so far as that conception has positive significance at all."

To this method, applied within limits and to suitable topics, there is no ground for objecting. On the contrary, it is wholesome to keep in touch with concrete facts, as far as possible, by remembering to bring our theories constantly into connection with them. The method, however, involves more than is stated in the extract which I quoted just now. It involves also the suggestion of the pragmatic criterion of truth: a belief is to be judged true in so far as the practical consequences of its adoption are good. Some pragmatists, for example, Le Roy (who has lately suffered Papal condemnation), regard the pragmatic test as giving *only* a criterion;[1] others, notably Dr. Schiller, regard it as giving the actual *meaning* of truth. William James agrees on this point with Dr. Schiller, though, like him, he does not enter into the question of criterion *versus* meaning.

The pragmatic theory of truth is the central doctrine of pragmatism, and we must consider it at some length. William James states it in various ways, some of which I shall now quote. He says: "Ideas (which themselves are but parts of our experience) become true just in so far as they help us to get into satisfactory relation with other parts of our experience." Again: "Truth is *one species of good*, and not, as is usually supposed, a category distinct from good, and co-ordinate with it. *The true is the name of whatever proves itself to be good in the way of belief, and good, too, for definite, assignable reasons.*" That truth means "agreement with reality" may be said by a pragmatist as well as by any one else, but the pragmatist differs from others as to what is meant by *agreement*, and also (it would seem) as to what is meant by *reality*. William James gives the following definition of agreement: "To 'agree' in the widest sense with a reality *can only mean to be guided either straight up to it or into its surroundings, or to be put into such working touch with it as to handle either it or something connected with it better than if we disagreed.*" This language is rather metaphorical, and a little puzzling; it is plain, however, that "agreement" is regarded as practical, not as merely intellectual. This emphasis on practice is, of course, one of the leading features of pragmatism.

In order to understand the pragmatic notion of truth, we have to be clear as to the basis of *fact* upon which truths are supposed to rest. Immediate sensible experience, for example, does not come under the alternative of *true* and *false*. "Day follows day," says James, "and its contents are simply added.

---

[1] Cf., e.g., Le Roy, "Comment se pose le problème de Dieu," *Revue de Métaphysique et de Morale*, xv. 4 (July, 1907), pp. 506, 507 *n*.

The new contents themselves are not true, they simply *come* and *are*. Truth is *what we say about* them." Thus when we are merely aware of sensible objects, we are not to be regarded as knowing any truth, although we have a certain kind of contact with reality. It is important to realise that the *facts* which thus lie outside the scope of truth and falsehood supply the material which is presupposed by the pragmatic theory. Our beliefs have to agree with matters of fact: it is an essential part of their "satisfactoriness" that they should do so. James also mentions what he calls "relations among purely mental ideas" as part of our stock-in-trade with which pragmatism starts. He mentions as instances "1 and 1 make 2," "white differs less from grey than it does from black," and so on. All such propositions as these, then, we are supposed to know for certain before we can get under way. As James puts it: "Between the coercions of the sensible order and those of the ideal order, our mind is thus wedged tightly. Our ideas must agree with realities, be such realities concrete or abstract, be they facts or be they principles, under penalty of endless inconsistency and frustration." Thus it is only when we pass beyond plain matters of fact and *a priori* truisms that the pragmatic notion of truth comes in. It is, in short, the notion to be applied to doubtful cases, but it is not the notion to be applied to cases about which there can be no doubt. And that there are cases about which there can be no doubt is presupposed in the very statement of the pragmatist position. 'Our account of truth," James tells us, "is an account . . . of processes of leading, realised *in rebus*, and having only this quality in common, that they *pay*." We may thus sum up the philosophy in the following definition: "A truth is anything which it pays to believe." Now, if this definition is to be useful, as pragmatism intends it to be, it must be possible to know that it pays to believe something without knowing anything that pragmatism would call a truth. Hence the knowledge that a certain belief pays must be classed as knowledge of a sensible fact or of a "relation among purely mental ideas," or as some compound of the two, and must be so easy to discover as not to be worthy of having the pragmatic test applied to it. There is, however, some difficulty in this view. Let us consider for a moment what it means to say that a belief "pays." We must suppose that this means that the consequences of entertaining the belief are better than those of rejecting it. In order to know this, we must know what are the consequences of entertaining it, and what are the consequences of rejecting it; we must know also what consequences are good, what bad, what consequences are better, and what worse. Take, say, belief in the Roman Catholic Faith. This, we may agree, causes a certain amount of happiness at the expense of a certain amount of stupidity and priestly domination. Such a view is disputable and disputed, but we will let that pass. But then comes the question whether, admitting the effects to be such, they are to be classed as on the whole good or on the whole bad; and this question is one which is so difficult that our test of truth becomes practically useless. It is far easier, it seems to me, to settle the plain question of fact: "Have Popes been always infallible?" than to settle the question whether the effects of thinking them infallible are on the whole good. Yet this question, of the truth of Roman Catholicism, is just the sort of question that pragmatists consider specially suitable to their method.

The notion that it is quite easy to know when the consequences of a belief are good, so easy, in fact, that a theory of knowledge need take no account of anything so simple—this notion, I must say, seems to me one of the strangest assumptions for a theory of knowledge to make. Let us take another illustration. Many of the men of the French Revolution were disciples of Rousseau, and their belief in his doctrines had far-reaching effects, which make Europe at this day a different place from what it would have been without that belief. If, on the whole, the effects of their belief have been good, we shall have to say that their belief was true; if bad, that it was false. But how are we to strike the balance? It is almost impossible to disentangle what the effects have been; and even if we could ascertain them, our judgment as to whether they have been good or bad would depend upon our political opinions. It is surely far easier to discover by direct investigation that the *Contrat Social* is a myth than to decide whether belief in it has done harm or good on the whole.

Another difficulty which I feel in regard to the pragmatic meaning of "truth" may be stated as follows: Suppose I accept the pragmatic criterion, and suppose you persuade me that a certain belief is useful. Suppose I thereupon conclude that the belief is true. Is it not obvious that there is a transition in my mind from seeing that the belief is useful to actually holding that the belief is true? Yet this could not be so if the pragmatic account of truth were valid. Take, say, the belief that other people exist. According to the pragmatists, to say "it is true that other people exist" *means* "it is useful to believe that other people exist." But if so, then these two phrases are merely different words for the same proposition; therefore when I believe the one I believe the other. If this were so, there could be no transition from the one to the other, as plainly there is. This shows that the word "true" represents for us a different idea from that represented by the phrase "useful to believe," and that, therefore, the pragmatic definition of truth ignores, without destroying, the meaning commonly given to the word "true," which meaning, in my opinion, is of fundamental importance, and can only be ignored at the cost of hopeless inadequacy.

This brings me to the difference between *criterion* and *meaning*—a point on which neither James nor Dr. Schiller is very clear. I may best explain the difference, to begin with, by an instance. If you wish to know whether a certain book is in a library, you consult the catalogue: books mentioned in the catalogue are presumably in the library, books not mentioned in it are presumably not in the library. Thus the catalogue affords a *criterion* of whether a book is in the library or not. But even supposing the catalogue perfect, it is obvious that when you say the book is in the library you do not *mean* that it is mentioned in the catalogue. You mean that the actual book is to be found somewhere in the shelves. It therefore remains an intelligible hypothesis that there are books in the library which are not yet catalogued, or that there are books catalogued which have been lost and are no longer in the library. And it remains an inference from the discovery that a book is mentioned in the catalogue to the conclusion that the book is in the library. Speaking abstractly, we may say that a property A is a *criterion* of a property B when the same objects possess both; and A is a *useful* criterion of B if it is easier to discover whether an object possesses the property A than whether it possesses the property B. Thus being mentioned in the catalogue is a *useful* criterion of being in the library, because it is easier to consult the catalogue than to hunt through the shelves.

Now if pragmatists only affirmed that utility is a *criterion* of truth, there would be much less to be said against their view. For there certainly seem to be few cases, if any, in which it is clearly useful to believe what is false. The chief criticism one would then have to make on pragmatism would be to deny that utility is a *useful* criterion, because it is so often harder to determine whether a belief is useful than whether it is true. The arguments of pragmatists are almost wholly directed to proving that utility is a *criterion;* that utility is the *meaning* of truth is then supposed to follow. But, to return to our illustration of the library, suppose we had conceded that there are no mistakes in the British Museum catalogue: would it follow that the catalogue would do without the books? We can imagine some person long engaged in a comparative study of libraries, and having, in the process, naturally lost all taste for reading, declaring that the catalogue is the only important thing—as for the books, they are useless lumber; no one ever wants them, and the principle of economy should lead us to be content with the catalogue. Indeed, if you consider the matter with an open mind, you will see that the catalogue *is* the library, for it tells you everything you can possibly wish to know about the library. Let us, then, save the taxpayers' money by destroying the books: allow free access to the catalogue, but condemn the desire to read as involving an exploded dogmatic realism.

This analogy of the library is not, to my mind, fantastic or unjust, but as close and exact an analogy as I have been able to think of. The point I am trying to make clear is concealed from pragmatists, I think, by the fact that their theories start very often from such things as the general hypotheses of science—ether, atoms, and the like. In such cases, we take little interest in the hypotheses themselves, which, as we well know, are liable to rapid change. What we care about are the inferences as to sensible phenomena which the hypotheses enable us to make. All we ask of the hypotheses is that they should "work"—though it should be observed that what constitutes "working" is not the general agreeableness of their results, but the conformity of these results with observed phenomena. But in the case of these general scientific hypotheses, no sensible man believes that they are true as they stand. They are believed to be true in part, and to work because of the part that is true; but it is expected that in time some element of falsehood will be discovered, and some truer theory will be substituted. Thus pragmatism would seem to derive its notion of what constitutes belief from cases in which, properly speaking, belief is absent, and in which—what is pragmatically important—there is but a slender interest in truth or falsehood as compared to the interest in what "works."

But when this method is extended to cases in which the proposition in question has an emotional interest on its own account, apart from its working, the pragmatic account becomes less satisfactory. This point has been well brought out by Prof. Stout in *Mind*,[2] and what I have to say is mostly contained in his remarks. Take the question whether other people exist. It seems perfectly possible to suppose that the hypothesis that they

[2] October, 1907, pp. 586–8. This criticism occurs in the course of a very sympathetic review of Dr. Schiller's *Studies in Humanism*.

exist will always work, even if they do not in fact exist. It is plain, also, that it makes for happiness to believe that they exist—for even the greatest misanthropist would not wish to be deprived of the objects of his hate. Hence the belief that other people exist is, pragmatically, a true belief. But if I am troubled by solipsism, the discovery that a belief in the existence of others is "true" in the pragmatist's sense is not enough to allay my sense of loneliness: the perception that I should profit by rejecting solipsism is not alone sufficient to make me reject it. For what I desire is not that the belief in solipsism should be false in the pragmatic sense, but that other people should in fact exist. And with the pragmatist's meaning of truth, these two do not necessarily go together. The belief in solipsism might be false even if I were the only person or thing in the universe.

This paradoxical consequence would, I presume, not be admitted by pragmatists. Yet it is an inevitable outcome of the divorce which they make between *fact* and *truth*. Returning to our illustration, we may say that "facts" are represented by the books, and "truths" by the entries in the catalogue. So long as you do not wish to read the books, the "truths" will do in place of the "facts," and the imperfections of your library can be remedied by simply making new entries in the catalogue. But as soon as you actually wish to read a book, the "truths" become inadequate, and the "facts" become all-important. The pragmatic account of truth assumes, so it seems to me, that no one takes any interest in facts, and that the truth of the proposition that your friend exists is an adequate substitute for the fact of his existence. "Facts," they tell us, are neither true nor false, therefore truth cannot be concerned with them. But the truth "A exists," if it is a truth, is concerned with A, who in that case is a fact; and to say that "A exists" may be true even if A does not exist is to give a meaning to "truth" which robs it of all interest. Dr. Schiller is fond of attacking the view that truth must correspond with reality; we may conciliate him by agreeing that *his* truth, at any rate, need not correspond with reality. But we shall have to add that reality is to us more interesting than such truth.

I am, of course, aware that pragmatists minimise the basis of "fact," and speak of the "making of reality" as proceeding *pari passu* with the "making of truth." It is easy to criticise the claim to "make reality" except within obvious limits. But when such criticisms are met by pointing to the pragmatist's admission that, after all, there must be a basis of "fact" for our creative activity to work upon, then the opposite line of criticism comes into play. Dr. Schiller, in his essay on "the making of reality," minimises the importance of the basis of "fact," on the ground (it would seem) that "facts" will not submit to pragmatic treatment, and that, if pragmatism is true, they are unknowable.[3] Hence, on pragmatistic principles, it is useless to think about facts. We therefore return to fictions with a sigh of relief, and soothe our scruples by calling them "realities." But it seems something of a *petitio principii* [begging of the question] to condemn "facts" because pragmatism, though it finds them necessary, is unable to deal with them. And William James, it should be said, makes less attempt than Dr. Schiller does to minimise facts. In this essay, therefore, I have considered the difficulties which pragmatism has to face if it admits "facts" rather than those (no less serious) which it has to face if it denies them.

[3] Cf. *Studies in Humanism*, pp. 434–6.

It is chiefly in regard to religion that the pragmatist use of "truth" seems to me misleading. Pragmatists boast much of their ability to reconcile religion and science, and William James, as we saw, professes to have discovered a position combining the merits of tender-mindedness and tough-mindedness. The combination is really effected, if I am not mistaken, in a way of which pragmatists are not themselves thoroughly aware. For their position, if they fully realised it, would, I think, be this: "We cannot know whether, in fact, there is a God or a future life, but we can know that the belief in God and a future life is true." This position, it is to be feared, would not afford much comfort to the religious if it were understood, and I cannot but feel some sympathy with the Pope in his condemnation of it.

"On pragmatic principles," James says, "we cannot reject any hypothesis if consequences useful to life flow from it." He proceeds to point out that consequences useful to life flow from the hypothesis of the Absolute, which is therefore so far a true hypothesis. But it should be observed that these useful consequences flow from the hypothesis that the Absolute is a fact, not from the hypothesis that useful consequences flow from belief in the Absolute. But we cannot believe the hypothesis that the Absolute is a fact merely because we perceive that useful consequences flow from this hypothesis. What we can believe on such grounds is that this hypothesis is what pragmatists call "true," i.e. that it is useful; but it is not from this belief that the useful consequences flow, and the grounds alleged do not make us believe that the Absolute is a fact, which is the useful belief. In other words, the useful belief is that the Absolute is a fact, and pragmatism shows that this belief is what it calls "true." Thus pragmatism persuades us that belief in the Absolute is "true," but does not persuade us that the Absolute is a fact. The belief which it persuades us to adopt is therefore not the one which is useful. In ordinary logic, if the belief in the Absolute is true, it follows that the Absolute is a fact. But with the pragmatist's meaning of "true" this does not follow; hence the proposition which he proves is not, as he thinks, the one from which comforting consequences flow.

In another place James says: "On pragmatistic principles, if the hypothesis of God works satisfactorily in the widest sense of the word, it is true." This proposition is, in reality, a mere tautology. For we have laid down the definition: "The word 'true' means 'working satisfactorily in the widest sense of the word.'" Hence the proposition stated by James is merely a verbal variant on the following: "On pragmatistic principles, if the hypothesis of God works satisfactorily in the widest sense of the word, then it works satisfactorily in the widest sense of the word." This would hold even on other than pragmatistic principles; presumably what is peculiar to pragmatism is the belief that this is an important contribution to the philosophy of religion. The advantage of the pragmatic method is that it decides the question of the truth of the existence of God by purely mundane arguments, namely, by the effects of belief in His existence upon our life in this world. But unfortunately this gives a merely mundane conclusion, namely, that belief in God is true, i.e. useful, whereas what religion desires is the conclusion that God exists, which pragmatism never even approaches. I infer, therefore, that the pragmatic philosophy of religion, like most philosophies whose conclusions are interesting, turns on an unconscious play upon words. A common word—in this case, the word "true"—is taken at the outset in an uncommon sense, but as the argument proceeds the usual sense of the word gradually slips back, and the conclusions arrived at seem, therefore, quite different from what they would be seen to be if the initial definition had been remembered.

The point is, of course, that, so soon as it is admitted that there are things that exist, it is impossible to avoid recognising a distinction, to which we may give what name we please, between believing in the existence of something that exists and believing in the existence of something that does not exist. It is common to call the one belief true, the other false. But if, with the pragmatists, we prefer to give a different meaning to the words "true" and "false," that does not prevent the distinction commonly called the distinction of "true" and "false" from persisting. The pragmatist attempt to ignore this distinction fails, as it seems to me, because a basis of fact cannot be avoided by pragmatism, and this basis of fact demands the *usual* antithesis of "true" and "false." It is hardly to be supposed that pragmatists will admit this conclusion. But it may be hoped that they will tell us in more detail how they propose to avoid it.

Pragmatism, if I have not misunderstood it, is largely a generalisation from the procedure of the inductive sciences. In so far as it lays stress upon the importance of induction, I find myself in agreement with it; and as to the nature of induction also, I think it is far more nearly right than are most of the traditional accounts. But on fundamental questions of philosophy I find myself wholly opposed to it, and unable to see that inductive procedure gives any warrant for its conclusions. To make this clear, I will very briefly explain how I conceive the nature and scope of induction.

When we survey our beliefs, we find that we hold different beliefs with very different degrees of conviction. Some—such as the belief that I am sitting in a chair, or that $2 + 2 = 4$—can be doubted by few except those who have had a long training in philosophy. Such beliefs are held so firmly that non-philosophers who deny them are put into lunatic asylums. Other beliefs, such as the facts of history, are held rather less firmly, but still in the main without much doubt where they are well authenticated. Beliefs about the future, as that the sun will rise to-morrow and that the trains will run approximately as in Bradshaw, may be held with almost as great conviction as beliefs about the past. Scientific laws are generally believed less firmly, and there is a gradation among them from such as seem nearly certain to such as have only a slight probability in their favour. Philosophical beliefs, finally, will, with most people, take a still lower place, since the opposite beliefs of others can hardly fail to induce doubt. Belief, therefore, is a matter of degree. To speak of belief, disbelief, doubt, and suspense of judgment as the only possibilities is as if, from the writing on the thermometer, we were to suppose that blood heat, summer heat, temperate, and freezing were the only temperatures. There is a continuous gradation in belief, and the more firmly we believe anything, the less willing we are to abandon it in case of conflict.

Besides the degree of our belief, there is another important respect in which a belief may vary, namely, in the extent to which it is *spontaneous* or *derivative*. A belief obtained by inference may be called *derivative;* one not so obtained, *spontaneous*. When we do not need any outside evidence to make us entertain a belief, we may say that what we believe is *obvious*. Our belief in the existence of sensible objects is of this nature: "seeing is believing," and we demand no further evidence. The same applies to certain logical principles, e.g. that whatever follows from a true proposition must be true. A proposition may be obvious in very varying degrees. For example, in matters of æsthetic taste we have to judge immediately whether a work of art is beautiful or not, but the degree of obviousness involved is probably small, so that we feel no very great confidence in our judgment. Thus our spontaneous beliefs are not necessarily stronger than derivative beliefs. Moreover, few beliefs, if any, are *wholly* spontaneous in an educated man. The more a man has organised his knowledge, the more his beliefs will be interdependent, and the more will obvious truths be reinforced by their connection with other obvious truths. In spite of this fact, however, obviousness remains always the ultimate source of our beliefs; for what is called verification or deduction consists always in being brought into relation with one or more obvious propositions. This process of verification is necessary even for propositions which seem obvious, since it appears on examination that two apparently obvious propositions may be inconsistent, and hence that apparent obviousness is not a sufficient guarantee of truth. We therefore have to subject our beliefs to a process of organisation, making groups of such as are mutually consistent, and when two such groups are not consistent with each other, selecting that group which seems to us to contain the most evidence, account being taken both of the degree of obviousness of the propositions it contains and of the number of such propositions. It is as the result of such a process, for example, that we are led, if we are led, to conclude that colours are not objective properties of things. Induction, in a broad sense, may be described as the process of selecting hypotheses which will organise our spontaneous beliefs, preserving as many of them as possible, and interconnecting them by general propositions which, as is said, "explain" them, i.e. give a ground from which they can be deduced. In this sense, all knowledge is inductive as soon as it is reflective and organised. In any science, there is a greater or less degree of obviousness about many of its propositions: those that are obvious are called *data;* other propositions are only accepted because of their connection with the data. This connection itself may be of two kinds, either that the propositions in question can be deduced from the data, or that the data can be deduced from the propositions in question, and we know of no way of deducing the data without assuming the propositions in question. The latter is the case of working hypotheses, which covers all the general laws of science and all the metaphysics both of common sense and of professed philosophy. It is, apparently, by generalising the conception of "working hypothesis" that pragmatism has arisen. But three points seem to me to have been overlooked in this generalisation. First, working hypotheses are only a small part of our beliefs, not the whole, as pragmatism seems to think. Secondly, prudent people give only a low degree of belief to working hypotheses; it is therefore a curious procedure to select them as the very types of beliefs in general. Thirdly, pragmatism seems to confound two very different conceptions of "working." When science says that a hypothesis works, it means that from this hypothesis we can deduce a number of propositions which are verifiable, i.e. obvious under suitable circumstances, and that we cannot deduce any propositions of which the contradictories are verifiable. But when *pragmatism* says that a hypothesis works, it means that the effects of believing it are good, including among the effects not only the beliefs which we deduce from it, but also the emotions entailed by it or its perceived consequences, and the actions to which we are prompted by it or its perceived consequences. This is a totally different conception of "working," and one for which the authority of scientific procedure cannot be invoked. I infer, therefore, that induction, rightly analysed, does not lead us to pragmatism, and that the inductive results which pragmatism takes as the very type of truth are precisely those among our beliefs which should be held with most caution and least conviction.

To sum up: while agreeing with the empirical temper of pragmatism, with its readiness to treat all philosophical tenets as "working hypotheses," we cannot agree that when we say a belief is true we mean that it is a hypothesis which "works," especially if we mean by this to take account of the excellence of its effects, and not merely of the truth of its consequences. If, to avoid disputes about words, we agree to accept the pragmatic definition of the word "truth," we find that the belief that A exists may be "true" even when A does not exist. This shows that the conclusions arrived at by pragmatism in the sphere of religion do not have the meaning which they appear to have, and are incapable, when rightly understood, of yielding us the satisfaction which they promise. The attempt to get rid of "fact" turns out to be a failure, and thus the old notion of truth reappears. And if the pragmatist states that utility is to be merely a *criterion* of truth, we shall reply first, that it is not a useful criterion, because it is usually harder to discover whether a belief is useful than whether it is true; secondly, that since no *a priori* reason is shown why truth and utility should always go together, utility can only be shown to be a criterion at all by showing inductively that it accompanies truth in all known instances, which requires that we should already know in many instances what things are true. Finally, therefore, the pragmatist theory of truth is to be condemned on the ground that it does not "work."

15

TRUTH

J. L. Austin

1. 'What is truth?' said jesting Pilate, and would not stay for an answer. Pilate was in advance of his time. For 'truth' itself is an abstract noun, a camel, that is, of a logical construction, which cannot get past the eye even of a grammarian. We approach it cap and categories in hand: we ask ourselves whether Truth is a substance (the Truth, the Body of Knowledge), or a quality (something like the colour red, inhering in truths), or a relation ('correspondence').[1] But philosophers should take something more nearly their own size to strain at. What needs discussing rather is the use, or certain uses, of the word 'true'. *In vino*, possibly, *'veritas'* ['truth'], but in a sober symposium *'verum'* ['true'].

2. What is it that we say is true or is false? Or, how does the phrase 'is true' occur in English sentences? The answers appear at first multifarious. We say (or are said to say) that beliefs are true, that descriptions or accounts are true, that propositions or assertions or statements are true, and that words or sentences are true: and this is to mention only a selection of the more obvious candidates. Again, we say (or are said to say) 'It is true that the cat is on the mat', or 'It is true to say that the cat is on the mat', or ' "The cat is on the mat" is true'. We also remark on occasion, when someone else has said something, 'Very true' or 'That's true' or 'True enough'.

Most (though not all) of these expressions, and others besides, certainly do occur naturally enough. But it seems reasonable to ask whether there is not some use of 'is true' that is primary, or some generic name for that which at bottom we are always saying 'is true'. Which, if any, of these expressions is to be taken *au pied de la lettre* [quite literally]? To answer this will not take us long, nor, perhaps, far: but in philosophy the foot of the letter is the foot of the ladder.

I suggest that the following are the primary forms of expression:

J. L. Austin, "Truth," *Proceedings of the Aristotelian Society*, Supplementary Vol. XXIV (1950), 111–128. Reprinted by courtesy of the Editor of The Aristotelian Society.
    [1] It is sufficiently obvious that 'truth' is a substantive, 'true' an adjective and 'of' in 'true of' a preposition.

It is true (to say) that the cat is on the mat.

That statement (of his, &c.) is true.

The statement that the cat is on the mat is true.

But first for the rival candidates.

(*a*) Some say that 'truth is primarily a property of beliefs'. But it may be doubted whether the expression 'a true belief' is at all common outside philosophy and theology: and it seems clear that a man is said to hold a true belief when and in the sense that he believes (in) *something which* is true, or believes that *something which* is true is true. Moreover if, as some also say, a belief is 'of the nature of a picture', then it is of the nature of what cannot be true, though it may be, for example, faithful.[2]

(*b*) True descriptions and true accounts are simply varieties of true statements or of collections of true statements, as are true answers and the like. The same applies to propositions too, in so far as they are genuinely said to be true (and not, as more commonly, sound, tenable and so on).[3] A proposition in law or in geometry is something portentous, usually a generalization, that we are invited to accept and that has to be recommended by argument: it cannot be a direct report on current observation— if you look and inform me that the cat is on the mat, that is not a proposition though it is a statement. In philosophy, indeed, 'proposition' is sometimes used in a special way for 'the meaning or sense of a sentence or family of sentences': but whether we think a lot or little of this usage, a proposition in this sense cannot, at any rate, be what we say is true or false. For we never say 'The meaning (or sense) of this sentence (or of these words) is true': what we do say is what the judge or jury says, namely that '*The words* taken in this sense, or if we assign to them such and such a meaning, or so interpreted or understood, *are true*'.

(*c*) Words and sentences are indeed said to be true, the former often, the latter rarely. But only in certain senses. Words as discussed by philologists, or by lexicographers, grammarians, linguists, phoneticians, printers, critics (stylistic or textual) and so on, are not true or false: they are wrongly formed, or ambiguous or defective or untranslatable or unpronounceable or mis-spelled or archaistic or corrupt or what not.[4] Sentences in similar contexts are elliptic or involved or alliterative or ungrammatical. We may, however, genuinely say 'His closing words were very true' or 'The third sentence on page 5 of his speech is quite false': but here 'words' and 'sentence' refer, as is shown by the demonstratives (possessive pronouns, temporal verbs, definite descriptions, &c.), which in this usage consistently accompany them, to the words or sentence *as used by a certain person on a*

---

[2] A likeness is true *to* life, but not true *of* it. A *word* picture can be true, just because it is *not* a picture.

[3] Predicates applicable also to 'arguments', which we likewise do not say are true, but, for example, valid.

[4] Peirce made a beginning by pointing out that there are two (or three) different senses of the word 'word', and adumbrated a technique ('counting' words) for deciding what is a 'different sense'. But his two senses are not well defined, and there are many more—the 'vocable' sense, the philologist's sense in which 'grammar' is the same word as 'glamour', the textual critic's sense in which the 'the' in l. 254 has been written twice, and so on. With all his 66 divisions of signs, Peirce does not, I believe, distinguish between a sentence and a statement.

certain occasion. That is, they refer (as does 'Many a true word spoken in jest') to *statements.*

A statement is made and its making is an historic event, the utterance by a certain speaker or writer of certain words (a sentence) to an audience with reference to an historic situation, event or what not.[5]

A sentence is made *up of* words, a statement is made *in* words. A sentence is not English or not good English, a statement is not in English or not in good English. Statements are made, words or sentences are used. We talk of *my* statement, but of *the English* sentence (if a sentence is mine, I coined it, but I do not coin statements). The *same* sentence is used in making *different* statements (I say 'It is mine', you say 'It is mine'): it may also be used on two occasions or by two persons in making the *same* statement, but for this the utterance must be made with reference to the same situation or event.[6] We speak of 'the statement that S,' but of 'the sentence "S" ', not of 'the sentence that S'.[7]

When I say that a statement is what is true, I have no wish to become wedded to one word. 'Assertion', for example, will in most contexts do just as well, though perhaps it is slightly wider. Both words share the weakness of being rather solemn (much more so than the more general 'what you said' or 'your words')—though perhaps we are generally being a little solemn when we discuss the truth of anything. Both have the merit of clearly referring to the historic use of a sentence by an utterer, and of being therefore precisely not equivalent to 'sentence'. For it is a fashionable mistake to take as primary '(The sentence) "S" is true (in the English language)'. Here the addition of the words 'in the English language' serves to emphasize that 'sentence' is not being used as equivalent to 'statement', so that it precisely is not what can be true or false (and moreover, 'true in the English language' is a solecism, mismodelled presumably, and with deplorable effect, on expressions like 'true in geometry').

3. When is a statement true? The temptation is to answer (at least if we confine ourselves to 'straightforward' statements): 'When it corresponds to the facts'. And as a piece of standard English this can hardly be wrong. Indeed, I must confess I do not really think it is wrong at all: the theory of truth is a series of truisms. Still, it can at least be misleading.

If there is to be communication of the sort that we achieve by language at all, there must be a stock of symbols of some kind which a communicator

---

[5] 'Historic' does not, of course, mean that we cannot speak of future or possible statements. A 'certain' speaker need not be any definite speaker. 'Utterance' need not be public utterance—the audience may be the speaker himself.

[6] 'The same' does not always mean the same. In fact it has no meaning in the way that an 'ordinary' word like 'red' or 'horse' has a meaning: it is a (the typical) device for establishing and distinguishing the meanings of ordinary words. Like 'real', it is part of our apparatus *in* words for fixing and adjusting the semantics *of* words.

[7] Inverted commas show that the words, though uttered (in writing), are not to be taken as a statement by the utterer. This covers two possible cases, (i) where what is to be discussed is the sentence, (ii) where what is to be discussed is a statement made elsewhere in the words 'quoted'. Only in case (i) is it correct to say simply that the token is doing duty for the type (and even here it is quite incorrect to say that 'The cat is on the mat' is the *name* of an English sentence—though possibly *The Cat is on the Mat* might be the title of a novel, or a bull might be known as *Catta est in matta*). Only in case (ii) is there something true or false, *viz.* (not the quotation but) the statement made in the words quoted.

('the speaker') can produce 'at will' and which a communicatee ('the audience') can observe: these may be called the 'words', though, of course, they need not be anything very like what we should normally call words—they might be signal flags, &c. There must also be something other than the words, which the words are to be used to communicate about: this may be called the 'world'. There is no reason why the world should not include the words, in every sense except the sense of the actual statement itself which on any particular occasion is being made about the world. Further, the world must exhibit (we must observe) similarities and dissimilarities (there could not be the one without the other): if everything were either absolutely indistinguishable from anything else or completely unlike anything else, there would be nothing to say. And finally (for present purposes—of course there are other conditions to be satisfied too) there must be two sets of conventions:

Descriptive conventions correlating the words (= sentences) with the *types* of situation, thing, event, &c., to be found in the world.

Demonstrative conventions correlating the words (= statements) with the *historic* situations, &c., to be found in the world.[8]

A statement is said to be true when the historic state of affairs to which it is correlated by the demonstrative conventions (the one to which it 'refers') is of a type[9] with which the sentence used in making it is correlated by the descriptive conventions.[10]

3a. Troubles arise from the use of the word 'facts' for the historic situations, events, &c., and in general, for the world. For 'fact' is regularly used in conjunction with 'that' in the sentences 'The fact is that S' or 'It is a fact that S' and in the expression 'the fact that S', all of which imply that it would be true to say that S.[11]

[8] Both sets of conventions may be included together under 'semantics'. But they differ greatly.

[9] 'Is of a type with which' means 'is sufficiently like those standard states of affairs with which'. Thus, for a statement to be true one state of affairs must be *like* certain others, which is a natural relation, but also *sufficiently* like to merit the same 'description', which is no longer a purely natural relation. To say 'This is red' is not the same as to say 'This is like those', nor even as to say 'This is like those which were called red'. That things are *similar*, or even 'exactly' similar, I may literally see, but that they are the *same* I cannot literally see—in calling them the same colour a convention is involved additional to the conventional choice of the name to be given to the colour which they are said to be.

[10] The trouble is that sentences contain words or verbal devices to serve both descriptive and demonstrative purposes (not to mention other purposes), often both at once. In philosophy we mistake the descriptive for the demonstrative (theory of universals) or the demonstrative for the descriptive (theory of monads). A sentence as normally distinguished from a mere word or phrase is characterized by its containing a minimum of verbal demonstrative devices (Aristotle's 'reference to time'); but many demonstrative conventions are non-verbal (pointing, &c.), and using these we can make a statement in a single word which is not a 'sentence'. Thus, 'languages' like that of (traffic, &c.) *signs* use quite distinct media for their descriptive and demonstrative elements (the sign on the post, the site of the post). And however many verbal demonstrative devices we use as auxiliaries, there must *always* be a non-verbal *origin* for these co-ordinates, which is the point of utterance of the statement.

[11] I use the following *abbreviations:*
S for the cat is on the mat.
ST for it is true that the cat is on the mat.
tst for the statement that.
I take tstS as my example throughout and not, say, tst Julius Caesar was bald or tst all

This may lead us to suppose that

  (i) 'fact' is only an alternative expression for 'true statement'. We note that
      when a detective says 'Let's look at the facts' he does not crawl round the
      carpet, but proceeds to utter a string of statements: we even talk of 'stating
      the facts';
 (ii) for every true statement there exists 'one' and its own precisely correspond-
      ing fact—for every cap the head it fits.

It is (i) which leads to some of the mistakes in 'coherence' or formalist
theories; (ii) to some of those in 'correspondence' theories. Either we
suppose that there is nothing there but the true statement itself, nothing to
which it corresponds, or else we populate the world with linguistic *Doppel-
gänger* [doubles] (and grossly overpopulate it—every nugget of 'positive'
fact overlaid by a massive concentration of 'negative' facts, every tiny
detailed fact larded with generous general facts, and so on).

When a statement is true, there is, *of course*, a state of affairs which makes
it true and which is *toto mundo* [entirely] distinct from the true statement
about it: but equally of course, we can only *describe* that state of affairs *in
words* (either the same or, with luck, others). I can only describe the
situation in which it is true to say that I am feeling sick by saying that it is
one in which I am feeling sick (or experiencing sensations of nausea):[12] yet
between stating, however truly, that I am feeling sick and feeling sick there
is a great gulf fixed.[13]

'Fact that' is a phrase designed for use in situations where the distinction
between a true statement and the state of affairs about which it is a truth is
neglected; as it often is with advantage in ordinary life, though seldom in
philosophy—above all in discussing truth, where it is precisely our business
to prise the words off the world and keep them off it. To ask 'Is the fact that
S the true statement that S or that which it is true of?' may beget absurd
answers. To take an analogy: although we may sensibly ask 'Do we *ride* the
word "elephant" or the animal?' and equally sensibly 'Do we *write* the word
or the animal?' it is nonsense to ask 'Do we *define* the word or the animal?'
For defining an elephant (supposing we ever do this) is a compendious
description of an operation involving both word and animal (do we focus the
image or the battleship?); and so speaking about 'the fact that' is a
compendious way of speaking about a situation involving both words and
world.[14]

---

mules are sterile, because these latter are apt in their different ways to make us overlook
the distinction between sentence and statement: we have, apparently, in the one case a
sentence capable of being used to refer to only one historic situation, in the other a
statement without reference to at least (or to any particular) one.

If space permitted other types of statement (existential, general, hypothetical, &c.)
should be dealt with: these raise problems rather of meaning than of truth, though I feel
uneasiness about hypotheticals.

[12] If this is what was meant by ' "It is raining" is true if and only if it is raining', so far
so good.

[13] It takes two to make a truth. Hence (obviously) there can be no criterion of truth
in the sense of some feature detectable in the statement itself which will reveal whether
it is true or false. Hence, too, a statement cannot without absurdity refer to itself.

[14] 'It is true that S' and 'It is a fact that S' are applicable in the same circumstances;

3*b*. 'Corresponds' also gives trouble, because it is commonly given too restricted or too colourful a meaning, or one which in this context it cannot bear. The only essential point is this: that the correlation between the words (= sentences) and the type of situation, event, &c. which is to be such that when a statement in those words is made with reference to an historic situation of that type the statement is then true, is *absolutely and purely* conventional. We are absolutely free to appoint *any* symbol to describe *any* type of situation, so far as merely being true goes. In a small one-spade language tst nuts might be true in exactly the same circumstances as the statement in English that the National Liberals are the people's choice.[15] There is no need whatsoever for the words used in making a true statement to 'mirror' in any way, however indirect, any feature whatsoever of the situation or event; a statement no more needs, in order to be true, to reproduce the 'multiplicity,' say, or the 'structure' or 'form' of the reality, than a word needs to be echoic or writing pictographic. To suppose that it does, is to fall once again into the error of reading back into the world the features of language.

The more rudimentary a language, the more, very often, it will tend to have a 'single' word for a highly 'complex' type of situation: this has such disadvantages as that the language becomes elaborate to learn and is incapable of dealing with situations which are non-standard, unforeseen, for which there may just be no word. When we go abroad equipped only with a phrase-book, we may spend long hours learning by heart—

$$A^1\text{-moest-fa}^1\text{nd-}^e\text{tschâ}^r\text{woum}^e\text{n,}$$
$$Ma^1\text{hwîl-iz-wau}^r\text{pt (bènt),}$$

and so on and so on, yet faced with the situation where we have the pen of our aunt, find ourselves quite unable to say so. The characteristics of a more developed language (articulation, morphology, syntax, abstractions, &c.), do not make statements in it any more capable of being true or capable of being any more true, they make it more adaptable, more learnable, more comprehensive, more precise, and so on; and *these* aims may no doubt be furthered by making the language (allowance made for the nature of the medium) 'mirror' in conventional ways features descried in the world.

Yet even when a language does 'mirror' such features very closely (and does it ever?) the truth of statements remains still a matter, as it was with the most rudimentary languages, of the words used being the ones *conventionally appointed* for situations of the type to which that referred to belongs. A picture, a copy, a replica, a photograph—these are *never* true in so far as they are reproductions, produced by natural or mechanical means: a reproduction can be accurate or lifelike (true *to* the original), as a gramophone recording or a transcription may be, but not true (*of*) as a record of proceedings can be. In the same way a (natural) sign *of* something

---

the cap fits when there is a head it fits. Other words can fill the same role as 'fact': we say, e.g. 'The situation is that S'.

[15] We could use 'nuts' even now as a code-word: but a code, as a transformation of a language, is distinguished from a language, and a code-word dispatched is not (called) 'true'.

can be infallible or unreliable but only an (artificial) sign *for* something can be right or wrong.[16]

There are many intermediate cases between a true account and a faithful picture, as here somewhat forcibly contrasted, and it is from the study of these (a lengthy matter) that we can get the clearest insight into the contrast. For example, maps: these may be called pictures, yet they are highly conventionalized pictures. If a map can be clear or accurate or misleading, like a statement, why can it not be true or exaggerated? How do the 'symbols' used in map-making differ from those used in statement-making? On the other hand, if an air-mosaic is not a map, why is it not? And when does a map become a diagram? These are the really illuminating questions.

4. Some have said that—

To say that an assertion is true is not to make any further assertion at all.
In all sentences of the form '*p* is true' the phrase 'is true' is logically superfluous.
To say that a proposition is true is just to assert it, and to say that it is false is just to assert its contradictory.

But wrongly. TstS (except in paradoxical cases of forced and dubious manufacture) refers to the world or any part of it exclusive of tstS, i.e. of itself.[17] TstST refers to the world or any part of it *inclusive* of tstS, though once again exclusive of itself, i.e. of tstST. That is, tstST refers to something to which tstS cannot refer. TstST does not, certainly, include any statement referring to the world exclusive of tstS which is not included already in tstS—more, it seems doubtful whether it does include that statement about the world exclusive of tstS which is made when we state that S. (If I state that tstS is true, should we really agree that I have stated that S? Only 'by implication'.)[18] But all this does not go any way to show that tstST is not a statement different from tstS. If Mr. Q writes on a notice-board 'Mr. W is a burglar', then a trial is held to decide whether Mr. Q's published statement that Mr. W is a burglar is a libel: finding 'Mr. Q's statement was true (in substance and in fact)'. Thereupon a second trial is held, to decide whether Mr. W. is a burglar, in which Mr. Q's statement is no longer under consideration: verdict 'Mr. W is a burglar'. It is an arduous business to hold a second trial: why is it done if the verdict is the same as the previous finding?[19]

What is felt is that the evidence considered in arriving at the one verdict is the same as that considered in arriving at the other. This is not strictly correct. It is more nearly correct that whenever tstS is true then tstST is also true and conversely, and that whenever tstS is false tstST is also false

---

[16] Berkeley confuses these two. There will not be books in the running brooks until the dawn of hydro-semantics.

[17] A statement may refer to 'itself' in the sense, for example, of the sentence used or the utterance uttered in making it ('statement' is not exempt from all ambiguity). But paradox does result if a statement purports to refer to itself in a more full-blooded sense, purports, that is, to state that it itself is true, or to state what it itself refers to ('This statement is about Cato').

[18] And 'by implication' tstST asserts something about the making of a statement which tstS certainly does not assert.

[19] This is not quite fair: there are many legal and personal reasons for holding two trials—which, however, do not affect the point that the issue being tried is not the same.

and conversely.[20] And it is argued that the words 'is true' are logically superfluous because it is believed that generally if any two statements are always true together and always false together then they must mean the same. Now whether this is in general a sound view may be doubted: but even if it is, why should it not break down in the case of so obviously 'peculiar' a phrase as 'is true'? Mistakes in philosophy notoriously arise through thinking that what holds of 'ordinary' words like 'red' or 'growls' must also hold of extraordinary words like 'real' or 'exists'. But that 'true' is just such another extraordinary word is obvious.[21]

There is something peculiar about the 'fact' which is described by tstST, something which may make us hesitate to call it a 'fact' at all; namely, that the relation between tstS and the world which tstST asserts to obtain is a *purely conventional* relation (one which 'thinking makes so'). For we are aware that this relation is one which we could alter at will, whereas we like to restrict the word 'fact' to *hard* facts, facts which are natural and unalterable, or anyhow not alterable at will. Thus, to take an analogous case, we may not like calling it a fact that the word elephant means what it does, though we can be induced to call it a (soft) fact—and though, of course, we have no hesitation in calling it a fact that contemporary English speakers use the word as they do.

An important point about this view is that it confuses falsity with negation: for according to it, it is the same thing to say 'He is not at home' as to say 'It is false that he is at home'. (But what if no one has said that he *is* at home? What if he is lying upstairs dead?) Too many philosophers maintain, when anxious to explain away negation, that a negation is just a second order affirmation (to the effect that a certain first order affirmation is false), yet, when anxious to explain away falsity, maintain that to assert that a statement is false is just to assert its negation (contradictory). It is impossible to deal with so fundamental a matter here.[22] Let me assert the

[20] Not *quite* correct, because tstST is only in place at all when tstS is envisaged as made and has been verified.

[21] *Unum, verum, bonum* [one, true, good]—the old favourites deserve their celebrity. There is something odd about each of them. Theoretical thelogy is a form of onomatolatry.

[22] The following two sets of logical axioms are, as Aristotle (though not his successors) makes them, quite distinct:
(*a*) No statement can be both true and false.
No statement can be neither true nor false.
(*b*) Of two contradictory statements—
Both cannot be true.
Both cannot be false.
The second set demands a definition of contradictories, and is usually joined with an unconscious postulate that for every statement there is one and only one other statement such that the pair are contradictories. It is doubtful how far any language does or must contain contradictories, however defined, such as to satisfy both this postulate and the set of axioms (*b*).
Those of the so-called 'logical paradoxes' (hardly a genuine class) which concern 'true' and 'false' are *not* to be reduced to cases of self-contradiction, any more than 'S but I do not believe it' is. A statement to the effect that it is itself true is every bit as absurd as one to the effect that it is itself false. There are *other* types of sentence which offend against the fundamental conditions of all communication in ways *distinct from* the way in which 'This is red and is not red' offends—e.g. 'This does (I do) not exist', or equally absurd 'This exists (I exist)'. There are more deadly sins than one; nor does the way to salvation lie through any hierarchy.

following merely. Affirmation and negation are exactly on a level, in this sense, that no language can exist which does not contain conventions for both and that both refer to the world equally directly, not to statements about the world: whereas a language can quite well exist without any device to do the work of 'true' and 'false'. Any satisfactory theory of truth must be able to cope equally with falsity:[23] but 'is false' can only be maintained to be logically superfluous by making this fundamental confusion.

5. There is another way of coming to see that the phrase 'is true' is not logically superfluous, and to appreciate what sort of a statement it is to say that a certain statement is true. There are numerous other adjectives which are in the same class as 'true' and 'false', which are concerned, that is, with the relations between the words (as uttered with reference to an historic situation) and the world, and which nevertheless no one would dismiss as logically superfluous. We say, for example, that a certain statement is exaggerated or vague or bald, a description somewhat rough or misleading or not very good, an account rather general or too concise. In cases like these it is pointless to insist on deciding in simple terms whether the statement is 'true or false'. Is it true or false that Belfast is north of London? That the galaxy is the shape of a fried egg? That Beethoven was a drunkard? That Wellington won the battle of Waterloo? There are various *degrees and dimensions* of success in making statements: the statements fit the facts always more or less loosely, in different ways on different occasions for different intents and purposes. What may score full marks in a general knowledge test may in other circumstances get a gamma. And even the most adroit of languages may fail to 'work' in an abnormal situation or to cope, or cope reasonably simply, with novel discoveries: is it true or false that the dog goes round the cow?[24] What, moreover, of the large class of cases where a statement is not so much false (or true) as out of place, *inept* ('All the signs of bread' said when the bread is before us)?

We become obsessed with 'truth' when discussing statements, just as we become obsessed with 'freedom' when discussing conduct. So long as we think that what has always and alone to be decided is whether a certain action was done freely or was not, we get nowhere: but so soon as we turn instead to the numerous other adverbs used in the same connexion ('accidentally', 'unwillingly', 'inadvertently', &c.), things become easier, and we come to see that no concluding inference of the form 'Ergo, it was done freely (or not freely)' is required. Like freedom, truth is a bare minimum or

[23] To be false is (not, of course, to correspond to a non-fact, but) to miscorrespond with a fact. Some have not seen how, then, since the statement which is false does not describe the fact with which it mis-corresponds (but mis-describes it), we know which fact to compare it with: this was because they thought of all linguistic conventions as descriptive—but it is the demonstrative conventions which fix which situation it is to which the statement refers. No statement can state what it itself refers to.

[24] Here there is much sense in 'coherence' (and pragmatist) theories of truth, despite their failure to appreciate the trite but central point that truth is a matter of the relation between words and world, and despite their wrong-headed *Gleichschaltung* [assimilation] of all varieties of statemental failure under the lone head of 'partly true' (thereafter wrongly equated with 'part of the truth'). 'Correspondence' theorists too often talk as one would who held that every map is either accurate or inaccurate; that accuracy is a single and the sole virtue of a map; that every country can have but one accurate map; that a map on a larger scale or showing different features must be a map of a different country; and so on.

an illusory ideal (the truth, the whole truth and nothing but the truth about, say, the battle of Waterloo or the *Primavera*).

6. Not merely is it jejune to suppose that all a statement aims to be is 'true', but it may further be questioned whether every 'statement' does aim to be true at all. The principle of Logic, that 'Every proposition must be true or false', has too long operated as the simplest, most persuasive and most pervasive form of the descriptive fallacy. Philosophers under its influence have forcibly interpreted all 'propositions' on the model of the statement that a certain thing is red, as made when the thing concerned is currently under observation.

Recently, it has come to be realized that many utterances which have been taken to be statements (merely because they are not, on grounds of grammatical form, to be classed as commands, questions, &c.) are not in fact descriptive, nor susceptible of being true or false. When is a statement not a statement? When it is a formula in a calculus: when it is a performatory utterance: when it is a value-judgement: when it is a definition: when it is part of a work of fiction—there are many such suggested answers. It is simply not the business of such utterances to 'correspond to the facts' (and even genuine statements have other businesses besides that of so corresponding).

It is a matter for decision how far we should continue to call such masqueraders 'statements' at all, and how widely we should be prepared to extend the uses of 'true' and 'false' in 'different senses'. My own feeling is that it is better, when once a masquerader has been unmasked, *not* to call it a statement and *not* to say it is true or false. In ordinary life we should not call most of them statements at all, though philosophers and grammarians may have come to do so (or rather, have lumped them all together under the term of art 'proposition'). We make a difference between 'You said you promised' and 'You stated that you promised': the former can mean that you said 'I promise', whereas the latter must mean that you said 'I promised': the latter, which we say you 'stated', is something which is true or false, whereas for the former, which is not true or false, we use the wider verb to 'say'. Similarly, there is a difference between 'You say this is (call this) a good picture' and 'You state that this is a good picture'. Moreover, it was only so long as the real nature of arithmetical formulae, say, or of geometrical axioms remained unrecognized, and they were thought to record information about the world, that it was reasonable to call them 'true' (and perhaps even 'statements'—though were they ever so called?): but, once their nature has been recognized, we no longer feel tempted to call them 'true' or to dispute about their truth or falsity.

In the cases so far considered the model 'This is red' breaks down because the 'statements' assimilated to it are not of a nature to correspond to facts at all—the words are not descriptive words, and so on. But there is also another type of case where the words *are* descriptive words and the 'proposition' does in a way have to correspond to facts, but precisely not in the way that 'This is red' and similar statements setting up to be true have to do.

In the human predicament, for use in which our language is designed, we may wish to speak about states of affairs which have not been observed or are not currently under observation (the future, for example). And although we *can* state anything 'as a fact' (which statement will then be true or false[25]) we need not do so: we need only say 'The cat *may be* on the mat'. This utterance is quite different from tstS—it is not a statement at all (it is not true or false; it is compatible with 'The cat may *not* be on the mat'). In the same way, the situation in which we discuss whether and state that tstS is *true* is different from the situation in which we discuss whether it is *probable* that S. Tst it is probable that S is out of place, inept, in the situation where we can make tstST, and, I think, conversely. It is not our business here to discuss probability: but is worth observing that the phrases 'It is true that' and 'It is probable that' are in the same line of business,[26] and in so far incompatibles.

7. In a recent article in *Analysis* Mr. Strawson has propounded a view of truth which it will be clear I do not accept. He rejects the 'semantic' account of truth on the perfectly correct ground that the phrase 'is true' is not used in talking about *sentences*, supporting this with an ingenious hypothesis as to how meaning may have come to be confused with truth: but this will not suffice to show what he wants—that 'is true' is not used in talking about (or that 'truth is not a property of') *anything*. For it *is* used in talking about *statements* (which in his article he does not distinguish clearly from sentences). Further, he supports the 'logical superfluity' view to this extent, that he agrees that to say that ST is not to make any further assertion at all, beyond the assertion that S: but he disagrees with it in so far as he thinks that to say that ST *is* to *do* something more than just to assert that S—it is namely to *confirm* or to *grant* (or something of that kind) the assertion, made or taken as made already, that S. It will be clear that and why I do not accept the first part of this: but what of the second part? I agree that to say that ST 'is' very often, and according to the all-important linguistic occasion, to confirm tstS or to grant it or what not; but this cannot show that to say that ST is not also and at the same time to make an assertion about tstS. To say that I believe you 'is' on occasion to accept your statement; but it is also to make an assertion, which is not made by the strictly performatory utterance 'I accept your statement'. It is common for quite ordinary statements to have a performatory 'aspect': to say that you are a cuckold may be to insult you, but it is also and at the same time to make a statement which is true or false. Mr. Strawson, moreover, seems to confine himself to the case where I *say* 'Your statement is true' or something similar—but what of the case where you state that S and I *say* nothing but '*look and see*' that your statement is true? I do not see how this critical case, to which nothing analogous occurs with strictly performatory utterances, could be made to respond to Mr. Strawson's treatment.

One final point: if it is admitted (*if*) that the rather boring yet satisfactory relation between words and world which has here been discussed does genuinely occur, why should the phrase 'is true' not be our way of describing it? And if it is not, what else is?

---

[25] Though it is not yet in place to call it either. For the same reason, one cannot lie or tell the truth about the future.

[26] Compare the odd behaviours of 'was' and 'will be' when attached to 'true' and to 'probable'.

16

TRUTH

P. F. Strawson

Mr. Austin offers us a purified version of the correspondence theory of truth. On the one hand he disclaims the semanticists' error of supposing that "true" is a predicate of sentences; on the other, the error of supposing that the relation of correspondence is other than purely conventional, the error which models the word on the world or the world on the word. His own theory is, roughly, that to say that a statement is true is to say that a certain speech-episode is related in a certain conventional way to something in the world exclusive of itself. But neither Mr. Austin's account of the two terms of the truth-conferring relation, nor his account of the relation itself, seems to me satisfactory. The correspondence theory requires, not purification, but elimination.

1. *Statements.*—It is, of course, indisputable that we use various substantival expressions as grammatical subjects of "true." These are, commonly, noun-phrases like "What he said" or "His statement"; or pronouns or noun-phrases, with a "that"-clause in apposition, *e.g.*, "It . . . that *p*" and "The statement that *p*." Austin proposes that we should use "statement" to do general duty for such expressions as these. I have no objection. This will enable us to say, in a philosophically non-committal way, that, in using "true," we are talking about statements. By "saying this in a non-committal way," I mean saying it in a way which does not commit us to any view about the nature of statements so talked about; which does not commit us, for example, to the view that statements so talked about are historic events.

The words "assertion" and "statement" have a parallel and convenient duplicity of sense. "My statement" may be either what I say or my saying it. My saying something is certainly an episode. What I say is not. It is the latter, not the former, we declare to be true. (Speaking the truth is not a manner of speaking: it is saying something true.) When we say "His statement was received with thunderous applause" or "His vehement asser-

P. F. Strawson, "Truth," *Proceedings of the Aristotelian Society*, Supplementary Vol. XXIV (1950), 129–156. Reprinted by courtesy of the Editor of The Aristotelian Society.

tion was followed by a startled silence," we are certainly referring to, characterising, a historic event, and placing it in the context of others. If I say that the same statement was first whispered by John and then bellowed by Peter, uttered first in French and repeated in English, I am plainly still making historical remarks about utterance-occasions; but the word "statement" has detached itself from reference to any particular speech-episode. The episodes I am talking about are the whisperings, bellowings, utterings and repetitions. The statement is not something that figures in all these episodes. Nor, when I say that the statement is true, as opposed to saying that it was, in these various ways, made, am I talking indirectly about these episodes or any episodes at all. (Saying of a statement that it is true is not related to saying of a speech-episode that it was true as saying of a statement that it was whispered is related to saying of a speech-episode that it was a whisper.) It is futile to ask what thing or event I *am* talking about (over and above the subject-matter of the statement) in declaring a statement to be true; for there is no such thing or event. The word "statement" and the phrase "What he said," like the conjunction "that" followed by a noun clause, are convenient, grammatically substantival, devices, which we employ, on certain occasions, for certain purposes, notably (but not only) the occasions on which we use the word "true." What these occasions are I shall try later to elucidate. To suppose that, whenever we use a singular substantive, we are, or ought to be, using it to refer to something, is an ancient, but no longer a respectable, error.

More plausible than the thesis that in declaring a statement to be true I am talking about a speech-episode is the thesis that in order for me to declare a statement true, there must have occurred, within my knowledge, at least one episode which was a making of that statement. This is largely, but (as Austin sees) not entirely, correct. The occasion of my declaring a statement to be true may be not that someone has made the statement, but that I am envisaging the possibility of someone's making it. For instance, in discussing the merits of the Welfare State, I might say: "It is true that the general health of the community has improved (that p), but this is due only to the advance in medical science." It is not necessary that anyone should have said that p, in order for this to be a perfectly proper observation. In making it, I am not talking *about* an actual or possible speech-episode. I am myself asserting that p, in a certain way, with a certain purpose. I am anticipatorily conceding, in order to neutralize, a possible objection. I forestall someone's making the statement that p by making it myself, with additions. It is of prime importance to distinguish the fact that the use of "true" always glances backwards or forwards to the actual or envisaged making of a statement by someone, from the theory that it is used to characterise such (actual or possible) episodes.

It is not easy to explain the non-episodic and non-committal sense of "statement" in which "statement" = "what is said to be true or false." But, at the risk of being tedious, I shall pursue the subject. For if Austin is right in the suggestion that it is basically of speech-episodes that we predicate "true," it should be possible to "reduce" assertions in which we say of a statement in the non-episodic sense that it is true to assertions in which we are predicating truth of episodes. Austin points out that the same sentence may be used to make different statements. He would no doubt agree that different sentences may be used to make the same statement. I am not thinking only of different languages or synonymous expressions in the same language; but also of such occasions as that on which you say of Jones "He is ill," I say *to* Jones "You are ill" and Jones says "I am ill." Using, not only different sentences, but sentences with different meanings, we all make "the same statement"; and this is the sense of "statement" we need to discuss, since it is, *prima facie*, of statements in this sense that we say that they are true or false (*e.g.*, "What they all said, namely, that Jones was ill, was quite true."). We could say: people make the same statement when the words they use in the situations in which they use them are such that they must (logically) either all be making a true statement or all be making a false statement. But this is to use "true" in the elucidation of "same statement." Or we could say, of the present case: Jones, you and I all make the same statement because, using the words we used in the situation in which we used them, we were all applying the same description to the same person at a certain moment in his history; anyone applying that description to that person (etc.), would be making that statement. Mr. Austin might then wish to analyse (A) "The statement that Jones was ill is true" in some such way as the following: "If anyone has uttered, or were to utter, words such that in the situation in which they are uttered, he is applying to a person the same description as I apply to that person when I now utter the words 'Jones was ill,' then the resulting speech-episode was, or would be, true." It seems plain, however, that nothing but the desire to find a metaphysically irreproachable first term for the correspondence relation could induce anyone to accept this analysis of (A) as an elaborate general hypothetical. It would be a plausible suggestion only if the grammatical subjects of "true" were *commonly* expressions referring to particular, uniquely dateable, speech-episodes. But the simple and obvious fact is that the expressions occurring as such grammatical subjects ("What they said," "It . . . that *p*" and so on) never do, in these contexts, stand for such episodes.[1] *What they said* has no date, though their several sayings of it are dateable. *The statement that p* is not an event, though it had to be made for the first time and made within my knowledge if I am to talk of its truth or falsity. If I endorse Plato's view, wrongly attributing it to Lord Russell ("Russell's view that *p* is quite true"), and am corrected, I have not discovered that I was talking of an event separated by centuries from the one I imagined I was talking of. (Corrected, I may say: "Well it's true, whoever said it.") My *implied* historical judgment is false; that is all.

2. *Facts.*—What of the second term of the correspondence relation? For this Mr. Austin uses the following words or phrases: "thing," "event," "situation," "state of affairs," "feature" and "fact." All these are words which should be handled with care. I think that through failing to discriminate sufficiently between them, Mr. Austin (1) encourages the assimilation of facts to things, or (what is approximately the same thing) of stating to

[1] And the cases where such phrases might most plausibly be exhibited as having an episode-referring rôle are precisely those which yield most readily to another treatment; *viz.*, those in which one speaker corroborates, confirms or grants what another has just said (*see* Section 4 below).

referring; (2) misrepresents the use of "true"; and (3) obscures another and more fundamental problem.

In section 3 of his paper, Mr. Austin says, or suggests, that all stating involves both referring ("demonstration") and characterizing ("description"). It is questionable whether all statements do involve both,[2] though it is certain that some do. The following sentences, for example, could all be used to make such statements; *i.e.*, statements in the making of which both the referring and describing functions are performed, the performance of the two functions being approximately (though not exclusively) assignable to different parts of the sentences as uttered:—

The cat has the mange.
That parrot talks a lot.
Her escort was a man of medium build, clean-shaven, well-dressed and with a North Country accent.

In using such sentences to make statements, we refer to a thing or person (object) in order to go on to characterize it: (we demonstrate in order to describe). A *reference* can be correct or incorrect. A *description* can fit, or fail to fit, the thing or person to which it is applied.[3] When we refer correctly, there certainly is a conventionally established relation between the words, so used, and the thing to which we refer. When we describe correctly, there certainly is a conventionally established relation between the words we use in describing and the type of thing or person we describe. These relations, as Mr. Austin emphasizes, are different. An expression used referringly has a different logical rôle from an expression used describingly. They are differently related to the object. And *stating* is different from referring, and different from describing; for it is (in such cases) both these at once. Statement (*some* statement) is reference-cum-description. To avoid cumbersome phrasing, I shall speak henceforward of *parts* of statements (the referring part and the describing part); though parts of statements are no more to be equated with parts of sentences (or parts of speech-episodes) than statements are to be equated with sentences (or speech-episodes).

That (person, thing, etc.) to which the referring part of the statement refers, and which the describing part of the statement fits or fails to fit, is that which the statement is *about*. It is evident that there is nothing else in the world for the statement itself to be related to either in some further way of its own or in either of the different ways in which these different parts of the statement are related to what the statement is about. And it is evident that the demand that there should be such a relatum is logically absurd: a logically fundamental type-mistake. But the demand for something in the world *which makes the statement true* (Mr. Austin's phrase), or *to which the statement corresponds when it is true*, is just this demand. And the answering theory that to say that a statement is true is to say that a speech-episode is conventionally related in a certain way to such a relatum repro-

---

[2] *See* Section 5 below. The thesis that all statements involve both demonstration and description is, roughly, the thesis that all statements are, or involve, subject-predicate statements (not excluding relational statements).

[3] *Cf.* the phrase "He is described as . . ." What fills the gap is not a sentence (expression which could normally be used to make a statement), but a phrase which could occur as a part of an expression so used.

duces the type-error embodied in this demand. For while we certainly say that a statement corresponds to (fits, is borne out by, agrees with) the facts, as a variant on saying that it is true, we *never* say that a statement corresponds to the thing, person, etc., it is about. What "makes the statement" that the cat has mange "true," is not the cat, but the *condition* of the cat, *i.e.*, the fact that the cat has mange. The only plausible candidate for the position of what (in the world) makes the statement true is the fact it states; but the fact it states is not something in the world.[4] It is not an object; not even (as some have supposed) a complex object consisting of one or more particular elements (constituents, parts) and a universal element (constituent, part). I can (perhaps) hand you, or draw a circle round, or time with a stop-watch the things or incidents that are referred to when a statement is made. Statements are about such objects; but they state facts. Mr. Austin seems to ignore the complete difference of type between, *e.g.*, "fact" and "thing"; to talk as if "fact" were just a very general word (with, unfortunately, some misleading features) for "event," "thing," etc., instead of being (as it is) both wholly different from these, and yet the only possible candidate for the desired non-linguistic correlate of "statement." Roughly: the thing, person, etc., referred to is the material correlate of the referring part of the statement; the quality or property the referent is said to "possess" is the *pseudo*-material correlate of its describing part; and the fact to which the statement "corresponds" is the *pseudo*-material correlate of the statement as a whole.

These points are, of course, reflected in the behaviour of the word "fact" in ordinary language; behaviour which Mr. Austin notes, but by which he is insufficiently warned. "Fact," like "true," "states" and "statement" is wedded to "that"-clauses; and there is nothing unholy about this union. Facts are known, stated, learnt, forgotten, overlooked, commented on, communicated or noticed. (Each of these verbs may be followed by a "that"-clause or a "the fact that"-clause.) Facts are what statements (when true) state; they are not what statements are about. They are not, like things or happenings on the face of the globe, witnessed or heard or seen, broken or overturned, interrupted or prolonged, kicked, destroyed, mended or noisy. Mr. Austin notes the expression "fact that," warns us that it may tempt us to identify facts with true statements and explains its existence by saying that for certain purposes in ordinary life we neglect, or take as irrelevant, the distinction between saying something true and the thing or episode of which we are talking. It would indeed be wrong—but not for Mr. Austin's reasons —to identify "fact" and "true statement"; for these expressions have different rôles in our language, as can be seen by the experiment of trying to interchange them in context. Nevertheless their rôles—or those of related expressions—overlap. There is no nuance, except of style, between "That's true" and "That's a fact"; nor between "Is it true that . . . ?" and "Is it a

[4] This is not, of course, to deny that there is that in the world which a statement of this kind is about (true or false *of*), which is *referred to* and *described* and which the description fits (if the statement is true) or fails to fit (if it is false). This truism is an inadequate introduction to the task of elucidating, not our use of "true," but a certain general way of using language, a certain type of discourse, *viz.*, the fact-stating type of discourse. What confuses the issue about the use of the word "true" is precisely its entanglement with this much more fundamental and difficult problem. (*See* (ii) of this section.)

fact that . . . ?"[5] But Mr. Austin's reasons for objecting to the identification seem mistaken, as does his explanation of the usage which (he says)
tempts us to make it. Because he thinks of a statement as something in the
world (a speech-episode) and a fact as something else in the world (what
the statement either "corresponds to" or "is about"), he conceives the
distinction as of overriding importance in philosophy, though (surprisingly)
sometimes negligible for ordinary purposes. But I can conceive of no
occasion on which I could possibly be held to be "neglecting or taking as
irrelevant" the distinction between, say, my wife's bearing me twins (at
midnight) and my saying (ten minutes later) that my wife had borne me
twins. On Mr. Austin's thesis, however, my announcing "The fact is that
my wife has borne me twins" would be just such an occasion.

Elsewhere in his paper, Mr. Austin expresses the fact that there is no
theoretical limit to what could truly be said about things in the world, while
there are very definite practical limits to what human beings actually can
and do say about them, by the remark that statements "always fit the facts
more or less loosely, in different ways for different purposes." But what
could fit more perfectly the fact that it is raining than the statement that it is
raining? Of course, statements and facts fit. They were made for each other.
If you prise the statements off the world you prise the facts off it too; but
the world would be none the poorer. (You don't also prise off the world
what the statements are about—for this you would need a different kind of
lever.)

A symptom of Mr. Austin's uneasiness about facts is his preference for the
expressions "situation" and "state of affairs"; expressions of which the
character and function are a little less transparent than those of "fact." They
are more plausible candidates for inclusion in the world. For while it is true
that situations and states of affairs are not seen or heard (any more than facts
are), but are rather *summed up* or *taken in at a glance* (phrases which stress
the connection with statement and "that"-clause respectively), it is also true
that there is a sense of "about" in which we do talk about, do describe,
situations and states of affairs. We say, for example, "The international
situation is serious" or "This state of affairs lasted from the death of the
King till the dissolution of Parliament." In the same sense of "about," we
talk about facts; as when we say "I am alarmed by the fact that kitchen
expenditure has risen by 50 per cent in the last year." But whereas "fact" in
such usages is linked with a "that"-clause (or connected no less obviously
with "statement," as when we "take down the facts" or hand someone the
facts on a sheet of paper), "situation" and "state of affairs" stand by themselves, states of affairs are said to have a beginning and an end, and so on.
Nevertheless, situations and states of affairs so talked of are (like facts so
talked of), abstractions that a logician, if not a grammarian, should be able
to see through. Being alarmed by a fact is not like being frightened by a
shadow. It is being alarmed because. . . . One of the most economical and
pervasive devices of language is the use of substantival expressions to

---

[5] I think in general the difference between them is that while the use of "true," as
already acknowledged, glances backwards or forwards at an actual or envisaged making
of a statement, the use of "fact" does not generally do this though it may do it
sometimes. It certainly does not do it in, *e.g.*, the phrase "The fact is that . . ." which
serves rather to prepare us for the unexpected and unwelcome.

abbreviate, summarize and connect. Having made a series of descriptive statements, I can comprehensively connect with these the remainder of my discourse by the use of such expressions as "this situation" or "this state of affairs"; just as, having produced what I regard as a set of reasons for a certain conclusion I allow myself to draw breath by saying "Since *these things* are so, then . . . ," instead of prefacing the entire story by the conjunction. A situation or state of affairs is, roughly, a set of facts not a set of things.

A point which it is important to notice in view of Mr. Austin's use of these expressions (in sections 3a and 3b of his paper) is that when we *do* "talk about" situations (as opposed to things and persons) the situation we talk about is not, as he seems to think it is, correctly identified with the fact we state (with "what makes the statement true"). If a situation is the "subject" of our statement, then what "makes the statement true" is not the situation, but the fact that the situation has the character it is asserted to have. I think much of the persuasiveness of the phrase "talking about situations" derives from that use of the word on which I have just commented. But if a situation is treated as the "subject" of a statement, then it will not serve as the non-linguistic term, for which Mr. Austin is seeking, of the "relation of correspondence"; and if it is treated as the non-linguistic term of this relation, it will not serve as the subject of the statement.

Someone might now say: "No doubt 'situation,' 'state of affairs,' 'facts' are related in this way to 'that'-clauses and assertive sentences; can serve, in certain ways and for certain purposes, as indefinite stand-ins for specific expressions of these various types. So also is 'thing' related to some nouns; 'event' to some verbs, nouns and sentences; 'quality' to some adjectives; 'relation' to some nouns, verbs and adjectives. Why manifest this prejudice in favour of things and events as alone being parts of the world or its history? Why not situations and facts as well?" The answer to this (implicit in what has gone before) is twofold.

(i) The first part of the answer[6] is that the whole charm of talking of situations, states of affairs or facts as included in, or parts of, the world, consists in thinking of them as things, and groups of things; that the temptation to talk of situations, etc., in the idiom appropriate to talking of things and events is, once this first step is taken, overwhelming. Mr. Austin does not withstand it. He significantly slips in the word "feature" (noses and hills are *features*, of faces and landscapes) as a substitute for "facts." He says that the reason why photographs and maps are not "true" in the way that statements are true is that the relation of a map or a photograph to what it is a map or a photograph of is not wholly (in the first case) and not all (in the second) a conventional relation. But this is not the only, or the fundamental, reason (The relation between the Prime Minister of England and the phrase "the Prime Minister of England" *is* conventional; but it doesn't make sense to say that someone uttering the phrase out of context is saying something true or false.) The (for present purposes) fundamental reason is that "being a map of" or "being a photograph of" *are* relations, of which the non-

---

[6] Which could be more shortly expressed by saying that if we read "world" (a sadly corrupted word) as "heavens and earth," talk of facts, situations and states of affairs, as "included in" or "parts of" the world is, obviously, metaphorical. The world is the totality of things, not of facts.

photographic, non-cartographical, relata are, say, personal or geographical *entities*. The trouble with correspondence theories of truth is not primarily the tendency to substitute non-conventional relations for what is really a wholly conventional relation. It is the misrepresentation of "correspondence between statement and fact" *as a relation, of any kind, between events or things or groups of things* that is the trouble. Correspondence theorists think of a statement as "describing that which makes it true" (fact, situation, state of affairs) in the way a descriptive predicate may be used to describe, or a referring expression to refer to, a thing.[7]

(ii) The second objection to Mr. Austin's treatment of facts, situations, states of affairs as "parts of the world" which we declare to stand in a certain relation to a statement when we declare that statement true, goes deeper than the preceding one but is, in a sense, its point. Mr. Austin rightly says or implies (section 3) that for some of the purposes for which we use language, there must be conventions correlating the words of our language with what is to be found in the world. Not all the linguistic purposes for which this necessity holds, however, are identical. Orders, as well as information, are conventionally communicated. Suppose "orange" always meant what we mean by "Bring me an orange" and "that orange" always meant what we mean by "Bring me that orange," and, in general, our language contained only sentences in some such way imperative. There would be no less need for a conventional correlation between the word and the world. Nor would there be any less to be found in the world. But those pseudo-entities which *make statements true* would not figure among the non-linguistic correlates. They would no more be found; (they never were found, and never did figure among the non-linguistic correlates). The point is that the word "fact" (and the "set-of-facts" words like "situation," "state of affairs") have, like the words "statement" and "true" themselves, a certain type of word-world-relating discourse (the informative) *built in* to them. The occurrence in ordinary discourse of the words "fact," "statement," "true" signalizes the occurrence of this type of discourse; just as the occurrence of the words "order," "obeyed" signalizes the occurrence of another kind of conventional communication (the imperative). If our task were to elucidate the nature of the first type of discourse, it would be futile to attempt to do it in terms of the words "fact," "statement," "true," for

---

[7] Suppose the pieces set on a chessboard, a game in progress. And suppose someone gives, in words, an exhaustive statement of the position of the pieces. Mr. Austin's objection (or one of his objections) to earlier correspondence theories is that they would represent the relation between the description and the board with the pieces on it as like, say, the relation between a newspaper diagram of a chess-problem and a board with the pieces correspondingly arranged. He says, rather, that the relation is a purely conventional one. My objection goes farther. It is that there is no thing or event called "a statement" (though there is the making of the statement) and there is no thing or event called "a fact" or "situation" (though there is the chessboard with the pieces on it) which stand to one another in any, even a purely conventional, relation as the newspaper diagram stands to the board-and-pieces. The facts (situation, state of affairs) cannot, like the chessboard-and-pieces, have coffee spilt on them or be upset by a careless hand. It is because Mr. Austin needs such events and things for his theory that he takes the making of the statement as the statement, and that which the statement is about as the fact which it states.

Events can be dated and things can be located. But the facts which statements (when true) state can be neither dated or located. (Nor can the statements, though the making of them can be.) Are they included in the world?

these words contain the problem, not its solution. It would, for the same reason, be equally futile to attempt to elucidate any one of these words (in so far as the elucidation of *that* word would be the elucidation of *this* problem) in terms of the others. And it is, indeed, very strange that people have so often proceeded by saying "Well, we're pretty clear what a statement is, aren't we? Now let us settle *the further question, viz.,* what it is for a statement to be true." This is like "Well, we're clear about what a command is: now what is it for a command to be obeyed?" As if one could divorce statements and commands from the point of making or giving them!

Suppose we had in our language the word "execution" meaning "action which is the carrying out of a command." And suppose someone asked the philosophical question: What is *obedience?* What is it for a command to be *obeyed?* A philosopher might produce the answer: "Obedience is a conventional relation between a command and an execution. A command is obeyed when it corresponds to an execution."

This is the Correspondence Theory of Obedience. It has, perhaps, a little less value as an attempt to elucidate the nature of one type of communication than the Correspondence Theory of Truth has as an attempt to elucidate that of another. In both cases, the words occurring in the solution incorporate the problem. And, of course, this intimate relation between "statement" and "fact" (which is understood when it is seen that they both incorporate this problem) explains why it is that when we seek to explain *truth* on the model of naming or classifying or any other kind of conventional or non-conventional relation between one thing and another, we always find ourselves landed with "fact," "situation," "state of affairs" as the non-linguistic terms of the relation.

But why should the problem of Truth (the problem about our use of "true") be seen as this problem of elucidating the fact-stating type of discourse? The answer is that it shouldn't be; but that the Correspondence Theory can only be fully seen through when it is seen as a barren attempt on this second problem. Of course, a philosopher concerned with the second problem, concerned to elucidate a certain general type of discourse, must stand back from language and talk about the different ways in which utterances are related to the world (though he must get beyond "correspondence of statement and fact" if his talk is to be fruitful). But—to recur to something I said earlier—the occurrence *in ordinary discourse* of the words "true," "fact," etc., signalizes, without commenting on, the occurrence of a certain way of using language. When we use these words in ordinary life, we are talking within, and not about, a certain frame of discourse; we are precisely not talking about the way in which utterances are, or may be, conventionally related to the world. We are talking about persons and things, but in a way in which we could not talk about them if conditions of certain kinds were not fulfilled. The problem about the use of "true" is to see how this word fits into that frame of discourse. The surest route to the wrong answer is to confuse this problem with the question: What type of discourse is this?[8]

---

[8] A parallel mistake would be to think that in our ordinary use (as opposed to a philosopher's use) of the word "quality," we were talking about people's uses of words; on the ground (correct in itself) that this word would have no use but for the occurrence of a certain general way of using words.

3. *Conventional Correspondence.*—It will be clear from the previous paragraph what I think wrong with Mr. Austin's account of the relation itself, as opposed to its terms. In section 4 of his paper he says that, when we declare a statement to be true, the relation between the statement and the world which our declaration "asserts to obtain" is "a purely conventional relation" and "one which we could alter at will." This remark reveals the fundamental confusion of which Mr. Austin is guilty between:—

(*a*) the semantic conditions which must be satisfied for the statement that a certain statement is true to be itself true; and

(*b*) what is asserted when a certain statement is stated to be true.

Suppose A makes a statement, and B declares A's statement to be true. Then for B's statement to be true, it is, *of course*, necessary that the words used by A in making the statement should stand in a certain conventional (semantical) relationship with the world; and that the "linguistic rules" underlying this relationship should be rules "observed" by both A and B. It should be remarked that these conditions (with the exception of the condition about B's observance of linguistic rules) are equally necessary conditions of A's having made a true statement in using the words he used. *It is no more and no less absurd to suggest that B, in making his statement, asserts that these semantic conditions are fulfilled than it is to suggest that A, in making his statement, asserts that these semantic conditions are fulfilled (i.e., that we can never use words without mentioning them).* If Mr. Austin is right in suggesting that to say that a statement is true is to say that "the historic state of affairs to which it [*i.e.*, for Mr. Austin, the episode of making it] is correlated by the demonstrative conventions (the one it 'refers to') is of a type with which the sentence used in making the statement is correlated by the descriptive conventions," *then* (and this is shown quite clearly by his saying that the relation we assert to obtain is a "purely conventional one" which "could be altered at will") in declaring a statement to be true, we are either:—

(*a*) talking about the meanings of the words used by the speaker whose making of the statement is the occasion for our use of "true" (*i.e.*, profiting by the occasion to give semantic rules); or

(*b*) saying that the speaker has used correctly the words he did use.

It is *patently* false that we are doing either of these things. Certainly, we use the word "true" when the semantic conditions described by Austin[9] are

---

[9] In what, owing to his use of the words "statement," "fact," "situation," etc., is a misleading form. The quoted account of the conditions of truthful statement is more nearly appropriate as an account of the conditions of correct descriptive reference. Suppose, in a room with a bird in a cage, I say "That parrot is very talkative." Then my use of the referring expression ("That parrot") with which my sentence begins is correct when the token-object (bird) with which my token-expression (event) is correlated by the conventions of demonstration is of a kind with which the type-expression is correlated by the conventions of description. Here we do have an event and a thing and a (type-mediated) conventional relation between them. If someone corrects me, saying "That's not a parrot; it's a cockatoo," he may be correcting either a linguistic or a factual error on my part. (The question of which he is doing is the question of whether I would have stuck to my story on a closer examination of the

fulfilled; but we do not, in using the word, *state* that they are fulfilled. (And this, incidentally, is the answer to the question with which Mr. Austin concludes his paper.) The damage is done (the two problems distinguished at the end of the previous section confused) by asking the question: *When* do we use the word "true"? instead of the question: *How* do we use the word "true"?

Someone says: "It's true that French Governments rarely last more than a few months, but the electoral system is responsible for that." Is the fact he states in the first part of his sentence alterable by changing the conventions of language? It is not.

4. *Uses of "that"-clauses; and of "statement," "true," "fact," "exaggerated," etc.*—(a) There are many ways of making an assertion about a thing, X, besides the bare use of the sentence-pattern "X is Y." Many of these involve the use of "that"-clauses. For example:—

> How often shall I have to tell you
> Today I learnt
> It is surprising
> The fact is
> I have just been reminded of the fact } that X is Y.
> It is indisputable
> It is true
> It is established beyond question

These are all ways of asserting, in very different context and circumstances, that X is Y.[10] Some of them involve autobiographical assertions as well; others do not. In the grammatical sense already conceded, all of them are "about" facts or statements. In no other sense is any of them about either, though some of them carry *implications* about the *making* of statements.

(b) There are many different circumstances in which the simple sentence-pattern "X is Y" may be used to do things which are not merely stating (though they all involve stating) that X is Y. In uttering words of this simple pattern we may be encouraging, reproving or warning someone; reminding someone; answering, or replying to, someone; denying what someone has said; confirming, granting, corroborating, agreeing with, admitting what someone has said. Which of these, if any, we are doing depends on the circumstances in which, using this simple sentence-pattern, we assert that X is Y.

(c) In many of the cases in which we are doing something besides merely stating that X is Y, we have available, for use in suitable contexts, certain abbreviatory devices which enable us to state that X is Y (to make our

---

bird.) Only in the former case is he declaring a certain semantic condition to be unfulfilled. In the latter case, he is talking about the bird. He asserts that it is a cockatoo and not a parrot. This he could have done whether I had spoken or not. He also *corrects* me, which he could not have done if I had not spoken.

[10] One might prefer to say that in some of these cases one was asserting only *by implication* that X is Y; though it seems to me more probable that in all these cases we should say, of the speaker, not "What he said implied that X is Y," but "He *said* that X was Y."

denial, answer, admission or whatnot) *without* using the sentence-pattern "X is Y." Thus, if someone asks us "Is X Y?", we may state (in the way of reply) that X is Y by saying "Yes." If someone says "X is Y," we may state (in the way of denial) that X is not Y, by saying "It is not" or by saying "That's not true"; or we may state (in the way of corroboration, agreement, granting, etc.) that X is Y by saying "It is indeed" or "That is true." In all these cases (of reply, denial and agreement) the context of our utterance, as well as the words we use, must be taken into account if it is to be clear what we are asserting, *viz.*, that X is (or is not) Y. It seems to me plain that in these cases "true" and "not true" (we rarely use "false") are functioning as abbreviatory statement-devices of the same general kind as the others quoted. And it seems also plain that the *only* difference between these devices which might tempt us, while saying of some ("Yes," "It is indeed," "It is not") that, in using them, we were talking about X, to say of others ("That's true," "That's not true") that, in using them, we were talking about something quite different, *viz.*, the utterance which was the occasion for our use of these devices, is their difference in grammatical structure, *i.e.*, the fact that "true" occurs as a grammatical predicate.[11] (It is obviously not a predicate of X.) If Mr. Austin's thesis, that in using the word "true" we make an assertion about a statement, were no more than the thesis that the word "true" occurs as a grammatical predicate, with, as grammatical subjects, such words and phrases as "That," "What he said," "His statement," etc., then, of course, it would be indisputable. It is plain, however, that he means more than this, and I have already produced my objections to the more that he means.

(*d*) It will be clear that, in common with Mr. Austin, I reject the thesis that the phrase "is true" is logically superfluous, together with the thesis that to say that a proposition is true is *just* to assert it and to say that it is false is *just* to assert its contradictory. "True" and "not true" have jobs of their own to do, *some*, but by no means all, of which I have characterized above. In using them, we are not *just* asserting that X is Y or that X is not Y. We are asserting this in a way in which we could not assert it unless certain conditions were fulfilled; we may also be granting, denying, confirming, etc. It will be clear also that the rejection of these two theses does not entail acceptance of Mr. Austin's thesis that in using "true" we are making an assertion about a statement. Nor does it entail the rejection of the thesis which Mr. Austin (in Section 4 of his paper) couples with these two, *viz.*, the thesis that to say that an assertion is true is not to make any further *assertion* at all. This thesis holds for many uses, but requires modification for others.

(*e*) The occasions for using "true" mentioned so far in this section are evidently not the only occasions of its use. There is, for example, the generally concessive employment of "It is true that *p* . . .", which it is difficult to see how Mr. Austin could accommodate. All these occasions

---

[11] Compare also the English habit of making a statement followed by an interrogative appeal for agreement in such forms as "isn't it?", "doesn't he?" etc., with the corresponding German and Italian idioms, "Nicht wahr?", "non è vero?" There is surely no significant difference between the phrases which do not employ the word for "true" and those which do: they all appeal for agreement in the same way.

have, however, a certain contextual immediacy which is obviously absent when we utter such sentences as "What John said yesterday is quite true" and "What La Rochefoucauld said about friendship is true." Here the context of our utterance does not identify for us the statement we are talking about (in the philosophically non-committal sense in which we *are* "talking about statements" when we use the word "true"), and so we use a descriptive phrase to do the job. But the descriptive phrase does not identify an event; though the statement we make carries the implication (in some sense of "implication") that there occurred an event which was John's making yesterday (or Rochefoucauld's making sometime) the statement that *p* (*i.e.*, the statement we declare to be true). We are certainly not telling our audience that the event occurred, *e.g.*, that John made the statement that *p*, for (i) we do not state, either by way of quotation or otherwise, what it was that John said yesterday, and (ii) our utterance achieves its main purpose (that of making, by way of confirmation or endorsement, the statement that *p*) only if our audience already knows that John yesterday made the statement that *p*. The abbreviatory function of "true" in cases such as these becomes clearer if we compare them with what we say in the case where (i) we want to assert that *p*; (ii) we want to indicate (or display our knowledge that) an event occurred which was John's making yesterday the statement that *p*; (iii) we believe our audience ignorant or forgetful of the fact that John said yesterday that *p*. We then use the formula "As John said yesterday, *p*" or "It is true, as John said yesterday, that *p*," or "What John said yesterday, namely that *p*, is true." (Of course the words represented by the letter *p*, which we use, may be—sometimes, if we are to make the same statement, must be—different from the words which John used.) Sometimes, to embarrass, or test, our audience, we use, in cases where the third of these conditions is fulfilled, the formula appropriate to its non-fulfilment, *viz.*, "What John said yesterday is true."

(*f*) In criticism of my view of truth put forward in *Analysis*,[12] and presumably in support of his own thesis that "true" is used to assert that a certain relation obtains between a speech-episode and something in the world exclusive of that episode, Mr. Austin makes, in Section 7 of his paper, the following point. He says: "Mr. Strawson seems to confine himself to the case when I say "Your statement is true" or something similar—but what of the case when you state that S and I say nothing, but *look and see* that your statement is true?" The point of the objection is, I suppose, that since I *say* nothing, I cannot be making any performatory use of "true"; yet I can see *that* your statement is true. The example, however, seems to have a force precisely contrary to what Mr. Austin intended. Of course, "true" has a different rôle in "X sees that Y's statement is true" from its rôle in "Y's statement is true." What is this rôle? Austin says in my hearing "There is a cat on the mat" and I look and see a cat on the mat. Someone (Z) reports: "Strawson saw that Austin's statement was true." What is he reporting? He is reporting that I have seen a cat on the mat; but he is reporting this in a way in which he could not report it except in certain circumstances, *viz.*, in the circumstances of Austin's having said in my hearing that there was a cat

12 Vol. 9, No. 6, June, 1949.

on the mat. Z's remark also carries the implication that Austin made a statement, but cannot be regarded as *reporting* this by implication since it fulfils its main purpose only if the audience already knows that Austin made a statement and what statement he made; and the implication (which *can* be regarded as an implied report) that I heard and understood what Austin said.[13] The man who looks and sees that the statement that there is a cat on the mat is true, sees no more and no less than the man who looks and sees that there is a cat on the mat, or the man who looks and sees that there is *indeed* a cat on the mat. But the *settings* of the first and third cases may be different from that of the second.

This example has value, however. It emphasizes the importance of the concept of the "occasion" on which we may make use of the assertive device which is the subject of this symposium (the word "true"); and minimizes (what I was inclined to over-emphasize) the performatory character of our uses of it.

(*g*) Mr. Austin stresses the differences between negation and falsity; rightly, in so far as to do so is to stress the difference (of occasion and context) between asserting that X is not Y and denying the assertion that X is Y. He also exaggerates the difference; for, if I have taken the point of his example, he suggests that there are cases in which "X is not Y" is inappropriate to a situation in which, if anyone stated that X was Y, it would be correct to say that the statement that X was Y was false. These are cases where the question of whether X is or is not Y does not arise (where the conditions of its arising are not fulfilled). They are equally, it seems to me, cases when the question of the truth or falsity of the statement that X is Y does not arise.

(*h*) A qualification of my general thesis, that in using "true" and "untrue" we are not talking about a speech-episode, is required to allow for those cases where our interest is not primarily in what the speaker asserts, but in the speaker's asserting it, in, say, the fact of his having *told the truth* rather than in the fact which he reported in doing so. (We may, of course, be interested in both; or our interest in a man's evident truthfulness on one occasion may be due to our concern with the degree of his reliability on others.)

But this case calls for no special analysis and presents no handle to any theorist of truth; for to use "true" in this way is simply to characterize a certain *event* as *the making*, by someone, of a true statement. The problem of analysis remains.

(*i*) Mr. Austin says that we shall find it easier to be clear about "true" if we consider other adjectives "in the same class," such as "exaggerated," "vague," "rough," "misleading," "general," "too concise." I do not think these words *are* in quite the same class as "true" and "false." In any language in which statements can be made at all, it must be possible to make true and false statements. But statements can suffer from the further defects Mr. Austin mentions only when language has attained a certain richness. Imagine one of Mr. Austin's rudimentary languages with "single words" for "com-

---

[13] If *I* report: "I see that Austin's statement is true," this is simply a first-hand corroborative report that there is a cat on the mat, made in a way in which it could not be made except in these circumstances.

plex situations" of totally different kinds. One could make true or false statements; but not statements which were exaggerated, over-concise, too general or rather rough. And even given a language as rich as you please, whereas all statements made in it could be true or false, not all statements could be exaggerated. When can we say that the statement that p is exaggerated? *One* of the conditions is this: that, if the sentence S_1 is used to make the statement that p, there should be some sentence S_2 (which could be used to make the statement that q) such that S_1 and S_2 are related somewhat as "There were 200 people there" is related to "There were 100 people there." (To the remark "We got married yesterday," you cannot, except as a joke, reply: "You're exaggerating.")

Mr. Austin's belief, then, that the word "exaggerated" stands for a relation between a statement and something in the world exclusive of the statement, would at least be an over-simplification, even if it were not objectionable in other ways. But it is objectionable in other ways. The difficulties about statement and fact recur; and the difficulties about the relation. Mr. Austin would not want to say that the relation between an exaggerated statement and the world was like that between a glove and a hand too small for it. He would say that the relation was a conventional one. But the fact that the statement that p is exaggerated is not in any sense a conventional fact. (It is, perhaps, the fact that there were 1,200 people there and not 2,000.) If a man says: "There were at least 2,000 people there," you may reply (A) "No, there were not so many (far more)," or you may reply (B) "That's an exaggeration (understatement)." (A) and (B) say the same thing. Look at the situation more closely. In saying (A), you are not merely asserting that there were fewer than 2,000 people there: you are also correcting the first speaker, and correcting him in a certain general way, which you could not have done if he had not spoken as he did, though you could merely have asserted that there were fewer than 2,000 there without his having spoken. Notice also that what is being asserted by the use of (A)—that there were fewer than 2,000 there—cannot be understood without taking into account the original remark which was the occasion for (A). (A) has both contextually-assertive and performatory features. (B) has the same features, and does the same job as (A), but more concisely and with greater contextual reliance.

Not all the words taken by Austin as likely to help us to be clear about "true" are in the same class as one another. "Exaggerated" is, of those he mentions, the one most relevant to his thesis; but has been seen to yield to my treatment. Being "over-concise" and "too general" are not ways of being "not quite true." These obviously relate to the specific purposes of specific makings of statements; to the unsatisfied wishes of specific audiences. No alteration in things in the world, nor any magical replaying of the course of events, could bring statements so condemned into line, in the way that an "exaggerated assessment" of the height of a building could be brought into line by inorganic growth. Whether the statement (that p) is true or false is a matter of the way things are (of whether p); whether a statement is exaggerated (if the question arises—which depends on the type of statement and the possibilities of the language) is a matter of the way things are (*e.g.*, of whether or not there were fewer than 2,000 there). But whether a statement is over-concise[14] or too general depends on what the hearer wants to know. The world does not demand to be described with one degree of detail rather than another.

5. *The scope of "statement," "true," "false" and "fact."*—Commands and questions, obviously do not claim to be statements of fact: they are not true or false. In Section 6 of his paper, Mr. Austin reminds us that there are many expressions neither interrogative nor imperative in form which we use for other purposes than that of reportage or forecast. From our employment of these expressions he recommends that we withhold (suspects that we do, in practice, largely withhold) the appellation "stating facts," the words "true" and "false." Philosophers, even in the sphere of language, are not legislators; but I have no wish to challenge the restriction, in some philosophical contexts, of the words "statement," "true," "false," to what I have myself earlier called the "fact-stating" type of discourse.

What troubles me more is Mr. Austin's own incipient analysis of this type of discourse. It seems to me such as to force him to carry the restriction further than he wishes or intends. And here there are two points which, though connected, need to be distinguished. First, there are difficulties besetting the relational theory of truth as such; second, there is the persistence of these difficulties in a different form when this "theory of truth" is revealed as, rather, an incipient analysis of the statement-making use of language.

First then, facts of the cat-on-the-mat-type are the favoured species for adherents of Mr. Austin's type of view. For here we have one thing (one chunk of reality) sitting on another: we can (if we are prepared to commit the errors commented on in Section (2) above) regard the two together as forming a single chunk, if we like, and call it a fact or state of affairs. The view may then seem relatively plausible that to say that the statement (made by me to you) that the cat is on the mat is true is to say that the three-dimensional state of affairs with which the episode of my making the statement is correlated by the demonstrative conventions is of a type with which the sentence I use is correlated by the descriptive conventions. Other species of fact, however, have long been known to present more difficulty: the fact that the cat is not on the mat, for example, or the fact that there are white cats, or that cats persecute mice, or that if you give my cat an egg, it will smash it and eat the contents. Consider the simplest of these cases, that involving negation. With what type of state-of-affairs (chunk of reality) is the sentence "The cat is not on the mat" correlated by conventions of description? With a mat *simpliciter* [merely]? With a dog on a mat? With a cat up a tree? The amendment of Mr. Austin's view to which one might be tempted for negative statements (*i.e.*, "S is true" = "The state of affairs to which S is correlated by the demonstrative conventions is *not* of a type with which *the affirmative form of* S is correlated by the descriptive conventions") destroys the simplicity of the story by creating the need for a

---

[14] "Concise" is perhaps less often used of what a man says than of the way he says it (*e.g.*, "concisely put," "concisely expressed," "a concise formulation"). A may take 500 words to say what B says in 200. Then I shall say that B's formulation was more concise than A's, meaning simply that he used fewer words.

different sense of "true" when we discuss negative statements. And worse is to follow. Not all statements employ conventions of demonstration. Existential statements don't, nor do statements of (even relatively) unrestricted generality. Are we to deny that these are statements, or create a further sense of "true"? And what has become of the non-linguistic correlate, the chunk of reality? Is this, in the case of existential or general statements, the entire world? Or, in the case of negatively existential statements, an ubiquitous non-presence?

As objections to a correspondence theory of truth, these are familiar points; though to advance them as such is to concede too much to the theory. What makes them of interest is their power to reveal how such a theory, in addition to its intrinsic defects, embodies too narrow a conception of the fact-stating use of language. Mr. Austin's description of the conditions under which a statement is true, regarded as an analysis of the fact-stating use, applies only to affirmative subject-predicate statements, *i.e.*, to statements in making which we refer to some one or more localized thing or group of things, event or set of events, and characterize it or them in some positive way (identify the object or objects and affix the label). It does not apply to negative, general and existential statements nor, straight-forwardly, to hypothetical and disjunctive statements. I agree that any language capable of the fact-stating use must have some devices for performing the function to which Mr. Austin exclusively directs his attention, and that other types of statements of fact can be understood only in relation to this type. But the other types *are* other types. For example, the word "not" can usefully be regarded as a kind of crystallizing-out of something *implicit* in all use of descriptive language (since no predicate would have any descriptive force if it were compatible with everything). But from this it does not follow that negation (*i.e.*, the *explicit* exclusion of some characteristic) is a kind of affirmation, that negative statements are properly discussed in the language appropriate to affirmative statements. Or take the case of existential statements. Here one needs to distinguish two kinds of demonstration or reference. There is, first, the kind whereby we enable our hearer to identify the thing or person or event or set of these which we then go on to characterize in some way. There is, second, the kind by which we simply indicate a locality. The first ("*Tabby* has the mange") answers the question "Who (which one, what) are you talking about?" The second ("*There's* a cat") the question "Where?" It is plain that no part of an existential statement performs the first function; though Austin's account of reference-cum-description is appropriate to reference of this kind rather than to that of the other. It is clear also that a good many existential statements do not answer the question "Where?" though they may license the enquiry. The difference between various types of statement, and their mutual relations, is a matter for careful description. Nothing is gained by lumping them all together under a description appropriate only to one, even though it be the basic, type.

6. *Conclusion.*—My central objection to Mr. Austin's thesis is this. He describes the conditions which must obtain if we are correctly to declare a statement true. His detailed description of these conditions is, with reserva-

tions, correct as far as it goes, though in several respects too narrow. The central mistake is to suppose that in using the word "true" we are asserting such conditions to obtain. That this is a mistake is shown by the detailed examination of the behaviour of such words as "statement," "fact," etc., and of "true" itself, and by the examination of various different types of statement. This also reveals some of the ways in which "true" actually functions as an assertive device. What supremely confuses the issue is the failure to distinguish between the task of elucidating the nature of a certain type of communication (the empirically informative) from the problem of the actual functioning of the word "true" within the framework of that type of communication.

Further References

Ayer, A. J. *The Problem of Knowledge.* Harmondsworth: Penguin Books, 1956.*

Ayer, A. J. (ed.). *Logical Positivisim.* New York: The Free Press, 1959.†

Barker, S. F. *Induction and Hypothesis.* Ithaca, N. Y.: Cornell University Press, 1957.

Benacerraf, P., and Putnam, H. (eds.). *Philosophy of Mathematics.* Englewood Cliffs, N. J.: Prentice-Hall, 1964.

Bouwsma, O. K. "Descartes' Skepticism of the Senses," *Mind,* LIV (1945), 313–322.

Chisholm, R. M. "Theory of Knowledge." In Chisholm, R. M. *et al. Philosophy.* Englewood Cliffs, N. J.: Prentice-Hall, 1964.

————. *Theory of Knowledge.* Englewood Cliffs, N. J.: Prentice-Hall, 1966.*

Copi, Irving M., and Gould, James A. (eds.). *Readings in Logic.* New York: Macmillan, 1964.*

Hintikka, Jaakko. *Knowledge and Belief.* Ithaca, N. Y.: Cornell University Press, 1962.

Kneale, William. *Probability and Induction.* Oxford: Clarendon Press, 1949.

Körner, S. *The Philosophy of Mathematics.* New York: Harper & Row, 1960.*

Kyburg, Henry E., Jr. "Recent Work in Inductive Logic," *American Philosophical Quarterly,* I (1964), 249–287.

Kyburg, Henry E., Jr., and Nagel, Ernest (eds.). *Induction: Some Current Issues.* Middletown, Conn.: Wesleyan University Press, 1963.

Malcolm, Norman. *Knowledge and Certainty.* Englewood Cliffs, N. J.: Prentice-Hall, 1963.

Nagel, Ernest. "Principles of the Theory of Probability." In *International Encyclopedia of Unified Science.* Vol. I, No. 6. Chicago: University of Chicago Press, 1939.*

Pitcher, George (ed.). *Truth.* Englewood Cliffs, N. J.: Prentice-Hall, 1964.*

Scheffler, Israel. *The Anatomy of Inquiry.* New York: Knopf, 1963. Pt. III.

Skyrms, Brian. *Choice and Chance.* Belmont, Calif.: Dickenson, 1966.*

Stroll, Avrum (ed.). *Epistemology.* New York: Harper & Row, 1967.*

Tarski, Alfred. "The Semantic Conception of Truth," *Philosophy and Phenomenological Research,* IV (1944), 341–375.

Wittgenstein, Ludwig. *Remarks on the Foundations of Mathematics.* Oxford: Basil Blackwell, 1956.

————. *Tractatus Logico-Philosophicus.* London, Routledge & Kegan Paul, 1962.

* Paperback edition.   † Also available in a paperback edition.

:VI:

Meaning
and Perception

INTRODUCTION

The problems of the theory of meaning, in spite of the obvious respects in which they pervade the entire history of philosophy, have been focused in a systematic way largely in our own century. In a very real sense, the distinctive work of contemporary philosophy has centered on the nature of language and on the respects in which we can, and cannot, speak of the relationship between language and the world. These were the issues that engaged C. S. Peirce, Gottlob Frege, Bertrand Russell, the Logical Positivists (or Logical Empiricists), and Ludwig Wittgenstein.

Peirce (VI: 1) is, in fact, often regarded as the first philosopher of importance to have made the analysis of meaning the pivotal question of his entire professional endeavor. His main philosophical contribution, pragmatism—which he regarded as having been misread by his followers as a theory of truth rather than of meaning—interestingly anticipates versions of the verifiability theory of meaning and, in particular, of operationalism. Peirce's account enables us to appreciate the strategy of testing proposed theories of meaning; ironically enough, his own difficulty with the management of dispositional terms points prophetically to the characteristic difficulties of the verifiability theory of meaning, not to mention Peirce's inoperable concept of "the long run."

The verifiability theory of meaning is, without question, the single most sustained (and cooperative) effort in the history of philosophy to puzzle out what we mean by the "meaning" of sentences. Actually, among the Logical Positivists and their close critics, two rather different questions have been, under the heading of that theory, regularly confused with each other: first, the question of criteria (no matter how formally or informally construed) of significance, that is, of conditions in accordance with which one can decide that given sentences are *meaningful;* and second, the question of sense itself, that is, of rules (no matter how formally or informally construed) by which to specify *the meaning* of given sentences. Considerations of both sorts have led to doctrines of what we mean by the "meaning" of sentences; although to give the meaning of sentences is to presuppose that the sentences so explicated are meaningful, to determine *that* sentences are meaningful is not at all to give their meaning.

Moritz Schlick (VI:2), who, with Rudolf Carnap, is the most prominent among the Logical Positivists, appears, in advancing his version of the verifiability theory of meaning, to be providing a rule for the specification of the meaning of sentences as well as a criterion for determining whether given sentences are meaningful. The most notable internal difficulty of his thesis, as contrasted with the general difficulties of the verifiability claim, concern his failure to make provision against would-be descriptions that are not self-contradictory yet are nevertheless nonsense. This failure draws our attention to the possible implications of being obliged to admit a number of sentences as paradigms of meaningful sentences, which verificationist claims about *other* sentences must presuppose.

As a matter of fact, Carnap had attempted to systematize a basic empiricist language in which the relationship between these two sets of sentences was fully articulated. But the inherent difficulties of *all* versions of the empiricist criterion of meaning—whether of the testability sort or of the translatability sort—have remained unaffected by this provision and, in some respects at least, are if anything intensified. Carl Hempel's resumé (VI:3) of the transformations in the empiricist criterion makes this abundantly clear; however sympathetic Hempel's account, it also makes clear the important sense in which we are not yet able to formulate adequate criteria of significance, notably for dispositional and theoretical terms. Friedrich Waismann (VI:4) attempts, from a point of view that may fairly be termed Wittgensteinian, to challenge the adequacy of the verifiability theory of meaning, considering, for instance, that to specify a method for verifying sentences presupposes that one has grasped the meaning of those sentences with respect to which a given method of verification is judged to be relevant.

If we grant that language does in some sense capture the distinctions of the world, the difference between the sense and the reference of linguistic expressions is very nearly the most important of all the questions concerning the relationship between language and the world. For the clarification of this difference bears essentially on the way in which we link questions of the meaning of what we say about the world with questions of the truth or falsity of what we say. This theme appears prominently in the pioneering work of Gottlob Frege (VI:5), where, working largely with puzzles about identity statements, he clearly delineates the irreducibility of sense to reference and of reference to sense. For example, in the well-known instance of the morning star and the evening star, Frege demonstrates that the *information* gained by the assertion of their identity requires the admission of a difference in sense (in "thoughts") between the descriptive predicates since the identity being a true one, their reference ("nominatum") must be the same. Again, such sentences as "Odysseus deeply asleep was disembarked at Ithaca," which must be admitted to have sense but no reference (as being neither true nor false, in fiction and in poetry), oblige us to distinguish between sense and reference.

The problem of the analysis of denoting expressions, in terms of sense and reference, becomes, in the work of Bertrand Russell (VI:6) central to the fortunes of ontology and the reconstruction of language. Working with specimen assertions such as "The King of France is bald," Russell sought to avoid the embarrassment of supposing that the expression "the King of France" refers to some nonexistent entity, even though the definite article is used and the expression appears in the subject position in the sentence. His strategy is to deny that the expression has a denoting function (even though it appears to have one), and he proposes to translate sentences such as "The King of France is bald" so that the offending expression will reappear, in its translation according to the canon of reconstruction, in the appropriate predicate position.

The adequacy of Russell's account, however, has been challenged by P. F. Strawson (VI:7), in what has come to be regarded as one of the critical exchanges in comparatively recent British philosophy. Strawson, rather in the spirit of Frege, distinguishes sharply between the sense and the reference of the expressions in question. Narrowly construed, his position is to object to Russell's regarding the sentence "The King of France is bald" as false. Strawson holds that since reference fails, the question of truth and falsity does not arise, even though the sentence is significant. More broadly construed, Strawson's position appeals to "ordinary-language" considerations against restricted views of what counts as a significant utterance for Russell and, on different grounds, for the Positivists. By insisting on the context-bound nature of reference itself, Strawson raises doubts about the entire program of proposing such ideal languages as Russell had in mind.

Of course, behind disputes of the sort considered lurks the larger issue of whether and in what way we can analyze the "real form" of ordinary sentences and "what it really means to say" when we say such and such. Often, there are critical ontological alternatives at stake in the attempt; sometimes, however, there are only questions of the proper logical characterization of given expressions to consider. Gilbert Ryle's relatively early paper on this issue (VI:8) shows striking affinities with Russell's account of denoting and Frege's distinction of sense and reference, in spite of Ryle's explicit attraction to Wittgenstein's mode of analysis. Ryle is extremely cautious about the relationship of understanding and using sentences in ordinary usage to the logical and ontological analysis of these sentences.

The issue has continued to exercise philosophers down to our own day. W. V. Quine (VI:9) attempts very boldly, in a manner quite sympathetic with Russell's venture, to provide a canon by which to account for the kinds of entities that there are in the world. But the problem stubbornly remains: we must ask ourselves whether Quine's ontological motto—To be is to be the value of a bound variable—is intended to *register* the ontic import of ordinary sentences or to *discover* or *posit* such ontic import. From the Wittgensteinian point of view, the underlying question has to do with whether we are, in ontological disputes, attempting the impossible, by seeking to pass beyond the analysis of language (as it is used to talk about the world) to an analysis of the world itself in some linguistically uninfected way. This is the concern of D. F. Pears (VI:10).

All these issues, however, raise questions about how it is that we come to have knowledge of the world at all. The master theme, admittedly not always adhered to in the history of philosophy and difficult to put correctly within acceptable limits, is that our knowledge of the world depends on sensory perception. Plato's *Theaetetus* (VI:11) is one of the great classical investigations of the distinction between knowledge and right opinion (this recalls the problems of Part V), with special attention to the sense in which perception may or may not be counted as knowledge.

The modern discussion of sensory perception achieves its first focusing in the British empiricist tradition. There we see the effort to demonstrate that all knowledge ultimately depends on sensory experience. The well-known puzzles that were the particular concern of John Locke (VI:12) and George Berkeley (VI:13) expose, by their very persistence, the inability of empiricism to account for the totality of knowledge in sensory terms. Berkeley's exposure of what he regards as Locke's inherent skepticism—in regard to the difficulties of material substance, the distinction between primary and secondary qualities, the use of universal terms, knowledge of one's self, the causal theory of perception—tend to reflect as much on the limitations of a modified empiricism as they do on the corrigibility of Locke's account.

Interest in perception theory has never really flagged in modern philosophy; it has flourished very remarkably, however, during our own century. Here, the key questions, posed in extremely sophisticated forms, have had to do largely with the adequacy of all versions of so-called sense-datum theories. G. E. Moore's account (VI:14) depends primarily on analyzing Berkeley's principle *esse est percipi* as being not an identity and, in any case, a false proposition; also, it depends on taking sensory perception as the "most primitive" way of knowing material objects, yet a way of knowing material objects that itself entails "directly apprehending" something even more elemental: sense data. Thus Moore generated, not altogether willingly, a whole series of puzzles that parallel those of classical empiricism, which was concerned with the differences between the sense data I perceive and those you perceive, as well as with the proper relationship between sense data and material objects. The opacity of Moore's remarks about sense data is amusingly exhibited in O. K. Bouwsma's essay (V:15).

A. J. Ayer's numerous and changing accounts of the analysis of sense-datum language make it difficult to assign him a single and simple thesis. In our selection (VI:16), he attempts to sketch the lines of a so-called phenomenalist position in which a sense-datum language is taken to be basic to perceptual knowledge and physical objects are construed as being theoretical entities with respect to sense data that are directly perceived. It has been seriously doubted by most philosophers that the phenomenalist program is logically possible. It has even been supposed by many to have been demonstrated that that program is impossible since a sense-datum language can be shown to be conceptually dependent on a physical-object language.

This theme is pursued, for example, by J. L. Austin (VI:17) within the confines of an "ordinary-language" approach and with particular attention to the use of such expressions as "looks," "appears," "really," and the like. A related inquiry, formulated not so much in linguistic terms as in terms of the priorities proper (say, to "being red" and "looking red") is advanced by Roderick Chisholm (VI:18). But Chisholm is interested in the analysis of "perceiving" itself. "Perceiving" is viewed as one among an entire range of verbs that have to do with knowledge and action and desire, and are said to be "intentional," in the sense that the perceiving subject has certain beliefs and expectations relating to the very conditions under which he perceives, or fails to perceive, an object.

If the argument is maintained, we are returned, of course, to the grave difficulties that inhere in the empiricist tradition with regard to the concepts of persons, perceiving selves, minds, in the analysis of perception and, more generally, knowledge. The value of this maneuver, beyond the technical issues that it raises, lies in the unexpected discovery of the unity of philosophical inquiry, in that the analysis of apparently restricted questions about sensory perception obliges us to reconsider the analysis of other critical, yet seemingly independent issues.

The Theory of Meaning

1
HOW TO MAKE OUR IDEAS CLEAR

C. S. Peirce

THE PRAGMATIC MAXIM

And what, then, is belief? It is the demi-cadence which closes a musical phrase in the symphony of our intellectual life. We have seen that it has just three properties: First, it is something that we are aware of; second, it appeases the irritation of doubt; and, third, it involves the establishment in our nature of a rule of action, or, say for short, a *habit*. As it appeases the irritation of doubt, which is the motive for thinking, thought relaxes, and comes to rest for a moment when belief is reached. But, since belief is a rule for action, the application of which involves further doubt and further thought, at the same time that it is a stopping-place, it is also a new starting-place for thought. That is why I have permitted myself to call it thought at rest, although thought is essentially an action. The *final* upshot of thinking is the exercise of volition, and of this thought no longer forms a part; but belief is only a stadium of mental action, an effect upon our nature due to thought, which will influence future thinking.

The essence of belief is the establishment of a habit; and different beliefs are distinguished by the different modes of action to which they give rise. If beliefs do not differ in this respect, if they appease the same doubt by producing the same rule of action, then no mere differences in the manner of consciousness of them can make them different beliefs, any more than playing a tune in different keys is playing different tunes. Imaginary distinctions are often drawn between beliefs which differ only in their mode of expression;—the wrangling which ensues is real enough, however. To believe that any objects are arranged among themselves as in Fig. 1, and to believe that they are arranged [as] in Fig. 2, are one and the same belief; yet it is conceivable that a man should assert one proposition and deny the other. Such false distinctions do as much harm as the confusion of beliefs really different, and are among the pitfalls of which we ought constantly to beware, especially when we are upon metaphysical ground. One singular deception of this sort, which often occurs, is to mistake the sensation

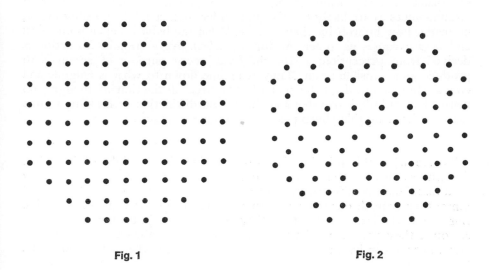

Fig. 1   Fig. 2

produced by our own unclearness of thought for a character of the object we are thinking. Instead of perceiving that the obscurity is purely subjective, we fancy that we contemplate a quality of the object which is essentially mysterious; and if our conception be afterward presented to us in a clear form we do not recognize it as the same, owing to the absence of the feeling of unintelligibility. So long as this deception lasts, it obviously puts an impassable barrier in the way of perspicuous thinking; so that it equally interests the opponents of rational thought to perpetuate it, and its adherents to guard against it.

Another such deception is to mistake a mere difference in the grammatical construction of two words for a distinction between the ideas they express. In this pedantic age, when the general mob of writers attend so much more to words than to things, this error is common enough. When I just said that thought is an *action*, and that it consists in a *relation*, although a person performs an action but not a relation, which can only be the result of an action, yet there was no inconsistency in what I said, but only a grammatical vagueness.

From all these sophisms we shall be perfectly safe so long as we reflect that the whole function of thought is to produce habits of action; and that whatever there is connected with a thought, but irrelevant to its purpose, is an accretion to it, but no part of it. If there be a unity among our sensations which has no reference to how we shall act on a given occasion, as when we listen to a piece of music, why we do not call that thinking. To develop its meaning, we have, therefore, simply to determine what habits it produces, for what a thing means is simply what habits it involves. Now, the identity of a habit depends on how it might lead us to act, not merely under such circumstances as are likely to arise, but under such as might possibly occur, no matter how improbable they may be. What the habit is depends on *when* and *how* it causes us to act. As for the *when*, every stimulus to action is derived from perception; as for the *how*, every purpose of action is to produce some sensible result. Thus, we come down to what is tangible and conceivably practical, as the root of every real distinction of thought, no matter how subtle it may be; and there is no distinction of meaning so fine as to consist in anything but a possible difference of practice.

To see what this principle leads to, consider in the light of it such a doctrine as that of transubstantiation. The Protestant churches generally hold that the elements of the sacrament are flesh and blood only in a tropical sense; they nourish our souls as meat and the juice of it would our bodies. But the Catholics maintain that they are literally just meat and blood; although they possess all the sensible qualities of wafer-cakes and diluted wine. But we can have no conception of wine except what may enter into a belief, either—

1. That this, that, or the other, is wine; or,
2. That wine possesses certain properties.

Such beliefs are nothing but self-notifications that we should, upon occasion, act in regard to such things as we believe to be wine according to the qualities which we believe wine to possess. The occasion of such action would be some sensible perception, the motive of it to produce some sensible result. Thus our action has exclusive reference to what affects the senses, our habit has the same bearing as our action, our belief the same as our habit, our conception the same as our belief; and we can consequently mean nothing by wine but what has certain effects, direct or indirect, upon our senses; and to talk of something as having all the sensible characters of wine, yet being in reality blood, is senseless jargon. Now, it is not my object to pursue the theological question; and having used it as a logical example I drop it, without caring to anticipate the theologian's reply. I only desire to point out how impossible it is that we should have an idea in our minds which relates to anything but conceived sensible effects of things. Our idea of anything *is* our idea of its sensible effects; and if we fancy that we have any other we deceive ourselves, and mistake a mere sensation accompanying

the thought for a part of the thought itself. It is absurd to say that thought
has any meaning unrelated to its only function. It is foolish for Catholics and
Protestants to fancy themselves in disagreement about the elements of the
sacrament, if they agree in regard to all their sensible effects, here and
hereafter.

It appears, then, that the rule for attaining . . . clearness of apprehension
is as follows: Consider what effects, that might conceivably have practical
bearings, we conceive the object of our conception to have. Then, our
conception of these effects is the whole of our conception of the object.

SOME APPLICATIONS OF THE PRAGMATIC MAXIM

Let us illustrate this rule by some examples; and, to begin with the simplest
one possible, let us ask what we mean by calling a thing *hard*. Evidently that
it will not be scratched by many other substances. The whole conception of
this quality, as of every other, lies in its conceived effects. There is absolutely no difference between a hard thing and a soft thing so long as they are
not brought to the test. Suppose, then, that a diamond could be crystallized
in the midst of a cushion of soft cotton, and should remain there until it was
finally burned up. Would it be false to say that that diamond was soft? This
seems a foolish question, and would be so, in fact, except in the realm of
logic. There such questions are often of the greatest utility as serving to
bring logical principles into sharper relief than real discussions ever could. In
studying logic we must not put them aside with hasty answers, but must
consider them with attentive care, in order to make out the principles
involved. We may, in the present case, modify our question, and ask what
prevents us from saying that all hard bodies remain perfectly soft until they
are touched, when their hardness increases with the pressure until they are
scratched. Reflection will show that the reply is this: there would be no
falsity in such modes of speech. They would involve a modification of our
present usage of speech with regard to the words hard and soft, but not of
their meanings. For they represent no fact to be different from what it is;
only they involve arrangements of facts which would be exceedingly
maladroit. This leads us to remark that the question of what would occur
under circumstances which do not actually arise is not a question of fact,
but only of the most perspicuous arrangement of them. For example, the
question of free-will and fate in its simplest form, stripped of verbiage, is
something like this: I have done something of which I am ashamed; could I,
by an effort of the will, have resisted the temptation, and done otherwise?
The philosophical reply is, that this is not a question of fact, but only of the
arrangement of facts. Arranging them so as to exhibit what is particularly
pertinent to my question—namely, that I ought to blame myself for having
done wrong—it is perfectly true to say that, if I had willed to do otherwise
than I did, I should have done otherwise. On the other hand, arranging the
facts so as to exhibit another important consideration, it is equally true that,
when a temptation has once been allowed to work, it will, if it has a certain
force, produce its effect, let me struggle how I may. There is no objection
to a contradiction in what would result from a false supposition. The *re-*

ductio ad absurdum consists in showing that contradictory results would follow from a hypothesis which is consequently judged to be false. Many questions are involved in the free-will discussion, and I am far from desiring to say that both sides are equally right. On the contrary, I am of opinion that one side denies important facts, and that the other does not. But what I do say is, that the above single question was the origin of the whole doubt; that, had it not been for this question, the controversy would never have arisen; and that this question is perfectly solved in the manner which I have indicated.

Let us next seek a clear idea of Weight. This is another very easy case. To say that a body is heavy means simply that, in the absence of opposing force, it will fall. This (neglecting certain specifications of how it will fall, etc., which exist in the mind of the physicist who uses the word) is evidently the whole conception of weight. It is a fair question whether some particular facts may not *account* for gravity; but what we mean by the force itself is completely involved in its effects.

This leads us to undertake an account of the idea of Force in general. This is the great conception which, developed in the early part of the seventeenth century from the rude idea of a cause, and constantly improved upon since, has shown us how to explain all the changes of motion which bodies experience, and how to think about all physical phenomena; which has given birth to modern science, and changed the face of the globe; and which, aside from its more special uses, has played a principal part in directing the course of modern thought, and in furthering modern social development. It is, therefore, worth some pains to comprehend it. According to our rule, we must begin by asking what is the immediate use of thinking about force; and the answer is, that we thus account for changes of motion. If bodies were left to themselves, without the intervention of forces, every motion would continue unchanged both in velocity and in direction. Furthermore, change of motion never takes place abruptly; if its direction is changed, it is always through a curve without angles; if its velocity alters, it is by degrees. The gradual changes which are constantly taking place are conceived by geometers to be compounded together according to the rules of the parallelogram of forces. If the reader does not already know what this is, he will find it, I hope, to his advantage to endeavor to follow the following explanation; but if mathematics are insupportable to him, pray let him skip three paragraphs rather than we should part company here.

A *path* is a line whose beginning and end are distinguished. Two paths are considered to be equivalent, which, beginning at the same point, lead to the same point. Thus the two paths, *A B C D E* and *A F G H E* (Fig. 3), are equivalent. Paths which do *not* begin at the same point are considered to be equivalent, provided that, on moving either of them without turning it, but keeping it always parallel to its original position, when its beginning coincides with that of the other path, the ends also coincide. Paths are considered as geometrically added together, when one begins where the other ends; thus the path *A E* is conceived to be a sum of *A B, B C, C D,* and

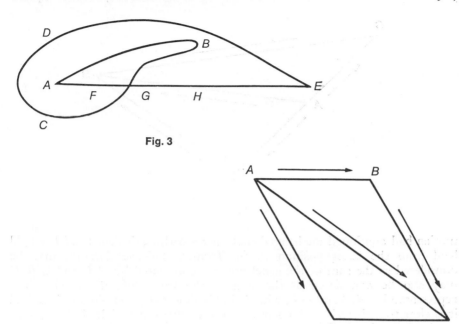

Fig. 3

Fig. 4

D E. In the parallelogram of Fig. 4 the diagonal *A C* is the sum of *A B* and *B C*; or, since *A D* is geometrically equivalent to *B C*, *A C* is the geometrical sum of *A B* and *A D*.

All this is purely conventional. It simply amounts to this: that we choose to call paths having the relations I have described equal or added. But, though it is a convention, it is a convention with a good reason. The rule for geometrical addition may be applied not only to paths, but to any other things which can be represented by paths. Now, as a path is determined by the varying direction and distance of the point which moves over it from the starting-point, it follows that anything which from its beginning to its end is determined by a varying direction and a varying magnitude is capable of being represented by a line. Accordingly, *velocities* may be represented by lines, for they have only directions and rates. The same thing is true of *accelerations*, or changes of velocities. This is evident enough in the case of velocities; and it becomes evident for accelerations if we consider that precisely what velocities are to positions—namely, states of change of them—that accelerations are to velocities.

The so-called "parallelogram of forces" is simply a rule for compounding accelerations. The rule is, to represent the accelerations by paths, and then to geometrically add the paths. The geometers, however, not only use the "parallelogram of forces" to compound different accelerations, but also to resolve one acceleration into a sum of several. Let *A B* (Fig. 5) be the path which represents a certain acceleration—say, such a change in the motion of a body that at the end of one second the body will, under the influence of that change, be in a position different from what it would have had if its

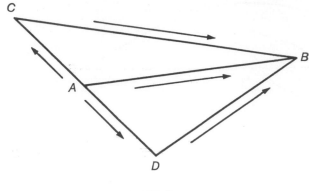

Fig. 5

motion had continued unchanged such that a path equivalent to $A\,B$ would lead from the latter position to the former. This acceleration may be considered as the sum of the accelerations represented by $A\,C$ and $C\,B$. It may also be considered as the sum of the very different accelerations represented by $A\,D$ and $D\,B$, where $A\,D$ is almost the opposite of $A\,C$. And it is clear that there is an immense variety of ways in which $A\,B$ might be resolved into the sum of two accelerations.

After this tedious explanation, which I hope, in view of the extraordinary interest of the conception of force, may not have exhausted the reader's patience, we are prepared at last to state the grand fact which this conception embodies. This fact is that if the actual changes of motion which the different particles of bodies experience are each resolved in its appropriate way, each component acceleration is precisely such as is prescribed by a certain law of Nature, according to which bodies, in the relative positions which the bodies in question actually have at the moment,[1] always receive certain accelerations, which, being compounded by geometrical addition, give the acceleration which the body actually experiences.

This is the only fact which the idea of force represents, and whoever will take the trouble clearly to apprehend what this fact is, perfectly comprehends what force is. Whether we ought to say that a force *is* an acceleration, or that it *causes* an acceleration, is a mere question of propriety of language, which has no more to do with our real meaning than the difference between the French idiom "*Il fait froid*" and its English equivalent "*It is cold.*" Yet it is surprising to see how this simple affair has muddled men's minds. In how many profound treatises is not force spoken of as a "mysterious entity," which seems to be only a way of confessing that the author despairs of ever getting a clear notion of what the word means! In a recent admired work on *Analytic Mechanics* it is stated that we understand precisely the effect of force, but what force itself is we do not understand! This is simply a self-contradiction. The idea which the word force excites in our minds has no other function than to affect our actions, and these actions can have no reference to force otherwise than through its effects. Consequently, if we know what the effects of force are, we are acquainted with every fact which is implied in saying that a force exists, and there is nothing

---

[1] Possibly the velocities also have to be taken into account.

more to know. The truth is, there is some vague notion afloat that a question may mean something which the mind cannot conceive; and when some hair-splitting philosophers have been confronted with the absurdity of such a view, they have invented an empty distinction between positive and negative conceptions, in the attempt to give their non-idea a form not obviously nonsensical. The nullity of it is sufficiently plain from the considerations given a few pages back; and, apart from those considerations, the quibbling character of the distinction must have struck every mind accustomed to real thinking.

.   .   .

2

MEANING AND VERIFICATION

Moritz Schlick

I

Philosophical questions, as compared with ordinary scientific problems, are always strangely paradoxical. But it seems to be an especially strange paradox that the question concerning the meaning of a proposition should constitute a serious philosophical difficulty. For is it not the very nature and purpose of every proposition to express its own meaning? In fact, when we are confronted with a proposition (in a language familiar to us) we usually know its meaning immediately. If we do not, we can have it explained to us, but the explanation will consist of a new proposition; and if the new one is capable of expressing the meaning, why should not the original one be capable of it? So that a snippy person when asked what he meant by a certain statement might be perfectly justified in saying, 'I meant exactly what I said!'.

It is logically legitimate and actually the normal way in ordinary life and even in science to answer a question concerning the meaning of a proposition by simply repeating it either more distinctly or in slightly different words. Under what circumstances, then, can there be any sense in asking for the meaning of a statement which is well before our eyes or ears?

Evidently the only possibility is that we have not *understood* it. And in this case what is actually before our eyes or ears is nothing but a series of words which we are unable to handle; we do not know how to use it, how to 'apply it to reality'. Such a series of words is for us simply a complex of signs 'without meaning', a mere sequel of sounds or a mere row of marks on paper, and we have no right to call it 'a proposition' at all; we may perhaps speak of it as 'a sentence'.

If we adopt this terminology we can now easily get rid of our paradox by saying that we cannot inquire after the meaning of a proposition, but can

From Moritz Schlick, "Meaning and Verification," *The Philosophical Review*, XLV (1936), 339–349, 352–353. Reprinted by permission of *The Philosophical Review* and the executors of Moritz Schlick's estate.

ask about the meaning of a sentence, and that this amounts to asking, 'What proposition does the sentence stand for?'. And this question is answered either by a proposition in a language with which we are already perfectly familiar; or by indicating the logical rules which will make a proposition out of the sentence, *i.e.*, will tell us exactly in what circumstances the sentence is to be *used*. These two methods do not actually differ in principle; both of them give meaning to the sentence (transform it into a proposition) by locating it, as it were, within the system of a definite language; the first method making use of a language which is already in our possession, the second one building it up for us. The first method represents the simplest kind of ordinary 'translation'; the second one affords a deeper insight into the nature of meaning, and will have to be used in order to overcome philosophical difficulties connected with the understanding of sentences.

The source of these difficulties is to be found in the fact that very often we do not know how to handle our own words; we speak or write without having first agreed upon a definite logical grammar which will constitute the signification of our terms. We commit the mistake of thinking that we know the meaning of a sentence (*i.e.*, understand it as a proposition) if we are familiar with all the words occurring in it. But this is not sufficient. It will not lead to confusion or error as long as we remain in the domain of everyday life by which our words have been formed and to which they are adapted, but it will become fatal the moment we try to think about abstract problems by means of the same terms without carefully fixing their signification for the new purpose. For every word has a definite signification only within a definite context into which it has been fitted; in any other context it will have no meaning unless we provide new rules for the use of the word in the new case, and this may be done, at least in principle, quite arbitrarily.

Let us consider an example. If a friend should say to me, 'Take me to a country where the sky is three times as blue as in England!' I should not know how to fulfill his wish; his phrase would appear nonsensical to me, because the word 'blue' is used in a way which is not provided for by the rules of our language. The combination of a numeral and the name of a color does not occur in it; therefore my friend's sentence has no meaning, although its exterior linguistic form is that of a command or a wish. But he can, of course, give it a meaning. If I ask him, 'What do you mean by "three times as blue"?', he can arbitrarily indicate certain definite physical circumstances concerning the serenity of the sky which he wants his phrase to be the description of. And then, perhaps, I shall be able to follow his directions; his wish will have become meaningful for me.

Thus, whenever we ask about a sentence, 'What does it mean?', what we expect is instruction as to the circumstances in which the sentence is to be used; we want a description of the conditions under which the sentence will form a *true* proposition, and of those which will make it *false*. The meaning of a word or a combination of words is, in this way, determined by a set of rules which regulate their use and which, following Wittgenstein, we may call the rules of their *grammar*, taking this word in its widest sense.

(If the preceding remarks about meaning are as correct as I am convinced they are, this will, to a large measure, be due to conversations with Wittgenstein which have greatly influenced my own views about these matters. I can hardly exaggerate my indebtedness to this philosopher. I do not wish to impute to him any responsibility for the contents of this article, but I have reason to hope that he will agree with the main substance of it.)

Stating the meaning of a sentence amounts to stating the rules according to which the sentence is to be used, and this is the same as stating the way in which it can be verified (or falsified). The meaning of a proposition is the method of its verification.

The 'grammatical' rules will partly consist of ordinary definitions, *i.e.*, explanations of words by means of other words, partly of what are called 'ostensive' definitions, *i.e.*, explanations by means of a procedure which puts the words to actual use. The simplest form of an ostensive definition is a pointing gesture combined with the pronouncing of the word, as when we teach a child the signification of the sound 'blue' by showing a blue object. But in most cases the ostensive definition is of a more complicated form; we cannot point to an object corresponding to words like 'because', 'immediate', 'chance', 'again', etc. In these cases we require the presence of certain complex situations, and the meaning of the words is defined by the way we use them in these different situations.

It is clear that in order to understand a verbal definition we must know the signification of the explaining words beforehand, and that the only explanation which can work without any previous knowledge is the ostensive definition. We conclude that there is no way of understanding any meaning without ultimate reference to ostensive definitions, and this means, in an obvious sense, reference to 'experience' or 'possibility of verification'.

This is the situation, and nothing seems to me simpler or less questionable. It is this situation and nothing else that we describe when we affirm that the meaning of a proposition can be given only by giving the rules of its verification in experience. (The addition, 'in experience', is really superfluous, as no other kind of verification has been defined.)

This view has been called the "experimental theory of meaning"; but it certainly is no theory at all, for the term 'theory' is used for a set of hypotheses about a certain subject-matter, and there are no hypotheses involved in our view, which proposes to be nothing but a simple statement of the way in which meaning is *actually* assigned to propositions, both in everyday life and in science. There has never been any other way, and it would be a grave error to suppose that we believe we have discovered a new conception of meaning which is contrary to common opinion and which we want to introduce into philosophy. On the contrary, our conception is not only entirely in agreement with, but even derived from, common sense and scientific procedure. Although our criterion of meaning has always been employed in practice, it has very rarely been formulated in the past, and this is perhaps the only excuse for the attempts of so many philosophers to deny its feasibility.

The most famous case of an explicit formulation of our criterion is Einstein's answer to the question, What do we mean when we speak of two events at distant places happening simultaneously? This answer consisted in a description of an experimental method by which the simultaneity of such events was actually ascertained. Einstein's philosophical opponents maintained—and some of them still maintain—that they knew the meaning of the above question independently of any method of verification. All I am trying to do is to stick consistently to Einstein's position and to admit no exceptions from it. (Professor Bridgman's book on *The Logic of Modern Physics* is an admirable attempt to carry out this program for all concepts of physics.) I am not writing for those who think that Einstein's philosophical opponents were right.

II

Professor C. I. Lewis, in a remarkable address on "Experience and Meaning" (published in . . . [*Philosophical*] *Review*, March 1934), has justly stated that the view developed above (he speaks of it as the "empirical-meaning requirement") forms the basis of the whole philosophy of what has been called the "logical positivism of the Viennese Circle". He criticizes this basis as inadequate chiefly on the ground that its acceptance would impose certain limitations upon "significant philosophic discussion" which, at some points, would make such discussion altogether impossible and, at other points, restrict it to an intolerable extent.

.   .   .

The mere statement that no sentence has meaning unless we are able to indicate a way of testing its truth or falsity is not very useful if we do not explain very carefully the signification of the phrases 'method of testing' and 'verifiability'.

.   .   .

How do we define verifiability?
In the first place I should like to point out that when we say that "a proposition has meaning only if it is verifiable" we are not saying ". . . if it is *verified*". This simple remark does away with one of the chief objections; the "here and now predicament", as Professor Lewis calls it, does not exist any more. We fall into the snares of this predicament only if we regard verification itself as the criterion of meaning, instead of 'possibility of verification' (= verifiability); this would indeed lead to a "reduction to absurdity of meaning". Obviously the predicament arises through some fallacy by which these two notions are confounded. I do not know if Russell's statement, "Empirical knowledge is confined to what we actually observe" (quoted by Professor Lewis), must be interpreted as containing this fallacy, but it would certainly be worth while to discover its genesis.
Let us consider the following argument which Professor Lewis discusses, but which he does not want to impute to anyone:

> Suppose it maintained that no issue is meaningful unless it can be put to the test of decisive verification. And no verification can take place except in the immediately present experience of the subject. Then nothing can be meant except what is actually present in the experience in which that meaning is entertained.

This argument has the form of a conclusion drawn from two premisses. Let us for the moment assume the second premiss to be meaningful and true. You will observe that even then the conclusion does *not* follow. For the first premiss assures us that the issue has meaning if it *can* be verified; the verification does not have to take place, and therefore it is quite irrelevant whether it can take place in the future or in the present only. Apart from this, the second premiss is, of course, nonsensical; for what fact could possibly be described by the sentence 'verification can take place only in present experience'? Is not verifying an act or process like hearing or feeling bored? Might we not just as well say that I can hear or feel bored only in the present moment? And what could I mean by this? The particular nonsense involved in such phrases will become clearer when we speak of the 'egocentric predicament' later on; at present we are content to know that our empirical-meaning postulate has nothing whatever to do with the now-predicament. 'Verifiable' does not even mean 'verifiable here now'; much less does it mean 'being verified now'.

Perhaps it will be thought that the only way of making sure of the verifiability of a proposition would consist in its actual verification. But we shall soon see that this is not the case.

There seems to be a great temptation to connect meaning and the 'immediately given' in the wrong way; and some of the Viennese positivists may have yielded to this temptation, thereby getting dangerously near to the fallacy we have just been describing. Parts of Carnap's *Logischer Aufbau der Welt* [*The Logical Structure of the World*], for instance, might be interpreted as implying that a proposition about future events did not really refer to the future at all but asserted only the present existence of certain expectations (and, similarly, speaking about the past would really mean speaking about present memories). But it is certain that the author of that book does not hold such a view now, and that it cannot be regarded as a teaching of the new positivism. On the contrary, we have pointed out from the beginning that our definition of meaning does not imply such absurd consequences, and when someone asked, "But how can you verify a proposition about a future event?", we replied, "Why, for instance, by waiting for it to happen! 'Waiting' is a perfectly legitimate method of verification".

. . .

III

Verifiability means possibility of verification. Professor Lewis justly remarks that to "omit all examination of the wide range of significance which could attach to 'possible verification', would be to leave the whole conception rather obscure". For our purpose it suffices to distinguish between two of the many ways in which the word 'possibility' is used. We shall call them 'empirical possibility' and 'logical possibility'. Professor Lewis describes two meanings of 'verifiability' which correspond exactly to this difference; he is fully aware of it, and there is hardly anything left for me to do but carefully to work out the distinction and show its bearing upon our issue.

I propose to call 'empirically possible' anything that does not contradict the laws of nature. This is, I think, the largest sense in which we may speak of empirical possibility; we do not restrict the term to happenings which are not only in accordance with the laws of nature but also with the actual state of the universe (where 'actual' might refer to the present moment of our own lives, or to the condition of human beings on this planet, and so forth). If we chose the latter definition (which seems to have been in Professor

Lewis's mind when he spoke of "possible experience as conditioned by the actual") we should not get the sharp boundaries we need for our present purpose. So 'empirical possibility' is to mean 'compatibility with natural laws'.

Now, since we cannot boast of a complete and sure knowledge of nature's laws, it is evident that we can never assert with certainty the empirical possibility of any fact, and here we may be permitted to speak of *degrees* of possibility. Is it possible for me to lift this book? Surely!—This table? I think so!—This billiard table? I don't think so!—This automobile? Certainly not!—It is clear that in these cases the answer is given by *experience*, as the result of experiments performed in the past. Any judgment about empirical possibility is based on experience and will often be rather uncertain; there will be no sharp boundary between possibility and impossibility.

Is the possibility of verification which we insist upon of this empirical sort? In that case there would be different degrees of verifiability, the question of meaning would be a matter of more or less, not a matter of yes or no. In many disputes concerning our issue it is the empirical possibility of verification which is discussed; the various examples of verifiability given by Professor Lewis, *e.g.*, are instances of different empirical circumstances in which the verification is carried out or prevented from being carried out. Many of those who refuse to accept our criterion of meaning seem to imagine that the procedure of its application in a special case is somewhat like this: A proposition is presented to us ready made, and in order to discover its meaning we have to try various methods of verifying or falsifying it, and if one of these methods works we have found the meaning of the proposition; but if not, we say it has no meaning. If we really had to proceed in this way, it is clear that the determination of meaning would be entirely a matter of experience, and that in many cases no sharp and ultimate decision could be obtained. How could we ever know that we had tried long enough, if none of our methods were successful? Might not future efforts disclose a meaning which we were unable to find before?

This whole conception is, of course, entirely erroneous. It speaks of meaning as if it were a kind of entity inherent in a sentence and hidden in it like a nut in its shell, so that the philosopher would have to crack the shell or sentence in order to reveal the nut or meaning. We know from our considerations in section I that a proposition cannot be given 'ready made'; that meaning does not inhere in a sentence where it might be discovered, but that it must be bestowed upon it. And this is done by applying to the sentence the rules of the logical grammar of our language, as explained in section I. These rules are not facts of nature which could be 'discovered', but they are prescriptions stipulated by acts of definition. And these definitions have to be known to those who pronounce the sentence in question and to those who hear or read it. Otherwise they are not confronted with any proposition at all, and there is nothing they could try to verify, because you can't verify or falsify a mere row of words. You cannot even start verifying before you know the meaning, *i.e.*, before you have established the possibility of verification.

In other words, the possibility of verification which is relevant to meaning cannot be of the empirical sort; it cannot be established *post festum* [after the fact]. You have to be sure of it before you can consider the empirical circumstances and investigate whether or no or under what conditions they will permit of verification. The empirical circumstances are all-important when you want to know if a proposition is *true* (which is the concern of the scientist), but they can have no influence on the *meaning* of the proposition (which is the concern of the philosopher). Professor Lewis has seen and expressed this very clearly, and our Vienna positivism, as far as I can answer for it, is in complete agreement with him on this point. It must be emphasized that when we speak of verifiability we mean *logical* possibility of verification, and nothing but this.

.   .   .

The dividing line between logical possibility and impossibility of verification is absolutely sharp and distinct; there is no gradual transition between meaning and nonsense. For either you have given the grammatical rules for verification, or you have not; *tertium non datur* [there is no third possibility].

Empirical possibility is determined by the laws of nature, but meaning and verifiability are entirely independent of them. Everything that I can describe or define is logically possible—and definitions are in no way bound up with natural laws. The proposition 'Rivers flow uphill' is meaningful, but happens to be false because the fact it describes is *physically* impossible. It will not deprive a proposition of its meaning if the conditions which I stipulate for its verification are incompatible with the laws of nature; I may prescribe conditions, for instance, which could be fulfilled only if the velocity of light were greater than it actually is, or if the Law of Conservation of Energy did not hold, and so forth.

An opponent of our view might find a dangerous paradox or even a contradiction in the preceding explanations, because on the one hand we insisted so strongly on what has been called the "*empirical*-meaning requirement", and on the other hand we assert most emphatically that meaning and verifiability do not depend on any empirical conditions whatever, but are determined by purely logical possibilities. The opponent will object: if meaning is a matter of experience, how can it be a matter of definition and logic?

In reality there is no contradiction or difficulty. The word 'experience' is ambiguous. Firstly, it may be a name for any so-called 'immediate data'— which is a comparatively modern use of the word—and secondly we can use it in the sense in which we speak *e.g.*, of an 'experienced traveller', meaning a man who has not only seen a great deal but also knows how to profit from it for his actions. It is in this second sense (by the way, the sense the word has in Hume's and Kant's philosophy) that verifiability must be declared to be independent of experience. The possibility of verification does not rest on any 'experiential truth', on a law of nature or any other true general proposition, but is determined solely by our definitions, by the rules which have been fixed for our language, or which we can fix arbitrarily at any moment. All of these rules ultimately point to ostensive definitions, as we have explained, and through them verifiability is linked to *experience* in the *first* sense of the word. No rule of expression presupposes any law or regularity in the world (which is the condition of 'experience' as Hume and Kant use the word), but it does presuppose data and situations, to which names can be attached. The rules of language are rules of the application of language; so there must be something to which it can be applied. Expressibility and verifiability are one and the same thing. There is no antagonism between logic and experience. Not only can the logician be an empiricist at the same time; he *must* be one if he wants to understand what he himself is doing.

.   .   .

3
EMPIRICIST CRITERIA OF COGNITIVE SIGNIFICANCE: PROBLEMS AND CHANGES

Carl G. Hempel

1. THE GENERAL EMPIRICIST CONCEPTION OF COGNITIVE AND EMPIRICAL SIGNIFICANCE

It is a basic principle of contemporary empiricism that a sentence makes a cognitively significant assertion, and thus can be said to be either true or false, if and only if either (1) it is analytic or contradictory—in which case it is said to have purely logical meaning or significance—or else (2) it is capable, at least potentially, of test by experiential evidence—in which case it is said to have empirical meaning or significance. The basic tenet of this principle, and especially of its second part, the so-called testability criterion of empirical meaning (or better: meaningfulness), is not peculiar to empiricism alone: it is characteristic also of contemporary operationism, and in a sense of pragmatism as well; for the pragmatist maxim that a difference must make a difference to be a difference may well be construed as insisting that a verbal difference between two sentences must make a difference in experiential implications if it is to reflect a difference in meaning.

How this general conception of cognitively significant discourse led to the rejection, as devoid of logical and empirical meaning, of various formulations in speculative metaphysics, and even of certain hypotheses offered within empirical science, is too well known to require recounting. I think that the general intent of the empiricist criterion of meaning is basically

From Carl G. Hempel, *Aspects of Scientific Explanation* (New York and London: 1965), Essay IV, pp. 101–119. Copyright © 1965 by the Free Press. This essay combines, with certain omissions and some other changes, the contents of two articles: "Problems and Changes in the Empiricist Criterion of Meaning," *Revue Internationale de Philosophie*, No. 11 (1950), 41–63; and "The Concept of Cognitive Significance: A Reconsideration," *Proceedings of the American Academy of Arts and Sciences*, 80 (1951), 61–77. Reprinted by permission of the Director of *Revue Internationale de Philosophie; Daedalus,* Journal of the American Academy of Arts and Sciences, Boston, Massachusetts; and the author.

sound, and that notwithstanding much oversimplification in its use, its critical application has been, on the whole, enlightening and salutary. I feel less confident, however, about the possibility of restating the general idea in the form of precise and general criteria which establish sharp dividing lines (a) between statements of purely logical and statements of empirical significance, and (b) between those sentences which do have cognitive significance and those which do not.

In the present paper, I propose to reconsider these distinctions as conceived in recent empiricism, and to point out some of the difficulties they present. The discussion will concern mainly the second of the two distinctions; in regard to the first, I shall limit myself to a few brief remarks.

2. THE EARLIER TESTABILITY CRITERIA OF MEANING AND THEIR SHORTCOMINGS

Let us note first that any general criterion of cognitive significance will have to meet certain requirements if it is to be at all acceptable. Of these, we note one, which we shall consider here as expressing a necessary, though by no means sufficient, *condition of adequacy* for criteria of cognitive significance.

(A) If under a given criterion of cognitive significance, a sentence N is nonsignificant, then so must be all truth-functional compound sentences in which N occurs nonvacuously as a component. For if N cannot be significantly assigned a truth value, then it is impossible to assign truth values to the compound sentences containing N; hence, they should be qualified as nonsignificant as well.

We note two corollaries of requirement (A):

(A1) If under a given criterion of cognitive significance, a sentence S is nonsignificant, then so must be its negation, $\sim S$.

(A2) If under a given criterion of cognitive significance, a sentence N is nonsignificant, then so must be any conjunction $N \cdot S$ and any disjunction $N \vee S$, no matter whether S is significant under the given criterion or not.

We now turn to the initial attempts made in recent empiricism to establish general criteria of cognitive significance. Those attempts were governed by the consideration that a sentence, to make an empirical assertion must be capable of being borne out by, or conflicting with, phenomena which are potentially capable of being directly observed. Sentences describing such potentially observable phenomena—no matter whether the latter do actually occur or not—may be called observation sentences. More specifically, an *observation sentence* might be construed as a sentence—no matter whether true or false—which asserts or denies that a specified object, or group of objects, of macroscopic size has a particular *observable characteristic*, i.e., a characteristic whose presence or absence can, under favorable circumstances, be ascertained by direct observation.

The task of setting up criteria of empirical significance is thus transformed into the problem of characterizing in a precise manner the relationship which obtains between a hypothesis and one or more observation sentences whenever the phenomena described by the latter either confirm or disconfirm the hypothesis in question. The ability of a given sentence to enter into that relationship to some set of observation sentences would then characterize its testability-in-principle, and thus its empirical significance. Let us now briefly examine the major attempts that have been made to obtain criteria of significance in this manner.

One of the earliest criteria is expressed in the so-called *verifiability requirement*. According to it, a sentence is empirically significant if and only if it is not analytic and is capable, at least in principle, of complete verification by observational evidence; i.e., if observational evidence can be described which, if actually obtained, would conclusively establish the truth of the sentence. With the help of the concept of observation sentence, we can restate this requirement as follows: A sentence S has empirical meaning if and only if it is possible to indicate a finite set of observation sentences, O_1, O_2, . . . , O_n, such that if these are true, then S is necessarily true, too. As stated, however, this condition is satisfied also if S is an analytic sentence or if the given observation sentences are logically incompatible with each other. By the following formulation, we rule these cases out and at the same time express the intended criterion more precisely:

(2.1) REQUIREMENT OF COMPLETE VERIFIABILITY IN PRINCIPLE. A sentence has empirical meaning if and only if it is not analytic and follows logically from some finite and logically consistent class of observation sentences. These observation sentences need not be true, for what the criterion is to explicate is testability by "potentially observable phenomena," or testability "in principle."

In accordance with the general conception of cognitive significance outlined earlier, a sentence will now be classified as cognitively significant if either it is analytic or contradictory, or it satisfies the verifiability requirement.

This criterion, however, has several serious defects. One of them has been noted by several writers:

a. Let us assume that the properties of being a stork and of being red-legged are both observable characteristics, and that the former does not logically entail the latter. Then the sentence

(S1)   All storks are red-legged

is neither analytic nor contradictory; and clearly, it is not deducible from a finite set of observation sentences. Hence, under the contemplated criterion, S1 is devoid of empirical significance; and so are all other sentences purporting to express universal regularities or general laws. And since sentences of this type constitute an integral part of scientific theories, the verifiability requirement must be regarded as overly restrictive in this respect.

Similarly, the criterion disqualifies all sentences such as 'For any substance there exists some solvent', which contain both universal and existential quantifiers (i.e., occurrences of the terms 'all' and 'some' or their equivalents); for no sentences of this kind can be logically deduced from any finite set of observation sentences.

Two further defects of the verifiability requirement do not seem to have been widely noticed:

b. As is readily seen, the negation of S1

(~S1)   There exists at least one stork that is not red-legged

is deducible from any two observation sentences of the type 'a is a stork' and 'a is not red-legged'. Hence, ~S1 is cognitively significant under our criterion, but S1 is not, and this constitutes a violation of condition (A1).

c. Let S be a sentence which does, and N a sentence which does not satisfy the verifiability requirement. Then S is deducible from some set of observation sentences; hence, by a familiar rule of logic, SvN is deducible from the same set, and therefore cognitively significant according to our criterion. This violates condition (A2) above.

Strictly analogous considerations apply to an alternative criterion, which makes complete falsifiability in principle the defining characteristic of empirical significance. Let us formulate this criterion as follows:

(2.2) REQUIREMENT OF COMPLETE FALSIFIABILITY IN PRINCIPLE. A sentence has empirical meaning if and only if its negation is not analytic and follows logically from some finite logically consistent class of observation sentences.

This criterion qualifies a sentence as empirically meaningful if its negation satisfies the requirements of complete verifiability; as it is to be expected, it is therefore inadequate on similar grounds as the latter:

(a) It denies cognitive significance to purely existential hypotheses, such as 'There exists at least one unicorn', and all sentences whose formulation calls for mixed—i.e., universal and existential—quantification, such as 'For every compound there exists some solvent', for none of these can possibly be conclusively falsified by a finite number of observation sentences.

(b) If 'P' is an observation predicate, then the assertion that all things have the property P is qualified as significant, but its negation, being equivalent to a purely existential hypothesis, is disqualified [cf. (a)]. Hence, criterion (2.2) gives rise to the same dilemma as (2.1).

(c) If a sentence S is completely falsifiable whereas N is a sentence which is not, then their conjunction, S·N (i.e., the expression obtained by connecting the two sentences by the word 'and') is completely falsifiable; for if the negation of S is entailed by a class of observation sentences, then the negation of S·N is, *a fortiori*, entailed by the same class. Thus, the criterion allows empirical significance to many sentences which an adequate empiricist criterion should rule out, such as 'All swans are white and the absolute is perfect.'

In sum, then, interpretations of the testability criterion in terms of complete verifiability or of complete falsifiability are inadequate because they are overly restrictive in one direction and overly inclusive in another, and because both of them violate the fundamental requirement A.

Several attempts have been made to avoid these difficulties by construing the testability criterion as demanding merely a partial and possibly indirect confirmability of empirical hypotheses by observational evidence.

A formulation suggested by Ayer is characteristic of these attempts to set up a clear and sufficiently comprehensive criterion of confirmability. It states, in effect, that a sentence S has empirical import if from S in conjunction with suitable subsidiary hypotheses it is possible to derive observation sentences which are not derivable from the subsidiary hypotheses alone.

This condition is suggested by a closer consideration of the logical structure of scientific testing; but it is much too liberal as it stands. Indeed, as Ayer himself has pointed out in the second edition of his book, *Language, Truth, and Logic*, his criterion allows empirical import to any sentence whatever. Thus, e.g., if S is the sentence 'The absolute is perfect', it suffices to choose as a subsidiary hypothesis the sentence 'If the absolute is perfect then this apple is red' in order to make possible the deduction of the observation sentence 'This apple is red', which clearly does not follow from the subsidiary hypothesis alone.

To meet this objection, Ayer proposed a modified version of his testability criterion. In effect, the modification restricts the subsidiary hypotheses mentioned in the previous version to sentences which either are analytic or can independently be shown to be testable in the sense of the modified criterion.

But it can readily be shown that this new criterion, like the requirement of complete falsifiability, allows empirical significance to any conjunction $S \cdot N$, where S satisfies Ayer's criterion while N is a sentence such as 'The absolute is perfect', which is to be disqualified by that criterion. Indeed, whatever consequences can be deduced from S with the help of permissible subsidiary hypotheses can also be deduced from $S \cdot N$ by means of the same subsidiary hypotheses; and as Ayer's new criterion is formulated essentially in terms of the deducibility of a certain type of consequence from the given sentence, it countenances $S \cdot N$ together with S. Another difficulty has been pointed out by Church, who has shown that if there are any three observation sentences none of which alone entails any of the others, then it follows for any sentence S whatsoever that either it or its denial has empirical import according to Ayer's revised criterion.

All the criteria considered so far attempt to explicate the concept of empirical significance by specifying certain logical connections which must obtain between a significant sentence and suitable observation sentences. It seems now that this type of approach offers little hope for the attainment of precise criteria of meaningfulness: this conclusion is suggested by the preceding survey of some representative attempts, and it receives additional support from certain further considerations, some of which will be presented in the following sections.

3. CHARACTERIZATION OF SIGNIFICANT SENTENCES BY CRITERIA FOR THEIR CONSTITUENT TERMS

An alternative procedure suggests itself which again seems to reflect well the general viewpoint of empiricism: It might be possible to characterize cognitively significant sentences by certain conditions which their constituent terms have to satisfy. Specifically, it would seem reasonable to say that all extralogical terms in a significant sentence must have experiential reference, and that therefore their meanings must be capable of explication by reference to observables exclusively. In order to exhibit certain analogies between this approach and the previous one, we adopt the following terminological conventions:

Any term that may occur in a cognitively significant sentence will be called a *cognitively significant term*. Furthermore, we shall understand by an *observation term* any term which either (a) is an *observation predicate*, i.e., signifies some observable characteristic (as do the terms 'blue', 'warm', 'soft', 'coincident with', 'of greater apparent brightness than') or (b) names some physical object of macroscopic size (as do the terms 'the needle of this instrument', 'the Moon', 'Krakatoa Volcano', 'Greenwich, England', 'Julius Caesar').

Now while the testability criteria of meaning aimed at characterizing the cognitively significant sentences by means of certain inferential connections in which they must stand to some observation sentences, the alternative approach under consideration would instead try to specify the vocabulary that may be used in forming significant sentences. This vocabulary, the class of significant terms, would be characterized by the condition that each of its elements is either a logical term or else a term with empirical significance; in the latter case, it has to stand in certain definitional or explicative connections to some observation terms. This approach certainly avoids any violations of our earlier conditions of adequacy. Thus, e.g., if S is a significant sentence, i.e., contains cognitively significant terms only, then so is its denial, since the denial sign, and its verbal equivalents, belong to the vocabulary of logic and are thus significant. Again, if N is a sentence containing a non-significant term, then so is any compound sentence which contains N.

But this is not sufficient, of course. Rather, we shall now have to consider a crucial question analogous to that raised by the previous approach: Precisely how are the logical connections between empirically significant terms and observation terms to be construed if an adequate criterion of cognitive significance is to result? Let us consider some possibilities.

(3.1) The simplest criterion that suggests itself might be called the *requirement of definability*. It would demand that any term with empirical significance must be explicitly definable by means of observation terms.

This criterion would seem to accord well with the maxim of operationism that all significant terms of empirical science must be introduced by operational definitions. However, the requirement of definability is vastly too restrictive, for many important terms of scientific and even pre-scientific discourse cannot be explicitly defined by means of observation terms.

In fact, as Carnap has pointed out, an attempt to provide explicit definitions in terms of observables encounters serious difficulties as soon as disposition terms, such as 'soluble', 'malleable', 'electric conductor', etc., have to be accounted for; and many of these occur even on the pre-scientific level of discourse.

Consider, for example, the word 'fragile'. One might try to define it by saying that an object x is fragile if and only if it satisfies the following condition: If at any time t the object is sharply struck, then it breaks at that time. But if the statement connectives in this phrasing are construed truth-functionally, so that the definition can be symbolized by

$$(D) \qquad Fx \equiv (t)(Sxt \supset Bxt)$$

then the predicate 'F' thus defined does not have the intended meaning. For let a be any object which is not fragile (e.g., a raindrop or a rubber band), but which happens not to be sharply struck at any time throughout its existence. Then 'Sat' is false and hence '$Sat \supset Bat$' is true for all values of 't'; consequently, 'Fa' is true though a is not fragile.

To remedy this defect, one might construe the phrase 'if . . . then . . .' in the original definiens as having a more restrictive meaning than the truth-functional conditional. This meaning might be suggested by the subjunctive phrasing 'If x were to be sharply struck at any time t, then x would break at t.' But a satisfactory elaboration of this construal would require a clarification of the meaning and the logic of counterfactual and subjunctive conditionals, which is a thorny problem.

An alternative procedure was suggested by Carnap in his theory of reduction sentences. These are sentences which, unlike definitions, specify the meaning of a term only conditionally or partially. The term 'fragile', for example, might be introduced by the following reduction sentence:

$$(R) \qquad (x)(t)[Sxt \supset (Fx \equiv Bxt)]$$

which specifies that if x is sharply struck at any time t, then x is fragile if and only if x breaks at t.

Our earlier difficulty is now avoided, for if a is a nonfragile object that is never sharply struck, then that expression in R which follows the quantifiers is true of a; but this does not imply that 'Fa' is true. But the reduction sentence R specifies the meaning of 'F' only for application to those objects which meet the "test condition" of being sharply struck at some time; for these it states that fragility then amounts to breaking. For objects that fail to meet the test condition, the meaning of 'F' is left undetermined. In this sense, reduction sentences have the character of partial or conditional definitions.

Reduction sentences provide a satisfactory interpretation of the experiential import of a large class of disposition terms and permit a more adequate formulation of so-called operational definitions, which, in general, are not complete definitions at all. These considerations suggest a greatly liberalized alternative to the requirement of definability:

(3.2) *The requirement of reducibility.* Every term with empirical significance must be capable of introduction, on the basis of observation terms, through chains of reduction sentences.

This requirement is characteristic of the liberalized versions of positivism and physicalism which, since about 1936, have superseded the older, overly narrow conception of a full definability of all terms of empirical science by means of observables, and it avoids many of the shortcomings of the latter. Yet, reduction sentences do not seem to offer an adequate means for the introduction of the central terms of advanced scientific theories, often referred to as theoretical constructs. This is indicated by the following considerations: A chain of reduction sentences provides a necessary and a sufficient condition for the applicability of the term it introduces. (When the two conditions coincide, the chain is tantamount to an explicit definition.) But now take, for example, the concept of length as used in classical physical theory. Here, the length in centimeters of the distance between two points may assume any positive real number as its value; yet it is clearly impossible to formulate, by means of observation terms, a sufficient condition for the applicability of such expressions as 'having a length of $\sqrt{2}$ cm' and 'having a length of $\sqrt{2} + 10^{-100}$ cm'; for such conditions would provide a possibility for discrimination, in observational terms, between two lengths which differ by only 10^{-100} cm.

It would be ill-advised to argue that for this reason, we ought to permit only such values of the magnitude, length, as permit the statement of sufficient conditions in terms of observables. For this would rule out, among others, all irrational numbers and would prevent us from assigning to the diagonal of a square with sides of length 1, the length $\sqrt{2}$, which is required by Euclidean geometry. Hence, the principles of Euclidean geometry would not be universally applicable in physics. Similarly, the principles of the calculus would become inapplicable, and the system of scientific theory as we know it today would be reduced to a clumsy, unmanageable torso. This, then, is no way of meeting the difficulty. Rather, we shall have to analyze more closely the function of constructs in scientific theories, with a view to obtaining through such an analysis a more adequate characterization of cognitively significant terms.

Theoretical constructs occur in the formulation of scientific theories. These may be conceived of, in their advanced stages, as being stated in the form of deductively developed axiomatized systems. Classical mechanics, or Euclidean or some Non-Euclidean form of geometry in physical interpretation, present examples of such systems. The extralogical terms used in a theory of this kind may be divided, in familiar manner, into primitive or basic terms, which are not defined within the theory, and defined terms, which are explicitly defined by means of the primitives. Thus, e.g., in Hilbert's axiomatization of Euclidean geometry, the terms 'point', 'straight line', 'between' are among the primitives, while 'line segment', 'angle', 'triangle', 'length' are among the defined terms. The basic and the defined terms together with the terms of logic constitute the vocabulary out of which all the sentences of the theory are constructed. The latter are divided, in an axiomatic presentation, into primitive statements (also called postulates or basic statements) which, in the theory, are not derived from any other statements, and derived ones, which are obtained by logical deduction from the primitive statements.

From its primitive terms and sentences, an axiomatized theory can be developed by means of purely formal principles of definition and deduction, without any consideration of the empirical significance of its extralogical terms. Indeed, this is the standard procedure employed in the axiomatic development of uninterpreted mathematical theories such as those of abstract groups or rings or lattices, or any form of pure (i.e., noninterpreted) geometry.

However, a deductively developed system of this sort can constitute a scientific theory only if it has received an empirical interpretation which renders it relevant to the phenomena of our experience. Such interpretation is given by assigning a meaning, in terms of observables, to certain terms or sentences of the formalized theory. Frequently, an interpretation is given not for the primitive terms or statements but rather for some of the terms definable by means of the primitives, or for some of the sentences deducible from the postulates. Furthermore, interpretation may amount to only a partial assignment of meaning. Thus, e.g., the rules for the measurement of length by means of a standard rod may be considered as providing a *partial* empirical interpretation for the term 'the length, in centimeters, of interval *i*', or alternatively, for some sentences of the form 'the length of interval *i* is *r* centimeters'. For the method is applicable only to intervals of a certain medium size, and even for the latter it does not constitute a full interpretation since the use of a standard rod does not constitute the only way of determining length: various alternative procedures are available involving the measurement of other magnitudes which are connected, by general laws, with the length that is to be determined.

This last observation, concerning the possibility of an indirect measurement of length by virtue of certain laws, suggests an important reminder. It is not correct to speak, as is often done, of "the experiential meaning" of a term or a sentence in isolation. In the language of science, and for similar reasons even in pre-scientific discourse, a single statement usually has no experiential implications. A single sentence in a scientific theory does not, as a rule, entail any observation sentences; consequences asserting the occurrence of certain observable phenomena can be derived from it only by conjoining it with a set of other, subsidiary, hypotheses. Of the latter, some will usually be observation sentences, others will be previously accepted theoretical statements. Thus, e.g., the relativistic theory of the deflection of light rays in the gravitational field of the sun entails assertions about observable phenomena only if it is conjoined with a considerable body of astronomical and optical theory as well as a large number of specific statements about the instruments used in those observations of solar eclipses which serve to test the hypothesis in question.

Hence, the phrase, 'the experiential meaning of expression E' is elliptical: What a given expression "means" in regard to potential empirical data is relative to two factors, namely:

I. *the linguistic framework L* to which the expression belongs. Its rules determine, in particular, what sentences—observational or otherwise—may be inferred from a given statement or class of statements;

II. the theoretical context in which the expression occurs, i.e., the class of those statements in L which are available as subsidiary hypotheses.

Thus, the sentence formulating Newton's law of gravitation has no experiential meaning by itself; but when used in a language whose logical apparatus permits the development of the calculus, and when combined with a suitable system of other hypotheses—including sentences which connect some of the theoretical terms with observation terms and thus establish a partial interpretation—then it has a bearing on observable phenomena in a large variety of fields. Analogous considerations are applicable to the term 'gravitational field', for example. It can be considered as having experiential meaning only within the context of a theory, which must be at least partially interpreted; and the experiential meaning of the term—as expressed, say, in the form of operational criteria for its application—will depend again on the theoretical system at hand, and on the logical characteristics of the language within which it is formulated.

4. COGNITIVE SIGNIFICANCE AS A CHARACTERISTIC OF INTERPRETED SYSTEMS

The preceding considerations point to the conclusion that a satisfactory criterion of cognitive significance cannot be reached through the second

avenue of approach here considered, namely by means of specific requirements for the terms which make up significant sentences. This result accords
with a general characteristic of scientific (and, in principle, even pre-scientific) theorizing: Theory formation and concept formation go hand in
hand; neither can be carried on successfully in isolation from the other.

If, therefore, cognitive significance can be attributed to anything, then
only to entire theoretical systems formulated in a language with a well-de-
termined structure. And the decisive mark of cognitive significance in such
a system appears to be the existence of an interpretation for it in terms of
observables. Such an interpretation might be formulated, for example, by
means of conditional or biconditional sentences connecting nonobservational
terms of the system with observation terms in the given language; the latter
as well as the connecting sentences may or may not belong to the theoretical
system.

But the requirement of partial interpretation is extremely liberal; it is satisfied, for example, by the system consisting of contemporary physical theory
combined with some set of principles of speculative metaphysics, even if the
latter have no empirical interpretation at all. Within the total system, these
metaphysical principles play the role of what K. Reach and also O. Neurath
liked to call *isolated sentences:* They are neither purely formal truths or
falsehoods, demonstrable or refutable by means of the logical rules of the
given language system; nor do they have any experiential bearing; i.e., their
omission from the theoretical system would have no effect on its explanatory
and predictive power in regard to potentially observable phenomena (i.e.,
the kind of phenomena described by observation sentences). Should we not,
therefore, require that a cognitively significant system contain no isolated
sentences? The following criterion suggests itself:

(4.1) A theoretical system is cognitively significant if and only if it is
partially interpreted to at least such an extent that none of its primitive
sentences is isolated.

But this requirement may bar from a theoretical system certain sentences
which might well be viewed as permissible and indeed desirable. By way of a
simple illustration, let us assume that our theoretical system T contains the
primitive sentence

$$(S1) \qquad (x) \, [P_1x \supset (Qx \equiv P_2x)]$$

where 'P_1' and 'P_2' are observation predicates in the given language L, while
'Q' functions in T somewhat in the manner of a theoretical construct and
occurs in only one primitive sentence of T, namely $S1$. Now $S1$ is not a truth
or falsehood of formal logic; and furthermore, if $S1$ is omitted from the set of
primitive sentences of T, then the resulting system, T', possesses exactly the
same systematic, i.e., explanatory and predictive, power as T. Our contemplated criterion would therefore qualify $S1$ as an isolated sentence which has
to be eliminated—excised by means of Occam's razor, as it were—if the
theoretical system at hand is to be cognitively significant.

But it is possible to take a much more liberal view of $S1$ by treating it as a
partial definition for the theoretical term 'Q'. Thus conceived, $S1$ specifies
that in all cases where the observable characteristic P_1 is present, 'Q' is ap-

plicable if and only if the observable characteristic P_2 is present as well. In fact, $S1$ is an instance of those partial, or conditional, definitions which Carnap calls bilateral reduction sentences. These sentences are explicitly qualified by Carnap as analytic (though not, of course, as truths of formal logic), essentially on the ground that all their consequences which are expressible by means of observation predicates (and logical terms) alone are truths of formal logic.

Let us pursue this line of thought a little further. This will lead us to some observations on analytic sentences and then back to the question of the adequacy of (4.1).

Suppose that we add to our system T the further sentence

$$(S2) \qquad (x)[P_3x \supset (Qx \equiv P_4x)]$$

where 'P_3', 'P_4' are additional observation predicates. Then, on the view that "every bilateral reduction sentence is analytic", $S2$ would be analytic as well as $S1$. Yet, the two sentences jointly entail non-analytic consequences which are expressible in terms of observation predicates alone, such as

$$(O) \qquad (x) [\sim (P_1x \cdot P_2x \cdot P_3x \cdot \sim P_4x) \cdot \sim (P_1x \cdot \sim P_2x \cdot P_3x \cdot P_4x)]$$

But one would hardly want to admit the consequence that the conjunction of two analytic sentences may be synthetic. Hence if the concept of analyticity can be applied at all to the sentences of interpreted deductive systems, then it will have to be relativized with respect to the theoretical context at hand. Thus, e.g., $S1$ might be qualified as analytic relative to the system T, whose remaining postulates do not contain the term 'Q', but as synthetic relative to the system T enriched by $S2$. Strictly speaking, the concept of analyticity has to be relativized also in regard to the rules of the language at hand, for the latter determine what observational or other consequences are entailed by a given sentence. This need for at least a twofold relativization of the concept of analyticity was almost to be expected in view of those considerations which required the same twofold relativization for the concept of experiential meaning of a sentence.

If, on the other hand, we decide not to permit $S1$ in the role of a partial definition and instead reject it as an isolated sentence, then we are led to an analogous conclusion: Whether a sentence is isolated or not will depend on the linguistic frame and on the theoretical context at hand: While $S1$ is isolated relative to T (and the language in which both are formulated), it acquires definite experiential implications when T is enlarged by $S2$.

Thus we find, on the level of interpreted theoretical systems, a peculiar rapprochement, and partial fusion, of some of the problems pertaining to the concepts of cognitive significance and of analyticity: Both concepts need to be relativized; and a large class of sentences may be viewed, apparently with equal right, as analytic in a given context, or as isolated, or nonsignificant, in respect to it.

In addition to barring, as isolated in a given context, certain sentences which could just as well be construed as partial definitions, the criterion (4.1) has another serious defect. Of two logically equivalent formulations of a theoretical system it may qualify one as significant while barring the other as containing an isolated sentence among its primitives. For assume that a certain theoretical system $T1$ contains among its primitive sentences S', S'',

. . . exactly one, S', which is isolated. Then $T1$ is not significant under (4.1). But now consider the theoretical system $T2$ obtained from $T1$ by replacing the two first primitive sentences, S', S'', by one, namely their conjunction. Then, under our assumptions, none of the primitive sentences of $T2$ is isolated, and $T2$, though equivalent to $T1$, is qualified as significant by (4.1). In order to do justice to the intent of (4.1), we would therefore have to lay down the following stricter requirement:

(4.2) A theoretical system is cognitively significant if and only if it is partially interpreted to such an extent that in no system equivalent to it at least one primitive sentence is isolated.

Let us apply this requirement to some theoretical system whose postulates include the two sentences $S1$ and $S2$ considered before, and whose other postulates do not contain 'Q' at all. Since the sentences $S1$ and $S2$ together entail the sentence O, the set consisting of $S1$ and $S2$ is logically equivalent to the set consisting of $S1$, $S2$ and O. Hence, if we replace the former set by the latter, we obtain a theoretical system equivalent to the given one. In this new system, both $S1$ and $S2$ are isolated since, as can be shown, their removal does not affect the explanatory and predictive power of the system in reference to observable phenomena. To put it intuitively, the systematic power of $S1$ and $S2$ is the same as that of O. Hence, the original system is disqualified by (4.2). From the viewpoint of a strictly sensationalist positivism as perhaps envisaged by Mach, this result might be hailed as a sound repudiation of theories making reference to fictitious entities, and as a strict insistence on theories couched exclusively in terms of observables. But from a contemporary vantage point, we shall have to say that such a procedure overlooks or misjudges the important function of constructs in scientific theory: The history of scientific endeavor shows that if we wish to arrive at precise, comprehensive, and well-confirmed general laws, we have to rise above the level of direct observation. The phenomena directly accessible to our experience are not connected by general laws of great scope and rigor. Theoretical constructs are needed for the formulation of such higher-level laws. One of the most important functions of a well-chosen construct is its potential ability to serve as a constituent in ever new general connections that may be discovered; and to such connections we would blind ourselves if we insisted on banning from scientific theories all those terms and sentences which could be "dispensed with" in the sense indicated in (4.2). In following such a narrowly phenomenalistic or positivistic course, we would deprive ourselves of the tremendous fertility of theoretical constructs, and we would often render the formal structure of the expurgated theory clumsy and inefficient.

Criterion (4.2), then, must be abandoned, and considerations such as those outlined in this paper seem to lend strong support to the conjecture that no adequate alternative to it can be found; i.e., that it is not possible to formulate general and precise criteria which would separate those partially interpreted systems whose isolated sentences might be said to have a significant function from those in which the isolated sentences are, so to speak, mere useless appendages.

We concluded earlier that cognitive significance in the sense intended by recent empiricism and operationism can at best be attributed to sentences forming a theoretical system, and perhaps rather to such systems as wholes. Now, rather than try to replace (4.2) by some alternative, we will have to recognize further that cognitive significance in a system is a matter of degree: Significant systems range from those whose entire extralogical vocabulary consists of observation terms, through theories whose formulation relies heavily on theoretical constructs, on to systems with hardly any bearing on potential empirical findings. Instead of dichotomizing this array into significant and nonsignificant systems it would seem less arbitrary and more promising to appraise or compare different theoretical systems in regard to such characteristics as these:

    a. the clarity and precision with which the theories are formulated, and with which the logical relationships of their elements to each other and to expressions couched in observational terms have been made explicit;

    b. the systematic, i.e., explanatory and predictive, power of the systems in regard to observable phenomena;

    c. the formal simplicity of the theoretical system with which a certain systematic power is attained;

    d. the extent to which the theories have been confirmed by experiential evidence.

Many of the speculative philosophical approaches to cosmology, biology, or history, for example, would make a poor showing on practically all of these counts and would thus prove no matches to available rival theories, or would be recognized as so unpromising as not to warrant further study or development.

If the procedure here suggested is to be carried out in detail, so as to become applicable also in less obvious cases, then it will be necessary, of course, to develop general standards, and theories pertaining to them, for the appraisal and comparison of theoretical systems in the various respects just mentioned. To what extent this can be done with rigor and precision cannot well be judged in advance. In recent years, a considerable amount of work has been done towards a definition and theory of the concept of degree of confirmation, or logical probability, of a theoretical system; and several contributions have been made towards the clarification of some of the other ideas referred to above. The continuation of this research represents a challenge for further constructive work in the logical and methodological analysis of scientific knowledge.

4

MEANING AND VERIFICATION

Friedrich Waismann

. . .

WHEN DO WE UNDERSTAND THE MEANING OF A SENTENCE?

In daily life this question causes us no difficulty. If a traveller reports to us that he has met dwarfs in the central regions of Africa, then we understand what is meant. There seems to be no further problem here which could disquiet us. Yet cases can arise where a thorough consideration of that which is meant in a sentence is absolutely necessary and where those who think that they are able to gather the meaning directly from the words of the sentence would go far astray. If a philosopher says to us 'Only the experience of the present moment has reality', and if another contradicts him, then it is by no means clear what the dispute is about; in fact, it is not even clear whether both the opponents mean anything with their words at all (and that is why the dispute can continue so long). In such cases it is necessary to find a criterion which indicates whether one has understood the meaning of a sentence. Such a criterion must already be contained in the normal use of language. We need only select it from ordinary language and express it in a clear sentence in order to find the answer to our question.

When are we *certain* that we understand the meaning of a sentence? Let us imagine that wave-mechanics is explained in a lecture. How can we ascertain whether a listener has understood the meaning of this theory? Is it sufficient that he can repeat it in his own words? Or that he has vivid images? Or that he can draw normal conclusions? All this would not prove to us that he has really understood the meaning. There is only one method which we must adopt in order to find the answer: we must ask him how he would set about investigating the truth of this theory. If he is unable to describe the conditions necessary to prove the truth of the theory, then we should say: 'he is mistaken, he has not really grasped what the theory states'.

From Friedrich Waismann, *The Principles of Linguistic Philosophy*, R. Harré, ed. (London and New York: 1965), Chap. XVI, Secs. 2–5, 7, pp. 324–332, 335–337. Reprinted by permission of St. Martin's Press Inc., The Macmillan Company of Canada Ltd., and Macmillan & Co. Ltd.

If, on the other hand, he can state some experiment which confirms or refutes the propositions of wave-mechanics, then he has understood the theory—even if it turns out that for practical reasons the experiment cannot be performed. It seems obvious that it is no new discovery, but only the formulation of a method used by everyone, when we say: 'the criterion of understanding a sentence is the knowledge of the method of its verification'.

In order, however, to avoid misunderstandings about what has been said two points must be added:

(i) Our criterion does not demand that we should know whether the proposition is true. It demands only that we should be able to describe theoretically a way in which the assertion could be examined. We can obviously understand a proposition without knowing whether it is true.

(ii) Our criterion is: can the sentence be theoretically verified? and *not:* can it be verified in practice? There are many propositions the truth of which at present cannot be verified—for example, the proposition whether there are mountains on the back of the moon. But we can describe now the observations which would make the proposition true.

ARE UNVERIFIABLE STATEMENTS MEANINGLESS?

The most controversial problem is this: have only those propositions meaning which are verifiable? If one answers with 'Yes', this answer has the air of an empirical statement which will arouse all sorts of opposition. For it could be objected: why should not facts exist which will always be inaccessible to us? If certain speculations of contemporary astronomy should prove true the expanding universe must finally separate into segments which are no longer causally connected. Under those circumstances we would not be able to have any knowledge of events outside our part of the universe. Another example: certain facts of quantum-mechanics could not be expressed at all in the language of classical physics, much less could they be verified—have these events because of this not occurred? Such an objection would be a complete misunderstanding. We do not say that everything which exists is accessible to our knowledge, or even to expression by ordinary language. We only say: if someone makes an assertion, then he must be able to state some possible method of verification, otherwise he is not clear about what he says. However, even this formulation still sounds dogmatic and may provoke opposition. Let us make the situation clear with the help of an example.

Let us imagine a man who says 'The universe has expanded to twice its original size this night'. How would the world appear to us on waking up in the morning? Well—just exactly as before. All things have become twice as large, consequently also the standard with which I measure, and thus I shall count with it the same number of metres. Our visual perceptions would also remain unchanged since that transformation leaves the angles unchanged. In short, this remarkable change of our world could not be verified in any way, it would remain completely unnoticed by us—at least, if we only consider spatial measurements. (It would, on the other hand, become manifest as soon as we measure the weight, the density, etc. We will for the sake of simplicity leave this possibility out of consideration.)

Now someone could say: 'we have seen that it is conceivable that the world should expand to twice its original size without our noticing it'. Perhaps it has really done so? And now it looks as if this proposition, though it could never be verified, nevertheless has a certain meaning: it states that the world has become twice as large. It might be said: 'if I want to put forward this hypothesis I can do so, and I am sure that no one can disprove it'.

Arguments of this kind could be used only because the logical situation remained obscure. The argument sounds as if an accidental combination of circumstances prevented me from getting knowledge of an event which in fact really has occurred. It lays stress upon the possibility that there could always be facts about which we can never know anything. The point in question, however, is not what we can know and what we cannot know, but only whether that sentence expresses a meaning.

Let us now investigate the meaning of the single words, in order to bring more clarity into the matter. We ask those who oppose us: You consider it possible that everything in the world has become twice as large as before. Clearly then also my hand is twice its original size. Now what does that mean? In daily life we understand the meaning of these words perfectly well. A thing has become twice as large means: if I measure it with a given standard, the number of linear units will be twice the number of units as measured before; or if I look at that thing it appears to me twice as large. We now ask: has the expression 'twice as large' the same significance in our case? Evidently not. According to the assumption it is not possible to determine the change either through applying a given standard or measuring the angles. Well, then, what does the expression mean? It has lost the old meaning; what is the new meaning? One might say ' "My hand has become twice as large" means: when measured with a standard measure which is not subject to the change, then it is twice as large as before'. We now ask the further question: 'And what does it mean to say the standard measure has remained unchanged? What is the criterion for this?' If I am to understand what is meant by a 'standard measure of unchangeable length', then the explanation of this phrase must give a criterion for ascertaining the invariability, or else I should not know when to use the expression and when not.

Let us sum up: either one explains the meaning of the words of the sentence; then the statement is verifiable, and the explanation shows the way to the verification; or, if the statement cannot be verified in any way, this is due to the fact that we have given no meaning to one of the expressions occurring in it. Though one is using words which have a clear meaning in ordinary language one is using them in a context, in which they lose this meaning. What we do here is merely to draw attention to the fact that they do lose their meaning.

Anyone who believes that he understands the meaning of the sentence 'The universe has expanded to twice its original size' is subject to a delusion. This delusion may be due to two circumstances: firstly, to the use of well-known words which are combined with each other in such a way that they sound like a familiar sentence; secondly, to the influence of images. If somebody says 'Certainly I can imagine that the world has expanded to twice its size', no doubt he thinks that he can do so because he can call up an image, say an image of the solar system expanding—while he himself remains unchanged in size. But he has not imagined the situation which would verify the proposition, namely, that he as well as the universe has changed in size—but an entirely different situation.

If thus we deny meaning to such a sentence we do not do this out of prejudice or on the basis of some philosophical 'theory', but merely because we see that in forming this sentence we have not fulfilled the conditions under which words acquire their meaning. The fact that this has often not been noticed has led to a great number of violent disputes to which the history of philosophy is a witness. We will place some examples side by side here which speak for themselves.

(i) Schopenhauer believed that Kant was mistaken when he said: 'It is not time itself which passes, it is only phenomena, occurring in time, which pass'. He put his argument in the following way: that this view is utterly false is proved by the fact that we all know with certainty that, even if everything in heaven and on earth came to a sudden standstill, time would pass on undisturbed; in such a way that, if subsequently nature started to work again, the question as to the length of the interval could be given an exact answer. If this were not the case, then time would have to stop with the stopping of the clock and move with the clock's movement.

(ii) Paul Mongré (Felix Hausdorff): 'If the movement of events in the Universe were suddenly to be a hundred times faster or slower than at present—this transcendental change in pace would remain completely unnoticed by us, since the standard of measurement would be subject to the same change as the periods of time which are measured by it. Or even past and future could be reversed if only our experiences and our memory remain unaltered.

'All this is transcendentally conceivable, because it is empirically unnoticeable; objectively admissible, because subjectively inaccessible'.

(iii) Otto v. Guericke considered air to be the scent of a substance which we do not perceive only because we have been used to it from our childhood.

(iv) Pierre d'Ailly, a late scholastic, believed it to be conceivable that our perceptions of reality should continue, even if reality itself had ceased to exist. How then, he asked, could we possibly know that physical objects exist?

'THE MEANING OF A STATEMENT IS THE METHOD
OF ITS VERIFICATION'

In such cases it is useful to say: 'the meaning of a statement is the method of its verification'. To say this is not to hold a theory which can be true or false—but it is rather a recommendation as to the way in which we should deal with certain sentences when they have no conventional meaning. We could also formulate it in this way: 'if you are not clear what the meaning of a statement is, or whether it has any meaning at all, then consider how it can be verified'. Once you realize how this can be done, then you will understand what the sentence means.

But if we were tempted to take the dictum 'The meaning of a statement is the method of its verification' as a *definition* of 'meaning', then it would not be difficult to raise various objections against it. I am now going to consider the meaning of imaginary sentences or of rules where it is quite obvious that this equation does not hold. The examples which I have in mind are, for instance: 'It rained yesterday', 'This man died five hours ago', 'Julius Caesar crossed the Alps'. Let us consider the first example. Surely this sentence seems to have a clear meaning straight away. However, if I were asked how it could be verified, I should perhaps in the first moment be at a loss and then make various suggestions: I could ask other persons, or look up the meteorological report of the previous day, I could examine the traces of moisture on the ground, or resort to my own memory. There is a vast number of possibilities which can hardly be exhausted. It is even possible that some discovery might be made by which the time of the last rain could be exactly ascertained. But do I *mean* by the statement the existence of any one of these facts? What I mean is surely that yesterday a definite occurrence took place of which the traces of moisture, etc., are only 'indications'. Now it seems that the meaning of a sentence has nothing whatsoever to do with its verification. One is inclined to say: 'I just do understand the sentence, I understand it because I know the English language'.

It looks now as if it were right to say: 'I can only suggest a method of verification *after* I have understood the meaning'. Usually, when considering such statements of daily life, I do not think of the verification, but could, if necessary, propose this or that procedure. By doing this, however, the meaning is, of course, not changed nor does it become *clearer* to me what I originally meant by the statement. On the contrary: the method of verification is irregular, loose, fluctuating, while the sentence always means the same.

Obviously I know what it means that it is now raining; I also know what the word 'yesterday' means; and now I understand the sentence 'It rained yesterday', and I understand it only because I understand the single words and know the usage of English syntax. This, however, does not mean that I know how the proposition is to be verified. If, subsequently, I learn to know one or the other method of verification, nothing is added to the meaning. What is it that leads me to suggest a particular method of verification? Well, I have learned from experience that rain leaves traces of moisture on the earth, or that the appearance of the plants is changed, etc. I remember such experiences and say that in this manner it can be determined whether it has rained yesterday. In such cases, therefore, to explain the method of verification is *not* to explain the meaning.

Let us take the second example: 'This man died five hours ago'. If I were asked whether I understood this sentence, I would truly answer: Of course I do; otherwise one could object that I do not know English. But if I were asked how I should verify it, I should not know what to say. Suppose it had been discovered how the moment of the death of the man can be precisely found out, say by examining the condition of the blood, I would not say, 'Ah, now at last I understand what the sentence means'. The meaning of the sentence had already been established before that discovery.

If a child does not understand a sentence, then what we explain to him is the meaning of the words, but not the method of its verification. In the normal use of language the questions 'What does this sentence mean?' and 'How do I find out whether this sentence is true?' are two entirely different questions, and everyone will refuse to regard them as alike.

Strange how irregular language is. Sometimes the meaning of a sentence is entirely clear to us while we do not know anything suitable to say about its verification or at least we hesitate between different possibilities. In other cases the meaning of a sentence is obscure to us, and only when the verification is given do we understand what the sentence expresses.

This shows that there are two ways of explaining the meaning of a sentence. One way is to give the meaning of the various words in the sentence and explain the way in which they are combined. The other consists in the description of the verification.

THE DESCRIPTION OF VERIFICATION

Let us now consider carefully the expression 'method of verification'. What are we doing when we describe the method of verification? In other words, what sort of an answer can we expect if we ask: how is a statement verified? Let us take an example: supposing that a metal ball is lying in front of me and someone says that it is charged with electricity—how can I verify this statement? I should connect the ball with an electroscope and observe whether the gold leaves diverge. The statement 'The gold leaves of the instrument diverge' describes the verification of the statement 'The ball is charged'. What, then, is it that I do when I describe the verification of the proposition p? I give a second proposition q, and determine that the second is to follow from the first. This is giving a rule of inference which connects these two propositions with each other. This rule is a part of the grammar of the expression p; and it must be determined *before* we can significantly apply the proposition p.

In ordinary language these two cases are not clearly distinguished. The question 'How do you tell whether his statement is true?' is answered now by giving a rule of inference, now by stating an empirical connection. And from this spring most of the confusions that disturb us in the question 'Is the meaning of a sentence the method of its verification?' Length can be measured in this way, or in that way, and we call the result of both measurements the 'length of the line'. Sometimes, however, we use the expression 'The length of a line' in such a way that it corresponds only to the result of one measurement. Then it is necessary for us to call to mind this convention. To make such a convention is, of course, nothing more than a grammatical procedure, and to give the method of verification is to give this rule.

Another example would be the question: under what conditions do we say that a human being is dead? Supposing we give the following explanation: a person is dead when his heart has stopped beating. Scarcely anyone would protest against such a definition. But if it were discovered that, given certain circumstances, human beings move, behave and act exactly as they do normally while their hearts have stopped beating, then the question would arise: shall we still say to them that they are dead?; or should we not rather speak of different meanings of the word 'dead' and distinguish between, say, 'heart-dead' and 'dead' in some other way? If now someone were to say that a person is dead, then we should ask him: 'What do you mean by "dead"? Heart-dead or dead in the other sense?' This question is a question as to the verification of the sentence, and the answer is a contribution to its grammar.

But there are cases where the situation is entirely different. Remember the example 'It rained yesterday', where the meaning is clear to start with and where there is a vast number of methods of verification. We are now in a position to explain the problem which has been troubling us in this chapter: how is it that sometimes the meaning of a sentence is absolutely certain while the method of verification is loose and variable—while in other cases the blurred meaning becomes clear and definite only when the method of verification is given. We must be aware of the fact that until now we have used the expression 'method of verification' in two entirely different senses. One could formulate the difference thus: when I say 'If it rained yesterday, the earth is moist today', then this is not a rule of inference, but an empirical statement. Empirical statements of this kind help us to find out the truth of the assertion, but they do not determine its meaning. The meaning was already established before a method of checking was even mentioned. Therefore the method of testing conforms to the meaning. On the other hand, when I say 'If the ball is charged, the leaves of the electroscope diverge' I am giving a rule of inference which explains the meaning of the first sentence. The meaning of the sentence is now dependent upon the method of verification. If I specify other rules for the expression, then I thereby change its meaning.

To give the method of verification is therefore only *one* aspect of the explanation of the meaning of the sentence. Another is, for example, the explanation of a word through demonstrative definition; another, to produce a drawing. The statement which expresses the method of verification of a proposition in the one sense is certainly a grammatical explanation and can explain the meaning of the sentence to us. We would not, however, call every explanation of the meaning an explanation of the verification, and thus the dictum: 'The meaning of a sentence is the method of its verification' is decidedly misleading.

. . .

THE MEANING AS SHADOW OF REALITY

What is the meaning of a sentence? The question, if put in this form, is misleading in many ways. It seems to us as if the meaning were a shadow which stands behind the signs, a shadow picture of the reality which the sentence represents. This view may be due to the fact that when we utter or hear a sentence we often have hovering in our minds an image of what the sentence represents. Now, is this image the meaning? But how can this image get us any further? How can it mediate between signs and reality?

The mental processes connected with speaking or hearing do not, for the purpose in hand, interest us. Everything inside our minds can, for our purposes, be replaced by something external—a mental calculation by one on paper, a conviction by a tone of voice and gesture, a memory picture by a painted picture, and so on. When we are puzzled as to whether the meaning is just the image evoked by the sentence, it is advisable to replace the image by a painted representation. For why should not the painted picture produce the same effect as the image? Of course, to make possible such a representation, we must confine our sentences to those which describe, for example, the position and colours of physical objects. If this suggestion were to be accepted, we should now have to say that the meaning of a 'sentence' is a painted picture. I have, indeed, here given a definite sense to the word 'meaning', though this sense does not quite correspond to what the word is usually expected to convey. For I might go on to ask 'And what is the meaning of such a picture?' And if we do speak of the meaning of a picture, is it not natural to speak too of the meaning of an image? Thus, to say that the meaning *is* the image does not get us any further.

What one would really like to say is that the meaning is certainly not a mere combination of sounds, but that there must be something behind it. But what lies 'behind' it is the system, the language of which the sentence is part. And here the idea of 'something behind' as an aethereal element is due to a delusion. In this sense the use of the word 'meaning' is misleading, and one can see in it a survival of a primitive and obsolete conception of language.

The position is similar when a command seems to anticipate its performance in some shadowy manner. One might ask: when I tell someone to fetch me an apple, how is it that he understands what I ask him to do? Surely the mere sound of the words does not tell him what it is that he will do when he obeys the command. There seems to be a gap between the expression and the performance. Do the signs in some queer way anticipate their translation into action like some dim shadow? But in what, then, does this shadow consist? If I tried to bring the expression of the command as near as possible to the performance expected, for instance, if I expressed the command by pointing at an apple and making a gesture of fetching—how is he to know what all this means? It seems as though the command must fail, whatever my efforts, to find adequate expression. Since it is not the mere verbal expression we are tempted to say it must be the *meaning* of the command which in some way contains its performance. And here again we return to thinking of the meaning as a shadow which stands behind the expression of the command. The meaning, or the thought, we say, is capable of doing things which no material sign can do—to anticipate what at the time of the command does not exist. That is one reason why thought is taken to have a specifically animate nature; and the psyche to have a life of its own with capacities different from those of the dead signs. In a certain sense a command does really anticipate its performance if by this we mean that the words in the command indicate what has to be done in order to carry it out. The command indicates that it is an *apple* and not a pear which is to be fetched; that the apple is to be *fetched* and not carried away. Here there seems to be some sense in asking, about this or any other explanation, 'What exactly does *it* purport?' But what sort of answer can we expect to this question? Any answer must be yet another sentence so that this form of question does not help us. One can no more go on asking for ever 'And what does *this* sentence mean?' than one can ask 'What sentence is it which is formed by these words?'

Let us replace the question 'What is the meaning of a sentence?' by the question 'How do we use the phrase "meaning of a sentence"?' For instance, in what circumstances should we say 'I understand the meaning of this

sentence', 'I explain the meaning of this sentence', 'These two sentences have
the same meaning', 'They differ in meaning', etc. To put the question in this
way immediately brings us down to earth. Moreover, we must be careful to
guard against the prejudice that there is one distinct use of the word
'meaning', whereas the use of 'meaning', like that of 'understanding', is a
fluctuating one. One could say that the use of the word 'meaning' is made up
of a large number of related games which are, metaphorically speaking, its
various facets. And it is just the interconnection of these facets, this related-
ness which forms the oneness of the concept, which leads us to speak of *the*
meaning. But, we wish to be precise, we can only give a piecemeal description of the grammar of 'meaning' and point out how the uses differ from one
another in different contexts.

Language and the World

5

ON SENSE AND NOMINATUM

Gottlob Frege

The idea of Sameness[1] challenges reflection. It raises questions which are not quite easily answered. Is Sameness a relation? A relation between objects? Or between names or signs of objects? I assumed the latter alternative in my *Begriffsschrift*. The reasons that speak in its favor are the following: "a = a" and "a = b" are sentences of obviously different cognitive significance: "a = a" is valid *a priori* and according to Kant is to be called analytic, whereas sentences of the form "a = b" often contain very valuable extensions of our knowledge and cannot always be justified in an *a priori* manner. The discovery that it is not a different and novel sun which rises every morning, but that it is the very same, certainly was one of the most consequential ones in astronomy. Even nowadays the re-cognition (identification) of a planetoid or a comet is not always a matter of self-evidence. If we wished to view identity as a relation between the objects designated by the names 'a' and 'b' then "a = b" and "a = a" would not seem different if "a = b" is true. This would express a relation of a thing to itself, namely, a relation such that it holds between everything and itself but never between one thing and another. What one wishes to express with "a = b" seems to be that the signs or names 'a' and 'b' name the same thing; and in that case we would be dealing with those signs: a relation between them would be asserted. But this relation could hold only inasmuch as they name or

From "On Sense and Nominatum" by Gottlob Frege, Herbert Feigl, trans., in *Readings in Philosophical Analysis,* Herbert Feigl and Wilfrid Sellars, eds. Copyright, 1949, Appleton-Century-Crofts, Inc. Reprinted by permission of the publisher.

[1] I use this word in the sense of identity and understand "a = b" in the sense of "a is the same as b" or "a and b coincide".

designate something. The relation, as it were, is mediated through the connection of each sign with the same nominatum. This connection, however, is arbitrary. You cannot forbid the use of an arbitrarily produced process or object as a sign for something else. Hence, a sentence like "a = b" would no longer refer to a matter of fact but rather to our manner of designation; no genuine knowledge would be expressed by it. But this is just what we do want to express in many cases. If the sign 'a' differs from the sign 'b' only as an object (here by its shape) but not by its rôle as a sign, that is to say, not in the manner in which it designates anything, then the cognitive significance of "a = a" would be essentially the same as that of "a = b", if "a = b" is true. A difference could arise only if the difference of the signs corresponds to a difference in the way in which the designated objects are given. Let a, b, c be straight lines which connect the corners of a triangle with the midpoints of the opposite sides. The point of intersection of a and b is then the same as that of b and c. Thus we have different designations of the same point and these names ('intersection of a and b', 'intersection of b and c') indicate also the manner in which these points are presented. Therefore the sentence expresses a genuine cognition.

Now it is plausible to connect with a sign (name, word combination, expression) not only the designated object, which may be called the nominatum of the sign, but also the sense (connotation, meaning) of the sign in which is contained the manner and context of presentation. Accordingly, in our examples the *nominata* of the expressions 'the point of intersection of a and b' and 'the point of intersection of b and c' would be the same;—not their senses. The nominata of 'evening star' and 'morning star' are the same but not their senses.

From what has been said it is clear that I here understand by 'sign' or 'name' any expression which functions as a proper name, whose nominatum accordingly is a definite object (in the widest sense of this word). But no concept or relation is under consideration here. These matters are to be dealt with in another essay. The designation of a single object may consist of several words or various signs. For brevity's sake, any such designation will be considered as a proper name.

The sense of a proper name is grasped by everyone who knows the language or the totality of designations of which the proper name is a part;[2] this, however, illuminates the nominatum, if there is any, in a very one-sided fashion. A complete knowledge of the nominatum would require that we could tell immediately in the case of any given sense whether it belongs to the nominatum. This we shall never be able to do.

The regular connection between a sign, its sense and its nominatum is such that there corresponds a definite sense to the sign and to this sense there corresponds again a definite nominatum; whereas not one sign only belongs to one nominatum (object). In different languages, and even in one language, the same sense is represented by different expressions. It is true, there

---

[2] In the case of genuinely proper names like 'Aristotle' opinions as regards their sense may diverge. As such may, e.g., be suggested: Plato's disciple and the teacher of Alexander the Great. Whoever accepts this sense will interpret the meaning of the statement "Aristotle was born in Stagira" differently from one who interpreted the sense of 'Aristotle' as the Stagirite teacher of Alexander the Great. As long as the nominatum remains the same, these fluctuations in sense are tolerable. But they should be avoided in the system of a demonstrative science and should not appear in a perfect language.

are exceptions to this rule. Certainly there should be a definite sense to each expression in a complete configuration of signs, but the natural languages in many ways fall short of this requirement. We must be satisfied if the same word, at least in the same context, has the same sense. It can perhaps be granted that an expression has a sense if it is formed in a grammatically correct manner and stands for a proper name. But as to whether there is a denotation corresponding to the connotation is hereby not decided. The words 'the heavenly body which has the greatest distance from the earth' have a sense; but it is very doubtful as to whether they have a nominatum. The expression 'the series with the least convergence' has a sense; but it can be proved that it has no nominatum, since for any given convergent series, one can find another one that is less convergent. Therefore the grasping of a sense does not with certainty warrant a corresponding nominatum.

When words are used in the customary manner then what is talked about are their nominata. But it may happen that one wishes to speak about the words themselves or about their senses. The first case occurs when one quotes someone else's words in direct (ordinary) discourse. In this case one's own words immediately name (denote) the words of the other person and only the latter words have the usual nominata. We thus have signs of signs. In writing we make use of quotes enclosing the word-icons. A word-icon in quotes must therefore not be taken in the customary manner.

If we wish to speak of the sense of an expression 'A' we can do this simply through the locution 'the sense of the expression 'A' '. In indirect (oblique) discourse we speak of the sense, e.g., of the words of someone else. From this it becomes clear that also in indirect discourse words do not have their customary nominata; they here name what customarily would be their sense. In order to formulate this succinctly we shall say: words in indirect discourse are used *indirectly*, or have *indirect* nominata. Thus we distinguish the *customary* from the *indirect* nominatum of a word; and similarly, its *customary* sense from its *indirect* sense. The indirect nominatum of a word is therefore its customary sense. Such exceptions must be kept in mind if one wishes correctly to comprehend the manner of connection between signs, senses and nominata in any given case.

.   .   .

The nominatum of a proper name is the object itself which is designated thereby; the image which we may have along with it is quite subjective; the sense lies in between, not subjective as is the image, but not the object either. . . .

We can now recognize three levels of differences of words, expressions and complete sentences. The difference may concern at most the imagery, or else the sense but not the nominatum, or finally also the nominatum. In regard to the first level, we must note that, owing to the uncertain correlation of images with words, a difference may exist for one person that another does not discover. The difference of a translation from the original should properly not go beyond the first level. Among the differences possible in this connection we mention the shadings and colorings which poetry seeks to impart to the senses. These shadings and colorings are not objective. Every listener or reader has to add them in accordance with the hints of the poet or speaker. Surely, art would be impossible without some kinship among human imageries; but just how far the intentions of the poet are realized can never be exactly ascertained.

We shall henceforth no longer refer to the images and picturizations; they were discussed only lest the image evoked by a word be confused with its sense or its nominatum.

In order to facilitate brief and precise expression we may lay down the following formulations:

A proper name (word, sign, sign-compound, expression) expresses its sense, and designates or signifies its nominatum. We let a *sign express* its sense and *designate* its nominatum.

. . .

Thus far we have considered sense and nominatum only of such expressions, words and signs which we called proper names. We are now going to inquire into the sense and the nominatum of a whole declarative sentence. Such a sentence contains a proposition.[3] Is this thought to be regarded as the sense or the nominatum of the sentence? Let us for the moment assume that the sentence has a nominatum! If we then substitute a word in it by another word with the same nominatum but with a different sense, then this substitution cannot affect the nominatum of the sentence. But we realize that in such cases the proposition is changed; e.g., the proposition of the sentence "the morning star is a body illuminated by the sun" is different from that of "the evening star is a body illuminated by the sun". Someone who did not know that the evening star is the same as the morning star could consider the one proposition true and the other false. The proposition can therefore not be the nominatum of the sentence; it will instead have to be regarded as its sense. But what about the nominatum? Can we even ask this question? A sentence as a whole has perhaps only sense and no nominatum? It may in any case be expected that there are such sentences, just as there are constituents of sentences which do have sense but no nominatum. Certainly, sentences containing proper names without nominata must be of this type. The sentence "Odysseus deeply asleep was disembarked at Ithaca" obviously has a sense. But since it is doubtful as to whether the name 'Odysseus' occurring in this sentence has a nominatum, so it is also doubtful that the whole sentence has one. However, it is certain that whoever seriously regards the sentence either as true or as false also attributes to the name 'Odysseus' a nominatum, not only a sense; for it is obviously the nominatum of this name to which the predicate is either ascribed or denied. He who does not acknowledge the nominatum cannot ascribe or deny a predicate to it. It might be urged that the consideration of the nominatum of the name is going farther than is necessary; one could be satisfied with the sense, if one stayed with the proposition. If all that mattered were only the sense of the sentence (i.e., the proposition) then it would be unnecessary to be concerned with the nominata of the sentence-components, for only the sense of the components can be relevant for the sense of the sentence. The proposition remains the same, no matter whether or not the name 'Odysseus' has a nominatum. The fact that we are at all concerned about the nominatum of a sentence-component indicates that we generally acknowledge or postulate a

[3] By 'proposition' I do not refer to the subjective activity of thinking but rather to its objective content which is capable of being the common property of many.

nominatum for the sentence itself. The proposition loses in interest as soon as we recognize that one of its parts is lacking a nominatum. We may therefore be justified to ask for a nominatum of a sentence, in addition to its sense. But why do we wish that every proper name have not only a sense but also a nominatum? Why is the proposition alone not sufficient? We answer: because what matters to us is the truth-value. This, however, is not always the case. In listening to an epic, for example, we are fascinated by the euphony of the language and also by the sense of the sentences and by the images and emotions evoked. In turning to the question of truth we disregard the artistic appreciation and pursue scientific considerations. Whether the name 'Odysseus' has a nominatum is therefore immaterial to us as long as we accept the poem as a work of art.[4] Thus, it is the striving for truth which urges us to penetrate beyond the sense to the nominatum.

We have realized that we are to look for the nominatum of a sentence whenever the nominata of the sentence-components are the thing that matters; and that is the case whenever and only when we ask for the truth value.

Thus we find ourselves persuaded to accept the *truth-value* of a sentence as its nominatum. By the truth-value of a sentence I mean the circumstance of its being true or false. There are no other truth-values. For brevity's sake I shall call the one the True and the other the False. Every declarative sentence, in which what matters are the nominata of the words, is therefore to be considered as a proper name; and its nominatum, if there is any, is either the True or the False. These two objects are recognized, even if only tacitly by everyone who at all makes judgments, holds anything as true, thus even by the skeptic. To designate truth-values as objects may thus far appear as a capricious idea or as a mere play on words, from which no important conclusion should be drawn. What I call an object can be discussed only in connection with the nature of concepts and relations. That I will reserve for another essay. But this might be clear even here: in every judgment[5]—no matter how obvious—a step is made from the level of propositions to the level of the nominata (the objective facts).

It may be tempting to regard the relation of a proposition to the True not as that of sense to nominatum but as that of the subject to the predicate. One could virtually say: "the proposition that 5 is a prime number is true". But on closer examination one notices that this does not say any more than is said in the simple sentence "5 is a prime number". This makes clear that the relation of a proposition to the True must not be compared with the relation of subject and predicate. Subject and predicate (interpreted logically) are, after all, components of a proposition; they are on the same level as regards cognition. By joining subject and predicate we always arrive only at a proposition; in this way we never move from a sense to a nominatum or from a proposition to its truth-value. We remain on the same level and never proceed from it to the next one. Just as the sun cannot be part of a proposi-

---

[4] It would be desirable to have an expression for signs which have sense only. If we call them 'icons' then the words of an actor on the stage would be icons; even the actor himself would be an icon.

[5] A judgment is not merely the apprehension of a thought or proposition but the acknowledgment of its truth.

tion, so the truth-value, because it is not the sense, but an object, cannot be either.

If our conjecture (that the nominatum of a sentence is its truth value) is correct, then the truth-value must remain unchanged if a sentence-component is replaced by an expression with the same nominatum but with a different sense. Indeed, Leibnitz declares: *"Eadem sunt, quae sibi mutuo substitui possunt, salva veritate"* ["Terms that are mutually replaceable, preserving truth, are the same"]. What else, except the truth-value, could be found, which quite generally belongs to every sentence and regarding which the nominata of the components are relevant and which would remain invariant for substitutions of the type indicated?

Now if the truth-value of a sentence is its nominatum, then all true sentences have the same nominatum, and likewise all false ones. This implies that all detail has been blurred in the nominatum of a sentence. What interests us can therefore never be merely the nominatum; but the proposition alone does not give knowledge; only the proposition together with its nominatum, i.e., its truth-value, does. Judging may be viewed as a movement from a proposition to its nominatum, i.e., its truth-value. Of course this is not intended as a definition. Judging is indeed something peculiar and unique. One might say that judging consists in the discerning of parts within the truth-value. This discernment occurs through recourse to the proposition. Every sense that belongs to a truth-value would correspond in its own manner to the analysis. I have, however, used the word 'part' in a particular manner here: I have transferred the relation of whole and part from the sentence to its nominatum. This I did by viewing the nominatum of a word as part of the nominatum of a sentence, when the word itself is part of the sentence. True enough, this way of putting things is objectionable since as regards the nominatum the whole and one part of it does not determine the other part; and also because the word 'part' in reference to bodies has a different customary usage. A special expression should be coined for what has been suggested above.

We shall now further examine the conjecture that the truth-value of a sentence is its nominatum. We have found that the truth-value of a sentence remains unaltered if an expression within the sentence is replaced by a synonymous one. But we have as yet not considered the case in which the expression-to-be-replaced is itself a sentence. If our view is correct, then the truth-value of a sentence, which contains another sentence as a part, must remain unaltered when we substitute for the part another of the same truth-value. Exceptions are to be expected if the whole or the part are either in direct or indirect discourse; for as we have seen, in that case the nominata of the words are not the usual ones. A sentence in direct discourse nominates again a sentence but in indirect discourse it nominates a proposition.

Our attention is thus directed to subordinate sentences (i.e., dependent clauses). These present themselves of course as parts of a sentence-structure which from a logical point of view appears also as a sentence, and indeed as if it were a main clause. But here we face the question whether in the case of dependent clauses it also holds that their nominata are truth-values. We know already that this is not the case with sentences in indirect discourse. The grammarians view clauses as representatives of sentence-parts and divide them accordingly into subjective, relative, and adverbial clauses. This might suggest that the nominatum of a clause is not a truth-value but rather that it is of similar nature as that of a noun or of an adjective or of an adverb; in short, of a sentence-part whose sense is not a proposition but only part thereof. Only a thorough investigation can provide clarity in this matter. We shall herein not follow strictly along grammatical lines, but rather group together what is logically of comparable type. Let us first seek out such instances in which, as we just surmised, the sense of a clause is not a self-sufficient proposition.

Among the abstract clauses beginning with 'that' there is also the indirect discourse, of which we have seen that in it the words have their indirect (oblique) nominata which coincide with what are ordinarily their senses. In this case then the clause has as its nominatum a proposition, not a truth-value; its sense is not a proposition but it is the sense of the words 'the proposition that . . .', which is only a part of the proposition corresponding to the total sentence-structure. This occurs in connection with 'to say', 'to hear', 'to opine', 'to be convinced', 'to infer' and similar words.[6] The situation is different, and rather complicated in connection with such words as 'to recognize', 'to know', 'to believe', a matter to be considered later.

One can see that in these cases the nominatum of the clause indeed consists in the proposition, because whether that proposition is true or false is immaterial for the truth of the whole sentence. Compare, e.g., the following two sentences: "Copernicus believed that the planetary orbits are circles" and "Copernicus believed that the appearance of the sun's motion is produced by the real motion of the earth". Here the one clause can be substituted for the other without affecting the truth. The sense of the principal sentence together with the clause is the single proposition; and the truth of the whole implies neither the truth nor the falsity of the clause. In cases of this type it is not permissible to replace in the clause one expression by another of the same nominatum. Such replacement may be made only by expressions of the same indirect nominatum, i.e., of the same customary sense. If one were to infer: the nominatum of a sentence is not its truth-value ("because then a sentence could always be replaced by another with the same truth-value"), he would prove too much; one could just as well maintain that the nominatum of the word 'morning star' is not Venus, for one cannot always substitute 'Venus' for 'morning star'. The only correct conclusion is that the nominatum of a sentence is *not always* its truth-value, and that 'morning star' does not always nominate the planet Venus; for this is indeed not the case when the word is used with its indirect nominatum. Such an exceptional case is before us in the clauses just considered, whose nominatum is a proposition.

When we say "it seems that . . ." then we mean to say "it seems to me that . . ." or "I opine that . . .". This is the same case over again. Similarly with expressions such as: 'to be glad', 'to regret', 'to approve', 'to disapprove', 'to hope', 'to fear'. When Wellington, toward the end of the battle of Belle-Alliance was glad that the Prussians were coming, the ground of his rejoicing was a conviction. Had he actually been deceived, he would not have been less glad, as long as his belief persisted; and before he arrived

---

[6] In "*A* lied, that he had seen *B*" the clause denotes a proposition of which it is said, firstly, that *A* asserted it as true, and, secondly, that *A* was convinced of its falsity.

at the conviction that the Prussians were coming he could not have been glad about it, even if in fact they were already approaching.

Just as a conviction or a belief may be the ground of a sentiment, so it can also be the ground of another conviction such as in inference. In the sentence "Columbus inferred from the roundness of the earth that he could, traveling westward, reach India" we have, as nominata of its parts two propositions: that the earth is round, and that Columbus traveling westward could reach India. What matters here is only that Columbus was convinced of the one as well as of the other and that the one conviction furnishes the ground for the other. It is irrelevant for the truth of our sentence whether the earth is really round and whether Columbus could have reached India in the manner he fancied. But it is not irrelevant whether for 'the earth' we substitute 'the planet accompanied by one satellite whose diameter is larger than one-fourth of its own diameter'. Here also we deal with the indirect nominata of the words.

Adverbial clauses of purpose with 'so that', likewise belong here; obviously the purpose is a proposition; therefore: indirect nominata of the words, expressed in subjunctive form.

The clause with 'that' after 'to command', 'to request', 'to forbid' would appear in imperative form in direct discourse. Imperatives have no nominata; they have only sense. It is true, commands or requests are not propositions, but they are of the same type as propositions. Therefore the words in the dependent clauses after 'to command', 'to request', etc. have indirect nominata. The nominatum of such a sentence is thus not a truth-value but a command, a request, and the like.

We meet a similar situation in the case of dependent questions in phrases like 'to doubt if', 'not to know what'. It is easy to see that the words, here too, have to be interpreted in terms of their indirect nominata. The dependent interrogatory clauses containing 'who', 'what', 'where', 'when', 'how', 'whereby', etc. often apparently approximate closely adverbial clauses in which the words have their ordinary nominata. These cases are linguistically distinguished through the mode of the verb. In the subjunctive we have a dependent question and the indirect nominata of the words, so that a proper name cannot generally be replaced by another of the same object.

In the instances thus far considered the words in the clause had indirect nominata; this made it intelligible that the nominatum of the clause itself is indirect, i.e., not a truth-value, but a proposition, a command, a request, a question. The clause could be taken as a noun; one might even say, as a proper name of that proposition, command, etc., in whose rôle it functions in the context of the sentence-structure.

We are now going to consider clauses of another type, in which the words do have their customary nominata although there does not appear a proposition as the sense or a truth-value as the nominatum. How this is possible will best be elucidated by examples.

"He who discovered the elliptical shape of the planetary orbits, died in misery".

If, in this example, the sense of the clause were a proposition, it would have to be expressible also in a principal sentence. But this cannot be done because the grammatical subject 'he who' has no independent sense. It merely mediates the relations to the second part of the sentence: 'died in misery'. Therefore the sense of the clause is not a complete proposition and its nominatum is not a truth-value, but Kepler. It might be objected that the sense of the whole does include a proposition as its part; namely, that there was someone who first recognized the elliptical shape of the planetary orbits; for if we accept the whole as true we cannot deny this part. Indubitably so; but only because otherwise the clause "he who discovered the elliptical shape, etc." would have no nominatum. Whenever something is asserted then the presupposition taken for granted is that the employed proper names, simple or compound, have nominata. Thus, if we assert "Kepler died in misery" it is presupposed that the name 'Kepler' designates something. However, the proposition that the name 'Kepler' designates something is, the foregoing notwithstanding, not contained in the sense of the sentence "Kepler died in misery". If that were the case the denial would not read "Kepler did not die in misery" but "Kepler did not die in misery, or the name 'Kepler' is without nominatum". That the name 'Kepler' designates something is rather the presupposition of the assertion "Kepler died in misery" as well as of its denial. Now, it is a defect of languages that expressions are possible within them, which, in their grammatical form, seemingly determined to designate an object, nevertheless do not fulfill this condition in special cases; because this depends on the truth of the sentence. Thus it depends upon the truth of the sentence "there was someone who discovered the ellipticity of the orbits" whether the clause 'he who discovered the ellipticity of the orbits' really designates an object, or else merely evokes the appearance thereof, while indeed being without nominatum. Thus it may seem as if our clause, as part of its sense, contained the proposition that there existed someone who discovered the ellipticity of the orbits. If this were so, then the denial would have to read "he who first recognized the ellipticity of the orbits did not die in misery, or there was no one who discovered the ellipticity of the orbits." This, it is obvious, hinges upon an imperfection of language of which, by the way, even the symbolic language of analysis is not entirely free; there, also, sign compounds may occur which appear as if they designated something, but which at least hitherto are without nominatum, e.g., divergent infinite series. This can be avoided, e.g., through the special convention that the nominatum of divergent infinite series be the number 0. It is to be demanded that in a logically perfect language (logical symbolism) every expression constructed as a proper name in a grammatically correct manner out of already introduced symbols, in fact designate an object; and that no symbol be introduced as a proper name without assurance that it have a nominatum. It is customary in logic texts to warn against the ambiguity of expressions as a source of fallacies. I deem it at least as appropriate to issue a warning against apparent proper names that have no nominata. The history of mathematics has many a tale to tell of errors which originated from this source. The demagogic misuse is close (perhaps closer) at hand as in the case of ambiguous expressions. 'The will of the people' may serve as an example in this regard; for it is easily established that there is no generally accepted nominatum of that expression. Thus it is obviously not without importance to obstruct once for all the source of these errors, at least as regards their occurrence in science. Then such objections as the one discussed above will become impossible, for then it will be seen that whether a proper name has a nominatum can never depend upon the truth of a proposition.

Our considerations may be extended from these subjective clauses to the logically related relative and adverbial clauses.

Relative clauses, too, are employed in the formation of compound proper names—even if, in contradistinction to subjective clauses, they are not sufficient by themselves for this purpose. These relative clauses may be regarded as equivalent to appositions. Instead of 'the square root of 4 which is smaller than 0' we can also say 'the negative square root of 4'. We have here a case in which out of a conceptual expression a compound proper name is formed, with the help of the definite article in the singular. This is at any rate permissible when one and only one object is comprised by the concept.[7] Conceptual expression can be formed in such a fashion that their characteristics are indicated through relative clauses as in our example through the clause 'which is smaller than 0'. Obviously, such relative clauses, just as the subjective clauses above, do not refer to a proposition as their sense nor to a truth-value as their nominatum. Their sense is only a part of a proposition, which in many cases, can be expressed by a simple apposition. As in the subjective clauses an independent subject is missing and it is therefore impossible to represent the sense of the clause in an independent principal sentence.

.   .   .

The sense of a subordinate clause is usually not a proposition but only part of one. Its nominatum is therefore not a truth-value. The reason for this is *either:* that the words in the subordinate clause have only indirect nominata, so that the nominatum, not the sense, of the clause is a proposition, *or,* that the clause, because of a contained indeterminately indicating constituent, is incomplete, such that only together with the principal clause does it express a proposition. However, there are also instances in which the sense of the dependent clause is a complete proposition, and in this case it can be replaced by another clause of the same truth-value without altering the truth-value of the whole; that is, inasmuch as there are no grammatical obstacles in the way.

.   .   .

It is difficult to exhaust all possibilities that present themselves in language; but I hope, in essence at least, to have disclosed the reasons why, in view of the invariance of the truth of a whole sentence, a clause cannot always be replaced by another of the same truth-value. These reasons are:

1. that the clause does not denote a truth-value in that it expresses only a part of a proposition;
2. that the clause, while it does denote a truth-value, is not restricted to this function in that its sense comprises, beside one proposition, also a part of another.

[7] According to our previous remarks such an expression should always be assured of a nominatum, e.g., through the special convention that the nominatum be the number 0 if there is no object or more than one object denoted by the expression.

The first case holds

    a. with the indirect nominata of the words;
    b. if a part of the sentence indicates only indirectly without being a proper name.

In the second case the clause is to be interpreted in a twofold manner; namely, once with its usual nominatum; the other time with its indirect nominatum; or else, the sense of a part of the clause may simultaneously be a constituent of another proposition which, together with the sense expressed in the dependent clause, amounts to the total sense of the main and the dependent clause.

This makes it sufficiently plausible that instances in which a clause is not replaceable by another of the same truth-value do not disprove our view that the nominatum of a sentence is its truth-value and its sense a proposition.

Let us return to our point of departure now.

When we discerned generally a difference in cognitive significance between "a = a" and "a = b" then this is now explained by the fact that for the cognitive significance of a sentence the sense (the proposition expressed) is no less relevant than its nominatum (the truth-value). If a = b, then the nominatum of 'a' and of 'b' is indeed the same and therefore also the truth-value of "a = b" is the same as that of "a = a". Nevertheless, the sense of 'b' may differ from the sense of 'a'; and therefore the proposition expressed by "a = b" may differ from the proposition expressed by "a = a"; in that case the two sentences do not have the same cognitive significance. Thus, if, as above, we mean by 'judgment' the transition from a proposition to its truth-value, then we can also say that the judgments differ from one another.

6

ON DENOTING

Bertrand Russell

By a "denoting phrase" I mean a phrase such as any one of the following: a man, some man, any man, every man, all men, the present King of England, the present King of France, the centre of mass of the Solar System at the first instant of the twentieth century, the revolution of the earth round the sun, the revolution of the sun round the earth. Thus a phrase is denoting solely in virtue of its *form*. We may distinguish three cases: (1) A phrase may be denoting, and yet not denote anything; *e.g.*, "the present King of France". (2) A phrase may denote one definite object; *e.g.*, "the present King of England" denotes a certain man. (3) A phrase may denote ambiguously; *e.g.*, "a man" denotes not many men, but an ambiguous man. The interpretation of such phrases is a matter of considerable difficulty; indeed, it is very hard to frame any theory not susceptible of formal refutation. All the difficulties with which I am acquainted are met, so far as I can discover, by the theory which I am about to explain.

The subject of denoting is of very great importance, not only in logic and mathematics, but also in theory of knowledge. For example, we know that the centre of mass of the Solar System at a definite instant is some definite point, and we can affirm a number of propositions about it; but we have no immediate *acquaintance* with this point, which is only known to us by description. The distinction between *acquaintance* and *knowledge about* is the distinction between the things we have presentations of, and the things we only reach by means of denoting phrases. It often happens that we know that a certain phrase denotes unambiguously, although we have no acquaintance with what it denotes; this occurs in the above case of the centre of mass. In perception we have acquaintance with the objects of perception, and in thought we have acquaintance with objects of a more abstract logical character; but we do not necessarily have acquaintance with the objects denoted by phrases composed of words with whose meanings we are acquainted. To take a very important instance: There seems no reason to

Bertrand Russell, "On Denoting," *Mind*, XIV (1905), 479–493. Reprinted by permission of the Editor of *Mind*, George Allen & Unwin Ltd., the Macmillan Company, and the author.

believe that we are ever acquainted with other people's minds, seeing that these are not directly perceived; hence what we know about them is obtained through denoting. All thinking has to start from acquaintance; but it succeeds in thinking *about* many things with which we have no acquaintance.

The course of my argument will be as follows. I shall begin by stating the theory I intend to advocate;[1] I shall then discuss the theories of Frege and Meinong, showing why neither of them satisfies me; then I shall give the grounds in favour of my theory; and finally I shall briefly indicate the philosophical consequences of my theory.

My theory, briefly, is as follows. I take the notion of the *variable* as fundamental; I use "C (x)" to mean a proposition[2] in which x is a constituent, where x, the variable, is essentially and wholly undetermined. Then we can consider the two notions "C (x) is always true" and "C (x) is sometimes true".[3] Then *everything* and *nothing* and *something* (which are the most primitive of denoting phrases) are to be interpreted as follows:—

C (everything) means "C (x) is always true";
C (nothing) means " 'C (x) is false' is always true";
C (something) means "It is false that 'C (x) is false' is always true".[4]

Here the notion "C (x) is always true" is taken as ultimate and indefinable, and the others are defined by means of it. *Everything, nothing*, and *something*, are not assumed to have any meaning in isolation, but a meaning is assigned to *every* proposition in which they occur. This is the principle of the theory of denoting I wish to advocate: that denoting phrases never have any meaning in themselves, but that every proposition in whose verbal expression they occur has a meaning. The difficulties concerning denoting are, I believe, all the result of a wrong analysis of propositions whose verbal expressions contain denoting phrases. The proper analysis, if I am not mistaken, may be further set forth as follows.

Suppose now we wish to interpret the proposition, "I met a man". If this is true, I met some definite man; but that is not what I affirm. What I affirm is, according to the theory I advocate:—

" 'I met x, and x is human' is not always false".

Generally, defining the class of men as the class of objects having the predicate *human*, we say that:—

"C (a man)" means " 'C (x) and x is human' is not always false".

This leaves "a man," by itself, wholly destitute of meaning, but gives a meaning to every proposition in whose verbal expression "a man" occurs.

---

[1] I have discussed this subject in *Principles of Mathematics*, chapter v., and § 476. The theory there advocated is very nearly the same as Frege's, and is quite different from the theory to be advocated in what follows.

[2] More exactly, a propositional function.

[3] The second of these can be defined by means of the first, if we take it to mean, "It is not true that 'C (x) is false' is always true".

[4] I shall sometimes use, instead of this complicated phrase, the phrase "C (x) is not always false," or "C (x) is sometimes true," supposed *defined* to mean the same as the complicated phrase.

Consider next the proposition "all men are mortal". This proposition[5] is really hypothetical and states that *if* anything is a man, it is mortal. That is, it states that if x is a man, x is mortal, whatever x may be. Hence, substituting 'x is human' for 'x is a man,' we find: —

"All men are mortal" means " 'If x is human, x is mortal' is always true".

This is what is expressed in symbolic logic by saying that "all men are mortal" means " 'x is human' implies 'x is mortal' for all values of x". More generally, we say: —

"C (all men)" means " 'If x is human, then C (x) is true' is always true".

Similarly

"C (no men)" means " 'If x is human, then C (x) is false' is always true".
"C (some men)" will mean the same as "C (a man),"[6] and
"C (a man)" means "It is false that 'C (x) and x is human' is always false".
"C (every man)" will mean the same as "C (all men)".

It remains to interpret phrases containing *the*. These are by far the most interesting and difficult of denoting phrases. Take as an instance "the father of Charles II. was executed". This asserts that there was an x who was the father of Charles II. and was executed. Now *the*, when it is strictly used, involves uniqueness; we do, it is true, speak of "*the* son of So-and-so" even when So-and-so has several sons, but it would be more correct to say "*a* son of So-and-so". Thus for our purposes we take *the* as involving uniqueness. Thus when we say "x was *the* father of Charles II." we not only assert that x had a certain relation to Charles II., but also that nothing else had this relation. The relation in question, without the assumption of uniqueness, and without any denoting phrases, is expressed by "x begat Charles II.". To get an equivalent of "x was the father of Charles II.," we must add, "If y is other than x, y did not beget Charles II.," or, what is equivalent, "If y begat Charles II., y is identical with x". Hence "x is the father of Charles II." becomes "x begat Charles II.; and 'if y begat Charles II., y is identical with x' is always true of y".

Thus "the father of Charles II. was executed" becomes: —

"It is not always false of x that x begat Charles II. and that x was executed and that 'if y begat Charles II., y is identical with x' is always true of y".

This may seem a somewhat incredible interpretation; but I am not at present giving reasons, I am merely *stating* the theory.

To interpret "C (the father of Charles II.)," where C stands for any statement about him, we have only to substitute C (x) for "x was executed"

---

[5] As has been ably argued in Mr. Bradley's *Logic*, book i., chap. ii.

[6] Psychologically "C (a man)" has a suggestion of *only one*, and "C (some men)" has a suggestion of *more than one*; but we may neglect these suggestions in a preliminary sketch.

in the above. Observe that, according to the above interpretation, whatever statement C may be, "C (the father of Charles II.)" implies:—

"It is not always false of x that 'if y begat Charles II., y is identical with x' is always true of y,"

which is what is expressed in common language by "Charles II. had one father and no more". Consequently if this condition fails, *every* proposition of the form "C (the father of Charles II.)" is false. Thus *e.g.* every proposition of the form "C (the present King of France)" is false. This is a great advantage in the present theory. I shall show later that it is not contrary to the law of contradiction, as might be at first supposed.

The above gives a reduction of all propositions in which denoting phrases occur to forms in which no such phrases occur. Why it is imperative to effect such a reduction, the subsequent discussion will endeavour to show.

The evidence for the above theory is derived from the difficulties which seem unavoidable if we regard denoting phrases as standing for genuine constituents of the propositions in whose verbal expressions they occur. Of the possible theories which admit such constituents the simplest is that of Meinong.[7] This theory regards any grammatically correct denoting phrase as standing for an *object*. Thus "the present King of France," "the round square," etc., are supposed to be genuine objects. It is admitted that such objects do not *subsist*, but nevertheless they are supposed to be objects. This is in itself a difficult view; but the chief objection is that such objects, admittedly, are apt to infringe the law of contradiction. It is contended, for example, that the existent present King of France exists, and also does not exist; that the round square is round, and also not round; etc. But this is intolerable; and if any theory can be found to avoid this result, it is surely to be preferred.

The above breach of the law of contradiction is avoided by Frege's theory. He distinguishes, in a denoting phrase, two elements, which we may call the *meaning* and the *denotation*.[8] Thus "the centre of mass of the Solar System at the beginning of the twentieth century" is highly complex in *meaning*, but its *denotation* is a certain point, which is simple. The Solar System, the twentieth century, etc., are constituents of the *meaning*; but the *denotation* has no constituents at all.[9] One advantage of this distinction is that it shows why it is often worth while to assert identity. If we say "Scott is the author of *Waverley*," we assert an identity of denotation with a difference of meaning. I shall, however, not repeat the grounds in favour of this theory, as I have urged its claims elsewhere (*loc. cit.*), and am now concerned to dispute those claims.

One of the first difficulties that confront us, when we adopt the view that

[7] See *Untersuchungen zur Gegenstandstheorie und Psychologie*, Leipzig, 1904, the first three articles (by Meinong, Ameseder and Mally respectively).

[8] See his "Ueber Sinn und Bedeutung," *Zeitschrift für Phil. und Phil. Kritik*, vol. 100.

[9] Frege distinguishes the two elements of meaning and denotation everywhere, and not only in complex denoting phrases. Thus it is the *meanings* of the constituents of a denoting complex that enter into its *meaning*, not their *denotation*. In the proposition "Mont Blanc is over 1,000 metres high," it is, according to him, the *meaning* of "Mont Blanc," not the actual mountain, that is a constituent of the *meaning* of the proposition.

denoting phrases *express* a meaning and *denote* a denotation,[10] concerns the cases in which the denotation appears to be absent. If we say "the King of England is bald," that is, it would seem, not a statement about the complex *meaning* "the King of England," but about the actual man denoted by the meaning. But now consider "the King of France is bald". By parity of form, this also ought to be about the denotation of the phrase "the King of France". But this phrase, though it has a *meaning* provided "the King of England" has a meaning, has certainly no denotation, at least in any obvious sense. Hence one would suppose that "the King of France is bald" ought to be nonsense; but it is not nonsense, since it is plainly false. Or again consider such a proposition as the following: "If *u* is a class which has only one member, then that one member is a member of *u*," or, as we may state it, "If *u* is a unit class, *the u* is a *u*". This proposition ought to be *always* true, since the conclusion is true whenever the hypothesis is true. But "the *u*" is a denoting phrase, and it is the denotation, not the meaning, that is said to be a *u*. Now if *u* is *not* a unit class, "the *u*" seems to denote nothing; hence our proposition would seem to become nonsense as soon as *u* is not a unit class.

Now it is plain that such propositions do *not* become nonsense merely because their hypotheses are false. The King in "The Tempest" might say, "If Ferdinand is not drowned, Ferdinand is my only son". Now "my only son" is a denoting phrase, which, on the face of it, has a denotation when, and only when, I have exactly one son. But the above statement would nevertheless have remained true if Ferdinand had been in fact drowned. Thus we must either provide a denotation in cases in which it is at first sight absent, or we must abandon the view that the denotation is what is concerned in propositions which contain denoting phrases. The latter is the course that I advocate. The former course may be taken, as by Meinong, by admitting objects which do not subsist, and denying that they obey the law of contradiction; this, however, is to be avoided if possible. Another way of taking the same course (so far as our present alternative is concerned) is adopted by Frege, who provides by definition some purely conventional denotation for the cases in which otherwise there would be none. Thus "the King of France," is to denote the null-class; "the only son of Mr. So-and-so" (who has a fine family of ten), is to denote the class of all his sons; and so on. But this procedure, though it may not lead to actual logical error, is plainly artificial, and does not give an exact analysis of the matter. Thus if we allow that denoting phrases, in general, have the two sides of meaning and denotation, the cases where there seems to be no denotation cause difficulties both on the assumption that there really is a denotation and on the assumption that there really is none.

A logical theory may be tested by its capacity for dealing with puzzles, and it is a wholesome plan, in thinking about logic, to stock the mind with as many puzzles as possible, since these serve much the same purpose as is served by experiments in physical science. I shall therefore state three puzzles which a theory as to denoting ought to be able to solve; and I shall show later that my theory solves them.

(1) If *a* is identical with *b*, whatever is true of the one is true of the

[10] In this theory, we shall say that the denoting phrase *expresses* a meaning; and we shall say both of the phrase and of the meaning that they *denote* a denotation. In the other theory, which I advocate, there is no *meaning*, and only sometimes a *denotation*.

other, and either may be substituted for the other in any proposition without altering the truth or falsehood of that proposition. Now George IV. wished to know whether Scott was the author of *Waverley;* and in fact Scott *was* the author of *Waverley.* Hence we may substitute *Scott* for *the author of "Waverley,"* and thereby prove that George IV. wished to know whether Scott was Scott. Yet an interest in the law of identity can hardly be attributed to the first gentleman of Europe.

(2) By the law of excluded middle, either "A is B" or "A is not B" must be true. Hence either "the present King of France is bald" or "the present King of France is not bald" must be true. Yet if we enumerated the things that are bald, and then the things that are not bald, we should not find the present King of France in either list. Hegelians, who love a synthesis, will probably conclude that he wears a wig.

(3) Consider the proposition "A differs from B". If this is true, there is a difference between A and B, which fact may be expressed in the form "the difference between A and B subsists". But if it is false that A differs from B, then there is no difference between A and B, which fact may be expressed in the form "the difference between A and B does not subsist". But how can a non-entity be the subject of a proposition? "I think, therefore I am" is no more evident than "I am the subject of a proposition, therefore I am," provided "I am" is taken to assert subsistence or being,[11] not existence. Hence, it would appear, it must always be self-contradictory to deny the being of anything; but we have seen, in connexion with Meinong, that to admit being also sometimes leads to contradictions. Thus if A and B do not differ, to suppose either that there is, or that there is not, such an object as "the difference between A and B" seems equally impossible.

The relation of the meaning to the denotation involves certain rather curious difficulties, which seem in themselves sufficient to prove that the theory which leads to such difficulties must be wrong.

When we wish to speak about the *meaning* of a denoting phrase, as opposed to its *denotation*, the natural mode of doing so is by inverted commas. Thus we say:—

The centre of mass of the Solar System is a point, not a denoting complex;
"The centre of mass of the Solar System" is a denoting complex, not a point.

Or again,

The first line of Gray's Elegy states a proposition.
"The first line of Gray's Elegy" does not state a proposition.

Thus taking any denoting phrase, say C, we wish to consider the relation between C and "C," where the difference of the two is of the kind exemplified in the above two instances.

We say, to begin with, that when C occurs it is the *denotation* that we are speaking about; but when "C" occurs, it is the *meaning*. Now the relation of meaning and denotation is not merely linguistic through the phrase: there must be a logical relation involved, which we express by saying that the

[11] I use these as synonyms.

meaning denotes the denotation. But the difficulty which confronts us is that we cannot succeed in *both* preserving the connexion of meaning and denotation *and* preventing them from being one and the same; also that the meaning cannot be got at except by means of denoting phrases. This happens as follows.

The one phrase C was to have both meaning and denotation. But if we speak of "the meaning of C," that gives us the meaning (if any) of the denotation. "The meaning of the first line of Gray's Elegy" is the same as "The meaning of 'The curfew tolls the knell of parting day,'" and is not the same as "The meaning of 'the first line of Gray's Elegy'". Thus in order to get the meaning we want, we must speak not of "the meaning of C," but of "the meaning of 'C,'" which is the same as "C" by itself. Similarly "the denotation of C" does not mean the denotation we want, but means something which, if it denotes at all, denotes what is denoted by the denotation we want. For example, let "C" be "the denoting complex occurring in the second of the above instances". Then

$$C = \text{"the first line of Gray's Elegy,"}$$

and the denotation of C = The curfew tolls the knell of parting day. But what we *meant* to have as the denotation was "the first line of Gray's Elegy". Thus we have failed to get what we wanted.

The difficulty in speaking of the meaning of a denoting complex may be stated thus: The moment we put the complex in a proposition, the proposition is about the denotation; and if we make a proposition in which the subject is "the meaning of C," then the subject is the meaning (if any) of the denotation, which was not intended. This leads us to say that, when we distinguish meaning and denotation, we must be dealing with the meaning: the meaning has denotation and is a complex, and there is not something other than the meaning, which can be called the complex, and be said to *have* both meaning and denotation. The right phrase, on the view in question, is that some meanings have denotations.

But this only makes our difficulty in speaking of meanings more evident. For suppose C is our complex; then we are to say that C *is* the meaning of the complex. Nevertheless, whenever C occurs without inverted commas, what is said is not true of the meaning, but only of the denotation, as when we say: The centre of mass of the Solar System is a point. Thus to speak of C itself, *i.e.*, to make a proposition about the meaning, our subject must not be C, but something which denotes C. Thus "C," which is what we use when we want to speak of the meaning, must be not the meaning, but something which denotes the meaning. And C must not be a constituent of this complex (as it is of "the meaning of C"); for if C occurs in the complex, it will be its denotation, not its meaning, that will occur, and there is no backward road from denotations to meanings, because every object can be denoted by an infinite number of different denoting phrases.

Thus it would seem that "C" and C are different entities, such that "C" denotes C; but this cannot be an explanation, because the relation of "C" to C remains wholly mysterious; and where are we to find the denoting complex "C" which is to denote C? Moreover, when C occurs in a proposition, it is not *only* the denotation that occurs (as we shall see in the next paragraph);

yet, on the view in question, C is only the denotation, the meaning being wholly relegated to "C". This is an inextricable tangle, and seems to prove that the whole distinction of meaning and denotation has been wrongly conceived.

That the meaning is relevant when a denoting phrase occurs in a proposition is formally proved by the puzzle about the author of *Waverley*. The proposition "Scott was the author of *Waverley*" has a property not possessed by "Scott was Scott," namely the property that George IV. wished to know whether it was true. Thus the two are not identical propositions; hence the meaning of "the author of *Waverley*" must be relevant as well as the denotation, if we adhere to the point of view to which this distinction belongs. Yet, as we have just seen, so long as we adhere to this point of view, we are compelled to hold that only the denotation can be relevant. Thus the point of view in question must be abandoned.

It remains to show how all the puzzles we have been considering are solved by the theory explained at the beginning of this article.

According to the view which I advocate, a denoting phrase is essentially *part* of a sentence, and does not, like most single words, have any significance on its own account. If I say "Scott was a man," that is a statement of the form "x was a man," and it has "Scott" for its subject. But if I say "the author of *Waverley* was a man," that is not a statement of the form "x was a man," and does not have "the author of *Waverley*" for its subject. Abbreviating the statement made at the beginning of this article, we may put, in place of "the author of *Waverley* was a man," the following: "One and only one entity wrote *Waverley*, and that one was a man". (This is not so strictly what is meant as what was said earlier; but it is easier to follow.) And speaking generally, suppose we wish to say that the author of *Waverley* had the property ϕ, what we wish to say is equivalent to "One and only one entity wrote *Waverley*, and that one had the property ϕ".

The explanation of *denotation* is now as follows. Every proposition in which "the author of *Waverley*" occurs being explained as above, the proposition "Scott was the author of *Waverley*" (*i.e.* "Scott was identical with the author of *Waverley*") becomes "One and only one entity wrote *Waverley*, and Scott was identical with that one"; or, reverting to the wholly explicit form: "It is not always false of x that x wrote *Waverley*, that it is always true of y that if y wrote *Waverley* y is identical with x, and that Scott is identical with x". Thus if "C" is a denoting phrase, it may happen that there is one entity x (there cannot be more than one) for which the proposition "x is identical with C" is true, this proposition being interpreted as above. We may then say that the entity x is the denotation of the phrase "C". Thus Scott is the denotation of "the author of *Waverley*". The "C" in inverted commas will be merely the *phrase*, not anything that can be called the *meaning*. The phrase *per se* has no meaning, because in any proposition in which it occurs the proposition, fully expressed, does not contain the phrase, which has been broken up.

The puzzle about George IV.'s curiosity is now seen to have a very simple solution. The proposition "Scott was the author of *Waverley*," which was written out in its unabbreviated form in the preceding paragraph, does not contain any constituent "the author of *Waverley*" for which we could substitute "Scott". This does not interfere with the truth of inferences resulting from making what is *verbally* the substitution of "Scott" for "the author of *Waverley*," so long as "the author of *Waverley*" has what I call a *primary* occurrence in the proposition considered. The difference of primary and secondary occurrences of denoting phrases is as follows: —

When we say: "George IV. wished to know whether so-and-so," or when we say "So-and-so is surprising" or "So-and-so is true," etc., the "so-and-so" must be a proposition. Suppose now that "so-and-so" contains a denoting phrase. We may either eliminate this denoting phrase from the subordinate proposition "so-and-so," or from the whole proposition in which "so-and-so" is a mere constituent. Different propositions result according to which we do. I have heard of a touchy owner of a yacht to whom a guest, on first seeing it, remarked, "I thought your yacht was larger than it is"; and the owner replied, "No, my yacht is not larger than it is". What the guest meant was, "The size that I thought your yacht was is greater than the size your yacht is"; the meaning attributed to him is, "I thought the size of your yacht was greater than the size of your yacht". To return to George IV. and *Waverley*, when we say, "George IV. wished to know whether Scott was the author of *Waverley*," we normally mean "George IV. wished to know whether one and only one man wrote *Waverley* and Scott was that man"; but we *may* also mean: "One and only one man wrote *Waverley*, and George IV. wished to know whether Scott was that man". In the latter, "the author of *Waverley*" has a *primary* occurrence; in the former, a *secondary*. The latter might be expressed by "George IV. wished to know, concerning the man who in fact wrote *Waverley*, whether he was Scott". This would be true, for example, if George IV. had seen Scott at a distance, and had asked "Is that Scott?" A *secondary* occurrence of a denoting phrase may be defined as one in which the phrase occurs in a proposition *p* which is a mere constituent of the proposition we are considering, and the substitution for the denoting phrase is to be effected in *p*, not in the whole proposition concerned. The ambiguity as between primary and secondary occurrences is hard to avoid in language; but it does no harm if we are on our guard against it. In symbolic logic it is of course easily avoided.

The distinction of primary and secondary occurrences also enables us to deal with the question whether the present King of France is bald or not bald, and generally with the logical status of denoting phrases that denote nothing. If "C" is a denoting phrase, say "the term having the property F," then

"C has the property ϕ" means "one and only one term has the property F, and that one has the property ϕ".[12]

If now the property F belongs to no terms, or to several, it follows that "C has the property ϕ" is false for *all* values of ϕ. Thus "the present King of France is bald" is certainly false; and "the present King of France is not bald" is false if it means

"There is an entity which is now King of France and is not bald,"

but is true if it means

---

[12] This is the abbreviated, not the stricter, interpretation.

"It is false that there is an entity which is now King of France and is bald".

That is, "the King of France is not bald" is false if the occurrence of "the King of France" is *primary*, and true if it is *secondary*. Thus all propositions in which "the King of France" has a primary occurrence are false; the denials of such propositions are true, but in them "the King of France" has a secondary occurrence. Thus we escape the conclusion that the King of France has a wig.

We can now see also how to deny that there is such an object as the difference between A and B in the case when A and B do not differ. If A and B do differ, there is one and only one entity *x* such that "*x* is the difference between A and B" is a true proposition; if A and B do not differ, there is no such entity *x*. Thus according to the meaning of denotation lately explained, "the difference between A and B" has a denotation when A and B differ, but not otherwise. This difference applies to true and false propositions generally. If "*a* R *b*" stands for "*a* has the relation R to *b*," then when *a* R *b* is true, there is such an entity as the relation R between *a* and *b*; when *a* R *b* is false, there is no such entity. Thus out of any proposition we can make a denoting phrase, which denotes an entity if the proposition is true, but does not denote an entity if the proposition is false. *E.g.*, it is true (at least we will suppose so) that the earth revolves round the sun, and false that the sun revolves round the earth; hence "the revolution of the earth round the sun" denotes an entity, while "the revolution of the sun round the earth" does not denote an entity.[13]

The whole realm of non-entities, such as "the round square," "the even prime other than 2," "Apollo," "Hamlet," etc., can now be satisfactorily dealt with. All these are denoting phrases which do not denote anything. A proposition about Apollo means what we get by substituting what the classical dictionary tells us is meant by Apollo, say "the sun-god". All propositions in which Apollo occurs are to be interpreted by the above rules for denoting phrases. If "Apollo" has a primary occurrence, the proposition containing the occurrence is false; if the occurrence is secondary, the proposition may be true. So again "the round square is round" means "there is one and only one entity *x* which is round and square, and that entity is round," which is a false proposition, not, as Meinong maintains, a true one. "The most perfect Being has all perfections; existence is a perfection; therefore the most perfect Being exists" becomes:—

"There is one and only one entity *x* which is most perfect; that one has all perfections; existence is a perfection; therefore that one exists".

As a proof, this fails for want of a proof of the premiss "there is one and only one entity *x* which is most perfect".[14]

[13] The propositions from which such entities are derived are not identical either with these entities or with the propositions that these entities have being.

[14] The argument can be made to prove validly that all members of the class of most perfect Beings exist; it can also be proved formally that this class cannot have *more* than one member; but, taking the definition of perfection as possession of all positive predicates, it can be proved almost equally formally that the class does not have even one member.

Mr. MacColl (MIND, N.S., No. 54, and again No. 55, p. 401) regards individuals as of two sorts, real and unreal; hence he defines the null-class as the class consisting of all unreal individuals. This assumes that such phrases as "the present King of France," which do not denote a real individual, do, nevertheless, denote an individual, but an unreal one. This is essentially Meinong's theory, which we have seen reason to reject because it conflicts with the law of contradiction. With our theory of denoting, we are able to hold that there are no unreal individuals; so that the null-class is the class containing no members, not the class containing as members all unreal individuals.

It is important to observe the effect of our theory on the interpretation of definitions which proceed by means of denoting phrases. Most mathematical definitions are of this sort: for example, "$m-n$ means the number which, added to n, gives m". Thus $m-n$ is defined as meaning the same as a certain denoting phrase; but we agreed that denoting phrases have no meaning in isolation. Thus what the definition really ought to be is: "Any proposition containing $m-n$ is to mean the proposition which results from substituting for '$m-n$' 'the number which, added to n, gives m'". The resulting proposition is interpreted according to the rules already given for interpreting propositions whose verbal expression contains a denoting phrase. In the case where m and n are such that there is one and only one number x which, added to n, gives m, there is a number x which can be substituted for $m-n$ in any proposition containing $m-n$ without altering the truth or falsehood of the proposition. But in other cases, all propositions in which "$m-n$" has a primary occurrence are false.

The usefulness of *identity* is explained by the above theory. No one outside a logic-book ever wishes to say "x is x," and yet assertions of identity are often made in such forms as "Scott was the author of *Waverley*" or "thou art the man". The meaning of such propositions cannot be stated without the notion of identity, although they are not simply statements that Scott is identical with another term, the author of *Waverly*, or that thou art identical with another term, the man. The shortest statement of "Scott is the author of *Waverley*" seems to be: "Scott wrote *Waverley*; and it is always true of y that if y wrote *Waverley*, y is identical with Scott". It is in this way that identity enters into "Scott is the author of *Waverley*"; and it is owing to such uses that identity is worth affirming.

One interesting result of the above theory of denoting is this: when there is anything with which we do not have immediate acquaintance, but only definition by denoting phrases, then the propositions in which this thing is introduced by means of a denoting phrase do not really contain this thing as a constituent, but contain instead the constituents expressed by the several words of the denoting phrase. Thus in every proposition that we can apprehend (*i.e.* not only in those whose truth or falsehood we can judge of, but in all that we can think about), all the constituents are really entities with which we have immediate acquaintance. Now such things as matter (in the sense in which matter occurs in physics) and the minds of other people are known to us only by denoting phrases, *i.e.*, we are not *acquainted* with them, but we know them as what has such and such properties. Hence, although we can form propositional functions C (x) which must hold of such and such a material particle, or of So-and-so's mind, yet we are not acquainted with the propositions which affirm these things that we know must be true, because we cannot apprehend the actual entities concerned. What we know is "So-and-so has a mind which has such and such properties" but we do not know "A has such and such properties," where A *is* the mind in question. In such a case, we know the properties of a thing without having acquaintance with the thing itself, and without, consequently, knowing any single proposition of which the thing itself is a constituent.

Of the many other consequences of the view I have been advocating, I will say nothing. I will only beg the reader not to make up his mind against the view—as he might be tempted to do, on account of its apparently excessive complication—until he has attempted to construct a theory of his own on the subject of denotation. This attempt, I believe, will convince him that, whatever the true theory may be, it cannot have such a simplicity as one might have expected beforehand.

7

ON REFERRING

P. F. Strawson

I

We very commonly use expressions of certain kinds to mention or refer to some individual person or single object or particular event or place or process, in the course of doing what we should normally describe as making a statement about that person, object, place, event, or process. I shall call this way of using expressions the "uniquely referring use". The classes of expressions which are most commonly used in this way are: singular demonstrative pronouns ("this" and "that"); proper names (*e.g.* "Venice", "Napoleon", "John"); singular personal and impersonal pronouns ("he", "she", "I", "you", "it"); and phrases beginning with the definite article followed by a noun, qualified or unqualified, in the singular (*e.g.* "the table", "the old man", "the king of France"). Any expression of any of these classes can occur as the subject of what would traditionally be regarded as a singular subject-predicate sentence; and would, so occurring, exemplify the use I wish to discuss.

I do not want to say that expressions belonging to these classes never have any other use than the one I want to discuss. On the contrary, it is obvious that they do. It is obvious that anyone who uttered the sentence, "The whale is a mammal", would be using the expression "the whale" in a way quite different from the way it would be used by anyone who had occasion seriously to utter the sentence, "The whale struck the ship". In the first sentence one is obviously *not* mentioning, and in the second sentence one obviously *is* mentioning, a particular whale. Again if I said, "Napoleon was the greatest French soldier", I should be using the word "Napoleon" to mention a certain individual, but I should not be using the phrase, "the greatest French soldier", to mention an individual, but to say something about an individual I had already mentioned. It would be natural to say that in using this sentence I was talking *about* Napoleon and that what I was *saying* about him was that he was the greatest French soldier. But of course I

From P. F. Strawson, "On Referring," *Mind*, LIX (1950), Secs. 1–3, 320–335. Reprinted by permission of the Editor of *Mind* and the author.

could use the expression, "the greatest French soldier", to mention an individual; for example, by saying: "The greatest French soldier died in exile". So it is obvious that at least some expressions belonging to the classes I mentioned *can* have uses other than the use I am anxious to discuss. Another thing I do not want to say is that in any given sentence there is never more than one expression used in the way I propose to discuss. On the contrary, it is obvious that there may be more than one. For example, it would be natural to say that, in seriously using the sentence, "The whale struck the ship", I was saying something about both a certain whale and a certain ship, that I was using each of the expressions "the whale" and "the ship" to mention a particular object; or, in other words, that I was using each of these expressions in the uniquely referring way. In general, however, I shall confine my attention to cases where an expression used in this way occurs as the grammatical subject of a sentence.

I think it is true to say that Russell's Theory of Descriptions, which is concerned with the last of the four classes of expressions I mentioned above (*i.e.* with expressions of the form "the so-and-so") is still widely accepted among logicians as giving a correct account of the use of such expressions in ordinary language. I want to show, in the first place, that this theory, so regarded, embodies some fundamental mistakes.

What question or questions about phrases of the form "the so-and-so" was the Theory of Descriptions designed to answer? I think that at least one of the questions may be illustrated as follows. Suppose some one were now to utter the sentence, "The king of France is wise". No one would say that the sentence which had been uttered was meaningless. Everyone would agree that it was significant. But everyone knows that there is not at present a king of France. One of the questions the Theory of Descriptions was designed to answer was the question: how can such a sentence as "The king of France is wise" be significant even when there is nothing which answers to the description it contains, *i.e.*, in this case, nothing which answers to the description "The king of France"? And one of the reasons why Russell thought it important to give a correct answer to this question was that he thought it important to show that another answer which might be given was wrong. The answer that he thought was wrong, and to which he was anxious to supply an alternative, might be exhibited as the conclusion of either of the following two fallacious arguments. Let us call the sentence "The king of France is wise" the sentence S. Then the first argument is as follows:

(1) The phrase, "the king of France", is the subject of the sentence S.

Therefore (2) if S is a significant sentence, S is a sentence *about* the king of France.

But (3) if there in no sense exists a king of France, the sentence is not about anything, and hence not about the king of France.

Therefore (4) since S is significant, there must in some sense (in some world) exist (or subsist) the king of France.

And the second argument is as follows:

(1) If S is significant, it is either true or false.

(2) S is true if the king of France is wise and false if the king of France is not wise.

(3) But the statement that the king of France is wise and the statement that the king of France is not wise are alike true only if there is (in some sense, in some world) something which is the king of France.

Hence (4) since S is significant, there follows the same conclusion as before.

These are fairly obviously bad arguments, and, as we should expect, Russell rejects them. The postulation of a world of strange entities, to which the king of France belongs, offends, he says, against "that feeling for reality which ought to be preserved even in the most abstract studies". The fact that Russell rejects these arguments is, however, less interesting than the extent to which, in rejecting their conclusion, he concedes the more important of their principles. Let me refer to the phrase, "the king of France", as the phrase D. Then I think Russell's reasons for rejecting these two arguments can be summarised as follows. The mistake arises, he says, from thinking that D, which is certainly the *grammatical* subject of S, is also the *logical* subject of S. But D is not the logical subject of S. In fact S, although grammatically it has a singular subject and a predicate, is not logically a subject-predicate sentence at all. The proposition it expresses is a complex kind of *existential* proposition, part of which might be described as a "uniquely existential" proposition. To exhibit the logical form of the proposition, we should re-write the sentence in a logically appropriate grammatical form; in such a way that the deceptive similarity of S to a sentence expressing a subject-predicate proposition would disappear, and we should be safeguarded against arguments such as the bad ones I outlined above. Before recalling the details of Russell's analysis of S, let us notice what his answer, as I have so far given it, seems to imply. His answer seems to imply that in the case of a sentence which is similar to S in that (1) it is grammatically of the subject-predicate form and (2) its grammatical subject does not refer to anything, then the only alternative to its being meaningless is that it should not really (*i.e.* logically) be of the subject-predicate form at all, but of some quite different form. And this in its turn seems to imply that if there are any sentences which are genuinely of the subject-predicate form, then the very fact of their being significant, having a meaning, guarantees that there *is* something referred to by the logical (and grammatical) subject. Moreover, Russell's answer seems to imply that there are such sentences. For if it is true that one may be misled by the grammatical similarity of S to other sentences into thinking that it is logically of the subject-predicate form, then surely there must be other sentences grammatically similar to S, which *are* of the subject-predicate form. To show not only that Russell's answer seems to imply these conclusions, but that he accepted at least the first two of them, it is enough to consider what he says about a class of expressions which he calls "logically proper names" and contrasts with expressions, like D, which he calls "definite descriptions". Of logically proper names Russell says or implies the following things:

(1) That they and they alone can occur as subjects of sentences which are genuinely of the subject-predicate form;

(2) that an expression intended to be a logically proper name is *meaningless*

unless there is some single object for which it stands: for the *meaning* of such an expression just is the individual object which the expression designates. To be a name at all, therefore, it *must* designate something.

It is easy to see that if anyone believes these two propositions, then the only way for him to save the significance of the sentence S is to deny that it is a logically subject-predicate sentence. Generally, we may say that Russell recognises only two ways in which sentences which seem, from their grammatical structure, to be about some particular person or individual object or event, can be significant:

(1) The first is that their grammatical form should be misleading as to their logical form, and that they should be analysable, like S, as a special kind of existential sentence;

(2) The second is that their grammatical subject should be a logically proper name, of which the meaning is the individual thing it designates.

I think that Russell is unquestionably wrong in this, and that sentences which are significant, and which begin with an expression used in the uniquely referring way fall into neither of these two classes. Expressions used in the uniquely referring way are never either logically proper names or descriptions, if what is meant by calling them "descriptions" is that they are to be analysed in accordance with the model provided by Russell's Theory of Descriptions.

There are no logically proper names and there are no descriptions (in this sense).

Let us now consider the details of Russell's analysis. According to Russell, anyone who asserted S would be asserting that:

(1) There is a king of France.
(2) There is not more than one king of France.
(3) There is nothing which is king of France and is not wise.

It is easy to see both how Russell arrived at this analysis, and how it enables him to answer the question with which we began, *viz.* the question: How can the sentence S be significant when there is no king of France? The way in which he arrived at the analysis was clearly by asking himself what would be the circumstances in which we would say that anyone who uttered the sentence S had made a true assertion. And it does seem pretty clear, and I have no wish to dispute, that the sentences (1)–(3) above do describe circumstances which are at least *necessary* conditions of anyone making a true assertion by uttering the sentence S. But, as I hope to show, to say this is not at all the same thing as to say that Russell has given a correct account of the use of the sentence S or even that he has given an account which, though incomplete, is correct as far as it goes; and is certainly not at all the same thing as to say that the model translation provided is a correct model for all (or for any) singular sentences beginning with a phrase of the form "the so-and-so".

It is also easy to see how this analysis enables Russell to answer the question of how the sentence S can be significant, even when there is no king of France. For, if this analysis is correct, anyone who utters the sentence S to-day would be jointly asserting three propositions, one of which (*viz.* that there is a king of France) would be false; and since the conjunction of three propositions, of which one is false, is itself false, the assertion as a whole would be significant, but false. So neither of the bad arguments for subsistent entities would apply to such an assertion.

II

As a step towards showing that Russell's solution of his problem is mistaken, and towards providing the correct solution, I want now to draw certain distinctions. For this purpose I shall, for the remainder of this section, refer to an expression which has a uniquely referring use as "an expression" for short; and to a sentence beginning with such an expression as "a sentence" for short. The distinctions I shall draw are rather rough and ready, and, no doubt, difficult cases could be produced which would call for their refinement. But I think they will serve my purpose. The distinctions are between:

(A1) a sentence,
(A2) a use of a sentence,
(A3) an utterance of a sentence,

and, correspondingly, between:

(B1) an expression,
(B2) a use of an expression,
(B3) an utterance of an expression.

Consider again the sentence, "The king of France is wise". It is easy to imagine that this sentence was uttered at various times from, say, the beginning of the seventeenth century onwards, during the reigns of each successive French monarch; and easy to imagine that it was also uttered during the subsequent periods in which France was not a monarchy. Notice that it was natural for me to speak of "the sentence" or "this sentence" being uttered at various times during this period; or, in other words, that it would be natural and correct to speak of *one and the same* sentence being uttered on all these various occasions. It is in the sense in which it would be correct to speak of one and the same sentence being uttered on all these various occasions that I want to use the expression (A1) "a sentence". There are, however, obvious differences between different *occasions of the use* of this sentence. For instance, if one man uttered it in the reign of Louis XIV and another man uttered it in the reign of Louis XV, it would be natural to say (to assume) that they were respectively talking about different people; and it might be held that the first man, in using the sentence, made a true assertion, while the second man, in using the same sentence, made a false assertion. If on the other hand two different men simultaneously uttered the sentence (*e.g.* if one wrote it and the other spoke it) during the reign of Louis XIV, it would be natural to say (assume) that they were both talking about the same person, and, in that case, in using the sentence, they *must* either both have made a true assertion or both have made a false assertion. And this illustrates what I mean by *a use* of a sentence. The two men who uttered the sentence, one in the reign of Louis XV and one in the reign of Louis XIV, each made a different use of the same sentence; whereas the two men who uttered the sentence simultaneously in the reign of Louis XIV, made the same use[1] of the same sentence. Obviously in the case of this sentence, and equally obviously in the case of many others, we cannot talk of *the sentence* being true or false, but only of its being used to make a true or false assertion, or (if this is preferred) to express a true or a false proposition. And equally obviously we cannot talk of *the sentence* being *about* a particular person, for the same sentence may be used at different times to talk about quite different particular persons, but only of *a use* of the sentence to talk about a particular person. Finally it will make sufficiently clear what I mean by an utterance of a sentence if I say that the two men who simultaneously uttered the sentence in the reign of Louis XIV made two different utterances of the same sentence, though they made the same *use* of the sentence.

If we now consider not the whole sentence, "The king of France is wise", but that part of it which is the expression, "the king of France", it is obvious that we can make analogous, though not identical distinctions between (1) the expression, (2) a use of the expression and (3) an utterance of the expression alone, that you can talk about a particular person. Instead, we correctly talk of the expression "the king of France" being used to express a true or false proposition, since in general only sentences can be used truly or falsely; and similarly it is only by using a sentence and not by using an expression alone, that you can talk about a particular person. Instead, we shall say in this case that you *use* the expression to *mention* or *refer to* a particular person in the course of using the sentence to talk about him. But obviously in this case, and a great many others, the *expression* (B1) cannot be said to mention, or refer to, anything, any more than the *sentence* can be said to be true or false. The same expression can have different mentioning-uses, as the same sentence can be used to make statements with different truth-values. "Mentioning", or "referring", is not something an expression does; it is something that some one can use an expression to do. Mentioning, or referring to, something is a characteristic of *a use* of an expression, just as "being about" something, and truth-or-falsity, are characteristics of *a use* of a sentence.

A very different example may help to make these distinctions clearer. Consider another case of an expression which has a uniquely referring use, *viz.* the expression "I"; and consider the sentence, "I am hot". Countless people may use this same sentence; but it is logically impossible for two different people to make *the same use* of this sentence: or, if this is preferred, to use it to express the same proposition. The expression "I" may correctly be used by (and only by) any one of innumerable people to refer to himself. To say this is to say something about the expression "I": it is, in a sense, to give its meaning. This is the sort of thing that can be said about *expressions*. But it makes no sense to say of the *expression* "I" that it refers to a particular person. This is the sort of thing that can be said only of a particular use of the expression.

Let me use "type" as an abbreviation for "sentence or expression". Then I am not saying that there are sentences and expressions (types), *and* uses of

---

[1] This usage of 'use' is, of course, different from (*a*) the current usage in which 'use' (of a particular word, phrase, sentence) = (roughly) 'rules for using' = (roughly) 'meaning'; and from (*b*) my own usage in the phrase "uniquely referring use of expressions" in which 'use' = (roughly) 'way of using'.

them, *and* utterances of them, as there are ships *and* shoes *and* sealing-wax. I am saying that we cannot say *the same things* about types, uses of types, and utterances of types. And the fact is that we do talk about types; and that confusion is apt to result from the failure to notice the differences between what we can say about these and what we can say only about the *uses* of types. We are apt to fancy we are talking about sentences and expressions when we are talking about the uses of sentences and expressions.

This is what Russell does. Generally, as against Russell, I shall say this. Meaning (in at least one important sense) is a function of the sentence or expression; mentioning and referring and truth or falsity, are functions of the use of the sentence or expression. To give the meaning of an expression (in the sense in which I am using the word) is to give *general directions* for its use to refer to or mention particular objects or persons; to give the meaning of a sentence is to give *general directions* for its use in making true or false assertions. It is not to talk about any particular occasion of the use of the sentence or expression. The meaning of an expression cannot be identified with the object it is used, on a particular occasion, to refer to. The meaning of a sentence cannot be identified with the assertion it is used, on a particular occasion, to make. For to talk about the meaning of an expression or sentence is not to talk about its use on a particular occasion, but about the rules, habits, conventions governing its correct use, on all occasions, to refer or to assert. So the question of whether a sentence or expression *is significant or not* has nothing whatever to do with the question of whether the sentence, *uttered on a particular occasion*, is, on that occasion, being used to make a true-or-false assertion or not, or of whether the expression is, on that occasion, being used to refer to, or mention, anything at all.

The source of Russell's mistake was that he thought that referring or mentioning, if it occurred at all, must be meaning. He did not distinguish B1 from B2; he confused expressions with their use in a particular context; and so confused meaning with mentioning, with referring. If I talk about my handkerchief, I can, perhaps, produce the object I am referring to out of my pocket. I can't produce the meaning of the expression, "my handkerchief", out of my pocket. Because Russell confused meaning with mentioning, he thought that if there were any expressions having a uniquely referring use, which were what they seemed (*i.e.* logical subjects) and not something else in disguise, their meaning must *be* the particular object which they were used to refer to. Hence the troublesome mythology of the logically proper name. But if some one asks me the meaning of the expression "this"—once Russell's favorite candidate for this status—I do not hand him the object I have just used the expression to refer to, adding at the same time that the meaning of the word changes every time it is used. Nor do I hand him all the objects it ever has been, or might be, used to refer to. I explain and illustrate the conventions governing the use of the expression. This *is* giving the meaning of the expression. It is quite different from giving (in any sense of giving) the object to which it refers; for the expression itself does not refer to anything; though it can be used, on different occasions, to refer to innumerable things. Now as a matter of fact there is, in English, a sense of the word "mean" in which this word does approximate to "indicate, mention or refer to"; *e.g.* when somebody (unpleasantly) says, "I mean you"; or when I point and say, "That's the one I mean". But *the one I meant* is quite different from *the meaning of the expression* I used to talk of it. In this special sense of "mean", it is people who mean, not expressions. People use expressions to refer to particular things. But the meaning of an expression is not the set of things or the single thing it may correctly be used to refer to: the meaning is the set of rules, habits, conventions for its use in referring.

It is the same with sentences: even more obviously so. Every one knows that the sentence, "The table is covered with books", is significant, and every one knows what it means. But if I ask, "What object is that sentence about?" I am asking an absurd question—a question which cannot be asked about the sentence, but only about some use of the sentence: and in this case the sentence hasn't been used, it has only been taken as an example. In knowing what it means, you are knowing how it could correctly be used to talk about things: so knowing the meaning hasn't anything to do with knowing about any particular use of the sentence to talk about anything. Similarly, if I ask: "Is the sentence true or false?" I am asking an absurd question, which becomes no less absurd if I add, "It must be one or the other since it's significant". The question is absurd, because the *sentence* is neither true nor false any more than it's *about* some object. Of course the fact that it's significant is the same as the fact that it *can* correctly be used to talk about something and that, in so using it, some one will be making a true or false assertion. And I will add that it will be used to make a true or false assertion *only* if the person using it *is* talking about something. If, when he utters it, he is not talking about anything, then his use is not a genuine one, but a spurious or pseudo-use: he is not making either a true or a false assertion, though he may think he is. And this points the way to the correct answer to the puzzle to which the Theory of Descriptions gives a fatally incorrect answer. The important point is that the question of whether the sentence is significant or not is quite independent of the question that can be raised about a particular use of it, *viz.* the question whether it is a genuine or a spurious use, whether it is being used to talk about something, or in make-believe, or as an example in philosophy. The question whether the sentence is significant or not is the question whether there exist such language habits, conventions or rules that the sentence logically could be used to talk about something; and is hence quite independent of the question whether it is being so used on a particular occasion.

III

Consider again the sentence, "The king of France is wise", and the true and false things Russell says about it.

There are at least two true things which Russell would say about the sentence:

(1) The first is that it is significant; that if anyone were now to utter it, he would be uttering a significant sentence.

(2) The second is that anyone now uttering the sentence would be making a true assertion only if there in fact at present existed one and only one king of France, and if he were wise.

What are the false things which Russell would say about the sentence? They are:

(1) That anyone now uttering it would be making a true assertion or a false assertion;

(2) That part of what he would be asserting would be that there at present existed one and only one king of France.

I have already given some reasons for thinking that these two statements are incorrect. Now suppose some one were in fact to say to you with a perfectly serious air: "The king of France is wise". Would you say, "That's untrue"? I think it's quite certain that you wouldn't. But suppose he went on to *ask* you whether you thought that what he had just said was true, or was false; whether you agreed or disagreed with what he had just said. I think you would be inclined, with some hesitation, to say that you didn't do either; that the question of whether his statement was true or false simply *didn't arise*, because there was no such person as the king of France.[2] You might, if he were obviously serious (had a dazed astray-in-the-centuries look), say something like: "I'm afraid you must be under a misapprehension. France is not a monarchy. There is no king of France." And this brings out the point that if a man seriously uttered the sentence, his uttering it would in some sense be *evidence* that he *believed* that there was a king of France. It would not be evidence for his believing this simply in the way in which a man's reaching for his raincoat is evidence for his believing that it is raining. But nor would it be evidence for his believing this in the way in which a man's saying, "It's raining" is evidence for his believing that it is raining. We might put it as follows. To say, "The king of France is wise" is, in some sense of "imply", to *imply* that there is a king of France. But this is a very special and odd sense of "imply". "Implies" in this sense is certainly not equivalent to "entails" (or "logically implies"). And this comes out from the fact that when, in response to his statement, we say (as we should) "There is no king of France", we should certainly *not* say we were *contradicting* the statement that the king of France is wise. We are certainly not saying that it's false. We are, rather, giving a reason for saying that the question of whether it's true or false simply doesn't arise.

And this is where the distinction I drew earlier can help us. The sentence, "The king of France is wise", is certainly significant; but this does not mean that any particular use of it is true or false. We use it truly or falsely when we use it to talk about some one; when, in using the expression, "The king of France", we are in fact mentioning some one. The fact that the sentence and the expression, respectively, are significant just is the fact that the sentence *could* be used, in certain circumstances, to say something true or false, that the expression *could* be used, in certain circumstances to mention a particular person; and to know their meaning is to know what sort of circumstances these are. So when we utter the sentence without in fact mentioning anybody by the use of the phrase, "The king of France", the sentence doesn't cease to be significant: we simply *fail* to say anything true or false because we simply fail to mention anybody by this particular use of that perfectly significant phrase. It is, if you like, a spurious use of the sentence, and a spurious use of the expression; though we may (or may not) mistakenly think it a genuine use.

[2] Since this article was written, there has appeared a clear statement of this point by Mr. Geach in *Analysis*, Vol. 10, No. 4, March, 1950.

And such spurious uses are very familiar. Sophisticated romancing, sophisticated fiction,[3] depend upon them. If I began, "The king of France is wise", and went on, "and he lives in a golden castle and has a hundred wives", and so on, a hearer would understand me perfectly well, without supposing *either* that I was talking about a particular person, *or* that I was making a false statement to the effect that there existed such a person as my words described. (It is worth adding that where the use of sentences and expressions is overtly fictional, the sense of the word "about" may change. As Moore said, it is perfectly natural and correct to say that some of the statements in *Pickwick Papers* are *about* Mr. Pickwick. But where the use of sentences and expressions is not overtly fictional, this use of "about" seems less correct; *i.e.* it would not *in general* be correct to say that a statement was about Mr. X or the so-and-so, unless there were such a person or thing. So it is where the romancing is in danger of being taken seriously that we might answer the question, "Who is he talking about?" with "He's not talking about anybody"; but, in saying this, we are not saying that what he is saying is either false or nonsense.)

Overtly fictional uses apart, however, I said just now that to use such an expression as "The king of France" at the beginning of a sentence was, in some sense of "imply", to imply that there was a king of France. When a man uses such an expression, he does not *assert*, nor does what he says *entail*, a uniquely existential proposition. But one of the conventional functions of the definite article is to act as a *signal* that a unique reference is being made—a signal, not a disguised assertion. When we begin a sentence with "the such-and-such" the use of "the" shows, but does not state, that we are, or intend to be, referring to one particular individual of the species "such-and-such". *Which* particular individual is a matter to be determined from context, time, place and any other features of the situation of utterance. Now, whenever a man uses any expression, the presumption is that he thinks he is using it correctly: so when he uses the expression, "the such-and-such", in a uniquely referring way, the presumption is that he thinks both that there is *some* individual of that species, and that the context of use will sufficiently determine which one he has in mind. To use the word "the" in this way is then to imply (in the relevant sense of "imply") that the existential conditions described by Russell are fulfilled. But to use "the" in this way is not to *state* that those conditions are fulfilled. If I begin a sentence with an expression of the form, "the so-and-so", and then am prevented from saying more, I have made no statement of any kind; but I may have succeeded in mentioning some one or something.

The uniquely existential assertion supposed by Russell to be part of any assertion in which a uniquely referring use is made of an expression of the form "the so-and-so" is, he observes, a compound of two assertions. To say that there is a ϕ is to say something compatible with there being several ϕs; to say there is not more than one ϕ is to say something compatible with there being none. To say there is one ϕ and one only is to compound these two assertions. I have so far been concerned mostly with the alleged assertion of existence and less with the alleged assertion of uniqueness. An example which throws the emphasis on to the latter will serve to bring out

[3] The unsophisticated kind begins: "Once upon a time there was . . .".

more clearly the sense of "implied" in which a uniquely existential assertion is implied, but not entailed, by the use of expressions in the uniquely referring way. Consider the sentence, "The table is covered with books". It is quite certain that in any normal use of this sentence, the expression "the table" would be used to make a unique reference, *i.e.* to refer to some one table. It is a quite strict use of the definite article, in the sense in which Russell talks on p. 30 of *Principia Mathematica*, of using the article "*strictly*, so as to imply uniqueness". On the same page Russell says that a phrase of the form "the so-and-so", used strictly, "will only have an application in the event of there being one so-and-so and no more". Now it is obviously quite false that the phrase "the table" in the sentence "the table is covered with books", used normally, will "only have an application in the event of there being one table and no more". It is indeed tautologically true that, in such a use, the phrase will have an application only in the event of there being one table and no more *which is being referred to*, and that it will be understood to have an application only in the event of there being one table and no more which it is understood as being used to refer to. To use the sentence is not to assert, but it is (in the special sense discussed) to imply, that there is only one thing which is *both* of the kind specified (*i.e.* a table) *and is being referred to* by the speaker. It is obviously not to assert this. To refer is not to say you are referring. To say there is *some table or other* to which you are referring is not the same as referring to a particular table. We should have no use for such phrases as "the individual I referred to" unless there were something which counted as referring. (It would make no sense to say you had pointed if there were nothing which counted as pointing.) So once more I draw the conclusion that referring to or mentioning a particular thing cannot be dissolved into any kind of assertion. To refer is not to assert, though you refer in order to go on to assert.

Let me now take an example of the uniquely referring use of an expression not of the form, "the so-and-so". Suppose I advance my hands, cautiously cupped, towards someone, saying, as I do so, "This is a fine red one". He, looking into my hands and seeing nothing there, may say: "What is? What are you talking about?" Or perhaps, "But there's nothing in your hands". Of course it would be absurd to say that in saying "But you've got nothing in your hands", he was *denying* or *contradicting* what I said. So "this" is not a disguised description in Russell's sense. Nor is it a logically proper name. For one must know what the sentence means in order to react in that way to the utterance of it. It is precisely because the significance of the word "this" is independent of any particular reference it may be used to make, though not independent of the way it may be used to refer, that I can, as in this example, use it to *pretend* to be referring to something.

The general moral of all this is that communication is much less a matter of explicit or disguised assertion than logicians used to suppose. The particular application of this general moral in which I am interested is its application to the case of making a unique reference. It is a part of the significance of expressions of the kind I am discussing that they can be used, in an immense variety of contexts, to make unique references. It is no part of their significance to assert that they are being so used or that the conditions of their being so used are fulfilled. So the wholly important distinction we are required to draw is between:

(1) using an expression to make a unique reference; and

(2) asserting that there is one and only one individual which has certain characteristics (*e.g.* is of a certain kind, or stands in a certain relation to the speaker, or both).

This is, in other words, the distinction between:

(1) sentences containing an expression used to indicate or mention or refer to a particular person or thing; and

(2) uniquely existential sentences.

What Russell does is progressively to assimilate more and more sentences of class (1) to sentences of class (2), and consequently to involve himself in insuperable difficulties about logical subjects, and about values for individual variables generally: difficulties which have led him finally to the logically disastrous theory of names developed in the *Enquiry* and in *Human Knowledge*. That view of the meaning of logical-subject-expressions which provides the whole incentive to the Theory of Descriptions at the same time precludes the possibility of Russell's ever finding any satisfactory substitutes for those expressions which, beginning with substantival phrases, he progressively degrades from the status of logical subjects.[4] It is not simply, as is sometimes said, the fascination of the relation between a name and its bearer, that is the root of the trouble. Not even names come up to the impossible standard set. It is rather the combination of two more radical misconceptions: first, the failure to grasp the importance of the distinction (section II above) between what may be said of an expression and what may be said of a particular use of it; second, a failure to recognise the uniquely referring use of expressions for the harmless, necessary thing it is, distinct from, but complementary to, the predicative or ascriptive use of expressions. The expressions which can in fact occur as singular logical subjects are expressions of the class I listed at the outset (demonstratives, substantival phrases, proper names, pronouns): to say this is to say that these expressions, together with context (in the widest sense) are what one uses to make unique references. The point of the conventions governing the uses of such expressions is, along with the situation of utterance, to secure uniqueness of reference. But to do this, enough is enough. We do not, and we cannot, while referring, attain the point of complete explicitness at which the referring function is no longer performed. The actual unique reference made, if any, is a matter of the particular use in the particular context; the significance of the expression used is the set of rules or conventions which permit such references to be made. Hence we can, using significant expressions, pretend to refer, in make-believe or in fiction, or mistakenly think we are referring when we are not referring to anything.

This shows the need for distinguishing two kinds (among many others) of linguistic conventions or rules: rules for referring, and rules for attributing and ascribing; and for an investigation of the former. If we recognise this distinction of use for what it is, we are on the way to solving a number of ancient logical and metaphysical puzzles.

.   .   .

---

[4] And this in spite of the danger-signal of that phrase, "*misleading* grammatical form".

SYSTEMATICALLY MISLEADING
EXPRESSIONS

Gilbert Ryle

Philosophical arguments have always largely, if not entirely, consisted in attempts to thrash out "what it means to say so and so." It is observed that men in their ordinary discourse, the discourse, that is, that they employ when they are not philosophizing, use certain expressions, and philosophers fasten on to certain more or less radical types or classes of such expressions and raise their question about all expressions of a certain type and ask what they really mean.

Sometimes philosophers say that they are analysing or clarifying the "concepts" which are embodied in the "judgments" of the plain man or of the scientist, historian, artist or who-not. But this seems to be only a gaseous way of saying that they are trying to discover what is meant by the general terms contained in the sentences which they pronounce or write. For, as we shall see, "*x* is a concept" and "*y* is a judgment" are themselves systematically misleading expressions.

But the whole procedure is very odd. For, if the expressions under consideration are intelligently used, their employers must already know what they mean and do not need the aid or admonition of philosophers before they can understand what they are saying. And if their hearers understand what they are being told, they too are in no such perplexity that they need to have this meaning philosophically "analysed" or "clarified" for them. And, at least, the philosopher himself must know what the expressions mean, since otherwise he could not know what it was that he was analysing.

.   .   .

Certainly expressions do occur for which better substitutes could be found and should be or should have been employed. (1) An expression may be a breach of, *e.g.*, English or Latin grammar. (2) A word may be a foreign word, or a rare word or a technical or trade term for which there exists a

Gilbert Ryle, "Systematically Misleading Expressions," *Proceedings of the Aristotelian Society*, XXXII (1931–1932), 139–152, 157–163, 165–169. Reprinted by courtesy of the Editor of The Aristotelian Society.

familiar synonym. (3) A phrase or sentence may be clumsy or unfamiliar in its structure. (4) A word or phrase may be equivocal and so be an instrument of possible puns. (5) A word or phrase may be ill-chosen as being general where it should be specific, or allusive where the allusion is not known or not obvious. (6) Or a word may be a malapropism or a misnomer. But the search for paraphrases which shall be more swiftly intelligible to a given audience or more idiomatic or stylish or more grammatically or etymologically correct is merely applied lexicography or philology—it is not philosophy.

We ought then to face the question: Is there such a thing as analysing or clarifying the meaning of the expressions which people use, except in the sense of substituting philologically better expressions for philologically worse ones? (We might have put the problem in the more misleading terminology of "concepts" and asked: How can philosophizing so operate by analysis and clarification, upon the concepts used by the plain man, the scientist or the artist, that after this operation the concepts are illumined where before they were dark? The same difficulties arise. For there can be no such thing as a confused concept, since either a man is conceiving, *i.e.*, knowing the nature of his subject-matter, or he is failing to do so. If he is succeeding, no clarification is required or possible; and if he is failing, he must find out more or think more about the subject-matter, the apprehension of the nature of which we call his "concept." But this will not be philosophizing about the concept, but exploring further the nature of the thing, and so will be economics, perhaps, or astronomy or history. But as I think that it can be shown that it is not true in any natural sense that "there are concepts," I shall adhere to the other method of stating the problem.)

· · ·

The gist of what I want to establish is this. There are many expressions[1] which occur in non-philosophical discourse which, though they are perfectly clearly understood by those who use them and those who hear or read them, are nevertheless couched in grammatical or syntactical forms which are in a demonstrable way *improper* to the states of affairs which they record (or the alleged states of affairs which they profess to record). Such expressions can be reformulated and for philosophy but *not* for non-philosophical discourse must be reformulated into expressions of which the syntactical form is proper to the facts recorded (or the alleged facts alleged to be recorded).

When an expression is of such a syntactical form that it is improper to the fact recorded, it is systematically misleading in that it naturally suggests to

---

[1] I use "expression" to cover single words, phrases and sentences. By "statement" I mean a sentence in the indicative. When a statement is true, I say it "records" a fact or state of affairs. False statements do not record. To know that a statement is true is to know that something is the case and that the statement records it. When I barely understand a statement I do not know that it records a fact, nor need I know the fact that it records, if it records one. But I know what state of affairs *would* obtain, if the statement recorded a state of affairs.

Every significant statement is a quasi-record, for it has both the requisite structure and constituents to be a record. But knowing these, we don't yet know that it is a record of a fact. False statements are pseudo-records and are no more records than pseudo-antiquities are antiquities. So the question, What do false statements state? is meaningless if "state" means "record." If it means, What *would* they record if they recorded something being the case? the question contains its own answer.

some people—though not to "ordinary" people—that the state of affairs recorded is quite a different sort of state of affairs from that which it in fact is.

I shall try to show what I am driving at by examples. I shall begin by considering a whole class of expressions of one type which occur and occur perfectly satisfactorily in ordinary discourse, but which are, I argue, *systematically misleading*, that is to say, that they are couched in a syntactical form improper to the facts recorded and proper to facts of quite another logical form than the facts recorded. (For simplicity's sake, I shall speak as if all the statements adduced as examples are true. For false statements are not formally different from true ones. Otherwise grammarians could become omniscient. And when I call a statement "systematically misleading" I shall not mean that it is false, and certainly not that it is senseless. By "systematically" I mean that all expressions of that grammatical form would be misleading in the same way and for the same reason.)

I. QUASI-ONTOLOGICAL STATEMENTS

Since Kant, we have, most of us, paid lip service to the doctrine that "existence is not a quality" and so we have rejected the pseudo-implication of the ontological argument; "God is perfect, being perfect entails being existent, ∴ God exists." For if existence is not a quality, it is not the sort of thing that can be entailed by a quality.

But until fairly recently it was not noticed that if in "God exists" "exists" is not a predicate (save in grammar), then in the same statement "God" cannot be (save in grammar) the subject of predication. The realization of this came from examining negative existential propositions like "Satan does not exist" or "unicorns are non-existent." If there is no Satan, then the statement "Satan does not exist" cannot be about Satan in the way in which "I am sleepy" is about me. Despite appearances the word "Satan" cannot be signifying a subject of attributes.

Philosophers have toyed with theories which would enable them to continue to say that "Satan does not exist" is none the less still somehow about Satan, and that "exists" still signifies some sort of attribute or character, although not a quality.

So some argued that the statement was about something described as "the idea of Satan," others that it was about a subsistent but non-actual entity called "Satan." Both theories in effect try to show that something may *be* (whether as being "merely mental" or as being in "the realm of subsistents"), but not be in existence. But as we can say "round squares do not exist," and "real nonentities do not exist," this sort of interpretation of negative existentials is bound to fill either the realm of subsistents or the realm of ideas with walking self-contradictions. So the theories had to be dropped and a new analysis of existential propositions had to begin.

Suppose I assert of (apparently) the general subject "carnivorous cows" that they "do not exist," and my assertion is true, I cannot really be talking about carnivorous cows, for there are none. So it follows that the expression "carnivorous cows" is not really being used, though the grammatical appearances are to the contrary, to denote the thing or things of which the predicate is being asserted. And in the same way as the verb "exists" is not signifying the character asserted, although grammatically it looks as if it was, the real predicate must be looked for elsewhere.

So the clue of the grammar has to be rejected and the analysis has been suggested that "carnivorous cows do not exist" means what is meant by "no cows are carnivorous" or "no carnivorous beasts are cows." But a further improvement seems to be required.

"Unicorns do not exist" seems to mean what is meant by "nothing is *both* a quadruped *and* herbivorous *and* the wearer of one horn" (or whatever the marks of being an unicorn are). And this does not seem to imply that there are some quadrupeds or herbivorous animals.

So "carnivorous cows do not exist" ought to be rendered "nothing is both a cow and carnivorous," which does not as it stands imply that anything is either.

Take now an apparently singular subject as in "God exists" or "Satan does not exist." If the former analysis was right, then here too "God" and "Satan" are in fact, despite grammatical appearance, predicative expressions. That is to say, they are that element in the assertion that something has or lacks a specified character or set of characters, which signifies the character or set of characters by which the subject is being asserted to be characterized. "God exists" must mean what is meant by "Something, and one thing only, is omniscient, omnipotent and infinitely good" (or whatever else are the characters summed in the compound character of being a god and the only god). And "Satan does not exist" must mean what is meant by "nothing is both devilish and alone in being devilish," or perhaps "nothing is both devilish and called 'Satan,' " or even " 'Satan' is not the proper name of anything." To put it roughly, "*x* exists" and "*x* does not exist" do not assert or deny that a given subject of attributes *x* has the attribute of existing, but assert or deny the attribute of being *x*-ish or being an *x* of something not named in the statement.

Now I can show my hand. I say that expressions such as "carnivorous cows do not exist" are systematically misleading and that the expressions by which we paraphrased them are not or are not in the same way or to the same extent systematically misleading. But they are not false, nor are they senseless. They are true, and they really do mean what their less systematically misleading paraphrases mean. Nor (save in a special class of cases) is the non-philosophical author of such expressions ignorant or doubtful of the nature of the state of affairs which his expression records. He is not a whit misled. There is a trap, however, in the form of his expression, but a trap which only threatens the man who has begun to generalize about sorts or types of states of affairs and assumes that every statement gives in its syntax a clue to the logical form of the fact that it records. I refer here not merely nor even primarily to the philosopher, but to any man who embarks on abstraction.

But before developing this theme I want to generalize the results of our examination of what we must now describe as "so-called existential statements." It is the more necessary that, while most philosophers are now forewarned by Kant against the systematic misleadingness of "God exists," few of them have observed that the same taint infects a whole host of other expressions.

If "God exists" means what we have said it means, then patently "God is an existent," "God is an entity," "God has being," or "existence" require the same analysis. So ". . . is an existent," ". . . is an entity" are only bogus predicates, and that of which (in grammar) they are asserted are only bogus subjects.

And the same will be true of all the items in the following pair of lists.

Mr. Baldwin—	Mr. Pickwick—
is a being.	is a nonentity.
is real, or a reality.	is unreal or an unreality, or an appearance.
is a genuine entity.	is a bogus or sham entity.
is a substance.	is not a substance.
is an actual object or entity.	is an unreal object or entity.
is objective.	is not objective or is subjective.
is a concrete reality.	is a fiction or figment.
is an object.	is an imaginary object.
is.	is not.
	is a mere idea.
	is an abstraction.
	is a logical construction.

None of these statements is really about Mr. Pickwick. For if they are true, there is no such person for them to be about. Nor is any of them about Mr. Baldwin. For if they were false, there would be no one for them to be about. Nor in any of them is the grammatical predicate that element in the statement which signifies the character that is being asserted to be characterizing or not to be characterizing something.

I formulate the conclusion in this rather clumsy way. There is a class of statements of which the grammatical predicate *appears* to signify not the having of a specified character but the having (or not having) of a specified *status*. But in all such statements the appearance is a purely grammatical one, and what the statements really record can be stated in statements embodying no such quasi-ontological predicates.

And, again, in all such quasi-ontological statements the grammatical subject-word or phrase *appears* to denote or refer to something as that of which the quasi-ontological predicate is being predicated; but in fact the apparent subject term is a concealed predicative expression, and what is really recorded in such statements can be re-stated in statements no part of which even appears to refer to any such subject.

In a word, all quasi-ontological statements are systematically misleading. (If I am right in this, then the conclusion follows, which I accept, that those metaphysical philosophers are the greatest sinners, who, as if they were saying something of importance, make "Reality" or "Being" the subject of their propositions, or "real" the predicate. For at best what they say is systematically misleading, which is the one thing which a philosopher's propositions have no right to be; and at worst it is meaningless.)

I must give warning again, that the naïve employer of such quasi-ontological expressions is not necessarily and not even probably misled. He has said what he wanted to say, and anyone who knew English would understand what he was saying. Moreover, I would add, in the cases that I have listed, the statements are not merely significant but true. Each of them records a real state of affairs. Nor *need* they mislead the philosopher. We, for instance, I hope are not misled. But the point is that anyone, the philosopher included, who abstracts and generalizes and so tries to consider what different facts of the same type (*i.e.*, facts of the same type about different things) have in common, is compelled to use the common grammatical form of the statements of those facts as handles with which to grasp the common logical form of the facts themselves. For (what we shall see later) as the way in which a fact *ought* to be recorded in expressions *would* be a clue to the form of that fact, we jump to the assumption that the way in which a fact *is* recorded *is* such a clue. And very often the clue is misleading and suggests that the fact is of a different form from what really is its form. "Satan is not a reality" from its grammatical form looks as if it recorded the same sort of fact as "Capone is not a philosopher," and so was just as much denying a character of a somebody called "Satan" as the latter does deny a character of a somebody called "Capone." But it turns out that the suggestion is a fraud; for the fact recorded would have been properly or less improperly recorded in the statement " 'Satan' is not a proper name" or "No one is called 'Satan' " or "No one is both called 'Satan' and is infinitely malevolent, etc.," or perhaps "Some people believe that someone is both called 'Satan' and infinitely malevolent, but their belief is false." And none of these statements even pretend to be "about Satan." Instead, they are and are patently about the noise "Satan" or else about people who misuse it.

In the same way, while it is significant, true and directly intelligible to say "Mr. Pickwick is a fiction," it is a systematically misleading expression (*i.e.*, an expression misleading in virtue of a formal property which it does or might share with other expressions); for it does not really record, as it appears to record, a fact of the same sort as is recorded in "Mr. Baldwin is a statesman." The world does not contain fictions in the way in which it contains statesmen. There is no subject of attributes of which we can say "*there* is a fiction." What we can do is to say of Dickens "*there* is a story-teller," or of Pickwick Papers "*there* is a pack of lies"; or of a sentence in that novel, which contains the pseudo-name "Mr. Pickwick" "*there* is a fable." And when we say things of this sort we are recording just what we recorded when we said "Mr. Pickwick is a fiction," only our new expressions do not suggest what our old one did that some subject of attributes has the two attributes of being called "Mr. Pickwick" and of being a fiction, but instead that some subject of attributes has the attributes of being called Dickens and being a coiner of false propositions and pseudo-proper names, or, on the other analysis, of being a book or a sentence which could only be true or false *if* someone was called "Mr. Pickwick." The proposition "Mr. Pickwick is a fiction" is really, despite its *prima facies*, about Dickens or else about Pickwick Papers. But the fact that it is so is concealed and not exhibited by the form of the expression in which it is said.

It must be noted that the sense in which such quasi-ontological statements are misleading is not that they are false and not even that any word in them is equivocal or vague, but only that they are formally improper to the facts of the logical form which they are employed to record and proper to facts of quite another logical form. What the implications are of these notions of formal propriety or formal impropriety we shall see later on.

II STATEMENTS SEEMINGLY ABOUT UNIVERSALS, OR QUASI-PLATONIC STATEMENTS

We often and with great convenience use expressions such as "Unpunctuality is reprehensible" and "Virtue is its own reward." And at first sight these seem to be on all fours with "Jones merits reproof" and "Smith has given himself the prize." So philosophers, taking it that what is meant by such statements as the former is precisely analogous to what is meant by such statements as the latter, have accepted the consequence that the world contains at least two sorts of objects, namely, particulars like Jones and Smith, and "universals" like Unpunctuality and Virtue.

But absurdities soon crop up. It is obviously silly to speak of an universal meriting reproof. You can no more praise or blame an "universal" than you can make holes in the Equator.

Nor when we say "unpunctuality is reprehensible" do we really suppose that unpunctuality ought to be ashamed of itself.

What we do mean is what is also meant but better expressed by "Whoever is unpunctual deserves that other people should reprove him for being unpunctual." For it is unpunctual men and not unpunctuality who can and should be blamed, since they are, what it is not, moral agents. Now in the new expression "whoever is unpunctual merits reproof" the word "unpunctuality" has vanished in favour of the predicative expression ". . . is unpunctual." So that while in the original expression "unpunctuality" seemed to denote the subject of which an attribute was being asserted, it now turns out to signify the having of an attribute. And we are really saying that anyone who has that attribute, has the other.

Again, it is not literally true that Virtue is a recipient of rewards. What is true is that anyone who is virtuous is benefited thereby. Whoever is good, gains something by being good. So the original statement was not "about Virtue" but about good men, and the grammatical subject-word "Virtue" meant what is meant by ". . . is virtuous" and so was, what it pretended not to be, a predicative expression.

I need not amplify this much. It is not literally true that "honesty compels me to state so and so," for "honesty" is not the name of a coercive agency. What is true is more properly put "because I am honest, or wish to be honest, I am bound to state so and so." "Colour involves extension" means what is meant by "Whatever is coloured is extended"; "hope deferred maketh the heart sick" means what is meant by "whoever for a long time hopes for something without getting it becomes sick at heart."

It is my own view that all statements which seem to be "about universals" are analysable in the same way, and consequently that general terms are never really the names of subjects of attributes. So "universals" are not objects in the way in which Mt. Everest is one, and therefore the age-old question what *sort* of objects they are is a bogus question. For general nouns, adjectives, etc., are not proper names, so we cannot speak of "the objects called 'equality,' 'justice,' and 'progress.' "

Platonic and anti-Platonic assertions, such as that "equality is, or is not, a real entity," are, accordingly, alike misleading, and misleading in two ways at once; for they are both quasi-ontological statements and quasi-Platonic ones.

However, I do not wish to defend this general position here, but only to show that in *some* cases statements which from their grammatical form seem to be saying that "honesty does so and so" or "equality is such and such," are really saying in a formally improper way (though one which is readily understandable and idiomatically correct) "anything which is equal to x is such and such" or "whoever is honest, is so and so." These statements state overtly what the others stated covertly that something's having one attribute necessitates its having the other.

Of course, the plain man who uses such quasi-Platonic expressions is not making a philosophical mistake. He is not philosophizing at all. He is not misled by and does not even notice the fraudulent pretence contained in such propositions that they are "about Honesty" or "about Progress." He knows what he means and will, very likely, accept our more formally proper restatement of what he means as a fair paraphrase, but he will not have any motive for desiring the more proper form of expression, nor even any grounds for holding that it is more proper. For he is not attending to the form of the fact in abstraction from the special subject matter that the fact is about. So for him the best way of expressing something is the way which is the most brief, the most elegant, or the most emphatic, whereas those who, like philosophers, must generalize about the *sorts* of statements that have to be made of *sorts* of facts about *sorts* of topics, cannot help treating as clues to the logical structures for which they are looking the grammatical forms of the common types of expressions in which these structures are recorded. And these clues are often misleading.

·   ·   ·

III SYSTEMATICALLY MISLEADING QUASI-REFERENTIAL "THE"-PHRASES

1. There frequently occur in ordinary discourse expressions which, though "the"-phrases, are not unique descriptions at all, although from their grammatical form they look as if they are. The man who does not go in for abstraction and generalization uses them without peril or perplexity and knows quite well what he means by the sentences containing them. But the philosopher has to re-state them in a different and formally more proper arrangement of words if he is not to be trapped.

When a descriptive phrase is used as the grammatical subject of a sentence in a formally non-misleading way, as in "the King went shooting to-day," we know that if the statement as a whole is true (or even false) then there must be in the world someone in particular to whom the description "the King" refers or applies. And we could significantly ask "Who is the King?" and "Are the father of the Prince of Wales and the King one and the same person?"

But we shall see that there are in common use quasi-descriptive phrases of the form "the so-and-so," in the cases of which there is in the world no one and nothing that could be described as that to which the phrase refers or applies, and thus that there is nothing and nobody about which or whom we could even ask "Is it the so-and-so?" or "Are he and the so-and-so one and the same person?"

It can happen in several ways. Take first the statement, which is true and clearly intelligible, "Poincaré is not the King of France." This at first sight looks formally analogous to "Tommy Jones is not (*i.e.*, is not identical with) the King of England." But the difference soon shows itself. For whereas if the latter is true then its converse "the King of England is not Tommy Jones" is true, it is neither true nor false to say "The King of France is not Poincaré." For there is no King of France and the phrase "the King of France" does not fit anybody—nor did the plain man who said "Poincaré is not the King of France" suppose the contrary. So "the King of France" in this statement is not analogous to "the King of England" in the others. It is not really being used referentially or as a unique description of somebody at all.

We can now redraft the contrasted propositions in forms of words which shall advertize the difference which the original propositions concealed between the forms of the facts recorded.

"Tommy Jones is not the same person as the King of England" means what is meant by (1) "Somebody and—of an unspecified circle—one person only is called Tommy Jones; (2) Somebody, and one person only has royal power in England; and (3) No one both is called Tommy Jones and is King of England." The original statement could not be true unless (1) and (2) were true.

Take now "Poincaré is not the King of France." This means what is meant by (1) Someone is called "Poincaré" and (2) Poincaré has not got the rank, being King of France. And this does not imply that anyone has that rank.

Sometimes this twofold use, namely the referential and the non-referential use of "the"-phrases troubles us in the mere practice of ordinary discourse. "Smith is not the only man who has ever climbed Mont Blanc" might easily be taken by some people to mean what is meant by "One man and one man only has climbed Mont Blanc, but Smith is not he," and by others, "Smith has climbed Mont Blanc but at least one other man has done so too." But I am not interested in the occasional ambiguity of such expressions, but in the fact that an expression of this sort which is really being used in the non-referential way is apt to be construed as if it *must* be referentially used, or as if any "the"-phrase was referentially used. Philosophers and others who have to abstract and generalize tend to be misled by the verbal similarity of "the"-phrases of the one sort with "the"-phrases of the other into "coining entities" in order to be able to show to what a given "the"-phrase refers.

Let us first consider the phrase "the top of that tree" or "the centre of that bush" as they occur in such statements as "an owl is perched on the top of that tree," "my arrow flew through the centre of the bush." These statements are quite unambiguous and convey clearly and correctly what they are intended to convey.

But as they are in syntax analogous to "a man is sitting next to the Vice-Chancellor" and "my arrow flew through the curtain," and as further an indefinite list could be drawn up of different statements having in common the "the"-phrases "the top of that tree" and "the centre of that bush," it is hard for people who generalize to escape the temptation of supposing or even believing that these "the"-phrases refer to objects in the way in which "the Vice-Chancellor" and "the curtain" refer to objects. And this is to suppose or believe that the top of that tree is a genuine subject of attributes in just the same way as the Vice-Chancellor is.

But (save in the case where the expression is being misused for the expression "the topmost branch" or "the topmost leaf of the tree") "the top of the tree" at once turns out not to be referring to any object. There is nothing in the world of which it is true (or even false) to say "that is the top of such and such a tree." It does not, for instance, refer to a bit of the tree, or it could be cut down and burned or put in a vase. "The top of the tree" does not refer to anything, but it signifies an attribute, namely, the having of a relative position, when it occurs in statements of the form "x is at or near or above or below the top of the tree." To put it crudely, it does not refer to a thing but signifies a thing's being in a certain place, or else signifies not a thing but the site or locus of a thing such as of the bough or leaf which is higher than any of the other boughs or leaves on the tree. Accordingly it makes sense to say that now one bough and now another is at the top of the tree. But "at the top of the tree" means no more than what is meant by "higher than any other part of the tree," which latter phrase no one could take for a referential phrase like "the present Vice-Chancellor."

The place of a thing, or the whereabouts of a thing is not a thing but the tail end of the fact that something is there. "Where the bee sucks, there suck I," but it is the clover flower that is there which holds the honey and not the whereabouts of the flower. All that this amounts to is that though we can use quasi-descriptive phrases to enable us to state where something is, that the thing is there is a relational character of the thing and not itself a subject of characters.

I suspect that a lot of Cartesian and perhaps Newtonian blunders about Space and Time originate from the systematically misleading character of the "the"-phrases which we use to date and locate things, such as "the region occupied by x," "the path followed by y," "the moment or date at which z happened." It was not seen that these are but hamstrung predicative expressions and are not and are not even ordinarily taken to be referentially used descriptive expressions, any more than "the King of France" in "Poincaré is not the King of France" is ordinarily treated as if it was a referentially used "the"-phrase.

Take another case. "Jones hates the thought of going to hospital," "the idea of having a holiday has just occurred to me." These quasi-descriptive phrases suggest that there is one object in the world which is what is referred to by the phrase "the thought of going to hospital" and another which is what is referred to by "the idea of having a holiday." And anyhow partly through accepting the grammatical *prima facies* [appearance] of such expressions, philosophers have believed as devoutly in the existence of "ideas," "conceptions" and "thoughts" or "judgments" as their predecessors did (from similar causes) in that of substantial forms or as children do (from similar causes) in that of the Equator, the sky and the North Pole.

But if we re-state them, the expressions turn out to be no evidence whatsoever in favour of the Lockean demonology. For "Jones hates the thought of going to hospital" only means what is meant by "Jones feels distressed when he thinks of what he will undergo if he goes to hospital."

The phrase "the thought of . . ." is transmuted into "whenever he thinks of . . .," which does not even seem to contain a reference to any other entity than Jones and, perhaps, the hospital. For it to be true, the world must contain a Jones who is sometimes thinking and sometimes, say, sleeping; but it need no more contain both Jones and "the thought or idea of so and so" than it need contain both someone called "Jones" and something called "Sleep."

Similarly, the statement "the idea of taking a holiday has just occurred to me" seems grammatically to be analogous to "that dog has just bitten me." And as, if the latter is true, the world must contain both me and the dog, so it would seem, if the former is true, the world must contain both me and the idea of taking a holiday. But the appearance is a delusion. For while I could not re-state my complaint against the dog in any sentence not containing a descriptive phrase referring to it, I can easily do so with the statement about "the idea of taking a holiday," *e.g.*, in the statement "I have just been thinking that I might take a holiday."

A host of errors of the same sort has been generated in logic itself and epistemology by the omission to analyse the quasi-descriptive phrase "the meaning of the expression 'x' ". I suspect that all the mistaken doctrines of concepts, ideas, terms, judgments, objective propositions, contents, objectives and the like derive from the same fallacy, namely, that there must be *something* referred to by such expressions as "the meaning of the word (phrase or sentence) 'x'," on all fours with the policeman who really is referred to by the descriptive phrase in "our village policeman is fond of football." And the way out of the confusion is to see that some "the"-phrases are only similar in grammar and not similar in function to referentially-used descriptive phrases, *e.g.*, in the case in point, "the meaning of 'x' " is like "the King of France" in "Poincaré is not the King of France," a predicative expression used non-referentially.

And, of course, the ordinary man does not pretend to himself or anyone else that when he makes statements containing such expressions as "the meaning of 'x'," he is referring to a queer new object: it does not cross his mind that his phrase might be misconstrued as a referentially used descriptive phrase. So he is not guilty of philosophical error or clumsiness. None the less his form of words is systematically misleading. For an important difference of logical form is disguised by the complete similarity of grammatical form between "the village policeman is reliable" and "the meaning of 'x' is doubtful" or again between "I have just met the village policeman" and "I have just grasped the meaning of 'x'."

(Consequently, as there is no object describable as that which is referred to by the expression "the meaning of 'x'," questions about the status of such objects are meaningless. It is as pointless to discuss whether word-meanings (*i.e.*, "concepts" or "universals") are subjective or objective, or whether sentence-meanings (*i.e.*, "judgments" or "objectives") are subjective or objective, as it would be to discuss whether the Equator or the sky is subjective or objective. For the questions themselves are not about anything.)

All this does not of course in the least prevent us from using intelligently and intelligibly sentences containing the expression "the meaning of 'x' " where this can be re-drafted as "what 'x' means." For here the "the"-phrase is being predicatively used and not as an unique description. "The meaning of 'x' is the same as the meaning of 'y' " is equivalent to " 'x' means what 'y' means," and that can be understood without any temptation to multiply entities.

                                    .   .   .

I have chosen these three main types of systematically misleading expressions because all alike are misleading in a certain direction. They all suggest the existence of new sorts of objects or, to put it in another way, they are all temptations to us to "multiply entities." In each of them, the quasi-ontological, the quasi-Platonic and the quasi-descriptive expressions, an expression is misconstrued as a denoting expression which in fact does not denote, but only looks grammatically like expressions which are used to denote. Occam's prescription was, therefore, in my view, "do not treat all expressions which are grammatically like proper names or referentially used "the"-phrases, as if they were therefore proper names or referentially used "the"-phrases."

                                    .   .   .

I wish now to raise, but not to solve, some consequential problems which arise.

1. Given that an expression of a certain grammatical form is proper (or anyhow approximates to being proper) to facts of a certain logical form and to those facts only, is this relation of propriety of grammatical to logical form *natural* or *conventional?*

I cannot myself credit what seems to be the doctrine of Wittgenstein and the school of logical grammarians who owe allegiance to him, that what makes an expression formally proper to a fact is some real and non-conventional one-one picturing relation between the composition of the expression and that of the fact. For I do not see how, save in a small class of specially-chosen cases, a fact or state of affairs can be deemed like or even unlike in structure a sentence, gesture or diagram. For a fact is not a collection—even an arranged collection—of bits in the way in which a sentence is an arranged collection of noises or a map an arranged collection of scratches. A fact is not a thing and so is not even an arranged thing. Certainly a map may be like a country or a railway system, and in a more general, or looser, sense a sentence, as an ordered series of noises might be a similar sort of series to a series of vehicles in a stream of traffic or the series of days in the week.

But in Socrates being angry or in the fact that either Socrates was wise or Plato was dishonest I can see no concatenation of bits such that a concatenation of parts of speech could be held to be of the same general architectural plan as it. But this difficulty may be just denseness on my part.

On the other hand, it is not easy to accept what seems to be the alternative that it is just by convention that a given grammatical form is specially dedicated to facts of a given logical form. For, in fact, customary usage is perfectly tolerant of systematically misleading expressions. And, moreover, it is hard to explain how in the genesis of languages our presumably non-philosophical forbears could have decided on or happened on the dedication of a given grammatical form to facts of a given logical form. For presumably the study of abstract logical form is later than the entry into common use of syntactical idioms.

It is, however, my present view that the propriety of grammatical to logical forms is more nearly conventional than natural: though I do not suppose it to be the effect of whim or of deliberate plan.

2. The next question is: How are we to discover in particular cases whether an expression is systematically misleading or not? I suspect that the answer to this will be of this sort. We meet with and understand and even believe a certain expression such as "Mr. Pickwick is a fictitious person" and "the Equator encircles the globe." And we know that if these expressions are saying what they seem to be saying, certain other propositions will follow. But it turns out that the naturally consequential propositions "Mr. Pickwick was born in such and such a year" and "the Equator is of such and such a thickness" are not merely false but, on analysis, in contradiction with something in that from which they seemed to be logical consequences. The only solution is to see that being a fictitious person is not to be a person of a certain sort, and that the sense in which the Equator girdles the earth is not that of being any sort of a ring or ribbon enveloping the earth. And this is to see that the original propositions were not saying what they seemed on first analysis to be saying. Paralogisms and antinomies are the evidence that an expression is systematically misleading.

None the less, the systematically misleading expressions as intended and as understood contain no contradictions. People do not really talk philosophical nonsense—unless they are philosophizing or, what is quite a different thing, unless they are being sententious. What they do is to use expressions which, from whatever cause—generally the desire for brevity and simplicity of discourse—disguise instead of exhibiting the forms of the facts recorded. And it is to reveal these forms that we abstract and generalize. These processes of abstraction and generalization occur before philosophical analysis begins. It seems indeed that their results are the subject matter of philosophy. Pre-philosophical abstract thinking is always misled by systematically misleading expressions, and even philosophical abstract thinking, the proper function of which is to cure this disease, is actually one of its worst victims.

3. I do not know any way of classifying or giving an exhaustive list of the possible types of systematically misleading expressions. I fancy that the number is in principle unlimited, but that the number of prevalent and obsessing types is fairly small.

4. I do not know any way of proving that an expression contains no systematic misleadingness at all. The fact that antinomies have not yet been shown to arise is no proof that they never will arise. We can know that of two expressions "x" and "y" which record the same fact, "x" is less misleading than "y"; but not that "x" cannot itself be improved upon.

5. Philosophy must then involve the exercise of systematic restatement. But this does not mean that it is a department of philology or literary criticism.

Its restatement is not the substitution of one noun for another or one verb for another. That is what lexicographers and translators excel in. Its restatements are transmutations of syntax, and transmutations of syntax controlled not by desire for elegance or stylistic correctness but by desire to exhibit the forms of the facts into which philosophy is the enquiry.

9

ON WHAT THERE IS

W. V. Quine

A curious thing about the ontological problem is its simplicity. It can be put in three Anglo-Saxon monosyllables: 'What is there?' It can be answered, moreover, in a word—'Everything'—and everyone will accept this answer as true. However, this is merely to say that there is what there is. There remains room for disagreement over cases; and so the issue has stayed alive down the centuries.

Suppose now that two philosophers, McX and I, differ over ontology. Suppose McX maintains there is something which I maintain there is not. McX can, quite consistently with his own point of view, describe our difference of opinion by saying that I refuse to recognize certain entities. I should protest, of course, that he is wrong in his formulation of our disagreement, for I maintain that there are no entities, of the kind which he alleges, for me to recognize; but my finding him wrong in his formulation of our disagreement is unimportant, for I am committed to considering him wrong in his ontology anyway.

When *I* try to formulate our difference of opinion, on the other hand, I seem to be in a predicament. I cannot admit that there are some things which McX countenances and I do not, for in admitting that there are such things I should be contradicting my own rejection of them.

It would appear, if this reasoning were sound, that in any ontological dispute the proponent of the negative side suffers the disadvantage of not being able to admit that his opponent disagrees with him.

This is the old Platonic riddle of nonbeing. Nonbeing must in some sense be, otherwise what is it that there is not? This tangled doctrine might be nicknamed *Plato's beard;* historically it has proved tough, frequently dulling the edge of Occam's razor.

It is some such line of thought that leads philosophers like McX to impute being where they might otherwise be quite content to recognize that there is nothing. Thus, take Pegasus. If Pegasus *were* not, McX argues, we should

---

not be talking about anything when we use the word; therefore it would be nonsense to say even that Pegasus is not. Thinking to show thus that the denial of Pegasus cannot be coherently maintained, he concludes that Pegasus is.

McX cannot, indeed, quite persuade himself that any region of space-time, near or remote, contains a flying horse of flesh and blood. Pressed for further details on Pegasus, then, he says that Pegasus is an idea in men's minds. Here, however, a confusion begins to be apparent. We may for the sake of argument concede that there is an entity, and even a unique entity (though this is rather implausible), which is the mental Pegasus-idea; but this mental entity is not what people are talking about when they deny Pegasus.

McX never confuses the Parthenon with the Parthenon-idea. The Parthenon is physical; the Parthenon-idea is mental (according anyway to McX's version of ideas, and I have no better to offer). The Parthenon is visible; the Parthenon-idea is invisible. We cannot easily imagine two things more unlike, and less liable to confusion, than the Parthenon and the Parthenon-idea. But when we shift from the Parthenon to Pegasus, the confusion sets in—for no other reason than that McX would sooner be deceived by the crudest and most flagrant counterfeit than grant the nonbeing of Pegasus.

The notion that Pegasus must be, because it would otherwise be nonsense to say even that Pegasus is not, has been seen to lead McX into an elementary confusion. Subtler minds, taking the same precept as their starting point, come out with theories of Pegasus which are less patently misguided than McX's, and correspondingly more difficult to eradicate. One of these subtler minds is named, let us say, Wyman. Pegasus, Wyman maintains, has his being as an unactualized possible. When we say of Pegasus that there is no such thing, we are saying, more precisely, that Pegasus does not have the special attribute of actuality. Saying that Pegasus is not actual is on a par, logically, with saying that the Parthenon is not red; in either case we are saying something about an entity whose being is unquestioned.

Wyman, by the way, is one of those philosophers who have united in ruining the good old word 'exist'. Despite his espousal of unactualized possibles, he limits the word 'existence' to actuality—thus preserving an illusion of ontological agreement between himself and us who repudiate the rest of his bloated universe. We have all been prone to say, in our common-sense usage of 'exist', that Pegasus does not exist, meaning simply that there is no such entity at all. If Pegasus existed he would indeed be in space and time, but only because the word 'Pegasus' has spatio-temporal connotations, and not because 'exists' has spatio-temporal connotations. If spatio-temporal reference is lacking when we affirm the existence of the cube root of 27, this is simply because a cube root is not a spatio-temporal kind of thing, and not because we are being ambiguous in our use of 'exist'.[1] However, Wyman, in

---

[1] The impulse to distinguish terminologically between existence as applied to objects actualized somewhere in space-time and existence (or subsistence or being) as applied to other entities arises in part, perhaps, from an idea that the observation of nature is relevant only to questions of existence of the first kind. But this idea is readily refuted by counter-instances such as 'the ratio of the number of centaurs to the number of unicorns'. If there were such a ratio, it would be an abstract entity, viz. a number. Yet it is only by studying nature that we conclude that the number of centaurs and the number of unicorns are both 0 and hence that there is no such ratio.

an ill-conceived effort to appear agreeable, genially grants us the non-existence of Pegasus and then, contrary to what *we* meant by nonexistence of Pegasus, insists that Pegasus *is*. Existence is one thing, he says, and subsistence is another. The only way I know of coping with this obfuscation of issues is to *give* Wyman the word 'exist'. I'll try not to use it again; I still have 'is'. So much for lexicography; let's get back to Wyman's ontology.

Wyman's overpopulated universe is in many ways unlovely. It offends the aesthetic sense of us who have a taste for desert landscapes, but this is not the worst of it. Wyman's slum of possibles is a breeding ground for disorderly elements. Take, for instance, the possible fat man in that doorway; and, again, the possible bald man in that doorway. Are they the same possible man, or two possible men? How do we decide? How many possible men are there in that doorway? Are there more possible thin ones than fat ones? How many of them are alike? Or would their being alike make them one? Are no *two* possible things alike? Is this the same as saying that it is impossible for two things to be alike? Or, finally, is the concept of identity simply inapplicable to unactualized possibles? But what sense can be found in talking of entities which cannot meaningfully be said to be identical with themselves and distinct from one another? These elements are well-nigh incorrigible. By a Fregean therapy of individual concepts, some effort might be made at rehabilitation; but I feel we'd do better simply to clear Wyman's slum and be done with it.

Possibility, along with the other modalities of necessity and impossibility and contingency, raises problems upon which I do not mean to imply that we should turn our backs. But we can at least limit modalities to whole statements. We may impose the adverb 'possibly' upon a statement as a whole, and we may well worry about the semantical analysis of such usage; but little real advance in such analysis is to be hoped for in expanding our universe to include so-called *possible entities*. I suspect that the main motive for this expansion is simply the old notion that Pegasus, for example, must be because otherwise it would be nonsense to say even that he is not.

Still, all the rank luxuriance of Wyman's universe of possibles would seem to come to naught when we make a slight change in the example and speak not of Pegasus but of the round square cupola on Berkeley College. If, unless Pegasus were, it would be nonsense to say that he is not, then by the same token, unless the round square cupola on Berkeley College were, it would be nonsense to say that it is not. But, unlike Pegasus, the round square cupola on Berkeley College cannot be admitted even as an unactualized *possible*. Can we drive Wyman now to admitting also a realm of unactualizable impossibles? If so, a good many embarrassing questions could be asked about them. We might hope even to trap Wyman in contradictions, by getting him to admit that certain of these entities are at once round and square. But the wily Wyman chooses the other horn of the dilemma and concedes that it is nonsense to say that the round square cupola on Berkeley College is not. He says that the phrase 'round square cupola' is meaningless.

Wyman was not the first to embrace this alternative. The doctrine of the meaninglessness of contradictions runs away back. The tradition survives, moreover, in writers who seem to share none of Wyman's motivations. Still, I wonder whether the first temptation to such a doctrine may not have been substantially the motivation which we have observed in Wyman. Certainly the doctrine has no intrinsic appeal; and it has led its devotees to such quixotic extremes as that of challenging the method of proof by *reductio ad absurdum* [the technique of deriving absurd consequences]—a challenge in which I sense a *reductio ad absurdum* of the doctrine itself.

Moreover, the doctrine of meaninglessness of contradictions has the severe methodological drawback that it makes it impossible, in principle, ever to devise an effective test of what is meaningful and what is not. It would be forever impossible for us to devise systematic ways of deciding whether a string of signs made sense—even to us individually, let alone other people— or not. For it follows from a discovery in mathematical logic, due to Church, that there can be no generally applicable test of contradictoriness.

I have spoken disparagingly of Plato's beard, and hinted that it is tangled. I have dwelt at length on the inconveniences of putting up with it. It is time to think about taking steps.

Russell, in his theory of so-called singular descriptions, showed clearly how we might meaningfully use seeming names without supposing that there be the entities allegedly named. The names to which Russell's theory directly applies are complex descriptive names such as 'the author of *Waverley*', 'the present King of France', 'the round square cupola on Berkeley College'. Russell analyzes such phrases systematically as fragments of the whole sentences in which they occur. The sentence 'The author of *Waverley* was a poet', for example, is explained as a whole as meaning 'Someone (better: something) wrote *Waverley* and was a poet, and nothing else wrote *Waverley*'. (The point of this added clause is to affirm the uniqueness which is implicit in the word 'the', in '*the* author of *Waverley*'.) The sentence 'The round square cupola on Berkeley College is pink' is explained as 'Something is round and square and is a cupola on Berkeley College and is pink, and nothing else is round and square and a cupola on Berkeley College'.

The virtue of this analysis is that the seeming name, a descriptive phrase, is paraphrased *in context* as a so-called incomplete symbol. No unified expression is offered as an analysis of the descriptive phase, but the statement as a whole which was the context of that phrase still gets its full quota of meaning—whether true or false.

The unanalyzed statement 'The author of *Waverley* was a poet' contains a part, 'the author of *Waverley*', which is wrongly supposed by McX and Wyman to demand objective reference in order to be meaningful at all. But in Russell's translation, 'Something wrote *Waverley* and was a poet and nothing else wrote *Waverley*', the burden of objective reference which had been put upon the descriptive phrase is now taken over by words of the kind that logicians call bound variables, variables of quantification, namely, words like 'something', 'nothing', 'everything'. These words, far from purporting to be names specifically of the author of *Waverley*, do not purport to be names at all; they refer to entities generally, with a kind of studied ambiguity peculiar to themselves. These quantificational words or bound variables are, of course a basic part of language, and their meaning-fulness, at least in context, is not to be challenged. But their meaningfulness in no way presupposes there being either the author of *Waverley* or the round square cupola on Berkeley College or any other specifically pre-assigned objects.

Where descriptions are concerned, there is no longer any difficulty in affirming or denying being. 'There *is* the author of *Waverley*' is explained by Russell as meaning 'Someone (or, more strictly, something) wrote *Waverley* and nothing else wrote *Waverley*'. 'The author of *Waverley* is not' is explained, correspondingly, as the alternation 'Either each thing failed to write *Waverley* or two or more things wrote *Waverley*'. This alternation is false, but meaningful; and it contains no expression purporting to name the author of *Waverley*. The statement 'The round square cupola on Berkeley College is not' is analyzed in similar fashion. So the old notion that statements of nonbeing defeat themselves goes by the board. When a statement of being or nonbeing is analyzed by Russell's theory of descriptions, it ceases to contain any expression which even purports to name the alleged entity whose being is in question, so that the meaningfulness of the statement no longer can be thought to presuppose that there be such an entity.

Now what of 'Pegasus'? This being a word rather than a descriptive phrase, Russell's argument does not immediately apply to it. However, it can easily be made to apply. We have only to rephrase 'Pegasus' as a description, in any way that seems adequately to single out our idea; say, 'the winged horse that was captured by Bellerophon'. Substituting such a phrase for 'Pegasus', we can then proceed to analyze the statement 'Pegasus is', or 'Pegasus is not', precisely on the analogy of Russell's analysis of 'The author of *Waverley* is' and 'The author of *Waverley* is not'.

In order thus to subsume a one-word name or alleged name such as 'Pegasus' under Russell's theory of description, we must, of course, be able first to translate the word into a description. But this is no real restriction. If the notion of Pegasus had been so obscure or so basic a one that no pat translation into a descriptive phrase had offered itself along familiar lines, we could still have availed ourselves of the following artificial and trivial-seeming device: we could have appealed to the *ex hypothesi* unanalyzable, irreducible attribute of *being Pegasus*, adopting, for its expression, the verb 'is-Pegasus', or 'pegasizes'. The noun 'Pegasus' itself could then be treated as derivative, and identified after all with a description: 'the thing that is-Pegasus', 'the thing that pegasizes'.

If the importing of such a predicate as 'pegasizes' seems to commit us to recognizing that there is a corresponding attribute, pegasizing, in Plato's heaven or in the minds of men, well and good. Neither we nor Wyman nor McX have been contending, thus far, about the being or nonbeing of universals, but rather about that of Pegasus. If in terms of pegasizing we can interpret the noun 'Pegasus' as a description subject to Russell's theory of descriptions, then we have disposed of the old notion that Pegasus cannot be said not to be without presupposing that in some sense Pegasus is.

Our argument is now quite general. McX and Wyman supposed that we could not meaningfully affirm a statement of the form 'So-and-so is not', with a simple or descriptive singular noun in place of 'so-and-so', unless so-and-so is. This supposition is now seen to be quite generally groundless, since the singular noun in question can always be expanded into a singular description, trivially or otherwise, and then analyzed out *à la* Russell.

We commit ourselves to an ontology containing numbers when we say there are prime numbers larger than a million; we commit ourselves to an ontology containing centaurs when we say there are centaurs; and we commit ourselves to an ontology containing Pegasus when we say Pegasus is. But we do not commit ourselves to an ontology containing Pegasus or the author of *Waverley* or the round square cupola on Berkeley College when we say that Pegasus or the author of *Waverley* or the cupola in question is *not*. We need no longer labor under the delusion that the meaningfulness of a statement containing a singular term presupposes an entity named by the term. A singular term need not name to be significant.

An inkling of this might have dawned on Wyman and McX even without benefit of Russell if they had only noticed—as so few of us do—that there is a gulf between *meaning* and *naming* even in the case of a singular term which is genuinely a name of an object. The following example from Frege will serve. The phrase 'Evening Star' names a certain large physical object of spherical form, which is hurtling through space some scores of millions of miles from here. The phrase 'Morning Star' names the same thing, as was probably first established by some observant Babylonian. But the two phrases cannot be regarded as having the same meaning; otherwise that Babylonian could have dispensed with his observations and contented himself with reflecting on the meanings of his words. The meanings, then, being different from one another, must be other than the named object, which is one and the same in both cases.

Confusion of meaning with naming not only made McX think he could not meaningfully repudiate Pegasus; a continuing confusion of meaning with naming no doubt helped engender his absurd notion that Pegasus is an idea, a mental entity. The structure of his confusion is as follows. He confused the alleged *named object* Pegasus with the *meaning* of the word 'Pegasus', therefore concluding that Pegasus must be in order that the word have meaning. But what sorts of things are meanings? This is a moot point; however, one might quite plausibly explain meanings as ideas in the mind, supposing we can make clear sense in turn of the idea of ideas in the mind. Therefore Pegasus, initially confused with a meaning, ends up as an idea in the mind. It is the more remarkable that Wyman, subject to the same initial motivation as McX, should have avoided this particular blunder and wound up with unactualized possibles instead.

Now let us turn to the ontological problem of universals: the question whether there are such entities as attributes, relations, classes, numbers, functions. McX, characteristically enough, thinks there are. Speaking of attributes, he says: "There are red houses, red roses, red sunsets; this much is prephilosophical common sense in which we must all agree. These houses, roses, and sunsets, then, have something in common; and this which they have in common is all I mean by the attribute of redness." For McX, thus, there being attributes is even more obvious and trivial than the obvious and trivial fact of there being red houses, roses, and sunsets. This, I think, is characteristic of metaphysics, or at least of that part of metaphysics called ontology: one who regards a statement on this subject as true at all must regard it as trivially true. One's ontology is basic to the conceptual scheme by which he interprets all experiences, even the most commonplace ones. Judged within some particular conceptual scheme—and how else is judgment possible?—an ontological statement goes without saying, standing in need of no separate justification at all. Ontological statements follow immediately from all manner of casual statements of commonplace fact, just as—from the point of view, anyway, of McX's conceptual scheme—'There is an attribute' follows from 'There are red houses, red roses, red sunsets'.

Judged in another conceptual scheme, an ontological statement which is axiomatic to McX's mind may, with equal immediacy and triviality, be adjudged false. One may admit that there are red houses, roses, and sunsets, but deny, except as a popular and misleading manner of speaking, that they have anything in common. The words 'houses', 'roses', and 'sunsets' are true of sundry individual entities which are houses and roses and sunsets, and the word 'red' or 'red object' is true of each of sundry individual entities which are red houses, red roses, red sunsets; but there is not, in addition, any entity whatever, individual or otherwise, which is named by the word 'redness', nor, for that matter, by the word 'househood', 'rosehood', 'sunsethood'. That the houses and roses and sunsets are all of them red may be taken as ultimate and irreducible, and it may be held that McX is no better off, in point of real explanatory power, for all the occult entities which he posits under such names as 'redness.'

One means by which McX might naturally have tried to impose his ontology of universals on us was already removed before we turned to the problem of universals. McX cannot argue that predicates such as 'red' or 'is-red', which we all concur in using, must be regarded as names each of a single universal entity in order that they be meaningful at all. For we have seen that being a name of something is a much more special feature than being meaningful. He cannot even charge us—at least not by *that* argument —with having posited an attribute of pegasizing by our adoption of the predicate 'pegasizes'.

However, McX hits upon a different stratagem. "Let us grant," he says, "this distinction between meaning and naming of which you make so much. Let us even grant that 'is red', 'pegasizes', etc., are not names of attributes. Still, you admit they have meanings. But these *meanings*, whether they are *named* or not, are still universals, and I venture to say that some of them might even be the very things that I call attributes, or something to much the same purpose in the end."

For McX, this is an unusually penetrating speech; and the only way I know to counter it is by refusing to admit meanings. However, I feel no reluctance toward refusing to admit meanings, for I do not thereby deny that words and statements are meaningful. McX and I may agree to the letter in our classification of linguistic forms into the meaningful and the meaningless, even though McX construes meaningfulness as the *having* (in some sense of 'having') of some abstract entity which he calls a meaning, whereas I do not. I remain free to maintain that the fact that a given linguistic utterance is meaningful (or *significant*, as I prefer to say so as not to invite hypostasis of meanings as entities) is an ultimate and irreducible matter of fact; or, I may undertake to analyze it in terms directly of what people do in the presence of the linguistic utterance in question and other utterances similar to it.

The useful ways in which people ordinarily talk or seem to talk about meanings boil down to two: the *having* of meanings, which is significance, and *sameness* of meaning, or synonymy. What is called *giving* the meaning of an utterance is simply the uttering of a synonym, couched, ordinarily, in clearer language than the original. If we are allergic to meanings as such, we can speak directly of utterances as significant or insignificant, and as synonymous or heteronymous one with another. The problem of explaining these adjectives 'significant' and 'synonymous' with some degree of clarity and rigor—preferably, as I see it, in terms of behavior—is as difficult as it is important. But the explanatory value of special and irreducible intermediary entities called meanings is surely illusory.

Up to now I have argued that we can use singular terms significantly in sentences without presupposing that there are the entities which those terms purport to name. I have argued further that we can use general terms, for example, predicates, without conceding them to be names of abstract entities. I have argued further that we can view utterances as significant, and as synonymous or heteronymous with one another, without countenancing a realm of entities called meanings. At this point McX begins to wonder whether there is any limit at all to our ontological immunity. Does *nothing* we may say commit us to the assumption of universals or other entities which we may find unwelcome?

I have already suggested a negative answer to this question, in speaking of bound variables, or variables of quantification, in connection with Russell's theory of descriptions. We can very easily involve ourselves in ontological commitments by saying, for example, that *there is something* (bound variable) which red houses and sunsets have in common; or that *there is something* which is a prime number larger than a million. But this is, essentially, the *only* way we can involve ourselves in ontological commitments: by our use of bound variables. The use of alleged names is no criterion, for we can repudiate their namehood at the drop of a hat unless the assumption of a corresponding entity can be spotted in the things we affirm in terms of bound variables. Names are, in fact, altogether immaterial to the ontological issue, for I have shown, in connection with 'Pegasus' and 'pegasize', that names can be converted to descriptions, and Russell has shown that descriptions can be eliminated. Whatever we say with the help of names can be said in a language which shuns names altogether. To be assumed as an entity is, purely and simply, to be reckoned as the value of a variable. In terms of the categories of traditional grammar, this amounts roughly to saying that to be is to be in the range of reference of a pronoun. Pronouns are the basic media of reference; nouns might better have been named propronouns. The variables of quantification, 'something', 'nothing', 'everything', range over our whole ontology, whatever it may be; and we are convicted of a particular ontological presupposition if, and only if, the alleged presuppositum has to be reckoned among the entities over which our variables range in order to render one of our affirmations true.

We may say, for example, that some dogs are white and not thereby commit ourselves to recognizing either doghood or whiteness as entities. 'Some dogs are white' says that some things that are dogs are white; and, in order that this statement be true, the things over which the bound variable 'something' ranges must include some white dogs, but need not include doghood or whiteness. On the other hand, when we say that some zoölogical species are cross-fertile we are committing ourselves to recognizing as entities the several species themselves, abstract though they are. We remain so committed at least until we devise some way of so paraphrasing the statement as to show that the seeming reference to species on the part of our bound variable was an avoidable manner of speaking.

Classical mathematics, as the example of primes larger than a million clearly illustrates, is up to its neck in commitments to an ontology of abstract entities. Thus it is that the great mediaeval controversy over universals has flared up anew in the modern philosophy of mathematics. The issue is clearer now than of old, because we now have a more explicit standard whereby to decide what ontology a given theory or form of discourse is committed to: a theory is committed to those and only those entities to which the bound variables of the theory must be capable of referring in order that the affirmations made in the theory be true.

Because this standard of ontological presupposition did not emerge clearly in the philosophical tradition, the modern philosophical mathematicians have not on the whole recognized that they were debating the same old problem of universals in a newly clarified form. But the fundamental cleavages among modern points of view on foundations of mathematics do come down pretty explicitly to disagreements as to the range of entities to which the bound variables should be permitted to refer.

The three main mediaeval points of view regarding universals are designated by historians as *realism, conceptualism,* and *nominalism.* Essentially these same three doctrines reappear in twentieth-century surveys of the philosophy of mathematics under the new names *logicism, intuitionism,* and *formalism.*

Realism, as the word is used in connection with the mediaeval controversy over universals, is the Platonic doctrine that universals or abstract entities have being independently of the mind; the mind may discover them but cannot create them. *Logicism,* represented by Frege, Russell, Whitehead, Church, and Carnap, condones the use of bound variables to refer to abstract entities known and unknown, specifiable and unspecifiable, indiscriminately.

Conceptualism holds that there are universals but they are mind-made. *Intuitionism,* espoused in modern times in one form or another by Poincaré, Brouwer, Weyl, and others, countenances the use of bound variables to refer to abstract entities only when those entities are capable of being cooked up individually from ingredients specified in advance. As Fraenkel has put it, logicism holds that classes are discovered while intuitionism holds that they are invented—a fair statement indeed of the old opposition between realism and conceptualism. This opposition is no mere quibble; it makes an essential difference in the amount of classical mathematics to which one is willing to subscribe. Logicists, or realists, are able on their assumptions to get Cantor's ascending orders of infinity; intuitionists are compelled to stop with the lowest order of infinity, and, as an indirect consequence, to abandon even some of the classical laws of real numbers. The modern controversy between logicism and intuitionism arose, in fact, from disagreements over infinity.

Formalism, associated with the name of Hilbert, echoes intuitionism in deploring the logicist's unbridled recourse to universals. But formalism also finds intuitionism unsatisfactory. This could happen for either of two opposite reasons. The formalist might, like the logicist, object to the crippling of classical mathematics; or he might, like the *nominalists* of old, object to admitting abstract entities at all, even in the restrained sense of mind-made entities. The upshot is the same: the formalist keeps classical mathematics as a play of insignificant notations. This play of notations can still be of utility—whatever utility it has already shown itself to have as a crutch for physicists and technologists. But utility need not imply significance, in any literal linguistic sense. Nor need the marked success of mathematicians in spinning out theorems, and in finding objective bases for agreement with one another's results, imply significance. For an adequate basis for agreement among mathematicians can be found simply in the rules which govern the manipulation of the notations—these syntactical rules being, unlike the notations themselves, quite significant and intelligible.

I have argued that the sort of ontology we adopt can be consequential—notably in connection with mathematics, although this is only an example. Now how are we to adjudicate among rival ontologies? Certainly the answer is not provided by the semantical formula "To be is to be the value of a variable"; this formula serves rather, conversely, in testing the conformity of a given remark or doctrine to a prior ontological standard. We look to bound variables in connection with ontology not in order to know what there is, but in order to know what a given remark or doctrine, ours or someone else's, *says* there is; and this much is quite properly a problem involving language. But what there is is another question.

In debating over what there is, there are still reasons for operating on a semantical plane. One reason is to escape from the predicament noted at the beginning of this essay: the predicament of my not being able to admit that there are things which McX countenances and I do not. So long as I adhere to my ontology, as opposed to McX's, I cannot allow my bound variables to refer to entities which belong to McX's ontology and not to mine. I can, however, consistently describe our disagreement by characterizing the statements which McX affirms. Provided merely that my ontology countenances linguistic forms, or at least concrete inscriptions and utterances, I can talk about McX's sentences.

Another reason for withdrawing to a semantical plane is to find common ground on which to argue. Disagreement in ontology involves basic disagreement in conceptual schemes; yet McX and I, despite these basic disagreements, find that our conceptual schemes converge sufficiently in their intermediate and upper ramifications to enable us to communicate successfully on such topics as politics, weather, and, in particular, language. In so far as our basic controversy over ontology can be translated upward into a semantical controversy about words and what to do with them, the collapse of the controversy into question-begging may be delayed.

It is no wonder, then, that ontological controversy should tend into controversy over language. But we must not jump to the conclusion that what there is depends on words. Translatability of a question into semantical terms is no indication that the question is linguistic. To see Naples is to bear a name which, when prefixed to the words 'sees Naples', yields a true sentence; still there is nothing linguistic about seeing Naples.

Our acceptance of an ontology is, I think, similar in principle to our acceptance of a scientific theory, say a system of physics: we adopt, at least in so far as we are reasonable, the simplest conceptual scheme into which the disordered fragments of raw experience can be fitted and arranged. Our ontology is determined once we have fixed upon the over-all conceptual scheme which is to accommodate science in the broadest sense; and the considerations which determine a reasonable construction of any part of that conceptual scheme, for example, the biological or the physical part, are not different in kind from the considerations which determine a reasonable construction of the whole. To whatever extent the adoption of any system of scientific theory may be said to be a matter of language, the same—but no more—may be said of the adoption of an ontology.

But simplicity, as a guiding principle in constructing conceptual schemes, is not a clear and unambiguous idea; and it is quite capable of presenting a double or multiple standard. Imagine, for example, that we have devised the most economical set of concepts adequate to the play-by-play reporting of immediate experience. The entities under this scheme—the values of bound variables—are, let us suppose, individual subjective events of sensation or reflection. We should still find, no doubt, that a physicalistic conceptual scheme, purporting to talk about external objects, offers great advantages in simplifying our over-all reports. By bringing together scattered sense events and treating them as perceptions of one object, we reduce the complexity of our stream of experience to a manageable conceptual simplicity. The rule of simplicity is indeed our guiding maxim in assigning sense data to objects: we associate an earlier and a later round sensum with the same so-called penny, or with two different so-called pennies, in obedience to the demands of maximum simplicity in our total world-picture.

Here we have two competing conceptual schemes, a phenomenalistic one and a physicalistic one. Which should prevail? Each has its advantages; each has its special simplicity in its own way. Each, I suggest, deserves to be developed. Each may be said, indeed, to be the more fundamental, though in different senses: the one is epistemologically, the other physically, fundamental.

The physical conceptual scheme simplifies our account of experience because of the way myriad scattered sense events come to be associated with single so-called objects; still there is no likelihood that each sentence about physical objects can actually be translated, however deviously and complexly, into the phenomenalistic language. Physical objects are postulated entities which round out and simplify our account of the flux of experience, just as the introduction of irrational numbers simplifies laws of arithmetic. From the point of view of the conceptual scheme of the elementary arithmetic of rational numbers alone, the broader arithmetic of rational and irrational numbers would have the status of a convenient myth, simpler than the literal truth (namely, the arithmetic of rationals) and yet containing that literal truth as a scattered part. Similarly, from a phenomenalistic point of view, the conceptual scheme of physical objects is a convenient myth, simpler than the literal truth and yet containing that literal truth as a scattered part.

Now what of classes or attributes of physical objects, in turn? A platonistic ontology of this sort is, from the point of view of a strictly physicalistic conceptual scheme, as much a myth as that physicalistic conceptual scheme itself is for phenomenalism. This higher myth is a good and useful one, in turn, in so far as it simplifies our account of physics. Since mathematics is an integral part of this higher myth, the utility of this myth for physical science is evident enough. In speaking of it nevertheless as a myth, I echo that philosophy of mathematics to which I alluded earlier under the name of formalism. But an attitude of formalism may with equal justice be adopted toward the physical conceptual scheme, in turn, by the pure aesthete or phenomenalist.

The analogy between the myth of mathematics and the myth of physics is, in some additional and perhaps fortuitous ways, strikingly close. Consider, for example, the crisis which was precipitated in the foundations of mathematics, at the turn of the century, by the discovery of Russell's paradox and other antinomies of set theory. These contradictions had to be obviated by unintuitive, *ad hoc* devices; our mathematical myth-making became deliberate and evident to all. But what of physics? An antinomy arose between the undular and the corpuscular accounts of light; and if this was not as out-and-out a contradiction as Russell's paradox, I suspect that the reason is that physics is not as out-and-out as mathematics. Again, the second great modern crisis in the foundations of mathematics—precipitated in 1931 by Gödel's proof that there are bound to be undecidable statements in arithmetic—has its companion piece in physics in Heisenberg's indeterminacy principle.

In earlier pages I undertook to show that some common arguments in favor of certain ontologies are fallacious. Further, I advanced an explicit standard whereby to decide what the ontological commitments of a theory are. But the question what ontology actually to adopt still stands open, and the obvious counsel is tolerance and an experimental spirit. Let us by all means see how much of the physicalistic conceptual scheme can be reduced to a phenomenalistic one; still, physics also naturally demands pursuing, irreducible *in toto* though it be. Let us see how, or to what degree, natural science may be rendered independent of platonistic mathematics; but let us also pursue mathematics and delve into its platonistic foundations.

From among the various conceptual schemes best suited to these various pursuits, one—the phenomenalistic—claims epistemological priority. Viewed from within the phenomenalistic conceptual scheme, the ontologies of physical objects and mathematical objects are myths. The quality of myth, however, is relative; relative, in this case, to the epistemological point of view. This point of view is one among various, corresponding to one among our various interests and purposes.

10

UNIVERSALS

D. F. Pears

'Do universals exist?' This question was debated so long and vehemently because it was mistaken for a factual question about some airy realm of being. But why was this mistake made? One diagnosis is that general words were tacitly assimilated to proper names,[1] and that, when this practice is exposed, it becomes harmless but pointless.[2] But this is a description of what happened rather than an explanation; it gives something more like a symptom than a cause. Could so many philosophers have been so silly in such a simple way? Even moderate scepticism on this point would lead to an attempt to supplement this suggestion. This article is such an attempt.

'Universals exist' has a deceptive logic. Realists offer it as the conclusion of many arguments: but unlike the premisses of these arguments, it cannot be understood as a verifiable statement of fact. On the other hand, if it is taken merely as an esoteric way of stating those premisses over again, the vehemence of the controversy becomes inexplicable. Faced with this difficulty of interpretation, some modern philosophers suggest that it is no good puzzling about its literal meaning, just as it is no good puzzling about the literal meaning of dreams. For traditional philosophy provided a small set of possible conclusions to arguments about the generality of thought and language, and tradition was strong. If a tribe educated its children to dream according to a tradition which restricted their manifest dream contents within narrow limits, it would be difficult to discover their much more varied latent dream contents.[3] Similarly, although realists are argumentative, it is difficult to answer the question why they maintain that universals exist. Any answer must be based on a selection from among the many reasons which they themselves proffer: and a good selection will be diagnostic; it

---

D. F. Pears "Universals," *The Philosophical Quarterly*, I (1950–1951), 218–227. Reprinted by permission of the publisher and the author.

[1] Cf. J. S. Mill, *Examination of Sir William Hamilton's Philosophy* (5th edn., London, 1878) chap. XVII, p. 381, and Berkeley, *Principles of Human Knowledge*, Introduction §18.

[2] Cf. M. Lazerowitz, 'The Existence of Universals' (*Mind*, 1946, pp. 1ff.).

[3] Cf. Freud, *The Interpretation of Dreams*, tr. A. A. Brill (London, 1913), p. 166.

will successfully explain the doctrine. There is no sharp boundary here between descriptions of the premisses of philosophical arguments and diagnoses of their conclusions: because success in explaining, which is the criterion of a diagnosis, is a matter of degree, and because the reasons which philosophers themselves give for their doctrines sometimes completely explain why they held them. Quine's remark, that realists find a universal for every property which can be existentially generalized,[4] is an extremely brief description. The thesis of Berkeley and Mill was more than this: it was a diagnosis, but an inadequate one. I shall try to provide a less inadequate diagnosis.

'Because universals exist' is the answer to at least two general questions: 'Why are things what they are'?[5] and 'Why are we able to name things as we do'? Though Plato and Aristotle sometimes distinguished these two questions, it was characteristic of Greek thought to confuse them. Yet they can be clearly distinguished, the first requiring a dynamic answer from scientists, and the second a static answer from logicians. Now philosophy has often staked premature claims in the territory of science by giving quick comprehensive answers to questions which really required laborious detailed answers. And clearly this is what happened to the first of the two questions. When detailed causal answers were provided to it, the comprehensive answer 'Because universals exist' was no longer acceptable or necessary.[6] But what would detailed answers to the second question be like? Presumably they would be explanations of the meanings of words. But philosophers are easily led to neglect such detailed progressive answers to the second question, and to seek instead a comprehensive and ultimate explanation of naming. For, though comprehensive answers to the first question are clearly futile, there are no obvious penalties attached to answering the second question in a comprehensive way. Yet, I shall argue—and this will be my first thesis—that any comprehensive explanation of naming is necessarily circular: and that philosophers think that, in spite of this disadvantage, such explanations have some point largely because they wrongly assimilate naming to natural processes. Yet surely naming cannot be utterly artificial? My second thesis will be that the desire to understand naming leads to a hunt for a completely satisfactory analogy: but that all other processes either already contain the very feature of naming which was puzzling, or else are too natural or too artificial to be really analogous; and that it was the inevitable oscillation between these three points which prolonged the controversy about universals.

It is unnecessary to produce evidence that philosophers who proposed the existence of universals thought that they were explaining the unity of classes and hence the possibility of naming. What is debatable is whether this was an important motive, and this can be decided only in the sequel. My first thesis, which I must now try to establish, is that realism is necessarily a circular explanation of naming. Now the answer to the question 'Why are

[4] Cf. 'Designation and Existence' in Feigl and Sellars, *Readings in Philosophical Analysis* (New York, 1949), p. 48.

[5] Aristotle criticized Plato's theory largely as an inadequate answer to this question.

[6] Socrates in the *Phaedo* (100d) says that it is the only acceptable answer to the first question. But the advance of science has undermined this thesis more thoroughly than the advance of logic has undermined the thesis that it is an acceptable answer to the second question.

we able to name things as we do?' is 'The reason varies'. For it is always possible with more or less ingenuity, depending on the degree of atomicity of the name, to give a detailed informative reason; and this reason will vary with the name. But ultimately there must be some exit from the maze of words, and wherever this exit is made, it will be impossible to give an informative reason except by pointing. For the only other way of giving an informative reason is to give a new word, and this would prevent the exit from the maze of words from being made at this place.[7] Still at the place where the exit is made it is always possible to give a detailed reason like 'We are able to call things red because they are red', which is too obviously circular even to look informative. Or alternatively it is possible to say 'We are able to call things ϕ because they are ϕ', and this is a general reason which is almost as obviously circular and uninformative. What philosophers who propose the existence of universals do is to propose a general reason which looks informative because it shifts to another level, but unfortunately is not. It merely marks time: but marking time can look very like marching if only the movements of the performers are watched, and not the ground which they profess to be covering. Yet this ground could not be covered. For the reason could not be informative even if it were detailed; since there could be a non-circular answer to the question 'What universal?' only if the exit from the maze of words were made at some different point, which would merely put off the moment of embarrassment from which in the end neither speech nor thought can be saved. Thus realism fails to escape the limitations of all explanations of naming; that they can be informative only if they are not general but detailed, and then only if they are not given at the point where an exit is made from the maze of words.

Uninformative answers have their point. They are silencing. What is wrong with realism is not this, but that it masquerades as an answer which advances knowledge one step further. The analytic machine acquires a momentum which carries it beyond the point where it ought to stop. And there is an inveterate philosophical habit which strengthens the tendency to go beyond this point, or rather to think that one has gone beyond it. 'A thing is called by a certain name because it instantiates a certain universal' is obviously circular when particularized, but it looks imposing when it is left in this general form. And it looks imposing in this general form largely because of the inveterate philosophical habit of treating the shadows cast by words and sentences as if they were separately identifiable. Universals, like facts and propositions, are such shadows; and too often philosophers by appealing to them in general terms have produced in their readers a feeling of satisfaction which ought to have been produced only by specifying them.[8] But universals are specifiable only by reference to words. Similarly

---

[7] Cf. the view sketched by Socrates in the *Theaetetus* 201e–202c, and Antisthenes' view given by Aristotle in *Met.* H, 1043 b 23–32; also L. Wittgenstein, *Tractatus* 5; M. Schlick, *Grundzüge der Naturphilosophie* (Vienna, 1948), p. 21; and A. J. Ayer, *Thinking and Meaning* (London, 1947), p. 28.

[8] The same trick is played by those who say that laws of nature exhibit connections between universals. This gives the impression that we could independently know the eternal framework in which temporal things move and change, rather as we independently know how a piston must move by looking at a cylinder: cf. what Köhler says about Aristotle's astronomy and Descartes' neurology (*Gestalt Psychology*, London, 1930, pp. 82–6).

facts may be brute and propositions may be definite, but what exactly it is about them which is brute or definite can be specified only by reference to the sentences which were the unacknowledged starting-points. In all these cases it is tacit re-duplication which makes philosophers think that they can enjoy the benefits of specifying without actually specifying. Yet the explanation of naming is incomplete until a particular universal is specified, and, when it is specified, the explanation immediately fails through circularity. Naming is hazardous,[9] and any attempt to make it foolproof by basing it on an independent foundation must fail in this way. It is impossible to cross the gap between language and things without really crossing it.[10]

Since the failure of realism to perform this feat is inevitable, its rivals fail too. Nominalism, conceptualism and imagism,[11] in so far as they are rivals of realism, are attempts to provide a unity which will explain naming. Nominalism says that a name is merely connected with a multitude of things, sometimes adding that these things are similar. Conceptualism says that the name is not directly connected with the things but only via a concept, thus changing the nodal point. Imagism says that the nodal point is an image. And realism says that there is really no nodal point, since a name, though it appears to be connected with a multitude of things is all the time connected with only one thing, a universal. This is an over-simplification of what these theories say about the One and the Many; but it is enough for my next purpose, which is to show that these rivals of realism cannot produce a non-circular explanation of naming at those points where an exit is made from the maze of words.

The two psychological theories say that one word can apply to many things only because of the mediation of a concept or of an image. Locke's abstract general idea is 'the workmanship of the understanding, but has its foundation in the similitudes of things'.[12] And Berkeley replaces it by an idea which 'considered in itself is particular but becomes general by being made to represent or stand for all other particular ideas of the same sort'.[13] But what similitudes, and what representation? In the end both Locke's concept and Berkeley's image are completely identifiable only by their use.[14] Of course we can partly identify images by describing their features: and in this way we may even almost completely identify them, since certain images most naturally stand for certain things. And the same could be said of concepts, if they were not merely philosophers' reifications of mental processes. But this will not completely identify either of them, since thought may not follow the most natural course; nor is it always clear which is the most natural course. It is not so much that thinking is speaking as that thinking is like speaking in the only way that matters: it uses one thing as a symbol to stand for many things. And the only tool which could not be used differently is the use. Even something which had its use written on it could

---

[9] Cf. Bradley, *Appearance and Reality*, p. 22 and p. 533; and C. S. Peirce, *Collected Papers* (vol. I, para. 145): 'Direct experience is neither certain nor uncertain, because it affirms nothing—it just is.'

[10] Cf. Stuart Hampshire, 'Scepticism and Meaning' (*Philosophy*, July 1950, p. 245).

[11] Cf. H. H. Price, *Thinking and Representation* (British Academy Lecture, 1946).

[12] Locke, *Essay concerning Human Understanding*, Bk. III, chap. III, § xiii.

[13] Berkeley, *Principles of Human Knowledge*, Introduction, § 12.

[14] This is due to Wittgenstein: cf. e.g. *Tractatus*, 3.326, 'In order to recognize the symbol in the sign we must consider the significant use'.

be used differently.[15] And, if the psychological tool, whether concept or image, can be completely identified only by the things on which it is used, it cannot explain naming without circularity. For, unless we point, the use can be specified only by backward reference to the name. Nor is this circularity surprising. For psychological tools have no advantage over words: they are like them in being symbols, and unlike them only in being shadowy symbols.

The type of nominalism which says that a name is applied to a number of things which are similar immediately falls into the same circularity. For 'similar' is an incomplete predicate, anything being similar to anything in some way, perhaps a negative way.[16] And in the end the kind of similarity which is meant can be specified only by a backward reference to the name. Equally the type of nominalism which merely says that a name is applied to a class of things cannot say which class without a backward reference to the name. Here the circularity is so obvious and there is so little to cushion the shock of the realization that naming is naming that this type of nominalism seems hardly tenable. For, however strongly nominalists react against realism, they can never quite escape its influence: once somebody had said that universals exist it could never be quite the same again. Surely, one wants to protest, there must be some way of giving the class besides reference to the name? Well there is, of course, enumeration. But this answer seems to fail to allow for the possibility of ever using the name correctly in any synthetic sentence. For, if the class is given by enumeration, surely every use of the name must be either incorrect or analytic? Since, if to call a thing 'ϕ' is to include it in the class of things called 'ϕ', then surely either it is incorrect to call it 'ϕ' or else the class cannot be given without reference to it? It is the example of realism which encourages these protests. But it is a bad example. Such neatness is not to be had. For, first of all, these classes cannot be given by enumeration of all their members, since, except for words belonging to dead languages, they are never complete. Nor is it true even that each member must either contribute or not contribute towards giving a class; since a name may be applied to the same thing twice, once analytically and

[15] W. T. Stace in 'Russell's Neutral Monism' in *The Philosophy of Bertrand Russell*, pp. 381–3, complains that neither Berkeley's precise image nor Russell's vague image (in *An Inquiry into Meaning and Truth*) succeeds in explaining the generality of thought. But no description of any item of mental furniture which included only its momentary properties and not its habitual use could possibly explain the generality of thought.

[16] Hence the point of many riddles. Cf. Stuart Hampshire, 'Scepticism and Meaning' (*Philosophy*, July 1950, p. 238). Also Plato, *Protagoras* 331 d. The Platonic theory avoids the 'similarity' difficulty, but not of course the general difficulty of which this is only one form. Speusippus, who abandoned the Platonic theory, seems to have held that, since every species is like every other species in some way, it is impossible to define one species without defining every other species. Cf. Aristotle, *Post. An.* 97 a 6–11. Cf. H. Cherniss, *Aristotle's Criticism of Plato and the Academy* (I. 60), quoted by W. D. Ross in his note on this passage. J. Stenzel, in Pauly-Wissowa Real-Encyclopädie, *s.v.* Speusippus, pp. 1650 and 1655, brings out the affinity between Speusippus' view and Post-Kantian Idealism. Cf. Brand Blanshard on individuals (not species). 'One never gets what is fully particular until one has specified its relations of every kind with everything else in the universe', *The Nature of Thought* (London, 1939), vol. I, p. 639. Curiously enough N. R. Campbell arrives independently at a similar conclusion about species, when he is discussing the definition of such substances as silver, mercury or lead (*Physics. The Elements*, Cambridge, 1920, p. 50). All attempts to explain the unity of a species by similarity—whether by similarity of the individuals to one another, or by similarities and differences between the species and other species—suffer from the same incompleteness.

once synthetically, and even a single use of a name may be synthetic for the speaker and analytic for the hearer. In fact the disjunction 'Analytic or Synthetic' cannot be applied simply to the addition of a member to a class without further caveats. But this in itself is not enough to remove the difficulty; it only makes it reappear in a new form. For if the addition of a member to a class can be synthetic for the speaker and analytic for a subsequent lexicographer, then to what class was the member added? Surely we now have two classes on our hands instead of one? An analogy will help us to deal with this new form of the difficulty. Naming is like electing the sort of member who makes a difference to a club. Strictly we cannot say without qualification to what club he was elected, since it was one club before he was elected and another club after he was elected. The club building might be pointed out, and of course there is no parallel move in the case of naming, although realism pretends that there is. But, even if there were no building or anything else of that kind, the puzzle about the two clubs would not be very perplexing. Similarly, when we reject the simple application of the dichotomy 'Analytic or Synthetic' the resulting puzzle about two classes is not very perplexing. All that is necessary is to point out that a class is incompletely given by a changing quorum. This may be untidy, but why not? There is something radically wrong with a request to be given a class which is not satisfied either with a reference to the name or with progressive enumeration. It is a request to be given something without being given it; as if somewhere, if only philosophers searched long enough, there could be found something which possessed all the advantages of a word and none of its disadvantages, an epistemological vehicle which carried all its destinations.

I now turn to my second thesis, that nothing is sufficiently like naming without being too like naming. Defenders of realism, like defenders of the other theories of naming, might object that the criticism contained in my first thesis is obvious, superficial and directed against a man of straw. For realism does not offer a non-circular detailed explanation of naming—how could it?—but simply gives a general characterization of the sort of unity which makes naming possible. But notice how very like a dream realism is. Taken literally it seems to be of little importance. But, if it is taken as the expression of a doctrine which, if *per impossibile* [assuming the impossible] it were true, would give it great importance, the suggestion is immediately repudiated. Yet it does express such a doctrine, even if its exponents intermittently deny that it does; and it is to the devious expression of this doctrine that it owes most of its attractiveness. Its manifest content is little more than a harmless caprice, but its latent content is a serious error.

But has realism no point when it is taken simply as a general characterization of the sort of unity which makes naming possible? One might answer that it has no point, and that it succeeds in appearing to have some point only by the device of inventing a new comprehensive term: and that this device is considered effective only in philosophy, since outside philosophy it is too obviously like making an impressive gesture in the direction of the interesting object, opening one's mouth and saying absolutely nothing. But such a denial would be tantamount to a denial that any general characterization of the sort of unity which makes naming possible could have a point. And surely such a denial would be wrong, since something can be done towards explaining the general possibility of naming by finding analogous processes? For instance, what makes naming possible is one thing which is in many things as an ingredient.[17] But does this analogy throw much light on naming? Any feature of logical mixing which is at all interesting seems to distinguish it from all other sorts of mixing. The values of an unrestricted variable are strange receptacles. What prevents contrary ingredients from being put in together, or an implicans from appearing without its implicate, is never the causal consequences. And anyway the whole notion of mixing ingredients which were not there before the mixing is peculiar. Could there be a logical conjuring trick?

Here defenders of realism might object that a new misunderstanding had replaced the old one. For, if realism is to be understood, not only must a general characterization of naming be allowed, but also the verification principle must not be applied too crudely. And anyway, if mixing is not a good analogy, this only means that some better analogy must be sought. This objection might lead to a tolerant examination of other analogies.[18] But fortunately it also opens up a short cut to the heart of the matter, which I shall soon take. Now it would be taking too short a cut to repeat the platitude that naming is *sui generis* [logically distinctive]. For it is natural to seek an analogy even if the search can never be completely successful. And anyway Butler's truism applies to everything. What is needed in order to explain the peculiar persistence of the debate about universals is something slightly longer, a demonstration that no analogy can be sufficiently close to satisfy philosophers without being too close.

It is most natural to seek a visible process as an analogy to naming, particularly for the Greeks who began this controversy.[19] Now previously I insisted that it is impossible in the end to give a detailed non-circular description of what makes it possible to name anything. Here, however, it would be unfair to object that, if naming in general is compared to a visible process, still that process itself must be named. For this sort of circularity is the inevitable result of the philosopher's predicament. However, it is dangerous to begin speaking at all where so little can be said. For it is fatally easy to think that one has separate access to what makes a name applicable just because one has separate access to whatever stands for this in the analogy. But, waiving this, let us now take the short cut and ask what sort of visible process could be analogous to naming. Let us try a rough analogy and say that one word is connected with many objects in the same way that the estuary of a river is connected with its many sources. But this analogy fails because this connection just happens naturally. We might then try to mend the analogy by saying that water follows the easiest course. But this could be called choice only anthropomorphically, in an extended and weak sense of 'choice'. In order to introduce choice in a restricted, strong sense, it is necessary to alter the analogy and say that people by directing the streams choose which sources shall feed the river. But, if the first process was too natural to be like naming, the second is too artificial, since, for the analogy

[17] Cf. A. N. Whitehead, *Science and the Modern World* (Cambridge, 1928), pp. 197ff. For a criticism of this analogy, cf. Bentham, *Works*, vol. VIII, p. 335.

[18] Metaphors must not be dismissed just because they are metaphors, as, e.g. 'copying' and 'participation' are by Aristotle, *Met.* 991 a 20.

[19] Cf. J. Stenzel, *Plato's Method of Dialectic* (Oxford, 1940), p. 37.

to work, the sources ought to have something in common besides the fact that the river is fed from them. And it is difficult to find an analogy which is neither too natural nor too artificial. The characteristic of naming which is difficult to match is that the objects have something in common besides being called by one name, but nothing in common which counts except that in virtue of which they are called by one name. And this characteristic can be matched only by allowing that something makes it convenient but not absolutely necessary for people to canalize streams into the river in the way they do, and that whatever it is which makes this choice convenient is the only thing common to the sources which counts. But this compromise between the two extremes introduces into the analogy the very feature which it was intended to explain. For just how something works in influencing usage was what was to be explained. Nor is there a fourth alternative. So after all even general analogical characterizations of naming do fall into a circularity which is closely related to the type of circularity which my first thesis exposed. Neither in detail nor in general is it possible to step outside language.

This short way with analogies looks too superficial. For suppose that it is granted that one of the things that metaphysicians do is to seek the unattainable: that they hunt for definitions which would in no way involve their definienda,[20] and for analogies which would in no way involve what they were intended to explain. Yet even so metaphysics is a natural and inevitable pursuit, since the easiest way to discover how far one can go is to try to go one stage farther. And anyway there is a difference between complete failure and partial success; since, so long as analogies do not reach the point of self-frustration they get better and better as they approach it. These two qualifications are just but they only serve to strengthen my thesis that it was oscillation between the three points which prolonged the controversy about universals. For unless the possible analogies are mapped out in this simple way, it seems always conceivable that some altogether better analogy might lurk in an unexplored corner.

And what more are the rival theories of naming doing than seeking a completely satisfactory analogy? It is only jargon which makes them appear to be doing something more. The type of nominalism which suggests that things which are called by one name have only their name in common represents the extreme of artificiality.[21] It suggests that there are never any ways of telling even approximately whether a word is used in one sense or two senses. At the other extreme stands the type of realism which suggests that there is always one method of getting a precise answer to this question. In between are all the other theories of naming, which allow that it is neither impossible for the lexicographer to succeed in answering this question nor impossible for him to fail. None of these middle theories is really wrong, since of course we do bestow common names on certain chosen groups of things which exhibit certain similarities (else why should we do it?) or instantiate certain universals (why else were they invented?). But on the other hand none of them goes deep enough to satisfy the true metaphysician who is in all of us; since though they take us to the bottom of

[20] Cf. J. Wisdom, 'Metaphysics and Verification' (*Mind*, 1938, pp. 465ff.)
[21] There are traces of such an extreme form of nominalism in Hobbes. Cf. *Leviathan*, Pt. I, chap. IV, p. 13 (Everyman edition).

naming, we were in a simpler way already there, and they do not succeed in showing us how naming is founded on something else which lies even deeper. Hence each of these middle theories (except imagism, which says something empirical which seems to be false) develops its own thesis with embarrassing success up to a point, and can discredit its rivals only by accusing them of not going beyond that point. But, since naming cannot be explained by anything which really goes beyond a reasoned choice of usage, this is an unfair accusation. And its unfairness is concealed from those who make it only because each tacitly and wrongly assumes that his own theory alone does go beyond this point. Thus moderate nominalists maintain that similarity is a better explanation of the unity of a class than the presence of a universal. (But why should people not *just* recognize the presence of universals?) And moderate realists retort that this admits the existence of at least one universal, similarity. (But why should the presence of a universal explain the recognition of similarity if it cannot explain the recognition of anything else? Why should people not *just* recognize similarity?) Really these are not two arguments but two bare assertions of superiority. They are manœuvres which are carried out in a way which suggests that they are difficult and that they must be advances: but both these suggestions are false. Yet these theories do seem to be striving towards something. And they are. Their goal is the unattainable completely satisfactory explanation of naming. And, as so often happens in metaphysics, progress is measured by distance from the starting-point and not by proximity to the goal whose unattainability each uses against its rivals without allowing it to deter itself.

Thus theories of naming, which seem to flout the verification principle without therefore saying nothing, can be interpreted as disguised analogies. And, though there is a common limit beyond which they cannot go, the success with which they stealthily approach this limit, camouflaged in the technical terms of epistemology, varies. But if this almost mechanical oscillation is avoided what else can be said about naming? Certainly as the first part of this article showed, detailed answers to the question why we name things as we do will in the end be circular. Only the trick of giving a general answer as if it were a detailed one cloaks their failure. If a word is explained ostensively, then however difficult this process may be it really is explained ostensively. It is no good trying to combine the concreteness of ostensive definition with the clarity of verbal definition. Verbal definitions have such an easy task just because ostensive definitions have such a difficult task. Surveyors find it easier to fix the positions of points which they can visit than to fix the positions of points which they cannot visit. Similarly it is easy to fix the relative positions of words: but the points in things to which words are related are in the end inaccessible to logicians.

Then what else can be said about naming? How *does* the lexicographer tell when a word is used in two senses rather than in one sense? Surely there must be something in common to all well constructed series of things? Yes, just that they *are* well constructed. For this question already contains the equivalent of any possible comprehensive answer which could be given to it. And, though in one way it is hard to see what detailed answers could be given to it, in another way it is only too easy to see. For we never reach a point where an exit *must* be made from the maze of words. Admittedly, if a verbal explanation is given at one point, it is only successful if at some other point a connection with things is already understood; and at some points it is more natural not to offer more words. But at no point is an exit obligatory. So, if detailed reasons why we call a thing what we do are required, it is easy to give them; but never ultimately or in the end, since here *ex vi termini* [by the very sense of the term] it is impossible to give them. But philosophers tend to ignore this kind of detailed answer and press on. But where to? Perhaps to experimental psychology, in order to discover how changes in the sense organs, in training and in interests alter the ways in which people group things. But this sort of investigation only gives the varying tests of the good construction of a series, and not its essence. But what could its essence be? When general analogical characterizations of naming have been mentioned, and detailed reasons why we call particular things by particular names, and the psychological background of all this, what is left? The desire to go on explaining naming is to some extent the result of the way these three fields have been confused, and to some extent the result of a natural feeling that in such a vast territory there might be something which lies outside these three fields. But above all it is the result of the Protean metaphysical urge to transcend language.

The Senses and Their Objects

11

KNOWLEDGE AND PERCEPTION

Plato

• • •

Socrates. Suppose now, that we ask Protagoras, or one of his disciples, a question:—O, Protagoras, we will say to him, Man is, as you declare, the measure of all things—white, heavy, light, and the whole class of such things; for he has the criterion of them in himself, and when he thinks that things are such as he experiences them to be, he thinks what is and is true to himself. Is it not so?

Theodorus. Yes.

Soc. What now of future events, Protagoras? we shall say. Has each man the criterion of these also within himself, so that they *will be* for him as he supposes that they will be? For example, take the case of heat:—When an ordinary man thinks that he is going to have a fever, and that this kind of heat is coming on, and another person, who is a physician, thinks the contrary, whose opinion about the future is likely to prove right? Or are they both right?—he will have both heat and fever in his own judgement and neither in the physician's judgement?

Theod. That would be ridiculous.

Soc. And the vinegrower, if I am not mistaken, is a better judge of the sweetness or dryness of the vintage which is not yet gathered than the harp-player?

Theod. Certainly.

From *Theaetetus*, in *The Dialogues of Plato*, 4th ed., B. Jowett, trans., pp. 277–279, 281–288. Copyright, 1953, by The Clarendon Press, reprinted by permission of The Clarendon Press, Oxford.

Soc. And in musical composition the musician will know better than the training master what the training master himself will hereafter think harmonious or the reverse?

Theod. Of course.

Soc. And the cook will be a better judge than the guest, who is not a cook, of the pleasure to be derived from the dinner which is in preparation; for of present or past pleasure we are not as yet arguing; the question is whether everyone is to himself the best judge of that which will seem to be and will be to him in the future?—nay, would not you, Protagoras, better guess which arguments in a court would convince any one of us than the ordinary man?

Theod. Certainly, Socrates, he used to profess in the strongest manner that he was the superior of all men in this respect.

Soc. To be sure, friend: who would have paid a large sum for the privilege of talking to him, if he had really persuaded his visitors that neither a prophet nor any other man was better able to judge what will be and seem to be in the future than everyone could for himself?

Theod. Who indeed?

Soc. But now legislation and expediency are all concerned with the future; and everyone will admit that states, in passing laws, must often fail of their highest interests?

Theod. Quite true.

Soc. Then we may fairly argue against your master, that he must admit one man to be wiser than another, and that the wiser is a measure: but I, who know nothing, am not at all obliged to accept the honour which the advocate of Protagoras was just now forcing upon me, whether I would or not, of being a measure of anything.

Theod. That is the best refutation of him, Socrates; although he is also caught when he ascribes truth to the opinions of others, who give the lie direct to his own opinion.

Soc. There are many ways, Theodorus, in which the doctrine that every opinion of every man is true may be refuted; but there is more difficulty in proving that states of feeling, which are present to a man, and out of which arise sensations and opinions in accordance with them, are sometimes not true. And very likely I have been talking nonsense about them; for they may be unassailable, and those who say that there is clear evidence of them, and that they are matters of knowledge, may probably be right; in which case our friend Theaetetus was not so far from the mark when he identified perception and knowledge. And therefore let us draw nearer, as the advocate of Protagoras desires, and give the truth of the universal flux a ring: is the theory sound or not? at any rate, no small war is raging about it, and there are combatants not a few.

Theod. No small war, indeed, for in Ionia the sect makes rapid strides; the disciples of Heracleitus are most energetic upholders of the doctrine.

.   .   .

Soc. . . . What do they mean when they say that all things are in motion? That is to say, do they assert that there is only one kind of motion, or, as I think, two? I should like to have your opinion upon this point in addition to my own, that I may err, if I must err, in your company; tell me, then, when a thing changes from one place to another, or goes round in the same place, is not that what is called motion?

Theod. Yes.

Soc. Here then we have one kind of motion. But when a thing, remaining on the same spot, grows old, or becomes black from being white, or hard from being soft, or undergoes any other change, may not this be properly called motion of another kind?

Theod. I think it must be so called.

Soc. Of motion then there are these two kinds, 'change', and 'motion in place'.

Theod. You are right.

Soc. And now, having made this distinction, let us address ourselves to those who say that all is motion, and ask them whether all things according to them have the two kinds of motion, and are changed as well as move in place, or is one thing moved in both ways, and another in one only?

Theod. Indeed, I do not know what to answer; but I think they would say that all things are moved in both ways.

Soc. Yes, comrade; for, if not, they would have to say that the same things are in motion and at rest, and there would be no more truth in saying that all things are in motion, than that all things are at rest.

Theod. To be sure.

Soc. And if they are to be in motion, and nothing is to be devoid of motion, all things must always have every sort of motion?

Theod. Most true.

Soc. Consider a further point: did we not understand them to explain the generation of heat, whiteness, or anything else, in some such manner as the following:—were they not saying that each of these is a movement which takes place at the time of perception between an agent and a patient, whereby the patient ceases to be a perceiving power and becomes a percipient, and the agent a quale instead of a quality? I suspect that quality may appear a strange and uncouth term to you, and that you do not understand the general expression. Then I will take particular instances: I mean to say that the producing power or agent becomes neither heat nor whiteness, but hot and white, and the like of other things. For I must repeat what I said before, that neither this agent and patient, nor anything else in the world, can exist in isolation, but when they come together and generate sensations and their objects, the one becomes a thing of a certain quality, and the other a percipient. You remember?

Theod. Of course.

Soc. We may leave the details of their theory unexamined, but we must not forget to ask them the only question with which we are concerned: Are all things in motion and flux?

Theod. Yes, they will reply.

Soc. And they are moved in both those ways which we distinguished; that is to say, they move in place and are also changed?

Theod. Of course, if the motion is to be perfect.

Soc. If they only moved in place and were not changed, we should be able to say what is the nature of the things which are in motion and flux?

Theod. Exactly.

Soc. But now, since not even white continues to flow white, and whiteness itself is a flux or change which is passing into another colour, and is never to be caught standing still, can the name of any colour be rightly used at all?

Theod. How is that possible, Socrates, either in the case of this or of any other quality—if while we are using the word the object is escaping in the flux?

Soc. And what would you say of perceptions, such as sight and hearing, or any other kind of perception? Is there any stopping in the act of seeing and hearing?

Theod. Certainly not, if all things are in motion.

Soc. Then we must not speak of seeing any more than of not-seeing, nor of any other perception more than of any non-perception, if all things partake of every kind of motion?

Theod. Certainly not.

Soc. Yet perception is knowledge: so at least Theaetetus and I were saying.

Theod. Very true.

Soc. Then when we were asked what is knowledge, we no more answered what is knowledge than what is not knowledge?

Theod. I suppose not.

Soc. Here, then, is a fine result: we corrected our first answer in our eagerness to prove that nothing is at rest and so save that answer. But now it is clear that if nothing is at rest, every answer upon whatever subject is equally right: you may say that a thing is or is not thus; or, if you prefer, 'becomes' thus; and if we say 'becomes', we shall not then hamper them with words expressive of rest.

Theod. Quite true.

Soc. Yes, Theodorus, except in saying 'thus' and 'not thus'. But you ought not to use the word 'thus', for there is no motion in 'thus' or in 'not thus'. The maintainers of the doctrine have as yet no words in which to express themselves, and must get a new language. I might suggest to them the phrase 'no how', which being perfectly indefinite might suit them best.

Theod. Yes, that is a manner of speaking in which they will be quite at home.

Soc. And so, Theodorus, we have done with your friend without assenting to his doctrine, that every man is the measure of all things—a wise man only is a measure; neither can we allow that knowledge is perception, at least on the hypothesis of a perpetual flux; but perhaps our friend Theaetetus intends it in some other sense.

.   .   .

. . . Theaetetus, take another view of the subject: you answered that knowledge is perception?

Theaetetus. I did.

Soc. And if any one were to ask you: With what does a man see black and white colours? and with what does he hear high and low sounds?—you would say, if I am not mistaken, 'With the eyes and with the ears.'

Theaet. I should.

Soc. The free use of words and phrases, rather than minute precision, is generally characteristic of a liberal education, and the opposite is pedantic; but sometimes precision is necessary, and I believe that the answer which you have just given is open to the charge of incorrectness; for which is more correct, to say that we see or hear with the eyes and with the ears, or through the eyes and through the ears.

Theaet. I should say 'through', Socrates, rather than 'with'.

Soc. Yes, my boy, for no one can suppose that in each of us, as in a sort of Trojan horse, there are perched a number of unconnected senses, which do not all meet in some one nature, the soul or whatever we please to call it, of which they are the instruments, and with which through them we perceive objects of sense.

Theaet. I agree with you in that opinion.

Soc. The reason why I am thus precise is, because I want to know whether, when we perceive black and white through the eyes, and again, other qualities through other organs, we do not perceive them with one and the same part of ourselves; and whether, if you were asked, you could refer all such perceptions to the body. Perhaps, however, I had better allow you to answer for yourself and not interfere. Tell me, then, are not the organs through which you perceive warm and hard and light and sweet, organs of the body?

Theaet. Of the body, certainly.

Soc. And you would admit that what you perceive through one faculty you cannot perceive through another; the objects of hearing, for example, cannot be perceived through sight, or the objects of sight through hearing?

Theaet. Of course not.

Soc. If you have any thought about both of them, this common perception cannot come to you, either through the one or the other organ?

Theaet. It cannot.

Soc. How about sounds and colours: in the first place you may reflect that they both *exist?*

Theaet. Yes.

Soc. And that either of them is different from the other, and the same with itself?

Theaet. Certainly.

Soc. And that both are two and each of them one?

Theaet. Yes.

Soc. You can further observe whether they are like or unlike one another?

Theaet. I dare say.

Soc. But through what do you perceive all this about them? for neither through hearing nor yet through seeing can you apprehend that which they have in common. Let me give you an illustration of the point at issue:—If there were any meaning in asking whether sounds and colours are saline or not, you would be able to tell me what faculty would consider the question. It would not be sight or hearing, but some other.

Theaet. Certainly; the faculty of taste.

Soc. Very good; and now tell me what is the power which discerns, not only in sensible objects, but in all things, universal properties, such as those which are called being and not-being, and those others about which we were just asking—what organs will you assign for the perception of these by the appropriate power in us?

Theaet. You are thinking of being and not-being, likeness and unlikeness, sameness and difference, and also of unity and any other number which occurs in our judgement of objects. And evidently your question applies to odd and even numbers and other arithmetical conceptions—through what bodily organ the soul perceives them.

Soc. You follow me excellently, Theaetetus; that is precisely what I am asking.

Theaet. Indeed, Socrates, I cannot answer; my only notion is, that these, unlike objects of sense, have no separate organ, but that the mind, by a power of her own, contemplates such common properties in all things.

Soc. You are a beauty, Theaetetus, and not ugly, as Theodorus was saying; for he who utters the beautiful is himself beautiful and good. And besides being beautiful, you have done me a kindness in releasing me from a very long discussion, if you believe that the soul views some things by herself and others through the bodily organs. For that was my own opinion, and I wanted you to agree with me.

Theaet. Indeed, I do believe it.

Soc. And to which class would you refer being or essence; for this, of all our notions, is the most universal?

Theaet. I should say, to that class which the soul aspires to know of herself.

Soc. And would you say this also of like and unlike, same and other?

Theaet. Yes.

Soc. And would you say the same of the noble and base, and of good and evil?

Theaet. These also I conceive to be among the chief instances of those relative terms whose nature the soul perceives by comparing in herself things past and present with the future.

Soc. Hold! does she not perceive the hardness of that which is hard by the touch, and the softness of that which is soft equally by the touch?

Theaet. Yes.

Soc. But their *being*, I mean the fact that they are, and their opposition to one another, and the being (to repeat that term) of this opposition, the soul herself endeavours to decide for us by the review and comparison of them?

Theaet. Certainly.

Soc. The simple sensations which reach the soul through the body are given at birth to men and animals by nature, but their reflections on the being and use of them are slowly and hardly gained, if they are ever gained, by education and long experience.

Theaet. Assuredly.

Soc. And can a man attain truth who fails of attaining being?

Theaet. Impossible.

Soc. And can he who misses the truth of anything, have a knowledge of that thing?

Theaet. He cannot.

Soc. Then knowledge does not consist in impressions of sense, but in reasoning about them; in that only, and not in the mere impression, truth and being can be attained?

Theaet. Apparently.

Soc. And would you call the two processes by the same name, when there is so great a difference between them?

Theaet. That would certainly not be right.

Soc. And what name would you give to seeing, hearing, smelling, being cold and being hot?

Theaet. I should call all of them perceiving—what other name could be given to them?

Soc. Perception would be the collective name of them?

Theaet. Certainly.

Soc. Which, as we say, has no part in the attainment of truth, since it does not attain to being?

Theaet. Certainly not.

Soc. And therefore not in knowledge?

Theaet. No.

Soc. Then perception, Theaetetus, can never be the same as knowledge?

Theaet. Apparently not, Socrates; and knowledge has now been most distinctly proved to be different from perception.

·   ·   ·

12

KNOWLEDGE AND PERCEPTION

John Locke

CHAPTER VIII. SIMPLE IDEAS OF SENSATION

. . .

To discover the nature of our *ideas* the better, and to discourse of them intelligibly, it will be convenient to distinguish them *as they are ideas or perceptions in our minds;* and *as they are modifications of matter in the bodies that cause such perceptions in us:* that so we may not think (as perhaps usually is done) that they are exactly the images and resemblances of something inherent in the subject; most of those of sensation being in the mind no more the likeness of something existing without us, than the names that stand for them are the likeness of our ideas, which yet upon hearing they are apt to excite in us.

Whatsoever the mind perceives *in itself*, or is the immediate object of perception, thought, or understanding, that I call *idea;* and the power to produce any idea in our mind, I call *quality* of the subject wherein that power is. Thus a snowball having the power to produce in us the ideas of white, cold, and round,—the power to produce those ideas in us, as they are in the snowball, I call qualities; and as they are sensations or perceptions in our understandings, I call them ideas; which *ideas,* if I speak of sometimes as in the things themselves, I would be understood to mean those qualities in the objects which produce them in us.

[Qualities thus considered in bodies are, *First,* such as are utterly inseparable from the body, in what state soever it be;] and such as in all the alterations and changes it suffers, all the force can be used upon it, it constantly keeps; and such as sense constantly finds in every particle of matter which has bulk enough to be perceived; and the mind finds inseparable from every particle of matter, though less than to make itself singly be perceived by our senses: v.g. Take a grain of wheat, divide it into two parts; each part has still solidity, extension, figure, and mobility: divide

---

From John Locke, *An Essay Concerning Human Understanding*, A. C. Fraser, ed. (Oxford: The Clarendon Press, 1894), Book II, Chap. VIII, Secs. 7–26, Vol. I, pp. 168–182; Book IV, Chap. XI, Secs. 1–10, Vol. II, pp. 325–336.

it again, and it retains still the same qualities; and so divide it on, till the parts become insensible; they must retain still each of them all those qualities. For division (which is all that a mill, or pestle, or any other body, does upon another, in reducing it to insensible parts) can never take away either solidity, extension, figure, or mobility from any body, but only makes two or more distinct separate masses of matter, of that which was but one before; all which distinct masses, reckoned as so many distinct bodies, after division, make a certain number. [These I call *original* or *primary qualities* of body, which I think we may observe to produce simple ideas in us, viz. solidity, extension, figure, motion or rest, and number.

Secondly, such qualities which in truth are nothing in the objects themselves but powers to produce various sensations in us by their primary qualities, i.e. by the bulk, figure, texture, and motion of their insensible parts, as colours, sounds, tastes, &c. These I call *secondary qualities*. To these might be added a *third* sort, which are allowed to be barely powers; though they are as much real qualities in the subject as those which I, to comply with the common way of speaking, call qualities, but for distinction, secondary qualities. For the power in fire to produce a new colour, or consistency, in *wax* or *clay*,—by its primary qualities, is as much a quality in fire, as the power it has to produce in *me* a new idea or sensation of warmth or burning, which I felt not before,—by the same primary qualities, viz. the bulk, texture, and motion of its insensible parts.]

[The next thing to be considered is, how bodies produce ideas in us; and that is manifestly by impulse, the only way which we can conceive bodies to operate in.]

If then external objects be not united to our minds when they produce ideas therein; and yet we perceive these *original* qualities in such of them as singly fall under our senses, it is evident that some motion must be thence continued by our nerves, or animal spirits, by some parts of our bodies, to the brains or the seat of sensation, there to produce in our minds the particular ideas we have of them. And since the extension, figure, number, and motion of bodies of an observable bigness, may be perceived at a distance by the sight, it is evident some singly imperceptible bodies must come from them to the eyes, and thereby convey to the brain some motion; which produces these ideas which we have of them in us.

After the same manner that the ideas of these original qualities are produced in us, we may conceive that the ideas of *secondary* qualities are also produced, viz. by the operation of insensible particles on our senses. For, it being manifest that there are bodies and good store of bodies, each whereof are so small, that we cannot by any of our senses discover either their bulk, figure, or motion,—as is evident in the particles of the air and water, and others extremely smaller than those; perhaps as much smaller than the particles of air and water, as the particles of air and water are smaller than peas or hail-stones;—let us suppose at present that the different motions and figures, bulk and number, of such particles, affecting the several organs of our senses, produce in us those different sensations which we have from the colours and smells of bodies; v.g. that a violet, by the impulse of such insensible particles of matter, of peculiar figures and bulks, and in different degrees and modifications of their motions, causes the ideas of the blue colour, and sweet scent of that flower to be produced in our minds. It being no more impossible to conceive that God should annex such ideas to such motions, with which they have no similitude, than that he should annex the idea of pain to the motion of a piece of steel dividing our flesh, with which that idea hath no resemblance.

What I have said concerning colours and smells may be understood also of tastes and sounds, and other the like sensible qualities; which, whatever reality we by mistake attribute to them, are in truth nothing in the objects themselves, but powers to produce various sensations in us; and depend on those primary qualities, viz. bulk, figure, texture, and motion of parts [as I have said].

From whence I think it easy to draw this observation,—that the ideas of primary qualities of bodies are resemblances of them, and their patterns do really exist in the bodies themselves, but the ideas produced in us by these secondary qualities have no resemblance of them at all. There is nothing like our ideas, existing in the bodies themselves. They are, in the bodies we denominate from them, only a power to produce those sensations in us: and what is sweet, blue, or warm in idea, is but the certain bulk, figure, and motion of the insensible parts, in the bodies themselves, which we call so.

Flame is denominated hot and light; snow, white and cold; and manna, white and sweet, from the ideas they produce in us. Which qualities are commonly thought to be the same in those bodies that those ideas are in us, the one the perfect resemblance of the other, as they are in a mirror, and it would by most men be judged very extravagant if one should say otherwise. And yet he that will consider that the same fire that, at one distance produces in us the sensation of warmth, does, at a nearer approach, produce in us the far different sensation of pain, ought to bethink himself what reason he has to say—that this idea of warmth, which was produced in him by the fire, is *actually in the fire;* and his idea of pain, which the same fire produced in him the same way, is *not* in the fire. Why are whiteness and coldness in snow, and pain not, when it produces the one and the other idea in us; and can do neither, but by the bulk, figure, number, and motion of its solid parts?

The particular bulk, number, figure, and motion of the parts of fire or snow are really in them,—whether any one's senses perceive them or no: and therefore they may be called *real* qualities, because they really exist in those bodies. But light, heat, whiteness, or coldness, are no more really in them than sickness or pain is in manna. Take away the sensation of them; let not the eyes see light or colours, nor the ears hear sounds; let the palate not taste, nor the nose smell, and all colours, tastes, odours, and sounds, *as they are such particular ideas,* vanish and cease, and are reduced to their causes, i.e. bulk, figure, and motion of parts.

A piece of manna of a sensible bulk is able to produce in us the idea of a round or square figure; and by being removed from one place to another, the idea of motion. This idea of motion represents it as it really is in manna moving: a circle or square are the same, whether in idea or existence, in the mind or in the manna. And this, both motion and figure, are really in the manna, whether we take notice of them or no: this everybody is ready to agree to. Besides, manna, by the bulk, figure, texture, and motion of its parts, has a power to produce the sensations of sickness, and sometimes of acute pains or gripings in us. That these ideas of sickness and pain are *not* in the manna, but effects of its operations on us, and are nowhere when we feel them not; this also every one readily agrees to. And yet men are hardly to be brought to think that sweetness and whiteness are not really in manna; which are but the effects of the operations of manna, by the motion, size, and figure of its particles, on the eyes and palate: as the pain and sickness caused by manna are confessedly nothing but the effects of its operations on the stomach and guts, by the size, motion, and figure of its insensible parts, (for by nothing else can a body operate, as has been proved): as if it could not operate on the eyes and palate, and thereby produce in the mind particular distinct ideas, which in itself it has not, as well as we allow it can operate on the guts and stomach, and thereby produce distinct ideas, which in itself it has not. These ideas, being all effects of the operations of manna on several parts of our bodies, by the size, figure, number, and motion of its parts;—why those produced by the eyes and palate should rather be thought to be really in the manna, than those produced by the stomach and guts; or why the pain and sickness, ideas that are the effect of manna, should be thought to be nowhere when they are not felt; and yet the sweetness and whiteness, effects of the same manna on other parts of the body, by ways equally as unknown, should be thought to exist in the manna, when they are not seen or tasted, would need some reason to explain.

Let us consider the red and white colours in porphyry. Hinder light from striking on it, and its colours vanish; it no longer produces any such ideas in us: upon the return of light it produces these appearances on us again. Can any one think any real alterations are made in the porphyry by the presence or absence of light; and that those ideas of whiteness and redness are really in porphyry in the light, when it is plain *it has no colour in the dark?* It has, indeed, such a configuration of particles, both night and day, as are apt, by the rays of light rebounding from some parts of that hard stone, to produce in us the idea of redness, and from others the idea of whiteness; but whiteness or redness are not in it at any time, but such a texture that hath the power to produce such a sensation in us.

Pound an almond, and the clear white colour will be altered into a dirty one, and the sweet taste into an oily one. What real alteration can the beating of the pestle make in any body, but an alteration of the texture of it?

Ideas being thus distinguished and understood, we may be able to give an account how the same water, at the same time, may produce the idea of cold by one hand and of heat by the other: whereas it is impossible that the same water, if those ideas were really in it, should at the same time be both hot and cold. For, if we imagine *warmth*, as it is in our hands, to be nothing but a certain sort and degree of motion in the minute particles of our nerves or animal spirits, we may understand how it is possible that the same water may, at the same time, produce the sensations of heat in one hand and cold in the other; which yet *figure* never does, that never producing the idea of a square by one hand which has produced the idea of a globe by another. But if the sensation of heat and cold be nothing but the increase or diminution of the motion of the minute parts of our bodies, caused by the corpuscles of any other body, it is easy to be understood, that if that motion be greater in one hand than in the other; if a body be applied to the two hands, which has in its minute particles a greater motion than in those of one of the hands, and a less than in those of the other, it will increase the motion of the one hand

and lessen it in the other; and so cause the different sensations of heat and cold that depend thereon.

I have in what just goes before been engaged in physical inquiries a little further than perhaps I intended. But, it being necessary to make the nature of sensation a little understood; and to make the difference between the *qualities* in bodies, and the *ideas* produced by them in the mind, to be distinctly conceived, without which it were impossible to discourse intelligibly of them;—I hope I shall be pardoned this little excursion into natural philosophy; it being necessary in our present inquiry to distinguish the *primary* and *real* qualities of bodies, which are always in them (viz. solidity, extension, figure, number, and motion, or rest, and are sometimes perceived by us, viz. when the bodies they are in are big enough singly to be discerned), from those *secondary* and *imputed* qualities, which are but the powers of several combinations of those primary ones, when they operate without being distinctly discerned,—whereby we may also come to know what ideas are, and what are not, resemblances of something really existing in the bodies we denominate from them.

The qualities, then, that are in bodies, rightly considered, are of three sorts:—

First, The bulk, figure, number, situation, and motion or rest of their solid parts. Those are in them, whether we perceive them or not; and when they are of that size that we can discover them, we have by these an idea of the thing as it is in itself; as is plain in artificial things. These I call *primary qualities.*

Secondly, The power that is in any body, by reason of its insensible primary qualities, to operate after a peculiar manner on any of our senses, and thereby produce in *us* the different ideas of several colours, sounds, smells, tastes, &c. These are usually called *sensible qualities.*

Thirdly, The power that is in any body, by reason of the particular constitution of its primary qualities, to make such a change in the bulk, figure, texture, and motion of *another body*, as to make it operate on our senses differently from what it did before. Thus the sun has a power to make wax white, and fire to make lead fluid. [These are usually called *powers.*]

The first of these, as has been said, I think may be properly called real, original, or primary qualities; because they are in the things themselves, whether they are perceived or not: and upon their different modifications it is that the secondary qualities depend.

The other two are only powers to act differently upon other things: which powers result from the different modifications of those primary qualities.

But, though the two latter sorts of qualities are powers barely, and nothing but powers, relating to several other bodies, and resulting from the different modifications of the original qualities, yet they are generally otherwise thought of. For the *second* sort, viz. the powers to produce several ideas in us, by our senses, are looked upon as real qualities in the things thus affecting us: but the *third* sort are called and esteemed barely powers. v.g. The idea of heat or light, which we receive by our eyes, or touch, from the sun, are commonly thought real qualities existing in the sun, and something more than mere powers in it. But when we consider the sun in reference to wax, which it melts or blanches, we look on the whiteness and softness produced in the wax, not as qualities in the sun, but effects produced by powers in it. Whereas, if rightly considered, these qualities of light and warmth, which are perceptions in me when I am warmed or enlightened by the sun, are no otherwise in the sun, than the changes made in the wax, when it is blanched or melted, are in the sun. They are all of them equally *powers in the sun, depending on its primary qualities;* whereby it is able, in the one case, so to alter the bulk, figure, texture, or motion of some of the insensible parts of my eyes or hands, as thereby to produce in me the idea of light or heat; and in the other, it is able so to alter the bulk, figure, texture, or motion of the insensible parts of the wax, as to make them fit to produce in me the distinct ideas of white and fluid.

The reason why the one are ordinarily taken for real qualities, and the other only for bare powers, seems to be, because the ideas we have of distinct colours, sounds, &c., containing nothing at all in them of bulk, figure, or motion, we are not apt to think them the effects of these primary qualities; which appear not, to our senses, to operate in their production, and with which they have not any apparent congruity or conceivable connexion. Hence it is that we are so forward to imagine, that those ideas are the resemblances of something really existing in the objects themselves: since sensation discovers nothing of bulk, figure, or motion of parts in their production; nor can reason show how bodies, *by their bulk, figure, and motion*, should produce in the mind the ideas of blue or yellow, &c. But, in the other case, in the operations of bodies changing the qualities one of another, we plainly discover that the quality produced hath commonly no resemblance with anything in the thing producing it; wherefore we look on it as a bare effect of power. For, through receiving the idea of heat or light from the sun, we are apt to think *it* is a perception and resemblance of such a quality in the sun; yet when we see wax, or a fair face, receive change of colour from the sun, we cannot imagine that to be the reception or resemblance of anything in the sun, because we find not those different colours in the sun itself. For, our senses being able to observe a likeness or unlikeness of sensible qualities in two different external objects, we forwardly enough conclude the production of any sensible quality in any subject to be an effect of bare power, and not the communication of any quality which was really in the efficient, when we find no such sensible quality in the thing that produced it. But our senses, not being able to discover any unlikeness between the idea produced in us, and the quality of the object producing it, we are apt to imagine that our ideas are resemblances of something in the objects, and not the effects of certain powers placed in the modification of their primary qualities, with which primary qualities the ideas produced in us have no resemblance.

To conclude. Beside those before-mentioned primary qualities in bodies, viz. bulk, figure, extension, number, and motion of their solid parts; all the rest, whereby we take notice of bodies, and distinguish them one from another, are nothing else but several powers in them, depending on those primary qualities; whereby they are fitted, either by immediately operating on our bodies to produce several different ideas in us; or else, by operating on other bodies, so to change their primary qualities as to render them capable of producing ideas in us different from what before they did. The former of these, I think, may be called secondary qualities *immediately perceivable:* the latter, secondary qualities, *mediately perceivable.*

CHAPTER XI. OF OUR KNOWLEDGE OF THE EXISTENCE
OF OTHER THINGS

The knowledge of our own being we have by intuition. The existence of a God, reason clearly makes known to us . . .

The knowledge of the existence of *any other thing* we can have only by *sensation:* for there being no necessary connexion of real existence with any *idea* a man hath in his memory; nor of any other existence but that of God with the existence of any particular man: no particular man can know the existence of any other being, but only when, by actual operating upon him, it makes itself perceived by him. For, the having the idea of anything in our mind, no more proves the existence of that thing, than the picture of a man evidences his being in the world, or the visions of a dream make thereby a true history.

It is therefore the *actual receiving* of ideas from without that gives us notice of the existence of other things, and makes us know, that something doth exist at that time without us, which causes that idea in us; though perhaps we neither know nor consider how it does it. For it takes not from the certainty of our senses, and the ideas we receive by them, that we know not the manner wherein they are produced: v.g. whilst I write this, I have, by the paper affecting my eyes, that idea produced in my mind, which, whatever object causes, I call *white;* by which I know that that quality or accident (i.e. whose appearance before my eyes always causes that idea) doth really exist, and hath a being without me. And of this, the greatest assurance I can possibly have, and to which my faculties can attain, is the testimony of my eyes, which are the proper and sole judges of this thing; whose testimony I have reason to rely on as so certain, that I can no more doubt, whilst I write this, that I see white and black, and that something really exists that causes that sensation in me, than that I write or move my hand; which is a certainty as great as human nature is capable of, concerning the existence of anything, but a man's self alone, and of God.

The notice we have by our senses of the existing of things without us, though it be not altogether so certain as our intuitive knowledge, or the deductions of our reason employed about the clear abstract ideas of our own minds; yet it is an assurance that deserves the name of *knowledge.* If we persuade ourselves that our faculties act and inform us right concerning the existence of those objects that affect them, it cannot pass for an ill-grounded confidence: for I think nobody can, in earnest, be so sceptical as to be uncertain of the existence of those things which he sees and feels. At least, he that can doubt so far, (whatever he may have with his own thoughts,) will never have any controversy with me; since he can never be sure I say anything contrary to his own opinion. As to myself, I think God has given me assurance enough of the existence of things without me: since, by their different application, I can produce in myself both pleasure and pain, which is one great concernment of my present state. This is certain: the confidence that our faculties do not herein deceive us, is the greatest assurance we are capable of concerning the existence of material beings. For we cannot act anything but by our faculties; nor talk of knowledge itself, but by the help of those faculties which are fitted to apprehend even what knowledge is.

But besides the assurance we have from our senses themselves, that they do not err in the information they give us of the existence of things without us, when they are affected by them, we are further confirmed in this assurance by other concurrent reasons:—

I. It is plain those perceptions are produced in us by exterior causes affecting our senses: because those that want the *organs* of any sense, never can have the ideas belonging to that sense produced in their minds. This is too evident to be doubted: and therefore we cannot but be assured that they come in by the organs of that sense, and no other way. The organs themselves, it is plain, do not produce them: for then the eyes of a man in the dark would produce colours, and his nose smell roses in the winter: but we see nobody gets the relish of a pineapple, till he goes to the Indies, where it is, and tastes it.

II. Because sometimes I find that *I cannot avoid the having those ideas produced in my mind*. For though, when my eyes are shut, or windows fast, I can at pleasure recall to my mind the ideas of light, or the sun, which former sensations had lodged in my memory; so I can at pleasure lay by *that* idea, and take into my view that of the smell of a rose, or taste of sugar. But, if I turn my eyes at noon towards the sun, I cannot avoid the ideas which the light or sun then produces in me. So that there is a manifest difference between the ideas laid up in my memory, (over which, if they were there only, I should have constantly the same power to dispose of them, and lay them by at pleasure,) and those which force themselves upon me, and I cannot avoid having. And therefore it must needs be some exterior cause, and the brisk acting of some objects without me, whose efficacy I cannot resist, that produces those ideas in my mind, whether I will or no. Besides, there is nobody who doth not perceive the difference in himself between contemplating the sun, as he hath the idea of it in his memory, and actually looking upon it: of which two, his perception is so distinct, that few of his ideas are more distinguishable one from another. And therefore he hath certain knowledge that they are not *both* memory, or the actions of his mind, and fancies only within him; but that actual seeing hath a cause without.

III. Add to this, that many of those ideas are *produced in us with pain*, which afterwards we remember without the least offence. Thus, the pain of heat or cold, when the idea of it is revived in our minds, gives us no disturbance; which, when felt, was very troublesome; and is again, when actually repeated: which is occasioned by the disorder the external object causes in our bodies when applied to them: and we remember the pains of hunger, thirst, or the headache, without any pain at all; which would either never disturb us, or else constantly do it, as often as we thought of it, were there nothing more but ideas floating in our minds, and appearances entertaining our fancies, without the real existence of things affecting us from abroad. The same may be said of *pleasure*, accompanying several actual sensations. And though mathematical demonstration depends not upon sense, yet the examining them by diagrams gives great credit to the evidence of our sight, and seems to give it a certainty approaching to that of demonstration itself. For, it would be very strange, that a man should allow it for an undeniable truth, that two angles of a figure, which he measures by lines and angles of a diagram, should be bigger one than the other, and yet doubt of the existence of those lines and angles, which by looking on he makes use of to measure that by.

IV. Our *senses* in many cases *bear witness to the truth of each other's report*, concerning the existence of sensible things without us. He that *sees* a fire, may, if he doubt whether it be anything more than a bare fancy, *feel* it too; and be convinced, by putting his hand in it. Which certainly could never be put into such exquisite pain by a bare idea or phantom, unless that the pain be a fancy too: which yet he cannot, when the burn is well, by raising the idea of it, bring upon himself again.

Thus I see, whilst I write this, I can change the appearance of the paper; and by designing the letters, tell *beforehand* what new idea it shall exhibit the very next moment, by barely drawing my pen over it: which will neither appear (let me fancy as much as I will) if my hands stand still; or though I move my pen, if my eyes be shut: nor, when those characters are once made on the paper, can I choose afterwards but see them as they are; that is, have the ideas of such letters as I have made. Whence it is manifest, that they are not barely the sport and play of my own imagination, when I find that the characters that were made at the pleasure of my own thoughts, do not obey them; nor yet cease to be, whenever I shall fancy it, but continue to affect my senses constantly and regularly, according to the figures I made them. To which if we will add, that the sight of those shall, from another man, draw such sounds as I beforehand design they shall stand for, there will be little reason left to doubt that those words I write do really exist without me, when they cause a long series of regular sounds to affect my ears, which could not be the effect of my imagination, nor could my memory retain them in that order.

But yet, if after all this any one will be so sceptical as to distrust his senses, and to affirm that all we see and hear, feel and taste, think and do, during our whole being, is but the series and deluding appearances of a long dream, whereof there is no reality; and therefore will question the existence of all things, or our knowledge of anything: I must desire him to consider, that, if all be a dream, then he doth but dream that he makes the question, and so it is not much matter that a waking man should answer him. But yet, if he pleases, he may dream that I make him this answer, That the certainty of things existing in *rerum natura* when we have the testimony of our senses for it is not only as great as our frame can attain to, but as our condition needs. For, our faculties being suited not to the full extent of being, nor to a perfect, clear, comprehensive knowledge of things free from all doubt and scruple; but to the preservation of us, in whom they are; and accommodated to the use of life: they serve to our purpose well enough, if they will but give us certain notice of those things, which are convenient or inconvenient to us. For he that sees a candle burning, and hath experimented the force of its flame by putting his finger in it, will little doubt that this is something existing without him, which does him harm, and puts him to great pain: which is assurance enough, when no man requires greater certainty to govern his actions by than what is as certain as his actions themselves. And if our dreamer pleases to try whether the glowing heat of a glass furnace be barely a wandering imagination in a drowsy man's fancy, by putting his hand into it, he may perhaps be wakened into a certainty greater than he could wish, that it is something more than bare imagination. So that this evidence is as great as we can desire, being as certain to us as our pleasure or pain, i.e. happiness or misery; beyond which we have no concernment, either of knowing or being. Such an assurance of the existence of things without us is sufficient to direct us in the attaining the good and avoiding the evil which is caused by them, which is the important concernment we have of being made acquainted with them.

In fine, then, when our senses do actually convey into our understandings any idea, we cannot but be satisfied that there doth something *at that time* really exist without us, which doth affect our senses, and by them give notice of itself to our apprehensive faculties, and actually produce that idea which we then perceive: and we cannot so far distrust their testimony, as to doubt that such *collections* of simple ideas as we have observed by our senses to be united together, do really exist together. But this knowledge extends as far as the present testimony of our senses, employed about particular objects that do then affect them, and no further. For if I saw such a collection of simple ideas as is wont to be called *man*, existing together one minute since, and am now alone, I cannot be certain that the same man exists now, since there is no *necessary connexion* of his existence a minute since with his existence now: by a thousand ways he may cease to be, since I had the testimony of my senses for his existence. And if I cannot be certain that the man I saw last to-day is now in being, I can less be certain that he is so who hath been longer removed from my senses, and I have not seen since yesterday, or since the last year: and much less can I be certain of the existence of men that I never saw. And, therefore, though it be highly probable that millions of men do now exist, yet, whilst I am alone, writing this, I have not that certainty of it which we strictly call knowledge; though the great likelihood of it puts me past doubt, and it be reasonable for me to do several things upon the confidence that there are men (and men also of my acquaintance, with whom I have to do) now in the world: but this is but probability, not knowledge.

Whereby yet we may observe how foolish and vain a thing it is for a man of a narrow knowledge, who having reason given him to judge of the different evidence and probability of things, and to be swayed accordingly; how vain, I say, it is to expect demonstration and certainty in things not capable of it; and refuse assent to very rational propositions, and act contrary to very plain and clear truths, because they cannot be made out so evident, as to surmount every the least (I will not say reason, but) pretence of doubting. He that, in the ordinary affairs of life, would admit of nothing but direct plain demonstration, would be sure of nothing in this world, but of perishing quickly. The wholesomeness of his meat or drink would not give him reason to venture on it: and I would fain know what it is he could do upon such grounds as are capable of no doubt, no objection.

.   .   .

13

THE REALITY OF SENSIBLE THINGS

George Berkeley

· · ·

Philonous. Shall we . . . examine which of us it is that denies the reality of sensible things, or professes the greatest ignorance of them; since, if I take you rightly, he is to be esteemed the greatest *sceptic?*

· · ·

Hylas. That is what I desire.

Philonous. What mean you by sensible things?

Hylas. Those things which are perceived by the senses. Can you imagine that I mean any thing else?

Philonous. Pardon me, Hylas, if I am desirous clearly to apprehend your notions, since this may much shorten our inquiry. Suffer me then to ask you this farther question. Are those things only perceived by the senses which are perceived immediately? Or may those things properly be said to be *sensible*, which are perceived mediately, or not without the intervention of others?

Hylas. I do not sufficiently understand you.

Philonous. In reading a book, what I immediately perceive are the letters, but mediately, or by means of these, are suggested to my mind the notions of God, virtue, truth, *&c*. Now, that the letters are truly sensible things, or perceived by sense, there is no doubt: but I would know whether you take the things suggested by them to be so too.

Hylas. No certainly, it were absurd to think *God* or *Virtue* sensible things, though they may be signified and suggested to the mind by sensible marks, with which they have an arbitrary connexion.

Philonous. It seems then, that by *sensible things* you mean those only which can be perceived immediately by sense.

Hylas. Right.

From *Three Dialogues between Hylas and Philonous*, in *The Works of George Berkeley, Bishop of Cloyne*, T. E. Jessop, ed. (London: Thomas Nelson & Sons Ltd., 1949), Vol. II, First Dialogue, pp. 173–191, 193–195. Reprinted by permission of the publisher.

Philonous. Doth it not follow from this, that though I see one part of the sky red, and another blue, and that my reason doth thence evidently conclude there must be some cause of that diversity of colours, yet that cause cannot be said to be a sensible thing, or perceived by the sense of seeing?

Hylas. It doth.

Philonous. In like manner, though I hear variety of sounds, yet I cannot be said to hear the causes of those sounds.

Hylas. You cannot.

Philonous. And when by my touch I perceive a thing to be hot and heavy, I cannot say with any truth or propriety, that I feel the cause of its heat or weight.

Hylas. To prevent any more questions of this kind, I tell you once for all, that by *sensible things* I mean those only which are perceived by sense, and that in truth the senses perceive nothing which they do not perceive immediately: for they make no inferences. The deducing therefore of causes or occasions from effects and appearances, which alone are perceived by sense, entirely relates to reason.

Philonous. The point then is agreed between us, that *sensible things are those only which are immediately perceived by sense.* You will farther inform me, whether we immediately perceive by sight any thing beside light, and colours, and figures: or by hearing, any thing but sounds: by the palate, any thing beside tastes: by the smell, beside odours: or by the touch, more than tangible qualities.

Hylas. We do not.

Philonous. It seems therefore, that if you take away all sensible qualities, there remains nothing sensible.

Hylas. I grant it.

Philonous. Sensible things therefore are nothing else but so many sensible qualities, or combinations of sensible qualities.

Hylas. Nothing else.

Philonous. Heat then is a sensible thing.

Hylas. Certainly.

Philonous. Doth the reality of sensible things consist in being perceived? or, is it something distinct from their being perceived, and that bears no relation to the mind?

Hylas. To *exist* is one thing, and to be *perceived* is another.

Philonous. I speak with regard to sensible things only: and of these I ask, whether by their real existence you mean a subsistence exterior to the mind, and distinct from their being perceived?

Hylas. I mean a real absolute being, distinct from, and without any relation to their being perceived.

Philonous. Heat therefore, if it be allowed a real being, must exist without the mind.

Hylas. It must.

Philonous. Tell me, Hylas, is this real existence equally compatible to all degrees of heat, which we perceive: or is there any reason why we should attribute it to some, and deny it others? And if there be, pray let me know that reason.

Hylas. Whatever degree of heat we perceive by sense, we may be sure the
same exists in the object that occasions it.

Philonous. What, the greatest as well as the least?

Hylas. I tell you, the reason is plainly the same in respect of both: they are
both perceived by sense; nay, the greater degree of heat is more
sensibly perceived; and consequently, if there is any difference, we are
more certain of its real existence than we can be of the reality of a lesser
degree.

Philonous. But is not the most vehement and intense degree of heat a very
great pain?

Hylas. No one can deny it.

Philonous. And is any unperceiving thing capable of pain or pleasure?

Hylas. No certainly.

Philonous. Is your material substance a senseless being, or a being endowed
with sense and perception?

Hylas. It is senseless, without doubt.

Philonous. It cannot therefore be the subject of pain.

Hylas. By no means.

Philonous. Nor consequently of the greatest heat perceived by sense, since
you acknowledge this to be no small pain.

Hylas. I grant it.

Philonous. What shall we say then of your external object; is it a material
substance, or no?

Hylas. It is a material substance with the sensible qualities inhering in it.

Philonous. How then can a great heat exist in it, since you own it cannot in a
material substance? I desire you would clear this point.

Hylas. Hold, Philonous, I fear I was out in yielding intense heat to be a pain.
It should seem rather, that pain is something distinct from heat, and the
consequence or effect of it.

Philonous. Upon putting your hand near the fire, do you perceive one
simple uniform sensation, or two distinct sensations?

Hylas. But one simple sensation.

Philonous. Is not the heat immediately perceived?

Hylas. It is.

Philonous. And the pain?

Hylas. True.

Philonous. Seeing therefore they are both immediately perceived at the same
time, and the fire affects you only with one simple, or uncompounded
idea, it follows that this same simple idea is both the intense heat
immediately perceived, and the pain; and consequently, that the intense
heat immediately perceived, is nothing distinct from a particular sort of
pain.

Hylas. It seems so.

Philonous. Again, try in your thoughts, Hylas, if you can conceive a
vehement sensation to be without pain, or pleasure.

Hylas. I cannot.

Philonous. Or can you frame to yourself an idea of sensible pain or pleasure
in general, abstracted from every particular idea of heat, cold, tastes,
smells? &c.

Hylas. I do not find that I can.

Philonous. Doth it not therefore follow, that sensible pain is nothing distinct from those sensations or ideas, in an intense degree?

Hylas. It is undeniable; and to speak the truth, I begin to suspect a very great heat cannot exist but in a mind perceiving it.

Philonous. What! are you then in that *sceptical* state of suspense, between affirming and denying?

Hylas. I think I may be positive in the point. A very violent and painful heat cannot exist without the mind.

Philonous. It hath not therefore, according to you, any real being.

Hylas. I own it.

Philonous. Is it therefore certain, that there is no body in nature really hot?

Hylas. I have not denied there is any real heat in bodies. I only say, there is no such thing as an intense real heat.

Philonous. But did you not say before, that all degrees of heat were equally real: or if there was any difference, that the greater were more undoubtedly real than the lesser?

Hylas. True: but it was, because I did not then consider the ground there is for distinguishing between them, which I now plainly see. And it is this: because intense heat is nothing else but a particular kind of painful sensation; and pain cannot exist but in a perceiving being; it follows that no intense heat can really exist in an unperceiving corporeal substance. But this is no reason why we should deny heat in an inferior degree to exist in such a substance.

Philonous. But how shall we be able to discern those degrees of heat which exist only in the mind, from those which exist without it?

Hylas. That is no difficult matter. You know, the least pain cannot exist unperceived; whatever therefore degree of heat is a pain, exists only in the mind. But as for all other degrees of heat, nothing obliges us to think the same of them.

Philonous. I think you granted before, that no unperceiving being was capable of pleasure, any more than of pain.

Hylas. I did.

Philonous. And is not warmth, or a more gentle degree of heat than what causes uneasiness, a pleasure?

Hylas. What then?

Philonous. Consequently it cannot exist without the mind in any unperceiving substance, or body.

Hylas. So it seems.

Philonous. Since therefore, as well those degrees of heat that are not painful, as those that are, can exist only in a thinking substance; may we not conclude that external bodies are absolutely incapable of any degree of heat whatsoever?

Hylas. On second thoughts, I do not think it so evident that warmth is a pleasure, as that a great degree of heat is a pain.

Philonous. I do not pretend that warmth is as great a pleasure as heat is a pain. But if you grant it to be even a small pleasure, it serves to make good my conclusion.

Hylas. I could rather call it an *indolence*. It seems to be nothing more than a privation of both pain and pleasure. And that such a quality or state as this may agree to an unthinking substance, I hope you will not deny.

Philonous. If you are resolved to maintain that warmth, or a gentle degree of heat, is no pleasure, I know not how to convince you otherwise, than by appealing to your own sense. But what think you of cold?

Hylas. The same that I do of heat. An intense degree of cold is a pain; for to feel a very great cold, is to perceive a great uneasiness: it cannot therefore exist without the mind; but a lesser degree of cold may, as well as a lesser degree of heat.

Philonous. Those bodies therefore, upon whose application to our own, we perceive a moderate degree of heat, must be concluded to have a moderate degree of heat or warmth in them: and those, upon whose application we feel a like degree of cold, must be thought to have cold in them.

Hylas. They must.

Philonous. Can any doctrine be true that necessarily leads a man into an absurdity?

Hylas. Without doubt it cannot.

Philonous. Is it not an absurdity to think that the same thing should be at the same time both cold and warm?

Hylas. It is.

Philonous. Suppose now one of your hands hot, and the other cold, and that they are both at once put into the same vessel of water, in an intermediate state; will not the water seem cold to one hand, and warm to the other?

Hylas. It will.

Philonous. Ought we not therefore by your principles to conclude, it is really both cold and warm at the same time, that is, according to your own concession, to believe an absurdity.

Hylas. I confess it seems so.

Philonous. Consequently, the principles themselves are false, since you have granted that no true principle leads to an absurdity.

Hylas. But after all, can any thing be more absurd than to say, *there is no heat in the fire?*

Philonous. To make the point still clearer; tell me, whether in two cases exactly alike, we ought not to make the same judgment?

Hylas. We ought.

Philonous. When a pin pricks your finger, doth it not rend and divide the fibres of your flesh?

Hylas. It doth.

Philonous. And when a coal burns your finger, doth it any more?

Hylas. It doth not.

Philonous. Since therefore you neither judge the sensation itself occasioned by the pin, nor any thing like it to be in the pin; you should not, conformably to what you have now granted, judge the sensation occasioned by the fire, or any thing like it, to be in the fire.

Hylas. Well, since it must be so, I am content to yield this point, and acknowledge, that heat and cold are only sensations existing in our minds: but there still remain qualities enough to secure the reality of external things.

Philonous. But what will you say, Hylas, if it shall appear that the case is the same with regard to all other sensible qualities, and that they can no more be supposed to exist without the mind, than heat and cold?

Hylas. Then indeed you will have done something to the purpose; but that is what I despair of seeing proved.

Philonous. Let us examine them in order. What think you of tastes, do they exist without the mind, or no?

Hylas. Can any man in his senses doubt whether sugar is sweet, or wormwood bitter?

Philonous. Inform me, Hylas. Is a sweet taste a particular kind of pleasure or pleasant sensation, or is it not?

Hylas. It is.

Philonous. And is not bitterness some kind of uneasiness or pain?

Hylas. I grant it.

Philonous. If therefore sugar and wormwood are unthinking corporeal substances existing without the mind, how can sweetness and bitterness, that is, pleasure and pain, agree to them?

Hylas. Hold, Philonous, I now see what it was deluded me all this time. You asked whether heat and cold, sweetness and bitterness, were not particular sorts of pleasure and pain; to which I answered simply, that they were. Whereas I should have thus distinguished: those qualities, as perceived by us, are pleasures or pains, but not as existing in the external objects. We must not therefore conclude absolutely, that there is no heat in the fire, or sweetness in the sugar, but only that heat or sweetness, as perceived by us, are not in the fire or sugar. What say you to this?

Philonous. I say it is nothing to the purpose. Our discourse proceeded altogether concerning sensible things, which you defined to be the things we *immediately perceive by our senses*. Whatever other qualities therefore you speak of, as distinct from these, I know nothing of them, neither do they at all belong to the point in dispute. You may indeed pretend to have discovered certain qualities which you do not perceive, and assert those insensible qualities exist in fire and sugar. But what use can be made of this to your present purpose, I am at a loss to conceive. Tell me then once more, do you acknowledge that heat and cold, sweetness and bitterness (meaning those qualities which are perceived by the senses) do not exist without the mind?

Hylas. I see it is to no purpose to hold out, so I give up the cause as to those mentioned qualities. Though I profess it sounds oddly, to say that sugar is not sweet.

Philonous. But for your farther satisfaction, take this along with you: that which at other times seems sweet, shall to a distempered palate appear bitter. And nothing can be plainer, than that divers persons perceive different tastes in the same food, since that which one man delights in, another abhors. And how could this be, if the taste was something really inherent in the food?

Hylas. I acknowledge I know not how.

Philonous. In the next place, odours are to be considered. And with regard to these, I would fain know, whether what hath been said of tastes doth not exactly agree to them? Are they not so many pleasing or displeasing sensations?

Hylas. They are.

.   .   .

Philonous. May we not therefore conclude of smells, as of the other fore-mentioned qualities, that they cannot exist in any but a perceiving substance or mind?

Hylas. I think so.

Philonous. Then as to sounds, what must we think of them: are they accidents really inherent in external bodies, or not?

Hylas. That they inhere not in the sonorous bodies, is plain from hence; because a bell struck in the exhausted receiver of an air-pump, sends forth no sound. The air therefore must be thought the subject of sound.

Philonous. What reason is there for that, Hylas?

Hylas. Because when any motion is raised in the air, we perceive a sound greater or lesser, in proportion to the air's motion; but without some motion in the air, we never hear any sound at all.

Philonous. And granting that we never hear a sound but when some motion is produced in the air, yet I do not see how you can infer from thence, that the sound itself is in the air.

Hylas. It is this very motion in the external air, that produces in the mind the sensation of *sound*. For, striking on the drum of the ear, it causeth a vibration, which by the auditory nerves being communicated to the brain, the soul is thereupon affected with the sensation called *sound*.

Philonous. What! is sound then a sensation?

Hylas. I tell you, as perceived by us, it is a particular sensation in the mind.

Philonous. And can any sensation exist without the mind?

Hylas. No certainly,

Philonous. How then can sound, being a sensation exist in the air, if by the *air* you mean a senseless substance existing without the mind?

Hylas. You must distinguish, Philonous, between sound as it is perceived by us, and as it is in itself; or (which is the same thing) between the sound we immediately perceive, and that which exists without us. The former indeed is a particular kind of sensation, but the latter is merely a vibrative or undulatory motion in the air.

Philonous. I thought I had already obviated that distinction by the answer I gave when you were applying it in a like case before. But to say no more of that; are you sure then that sound is really nothing but motion?

Hylas. I am.

Philonous. Whatever therefore agrees to real sound, may with truth be attributed to motion.

Hylas. It may.

Philonous. It is then good sense to speak of *motion*, as of a thing that is *loud*, *sweet*, *acute*, or *grave*.

Hylas. I see you are resolved not to understand me. Is it not evident, those accidents or modes belong only to sensible sound, or *sound* in the common acceptation of the word, but not to *sound* in the real and philosophic sense, which, as I just now told you, is nothing but a certain motion of the air?

Philonous. It seems then there are two sorts of sound, the one vulgar, or that which is heard, the other philosophical and real.

Hylas. Even so.

Philonous. And the latter consists in motion.

Hylas. I told you so before.

Philonous. Tell me, Hylas, to which of the senses think you, the idea of motion belongs: to the hearing?

Hylas. No certainly, but to the sight and touch.

Philonous. It should follow then, that according to you, real sounds may possibly be *seen* or *felt*, but never *heard*.

Hylas. Look you, Philonous, you may if you please make a jest of my opinion, but that will not alter the truth of things. I own indeed, the inferences you draw me into, sound something oddly; but common language, you know, is framed by, and for the use of the vulgar: we must not therefore wonder, if expressions adapted to exact philosophic notions, seem uncouth and out of the way.

Philonous. Is it come to that? I assure you, I imagine myself to have gained no small point, since you make so light of departing from common phrases and opinions; it being a main part of our inquiry, to examine whose notions are widest of the common road, and most repugnant to the general sense of the world. But can you think it no more than a philosophical paradox, to say that *real sounds are never heard*, and that the idea of them is obtained by some other sense. And is there nothing in this contrary to nature and the truth of things?

Hylas. To deal ingenuously, I do not like it. And after the concessions already made, I had as well grant that sounds too have no real being without the mind.

Philonous. And I hope you will make no difficulty to acknowledge the same of colours.

Hylas. Pardon me: the case of colours is very different. Can any thing be plainer, than that we see them on the objects?

Philonous. The objects you speak of are, I suppose, corporeal substances existing without the mind.

Hylas. They are.

Philonous. And have true and real colours inhering in them?

Hylas. Each visible object hath that colour which we see in it.

Philonous. How! Is there any thing visible but what we perceive by sight?

Hylas. There is not.

Philonous. And do we perceive anything by sense, which we do not perceive immediately?

Hylas. How often must I be obliged to repeat the same thing? I tell you, we do not.

Philonous. Have patience, good Hylas; and tell me once more, whether there is any thing immediately perceived by the senses, except sensible qualities. I know you asserted there was not: but I would now be informed, whether you still persist in the same opinion.

Hylas. I do.

Philonous. Pray, is your corporeal substance either a sensible quality, or made up of sensible qualities?

Hylas. What a question that is! who ever thought it was?

Philonous. My reason for asking was, because in saying, *each visible object hath that colour which we see in it,* you make visible objects to be corporeal substances; which implies either that corporeal substances are sensible qualities, or else that there is something beside sensible qualities perceived by sight: but as this point was formerly agreed between us, and is still maintained by you, it is a clear consequence, that your corporeal substance is nothing distinct from sensible qualities.

Hylas. You may draw as many absurd consequences as you please, and endeavour to perplex the plainest things; but you shall never persuade me out of my senses. I clearly understand my own meaning.

Philonous. I wish you would make me understand it too. But since you are unwilling to have your notion of corporeal substance examined, I shall urge that point no farther. Only be pleased to let me know, whether the same colours which we see, exist in external bodies, or some other.

Hylas. The very same.

Philonous. What! are then the beautiful red and purple we see on yonder clouds, really in them? Or do you imagine they have in themselves any other form, than that of a dark mist or vapour?

Hylas. I must own, Philonous, those colours are not really in the clouds as they seem to be at this distance. They are only apparent colours.

Philonous. Apparent call you them? how shall we distinguish these apparent colours from real?

Hylas. Very easily. Those are to be thought apparent, which appearing only at a distance, vanish upon a nearer approach.

Philonous. And those I suppose are to be thought real, which are discovered by the most near and exact survey.

Hylas. Right.

Philonous. Is the nearest and exactest survey made by the help of a microscope, or by the naked eye?

Hylas. By a microscope, doubtless.

Philonous. But a microscope often discovers colours in an object different from those perceived by the unassisted sight. And in case we had microscopes magnifying to any assigned degree; it is certain, that no object whatsoever viewed through them, would appear in the same colour which it exhibits to the naked eye.

Hylas. And what will you conclude from all this? You cannot argue that there are really and naturally no colours on objects: because by artificial managements they may be altered, or made to vanish.

Philonous. I think it may evidently be concluded from your own concessions, that all the colours we see with our naked eyes, are only apparent as those on the clouds, since they vanish upon a more close and accurate inspection, which is afforded us by a microscope. Then as to what you say by way of prevention: I ask you, whether the real and natural state of an object is better discovered by a very sharp and piercing sight, or by one which is less sharp?

Hylas. By the former without doubt.

Philonous. Is it not plain from *dioptrics*, that microscopes make the sight more penetrating, and represent objects as they would appear to the eye, in case it were naturally endowed with a most exquisite sharpness?

Hylas. It is.

Philonous. Consequently the microscopical representation is to be thought that which best sets forth the real nature of the thing, or what it is in itself. The colours therefore by it perceived, are more genuine and real, than those perceived otherwise.

Hylas. I confess there is something in what you say.

Philonous. Besides, it is not only possible but manifest, that there actually are animals, whose eyes are by Nature framed to perceive those things, which by reason of their minuteness escape our sight. What think you of those inconceivably small animals perceived by glasses? Must we suppose they are all stark blind? Or, in case they see, can it be imagined their sight hath not the same use in preserving their bodies from injuries, which appears in that of all other animals? And if it hath, is it not evident, they must see particles less than their own bodies, which will present them with a far different view in each object, from that which strikes our senses? Even our own eyes do not always represent objects to us after the same manner. In the *jaundice*, every one knows that all things seem yellow. Is it not therefore highly probable, those animals in whose eyes we discern a very different texture from that of ours, and whose bodies abound with different humours, do not see the same colours in every object that we do? From all which, should it not seem to follow, that all colours are equally apparent, and that none of those which we perceive are really inherent in any outward object?

Hylas. It should.

Philonous. The point will be past all doubt, if you consider, that in case colours were real properties or affections inherent in external bodies, they could admit of no alteration, without some change wrought in the very bodies themselves: but is it not evident from what hath been said, that upon the use of microscopes, upon a change happening in the humours of the eye, or a variation of distance, without any manner of real alteration in the thing itself, the colours of any object are either changed, or totally disappear? Nay all other circumstances remaining the same, change but the situation of some objects, and they shall present different colours to the eye. The same thing happens upon viewing an object in various degrees of light. And what is more known, than that the same bodies appear differently coloured by candle-light, from what they do in the open day? Add to these the experiment of a prism, which separating the heterogeneous rays of light, alters the colour of any object; and will cause the whitest to appear of a deep blue or red to the naked eye. And now tell me, whether you are still of opinion, that every body hath its true real colour inhering in it; and if you think it hath, I would fain know farther from you, what certain distance and position of the object, what peculiar texture and formation of the eye, what degree or kind of light is necessary for ascertaining that true colour, and distinguishing it from apparent ones.

Hylas. I own myself entirely satisfied, that they are all equally apparent; and that there is no such thing as colour really inhering in external bodies, but that it is altogether in the light. And what confirms me in this opinion is, that in proportion to the light, colours are still more or less vivid; and if there be no light, then are there no colours perceived. Besides, allowing there are colours on external objects, yet how is it possible for us to perceive them? For no external body affects the mind, unless it act first on our organs of sense. But the only action of bodies is motion; and motion cannot be communicated otherwise than by impulse. A distant object therefore cannot act on the eye, nor consequently make itself or its properties perceivable to the soul. Whence it plainly follows, that it is immediately some contiguous substance, which operating on the eye occasions a perception of colours: and such is light.

Philonous. How! is light then a substance?

Hylas. I tell you, Philonous, external light is nothing but a thin fluid substance, whose minute particles being agitated with a brisk motion, and in various manners reflected from the different surfaces of outward objects to the eyes, communicate different motions to the optic nerves; which being propagated to the brain, cause therein various impressions: and these are attended with the sensations of red, blue, yellow, &c.

Philonous. It seems then, the light doth no more than shake the optic nerves.

Hylas. Nothing else.

Philonous. And consequent to each particular motion of the nerves the mind is affected with a sensation, which is some particular colour.

Hylas. Right.

Philonous. And these sensations have no existence without the mind.

Hylas. They have not.

Philonous. How then do you affirm that colours are in the light, since by *light* you understand a corporeal substance external to the mind?

Hylas. Light and colours, as immediately perceived by us, I grant cannot exist without the mind. But in themselves they are only the motions and configurations of certain insensible particles of matter.

Philonous. Colours then in the vulgar sense, or taken for the immediate objects of sight, cannot agree to any but a perceiving substance.

Hylas. That is what I say.

Philonous. Well then, since you give up the point as to those sensible qualities, which are alone thought colours by all mankind beside, you may hold what you please with regard to those invisible ones of the philosophers. It is not my business to dispute about them; only I would advise you to bethink your self, whether considering the inquiry we are upon, it be prudent for you to affirm, *the red and blue which we see are not real colours, but certain unknown motions and figures which no man ever did or can see, are truly so*. Are not these shocking notions, and are not they subject to as many ridiculous inferences, as those you were obliged to renounce before in the case of sounds?

Hylas. I frankly own, Philonous, that it is in vain to stand out any longer. Colours, sounds, tastes, in a word, all those termed *secondary qualities*, have certainly no existence without the mind. But by this acknowledgment I must not be supposed to derogate any thing from the reality of matter or external objects, seeing it is no more than several philosophers maintain, who nevertheless are the farthest imaginable from denying matter. For the clearer understanding of this, you must know sensible qualities are by philosophers divided into *primary* and *secondary*. The former are extension, figure, solidity, gravity, motion, and rest. And these they hold exist really in bodies. The latter are those above enumerated; or briefly, all sensible qualities beside the primary, which they assert are only so many sensations or ideas existing no where but in the mind. But all this, I doubt not, you are already apprised of. For my part, I have been a long time sensible there was such an opinion current among philosophers, but was never thoroughly convinced of its truth till now.

Philonous. You are still then of opinion, that extension and figures are inherent in external unthinking substances.

Hylas. I am.

Philonous. But what if the same arguments which are brought against secondary qualities, will hold good against these also?

Hylas. Why then I shall be obliged to think, they too exist only in the mind.

Philonous. Is it your opinion, the very figure and extension which you perceive by sense, exist in the outward object or material substance?

Hylas. It is.

Philonous. Have all other animals as good grounds to think the same of the figure and extension which they see and feel?

Hylas. Without doubt, if they have any thought at all.

Philonous. Answer me, Hylas. Think you the senses were bestowed upon all animals for their preservation and well-being in life? or were they given to men alone for this end?

Hylas. I make no question but they have the same use in all other animals.

Philonous. If so, is it not necessary they should be enabled by them to perceive their own limbs, and those bodies which are capable of harming them?

Hylas. Certainly.

Philonous. A mite therefore must be supposed to see his own foot, and things equal or even less than it, as bodies of some considerable dimension; though at the same time they appear to you scarce discernible, or at best as so many visible points.

Hylas. I cannot deny it.

Philonous. And to creatures less than the mite they will seem yet larger.

Hylas. They will.

Philonous. Insomuch that what you can hardly discern, will to another extremely minute animal appear as some huge mountain.

Hylas. All this I grant.

Philonous. Can one and the same thing be at the same time in itself of different dimensions?

Hylas. That were absurd to imagine.

Philonous. But from what you have laid down it follows, that both the extension by you perceived, and that perceived by the mite itself, as likewise all those perceived by lesser animals, are each of them the true extension of the mite's foot, that is to say, by your own principles you are led into an absurdity.

Hylas. There seems to be some difficulty in the point.

Philonous. Again, have you not acknowledged that no real inherent property of any object can be changed, without some change in the thing itself?

Hylas. I have.

Philonous. But as we approach to or recede from an object, the visible extension varies, being at one distance ten or an hundred times greater than at another. Doth it not therefore follow from hence likewise, that it is not really inherent in the object?

Hylas. I own I am at a loss what to think.

Philonous. Your judgment will soon be determined, if you will venture to think as freely concerning this quality, as you have done concerning the rest. Was it not admitted as a good argument, that neither heat nor cold was in the water, because it seemed warm to one hand, and cold to the other?

Hylas. It was.

Philonous. Is it not the very same reasoning to conclude, there is no extension or figure in an object, because to one eye it shall seem little, smooth, and round, when at the same time it appears to the other, great, uneven, and angular?

Hylas. The very same. But doth this latter fact ever happen?

Philonous. You may at any time make the experiment, by looking with one eye bare, and with the other through a microscope.

Hylas. I know not how to maintain it, and yet I am loth to give up *extension*, I see so many odd consequences following upon such a concession.

Philonous. Odd, say you? After the concessions already made, I hope you will stick at nothing for its oddness. But on the other hand should it not seem very odd, if the general reasoning which includes all other sensible qualities did not also include extension? If it be allowed that no idea nor any thing like an idea can exist in an unperceiving substance, then surely it follows, that no figure or mode of extension, which we can either perceive or imagine, or have any idea of, can be really inherent in matter; not to mention the peculiar difficulty there must be, in conceiving a material substance, prior to and distinct from extension, to be the *substratum* of extension. Be the sensible quality what it will, figure, or sound, or colour; it seems alike impossible it should subsist in that which doth not perceive it.

Hylas. I give up the point for the present, reserving still a right to retract my opinion, in case I shall hereafter discover any false step in my progress to it.

Philonous. That is a right you cannot be denied. Figures and extension being dispatched, we proceed next to *motion*. Can a real motion in any external body be at the same time both very swift and very slow?

Hylas. It cannot.

Philonous. Is not the motion of a body swift in a reciprocal proportion to the time it takes up in describing any given space? Thus a body that describes a mile in an hour, moves three times faster than it would in case it described only a mile in three hours.

Hylas. I agree with you.

Philonous. And is not time measured by the succession of ideas in our minds?

Hylas. It is.

Philonous. And is it not possible ideas should succeed one another twice as fast in your mind, as they do in mine, or in that of some spirit of another kind.

Hylas. I own it.

Philonous. Consequently the same body may to another seem to perform its motion over any space in half the time that it doth to you. And the same reasoning will hold as to any other proportion: that is to say, according to your principles (since the motions perceived are both really in the object) it is possible one and the same body shall be really moved the same way at once, both very swift and very slow. How is this consistent either with common sense, or with what you just now granted?

Hylas. I have nothing to say to it.

Philonous. Then as for *solidity;* either you do not mean any sensible quality by that word, and so it is beside our inquiry: or if you do, it must be either hardness or resistance. But both the one and the other are plainly relative to our senses: it being evident, that what seems hard to one animal, may appear soft to another, who hath greater force and firmness of limbs. Nor is it less plain, that the resistance I feel is not in the body.

.   .   .

Hylas. I wonder, Philonous, if what you say be true, why those philosophers who deny the secondary qualities any real existence, should yet attribute it to the primary. If there is no difference between them, how can this be accounted for?

.   .   .

Philonous. Can you even separate the ideas of extension and motion, from the ideas of all those qualities which they who make the distinction, term *secondary*.

.   .   .

. . . Since therefore it is impossible even for the mind to disunite the ideas of extension and motion from all other sensible qualities, doth it not follow, that where the one exist, there necessarily the other exist likewise?

Hylas. It should seem so.

Philonous. Consequently the very same arguments which you admitted, as conclusive against the secondary qualities, are without any farther application of force against the primary too. Besides, if you will trust your senses, is it not plain all sensible qualities coexist, or to them, appear as being in the same place? Do they ever represent a motion, or figure, as being divested of all other visible and tangible qualities?

Hylas. You need say no more on this head. I am free to own, if there be no secret error or oversight in our proceedings hitherto, that all sensible qualities are alike to be denied existence without the mind. But my fear is, that I have been too liberal in my former concessions, or overlooked some fallacy or other. In short, I did not take time to think.

Philonous. For that matter, Hylas, you may take what time you please in reviewing the progress of our inquiry. You are at liberty to recover any slips you might have made, or offer whatever you have omitted, which makes for your first opinion.

Hylas. One great oversight I take to be this: that I did not sufficiently distinguish the *object* from the *sensation.* Now though this latter may not exist without the mind, yet it will not thence follow that the former cannot.

Philonous. What object do you mean? the object of the senses?

Hylas. The same.

Philonous. It is then immediately perceived.

Hylas. Right.

Philonous. Make me to understand the difference between what is immediately perceived, and a sensation.

Hylas. The sensation I take to be an act of the mind perceiving; beside which, there is something perceived; and this I call the *object.* For example, there is red and yellow on that tulip. But then the act of perceiving those colours is in me only, and not in the tulip.

Philonous. What tulip do you speak of? is it that which you see?

Hylas. The same.

Philonous. And what do you see beside colour, figure, and extension?

Hylas. Nothing.

Philonous. What you would say then is, that the red and yellow are coexistent with the extension; is it not?

Hylas. That is not all; I would say, they have a real existence without the mind, in some unthinking substance.

Philonous. That the colours are really in the tulip which I see, is manifest. Neither can it be denied, that this tulip may exist independent of your mind or mine; but that any immediate object of the senses, that is, any idea, or combination of ideas, should exist in an unthinking substance, or exterior to all minds, is in itself an evident contradiction. Nor can I imagine how this follows from what you said just now, to wit that the red and yellow were on the tulip *you saw*, since you do not pretend to *see* that unthinking substance.

.   •   •

14
SENSE-DATA

G. E. Moore

. . . I shall . . . begin discussing the various ways in which we know of the existence of material objects—*supposing* that we do know of their existence. I do not want to assume, to begin with, that we *certainly do* know that they exist. I only want to consider what sort of a thing our knowledge of them is, *supposing* that it is really knowledge. . . .

And I . . . should begin with the most primitive sort of way in which we commonly suppose that we have knowledge of them—namely, that kind of knowledge, which we should call knowledge *by means of the senses*—the knowledge which we have, for instance, by seeing and feeling, as when we feel an object over with our hands. This way of knowing material objects, by means of the senses, is, of course, by no means the only way in which we commonly suppose we know of their existence. For instance, each of us knows of the past existence of many material objects by means of memory; we remember the existence of objects which we are no longer perceiving by any of our senses. We know of others again, which we ourselves have never perceived by our senses and cannot therefore remember, by the testimony of other persons who *have* perceived them by their senses. And we know also, we suppose, by means of inference, of others which nobody has ever perceived by his senses: we know, for instance, in this way that there is another surface of the moon, different from that which is constantly turned to the earth. All these other ways of knowing material objects, I shall have presently to consider, and to contrast them with sense-perception. But all these other ways do seem, in a sense, to be *based* upon sense-perception, so that *it* is, in a sense, the most primitive way of knowing material objects: it seems, in fact, to be true, that if I had not known of *some* material objects by means of sense-perception, I could never possibly have known of any others in any of these other ways; and this seems to be true universally: no man could ever know of the existence of any material objects at all, unless he first knew of *some* by means of his senses. The evidence of the senses is,

From G. E. Moore, *Some Main Problems of Philosophy* (London: George Allen & Unwin Ltd., 1953), Chap. II, pp. 28–38, 40, 42–44. Reprinted by permission of the publisher.

therefore, the evidence upon which all our other ways of knowing material objects seems to be based.

And what I want first to consider is what sort of a thing this evidence of the senses is; or in other words what it is that happens when (as we should say) we see, or feel, a material object, or perceive one by any other sense. And I propose to take as an instance, for the sake of simplicity, a single sense *only*—namely, the sense of sight: I shall use what happens when we *see*, as an illustration of what happens in sense-perception generally. All the general principles which I point out with regard to the sense of seeing, will, I think, be easily transferable, *mutatis mutandis*, to all the other senses by which we can be said to perceive material objects.

My first question is, then: What exactly is it that happens, when (as we should say) we *see* a material object? And I should explain, perhaps, to avoid misunderstanding, that the occurrence which I mean here to analyse is merely the *mental* occurrence—the act of consciousness—which we call *seeing*. I do not mean to say anything at all about the bodily processes which occur in the eye and the optic nerves and the brain. I have no doubt, myself, that these bodily processes *do* occur, when we see; and that physiologists really do *know* a great deal about them. But all that I shall mean by '*seeing*', and all that I wish to talk about, is the mental occurrence—the act of consciousness—which occurs (as is supposed) as a consequence of or accompaniment of these bodily processes. This mental occurrence, which I call 'seeing', is known to us in a much more simple and direct way, than are the complicated physiological processes which go on in our eyes and nerves and brains. A man cannot directly observe the minute processes which go on in his own eyes and nerves and brain when he sees; but all of us who are not blind can directly observe this mental occurrence, which we mean by seeing. And it is solely with *seeing*, in this sense—seeing, as an act of consciousness which we can all of us directly observe as happening in our own minds—that I am now concerned.

And I wish to illustrate what I have to say about seeing by a direct practical example; because, though I dare say many of you are perfectly familiar with the sort of points I wish to raise, it is, I think, very important for every one, in these subjects, to consider carefully single concrete instances, so that there may be no mistake as to exactly what it is that is being talked about. Such mistakes are, I think, very apt to happen, if one talks merely in generalities; and moreover one is apt to overlook important points. I propose, therefore, to hold up an envelope in my hand, and to ask you all to look at it for a moment; and then to consider with me exactly what it is that happens, when you see it: *what* this occurrence, which we call the *seeing* of it, *is*.

I hold up this envelope, then: I look at it, and I hope you all will look at it. And now I put it down again. Now what has happened? We should certainly say (if you have looked at it) that we all *saw* that envelope, that we all saw *it, the same* envelope: *I* saw it, and you all saw it. We all saw *the same* object. And by the *it*, which we all saw, we mean an object, which, at any one of the moments when we were looking at it, occupied just *one* of the many places that constitute the whole of space. Even during the short time in which we were looking at it, it may have moved—occupied successively several different places; for the earth, we believe, is constantly going round on its axis, and carrying with it all the objects on its surface, so that, even while we looked at the envelope, it probably moved and changed its position in space, though we did not see it move. But at any *one* moment, we should say, this *it,* the envelope, which we say we all saw, was at some *one* definite place in space.

But now, what happened to each of us, when we saw that envelope? I will begin by describing *part* of what happened to me. I saw a patch[1] of a particular whitish colour, having a certain size, and a certain shape, a shape with rather sharp angles or corners and bounded by fairly straight lines. These things: this patch of a whitish colour, and its size and shape I did actually see. And I propose to call these things, the colour and size and shape, *sense-data,*[2] things *given* or presented by the senses—given, in this case, by my sense of sight. Many philosophers have called these things which I call sense-data, *sensations.* They would say, for instance, that that particular patch of colour was a sensation. But it seems to me that this term 'sensation' is liable to be misleading. We should certainly say that I *had* a sensation, when I saw that colour. But when we say that I *had* a sensation, what we mean is, I think, that I had the experience which consisted in my *seeing* the colour. That is to say, what we mean by a 'sensation' in this phrase, is my *seeing* of the colour, not the colour which I saw: this colour does not seem to be what I mean to say that I *had,* when I say I *had* a sensation of colour. It is very unnatural to say that I *had* the colour, that I *had* that particular whitish grey or that I *had* the patch which was of that colour. What I certainly did *have* is the experience which consisted in my seeing the colour and the patch. And when, therefore, we talk of *having* sensations, I think what we mean by 'sensations' is the experiences which consist in apprehending certain sense-data, *not* these sense-data themselves. I think, then, that the term 'sensation' is liable to be misleading, because it may be used in two different senses, which it is very important to distinguish from one another. It may be used *either* for the colour which I saw or for the experience which consisted in my seeing it. And it is, I think very important, for several reasons, to distinguish these two things. I will mention only two of these reasons. In the first place, it is, I think, quite conceivable (I do not say it is actually true) but *conceivable* that the patch of colour which I saw may have continued to exist after I saw it: whereas, of course, when I ceased to see it, *my seeing* of it ceased to exist. I will illustrate what I mean, by holding up the envelope again, and looking at it. I look at it, and I again see a *sense-datum,* a patch of a whitish colour. But now I immediately turn away my eyes, and I no longer see that sense-datum: my seeing of it has ceased to exist. But I am by no means sure that the sense-datum—that very same patch of whitish colour which I saw—is not still *existing* and still there. I do not say, for certain, that it is: I think very likely it is not. But I have a strong inclination to believe that it is. And it seems to me at least *conceivable*

---

[1] I am so extending the use of the word 'patch' that, *e.g.,* the very small black dot which I directly apprehend when I see a full-stop, or the small black line which I directly apprehend when I see a hyphen, are, each of them, in the sense in which I am using the word, a 'patch of colour'. (1952).

[2] I should now make, and have for many years made, a sharp distinction between what I have called the 'patch', on the one hand, and the colour, size and shape, *of* which it is, on the other; and should call, and have called, *only* the patch, *not* its colour, size or shape, a 'sense-datum'. (1952).

that it should be still existing, whereas my *seeing* of it certainly has ceased to exist. This is one reason for distinguishing between the sense-data which I see, and my seeing of them. And here is another. It seems to me *conceivable* —here again I do not say it is true but *conceivable*—that some sense-data —this whitish colour for instance—are in the place in which the material object—the envelope, is. It seems to me *conceivable* that this whitish colour is really on the surface of the material envelope. Whereas it does not seem to me that my *seeing* of it is in that place. My seeing of it is in another place—somewhere within my body. Here, then, are two reasons for distinguishing between the *sense-data* which I see, and my *seeing* of them. And it seems to me that both of these two very different things are often meant when people talk about 'sensations'. In fact, when you are reading any philosopher who is talking about sensations (or about sense-*impressions* or *ideas* either), you need to look very carefully to see which of the two he is talking about in any particular passage—whether of the sense-data them-selves or of our apprehension of them: you will, I think, almost invariably find that he is talking now of the one and now of the other, and very often that he is assuming that what is true of the one must also be true of the other—an assumption which does not seem to be at all justified. I think, there-fore, that the term 'sensation' is liable to be very misleading. And I shall, therefore, never use it. I shall always talk of *sense-data*, when what I mean is such things as this colour and size and shape or the patch which is *of* this colour and size and shape, which I actually see. And when I want to talk of my seeing of them, I shall expressly call this the seeing of sense-data; or, if I want a term which will apply equally to all the senses, I shall speak of the *direct apprehension of* sense-data. Thus when I see this whitish colour, I am *directly apprehending* this whitish colour: my seeing of it, as a mental act, an act of consciousness, just consists in my direct apprehension of it;—so too when I hear a sound, I directly apprehend the sound; when I feel a tooth-ache I directly apprehend the ache: and all these things—the whitish colour, the sound and the ache are *sense-data*.

To return, then, to what happened to us, when we all saw the same envelope. Part, at least, of what happened to me, I can now express by saying that I saw certain sense-data: I saw a whitish patch of colour, of a particular size and shape. And I have no doubt whatever that this is part, at least, of what happened to all of you. You also saw certain sense-data; and I expect also that the sense-data which you saw were more or less similar to those which I saw. You also saw a patch of colour which might be described as whitish, of a size not very different from the size of the patch which I saw, and of a shape similar at least in this that it had rather sharp corners and was bounded by fairly straight lines. But now, what I want to emphasize is this. Though we all did (as we should say) see *the same* envelope, no two of us, in all probability, saw exactly the *same sense-data*. Each of us, in all probability, saw, to begin with, a slightly different shade of colour. All these colours may have been whitish; but each was probably at least slightly different from all the rest, according to the way in which the light fell upon the paper, relatively to the different positions you are sitting in; and again according to differences in the strength of your eye-sight, or your distance from the paper. And so too, with regard to the size of the patch of colour which you saw: differences in the strength of your eyes and in your distance from the envelope probably made slight differences in the size of the patch of colour, which you saw. And so again with regard to the shape. Those of you on that side of the room will have seen a rhomboidal figure, while those in front of me will have seen a figure more nearly rectangular. Those on my left will have seen a figure more like this which you in front now see, and which you see is different from *this* which you then saw. And those in front of me will have seen a figure like that which you on the left now see, and which, you see, is different from *this*, which you saw before. Those directly in front of me, may, indeed, have all seen very nearly the same figure—perhaps, even, exactly the same. But we should not say we *knew* that any two did; whereas we should say we did *know* that we all saw the *same* envelope. That you did all see the same envelope, would, indeed, be accepted in ordinary life as a certainty of the strongest kind. Had you all seen me commit a murder, as clearly as you all saw this envelope, your evidence would be accepted by any jury as sufficient to hang me. Such evidence would be accepted in any court of law as quite conclusive; we should take such a responsibility as that of hanging a man, upon it. It would be accepted, that is, that you had all seen me, *the same man*, commit a murder; and not merely that you had all seen some man or other, possibly each of you a different man in each case, commit one. And yet, in this case, as in the case of the envelope, the sense-data which you had all seen, would have been different sense-data: you could not swear in a court of law that you had all seen exactly the *same sense-data*.

Now all this seems to me to shew very clearly, that, *if* we *did* all see the same envelope, the envelope which we saw was not *identical with* the sense-data which we saw: the envelope cannot be exactly the same thing as each of the sets of sense-data, which we each of us saw; for these were in all probability each of them slightly different from all the rest, and they cannot, therefore, *all* be exactly the same thing as the envelope.

But it might be said: Of course, when we say that we all saw the envelope, we do not mean that we all saw the *whole* of it. I, for instance, only saw *this* side of it, whereas all of you only saw *that* side. And generally, when we talk of seeing an object we only mean seeing some *part* of it. There is always more in any object which we see, than the *part* of it which we see.

And this, I think, is quite true. Whenever we talk roughly of seeing any object, it is true that, in another and stricter sense of the word *see*, we only see *a part of* it. And it might, therefore, be suggested that why we say we all saw this envelope, when we each, in fact, saw a different set of sense-data, is because each of these *sets of sense-data* is, in fact, a *part* of the envelope.

But it seems to me there is a great difficulty even in maintaining that the different sense-data we all saw are parts of the envelope. What do we mean by a *part* of a material object? We mean, I think, at least this. What we call a part of a material object must be something which occupies a part of the volume in space occupied by the whole object. For instance, this envelope occupies a certain volume in space: that is to say, it occupies a space which has breadth and thickness as well as length. And anything which is a *part* of the envelope at any moment, must be *in* some part of the volume of space occupied by the whole envelope at that moment: it must be somewhere within that volume, or at some point in the surfaces bounding that volume.

Are, then, any of the sense-data we saw *parts* of the envelope in this sense?

The sense-data I mentioned were these three—the colour—the whitish colour; the *size* of this colour; its *shape*.[3] And of these three it is only the colour, which could, in the sense defined, possibly be supposed to be a *part* of the envelope. The colour might be supposed to occupy a *part* of the volume occupied by the envelope—one of its bounding surfaces,[4] for instance. But the size and shape could hardly be said to *occupy* any part of this volume. What might be true of them is that the size I saw *is* the size of one surface of the envelope; and that the shape *is* the shape of this surface of the envelope. The side of the envelope which I say I saw certainly *has* some size and some shape; and the sense-data—the size and shape, which I saw as the size and shape of a patch of colour—might possibly *be* the size and shape of this side of the envelope.

Let us consider whether these things are so.

And, first, as to the colours. Can these possibly be parts of the envelope? What we supposed is that each of you probably saw a slightly different colour. And if we are to suppose that *all* those colours are parts of the envelope, then we must suppose that *all* of them are in the same place. We must suppose that ever so many different colours all of them occupy the same surface—this surface of the envelope which you now see. And I think it is certainly difficult to suppose this, though not absolutely impossible. It is not absolutely impossible, I think, that all the different colours which you see are really all of them in the same place. But I myself find it difficult to believe that this is so; and you can understand, I think, why most philosophers should have declared it to be impossible. They have declared, chiefly, I think, on grounds like this, that none of the colours which any of us ever see are ever parts of material objects: they have declared that none of them are ever in any part of the places where material objects (if there are any material objects) are. This conclusion does, indeed, go beyond what the premisses justify, even if we accept the premiss that several different colours cannot all be in exactly the same place. For it remains possible that the colour, which some *one* of you sees, is really on the surface of the envelope; whereas the colours which all the rest of you see are *not* there. But if so, then we must say that though all of you are seeing the same side of the envelope, yet only one of you is seeing a sense-datum which is a part of that side: the sense-data seen by all the rest are *not* parts of the envelope. And this also, I think, is difficult to believe. It might be, indeed, that those of you who are seeing a colour, which is *not* a part of the envelope, might yet be seeing a size and a shape which really *is* the size and shape of one side of the envelope; and we will go on to consider whether *this* is so.

And, first, as to the size. I assumed that the sense-given sizes, which you see, are all of them probably slightly different from one another. And, if this be so, then certainly it seems to be absolutely impossible that they should *all*

---

[3] I had here forgotten that one of the sense-data mentioned was the *patch* which *has* that colour and shape and size—the *patch* which, I should now say, is the *only* 'sense-datum', having to do with the envelope, which I then saw. (1952).

[4] I should now say that any part of the *surface* of a volume is *not* a part of the volume, because it is not itself a volume. (1952).

of them be the size of this side of the envelope. This side of the envelope can only really have *one* size; it cannot have several different sizes. But it may not seem quite clear, that you all do see different sizes; the differences between the different distances at which you are from the envelope are not so great, but what the patches of colour you all see might be, at least, of *much the same* size. So I will give a hypothetical instance to make my point clearer. Suppose this room were so large that I could carry the envelope two or three hundred yards away from you. The sense-given size which you would then see, when I was three hundred yards off, would certainly be appreciably smaller than what you see now. And yet you would still be seeing this same envelope. It seems quite impossible that these two very different sizes should both of them be *the* size of the envelope. So that here the *only* possibility is that the size which you see at some *one* definite distance or set of distances, should be the envelope's real size, *if* you ever see its real size at all. This may be so: it may be that some one of the sense-given sizes which we see is the envelope's real size. But it seems also possible that none of them are; and in any case we all see the envelope, just the same, *whether* we see its real size or not.

And now for the shape. Here again it seems quite impossible that *all* the shapes we see can be the envelope's real shape. This side of the envelope can have but *one* shape: it cannot be both rhomboidal, as is the shape which you on the left see, and also rectangular, as is the shape seen by those in front; the angles at its corners cannot be both right angles and also very far from right angles. Certainly, therefore, the sense-given shape which some of you see is *not* the shape of this side of the envelope. But here it may be said, it is plain enough that one of the sense-given shapes seen *is* its real shape. You may say: The shape seen by those in front *is* its real shape; the envelope *is* rectangular. And I quite admit that this is so: I think we do know, in fact, that the envelope really is *roughly* rectangular. But here I want to introduce a distinction. There are two different senses in which we may talk of *the* shape of anything. A rectangle of the size of this envelope, and a rectangle of the size of this blackboard, may both, in a sense, have exactly *the same* shape. They may have the same shape in the sense, that all the angles of both are right angles, and that the proportions between the sides of the one, and those between the sides of the other, are the same. They may, in fact, have the same shape, in the sense in which a big square always has the same shape as a small square, however big the one may be and however small the other. But there is another sense in which *the* shape of a big square is obviously not *the same* as that of a small square. We may mean by *the* shape of a big square the actual lines bounding it; and if we mean this, *the* shape of a big square cannot possibly be the *same* as *the* shape of a smaller one. The lines bounding the two cannot possibly be the *same* lines. And the same thing may be true, even when there is no difference in size between two shapes. Imagine *two* squares, of the same size, side by side. The lines bounding the one are *not* the same lines as those bounding the other: though each is both *of* the same shape and *of* the same size as the other. The difference between these two senses in which we may talk of *the* shape of anything, may be expressed by saying that the shape of the big square is the same *in quality*—qualitatively identical—with that of the small square, but is not *numerically* the same—not numerically identical: the shape of the big square is *numerically* different from that of the small, in the sense that they are *two* shapes, and not one only, of which we are talking, though both are the same in quality: both are *squares*, but the one is *one* square and the other is *another* square. There is, then, a difference between two different kinds of identity: qualitative identity and numerical identity; and we are all perfectly familiar with the difference between the two, though the names may sound strange. I shall in future use these names: qualitative identity and numerical identity. And now to return to the case of the envelope. Even supposing that the sense-given shape which you in front see is rectangular, and that the real shape of the envelope is also rectangular, and that both are rectangles of exactly the same shape; it still does not follow that the sense-given shape which you see is *the* shape of the envelope. The sense-given shape and the shape of the envelope, even if they are qualitatively the same, *must* still be *two* different shapes, *numerically* different, unless they are *of the same size;* just as *the* shape of a large square must be numerically different from *the* shape of a smaller one. And we saw before how difficult it was to be sure that any of the sizes which you saw were the *real* size of the envelope. And even if the sense-given size which some one of you sees *is* the real size of the envelope, it still does not follow that the sense-given *shape* which you see is numerically the same as the shape of the envelope. The two may be numerically different, just as in the case of two different squares, side by side, of the same shape and size, *the* shape of the one *is* not *the* shape of the other; they are two numerically different shapes. We may say, then, that if those of you who see rectangular shapes, do see rectangular shapes of different sizes, only one of these can possibly be *the* shape of the envelope: all the others may be *of* the same shape—the same in quality—but they cannot be *the* shape of the envelope. And even if some *one* of you does see a shape, which is of the same size as *the* shape of the envelope, as well as being of the same shape (and it is very doubtful whether any of you does) it would yet be by no means certain that this sense-given shape which you saw was *the* shape of the envelope. It might be a shape *numerically* different from *the* shape of the envelope, although exactly similar both in shape and size. And finally there is some reason to suppose that none of the sense-given shapes which any of you see are *exactly* the same, even in quality, as *the* shape of the envelope. The envelope itself probably has a more or less irregular edge; there are probably ups and downs in the line bounding its side, which you at that distance cannot see.

Of the three kinds of sense-data,[5] then, which you all of you saw, when I held up the envelope, namely, the whitish colour, its size, and its shape, the following things seem to be true. First, as regards the colour, no one of you can be sure that the exact colour which you saw was really a part of the envelope—was really in any part of the space, which the real envelope (if there was a real envelope) occupied. Then as regards the size, no one of you can be sure that the size which you saw was the real size of the envelope. And finally as regards the shape, no one of you can be sure that the shape which you saw was really of exactly the same shape as that of the envelope; still less can you be sure that it *was the* shape of the envelope, that the bounding lines which composed it were numerically the same bounding lines as those which enclosed the envelope. And not only can none of you be sure

[5] The *patch* itself, which *has* that colour and shape and size, again forgotten! (1952).

of these things. As regards the sizes and shapes which you saw, it seems quite certain that some of you saw sizes and shapes which were *not* the real size and shape of the envelope; because it seems quite certain that some of you saw sizes and shapes different from those seen by others, and that these different sizes and shapes cannot possibly *all* be *the* size and shape of the envelope. And as regards the colours it seems fairly certain, that the colours which you saw cannot all have been *in* the envelope; since it seems fairly certain that you all saw slightly different colours, and it is difficult to believe, though not absolutely impossible, that all these different colours were really in the same place at the same time.

This seems to be the state of things with regard to these sense-data—the colour, the size and the shape. They seem, in a sense, to have had very little to do with the real envelope, if there *was* a real envelope. It seems very probable that *none* of the colours seen was really a part of the envelope; and that *none* of the sizes and shapes seen were the size or the shape of the real envelope.

.   .   .

Well now: Chiefly, I think, for reasons of the sort which I have given you, an overwhelming majority of philosophers have adopted the following views.

.   .   .

. . . They have held, that is (1) that absolutely every sense-datum that any person ever directly apprehends exists only so long as he apprehends it, (2) that no sense-datum which any one person directly apprehends ever is directly apprehended by any other person, and (3) that no sense-datum that is directly apprehended by one person can be in *the same space with* any sense-datum apprehended by any other person—that no sense-datum that is seen or heard or felt by me can possibly be either in the same place with or at any distance from any that is seen or heard or felt by any one else. These three things are, I think, the chief things that are meant, when it is said that all sense-data exist only *in the mind of* the person who apprehends them; and it is certainly the common view in philosophy that all sense-data do only exist *in our minds*. I do not think myself that this is a good way of expressing what is meant. Even if all these three things are true of all the sense-data which I ever directly apprehend; it does not seem to me to follow that they exist only in my mind, or indeed are *in* my mind in any sense at all except that they are apprehended by me. They are, so far as I can see, not in my mind in the sense in which my apprehension of them is in my mind: for instance, this whitish colour, even if it does only exist while I see it, and cannot be seen by any one else, does not seem to me to be *in* my mind in the sense in which my seeing of it is *in my mind*. My seeing of it is, it seems to me, related to my mind in a way in which this which I see is not related to it: and I should prefer to confine the phrase 'in the mind' to those things which are related to my mind, in the way in which my seeing of this colour, and my other acts of consciousness are related to it. But whether they could be properly said to be in my mind or not, certainly all the sense-data, which I ever directly apprehend, are, if these three things are true of them, *dependent* upon my mind in a most intimate sense. If it is really true of all of them that they exist only while I am conscious of them, that nobody else ever is directly conscious of them, and that they are situated only in a private space of my own, which also exists only while I am conscious of it, and of which no one else is ever directly conscious—then certainly nothing could well be more thoroughly dependent on my mind than they are. Most philosophers have, I think, certainly held that all sense-data are dependent on our minds in this sense. This has been held both by philosophers who believe that there are material objects and that we know of their existence, and by those who believe that there are no such things as material objects, or, that, if there are, we do not know it. It has, in fact, an overwhelming weight of authority in its favour. And I am going to call if for the moment *the accepted view.*

And as regards the question whether this accepted view is true or not, I confess I cannot make up my mind. I think it may very likely be true. But I have never seen any arguments in its favour which seem to me to be absolutely conclusive. . . .

.　　　.　　　.

15

MOORE'S THEORY OF SENSE-DATA

O. K. Bouwsma

I

I want in this essay to discuss a few sentences from Professor Moore's "A Defence of Common Sense," published in the volume containing the second series of contributions to *Contemporary British Philosophy*. These sentences are contained in part IV of that contribution. In this part Professor Moore is expounding what he regards as the correct analysis of such sentences as "This is a hand," "That is the sun," "This is a dog," etc. Involved in this exposition is the assertion: "whenever I know or judge such a proposition to be true, there is always some sense-datum about which the proposition in question is a proposition—some sense-datum which is a subject of the proposition in question."[1] Professor Moore goes on to recognize "that some philosophers have . . . doubted whether there are any such things as other philosophers have meant by 'sense-data',"[2] and in order to make sure that his readers may be persuaded, he goes on with the following attempt at definition, which I quote.

Professor Moore writes:

And in order to point out to the reader what sort of things I mean by sense-data, I need only ask him to look at his own right hand. If he does this he will be able to pick out something (and unless he is seeing double, only one thing) with regard to which he will see that it is, at first sight, a natural view to take, that that thing is identical, not indeed, with his whole right hand, but with that part of its surface which he is actually seeing, but will also (on a little reflection) be able to see that it is doubtful whether it can be identical with the part of the surface of his hand in question. Things *of the sort* (in a certain respect)

O. K. Bouwsma, in *The Philosophy of G. E. Moore*, P. A. Schilpp, ed. (Evanston, Ill.: Northwestern University Press, 1942). Now published by The Open Court Publishing Company, La Salle, Illinois, pp. 1–20. Reprinted by permission of The Open Court Publishing Company.

[1] J. H. Muirhead, ed., *Contemporary British Philosophy*, Second Series (New York: Macmillan, 1924), p. 217.

[2] *Ibid.*, p. 217.

of which this thing is, which he sees in looking at his hand, and with regard to which he can understand how some philosopher should have supposed it to be the part of the surface of his hand which he is seeing, while others have supposed that it can't be, are what I mean by sense-data. I therefore define the term in such a way that it is an open question whether the sense-datum which I now see in looking at my hand and which is a sense-datum of my hand, is or is not identical with that part of its surface which I am now actually seeing.[3]

I propose first to discuss some difficulties in this paragraph. Professor Moore invites his readers to pick out something, but his directions for doing this are not clear. Commonly if one is asked to pick out something, the something is described. Out of this bowl, pick out the red flower; out of this sheaf pick out the longest straw. We should all know how to follow these directions. But Professor Moore's directions are not like this. Apparently you simply pick out something; that is, as you are looking at your hand, and keeping your eye on your hand, you pick out something. Suppose you pick out your knuckles. Certainly that is something you can pick out. Well, is that the sort of thing Professor Moore intended that you should pick out? It is not. And this is the test which what you pick out must satisfy in order to meet Professor Moore's requirement. You must pick out something "with regard to which . . . it is, at first sight, a natural view to take, that that thing is identical with that part of its surface which (you are) actually seeing." So of course, the knuckles won't do. Even the surface of the knuckles won't do. What better could one do, than pick out the surface of the hand one is seeing? Certainly you can pick this out and it would be a natural view to take that that thing is identical with that part of the surface which you are actually seeing. This is a bit doubtful however, since you would scarcely be expected to pick out the whole of the surface which you are seeing, for picking out is selecting, and after selection there would be a remainder, which in this case there would not be. Furthermore if you do pick out the surface of the hand which you are seeing, could you then (on a little reflection) doubt that it is the surface of the hand you are seeing? For until you manage to do this too you would not have picked out what Professor Moore means by a sense-datum.

I confess that I am unable with these directions to attain the desired result. Looking at my hand I can pick out knuckles, finger-tips, nails, lines, veins, etc., but to none of them does the description which Professor Moore gives apply. If I pick out the knuckles, I am not seized with any doubts that they are the surface of my hand; and so with the finger-tips, nails, etc. And how I should ever be in a position to anticipate that what I do pick out would satisfy the given conditions I do not understand. I can see how if yesterday I had been asked to pick out my thumb, and then a little later doubted that what I had picked out was my thumb (for I had my fingers crossed in an unusual way) then today I might, remembering, pick out what yesterday it seemed very natural to take to be identical with my thumb and then what later I came to doubt was identical with my thumb. But Professor Moore's directions are not like this. He says that there is something which you may pick out and with respect to it, you will have the described difficulty. I have not been able to pick it out.

[3] *Ibid.*, p. 218.

This, then, is one peculiarity of Professor Moore's directions. One who is unacquainted with sense-data, and so has no information with regard to what to pick out, must resort to random picking, and wish for luck. Professor Moore's directions are something like this: Pick out of this basket something of which you will see that it is, at first sight, a natural view to take that that thing is identical with a red marble, but of which you will also see that it is doubtful whether it can be identical with the red marble. Now one might look at the basket and notice what there is in it. Here is a red marble, here a red pepper, here a red rubber ball, etc. One might notice all these things, and turn away, saying that there was nothing there which seemed at first glance to be a red marble, and then a moment later seemed not to be a red marble. So there was nothing to pick out. On the other hand, there might be something red and round in that basket which did at first appear to be a red marble, and then upon closer inspection turned out to be a red rubber ball. And picking out the red rubber ball would satisfy the directions. I am trying by these analogies to figure out just what sort of directions these are that Professor Moore is giving, in order to show why I have been unable in looking at my hand to discover anything which I should have some reason to suppose met with Professor Moore's directions.

But this is a general comment. Professor Moore says that there is something about which you first feel sure and then about which you doubt. In seeking for this I do not see how in feeling sure one could anticipate the doubting. But I should like further to notice some peculiarities concerning what it is one is at first to be sure of, and then is to doubt. I have in mind Professor Moore's use of the following types of sentence, in which X symbolizes the something which you are able to pick out:

1. X is identical with the surface of my right hand.
2. X can be identical with the surface of my right hand.
3. X cannot be identical with the surface of my right hand.

I want first to consider the first type of sentence in order to make clear the context in which we should commonly understand it. And for this purpose I am going to define a certain word, parodying the definition which Moore gives of the word sense-datum. This is the parody:

> And in order to point out to the reader what sort of thing I mean by———, I need only ask him to look at the cook's right hand. If he does this he will be able to pick out something with regard to which he will see that it is at first a natural view to take that that thing is identical not indeed with the cook's whole right hand, but with that part of its surface which one is actually (?) seeing but will also (on a little inspection) be able to see that it is doubtful whether it can be identical with the part of the hand in question. Things of the sort of which this thing is, which he sees in looking at the cook's hand, and with regard to which he can understand how some kitchen visitors should have supposed it to be the part of the surface of the cook's hand at which he was looking, while others have supposed that it can't be, are what I mean by rubber gloves.

This experiment, I think, might do very well for all kitchen visitors. But obviously its success depends upon a familiarity with the use of the expression "human hand" by which the inspection is guided. Look closely at the hand; does it look like a hand? pinch it, smell it, etc. Does the surface stretch like taffy, is it very smooth, etc.? Apparently in a case such as this there is no difficulty in distinguishing the surface of a hand from the surface of rubber gloves. Now then, when the reader in Professor Moore's experiment looks at his hand, and sees the surface of his hand, what happens? Does he think that some new kind of gloves, made to resemble the hand, have come to be worn, and that these gloves are, to smell, and touch, and sight, indistinguishable from the surface of the hand, gloves which you may not know you are wearing unless you remember that you put them on? If in a case of this sort one forgot, would one then be sensing, directly perceiving, a sense-datum? The answer is: No. For what distinguishes the doubt in terms of which Professor Moore defines the sense-datum, is that it cannot be resolved. Once the doubt arises, there is no way of settling the question whether the thing one can pick out is identical with the surface of one's hand or not. It must be remembered that Professor Moore does not say that the sense-datum is not identical with the surface of the hand. He only says that in looking at one's hand one comes to doubt that something, which may be the surface of one's hand, is the surface of one's hand. But, unlike the doubt about the surface of the hand and the rubber gloves, it cannot be settled. Once the doubt has arisen, there's nothing to do but to go on doubting. Scratching, smelling, looking more closely, do not give relief.

I can imagine someone in a facetious vein suggesting that the situation which Professor Moore describes is more like trying to distinguish identical twins occupying the same space. It's as though someone had been told: "He's identical twins," and then whenever that someone saw him, he would shake his head, looking, wondering, asking himself: Am I seeing Hans or Fritz? or when I am directly perceiving Hans, am I indirectly perceiving Fritz? He cannot decide. If someone says: You're seeing Hans (that seems the natural view to take) he proceeds to doubt: "Maybe it's Fritz." He might in this situation easily come to see that some people would hold that Hans was not twins, and that Fritz is either an alternative notation for Fritz, or a meaningless expression.

Now I want to try a further experiment, again to exhibit the misleading familiarity of Professor Moore's language. In the experiment designed to test for rubber gloves, the point made was that Moore's language is applicable to such things as hands and gloves. I want now to show that it is also applicable to mirror-images. This is the experiment:

> And in order to point out to the reader what I mean by————, I need only ask him to look into the mirror, holding up his right hand to the glass. If he does this, he will be able to pick out something with regard to which he will see, that it is, at first sight, a natural view to take, that that thing is identical, not indeed with his whole right hand, but with that part of the surface which is reflected there, but will also (smiling to himself) be able to see that it is doubtful whether it can be identical with the part of the surface of his hand in question. Things of this sort of which this thing is, which he sees in looking at the reflection of his hand, and with regard to which he can understand how some creatures, little people and puppies, should have supposed it to be the part of the surface of his hand, while grown-ups supposed that it can't be, are what I mean by hand-mirror-images.

Now the point of these two analogous experiments is this: If you are among those philosophers who doubt that there are any such things as some philosophers have meant by sense-data, and if you try to understand Professor Moore's directions in the attempt to identify a sense-datum, then further if you interpret a philosopher's language as so much English, you are certain to fail. If you look at your hand and try to stir up doubts about what you are seeing, you may object to yourself: But maybe I am wearing rubber gloves. Well, you know how to take care of that. Or you may object: But maybe I am looking into a mirror, and what I see, is just an image. You also know how to take care of that. What other misgiving suggestion remains then? It must be remembered that Professor Moore says that the doubt arises "on a little reflection" though he does not, in this context at least, tell us at all what reflection induces the doubt. It won't do, of course, to object: But maybe there are sense-data, and it is a property of sense-data to pass for the surface of things we look at, both when and if they are, and when and if they are not, the surfaces of objects. For it is by means of some reflection which does not involve that there are sense-data, but that leads to the requisite doubt concerning the surface of one's hand, that one is persuaded that there are sense-data. What I mean to point out here is that the language of the experiment is strange language so long as we are not acquainted with sense-data. Once we distinguish a sense-datum we may come to see how it applies. But before we can do this we must come to doubt. And before we come to doubt we must indulge in a "little reflection." The question is: what reflection? What is it that led Professor Moore and some other philosophers to come to that pass where, when each looks at his hand, he may ask without the slightest perturbation: And is this the surface of a hand? If, actually seeing the surface of his hand, he says: "Maybe not," then he is aware of a sense-datum. The question is: What thoughts lead him to this doubt?

Before I go on to consider what these reflections may be, I should like to discuss the second and third kinds of sentences above:

2. X can be identical with the surface of my right hand.
3. X cannot be identical with the surface of my right hand.

For this, notice a case of doubt in which one might have employed language of the sort which Professor Moore uses. Isaac on the day when he was deceived might have asked: Is this the hand of Jacob or the hand of Esau? Isaac was touching the hand and hearing the voice. The voice led him to doubt. We all understand this. And he might, had he attended Cambridge, have said: The hand that I am touching (and which I have picked out) is identical with the hand that is Esau's. I suppose that generally no one ever bothers to say a thing like this unless some doubt has preceded the assertion. So Isaac expected that this was the hand of Esau, but the voice made him doubtful. How could this be Esau's hand, when the voice which accompanied it sounded like Jacob's voice? In a dispute then, and to settle the matter (Isaac was very old!), Isaac may have said: This hand is identical with Esau's hand. He was wrong of course, but the confusion was one of hands; he mistook Jacob's hand for Esau's hand. The occasion for the use of the sentence arises after doubt and after denial. "What do you see?" "My right hand." "Oh, no you don't." "I say (temper rising) that what I see, is identical with my right hand. It is my right hand." It follows, of course, that we also have a use for: X is not identical with my right hand. If Rebecca on that occasion long ago, had had a mind to, she might have interrupted with: "You're wrong, Isaac. That hand is not identical with the hand of Esau. It's Jacob's hand."

Now we can also make a case for "This hand can be the hand of Esau," and so with "This hand cannot be the hand of Esau." Rebecca might have said: "It can't be." And then she would have given reasons, for such statements as "It can be" and "It can't be" have this sort of reference. So Isaac might have asked: Why can't it be? And the answer might have been: See here: You know that Esau's is a hairy hand. If you pull at the hairs on his hand, it pains him and you can see it on his face. And what is more the hair does not pull out. Try that experiment on this hand. There is no pain. The hair easily pulls off, and under the layer of hair, you will find paste. That's why this cannot be Esau's hand. Esau's hand is a genuine hairy, but this hand is a wolf's hand in sheep's clothing. To which Isaac might have lamented: But I thought it was Esau's. And it could have been for all I knew. The hand was hairy, it smelled of the field and of game, like Esau's hand. And it seemed like a large hand to me. So you see it could have been Esau's hand.

It is clearly, I think, situations such as these which we have in mind in the use of the expressions which Professor Moore employs. There is mistaking one thing for another thing, Jacob's hand for Esau's hand. There are also considerations which are involved in making the mistake, and other considerations which are involved in correcting the mistake. These considerations are of two kinds. If we are clear about what Jacob's hand is like, and clear about what Esau's hand is like, then the respects in which they are similar are likely to involve us in mistaking one for the other. The respects in which they are dissimilar, are the considerations which we draw upon when we correct our mistake, or when we come to say that "This cannot be so and so."

Accordingly, when Professor Moore says that you can pick out something about which you are inclined to say that it is identical with the surface of your hand, and this arises in a context in which you are inclined to say both that it can be, and that it cannot be, one would expect that some reasons would be at hand in respect to both. What makes you think that what you can pick out, can be identical with the surface of your hand and what makes you think that it cannot be identical with it? Is what you picked out similar in certain respects to the surface of your right hand, and dissimilar in certain other respects to that surface? Professor Moore has said that one would come to doubt by way of "a little reflection," as I noticed before, and the analysis which we have just made would lead one to expect that the reflection would consist in noticing similarities and dissimilarities between what you picked out and the surface of your right hand. Of course, if any dissimilarities were noticed, that ought to settle the matter. If the something is dissimilar, then of course, it is not the surface of one's hand. It looks as though one is aware of nothing but similarities, supposing one has picked out something, and yet that one is suspicious that there may be dissimilarities of which one is unaware. It's as though one were looking at one's hand, and had a suspicion that what one was seeing was not one's hand at all. So one examined one's hand carefully, found out that it was exactly what one expected one's hand to be like and yet concluded: "But maybe there is something I am not seeing, maybe there's a difference I am missing. So maybe after all, this is not my hand." What then planted this suspicion?

There is one further point that I should like to make. The experiment which Professor Moore proposes, takes for granted that each of us knows how to identify the surface of his hand. It is in terms of this identification that we are to come to recognize the something we pick out. Now then, each of us is able to describe his own hand. One might take a print of it, study it carefully for color shadings, shape and surface markings. If then one is well-informed about the surface of one's own hand, the doubt which Professor Moore describes does not arise because of any lack of information about one's hand. Apparently then the something which you pick out has the same characteristics which the surface of your hand has. If it did not have the same characteristics, obviously it would be different from the surface of your hand, and if it had the same and some others, it would also be different. So, if it has any characteristics at all, it must have the same characteristics as the surface of your hand. How then explain the suggestion that they are different? Are they in different places? This is also out of the question. We do not see the surface of the hand in one place, and pick out the something in a different place. If we did the doubt that the "something" and the surface of my hand are identical, would be settled. This too does not explain the suggestion that the something and the surface of my hand are identical. What then?

If what I have just suggested about knowing the surface of one's hand is not admitted, then what? Then certainly we are at a loss. The experiment presupposes that we know something, and that by way of this we may become aware of something else. If you know the surface of your hand, you can become acquainted with your knuckles. You certainly can, if you look at your hand, pick out your knuckles. In some such way as this you also become acquainted with "a sense-datum." Suppose however that, in a situation in which you did pick out your knuckles, you were seized with a doubt as to whether your knuckles were identical with the surface of your right hand which you are seeing, how would you account for this? If nothing very serious has happened, one might suggest that you had now come to use the expression "the surface of my hand" in a very unusual way. I have an inkling that something of this sort has happened in the sentences from Professor Moore's exposition. If one can think that "the something which one can pick out" is identical with the surface of one's hand, then either one must take for granted the use of the expression "the surface of one's hand" which applies then to something one can see, smell, touch, kiss, etc., and so grant that what one can pick out is also something which one can see, smell, touch, kiss, etc., or otherwise one takes for granted the use of the expression "what one can pick out" knowing well what this is like that one can pick out, and that for instance one cannot touch, taste, smell, etc., what one can pick out, and so grant also that "the surface of my hand" is something which, like what one can pick out, can be seen, but cannot be touched, tasted, smelled, etc. Either, then, Professor Moore is in effect saying that you can pick out a physical object which is identical with the surface of your hand, or you can pick out something which is not a physical object at all, and that is identical with the surface of your hand. The puzzle is as to how a non-physical object (a sense-datum) can be identical with a physical object. It seems at any rate inevitable that if anything can be conceived to be the surface of my hand, it must be physical; and that if the surface of my hand can be conceived to be a sense-datum, the surface of my hand is not physical. But in that case what has happened to the expression: "the surface of my hand?"

II

I have tried, in what preceded, to point out some of the difficulties which I have met in trying to follow Professor Moore's directions. And I regard as crucial in this respect the three sentences which I discussed, and the use of the phrase: "the surface of my hand." I also noticed that what leads to the doubt in Professor Moore's experiment, is a "little reflection." My suggestion is that it is the same "little reflection" which leads us to use these sentences, and the phrase just noticed. And I want now to describe the reflections which, in my own case, seems to lead me in that direction.

There are especially three sets of facts which lead me to try to distinguish a sense-datum in the prescribed way. One is certain facts concerning sounds, odors and tastes. Another is facts concerning mirror reflections, images, echoes, etc. And a third is the use of such expressions as: It looks like . . . , This looks like . . . , etc. There may be other facts which are relevant as these are. But I have noticed that when I, at any rate, meet the expression sense-data, these are the sorts of fact which come to my mind.

I want, before I go on, to notice how narrowly Professor Moore has conceived the problem of sense-data. It is common among those who say that there are sense-data to say that sounds, odors, tastes, etc., are sense-data; but it appears, apart from the tell-no-tale phrase "in a certain respect," that Professor Moore means by a sense-datum only that sort of thing which may be taken to be the surface of something or other. In other words, Professor Moore confines his use of the phrase sense-datum only to what others would describe as *visual* sense-data. I find Professor Moore's definition unusual in this respect, or misleading. If he does define "sense-data" in such a way as to include only "visual sense-data" then he defines the term in a way inconsistent with his own use of the term, for in a previous sentence he says, referring to sense-data: "I am at present seeing a great number of them and feeling others." At any rate his exposition excludes smells, tastes, and sounds. However that may be, the problem here is: What reflections would lead one to distinguish something which one would then say can or cannot be identical with the surface of one's hand which one is seeing?

The fact with respect to sounds, smells, and tastes is that they function in perceptual experiences in two ways. I can illustrate this best by a few pairs of sentences. Notice these:

I hear a gnawing sound.
I hear a rat.

I smell an odor.
I smell a rat.

I taste a sour taste.
I taste lemon.

The first of each of these pairs functions independently of the second, and one can describe sounds, odors, and tastes, without committing oneself to any sentence of the sort which is second in each pair. But the second does not function independently of the first. If you say: I hear a rat, then the question: What was the sound like?, is pertinent. In each case one may ask: What was the sound, or the odor, or the taste like? We are all acquainted with the descriptions of sounds, odors, and tastes. I need not, I think, enlarge upon this. If now someone held that there were sense-data and he meant by this that there were sounds, odors, and tastes, and that these are descriptively independent of rats and lemons, etc., there would, I think, be no controversy about this. There is no such question as: Is the sound or the odor of the rat identical with the surface of a rat, or the taste of a lemon identical with the surface of a lemon, or of that part of the lemon which I am tasting?

But now there are also certain similarities among facts of this following sort:

I hear a rat.
I smell a rat.
I taste a lemon.
I see a cloud.
I touch velvet.

And here, I take it, one is likely by reflection upon these sets of similarities to suppose that there must be some fact which corresponds to: I see a cloud, as: I hear a sound corresponds to: I hear a rat. And so too with: I touch velvet. Since, in other words, to hearing there corresponds a hearing sense-datum, and to smelling a smelling sense-datum, etc., so to seeing and to touching there must correspond seeing and touching sense-data. Actually, of course, there need not be such; and one part of the suggested parallel between hearing, smelling, and tasting, on the one hand, and seeing and touching, on the other, is missing. There are no descriptions of "sights" and "touches" which are independent conceptually of the descriptive characteristics of rats, lemons, clouds, velvet, etc. If you attempt to describe what you see, the same words which you use to describe the lemon or the cloud, will also serve to describe the purported sense-datum. So, if there is a sense-datum in these last cases, a new vocabulary will have to be engaged to perform the service. And so we get two different meanings for "is red" in the sentences "This (sense-datum) is red," and "This rose is red." This sort of accommodation is the consequence of the assumption that just as there are auditory sense-data so there must be visual sense-data. We make up for the deficiency in the facts from which we start by inventing a new vocabulary. Unfortunately we are compelled to use the same words which have otherwise performed an unambiguous service. It also follows that, if in the respect noted, seeing is like hearing, then as one is able, in hearing a bird, to distinguish the sound of the bird, so in seeing a hand one is able to pick out a corresponding visual sense-datum. The effect of these analogies may be so strong as to lead one to say that there must be a sense-datum.

These analogies do not however provide the only motive. Consider mirror reflections. Mirror reflections are like sounds and odors and tastes in a certain respect, and they are like lemons and clouds and velvet in another respect. The image of a lemon or a cloud is like a sound or an odor, in that the image is descriptively independent of the description of any lemon or cloud. On the other hand, the description of an image of a lemon or cloud is unlike the description of a sound or odor, in that the descriptive items which compose it are engaged also in describing lemons and clouds. Now how do these facts about images incline one to the belief that when one is looking at one's hand one is seeing a sense-datum, as one hears a sound? Perhaps in this way: If one is already impressed with the analogy between hearing and seeing, then one is inclined to believe that there is something which one is seeing which is distinguishable as the sound is from the bird one hears. Now if you look at your hand and try to discover this corresponding element, you may find your effort encouraged by the fact that there are things which are descriptively identical with what you are seeing which are nevertheless not the surfaces of lemons and clouds at all. That is, here you have in reflections what, since they are described in the same way in which lemons and clouds and hands are described, may very well be taken to be "the surfaces of lemons and clouds." So when you look at your hand, you may describe what you see just as you would describe the reflection of it in the mirror. Since then what you see is taken to be the surface of your hand, you at once understand how something might be described in this same way, and yet not be the surface of your hand at all. For the image in the mirror is not the surface of your hand. It is clear certainly that with this in mind you can, if you look at your hand, pick out something which is like what you saw in the mirror, when you raised your hand to the mirror.

There is one further set of facts which disposes us in the same way. Notice such sentences as these:

This sounds like a horse.
This smells like an onion.
This tastes like a peppermint.
This looks like a million dollars.
This feels like a sponge.

The use of these expressions is parallel to the first set described above. The first three are admittedly statements about a sound, a smell, and a taste. Now how about the fourth and the fifth? Well, they must also be about a "look" and about a "feel," the corresponding sense-data of seeing and touching, respectively. This does not now seem to me at all persuasive, and of course, for the same reason which I gave in discussing sounds, smells, etc. If one wished, for instance, to identify by description or by some other form of direction, the sound or smell in question, as distinguished from the horse or the onion, this is a simple matter. But if you wish to call attention to the "look" or to the "feel" in question there is no resort to doing this, save pointing out or identifying the "million dollars" or "the sponge" or whatever the object may be. In other words, what is called the "look" or the "feel" is not identifiable in the way in which the sound, or smell are identifiable. The use of the word "this" is commonly defined so as to apply to such uses as are involved in these first three sentences. But it is only by analogy that one comes to suppose that in the last two sentences the use is like that in the first three. Of course such a sentence as: "This looks like a million dollars," may apply also to a mirror-image, and we have already noticed what this means. The image of a girl who looks like a million dollars would also look like a million dollars. This means simply that they are described in the same way. Certainly from such facts as these, which we all admit, it does not follow that when you look at your hand, you can pick out something which is not your hand, of which you now say that it looks like your hand.

These are some of the facts upon which I reflect a little, when I am led to the view that what Professor Moore has tried to persuade us is true. I want now to show that, if one does follow the lead of these facts, one is likely to use precisely the sort of language about "sense-data" which Professor Moore does use. If the analogy between seeing and hearing holds, then it follows in the first place that if you look at your right hand you will be able to pick out something, something which on the assumption given, corresponds to the sound in hearing. But this is a strange sort of direction, for, if I look at my right hand, nothing at all corresponds to the sound in case of hearing. There is simply my hand, or more conveniently as you will see in a moment, the surface of my hand. So I pick that out. Now I reflect, and describe what I see, reminded that what I see is like reflections in mirrors. I know, of course, that mirror-reflections are not identical with the surfaces of any hands, no matter how perfect the image may be. Now, since this is like an image in all these respects, it can't be the surface of my hand at all, and this in spite of the fact that I thought at the outset that I was picking out the surface of my hand. If the only thing I could pick out was what I took to be the surface of my hand, and that is the sense-datum, and this is like the image in the mirror, then see what follows. The reflection in the mirror has no depth. I cannot prick it with a pin. Now then does the surface of my hand have depth? If you say that what you picked out is like the reflection in the mirror, and it has no depth, then if it is identical with the surface of my hand, then the surface of my hand also has no depth. Can that be? On the other hand, if you say that what I picked out is identical with the surface of my hand, and the surface of my hand has depth, are we then to allow that the sense-datum, like a hand's surface, has depth? Can I prick a sense-datum with a pin? This is the puzzle which I noticed previously when I discussed Professor Moore's use of the phrase "surface of my hand," and it arises from conceiving of the sense-datum as like a mirror-reflection, and at the same time as something which one can pick out. If when, on this basis, I look at my hand, and try to pick out a sense-datum, I must be surprised to discover something which, though it may be in certain respects like the image in the mirror, is also remarkably unlike it. For, in spite of what all these facts already noticed lead me to expect, I discover nothing but my hand.

I should like to labour this last point. Imagine the sort of situation you would be in, if, upon the basis of such facts as I have noticed, you were disposed to expect a sense-datum. What would you say in trying to describe what you expect? First of all, you might tell someone to look at his hand, on the expectation that just as if he heard a bird, there would be a sound to identify, so here there would be something corresponding to the sound. It also follows from the character of what you see, that if there is something corresponding to the sound, that you could pick it out. If this were all, one would be inclined to describe what you might pick out as "a yellow patch," "a red patch," "a canoid patch of brown," etc., and it is easy to see what in a case of this sort has happened. People who invent expressions of this sort are trying to find some expressions which parallel the descriptions of sounds, but the parallel is deceptive. For, if in looking at your hand you now try to pick out "a hand-shape of pink," you will find yourself picking out the surface of your hand, whereas in the case of a sound the relations between the sound and the bird are obviously different. The description of the sound is not a description of the bird. But there is no necessity for pursuing this. It is only necessary that what you pick out should, like the sound, be distinguishable from your hand, or the surface of your hand. As it is, you know that reflections in mirrors and images otherwise are distinguishable from what they reflect and image, though they are not descriptively distinguishable from what they reflect and image. So we formulate a description accordingly: Pick out what has the characteristics of a mirror-reflection. Looking into the mirror, holding your hand to the mirror, I might ask: What do you see?, and what you would then give me as a description would equally apply to your hand. Now then you look at your hand, and describe your hand, for what will satisfy my request is just that. Further, if you have already committed yourself to saying that there is something here which corresponds to the sound in the case of hearing the bird, then you will feel pretty sure that you have picked that out. But you will nevertheless be puzzled. For if you have picked out the sense-datum, then if someone says: Now pick out the surface of your hand, you will be unable to do so unless the sense-datum and the surface of your hand are identical. And if you then ask: Did I pick out the surface of my hand?, already assured that you did pick out the sense-datum, you will be inclined to say: That may be, for a sense-datum can be the surface of a hand. And you will be inclined to say this because, as I said before, the reflection and the surface of my hand are similar. But you will also be inclined to say that a sense-datum cannot be the surface.

III

I have tried, in the preceding sections, first of all to explore certain difficulties in the directions which Professor Moore gives for discovering what it is he means by a sense-datum, and second to try to discover what motives there are which lead us to expect that there are sense-data, and which lead us also to such curious descriptions of them. My thesis has been this: The obvious distinction between sounds, tastes, and smells in hearing, tasting, and smelling leads us to expect a corresponding something or other in the case of seeing and touching. So when I look at my hand, I am led to expect that there is a sense-datum in this case. So I may say that I can pick it out. But when I try to pick it out I am at a loss. There is only my hand. Now if I still persist in holding that there is a sense-datum present, I am bound to describe it in a peculiar way. I am likely to describe it in analogy with an image or mirror-reflection. I may go on to think of the sense-datum which must be there, as spread exceedingly thin over the surface of my hand, a kind of epi-epidermis, and at the same time as looking just like my hand when the sense-datum has been removed. Now if I keep this fixed in my mind, and look at my hand, and if I am asked: What do you see?, I am supposed not to know what to say. Do I see just an image spread over the surface of my hand like so much surfacing surfaceless paint, or do I see the surface of my hand? I think I can tell an image from the surface of my hand, but I confess that I should be much distressed in the attempt to distinguish the image of the surface of my hand laid neatly on the surface of my hand and defined in such a way as to be indistinguishable from the surface of my hand, from the surface of my hand. But fortunately, as I think, at least, I am not led to expect anything like images spread over the surface of my hand, and if I did, I should try pricking the epidermis. As I have noticed before, that the attempt to describe what "must" be present is desperate is also apparent in the consequent use of the expression "the surface of his hand." For we do not as a matter of fact have any difficulty in identifying the surface of our hands. If then there is some difficulty, that difficulty has not been properly described. And the point of my essay is that the supposed entity which is defined in terms of a confusion, which is generated by sentential likenesses, misleads us and catches us in linguistic pockets.

Rubber gloves, the image of my hand, another man's hand, all of these I know how to distinguish from my hand, when I look at my hand, and when I am in doubt. But I am not moved by the suggestion that whenever I look at my hand an image of my hand may be interposed between my hand and my eye. In that case we should need to invent the theory of the Pre-Established Harmony between the hand and the sense-datum. But why suggest it?

Having come to the end of my essay I am now full of misgivings. I know that I have not refuted Professor Moore's view. I have tried, however, teasing the words of Professor Moore's exposition, to get the matter straight. And this is what has come of it. May my betters rob me of my "darling follies," among which betters I have long counted first Professor Moore.

16

CONCERNING PHENOMENALISM

A. J. Ayer

The problem of specifying the relationship of material things to sense-data . . . is apt to be obscured by being represented as a problem about the inter-relationship of two different classes of objects. There is, indeed, a sense in which it is correct to say that both sense-data and material things exist, inasmuch as sentences that are used to describe sense-data and sentences that are used to describe material things both very frequently express true propositions. But it would not be correct to infer from this that there really were both material things and sense-data, in the sense in which it can truly be said that there really are chairs as well as tables, or that there are tastes as well as sounds. For whereas, in these cases, the existential propositions refer to different empirical "facts", this does not hold good in the case of sense-data and material things. All the same, the term "material thing" is not synonymous with any term or set of terms that stand for species of sense-data. It is indeed logically necessary that any situation that in any degree establishes the existence of a material thing should also establish the existence of a sense-datum; for we have constructed the sense-datum language in such a way that whenever it is true that a material thing is perceived, it must also be true that a sense-datum is sensed; and this applies also to the cases where the existence of the material thing is inferred from observations of its "physical effects". But it is not wholly a matter of convention that a situation which establishes the existence of a sense-datum should also be evidence in some degree for the existence of a material thing. For this depends . . . upon certain special features of our sensory experience, which it might conceivably not have possessed. Moreover, while a situation which directly establishes the existence of a sense-datum does so conclusively, no such situations can conclusively establish the existence of a material thing. The degree to which the existence of the material thing is established will depend upon the character of the sense-data in question, and especially upon the nature of the contexts in which they occur; but whatever the strength

From A. J. Ayer, *The Foundations of Empirical Knowledge* (London: 1940), Chap. V, Sec. 22, pp. 229–243. Reprinted by permission of St. Martin's Press Inc., The Macmillan Company of Canada Ltd., and Macmillan & Co. Ltd.

of this evidence may be, it will always be logically compatible with the hypothesis that this material thing is not in all respects what it appears to be, or even that it does not exist at all. Additional evidence may weaken this hypothesis to an extent that makes it very foolish still to entertain it; but it may also substantiate it, as the fact that there are illusions shows. At the same time, it is to be remarked that this additional evidence, whether favourable or not, will always consist in the occurrence of further sense-data. Indeed there is nothing else in which one can legitimately suppose it to consist, once one has accepted the rule that the word "sense-datum" is to be used to stand for whatever is, in fact, observed. And since it is impossible, by any valid process of inference, to make a transition from what is observed to anything that is conceived as being, in principle, unobservable, all that the evidence in question will be evidence for or against is the possible occurrence of further sense-data still. And from this it seems to follow that, even though the term "material thing" is not synonymous with any set of terms that stand for species of sense-data, any proposition that refers to a material thing must somehow be expressible in terms of sense-data, if it is to be empirically significant.

A common way of expressing this conclusion is to say that material things are nothing but collections of actual and possible sense-data. But this is a misleading formula and one that provokes objections which a more accurate way of speaking might avoid. Thus, it is sometimes argued, by those who reject this "phenomenalistic" analysis of the nature of material things, that to conceive of such things as houses or trees or stones as mere collections of actual and possible sense-data is to ignore their "unity" and "substantiality", and that, in any case, it is hard to see how anything can be composed of so shadowy a being as a possible sense-datum. But these objections are founded upon the mistaken assumption that a material thing is supposed to consist of sense-data, as a patchwork quilt consists of different coloured pieces of silk. To remove this misconception, it must be made clear that what the statement that material things consist of sense-data must be understood to designate is not a factual but a linguistic relationship. What is being claimed is simply that the propositions which are ordinarily expressed by sentences which refer to material things could also be expressed by sentences which referred exclusively to sense-data; and the inclusion of possible as well as actual sense-data among the elements of the material things must be taken only to imply a recognition that some of these statements about sense-data will have to be hypothetical. As for the belief in the "unity" and "substantiality" of material things, . . . it may be correctly represented as involving no more than the attribution to visual and tactual sense-data of certain relations which do, in fact, obtain in our experience. And . . . it is only the contingent fact that there are these relations between sense-data that makes it profitable to describe the course of our experience in terms of the existence and behaviour of material things.

It may seem that an attempt to carry out this plan of "reducing" material things to sense-data would be at variance with my previous attempt to draw a sharp distinction between them. But the purpose of making this distinction was simply to increase the utility and clarity of the sense-datum language by ensuring that its sentences should not be of the same logical form as those that refer to material things. And here it may be explained that two sentences may be said to have the same logical form if they can be correlated in such a way that to each expression that occurs in either one of them there corresponds in the other an expression of the same logical type; and that two expressions may be said to be of the same logical type if any sentence that significantly contains either one of them remains significant when the other is put in its place. It follows that if sentences referring to sense-data are of a different logical form from sentences referring to material things, it must not be assumed that precisely the same things can be said about them. To say, for example, that this was being written with a "pennish" group of sense-data, instead of saying that it was being written with a pen, would be neither true nor false but nonsensical. But this does not rule out the possibility that a proposition which is expressed by a sentence referring to a material thing can equally well be expressed by an entirely different set of sentences, which refer to sense-data; and this is what those who assert that material things are "logical constructions" out of sense-data must be understood to claim. Their view is sometimes put in the form of an assertion that "to say anything about a material thing is to say something, but not the same thing about classes of sense-data";[1] but if this is taken to imply that any significant statement about a material thing can actually be translated, without alteration of meaning, into a definite set of statements about sense-data, it is not strictly accurate, for a reason I shall presently give.

An objection which is often brought against phenomenalists is that they begin with a false conception of the nature of "perceptual situations". Thus, it is held by some philosophers that what is directly observed is usually not a sense-datum at all, but a material thing; so that the view that material things must be reducible to sense-data, on the ground that these alone are observable, is fundamentally erroneous. But this . . . is not the expression of a disagreement about any matter of fact, but only of a preference for a different form of language. It is indeed legitimate to use the phrase "direct observation" in such a way that things like houses and trees and stones can properly be said to be directly observable; and this usage can perfectly well be made to cover the case of delusive as well as veridical perceptions, provided that it is allowed that what is "directly observed" may not in fact exist, and that it may not really have the properties that it appears to have. But . . . it is also legitimate to use the phrase "direct observation" in such a way that it is only what is designated by the term "sense-datum", or some equivalent term, that can be said to be directly observable; and that it is this usage that, for my present purpose, is to be preferred. And one reason why it is to be preferred is to be found in the fact, which I have already mentioned, that whereas the proposition that a sense-datum is veridically sensed does not entail that any material thing is veridically perceived, the proposition that a material thing is veridically perceived can always be represented as entailing that some sense-datum or other is veridically sensed. Indeed, it is inconceivable that any sense-datum should not be sensed veridically, since it has been made self-contradictory to say of an experienced sense-datum that it does not exist or that it does not really have the properties that it appears to have. And because there is this logical relationship between "perceiving a material thing" and "sensing a sense-datum", it follows that, while a refer-

---

[1] *Vide* A. E. Duncan-Jones, "Does Philosophy Analyse Common Sense?" *Aristotelian Society Supplementary Proceedings*, 1937, pp. 140–41.

ence to a material thing will not elucidate the meaning of a sentence which is used to describe a sense-datum, except in so far as the poverty of our language may make it convenient to identify this sense-datum as one of a type that is ordinarily associated with a special sort of material thing, a reference to sense-data will provide a general elucidation of the meaning of statements about material things by showing what is the kind of evidence by which they may be verified. And this may be regarded as the purpose of the phenomenalist analysis.

Besides the philosophers who maintain that material things are themselves "directly observed", there are others who object to phenomenalism on the ground that even if the occurrence of illusions shows that what is directly observed is not a material thing, it is still not just a sense-datum. Thus Professor Stout, for one, has argued that "the evidence of sense-perception flatly contradicts phenomenalism", on the ground that to regard what is immediately experienced as being just a sensible appearance is to ignore an essential factor which he calls "perceptual seeming".[2] According to him, it is because of "perceptual seeming" that one is able to "perceive one thing as behind another, although it is so hidden that there is no sensible appearance of it", or that one can "perceive things as having insides, when they are not transparent".[3] But while this line of argument may have some force against those who employ a physiological criterion for determining the character of sense-data, it does not affect us at all, inasmuch as our use of the word sense-datum is not bound up with any special empirical theory about the nature of what is given. If one accepts the view of certain psychologists that there are experiences that may properly be described as experiences of "seeing the inside of a solid object" or "seeing an object when it is screened by another", then the inference one must draw is not that what is observed on such occasions is "more than a mere sense-datum", but that the character of people's visual sense-fields is empirically different from what a misplaced attention to the laws of physiology might lead one to suppose. It is true that the terms in which the psychologists describe such experiences are not purely sensory; but the reason for this is that it is only by referring to material things that they can actually expect to make their meaning under-stood. We must not, therefore, be misled into supposing that what they are intending to describe is anything more than a sensory phenomenon. The statement that someone is having the experience of "seeing the inside of a solid object" must not, in this context, be taken to exclude the possibility that no such physical object is actually there.

It may, however, be admitted that not only in cases of this sort, but in the vast majority of cases in which one senses a visual or tactual sense-datum, one tends to take it for granted that there is a physical object "there"; and it may be that this is what Professor Stout is referring to when he talks of "perceptual seeming". But this is a fact that I do not think any phenome-nalist would wish to deny. The view that material things are, in the sense I have just explained, logical constructions out of sense-data does not imply that "perceiving a material thing" need involve any conscious process of inference from the occurrence of one sense-datum to the possible occur-rence of another. The phenomenalist is perfectly free to admit that the

[2] "Phenomenalism", *Proceedings of the Aristotelian Society*, 1938–39, pp. 1–18.
[3] *Loc. cit.*, pp. 10–11.

sensing of a visual or tactual sense-datum is, in most cases, accompanied by an unreflecting assumption of the existence of some material thing. But the question in which he is interested is, What exactly is it that is here unreflectingly assumed? And his answer, which certainly cannot be refuted by any such appeal to psychology as Professor Stout relies on, is that it is the possibility of obtaining further sense-data.

It would seem that the best way to justify the claim that "to say anything about a material thing is always to say something, though not the same thing, about certain sense-data", would be to provide a number of specimen translations. But this is what no one has ever yet been able to do. It may be suggested that the reason why it has never been done is that no one has yet devised a sufficiently elaborate vocabulary. With our current resources of language we are able to classify visual sense-data only in a very general way, tactual data even less specifically, and kinaesthetic data hardly at all: and the result is that when we wish to distinguish the sense-data that belong to one sort of material thing from those that belong to another we are unable to achieve it except by referring to the material things in question. But suppose that someone took the trouble to name all the different varieties of sensible characteristics with which he was acquainted. Even so, he would still not be able to translate any statement about a material thing into a finite set of statements about sense-data. It is not inconceivable that someone should construct and make use of such a sensory language, though in practice he would find it very difficult to make himself understood; but what he succeeded in expressing by these means would never be precisely equivalent even to the singular statements that we make about material things. For when statements are equivalent to one another, they can always be represented as standing in a relationship of mutual entailment. And, in the case I am now considering, this condition cannot be fulfilled.

I have indeed already admitted that no finite set of singular statements about sense-data can ever formally entail a statement about a material thing, inasmuch as I have recognized that statements about material things are not conclusively verifiable. For when we try to reproduce the content of a statement about a material thing by specifying the empirical situations that would furnish us with direct tests of its validity, we find that the number of these possible tests is infinite. Admittedly, when someone makes a statement of this kind he does not actually envisage an infinite series of possible verifications. He may very well be satisfied, in familiar circumstances, with the single sense-experience on which his statement is based; and if he does think it necessary to test it further, the subsequent occurrence, in the appropriate conditions, of only a limited number of "favourable" sense-data will be sufficient, in the absence of contrary evidence, to convince him that it is true. And this is an entirely reasonable procedure . . . But the fact remains that however many favourable tests he may make he can never reach a stage at which it ceases to be conceivable that further sense-experience will reverse the verdict of the previous evidence. He will never be in a position to demonstrate that he will not subsequently have experiences that will entitle him to conclude that his original statement was false after all. And this implies that the content of a statement about a material thing cannot be exhaustively specified by any finite number of references to sense-data. This difficulty could indeed be met by introducing into the sense-datum language a suitable set of expressions which would be understood to refer to infinite series of sense-data. But I am afraid that most philosophers would not admit that this gave them the sort of translation that they wanted. For all that would seem to be achieved by the introduction of these new expressions would be a mere renaming of material things.

But not only is the occurrence of any one particular, finite series of sense-data never formally sufficient to establish the truth of a statement about a material thing; it is never even necessary. There is, indeed, a sense in which it can be said that every statement about a material thing entails some set of statements or other about sense-data, inasmuch as it is only by the occurrence of some sense-datum that any statement about a material thing is ever in any degree verified. But there is no set of statements about the occurrence of particular sense-data of which it can truly be said that precisely this is entailed by a given statement about a material thing. And the reason for this is that what is required to verify a statement about a material thing is never just the occurrence of a sense-datum of an absolutely specific kind, but only the occurrence of one or other of the sense-data that fall within a fairly indefinite range. In other words, not only can we go on testing a statement about a material thing as long as we like without being able to arrive at a formal demonstration of its truth; but for any test that we actually do carry out there are always an indefinite number of other tests, differing to some extent either in respect of their conditions or their results, which would have done just as well. And this means that if we try to describe what at any given moment would afford us direct evidence for the truth of a statement about a material thing by putting forward a disjunction of statements about sense-data, we shall find once again that this disjunction will have to be infinite.[4]

But if one infers from this that sentences referring to material things cannot be translated, without alteration of meaning, into sentences referring to sense-data, one must not then conclude that to speak about a material thing is to speak about something altogether different from sense-data, or that it is to speak about sense-data but about something else besides. For that would be a mistake analogous to that of supposing that because sentences referring indefinitely to what is red cannot be translated into a finite number of sentences referring to particular red things, therefore "redness" is the name of an object with a distinct existence of its own, or that because sentences referring to "someone" cannot be translated into a finite disjunction of sentences referring to particular persons, therefore "someone" is the name of a peculiar being, a "subsistent entity" perhaps, who is distinct from any person that one can actually meet. If we cannot produce the required translations of sentences referring to material things into sentences referring to sense-data, the reason is not that it is untrue that "to say anything about a material thing is always to say something about sense-data", but only that one's references to material things are vague in their application to phenomena and that the series of sense-data that they may be understood to specify are composed of infinite sets of terms.

This does not mean, however, that nothing can be done in the way of "analysing material things in terms of sense-data". It would not, indeed, be profitable to seek in any such analysis a means of distinguishing one material

[4] Cf. John Wisdom, "Metaphysics and Verification", *Mind*, October 1938, pp. 478–81.

thing from another. It is not by a verbal analysis in terms of sense-data that one can hope to make clear what is meant, for example, by "a pen" as opposed to "a pencil", or by "a steamship" as opposed to "a canoe". One can give a verbal, as well as an ostensive, indication of the meaning of such words; but it will not exclude the use of other expressions that belong to a physical rather than to a purely sensory terminology. At the same time, there are certain general features about the way in which any expression referring to a material thing applies to phenomena that one can profitably undertake to analyse. That is to say, one may be able to explain what are the relations between sense-data that make it possible for us successfully to employ the physical terminology that we do. If I may now use the metaphor of construction without being misunderstood, I can describe the task [in question] as that of showing what are the general principles on which, from our resources of sense-data, we "construct" the world of material things.

17

THE ARGUMENT FROM ILLUSION

J. L. Austin

The primary purpose of the argument from illusion is to induce people to accept 'sense-data' as the proper and correct answer to the question what they perceive on certain *abnormal, exceptional* occasions; but in fact it is usually followed up with another bit of argument intended to establish that they *always* perceive sense-data. Well, what is the argument?

In Ayer's statement[1] it runs as follows. It is 'based on the fact that material things may present different appearances to different observers, or to the same observer in different conditions, and that the character of these appearances is to some extent causally determined by the state of the conditions and the observer'. As illustrations of this alleged fact Ayer proceeds to cite perspective ('a coin which looks circular from one point of view may look elliptical from another'); refraction ('a stick which normally appears straight looks bent when it is seen in water'); changes in colour-vision produced by drugs ('such as mescal'); mirror-images; double vision; hallucination; apparent variations in tastes; variations in felt warmth ('according as the hand that is feeling it is itself hot or cold'); variations in felt bulk ('a coin seems larger when it is placed on the tongue than when it is held in the palm of the hand'); and the oft-cited fact that 'people who have had limbs amputated may still continue to feel pain in them'.

He then selects three of these instances for detailed treatment. First, refraction—the stick which normally 'appears straight' but 'looks bent' when seen in water. He makes the 'assumptions' (*a*) that the stick does not *really change its shape* when it is placed in water, and (*b*) that it *cannot be* both crooked and straight.[2] He then concludes ('it follows') that 'at least

From J. L. Austin, *Sense and Sensibilia* (Oxford: 1962), Chap. III, pp. 20–32. Reprinted by permission of The Clarendon Press, Oxford.

[1] Ayer, *The Foundations of Empirical Knowledge*, pp. 3–5.

[2] It is not only strange, but also important, that Ayer calls these 'assumptions'. Later on he is going to take seriously the notion of denying at least one of them, which he could hardly do if he had recognized them here as the plain and incontestable facts that they are.

one of the *visual appearances* of the stick is *delusive'*. Nevertheless, even when 'what we see is not the *real quality* of a *material thing*, it is supposed that we are still seeing something'—and this something is to be called a 'sense-datum'. A sense-datum is to be 'the object of which we are *directly* aware, in perception, if it is not *part* of any *material thing'*. (The italics are mine throughout this and the next two paragraphs.)

Next, mirages. A man who sees a mirage, he says, is 'not perceiving any material thing; for the oasis which he thinks he is perceiving *does not exist'*. But 'his *experience* is not an experience of nothing'; thus 'it is said that he is experiencing sense-data, which are similar in character to what he would be experiencing if he were seeing a real oasis, but are delusive in the sense that *the material thing which they appear to present* is not *really there'*.

Lastly, reflections. When I look at myself in a mirror 'my body *appears to be* some distance behind the glass'; but it cannot actually be in two places at once; thus, my perceptions in this case 'cannot all be *veridical'*. But I do see *something;* and if 'there really is no such material thing as my body in the place where it appears to be, what is it that I am seeing?' Answer—a sense-datum. Ayer adds that 'the same conclusion may be reached by taking any other of my examples'.

Now I want to call attention, first of all, to the name of this argument— the 'argument from *illusion'*, and to the fact that it is produced as establishing the conclusion that some at least of our 'perceptions' are *delusive*. For in this there are two clear implications—(*a*) that all the cases cited in the argument are cases of *illusions;* and (*b*) that *illusion* and *delusion* are the same thing. But both of these implications, of course, are quite wrong; and it is by no means unimportant to point this out, for, as we shall see, the argument trades on confusion at just this point.

What, then, would be some genuine examples of illusion? (The fact is that hardly any of the cases cited by Ayer is, at any rate without stretching things, a case of illusion at all.) Well, first, there are some quite clear cases of *optical* illusion—for instance the case we mentioned earlier in which, of two lines of equal length, one is made to look longer than the other. Then again there are illusions produced by professional 'illusionists', conjurors—for instance the Headless Woman on the stage, who is made to look headless, or the ventriloquist's dummy which is made to appear to be talking. Rather different—not (usually) produced on purpose—is the case where wheels rotating rapidly enough in one direction may look as if they were rotating quite slowly in the opposite direction. Delusions, on the other hand, are something altogether different from this. Typical cases would be delusions of persecution, delusions of grandeur. These are primarily a matter of grossly disordered beliefs (and so, probably, behaviour) and may well have nothing in particular to do with perception.[3] But I think we might also say that the patient who sees pink rats has (suffers from) delusions—particularly, no doubt, if, as would probably be the case, he is not clearly aware that his pink rats aren't real rats.[4]

The most important differences here are that the term 'an illusion' (in a perceptual context) does not suggest that something totally unreal is *con-*

---

[3] The latter point holds, of course, for *some* uses of "illusion" too; there are the illusions which some people (are said to) lose as they grow older and wiser.

[4] Cp. the white rabbit in the play called *Harvey*.

jured up—on the contrary, there just is the arrangement of lines and arrows on the page, the woman on the stage with her head in a black bag, the rotating wheels; whereas the term 'delusion' *does* suggest something totally unreal, not really there at all. (The convictions of the man who has delusions of persecution can be *completely* without foundation.) For this reason delusions are a much more serious matter—something is really wrong, and what's more, wrong *with* the person who has them. But when I see an optical illusion, however well it comes off, there is nothing wrong with me personally, the illusion is not a little (or a large) peculiarity or idiosyncrasy of my own; it is quite public, anyone can see it, and in many cases standard procedures can be laid down for producing it. Furthermore, if we are not actually to be taken in, we need to be *on our guard;* but it is no use to tell the sufferer from delusions to be on his guard. He needs to be cured.

Why is it that we tend—if we do—to confuse illusions with delusions? Well, partly, no doubt the terms are often used loosely. But there is also the point that people may have, without making this explicit, different views or theories about the facts of some cases. Take the case of seeing a ghost, for example. It is not generally known, or agreed, what seeing ghosts *is*. Some people think of seeing ghosts as a case of something being conjured up, perhaps by the disordered nervous system of the victim; so in their view seeing ghosts is a case of delusion. But other people have the idea that what is called seeing ghosts is a case of being taken in by shadows, perhaps, or reflections, or a trick of the light—that is, they assimilate the case in their minds to illusion. In this way, seeing ghosts, for example, may come to be labelled sometimes as 'delusion', sometimes as 'illusion'; and it may not be noticed that it makes a difference which label we use. Rather, similarly, there seem to be different doctrines in the field as to what mirages are. Some seem to take a mirage to be a vision conjured up by the crazed brain of the thirsty and exhausted traveller (delusion), while in other accounts it is a case of atmospheric refraction, whereby something below the horizon is made to appear above it (illusion). (Ayer, you may remember, takes the delusion view, although he cites it along with the rest as a case of illusion. He says not that the oasis appears to be where it is not, but roundly that 'it does not exist'.)

The way in which the 'argument from illusion' positively trades on not distinguishing illusions from delusions is, I think, this. So long as it is being suggested that the cases paraded for our attention are cases of *illusion*, there is the implication (from the ordinary use of the word) that there really is something there that we perceive. But then, when these cases begin to be quietly called delusive, there comes in the very different suggestion of something being conjured up, something unreal or at any rate 'immaterial'. These two implications taken together may then subtly insinuate that in the cases cited there really is something that we are perceiving, but that this is an immaterial something; and this insinuation, even if not conclusive by itself, is certainly well calculated to edge us a little closer towards just the position where the sense-datum theorist wants to have us.

So much, then—though certainly there could be a good deal more—about the differences between illusions and delusions and the reasons for not obscuring them. Now let us look briefly at some of the other cases Ayer lists. Reflections, for instance. No doubt you *can* produce illusions with mirrors, suitably disposed. But is just *any* case of seeing something in a mirror an illusion, as he implies? Quite obviously not. For seeing things in mirrors is a perfectly *normal* occurrence, completely familiar, and there is usually no question of anyone being taken in. No doubt, if you're an infant or an aborigine and have never come across a mirror before, you may be pretty baffled, and even visibly perturbed, when you do. But is that a reason why the rest of us should speak of illusion here? And just the same goes for the phenomena of perspective—again, one *can* play tricks with perspective, but in the ordinary case there is no question of illusion. That a round coin should 'look elliptical' (in one sense) from some points of view is exactly what we expect and what we normally find; indeed, we should be badly put out if we ever found this not to be so. Refraction again—the stick that looks bent in water—is far too familiar a case to be properly called a case of illusion. We may perhaps be prepared to agree that the stick looks bent; but then we can see that it's partly submerged in water, so that is exactly how we should expect it to look.

It is important to realize here how familiarity, so to speak, takes the edge off illusion. Is the cinema a case of illusion? Well, just possibly the first man who ever saw moving pictures may have felt inclined to say that here was a case of illusion. But in fact it's pretty unlikely that even he, even momentarily, was actually taken in; and by now the whole thing is so ordinary a part of our lives that it never occurs to us even to raise the question. One might as well ask whether producing a photograph is producing an illusion —which would plainly be just silly.

Then we must not overlook, in all this talk about illusions and delusions, that there are plenty of more or less unusual cases, not yet mentioned, which certainly aren't either. Suppose that a proof-reader makes a mistake—he fails to notice that what ought to be 'causal' is printed as 'casual'; does he have a delusion? Or is there an illusion before him? Neither, of course; he simply *misreads*. Seeing after-images, too, though not a particularly frequent occurrence and not just an ordinary case of seeing, is neither seeing illusions nor having delusions. And what about dreams? Does the dreamer see illusions? Does he have delusions? Neither; dreams are *dreams*.

Let us turn for a moment to what Price has to say about illusions. He produces,[5] by way of saying 'what the term "illusion" means', the following 'provisional definition': 'An illusory sense-datum of sight or touch is a sense-datum which is such that we tend to take it to be part of the surface of a material object, but if we take it so we are wrong.' It is by no means clear, of course, what this dictum itself means; but still, it seems fairly clear that the definition doesn't actually fit all the cases of illusion. Consider the two lines again. Is there anything here which we tend to take, wrongly, to be part of the surface of a material object? It doesn't seem so. We just see the two lines, we don't think or even tend to think that we see anything else, we aren't even raising the question whether anything is or isn't 'part of the surface' of—what, anyway? the lines? the page?—the trouble is just that one line looks longer than the other, though it isn't. Nor surely, in the case of the Headless Woman, is it a question whether anything is or isn't part of her surface; the trouble is just that she looks as if she had no head.

[5] *Perception*, p. 27.

It is noteworthy, of course, that, before he even begins to consider the 'argument from illusion', Price has already incorporated in this 'definition' the idea that in such cases there is something to be seen *in addition to* the ordinary things—which is part of what the argument is commonly used, and not uncommonly taken, to *prove*. But this idea surely has no place in an attempt to say what 'illusion' *means*. It comes in again, improperly I think, in his account of perspective (which incidentally he also cites as a species of illusion)—'a distant hillside which is full of protuberances, and slopes upwards at quite a gentle angle, will appear flat and vertical. . . . This means that the sense-datum, the colour-expanse which we sense, actually *is* flat and vertical.' But why should we accept this account of the matter? Why should we say that there is *anything* we see which *is* flat and vertical, though not 'part of the surface' of any material object? To speak thus is to assimilate all such cases to cases of delusion, where there *is* something not 'part of any material thing'. But we have already discussed the undesirability of this assimilation.

Next, let us have a look at the account Ayer himself gives of some at least of the cases he cites. (In fairness we must remember here that Ayer has a number of quite substantial reservations of his own about the merits and efficacy of the argument from illusion, so that it is not easy to tell just how seriously he intends his exposition of it to be taken; but this is a point we shall come back to.)

First, then, the familiar case of the stick in water. Of this case Ayer says (*a*) that since the stick looks bent but is straight, 'at least one of the visual appearances of the stick is *delusive*'; and (*b*) that 'what we see [directly anyway] is not the real quality of [a few lines later, not part of] a material thing'. Well now: does the stick 'look bent' to begin with? I think we can agree that it does, we have no better way of describing it. But of course it does *not* look *exactly* like a bent stick, a bent stick out of water—at most, it may be said to look rather like a bent stick partly immersed *in* water. After all, we can't help seeing the water the stick is partly immersed in. So exactly what in this case is supposed to be *delusive?* What is wrong, what is even faintly surprising, in the idea of a stick's being straight but looking bent sometimes? Does anyone suppose that if something is straight, then it jolly well has to *look* straight at all times and in all circumstances? Obviously no one seriously supposes this. So what mess are we supposed to get into here, what is the difficulty? For of course it has to be suggested that there *is* a difficulty—a difficulty, furthermore, which calls for a pretty radical solution, the introduction of sense-data. But what is the problem we are invited to solve in this way?

Well, we are told, in this case you are seeing *something;* and what is this something 'if it is not part of any material thing'? But this question is, really, completely mad. The straight part of the stick, the bit not under water, is presumably part of a material thing; don't we see that? And what about the bit *under* water?—we can see that too. We can see, come to that, the water itself. In fact what we see is *a stick partly immersed in water;* and it is particularly extraordinary that this should appear to be called in question— that a question should be raised about *what* we are seeing—since this, after all, is simply the description of the situation with which we started. It was, that is to say, agreed at the start that we were looking at a stick, 'a material thing', part of which was under water. If, to take a rather different case, a church were cunningly camouflaged so that it looked like a barn, how could any serious question be raised about what we see when we look at it? We see, of course, *a church* that now *looks like a barn*. We do *not* see an immaterial barn, an immaterial church, or an immaterial anything else. And what in this case could seriously tempt us to say that we do?

Notice, incidentally, that in Ayer's description of the stick-in-water case, which is supposed to be prior to the drawing of any philosophical conclusions, there has already crept in the unheralded but important expression 'visual appearances'—it is, of course, ultimately to be suggested that all we *ever* get when we see is a visual appearance (whatever that may be).

Consider next the case of my reflection in a mirror. My body, Ayer says, 'appears to be some distance behind the glass'; but as it's in front, it can't really be behind the glass. So what am I seeing? A sense-datum. What about this? Well, once again, although there is no objection to saying that my body 'appears to be some distance behind the glass', in saying this we must remember what sort of situation we are dealing with. It does not 'appear to be' there in a way which might tempt me (though it might tempt a baby or a savage) to go round the back and look for it, and be astonished when this enterprise proved a failure. (To say that A is *in* B doesn't always mean that if you open B you will find A, just as to say that A is *on* B doesn't always mean that you could pick it off—consider 'I saw my face in the mirror', 'There's a pain in my toe', 'I heard him on the radio', 'I saw the image on the screen', &c. Seeing something in a mirror is not like seeing a bun in a shop-window.) But does it follow that, since my body is not actually located behind the mirror, I am not seeing a material thing? Plainly not. For one thing, I can see the mirror (nearly always anyway). I can see my own body 'indirectly', *sc.* in the mirror. I can also see the reflection of my own body or, as some would say, a mirror-image. And a mirror-image (if we choose this answer) is not a 'sense-datum'; it can be photographed, seen by any number of people, and so on. (Of course there is no question here of either illusion or delusion.) And if the question is pressed, what actually *is* some distance, five feet say, behind the mirror, the answer is, not a sense-datum, but some region of the adjoining room.

The mirage case—at least if we take the view, as Ayer does, that the oasis the traveller thinks he can see 'does not exist'—is significantly more amenable to the treatment it is given. For here we are supposing the man to be genuinely deluded, he is *not* 'seeing a material thing'.[6] We don't actually have to say, however, even here that he is 'experiencing sense-data'; for though, as Ayer says above, 'it is convenient to give a name' to what he is experiencing, the fact is that it already has a name—a *mirage*. Again, we should be wise not to accept too readily the statement that what he is experiencing is *'similar in character* to what he would be experiencing if he were seeing a real oasis'. For is it at all likely, really, to be very similar? And, looking ahead, if we were to concede this point we should find the concession being used against us at a later stage—namely, at the stage where we shall be invited to agree that we see sense-data always, in normal cases too.

---

[6] Not even 'indirectly', no such thing is 'presented'. Doesn't this seem to make the case, though more amenable, a good deal less useful to the philosopher? It's hard to see how normal cases could be said to be *very like* this.

18

"INTENTIONAL INEXISTENCE"

Roderick M. Chisholm

I

I have suggested that the locution "There is something that S *perceives* to be *f*" may be defined as meaning: there is something such that it is *f*, it appears to S in some way, S takes it to be *f*, and S has adequate evidence for so doing. And I have suggested that "S *takes* something to be *f*" may be defined by reference to what S assumes, or accepts. I have now said all that I can about the philosophic questions which the concepts of *adequate evidence* and of *appearing* involve. Let us finally turn, then, to the concept of *assuming*, or *accepting*. The principal philosophic questions which this concept involves may be formulated by reference to a thesis proposed by Franz Brentano.

Psychological phenomena, according to Brentano, are characterized "by what the scholastics of the Middle Ages referred to as the intentional (also the mental) inexistence of the object, and what we, although with not quite unambiguous expressions, would call relation to a content, direction upon an object (which is not here to be understood as a reality), or immanent objectivity."[1] This "intentional inexistence," Brentano added, is peculiar to what is psychical; things which are merely physical show nothing like it.

Assuming, or *accepting*, is one of the phenomena Brentano would have called intentional. I will first try to formulate Brentano's thesis somewhat more exactly; then I will ask whether it is true of assuming.

II

The phenomena most clearly illustrating the concept of "intentional inexistence" are what are sometimes called psychological attitudes; for example, desiring, hoping, wishing, seeking, believing, and assuming. When

From Roderick M. Chisholm, *Perceiving* (Ithaca, N.Y.: 1957), Chap. XI, pp. 168–185. © 1957 by Cornell University. Used by permission of Cornell University Press.
[1] Franz Brentano, *Psychologie vom empirischen Standpunkte* (Leipzig, 1924), I, 124–125.

Brentano said that these attitudes "intentionally contain an object in themselves," he was referring to the fact that they can be truly said to "have objects" even though the objects which they can be said to have do not in fact exist. Diogenes could have looked for an honest man even if there hadn't been any honest men. The horse can desire to be fed even though he won't be fed. James could believe there are tigers in India, and *take* something there to be a tiger, even if there aren't any tigers in India.

But *physical*—or nonpsychological—phenomena, according to Brentano's thesis, cannot thus "intentionally contain objects in themselves." In order for Diogenes to sit in his tub, for example, there must be a tub for him to sit in; in order for the horse to eat his oats, there must be oats for him to eat; and in order for James to shoot a tiger, there must be a tiger there to shoot.

The statements used in these examples seem to have the form of relational statements. "Diogenes sits in his tub" is concerned with a relation between Diogenes and his tub. Syntactically, at least, "Diogenes looks for an honest man" is similar: Diogenes' quest seems to relate him in a certain way to honest men. But the relations described in this and in our other psychological statements, if they can properly be called "relations," are of a peculiar sort. They can hold even though one of their terms, if it can properly be called a "term," does not exist. It may seem, therefore, that one can be "intentionally related" to something which does not exist.[2]

These points can be put somewhat more precisely by referring to the language we have used. We may say that, in our language, the expressions "looks for," "expects," and "believes" occur in sentences which are intentional, or are used intentionally, whereas "sits in" "eats," and "shoots" do not. We can formulate a working criterion by means of which we can distinguish sentences that are intentional, or are used intentionally, in a certain language from sentences that are not. It is easy to see, I think, what this criterion would be like, if stated for ordinary English.

First, let us say that a simple declarative sentence is intentional if it uses a substantival expression—a name or a description—in such a way that neither the sentence nor its contradictory implies either that there is or that there isn't anything to which the substantival expression truly applies. "Diogenes looked for an honest man" is intentional by this criterion. Neither "Diogenes looked for an honest man" nor its contradictory—"Diogenes did *not* look for an honest man"—implies either that there are, or that there are not, any honest men. But "Diogenes sits in his tub" is not intentional by this criterion, for it implies that there *is* a tub in which he sits.

Secondly, let us say, of any noncompound sentence which contains a propositional clause, that it is intentional provided that neither the sentence nor its contradictory implies either that the propositional clause is true or that it is false. "James believes there are tigers in India" is intentional by this criterion, because neither it nor its contradictory implies either that there are, or that there are not, any tigers in India. "He succeeded in visiting

---

[2] But the point of talking about "intentionality" is not that there is a peculiar type of "inexistent" object; it is rather that there is a type of psychological phenomenon which is unlike anything purely physical. In his later writings Brentano explicitly rejected the view that there are "inexistent objects"; see his *Psychologie,* II, 133 ff., and *Wahrheit und Evidenz* (Leipzig, 1930), pp. 87, 89.

India," since it implies that he did visit India, is not intentional. "He is able to visit India," although it does not imply that he will visit India, is also not intentional. For its contradictory—"He is not able to visit India"—implies that he does *not* visit India.

A third mark of intentionality may be described in this way. Suppose there are two names or descriptions which designate the same things and that E is a sentence obtained merely by separating these two names or descriptions by means of "is identical with" (or "are identical with" if the first word is plural). Suppose also that A is a sentence using one of those names or descriptions and that B is like A except that, where A uses the one, B uses the other. Let us say that A is intentional if the conjunction of A and E does not imply B.[3] We can now say of certain cognitive sentences— sentences using "know," "see," "perceive," and the like in one of the ways which have interested us here—that they, too, are intentional. Most of us knew in 1944 that Eisenhower was the one in command (A); but although he was (identical with) the man who was to succeed Truman (E), it is not true that we knew in 1944 that the man who was to succeed Truman was the one in command (B).

Let us say that a *compound* sentence is one compounded from two or more sentences by means of propositional connectives, such as "and," "or," "if-then," "although," "because," and the like. The three foregoing marks of intentionality apply to sentences which are *not* compound. We may now say that a compound declarative sentence is intentional if and only if one or more of its component sentences is intentional. Thus the antecedent of "If Parsifal sought the Holy Grail, he was a Christian" enables us to say that the whole statement is intentional.

When we use perception words propositionally, our sentences display the third of the above marks of intentionality. I may see that John is the man in the corner and John may be someone who is ill; but I do not now *see* that John is someone who is ill. Perception sentences, as we have seen, entail sentences about taking and assuming. And sentences about taking and assuming display the second of the above marks of intentionality. "He takes—and therefore assumes—those rocks to be the reef" does not imply that the rocks *are* the reef and it does not imply that they are not. And similarly for its contradiction: "He does not take—or assume—those rocks to be the reef."

We may now re-express Brentano's thesis—or a thesis resembling that of Brentano—by reference to intentional sentences. Let us say (1) that we do not need to use intentional sentences when we describe nonpsychological phenomena; we can express all of our beliefs about what is merely "physical" in sentences which are not intentional.[4] But (2) when we wish to

---

[3] This third mark is essentially the same as Frege's concept of "indirect reference." See Gottlob Frege, "Über Sinn und Bedeutung," *Zeitschrift für Philosophie und Philosophische Kritik*, n.s. C (1892), 25–50, especially 38; reprinted in Herbert Feigl and W. S. Sellars, eds., *Readings in Philosophical Analysis* (New York, 1949), and Peter Geach and Max Black, eds., *Philosophical Writings of Gottlob Frege* (Oxford, 1952).

[4] There are sentences describing relations of comparison—for example, "Some lizards look like dragons"—which may constitute an exception to (1). If they are exceptions, then we may qualify (1) to read: "We do not need any intentional sentences, other than those describing relations of comparison, when we describe nonpsychological phenomena." This qualification would not affect any of the points to be made here.

describe perceiving, assuming, believing, knowing, wanting, hoping, and other such attitudes, then either (a) we must use sentences which are intentional or (b) we must use terms we do not need to use when we describe nonpsychological phenomena.

In describing nonpsychological phenomena, we do, on occasion, use sentences which are intentional by one or more of the above criteria. One may say, "This weapon, suitably placed, is capable of causing the destruction of Boston" and "The cash register knows that 7 and 5 are 12." But although these sentences are intentional according to our criteria, we can readily transform them into others which are not: "If this weapon were suitably placed, then Boston would be destroyed" and "If you press the key marked '7' and the one marked '5', the cash register will yield a slip marked '12.'"

It would be an easy matter, of course, to invent a psychological terminology enabling us to describe perceiving, taking, and assuming in sentences which are not intentional. Instead of saying, for example, that a man *takes* something to be a deer, we could say "His perceptual environment is deer-inclusive." But in so doing, we are using technical terms—"perceptual environment" and "deer-inclusive"—which, presumably, are not needed for the description of nonpsychological phenomena. And unless we can re-express the deer-sentence once again, this time as a nonintentional sentence containing no such technical terms, what we say about the man and the deer will conform to our present version of Brentano's thesis.

How would we go about showing that Brentano was wrong? I shall consider the three most likely methods. None of them seems to be satisfactory.

III

Some philosophers have tried to describe psychological attitudes in terms of *linguistic* behavior. In his inaugural lecture, *Thinking and Meaning*, Professor Ayer tried to define the locution "thinking of *x*" by reference to the use of symbols which designate *x*. A man is *thinking of* a unicorn, Ayer suggested, if (among other things) the man is disposed to use symbols which *designate* unicorns; he *believes* that there are unicorns if (among other things) he is disposed to utter sentences containing words which *designate* or *refer* to unicorns.[5] And perhaps one might try to define "taking" and "assuming" in a similar way. But this type of definition leaves us with our problem.

When we talk about what is "designated" or "referred to" by words or sentences, our own sentences are intentional. When we affirm the sentence "In German, *Einhorn* designates, or refers to, unicorns," we do not imply that there are any unicorns and we do not imply that there are not; and similarly when we deny the sentence. If we think of words and sentences as

---

[5] A. J. Ayer, *Thinking and Meaning*, p. 13. Compare W. S. Sellars, "Mind, Meaning, and Behavior," *Philosophical Studies*, III (1952), 83–95; "A Semantical Solution of the Mind-Body Problem," *Methodos* (1953), pp. 45–85; and "Empiricism and the Philosophy of Mind," in Herbert Feigl and Michael Scriven, eds., *The Foundations of Science and the Concepts of Psychology and Psychoanalysis* (Minneapolis, 1956). See also Leonard Bloomfield, *Linguistic Aspects of Science* (Chicago, 1939), pp. 17–19.

classes of noises and marks, then we may say that words and sentences are "physical" (nonpsychological) phenomena. But we must not suppose the meaning of words and sentences to be a property which they have apart from their relations to the psychological attitudes of the people who *use* them.

For we know, as Schlick once put it, "that meaning does not inhere in a sentence where it might be discovered"; meaning "must be bestowed upon" the sentence.[6] Instead of saying, "In German, *Einhorn* designates, or refers to, unicorns," we could say, less misleadingly, "German-speaking people use the word *Einhorn* in order to designate, or refer to, unicorns." A word or sentence designates so-and-so only if people *use* it to designate so-and-so.

Or can we describe "linguistic behavior" by means of sentences which are not intentional? Can we define such locutions as "the word 'Q' designates so-and-so" in language which is not intentional? If we can do these things, and if, as Ayer suggested, we can define "believing," or "assuming," in terms of linguistic behavior, then we must reject our version of Brentano's thesis. But I do not believe that we can do these things; I do not believe that we can define such locutions as "The word 'Q' designates so-and-so" or "The word 'Q' has such-and-such a *use*" in language which is not intentional.

Let us consider, briefly, the difficulties involved in one attempt to formulate such a definition.

Instead of saying, of a certain word or predicate "Q," that it designates or refers to so-and-so's, we may say that, if there were any so-and-so's, they would satisfy or fulfill the *intension* of the predicate "Q." But how are we to define "intension"? Professor Carnap once proposed a behavioristic definition of this use of "intension" which, if it were adequate, might enable us to formulate a behavioristic, nonintentional definition of "believe" and "assume." Although Carnap later conceded that his account was over-simplified, it is instructive, I think, to note the difficulties which stand in the way of defining "intension"—as well as "designates" and "refers to"—in nonintentional terms.[7]

Carnap had suggested that the "intension" of a predicate in a natural language may be defined in essentially this way: "The intension of a predicate 'Q' for a speaker X is the general condition which an object y must fulfill in order for X to be willing to ascribe the predicate 'Q' to y." Carnap did not define the term "ascribe" which appears in this definition, but from his general discussion we can see, I think, that he would have said something very much like this: "A person X ascribes 'Q' to an object y, provided that, in the presence of y, X gives an affirmative response to the question 'Q?' "

[6] Moritz Schlick, "Meaning and Verification," *Philosophical Review*, XLV (1936), 348; reprinted in Feigl and Sellars, eds., *Readings in Philosophical Analysis*. Compare this analogy, in "Meaning and Free Will," by John Hospers: "Sentences in themselves do not possess meaning; it is misleading to speak of 'the meaning of sentences' at all; meaning being conferred in every case by the speaker, the sentence's meaning is only like the light of the moon: without the sun to give it light, it would possess none. And for an analysis of the light we must go to the sun" (*Philosophy and Phenomenological Research*, X [1950], 308).

[7] Carnap's definition appeared on p. 42 of "Meaning and Synonymy in Natural Languages," *Philosophical Studies*, IV (1955), 33–47. In "On Some Concepts of Pragmatics," *Philosophical Studies*, VI, 89–91, he conceded that "designates" should be defined in terms of "believes." The second article was written in reply to my "A Note on Carnap's Meaning Analysis," which appeared in the same issue (pp. 87–89).

(Let us assume that the expressions "is willing to," "in the presence of," "affirmative response," and "question" present no difficulties.)

Such a definition of "intension" is adequate only if it allows us to say of Karl, who speaks German, that an object *y* fulfills the intension of *"Hund"* for Karl if and only if *y* is a dog. Let us consider, then, a situation in which Karl mistakes something for a dog; he is in the presence of a fox, say, and takes it to be a dog. In this case, Karl would be willing to give an affirmative response to the question *"Hund?"* Hence the fox fulfills the condition which an object must fulfill for Karl to be willing to ascribe *"Hund"* to it. And therefore the definition is inadequate.

Perhaps we can assume that Karl is usually right when he takes something to be a dog. And perhaps, therefore, we can say this: "The intension of '*Hund*' for Karl is the general condition which, more often than not, an object *y* must fulfill in order for Karl to be willing to ascribe '*Hund*' to *y*." But if the occasion we have considered is the only one on which Karl has been in the presence of a *fox*, then, according to the present suggestion, we must say, falsely, that the fox does not fulfill the intension of Karl's word *"Fuchs."* Moreover, if Karl believes there are unicorns and, on the sole occasion when he thinks he sees one, mistakes a horse for a unicorn, then the present suggestion would require us to say, falsely, that the horse fulfills the intension, for Karl, of his word *"Einhorn."*

The obvious way to qualify Carnap's definition would be to reintroduce the term "believe" and say something of this sort: "The intension of a predicate '*Q*' for a speaker X is the general condition which X must *believe* an object *y* to fulfill in order for X to be willing to ascribe the predicate '*Q*' to *y*." And, in general, when we say, "People use such and such a word to refer to so-and-so," at least part of what we mean to say is that people use that word when they wish to express or convey something they *know* or *believe*—or *perceive* or *take*—with respect to so-and-so. But if we define "intension" and "designates" in terms of "believe" and "assume," we can no longer hope, of course, to define "believe" and "assume" in terms of "intension" or "designates."

IV

The second way in which we might try to show that Brentano was wrong may be described by reference to a familiar conception of "sign behavior." Many philosophers and psychologists have suggested, in effect, that a man may be said to *perceive* an object *x*, or to *take* some object *x* to have a certain property *f*, provided only that there is something which *signifies* *x* to him, or which signifies to him that *x* is *f*. But what does "signify" mean?

We cannot be satisfied with the traditional descriptions of "sign behavior," for these, almost invariably, define such terms as "sign" by means of intentional concepts. We cannot say, for instance, that an object is a sign provided it causes someone to *believe*, or *expect*, or *think of* something; for sentences using "believe," "expect," and "think of" are clearly intentional. Nor can we say merely that an object is a sign provided it causes someone to be *set for*, or to be *ready for*, or to *behave appropriately to* something, for sentences using "set for," "ready for," and "behave appropriately to," despite their behavioristic overtones, are also intentional. Similar objections apply to such statements as "One object is a sign of another provided it *introduces* the other object *into the behavioral environment,* as contrasted with the physical environment, of some organism."

If we are to show that Brentano's thesis as applied to *sign* phenomena is mistaken, then we must not introduce any new technical terms into our analysis of sign behavior unless we can show that these terms apply also to nonpsychological situations.

Most attempts at nonintentional definitions of "sign" make use of the concept of *substitute stimulus.* If we use "referent" as short for "what is signified," we may say that, according to such definitions, the sign is described as a substitute for the referent. It is a substitute in the sense that, as stimulus, it has effects upon the subject which are similar to those the referent would have had. Such definitions usually take this form: V is a *sign* of R for a subject S if and only if V affects S in a manner similar to that in which R would have affected S.[8] The bell is a sign of food to the dog, because the bell affects the dog's responses, or his dispositions to respond, in a way similar to that in which the food would have affected them.

This type of definition involves numerous difficulties of which we need mention but one—that of specifying the respect or degree of similarity which must obtain between the effects attributed to the sign and those attributed to the referent. This difficulty is involved in every version of the substitute-stimulus theory. Shall we say that, given the conditions in the above definition, V is a sign of R to a subject S provided only that those responses of S which are stimulated by V are similar in *some* respect to those which have been (or would be) stimulated by R? In other words, should we say that V is a sign of R provided that V has some of the effects which R has had or would have had? This would have the unacceptable consequence that all stimuli signify each other, since any two stimuli have at least some effect in common. Every stimulus causes neural activity, for example; hence, to that extent at least, any two stimuli will have similar effects. Shall we say that V is a sign of R provided that V has *all* the effects which R would have had? If the bell is to have all the effects which the food would have had, then, as Morris notes, the dog must start to eat the bell.[9] Shall we say that V is a sign of R provided that V has the effects which *only* R would have had? If the sign has effects which only the referent can have, then the sign *is* the referent and only food can be a sign of food. The other methods of specify-

---

[8] Compare Charles E. Osgood, *Method and Theory in Experimental Psychology* (New York, 1953), p. 696: "A pattern of stimulation which is not the object is a sign of the object if it evokes in an organism a mediating reaction, this (a) being some fractional part of the total behavior elicited by the object and (b) producing distinctive self-stimulation that mediates responses which would not occur without the previous associa-tion of non-object and object patterns of stimulation. All of these limiting conditions seem necessary. The mediation process must include part of the same behavior made to the object if the sign is to have its representing property." Some of the difficulties of the substitute stimulus concept [qualification (a) in this definition] are met by qualification (b), which implies that the subject must once have perceived the thing signified. But (b) introduces new difficulties. Since I have never seen the President of the United States, no announcement, according to this definition, could signify to me that the President is about to arrive.

[9] See Charles Morris, *Signs, Language, and Behavior,* p. 12, and Max Black, "The Limitations of a Behavioristic Semiotic," *Philosophical Review,* LVI (1947), 258–272.

ing the degree or respect of similarity required by the substitute-stimulus definition, so far as I can see, have equally unacceptable consequences.

Reichenbach, in his *Elements of Symbolic Logic*, has applied this type of analysis to the concept of taking; but the consequences are similar. To say of a subject S, according to Reichenbach, that S *takes* something to be a dog is to say: "There is a z which is a bodily state of S and which is such that, whenever S is sensibly stimulated by a dog, S is in this bodily state z."[10] In other words, there are certain bodily conditions which S must fulfill in order for S to be sensibly stimulated by a dog; and whenever S satisfies any of these conditions, then S is taking something to be a dog.

But among the many conditions one must fulfill if one is to be sensibly stimulated by a dog is that of being alive. Hence if we know that S is alive, we can say that S is taking something to be a dog. The difficulty is that the bodily state z, of Reichenbach's formula, is not specified strictly enough. And the problem is to find an acceptable modification.

In reply to this objection, Reichenbach suggested, in effect, that "S takes something to be a dog" means that S's bodily state has all those neural properties which it must have—which are "physically necessary" for it to have—whenever S is sensibly stimulated by a dog.[11] But this definition has the unacceptable consequence that, whenever S is sensibly stimulated by a dog, then S *takes* the thing to be a dog. Thus, although we can say that a man may be stimulated by a fox and yet take it to be a dog, we can never say that he may be stimulated by a dog and *not* take it to be a dog.[12]

Similar objections apply to definitions using such expressions as "dog responses," "responses specific to dogs," "responses appropriate to dogs," and the like. For the problem of specifying what a man's "dog responses" might be is essentially that of specifying the bodily state to which Reichenbach referred.

V

Of all intentional phenomena, expectation is one of the most simple and, I think, one which is most likely to be definable in terms which are not intentional. If we could define, in nonintentional terms, what it means to say of a man, or an animal, that he expects something—that he expects some

[10] This is a paraphrase of what Hans Reichenbach formulated in special symbols on p. 275 of *Elements of Symbolic Logic* (New York, 1947).

[11] Reichenbach suggests this modification in "On Observing and Perceiving," *Philosophical Studies*, II (1951), pp. 92–93. This paper was written in reply to my "Reichenbach on Observing and Perceiving" (*Philosophical Studies*, II, 45–48), which contains some of the above criticisms. In these papers, as well as in Reichenbach's original discussion, the word "perceive" was used in the way in which we have been using "take." Reichenbach used the term "immediate existence" in place of Brentano's "intentional inexistence"; see *Elements of Symbolic Logic*, p. 274.

[12] This sort of modification may suggest itself: Consider those bodily states which are such that (i) S is in those states whenever he is sensibly stimulated by a dog and (ii) S cannot be in those states whenever he is *not* being stimulated by a dog. Shall we say "S takes something to be a dog" means that S is in this particular class of states? If we define "taking" in this way, then, we must say that, in the present state of psychology and physiology, we have no way of knowing whether anyone ever *does* take anything to be a dog, much less whether people take things to be dogs on just those occasions on which we want to be able to *say* that they take things to be dogs.

state of affairs to come about—then, perhaps, we could define "believing" and "assuming," nonintentionally, in terms of this sense of "expecting." If we are to show that Brentano is wrong, our hope lies here, I think.

For every expectancy, there is some possible state of affairs which would *fulfill* or *satisfy* it, and another possible state of affairs which would *frustrate* or *disrupt* it. If I expect the car to stop, then, it would seem, I am in a state which would be fulfilled or satisfied if and only if the car were to stop—and which would be frustrated or disrupted if and only if the car were not to stop. Hence we might consider defining "expects" in this way:

"S *expects E* to occur" means that S is in a bodily state *b* such that either (i) *b* would be fulfilled if and only if *E* were to occur or (ii) *b* would be disrupted if and only if *E* were not to occur.

Our problem now becomes that of finding appropriate meanings for "fulfill" and "disrupt."

Perhaps there is a way of defining "fulfill" in terms of the psychological concept of *re-enforcement* and of defining "disrupt" in terms of *dis-equilibration, surprise,* or *shock.* And perhaps we can then provide an account of the dog and the bell and the food in terms which will show that this elementary situation is not intentional. It is possible that the dog, because of the sound of the bell, is in a state which is such that either (i) his state will be re-enforced if he receives food or (ii) it will be disequilibrated if he does not. And it is possible that this state can be specified in physiological terms. Whether this is so, of course, is a psychological question which no one, apparently, is yet in a position to answer. But even if it is so, there are difficulties in principle which appear when we try to apply this type of definition to human behavior.

If we apply "expects," as defined, to human behavior, then we must say that the appropriate fulfillments or disruptions must be caused by the occurrence, or nonoccurrence, of the "intentional object"—of *what* it is that is expected. But it is easy to think of situations which, antecedently, we should want to describe as instances of expectation, but in which the fulfillments or disruptions do not occur in the manner required. And to accommodate our definition to such cases, we must make qualifications which can be expressed only by reintroducing the intentional concepts we are trying to eliminate.

This difficulty may be illustrated as follows: Jones, let us suppose, *expects* to meet his aunt at the railroad station within twenty-five minutes. Our formulation, as applied to this situation, would yield: "Jones is in a bodily state which would be fulfilled if he were to meet his aunt at the station within twenty-five minutes or which would be disrupted if he were not to meet her there within that time." But what if he were to meet his aunt and yet *take* her to be someone else? Or if he were to meet someone else and yet *take* her to be his aunt? In such cases, the fulfillments and disruptions would not occur in the manner required by our definition.

If we introduce the intentional term "perceives" or "takes" into our definition of "expects," in order to say, in this instance, that Jones *perceives* his aunt, or *takes* someone to be his aunt, then, of course, we can no longer define "assume"—or "perceive" and "take"—in terms of "expects." It is worth noting, moreover, that even if we allow ourselves the intentional term "perceive" our definition will be inadequate. Suppose that Jones were to visit the bus terminal, believing it to be the railroad station, or that he were to visit the railroad station believing it to be the bus terminal. If he met his aunt at the railroad station, believing it to be the bus terminal, then, contrary to our formula, he may be frustrated or surprised, and, if he fails to meet her there, his state may be fulfilled. Hence we must add further qualifications about what he believes or doesn't believe.[13]

If his visit to the station is brief and if he is not concerned about his aunt, the requisite re-enforcement or frustration may still fail to occur. Shall we add ". . . provided he *looks for* his aunt"? But now we have an intentional expression again. And even if we allow him to look for her, the re-enforcement or frustration may fail to occur if he finds himself able to satisfy desires which are more compelling than that of finding his aunt.

We seem to be led back, then, to the intentional language with which we began. In attempting to apply our definition of "expects" to a situation in which "expects" is ordinarily applicable, we find that we must make certain qualifications and that these qualifications can be formulated only by using intentional terms. We have had to introduce qualifications wherein we speak of the subject *perceiving* or *taking* something to be the object expected; hence we cannot now define "perceive" and "assume" in terms of "expect." We have had to add that the subject has certain *beliefs* concerning the nature of the conditions under which he perceives, or fails to perceive, the object. And we have referred to what he is *looking for* and to his other possible *desires*.

It may be that some of the simple "expectancies" we attribute to infants or to animals can be described, nonintentionally, in terms of re-enforcement or frustration. And possibly, as Ogden and Richards intimated, someone may yet find a way of showing that believing, perceiving, and taking are somehow "theoretically analysable" into such expectancies.[14] But until such programs are carried out, there is, I believe, some justification for saying that Brentano's thesis does apply to the concept of *perceiving*.

[13] R. B. Braithwaite in "Belief and Action" (*Aristotelian Society*, suppl. vol. XX [1946] p. 10) suggests that a man may be said to believe a proposition *p* provided this condition obtains: "If at a time when an occasion arises relevant to *p*, his springs of action are *s*, he will perform an action which is such that, if *p* is true, it will tend to fulfill *s*, and which is such that, if *p* is false, it will not tend to satisfy *s*." But the definition needs qualifications in order to exclude those people who, believing truly (*p*) that the water is deep at the base of Niagara Falls and wishing (*s*) to survive a trip over the falls, have yet acted in a way which has not tended to satisfy *s*. Moreover, if we are to use such a definition to show that Brentano was wrong, we must provide a non-intentional definition of the present use of "wish" or "spring of action." And, with Braithwaite's definition of "believe," it would be difficult to preserve the distinction which, apparently, we ought to make between *believing* a proposition and *acting upon* it (see Chapter One, Section 2). I have proposed detailed criticisms of a number of such definitions of "believe" in "Sentences about Believing," *Proceedings of the Aristotelian Society*, LVI (1955–1956), 125–148. Some of the difficulties involved in defining *purpose* nonintentionally are pointed out by Richard Taylor in "Comments on a Mechanistic Conception of Purpose," *Philosophy of Science*, XVII (1950), 310–317, and "Purposeful and Non-purposeful Behavior: A Rejoinder," *ibid.*, 327–332.

[14] C. K. Ogden and I. A. Richards, *The Meaning of Meaning*, 5th ed. (London, 1938), p. 71.

Further References

Alston, William P. *Philosophy of Language.* Englewood Cliffs, N. J.: Prentice-Hall, 1964.*

Armstrong, D. M. *Perception and the Physical World.* London: Routledge & Kegan Paul, 1961.

Austin, J. L. *How to Do Things with Words.* J. O. Urmson (ed.). London: Oxford University Press, 1962.†

———. *Sense and Sensibilia.* G. J. Warnock (ed.). Oxford: Clarendon Press, 1962.†

Ayer, A. J. *The Foundations of Empirical Knowledge.* London: Macmillan, 1940.*

———. *Language, Truth and Logic.* Rev. ed. New York: Dover, 1946.*

Ayer, A. J. (ed.). *Logical Positivism.* New York: The Free Press, 1959.†

Black, Max. *Language and Philosophy.* Ithaca, N. Y. : Cornell University Press, 1949.

———. *Models and Metaphors.* Ithaca, N. Y.: Cornell University Press, 1962.

Black, Max (ed.). *The Importance of Language.* Englewood Cliffs, N. J.: Prentice-Hall, 1962.*

Caton, Charles E. (ed.). *Philosophy and Ordinary Language.* Urbana: University of Illinois Press, 1963.*

Chappell, V. C. (ed.). *Ordinary Language.* Englewood Cliffs, N. J.: Prentice-Hall, 1964.*

Chisholm, Roderick M. *Perceiving.* Ithaca, N. Y.: Cornell University Press, 1957.

———. *Theory of Knowledge.* Englewood Cliffs, N. J.: Prentice-Hall, 1966.*

Feigl, Herbert, and Sellars, Wilfrid (eds.). *Readings in Philosophical Analysis.* New York: Appleton-Century-Crofts, 1949.

Flew, A. G. N. (ed.). *Logic and Language.* Oxford: Basil Blackwell, First Series, 1951, Second Series, 1953.†

Fodor, Jerry A., and Katz, Jerrold J. (eds.). *The Structure of Language.* Englewood Cliffs, N. J.: Prentice-Hall, 1964.

Hamlyn, D. W. *Sensation and Perception.* London: Routledge & Kegan Paul, 1961.

Hill, T. E. *Contemporary Theories of Knowledge.* New York: Ronald Press, 1961.

Hirst, R. J. *The Problems of Perception.* London: Allen & Unwin, 1959.

Hirst, R. J. (ed.). *Perception and the External World.* New York: Macmillan, 1965.*

Katz, Jerrold J. *Philosophy of Language.* New York: Harper & Row, 1966.

Linsky, Leonard (ed.). *Semantics and the Philosophy of Language.* Urbana: University of Illinois Press, 1952.

Macdonald, Margaret (ed.). *Philosophy and Analysis.* Oxford: Basil Blackwell, 1954.

Moore, G. E. *Some Main Problems of Philosophy.* London: Allen & Unwin, 1953.†

Pap, Arthur. *Elements of Analytic Philosophy.* New York: Macmillan, 1949.

Price, H. H. *Perception.* 2nd ed. London: Methuen, 1950.

Quine, W. F. *From a Logical Point of View.* Cambridge: Harvard University Press, 1953.†

———. *Word and Object.* Cambridge: MIT Press, 1960.†

Rollins, C. D. (ed.). *Knowledge and Experience.* Pittsburgh: University of Pittsburgh Press, 1963.

Russell, Bertrand. *An Inquiry into Meaning and Truth.* London: Allen & Unwin, 1940.†

Ryle, Gilbert. *Dilemmas.* Cambridge: Cambridge University Press, 1954.†

Smythies, J. R. *Analysis of Perception.* London: Routledge & Kegan Paul, 1956.

Strawson, P. F. *Individuals.* London: Methuen, 1959.†

Swartz, R. J. (ed.). *Perceiving, Sensing, and Knowing.* New York: Doubleday, 1965.*

Urmson, J. O. *Philosophical Analysis.* London: Oxford University Press, 1956.

Waismann, Friedrich. *The Principles of Linguistic Philosophy.* London: Macmillan, 1965.

Weinberg, J. R. *An Examination of Logical Positivism.* London: Routledge & Kegan Paul, 1936.†

Wittgenstein, Ludwig. *The Blue & Brown Books.* Oxford: Basil Blackwell, 1958.†

———. *Philosophical Investigations.* G. E. M. Anscombe (trans.). Oxford: Basil Blackwell, 1953.

Ziff, Paul. *Semantic Analysis.* Ithaca, N. Y.: Cornell University Press, 1960.

* Paperback edition.   † Also available in a paperback edition.

:VII:

---

*Conduct
and Values*

INTRODUCTION

The history of moral philosophy has been primarily concerned with conceptual questions about the proper norms of human conduct: nearly all discussions of ethical issues from Plato to G. E. Moore have focused on what men ought to do with their lives or on what the good life may be supposed to be. There is a natural conservatism in such an outlook; fresh contributions will depend heavily on a close scanning of the classics of the past, and one is bound to suppose that the true values cannot be very different from those that the masters of the tradition have supported. The continuity of ancient and modern texts is particularly striking: Aristotle's *Ethics*, for instance, is oddly up-to-date, however much one may disagree with its details.

A noticeable discontinuity in the tradition has appeared only very recently, and for a reason that bears directly on the evolution of philosophical investigation in other areas. To whatever extent they disagreed with one another about the proprieties of human conduct, the classical writers of the moral, legal, and political tradition were at least tacitly in agreement that the norms themselves and the claims made with respect to them were open to rational inspection and discovery. In a word, the tradition has been confidently committed to the belief, even though it had been hardly explored, that we can have knowledge of the norms of human conduct.

In our own time—largely through the effectiveness of Moore's analysis of the naturalistic fallacy (although ironically, contrary to his own intention)—the question of whether and in what sense we can be said to have moral knowledge has become the principal focus of debate. This is not to say that the possibility of moral knowledge is in doubt, although such reactions to Moore's account as the emotivism of A. J. Ayer (VII:12) and C. L. Stevenson have raised even that challenge. It is rather to say that in our own time moral philosophy has made certain so-called metaethical issues—as distinct from the substantive issues of what, normatively, one ought to do or what the good life is—the dominant philosophical issues. By this shift, moral philosophy has come to bear a noticeable resemblance to philosophy of language and to epistemology. Advice and direction, important as they obviously are, have inevitably dwindled as philosophical concerns.

The literature that antedated the strongly metaethical drift of recent work cannot be neatly compartmentalized as ethical or political or legal. Often, as in Plato's *Republic* (VII:1), which stands nearly at the beginning of systematic philosophy, questions of responsible conduct are viewed as having both personal (but not private) and communal implications. In fact, much of the charm and fascination of Plato's *Republic* depends on the close analogy that is posited by Socrates between the state and the soul. Even Aristotle's *Ethics* (VII:2), which is explicitly concerned with the well-being of individual men, presupposes an ordered community of a preferred sort. Leaving aside narrow questions of government and constitutionality, we must admit that for relatively large groups of men there is an inescapable continuity between normative questions of ethics, politics, and law.

Broadly speaking, ethical literature is classified with respect to whether the norms of conduct are thought to be governed by considerations of goodness or of rightness, as well as with respect to the dependence or independence of these concepts. Book I of Plato's *Republic*, for instance, draws our attention to the puzzling way in which considerations of goodness and rightness find their way into the simplest, most characteristic ethical reflection. Plato does not allow his characters properly to debate the nature of ethical rules—a typically metaethical question—but sets them instead the task of elaborating the vision of the good life. The resultant picture, whether it is construed ethically or politically, presupposes the discovery of the essential nature of man, in the sense of the discovery of his essential function or functions.

The theory of the good life thus proposed, which Plato shares with Aristotle (although they disagree about the detailed plan of the good life) and which, in a curious sense, the Greeks share with certain of the great Christian authors (witness St. Thomas Aquinas [VII:3]), has come to be called eudaimonism: this is the view that the good life is simply the proper functioning of man, the fulfilment of man's natural gifts. The somewhat conditional sense in which this view may be ascribed to such Christian thinkers as St. Augustine and even St. Thomas reflects their conception of the role of divinely ordained obligations and laws. Although these obligations and laws may be construed somewhat eudaimonistically (as in Thomism), they nevertheless provide historically influential grounds for the development of deontological ethics, that is, the ethics of obligation (and therefore of what is right), which is assumed to be logically independent of, and morally prior to, considerations of goodness and happiness.

A good deal of the history of ethical theory contains variations on the theme of human happiness. In Thomas Hobbes (VII:4), for instance, a type of psychological drive theory replaces the classical accounts of the organization of the soul. Hobbes thought of life, in moral and political terms, as being concerned with the gratification and frustration of conative forces; what he proposed was not a model of the good life in terms of human talents but a set of rational rules of conduct, given our nature, to which *any* proposed moral or political program must subscribe.

We find in Hobbes, therefore, the beginnings of utilitarian planning (at once personal and communal) with a decidedly hedonistic bent: obligation, which is rational enough, is conceptually dependent on what is good for men. On the other hand, the paradoxes of hedonism—in which pleasures and pains are not qualitatively, but only quantitatively, graded—oblige John Stuart Mill (VII:6), against his own training, to lead the theme of human happiness back to a version of eudaimonism, with its emphasis on the difference between the lower and higher parts of human nature. And in the work of John Dewey (VII:8) we find a relativizing and evolutionizing of human nature, with the result that both eudaimonism and hedonism are given a loosely biological appearance that adjusts them to the democratic expression of interests (as also, to some extent, in the view of R. B. Perry [VII:11]).

The great secular tradition of deontological ethics counts Immanuel Kant, without a doubt, as its patron saint. Kant (VII:5) sought to explicate the injunction that one ought to act rationally, in such a way that the logical form of would-be maxims of action might alone decide the morality (and rationality) of our conduct. The pursuit of happiness he recognizes to be natural—that to which we are by nature inclined—not necessarily in opposition to morality but not at all concerned with morality per se. Yet even Kant's exploration of types of duties, although it remains steadfastly deontological in form, must make certain assumptions about human nature—assumptions that may be broadly termed teleological. With respect to Kant's account, these assumptions raise doubts about the possibility or reasonableness of separating sharply the formal and material aspects of alleged duties.

In F. H. Bradley (VII:7) deontological preferences are construed in historical terms (through the same Hegelian influences that ultimately affected, although not so obviously, the teleological account of Dewey) and personal and communal concerns are brought together. Historical development and emergence provide the basis for rational conduct and duties, which are no longer assumed to be fixed for rational beings, but which may be discerned through insight into the essential nature of the society in which men find themselves. By this maneuver, the duties to which we are bound are able, for Bradley, to have at one and the same time the formal credentials of duties that are advocated rationally and the full, concrete content of policies that bear on the complex, actual life of interested human beings. Bradley sees his own efforts, therefore, as offering a corrective both to Kant's formalism and to the subjective criteria of utilitarianism.

Throughout the entire history of ethical theory, from the views of Thrasymachus in the *Republic* down to the scrupulous investigations of Henry Sidgwick, the question of whether rational conduct can be formulated as an egoistic program, or whether it is, by its very nature, bound to posit the same rules for all human agents, has been particularly intriguing, although not, curiously enough, systematically pursued. Historically, classical utilitarian theory has forced attention to the issue because of the self-centered nature of psychological hedonism and the intended altruism and universality of its ethical theorems. Brian Medlin's account (VII:9) of the logical difficulties of ethical egoism is one of the very few efforts pointedly addressed to the issue.

G. E. Moore (VII:10) ushers in an entirely new development in the history of ethical theory. Following Sidgwick, Moore explores the possibility of refinements in utilitarianism. But, in advancing his own account, he pauses to consider the logical properties of ethical predicates—in particular, "good." His discussion of the so-called naturalistic fallacy and of the "open-question" argument marks the beginning of the metaethical tradition. No philosophically relevant discussion of ethical issues since the appearance of *Principia Ethica* has been able to avoid coming to grips with Moore's challenge, although most accounts have shown no great interest in his normative convictions. R. B. Perry, in spite of his familiarity with Moore's challenge, has remained committed to a so-called naturalistic position. And indeed, Moore's account of the fallacy may be seen, on inspection, to be indecisive.

More characteristically, in our own time, A. J. Ayer has been inclined, like others (C. L. Stevenson, R. M. Hare), to reject Moore's incipient intuitionism—that is, Moore's adjustment to the fact that we grasp ethical values in a way quite different from the way in which we perceive sensible qualities—and has turned instead to the consideration of noncognitive interpretations of ethical discourse. This sort of reaction, however understandable and relevant to an analysis of the rich uses of ethical discourse, is simply too extreme. The pendulum has begun to swing back again: moral judgments are taken to be capable of being true or false, and it is no longer considered naive or uninformed to speak about moral knowledge. Kurt Baier's view (VII:13), for example, is in accord with this most recent development within moral theory.

Community, Interest, and Responsibility

1

JUSTICE AND THE GOOD LIFE

Plato

I

CEPHALUS: JUSTICE AS HONESTY IN WORD AND DEED

. . . . . .

Socrates. To tell the truth, Cephalus, I enjoy talking with very old people. They have gone before us on a road by which we too may have to travel, and I think we do well to learn from them what it is like, easy or difficult, rough or smooth. And now that you have reached an age when your foot, as the poets say, is on the threshold, I should like to hear what report you can give and whether you find it a painful time of life.

. . . . . .

. . . was your wealth, Cephalus, mostly inherited or have you made your own fortune?

Made my fortune, Socrates? As a man of business I stand somewhere between my grandfather and my father. My grandfather, who was my namesake, inherited about as much property as I have now and more than doubled it; whereas my father Lysanias reduced it below its present level. I shall be content if I can leave these sons of mine not less than I inherited, and perhaps a little more.

I asked, said I, because you strike me as not caring overmuch about money; and that is generally so with men who have not made their own fortune. . . . one more question: what do you take to be the greatest advantage you have got from being wealthy?

From *The Republic of Plato*, F. M. Cornford, trans. (Oxford: 1941), Book I, Chaps. I–IV, pp. 4, 5, 6–7, 9–40. Reprinted by permission of The Clarendon Press, Oxford.

One that perhaps not many people would take my word for. I can tell you, Socrates, that, when the prospect of dying is near at hand, a man begins to feel some alarm about things that never troubled him before. He may have laughed at those stories they tell of another world and of punishments there for wrongdoing in this life; but now the soul is tormented by a doubt whether they may not be true. Maybe from the weakness of old age, or perhaps because, now that he is nearer to what lies beyond, he begins to get some glimpse of it himself—at any rate he is beset with fear and misgiving; he begins thinking over the past: is there anyone he has wronged? If he finds that his life has been full of wrongdoing, he starts up from his sleep in terror like a child, and his life is haunted by dark forebodings; whereas, if his conscience is clear, that 'sweet Hope' that Pindar speaks of is always with him to tend his age. Indeed, Socrates, there is great charm in those lines describing the man who has led a life of righteousness:

> Hope is his sweet companion, she who guides
> Man's wandering purpose, warms his heart
> And nurses tenderly his age.

That is admirably expressed, admirably. Now in this, as I believe, lies the chief value of wealth, not for everyone, perhaps, but for the right-thinking man. It can do much to save us from going to that other world in fear of having cheated or deceived anyone even unintentionally or of being in debt to some god for sacrifice or to some man for money. Wealth has many other uses, of course; but, taking one with another, I should regard this as the best use that can be made of it by a man of sense.

You put your case admirably, Cephalus, said I. But take this matter of doing right: can we say that it really consists in nothing more nor less than telling the truth and paying back anything we may have received? Are not these very actions sometimes right and sometimes wrong? Suppose, for example, a friend who had lent us a weapon were to go mad and then ask for it back, surely anyone would say we ought not to return it. It would not be 'right' to do so; nor yet to tell the truth without reserve to a madman.

No, it would not.

Right conduct, then, cannot be defined as telling the truth and restoring anything we have been trusted with.

Yes, it can, Polemarchus broke in, at least if we are to believe Simonides.

Well, well, said Cephalus, I will bequeath the argument to you. It is time for me to attend to the sacrifice.

Your part, then, said Polemarchus, will fall to me as your heir.

By all means, said Cephalus with a smile; and with that he left us, to see to the sacrifice.

II

POLEMARCHUS: JUSTICE AS HELPING FRIENDS
AND HARMING ENEMIES

.   .   .

Then, said I, if you are to inherit this discussion, tell me, what is this saying of Simonides about right conduct which you approve?

That it is just to render every man his due. That seems to me a fair statement.

It is certainly hard to question the inspired wisdom of a poet like Simonides; but what this saying means you may know, Polemarchus, but I do not. Obviously it does not mean what we were speaking of just now—returning something we have been entrusted with to the owner even when he has gone out of his mind. And yet surely it is his due, if he asks for it back?

Yes.

But it is out of the question to give it back when he has gone mad?

True.

Simonides, then, must have meant something different from that when he said it was just to render a man his due.

Certainly he did; his idea was that, as between friends, what one owes to another is to do him good, not harm.

I see, said I; to repay money entrusted to one is not to render what is due, if the two parties are friends and the repayment proves harmful to the lender. That is what you say Simonides meant?

Yes, certainly.

And what about enemies? Are we to render whatever is their due to them?

Yes certainly, what really is due to them; which means, I suppose, what is appropriate to an enemy—some sort of injury.

It seems, then, that Simonides was using words with a hidden meaning, as poets will. He really meant to define justice as rendering to everyone what is appropriate to him; only he called that his 'due.'

Well, why not?

But look here, said I. Suppose we could question Simonides about the art of medicine—whether a physician can be described as rendering to some object what is due or appropriate to it; how do you think he would answer?

That the physician administers the appropriate diet or remedies to the body.

And the art of cookery—can that be described in the same way?

Yes; the cook gives the appropriate seasoning to his dishes.

Good. And the practice of justice?

If we are to follow those analogies, Socrates, justice would be rendering services or injuries to friends or enemies.

So Simonides means by justice doing good to friends and harm to enemies?

I think so.

And in matters of health who would be the most competent to treat friends and enemies in that way?

A physician.

And on a voyage, as regards the dangers of the sea?

A ship's captain.

In what sphere of action, then, will the just man be the most competent to do good or harm?

In war, I should imagine; when he is fighting on the side of his friends and against his enemies.

I see. But when we are well and staying on shore, the doctor and the ship's captain are of no use to us.

True.

Is it also true that the just man is useless when we are not at war?

I should not say that.

So justice has its uses in peace-time too?

Yes.

Like farming, which is useful for producing crops, or shoemaking, which is useful for providing us with shoes. Can you tell me for what purposes justice is useful or profitable in time of peace?

For matters of business, Socrates.

In a partnership, you mean?

Yes.

But if we are playing draughts, or laying bricks, or making music, will the just man be as good and helpful a partner as an expert draught-player, or a builder, or a musician?

No.

Then in what kind of partnership will he be more helpful?

Where money is involved, I suppose.

Except, perhaps, Polemarchus, when we are putting our money to some use. If we are buying or selling a horse, a judge of horses would be a better partner; or if we are dealing in ships, a ship-wright or a sea-captain.

I suppose so.

Well, when will the just man be specially useful in handling our money?

When we want to deposit it for safe-keeping.

When the money is to lie idle, in fact?

Yes.

So justice begins to be useful only when our money is out of use?

Perhaps so.

And in the same way, I suppose, if a pruning-knife is to be used, or a shield, or a lyre, then a vine-dresser, or a soldier, or a musician will be of service; but justice is helpful only when these things are to be kept safe. In fact justice is never of any use in using things; it becomes useful when they are useless.

That seems to follow.

If that is so, my friend, justice can hardly be a thing of much value. And here is another point. In boxing or fighting of any sort skill in dealing blows goes with skill in keeping them off; and the same doctor that can keep us from disease would also be clever at producing it by stealth; or again, a general will be good at keeping his army safe, if he can also cheat the enemy and steal his plans and dispositions. So a man who is expert in keeping things will always make an expert thief.

Apparently.

The just man, then, being good at keeping money safe, will also be good at stealing it.

That seems to be the conclusion, at any rate.

So the just man turns out to be a kind of thief. You must have learnt that from Homer, who showed his predilection for Odysseus' grandfather Autolycus by remarking that he surpassed all men in cheating and perjury. Justice, according to you and Homer and Simonides, turns out to be a form of skill in cheating, provided it be to help a friend or harm an enemy. That was what you meant?

Good God, no, he protested; but I have forgotten now what I did mean. All the same, I do still believe that justice consists in helping one's friends and harming one's enemies.

.   .   .

Which do you mean by a man's friends and enemies—those whom he believes to be good honest people and the reverse, or those who really are, though they may not seem so?

Naturally, his loves and hates depend on what he believes.

But don't people often mistake an honest man for a rogue, or a rogue for an honest man; in which case they regard good people as enemies and bad people as friends?

No doubt.

But all the same, it will then be right for them to help the rogue and to injure the good man?

Apparently.

And yet a good man is one who is not given to doing wrong.

True.

According to your account, then, it is right to ill-treat a man who does no wrong.

No, no, Socrates; that can't be sound doctrine.

It must be the wrongdoers, then, that it is right to injure, and the honest that are to be helped.

That sounds better.

Then, Polemarchus, the conclusion will be that for a bad judge of character it will often be right to injure his friends, when they really are rogues, and to help his enemies, when they really are honest men—the exact opposite of what we took Simonides to mean.

That certainly does follow, he said. We must shift our ground. Perhaps our definition of friend and enemy was wrong.

What definition, Polemarchus?

We said a friend was one whom we believe to be an honest man.

And how are we to define him now?

As one who really is honest as well as seeming so. If he merely seems so, he will be only a seeming friend. And the same will apply to enemies.

On this showing, then, it is the good people that will be our friends, the wicked our enemies.

Yes.

You would have us, in fact, add something to our original definition of justice: it will not mean merely doing good to friends and harm to enemies, but doing good to friends who are good, and harm to enemies who are wicked.

Yes, I think that is all right.

Can it really be a just man's business to harm any human being?

Certainly; it is right for him to harm bad men who are his enemies.

But does not harming a horse or a dog mean making it a worse horse or dog, so that each will be a less perfect creature in its own special way?

Yes.

Isn't that also true of human beings—that to harm them means making them worse men by the standard of human excellence?

Yes.

And is not justice a peculiarly human excellence?

Undoubtedly.

To harm a man, then, must mean making him less just.

I suppose so.

But a musician or a riding-master cannot be exercising his special skill, if he makes his pupils unmusical or bad riders.

No.

Whereas the just man is to exercise his justice by making men unjust? Or, in more general terms, the good are to make men bad by exercising their virtue? Can that be so?

No, it cannot.

It can no more be the function of goodness to do harm than of heat to cool or of drought to produce moisture. So if the just man is good, the business of harming people, whether friends or not, must belong to his opposite, the unjust.

I think that is perfectly true, Socrates.

So it was not a wise saying that justice is giving every man his due, if that means that harm is due from the just man to his enemies, as well as help to his friends. That is not true; because we have found that it is never right to harm anyone.

I agree.

Then you and I will make common cause against anyone who attributes that doctrine to Simonides or to any of the old canonical sages, like Bias or Pittacus.

Yes, he said, I am prepared to support you.

Do you know, I think that account of justice, as helping friends and harming enemies, must be due to some despot, so rich and powerful that he thought he could do as he liked—someone like Periander, or Perdiccas, or Xerxes, or Ismenias of Thebes.

That is extremely probable.

Very good, said I; and now that we have disposed of that definition of justice, can anyone suggest another?

III

THRASYMACHUS: JUSTICE AS THE INTEREST OF THE STRONGER

.   .   .

All this time Thrasymachus had been trying more than once to break in upon our conversation; but his neighbours had restrained him, wishing to hear the argument to the end. In the pause after my last words he could keep quiet no longer; but gathering himself up like a wild beast he sprang at us as if he would tear us in pieces. Polemarchus and I were frightened out of our wits, when he burst out to the whole company:

What is the matter with you two, Socrates? Why do you go on in this imbecile way, politely referring to each other's nonsense? If you really want to know what justice means, stop asking questions and scoring off the answers you get. You know very well it is easier to ask questions than to answer them. Answer yourself, and tell us what you think justice means. I won't have you telling us it is the same as what is obligatory or useful or advantageous or profitable or expedient; I want a clear and precise statement; I won't put up with that sort of verbiage.

. . . . . .

. . . Thrasymachus was evidently longing to win credit, for he was sure he had an admirable answer ready, though he made a show of insisting that I should be the one to reply. In the end he gave way and exclaimed:

So this is what Socrates' wisdom comes to! He refuses to teach, and goes about learning from others without offering so much as thanks in return.

I do learn from others, Thrasymachus; that is quite true; but you are wrong to call me ungrateful. I give in return all I can—praise; for I have no money. And how ready I am to applaud any idea that seems to me sound, you will see in a moment, when you have stated your own; for I am sure that will be sound.

Listen then, Thrasymachus began. What I say is that 'just' or 'right' means nothing but what is to the interest of the stronger party. Well, where is your applause? You don't mean to give it me.

I will, as soon as I understand, I said. I don't see yet what you mean by right being the interest of the stronger party. For instance, Polydamas, the athlete, is stronger than we are, and it is to his interest to eat beef for the sake of his muscles; but surely you don't mean that the same diet would be good for weaker men and therefore be right for us?

You are trying to be funny, Socrates. It's a low trick to take my words in the sense you think will be most damaging.

No, no, I protested; but you must explain.

Don't you know, then, that a state may be ruled by a despot, or a democracy, or an aristocracy?

Of course.

And that the ruling element is always the strongest?

Yes.

Well then, in every case the laws are made by the ruling party in its own interest; a democracy makes democratic laws, a despot autocratic ones, and so on. By making these laws they define as 'right' for their subjects whatever is for their own interest, and they call anyone who breaks them a 'wrong-doer' and punish him accordingly. That is what I mean: in all states alike 'right' has the same meaning, namely what is for the interest of the party established in power, and that is the strongest. So the sound conclusion is that what is 'right' is the same everywhere: the interest of the stronger party.

Now I see what you mean, said I; whether it is true or not, I must try to make out. When you define right in terms of interest, you are yourself giving one of those answers you forbade to me; though, to be sure, you add 'to the stronger party.'

An insignificant addition, perhaps!

Its importance is not clear yet; what is clear is that we must find out whether your definition is true. I agree myself that right is in a sense a matter of interest; but when you add 'to the stronger party,' I don't know about that. I must consider.

Go ahead, then.

I will. Tell me this. No doubt you also think it is right to obey the men in power?

I do.

Are they infallible in every type of state, or can they sometimes make a mistake?

Of course they can make a mistake.

In framing laws, then, they may do their work well or badly?

No doubt.

Well, that is to say, when the laws they make are to their own interest; badly, when they are not?

Yes.

But the subjects are to obey any law they lay down, and they will then be doing right?

Of course.

If so, by your account, it will be right to do what is not to the interest of the stronger party, as well as what is so.

What's that you are saying?

Just what you said, I believe; but let us look again. Haven't you admitted that the rulers, when they enjoin certain acts on their subjects, sometimes mistake their own best interests, and at the same time that it is right for the subjects to obey, whatever they may enjoin?

Yes, I suppose so.

Well, that amounts to admitting that it is right to do what is not to the interest of the rulers or the stronger party. They may unwittingly enjoin what is to their own disadvantage; and you say it is right for the others to do as they are told. In that case, their duty must be the opposite of what you said, because the weaker will have been ordered to do what is against the interest of the stronger. You with your intelligence must see how that follows.

Yes, Socrates, said Polemarchus, that is undeniable.

No doubt, Cleitophon broke in, if you are to be a witness on Socrates' side.

No witness is needed, replied Polemarchus; Thrasymachus himself admits that rulers sometimes ordain acts that are to their own disadvantage, and that it is the subjects' duty to do them.

That is because Thrasymachus said it was right to do what you are told by the men in power.

Yes, but he also said that what is to the interest of the stronger party is right; and, after making both these assertions, he admitted that the stronger sometimes command the weaker subjects to act against their interests. From all which it follows that what is in the stronger's interest is no more right than what is not.

No, said Cleitophon; he meant whatever the stronger *believes* to be in his own interest. That is what the subject must do, and what Thrasymachus meant to define as right.

That was not what he said, rejoined Polemarchus.

No matter, Polemarchus, said I; if Thrasymachus says so now, let us take him in that sense. Now, Thrasymachus, tell me, was that what you intended to say—that right means what the stronger thinks is to his interest, whether it really is so or not?

Most certainly not, he replied. Do you suppose I should speak of a man as 'stronger' or 'superior' at the very moment when he is making a mistake?

I did think you said as much when you admitted that rulers are not always infallible.

That is because you are a quibbler, Socrates. Would you say a man deserves to be called a physician at the moment when he makes a mistake in treating his patient and just in respect of that mistake; or a mathematician, when he does a sum wrong and just in so far as he gets a wrong result? Of course we do commonly speak of a physician or a mathematician or a scholar having made a mistake; but really none of these, I should say, is ever mistaken, in so far as he is worthy of the name we give him. So strictly speaking—and you are all for being precise—no one who practises a craft makes mistakes. A man is mistaken when his knowledge fails him; and at that moment he is no craftsman. And what is true of craftsmanship or any sort of skill is true of the ruler: he is never mistaken so long as he is acting as a ruler; though anyone might speak of a ruler making a mistake, just as he might of a physician. You must understand that I was talking in that loose way when I answered your question just now; but the precise statement is this. The ruler, in so far as he is acting as a ruler, makes no mistakes and consequently enjoins what is best for himself; and that is what the subject is to do. So, as I said at first, 'right' means doing what is to the interest of the stronger.

Very well, Thrasymachus, said I. So you think I am quibbling?

I am sure you are.

You believe my questions were maliciously designed to damage your position?

I know it. But you will gain nothing by that. You cannot outwit me by cunning, and you are not the man to crush me in the open.

Bless your soul, I answered, I should not think of trying. But, to prevent any more misunderstanding, when you speak of that ruler or stronger party whose interest the weaker ought to serve, please make it clear whether you are using the words in the ordinary way or in that strict sense you have just defined.

I mean a ruler in the strictest possible sense. Now quibble away and be as malicious as you can. I want no mercy. But you are no match for me.

Do you think me mad enough to beard a lion or try to outwit a Thrasymachus?

You did try just now, he retorted, but it wasn't a success.

.   .   .

Enough of this, said I. Now tell me about the physician in that strict sense you spoke of: is it his business to earn money or to treat his patients? Remember, I mean your physician who is worthy of the name.

To treat his patients.

And what of the ship's captain in the true sense? Is he a mere seaman or the commander of the crew?

The commander.

Yes, we shall not speak of him as a seaman just because he is on board a ship. That is not the point. He is called captain because of his skill and authority over the crew.

Quite true.

And each of these people has some special interest?

No doubt.

And the craft in question exists for the very purpose of discovering that interest and providing for it?

Yes.

Can it equally be said of any craft that it has an interest, other than its own greatest possible perfection?

What do you mean by that?

Here is an illustration. If you ask me whether it is sufficient for the human body just to be itself, with no need of help from without, I should say, Certainly not; it has weaknesses and defects, and its condition is not all that it might be. That is precisely why the art of medicine was invented: it was designed to help the body and provide for its interest. Would not that be true?

It would.

But now take the art of medicine itself. Has that any defects or weaknesses? Does any art stand in need of some further perfection, as the eye would be imperfect without the power of vision or the ear without hearing, so that in their case an art is required that will study their interests and provide for their carrying out those functions? Has the art itself any corresponding need of some further art to remedy its defects and look after its interests; and will that further art require yet another, and so on for ever? Or will every art look after its own interests? Or, finally, is it not true that no art needs to have its weaknesses remedied or its interests studied either by another art or by itself, because no art has in itself any weakness or fault, and the only interest it is required to serve is that of its subject-matter? In itself, an art is sound and flawless, so long as it is entirely true to its own nature as an art in the strictest sense—and it is the strict sense that I want you to keep in view. Is not that true?

So it appears.

Then, said I, the art of medicine does not study its own interest, but the needs of the body, just as a groom shows his skill by caring for horses, not for the art of grooming. And so every art seeks, not its own advantage—for it has no deficiencies—but the interest of the subject on which it is exercised.

It appears so.

But surely, Thrasymachus, every art has authority and superior power over its subject.

To this he agreed, though very reluctantly.

So far as arts are concerned, then, no art ever studies or enjoins the interest of the superior or stronger party, but always that of the weaker over which it has authority.

Thrasymachus assented to this at last, though he tried to put up a fight. I then went on:

So the physician, as such, studies only the patient's interest, not his own. For as we agreed, the business of the physician, in the strict sense, is not to make money for himself, but to exercise his power over the patient's body; and the ship's captain, again, considered strictly as no mere sailor, but in command of the crew, will study and enjoin the interest of his subordinates, not his own.

He agreed reluctantly.

And so with government of any kind: no ruler, in so far as he is acting as ruler, will study or enjoin what is for his own interest. All that he says and does will be said and done with a view to what is good and proper for the subject for whom he practises his art.

.   .   .

At this point, when everyone could see that Thrasymachus' definition of justice had been turned inside out, instead of making any reply, he said:

Socrates, have you a nurse?

Why do you ask such a question as that? I said. Wouldn't it be better to answer mine?

Because she lets you go about sniffling like a child whose nose wants wiping. She hasn't even taught you to know a shepherd when you see one, or his sheep either.

What makes you say that?

Why, you imagine that a herdsman studies the interests of his flocks or cattle, tending and fattening them up with some other end in view than his master's profit or his own; and so you don't see that, in politics, the genuine ruler regards his subjects exactly like sheep, and thinks of nothing else, night and day, but the good he can get out of them for himself. You are so far out in your notions of right and wrong, justice and injustice, as not to know that 'right' actually means what is good for someone else, and to be 'just' means serving the interest of the stronger who rules, at the cost of the subject who obeys; whereas injustice is just the reverse, asserting its authority over those innocents who are called just, so that they minister solely to their master's advantage and happiness, and not in the least degree to their own. Innocent as you are yourself, Socrates, you must see that a just man always has the worst of it. Take a private business: when a partnership is wound up, you will never find that the more honest of two partners comes off with the larger share; and in their relations to the state, when there are taxes to be paid, the honest man will pay more than the other on the same amount of property; or if there is money to be distributed, the dishonest will get it all. When either of them hold some public office, even if the just man loses in no other way, his private affairs at any rate will suffer from neglect, while his principles will not allow him to help himself from the public funds; not to mention the offence he will give to his friends and relations by refusing to sacrifice those principles to do them a good turn. Injustice has all the opposite advantages. I am speaking of the type I described just now, the man who can get the better of other people on a large scale: you must fix your eye on him, if you want to judge how much it is to one's own interest not to be just. You can see that best in the most consummate form of injustice, which rewards wrongdoing with supreme welfare and happiness and re- duces its victims, if they won't retaliate in kind, to misery. That form is despotism, which uses force or fraud to plunder the goods of others, public or private, sacred or profane, and to do it in a wholesale way. If you are

caught committing any one of these crimes on a small scale, you are
punished and disgraced; they call it sacrilege, kidnapping, burglary, theft
and brigandage. But if, besides taking their property, you turn all your
countrymen into slaves, you will hear no more of those ugly names; your
countrymen themselves will call you the happiest of men and bless your
name, and so will everyone who hears of such a complete triumph of
injustice; for when people denounce injustice, it is because they are afraid of
suffering wrong, not of doing it. So true is it, Socrates, that injustice, on a
grand enough scale, is superior to justice in strength and freedom and autocratic power; and 'right,' as I said at first, means simply what serves the
interest of the stronger party; 'wrong' means what is for the interest and
profit of oneself.

.   .   .

. . . [My good Thrasymachus, said I,] what is your opinion? Do you
think that the men who govern states—I mean rulers in the strict sense—
have no reluctance to hold office?

I don't think so, he replied; I know it.

Well, but haven't you noticed, Thrasymachus, that in other positions of
authority no one is willing to act unless he is paid wages, which he demands
on the assumption that all the benefit of his action will go to his charges?
Tell me: Don't we always distinguish one form of skill from another by its
power to effect some particular result? Do say what you really think, so that
we may get on.

Yes, that is the distinction.

And also each brings us some benefit that is peculiar to it: medicine gives
health, for example; the art of navigation, safety at sea; and so on.

Yes.

And wage-earning brings us wages; that is its distinctive product. Now,
speaking with that precision which you proposed, you would not say that
the art of navigation is the same as the art of medicine, merely on the
ground that a ship's captain regained his health on a voyage, because the sea
air was good for him. No more would you identify the practice of medicine
with wage-earning because a man may keep his health while earning wages,
or a physician attending a case may receive a fee.

No.

And, since we agreed that the benefit obtained by each form of skill is
peculiar to it, any common benefit enjoyed alike by all these practitioners
must come from some further practice common to them all?

It would seem so.

Yes, we must say that if all earn wages, they get that benefit in so far
as they are engaged in wage-earning as well as in practising their several
arts.

He agreed reluctantly.

This benefit, then—the receipt of wages—does not come to a man from
his special art. If we are to speak strictly, the physician, as such, produces
health; the builder, a house; and then each, in his further capacity of wage-
earner, gets his pay. Thus every art has its own function and benefits its
proper subject. But suppose the practitioner is not paid; does he then get any
benefit from his art?

Clearly not.

And is he doing no good to anyone either, when he works for nothing?

No, I suppose he does some good.

Well then, Thrasymachus, it is now clear that no form of skill or authority provides for its own benefit. As we were saying some time ago, it always studies and prescribes what is good for its subject—the interest of the weaker party, not of the stronger. And that, my friend, is why I said that no one is willing to be in a position of authority and undertake to set straight other men's troubles, without demanding to be paid; because, if he is to do his work well, he will never, in his capacity of ruler, do, or command others to do, what is best for himself, but only what is best for the subject. For that reason, if he is to consent, he must have his recompense, in the shape of money or honour, or of punishment in case of refusal.

What do you mean, Socrates? asked Glaucon. I recognize two of your three kinds of reward; but I don't understand what you mean by speaking of punishment as a recompense.

Then you don't understand the recompense required by the best type of men, or their motive for accepting authority when they do consent. You surely know that a passion for honours or for money is rightly regarded as something to be ashamed of.

Yes I do.

For that reason, I said, good men are unwilling to rule, either for money's sake or for honour. They have no wish to be called mercenary for demanding to be paid, or thieves for making a secret profit out of their office; nor yet will honours tempt them, for they are not ambitious. So they must be forced to consent under threat of penalty; that may be why a readiness to accept power under no such constraint is thought discreditable. And the heaviest penalty for declining to rule is to be ruled by someone inferior to yourself. That is the fear, I believe, that makes decent people accept power; and when they do so, they face the prospect of authority with no idea that they are coming into the enjoyment of a comfortable berth; it is forced upon them because they can find no one better than themselves, or even as good, to be entrusted with power. If there could ever be a society of perfect men, there might well be as much competition to evade office as there now is to gain it; and it would then be clearly seen that the genuine ruler's nature is to seek only the advantage of the subject, with the consequence that any man of understanding would sooner have another to do the best for him than be at the pains to do the best for that other himself. On this point, then, I entirely disagree with Thrasymachus' doctrine that right means what is to the interest of the stronger.

IV

THRASYMACHUS: IS INJUSTICE MORE PROFITABLE THAN JUSTICE?

.   .   .

However, . . . we may return to that question later. Much more important is the position Thrasymachus is asserting now: that a life of injustice is to be preferred to a life of justice. Which side do you take, Glaucon? Where do you think the truth lies?

I should say that the just life is the better worth having.

You heard Thrasymachus' catalogue of all the good things in store for injustice?

I did, but I am not convinced.

Shall we try to convert him, then, supposing we can find some way to prove him wrong?

By all means.

We might answer Thrasymachus' case in a set speech of our own, drawing up a corresponding list of the advantages of justice; he would then have the right to reply, and we should make our final rejoinder; but after that we should have to count up and measure the advantages on each list, and we should need a jury to decide between us. Whereas, if we go on as before, each securing the agreement of the other side, we can combine the functions of advocate and judge. We will take whichever course you prefer.

I prefer the second, said Glaucon.

Come then, Thrasymachus, said I, let us start afresh with our questions. You say that injustice pays better than justice, when both are carried to the furthest point?

I do, he replied; and I have told you why.

And how would you describe them? I suppose you would call one of them an excellence and the other a defect?

Of course.

Justice an excellence, and injustice a defect?

Now is that likely, when I am telling you that injustice pays, and justice does not?

Then what do you say?

The opposite.

That justice is a defect?

No; rather the mark of a good-natured simpleton.

Injustice, then, implies being ill-natured?

No; I should call it good policy.

Do you think the unjust are positively superior in character and intelligence, Thrasymachus?

Yes, if they are the sort that can carry injustice to perfection and make themselves masters of whole cities and nations. Perhaps you think I was talking of pickpockets. There is profit even in that trade, if you can escape detection; but it doesn't come to much as compared with the gains I was describing.

I understand you now on that point, I replied. What astonished me was that you should class injustice with superior character and intelligence and justice with the reverse.

Well, I do, he rejoined.

That is a much more stubborn position, my friend; and it is not so easy to see how to assail it. If you would admit that injustice, however well it pays, is nevertheless, as some people think, a defect and a discreditable thing, then we could argue on generally accepted principles. But now that you have gone so far as to rank it with superior character and intelligence, obviously you will say it is an admirable thing as well as a source of strength, and has all the other qualities we have attributed to justice.

You read my thoughts like a book, he replied.

However, I went on, it is no good shirking. I must go through with the argument, so long as I can be sure you are really speaking your mind. I do believe you are not playing with us now, Thrasymachus, but stating the truth as you conceive it.

Why not refute the doctrine? he said. What does it matter to you whether I believe it or not?

It does not matter, I replied.

.   .   .

[. . . *The musician, tuning an instrument, knows that there is for each string a certain pitch which is absolutely right. He shows his excellence and mastery of the art by aiming at that 'limit' or 'measure' (as the Greeks would call it), and he would be satisfied if he could attain it. In doing so he would be outdoing or 'going one better than' less skilful musicians or the unmusical; but he would not be showing superior skill if he tried to outdo a musician who acknowledged the same measure and had actually attained it. Socrates holds that in moral conduct also there is a measure which is absolutely right, whether we recognize it or not. The just man, who does recognize it, shows a wisdom and virtue corresponding to the skill of the good musician. The unjust, who acknowledges no measure or limit, because there is no limit to getting more and more for yourself at others' expense and that is his object, is, by all analogy, exhibiting rather a lack of intelligence and character . . . Socrates concludes: 'It is evident, then, that it is the just man that is wise and good (superior in character and intelligence), the unjust that is ignorant and bad.'*]

Thrasymachus' assent was dragged out of him with a reluctance of which my account gives no idea. He was sweating at every pore, for the weather was hot; and I saw then what I had never seen before—Thrasymachus blushing. However, now that we had agreed that justice implies superior character and intelligence, injustice a deficiency in both respects, I went on:

Good; let us take that as settled. But we were also saying that injustice was a source of strength. Do you remember, Thrasymachus?

I do remember; only your last argument does not satisfy me, and I could say a good deal about that. But if I did, you would tell me I was haranguing you like a public meeting. So either let me speak my mind at length, or else, if you want to ask questions, ask them, and I will nod or shake my head, and say 'Hm?' as we do to encourage an old woman telling us a story.

No, please, said I; don't give your assent against your real opinion.

Anything to please you, he rejoined, since you won't let me have my say. What more do you want?

Nothing. I replied. If that is what you mean to do, I will go on with my questions.

Go on, then.

Well, to continue where we left off. I will repeat my question: What is the nature and quality of justice as compared with injustice? It was suggested, I believe, that injustice is the stronger and more effective of the two; but now we have seen that justice implies superior character and intelligence, it will not be hard to show that it will also be superior in power to injustice, which implies ignorance and stupidity; that must be obvious to anyone. However, I would rather look deeper into this matter than take it as settled off-hand. Would you agree that a state may be unjust and may try to enslave other states or to hold a number of others in subjection unjustly?

Of course it may, he said; above all if it is the best sort of state, which carries injustice to perfection.

I understand, said I; that was your view. But I am wondering whether a state can do without justice when it is asserting its superior power over another in that way.

Not if you are right, that justice implies intelligence; but if I am right, injustice will be needed.

I am delighted with your answer, Thrasymachus; this is much better than just nodding and shaking your head.

It is all to oblige you.

Thank you. Please add to your kindness by telling me whether any set of men—a state or an army or a band of robbers or thieves—who were acting together for some unjust purpose would be likely to succeed, if they were always trying to injure one another. Wouldn't they do better, if they did not?

Yes, they would.

Because, of course, such injuries must set them quarrelling and hating each other. Only fair treatment can make men friendly and of one mind.

Be it so, he said; I don't want to differ from you.

Thank you once more, I replied. But don't you agree that, if injustice has this effect of implanting hatred wherever it exists, it must make any set of people, whether freemen or slaves, split into factions, at feud with one another and incapable of any joint action?

Yes.

And so with any two individuals: injustice will set them at variance and make them enemies to each other as well as to everyone who is just.

It will.

And will it not keep its character and have the same effect, if it exists in a single person?

Let us suppose so.

The effect being, apparently, wherever it occurs—in a state or a family or an army or anywhere else—to make united action impossible because of factions and quarrels, and moreover to set whatever it resides in at enmity with itself as well as with any opponent and with all who are just.

Yes, certainly.

Then I suppose it will produce the same natural results in an individual. He will have a divided mind and be incapable of action, for lack of single-ness of purpose; and he will be at enmity with all who are just as well as with himself?

Yes.

And 'all who are just' surely includes the gods?

Let us suppose so.

The unjust man, then, will be a god-forsaken creature; the good-will of heaven will be for the just.

Enjoy your triumph, said Thrasymachus. You need not fear my contra-dicting you. I have no wish to give offence to the company.

.   .   .

You will make my enjoyment complete, I replied, if you will answer my further questions in the same way. We have made out so far that just men are superior in character and intelligence and more effective in action. Indeed without justice men cannot act together at all; it is not strictly true to speak of such people as ever having effected any strong action in common. Had they been thoroughly unjust, they could not have kept their hands off one another; they must have had some justice in them, enough to keep them from injuring one another at the same time with their victims. This it was that enabled them to achieve what they did achieve: their injustice only partially incapacitated them for their career of wrongdoing; if perfect, it would have disabled them for any action whatsoever. I can see that all this is true, as against your original position. But there is a further question which we postponed: Is the life of justice the better and happier life? What we have said already leaves no doubt in my mind; but we ought to consider more carefully, for this is no light matter: it is the question, what is the right way to live?

Go on, then.

I will, said I. Some things have a function; a horse, for instance, is useful for certain kinds of work. Would you agree to define a thing's function in general as the work for which that thing is the only instrument or the best one?

I don't understand.

Take an example. We can see only with the eyes, hear only with the ears; and seeing and hearing might be called the functions of those organs.

Yes.

Or again, you might cut vine-shoots with a carving-knife or a chisel or many other tools, but with none so well as with a pruning-knife made for the purpose; and we may call that its function.

True.

Now, I expect, you see better what I meant by suggesting that a thing's function is the work that it alone can do, or can do better than anything else.

Yes, I will accept that definition.

Good, said I; and to take the same examples, the eye and the ear, which we said have each its particular function: have they not also a specific excellence or virtue? Is not that always the case with things that have some appointed work to do?

Yes.

Now consider: is the eye likely to do its work well, if you take away its peculiar virtue and substitute the corresponding defect?

Of course not, if you mean substituting blindness for the power of sight.

I mean whatever its virtue may be; I have not come to that yet. I am only asking, whether it is true of things with a function—eyes or ears or anything else—that there is always some specific virtue which enables them to work well; and if they are deprived of that virtue, they work badly.

I think that is true.

Then the next point is this. Has the soul a function that can be performed by nothing else? Take for example such actions as deliberating or taking charge and exercising control: is not the soul the only thing of which you can say that these are its proper and peculiar work?

That is so.

And again, living—is not that above all the function of the soul?

No doubt.

And we also speak of the soul as having a certain specific excellence or virtue?

Yes.

Then, Thrasymachus, if the soul is robbed of its peculiar virtue, it cannot possibly do its work well. It must exercise its power of controlling and taking charge well or ill according as it is itself in a good or a bad state.

That follows.

And did we not agree that the virtue of the soul is justice, and injustice its defect?

We did.

So it follows that a just soul, or in other words a just man, will live well; the unjust will not.

Apparently, according to your argument.

But living well involves well-being and happiness.

Naturally.

Then only the just man is happy; injustice will involve unhappiness.

Be it so.

But you cannot say it pays better to be unhappy.

Of course not.

Injustice then, my dear Thrasymachus, can never pay better than justice.

Well, he replied, this is a feast-day, and you may take all this as your share of the entertainment.

For which I have to thank you, Thrasymachus; you have been so gentle with me since you recovered your temper. It is my own fault if the entertainment has not been satisfactory. I have been behaving like a greedy guest, snatching a taste of every new dish that comes round before he has properly enjoyed the last. We began by looking for a definition of justice; but before we had found one, I dropped that question and hurried on to ask whether or not it involved superior character and intelligence; and then, as soon as another idea cropped up, that injustice pays better, I could not refrain from pursuing that.

So now the whole conversation has left me completely in the dark; for so long as I do not know what justice is, I am hardly likely to know whether or not it is a virtue, or whether it makes a man happy or unhappy.

2
VIRTUE

Aristotle

Virtue, . . . being of two kinds, intellectual and moral, intellectual virtue in the main owes both its birth and its growth to teaching (for which reason it requires experience and time), while moral virtue comes about as a result of habit, whence also its name *ethike* is one that is formed by a slight variation from the word *ethos* (habit). From this it is also plain that none of the moral virtues arises in us by nature; for nothing that exists by nature can form a habit contrary to its nature. For instance the stone which by nature moves downwards cannot be habituated to move upwards, not even if one tries to train it by throwing it up ten thousand times; nor can fire be habituated to move downwards, nor can anything else that by nature behaves in one way be trained to behave in another. Neither by nature, then, nor contrary to nature do the virtues arise in us; rather we are adapted by nature to receive them, and are made perfect by habit.

Again, of all the things that come to us by nature we first acquire the potentiality and later exhibit the activity (this is plain in the case of the senses; for it was not by often seeing or often hearing that we got these senses, but on the contrary we had them before we used them, and did not come to have them by using them); but the virtues we get by first exercising them, as also happens in the case of the arts as well. For the things we have to learn before we can do them, we learn by doing them, e.g. men become builders by building and lyre-players by playing the lyre; so too we become just by doing just acts, temperate by doing temperate acts, brave by doing brave acts.

This is confirmed by what happens in states; for legislators make the citizens good by forming habits in them, and this is the wish of every legislator, and those who do not effect it miss their mark, and it is in this that a good constitution differs from a bad one.

Again, it is from the same causes and by the same means that every virtue is both produced and destroyed, and similarly every art; for it is from playing the lyre that both good and bad lyre-players are produced. And the

From *Nicomachean Ethics*, W. D. Ross, trans., in *The Works of Aristotle* (Oxford: 1938), Book II, Secs. 1–9, pp. 331–347. Reprinted by permission of The Clarendon Press, Oxford.

corresponding statement is true of builders and of all the rest; men will be good or bad builders as a result of building well or badly. For if this were not so, there would have been no need of a teacher, but all men would have been born good or bad at their craft. This, then, is the case with the virtues also; by doing the acts that we do in our transactions with other men we become just or unjust, and by doing the acts that we do in the presence of danger, and being habituated to feel fear or confidence, we become brave or cowardly. The same is true of appetites and feelings of anger; some men become temperate and good-tempered, others self-indulgent and irascible, by behaving in one way or the other in the appropriate circumstances. Thus, in one word, states of character arise out of like activities. This is why the activities we exhibit must be of a certain kind; it is because the states of character correspond to the differences between these. It makes no small difference, then, whether we form habits of one kind or of another from our very youth; it makes a very great difference, or rather *all* the difference.

Since, then, the present inquiry does not aim at theoretical knowledge like the others (for we are inquiring not in order to know what virtue is, but in order to become good, since otherwise our inquiry would have been of no use), we must examine the nature of actions, namely how we ought to do them; for these determine also the nature of the states of character that are produced, . . . Now, that we must act according to the right rule is a common principle and must be assumed . . . i.e. both what the right rule is, and how it is related to the other virtues. But this must be agreed upon beforehand, that the whole account of matters of conduct must be given in outline and not precisely; . . . matters concerned with conduct and questions of what is good for us have no fixity, any more than matters of health. The general account being of this nature, the account of particular cases is yet more lacking in exactness; for they do not fall under any art or precept but the agents themselves must in each case consider what is appropriate to the occasion, as happens also in the art of medicine or of navigation.

But though our present account is of this nature we must give what help we can. First, then, let us consider this, that it is the nature of such things to be destroyed by defect and excess, as we see in the case of strength and of health (for to gain light on things imperceptible we must use the evidence of sensible things); both excessive and defective exercise destroys the strength, and similarly drink or food which is above or below a certain amount destroys the health, while that which is proportionate both produces and increases and preserves it. So too is it, then, in the case of temperance and courage and the other virtues. For the man who flies from and fears everything and does not stand his ground against anything becomes a coward, and the man who fears nothing at all but goes to meet every danger becomes rash; and similarly the man who indulges in every pleasure and abstains from none becomes self-indulgent, while the man who shuns every pleasure, as boors do, becomes in a way insensible; temperance and courage, then, are destroyed by excess and defect, and preserved by the mean.

But not only are the sources and causes of their origination and growth the same as those of their destruction, but also the sphere of their actualization will be the same; for this is also true of the things which are more evident to sense, e.g. of strength; it is produced by taking much food and undergoing much exertion, and it is the strong man that will be most able to do these things. So too is it with the virtues; by abstaining from pleasures we become temperate, and it is when we have become so that we are most able to abstain from them; and similarly too in the case of courage; for by being habituated to despise things that are terrible and to stand our ground against them we become brave, and it is when we have become so that we shall be most able to stand our ground against them.

We must take as a sign of states of character the pleasure or pain that ensues on acts; for the man who abstains from bodily pleasures and delights in this very fact is temperate, while the man who is annoyed at it is self-indulgent, and he who stands his ground against things that are terrible and delights in this or at least is not pained is brave, while the man who is pained is a coward. For moral excellence is concerned with pleasures and pains; it is on account of the pleasure that we do bad things, and on account of the pain that we abstain from noble ones. Hence we ought to have been brought up in a particular way from our very youth, as Plato says, so as both to delight in and to be pained by the things that we ought; for this is the right education.

Again, if the virtues are concerned with actions and passions, and every passion and every action is accompanied by pleasure and pain, for this reason also virtue will be concerned with pleasures and pains. This is indicated also by the fact that punishment is inflicted by these means; for it is a kind of cure, and it is the nature of cures to be effected by contraries.

Again, . . . every state of soul has a nature relative to and concerned with the kind of things by which it tends to be made worse or better; but it is by reason of pleasures and pains that men become bad, by pursuing and avoiding these—either the pleasures and pains they ought not or when they ought not or as they ought not, or by going wrong in one of the other similar ways that may be distinguished. Hence men even define the virtues as certain states of impassivity and rest; not well, however, because they speak absolutely, and do not say 'as one ought' and 'as one ought not' and 'when one ought or ought not', and the other things that may be added. We assume, then, that this kind of excellence tends to do what is best with regard to pleasures and pains, and vice does the contrary.

The following facts also may show us that virtue and vice are concerned with these same things. There being three objects of choice and three of avoidance, the noble, the advantageous, the pleasant, and their contraries, the base, the injurious, the painful, about all of these the good man tends to go right and the bad man to go wrong, and especially about pleasure; for this is common to the animals, and also it accompanies all objects of choice; for even the noble and the advantageous appear pleasant.

Again, it has grown up with us all from our infancy; this is why it is difficult to rub off this passion, engrained as it is in our life. And we measure even our actions, some of us more and others less, by the rule of pleasure and pain. For this reason, then, our whole inquiry must be about these; for to feel delight and pain rightly or wrongly has no small effect on our actions.

Again, it is harder to fight with pleasure than with anger, to use Hera-clitus' phrase, but both art and virtue are always concerned with what is harder; for even the good is better when it is harder. Therefore for this reason also the whole concern both of virtue and of political science is with pleasures and pains; for the man who uses these well will be good, he who uses them badly bad.

That virtue, then, is concerned with pleasures and pains, and that by the acts from which it arises it is both increased and, if they are done differ-ently, destroyed, and that the acts from which it arose are those in which it actualizes itself—let this be taken as said.

The question might be asked, what we mean by saying that we must become just by doing just acts, and temperate by doing temperate acts; for if men do just and temperate acts, they are already just and temperate, exactly as, if they do what is in accordance with the laws of grammar and of music, they are grammarians and musicians.

Or is this not true even of the arts? It is possible to do something that is in accordance with the laws of grammar, either by chance or at the suggestion of another. A man will be a grammarian, then, only when he has both done something grammatical and done it grammatically; and this means doing it in accordance with the grammatical knowledge in himself.

Again, the case of the arts and that of the virtues are not similar; for the products of the arts have their goodness in themselves, so that it is enough that they should have a certain character, but if the acts that are in accordance with the virtues have themselves a certain character it does not follow that they are done justly or temperately. The agent also must be in a certain condition when he does them; in the first place he must have knowledge, secondly he must choose the acts, and choose them for their own sakes, and thirdly his action must proceed from a firm and unchange-able character. These are not reckoned in as conditions of the possession of the arts, except the bare knowledge; but as a condition of the possession of the virtues knowledge has little or no weight, while the other conditions count not for a little but for everything, i.e. the very conditions which result from often doing just and temperate acts.

Actions, then, are called just and temperate when they are such as the just or the temperate man would do; but it is not the man who does these that is just and temperate, but the man who does them *as* just and temperate men do them. It is well said, then, that it is by doing just acts that the just man is produced, and by doing temperate acts the temperate man; without doing these no one would have even a prospect of becoming good.

But most people do not do these, but take refuge in theory and think they are being philosophers and will become good in this way, behaving some-what like patients who listen attentively to their doctors, but do none of the things they are ordered to do. As the latter will not be made well in body by such a course of treatment, the former will not be made well in soul by such a course of philosophy.

Next we must consider what virtue is. Since things that are found in the soul are of three kinds—passions, faculties, states of character, virtue must be one of these. By passions I mean appetite, anger, fear, confidence, envy, joy, friendly feeling, hatred, longing, emulation, pity, and in general the feelings that are accompanied by pleasure or pain; by faculties the things in virtue of which we are said to be capable of feeling these, e.g. of becoming angry or being pained or feeling pity; by states of character the things in virtue of which we stand well or badly with reference to the passions, e.g. with reference to anger we stand badly if we feel it violently or too weakly, and well if we feel it moderately; and similarly with reference to the other passions.

Now neither the virtues nor the vices are *passions*, because we are not called good or bad on the ground of our passions, but are so called on the ground of our virtues and our vices, and because we are neither praised nor blamed for our passions (for the man who feels fear or anger is not praised, nor is the man who simply feels anger blamed, but the man who feels it in a certain way), but for our virtues and our vices we *are* praised or blamed.

Again, we feel anger and fear without choice, but the virtues are modes of choice or involve choice. Further, in respect of the passions we are said to be moved, but in respect of the virtues and the vices we are said not to be moved but to be disposed in a particular way.

For these reasons also they are not *faculties;* for we are neither called good nor bad, nor praised nor blamed, for the simple capacity of feeling the passions; again, we have the faculties by nature, but we are not made good or bad by nature . . .

If, then, the virtues are neither passions nor faculties, all that remains is that they should be *states of character.*

Thus we have stated what virtue is in respect of its genus.

We must, however, not only describe virtue as a state of character, but also say what sort of state it is. We may remark, then, that every virtue or excellence both brings into good condition the thing of which it is the excellence and makes the work of that thing be done well; e.g. the excellence of the eye makes both the eye and its work good; for it is by the excellence of the eye that we see well. Similarly the excellence of the horse makes a horse both good in itself and good at running and at carrying its rider and at awaiting the attack of the enemy. Therefore, if this is true in every case, the virtue of man also will be the state of character which makes a man good and which makes him do his own work well.

. . . In everything that is continuous and divisible it is possible to take more, less, or an equal amount, and that either in terms of the thing itself or relatively to us; and the equal is an intermediate between excess and defect. By the intermediate in the object I mean that which is equidistant from each of the extremes, which is one and the same for all men; by the intermediate relatively to us that which is neither too much nor too little—and this is not one, nor the same for all. For instance, if ten is many and two is few, six is the intermediate, taken in terms of the object; for it exceeds and is exceeded by an equal amount; this is intermediate according to arithmetical proportion. But the intermediate relatively to us is not to be taken so; if ten pounds are too much for a particular person to eat and two too little, it does not follow that the trainer will order six pounds; for this also is perhaps too much for the person who is to take it, or too little—too little for Milo, too much for the beginner in athletic exercises. The same is true of running and wrestling. Thus a master of any art avoids excess and defect, but seeks the intermediate and chooses this—the intermediate not in the object but relatively to us.

If it is thus, then, that every art does its work well—by looking to the intermediate and judging its works by this standard (so that we often say of good works of art that it is not possible either to take away or to add anything, implying that excess and defect destroy the goodness of works of art, while the mean preserves it; and good artists, as we say, look to this in their work), and if, further, virtue is more exact and better than any art, as nature also is, then virtue must have the quality of aiming at the intermediate. I mean moral virtue; for it is this that is concerned with passions and actions, and in these there is excess, defect, and the intermediate. For instance, both fear and confidence and appetite and anger and pity and in general pleasure and pain may be felt both too much and too little, and in both cases not well; but to feel them at the right times, with reference to the right objects, towards the right people, with the right motive, and in the right way, is what is both intermediate and best, and this is characteristic of virtue. Similarly with regard to actions also there is excess, defect, and the intermediate. Now virtue is concerned with passions and actions, in which excess is a form of failure, and so is defect, while the intermediate is praised and is a form of success; and being praised and being successful are both characteristics of virtue. Therefore virtue is a kind of mean, since, as we have seen, it aims at what is intermediate.

Again, it is possible to fail in many ways (for evil belongs to the class of the unlimited, as the Pythagoreans conjectured, and good to that of the limited), while to succeed is possible only in one way (for which reason also one is easy and the other difficult—to miss the mark easy, to hit it difficult); for these reasons also, then, excess and defect are characteristic of vice, and the mean of virtue;

For men are good in but one way, but bad in many.

Virtue, then, is a state of character concerned with choice, lying in a mean, i.e. the mean relative to us, this being determined by a rational principle, and by that principle by which the man of practical wisdom would determine it. Now it is a mean between two vices, that which depends on excess and that which depends on defect; and again it is a mean because the vices respectively fall short of or exceed what is right in both passions and actions, while virtue both finds and chooses that which is intermediate. Hence in respect of its substance and the definition which states its essence virtue is a mean, with regard to what is best and right an extreme.

But not every action nor every passion admits of a mean; for some have names that already imply badness, e.g. spite, shamelessness, envy, and in the case of actions adultery, theft, murder; for all of these and suchlike things imply by their names that they are themselves bad, and not the excesses or deficiencies of them. It is not possible, then, ever to be right with regard to them; one must always be wrong. Nor does goodness or badness with regard to such things depend on committing adultery with the right woman, at the right time, and in the right way, but simply to do any of them is to go wrong. It would be equally absurd, then, to expect that in unjust, cowardly, and voluptuous action there should be a mean, an excess, and a deficiency; for at that rate there would be a mean of excess and of deficiency, an excess of excess, and a deficiency of deficiency. But as there is no excess and deficiency of temperance and courage because what is intermediate is in a sense an extreme, so too of the actions we have mentioned there is no mean nor any excess and deficiency, but however they are done they are wrong; for in general there is neither a mean of excess and deficiency, nor excess and deficiency of a mean.

We must, however, not only make this general statement, but also apply it to the individual facts. For among statements about conduct those which are general apply more widely, but those which are particular are more genuine, since conduct has to do with individual cases, and our statements must harmonize with the facts in these cases. We may take these cases from our table. With regard to feelings of fear and confidence courage is the mean; of the people who exceed, he who exceeds in fearlessness has no name (many of the states have no name), while the man who exceeds in confidence is rash, and he who exceeds in fear and falls short in confidence is a coward. With regard to pleasures and pains—not all of them, and not so much with regard to the pains—the mean is temperance, the excess self-indulgence. Persons deficient with regard to the pleasures are not often found; hence such persons also have received no name. But let us call them 'insensible'.
With regard to giving and taking of money the mean is liberality, the excess and the defect prodigality and meanness. In these actions people exceed and fall short in contrary ways; the prodigal exceeds in spending and falls short in taking, while the mean man exceeds in taking and falls short in spending. . . . With regard to money there are also other dispositions—a mean, magnificence (for the magnificent man differs from the liberal man; the former deals with large sums, the latter with small ones), and excess, tastelessness and vulgarity, and a deficiency, niggardliness; these differ from the states opposed to liberality. . . .
With regard to honour and dishonour the mean is proper pride, the excess is known as a sort of 'empty vanity', and the deficiency is undue humility; . . . liberality [is] related to magnificence, differing from it by dealing with small sums, so there is a state similarly related to proper pride, being concerned with small honours while that is concerned with great. For it is possible to desire honour as one ought, and more than one ought, and less, and the man who exceeds in his desires is called ambitious, the man who falls short unambitious, while the intermediate person has no name. The dispositions also are nameless, except that that of the ambitious man is called ambition. Hence the people who are at the extremes lay claim to the middle place; and we ourselves sometimes call the intermediate person ambitious and sometimes unambitious, and sometimes praise the ambitious man and sometimes the unambitious. . . . now let us speak of the remaining states according to the method which has been indicated.
With regard to anger also there is an excess, a deficiency, and a mean.

Although they can scarcely be said to have names, yet since we call the intermediate person good-tempered let us call the mean good temper; of the persons at the extremes let the one who exceeds be called irascible, and his vice irascibility, and the man who falls short an inirascible sort of person, and the deficiency inirascibility.

There are also three other means, which have a certain likeness to one another, but differ from one another: for they are all concerned with intercourse in words and actions, but differ in that one is concerned with truth in this sphere, the other two with pleasantness; and of this one kind is exhibited in giving amusement, the other in all the circumstances of life. We must therefore speak of these too, that we may the better see that in all things the mean is praiseworthy, and the extremes neither praiseworthy nor right, but worthy of blame. Now most of these states also have no names, but we must try, as in the other cases, to invent names ourselves so that we may be clear and easy to follow. With regard to truth, then, the intermediate is a truthful sort of person and the mean may be called truthfulness, while the pretence which exaggerates is boastfulness and the person characterized by it a boaster, and that which understates is mock modesty and the person characterized by it mock-modest. With regard to pleasantness in the giving of amusement the intermediate person is ready-witted and the disposition ready wit, the excess is buffoonery and the person characterized by it a buffoon, while the man who falls short is a sort of boor and his state is boorishness. With regard to the remaining kind of pleasantness, that which is exhibited in life in general, the man who is pleasant in the right way is friendly and the mean is friendliness, while the man who exceeds is an obsequious person if he has no end in view, a flatterer if he is aiming at his own advantage, and the man who falls short and is unpleasant in all circumstances is a quarrelsome and surly sort of person.

There are also means in the passions and concerned with the passions; since shame is not a virtue, and yet praise is extended to the modest man. For even in these matters one man is said to be intermediate, and another to exceed, as for instance the bashful man who is ashamed of everything; while he who falls short or is not ashamed of anything at all is shameless, and the intermediate person is modest. Righteous indignation is a mean between envy and spite, and these states are concerned with the pain and pleasures that are felt at the fortunes of our neighbours; the man who is characterized by righteous indignation is pained at undeserved good fortune, the envious man, going beyond him, is pained at all good fortune, and the spiteful man falls so far short of being pained that he even rejoices. . . .

There are three kinds of disposition, then, two of them vices, involving excess and deficiency respectively, and one a virtue, viz. the mean, and all are in a sense opposed to all; for the extreme states are contrary both to the intermediate state and to each other, and the intermediate to the extremes; as the equal is greater relatively to the less, less relatively to the greater, so the middle states are excessive relatively to the deficiencies, deficient relatively to the excesses, both in passions and in actions. For the brave man appears rash relatively to the coward, and cowardly relatively to the rash man; and similarly the temperate man appears self-indulgent relatively to the insensible man, insensible relatively to the self-indulgent, and the liberal man prodigal relatively to the mean man, mean relatively to the prodigal. Hence also the people at the extremes push the intermediate man each over to the other, and the brave man is called rash by the coward, cowardly by the rash man, and correspondingly in the other cases.

These states being thus opposed to one another, the greatest contrariety is that of the extremes to each other, rather than to the intermediate; for these are further from each other than from the intermediate, as the great is further from the small and the small from the great than both are from the equal. Again, to the intermediate some extremes show a certain likeness, as that of rashness to courage and that of prodigality to liberality; but the extremes show the greatest unlikeness to each other; now contraries are defined as the things that are furthest from each other, so that things that are further apart are more contrary.

To the mean in some cases the deficiency, in some the excess is more opposed; e.g. it is not rashness, which is an excess, but cowardice, which is a deficiency, that is more opposed to courage, and not insensibility, which is a deficiency, but self-indulgence, which is an excess, that is more opposed to temperance. This happens from two reasons, one being drawn from the thing itself; for because one extreme is nearer and liker to the intermediate, we oppose not this but rather its contrary to the intermediate. E.g., since rashness is thought liker and nearer to courage, and cowardice more unlike, we oppose rather the latter to courage; for things that are further from the intermediate are thought more contrary to it. This, then, is one cause, drawn from the thing itself; another is drawn from ourselves; for the things to which we ourselves more naturally tend seem more contrary to the intermediate. For instance, we ourselves tend more naturally to pleasures, and hence are more easily carried away towards self-indulgence than towards propriety. We describe as contrary to the mean, then, rather the directions in which we more often go to great lengths; and therefore self-indulgence, which is an excess, is the more contrary to temperance.

That moral virtue is a mean, then, and in what sense it is so, and that it is a mean between two vices, the one involving excess, the other deficiency, and that it is such because its character is to aim at what is intermediate in passions and in actions, has been sufficiently stated. Hence also it is no easy task to be good. For in everything it is no easy task to find the middle, e.g. to find the middle of a circle is not for every one but for him who knows; so too, any one can get angry—that is easy—or give or spend money; but to do this to the right person, to the right extent, at the right time, with the right motive, and in the right way, *that* is not for every one, nor is it easy; wherefore goodness is both rare and laudable and noble.

Hence he who aims at the intermediate must first depart from what is the more contrary to it, as Calypso advises—

Hold the ship out beyond that surf and spray.

For of the extremes one is more erroneous, one less so; therefore, since to hit the mean is hard in the extreme, we must as a second best, as people say, take the least of the evils; and this will be done best in the way we describe.

But we must consider the things towards which we ourselves also are easily carried away; for some of us tend to one thing, some to another; and this will be recognizable from the pleasure and the pain we feel. We must drag ourselves away to the contrary extreme; for we shall get into the intermediate state by drawing well away from error, as people do in straightening sticks that are bent.

Now in everything the pleasant or pleasure is most to be guarded against; for we do not judge it impartially. We ought, then, to feel towards pleasure as the elders of the people felt towards Helen, and in all circumstances repeat their saying; for if we dismiss pleasure thus we are less likely to go astray. It is by doing this, then (to sum the matter up) that we shall best be able to hit the mean.

But this is no doubt difficult, and especially in individual cases; for it is not easy to determine both how and with whom and on what provocation and how long one should be angry; for we too sometimes praise those who fall short and call them good-tempered, but sometimes we praise those who get angry and call them manly. The man, however, who deviates little from goodness is not blamed, whether he do so in the direction of the more or of the less, but only the man who deviates more widely; for he does not fail to be noticed. But up to what point and to what extent a man must deviate before he becomes blameworthy it is not easy to determine by reasoning, any more than anything else that is perceived by the senses; such things depend on particular facts, and the decision rests with perception. So much, then, is plain, that the intermediate state is in all things to be praised, but that we must incline sometimes towards the excess, sometimes towards the deficiency; for so shall we most easily hit the mean and what is right.

3

THE NATURE OF LAW

St. Thomas Aquinas

ON THE ESSENCE OF LAW

.   .   .

First Article: Whether Law Is Something Pertaining to Reason?

We proceed thus to the First Article:—
Objection 1. It would seem that law is not something pertaining to reason. For the Apostle says (*Rom.* vii. 23): *I see another law in my members*, etc. But nothing pertaining to reason is in the members, since the reason does not make use of a bodily organ. Therefore law is not something pertaining to reason.

Obj. 2. Further, in the reason there is nothing else but power, habit and act. But law is not the power itself of reason. In like manner, neither is it a habit of reason, because the habits of reason are the intellectual virtues, . . . Nor again is it an act of reason, because then law would cease when the act of reason ceases, for instance while we are asleep. Therefore law is nothing pertaining to reason.

Obj. 3. Further, the law moves those who are subject to it to act rightly. But it belongs properly to the will to move to act. . . . Therefore law pertains, not to the reason, but to the will, according to the words of the Jurist: *Whatsoever pleaseth the sovereign has the force of law.*

On the contrary, It belongs to the law to command and to forbid. But it belongs to reason to command, . . . Therefore law is something pertaining to reason.

I answer that, Law is a rule and measure of acts, whereby man is induced to act or is restrained from acting; for *lex* [*law*] is derived from *ligare* [*to bind*], because it binds one to act. Now the rule and measure of human acts

From *Summa Theologica*, in Anton C. Pegis, ed., *Basic Writings of St. Thomas Aquinas* (New York: Random House, Inc., 1945), First Part of the Second Part, QQ. 90, 91, 94, pp. 742–745, 748–752, 755–757, 772–781. Reprinted by permission of Random House, Inc., and Burns & Oates Ltd.

is the reason, which is the first principle of human acts. . . . For it belongs
to the reason to direct to the end, which is the first principle in all matters of
action, according to the Philosopher. Now that which is the principle in any
genus is the rule and measure of that genus: for instance, unity in the genus
of numbers, and the first movement in the genus of movements. Consequently, it follows that law is something pertaining to reason.

Reply Obj. 1. Since law is a kind of rule and measure, it may be in
something in two ways. First, as in that which measures and rules; and since
this is proper to reason, it follows that, in this way, law is in the reason
alone.— Secondly, as in that which is measured and ruled. In this way, law is
in all those things that are inclined to something because of some law; so that
any inclination arising from a law may be called a law, not essentially, but
by participation as it were. And thus the inclination of the members to
concupiscence is called *the law of the members.*

Reply Obj. 2. Just as, in external acts, we may consider the work and the
work done, for instance, the work of building and the house built, so in the
acts of reason, we may consider the act itself of reason, *i.e.*, to understand
and to reason, and something produced by this act. With regard to the
speculative reason, this is first of all the definition; secondly, the proposition;
thirdly, the syllogism or argument. And since the practical reason also makes
use of the syllogism in operable matters, . . . as the Philosopher teaches,
hence we find in the practical reason something that holds the same position
in regard to operations as, in the speculative reason, the proposition holds in
regard to conclusions. Such universal propositions of the practical reason
that are directed to operations have the nature of law. And these propositions are sometimes under our actual consideration, while sometimes they
are retained in the reason by means of a habit.

Reply Obj. 3. Reason has its power of moving from the will; . . . for it
is due to the fact that one wills the end, that the reason issues its commands
as regards things ordained to the end. But in order that the volition of what
is commanded may have the nature of law, it needs to be in accord with
some rule of reason. And in this sense is to be understood the saying that the
will of the sovereign has the force of law; or otherwise the sovereign's will
would savor of lawlessness rather than of law.

Second Article: Whether Law Is Always Directed to the Common Good?

We proceed thus to the Second Article:—

Objection 1. It would seem that law is not always directed to the
common good as to its end. For it belongs to law to command and to forbid.
But commands are directed to certain individual goods. Therefore the end
of law is not always the common good.

Obj. 2. Further, law directs man in his actions. But human actions are
concerned with particular matters. Therefore law is directed to some
particular good.

Obj. 3. Further, Isidore says: *If law is based on reason, whatever is
based on reason will be a law.* But reason is the foundation not only of what
is ordained to the common good, but also of that which is directed to private
good. Therefore law is not directed only to the good of all, but also to the
private good of an individual.

On the contrary, Isidore says that *laws are enacted for no private profit, but for the common benefit of the citizens.*

I answer that, As we have stated above, law belongs to that which is a principle of human acts, because it is their rule and measure. Now as reason is a principle of human acts, so in reason itself there is something which is the principle in respect of all the rest. Hence to this principle chiefly and mainly law must needs be referred. Now the first principle in practical matters, which are the object of the practical reason, is the last end: and the last end of human life is happiness or beatitude, . . . Consequently, law must needs concern itself mainly with the order that is in beatitude. Moreover, since every part is ordained to the whole as the imperfect to the perfect, and since one man is a part of the perfect community, law must needs concern itself properly with the order directed to universal happiness. Therefore the Philosopher, in the above definition of legal matters, mentions both happiness and the body politic, since he says that we call those legal matters *just which are adapted to produce and preserve happiness and its parts for the body politic.* For the state is a perfect community, as he says in *Politics* i.

Now, in every genus, that which belongs to it chiefly is the principle of the others, and the others belong to that genus according to some order towards that thing. Thus fire, which is chief among hot things, is the cause of heat in mixed bodies, and these are said to be hot in so far as they have a share of fire. Consequently, since law is chiefly ordained to the common good, any other precept in regard to some individual work must needs be devoid of the nature of a law, save in so far as it regards the common good. Therefore every law is ordained to the common good.

Reply Obj. 1. A command denotes the application of a law to matters regulated by law. Now the order to the common good, at which law aims, is applicable to particular ends. And in this way commands are given even concerning particular matters.

Reply Obj. 2. Actions are indeed concerned with particular matters, but those particular matters are referable to the common good, not as to a common genus or species, but as to a common final cause, according as the common good is said to be the common end.

. Reply Obj. 3. Just as nothing stands firm with regard to the speculative reason except that which is traced back to the first indemonstrable principles, so nothing stands firm with regard to the practical reason, unless it be directed to the last end which is the common good. Now whatever stands to reason in this sense has the nature of a law.

. . .

ON THE VARIOUS KINDS OF LAW

. . .

First Article: Whether There Is an Eternal Law?

We proceed thus to the First Article:—
Objection 1. It would seem that there is no eternal law. For every law is imposed on someone. But there was not someone from eternity on whom a

law could be imposed, since God alone was from eternity. Therefore no law
is eternal.

Obj. 2. Further, promulgation is essential to law. But promulgation could
not be from eternity, because there was no one to whom it could be
promulgated from eternity. Therefore no law can be eternal.

Obj. 3. Further, law implies order to an end. But nothing ordained to an
end is eternal, for the last end alone is eternal. Therefore no law is eternal.

On the contrary, Augustine says: *That Law which is the Supreme Reason
cannot be understood to be otherwise than unchangeable and eternal.*

I answer that, . . . law is nothing else but a dictate of practical reason
emanating from the ruler who governs a perfect community. Now it is
evident, granted that the world is ruled by divine providence, . . . that the
whole community of the universe is governed by the divine reason. Therefore the very notion of the government of things in God, the ruler of the
universe, has the nature of a law. And since the divine reason's conception of
things is not subject to time, but is eternal, according to *Prov.* viii. 23,
therefore it is that this kind of law must be called eternal.

Reply Obj. 1. Those things that do not exist in themselves exist in God,
inasmuch as they are known and preordained by Him, according to *Rom.* iv.
17: *Who calls those things that are not, as those that are.* Accordingly, the
eternal concept of the divine law bears the character of an eternal law in so
far as it is ordained by God to the government of things foreknown by
Him.

Reply Obj. 2. Promulgation is made by word of mouth or in writing, and
in both ways the eternal law is promulgated, because both the divine Word
and the writing of the Book of Life are eternal. But the promulgation cannot
be from eternity on the part of the creature that hears or reads.

Reply Obj. 3. Law implies order to the end actively, namely, in so far as
it directs certain things to the end; but not passively,—that is to say, the law
itself is not ordained to the end, except accidentally, in a governor whose
end is extrinsic to him, and to which end his law must needs be ordained.
But the end of the divine government is God Himself, and His law is not
something other than Himself. Therefore the eternal law is not ordained to
another end.

Second Article: Whether There Is in Us a Natural Law?

We proceed thus to the Second Article:—

Objection 1. It would seem that there is no natural law in us. For man is
governed sufficiently by the eternal law, since Augustine says that *the
eternal law is that by which it is right that all things should be most orderly.*
But nature does not abound in superfluities as neither does she fail in
necessaries. Therefore man has no natural law.

Obj. 2. Further, by the law man is directed, in his acts, to the end, . . .
But the directing of human acts to their end is not a function of nature, as is
the case in irrational creatures, which act for an end solely by their natural
appetite; whereas man acts for an end by his reason and will. Therefore man
has no natural law.

Obj. 3. Further, the more a man is free, the less is he under the law. But
man is freer than all the animals because of his free choice, with which he is

endowed in distinction from all other animals. Since, therefore, other animals are not subject to a natural law, neither is man subject to a natural law.

On the contrary, the *Gloss* on *Rom*. ii. 14 (*When the Gentiles, who have not the law, do by nature those things that are of the law*) comments as follows: *Although they have no written law, yet they have the natural law, whereby each one knows, and is conscious of, what is good and what is evil.*

I answer that, . . . law, being a rule and measure, can be in a person in two ways: in one way, as in him that rules and measures; in another way, as in that which is ruled and measured, since a thing is ruled and measured in so far as it partakes of the rule or measure. Therefore, since all things subject to divine providence are ruled and measured by the eternal law, as was stated above, it is evident that all things partake in some way in the eternal law, in so far as, namely, from its being imprinted on them, they derive their respective inclinations to their proper acts and ends. Now among all others, the rational creature is subject to divine providence in a more excellent way, in so far as it itself partakes of a share of providence, by being provident both for itself and for others. Therefore it has a share of the eternal reason, whereby it has a natural inclination to its proper act and end; and this participation of the eternal law in the rational creature is called the natural law. Hence the Psalmist, after saying (*Ps*. iv. 6): *Offer up the sacrifice of justice*, as though someone asked what the works of justice are, adds: *Many say, Who showeth us good things?* in answer to which question he says: *The light of Thy countenance, O Lord, is signed upon us.* He thus implies that the light of natural reason, whereby we discern what is good and what is evil, which is the function of the natural law, is nothing else than an imprint on us of the divine light. It is therefore evident that the natural law is nothing else than the rational creature's participation of the eternal law.

Reply Obj. 1. This argument would hold if the natural law were something different from the eternal law; whereas it is nothing but a participation thereof, as we have stated above.

Reply Obj. 2. Every act of reason and will in us is based on that which is according to nature, . . . For every act of reasoning is based on principles that are known naturally, and every act of appetite in respect of the means is derived from the natural appetite in respect of the last end. Accordingly, the first direction of our acts to their end must needs be through the natural law.

Reply Obj. 3. Even irrational animals partake in their own way of the eternal reason, just as the rational creature does. But because the rational creature partakes thereof in an intellectual and rational manner, therefore the participation of the eternal law in the rational creature is properly called a law, since a law is something pertaining to reason, . . . Irrational creatures, however, do not partake thereof in a rational manner, and therefore there is no participation of the eternal law in them, except by way of likeness.

Third Article: Whether There Is a Human Law?

We proceed thus to the Third Article:—

Objection 1. It would seem that there is not a human law. For the natural law is a participation of the eternal law, as was stated above. Now through the eternal law *all things are most orderly,* as Augustine states. Therefore the natural law suffices for the ordering of all human affairs. Consequently there is no need for a human law.

Obj. 2. Further, law has the character of a measure, . . . But human reason is not a measure of things, but *vice versa,* as is stated in *Metaph.* x. Therefore no law can emanate from the human reason.

Obj. 3. Further, a measure should be most certain, as is stated in *Metaph.* x. But the dictates of the human reason in matters of conduct are uncertain, according to *Wis.* ix. 14: *The thoughts of mortal men are fearful, and our counsels uncertain.* Therefore no law can emanate from the human reason.

On the contrary, Augustine distinguishes two kinds of law, the one eternal, the other temporal, which he calls human.

I answer that, . . . a law is a dictate of the practical reason. Now it is to be observed that the same procedure takes place in the practical and in the speculative reason, for each proceeds from principles to conclusions, . . . Accordingly, we conclude that, just as in the speculative reason, from naturally known indemonstrable principles we draw the conclusions of the various sciences, the knowledge of which is not imparted to us by nature, but acquired by the efforts of reason, so too it is that from the precepts of the natural law, as from common and indemonstrable principles, the human reason needs to proceed to the more particular determination of certain matters. These particular determinations, devised by human reason, are called human laws, provided that the other essential conditions of law be observed, . . . Therefore Tully says in his *Rhetoric* that *justice has its source in nature; thence certain things came into custom by reason of their utility; afterwards these things which emanated from nature, and were approved by custom, were sanctioned by fear and reverence for the law.*

Reply Obj. 1. The human reason cannot have a full participation of the dictate of the divine reason, but according to its own mode, and imperfectly. Consequently, just as on the part of the speculative reason, by a natural participation of divine wisdom, there is in us the knowledge of certain common principles, but not a proper knowledge of each single truth, such as that contained in the divine wisdom, so, too, on the part of the practical reason, man has a natural participation of the eternal law, according to certain common principles, but not as regards the particular determinations of individual cases, which are, however, contained in the eternal law. Hence the need for human reason to proceed further to sanction them by law.

Reply Obj. 2. Human reason is not, of itself, the rule of things. But the principles impressed on it by nature are the general rules and measures of all things relating to human conduct, of which the natural reason is the rule and measure, although it is not the measure of things that are from nature.

Reply Obj. 3. The practical reason is concerned with operable matters, which are singular and contingent, but not with necessary things, with which the speculative reason is concerned. Therefore human laws cannot have that inerrancy that belongs to the demonstrated conclusions of the sciences. Nor is it necessary for every measure to be altogether unerring and certain, but according as it is possible in its own particular genus.

.   .   .

Sixth Article: Whether There Is a Law in the *FOMES* of Sin?

We proceed thus to the Sixth Article:—

Objection 1. It would seem that there is no law of the 'fomes' [the disposition or inclination] of sin. For Isidore says that the *law is based on reason.* But the 'fomes' of sin is not based on reason, but deviates from it. Therefore the 'fomes' has not the nature of a law.

Obj. 2. Further, every law is binding, so that those who do not obey it are called transgressors. But man is not called a transgressor from not following the instigations of the 'fomes,' but rather from his following them. Therefore the 'fomes' has not the nature of a law.

Obj. 3. Further, law is ordained to the common good, . . . But the 'fomes' inclines us, not to the common good, but to our own private good. Therefore the 'fomes' has not the nature of law.

On the contrary, The Apostle says (*Rom.* vii. 23): *I see another law in my members, fighting against the law of my mind.*

I answer that, . . . law, as to its essence, resides in him that rules and measures, but, by way of participation, in that which is ruled and measured; so that every inclination or ordination which may be found in things subject to law is called a law by participation, . . . Now those who are subject to law may receive a twofold inclination from the lawgiver. First, in so far as he directly inclines his subjects to something. According to this, he directs different subjects to different acts; and in this way we may say that there is a military law and a mercantile law. Secondly, indirectly, and thus by the very fact that a lawgiver deprives a subject of some dignity, the latter passes into another order, so as to be under another law, as it were. For example, if a soldier be turned out of the army, he will become a subject of rural or of mercantile legislation.

Accordingly, under the divine Lawgiver, various creatures have various natural inclinations, so that what is, as it were, a law for one, is against the law for another. Thus, I might say that fierceness is, in a way, the law of a dog, but against the law of a sheep or another meek animal. And so the law of man, which, by the divine ordinance, is allotted to him according to his proper natural condition, is that he should act in accordance with reason; and this law was so effective in man's first state, that nothing either outside or against reason could take man unawares. But when man turned his back on God, he fell under the influence of his sensual impulses. In fact, this happens to each one individually, according as he has the more departed from the path of reason; so that, after a fashion, he is likened to the beasts that are led by the impulse of sensuality, according to *Ps.* xlviii. 21: *Man, when he was in honor, did not understand: he hath been compared to senseless beasts, and made like to them.*

Accordingly, then, this very inclination of sensuality, which is called the 'fomes,' in other animals has absolutely the nature of law, yet only in so far as we may consider as law what is an inclination subject to law. But in man, it has not the nature of law in this way; rather is it a deviation from the law of reason. But since, by the just sentence of God, man is deprived of original justice, and his reason bereft of its vigor, this impulse of sensuality, whereby he is led, has the nature of a law in so far as it is a penalty following from the divine law depriving man of his proper dignity.

Reply Obj. 1. This argument considers the 'fomes' in itself as an incentive to evil. It is not thus that it has the nature of a law, as we have stated above, but according as it results from the justice of the divine law; much as though we were to say that it is a law that a nobleman should be made subject to menial labor because of some misdeed.

Reply Obj. 2. This argument considers law in the light of a rule or measure; for it is in this sense that those who deviate from the law become transgressors. But the 'fomes' is not a law in this respect, but by a kind of participation, as was stated above.

Reply Obj. 3. This argument considers the 'fomes' as to its proper inclination, and not as to its origin. And yet if the inclination of sensuality be considered as it is in other animals, thus it is ordained to the common good, namely, to the preservation of nature in the species or in the individual. This is true in man also, in so far as sensuality is subject to reason. But it is called the 'fomes' in so far as it departs from the order of reason.

THE NATURAL LAW

.   .   .

First Article: Whether the Natural Law Is a Habit?

We proceed thus to the First Article:—
Objection 1. It would seem that the natural law is a habit. For, as the Philosopher says, *there are three things in the soul, power, habit and passion.* But the natural law is not one of the soul's powers, nor is it one of the passions, as we may see by going through them one by one. Therefore the natural law is a habit.

Obj. 2. Further, Basil says that the *conscience or synderesis is the law of our mind;* which can apply only to the natural law. But *synderesis* is a habit, . . . Therefore the natural law is a habit.

Obj. 3. Further, the natural law abides in man always, as will be shown further on. But man's reason, which the law regards, does not always think about the natural law. Therefore the natural law is not an act, but a habit.

On the contrary, Augustine says that *a habit is that whereby something is done when necessary.* But such is not the natural law, since it is in infants and in the damned who cannot act by it. Therefore the natural law is not a habit.

I answer that, A thing may be called a habit in two ways. First, properly and essentially, and thus the natural law is not a habit. For . . . the natural law is something appointed by reason, just as a proposition is a work of reason. Now that which a man does is not the same as that whereby he does it, for he makes a becoming speech by the habit of grammar. Since, then, a habit is that by which we act, a law cannot be a habit properly and essentially.

Secondly, the term habit may be applied to that which we hold by a habit. Thus *faith* may mean *that which we hold by faith.* Accordingly, since the precepts of the natural law are sometimes considered by reason actually, while sometimes they are in the reason only habitually, in this way the natural law may be called a habit. So, too, in speculative matters, the indemonstrable principles are not the habit itself whereby we hold these principles; they are rather the principles of which we possess the habit.

Reply Obj. 1. The Philosopher proposes there to discover the genus of virtue; and since it is evident that virtue is a principle of action, he mentions only those things which are principles of human acts, viz., powers, habits and passions. But there are other things in the soul besides these three: *e.g.*, acts, as *to will* is in the one that wills; again, there are things known in the knower; moreover its own natural properties are in the soul, such as immortality and the like.

Reply Obj. 2. *Synderesis* is said to be the law of our intellect because it is a habit containing the precepts of the natural law, which are the first principles of human actions.

Reply Obj. 3. This argument proves that the natural law is held habitually; and this is granted.

To the argument advanced in the contrary sense we reply that sometimes a man is unable to make use of that which is in him habitually, because of some impediment. Thus, because of sleep, a man is unable to use the habit of science. In like manner, through the deficiency of his age, a child cannot use the habit of the understanding of principles, or the natural law, which is in him habitually.

Second Article: Whether the Natural Law Contains Several
Precepts, Or Only one?

We proceed thus to the Second Article:—

Objection 1. It would seem that the natural law contains, not several precepts, but only one. For law is a kind of precept, . . . If therefore there were many precepts of the natural law, it would follow that there are also many natural laws.

Obj. 2. Further, the natural law is consequent upon human nature. But human nature, as a whole, is one, though, as to its parts, it is manifold. Therefore, either there is but one precept of the law of nature because of the unity of nature as a whole, or there are many by reason of the number of parts of human nature. The result would be that even things relating to the inclination of the concupiscible power would belong to the natural law.

Obj. 3. Further, law is something pertaining to reason, . . . Now reason is but one in man. Therefore there is only one precept of the natural law.

On the contrary, The precepts of the natural law in man stand in relation to operable matters as first principles do to matters of demonstration. But there are several first indemonstrable principles. Therefore there are also several precepts of the natural law.

I answer that, . . . the precepts of the natural law are to the practical reason what the first principles of demonstrations are to the speculative reason, because both are self-evident principles. Now a thing is said to be self-evident in two ways: first, in itself; secondly, in relation to us. Any proposition is said to be self-evident in itself, if its predicate is contained in the notion of the subject; even though it may happen that to one who does not know the definition of the subject, such a proposition is not self-evident. For instance, this proposition, *Man is a rational being*, is, in its very nature, self-evident, since he who says *man*, says *a rational being;* and yet to one who does not know what a man is, this proposition is not self-evident. Hence it is that, as Boethius says, certain axioms or propositions are universally self-evident to all; and such are the propositions whose terms are known to all, as, *Every whole is greater than its part*, and, *Things equal to one and the same are equal to one another.* But some propositions are self-evident only to the wise, who understand the meaning of the terms of such propositions. Thus to one who understands that an angel is not a body, it is self-evident that an angel is not circumscriptively in a place. But this is not evident to the unlearned, for they cannot grasp it.

Now a certain order is to be found in those things that are apprehended by men. For that which first falls under apprehension is *being*, the understanding of which is included in all things whatsoever a man apprehends. Therefore the first indemonstrable principle is that *the same thing cannot be affirmed and denied at the same time*, which is based on the notion of *being* and *not-being:* and on this principle all others are based, as is stated in *Metaph.* iv. Now as *being* is the first thing that falls under the apprehension absolutely, so *good* is the first thing that falls under the apprehension of the practical reason, which is directed to action (since every agent acts for an end, which has the nature of good). Consequently, the first principle in the practical reason is one founded on the nature of good, viz., that *good is that which all things seek after*. Hence this is the first precept of law, that *good is to be done and promoted, and evil is to be avoided.* All other precepts of the natural law are based upon this; so that all the things which the practical reason naturally apprehends as man's good belong to the precepts of the natural law under the form of things to be done or avoided.

Since, however, good has the nature of an end, and evil, the nature of the contrary, hence it is that all those things to which man has a natural inclination are naturally apprehended by reason as being good, and consequently as objects of pursuit, and their contraries as evil, and objects of avoidance. Therefore, the order of the precepts of the natural law is according to the order of natural inclinations. For there is in man, first of all, an inclination to good in accordance with the nature which he has in common with all substances, inasmuch, namely, as every substance seeks the preservation of its own being, according to its nature; and by reason of this inclination, whatever is a means of preserving human life, and of warding off its obstacles, belongs to the natural law. Secondly, there is in man an inclination to things that pertain to him more specially, according to that nature which he has in common with other animals; and in virtue of this inclination, those things are said to belong to the natural law *which nature has taught to all animals*, such as sexual intercourse, the education of offspring and so forth. Thirdly, there is in man an inclination to good according to the nature of his reason, which nature is proper to him. Thus man has a natural inclination to know the truth about God, and to live in society; and in this respect, whatever pertains to this inclination belongs to the natural law: *e.g.*, to shun ignorance, to avoid offending those among whom one has to live, and other such things regarding the above inclination.

Reply Obj. 1. All these precepts of the law of nature have the character of one natural law, inasmuch as they flow from one first precept.

Reply Obj. 2. All the inclinations of any parts whatsoever of human nature, *e.g.*, of the concupiscible and irascible parts, in so far as they are ruled by reason, belong to the natural law, and are reduced to one first precept, as was stated above. And thus the precepts of the natural law are many in themselves, but they are based on one common foundation.

Reply Obj. 3. Although reason is one in itself, yet it directs all things regarding man; so that whatever can be ruled by reason is contained under the law of reason.

Third Article: Whether All the Acts of the Virtues Are Prescribed by the Natural Law?

We proceed thus to the Third Article:—

Objection 1. It would seem that not all the acts of the virtues are prescribed by the natural law. For, . . . it is of the nature of law that it be ordained to the common good. But some acts of the virtues are ordained to the private good of the individual, as is evident especially in regard to acts of temperance. Therefore, not all the acts of the virtues are the subject of natural law.

Obj. 2. Further, every sin is opposed to some virtuous act. If therefore all the acts of the virtues are prescribed by the natural law, it seems to follow that all sins are against nature; whereas this applies to certain special sins.

Obj. 3. Further, those things which are according to nature are common to all. But the acts of the virtues are not common to all, since a thing is virtuous in one, and vicious in another. Therefore, not all the acts of the virtues are prescribed by the natural law.

On the contrary, Damascene says that *virtues are natural.* Therefore virtuous acts also are subject to the natural law.

I answer that, We may speak of virtuous acts in two ways: first, in so far as they are virtuous; secondly, as such and such acts considered in their proper species. If, then, we are speaking of the acts of the virtues in so far as they are virtuous, thus all virtuous acts belong to the natural law. For it has been stated that to the natural law belongs everything to which a man is inclined according to his nature. Now each thing is inclined naturally to an operation that is suitable to it according to its form: *e.g.*, fire is inclined to give heat. Therefore, since the rational soul is the proper form of man, there is in every man a natural inclination to act according to reason; and this is to act according to virtue. Consequently, considered thus, all the acts of the virtues are prescribed by the natural law, since each one's reason naturally dictates to him to act virtuously. But if we speak of virtuous acts, considered in themselves, *i.e.*, in their proper species, thus not all virtuous acts are prescribed by the natural law. For many things are done virtuously, to which nature does not primarily incline, but which, through the inquiry of reason, have been found by men to be conducive to well-living.

Reply Obj. 1. Temperance is about the natural concupiscences of food, drink and sexual matters, which are indeed ordained to the common good of nature, just as other matters of law are ordained to the moral common good.

Reply Obj. 2. By human nature we may mean either that which is proper to man, and in this sense all sins, as being against reason, are also against nature, as Damascene states; or we may mean that nature which is common to man and other animals, and in this sense, certain special sins are said to be against nature: *e.g.* contrary to sexual intercourse, which is natural to all animals, is unisexual lust, which has received the special name of the unnatural crime.

Reply Obj. 3. This argument considers acts in themselves. For it is owing to the various conditions of men that certain acts are virtuous for some, as being proportioned and becoming to them, while they are vicious for others, as not being proportioned to them.

Fourth Article: Whether the Natural Law Is the Same in All Men?

We proceed thus to the Fourth Article:—

Objection 1. It would seem that the natural law is not the same in all. For it is stated in the *Decretals* that *the natural law is that which is contained in the Law and the Gospel.* But this is not common to all men, because, as it is written (*Rom.* x. 16), *all do not obey the gospel.* Therefore the natural law is not the same in all men.

Obj. 2. Further, *Things which are according to the law are said to be just,* as is stated in *Ethics* v. But it is stated in the same book that nothing is so just for all as not to be subject to change in regard to some men. Therefore even the natural law is not the same in all men.

Obj. 3. Further, as was stated above, to the natural law belongs everything to which a man is inclined according to his nature. Now different men are naturally inclined to different things,—some to the desire of pleasures, others to the desire of honors, and other men to other things. Therefore, there is not one natural law for all.

On the contrary, Isidore says: *The natural law is common to all nations.*

I answer that, . . . to the natural law belong those things to which a man is inclined naturally; and among these it is proper to man to be inclined to act according to reason. Now it belongs to the reason to proceed from what is common to what is proper, as is stated in *Physics* i. The speculative reason, however, is differently situated, in this matter, from the practical reason. For, since the speculative reason is concerned chiefly with necessary things, which cannot be otherwise than they are, its proper conclusions, like the universal principles, contain the truth without fail. The practical reason, on the other hand, is concerned with contingent matters, which is the domain of human actions; and, consequently, although there is necessity in the common principles, the more we descend towards the particular, the more frequently we encounter defects. Accordingly, then, in speculative matters truth is the same in all men, both as to principles and as to conclusions; although the truth is not known to all as regards the conclusions, but only as regards the principles which are called *common notions.* But in matters of action, truth or practical rectitude is not the same for all as to what is particular, but only as to the common principles; and where there is the same rectitude in relation to particulars, it is not equally known to all.

It is therefore evident that, as regards the common principles whether of speculative or of practical reason, truth or rectitude is the same for all, and is equally known by all. But as to the proper conclusions of the speculative reason, the truth is the same for all, but it is not equally known to all. Thus, it is true for all that the three angles of a triangle are together equal to two right angles, although it is not known to all. But as to the proper conclusions of the practical reason, neither is the truth or rectitude the same for all, nor, where it is the same, is it equally known by all. Thus, it is right and true for all to act according to reason, and from this principle it follows, as a proper conclusion, that goods entrusted to another should be restored to their owner. Now this is true for the majority of cases. But it may happen in a particular case that it would be injurious, and therefore unreasonable, to restore goods held in trust; for instance, if they are claimed for the purpose of fighting against one's country. And this principle will be found to fail the more, according as we descend further towards the particular, *e.g.*, if one were to say that goods held in trust should be restored with such and such a guarantee, or in such and such a way; because the greater the number of conditions added, the greater the number of ways in which the principle may fail, so that it be not right to restore or not to restore.

Consequently, we must say that the natural law, as to the first common principles, is the same for all, both as to rectitude and as to knowledge. But as to certain more particular aspects, which are conclusions, as it were, of those common principles, it is the same for all in the majority of cases, both as to rectitude and as to knowledge; and yet in some few cases it may fail, both as to rectitude, by reason of certain obstacles (just as natures subject to degeneration and corruption fail in some few cases because of some obstacle), and as to knowledge, since in some the reason is perverted by passion, or evil habit, or an evil disposition of nature. Thus at one time theft, although it is expressly contrary to the natural law, was not considered wrong among the Germans, as Julius Cæsar relates.

Reply Obj. 1. The meaning of the sentence quoted is not that whatever is contained in the Law and the Gospel belongs to the natural law, since they contain many things that are above nature; but that whatever belongs to the natural law is fully contained in them. Therefore Gratian, after saying that *the natural law is what is contained in the Law and the Gospel*, adds at once, by way of example, *by which everyone is commanded to do to others as he would be done by*.

Reply Obj. 2. The saying of the Philosopher is to be understood of things that are naturally just, not as common principles, but as conclusions drawn from them, having rectitude in the majority of cases, but failing in a few.

Reply Obj. 3. Just as in man reason rules and commands the other powers, so all the natural inclinations belonging to the other powers must needs be directed according to reason. Therefore it is universally right for all men that all their inclinations should be directed according to reason.

Fifth Article: Whether the Natural Law Can Be Changed?

We proceed thus to the Fifth Article:—

Objection 1. It would seem that the natural law can be changed. For on *Eccles.* xvii. 9 (*He gave them instructions, and the law of life*) the *Gloss* says: *He wished the law of the letter to be written, in order to correct the law of nature*. But that which is corrected is changed. Therefore the natural law can be changed.

Obj. 2. Further, the slaying of the innocent, adultery and theft are against the natural law. But we find these things changed by God: as when God

commanded Abraham to slay his innocent son (*Gen.* xxii. 2); and when He
ordered the Jews to borrow and purloin the vessels of the Egyptians (*Exod.*
xii. 35); and when He commanded Osee to take to himself *a wife of fornica-
tions* (*Osee* i. 2). Therefore the natural law can be changed.

Obj. 3. Further, Isidore says that *the possession of all things in common,
and universal freedom, are matters of natural law*. But these things are seen
to be changed by human laws. Therefore it seems that the natural law is
subject to change.

On the contrary, It is said in the *Decretals: The natural law dates from the
creation of the rational creature. It does not vary according to time, but
remains unchangeable*.

I answer that, A change in the natural law may be understood in two
ways. First, by way of addition. In this sense, nothing hinders the natural
law from being changed, since many things for the benefit of human life
have been added over and above the natural law, both by the divine law and
by human laws.

Secondly, a change in the natural law may be understood by way of
subtraction, so that what previously was according to the natural law, ceases
to be so. In this sense, the natural law is altogether unchangeable in its first
principles. But in its secondary principles, which, as we have said, are certain
detailed proximate conclusions drawn from the first principles, the natural
law is not changed so that what it prescribes be not right in most cases. But
it may be changed in some particular cases of rare occurrence, through some
special causes hindering the observance of such precepts, as was stated
above.

Reply Obj. 1. The written law is said to be given for the correction of
the natural law, either because it supplies what was wanting to the natural
law, or because the natural law was so perverted in the hearts of some men,
as to certain matters, that they esteemed those things good which are
naturally evil; which perversion stood in need of correction.

Reply Obj. 2. All men alike, both guilty and innocent, die the death of
nature; which death of nature is inflicted by the power of God because of
original sin, according to *I Kings* ii. 6: *The Lord killeth and maketh alive*.
Consequently, by the command of God, death can be inflicted on any man,
guilty or innocent, without any injustice whatever.—In like manner, adultery is intercourse with another's wife; who is allotted to him by the law
emanating from God. Consequently intercourse with any woman, by the
command of God, is neither adultery nor fornication.—The same applies to
theft, which is the taking of another's property. For whatever is taken by
the command of God, to Whom all things belong, is not taken against the
will of its owner, whereas it is in this that theft consists.—Nor is it only in
human things that whatever is commanded by God is right; but also in
natural things, whatever is done by God is, in some way, natural, . . .

Reply Obj. 3. A thing is said to belong to the natural law in two ways.
First, because nature inclines thereto: *e.g.*, that one should not do harm to
another. Secondly, because nature did not bring with it the contrary. Thus,
we might say that for man to be naked is of the natural law, because nature
did not give him clothes, but art invented them. In this sense, *the possession
of all things in common and universal freedom* are said to be of the natural
law, because, namely, the distinction of possessions and slavery were not

brought in by nature, but devised by human reason for the benefit of human life. Accordingly, the law of nature was not changed in this respect, except by addition.

Sixth Article: Whether the Natural Law Can Be Abolished from the Heart of Man?

We proceed thus to the Sixth Article:—

Objection 1. It would seem that the natural law can be abolished from the heart of man. For on *Rom.* ii. 14 (*When the Gentiles who have not the law,* etc.) the *Gloss* says that *the law of justice, which sin had blotted out, is graven on the heart of man when he is restored by grace.* But the law of justice is the law of nature. Therefore the law of nature can be blotted out.

Obj. 2. Further, the law of grace is more efficacious than the law of nature. But the law of grace is blotted out by sin. Much more, therefore, can the law of nature be blotted out.

Obj. 3. Further, that which is established by law is proposed as something just. But many things are enacted by men which are contrary to the law of nature. Therefore the law of nature can be abolished from the heart of man.

On the contrary, Augustine says: *Thy law is written in the hearts of men, which iniquity itself effaces not.* But the law which is written in men's hearts is the natural law. Therefore the natural law cannot be blotted out.

I answer that, . . . there belong to the natural law, first, certain most common precepts that are known to all; and secondly, certain secondary and more particular precepts, which are, as it were, conclusions following closely from first principles. As to the common principles, the natural law, in its universal meaning, cannot in any way be blotted out from men's hearts. But it is blotted out in the case of a particular action, in so far as reason is hindered from applying the common principle to the particular action because of concupiscence or some other passion, . . . —But as to the other, *i.e.*, the secondary precepts, the natural law can be blotted out from the human heart, either by evil persuasions, just as in speculative matters errors occur in respect of necessary conclusions; or by vicious customs and corrupt habits, as, among some men, theft, and even unnatural vices, as the Apostle states (*Rom.* i. 24), were not esteemed sinful.

Reply Obj. 1. Sin blots out the law of nature in particular cases, not universally, except perchance in regard to the secondary precepts of the natural law, in the way stated above.

Reply Obj. 2. Although grace is more efficacious than nature, yet nature is more essential to man, and therefore more enduring.

Reply Obj. 3. This argument is true of the secondary precepts of the natural law, against which some legislators have framed certain enactments which are unjust.

4

LAWS OF NATURE

Thomas Hobbes

OF THE NATURAL CONDITION OF MANKIND AS CONCERNING THEIR FELICITY AND MISERY

Men by nature equal. Nature hath made men so equal, in the faculties of the body, and mind; as that though there be found one man sometimes manifestly stronger in body, or of quicker mind than another; yet when all is reckoned together, the difference between man, and man, is not so considerable, as that one man can thereupon claim to himself any benefit, to which another may not pretend, as well as he. For as to the strength of body, the weakest has strength enough to kill the strongest, either by secret machination, or by confederacy with others, that are in the same danger with himself.

And as to the faculties of the mind, setting aside the arts grounded upon words, and especially that skill of proceeding upon general, and infallible rules, called science; which very few have, and but in few things; as being not a native faculty, born with us; nor attained, as prudence, while we look after somewhat else, I find yet a greater equality amongst men, than that of strength. For prudence, is but experience; which equal time, equally bestows on all men, in those things they equally apply themselves unto. That which may perhaps make such equality incredible, is but a vain conceit of one's own wisdom, which almost all men think they have in a greater degree, than the vulgar; that is, than all men but themselves, and a few others, whom by fame, or for concurring with themselves, they approve. For such is the nature of men, that howsoever they may acknowledge many others to be more witty, or more eloquent, or more learned; yet they will hardly believe there be many so wise as themselves; for they see their own wit at hand, and other men's at a distance. But this proveth rather that men are in that point equal, than unequal. For there is not ordinarily a greater sign of the equal distribution of any thing, than that every man is contented with his share.

From equality proceeds diffidence. From this equality of ability, ariseth equality of hope in the attaining of our ends. And therefore if any two men

From Thomas Hobbes, *Leviathan*, in *The English Works of Thomas Hobbes*, William Molesworth, ed., Vol. III (London: John Bohn, 1839), Part I, Chaps. XIII–XV, pp. 110–138, 147.

desire the same thing, which nevertheless they cannot both enjoy, they
become enemies; and in the way to their end, which is principally their own
conservation, and sometimes their delectation only, endeavour to destroy, or
subdue one another. And from hence it comes to pass, that where an invader
hath no more to fear, than another man's single power; if one plant, sow,
build, or possess a convenient seat, others may probably be expected to
come prepared with forces united, to dispossess, and deprive him, not only
of the fruit of his labour, but also of his life, or liberty. And the invader
again is in the like danger of another.

From diffidence war. And from this diffidence of one another, there is no
way for any man to secure himself, so reasonable, as anticipation; that is, by
force, or wiles, to master the persons of all men he can, so long, till he see no
other power great enough to endanger him: and this is no more than his
own conservation requireth, and is generally allowed. Also because there be
some, that taking pleasure in contemplating their own power in the acts of
conquest, which they pursue farther than their security requires; if others,
that otherwise would be glad to be at ease within modest bounds, should not
by invasion increase their power, they would not be able, long time, by
standing only on their defence, to subsist. And by consequence, such
augmentation of dominion over men being necessary to a man's conservation, it ought to be allowed him.

Again, men have no pleasure, but on the contrary a great deal of grief, in
keeping company, where there is no power able to over-awe them all. For
every man looketh that his companion should value him, at the same rate he
sets upon himself: and upon all signs of contempt, or undervaluing, naturally
endeavours, as far as he dares (which amongst them that have no common
power to keep them in quiet, is far enough to make them destroy each
other), to extort a greater value from his contemners, by damage; and from
others, by the example.

So that in the nature of man, we find three principal causes of quarrel.
First, competition; secondly, diffidence; thirdly, glory.

The first, maketh men invade for gain; the second, for safety; and the
third, for reputation. The first use violence, to make themselves masters of
other men's persons, wives, children, and cattle; the second, to defend them;
the third, for trifles, as a word, a smile, a different opinion, and any other
sign of undervalue, either direct in their persons, or by reflection in their
kindred, their friends, their nation, their profession, or their name.

Out of civil states, there is always war of every one against every one.
Hereby it is manifest, that during the time men live without a common
power to keep them all in awe, they are in that condition which is called
war; and such a war, as is of every man, against every man. For WAR,
consisteth not in battle only, or the act of fighting; but in a tract of time,
wherein the will to contend by battle is sufficiently known: and therefore
the notion of *time*, is to be considered in the nature of war; as it is in the
nature of weather. For as the nature of foul weather, lieth not in a shower or
two of rain; but in an inclination thereto of many days together: so the
nature of war, consisteth not in actual fighting; but in the known disposition
thereto, during all the time there is no assurance to the contrary. All other
time is PEACE.

The incommodities of such a war. Whatsoever therefore is consequent to a time of war, where every man is enemy to every man; the same is consequent to the time, wherein men live without other security, than what their own strength, and their own invention shall furnish them withal. In such condition, there is no place for industry; because the fruit thereof is uncertain: and consequently no culture of the earth; no navigation, nor use of the commodities that may be imported by sea; no commodious building; no instruments of moving, and removing, such things as require much force; no knowledge of the face of the earth; no account of time; no arts; no letters; no society; and which is worst of all, continual fear, and danger of violent death; and the life of man, solitary, poor, nasty, brutish, and short.

It may seem strange to some man, that has not well weighed these things; that nature should thus dissociate, and render men apt to invade, and destroy one another: and he may therefore, not trusting to this inference, made from the passions, desire perhaps to have the same confirmed by experience. Let him therefore consider with himself, when taking a journey, he arms himself, and seeks to go well accompanied; when going to sleep, he locks his doors; when even in his house he locks his chests; and this when he knows there be laws, and public officers, armed, to revenge all injuries shall be done him; what opinion he has of his fellow-subjects, when he rides armed; of his fellow citizens, when he locks his doors; and of his children, and servants, when he locks his chests. Does he not there as much accuse mankind by his actions, as I do by my words? But neither of us accuse man's nature in it. The desires, and other passions of man, are in themselves no sin. No more are the actions, that proceed from those passions, till they know a law that forbids them: which till laws be made they cannot know: nor can any law be made, till they have agreed upon the person that shall make it.

It may peradventure be thought, there was never such a time, nor condition of war as this; and I believe it was never generally so, over all the world: but there are many places, where they live so now. For the savage people in many places of America, except the government of small families, the concord whereof dependeth on natural lust, have no government at all; and live at this day in that brutish manner, as I said before. Howsoever, it may be perceived what manner of life there would be, where there were no common power to fear, by the manner of life, which men that have formerly lived under a peaceful government, use to degenerate into, in a civil war.

But though there had never been any time, wherein particular men were in a condition of war one against another; yet in all times, kings, and persons of sovereign authority, because of their independency, are in continual jealousies, and in the state and posture of gladiators; having their weapons pointing, and their eyes fixed on one another; that is, their forts, garrisons, and guns upon the frontiers of their kingdoms; and continual spies upon their neighbours; which is a posture of war. But because they uphold thereby, the industry of their subjects; there does not follow from it, that misery, which accompanies the liberty of particular men.

In such a war nothing is unjust. To this war of every man, against every man, this also is consequent; that nothing can be unjust. The notions of right and wrong, justice and injustice have there no place. Where there is no common power, there is no law: where no law, no injustice. Force, and fraud, are in war the two cardinal virtues. Justice, and injustice are none of the faculties neither of the body, nor mind. If they were, they might be in a man that were alone in the world, as well as his senses, and passions. They are qualities, that relate to men in society, not in solitude. It is consequent also to the same condition, that there be no propriety, no dominion, no *mine* and *thine* distinct; but only that to be every man's, that he can get: and for so long, as he can keep it. And thus much for the ill condition, which man by mere nature is actually placed in; though with a possibility to come out of it, consisting partly in the passions, partly in his reason.

The passions that incline men to peace. The passions that incline men to peace, are fear of death; desire of such things as are necessary to commodious living; and a hope by their industry to obtain them. And reason suggesteth convenient articles of peace, upon which men may be drawn to agreement. These articles, are they, which otherwise are called the Laws of Nature . . .

OF THE FIRST AND SECOND NATURAL LAWS, AND OF CONTRACTS

Right of nature what. THE RIGHT OF NATURE, which writers commonly call *jus naturale*, is the liberty each man hath, to use his own power, as he will himself, for the preservation of his own nature; that is to say, of his own life; and consequently, of doing any thing, which in his own judgment, and reason, he shall conceive to be the aptest means thereunto.

Liberty what. BY LIBERTY, is understood, according to the proper signification of the word, the absence of external impediments: which impediments, may oft take away part of a man's power to do what he would; but cannot hinder him from using the power left him, according as his judgment, and reason shall dictate to him.

A law of nature what. Difference of right and law. A LAW OF NATURE, *lex naturalis*, is a precept or general rule, found out by reason, by which a man is forbidden to do that, which is destructive of his life, or taketh away the means of preserving the same; and to omit that, by which he thinketh it may be best preserved. For though they that speak of this subject, use to confound *jus*, and *lex*, *right* and *law:* yet they ought to be distinguished; because RIGHT, consisteth in liberty to do, or to forbear: whereas LAW, determineth, and bindeth to one of them: so that law, and right, differ as much, as obligation, and liberty; which in one and the same matter are inconsistent.

Naturally every man has right to every thing. The fundamental law of nature. And because the condition of man, as hath been declared in the precedent chapter, is a condition of war of every one against every one; in which case every one is governed by his own reason; and there is nothing he can make use of, that may not be a help unto him, in preserving his life against his enemies; it followeth, that in such a condition, every man has a right to every thing; even to one another's body. And therefore, as long as this natural right of every man to every thing endureth, there can be no security to any man, how strong or wise soever he be, of living out the time, which nature ordinarily alloweth men to live. And consequently it is a precept, or general rule of reason, *that every man, ought to endeavour peace, as far as he has hope of obtaining it; and when he cannot obtain it, that he may seek, and use, all helps, and advantages of war.* The first branch of which rule, containeth the first, and fundamental law of nature; which is, *to seek peace, and follow it*. The second, the sum of the right of nature; which is, *by all means we can, to defend ourselves*.

The second law of nature. From this fundamental law of nature, by which men are commanded to endeavour peace, is derived this second law; *that a man be willing, when others are so too, as far-forth, as for peace, and defence of himself he shall think it necessary, to lay down this right to all things; and be contented with so much liberty against other men, as he would allow other men against himself*. For as long as every man holdeth this right, of doing any thing he liketh; so long are all men in the condition of war. But if other men will not lay down their right, as well as he; then there is no reason for any one, to divest himself of his: for that were to expose himself to prey, which no man is bound to, rather than to dispose himself to peace. This is that law of the Gospel; *whatsoever you require that others should do to you, that do ye to them*. And that law of all men, *quod tibi fieri non vis, alteri ne feceris* [do not to others what you would not have done to yourself].

What it is to lay down a right. To *lay down* a man's *right* to any thing, is to *divest* himself of the *liberty*, of hindering another of the benefit of his own right to the same. For he that renounceth, or passeth away his right, giveth not to any other man a right which he had not before; because there is nothing to which every man had not right by nature: but only standeth out of his way, that he may enjoy his own original right, without hindrance from him; not without hindrance from another. So that the effect which redoundeth to one man, by another man's defect of right, is but so much diminution of impediments to the use of his own right original.

Renouncing a right, what it is. Transferring right what. Obligation. Duty. Injustice. Right is laid aside, either by simply renouncing it; or by transferring it to another. By *simply* RENOUNCING; when he cares not to whom the benefit thereof redoundeth. By TRANSFERRING; when he intendeth the benefit thereof to some certain person, or persons. And when a man hath in either manner abandoned, or granted away his right; then he is said to be OBLIGED, or BOUND, not to hinder those, to whom such right is granted, or abandoned, from the benefit of it: and that he *ought*, and it is his DUTY, not to make void that voluntary act of his own: and that such hindrance is INJUSTICE, and INJURY, as being *sine jure*; the right being before renounced, or transferred. So that *injury*, or *injustice*, in the controversies of the world, is somewhat like to that, which in the disputations of scholars is called *absurdity*. For as it is there called an absurdity, to contradict what one maintained in the beginning: so in the world, it is called injustice, and injury, voluntarily to undo that, which from the beginning he had voluntarily done. The way by which a man either simply renounceth, or transferreth his right, is a declaration, or signification, by some voluntary and sufficient sign, or signs, that he doth so renounce, or transfer; or hath so renounced, or transferred the same, to him that accepteth it. And these signs are either words only, or actions only; or, as it happeneth most often, both words, and actions. And the same are the BONDS, by which men are bound, and obliged: bonds, that have their strength, not from their own nature, for nothing is more easily broken than a man's word, but from fear of some evil consequence upon the rupture.

Not all rights are alienable. Whensoever a man transferreth his right, or renounceth it; it is either in consideration of some right reciprocally transferred to himself; or for some other good he hopeth for thereby. For it is a voluntary act: and of the voluntary acts of every man, the object is some *good to himself.* And therefore there be some rights, which no man can be understood by any words, or other signs, to have abandoned, or transferred. As first a man cannot lay down the right of resisting them, that assault him by force, to take away his life; because he cannot be understood to aim thereby, at any good to himself. The same may be said of wounds, and chains, and imprisonment; both because there is no benefit consequent to such patience; as there is to the patience of suffering another to be wounded, or imprisoned: as also because a man cannot tell, when he seeth men proceed against him by violence, whether they intend his death or not. And lastly the motive, and end for which this renouncing, and transferring of right is introduced, is nothing else but the security of a man's person, in his life, and in the means of so preserving life, as not to be weary of it. And therefore if a man by words, or other signs, seem to despoil himself of the end, for which those signs were intended; he is not to be understood as if he meant it, or that it was his will; but that he was ignorant of how such words and actions were to be interpreted.

Contract what. The mutual transferring of right, is that which men call CONTRACT.

There is difference between transferring of right to the thing; and transferring, or tradition, that is delivery of the thing itself. For the thing may be delivered together with the translation of the right; as in buying and selling with ready-money; or exchange of goods, or lands: and it may be delivered some time after.

Covenant what. Again, one of the contractors, may deliver the thing contracted for on his part, and leave the other to perform his part at some determinate time after, and in the mean time be trusted; and then the contract on his part, is called PACT, or COVENANT: or both parts may contract now, to perform hereafter: in which cases, he that is to perform in time to come, being trusted, his performance is called *keeping of promise,* or faith; and the failing of performance, if it be voluntary, *violation of faith.*

Free-gift. When the transferring of right, is not mutual: but one of the parties transferreth, in hope to gain thereby friendship, or service from another, or from his friends; or in hope to gain the reputation of charity, or magnanimity; or to deliver his mind from the pain of compassion; or in hope of reward in heaven; this is not contract, but GIFT, FREE-GIFT, GRACE: which words signify one and the same thing.

Signs of contract express. Promise. Signs of contract, are either *express,* or *by inference.* Express, are words spoken with understanding of what they signify: and such words are either of the time *present,* or *past;* as, *I give, I grant, I have given, I have granted, I will that this be yours:* or of the future; as, *I will give, I will grant:* which words of the future are called PROMISE.

Signs of contract by inference. Signs by inference, are sometimes the consequence of words; sometimes the consequence of silence; sometimes the consequence of actions; sometimes the consequence of forbearing an action: and generally a sign by inference, of any contract, is whatsoever sufficiently argues the will of the contractor.

Free-gift passeth by words of the present or past. Words alone, if they be of the time to come, and contain a bare promise, are an insufficient sign of a free-gift, and therefore not obligatory. For if they be of the time to come, as *to-morrow I will give,* they are a sign I have not given yet, and consequently that my right is not transferred, but remaineth till I transfer it by some other act. But if the words be of the time present, or past, as, *I have given,* or, *do give to be delivered to-morrow,* then is my to-morrow's right given away to-day; and that by the virtue of the words, though there were no other argument of my will. And there is a great difference in the significa-tion of these words, *volo hoc tuum esse cras,* and *cras dabo;* that is, between *I will that this be thine to-morrow,* and, *I will give it thee to-morrow:* for the word *I will,* in the former manner of speech, signifies an act of the will present; but in the latter, it signifies a promise of an act of the will to come: and therefore the former words, being of the present, transfer a future right; the latter, that be of the future, transfer nothing. But if there be other signs of the will to transfer a right, besides words; then, though the gift be free, yet may the right be understood to pass by words of the future: as if a man propound a prize to him that comes first to the end of a race, the gift is free; and though the words be of the future, yet the right passeth: for if he would not have his words so be understood, he should not have let them run.

Signs of contract are words both of the past, present, and future. In contracts, the right passeth, not only where the words are of the time present, or past, but also where they are of the future: because all contract is mutual translation, or change of right; and therefore he that promiseth only, because he hath already received the benefit for which he promiseth, is to be understood as if he intended the right should pass: for unless he had been content to have his words so understood, the other would not have performed his part first. And for that cause, in buying, and selling, and other acts of contract, a promise is equivalent to a covenant; and therefore obligatory.

Merit what. He that performeth first in the case of a contract, is said to MERIT that which he is to receive by the performance of the other; and he hath it as *due.* Also when a prize is propounded to many, which is to be given to him only that winneth; or money is thrown amongst many, to be enjoyed by them that catch it; though this be a free gift; yet so to win, or so to catch, is to *merit,* and to have it as DUE. For the right is transferred in the propounding of the prize, and in throwing down the money; though it be not determined to whom, but by the event of the contention. But there is between these two sorts of merit, this difference, that in contract, I merit by virtue of my own power, and the contractor's need; but in this case of free gift, I am enabled to merit only by the benignity of the giver: in contract, I merit at the contractor's hand that he should depart with his right; in this case of gift, I merit not that the giver should part with his right; but that when he has parted with it, it should be mine, rather than another's. And this I think to be the meaning of that distinction of the Schools, between *meritum congrui* and *meritum condigni.* For God Almighty, having prom-ised Paradise to those men, hoodwinked with carnal desires, that can walk through this world according to the precepts, and limits prescribed by him; they say, he that shall so walk, shall merit Paradise *ex congruo.* But because no man can demand a right to it, by his own righteousness, or any other power in himself, but by the free grace of God only; they say, no man can merit Paradise *ex condigno*. This I say, I think is the meaning of that distinction; but because disputers do not agree upon the signification of their own terms of art, longer than it serves their turn; I will not affirm any thing of their meaning: only this I say; when a gift is given indefinitely, as a prize to be contended for, he that winneth meriteth, and may claim the prize as due.

Covenants of mutual trust, when invalid. If a covenant be made, wherein neither of the parties perform presently, but trust one another; in the condition of mere nature, which is a condition of war of every man against every man, upon any reasonable suspicion, it is void: but if there be a common power set over them both, with right and force sufficient to compel performance, it is not void. For he that performeth first, has no assurance the other will perform after; because the bonds of words are too weak to bridle men's ambition, avarice, anger, and other passions, without the fear of some coercive power; which in the condition of mere nature, where all men are equal, and judges of the justness of their own fears, cannot possibly be supposed. And therefore he which performeth first, does but betray himself to his enemy; contrary to the right, he can never abandon, of defending his life, and means of living.

But in a civil estate, where there is a power set up to constrain those that would otherwise violate their faith, that fear is no more reasonable; and for that cause, he which by the covenant is to perform first, is obliged so to do.

The cause of fear, which maketh such a covenant invalid, must be always something arising after the covenant made; as some new fact, or other sign of the will not to perform: else it cannot make the covenant void. For that which could not hinder a man from promising, ought not to be admitted as a hindrance of performing.

Right to the end, containeth right to the means. He that transferreth any right, transferreth the means of enjoying it, as far as lieth in his power. As he that selleth land, is understood to transfer the herbage, and whatsoever grows upon it: nor can he that sells a mill turn away the stream that drives it. And they that give to a man the right of government in sovereignty, are understood to give him the right of levying money to maintain soldiers; and of appointing magistrates for the administration of justice.

No covenant with beasts. To make covenants with brute beasts, is impossible; because not understanding our speech, they understand not, nor accept of any translation of right; nor can translate any right to another: and without mutual acceptation, there is no covenant.

Nor with God without special revelation. To make covenant with God, is impossible, but by mediation of such as God speaketh to, either by revelation supernatural, or by his lieutenants that govern under him, and in his name: for otherwise we know not whether our covenants be accepted, or not. And therefore they that vow anything contrary to any law of nature, vow in vain; as being a thing unjust to pay such vow. And if it be a thing commanded by the law of nature, it is not the vow, but the law that binds them.

No covenant, but of possible and future. The matter, or subject of a covenant, is always something that falleth under deliberation; for to cove-

nant, is an act of the will; that is to say, an act, and the last act of deliberation; and is therefore always understood to be something to come; and
which is judged possible for him that covenanteth, to perform.

And therefore, to promise that which is known to be impossible, is no
covenant. But if that prove impossible afterwards, which before was
thought possible, the covenant is valid, and bindeth, though not to the thing
itself, yet to the value; or, if that also be impossible, to the unfeigned
endeavour of performing as much as is possible: for to more no man can be
obliged.

Covenants how made void. Men are freed of their covenants two ways;
by performing; or by being forgiven. For performance, is the natural end of
obligation; and forgiveness, the restitution of liberty; as being a retransfer-
ring of that right, in which the obligation consisted.

Covenants extorted by fear are valid. Covenants entered into by fear, in
the condition of mere nature, are obligatory. For example, if I covenant to
pay a ransom, or service for my life, to an enemy; I am bound by it: for it is
a contract, wherein one receiveth the benefit of life; the other is to receive
money, or service for it; and consequently, where no other law, as in the
condition of mere nature, forbiddeth the performance, the covenant is valid.
Therefore prisoners of war, if trusted with the payment of their ransom, are
obliged to pay it: and if a weaker prince, make a disadvantageous peace with
a stronger, for fear; he is bound to keep it; unless, as hath been said before,
there ariseth some new, and just cause of fear, to renew the war. And even
in commonwealths, if I be forced to redeem myself from a thief by promising him money, I am bound to pay it, till the civil law discharge me. For
whatsoever I may lawfully do without obligation, the same I may lawfully
covenant to do through fear: and what I lawfully covenant, I cannot lawfully break.

The former covenant to one, makes void the later to another. A former
covenant, makes void a later. For a man that hath passed away his right to
one man to-day, hath it not to pass to-morrow to another: and therefore the
later promise passeth no right, but is null.

A man's covenant not to defend himself is void. A covenant not to defend
myself from force, by force, is always void. For, as I have showed before,
no man can transfer, or lay down his right to save himself from death,
wounds, and imprisonment, the avoiding whereof is the only end of laying
down any right; and therefore the promise of not resisting force, in no
covenant transferreth any right; nor is obliging. For though a man may
covenant thus, *unless I do so, or so, kill me;* he cannot covenant thus, *unless I
do so, or so, I will not resist you, when you come to kill me.* For man by
nature chooseth the lesser evil, which is danger of death in resisting; rather
than the greater, which is certain and present death in not resisting. And this
is granted to be true by all men, in that they lead criminals to execution, and
prison, with armed men, notwithstanding that such criminals have consented
to the law, by which they are condemned.

No man obliged to accuse himself. A covenant to accuse oneself, without
assurance of pardon, is likewise invalid. For in the condition of nature,
where every man is judge, there is no place for accusation: and in the civil
state, the accusation is followed with punishment; which being force, a man
is not obliged not to resist. The same is also true, of the accusation of those,

by whose condemnation a man falls into misery; as of a father, wife, or benefactor. For the testimony of such an accuser, if it be not willingly given, is presumed to be corrupted by nature; and therefore not to be received: and where a man's testimony is not to be credited, he is not bound to give it. Also accusations upon torture, are not to be reputed as testimonies. For torture is to be used as means of conjecture, and light, in the further examination, and search of truth: and what is in that case confessed, tendeth to the ease of him that is tortured; not to the informing of the torturers: and therefore ought not to have the credit of a sufficient testimony: for whether he deliver himself by true, or false accusation, he does it by the right of preserving his own life.

The end of an oath. The form of an oath. The force of words, being, as I have formerly noted, too weak to hold men to the performance of their covenants; there are in man's nature, but two imaginable helps to strengthen it. And those are either a fear of the consequence of breaking their word; or a glory, or pride in appearing not to need to break it. This latter is a generosity too rarely found to be presumed on, especially in the pursuers of wealth, command, or sensual pleasure; which are the greatest part of mankind. The passion to be reckoned upon, is fear; whereof there be two very general objects: one, the power of spirits invisible; the other, the power of those men they shall therein offend. Of these two, though the former be the greater power, yet the fear of the latter is commonly the greater fear. The fear of the former is in every man, his own religion: which hath place in the nature of man before civil society. The latter hath not so; at least not place enough, to keep men to their promises; because in the condition of mere nature, the inequality of power is not discerned, but by the event of battle. So that before the time of civil society, or in the interruption thereof by war, there is nothing can strengthen a covenant of peace agreed on, against the temptations of avarice, ambition, lust, or other strong desire, but the fear of that invisible power, which they every one worship as God; and fear as a revenger of their perfidy. All therefore that can be done between two men not subject to civil power, is to put one another to swear by the God he feareth: which *swearing*, or OATH, is a *form of speech, added to a promise; by which he that promiseth, signifieth, that unless he perform, he renounceth the mercy of his God, or calleth to him for vengeance on himself.* Such was the heathen form, *Let* Jupiter *kill me else, as I kill this beast.* So is our form, *I shall do thus, and thus, so help me God.* And this, with the rites and ceremonies, which every one useth in his own religion, that the fear of breaking faith might be the greater.

No oath but by God. By this it appears, that an oath taken according to any other form, or rite, than his, that sweareth, is in vain; and no oath: and that there is no swearing by any thing which the swearer thinks not God. For though men have sometimes used to swear by their kings, for fear, or flattery; yet they would have it thereby understood, they attributed to them divine honour. And that swearing unnecessarily by God, is but profaning of his name: and swearing by other things, as men do in common discourse, is not swearing, but an impious custom, gotten by too much vehemence of talking.

An oath adds nothing to the obligation. It appears also, that the oath adds nothing to the obligation. For a covenant, if lawful, binds in the sight of

God, without the oath, as much as with it: if unlawful, bindeth not at all; though it be confirmed with an oath.

OF OTHER LAWS OF NATURE

The third law of nature, justice. From that law of nature, by which we are obliged to transfer to another, such rights, as being retained, hinder the peace of mankind, there followeth a third; which is this, *that men perform their covenants made:* without which, covenants are in vain, and but empty words; and the right of all men to all things remaining, we are still in the condition of war.

Justice and injustice what. And in this law of nature, consisteth the fountain and original of JUSTICE. For where no covenant hath preceded, there hath no right been transferred, and every man has right to every thing; and consequently, no action can be unjust. But when a covenant is made, then to break it is *unjust:* and the definition of INJUSTICE, is no other than *the not performance of covenant.* And whatsoever is not unjust, is *just.*

Justice and propriety begin with the constitution of commonwealth. But because covenants of mutual trust, where there is a fear of not performance on either part, as hath been said in the former chapter, are invalid; though the original of justice be the making of covenants; yet injustice actually there can be none, till the cause of such fear be taken away; which while men are in the natural condition of war, cannot be done. Therefore before the names of just, and unjust can have place, there must be some coercive power, to compel men equally to the performance of their covenants, by the terror of some punishment, greater than the benefit they expect by the breach of their covenant; and to make good that propriety, which by mutual contract men acquire, in recompense of the universal right they abandon: and such power there is none before the erection of a common-wealth. And this is also to be gathered out of the ordinary definition of justice in the Schools: for they say, that *justice is the constant will of giving to every man his own.* And therefore where there is no *own,* that is no propriety, there is no injustice; and where there is no coercive power erected, that is, where there is no commonwealth, there is no propriety; all men having right to all things: therefore where there is no commonwealth, there nothing is unjust. So that the nature of justice, consisteth in keeping of valid covenants: but the validity of covenants begins not but with the constitution of a civil power, sufficient to compel men to keep them: and then it is also that propriety begins.

Justice not contrary to reason. The fool hath said in his heart, there is no such thing as justice; and sometimes also with his tongue; seriously alleging, that every man's conservation, and contentment, being committed to his own care, there could be no reason, why every man might not do what he thought conduced thereunto: and therefore also to make, or not make; keep, or not keep covenants, was not against reason, when it conduced to one's benefit. He does not therein deny, that there be covenants; and that they are sometimes broken, sometimes kept; and that such breach of them may be called injustice, and the observance of them justice: but he questioneth, whether injustice, taking away the fear of God, for the same fool hath said in his heart there is no God, may not sometimes stand with that reason, which dictateth to every man his own good; and particularly then, when it conduceth to such a benefit, as shall put a man in a condition, to neglect not only the dispraise, and revilings, but also the power of other men. The kingdom of God is gotten by violence: but what if it could be gotten by unjust violence? were it against reason so to get it, when it is impossible to receive hurt by it? and if it be not against reason, it is not against justice; or else justice is not to be approved for good. From such reasoning as this, successful wickedness hath obtained the name of virtue: and some that in all other things have disallowed the violation of faith; yet have allowed it, when it is for the getting of a kingdom. And the heathen that believed, that Saturn was deposed by his son Jupiter, believed nevertheless the same Jupiter to be the avenger of injustice: somewhat like to a piece of law in Coke's *Commentaries on Littleton;* where he says, if the right heir of the crown be attainted of treason; yet the crown shall descend to him, and *eo instante* [in that very instant] the attainder be void: from which instances a man will be very prone to infer; that when the heir apparent of a kingdom, shall kill him that is in possession, though his father; you may call it injustice, or by what other name you will; yet it can never be against reason, seeing all the voluntary actions of men tend to the benefit of themselves; and those actions are most reasonable, that conduce most to their ends. This specious reasoning is nevertheless false.

For the question is not of promises mutual, where there is no security of performance on either side; as when there is no civil power erected over the parties promising; for such promises are no covenants: but either where one of the parties has performed already; or where there is a power to make him perform; there is the question whether it be against reason, that is, against the benefit of the other to perform, or not. And I say it is not against reason. For the manifestation whereof, we are to consider; first, that when a man doth a thing, which notwithstanding any thing can be foreseen, and reckoned on, tendeth to his own destruction, howsoever some accident which he could not expect, arriving may turn it to his benefit; yet such events do not make it reasonably or wisely done. Secondly, that in a condition of war, wherein every man to every man, for want of a common power to keep them all in awe, is an enemy, there is no man who can hope by his own strength, or wit, to defend himself from destruction, without the help of confederates; where every one expects the same defence by the confederation, that any one else does: and therefore he which declares he thinks it reason to deceive those that help him, can in reason expect no other means of safety, than what can be had from his own single power. He therefore that breaketh his covenant, and consequently declareth that he thinks he may with reason do so, cannot be received into any society, that unite themselves for peace and defence, but by the error of them that receive him; nor when he is received, be retained in it, without seeing the danger of their error; which errors a man cannot reasonably reckon upon as the means of his security: and therefore if he be left, or cast out of society, he perisheth; and if he live in society, it is by the errors of other men, which he could not foresee, nor reckon upon; and consequently against the reason of his preservation; and so, as all men that contribute not to his destruction, forbear him only out of ignorance of what is good for themselves.

As for the instance of gaining the secure and perpetual felicity of heaven, by any way; it is frivolous: there being but one way imaginable; and that is not breaking, but keeping of covenant.

And for the other instance of attaining sovereignty by rebellion; it is manifest, that though the event follow, yet because it cannot reasonably be expected, but rather the contrary; and because by gaining it so, others are taught to gain the same in like manner, the attempt thereof is against reason. Justice therefore, that is to say, keeping of covenant, is a rule of reason, by which we are forbidden to do any thing destructive to our life; and consequently a law of nature.

There be some that proceed further; and will not have the law of nature, to be those rules which conduce to the preservation of man's life on earth; but to the attaining of an eternal felicity after death; to which they think the breach of covenant may conduce; and consequently be just and reasonable such are they that think it a work of merit to kill, or depose, or rebel against, the sovereign power constituted over them by their own consent. But because there is no natural knowledge of man's estate after death; much less of the reward that is then to be given to breach of faith; but only a belief grounded upon other men's saying, that they know it supernaturally, or that they know those, that knew them, that knew others, that knew it supernaturally; breach of faith cannot be called a precept of reason, or nature.

Covenants not discharged by the vice of the person to whom they are made. Others, that allow for a law of nature, the keeping of faith, do nevertheless make exception of certain persons; as heretics, and such as use not to perform their covenant to others: and this also is against reason. For if any fault of a man, be sufficient to discharge our covenant made; the same ought in reason to have been sufficient to have hindered the making of it.

Justice of men and justice of actions what. The names of just, and unjust, when they are attributed to men, signify one thing; and when they are attributed to actions, another. When they are attributed to men, they signify conformity, or inconformity of manners, to reason. But when they are attributed to actions, they signify the conformity, or inconformity to reason, not of manners, or manner of life, but of particular actions. A just man therefore, is he that taketh all the care he can, that his actions may be all just: and an unjust man, is he that neglecteth it. And such men are more often in our language styled by the names of righteous, and unrighteous; than just, and unjust; though the meaning be the same. Therefore a righteous man, does not lose that title, by one, or a few unjust actions, that proceed from sudden passion, or mistake of things, or persons: nor does an unrighteous man, lose his character, for such actions, as he does, or forbears to do, for fear: because his will is not framed by the justice, but by the apparent benefit of what he is to do. That which gives to human actions the relish of justice, is a certain nobleness or gallantness of courage, rarely found, by which a man scorns to be beholden for the contentment of his life, to fraud, or breach of promise. This justice of the manners, is that which is meant, where justice is called a virtue; and injustice a vice.

But the justice of actions denominates men, not just, but *guiltless:* and the injustice of the same, which is also called injury, gives them but the name of *guilty.*

Justice of manners, and justice of actions. Again, the injustice of manners, is the disposition, or aptitude to do injury; and is injustice before it proceed to act; and without supposing any individual person injured. But the injustice of an action, that is to say injury, supposeth an individual person injured; namely him, to whom the covenant was made: and therefore many times the injury is received by one man, when the damage redoundeth to another. As when the master commandeth his servant to give money to a stranger; if it be not done, the injury is done to the master, whom he had before covenanted to obey; but the damage redoundeth to the stranger, to whom he had no obligation; and therefore could not injure him. And so also in commonwealths, private men may remit to one another their debts; but not robberies or other violences, whereby they are endamaged; because the detaining of debt, is an injury to themselves; but robbery and violence, are injuries to the person of the commonwealth.

Nothing done to a man by his own consent can be injury. Whatsoever is done to a man, comformable to his own will signified to the doer, is no injury to him. For if he that doeth it, hath not passed away his original right to do what he please, by some antecedent covenant, there is no breach of covenant; and therefore no injury done him. And if he have; then his will to have it done being signified, is a release of that covenant: and so again there is no injury done him.

Justice commutative and distributive. Justice of actions, is by writers divided into *commutative, and distributive:* and the former they say consisteth in proportion arithmetical; the latter in proportion geometrical. Commutative therefore, they place in the equality of value of the things contracted for; and distributive, in the distribution of equal benefit, to men of equal merit. As if it were injustice to sell dearer than we buy; or to give more to a man than he merits. The value of all things contracted for, is measured by the appetite of the contractors: and therefore the just value, is that which they be contented to give. And merit (besides that which is by covenant, where the performance on one part, meriteth the performance on the other part, and falls under justice commutative, not distributive) is not due to justice; but is rewarded of grace only. And therefore this distinction, in the sense wherein it useth to be expounded, is not right. To speak properly, commutative justice, is the justice, of a contractor; that is, a performance of covenant, in buying, and selling, hiring, and letting to hire; lending, and borrowing; exchanging, bartering, and other acts of contract.

And distributive justice, the justice of an arbitrator; that is to say, the act of defining what is just. Wherein, being trusted by them that make him arbitrator, if he perform his trust, he is said to distribute to every man his own: and this is indeed just distribution, and may be called, though improperly, distributive justice; but more properly equity; which also is a law of nature . . .

These dictates of reason, men used to call by the names of laws, but improperly: for they are but conclusions, or theorems concerning what conduceth to the conservation and defence of themselves; whereas law, properly, is the word of him, that by right hath command over others. But yet if we consider the same theorems, as delivered in the word of God, that by right commandeth all things; then are they properly called laws.

5

MORAL IMPERATIVES

Immanuel Kant

. . .

Everything in nature works according to laws. Only a rational being has the capacity of acting according to the conception of laws, i.e., according to principles. This capacity is will. Since reason is required for the derivation of actions from laws, will is nothing else than practical reason. If reason infallibly determines the will, the actions which such a being recognizes as objectively necessary are also subjectively necessary. That is, the will is a faculty of choosing only that which reason, independently of inclination, recognizes as practically necessary, i.e., as good. But if reason of itself does not sufficiently determine the will, and if the will is subjugated to subjective conditions (certain incentives) which do not always agree with objective conditions; in a word, if the will is not of itself in complete accord with reason (the actual case of men), then the actions which are recognized as objectively necessary are subjectively contingent, and the determination of such a will according to objective laws is constraint. That is, the relation of objective laws to a will which is not completely good is conceived as the determination of the will of a rational being by principles of reason to which this will is not by nature necessarily obedient.

The conception of an objective principle, so far as it constrains a will, is a command (of reason), and the formula of this command is called an *imperative*.

All imperatives are expressed by an "ought" and thereby indicate the relation of an objective law of reason to a will which is not in its subjective constitution necessarily determined by this law. This relation is that of constraint. Imperatives say that it would be good to do or to refrain from doing something, but they say it to a will which does not always do something simply because it is presented as a good thing to do. Practical good is what determines the will by means of the conception of reason and hence

From Immanuel Kant, *Foundations of the Metaphysics of Morals*, translated by Lewis White Beck, Sec. 2, pp. 29–51, 54–56. Copyright © 1959, by The Liberal Arts Press, Inc., reprinted by permission of The Liberal Arts Press Division of The Bobbs-Merrill Company, Inc.

not by subjective causes but, rather, objectively, i.e., on grounds which are valid for every rational being as such. It is distinguished from the pleasant as that which has an influence on the will only by means of a sensation from merely subjective causes, which hold only for the senses of this or that person and not as a principle of reason which holds for everyone.

A perfectly good will, therefore, would be equally subject to objective laws (of the good), but it could not be conceived as constrained by them to act in accord with them, because, according to its own subjective constitution, it can be determined to act only through the conception of the good. Thus no imperatives hold for the divine will or, more generally, for a holy will. The "ought" is here out of place, for the volition of itself is necessarily in unison with the law. Therefore imperatives are only formulas expressing the relation of objective laws of volition in general to the subjective imperfection of the will of this or that rational being, e.g., the human will.

All imperatives command either hypothetically or categorically. The former present the practical necessity of a possible action as a means to achieving something else which one desires (or which one may possibly desire). The categorical imperative would be one which presented an action as of itself objectively necessary, without regard to any other end.

Since every practical law presents a possible action as good and thus as necessary for a subject practically determinable by reason, all imperatives are formulas of the determination of action which is necessary by the principle of a will which is in any way good. If the action is good only as a means to something else, the imperative is hypothetical; but if it is thought of as good in itself, and hence as necessary in a will which of itself conforms to reason as the principle of this will, the imperative is categorical.

The imperative thus says what action possible to me would be good, and it presents the practical rule in relation to a will which does not forthwith perform an action simply because it is good, in part because the subject does not always know that the action is good and in part (when he does know it) because his maxims can still be opposed to the objective principles of practical reason.

The hypothetical imperative, therefore, says only that the action is good to some purpose, possible or actual. In the former case it is a problematical, in the latter an assertorical, practical principle. The categorical imperative, which declares the action to be of itself objectively necessary without making any reference to a purpose, i.e., without having any other end, holds as an apodictical (practical) principle.

We can think of that which is possible through the mere powers of some rational being as a possible purpose of any will. As a consequence, the principles of action, in so far as they are thought of as necessary to attain a possible purpose which can be achieved by them, are in reality infinitely numerous. All sciences have some practical part which consists of problems of some end which is possible for us and of imperatives as to how it can be reached. These can therefore generally be called imperatives of skill. Whether the end is reasonable and good is not in question at all, for the question is only of what must be done in order to attain it. The precepts to be followed by a physician in order to cure his patient and by a poisoner in order to bring about certain death are of equal value in so far as each does that which will perfectly accomplish his purpose. Since in early youth we do not know what ends may occur to us in the course of life, parents seek to let their children learn a great many things and provide for skill in the use of means to all sorts of arbitrary ends among which they cannot determine whether any one of them may later become an actual purpose of their pupil, though it is possible that he may some day have it as his actual purpose. And this anxiety is so great that they commonly neglect to form and correct their judgment on the worth of things which they may make their ends.

There is one end, however, which we may presuppose as actual in all rational beings so far as imperatives apply to them, i.e., so far as they are dependent beings; there is one purpose not only which they *can* have but which we can presuppose that they all *do* have by a necessity of nature. This purpose is happiness. The hypothetical imperative which represents the practical necessity of action as means to the promotion of happiness is an assertorical imperative. We may not expound it as merely necessary to an uncertain and a merely possible purpose, but as necessary to a purpose which we can a priori and with assurance assume for everyone because it belongs to his essence. Skill in the choice of means to one's own highest welfare can be called prudence in the narrowest sense. Thus the imperative which refers to the choice of means to one's own happiness, i.e., the precept of prudence, is still only hypothetical; the action is not absolutely commanded but commanded only as a means to another end.

Finally, there is one imperative which directly commands a certain conduct without making its condition some purpose to be reached by it. This imperative is categorical. It concerns not the material of the action and its intended result but the form and the principle from which it results. What is essentially good in it consists in the intention, the result being what it may. This imperative may be called the imperative of morality.

Volition according to these three principles is plainly distinguished by dissimilarity in the constraint to which they subject the will. In order to clarify this dissimilarity, I believe that they are most suitably named if one says that they are either rules of skill, counsels of prudence, or commands (laws) of morality, respectively. For law alone implies the concept of an unconditional and objective and hence universally valid necessity, and commands are laws which must be obeyed, even against inclination. Counsels do indeed involve necessity, but a necessity that can hold only under a subjectively contingent condition, i.e., whether this or that man counts this or that as part of his happiness; but the categorical imperative, on the other hand, is restricted by no condition. As absolutely, though practically, necessary it can be called a command in the strict sense. We could also call the first imperative technical (belonging to art), the second pragmatic (belonging to welfare), and the third moral (belonging to free conduct as such, i.e., to morals).

The question now arises: how are all these imperatives possible? This question does not require an answer as to how the action which the imperative commands can be performed but merely as to how the constraint of the will, which the imperative expresses in the problem, can be conceived. How an imperative of skill is possible requires no particular discussion. Whoever wills the end, so far as reason has decisive influence on his action, wills also the indispensably necessary means to it that lie in his power. This proposition, in what concerns the will, is analytical; for, in willing an object as my effect, my causality as an acting cause, i.e., the use of the means, is already thought, and the imperative derives the concept of necessary actions to this end from the concept of willing this end. Synthetical propositions undoubtedly are necessary in determining the means to a proposed end, but they do not concern the ground, the act of the will, but only the way to make the object real. Mathematics teaches, by synthetical propositions only, that in order to bisect a line according to an infallible principle I must make two intersecting arcs from each of its extremities; but if I know the proposed result can be obtained only by such an action, then it is an analytical proposition that, if I fully will the effect, I must also will the action necessary to produce it. For it is one and the same thing to conceive of something as an effect which is in a certain way possible through me and to conceive of myself as acting in this way.

If it were only easy to give a definite concept of happiness, the imperatives of prudence would completely correspond to those of skill and would be likewise analytical. For it could be said in this case as well as in the former that whoever wills the end wills also (necessarily according to reason) the only means to it which are in his power. But it is a misfortune that the concept of happiness is so indefinite that, although each person wishes to attain it, he can never definitely and self-consistently state what it is he really wishes and wills. The reason for this is that all elements which belong to the concept of happiness are empirical, i.e., they must be taken from experience, while for the idea of happiness an absolute whole, a maximum, of well-being is needed in my present and in every future condition. Now it is impossible even for a most clear-sighted and most capable but finite being to form here a definite concept of that which he really wills. If he wills riches, how much anxiety, envy, and intrigue might he not thereby draw upon his shoulders! If he wills much knowledge and vision, perhaps it might become only an eye that much sharper to show him as more dreadful the evils which are now hidden from him and which are yet unavoidable, or to burden his desires—which already sufficiently engage him—with even more needs! If he wills a long life, who guarantees that it will not be long misery? If he wills at least health, how often has not the discomfort of the body restrained him from excesses into which perfect health would have led him? In short, he is not capable, on any principle and with complete certainty, of ascertaining what would make him truly happy; omniscience would be needed for this. He cannot, therefore, act according to definite principles so as to be happy, but only according to empirical counsels, e.g., those of diet, economy, courtesy, restraint, etc., which are shown by experience best to promote welfare on the average. Hence the imperatives of prudence cannot, in the strict sense, command, i.e., present actions objectively as practically necessary; thus they are to be taken as counsels (*consilia*) rather than as commands (*praecepta*) of reason, and the task of determining infallibly and universally what action will promote the happiness of a rational being is completely unsolvable. There can be no imperative which would, in the strict sense, command us to do what makes for happiness, because happiness is an ideal not of reason but of imagination, depending only on empirical grounds which one would expect in vain to determine an action through which the totality of consequences—which is in fact infinite—could be achieved. Assuming that the means to happiness could be infallibly stated, this imperative of prudence would be an analytical proposition, for it differs from the imperative of skill only in that its end is given while in the latter case it is merely possible. Since both, however, only command the means to that which one presupposes, the imperative which commands the willing of the means to him who wills the end is in both cases analytical. There is, consequently, no difficulty in seeing the possibility of such an imperative.

To see how the imperative of morality is possible is, then, without doubt the only question needing an answer. It is not hypothetical, and thus the objectively conceived necessity cannot be supported by any presupposition, as was the case with the hypothetical imperatives. But it must not be overlooked that it cannot be shown by any example (i.e., it cannot be empirically shown) whether or not there is such an imperative; it is rather to be suspected that all imperatives which appear to be categorical may yet be hypothetical, but in a hidden way. For instance, when it is said, "Thou shalt not make a false promise," we assume that the necessity of this avoidance is not a mere counsel for the sake of escaping some other evil, so that it would read, "Thou shalt not make a false promise so that, if it comes to light, thou ruinest thy credit"; we assume rather that an action of this kind must be regarded as of itself bad and that the imperative of the prohibition is categorical. But we cannot show with certainty by any example that the will is here determined by the law alone without any other incentives, even though this appears to be the case. For it is always possible that secret fear of disgrace, and perhaps also obscure apprehension of other dangers, may have had an influence on the will. Who can prove by experience the non-existence of a cause when experience shows us only that we do not perceive the cause? But in such a case the so-called moral imperative, which as such appears to be categorical and unconditional, would be actually only a pragmatic precept which makes us attentive to our own advantage and teaches us to consider it.

Thus we shall have to investigate purely a priori the possibility of a categorical imperative, for we do not have the advantage that experience would give us the reality of this imperative, so that the [demonstration of its] possibility would be necessary only for its explanation and not for its establishment. In the meantime, this much may at least be seen: the categorical imperative alone can be taken as a practical *law*, while all the others may be called principles of the will but not laws. This is because what is necessary merely for the attainment of an arbitrary purpose can be regarded as itself contingent, and we get rid of the precept once we give up the purpose, whereas the unconditional command leaves the will no freedom to choose the opposite. Thus it alone implies the necessity which we require of a law.

Secondly, in the case of the categorical imperative or law of morality, the cause of difficulty in discerning its possibility is very weighty. This imperative is an a priori synthetical practical proposition, and, since to discern the possibility of propositions of this sort is so difficult in theoretical knowledge, it may well be gathered that it will be no less difficult in the practical.

In attacking this problem, we will first inquire whether the mere concept of a categorical imperative does not also furnish the formula containing the proposition which alone can be a categorical imperative. For even when we know the formula of the imperative, to learn how such an absolute law is possible will require difficult and special labors . . .

If I think of a hypothetical imperative as such, I do not know what it will contain until the condition is stated [under which it is an imperative]. But if I think of a categorical imperative, I know immediately what it contains. For since the imperative contains besides the law only the necessity that the maxim should accord with this law, while the law contains no condition to which it is restricted, there is nothing remaining in it except the universality of law as such to which the maxim of the action should conform; and in effect this conformity alone is represented as necessary by the imperative.

There is, therefore, only one categorical imperative. It is: Act only according to that maxim by which you can at the same time will that it should become a universal law.

Now if all imperatives of duty can be derived from this one imperative as a principle, we can at least show what we understand by the concept of duty and what it means, even though it remain undecided whether that which is called duty is an empty concept or not.

The universality of law according to which effects are produced constitutes what is properly called nature in the most general sense (as to form), i.e., the existence of things so far as it is determined by universal laws. [By analogy], then, the universal imperative of duty can be expressed as follows: Act as though the maxim of your action were by your will to become a universal law of nature.

We shall now enumerate some duties, adopting the usual division of them into duties to ourselves and to others and into perfect and imperfect duties.

1. A man who is reduced to despair by a series of evils feels a weariness with life but is still in possession of his reason sufficiently to ask whether it would not be contrary to his duty to himself to take his own life. Now he asks whether the maxim of his action could become a universal law of nature. His maxim, however, is: For love of myself, I make it my principle to shorten my life when by a longer duration it threatens more evil than satisfaction. But it is questionable whether this principle of self-love could become a universal law of nature. One immediately sees a contradiction in a system of nature whose law would be to destroy life by the feeling whose special office is to impel the improvement of life. In this case it would not exist as nature; hence that maxim cannot obtain as a law of nature, and thus it wholly contradicts the supreme principle of all duty.

2. Another man finds himself forced by need to borrow money. He well knows that he will not be able to repay it, but he also sees that nothing will be loaned him if he does not firmly promise to repay it at a certain time. He desires to make such a promise, but he has enough conscience to ask himself whether it is not improper and opposed to duty to relieve his distress in such a way. Now, assuming he does decide to do so, the maxim of his action would be as follows: When I believe myself to be in need of money, I will borrow money and promise to repay it, although I know I shall never do so. Now this principle of self-love or of his own benefit may very well be compatible with his whole future welfare, but the question is whether it is right. He changes the pretension of self-love into a universal law and then

puts the question: How would it be if my maxim became a universal law? He immediately sees that it could never hold as a universal law of nature and be consistent with itself; rather it must necessarily contradict itself. For the universality of a law which says that anyone who believes himself to be in need could promise what he pleased with the intention of not fulfilling it would make the promise itself and the end to be accomplished by it impossible; no one would believe what was promised to him but would only laugh at any such assertion as vain pretense.

3. A third finds in himself a talent which could, by means of some cultivation, make him in many respects a useful man. But he finds himself in comfortable circumstances and prefers indulgence in pleasure to troubling himself with broadening and improving his fortunate natural gifts. Now, however, let him ask whether his maxim of neglecting his gifts, besides agreeing with his propensity to idle amusement, agrees also with what is called duty. He sees that a system of nature could indeed exist in accordance with such a law, even though man (like the inhabitants of the South Sea Islands) should let his talents rust and resolve to devote his life merely to idleness, indulgence, and propagation—in a word, to pleasure. But he cannot possibly will that this should become a universal law of nature or that it should be implanted in us by a natural instinct. For, as a rational being, he necessarily wills that all his faculties should be developed, inasmuch as they are given to him for all sorts of possible purposes.

4. A fourth man, for whom things are going well, sees that others (whom he could help) have to struggle with great hardships, and he asks, "What concern of mine is it? Let each one be as happy as heaven wills, or as he can make himself; I will not take anything from him or even envy him; but to his welfare or to his assistance in time of need I have no desire to contribute." If such a way of thinking were a universal law of nature, certainly the human race could exist, and without doubt even better than in a state where everyone talks of sympathy and good will, or even exerts himself occasionally to practice them while, on the other hand, he cheats when he can and betrays or otherwise violates the rights of man. Now although it is possible that a universal law of nature according to that maxim could exist, it is nevertheless impossible to will that such a principle should hold everywhere as a law of nature. For a will which resolved this would conflict with itself, since instances can often arise in which he would need the love and sympathy of others, and in which he would have robbed himself, by such a law of nature springing from his own will, of all hope of the aid he desires.

The foregoing are a few of the many actual duties, or at least of duties we hold to be actual, whose derivation from the one stated principle is clear. We must be able to will that a maxim of our action become a universal law; this is the canon of the moral estimation of our action generally. Some actions are of such a nature that their maxim cannot even be *thought* as a universal law of nature without contradiction, far from it being possible that one could will that it should be such. In others this internal impossibility is not found, though it is still impossible to *will* that their maxim should be raised to the universality of a law of nature, because such a will would contradict itself. We easily see that that the former maxim conflicts with the stricter or narrower (imprescriptible) duty, the latter with broader (meritorious) duty. Thus all duties, so far as the kind of obligation (not the object of their action) is concerned, have been completely exhibited by these examples in their dependence on the one principle.

When we observe ourselves in any transgression of a duty, we find that we do not actually will that our maxim should become a universal law. That is impossible for us; rather, the contrary of this maxim should remain as a law generally, and we only take the liberty of making an exception to it for ourselves or for the sake of our inclination, and for this one occasion. Consequently, if we weighed everything from one and the same standpoint, namely, reason, we would come upon a contradiction in our own will, viz., that a certain principle is objectively necessary as a universal law and yet subjectively does not hold universally but rather admits exceptions. However, since we regard our action at one time from the point of view of a will wholly conformable to reason and then from that of a will affected by inclinations, there is actually no contradiction, but rather an opposition of inclination to the precept of reason (*antagonismus*). In this the universality of the principle (*universalitas*) is changed into mere generality (*generalitas*), whereby the practical principle of reason meets the maxim halfway. Although this cannot be justified in our own impartial judgment, it does show that we actually acknowledge the validity of the categorical imperative and allow ourselves (with all respect to it) only a few exceptions which seem to us to be unimportant and forced upon us.

We have thus at least established that if duty is a concept which is to have significance and actual legislation for our actions, it can be expressed only in categorical imperatives and not at all in hypothetical ones. For every application of it we have also clearly exhibited the content of the categorical imperative which must contain the principle of all duty (if there is such). This is itself very much. But we are not yet advanced far enough to prove a priori that that kind of imperative really exists, that there is a practical law which of itself commands absolutely and without any incentives, and that obedience to this law is duty.

With a view to attaining this, it is extremely important to remember that we must not let ourselves think that the reality of this principle can be derived from the particular constitution of human nature. For duty is practical unconditional necessity of action; it must, therefore, hold for all rational beings (to which alone an imperative can apply), and only for that reason can it be a law for all human wills. Whatever is derived from the particular natural situation of man as such, or from certain feelings and propensities, or even from a particular tendency of the human reason which might not hold necessarily for the will of every rational being (if such a tendency is possible), can give a maxim valid for us but not a law; that is, it can give a subjective principle by which we might act only if we have the propensity and inclination, but not an objective principle by which we would be directed to act even if all our propensity, inclination, and natural tendency were opposed to it. This is so far the case that the sublimity and intrinsic worth of the command is the better shown in a duty the fewer subjective causes there are for it and the more there are against it; the latter do not weaken the constraint of the law or diminish its validity.

Here we see philosophy brought to what is, in fact, a precarious position, which should be made fast even though it is supported by nothing in either heaven or earth. Here philosophy must show its purity as the absolute sustainer of its laws, and not as the herald of those which an implanted sense or who knows what tutelary nature whispers to it. Those may be better than no laws at all, but they can never afford fundamental principles, which reason alone dictates. These fundamental principles must originate entirely a priori and thereby obtain their commanding authority; they can expect nothing from the inclination of men but everything from the supremacy of the law and due respect for it. Otherwise they condemn man to self-contempt and inner abhorrence.

Thus everything empirical is not only wholly unworthy to be an ingredient in the principle of morality but is even highly prejudicial to the purity of moral practices themselves. For, in morals, the proper and inestimable worth of an absolutely good will consists precisely in the freedom of the principle of action from all influences from contingent grounds which only experience can furnish. We cannot too much or too often warn against the lax or even base manner of thought which seeks principles among empirical motives and laws, for human reason in its weariness is glad to rest on this pillow. In a dream of sweet illusions (in which it embraces not Juno but a cloud), it substitutes for morality a bastard patched up from limbs of very different parentage, which looks like anything one wishes to see in it, but not like virtue to anyone who has ever beheld her in her true form.

The question then is: Is it a necessary law for all rational beings that they should always judge their actions by such maxims as they themselves could will to serve as universal laws? If it is such a law, it must be connected (wholly a priori) with the concept of the will of a rational being as such. But in order to discover this connection we must, however reluctantly, take a step into metaphysics, although into a region of it different from speculative philosophy, i.e., into metaphysics of morals. In a practical philosophy it is not a question of assuming grounds for what happens but of assuming laws of what ought to happen even though it may never happen—that is to say, objective, practical laws. Hence in practical philosophy we need not inquire into the reasons why something pleases or displeases, how the pleasure of mere feeling differs from taste, and whether this is distinct from a general satisfaction of reason. Nor need we ask on what the feeling of pleasure or displeasure rests, how desires and inclinations arise, and how, finally, maxims arise from desires and inclination under the co-operation of reason. For all these matters belong to an empirical psychology, which would be the second part of physics if we consider it as philosophy of nature so far as it rests on empirical laws. But here it is a question of objectively practical laws and thus of the relation of a will to itself so far as it determines itself only by reason; for everything which has a relation to the empirical automatically falls away, because if reason of itself alone determines conduct it must necessarily do so a priori. The possibility of reason thus determining conduct must now be investigated.

The will is thought of as a faculty of determining itself to action in accordance with the conception of certain laws. Such a faculty can be found only in rational beings. That which serves the will as the objective ground of its self-determination is an end, and, if it is given by reason alone, it must hold alike for all rational beings. On the other hand, that which contains the ground of the possibility of the action, whose result is an end, is called the means. The subjective ground of desire is the incentive, while the objective ground of volition is the motive. Thus arises the distinction between subjective ends, which rest on incentives, and objective ends, which depend on motives valid for every rational being. Practical principles are formal when they disregard all subjective ends; they are material when they have subjective ends, and thus certain incentives, as their basis. The ends which a rational being arbitrarily proposes to himself as consequences of his action are material ends and are without exception only relative, for only their relation to a particularly constituted faculty of desire in the subject gives them their worth. And this worth cannot, therefore, afford any universal principles for all rational beings or valid and necessary principles for every volition. That is, they cannot give rise to any practical laws. All these relative ends, therefore, are grounds for hypothetical imperatives only.

But suppose that there were something the existence of which in itself had absolute worth, something which, as an end in itself, could be a ground of definite laws. In it and only in it could lie the ground of a possible categorical imperative, i.e., of a practical law.

Now, I say, man and, in general, every rational being exists as an end in himself and not merely as a means to be arbitrarily used by this or that will. In all his actions, whether they are directed to himself or to other rational beings, he must always be regarded at the same time as an end. All objects of inclinations have only a conditional worth, for if the inclinations and the needs founded on them did not exist, their object would be without worth. The inclinations themselves as the sources of needs, however, are so lacking in absolute worth that the universal wish of every rational being must be indeed to free himself completely from them. Therefore, the worth of any objects to be obtained by our actions is at all times conditional. Beings whose existence does not depend on our will but on nature, if they are not rational beings, have only a relative worth as means and are therefore called "things"; on the other hand, rational beings are designated "persons" because their nature indicates that they are ends in themselves, i.e., things which may not be used merely as means. Such a being is thus an object of respect and, so far, restricts all [arbitrary] choice. Such beings are not merely subjective ends whose existence as a result of our action has a worth for us, but are objective ends, i.e., beings whose existence in itself is an end. Such an end is one for which no other end can be substituted, to which these beings should serve merely as means. For, without them, nothing of absolute worth could be found, and if all worth is conditional and thus contingent, no supreme practical principle for reason could be found anywhere.

Thus if there is to be a supreme practical principle and a categorical imperative for the human will, it must be one that forms an objective principle of the will from the conception of that which is necessarily an end for everyone because it is an end in itself. Hence this objective principle can serve as a universal practical law. The ground of this principle is: rational nature exists as an end in itself. Man necessarily thinks of his own existence in this way; thus far it is a subjective principle of human actions. Also every other rational being thinks of his existence by means of the same rational ground which holds also for myself; thus it is at the same time an objective principle from which, as a supreme practical ground, it must be possible to derive all laws of the will. The practical imperative, therefore, is the following: Act so that you treat humanity, whether in your own person or in that of another, always as an end and never as a means only. Let us now see whether this can be achieved.

To return to our previous examples:

First, according to the concept of necessary duty to one's self, he who contemplates suicide will ask himself whether his action can be consistent with the idea of humanity as an end in itself. If, in order to escape from burdensome circumstances, he destroys himself, he uses a person merely as a means to maintain a tolerable condition up to the end of life. Man, however, is not a thing, and thus not something to be used merely as a means; he must always be regarded in all his actions as an end in himself. Therefore, I cannot dispose of man in my own person so as to mutilate, corrupt, or kill him. (It belongs to ethics proper to define more accurately this basic principle so as to avoid all misunderstanding, e.g., as to the amputation of limbs in order to preserve myself, or to exposing my life to danger in order to save it; I must, therefore, omit them here.)

Second, as concerns necessary or obligatory duties to others, he who intends a deceitful promise to others sees immediately that he intends to use another man merely as a means, without the latter containing the end in himself at the same time. For he whom I want to use for my own purposes by means of such a promise cannot possibly assent to my mode of acting against him and cannot contain the end of this action in himself. This conflict against the principle of other men is even clearer if we cite examples of attacks on their freedom and property. For then it is clear that he who transgresses the rights of men intends to make use of the persons of others merely as a means, without considering that, as rational beings, they must always be esteemed at the same time as ends, i.e., only as beings who must be able to contain in themselves the end of the very same action.

Third, with regard to contingent (meritorious) duty to one's self, it is not sufficient that the action not conflict with humanity in our person as an end in itself; it must also harmonize with it. Now in humanity there are capacities for greater perfection which belong to the end of nature with respect to humanity in our own person; to neglect these might perhaps be consistent with the preservation of humanity as an end in itself but not with the furtherance of that end.

Fourth, with regard to meritorious duty to others, the natural end which all men have is their own happiness. Humanity might indeed exist if no one contributed to the happiness of others, provided he did not intentionally detract from it; but this harmony with humanity as an end in itself is only negative rather than positive if everyone does not also endeavor, so far as he can, to further the ends of others. For the ends of any person, who is an end in himself, must as far as possible also be my end, if that conception of an end in itself is to have its full effect on me.

This principle of humanity and of every rational creature as an end in itself is the supreme limiting condition on freedom of the actions of each man. It is not borrowed from experience, first, because of its universality, since it applies to all rational beings generally and experience does not suffice to determine anything about them; and, secondly, because in experience humanity is not thought of (subjectively) as the end of men, i.e., as an object which we of ourselves really make our end. Rather it is thought of as the objective end which should constitute the supreme limiting condition of all subjective ends, whatever they may be. Thus this principle must arise from pure reason. Objectively the ground of all practical legislation lies (according to the first principle) in the rule and in the form of universality, which makes it capable of being a law (at most a natural law); subjectively, it lies in the end. But the subject of all ends is every rational being as an end in itself (by the second principle); from this there follows the third practical principle of the will as the supreme condition of its harmony with universal practical reason, viz., the idea of the will of every rational being as making universal law.

By this principle all maxims are rejected which are not consistent with the universal lawgiving of will. The will is thus not only subject to the law but subject in such a way that it must be regarded also as self-legislative and only for this reason as being subject to the law (of which it can regard itself as the author).

In the foregoing mode of conception, in which imperatives are conceived universally either as conformity to law by actions—a conformity which is similar to a natural order—or as the prerogative of rational beings as such, the imperatives exclude from their legislative authority all admixture of any interest as an incentive. They do so because they were conceived as categorical. They were only assumed to be categorical, however, because we had to make such an assumption if we wished to explain the concept of duty. But that there were practical propositions which commanded categorically could not here be proved independently, just as little as it can be proved anywhere in this section. One thing, however, might have been done: to indicate in the imperative itself, by some determination which it contained, that in volition from duty the renunciation of all interest is the specific mark of the categorical imperative, distinguishing it from the hypothetical. And this is now being done in the third formulation of the principle, i.e., in the idea of the will of every rational being as a will giving universal law. A will which stands under laws can be bound to this law by an interest. But if we think of a will giving universal laws, we find that a supreme legislating will cannot possibly depend on any interest, for such a dependent will would itself need still another law which would restrict the interest of its self-love to the condition that [the maxims of this will] should be valid as universal law.

Thus the principle of every human will as a will giving universal laws in all its maxims is very well adapted to being a categorical imperative, provided it is otherwise correct. Because of the idea of universal lawgiving, it is based on no interest, and, thus of all possible imperatives, it alone can be unconditional. Or, better, converting the proposition: if there is a categorical imperative (a law for the will of every rational being), it can only command that everything be done from the maxim of its will as one which could have as its object only itself considered as giving universal laws. For only in this case are the practical principle and the imperative which the will obeys unconditional, because the will can have no interest as its foundation.

.   .   .

. . . All maxims have:

1. A form, which consists in universality; and in this respect the formula of the moral imperative requires that the maxims be chosen as though they should hold as universal laws of nature.

2. A material, i.e., an end; in this respect the formula says that the rational being, as by its nature an end and thus as an end in itself, must serve in every maxim as the condition restricting all merely relative and arbitrary ends.

3. A complete determination of all maxims by the formula that all maxims which stem from autonomous legislation ought to harmonize with a possible realm of ends as with a realm of nature.

There is a progression here like that through the categories of the unity of the form of the will (its universality), the plurality of material (the objects, i.e., the ends), and the all-comprehensiveness or totality of the system of ends. But it is better in moral evaluation to follow the rigorous method and to make the universal formula of the categorical imperative the basis: Act according to the maxim which can at the same time make itself a universal law. But if one wishes to gain a hearing for the moral law, it is very useful to bring one and the same action under the three stated principles and thus, so far as possible, to bring it nearer to intuition.

We can now end where we started, with the concept of an unconditionally good will. That will is absolutely good which cannot be bad, and thus it is a will whose maxim, when made a universal law, can never conflict with itself. Thus this principle is also its supreme law: Always act according to that maxim whose universality as a law you can at the same time will. This is the only condition under which a will can never come into conflict with itself, and such an imperative is categorical. Because the validity of the will, as a universal law for possible actions, has an analogy with the universal connection of the existence of things under universal laws, which is the formal element of nature in general, the categorical imperative can also be expressed as follows: Act according to maxims which can at the same time have themselves as universal laws of nature as their object. Such, then, is the formula of an absolutely good will.

·   ·   ·

6

WHAT UTILITARIANISM IS

John Stuart Mill

A passing remark is all that needs be given to the ignorant blunder of supposing that those who stand up for utility as the test of right and wrong use the term in that restricted and merely colloquial sense in which utility is opposed to pleasure. An apology is due to the philosophical opponents of utilitarianism, for even the momentary appearance of confounding them with anyone capable of so absurd a misconception; which is the more extraordinary, inasmuch as the contrary accusation, of referring everything to pleasure, and that, too, in its grossest form, is another of the common charges against utilitarianism: and, as has been pointedly remarked by an able writer, the same sort of persons, and often the very same persons, denounce the theory "as impracticably dry when the word 'utility' precedes the word 'pleasure,' and as too practicably voluptuous when the word 'pleasure' precedes the word 'utility'." Those who know anything about the matter are aware that every writer, from Epicurus to Bentham, who maintained the theory of utility, meant by it, not something to be contradistinguished from pleasure, but pleasure itself, together with exemption from pain; and instead of opposing the useful to the agreeable or the ornamental, have always declared that the useful means these, among other things. Yet the common herd, including the herd of writers, not only in newspapers and periodicals, but in books of weight and pretension, are perpetually falling into this shallow mistake. Having caught up the word "utilitarian," while knowing nothing whatever about it but its sound, they habitually express by it the rejection or the neglect of pleasure in some of its forms: of beauty, of ornament, or of amusement. Nor is the term thus ignorantly misapplied solely in disparagement, but occasionally in compliment, as though it implied superiority to frivolity and the mere pleasures of the moment. And this perverted use is the only one in which the word is popularly known, and the one from which the new generation are acquiring their sole notion of its meaning. Those who introduced the word, but who had for many years discontinued it as a distinctive appellation, may well feel themselves

From John Stuart Mill, *Utilitarianism*, 15th ed. (London: Longmans, Green, 1907), Chap. II, pp. 8–38.

called upon to resume it if by doing so they can hope to contribute anything towards rescuing it from this utter degradation.

The creed which accepts as the foundation of morals "utility" or the "greatest happiness principle" holds that actions are right in proportion as they tend to promote happiness, wrong as they tend to produce the reverse of happiness. By happiness is intended pleasure, and the absence of pain; by unhappiness, pain, and the privation of pleasure. To give a clear view of the moral standard set up by the theory, much more requires to be said; in particular what things it includes in the ideas of pain and pleasure; and to what extent this is left an open question. But these supplementary explanations do not affect the theory of life on which this theory of morality is grounded—namely, that pleasure and freedom from pain are the only things desirable as ends; and that all desirable things (which are as numerous in the utilitarian as in any other scheme) are desirable either for the pleasure inherent in themselves, or as means to the promotion of pleasure and the prevention of pain.

Now such a theory of life excites in many minds, and among them in some of the most estimable in feeling and purpose, inveterate dislike. To suppose that life has (as they express it) no higher end than pleasure—no better and nobler object of desire and pursuit—they designate as utterly mean and groveling; as a doctrine worthy only of swine, to whom the followers of Epicurus were, at a very early period, contemptuously likened; and modern holders of the doctrine are occasionally made the subject of equally polite comparisons by its German, French, and English assailants.

When thus attacked, the Epicureans have always answered that it is not they, but their accusers, who represent human nature in a degrading light, since the accusation supposes human beings to be capable of no pleasures except those of which swine are capable. If this supposition were true, the charge could not be gainsaid, but would then be no longer an imputation; for if the sources of pleasure were precisely the same to human beings and to swine, the rule of life which is good enough for the one would be good enough for the other. The comparison of the Epicurean life to that of beasts is felt as degrading precisely because a beast's pleasures do not satisfy a human being's conceptions of happiness. Human beings have faculties more elevated than the animal appetites and, when once made conscious of them, do not regard anything as happiness which does not include their gratification. I do not, indeed, consider the Epicureans to have been by any means faultless in drawing out their scheme of consequences from the utilitarian principle. To do this in any sufficient manner, many Stoic, as well as Christian, elements require to be included. But there is no known Epicurean theory of life which does not assign to the pleasures of the intellect, of the feelings and imagination, and of the moral sentiments, a much higher value of pleasures than to those of mere sensation. It must be admitted, however, that utilitarian writers in general have placed the superiority of mental over bodily pleasures chiefly in the greater permanency, safety, uncostliness, etc., of the former—that is, in their circumstantial advantages rather than in their intrinsic nature. And on all these points utilitarians have fully proved their case; but they might have taken the other and, as it may be called, higher ground with entire consistency. It is quite compatible with the principle of utility to recognize the fact that some kinds of pleasure are more desirable and more valuable than others. It would be absurd that, while, in estimating all other things, quality is considered as well as quantity, the estimation of pleasures should be supposed to depend on quantity alone.

If I am asked what I mean by difference of quality in pleasures, or what makes one pleasure more valuable than another, merely as a pleasure, except its being greater in amount, there is but one possible answer. Of two pleasures, if there be one to which all or almost all who have experience of both give a decided preference, irrespective of a feeling of moral obligation to prefer it, that is the more desirable pleasure. If one of the two is, by those who are competently acquainted with both, placed so far above the other that they prefer it, even though knowing it to be attended with a greater amount of discontent, and would not resign it for any quantity of the other pleasure which their nature is capable of, we are justified in ascribing to the preferred enjoyment a superiority in quality so far outweighing quantity as to render it, in comparison, of small account.

Now it is an unquestionable fact that those who are equally acquainted with and equally capable of appreciating and enjoying both, do give a most marked preference to the manner of existence which employs their higher faculties. Few human creatures would consent to be changed into any of the lower animals for a promise of the fullest allowance of a beast's pleasures; no intelligent human being would consent to be a fool, no instructed person would be an ignoramus, no person of feeling and conscience would be selfish and base, even though they should be persuaded that the fool, the dunce, or the rascal is better satisfied with his lot than they are with theirs. They would not resign what they possess more than he for the most complete satisfaction of all the desires which they have in common with him. If they ever fancy they would, it is only in cases of unhappiness so extreme that to escape from it they would exchange their lot for almost any other, however undesirable in their own eyes. A being of higher faculties requires more to make him happy, is capable probably of more acute suffering, and certainly accessible to it at more points, than one of an inferior type; but in spite of these liabilities, he can never really wish to sink into what he feels to be a lower grade of existence. We may give what explanation we please of this unwillingness; we may attribute it to pride, a name which is given indiscriminately to some of the most and to some of the least estimable feelings of which mankind are capable: we may refer it to the love of liberty and personal independence, an appeal to which was with the Stoics one of the most effective means for the inculcation of it; to the love of power or to the love of excitement, both of which do really enter into and contribute to it; but its most appropriate appellation is a sense of dignity, which all human beings possess in one form or other, and in some, though by no means in exact, proportion to their higher faculties, and which is so essential a part of the happiness of those in whom it is strong that nothing which conflicts with it could be otherwise than momentarily an object of desire to them. Whoever supposes that this preference takes place at a sacrifice of happiness —that the superior being, in anything like equal circumstances, is not happier than the inferior—confounds the two very different ideas of happiness and content. It is indisputable that the being whose capacities of enjoyment are low has the greatest chance of having them fully satisfied; and a highly endowed being will always feel that any happiness which he can look for, as the world is constituted, is imperfect. But he can learn to bear its imperfections, if they are at all bearable; and they will not make him envy the being who is indeed unconscious of the imperfections, but only because he feels not at all the good which those imperfections qualify. It is better to be a human being dissatisfied than a pig satisfied; better to be Socrates dissatisfied than a fool satisfied. And if the fool, or the pig, are of a different opinion, it is because they only know their own side of the question. The other party to the comparison knows both sides.

It may be objected that many who are capable of the higher pleasures occasionally, under the influence of temptation, postpone them to the lower. But this is quite compatible with a full appreciation of the intrinsic superiority of the higher. Men often, from infirmity of character, make their election for the nearer good, though they know it to be the less valuable; and this no less when the choice is between two bodily pleasures than when it is between bodily and mental. They pursue sensual indulgences to the injury of health, though perfectly aware that health is the greater good. It may be further objected that many who begin with youthful enthusiasm for everything noble, as they advance in years, sink into indolence and selfishness. But I do not believe that those who undergo this very common change voluntarily choose the lower description of pleasures in preference to the higher. I believe that, before they devote themselves exclusively to the one, they have already become incapable of the other. Capacity for the nobler feelings is in most natures a very tender plant, easily killed, not only by hostile influences, but by mere want of sustenance; and in the majority of young persons it speedily dies away if the occupations to which their position in life has devoted them, and the society into which it has thrown them, are not favorable to keeping that higher capacity in exercise. Men lose their high aspirations as they lose their intellectual tastes, because they have not time or opportunity for indulging them; and they addict themselves to inferior pleasures, not because they deliberately prefer them, but because they are either the only ones to which they have access, or the only ones which they are any longer capable of enjoying. It may be questioned whether any one who has remained equally susceptible to both classes of pleasures, ever knowingly and calmly preferred the lower, though many, in all ages, have broken down in an ineffectual attempt to combine both.

From this verdict of the only competent judges, I apprehend there can be no appeal. On a question which is the best worth having of two pleasures, or which of two modes of existence is the most grateful to the feelings, apart from its moral attributes and from its consequences, the judgment of those who are qualified by knowledge of both, or, if they differ, that of the majority of them, must be admitted as final. And there needs be the less hesitation to accept this judgment respecting the quality of pleasures, since there is no other tribunal to be referred to even on the question of quantity. What means are there of determining which is the acutest of two pains, or the intensest of two pleasurable sensations, except the general suffrage of those who are familiar with both? Neither pains nor pleasures are homogeneous, and pain is always heterogeneous with pleasure. What is there to decide whether a particular pleasure is worth purchasing at the cost of a particular pain, except the feelings and judgment of the experienced? When, therefore, those feelings and judgment declare the pleasures derived from the higher faculties to be preferable *in kind*, apart from the question of intensity, to those of which the animal nature, disjoined from the higher faculties, is susceptible, they are entitled on this subject to the same regard.

I have dwelt on this point, as being a necessary part of a perfectly just conception of utility or happiness considered as the directive rule of human conduct. But it is by no means an indispensable condition to the acceptance of the utilitarian standard; for that standard is not the agent's own greatest happiness, but the greatest amount of happiness altogether; and if it may possibly be doubted whether a noble character is always the happier for its nobleness, there can be no doubt that it makes other people happier, and that the world in general is immensely a gainer by it. Utilitarianism, therefore, could only attain its end by the general cultivation of nobleness of character, even if each individual were only benefited by the nobleness of others, and his own, so far as happiness is concerned, were a sheer deduction from the benefit. But the bare enunciation of such an absurdity as this last renders refutation superfluous.

According to the greatest happiness principle, as above explained, the ultimate end, with reference to and for the sake of which all other things are desirable—whether we are considering our own good or that of other people—is an existence exempt as far as possible from pain, and as rich as possible in enjoyments, both in point of quantity and quality; the test of quality and the rule for measuring it against quantity being the preference felt by those who, in their opportunities of experience, to which must be added their habits of self-consciousness and self-observation, are best furnished with the means of comparison. This, being, according to the utilitarian opinion, the end of human action, is necessarily also the standard of morality, which may accordingly be defined "the rules and precepts for human conduct," by the observance of which an existence such as has been described might be, to the greatest extent possible, secured to all mankind; and not to them only, but, so far as the nature of things admits, to the whole sentient creation.

Against this doctrine, however, arises another class of objectors who say that happiness, in any form, cannot be the rational purpose of human life and action; because, in the first place, it is unattainable; and they contemptuously ask, What right hast thou to be happy?—a question which Mr. Carlyle clenches by the addition, What right, a short time ago, hadst thou even *to be?* Next they say that men can do *without* happiness; that all noble human beings have felt this, and could not have become noble but by learning the lesson of *Entsagen*, or renunciation; which lesson, thoroughly learnt and submitted to, they affirm to be the beginning and necessary condition of all virtue.

The first of these objections would go to the root of the matter were it well founded; for if no happiness is to be had at all by human beings, the attainment of it cannot be the end of morality or of any rational conduct. Though, even in that case, something might still be said for the utilitarian theory, since utility includes not solely the pursuit of happiness, but the prevention or mitigation of unhappiness; and if the former aim be chimerical, there will be all the greater scope and more imperative need for the latter, so long at least as mankind think fit to live, and do not take refuge in the simultaneous act of suicide recommended under certain conditions by

Novalis. When, however, it is thus positively asserted to be impossible that human life should be happy, the assertion, if not something like a verbal quibble, is at least an exaggeration. If by happiness be meant a continuity of highly pleasurable excitement, it is evident enough that this is impossible. A state of exalted pleasure lasts only moments or in some cases, and with some intermissions, hours or days, and is the occasional brilliant flash of enjoyment, not its permanent and steady flame. Of this the philosophers who have taught that happiness is the end of life were as fully aware as those who taunt them. The happiness which they meant was not a life of rapture; but moments of such, in an existence made up of few and transitory pains, many and various pleasures, with a decided predominance of the active over the passive, and having as the foundation of the whole not to expect more from life than it is capable of bestowing. A life thus composed, to those who have been fortunate enough to obtain it, has always appeared worthy of the name of happiness. And such an existence is even now the lot of many, during some considerable portion of their lives. The present wretched education and wretched social arrangements are the only real hindrance to its being attainable by almost all.

The objectors perhaps may doubt whether human beings, if taught to consider happiness as the end of life, would be satisfied with such a moderate share of it. But great numbers of mankind have been satisfied with much less. The main constituents of a satisfied life appear to be two, either of which by itself is often found sufficient for the purpose: tranquility and excitement. With much tranquility, many find that they can be content with very little pleasure; with much excitement, many can reconcile themselves to a considerable quantity of pain. There is assuredly no inherent impossibility of enabling even the mass of mankind to unite both, since the two are so far from being incompatible that they are in natural alliance, the prolongation of either being a preparation for, and exciting a wish for, the other. It is only those in whom indolence amounts to a vice that do not desire excitement after an interval of repose; it is only those in whom the need of excitement is a disease that feel the tranquility which follows excitement dull and insipid, instead of pleasurable in direct proportion to the excitement which preceded it. When people who are tolerably fortunate in their outward lot do not find in life sufficient enjoyment to make it valuable to them, the cause generally is caring for nobody but themselves. To those who have neither public nor private affections, the excitements of life are much curtailed, and in any case dwindle in value as the time approaches when all selfish interests must be terminated by death; while those who leave after them objects of personal affection, and especially those who have also cultivated a fellow-feeling with the collective interests of mankind, retain as lively an interest in life on the eve of death as in the vigor of youth and health. Next to selfishness, the principal cause which makes life unsatisfactory is want of mental cultivation. A cultivated mind—I do not mean that of a philosopher, but any mind to which the fountains of knowledge have been opened, and which has been taught, in any tolerable degree, to exercise its faculties—finds sources of inexhaustible interest in all that surrounds it: in the objects of nature, the achievements of art, the imaginations of poetry, the incidents of history, the ways of mankind, past and present, and their prospects in the future. It is possible, indeed, to become indifferent to all this, and that too without having exhausted a thousandth part of it, but only when one has had from the beginning no moral or human interest in these things, and has sought in them only the gratification of curiosity.

Now there is absolutely no reason in the nature of things why an amount of mental culture sufficient to give an intelligent interest in these objects of contemplation should not be the inheritance of every one born in a civilized country. As little is there an inherent necessity that any human being should be a selfish egotist, devoid of every feeling or care but those which center in his own miserable individuality. Something far superior to this is sufficiently common even now, to give ample earnest of what the human species may be made. Genuine private affections and a sincere interest in the public good are possible, though in unequal degrees, to every rightly brought up human being. In a world in which there is so much to interest, so much to enjoy, and so much also to correct and improve, every one who has this moderate amount of moral and intellectual requisites is capable of an existence which may be called enviable: and unless such a person, through bad laws or subjection to the will of others, is denied the liberty to use the sources of happiness within his reach, he will not fail to find this enviable existence, if he escape the positive evils of life, the great sources of physical and mental suffering—such as indigence, disease, and the unkindness, worthlessness, or premature loss of objects of affection. The main stress of the problem lies, therefore, in the contest with these calamities from which it is a rare good fortune entirely to escape; which, as things now are, cannot be obviated, and often cannot be in any material degree mitigated. Yet no one whose opinion deserves a moment's consideration can doubt that most of the great positive evils of the world are in themselves removable, and will, if human affairs continue to improve, be in the end reduced within narrow limits. Poverty, in any sense implying suffering, may be completely extinguished by the wisdom of society combined with the good sense and providence of individuals. Even that most intractable of enemies, disease, may be indefinitely reduced in dimensions by good physical and moral education and proper control of noxious influences, while the progress of science holds out a promise for the future of still more direct conquests over this detestable foe. And every advance in that direction relieves us from some, not only of the chances which cut short our own lives, but, what concerns us still more, which deprive us of those in whom our happiness is wrapt up. As for vicissitudes of fortune and other disappointments connected with worldly circumstances, these are principally the effect either of gross imprudence, of ill-regulated desires, or of bad or imperfect social institutions. All the grand sources, in short, of human suffering are in a great degree, many of them almost entirely, conquerable by human care and effort; and though their removal is grievously slow—though a long succession of generations will perish in the breach before the conquest is completed, and this world becomes all that, if will and knowledge were not wanting, it might easily be made—yet every mind sufficiently intelligent and generous to bear a part, however small and inconspicuous, in the endeavour will draw a noble enjoyment from the contest itself, which he would not for any bribe in the form of selfish indulgence consent to be without.

And this leads to the true estimation of what is said by the objectors concerning the possibility and the obligation of learning to do without happiness. Unquestionably it is possible to do without happiness; it is done involuntarily by nineteen-twentieths of mankind, even in those parts of our present world which are least deep in barbarism; and it often has to be done voluntarily by the hero or the martyr, for the sake of something which he prizes more than his individual happiness. But this something, what is it, unless the happiness of others or some of the requisites of happiness? It is noble to be capable of resigning entirely one's own portion of happiness, or chances of it; but, after all, this self-sacrifice must be for some end; it is not its own end; and if we are told that its end is not happiness but virtue, which is better than happiness, I ask, would the sacrifice be made if the hero or martyr did not believe that it would earn for others immunity from similar sacrifices? Would it be made if he thought that his renunciation of happiness for himself would produce no fruit for any of his fellow creatures, but to make their lot like his, and place them also in the condition of persons who have renounced happiness? All honor to those who can abnegate for themselves the personal enjoyment of life when by such renunciation they contribute worthily to increase the amount of happiness in the world; but he who does it or professes to do it for any other purpose is no more deserving of admiration than the ascetic mounted on his pillar. He may be an inspiriting proof of what men *can* do, but assuredly not an example of what they *should*.

Though it is only in a very imperfect state of the world's arrangements that any one can best serve the happiness of others by the absolute sacrifice of his own, yet, so long as the world is in that imperfect state, I fully acknowledge that the readiness to make such a sacrifice is the highest virtue which can be found in man. I will add that in this condition of the world, paradoxical as the assertion may be, the conscious ability to do without happiness gives the best prospect of realizing such happiness as is attainable. For nothing except that consciousness can raise a person above the chances of life, by making him feel that, let fate and fortune do their worst, they have not power to subdue him; which, once felt, frees him from excess of anxiety concerning the evils of life, and enables him, like many a Stoic in the worst times of the Roman Empire, to cultivate in tranquility the sources of satisfaction accessible to him, without concerning himself about the uncertainty of their duration any more than about their inevitable end.

Meanwhile, let utilitarians never cease to claim the morality of self-devotion as a possession which belongs by as good a right to them as either to the Stoic or to the Transcendentalist. The utilitarian morality does recognize in human beings the power of sacrificing their own greatest good for the good of others. It only refuses to admit that the sacrifice is itself a good. A sacrifice which does not increase or tend to increase the sum total of happiness, it considers as wasted. The only self-renunciation which it applauds is devotion to the happiness, or to some of the means of happiness, of others, either of mankind collectively or of individuals within the limits imposed by the collective interests of mankind.

I must again repeat what the assailants of utilitarianism seldom have the justice to acknowledge, that the happiness which forms the utilitarian standard of what is right in conduct is not the agent's own happiness but that of all concerned. As between his own happiness and that of others, utilitarianism requires him to be as strictly impartial as a disinterested and benevolent spectator. In the golden rule of Jesus of Nazareth, we read the complete spirit of the ethics of utility. "To do as you would be done by," and "to love your neighbor as yourself," constitute the ideal perfection of utilitarian morality. As the means of making the nearest approach to this ideal, utility would enjoin, first, that laws and social arrangements should place the happiness or (as, speaking practically, it may be called) the interest of every individual as nearly as possible in harmony with the interest of the whole; and, secondly, that education and opinion, which have so vast a power over human character should so use that power as to establish in the mind of every individual an indissoluble association between his own happiness and the good of the whole, especially between his own happiness and the practice of such modes of conduct, negative and positive, as regard for the universal happiness prescribes; so that not only he may be able to conceive the possibility of happiness to himself, consistently with conduct opposed to the general good, but also that a direct impulse to promote the general good may be in every individual one of the habitual motives of action, and the sentiments connected therewith may fill a large and prominent place in every human being's sentient existence. If the impugners of the utilitarian morality represented it to their own minds in this its true character, I know not what recommendation possessed by any other morality they could possibly affirm to be wanting to it; what more beautiful or more exalted developments of human nature any other ethical system can be supposed to foster, or what springs of action, not accessible to the utilitarian, such systems rely on for giving effect to their mandates.

The objectors to utilitarianism cannot always be charged with representing it in a discreditable light. On the contrary, those among them who entertain anything like a just idea of its disinterested character sometimes find fault with its standard as being too high for humanity. They say it is exacting too much to require that people shall always act from the inducement of promoting the general interests of society. But this is to mistake the very meaning of a standard of morals, and confound the business of ethics to tell us what are our duties, or by what test we may know them; but no system of ethics requires that the sole motive of all we do shall be a feeling of duty; on the contrary, ninety-nine hundredths of all our actions are done from other motives, and rightly so done if the rule of duty does not condemn them. It is the more unjust to utilitarianism that this particular misapprehension should be made a ground of objection to it, inasmuch as utilitarian moralists have gone beyond almost all others in affirming that the motive has nothing to do with the morality of the action, though much with the worth of the agent. He who saves a fellow creature from drowning does what is morally right, whether his motive be duty or the hope of being paid for his trouble; he who betrays the friend that trusts him is guilty of a crime, even if his object be to serve another friend to whom he is under greater obligations. But to speak only of actions done from the motive of duty, and in direct obedience to principle: it is a misapprehension of the utilitarian mode of thought to conceive it as implying that people should fix their minds upon so wide a generality as the world, or society at large. The great majority of good actions are intended not for the benefit of the world, but for that of individuals, of which the good of the world is made up; and the thoughts of the most virtuous man need not on these occasions travel beyond the particular persons concerned, except so far as is necessary to assure himself that in benefiting them he is not violating the rights, that is, the legitimate and authorized expectations, of any one else. The multiplication of happiness is, according to the utilitarian ethics, the object of virtue: the occasions on which any person (except one in a thousand) has it in his power to do this on an extended scale, in other words, to be a public benefactor, are but exceptional; and on these occasions alone is he called on to consider public utility; in every other case, private utility, the interest or happiness of some few persons, is all he has to attend to. Those alone the influence of whose actions extends to society in general need concern themselves habitually about so large an object. In the case of abstinences indeed—of things which people forbear to do from moral considerations, though the consequences in the particular case might be beneficial—it would be unworthy of an intelligent agent not to be consciously aware that the action is of a class which, if practiced generally, would be generally injurious, and that this is the ground of the obligation to abstain from it. The amount of regard for the public interest implied in this recognition is no greater than is demanded by every system of morals, for they all enjoin to abstain from whatever is manifestly pernicious to society.

The same considerations dispose of another reproach against the doctrine of utility, founded on a still grosser misconception of the purpose of a standard of morality, and of the very meaning of the words "right" and "wrong." It is often affirmed that utilitarianism renders men cold and unsympathizing; that it chills their moral feelings towards individuals; that it makes them regard only the dry and hard consideration of the consequences of actions, not taking into their moral estimate the qualities from which those actions emanate. If the assertion means that they do not allow their judgment respecting the rightness or wrongness of an action to be influenced by their opinion of the qualities of the person who does it, this is a complaint not against utilitarianism, but against any standard of morality at all; for certainly no known ethical standard decides an action to be good or bad because it is done by a good or a bad man, still less because done by an amiable, a brave, or a benevolent man, or the contrary. These considerations are relevant, not to the estimation of actions, but of persons; and there is nothing in the utilitarian theory inconsistent with the fact that there are other things which interest us in persons besides the rightness and wrongness of their actions. The Stoics, indeed, with the paradoxical misuse of language which was part of their system, and by which they strove to raise themselves above all concern about anything but virtue, were fond of saying that he who has that has everything; that he, and only he, is rich, is beautiful, is a king. But no claim of this description is made for the virtuous man by the utilitarian doctrine. Utilitarians are quite aware that there are other desirable possessions and qualities besides virtue, and are perfectly willing to allow to all of them their full worth. They are also aware that a right action does not necessarily indicate a virtuous character, and that actions which are blamable often proceed from qualities entitled to praise. When this is apparent in any particular case, it modifies their estimation, not certainly of the act, but of the agent. I grant that they are, notwithstanding, of opinion that in the long run the best proof of a good character is good actions; and resolutely refuse to consider any mental disposition as good of which the predominant tendency is to produce bad conduct. This makes them unpopular with many people; but it is an unpopularity which they must share with every one who regards the distinction between right and wrong in a serious light; and the reproach is not one which a conscientious utilitarian need be anxious to repel.

If no more be meant by the objection than that many utilitarians look on the morality of actions, as measured by the utilitarian standards, with too exclusive a regard, and do not lay sufficient stress upon the other beauties of character which go towards making a human being lovable or admirable, this may be admitted. Utilitarians who have cultivated their moral feelings, but not their sympathies, nor their artistic perceptions, do fall into this mistake; and so do all other moralists under the same conditions. What can be said in excuse for other moralists is equally available for them, namely, that, if there is to be any error, it is better that it should be on that side. As a matter of fact, we may affirm that among utilitarians, as among adherents of other systems, there is every imaginable degree of rigidity and of laxity in the application of their standard; some are even puritanically rigorous, while others are as indulgent as can possibly be desired by sinner or by sentimentalist. But on the whole, a doctrine which brings prominently forward the interest that mankind have in the repression and prevention of conduct which violates the moral law, is likely to be inferior to no other in turning the sanctions of opinion against such violations. It is true, the question, "What does violate the moral law?" is one on which those who recognize different standards of morality are likely now and then to differ. But difference of opinion on moral questions was not first introduced into the world by utilitarianism, while that doctrine does supply, if not always an easy, at all events a tangible and intelligible, mode of deciding such differences.

It may not be superfluous to notice a few more of the common misapprehensions of utilitarian ethics, even those which are so obvious and gross that it might appear impossible for any person of candor and intelligence to fall into them; since persons even of considerable mental endowment, often give themselves so little trouble to understand the bearings of any opinion against which they entertain a prejudice and men are in general so little conscious of this voluntary ignorance as a defect, that the vulgarest misunderstandings of ethical doctrines are continually met with in the deliberate writings of persons of the greatest pretensions both to high principle and to philosophy. We not uncommonly hear the doctrine of utility inveighed against as a *godless* doctrine. If it be necessary to say anything at all against so mere an assumption, we may say that the question depends upon what idea we have formed of the moral character of the Deity. If it be a true belief that God desires, above all things, the happiness of his creatures, and that this was his purpose in their creation, utility is not only not a godless doctrine, but more profoundly religious than any other. If it be meant that utilitarianism does not recognize the revealed will of God as the supreme law of morals, I answer that a utilitarian who believes in the perfect goodness and wisdom of God necessarily believes that whatever God has thought fit to reveal on the subject of morals must fulfil the requirements of utility in a supreme degree. But others besides utilitarians have been of opinion that the Christian revelation was intended, and is fitted, to inform the hearts and minds of mankind with a spirit which should enable them to find for themselves what is right, and incline them to do it when found, rather than to tell them, except in a very general way, what it is; and that we need a doctrine of ethics, carefully followed out, to *interpret* to us the will of God. Whether this opinion is correct or not, it is superfluous here to discuss; since whatever aid religion, either natural or revealed, can afford to ethical investigation, is as open to the utilitarian moralist as to any other. He can use it as the testimony of God to the usefulness or hurtfulness of any given course of action, by as good a right as others can use it for the indication of a transcendental law, having no connection with usefulness or with happiness.

Again, utility is often summarily stigmatized as an immoral doctrine by giving it the name of "expediency," and taking advantage of the popular use of that term to contrast it with principle. But the expedient, in the sense in which it is opposed to the right, generally means that which is expedient for the particular interest of the agent himself; as when a minister sacrifices the interests of his country to keep himself in place. When it means anything better than this, it means that which is expedient for some immediate object, some temporary purpose, but which violates a rule whose observance is expedient in a much higher degree. The expedient, in this sense, instead of being the same thing with the useful, is a branch of the hurtful. Thus it would often be expedient, for the purpose of getting over some momentary embarrassment, or attaining some object immediately useful to ourselves or others, to tell a lie. But inasmuch as the cultivation in ourselves of a sensitive feeling on the subject of veracity is one of the most useful, and the enfeeblement of that feeling one of the most hurtful, things to which our conduct can be instrumental; and inasmuch as any, even unintentional, deviation from truth does that much towards weakening the trustworthiness of human assertion, which is not only the principal support of all present social wellbeing, but the insufficiency of which does more than any one thing that can be named to keep back civilization, virtue, everything on which human happiness on the largest scale depends—we feel that the violation, for a present advantage, of a rule of such transcendent expediency is not expedient, and that he who, for the sake of convenience to himself or to some other individual, does what depends on him to deprive mankind of the good, and inflict upon them the evil, involved in the greater or less reliance which they can place in each other's word, acts the part of one of their worst enemies. Yet that even this rule, sacred as it is, admits of possible exceptions is acknowledged by all moralists; the chief of which is when the withholding of some fact (as of information from a malefactor, or of bad news from a person dangerously ill)would save an individual (especially an individual other than oneself) from great and unmerited evil, and when the withholding can only be effected by denial. But in order that the exception may not extend itself beyond the need, and may have the least possible effect in weakening reliance on veracity, it ought to be recognized and, if possible, its limits defined; and, if the principle of utility is good for anything, it must be good for weighing these conflicting utilities against one another, and marking out the region within which one or the other preponderates.

Again, defenders of utility often find themselves called upon to reply to such objections as this—that there is not time, previous to action, for calculating and weighing the effects of any line of conduct on the general happiness. This is exactly as if any one were to say that it is impossible to guide our conduct by Christianity because there is not time, on every occasion on which anything has to be done, to read through the Old and New Testaments. The answer to the objection is that there has been ample time, namely, the whole past duration of the human species. During all that time, mankind have been learning by experience the tendencies of actions; on which experience all the prudence, as well as all the morality, of life are dependent. People talk as if the commencement of this course of experience had hitherto been put off, and as if, at the moment when some man feels tempted to meddle with the property or life of another, he had to begin considering for the first time whether murder and theft are injurious to human happiness. Even then I do not think that he would find the question very puzzling; but, at all events, the matter is now done to his hand. It is truly a whimsical supposition that, if mankind were agreed in considering utility to be the test of morality, they would remain without any agreement as to what *is* useful, and would take no measures for having their notions on the subject taught to the young, and enforced by law and opinion. There is no difficulty in proving any ethical standard whatever to work ill if we suppose universal idiocy to be conjoined with it; but on any hypothesis short of that, mankind must by this time have acquired positive beliefs as to the effects of some actions on their happiness; and the beliefs which have thus come down are the rules of morality for the multitude, and for the philosopher until he has succeeded in finding better. That philosophers might easily do this, even now, on many subjects; that the received code of ethics is by no means of divine right; and that mankind have still much to learn as to the effects of actions on the general happiness, I admit or rather earnestly maintain. The corollaries from the principle of utility, like the precepts of every practical art, admit of indefinite improvement, and, in a progressive state of the human mind, their improvement is perpetually going on. But to consider the rules of morality as improveable is one thing; to pass over the intermediate generalization entirely and endeavor to test each individual action directly by the first principle is another. It is a strange notion that the acknowledgement of a first principle is inconsistent with the admission of secondary ones. To inform a traveller respecting the place of his ultimate destination is not to forbid the use of landmarks and direction-posts on the way. The proposition that happiness is the end and aim of morality does not mean that no roads ought to be laid down to that goal, or that persons going thither should not be advised to take one direction rather than another. Men really ought to leave off talking a kind of nonsense on this subject, which they would neither talk nor listen to on other matters of practical concernment. Nobody argues that the art of navigation is not founded on astronomy because sailors cannot wait to calculate the Nautical Almanac. Being rational creatures, they go to sea with it ready calculated; and all rational creatures go out upon the sea of life with their minds made up on the common questions of right and wrong, as well as on many of the far more difficult questions of wise and foolish. And this, as long as foresight is a human quality, it is to be presumed they will continue to do. Whatever we adopt as the fundamental principle of morality, we require subordinate principles to apply it by; the impossibility of doing without them, being common to all systems, can afford no argument against any one in particular; but gravely to argue as if no such secondary principles could be had, and as if mankind had remained till now, and always must remain, without drawing any general conclusions from the experience of human life, is as high a pitch, I think, as absurdity has ever reached in philosophical controversy.

The remainder of the stock arguments against utilitarianism mostly consist in laying to its charge the common infirmities of human nature, and the general difficulties which embarrass conscientious persons in shaping their course through life. We are told that a utilitarian will be apt to make his own particular case an exception to moral rules, and, when under temptation, will see a utility in the breach of a rule, greater than he will see in its observance. But is utility the only creed which is able to furnish us with excuses for evil doing, and means of cheating our own conscience? They are afforded in abundance by all doctrines which recognize as a fact in morals the existence of conflicting considerations, which all doctrines do that have been believed by sane persons. It is not the fault of any creed, but of the complicated nature of human affairs, that rules of conduct cannot be so framed as to require no exceptions, and that hardly any kind of action can safely be laid down as either always obligatory or always condemnable. There is no ethical creed which does not temper the rigidity of its laws by giving a certain latitude, under the moral responsibility of the agent, for accommodation to peculiarities of circumstances; and under every creed, at the opening thus made, self-deception and dishonest casuistry get in. There exists no moral system under which there do not arise unequivocal cases of conflicting obligation. These are the real difficulties, the knotty points both in the theory of ethics and in the conscientious guidance of personal conduct. They are overcome practically, with greater or with less success, according to the intellect and virtue of the individual; but it can hardly be pretended that anyone will be the less qualified for dealing with them, from possessing an ultimate standard to which conflicting rights and duties can be referred. If utility is the ultimate source of moral obligations, utility may be invoked to decide between them when their demands are incompatible. Though the application of the standard may be difficult, it is better than none at all; while in other systems the moral laws all claiming independent authority, there is no common umpire entitled to interfere between them; their claims to precedence one over another rest on little better than sophistry, and, unless determined, as they generally are, by the unacknowledged influence of considerations of utility, afford a free scope for the action of personal desires and partialities. We must remember that only in these cases of conflict between secondary principles is it requisite that first principles should be appealed to. There is no case of moral obligation in which some secondary principle is not involved; and if only one, there can seldom be any real doubt which one it is, in the mind of any person by whom the principle itself is recognized.

7

MY STATION AND ITS DUTIES

F. H. Bradley

. . .

We have learned that the self to be realized is not the self as this or that feeling, or as any series of the particular feelings of our own or others' streams or trains of consciousness. It is, in short, not the self to be pleased. The greatest sum of units of pleasure we found to be the idea of a mere collection, whereas, if we wanted morality, it was something like a universal that we wanted. Happiness, as the effort to construct that universal by the addition of particulars, gave us a futile and bastard product which carried its self-destruction within it, in the continual assertion of its own universality, together with its unceasing actual particularity and finitude; so that happiness was, if we chose, nowhere not realized; or again, if we chose, not anywhere realizable. And passing then to the opposite pole, to the universal as the negative of the particulars, to the supposed pure will or duty for duty's sake, we found that too was an unreal conception. It was a mere form which, to be will, must give itself a content, and which could give itself a content only at the cost of a self-contradiction. We saw, further, that any such content was in addition arbitrarily postulated and that, even then, the form was either never realized, because real in no particular content, or always and everywhere realized, because equally reconcilable with any content. And so, as before with happiness, we perceived that morality could have no existence if it meant anything more than the continual asseveration of an empty formula. And, if we had chosen, we might have gone on to exhibit the falsity of asceticism, to see that the self cannot be realized as its own mere negation, since morality is practice, is will to do something, is self-affirmation; and that a will to deny one's will is not self-realization, but rather is, strictly speaking, a psychical impossibility, a self-contradictory illusion. And the possibility, again, of taking as the self to be realized the self which I happen to have, my natural being, and of making life the end of life in the sense that each should live his life as he happens to find it in his own

From F. H. Bradley, *Ethical Studies*, 2nd ed. (London: Oxford University Press, 1927), Essay V, pp. 160–163, 174–192. Reprinted by permission of the publisher.

nature, has been precluded beforehand by the result derived from the consideration of the moral consciousness, viz., that morality implies a superior, a higher self, or at all events a universal something which is above this or that self and so above mine. And, to complete the account of our negations, we saw further, with respect to duty for duty's sake, that even were it possible (as it is not) to create a content from the formula and to elaborate in this manner a system of duties, yet even then the practice required by the theory would be impossible, and so too morality, since in practice particular duties must collide and the collision of duties, if we hold to duty for duty's sake, is the destruction of all duty save the unrealized form of duty in general.

But let us view this result, which seems so unsatisfactory, from the positive side; let us see after all with what we are left. We have self-realization left as the end, the self so far being defined as neither a collection of particular feelings nor an abstract universal. The self is to be realized as something not simply one or the other; it is to be realized further as will, will not being merely the natural will, or the will as it happens to exist and finds itself here or there, but the will as the *good* will, *i.e.*, the will that realizes an end which is above this or that man, superior to them, and capable of confronting them in the shape of a law or an ought. This superior something further, which is a possible law or ought to the individual man, does not depend for its existence on his choice or opinion. Either there is no morality, so says the moral consciousness, or moral duties exist independently of their position by this or that person—my duty may be mine and no other man's, but I do not make it mine. If it is duty, it would be the duty of any person in my case and condition, whether they thought so or not—in a word, duty is "objective," in the sense of not being contingent on the opinion or choice of this or that subject.

What we have left then (to resume it) is this—the end is the realization of the good will which is superior to ourselves; and again the end is self-realization. Bringing these together we see the end is the realization of ourselves as the will which is above ourselves. And this will (if morality exists) we saw must be "objective," because not dependent on "subjective" liking; and "universal," because not identifiable with any particular, but standing above all actual and possible particulars. Further, though universal it is not abstract since it belongs to its essence that it should be realized, and it has no real existence except in and through its particulars. The good will (for morality) is meaningless, if, whatever else it be, it be not the will of living human beings. It is a concrete universal because it not only is above but is within and throughout its details, and is so far only as they are. It is the life which can live only in and by them, as they are dead unless within it; it is the whole soul which lives so far as the body lives, which makes the body a living body and which without the body is as unreal an abstraction as the body without it. It is an organism and a moral organism; and it is conscious self-realization because only by the will of its self-conscious members can the moral organism give itself reality. It is the self-realization of the whole body because it is one and the same will which lives and acts in the life and action of each. It is the self-realization of each member because each member cannot find the function which makes him himself, apart from the whole to which he belongs; to be himself he must go beyond himself, to live his life he must live a life which is not *merely* his own, but which, none the less, but on the contrary all the more, is intensely and emphatically his own individuality. Here, and here first, are the contradictions which have beset us solved—here is a universal which can confront our wandering desires with a fixed and stern imperative, but which yet is no unreal form of the mind but a living soul that penetrates and stands fast in the detail of actual existence. It is real, and real for me. It is in its affirmation that I affirm myself, for I am but as a "heart-beat in its system." And I am real in it, for, when I give myself to it, it gives me the fruition of my own personal activity, the accomplished ideal of my life which is happiness. In the realized idea which, superior to me and yet here and now in and by me, affirms itself in a continuous process, we have found the end, we have found self-realization, duty, and happiness in one—yes, we have found ourselves when we have found our station and its duties, our function as an organ in the social organism.

. . .

Let us now in detail compare the advantages of our present view with the defects of "duty for duty's sake." The objections we found fatal to that view may be stated as follows: (1) The universal was abstract. There was no content which belonged to it and was one with it; and the consequence was that either nothing could be willed, or what was willed was willed not because of the universal, but capriciously. (2) The universal was "subjective." It certainly gave itself out as "objective," in the sense of being independent of this or that person, but still it was not real in the world. It did not come to us as what *was*, it came as what (merely) was to be, an inner notion in moral persons, which had not power to carry itself out and transform the world. And self-realization, if it means will, does mean that we put ourselves forth and see ourselves actual in outer existence. Hence, by identifying ourselves with that which has not this existence, which is not master of the outer world, we cannot secure our self-realization; since, when we have identified ourselves with the end, the end may still remain a mere inner end which does not accomplish itself, and so does not satisfy us. (3) The universal left a part of ourselves outside it. However much we tried to be good, however determined we were to make our will one with the good will, yet we never succeeded. There was always something left in us which was in contradiction with the good. And this we saw was even necessary because morality meant and implied this contradiction, unless we accepted that form of conscientiousness which consists in the simple identification of one's conscience with one's own self (unless, *i.e.*, the consciousness of the relation of my private self to myself as the good self be degraded into my self-consciousness of my mere private self as the good self); and this cannot be if we are in earnest with morality. There thus remains a perpetual contradiction in myself, no less than in the world, between the "is to be" and the "is," a contradiction that cannot be got rid of without getting rid of morality; for, as we saw, it is inherent in morality. The man cannot realize himself in himself as moral because the conforming of his sensuous nature to the universal would be the entire suppression of it, and hence not only of himself but also of the morality which is constituted by the relation of himself to the universal law. The man then cannot find self-realization in the morality of pure duty because (1) he cannot look on his subjective self as the realized moral law; (2) he cannot look on the objective world as the realization of the moral law; (3) he cannot realize the moral law at all because it is defined as that which has no particular content, and therefore no reality; or, if he gives it a content, then it is not the law he realizes, since the content is got not from the law but from elsewhere. In short, duty for duty's sake is an unsolved contradiction, the standing "is to be," which, therefore, because it is to be, is *not;* and in which, therefore, since it is *not,* he cannot find himself realized nor satisfy himself.

These are serious defects. Let us see how they are mended by "my station and its duties." In that (1) the universal is concrete, (2) it is objective, (3) it leaves nothing of us outside it.

(1) It is concrete, and yet not given by caprice. Let us take the latter first. It is not given by caprice for, although within certain limits I may choose my station according to my own liking, yet I and everyone else must have some station with duties pertaining to it, and those duties do not depend on our opinion or liking. Certain circumstances, a certain position, call for a certain course. How I in particular know what my right course is, is a question we shall recur to hereafter—but at present we may take it as an obvious fact that in my station my particular duties are prescribed to me, and I have them whether I wish to or not. And secondly, it is concrete. The universal to be realized is no abstraction, but an organic whole; a system where many spheres are subordinated to one sphere, and particular actions to spheres. This system is real in the detail of its functions, not out of them, and lives in its vital processes, not away from them. The organs are always at work for the whole, the whole is at work in the organs. And I am one of the organs. The universal then which I am to realize is the system which penetrates and subordinates to itself the particulars of all lives, and here and now in my life has this and that function in this and that case, in exercising which through my will it realizes itself as a whole, and me in it.

(2) It is "objective"; and this means that it does not stand over against the outer world as mere "subject" confronted by mere "object." In that sense of the words it is neither merely "objective" nor merely "subjective"; but it is that real identity of subject and object, which, as we have seen, is the only thing that satisfies our desires. The inner side does exist, but it is no more than the inside; it is one factor in the whole and must not be separated from the other factor; and the mistake which is made by the morality which confines itself to the individual man is just this attempt at the separation of what cannot be separated. The inner side certainly is a fact, and it can be distinguished from the rest of the whole; but it really is one element of the whole, depends on the whole for its being, and cannot be divided from it. Let us explain. The moral world, as we said, is a whole, and has two sides. There is an outer side, systems and institutions, from the family to the nation; this we may call the body of the moral world. And there must also be a soul, or else the body goes to pieces; everyone knows that institutions without the spirit of them are dead. In the moral organism this spirit is in the will of the organs as the will of the whole which, in and by the organs, carries out the organism and makes it alive, and which also (and this is the point to which attention is requested) is and must be felt or known in each organ as his own inward and personal will. It is quite clear that a nation is

not strong without public spirit, and is not public spirited unless the members of it are public spirited, *i.e.*, feel the good of the public as a personal matter, or have it at their hearts. The point here is that you cannot have the moral world unless it is willed; that to be willed it must be willed by persons; and that these persons not only have the moral world as the content of their wills, but also must in some way be aware of themselves as willing this content. This being inwardly aware of oneself as willing the good will falls in the inside of the moral whole; we may call it the soul; and it is the sphere of personal morality, or morality in the narrower sense of the consciousness of the relation of my private self to the inwardly presented universal will, my being aware of and willing myself as one with that or contrary to that, as dutiful or bad. We must never let this out of our sight, that, where the moral world exists, you have and you must have these two sides; neither will stand apart from the other; moral institutions are carcasses without personal morality, and personal morality apart from moral institutions is an unreality, a soul without a body.

Now this inward, this "subjective," this personal side, this knowing in himself by the subject of the relation in which the will of him as this or that man stands to the will of the whole within him, or (as was rightly seen by "duty for duty's sake") this consciousness in the one subject of himself as two selves, is, as we said, necessary for all morality. But the form in which it is present may vary very much, and, beginning with the stage of mere feeling, goes on to that of explicit reflection. The reader who considers the matter will perceive that (whether in the life of mankind or of this or that man) we do not begin with a consciousness of good and evil, right and wrong, as such, or in the strict sense. The child is taught to will a content which is universal and good, and he learns to identify his will with it so that he feels pleasure when he feels himself in accord with it, uneasiness or pain when his will is contrary thereto and he feels that it is contrary. This is the beginning of personal morality, and from this we may pass to consider the end . . . It consists [as far as form goes] in the explicit consciousness in myself of two elements which, even though they exist in disunion, are felt to be really one; these are myself as the will of this or that self, and again the universal will as the will for good; and this latter I feel to be my true self, and desire my other self to be subordinated to and so identified with it; in which case I feel the satisfaction of an inward realization. That so far as form goes is correct. But the important point on which "duty for duty's sake" utterly failed us was as to the content of the universal will. We have seen that for action this must have a content, and now we see where the content comes from. The universal side in personal morality is, in short, the reflection of the objective moral world into ourselves (or into itself). The outer universal which I have been taught to will as my will, and which I have grown to find myself in, is now presented by me inwardly to myself as the universal which is my true being, and which by my will I must realize, if need be, against my will as this or that man. So this inner universal has the same content as the outer universal, for it *is* the outer universal in another sphere; it is the inside *of* the outside. *There* was the whole system as an objective will, including my station, and realizing itself here and now in my function. *Here* is the same system presented as a will in me, standing above my will, which wills a certain act to be done by me as a will which is one with the universal will. This universal will is not a blank, but is filled by the consideration of my station in the whole with reference to habitual and special acts. The ideal self appealed to by the moral man is an ideally presented will, in his position and circumstances, which rightly particularizes the general laws which answer to the general functions and system of spheres of the moral organism. That is the content, and therefore, as we saw, it is concrete and filled. And therefore also (which is equally important) it is not merely "subjective."

If, on the inner side of the moral whole, the universal factor were (as in would-be morality it is) filled with a content which is not the detail of the objective will particularizing itself in such and such functions, then there would be no true identity of subject and object, no need why that which is moral should be that which is real, and we should never escape from a practical postulate, which, as we saw, is a practical standing contradiction. But if, as we have seen, the universal on the inside is the universal on the outside reflected in us, or (since we cannot separate it and ourselves) into itself in us; if the objective will of the moral organism is real only in the will of its organs, and if, in willing morally, we will ourselves as that will, and that will wills itself in us—then we must hold that this universal on the inner side is the will of the whole, which is self-conscious in us, and wills itself in us against the actual or possible opposition of the false private self. This being so, when we will morally, the will of the objective world wills itself in us, and carries both us and itself out into the world of the moral will, which is its own realm. We see thus that when morals are looked at as a whole, the will of the inside, so far as it is moral, *is* the will of the outside, and the two are one and cannot be torn apart without *ipso facto* destroying the unity in which morality consists. To be moral I must will my station and its duties; that is, I will to particularize the moral system truly in a given case; and the other side to this act is that the moral system wills to particularize itself in a given station and functions, *i.e.*, in my actions and by my will. In other words, my moral self is not simply mine; it is not an inner which belongs simply to me; and further, it is not a mere inner at all, but it is the soul which animates the body and lives in it, and would not be the soul if it had not a body and *its* body. The objective organism, the systematized moral world, is the reality of the moral will; my duties on the inside answer to due functions on the outside. There is no need here for a pre-established or a postulated harmony, for the moral whole is the identity of both sides; my private choice, so far as I am moral, is the mere form of bestowing myself on and identifying myself with the will of the moral organism, which realizes in its process both itself and myself. Hence we see that what I have to do I have not to force on a recalcitrant world; I have to fill my place—the place that waits for me to fill it; to make my private self the means, my life the sphere and the function of the soul of the whole, which thus, personal in me, externalizes both itself and me into a solid reality, which is both mine and its.

(3) What we come to now is the third superiority of "my station and its duties." The universal which is the end, and which we have seen is concrete and does realize itself, does also more. It gets rid of the contradiction between duty and the "empirical" self; it does not in its realization leave me forever outside and unrealized.

In "duty for duty's sake" we were always unsatisfied, no nearer our goal at the end than at the beginning. There we had the fixed antithesis of the sensuous self on one side, and a nonsensuous moral ideal on the other—a standing contradiction which brought with it a perpetual self-deceit, or the depressing perpetual confession that I am not what I ought to be in my inner heart, and that I never can be so. Duty, we thus saw, was an infinite process, an unending "not-yet"; a continual "not" with an everlasting "to be," or an abiding "to be" with a ceaseless "not."

From this last peevish enemy we are again delivered by "my station and its duties." There I realize myself morally, so that not only what ought to be in the world is, but I am what I ought to be, and find so my contentment and satisfaction. If this were not the case, when we consider that the ordinary moral man is self-contented and happy, we should be forced to accuse him of immorality, and we do not do this; we say he most likely might be better, but we do not say that he is bad, or need consider himself so. Why is this? It is because "my station and its duties" teaches us to identify others and ourselves with the station we fill; to consider that as good, and by virtue of that to consider others and ourselves good too. It teaches us that a man who does his work in the world is good, notwithstanding his faults, if his faults do not prevent him from fulfilling his station. It tells us that the heart is an idle abstraction; we are not to think of it, nor must we look at our insides, but at our work and our life, and say to ourselves, Am I fulfilling my appointed function or not? Fulfill it we can, if we will. What we have to do is not so much better than the world that we cannot do it: the world is there waiting for it; my duties are my rights. On the one hand, I am not likely to be much better than the world asks me to be; on the other hand, if I can take my place in the world I ought not to be discontented. Here we must not be misunderstood; we do not say that the false self, the habits and desires opposed to the good will, are extinguished. Though negated, they never are all of them entirely suppressed, and cannot be. Hence we must not say that any man really does fill his station to the full height of his capacity; nor must we say of any man that he cannot perform his function better than he does, for we all can do so, and should try to do so. We do not wish to deny what are plain moral facts, nor in any way to slur them over.

How then does the contradiction disappear? It disappears by my identifying myself with the good will that I realize in the world, by my refusing to identify myself with the bad will of my private self. So far as I am one with the good will, living as a member in the moral organism, I am to consider myself real and I am not to consider the false self real. That cannot be attributed to me in my character of member in the organism. Even in me the false existence of it has been partly suppressed by that organism; and, so far as the organism is concerned, it is wholly suppressed because contradicted in its results, and allowed no reality. Hence, not existing for the organism, it does not exist for me as a member thereof; and only as a member thereof do I hold myself to be real. And yet this is not justification by faith, for we not only trust, but see, that despite our faults the moral world stands fast, and we in and by it. It is like faith, however, in this, that not merely by thinking ourselves, but by willing ourselves as such, can we look on ourselves as organs in a good whole, and so ourselves good. And further, the knowledge that as members of the system we are real, and not otherwise, encourages us more and more to identify ourselves with that system; to make ourselves better, and so more real, since we see that the good is real, and that nothing else is.

Or, to repeat it, in education my self by habituation has been growing into one with the good self around me, and by my free acceptance of my lot hereafter I consciously make myself one with the good, so that, though bad habits cling to and even arise in me, yet I cannot but be aware of myself as the reality of the good will. That is my essential side; my imperfections are not, and practically they do not matter. The good will in the world realizes itself by and in imperfect instruments, and in spite of them. The work is done, and so long as I will my part of the work and do it (as I do), I feel that, if I perform the function, I *am* the organ, and that my faults, if they do not matter to my station, do not matter to me. My heart I am not to think of, except to tell by my work whether it is in my work, and one with the moral whole; and if that is so, I have the consciousness of absolute reality in the good because of and by myself, and in myself because of and through the good; and with that I am satisfied, and have no right to be dissatisfied.

The individual's consciousness of himself is inseparable from the knowing himself as an organ of the whole; and the residuum falls more and more into the background, so that he thinks of it, if at all, not as himself, but as an idle appendage. For his nature now is not distinct from his "artificial self." He is related to the living moral system not as to a foreign body; his relation to it is "too inward even for faith," since faith implies a certain separation. It is no other-world that he cannot see but must trust to: he feels himself in it, and it in him; in a word, the self-consciousness of himself *is* the self-consciousness of the whole in him, and his will is the will which sees in him its accomplishment by him; it is the free will which knows itself as the free will, and as this beholds its realization and is more than content.

The non-theoretical person, if he be not immoral, is at peace with reality; and the man who in any degree has made this point of view his own becomes more and more reconciled to the world and to life, and the theories of "advanced thinkers" come to him more and more as the thinnest and most miserable abstractions. He sees evils which cannot discourage him, since they point to the strength of the life which can endure such parasites and flourish in spite of them. If the popularizing of superficial views inclines him to bitterness, he comforts himself when he sees that they live in the head, and but little, if at all, in the heart and life; that still at the push the doctrinaire and the quacksalver go to the wall, and that even that too is as it ought to be. He sees the true account of the state (which holds it to be neither mere force nor convention, but the moral organism, the real identity of might and right) unknown or "refuted," laughed at and despised, but he sees the state every day in its practice refute every other doctrine, and do with the moral approval of all what the explicit theory of scarcely one will morally justify. He sees instincts are better and stronger than so-called "principles." He sees in the hour of need what are called "rights" laughed at, "freedom," the liberty to do what one pleases, tramped on, the claims of the individual trodden under foot, and theories burst like cobwebs. And he sees, as of old, the heart of a nation rise high and beat in the breast of each one of her citizens till her safety and her honor are dearer to each than life, till to those who live her shame and sorrow, if such is allotted, outweigh their loss, and death seems a little thing to those who go for her to their common and nameless grave. And he knows that what is stronger than death is hate or love, hate here for love's sake, and that love does not fear death because already it is the death into life of what our philosophers tell us is the only life and reality.

Yes, the state is not put together, but it lives; it is not a heap nor a machine; it is no mere extravagance when a poet talks of a nation's soul. It is the objective mind which is subjective and self-conscious in its citizens—it feels and knows itself in the heart of each. It speaks the word of command and gives the field of accomplishment, and in the activity of obedience it has and bestows individual life and satisfaction and happiness.

First in the community is the individual realized. He is here the embodiment of beauty, goodness, and truth—of truth because he corresponds to his universal conception, of beauty because he realizes it in a single form to the senses or imagination, of goodness because his will expresses and is the will of the universal.

"The realm of morality is nothing but the absolute spiritual unity of the essence of individuals, which exists in the independent reality of them. . . . The moral substance, looked at abstractedly from the mere side of its universality, is the law, and, as this, is only thought; but nonetheless is it, from another point of view, immediate real self-consciousness or custom: and conversely the individual exists as this single unit, inasmuch as it is conscious in its individuality of the universal consciousness as its own being, inasmuch as its action and existence are the universal Ethos. . . . They (the individuals) are aware in themselves that they possess this individual independent being because of the sacrifice of their individuality, because the universal substance is their soul and essence: and, on the other side, this universal is their individual action, the work that they as individuals have produced.

"The merely individual action and business of the separate person is concerned with the needs he is subject to as a natural being, as an individuality which exists. That even these his commonest functions do not come to nothing, but possess reality, is effected solely by the universal maintaining medium, by the power of the whole people. But it is not simply the form of persistence which the universal substance confers on his action; it gives also the content—what he does *is* the universal skill and custom of all. This content, just so far as it completely individualizes itself, is in its reality interlaced with the action of all. The work of the individual for his needs is a satisfaction of the needs of others as much as of his own; and he attains the satisfaction of his own only through the work of the others. The individual in his individual work thus accomplishes a universal work—he does so here *unconsciously;* but he also further accomplishes it as his *conscious* object: the whole as the whole is his work for which he sacrifices himself, and from which by that very sacrifice he gets again his self restored. Here there is nothing taken which is not given, nothing wherein the independent individual, by and in the resolution of his atomic existence, by and in the negation of his self, fails to give himself the positive significance of a being which exists by and for itself. The unity—on the one side of the being for another, or the making oneself into an outward thing, and on the other side of the being for oneself—this universal substance speaks its universal language in the usages and laws of his people: and yet this unchanging essence is itself nought else than the expression of the single individuality, which seems at first sight its mere opposite; the laws pronounce nothing but what everyone *is* and does. The individual recognizes the substance not only as his universal outward existence, but he recognizes also himself in it, particularized in his own individuality and in that of each of his fellow citizens. And so in the universal mind each one has nothing but self-certainty, the assurance of finding in existing reality nothing but himself. In all I contemplate independent beings, that are such, and are for themselves, only in the very same way that I am for myself; in them I see existing free unity of self with others, and existing by virtue of me and by virtue of the others alike. Them as myself, myself as them.

> In a free people, therefore, reason is realized in truth; it is present living mind, and in this not only does the individual find his destination, *i.e.*, his universal and singular essence, promulgated and ready to his hand as an outward existence, but he himself is this essence, and has also reached and fulfilled his destination. Hence the wisest men of antiquity have given judgment that wisdom and virtue consist in living agreeably to the Ethos of one's people.[1]

Once let us take the point of view which regards the community as the real moral organism, which in its members knows and wills itself and sees the individual to be real just so far as the universal self is in his self, as he in it, and we get the solution of most, if not all, of our previous difficulties. There is here no need to ask and by some scientific process find out what is moral, for morality exists all round us, and faces us, if need be, with a categorical imperative, while it surrounds us on the other side with an atmosphere of love.

The belief in this real moral organism is the one solution of ethical problems. It breaks down the antithesis of despotism and individualism; it denies them, while it preserves the truth of both. The truth of individualism is saved, because unless we have intense life and self-consciousness in the members of the state, the whole state is ossified. The truth of despotism is saved, because unless the member realizes the whole by and in himself, he fails to reach his own individuality. Considered in the main, the best communities are those which have the best men for their members, and the best men are the members of the best communities. Circle as this is, it is not a vicious circle. The two problems of the best man and best state are two sides, two distinguishable aspects of the one problem, how to realize in human nature the perfect unity of homogeneity and specification; and when we see that each of these without the other is unreal, then we see that (speaking in general) the welfare of the state and the welfare of its individuals are questions which it is mistaken and ruinous to separate. Personal morality and political and social institutions cannot exist apart, and (in general) the better the one the better the other. The community is moral because it realizes personal morality; personal morality is moral because and in so far as it realizes the moral whole.

1 Hegel, *Phänomenologie des Geistes* (1807), II, 256–8.

It is here we find an answer to the complaint of our day on the dwindling of human nature. The higher the organism (we are told), the more are its functions specified, and hence narrowed. The man becomes a machine, or the piece of a machine; and, though the world grows, "the individual withers." On this we may first remark that, if what is meant is that the more centralized the system, the more narrow and monotonous is the life of the member, that is a very questionable assertion. If it be meant that the individual's life can be narrowed to "file-packing," or the like, without detriment to the intensity of the life of the whole, that is even more questionable. If again it be meant that in many cases we have a one-sided specification, which, despite the immediate stimulus of particular function implies ultimate loss of life to the body, that, I think, probably is so, but it is doubtful if we are compelled to think it always must be so. But the root of the whole complaint is a false view of things, . . . The moral organism is not a mere animal organism. In the latter (it is no novel remark) the member is not aware of itself as such, while in the former it knows itself, and therefore knows the whole in itself. The narrow external function of the man is not the whole man. He has a life which we cannot see with our eyes; and there is no duty so mean that it is not the realization of this, and knowable as such. What counts is not the visible outer work so much as the spirit in which it is done. The breadth of my life is not measured by the multitude of my pursuits, nor the space I take up amongst other men, but by the fullness of the whole life which I know as mine. It is true that less now depends on each of us, as this or that man; it is not true that our individuality is therefore lessened, that therefore we have less in us.

Let us now consider our point of view in relation to . . . the common error that there is something "right in itself" for me to do, in the sense that either there must be some absolute rule of morality the same for all persons without distinction of times and places, or else that all morality is "relative," and hence no morality. Let us begin by remarking that there is no such fixed code or rule of right. It is abundantly clear that the morality of one time is not that of another time, that the men considered good in one age might in another age not be thought good, that what would be right for us here might be mean and base in another country, and what would be wrong for us here might there be our bounden duty. This is clear fact which is denied only in the interest of a foregone conclusion. The motive to deny it is the belief that it is fatal to morality. If what is right here is wrong there, then all morality (such is the notion) becomes chance and convention, and so ceases. But "my station and its duties" holds that *unless* morals varied, there could be no morality; that a morality which was *not* relative would be futile, and I should have to ask for something "more relative than this."

Let us explain. We hold that man is φύσει πολιτικός [political by nature], that apart from the community he is θεὸς ʼη̈ θηρίον [a god or beast], no man at all. We hold again that the true nature of man, the oneness of homogeneity and specification, is being wrought out in history; in short, we believe in evolution. The process of evolution is the humanizing of the bestial foundation of man's nature by carrying out in it the true idea of man—in other words, by realizing man as an infinite whole. This realization is possible only by the individual's living as member in a higher life, and this higher life is slowly developed in a series of stages. Starting from and on the basis of animal nature, humanity has worked itself out by gradual advances of specification and systematization, and any other progress would, in the world we know, have been impossible. The notion that full-fledged moral ideas fell down from heaven is contrary to all the facts with which we are acquainted. If they had done so, it would have been for their own sake; for by us they certainly could not have been perceived, much less applied. At any given period to know more than he did, man must have been more than he was; for a human being is nothing if he is not the son of his time, and he must realize himself as that, or he will not do it at all.

Morality is "relative," but is nonetheless real. At every stage there is the solid fact of a world so far moralized. There is an objective morality in the accomplished will of the past and present, a higher self worked out by the infinite pain, the sweat and blood of generations, and now given to me by free grace and in love and faith as a sacred trust. It comes to me as the truth of my own nature, and the power and the law, which is stronger and higher than any caprice or opinion of my own.

"Evolution," in this sense of the word, gives us over neither to chance nor alien necessity, for it is that self-realization which is the progressive conquest of both. But, on another understanding of the term, we cannot help asking, Is this still the case, and is "my station" a tenable point of view?

Wholly tenable, in the form in which we have stated it, it is not. For if, in saying Morality has developed, all we mean is that something has happened different from earlier events, that human society has changed, and that the alterations, so far as we know them, are more or less of a certain sort; if "progress" signifies that an advance has been set going and is kept up by chance in an unknown direction; that the higher is, in short, what *is* and what before was not, and that what will be, of whatever sort it is, will still be a step in progress; if, in short, the movement of history toward a goal is mere illusion, and the stages of that movement are nothing but the successes of what from time to time somehow happens to be best suited to the chance of circumstances—then it is clear in the first place that, teleology being banished, such words as evolution and progress have lost their own meaning, and that to speak of humanity realizing itself in history, and of myself finding in that movement the truth of myself worked out, would be simply to delude oneself with hollow phrases.

Thus far we must say that on such a view of "development" the doctrine of "my station" is grievously curtailed. But is it destroyed? Not wholly; though sorely mutilated, it still keeps its ground. We have rejected teleology but have not yet embraced individualism. We still believe that the universal self is more than a collection or an idea, that it is reality, and that apart from it the "individuals" are the fictions of a theory. We have still the fact of the one self particularized in its many members; and the right and duty of gaining self-realization through the real universal is still as certain as is the impossibility of gaining it otherwise. And so "my station" is after all a position, not indeed satisfactory, but not yet untenable.

But if the larger doctrine be the truth, if evolution is more than a tortured phrase, and progress to a goal no mere idea but an actual fact, then history is the working out of the true human nature through various incomplete stages toward completion, and "my station" is the one satisfactory view of morals. Here (as we have seen) all morality is and must be "relative" because the essence of realization is evolution through stages, and hence existence in some one stage which is not final; here, on the other hand, all morality is "absolute" because in every stage the essence of man *is* realized, however imperfectly; and yet again the distinction of right in itself against relative morality is not banished, because, from the point of view of a higher stage, we can see that lower stages failed to realize the truth completely enough, and also, mixed and one with their realization, did present features contrary to the true nature of man as we now see it. Yet herein the morality of every stage is justified for that stage; and the demand for a code of right in itself, apart from any stage, is seen to be the asking for an impossibility.

.   .   .

PROPOSITIONS OF APPRAISAL

John Dewey

Since desires and interests are activities which take place in the world and which have effects in the world, they are observable in themselves and in connection with their observed effects. It might seem then as if, upon any theory that relates valuation with desire and interest, we had now come within sight of our goal—the discovery of valuation-propositions. Propositions *about* valuations have, indeed, been shown to be possible. But they are valuation-propositions only in the sense in which propositions about potatoes are potato-propositions. They are propositions about matters-of-fact. The fact that these occurrences happen to be valuations does not make the propositions valuation-propositions in any distinctive sense. Nevertheless, the fact that such matter-of-fact propositions can be made is of importance. For, unless they exist, it is doubly absurd to suppose that valuation-propositions in a *distinctive* sense can exist. It has also been shown that the subject matter of personal activities forms no theoretical barrier to [the] institution of matter-of-fact propositions, for the behavior of human beings is open to observation. While there are practical obstacles to the establishment of valid general propositions about such behavior (i.e., about the relations of its constituent acts), its conditions and effects may be investigated. Propositions about valuations made in terms of their conditions and consequences delimit the problem as to existence of valuation-propositions in a *distinctive* sense. Are propositions about existent valuations themselves capable of being appraised, and can the appraisal when made enter into the constitution of further valuations? That a mother prizes or holds dear her child, we have seen, may be determined by observation; and the conditions and effects of different kinds of prizing or caring for may, in theory, be compared and contrasted with one another. In case the final outcome is to show that some kinds of acts of prizing are *better* than others, valuation-acts are themselves evaluated, and the evaluation may modify further direct acts of prizing. If this condition is satisfied, then propositions about valuations that actually take place become the subject matter of valuations in a distinctive sense, that is, a sense that marks them off both from propositions of physics and from historical propositions about what human beings have in fact done.

We are brought thus to the problem of the nature of appraisal or evaluation which, as we saw, is one of the two recognized significations of 'valuation.' Take such an elementary appraisal proposition as "This plot of ground is worth $200 a front foot." It is different in form from the proposition, "It has a frontage of 200 feet." The latter sentence states a matter of accomplished fact. The former sentence states a rule for determination of an act to be performed, its reference being to the future and not to something already accomplished or done. If stated in the context in which a tax-assessor operates, it states a regulative condition for levying a tax against the owner; if stated by the owner to a real estate dealer, it sets forth a regulative condition to be observed by the latter in offering the property for sale. The future act or state is not set forth as a prediction of what will happen but as something which *shall* or *should* happen. Thus the proposition may be said to lay down a norm, but "norm" must be understood simply in the sense of a condition *to be* conformed to in definite forms of future action. That rules are all but omnipresent in every mode of human relationship is too obvious to require argument. They are in no way confined to activities to which the name 'moral' is applied. Every recurrent form of activity, in the arts and professions, develops rules as to the best way in which to accomplish the ends in view. Such rules are used as criteria or "norms" for judging the value of proposed modes of behavior. The existence of rules for valuation of modes of behavior in different fields as wise or unwise, economical or extravagant, effective or futile, cannot be denied. The problem concerns not their existence as general propositions (since every rule of action is general) but whether they express only custom, convention, tradition, or are capable of stating relations between things as means and other things as consequences, which relations are themselves grounded in empirically ascertained and tested existential relations such as are usually termed those of cause and effect.

In the case of some crafts, arts, and technologies, there can be no doubt which of these alternatives is correct. The medical art, for example, is approaching a state in which many of the rules laid down for a patient by a physician as to what it is *better* for him to do, not merely in the way of medicaments but of diet and habits of life, are based upon experimentally ascertained principles of chemistry and physics. When engineers say that certain materials subjected to certain technical operations are *required* if a bridge capable of supporting certain loads is to be built over the Hudson River at a certain point, their advice does not represent their personal opinions or whims but is backed by acknowledged physical laws. It is commonly believed that such devices as radios and automobiles have been greatly improved (bettered) since they were first invented, and that the betterment in the relation of means to consequences is due to more adequate scientific knowledge of underlying physical principles. The argument does not demand the belief that the influence of custom and convention is entirely eliminated. It is enough that such cases show that it is possible for rules of appraisal or evaluation to rest upon scientifically warranted physical generalizations and that the ratio of rules of this type to those expressing mere customary habits is on the increase.

In medicine a quack may cite a number of alleged cures as evidential ground for taking the remedies he offers. Only a little examination is needed to show in what definite respects the procedures he recommends differ from those said to be "good" or to be "required" by competent physicians. There is, for example, no analysis of the cases presented as evidence to show that they are actually like the disease for the cure of which the remedy is urged; and there is no analysis to show that the recoveries which are said (rather than proved) to have taken place were in fact due to taking the medicine in question rather than to any one of an indefinite number of other causes. Everything is asserted wholesale with no analytic control of conditions. Furthermore, the first requirement of scientific procedure—namely, full publicity as to materials and processes—is lacking. The sole justification for citing these familiar facts is that their contrast with competent medical practice shows the extent to which the rules of procedure in the latter art have the warrant of tested empirical propositions. Appraisals of courses of action as better and worse, more and less serviceable, are as experimentally justified as are nonvaluative propositions about impersonal subject matter. In advanced engineering technologies propositions that state the *proper* courses of action to be adopted are evidently grounded in generalizations of physical and chemical science; they are often referred to as *applied* science. Nevertheless, propositions which lay down rules for procedures as being fit and good, as distinct from those that are inept and bad, are different in form from the scientific propositions upon which they rest. For they are rules for the use, in and by human activity, of scientific generalizations as means for accomplishing certain desired and intended ends.

Examination of these appraisals discloses that they have to do with things as they sustain to each other the relation of *means to ends or consequences.* Wherever there is an appraisal involving a rule as to better or as to needed action, there is an end to be reached: the appraisal is a valuation of things with respect to their serviceability or needfulness. If we take the examples given earlier, it is evident that real estate is appraised for the purpose of levying taxes or fixing a selling price; that medicinal treatments are appraised with reference to the end of effecting recovery of health; that materials and techniques are valued with respect to the building of bridges, radios, motor-cars, etc. If a bird builds its nest by what is called pure "instinct," it does not have to appraise materials and processes with respect to their fitness for an end. But if the result—the nest—is contemplated as an object of desire, then either there is the most arbitrary kind of trial-and-error operations or there is consideration of the fitness and usefulness of materials and processes to bring the desired object into existence. And this process of weighing obviously involves comparison of different materials and operations as alternative possible means. In every case, except those of sheer "instinct" and complete trial and error, there are involved observation of actual materials and estimate of their potential force in production of a particular result. There is always some observation of the *outcome attained* in comparison and contrast with that intended, such that the comparison throws light upon the actual fitness of the things employed as means. It thus makes possible a better judgment in the future as to their fitness and usefulness. On the basis of such observations certain modes of conduct are adjudged silly, imprudent, or unwise, and other modes of conduct sensible, prudent, or wise, the discrimination being made upon the basis of the validity of the estimates reached about the relation of things as means to the end or consequence actually reached.

The standing objection raised against this view of valuation is that it applies only to things *as means*, while propositions that are genuine valuations apply to things as *ends*. This point will be shortly considered at length. But it may be noted here that ends are appraised in the same evaluations in which things as means are weighed. For example, an end suggests itself. But, when things are weighed as means toward that end, it is found that it will take too much time or too great an expenditure of energy to achieve it, or that, if it were attained, it would bring with it certain accompanying inconveniences and the promise of future troubles. It is then appraised and rejected as a "bad" end.

The conclusions reached may be summarized as follows: (1) There are propositions which are not merely about valuations that have actually occurred (about, i.e., prizings, desires, and interests that have taken place in the past) but which describe and define certain things as good, fit, or proper in a definite existential relation: these propositions, moreover, are *generalizations*, since they form rules for the proper use of materials. (2) The existential relation in question is that of means-ends or means-consequences. (3) These propositions in their generalized form may rest upon scientifically warranted empirical propositions and are themselves capable of being tested by observation of results actually attained as compared with those intended.

The objection brought against the view just set forth is that it fails to distinguish between things that are good and right in and of themselves, immediately, intrinsically, and things that are simply good *for* something else. In other words, the latter are useful for attaining the things which have, so it is said, value in and of themselves, since they are prized for their own sake and not as means to something else. This distinction between two different meanings of 'good' (and 'right') is, it is claimed, so crucial for the whole theory of valuation and values that failure to make the distinction destroys the validity of the conclusions that have been set forth. This objection definitely puts before us for consideration the question of the relations to each other of the categories of *means* and *end*. In terms of the dual meaning of 'valuation' already mentioned, the question of the relation of *prizing* and *appraising* to one another is explicitly raised. For, according to the objection, appraising applies only to *means*, while prizing applies to things that are *ends*, so that a difference must be recognized between valuation in its full pregnant sense and evaluation as a secondary and derived affair.

Let the connection between prizing and valuation be admitted and also the connection between desire (and interest) and prizing. The problem as to the relation between appraisal of things as means and prizing of things as ends then takes the following form: Are desires and interests ('likings,' if one prefers that word), which directly effect an institution of end-values, independent of the appraisal of things as means or are they intimately influenced by this appraisal? If a person, for example, finds after due investigation that an immense amount of effort is required to procure the conditions that are the means required for realization of a desire (including perhaps sacrifice of other end-values that might be obtained by the same expenditure of effort), does that fact react to modify his original desire and hence, by definition, his valuation? A survey of what takes place in any deliberate activity provides an affirmative answer to this question. For what is deliberation except weighing of various alternative desires (and hence end-values) in terms of the conditions that are the means of their execution, and which, as means, determine the consequences actually arrived at? There can be no control of the operation of foreseeing consequences (and hence of forming ends-in-view) save in terms of conditions that operate as the causal conditions of their attainment. The proposition in which any object adopted as an end-in-view is statable (or explicitly stated) is *warranted* in just the degree to which existing conditions have been surveyed and appraised in their capacity as means. The sole alternative to this statement is that no deliberation whatsoever occurs, no ends-in-view are formed, but a person acts directly upon whatever impulse happens to present itself.

Any survey of the experiences in which ends-in-view are formed, and in which earlier impulsive tendencies are shaped through deliberation into a *chosen* desire, reveals that the object finally valued as an end to be reached is determined in its concrete makeup by appraisal of existing conditions as means. However, the habit of completely separating the conceptions of ends from that of means is so ingrained because of a long philosophical tradition that further discussion is required.

1. The common assumption that there is a sharp separation between things, on the one hand, as useful or helpful, and, on the other hand, as *intrinsically* good, and hence that there exists a separation between propositions as to what is expedient, prudent, or advisable and what is inherently desirable, does not, in any case, state a *self-evident* truth. The fact that such words as 'prudent,' 'sensible,' and 'expedient,' in the long run, or after survey of all conditions, merge so readily into the word 'wise' suggests (though, of course, it does not prove) that ends framed in separation from consideration of things as means are foolish to the point of irrationality.

2. Common sense regards some desires and interests as short-sighted, "blind," and others, in contrast, as enlightened, far-sighted. It does not for a moment lump all desires and interests together as having the same status with respect to end-values. Discrimination between their respective short-sightedness and farsightedness is made precisely on the ground of whether the object of a given desire is viewed as, in turn, itself a conditioning means of further consequences. Instead of taking a laudatory view of "immediate" desires and valuations, common sense treats refusal to mediate as the very essence of short-view judgment. For treating the end as *merely* immediate and exclusively final is equivalent to refusal to consider what will happen after and because a particular end is reached.

3. The words 'inherent,' 'intrinsic,' and 'immediate' are used ambiguously, so that a fallacious conclusion is reached. Any quality or property that actually belongs to any object or event is properly said to be immediate, inherent, or intrinsic. The fallacy consists in interpreting what is designated by these terms as out of relation to anything else and hence as absolute. For example, *means* are by definition relational, mediated, and mediating, since

they are intermediate between an existing situation and a situation that is to be brought into existence by their use. But the relational character of the *things* that are employed as means does not prevent the things from having their own immediate qualities. In case the things in question are prized and cared for, then, according to the theory that connects the property of value with prizing, they necessarily have an immediate quality of value. The notion that, when means and instruments are valued, the value-qualities which result are only instrumental is hardly more than a bad pun. There is nothing in the nature of prizing or desiring to prevent their being directed to things which are means, and there is nothing in the nature of means to militate against their being desired and prized. In empirical fact, the measure of the value a person attaches to a given end is not what he *says* about its preciousness but the care he devotes to obtaining and using the *means* without which it cannot be attained. No case of notable achievement can be cited in any field (save as a matter of sheer accident) in which the persons who brought about the end did not give loving care to the instruments and agencies of its production. The dependence of ends attained upon means employed is such that the statement just made reduces in fact to a tautology. Lack of desire and interest are proved by neglect of, and indifference to, required means. As soon as an attitude of desire and interest has been developed, then, because without full-hearted attention an end which is professedly prized will not be attained, the desire and interest in question automatically attach themselves to whatever other things are seen to be required means of attaining the end.

The considerations that apply to 'immediate' apply also to 'intrinsic' and 'inherent.' A quality, including that of value, is inherent if it actually belongs to something, and the question of whether or not it belongs is one of *fact* and not a question that can be decided by dialectical manipulation of the concept of inherency. If one has an ardent desire to obtain certain things as means, then the quality of value belongs to, or inheres in, those things. For the time being, producing or obtaining those means *is* the end-in-view. The notion that only that which is out of relation to everything else can justly be called *inherent* is not only itself absurd but is contradicted by the very theory that connects the value of objects as ends with desire and interest, for this view expressly makes the value of the end-object relational, so that, if the inherent is identified with the nonrelational, there are, according to this view, no inherent values at all. On the other hand, if it is the fact that the quality exists in this case, because that to which it belongs is conditioned by a relation, then the relational character of means cannot be brought forward as evidence that their value is not inherent. The same considerations apply to the terms 'intrinsic' and 'extrinsic' as applied to value-qualities. Strictly speaking, the phrase 'extrinsic value' involves a contradiction in terms. Relational properties do not lose their intrinsic quality of being just what they are because their coming into being is *caused* by something 'extrinsic.' The theory that such is the case would terminate logically in the view that there are no intrinsic qualities whatever, since it can be shown that such intrinsic qualities as *red, sweet, hard*, etc., are causally conditioned as to their occurrence. The trouble, once more, is that a dialectic of concepts has taken the place of examination of actual empirical facts. The extreme instance of the view that to be intrinsic is to be out of any relation is found in those writers who hold that, since values *are* intrinsic, they cannot depend upon *any* relation whatever, and certainly not upon a relation to human beings. Hence this school attacks those who connect value-properties with desire and interest on exactly the same ground that the latter equate the distinction between the values of means and ends with the distinction between instrumental and intrinsic values. The views of this extreme nonnaturalistic school may, accordingly, be regarded as a definite exposure of what happens when an analysis of the abstract concept of 'intrinsicalness' is substituted for analysis of empirical occurrences.

The more overtly and emphatically the valuation of objects as ends is connected with desire and interest, the more evident it should be that, since desire and interest are ineffectual save as they co-operatively interact with environing conditions, valuation of desire and interest, as means correlated with other means, is the sole condition for valid appraisal of objects as ends. If the lesson were learned that the object of scientific knowledge is *in any case* an ascertained correlation of changes, it would be seen, beyond the possibility of denial, that anything taken *as end* is in its own content or constituents a correlation of the energies, personal and extra-personal, which operate as means. An end as an *actual* consequence, as an existing outcome, is, like any other occurrence which is scientifically analyzed, nothing but the interaction of the conditions that bring it to pass. Hence it follows necessarily that the *idea* of the object of desire and interest, the *end-in-view* as distinct from the end or outcome actually effected, is warranted in the precise degree in which it is formed in terms of these operative conditions.

4. The chief weakness of current theories of valuation which relate the latter to desire and interest is due to failure to make an empirical analysis of concrete desires and interests as they actually exist. When such an analysis is made, certain relevant considerations at once present themselves.

(i) Desires are subject to frustration and interests are subject to defeat. The likelihood of the occurrence of failure in attaining desired ends is in direct ratio to failure to form desire and interest (and the objects they involve) on the basis of conditions that operate either as obstacles (negatively valued) or as positive resources. The difference between reasonable and unreasonable desires and interests is precisely the difference between those which arise casually and are not reconstituted through consideration of the conditions that will actually decide the outcome and those which are formed on the basis of existing liabilities and potential resources. That desires as they first present themselves are the product of a mechanism consisting of native organic tendencies and acquired habits is an undeniable fact. All growth in maturity consists in *not* immediately giving way to such tendencies but in remaking them in their first manifestation through consideration of the consequences they will occasion *if* they are acted upon—an operation which is equivalent to judging or evaluating them as means operating in connection with extra-personal conditions as also means. Theories of valuation which relate it to desire and interest cannot both eat their cake and have it. They cannot continually oscillate between a view of desire and interest that identifies the latter with impulses just as they happen to occur (as products of organic mechanisms) and a view of desire as a modification of a raw impulse through foresight of its outcome; the latter alone being desire, the whole difference between impulse and desire is made by the presence in desire of an end-in-view, of objects *as* foreseen consequences. The foresight will be dependable in the degree in which it is constituted by examination of the conditions that will in fact decide the outcome. If it seems that this point is being hammered in too insistently, it is because the issue at stake is nothing other and nothing less than the possibility of distinctive valuation-propositions. For it cannot be denied that propositions having evidential warrant and experimental test are possible in the case of evaluation of things as means. Hence it follows that, if these propositions enter into the formation of the interests and desires which are valuations of ends, the latter are thereby constituted the subject matter of authentic empirical affirmations and denials.

(ii) We commonly speak of "learning from experience" and the "maturity" of an individual or a group. What do we mean by such expressions? At the very least, we mean that in the history of individual persons and of the human race there takes place a change from original, comparatively unreflective, impulses and hard-and-fast habits to desires and interests that incorporate the results of critical inquiry. When this process is examined, it is seen to take place chiefly on the basis of careful observation of differences found between desired and proposed ends (*ends-in-view*) and attained ends or actual consequences. Agreement between what is wanted and anticipated and what is actually obtained confirms the selection of conditions which operate as means to the desired end; discrepancies, which are experienced as frustrations and defeats, lead to an inquiry to discover the causes of failure. This inquiry consists of more and more thorough examination of the conditions under which impulses and habits are formed and in which they operate. The result is formulation of desires and interests which are what they are through the union of the affective-motor conditions of action with the intellectual or ideational. The latter is there in any case if there is an end-in-view of any sort, no matter how casually formed, while it is adequate in just the degree in which the end is constituted in terms of the conditions of its actualization. For, wherever there is an *end-in-view* of any sort whatever, there is affective-*ideational*-motor activity; or, in terms of the dual meaning of valuation, there is union of prizing and appraising. Observation of results obtained, of *actual* consequences in their agreement with and difference from ends anticipated or held in view, thus provides the conditions by which desires and interests (and hence valuations) are matured and tested. Nothing more contrary to common sense can be imagined than the notion that we are incapable of changing our desires and interests by means of learning what the consequences of acting upon them are, or, as it is sometimes put, of *indulging* them. It should not be necessary to point in evidence to the spoiled child and the adult who cannot "face reality." Yet, as far as valuation and the theory of values are concerned, any theory which isolates valuation of ends from appraisal of means equates the spoiled child and the irresponsible adult to the mature and sane person.

(iii) Every person in the degree in which he is capable of learning from experience draws a distinction between what is desired and what is desirable whenever he engages in formation and choice of competing desires and interests. There is nothing far-fetched or "moralistic" in this statement. The contrast referred to is simply that between the object of a desire as it first presents itself (because of the existing mechanism of impulses and habits) and the object of desire which emerges as a revision of the first-appearing impulse, after the latter is critically judged in reference to the conditions which will decide the actual result. The "desirable," or the object which *should* be desired (valued), does not descend out of the a priori blue nor descend as an imperative from a moral Mount Sinai. It presents itself because past experience has shown that hasty action upon uncriticized desire leads to defeat and possibly to catastrophe. The "desirable" as distinct from the "desired" does not then designate something at large or a priori. It points to the difference between the operation and consequences of unexamined impulses and those of desires and interests that are the product of investigation of conditions and consequences. Social conditions and pressures are part of the conditions that affect the execution of desires. Hence they have to be taken into account in framing ends in terms of available means. But the distinction between the "is" in the sense of the object of a casually emerging desire and the "should be" of a desire framed in relation to actual conditions is a distinction which in any case is bound to offer itself as human beings grow in maturity and part with the childish disposition to "indulge" every impulse as it arises.

Desires and interests are, as we have seen, themselves causal conditions of results. As such they are potential means and have to be appraised as such. This statement is but a restatement of points already made. But it is worth making because it forcibly indicates how far away some of the theoretical views of valuation are from practical common-sense attitudes and beliefs. There is an indefinite number of proverbial sayings which in effect set forth the necessity of not treating desires and interests as final in their first appearance but of treating them as means—that is, of appraising them and forming objects or ends-in-view on the ground of what consequences they will tend to produce in practice. "Look before you leap"; "Act in haste, repent at leisure"; "A stitch in time saves nine"; "When angry count ten"; "Do not put your hand to the plow until the cost has been counted"—are but a few of the many maxims. They are summed up in the old saying, "*Respice finem*" ["Consider the outcome"]—a saying which marks the difference between simply *having* an end-in-view for which *any* desires suffice, and *looking*, examining, to make sure that the consequences that will actually result are such as will be actually prized and valued when they occur. Only the exigencies of a preconceived theory (in all probability one seriously infected by the conclusions of an uncritically accepted "subjectivistic" psychology) will ignore the concrete differences that are made in the content of "likings" and "prizings," and of desires and interests, by evaluating them in their respective causal capacities when they are taken as means.

·   ·   ·

9

ULTIMATE PRINCIPLES AND ETHICAL EGOISM

Brian Medlin

I believe that it is now pretty generally accepted by professional philosophers that ultimate ethical principles must be arbitrary. One cannot derive conclusions about what should be merely from accounts of what is the case; one cannot decide how people ought to behave merely from one's knowledge of how they do behave. To arrive at a conclusion in ethics one must have at least one ethical premiss. This premiss, if it be in turn a conclusion, must be the conclusion of an argument containing at least one ethical premiss. And so we can go back, indefinitely but not for ever. Sooner or later, we must come to at least one ethical premiss which is not deduced but baldly asserted. Here we must be a-rational; neither rational nor irrational, for here there is no room for reason even to go wrong.

But the triumph of Hume in ethics has been a limited one. What appears quite natural to a handful of specialists appears quite monstrous to the majority of decent intelligent men. At any rate, it has been my experience that people who are normally rational resist the above account of the logic of moral language, not by argument—for that can't be done—but by tooth and nail. And they resist from the best motives. They see the philosopher wantonly unravelling the whole fabric of morality. If our ultimate principles are arbitrary, they say, if those principles came out of thin air, then anyone can hold any principle he pleases. Unless moral assertions are statements of fact about the world and either true or false, we can't claim that any man is wrong, whatever his principles may be, whatever his behaviour. We have to surrender the luxury of calling one another scoundrels. That this anxiety flourishes because its roots are in confusion is evident when we consider that we don't call people scoundrels, anyhow, for being mistaken about their facts. Fools, perhaps, but that's another matter. Nevertheless, it doesn't become us to be high-up. The layman's uneasiness, however irrational it may be, is very natural and he must be reassured.

Brian Medlin, "Ultimate Principles and Ethical Egoism," *Australasian Journal of Philosophy*, XXXV (1957), 111–118. Reprinted by permission of the Editor of the *Australasian Journal of Philosophy*.

People cling to objectivist theories of morality from moral motives. It's a very queer thing that by doing so they often thwart their own purposes. There are evil opinions abroad, as anyone who walks abroad knows. The one we meet with most often, whether in pub or parlour, is the doctrine that everyone should look after himself. However refreshing he may find it after the high-minded pomposities of this morning's editorial, the good fellow knows this doctrine is wrong and he wants to knock it down. But while he believes that moral language is used to make statements either true or false, the best he can do is to claim that what the egoist says is false. Unfortunately, the egoist can claim that it's true. And since the supposed fact in question between them is not a publicly ascertainable one, their disagreement can never be resolved. And it is here that even good fellows waver, when they find they have no refutation available. The egoist's word seems as reliable as their own. Some begin half to believe that perhaps it is possible to supply an egoistic basis for conventional morality, some that it may be impossible to supply any other basis. I'm not going to try to prop up our conventional morality, which I fear to be a task beyond my strength, but in what follows I do want to refute the doctrine of ethical egoism. I want to resolve this disagreement by showing that what the egoist says is inconsistent. It is true that there are moral disagreements which can never be resolved, but this isn't one of them. The proper objection to the man who says 'Everyone should look after his own interests regardless of the interests of others' is not that he isn't speaking the truth, but simply that he isn't speaking.

We should first make two distinctions. This done, ethical egoism will lose much of its plausibility.

UNIVERSAL AND INDIVIDUAL EGOISM

Universal egoism maintains that everyone (including the speaker) ought to look after his own interests and to disregard those of other people except in so far as their interests contribute towards his own.

Individual egoism is the attitude that the egoist is going to look after himself and no one else. The egoist cannot promulgate that he is going to look after himself. He can't even preach that he *should* look after himself and preach this alone. When he tries to convince me that he should look after himself, he is attempting so to dispose me that I shall approve when he drinks my beer and steals Tom's wife. I cannot approve of his looking after himself and himself alone without so far approving of his achieving his happiness, regardless of the happiness of myself and others. So that when he sets out to persuade me that he should look after himself regardless of others, he must also set out to persuade me that I should look after him regardless of myself and others. Very small chance he has! And if the individual egoist cannot promulgate his doctrine without enlarging it, what he has is no doctrine at all.

A person enjoying such an attitude may believe that other people are fools not to look after themselves. Yet he himself would be a fool to tell them so. If he did tell them, though, he wouldn't consider that he was giving them *moral* advice. Persuasion to the effect that one should ignore the claims of morality because morality doesn't pay, to the effect that one has insufficient selfish motive and, therefore, insufficient motive for moral behaviour is not moral persuasion. For this reason I doubt that we should call the individual egoist's attitude an ethical one. And I don't doubt this in the way someone may doubt whether to call the ethical standards of Satan "ethical" standards. A malign morality is none the less a morality for being malign. But the attitude we're considering is one of mere contempt for all moral considerations whatsoever. An indifference to morals may be wicked, but it is not a perverse morality. So far as I am aware, most egoists imagine that they are putting forward a doctrine in ethics, though there may be a few who are prepared to proclaim themselves individual egoists. If the good fellow wants to know how he should justify conventional morality to an individual egoist, the answer is that he shouldn't and can't. Buy your car elsewhere, blackguard him whenever you meet, and let it go at that.

CATEGORICAL AND HYPOTHETICAL EGOISM

Categorical egoism is the doctrine that we all ought to observe our own interests, *because that is what we ought to do*. For the categorical egoist the egoistic dogma is the ultimate principle in ethics.

The hypothetical egoist, on the other hand, maintains that we all ought to observe our own interests, because. . . . If we want such and such an end, we must do so and so (look after ourselves). The hypothetical egoist is not a real egoist at all. He is very likely an unwitting utilitarian who believes mistakenly that the general happiness will be increased if each man looks wisely to his own. Of course, a man may believe that egoism is enjoined on us by God and he may therefore promulgate the doctrine and observe it in his conduct, not in the hope of achieving thereby a remote end, but simply in order to obey God. But neither is *he* a real egoist. He believes, ultimately, that we should obey God, even should God command us to altruism.

An ethical egoist will have to maintain the doctrine in both its universal and categorical forms. Should he retreat to hypothetical egoism he is no longer an egoist. Should he retreat to individual egoism his doctrine, while logically impregnable, is no longer ethical, no longer even a doctrine. He may wish to quarrel with this and if so, I submit peacefully. Let him call himself what he will, it makes no difference. I'm a philosopher, not a rat-catcher, and I don't see it as my job to dig vermin out of such burrows as individual egoism.

Obviously something strange goes on as soon as the ethical egoist tries to promulgate his doctrine. What is he doing when he urges upon his audience that they should each observe his own interests and those interests alone? Is he not acting contrary to the egoistic principle? It cannot be to his advantage to convince them, for seizing always their own advantage they will impair his. Surely if he does believe what he says, he should try to persuade them otherwise. Not perhaps that they should devote themselves to his interests, for they'd hardly swallow that; but that everyone should devote himself to the service of others. But is not to believe that someone should act in a certain way to try to persuade him to do so? Of course, we don't always try to persuade people to act as we think they should act. We may be lazy, for instance. But in so far as we believe that Tom should do so and so, we have a tendency to induce him to do so and so. Does it make sense to say: "Of course you should do this, but for goodness' sake don't"? Only where we mean: "You should do this for certain reasons, but here are even more persuasive reasons for not doing it." If the egoist believes ultimately that others should mind themselves alone, then, he must persuade them accordingly. If he doesn't persuade them, he is no universal egoist. It certainly makes sense to say: "I know very well that Tom should act in such and such a way. But I know also that it's not to my advantage that he should so act. So I'd better dissuade him from it." And this is just what the egoist must say, if he is to consider his own advantage and disregard everyone else's. That is, he must behave as an individual egoist, if he is to be an egoist at all.

He may want to make two kinds of objection here:

1. That it will not be to his disadvantage to promulgate the doctrine, provided that his audience fully understand what is to their ultimate advantage. This objection can be developed in a number of ways, but I think that it will always be possible to push the egoist into either individual or hypothetical egoism.

2. That it is to the egoist's advantage to preach the doctrine if the pleasure he gets out of doing this more than pays for the injuries he must endure at the hands of his converts. It is hard to believe that many people would be satisfied with a doctrine which they could only consistently promulgate in very special circumstances. Besides, this looks suspiciously like individual egoism in disguise.

I shall say no more on these two points because I want to advance a further criticism which seems to me at once fatal and irrefutable.

Now it is time to show the anxious layman that we have means of dealing with ethical egoism which are denied him; and denied him by just that objectivism which he thinks essential to morality. For the very fact that our ultimate principles must be arbitrary means they can't be anything we please. Just because they come out of thin air they can't come out of hot air. Because these principles are not propositions about matters of fact and cannot be deduced from propositions about matters of fact, they must be the fruit of our own attitudes. We assert them largely to modify the attitudes of our fellows but by asserting them we express our own desires and purposes. This means that we cannot use moral language cavalierly. Evidently, we cannot say something like 'All human desires and purposes are bad'. This would be to express our own desires and purposes, thereby committing a kind of absurdity. Nor, I shall argue, can we say 'Everyone should observe his own interests regardless of the interests of others'.

Remembering that the principle is meant to be both universal and categorical, let us ask what kind of attitude the egoist is expressing. Wouldn't that attitude be equally well expressed by the conjunction of an infinite number of avowals thus?—

I want myself to come out on top	and	I don't care about Tom, Dick, Harry . . .
and		and
I want Tom to come out on top	and	I don't care about myself, Dick, Harry . . .
and		and
I want Dick to come out on top	and	I don't care about myself, Tom, Harry . . .

and		and
I want Harry to come out on top	and	I don't care about myself, Dick, Tom . . .
etc.		etc.

From this analysis it is obvious that the principle expressing such an attitude must be inconsistent.

But now the egoist may claim that he hasn't been properly understood. When he says 'Everyone should look after himself and himself alone', he means 'Let each man do what he wants regardless of what anyone else wants'. The egoist may claim that what he values is merely that he and Tom and Dick and Harry should each do what he wants and not care about what anyone else may want and that this doesn't involve his principle in any inconsistency. Nor need it. But even if it doesn't, he's no better off. Just what does he value? Is it the well-being of himself, Tom, Dick and Harry or merely their going on in a certain way regardless of whether or not this is going to promote their well-being? When he urges Tom, say, to do what he wants, is he appealing to Tom's self-interest? If so, his attitude can be expressed thus:

I want myself to be happy		I want myself not to care about
and	and	Tom, Dick, Harry . . .
I want Tom to be happy		

We need go no further to see that the principle expressing such an attitude must be inconsistent. I have made this kind of move already. What concerns me now is the alternative position the egoist must take up to be safe from it. If the egoist values merely that people should go on in a certain way, regardless of whether or not this is going to promote their well-being, then he is not appealing to the self-interest of his audience when he urges them to regard their own interests. If Tom has any regard for himself at all, the egoist's blandishments will leave him cold. Further, the egoist doesn't even have his own interest in mind when he says that, like everyone else, he should look after himself. A funny kind of egoism this turns out to be.

Perhaps now, claiming that he is indeed appealing to the self-interest of his audience, the egoist may attempt to counter the objection of the previous paragraph. He may move into "Let each man do what he wants and let each man disregard what others want when their desires clash with his own". Now his attitude may be expressed thus:

I want everyone to be happy		I want everyone to disregard the happiness of others when their happiness clashes with his own.
	and	

The egoist may claim justly that a man can have such an attitude and also that in a certain kind of world such a man could get what he wanted. Our objection to the egoist has been that his desires are incompatible. And this is still so. If he and Tom and Dick and Harry did go on as he recommends by saying 'Let each man disregard the happiness of others, when their happiness conflicts with his own', then assuredly they'd all be completely miserable. Yet he wants them to be happy. He is attempting to counter this by saying that it is merely a fact about the world that they'd make one another miserable by going on as he recommends. The world could conceivably have been different. For this reason, he says, this principle is not inconsistent. This argument may not seem very compelling, but I advance it on the egoist's behalf because I'm interested in the reply to it. For now we don't even need to tell him that the world isn't in fact like that. (What it's like makes no difference.) Now we can point out to him that he is arguing not as an egoist but as a utilitarian. He has slipped into hypothetical egoism to save his principle from inconsistency. If the world were such that we always made ourselves and others happy by doing one another down, then we could find good utilitarian reasons for urging that we should do one another down.

If, then, he is to save his principle, the egoist must do one of two things. He must give up the claim that he is appealing to the self-interest of his audience, that he has even his own interest in mind. Or he must admit that . . . although 'I want everyone to be happy' refers to ends, nevertheless 'I want everyone to disregard the happiness of others when their happiness conflicts with his own' can refer only to means. That is, his so-called ultimate principle is really compounded of a principle and a moral rule subordinate to that principle. That is, he is really a utilitarian who is urging everyone to go on in a certain way so that everyone may be happy. A utilitarian, what's more, who is ludicrously mistaken about the nature of the world. Things being as they are, his moral rule is a very bad one. Things being as they are, it can only be deduced from his principle by means of an empirical premiss which is manifestly false. Good fellows don't need to fear him. They may rest easy that the world is and must be on their side and the best thing they can do is be good.

It may be worth pointing out that objections similar to those I have brought against the egoist can be made to the altruist. The man who holds that the principle 'Let everyone observe the interests of others' is both universal and categorical can be compelled to choose between two alternatives, equally repugnant. He must give up the claim that he is concerned for the well-being of himself and others. Or he must admit that, though 'I want everyone to be happy' refers to ends, nevertheless 'I want everyone to disregard his own happiness when it conflicts with the happiness of others' can refer only to means.

I have said from time to time that the egoistic principle is inconsistent. I have not said it is contradictory. This for the reason that we can, without contradiction, express inconsistent desires and purposes. To do so is not to say anything like 'Goliath was ten feet tall and not ten feet tall'. Don't we all want to eat our cake and have it too? And when we say we do we aren't asserting a contradiction. We are not asserting a contradiction whether we be making an avowal of our attitudes or stating a fact about them. We all have conflicting motives. As a utilitarian exuding benevolence I want the man who mows my landlord's grass to be happy, but as a slug-a-bed I should like to see him scourged. None of this, however, can do the egoist any good. For we assert our ultimate principles not only to express our own attitudes but also to induce similar attitudes in others, to dispose them to conduct themselves as we wish. In so far as their desires conflict, people don't know what to do. And, therefore, no expression of incompatible desires can ever serve for an ultimate principle of human conduct.

Metaethics

10
THE SUBJECT-MATTER OF ETHICS

G. E. Moore

I

It is very easy to point out some among our every-day judgments, with the truth of which Ethics is undoubtedly concerned. Whenever we say, 'So and so is a good man,' or 'That fellow is a villain'; whenever we ask, 'What ought I to do?' or 'Is it wrong for me to do like this?'; whenever we hazard such remarks as 'Temperance is a virtue and drunkenness a vice'—it is undoubtedly the business of Ethics to discuss such questions and such statements; to argue what is the true answer when we ask what it is right to do, and to give reasons for thinking that our statements about the character of persons or the morality of actions are true or false. In the vast majority of cases, where we make statements involving any of the terms 'virtue,' 'vice,' 'duty,' 'right,' 'ought,' 'good,' 'bad,' we are making ethical judgments; and if we wish to discuss their truth, we shall be discussing a point of Ethics.

So much as this is not disputed; but it falls very far short of defining the province of Ethics. That province may indeed be defined as the whole truth about that which is at the same time common to all such judgments and peculiar to them. But we have still to ask the question: What is it that is thus common and peculiar? And this is a question to which very different answers have been given by ethical philosophers of acknowledged reputation, and none of them, perhaps, completely satisfactory.

II

If we take such examples as those given above, we shall not be far wrong in saying that they are all of them concerned with the question of 'conduct'— with the question, what, in the conduct of us, human beings, is good, and

From G. E. Moore, *Principia Ethica* (Cambridge: Cambridge University Press, 1903), Chap. I, Secs. 1–14, pp. 1–21. Reprinted by permission of the publisher.

what is bad, what is right, and what is wrong. For when we say that a man is good, we commonly mean that he acts rightly; when we say that drunkenness is a vice, we commonly mean that to get drunk is a wrong or wicked action. And this discussion of human conduct is, in fact, that with which the name 'Ethics' is most intimately associated. It is so associated by derivation; and conduct is undoubtedly by far the commonest and most generally interesting object of ethical judgments.

Accordingly, we find that many ethical philosophers are disposed to accept as an adequate definition of 'Ethics' the statement that it deals with the question what is good or bad in human conduct. They hold that its enquiries are properly confined to 'conduct' or to 'practice'; they hold that the name 'practical philosophy' covers all the matter with which it has to do. Now, without discussing the proper meaning of the word (for verbal questions are properly left to the writers of dictionaries and other persons interested in literature; philosophy, as we shall see, has no concern with them), I may say that I intend to use 'Ethics' to cover more than this—a usage, for which there is, I think, quite sufficient authority. I am using it to cover an enquiry for which, at all events, there is no other word: the general enquiry into what is good.

Ethics is undoubtedly concerned with the question what good conduct is; but, being concerned with this, it obviously does not start at the beginning, unless it is prepared to tell us what is good as well as what is conduct. For 'good conduct' is a complex notion: all conduct is not good; for some is certainly bad and some may be indifferent. And on the other hand, other things, beside conduct, may be good; and if they are so, then, 'good' denotes some property, that is common to them and conduct; and if we examine good conduct alone of all good things, then we shall be in danger of mistaking for this property, some property which is not shared by those other things; and thus we shall have made a mistake about Ethics even in this limited sense; for we shall not know what good conduct really is. This is a mistake which many writers have actually made, from limiting their enquiry to conduct. And hence I shall try to avoid it by considering first what is good in general; hoping, that if we can arrive at any certainty about this, it will be much easier to settle the question of good conduct: for we all know pretty well what 'conduct' is. This, then, is our first question: What is good? and What is bad? and to the discussion of this question (or these questions) I give the name of Ethics, since that science must, at all events, include it.

III

But this is a question which may have many meanings. If, for example, each of us were to say 'I am doing good now' or 'I had a good dinner yesterday,' these statements would each of them be some sort of answer to our question, although perhaps a false one. So, too, when A asks B what school he ought to send his son to, B's answer will certainly be an ethical judgment. And similarly all distribution of praise or blame to any personage or thing that has existed, now exists, or will exist, does give some answer to the question 'What is good?' In all such cases some particular thing is judged to be good or bad: the question 'What?' is answered by 'This.' But this is not the sense in which a scientific Ethics asks the question. Not one, of all the many million answers of this kind, which must be true, can form a part of an ethical system; although that science must contain reasons and principles sufficient for deciding on the truth of all of them. There are far too many persons, things and events in the world, past, present, or to come, for a discussion of their individual merits to be embraced in any science. Ethics, therefore, does not deal at all with facts of this nature, facts that are unique, individual, absolutely particular; facts with which such studies as history, geography, astronomy, are compelled, in part at least, to deal. And, for this reason, it is not the business of the ethical philosopher to give personal advice or exhortation.

IV

But there is another meaning which may be given to the question 'What is good?' 'Books are good' would be an answer to it, though an answer obviously false; for some books are very bad indeed. And ethical judgments of this kind do indeed belong to Ethics; though I shall not deal with many of them. Such is the judgment 'Pleasure is good'—a judgment, of which Ethics should discuss the truth, although it is not nearly as important as that other judgment, with which we shall be much occupied presently—'Pleasure *alone* is good.' It is judgments of this sort, which are made in such books on Ethics as contain a list of 'virtues'—in Aristotle's 'Ethics' for example. But it is judgments of precisely the same kind, which form the substance of what is commonly supposed to be a study different from Ethics, and one much less respectable—the study of Casuistry. We may be told that Casuistry differs from Ethics, in that it is much more detailed and particular, Ethics much more general. But it is most important to notice that Casuistry does not deal with anything that is absolutely particular—particular in the only sense in which a perfectly precise line can be drawn between it and what is general. It is not particular in the sense just noticed, the sense in which this book is a particular book, and A's friend's advice particular advice. Casuistry may indeed be *more* particular and Ethics *more* general; but that means that they differ only in degree and not in kind. And this is universally true of 'particular' and 'general,' when used in this common, but inaccurate, sense. So far as Ethics allows itself to give lists of virtues or even to name constituents of the Ideal, it is indistinguishable from Casuistry. Both alike deal with what is general, in the sense in which physics and chemistry deal with what is general. Just as chemistry aims at discovering what are the properties of oxygen, *wherever it occurs*, and not only of this or that particular specimen of oxygen; so Casuistry aims at discovering what actions are good, *whenever they occur*. In this respect Ethics and Casuistry alike are to be classed with such sciences as physics, chemistry and physiology, in their absolute distinction from those of which history and geography are instances. And it is to be noted that, owing to their detailed nature, casuistical investigations are actually nearer to physics and to chemistry than are the investigations usually assigned to Ethics. For just as physics cannot rest content with the discovery that light is propagated by waves of ether, but must go on to discover the particular nature of the ether-waves corresponding to each several colour; so Casuistry, not content with the general law that charity is a virtue must attempt to discover the relative merits of every different form of charity. Casuistry forms, therefore, part of the ideal of ethical science: Ethics cannot be complete without it. The defects of Casuistry are not defects of principle; no objection can be taken to its aim and object. It has failed only because it is far too difficult a subject to be treated adequately in our present state of knowledge. The casuist has been unable to distinguish, in the cases which he treats, those elements upon which their value depends. Hence he often thinks two cases to be alike in respect of value, when in reality they are alike only in some other respect. It is to mistakes of this kind that the pernicious influence of such investigations has been due. For Casuistry is the goal of ethical investigation. It cannot be safely attempted at the beginning of our studies, but only at the end.

V

But our question 'What is good?' may have still another meaning. We may, in the third place, mean to ask, not what thing or things are good, but how 'good' is to be defined. This is an enquiry which belongs only to Ethics, not to Casuistry; and this is the enquiry which will occupy us first.

It is an enquiry to which most special attention should be directed; since this question, how 'good' is to be defined, is the most fundamental question in all Ethics. That which is meant by 'good' is, in fact, except its converse 'bad,' the *only* simple object of thought which is peculiar to Ethics. Its definition is, therefore, the most essential point in the definition of Ethics; and moreover a mistake with regard to it entails a far larger number of erroneous ethical judgments than any other. Unless this first question be fully understood, and its true answer clearly recognised, the rest of Ethics is as good as useless from the point of view of systematic knowledge. True ethical judgments, of the two kinds last dealt with, may indeed be made by those who do not know the answer to this question as well as by those who do; and it goes without saying that the two classes of people may lead equally good lives. But it is extremely unlikely that the *most general* ethical judgments will be equally valid, in the absence of a true answer to this question: I shall presently try to shew that the gravest errors have been largely due to beliefs in a false answer. And, in any case, it is impossible that, till the answer to this question be known, any one should know *what is the evidence* for any ethical judgment whatsoever. But the main object of Ethics, as a systematic science, is to give correct *reasons* for thinking that this or that is good; and, unless this question be answered, such reasons cannot be given. Even, therefore, apart from the fact that a false answer leads to false conclusions, the present enquiry is a most necessary and important part of the science of Ethics.

VI

What, then, is good? How is good to be defined? Now, it may be thought that this is a verbal question. A definition does indeed often mean the expressing of one word's meaning in other words. But this is not the sort of definition I am asking for. Such a definition can never be of ultimate importance in any study except lexicography. If I wanted that kind of definition I should have to consider in the first place how people generally used the word 'good'; but my business is not with its proper usage, as established by custom. I should, indeed, be foolish, if I tried to use it for something which it did not usually denote: if, for instance, I were to announce that, whenever I used the word 'good,' I must be understood to be thinking of that object which is usually denoted by the word 'table.' I shall, therefore, use the word in the sense in which I think it is ordinarily used; but at the same time I am not anxious to discuss whether I am right in thinking that it is so used. My business is solely with that object or idea, which I hold, rightly or wrongly, that the word is generally used to stand for. What I want to discover is the nature of that object or idea, and about this I am extremely anxious to arrive at an agreement.

But, if we understand the question in this sense, my answer to it may seem a very disappointing one. If I am asked 'What is good?' my answer is that good is good, and that is the end of the matter. Or if I am asked 'How is good to be defined?' my answer is that it cannot be defined, and that is all I have to say about it. But disappointing as these answers may appear, they are of the very last importance. To readers who are familiar with philosophic terminology, I can express their importance by saying that they amount to this: That propositions about the good are all of them synthetic and never analytic; and that is plainly no trivial matter. And the same thing may be expressed more popularly, by saying that, if I am right, then nobody can foist upon us such an axiom as that 'Pleasure is the only good' or that 'The good is the desired' on the pretence that this is 'the very meaning of the word.'

VII

Let us, then, consider this position. My point is that 'good' is a simple notion, just as 'yellow' is a simple notion; that, just as you cannot, by any manner of means, explain to any one who does not already know it, what yellow is, so you cannot explain what good is. Definitions of the kind that I was asking for, definitions which describe the real nature of the object or notion denoted by a word, and which do not merely tell us what the word is used to mean, are only possible when the object or notion in question is something complex. You can give a definition of a horse, because a horse has many different properties and qualities, all of which you can enumerate. But when you have enumerated them all, when you have reduced a horse to his simplest terms, then you can no longer define those terms. They are simply something which you think of or perceive, and to any one who cannot think of or perceive them, you can never, by any definition, make their nature known. It may perhaps be objected to this that we are able to describe to others, objects which they have never seen or thought of. We can, for instance, make a man understand what a chimaera is, although he has never heard of one or seen one. You can tell him that it is an animal with a lioness's head and body, with a goat's head growing from the middle of its back, and with a snake in place of a tail. But here the object which you are describing is a complex object; it is entirely composed of parts, with which we are all perfectly familiar—a snake, a goat, a lioness; and we know, too, the manner in which those parts are to be put together, because we know what is meant by the middle of a lioness's back, and where her tail is wont to grow. And so it is with all objects, not previously known, which we are able to define: they are all complex; all composed of parts, which may themselves, in the first instance, be capable of similar definition, but which must in the end be reducible to simplest parts, which can no longer be defined. But yellow and good, we say, are not complex: they are notions of that simple kind, out of which definitions are composed and with which the power of further defining ceases.

VIII

When we say, as Webster says, 'The definition of horse is "A hoofed quadruped of the genus Equus,"' we may, in fact, mean three different things. (1) We may mean merely: 'When I say "horse," you are to understand that I am talking about a hoofed quadruped of the genus Equus.' This might be called the arbitrary verbal definition: and I do not mean that good is indefinable in that sense. (2) We may mean, as Webster ought to mean: 'When most English people say "horse," they mean a hoofed quadruped of the genus Equus.' This may be called the verbal definition proper, and I do not say that good is indefinable in this sense either; for it is certainly possible to discover how people use a word: otherwise, we could never have known that 'good' may be translated by 'gut' in German and by 'bon' in French. But (3) we may, when we define horse, mean something much more important. We may mean that a certain object, which we all of us know, is composed in a certain manner: that it has four legs, a head, a heart, a liver, etc., etc., all of them arranged in definite relations to one another. It is in this sense that I deny good to be definable. I say that it is not composed of any parts, which we can substitute for it in our minds when we are thinking of it. We might think just as clearly and correctly about a horse, if we thought of all its parts and their arrangement instead of thinking of the whole: we could, I say, think how a horse differed from a donkey just as well, just as truly, in this way, as now we do, only not so easily; but there is nothing whatsoever which we could so substitute for good; and that is what I mean, when I say that good is indefinable.

IX

But I am afraid I have still not removed the chief difficulty which may prevent acceptance of the proposition that good is indefinable. I do not mean to say that *the* good, that which is good, is thus indefinable; if I did think so, I should not be writing on Ethics, for my main object is to help towards discovering that definition. It is just because I think there will be less risk of error in our search for a definition of 'the good,' that I am now insisting that *good* is indefinable. I must try to explain the difference between these two. I suppose it may be granted that 'good' is an adjective. Well 'the good,' 'that which is good,' must therefore be the substantive to which the adjective 'good' will apply: it must be the whole of that to which the adjective will apply, and the adjective must *always* truly apply to it. But if it is that to which the adjective will apply, it must be something different from that adjective itself; and the whole of that something different, whatever it is, will be our definition of *the* good. Now it may be that this something will have other adjectives, beside 'good,' that will apply to it. It may be full of pleasure, for example; it may be intelligent: and if these two adjectives are really part of its definition, then it will certainly be true, that pleasure and intelligence are good. And many people appear to think that, if we say 'Pleasure and intelligence are good,' or if we say 'Only pleasure and intelligence are good,' we are defining 'good.' Well, I cannot deny that propositions of this nature may sometimes be called definitions; I do not know well enough how the word is generally used to decide upon this point. I only wish it to be understood that that is not what I mean when I say there is no possible definition of good, and that I shall not mean this if I use the word again. I do most fully believe that some true proposition of the form 'Intelligence is good and intelligence alone is good' can be found; if none could be found, our definition of *the* good would be impossible. As it is, I believe *the* good to be definable; and yet I still say that good itself is indefinable.

X

'Good,' then, if we mean by it that quality which we assert to belong to a thing, when we say that the thing is good, is incapable of any definition, in the most important sense of that word. The most important sense of 'definition' is that in which a definition states what are the parts which invariably compose a certain whole; and in this sense 'good' has no definition because it is simple and has no parts. It is one of those innumerable objects of thought which are themselves incapable of definition, because they are the ultimate terms by reference to which whatever *is* capable of definition must be defined. That there must be an indefinite number of such terms is obvious, on reflection; since we cannot define anything except by an analysis, which, when carried as far as it will go, refers us to something, which is simply different from anything else, and which by that ultimate difference explains the peculiarity of the whole which we are defining: for every whole contains some parts which are common to other wholes also. There is, therefore, no intrinsic difficulty in the contention that 'good' denotes a simple and indefinable quality. There are many other instances of such qualities.

Consider yellow, for example. We may try to define it, by describing its physical equivalent; we may state what kind of light-vibrations must stimulate the normal eye, in order that we may perceive it. But a moment's reflection is sufficient to shew that those light-vibrations are not themselves what we mean by yellow. *They* are not what we perceive. Indeed we should never have been able to discover their existence, unless we had first been struck by the patent difference of quality between the different colours. The most we can be entitled to say of those vibrations is that they are what corresponds in space to the yellow which we actually perceive.

Yet a mistake of this simple kind has commonly been made about 'good.' It may be true that all things which are good are also something else, just as it is true that all things which are yellow produce a certain kind of vibration in the light. And it is a fact, that Ethics aims at discovering what are those other properties belonging to all things which are good. But far too many philosophers have thought that when they named those other properties they were actually defining good; that these properties, in fact, were simply not 'other,' but absolutely and entirely the same with goodness. This view I propose to call the 'naturalistic fallacy' and of it I shall now endeavour to dispose.

XI

Let us consider what it is such philosophers say. And first it is to be noticed that they do not agree among themselves. They not only say that they are right as to what good is, but they endeavour to prove that other people who say that it is something else, are wrong. One, for instance, will affirm that good is pleasure, another, perhaps, that good is that which is desired; and each of these will argue eagerly to prove that the other is wrong. But how is that possible? One of them says that good is nothing but the object of desire, and at the same time tries to prove that it is not pleasure. But from his first assertion, that good just means the object of desire, one of two things must follow as regards his proof:

(1) He may be trying to prove that the object of desire is not pleasure. But, if this be all, where is his Ethics? The position he is maintaining is merely a psychological one. Desire is something which occurs in our minds, and pleasure is something else which so occurs; and our would-be ethical philosopher is merely holding that the latter is not the object of the former. But what has that to do with the question in dispute? His opponent held the ethical proposition that pleasure was the good, and although he should prove a million times over the psychological proposition that pleasure is not the object of desire, he is no nearer proving his opponent to be wrong. The position is like this. One man says a triangle is a circle: another replies 'A triangle is a straight line, and I will prove to you that I am right: *for*' (this is the only argument) 'a straight line is not a circle.' 'That is quite true,' the other may reply; 'but nevertheless a triangle is a circle, and you have said nothing whatever to prove the contrary. What is proved is that one of us is wrong, for we agree that a triangle cannot be both a straight line and a circle: but which is wrong, there can be no earthly means of proving, since you define triangle as straight line and I define it as circle.'—Well, that is one alternative which any naturalistic Ethics has to face; if good is *defined* as something else, it is then impossible either to prove that any other definition is wrong or even to deny such definition.

(2) The other alternative will scarcely be more welcome. It is that the discussion is after all a verbal one. When A says 'Good means pleasant' and B says 'Good means desired,' they may merely wish to assert that most people have used the word for what is pleasant and for what is desired respectively. And this is quite an interesting subject for discussion: only it is not a whit more an ethical discussion than the last was. Nor do I think that any exponent of naturalistic Ethics would be willing to allow that this was all he meant. They are all so anxious to persuade us that what they call the good is what we really ought to do. 'Do, pray, act so, because the word "good" is generally used to denote actions of this nature': such, on this view, would be the substance of their teaching. And in so far as they tell us how we ought to act, their teaching is truly ethical, as they mean it to be. But

how perfectly absurd is the reason they would give for it! 'You are to do this, because most people use a certain word to denote conduct such as this.' 'You are to say the thing which is not, because most people call it lying.' That is an argument just as good!—My dear sirs, what we want to know from you as ethical teachers, is not how people use a word; it is not even, what kind of actions they approve, which the use of this word 'good' may certainly imply: what we want to know is simply what *is* good. We may indeed agree that what most people do think good, is actually so; we shall at all events be glad to know their opinions: but when we say their opinions about what *is* good, we do mean what we say; we do not care whether they call that thing which they mean 'horse' or 'table' or 'chair,' 'gut' or 'bon' or 'ἀγαθός'; we want to know what it is that they so call. When they say 'Pleasure is good," we cannot believe that they merely mean 'Pleasure is pleasure' and nothing more than that.

XII

Suppose a man says 'I am pleased'; and suppose that is not a lie or a mistake but the truth. Well, if it is true, what does that mean? It means that his mind, a certain definite mind, distinguished by certain definite marks from all others, has at this moment a certain definite feeling called pleasure. 'Pleased' *means* nothing but having pleasure, and though we may be more pleased or less pleased, and even, we may admit for the present, have one or another kind of pleasure; yet in so far as it is pleasure we have, whether there be more or less of it, and whether it be of one kind or another, what we have is one definite thing, absolutely indefinable, some one thing that is the same in all the various degrees and in all the various kinds of it that there may be. We may be able to say how it is related to other things: that, for example, it is in the mind, that it causes desire, that we are conscious of it, etc., etc. We can, I say, describe its relations to other things, but define it we can *not*. And if anybody tried to define pleasure for us as being any other natural object; if anybody were to say, for instance, that pleasure *means* the sensation of red, and were to proceed to deduce from that that pleasure is a colour, we should be entitled to laugh at him and to distrust his future statements about pleasure. Well, that would be the same fallacy which I have called the naturalistic fallacy. That 'pleased' does not mean 'having the sensation of red,' or anything else whatever, does not prevent us from understanding what it does mean. It is enough for us to know that 'pleased' does mean 'having the sensation of pleasure,' and though pleasure is absolutely indefinable, though pleasure is pleasure and nothing else whatever, yet we feel no difficulty in saying that we are pleased. The reason is, of course, that when I say 'I am pleased,' I do *not* mean that 'I' am the same thing as 'having pleasure.' And similarly no difficulty need be found in my saying that 'pleasure is good' and yet not meaning that 'pleasure' is the same thing as 'good,' that pleasure *means* good, and that good *means* pleasure. If I were to imagine that when I said 'I am pleased,' I meant that I was exactly the same thing as 'pleased,' I should not indeed call that a naturalistic fallacy, although it would be the same fallacy as I have called naturalistic with reference to Ethics. The reason of this is obvious enough. When a man confuses two natural objects with one another, defining the one by the

other, if for instance, he confuses himself, who is one natural object, with
'pleased' or with 'pleasure' which are others, then there is no reason to call
the fallacy naturalistic. But if he confuses 'good,' which is not in the same
sense a natural object, with any natural object whatever, then there is a
reason for calling that a naturalistic fallacy; its being made with regard to
'good' marks it as something quite specific, and this specific mistake deserves
a name because it is so common. As for the reasons why good is not to be
considered a natural object, they may be reserved for discussion in another
place. But, for the present, it is sufficient to notice this: Even if it were a
natural object, that would not alter the nature of the fallacy nor diminish its
importance one whit. All that I have said about it would remain quite
equally true: only the name which I have called it would not be so appropriate as I think it is. And I do not care about the name: what I do care
about is the fallacy. It does not matter what we call it, provided we
recognise it when we meet with it. It is to be met with in almost every book
on Ethics; and yet it is not recognised: and that is why it is necessary to
multiply illustrations of it, and convenient to give it a name. It is a very
simple fallacy indeed. When we say that an orange is yellow, we do not
think our statement binds us to hold that 'orange' means nothing else than
'yellow,' or that nothing can be yellow but an orange. Supposing the orange
is also sweet! Does that bind us to say that 'sweet' is exactly the same thing
as 'yellow,' that 'sweet' must be defined as 'yellow'? And supposing it be
recognised that 'yellow' just means 'yellow' and nothing else whatever, does
that make it any more difficult to hold that oranges are yellow? Most
certainly it does not: on the contrary, it would be absolutely meaningless to
say that oranges were yellow, unless yellow did in the end mean just
'yellow' and nothing else whatever—unless it was absolutely indefinable. We
should not get any very clear notion about things, which are yellow—we
should not get very far with our science, if we were bound to hold that
everything which was yellow, *meant* exactly the same thing as yellow. We
should find we had to hold that an orange was exactly the same thing as a
stool, a piece of paper, a lemon, anything you like. We could prove any
number of absurdities; but should we be the nearer to the truth? Why, then,
should it be different with 'good'? Why, if good is good and indefinable,
should I be held to deny that pleasure is good? Is there any difficulty in
holding both to be true at once? On the contrary, there is no meaning in
saying that pleasure is good, unless good is something different from
pleasure. It is absolutely useless, so far as Ethics is concerned, to prove, as
Mr. Spencer tries to do, that increase of pleasure coincides with increase of
life, unless good *means* something different from either life or pleasure. He
might just as well try to prove that an orange is yellow by shewing that it
always is wrapped up in paper.

XIII

In fact, if it is not the case that 'good' denotes something simple and
indefinable, only two alternatives are possible: either it is a complex, a given
whole, about the correct analysis of which there may be disagreement; or
else it means nothing at all, and there is no such subject as Ethics. In general,
however, ethical philosophers have attempted to define good, without

recognising what such an attempt must mean. They actually use arguments which involve one or both of the absurdities considered in §II. We are, therefore, justified in concluding that the attempt to define good is chiefly due to want of clearness as to the possible nature of definition. There are, in fact, only two serious alternatives to be considered, in order to establish the conclusion that 'good' does denote a simple and indefinable notion. It might possibly denote a complex, as 'horse' does; or it might have no meaning at all. Neither of these possibilities has, however, been clearly conceived and seriously maintained, as such, by those who presume to define good; and both may be dismissed by a simple appeal to facts.

(1) The hypothesis that disagreement about the meaning of good is disagreement with regard to the correct analysis of a given whole, may be most plainly seen to be incorrect by consideration of the fact that, whatever definition be offered, it may be always asked, with significance, of the complex so defined, whether it is itself good. To take, for instance, one of the more plausible, because one of the more complicated, of such proposed definitions, it may easily be thought, at first sight, that to be good may mean to be that which we desire to desire. Thus if we apply this definition to a particular instance and say 'When we think that A is good, we are thinking that A is one of the things which we desire to desire,' our proposition may seem quite plausible. But, if we carry the investigation further, and ask ourselves 'Is it good to desire to desire A?' it is apparent, on a little reflection, that this question is itself as intelligible, as the original question 'Is A good'—that we are, in fact, now asking for exactly the same information about the desire to desire A, for which we formerly asked with regard to A itself. But it is also apparent that the meaning of this second question cannot be correctly analysed into 'Is the desire to desire A one of the things which we desire to desire?': we have not before our minds anything so complicated as the question 'Do we desire to desire to desire to desire A?' Moreover any one can easily convince himself by inspection that the predicate of this proposition—'good'—is positively different from the notion of 'desiring to desire' which enters into its subject: 'That we should desire to desire A is good' is *not* merely equivalent to 'That A should be good is good.' It may indeed be true that what we desire to desire is always also good; perhaps, even the converse may be true: but it is very doubtful whether this is the case, and the mere fact that we understand very well what is meant by doubting it, shews clearly that we have two different notions before our minds.

(2) And the same consideration is sufficient to dismiss the hypothesis that 'good' has no meaning whatsoever. It is very natural to make the mistake of supposing that what is universally true is of such a nature that its negation would be self-contradictory: the importance which has been assigned to analytic propositions in the history of philosophy shews how easy such a mistake is. And thus it is very easy to conclude that what seems to be a universal ethical principle is in fact an identical proposition; that, if, for example, whatever is called 'good' seems to be pleasant, the proposition 'Pleasure is the good' does not assert a connection between two different notions, but involves only one, that of pleasure, which is easily recognised as a distinct entity. But whoever will attentively consider with himself what is actually before his mind when he asks the question 'Is pleasure (or whatever

it may be) after all good?' can easily satisfy himself that he is not merely wondering whether pleasure is pleasant. And if he will try this experiment with each suggested definition in succession, he may become expert enough to recognise that in every case he has before his mind a unique object, with regard to the connection of which with any other object, a distinct question may be asked. Every one does in fact understand the question 'Is this good?' When he thinks of it, his state of mind is different from what it would be, were he asked 'Is this pleasant, or desired, or approved?' It has a distinct meaning for him, even though he may not recognise in what respect it is distinct. Whenever he thinks of 'intrinsic value,' or 'intrinsic worth,' or says that a thing 'ought to exist,' he has before his mind the unique object—the unique property of things—which I mean by 'good.' Everybody is constantly aware of this notion, although he may never become aware at all that it is different from other notions of which he is also aware. But, for correct ethical reasoning, it is extremely important that he should become aware of this fact; and, as soon as the nature of the problem is clearly understood, there should be little difficulty in advancing so far in analysis.

XIV

'Good,' then, is indefinable; and yet, so far as I know, there is only one ethical writer, Prof. Henry Sidgwick, who has clearly recognised and stated this fact. We shall see, indeed, how far many of the most reputed ethical systems fall short of drawing the conclusions which follow from such a recognition. At present I will only quote one instance, which will serve to illustrate the meaning and importance of this principle that 'good' is indefinable, or, as Prof. Sidgwick says, an 'unanalysable notion.' It is an instance to which Prof. Sidgwick himself refers in a note on the passage, in which he argues that 'ought' is unanalysable[1].

'Bentham,' says Sidgwick, 'explains that his fundamental principle "states the greatest happiness of all those whose interest is in question as being the right and proper end of human action" '; and yet 'his language in other passages of the same chapter would seem to imply' that he *means* by the word "right" "conducive to the general happiness." Prof. Sidgwick sees that, if you take these two statements together, you get the absurd result that 'greatest happiness is the end of human action, which is conducive to the general happiness'; and so absurd does it seem to him to call this result, as Bentham calls it, 'the fundamental principle of a moral system,' that he suggests that Bentham cannot have meant it. Yet Prof. Sidgwick himself states elsewhere[2] that Psychological Hedonism is 'not seldom confounded with Egoistic Hedonism'; and that confusion, as we shall see, rests chiefly on that same fallacy, the naturalistic fallacy, which is implied in Bentham's statements. Prof. Sidgwick admits therefore that this fallacy is sometimes committed, absurd as it is; and I am inclined to think that Bentham may really have been one of those who committed it. Mill, as we shall see, certainly did commit it. In any case, whether Bentham committed it or not, his doctrine, as above quoted, will serve as a very good illustration of this

[1] *Methods of Ethics,* Bk. I, Chap. iii, § 1 (6th edition).
[2] *Methods of Ethics,* Bk. I, Chap. iv, § 1.

fallacy, and of the importance of the contrary proposition that good is indefinable.

Let us consider this doctrine. Bentham seems to imply, so Prof. Sidgwick says, that the word 'right' *means* 'conducive to general happiness.' Now this, by itself, need not necessarily involve the naturalistic fallacy. For the word 'right' is very commonly appropriated to actions which lead to the attainment of what is good; which are regarded as *means* to the ideal and not as ends-in-themselves. This use of 'right,' as denoting what is good as a means, whether or not it be also good as an end, is indeed the use to which I shall confine the word. Had Bentham been using 'right' in this sense, it might be perfectly consistent for him to *define* right as 'conducive to the general happiness,' *provided only* (and notice this proviso) he had already proved, or laid down as an axiom, that general happiness was *the* good, or (what is equivalent to this) that general happiness alone was good. For in that case he would have already defined *the* good as general happiness (a position perfectly consistent, as we have seen, with the contention that 'good' is indefinable), and, since right was to be defined as 'conducive to *the* good,' it would actually *mean* 'conducive to general happiness.' But this method of escape from the charge of having committed the naturalistic fallacy has been closed by Bentham himself. For his fundamental principle is, we see, that the greatest happiness of all concerned is the *right* and proper *end* of human action. He applies the word 'right,' therefore, to the end, as such, not only to the means which are conducive to it; and, that being so, right can no longer be defined as 'conducive to the general happiness,' without involving the fallacy in question. For now it is obvious that the definition of right as conducive to general happiness can be used by him in support of the fundamental principle that general happiness is the right end; instead of being itself derived from that principle. If right, by definition, means conducive to general happiness, then it is obvious that general happiness is the right end. It is not necessary now first to prove or assert that general happiness is the right end, before right is defined as conducive to general happiness—a perfectly valid procedure; but on the contrary the definition of right as conducive to general happiness proves general happiness to be the right end—a perfectly invalid procedure, since in this case the statement that 'general happiness is the right end of human action' is not an ethical principle at all, but either, as we have seen, a proposition about the meaning of words, or else a proposition about the *nature* of general happiness, not about its rightness or goodness.

Now, I do not wish the importance I assign to this fallacy to be misunderstood. The discovery of it does not at all refute Bentham's contention that greatest happiness is the proper end of human action, if that be understood as an ethical proposition, as he undoubtedly intended it. That principle may be true all the same; we shall consider whether it is so in succeeding chapters. Bentham might have maintained it, as Prof. Sidgwick does, even if the fallacy had been pointed out to him. What I am maintaining is that the *reasons* which he actually gives for his ethical proposition are fallacious ones so far as they consist in a definition of right. What I suggest is that he did not perceive them to be fallacious; that, if he had done so, he would have been led to seek for other reasons in support of his Utilitarianism; and that, had he sought for other reasons, he *might* have found none which he thought to be sufficient. In that case he would have changed his whole system—a most important consequence. It is undoubtedly also possible that he would have thought other reasons to be sufficient, and in that case his ethical system, in its main results, would still have stood. But, even in this latter case, his use of the fallacy would be a serious objection to him as an ethical philosopher. For it is the business of Ethics, I must insist, not only to obtain true results, but also to find valid reasons for them. The direct object of Ethics is knowledge and not practice; and any one who uses the naturalistic fallacy has certainly not fulfilled this first object, however correct his practical principles may be.

My objections to Naturalism are then, in the first place, that it offers no reason at all, far less any valid reason, for any ethical principle whatever; and in this it already fails to satisfy the requirements of Ethics, as a scientific study. But in the second place I contend that, though it gives a reason for no ethical principle, it is a *cause* of the acceptance of false principles—it deludes the mind into accepting ethical principles, which are false; and in this it is contrary to every aim of Ethics. It is easy to see that if we start with a definition of right conduct as conduct conducive to general happiness; then, knowing that right conduct is universally conduct conducive to the good, we very easily arrive at the result that the good is general happiness. If, on the other hand, we once recognise that we must start our Ethics without a definition, we shall be much more apt to look about us, before we adopt any ethical principle whatever; and the more we look about us, the less likely are we to adopt a false one. It may be replied to this: Yes, but we shall look about us just as much, before we settle on our definition, and are therefore just as likely to be right. But I will try to shew that this is not the case. If we start with the conviction that a definition of good can be found, we start with the conviction that good *can mean* nothing else than some one property of things; and our only business will then be to discover what that property is. But if we recognise that, so far as the meaning of good goes, anything whatever may be good, we start with a much more open mind. Moreover, apart from the fact that, when we think we have a definition, we cannot logically defend our ethical principles in any way whatever, we shall also be much less apt to defend them well, even if illogically. For we shall start with the conviction that good must mean so and so, and shall therefore be inclined either to misunderstand our opponent's arguments or to cut them short with the reply, 'This is not an open question: the very meaning of the word decides it; no one can think otherwise except through confusion.'

xv

Our first conclusion as to the subject-matter of Ethics is, then, that there is a simple, indefinable, unanalysable object of thought by reference to which it must be defined. . . .

THE DEFINITION OF VALUE
IN TERMS OF INTEREST

R. B. Perry

One can generally tell a man's special field of investigation by the words which he uses carefully and the words he uses carelessly. The physicist now uses the word 'atom' carefully; that is, he is prepared to say what he means by it. The geneticist is careful with such words as 'heredity' and 'environment'; the theologian with the word 'god'; the logician with 'proposition' and 'implication'; the mathematician with the word 'number'; the economist with the words 'price' and 'demand'; the political scientist with the word 'sovereignty.' Everyone except the specialist uses these words carelessly. The philosopher who is engaged in that branch of philosophy now known as "theory of value" is distinguished by the fact that the word which he is most careful about is the word 'value.'

Everyone else uses this word carelessly. There is a usage of common sense, as when it is said that men lose sight of "higher value" when they practice power politics, or lose sight of "values" altogether in the machine age; or when it is said that it is the task of a humanistic education to make students aware of the "values" of life. 'Value' is now a favorite word among the sociologists, psychologists, and psychiatrists. The word is scattered through the text, and even mentioned in the index; but it is used like 'and,' 'but,' and the nouns and adjectives of everyday speech, as though its meaning were so well understood as to require no examination. The theorist of value, on the other hand, is one who asks, of himself and of others, "Precisely what is meant by 'value'?" It is his business to have an answer to that question. In other words, 'value' is his *careful* word.

The question, "What does 'value' mean?" is not the same as the question "What things have value?" Though the two questions are often confused, the difference is evident when attention is called to it. The statement that "a sphere is a body of space bounded by one surface all points of which are equally distant from a point within called its center" is different from the

---

statement that "the earth is (or is not) a sphere." The statement that peace is a condition in which societies abstain from the use of violence in settling their disputes, is different from the statement that the world is (or is not) now at peace. And similarly, a statement, such as is proposed below, of what value is, differs from the statement that peace is valuable.

If the second of each of these pairs of statements is to be definitive and accurate it is clearly advisable to have in mind the first. If, in other words, one is to know whether peace is or is not valuable, it is well to know what 'valuable' is: in other words, to know what it is that is stated about peace when it is stated that it is valuable. But while the question raised by the second statement depends on an answer to the question raised by the first, the two questions are not the same question. And it is the first question with which the present inquiry is primarily concerned. In other words, theory of value ascribes value to things only in the light of what 'value' means.

Some philosophers, unfortunately, put the question concerning value in the form "What *is* meant by 'value'?" or "What *does* one mean by 'value'?" as though that meaning were already determined, and it was only necessary to call attention to it. Those who approach the matter in this way are accustomed to challenge a proposed definition of value by saying, "But this is not what is meant by 'value' " or "This is not what one means by 'value.' " The fact is, however, that there is no such established and universal meaning. Different people mean different things in different contexts. The problem is not to discover a present meaning—there are only too many meanings.

The problem is not solved, however, by simply enumerating these many meanings. This job is already done by the unabridged dictionaries which list, in fine print, all the varieties of meaning which appear in literature and ordinary speech. Theory of value is in search of a preferred meaning. The problem is to define, that is, *give* a meaning to the term, either by selecting from its existing meanings, or by creating a new meaning.

But one must not then leap to the conclusion that this giving of a meaning to the term 'value' is an arbitrary matter, dictated by the caprice, or mere personal convenience, of the author. One can, it is true, make the term mean "anything one likes," but this would not advance knowledge, or be of the slightest importance, or be capable either of proof or of disproof. The man who said "When I say 'value' I mean a purple cow" would not even be listened to, unless by a psychiatrist or a kindergarten teacher. There must, in other words, be a control or set of criteria, by which the definition is justified or rejected.

According to the definition of value here proposed, *a thing—any thing— has value, or is valuable, in the original and generic sense when it is the object of an interest—any interest. Or, whatever is [an] object of interest is ipso facto valuable.* Thus the valuableness of peace is the characteristic conferred on peace by the interest which is taken in it, for what it is, or for any of its attributes, effects, or implications.

Value is thus defined in terms of interest, and its meaning thus depends on another definition, namely, a definition of interest. The following is here proposed: interest is *a train of events determined by expectation of its outcome.* Or, *a thing is an object of interest when its being expected induces actions looking to its realization or non-realization.* Thus peace is an object of interest when acts believed to be conducive to peace, or preventive of peace, are performed on that account, or when events are selected or rejected because peace is expected of them.

Both of these definitions require clarification and elaboration; but these summary statements will suffice for the present purpose of indicating the criterion by which the definitions are to be justified. These criteria are three in number, namely, *linguistic, formal,* and *empirical.* When the definition is challenged it must defend itself on three grounds: its use of words; the clarity, definiteness, tenability, and fruitfulness of the concepts which it employs; and its capacity to describe certain facts of life, to which it refers, and by which it is verified. The definition is designed, in other words, to be at one and the same time, a nominal definition, an abstract or *a priori* definition, and a "real" definition.

2

In the first place, then, definition names, or affixes a verbal label; and in thus creating a verbal usage it has to take account of existing verbal usage. The fundamental purpose of naming is "ostensive"; that is to say, it identifies some object (thing, quality, act, relation, region, event) so that it may be subsequently recovered, and referred to in communication with others. It serves the purpose of directing the attention of several minds, or of the same mind at different times, to the same locus in the mind's environment.

Pure naming is conventional, that is, no account need be taken of any antecedent ostensive meaning, but only of brevity, euphony, and duplication. But naming is rarely, if ever, pure. In order that it should be pure the name would have to be new, that is, an arbitrary symbol invented on the spot. Verbal names, however, are usually secondhand; that is, the name has an antecedent usage, which renders its present usage appropriate or inappropriate. Even proper names, such as 'Rose' and 'Violet,' are commonly secondhand names. It is true that their use as proper names may become wholly, or almost wholly, divested of their original meanings; so that it would be absurd to dispute their application to a given person on the ground that she was in fact not rose or violet in color, but white or brown. But there is nevertheless a suggestion of flowerlike fragility which would render it inappropriate to give the name of 'Rose' or 'Violet,' except in an ironic sense, to a heavyweight prize fighter. Place names—of mountains, rivers, cities, and countries—arise from mixed motives. They are not merely labels by which the place is marked on the map for future reference, but, like 'Rocky Mountains,' ascribe to it the characteristics already designated by some common name; or, like 'America,' they say something about its history by borrowing the antecedent name of its supposed discoverer.

The words 'value' and 'interest' which are used in the present definition are secondhand names. Although they are here given a sharper meaning, to be consistently maintained, their appropriateness must be judged by their history and suggestiveness. In the light of existing usage do they serve well as pointers to focus the discussion on a certain region of inquiry?

In the present writer's early Harvard days the word 'value' was first beginning to become current in American philosophy, largely through the influence of Hugo Münsterberg, who, in addition to being a psychologist, was also a follower of the neo-Fichtean school of Windelband and Rickert. In fact, since Münsterberg learned to speak English fluently before he learned to pronounce it correctly, his students heard of "walues" before they heard of "values." Münsterberg would be scandalized by the liberties which have been taken with the word since his day. For with Münsterberg and his school, "values" possessed an exalted dignity transcending both nature and sense-perception. They have since become completely secularized, mingling with the affairs of everyday life, and consorting intimately with the vulgar facts of sense-experience. They have even been desecrated by psychologists, in violation of that *Anti-Psychologismus* [Anti-Psychologism] which was once with German philosophers a sort of Oath of Hippocrates.

Before the word 'value' could acquire that generality of meaning required for a philosophical theory of value, it was necessary to overrule the economists who had become accustomed to claim its exclusive use. But Adam Smith and John Stuart Mill had distinguished "value in use" from "value in exchange," and, in so using the same word twice, had already broadened its meaning to apply to a field of which economic value was only a circumscribed part.

Since the beginning of the present century, the word 'value' has acquired a popular use which has eclipsed its transcendental use by neo-Fichtean philosophers and its technical use by economists. The conscious employment of propaganda has called attention to the diversity of creeds and codes by which different human societies are governed, and these are frequently referred to as different beliefs concerning what has "value," or "supreme value." At the same time the word 'ideology' has acquired vogue as the name for a set of ideas which concern "values" as distinguished from matters of fact. The signal failure of natural science to save mankind from war and its destructive effects is often attributed to the fact that science ignores "values"; and the world looks to religion or liberal education to restore them.

The word 'value' is, then, a good name, because its history suggests that there is something common to duty and piety, price and utility, ideals and codes. At the same time it points toward that aspect of human life for which it is customary to employ the eulogistic-dyslogistic vocabulary. It points to other pointers, and borrows the ostensive meaning of such adjectives as 'good,' 'best,' 'right,' 'ought,' 'worthy,' 'beautiful,' 'sacred,' 'just,' and such nouns as 'happiness,' 'well-being,' and 'civilization.' As a common name for what these words name, it suggests a common meaning, or the attempt to find a common meaning. Of the words which already have such ostensive meaning, and which will therefore serve as guideposts, 'value' best combines specific reference with breadth and flexibility.

The word 'value' has also a grammatical convenience, in that it possesses substantive, adjectival, and verbal variants. We can speak of "values," of "valuable," and of the act of "valuing." This is, however, a dubious advantage, since it has given rise to serious ambiguities. Thus *a* value, in the substantive sense, may mean either *that which* has value, such as gold or justice; or a *kind* of value which it has, such as economic or moral. These distinctions are analogous to those between the determinable 'color,' the determinant 'red,' and the instance, such as 'the rose.'

'Valuable' like 'value' suffers from the defect that it is sometimes taken to refer only to what is "good," "right," etc., and to exclude the opposites, 'bad,' 'wrong,' etc., which clearly belong to the same field of discourse. There is no way of escaping this difficulty except by the awkward expedient of distinguishing the "positively" and "negatively," or "eulogistically" and "dyslogistically," valuable, thus giving a broader meaning to the unmodified adjective when it refers to both.

Most insidious and disastrous of all is the ambiguity attaching to the verb 'to value,' which may mean *making* valuable, or *judging* to be valuable. Similarly, to "value a thing highly" may mean either to care greatly for it, and thus to *give* it great value, as when one loves money; or it may mean to *ascribe* great value to it in some scale of comparative magnitude, as when one judges money to be more precious than sleep. And sometimes 'to value,' or 'to evaluate,' means to assign value to an object for *reasons*, that is, because it possesses certain characteristics, as when one values money for what it will buy. These differences must not be overlooked as a result of economy of speech.

3

The second of the words employed in the proposed definition of value is the word 'interest.' Here, again, the word selected is an old word, already used as a name, but selected because of all the old words it seems the best word to substitute for a class of words—'liking,' 'desiring,' 'willing,' 'loving,' 'hoping,' etc., and their opposites; and to suggest a common ostensive meaning as distinguished from that of another class of words embracing 'sensing,' 'perceiving,' 'thinking,' 'judging,' etc. If the word is to be used in this sense, however, it is necessary to exclude certain senses which are either too broad or too narrow.

In its broader use 'interest' is a synonym of attention; and the adjective 'interesting' is applied to any object or topic which attracts attention or excites curiosity, such as the sudden, novel, surprising, or contrasting. In this sense, a noise breaking into silence, or one's own name unexpectedly pronounced, immediately draws attention to itself and alerts the hearer. No doubt interest in this sense is commonly associated with feeling, desire, etc., but there is a difference nonetheless between sheer attentiveness—the turn of the head, shift of the eye, or focusing of consciousness—and the liking, desiring, etc., by which this may be conditioned, accompanied, or followed. This broader reference being eliminated, the word 'interest' points to attitudes of *for* and *against*, or what are sometimes called "motor-affective" attitudes, as when one says, "I am interested in the outcome," or "all interested parties should be excluded."

But here we encounter a sense of the word that is excessively narrow, its reference, namely, to self-interest or selfishness, which is a special case of interest. We need a use of the word such that the nurse's interest in her patient's recovery or relief from pain is as much an interest as her interest in gainful employment. The latter, or selfish, meaning is reflected in the use of the word 'disinterestedness' to signify interest directed to others. This word involves a flagrant ambiguity. There is a crucial difference between the absence or subordination of self-interest, and that state of apathy in which there is no interest at all. It is unfortunate that the word 'disinterested,' as when we speak of the disinterested judge, is used to mean breadth and inclusiveness of interest. It would be less misleading to say 'all-interested.'

A second excessively narrow use of the word 'interest' is that in which it refers to the collective, and more or less permanent, interest of a social group, as when one speaks of "the interest of labor" or "the interest of the consumer." The expression '*the* interests,' used in a political context, suggests interest that is both selfish and collective or permanent. But if the word is to be used in these restricted senses, then there is need of another and broader use which makes it possible to speak of interests which are generous, or fleeting and individual.

Despite these ambiguities, the word 'interest' is the least misleading name for a certain class of acts or states which have the common characteristic of *being for or against*. The expressions 'motor-affective attitudes' or 'attitudes of favor and disfavor' serve as its best paraphrases. 'Caring' and 'concern' are also convenient synonyms. The absence of interest is indifference, as when one says, "It makes no difference to me," "I do not care," or "It is of no concern to me." Indifference is to be distinguished from negative interest. Thus one speaks of not caring, or of its making no difference "one way or the other," implying that interest embraces both ways. It is especially significant to note that the words for which 'interest' is substituted come in pairs of opposites, which are not related simply as grammatical positives and negatives.

'Interest,' then, is to be taken as a class name for such names as 'liking'–'disliking,' 'loving'–'hating,' 'hoping'–'fearing,' 'desiring'–'avoiding,' and countless other kindred names. What they all ostensibly mean is what *it* ostensibly means. It invites attention to that to which they in their severalty and community already invite our attention. It will occasionally, for reasons of diction, be convenient to use some one of these more restricted names to stand for the rest. But if the term 'interest' is used with reasonable consistency to stand for them all then these richer words can be used as names for the different species of the genus which will be introduced in the further elaboration of the subject.

4

Definition does not merely name, it also *conceives*. It fixes upon an intelligible meaning. It may put together old meanings, so as to create new meanings. Although the mind may conceive freely—that is, may conceive or not, and may conceive an infinite variety of abstract or ideal objects—when it does conceive, and whatever it conceives, it is subject to certain requirements which are inherent in the nature of conceiving. These may be referred to as the "formal" requirements of a definition. They are the conditions which a theory must satisfy *qua* theory; that is, in advance of being verified. Are the concepts here employed "intelligible?" How are statements about interest as here conceived to be translated into statements about value? Does such a translation result in contradiction, confusion, and sterility? Is it fruitful and illuminating? Does it violate any fundamental logical or epistemological requirement? But at this point it is appropriate to introduce certain objections which, if valid, would save the trouble of proceeding further.

It has been objected, in the first place, that all or most of the words of the class here represented by the word 'value' (words such as 'good,' 'bad,' etc.) have *no* conceptual meaning, but only a so-called "emotive" meaning.[1] In other words, statements in which such words appear as predicates are not statements at all, but utterances. They have no objectivity, and are neither true nor false; but merely express the attitude of the person who makes them, and his desire to convert others to the same attitude. They are communicative and persuasive, but they are not cognitive and informative. Thus it is held that the word 'good' in the judgment that "Francis of Assisi was good," refers to no Franciscan characteristic, actual or alleged, but merely reflects the fact that the maker of the judgment esteems Saint Francis, and desires that others shall also esteem him.

There is no doubt of the fact that words are commonly used with an expressive, commendatory, or disparaging intent. A love poem or a political diatribe is not the same thing as a mathematical theorem or scientific statement. Words such as 'fascist' and 'red' lose their conceptual meaning and degenerate into smear words; "the land of the free and the home of the brave" may serve only to express and arouse a love of country. Most verbal statements, however, have *both* an objective and an emotive meaning. The mixture of meanings appears in the fact that either of two retorts is appropriate. Thus if a man is called a "red" in a community in which this word is offensive, he may either become angry, or affirm his belief in capitalism. Ordinarily he will do both: that is, angrily affirm his belief in capitalism. If a man is called a "reactionary" he is no doubt condemned; but he is also conceived as wedded to the past. He can defend himself either by retaliating upon his accuser with the word 'radical,' or by pointing to his interest in the future.

A word having only an emotive meaning like the word 'fie!' is the extreme opposite of a word having only a conceptual meaning, like the word 'ellipse.' The great body of human discourse, however, lies between these extremes. If verbal usage were to be so amended as to leave only exclamations, exhortations, compliments, and insults, on the one hand, and rigorous scientific concepts, on the other hand, most persons all of the time, and all persons, including scientists, most of the time, would have to remain mute. Statements which employ such terms as 'good' and 'bad' may, and usually do, convey objectively meaningful concepts, either expressly or by implication. Thus when Saint Francis is judged to be good, the fact that he fed the birds, and thus manifested loving-kindness to living things, is taken as *constituting* his goodness. Or, suppose that *A*, addressing himself to *B*, states that Lincoln was a "good" man *in that* he hated war, felt compassion for soldiers, and emancipated the slaves. *A* is not simply expressing his admiration for the kind of man Lincoln was, and his desire that *B* shall feel likewise. He is identifying the concept of good with the concept of

[1] Cf. C. L. Stevenson, *Ethics and Language*, 1948, *passim*. Much of the ethical controversy which this book has excited would have been avoided if the book had held strictly to its title. It would then have been treated like a book on "physics and language"—interesting, but not physics.

humanity, and ascribing it to Lincoln on the objective evidence of Lincoln's behavior.

The fact is that what force the argument has arises not from the absence of objective conceptual meanings, but from their abundance and variety. The argument reduces, then, to this: that there are no *invariable* objective meanings attaching to such terms as 'good' and 'bad' in common usage. Sometimes they mean one thing, sometimes another. Well, what of it? It is the business of theory of value to define such an invariable meaning. It is unlikely that because the word 'matter' has no common objective meaning as currently used it therefore has only a subjective or social meaning. Similarly, there is not the slightest reason why theory of value should be limited to ready-made meanings; should, in other words, be content to be a contemporary history of ideas, instead of undertaking that systematization of concepts which is the essential task of theory of value, of physical and chemical theory, in short, of all theory.

To reject the extravagances of the emotivist theory does not imply that judgments employing value terms are not peculiarly likely to be imbued with emotive meaning; nor does it forbid the supposition that judgments employing these terms may, in certain contexts, be wholly, or almost wholly, expressive and persuasive in their intent.

5

It may be objected, secondly, that while the word 'value' does have an objective, conceptual meaning, that meaning is indefinable. According to one variety of this view, value, or some equivalent, such as good or right, is a specific, irreducible, "non-natural" characteristic.[2] Its being "non-natural" means that it is neither physical nor mental, and therefore cannot be empirically observed. It can, however, so it is alleged, be seen by the eye of the mind, and, when so seen, it is seen to be unique and unanalyzable.

Although volumes have been written for and against this contention, it should require no argument whatever. If unanalyzable value is *there* within the range of intellectual vision, it should be possible, after a reasonable amount of effort, to bring it into focus. He who fails to find it cannot but conclude that there is no such thing; especially when the authors of the doctrine do not agree among themselves on what they find.

According to another variety of the view, value is an indefinable empirical quality, or a class of indefinable qualities such as pleasant, enticing, fascinating, awesome, revolting, etc.[3] These qualities are in some way connected with feelings—either they consist in feeling, or are apprehended through feeling—hence they may be designated "affective qualities." Since, like the "secondary qualities" color and sound, they have a *prima facie* objectivity, they are sometimes called "tertiary qualities."

This is not the place to examine the merits of this view, except as concerns the question of analyzability. As sensation blends with sensation to create a new quality (such as a fused tone or color), so sensation blended with

---

[2] This is the position taken by G. E. Moore, W. D. Ross and others of the so-called "Cambridge" or "Intuitionist" school.

[3] This view is to be found in G. Santayana, *Sense of Beauty*, 1899; and in J. Laird, *Study in Realism*, 1920.

feeling possesses an integral character which is distinguishable from the characters of its constituents. But this can scarcely be cited as evidence against analyzability since it is a statement of precisely what, in the field of sense-perception, analysis is. The problem presented is the problem presented by all analysis. There is a sense in which nothing is analyzable— namely, if it is assumed that analysis must leave things precisely as it finds them. Analysis here as elsewhere destroys beyond recovery the first blush of the immediately presented. But if all this be true, and if it applies to value, it is already too late to speak of value as unanalyzable or indefinable.[4]

The history of human knowledge creates a presumption against indefinables. At the outset of any inquiry its subject matter is, as yet, undefined; nothing is, as yet, said about it; it possesses the character of a questionable vagueness located in a certain indefinitely bounded quarter of the field. When the definition takes place, this pseudo-simplicity of ignorance is superseded by articulate complexity. There is always something which escapes the final knowledge of a given subject matter, namely, the antecedent phases of ignorance. But to allow this to deter us from definition would be a cognitive defeatism. Self, activity, causality, substance, matter, force, heat, have all appeared in the role of indefinables only to prove definable. The history of thought is strewn with abandoned indefinables; and it seems highly probable that the value-indefinable will shortly come to rest among these relics of man's unfinished business.

There is a further meaning of 'indefinability' which can, for present purposes, be eliminated. Logic and mathematics employ so-called indefinables in a sense which is relative to their own systematic procedures. Certain terms are *taken* as indefinable. The choice of the word 'indefinable' in this sense is unfortunate, since it appears to say that the concepts in question *can* not be defined, when it really means only that they *are* not defined. Their selection as indefinables within the system is quite independent of definable meanings which they may or may not have outside the system.

The final proof that a conceptual definition of value is possible is to provide such a definition. The definition here proposed must satisfy two sets of requirements. In the end it will appear that it must be descriptive, that is, must fit a certain selected body of facts. But in advance of this empirical test the definition must satisfy certain formal, that is, logical and epistemological, requirements. These requirements have to do with the *framing* of the theory—with its internal structure. It must be "theoretically" acceptable. The concepts which it employs must not only be clear and intelligible, but must lend themselves to judgments which are capable of systematization and elaboration. More specifically, the present definition must be capable of defending itself against charges of circularity, self-contradiction, and sceptical relativism.

6

The charge that the definition is *circular* consists in pointing out that when a thing is affirmed to be good because it is an object of positive interest, it is always possible to raise the question of the goodness of the interest. Thus it

---

[4] The author has discussed this question in "Value as Simply Value," *Journal of Philosophy, 28* (1931), pp. 522–6.

is generally agreed that the goodness of drugs is questionable despite the intense craving of the addict; and it is usually concluded that the drug is bad because the craving is bad. It would seem to follow that in order that a thing shall be good it must be the object of a good interest, in which case 'good' is defined in terms of good.

But this objection loses its force altogether when it is recognized that an interest may itself possess value, positive or negative, by the application of the same definition as that which is applied to its object. While the craving does invest its object with positive value, the craving may be invested with negative value from the standpoint of other interests; and this second value may be considered as overruling the positive value owing to its taking the higher ground of health or morals. The appetitive goodness of the drug does not include or imply the hygienic or moral goodness of the appetite. There are two goods, one of which is, in some sense yet to be examined, superior to the other. In other words, the definition does not state that a thing is good only when it is the object of a good interest, but when it is the object of any interest, good or bad. When the interest is good, its object is thereby enhanced, but there is no circularity.

But in escaping circularity does one not fall into *contradiction?* Is it not contradictory to affirm that the same object is both good and bad? The charge of contradiction is lightly made and, as a rule, superficially examined. The important thing is to discover just what propositions would, and what propositions would not, be contradictory. It is sometimes supposed that the expression 'one man's meat is another man's poison' involves a contradiction. But there would be a contradiction only provided the same proposition was both affirmed and denied. Thus it would be contradictory to say that one man's meat was not that man's meat, or that another man's poison was not his poison. Meat to one man and poison to another are not contradictories, but are two different and consistent propositions.

By a kind of grammatical license the term 'contradiction' is sometimes applied to interests. Strictly speaking, interests do not contradict, but *conflict.* Only propositions contradict. But interests are sometimes allowed to borrow the contradictoriness or consistency of their objects when these are stated as propositions. Thus the interests in preserving and in destroying the life of the same individual are said to be contradictory, because the will of one can be expressed by the resolve "he shall live" and the will of the other by the resolve "he shall not live." But to speak of interests themselves as contradictory is confusing and misleading. Two contradictories cannot both be true, but two conflicting forces can coexist.

To assert of the same object that it is good and that it is bad *seems* to be contradictory, because the two assertions are elliptical, that is, because of the omission of the axis of reference. It may seem to be contradictory to assert of the same body that it is "above" and "below" when one fails to specify *what* it is above and below. Similarly, it seems to be contradictory to say of the same thing that it is both good and bad when one omits to specify the interests from which it derives its goodness and badness. The interests being specified, there is no contradiction whatever in asserting that the same object is practically useful and aesthetically ugly, or that the same act is selfishly beneficent and socially injurious.

But is not contradiction escaped only by falling into *relativism?* Well, if one may be permitted a vulgarism, and so what? The word 'relativism' has a bad sound; even the word 'relativity,' despite its association with the latest physics, conveys a suggestion of philosophical untenability. But suppose that one substitute the more colorless word 'relational' and, instead of rejecting it as a fault, boldly affirm it as a merit; since it provides not only for value, but for ambivalence and multi-valence.

Many of the most familiar characteristics of things are relational. There is no disputing the fact that brother and son are relational characteristics. In other words, when one describes a man as a brother or a son, one states his relation to another human being. For any man, there is someone to whom he is related: "God gives us relations." So, according to the theory here proposed, when one describes a thing as good or bad one describes it in terms of its relation, direct or indirect, to a second thing, namely, an interest.

This, be it noted, is not the same as to say that one value is definable only by its relation to another *value*, which may or may not be the case. There is nothing in the relational view which forbids a thing's being conceived as absolutely valuable; that is, valuable regardless of the value of anything else.

There is only one kind of relativism which is epistemologically objectionable, and which is commonly known as "vicious relativism." The viciousness lies in its scepticism. It consists in the doctrine that all statements are elliptical unless they are introduced by the words "it seems to me at this moment." Were this the case I should not even be stating what I am saying now. I should say, "it seems to me that it seems to me that it seems to me," etc. *ad infinitum;* in which case I would never get to *what* seems to me, and I might as well have saved myself the trouble of making any statement at all.

Suffice it to say that the theory of value here proposed is no more relativistic in this vicious sense than any other theory, whether of value or of any other matter. The supposition that a relational theory of value is peculiarly vicious in its relativism rests on a confusion. It is mistakenly supposed that because objects derive their value, positive and negative, from interest it is implied that the interest from which they derive value is the interest of the knower or judge. This would mean that if I am to judge that an object possesses positive value to me *I* must like, desire, will, or love it. When, however, value is defined in terms of interest, then *any* interest will satisfy the definition; and if I observe that anyone else likes, desires, loves or wills a thing, then I am bound by the definition to judge it good. The evidence of its goodness or badness is the observable fact of interest, which is just as objective, and just as open to agreement, as any other fact of life or history.

7

The present definition of value is proposed not only as a nominal and conceptual, but as a "real" or "descriptive," definition.[5] Its justification

[5] Cf. S. C. Pepper, "The Descriptive Definition," *Journal of Philosophy, 43* (1946); A. Kaplan, "Definition and Specification of Meaning," *ibid., 43* (1946); M. Weitz, "Analysis and Real Definition," *Philosophical Studies, 1* (1950).

requires that the names which it employs shall be well selected in the light of verbal usage; and that its concepts shall yield judgments which are free from circularity, contradiction, and sceptical relativism. But these are only preliminary considerations. A descriptive definition, in short, is an hypothesis. Its crucial test is its bringing to light the systematic structure of some realm of fact—some state of affairs *of* which it is true. As will appear more clearly in the sequel, this does not imply any fundamental antithesis between the descriptive and the normative, but rather that norms themselves are also describable.

As here conceived, theory of value refers to a peculiarly pervasive feature of human existence and history, namely, the emergence of interests having objects; in which interests combine, wax, wane, and disappear; in which certain things are qualified to become objects of interests; and in which there are things and events which promote or defeat objects of interest. It does not deal, except for purposes of illustration, with particular historic societies and epochs, but with general types and structures of interest.

But while the field of personal and social events, like that of physical events, is inexhaustible, it is proper to select major events, or certain human enterprises and pursuits that have a claim to special attention because of their universality or importance. Referring to these as "pursuits," "enterprises," or "institutions," one may then test the theory by its providing a systematic description of morality, conscience, politics, law, economy, art, science, education, and religion. When the master concept of such a description is given the name of 'value,' then these major realms of human life are specifically describable as realms of value. In their aggregate these realms constitute what may properly be given the name of 'civilization,' that total human adventure whose rising and declining fortunes give significance to human life upon this planet.

Theory of value so conceived is a bold and far-flung program which cannot be undertaken without a humble awareness of its immense complexity. It requires the philosopher to enter fields in which specialists have already staked their special claims, and where the philosopher finds himself an amateur among professionals. He cannot hope to do their special work better than they do it, but only to incorporate their results and add items and relationships. The philosopher is accustomed to this somewhat shameless role. He does not, however, undertake the task arrogantly or overconfidently. For it is the philosopher who, having undertaken the task, is most acutely aware of its difficulty.

.   .   .

12

CRITIQUE OF ETHICS

A. J. Ayer

There is still one objection to be met before we can claim to have justified our view that all synthetic propositions are empirical hypotheses. This objection is based on the common supposition that our speculative knowledge is of two distinct kinds—that which relates to questions of empirical fact, and that which relates to questions of value. It will be said that "statements of value" are genuine synthetic propositions, but that they cannot with any show of justice be represented as hypotheses, which are used to predict the course of our sensations; and, accordingly, that the existence of ethics and æsthetics as branches of speculative knowledge presents an insuperable objection to our radical empiricist thesis.

In face of this objection, it is our business to give an account of "judgements of value" which is both satisfactory in itself and consistent with our general empiricist principles. We shall set ourselves to show that in so far as statements of value are significant, they are ordinary "scientific" statements; and that in so far as they are not scientific, they are not in the literal sense significant, but are simply expressions of emotion which can be neither true nor false. In maintaining this view, we may confine ourselves for the present to the case of ethical statements. What is said about them will be found to apply, *mutatis mutandis*, to the case of æsthetic statements also.

The ordinary system of ethics, as elaborated in the works of ethical philosophers, is very far from being a homogeneous whole. Not only is it apt to contain pieces of metaphysics, and analyses of non-ethical concepts: its actual ethical contents are themselves of very different kinds. We may divide them, indeed, into four main classes. There are, first of all, propositions which express definitions of ethical terms, or judgements about the legitimacy or possibility of certain definitions. Secondly, there are propositions describing the phenomena of moral experience, and their causes. Thirdly, there are exhortations to moral virtue. And, lastly, there are actual ethical judgements. It is unfortunately the case that the distinction between these four classes, plain as it is, is commonly ignored by ethical philosophers;

From A. J. Ayer, *Language, Truth and Logic*, rev. ed. (1946), Chap. VI, pp. 102–114. Reprinted by permission of Victor Gollancz, Ltd., and Dover Publications, Inc.

with the result that it is often very difficult to tell from their works what it is that they are seeking to discover or prove.

In fact, it is easy to see that only the first of our four classes, namely that which comprises the propositions relating to the definitions of ethical terms, can be said to constitute ethical philosophy. The propositions which describe the phenomena of moral experience, and their causes, must be assigned to the science of psychology, or sociology. The exhortations to moral virtue are not propositions at all, but ejaculations or commands which are designed to provoke the reader to action of a certain sort. Accordingly, they do not belong to any branch of philosophy or science. As for the expressions of ethical judgements, we have not yet determined how they should be classified. But inasmuch as they are certainly neither definitions nor comments upon definitions, nor quotations, we may say decisively that they do not belong to ethical philosophy. A strictly philosophical treatise on ethics should therefore make no ethical pronouncements. But it should, by giving an analysis of ethical terms, show what is the category to which all such pronouncements belong. And this is what we are now about to do.

A question which is often discussed by ethical philosophers is whether it is possible to find definitions which would reduce all ethical terms to one or two fundamental terms. But this question, though it undeniably belongs to ethical philosophy, is not relevant to our present enquiry. We are not now concerned to discover which term, within the sphere of ethical terms, is to be taken as fundamental; whether, for example, "good" can be defined in terms of "right" or "right" in terms of "good," or both in terms of "value." What we are interested in is the possibility of reducing the whole sphere of ethical terms to non-ethical terms. We are enquiring whether statements of ethical value can be translated into statements of empirical fact.

That they can be so translated is the contention of those ethical philosophers who are commonly called subjectivists, and of those who are known as utilitarians. For the utilitarian defines the rightness of actions, and the goodness of ends, in terms of the pleasure, or happiness, or satisfaction, to which they give rise; the subjectivist, in terms of the feelings of approval which a certain person, or group of people, has towards them. Each of these types of definition makes moral judgements into a sub-class of psychological or sociological judgements; and for this reason they are very attractive to us. For, if either was correct, it would follow that ethical assertions were not generically different from the factual assertions which are ordinarily contrasted with them; and the account which we have already given of empirical hypotheses would apply to them also.

Nevertheless we shall not adopt either a subjectivist or a utilitarian analysis of ethical terms. We reject the subjectivist view that to call an action right, or a thing good, is to say that it is generally approved of, because it is not self-contradictory to assert that some actions which are generally approved of are not right, or that some things which are generally approved of are not good. And we reject the alternative subjectivist view that a man who asserts that a certain action is right, or that a certain thing is good, is saying that he himself approves of it, on the ground that a man who confessed that he sometimes approved of what was bad or wrong would not be contradicting himself. And a similar argument is fatal to utilitarianism. We cannot agree that to call an action right is to say that of all the actions possible in the circumstances it would cause, or be likely to cause, the greatest happiness, or the greatest balance of pleasure over pain, or the greatest balance of satisfied over unsatisfied desire, because we find that it is not self-contradictory to say that it is sometimes wrong to perform the action which would actually or probably cause the greatest happiness, or the greatest balance of pleasure over pain, or of satisfied over unsatisfied desire. And since it is not self-contradictory to say that some pleasant things are not good, or that some bad things are desired, it cannot be the case that the sentence "*x* is good" is equivalent to "*x* is pleasant," or to "*x* is desired." And to every other variant of utilitarianism with which I am acquainted the same objection can be made. And therefore we should, I think, conclude that the validity of ethical judgements is not determined by the felicific tendencies of actions, any more than by the nature of people's feelings; but that it must be regarded as "absolute" or "intrinsic," and not empirically calculable.

If we say this, we are not, of course, denying that it is possible to invent a language in which all ethical symbols are definable in non-ethical terms, or even that it is desirable to invent such a language and adopt it in place of our own; what we are denying is that the suggested reduction of ethical to non-ethical statements is consistent with the conventions of our actual language. That is, we reject utilitarianism and subjectivism, not as proposals to replace our existing ethical notions by new ones, but as analyses of our existing ethical statements is consistent with the conventions of our actual language. which contain normative ethical symbols are not equivalent to sentences which express psychological propositions, or indeed empirical propositions of any kind.

It is advisable here to make it plain that it is only normative ethical symbols, and not descriptive ethical symbols, that are held by us to be indefinable in factual terms. There is a danger of confusing these two types of symbols, because they are commonly constituted by signs of the same sensible form. Thus a complex sign of the form "*x* is wrong" may constitute a sentence which expresses a moral judgement concerning a certain type of conduct, or it may constitute a sentence which states that a certain type of conduct is repugnant to the moral sense of a particular society. In the latter case, the symbol "wrong" is a descriptive ethical symbol, and the sentence in which it occurs expresses an ordinary sociological proposition; in the former case, the symbol "wrong" is a normative ethical symbol, and the sentence in which it occurs does not, we maintain, express an empirical proposition at all. It is only with normative ethics that we are at present concerned; so that whenever ethical symbols are used in the course of this argument without qualification, they are always to be interpreted as symbols of the normative type.

In admitting that normative ethical concepts are irreducible to empirical concepts, we seem to be leaving the way clear for the "absolutist" view of ethics—that is, the view that statements of value are not controlled by observation, as ordinary empirical propositions are, but only by a mysterious "intellectual intuition." A feature of this theory, which is seldom recognized by its advocates, is that it makes statements of value unverifiable. For it is notorious that what seems intuitively certain to one person may seem doubtful, or even false, to another. So that unless it is possible to provide some criterion by which one may decide between conflicting intuitions, a mere appeal to intuition is worthless as a test of a proposition's validity. But in the case of moral judgements, no such criterion can be given. Some moralists claim to settle the matter by saying that they "know" that their own moral judgements are correct. But such an assertion is of purely psychological interest, and has not the slightest tendency to prove the validity of any moral judgement. For dissentient moralists may equally well "know" that their ethical views are correct. And, as far as subjective certainty goes, there will be nothing to choose between them. When such differences of opinion arise in connection with an ordinary empirical proposition, one may attempt to resolve them by referring to, or actually carrying out, some relevant empirical test. But with regard to ethical statements, there is, on the "absolutist" or "intuitionist" theory, no relevant empirical test. We are therefore justified in saying that on this theory ethical statements are held to be unverifiable. They are, of course, also held to be genuine synthetic propositions.

Considering the use which we have made of the principle that a synthetic proposition is significant only if it is empirically verifiable, it is clear that the acceptance of an "absolutist" theory of ethics would undermine the whole of our main argument. And as we have already rejected the "naturalistic" theories which are commonly supposed to provide the only alternative to "absolutism" in ethics, we seem to have reached a difficult position. We shall meet the difficulty by showing that the correct treatment of ethical statements is afforded by a third theory, which is wholly compatible with our radical empiricism.

We begin by admitting that the fundamental ethical concepts are un-analysable, inasmuch as there is no criterion by which one can test the validity of the judgements in which they occur. So far we are in agreement with the absolutists. But, unlike the absolutists, we are able to give an explanation of this fact about ethical concepts. We say that the reason why they are unanalysable is that they are mere pseudo-concepts. The presence of an ethical symbol in a proposition adds nothing to its factual content. Thus if I say to someone, "You acted wrongly in stealing that money," I am not stating anything more than if I had simply said, "You stole that money." In adding that this action is wrong I am not making any further statement about it. I am simply evincing my moral disapproval of it. It is as if I had said, "You stole that money," in a peculiar tone of horror, or written it with the addition of some special exclamation marks. The tone, or the exclamation marks, adds nothing to the literal meaning of the sentence. It merely serves to show that the expression of it is attended by certain feelings in the speaker.

If now I generalise my previous statement and say, "Stealing money is wrong," I produce a sentence which has no factual meaning—that is, expresses no proposition which can be either true or false. It is as if I had written "Stealing money!!"—where the shape and thickness of the exclamation marks show, by a suitable convention, that a special sort of moral disapproval is the feeling which is being expressed. It is clear that there is nothing said here which can be true or false. Another man may disagree with me about the wrongness of stealing, in the sense that he may not have the same feelings about stealing as I have, and he may quarrel with me on account of my moral sentiments. But he cannot, strictly speaking, contradict me. For in saying that a certain type of action is right or wrong, I am not making any factual statement, not even a statement about my own state of mind. I am merely expressing certain moral sentiments. And the man who is ostensibly contradicting me is merely expressing his moral sentiments. So that there is plainly no sense in asking which of us is in the right. For neither of us is asserting a genuine proposition.

What we have just been saying about the symbol "wrong" applies to all normative ethical symbols. Sometimes they occur in sentences which record ordinary empirical facts besides expressing ethical feeling about those facts: sometimes they occur in sentences which simply express ethical feeling about a certain type of action, or situation, without making any statement of fact. But in every case in which one would commonly be said to be making an ethical judgement, the function of the relevant ethical word is purely "emotive." It is used to express feeling about certain objects, but not to make any assertion about them.

It is worth mentioning that ethical terms do not serve only to express feeling. They are calculated also to arouse feeling, and so to stimulate action. Indeed some of them are used in such a way as to give the sentences in which they occur the effect of commands. Thus the sentence "It is your duty to tell the truth" may be regarded both as the expression of a certain sort of ethical feeling about truthfulness and as the expression of the command "Tell the truth." The sentence "You ought to tell the truth" also involves the command "Tell the truth," but here the tone of the command is less emphatic. In the sentence "It is good to tell the truth" the command has become little more than a suggestion. And thus the "meaning" of the word "good," in its ethical usage, is differentiated from that of the word "duty" or the word "ought." In fact we may define the meaning of the various ethical words in terms both of the different feelings they are ordinarily taken to express, and also the different responses which they are calculated to provoke.

We can now see why it is impossible to find a criterion for determining the validity of ethical judgements. It is not because they have an "absolute" validity which is mysteriously independent of ordinary sense-experience, but because they have no objective validity whatsoever. If a sentence makes no statement at all, there is obviously no sense in asking whether what it says is true or false. And we have seen that sentences which simply express moral judgements do not say anything. They are pure expressions of feeling and as such do not come under the category of truth and falsehood. They are unverifiable for the same reason as a cry of pain or a word of command is unverifiable—because they do not express genuine propositions.

Thus, although our theory of ethics might fairly be said to be radically subjectivist, it differs in a very important respect from the orthodox subjectivist theory. For the orthodox subjectivist does not deny, as we do, that the sentences of a moralizer express genuine propositions. All he denies is that they express propositions of a unique non-empirical character. His own view is that they express propositions about the speaker's feelings. If this were so, ethical judgements clearly would be capable of being true or false. They would be true if the speaker had the relevant feelings, and false if he had not. And this is a matter which is, in principle, empirically verifiable. Furthermore they could be significantly contradicted. For if I say, "Tolerance is a virtue," and someone answers, "You don't approve of it," he would, on the ordinary subjectivist theory, be contradicting me. On our theory, he would not be contradicting me, because, in saying that tolerance was a virtue, I should not be making any statement about my own feelings or about anything else. I should simply be evincing my feelings, which is not at all the same thing as saying that I have them.

The distinction between the expression of feeling and the assertion of feeling is complicated by the fact that the assertion that one has a certain feeling often accompanies the expression of that feeling, and is then, indeed, a factor in the expression of that feeling. Thus I may simultaneously express boredom and say that I am bored, and in that case my utterance of the words, "I am bored," is one of the circumstances which make it true to say that I am expressing or evincing boredom. But I can express boredom without actually saying that I am bored. I can express it by my tone and gestures, while making a statement about something wholly unconnected with it, or by an ejaculation, or without uttering any words at all. So that even if the assertion that one has a certain feeling always involves the expression of that feeling, the expression of a feeling assuredly does not always involve the assertion that one has it. And this is the important point to grasp in considering the distinction between our theory and the ordinary subjectivist theory. For whereas the subjectivist holds that ethical statements actually assert the existence of certain feelings, we hold that ethical statements are expressions and excitants of feeling which do not necessarily involve any assertions.

We have already remarked that the main objection to the ordinary subjectivist theory is that the validity of ethical judgements is not determined by the nature of their author's feelings. And this is an objection which our theory escapes. For it does not imply that the existence of any feelings is a necessary and sufficient condition of the validity of an ethical judgement. It implies, on the contrary, that ethical judgements have no validity.

There is, however, a celebrated argument against subjectivist theories which our theory does not escape. It has been pointed out by Moore that if ethical statements were simply statements about the speaker's feelings, it would be impossible to argue about questions of value.[1] To take a typical example: if a man said that thrift was a virtue, and another replied that it was a vice, they would not, on this theory, be disputing with one another. One would be saying that he approved of thrift, and the other that *he* didn't; and there is no reason why both these statements should not be true. Now Moore held it to be obvious that we do dispute about questions of value, and accordingly concluded that the particular form of subjectivism which he was discussing was false.

It is plain that the conclusion that it is impossible to dispute about questions of value follows from our theory also. For as we hold that such sentences as "Thrift is a virtue" and "Thrift is a vice" do not express propositions at all, we clearly cannot hold that they express incompatible propositions. We must therefore admit that if Moore's argument really refutes the ordinary subjectivist theory, it also refutes ours. But, in fact, we

[1] Cf. *Philosophical Studies*, "The Name of Moral Philosophy."

deny that it does refute even the ordinary subjectivist theory. For we hold that one really never does dispute about questions of value.

This may seem, at first sight, to be a very paradoxical assertion. For we certainly do engage in disputes which are ordinarily regarded as disputes about questions of value. But, in all such cases, we find, if we consider the matter closely, that the dispute is not really about a question of value, but about a question of fact. When someone disagrees with us about the moral value of a certain action or type of action, we do admittedly resort to argument in order to win him over to our way of thinking. But we do not attempt to show by our arguments that he has the "wrong" ethical feeling towards a situation whose nature he has correctly apprehended. What we attempt to show is that he is mistaken about the facts of the case. We argue that he has misconceived the agent's motive: or that he has misjudged the effects of the action, or its probable effects in view of the agent's knowledge; or that he has failed to take into account the special circumstances in which the agent was placed. Or else we employ more general arguments about the effects which actions of a certain type tend to produce, or the qualities which are usually manifested in their performance. We do this in the hope that we have only to get our opponent to agree with us about the nature of the empirical facts for him to adopt the same moral attitude towards them as we do. And as the people with whom we argue have generally received the same moral education as ourselves, and live in the same social order, our expectation is usually justified. But if our opponent happens to have undergone a different process of moral "conditioning" from ourselves, so that, even when he acknowledges all the facts, he still disagrees with us about the moral value of the actions under discussion, then we abandon the attempt to convince him by argument. We say that it is impossible to argue with him because he has a distorted or undeveloped moral sense; which signifies merely that he employs a different set of values from our own. We feel that our own system of values is superior, and therefore speak in such derogatory terms of his. But we cannot bring forward any arguments to show that our system is superior. For our judgement that it is so is itself a judgement of value, and accordingly outside the scope of argument. It is because argument fails us when we come to deal with pure questions of value, as distinct from questions of fact, that we finally resort to mere abuse.

In short, we find that argument is possible on moral questions only if some system of values is presupposed. If our opponent concurs with us in expressing moral disapproval of all actions of a given type *t*, then we may get him to condemn a particular action A, by bringing forward arguments to show that A is of type *t*. For the question whether A does or does not belong to that type is a plain question of fact. Given that a man has certain moral principles, we argue that he must, in order to be consistent, react morally to certain things in a certain way. What we do not and cannot argue about is the validity of these moral principles. We merely praise or condemn them in the light of our own feelings.

If anyone doubts the accuracy of this account of moral disputes, let him try to construct even an imaginary argument on a question of value which does not reduce itself to an argument about a question of logic or about an empirical matter of fact. I am confident that he will not succeed in producing a single example. And if that is the case, he must allow that its involving the impossibility of purely ethical arguments is not, as Moore thought, a ground of objection to our theory, but rather a point in favour of it.

Having upheld our theory against the only criticism which appeared to threaten it, we may now use it to define the nature of all ethical enquiries. We find that ethical philosophy consists simply in saying that ethical concepts are pseudo-concepts and therefore unanalysable. The further task of describing the different feelings that the different ethical terms are used to express, and the different reactions that they customarily provoke, is a task for the psychologist. There cannot be such a thing as ethical science, if by ethical science one means the elaboration of a "true" system of morals. For we have seen that, as ethical judgements are mere expressions of feeling, there can be no way of determining the validity of any ethical system, and, indeed, no sense in asking whether any such system is true. All that one may legitimately enquire in this connection is, What are the moral habits of a given person or group of people, and what causes them to have precisely those habits and feelings? And this enquiry falls wholly within the scope of the existing social sciences.

It appears, then, that ethics, as a branch of knowledge, is nothing more than a department of psychology and sociology. And in case anyone thinks that we are overlooking the existence of casuistry, we may remark that casuistry is not a science, but is a purely analytical investigation of the structure of a given moral system. In other words, it is an exercise in formal logic.

When one comes to pursue the psychological enquiries which constitute ethical science, one is immediately enabled to account for the Kantian and hedonistic theories of morals. For one finds that one of the chief causes of moral behaviour is fear, both conscious and unconscious, of a god's displeasure, and fear of the enmity of society. And this, indeed, is the reason why moral precepts present themselves to some people as "categorical" commands. And one finds, also, that the moral code of a society is partly determined by the beliefs of that society concerning the conditions of its own happiness—or, in other words, that a society tends to encourage or discourage a given type of conduct by the use of moral sanctions according as it appears to promote or detract from the contentment of the society as a whole. And this is the reason why altruism is recommended in most moral codes and egotism condemned. It is from the observation of this connection between morality and happiness that hedonistic or eudæmonistic theories of morals ultimately spring, just as the moral theory of Kant is based on the fact, previously explained, that moral precepts have for some people the force of inexorable commands. As each of these theories ignores the fact which lies at the root of the other, both may be criticized as being onesided; but this is not the main objection to either of them. Their essential defect is that they treat propositions which refer to the causes and attributes of our ethical feelings as if they were definitions of ethical concepts. And thus they fail to recognise that ethical concepts are pseudo-concepts and consequently indefinable.

As we have already said, our conclusions about the nature of ethics apply to æsthetics also. Æsthetic terms are used in exactly the same way as ethical terms. Such æsthetic words as "beautiful" and "hideous" are employed, as ethical words are employed, not to make statements of fact, but simply to express certain feelings and evoke a certain response. It follows, as in ethics, that there is no sense in attributing objective validity to æsthetic judgements, and no possibility of arguing about questions of value in æsthetics, but only about questions of fact. A scientific treatment of æsthetics would show us what in general were the causes of æsthetic feeling, why various societies produced and admired the works of art they did, why taste varies as it does within a given society, and so forth. And these are ordinary psychological or sociological questions. They have, of course, little or nothing to do with æsthetic criticism as we understand it. But that is because the purpose of æsthetic criticism is not so much to give knowledge as to communicate emotion. The critic, by calling attention to certain features of the work under review, and expressing his own feelings about them, endeavours to make us share his attitude towards the work as a whole. The only relevant propositions that he formulates are propositions describing the nature of the work. And these are plain records of fact. We conclude, therefore, that there is nothing in æsthetics, any more than there is in ethics, to justify the view that it embodies a unique type of knowledge.

It should now be clear that the only information which we can legitimately derive from the study of our æsthetic and moral experiences is information about our own mental and physical make-up. We take note of these experiences as providing data for our psychological and sociological generalisations. And this is the only way in which they serve to increase our knowledge. It follows that any attempt to make our use of ethical and æsthetic concepts the basis of a metaphysical theory concerning the existence of a world of values, as distinct from the world of facts, involves a false analysis of these concepts.

.   .   .

13

MORAL REASONS

Kurt Baier

We can now turn to the question of what are moral reasons or considerations. . . . They are obviously those which occur in moral deliberation and the occurrence of which makes deliberation moral. We say of someone that he is a person of good will if he is always prepared (should it be necessary) to enter, before acting, into moral deliberation, that is to say, to work out what is, morally speaking, the best course open to him, that is, the course supported by the best moral reasons, and also prepared to act in accordance with the outcome of such deliberations.

What we normally call our moral convictions function as moral rules of reason, as moral consideration-making beliefs. Ordinarily, of course, our moral convictions are formulated simply as 'Stealing is wrong,' 'Lying is wrong,' and so on. They are not normally stated in the form I have given them, namely, 'The fact that stealing is wrong is a reason against stealing.' Nevertheless, although they are not formulated in this way, they are used as moral rules of reason. Just as we call those things dictated by self-interest reasons of self-interest, so we call those things dictated by morality moral reasons. To say that something is morally wrong is merely another way of saying that it is prohibited by, that it is against or contrary to, morality. Hence in the fact that something is wrong one has a reason (a moral one) against doing it. If something is a case of stealing and if stealing is wrong, that is, contrary to morality, then one has a moral reason against doing that thing.

MORAL CONVICTIONS CAN BE TRUE OR FALSE

It is often argued that our moral convictions are merely expressions of our feelings, emotions, or attitudes, or that they are commands or pseudo commands, and that, therefore, they cannot be true or false. It might be added that they must have some kind of imperatival force, for it must be

From Kurt Baier, *The Moral Point of View: A Rational Basis of Ethics*, abridged ed. (New York: Random House, Inc., 1965), Chap. V, pp. 82–109. Reprinted by permission of the publisher.

possible to act in accordance with or contrary to them. But one cannot act in accordance with or contrary to truths or facts. Truths or facts are compatible with any sort of behavior. Truths are, therefore, useless in morality. There we need something in the nature of precepts.

This argument is unsound. It is not impossible for a remark to be true or false and also imperatival. If, in a train, I say to my neighbor, 'No smoking in here,' I say something which can be true or false (for it may or may not be a nonsmokers') and also imperatival (for if it is a nonsmokers', then there is a rule forbidding smoking in the compartment). Thus, what makes 'No smoking in here' and 'Smoking prohibited' capable of being true or false is the fact that these remarks imply the existence and authority of certain orders or rules. Thus 'No smoking in here' can be true (or false), because the rule 'No smoking in this compartment' may be properly laid down by the Railway Company which may be entitled to do so. Our main task will, of course, be to show what are the appropriate tests which a moral rule must pass in order that remarks implying its existence should be said to be true. We have to answer questions such as what are the tests which the rule 'Thou shalt not kill' must pass if it is to be true that killing is wrong.

The proof that moral convictions could be true or false and also imperatival seems to me to constitute quite a strong argument in favor of saying that they actually are true or false, for this is what we all naturally think. The only reason why we have doubts is that philosophers have various reasons for saying that propositions cannot be both imperatival and true or false. However, in view of the great popularity of the emotive and imperativalist theories, it is perhaps not out of place to devote some additional space to establishing this conclusion.

My main contention is that we could not properly speak of *a morality*, as opposed to a system of conventions, customs, or laws, unless the question of the correctness or incorrectness, truth or falsity, of the rules prevalent in a community is asked, unless, in other words, the prevalent rules are subjected to certain tests. It is only when the current rules are no longer regarded as sacrosanct, as incapable of alteration or improvement, only when the current rules are contrasted with other possible, improved, ideal rules, that a group can be said to have a morality as opposed to a mere set of taboos.

We distinguish a great many different moralities—Greek, Roman, Arapesh, Christian, Mohammedan, Communist, feudal, bourgeois, proletarian, and so on. Moralities are always someone's, whether an individual's or a group's. In these respects, moralities are like customs and legal systems. But in another respect, moralities on the one hand and legal systems and customs on the other differ radically. When we have settled whether a line of action is in accordance with or contrary to the law or the customs of the group in question, we have settled conclusively whether this line of action is lawful or unlawful, customary or not customary. We cannot go on to ask, 'Well, perhaps it is legal here or customary there, but is it *really* legal, is it *really* customary?' Nor does it make sense to say, 'There is no law or custom against this sort of thing anywhere, but perhaps this sort of thing is *really* illegal or *really* contrary to custom.' By contrast, this kind of distinction can be and is drawn in moral matters. When we hear that in certain countries virginity above a certain age is regarded as selfish and immoral, or that not having scalped anyone by a certain age is regarded as cowardly or slothful, or that it is "wrong" for women to pass a certain stone without veiling their faces, we do not think that the question whether these sorts of conduct are *really* wrong has been decisively settled. Even whether these things are *wrong in that country* has not been answered. It has only been established that these types of conduct are *believed wrong in that country*.

When we have settled that something is against the customs or laws of a certain group, we cannot go on to ask whether it is merely believed or actually known to be illegal or contrary to custom. A person who goes on to ask that question must be said not to know what he is talking about. On the other hand, a person likewise does not know what he is talking about if he believes that finding out whether some course of action is contrary to the morality of a certain group settles the question whether this course of action is morally wrong. For he ignores the crucial question 'Is what the morality of that group forbids *really* wrong?' or, put differently, 'Are the moral convictions of that group true?' I take it for granted, then, that ordinary usage draws just that distinction between morality on the one hand and the custom and law on the other.

But, it might be asked, what does that prove? Our language might be confused. Perhaps we allow that question without having provided a method of answering it. Our moral locutions may be the embodiment of wishful thinking. It is not enough to point out that we *ask*, 'But are the moral convictions of this group really true?' If that question is to make sense, a procedure for answering it has to exist and it must be a sensible one.

I agree with the principle behind this objection. It is not enough to show, for instance, that we frequently do ask the question 'But is this religion true?' If it were enough, certain modern analyses of religious language would be obviously false. Certain philosophers who say that religious language is purely evocative could then be refuted simply by the reminder "But we do ask the question 'Is his religion true?' and your analysis does not permit it to be asked." Or when other philosophers say that the claim 'God exists' is a complex empirical assertion implying that things will not go from bad to worse in the future, but will in the end be all right, they could be refuted simply by saying that this is not implied in the religious assertion that God exists. I do not think that such philosophers can be so easily refuted. A refutation would have to show not only that we all *think* that this is not implied in such remarks or that we all wish to ask whether such remarks are true, but also that what we imply or what we wish to ask is sensible, that there is room for this question, that we can sensibly imply what we intend to, that we can ask this question and imply what we intend without making nonsense of our religious assertions. It is just because this is so difficult that some philosophers have been driven into these alternative analyses of religious assertions.

This is true of moral claims also. It is not enough to say, 'But we *do* ask whether our moral convictions are true.' We must also show what exactly is the sense of this question and how exactly it can be answered. When this is shown, . . . our original claim has been made good. Since we want to ask whether our moral convictions are true and since it can be explained what this question means and how it is answered and since it can be shown that it is an eminently sensible question, there can no longer be any objection to allowing it.

It follows from this that one of the most popular models of the nature of morality, the conception of it as divine or natural law, is inappropriate. Admittedly, at first sight, the notion of law looks promising. Like its moral analogue, the question whether something is in accordance with or contrary to law is completely objective: everybody within or outside a given society could be wrong about the legality or illegality of a given line of conduct. An enterprising lawyer may unearth an old law that is relevant. Before his find everyone including himself might well have considered that line of action lawful. His discovery shows that this universal belief was false. In this respect law is much closer to morality than custom. For if everyone in a certain society *believes* that something is contrary to custom, then it *necessarily* is. We all think it customary for gentlemen to take off their hats when the national anthem is played, hence it *is* customary. Not so with law, or with morality.

Nevertheless, the concept of law does not fit the case of morality. The very feature that makes it so attractive to religious persons renders it unsuitable as a model of morality. Religious people like to think of morality as a sort of law, because law implies or at any rate strongly suggests a legislator. If morality is a perfect law, then there must be a perfect legislator: God. But this is precisely the objection to law as a model of morality. For a legislator authoritatively settles the question whether a type of conduct is lawful or otherwise: *he makes it so.* The legality or illegality of a type of action is the logical consequence of the legislator's decision. It is the very function of the legislator to bring into being or abolish the illegality of something, as he thinks fit. However, the rightness or wrongness of a type of action cannot be the logical consequence of anyone's decision. An omniscient person would indeed *know* the difference between right and wrong and could reliably inform us of it, but he can only show us where the line runs—he cannot draw it. It is nonsense to say, 'Yesterday God decreed that killing shall no longer be morally wrong' or 'The moral law against lying was promulgated on May 1st.' Morality, therefore, cannot be any sort of law.

It must not be inferred from this that legal systems cannot be criticized on moral grounds. Even though the legislator is entitled to make whatever laws he thinks fit and even though whatever he enacts is really law, and even though it is true that there is no super-law with which the legislator must attempt to make his own enactments agree, nevertheless the legal enactments are open to criticism *from the moral point of view.*

The same point can also be made in the following way. Law and morality have this in common: everyone in this country can be wrong about this or that type of action being legal or illegal, right or wrong. This distinguishes both law and morality from mere custom. It is therefore more plausible to say that morality is a sort of law than to say that it is just convention. All the same, it is misleading. For when it has been established that adultery, say, is permitted by our law, then no further mistake is logically possible, in the field of law. It is then certain that in our country adultery is not unlawful. Incorporation of a rule in the legal system of a country is a final guarantee of the legality or illegality of the type of conduct in question. The law of the group cannot be illegal. It might perhaps be said against this that the law can be illegal when there is a constitution. But then my point can be made by saying that the constitution can't be unconstitutional. On the other hand, embodiment in the morality of the group is no final guarantee of the morality or immorality of the type of conduct in question. The morality of the group may be wrong. The moral convictions of the group may be mistaken.

I take it as established, then, that it is the very meaning of a 'morality' that it should contain a body of moral convictions which can be true or false, that is, a body of rules or precepts for which there are certain tests. If this is true, then morality is a comparatively sophisticated system of rules, and we have to admit the possibility of nonmoral or premoral societies, just as there are nonpolitical or prepolitical societies, such as the Australian aborigines. I believe that, as a matter of fact, moralities have appeared for the first time at roughly the stage when religion superseded magic (or whatever else may have preceded it) and law began to be added to custom. At that time, I believe, morality developed out of taboo. The main step in that direction is the dim realization, expressed in the powers given to a legislator, that the group's way of life is not altogether sacrosanct. The slow, unthought-out, uncontrolled way of social change is superseded by the method of deliberate, thought-out, sudden changes introduced by the legislator. At the same time, it is understood that the legislator is capable of making mistakes, that his legislation is not arbitrary, but is supposed to aim at certain things. In the absence of a clear understanding of what he is supposed to be aiming at, it seems a plausible thing to say that he is aiming at The Perfect Law which is laid up in heaven. But, as we have seen, on closer inspection, this is not satisfactory. As long as we are dealing with a legislator and his law, the same question necessarily arises: what are the grounds on which the legislator, however perfect he may be, is drawing up his legislation? Until these grounds are found, we cannot tell of any piece of legislation or its author whether it or he is perfect. And when we know the grounds, we no longer need, as a sitter for our legislative portrait, the perfect legislator and his law.

THE MORAL POINT OF VIEW

What, then, is the test which a moral conviction must pass in order to be called true? Many philosophers have held that there is not and cannot be such a test. They would perhaps admit that we may reduce our moral convictions to a few basic moral principles, or perhaps even only one, from which all others can be derived, but they would hold that at least one such principle must simply be selected as we please. Such basic principles, they would say, are matters for deciding, not for finding out.

I shall argue, on the contrary, that our moral convictions are true if they can be seen to be required or acceptable *from the moral point of view*. It is indeed true that a person must adopt the moral point of view if he is to be moral. But it is not true that this is an arbitrary decision. On the contrary, . . . there are the very best reasons for adopting this point of view.

Answers to practical questions can be arrived at by reference to a point of view, which may be defined by a principle. When we adopt a certain point of view, we adopt its defining principle. To look at practical problems from that point of view is to be prepared to answer practical questions of the form 'What shall I do?' 'What should be done?' by reference to its defining principle.

Suppose the problem under discussion is whether or not a certain traffic roundabout should be erected at a certain intersection. I can look at this from various points of view, that of a pedestrian or a motorist, a local politician or a manufacturer of roundabouts, and so on. In cases such as these, we have in mind the demands, goals, or aims of persons holding certain special positions or jobs or functions in a society. To look at our problem from the point of view of a motorist is to ask whether the erection of a roundabout at this intersection is in the interest of a motorist. For different points of view there may, of course, be different, even opposing, answers to the same practical questions. The roundabout may be in the interest of a motorist but not of a pedestrian, in the interest of a manufacturer of roundabouts but not of a local politician who depends for his votes on the poorer section (the pedestrians) of the population.

A point of view is not necessarily defined by the principle of self-interest or its more specific application to a particular position in society. We can, for instance, look at this problem from the point of view of town planners or traffic experts, who may favor the roundabout because their special task is to solve traffic problems. Their point of view is defined by the principle 'Favor anything that keeps the traffic flowing; oppose anything that is likely to cause traffic holdups.' But the erection of the roundabout can hardly be said to be *in their interest*. They do not derive any personal advantage or benefit from the scheme. There are many such disinterested points of view, for example, the point of view of a social worker, a social reformer, an advocate of public health schemes, a missionary.

A person is of good will if he adopts the moral point of view as supreme, that is, as overriding all other points of view. When asking the question 'What shall I do?' or 'What is to be done?' such a person will always engage in moral deliberation, survey and weigh the moral considerations, and give them greater weight than any others. A person has adopted the moral point of view when he reviews the facts in the light of *his* moral convictions. We do not require him to test his moral convictions every time, but only because we presume that he already has true moral convictions. This presumption may be false. He may simply have accepted without much questioning the moral convictions of his group, or he may have departed from them without getting any nearer the truth. In such a case, he merely *means* to adopt the moral point of view, but has not succeeded. He has adopted something which he wrongly believes to be the moral point of view. He must still be called a person of good will because of his intentions, but he cannot arrive at true answers to his question. Clearly, our central problem is to define the moral point of view.

SELF-INTEREST AND MORALITY

Throughout the history of philosophy, by far the most popular candidate for the position of the moral point of view has been self-interest. There are obvious parallels between these two standpoints. Both aim at the good. Both are rational. Both involve deliberation, the surveying and weighing of reasons. The adoption of either yields statements containing the word 'ought.' Both involve the notion of self-mastery and control over the desires. It is, moreover, plausible to hold that a person could not have a reason for doing anything whatsoever unless his behavior was designed to promote his own good. Hence, if morality is to have the support of reason, moral reasons must be self-interested, hence the point of view of morality and self-interest must be the same. On the other hand, it seems equally obvious that morality and self-interest are very frequently opposed. Morality often requires us to refrain from doing what self-interest recommends or to do what self-interest forbids. Hence it seems that morality and self-interest cannot be the same points of view.

Can we save the doctrine that the moral point of view is that of self-interest? One way of circumventing the difficulty just mentioned is to draw a distinction between two senses of 'self-interest,' shortsighted and enlightened. The shortsighted egoist always follows his short-range interest without taking into consideration how this will affect others and how their reactions will affect him. The enlightened egoist, on the other hand, knows that he cannot get the most out of life unless he pays attention to the needs of others on whose good will he depends. On this view, the standpoint of (immoral) egoism differs from that of morality in that it fails to consider the interests of others even when the long-range benefits to oneself are likely to be greater than the short-range sacrifices.

This view can be made more plausible still if we distinguish between those egoists who consider each course of action on its own merits and those who, for convenience, adopt certain rules of thumb which they have found will promote their long-range interest. Slogans such as 'Honesty is the best policy,' 'Give to charity rather than to the Department of Internal Revenue,' 'Always give a penny to a beggar when you are likely to be watched by your acquaintances,' 'Treat your servants kindly and they will work for you like slaves,' 'Never be arrogant to anyone—you may need his services one day,' are maxims of this sort. They embody the "wisdom" of a given society. The enlightened long-range egoist may adopt these as rules of thumb, that is, as *prima-facie* maxims, as rules which he will observe unless he has good evidence that departing from them will pay him better than abiding by them. It is obvious that the rules of behavior adopted by the enlightened egoist will be very similar to those of a man who rigidly follows our own moral code.

Moreover, this sort of egoism does not appear to be contrary to reason but, rather, to be required by it. For in the first place, the consistent enlightened egoist satisfies the categorical imperative, or at least one version of it, 'Act only on that maxim whereby thou canst at the same time will that it should become a universal law.' And in the second place, it seems to be superior to other forms of reasoning. For, as Sidgwick puts it, "I quite admit that when the painful necessity comes for another man to choose between his own happiness and the general happiness, he must as a reasonable being prefer his own, i.e. it is right for him to do this on my principle."[1]

Nevertheless it can be shown that this is not the point of view of morality. For those who adopt consistent egoism cannot make moral judgments.

---

[1] Henry Sidgwick, *The Methods of Ethics*, 7th ed. (London: Macmillan and Co., 1907), pref. to the 6th ed., p. xvii.

Moral talk is impossible for consistent egoists. But this amounts to a reductio ad absurdum of consistent egoism.

Let B and K be candidates for the presidency of a certain country and let it be granted that it is in the interest of either to be elected, but that only one can succeed. It would then be in the interest of B but against the interest of K if B were elected, and vice versa, and therefore in the interest of B but against the interest of K if K were liquidated, and vice versa. But from this it would follow that B ought to liquidate K, that it is wrong for B not to do so, that B has not "done his duty" until he has liquidated K; and vice versa. Similarly K, knowing that his own liquidation is in the interest of B and therefore anticipating B's attempts to secure it, ought to take steps to foil B's endeavors. It would be wrong for him not to do so. He would "not have done his duty" until he had made sure of stopping B. It follows that if K prevents B from liquidating him, his act must be said to be both wrong and not wrong—wrong because it is the prevention of what B ought to do, his duty, and wrong for B not to do it; not wrong because it is what K ought to do, his duty, and wrong for K not to do it. But one and the same act (logically) cannot be both morally wrong and not morally wrong. Hence in cases like these no moral judgments apply.

This is obviously absurd. For morality is designed to apply in just such cases, namely, those where interests conflict. But if the point of view of morality were that of self-interest, then there could *never* be moral solutions of conflicts of interest. However, when there are conflicts of interest, we always look for a "higher" point of view, one from which such conflicts can be settled. Consistent egoism makes everyone's private interest the "highest court of appeal." But by 'the moral point of view' we *mean* a point of view which furnishes a court of arbitration for conflicts of interest. Hence it cannot (logically) be identical with the point of view of the interest of any particular person or group of persons.

RULES AND EXCEPTIONS

A consistent egoist has only one supreme principle to which he does not make exceptions, namely, to do whatever is necessary for the promotion of his interest. All his other more specific maxims are merely rules of thumb designed to apply this principle to particular circumstances. If, in a particular case, they do not serve this end, then the consistent egoist would make an exception in his favor. A person who has adopted the moral point of view acts on a different supreme principle, namely, to do whatever is required by moral rules. All his other maxims are merely more specific rules of thumb designed to apply this principle to particular circumstances. The egoist's supreme principle requires him to make exceptions "in his favor," the moral person's supreme principle requires him not to make such exceptions.

Kant grasped this point even if only obscurely. He saw that adopting the moral point of view involves "acting on principle." It involves conforming to rules even when doing so is unpleasant, painful, costly, or ruinous to oneself. Kant, furthermore, argued that, since moral action is action on principle (and not merely in accordance with rules of thumb), moral rules are absolutely inflexible and without exceptions. Accordingly he concluded that if 'Thou shalt not kill' states a moral rule, then any and every act correctly describable as an act of killing someone must be said to be morally wrong.

Kant also saw that this view required him to reject some of our deepest moral convictions; we certainly think that the killing of a man in self-defense or by the hangman is not morally wrong. Kant was prepared to say that our moral convictions are wrong on this point. Can we salvage these moral convictions? The only alternative, to say that acting on principle does not require us not to make exceptions in our own favor, seems to be equally untenable.

It is therefore not surprising that many philosophers have abandoned Kant's (and the commonsense) view that the moral rightness of an act is its property of being in accordance with a moral rule or principle.

However, this whole problem arises only because of a misunderstanding of the expression 'making an exception in one's favor.' As soon as this is cleared up, it can be seen that Kant is right in saying that acting on principle implies making no exception in anyone's favor, but wrong in thinking that therefore all moral rules must be absolutely without exception.

'No parking in the city' has a number of recognized exceptions which are part of the rule itself, for example, 'except in the official parking areas,' 'except in front of a parking meter,' 'except on Saturday mornings and after 8 P.M. every day.' A person who does not know the recognized exceptions does not completely know the rule, for these exceptions more precisely delimit its range of application. A policeman who is not booking a motorist parking in front of a parking meter is not granting exemption to (making an exception in favor of) this motorist. On the contrary, he is administering the rule correctly. If he did apply the no-parking rule to the motorist, *he* would be applying it where *it* does not apply, because this is one of the recognized exceptions which are *part of the rule*. On the other hand, a policeman who does not book a motorist parking his vehicle in a prohibited area at peak hour on a busy day is making an exception in the motorist's favor. If he does so because the man is his friend, he illegitimately grants an exemption. If he does so because the motorist is a doctor who has been called to attend to a man lying unconscious on the pavement, this is a "deserving case" and he grants the exemption legitimately.

Apply this distinction to the rules of a given morality. Notice first that moral rules differ from laws and regulations in that they are not administered by special administrative organs such as policemen and magistrates. Everyone "administers" them himself. Nevertheless, it makes sense to speak of making exceptions in one's own favor. For one may refuse to apply the rule to oneself when one knows that it does apply, that is to say, one may refuse to observe it even when one knows one should. And what is true of making exceptions in one's own favor is true also of making them in favor of someone else. It is almost as immoral to make exceptions in favor of one's wife, son, or nephew as in favor of oneself.

When we say, therefore, that a person who has killed a burglar in self-defense has not done anything wrong, we are not making an exception in the houseowner's favor. It is much nearer the truth to say that, in our morality, the rule 'Thou shalt not kill' *has several recognized exceptions*, among them them 'in self-defense.' We can say that a man does not know fully our moral rule 'Thou shalt not kill' if he does not know that it has, among others, this "exception," i.e., limit of application.

Like other rules of reason, our moral convictions hold only *presumptively*. Killing is wrong *unless* it is killing in self-defense, killing by the hangman, killing of an enemy in wartime, accidental killing, and possibly mercy killing. If it is one of these types of killing, then it is *not* wrong.

Even if it is one of the wrongful acts of killing, it is so only *prima facie*, other things being equal. For there may have been an overriding moral reason in favor of killing the man, for example, that he is about to blow up a train and that this is the only way of stopping him.

One further point should be made to avoid misunderstanding. Unlike laws and regulations, moral rules have not been laid down by anyone. Knowing moral rules cannot, therefore, involve knowing exactly what a certain person has enjoined and forbidden and what exceptions he has allowed, because there is no such person. In the case of regulations and laws, it was precisely this knowledge which enabled us to draw the distinction between saying that someone was granting an exception and saying that he was merely applying the rule which, for cases of this sort, provided for an exception. Our distinction seems to collapse for moral rules.

However, the answer to this is simple. When a magistrate is empowered to make exceptions or grant exemptions in "deserving cases," the question of what is a "deserving case" is not of course answered in the regulation itself. If it were, the magistrate would not be exercising his power to grant exemption, but would simply apply the regulation as provided in it. How, then, does the magistrate or policeman know what is a deserving case? The doctor who parks his car in a prohibited spot in order to attend to an injured man is such a case, namely, a *morally deserving* case. The principles in accordance with which policemen or magistrates grant exemptions to existing regulations are moral principles. In the case of moral rules, there cannot be any distinction between exceptions which are part of the rule and deserving cases. *Only* deserving cases can be part of the moral rule, and *every* deserving case is properly part of it. Hence while in the case of laws and regulations there is a reason for going beyond the exceptions allowed in the regulation itself (when there is a morally deserving instance), in the case of moral rules there is no such reason. For all deserving cases are, from the nature of the case, part of the moral rule itself. Hence it is never right to make an exception to a moral rule in anyone's favor. Kant is therefore quite right in saying that it is always wrong to make exceptions to moral rules in one's own favor (and for that matter in anyone else's), but he is wrong in thinking that this makes moral rules inflexible. For the fact that departing from it would be in the agent's interest is simply not a legitimate ground for making an exception to a moral rule, as it is for exceptions to a rule of self-interest.

MORAL RULES ARE MEANT FOR EVERYBODY

The point of view of morality is inadequately characterized by saying that *I* have adopted it if *I* act on principles, that is, on rules to which I do not make exceptions whenever acting on them would frustrate one or the other of my purposes or desires. It is characterized by greater universality than that. It must be thought of as a standpoint from which rules are considered as being acted on *by everyone*. Moral rules are not merely rules to which a person must not make exceptions in his favor but they are principles *meant for everybody*.

The teaching of morality must be completely universal and open. Morality is not the preserve of an oppressed or privileged class or individual. People are neglecting their duties if they do not teach the moral rules to their children. Children are removed from the homes of criminals because they are not likely to be taught the moral rules there. An esoteric code, a set of precepts known only to the initiated and perhaps jealously concealed from outsiders, can at best be a religion, not a morality. 'Thou shalt not eat beans and this is a secret' or 'Always leave the third button of your waist-coat undone, but don't tell anyone except the initiated members' may be part of an estoeric religion, but not of a morality. 'Thou shalt not kill, but it is a strict secret' is absurd. 'Esoteric morality' is a contradiction in terms. It is no accident that the so-called higher religions were imbued with the missionary spirit, for they combine the beliefs of daemons and gods and spirits characteristic of primitive religions with *a system of morality*. Primitive religions are not usually concerned to proselytize. On the contrary, they are imbued with the spirit of the exclusive trade secret. If one thinks of one's religion as concentrated wisdom of life revealed solely to the *chosen* people, one will regard it as the exclusive property of the club, to be confined to the elect. If, on the other hand, the rules are thought to be for everyone to obey, one must in consistency want to spread the message.

The condition of universal teachability yields three other criteria of moral rules. They must not, in the first place, be "self-frustrating." They are so if their purpose is frustrated as soon as everybody acts on them, if they have a point only when a good many people act on the opposite principle. Someone might, for instance, act on the maxim 'When you are in need, ask for help, but never help another man when he is in need." If everybody adopted this principle, then their adoption of the second half would frustrate what obviously is the point of the adoption of the first half, namely, to get help when one is in need. Although such a principle is not self-contradictory—for anybody could consistently adopt it—it is nevertheless objectionable from the moral point of view, for it could not be taught openly to everyone. It would then lose its point. It is a parasitic principle, useful to anyone only if many people act on its opposite.

The same is true of "self-defeating" and "morally impossible" rules. A principle is self-defeating if its point is defeated as soon as a person lets it be known that he has adopted it, for example, the principle 'Give a promise even when you know or think that you can never keep it, or when you don't intend to keep it.' The very point of giving promises is to reassure and furnish a guarantee to the promisee. Hence any remark that throws doubt on the sincerity of the promiser will defeat the purpose of making a promise. And clearly to *let it be known* that one gives promises even when one knows or thinks one cannot, or when one does not intend to keep them, is to raise such doubts. And to say that one acts on the above principle is to imply that one may well give promises in these cases. Hence to reveal that one acts on this principle will tend to defeat one's own purpose.

It has already been said that moral rules must be capable of being taught openly, but this rule is self-defeating when taught openly, for then everyone would be known to act on it. Hence it cannot belong to the morality of any group.

Lastly, there are some rules which it is literally impossible to teach in the way the moral rules of a group must be capable of being taught, for example, the rule 'Always assert what you think not to be the case.' Such *morally impossible* rules differ from self-frustrating and self-defeating rules in that the latter could have been taught in this way, although it would have been quite senseless to do so, whereas the former literally cannot be so taught. The reason why the above rule cannot be taught in this way is that the only possible case of acting on it, doing so secretly, is ruled out by the conditions of *moral teaching.*

(1) Consider first someone secretly adopting this rule. His remarks will almost always mislead people, for *he will be taken to be saying what he thinks true*, whereas he *is* saying the opposite. Moreover, in most cases what he thinks (and not what he says) will be true. Thus, it will usually be the case that p is true when he says 'not-p,' and not-p when he says 'p,' whereas people will take it that p is true when he says 'p,' and not-p when he says 'not-p.' Thus communication between him and other people breaks down, since they will almost always be misled by him whether he wishes to mislead them or not. The possibility of communication depends on a speaker's ability *at will* to say either what he thinks to be the case or what he thinks not to be the case. Our speaker cannot communicate because by his principle he is forced to mislead his hearers.

Thus, anyone secretly adopting the principle 'Always assert what you think not to be the case' cannot communicate with others since he is bound to mislead them whether he wants to or not. Hence he cannot possibly teach the principle to anybody. And if he were to teach the principle without having adopted it himself, then, although he would be understood, those who adopted it would not. At any rate, since moral teaching involves teaching rules such as the taught may openly avow to be observing, this case is ruled out. A principle which is taught for secret acceptance only cannot be embodied in a *moral* rule of the group.

(2) Of course, people might soon come to realize what is the matter with our man. They may discover that in order not to be misled by what he says they have only to substitute 'p' for 'not-p' and vice versa. But if they do this, then they have interpreted his way of speaking, not as a reversal of the general presumption that one says what one thinks is the case (and not the opposite), but as a change of the use of 'not.' In his language, it will be said, 'not' has become an affirmation sign, negation being effected by omitting it. Thus, if communication is to be possible, we must interpret as a change in usage what is intended as the reversal of the presumption that every assertion conveys what the assertor believes to be the case.

If everyone were, by accident, to adopt simultaneously and secretly our principle 'Always assert what you think is not the case,' then, for some time at least, communication would be impossible. If, on the other hand, it were adopted openly, then communication would be possible, but only if the adoption of this principle were to be accompanied by a change in the use of "not" which would completely cancel the effect of the adoption of the principle. In that case, however, it can hardly be said that the principle has been adopted.

(3) The case we are considering is neither (1) nor (2). We are considering the open teaching of the principle 'Always assert what you think is not the case,' for open acceptance by everybody, an acceptance which is not to be interpreted as a change in the use of 'not.' But this is nonsense. We cannot all *openly* tell one another that we are always going to mislead one another in a certain way and insist that we must continue to be misled, though we know how we could avoid being misled. I conclude that this principle could not be embodied in a rule belonging to the morality of any group.

These points are of general interest in that they clarify some valuable remarks contained in Kant's doctrine of the categorical imperative. In particular they clarify the expression "can will" contained in the formulation 'Act so that thou *canst will* thy maxim to become a universal law of nature.' "Canst will" in one sense means what I have called "morally possible." Your maxim must be a formula which is morally possible, that is, which is logically capable of being a rule belonging to the morality of some group, as the maxim "Always lie" is not. No one *can* wish that maxim to be a rule *of some morality*. To say that one is wishing it is to contradict oneself. One cannot wish it any more than one can wish that time should move backwards.

The second sense of "can will" is that in which no rational person can will certain things. Self-frustrating and self-defeating moral rules are not morally impossible, they are merely senseless. No rational person could wish such rules to become part of any morality. That is to say, anyone wishing that they should, would thereby expose himself to the charge of irrationality, like the person who wishes that he should never attain his ends or that he should (for no reason at all) be plagued by rheumatic pains throughout his life.

The points just made also show the weakness of Kant's doctrine. For while it is true that someone who acts on the maxim 'Always lie' acts on a morally impossible one, it is not true that every liar necessarily acts on that maxim. If he acts on a principle at all, it may, for instance, be 'Lie when it is the only way to avoid harming someone,' or 'Lie when it is helpful to you and harmful to no one else,' or 'Lie when it is entertaining and harmless.' Maxims such as these can, of course, be willed in either of the senses explained.

MORAL RULES MUST BE FOR THE GOOD OF EVERYONE ALIKE

The conditions so far mentioned are merely formal. They exclude certain sorts of rule as not coming up to the formal requirements. But moral rules should also have a certain sort of content. Observation of these rules should be *for the good of everyone alike*. Thrasymachus' view that justice is the advantage of the stronger, if true of the societies of his day, is an indictment of their legal systems from the moral point of view. It shows that what goes by the name of morality in these societies is no more than a set of rules and laws which enrich the ruling class at the expense of the masses. But this is wrong because unjust, however much the rules satisfy the formal criteria.

For given certain initial social conditions, formal equality before the law may favor certain groups and exploit others.

There is one obvious way in which something may be for the good of everyone alike, namely, if it furthers the common good. When I am promoted and my salary is raised, this is to my advantage. It will also be to the advantage of my wife and my family and possibly of a few other people—it will not be to the advantage of my colleague who had hoped for promotion but is now excluded. It may even be to his detriment if his reputation suffers as a result. If the coal miners obtain an increase in their wages, then this is to the advantage of coal miners. It is for their common good. But it may not be to the advantage of anyone else. On the other hand, if production is raised and with it everyone's living standard, that is literally to everyone's advantage. The rule 'Work harder,' if it has these consequences, is for the common good of all.

Very few rules, if any, will be for the common good of everyone. But a rule may be in the interest of everyone alike, even though the results of the observation of the rule are not for the common good in the sense explained. Rules such as 'Thou shalt not kill,' 'Thou shalt not be cruel,' 'Thou shalt not lie' are obviously, in some other sense, for the good of everyone alike. What is this sense? It becomes clear if we look at these rules from the moral point of view, that is, that of an independent, unbiased, impartial, objective, dispassionate, disinterested judge. Taking such a God's-eye point of view, we can see that it is in the interest of everyone alike that everyone should abide by the rule 'Thou shalt not kill.' From the moral point of view, it is clear that it is in the interest of everyone alike if everyone alike should be allowed to pursue his own interests provided this does not adversely affect someone else's interests. Killing someone in the pursuit of my interests would interfere with his.

There can be no doubt that such a God's-eye point of view is involved in the moral standpoint. The most elementary teaching is based on it. The negative version of the so-called Golden Rule sums it up: 'Don't do unto others as you would not have them do unto you.' When we teach children the moral point of view, we try to explain it to them by getting them to put themselves in another person's place: 'How would you like to have that done to you!' 'Don't do evil,' the most readily accepted moral rule of all, is simply the most general form of stating this prohibition. For doing evil is the opposite of doing good. Doing good is doing for another person what, if he were able to follow (self-interested) reason, he would do for himself. Doing evil is doing to another person what it would be contrary to reason for him to do to himself. Harming another, hurting another, doing to another what he dislikes having done to him are the specific forms this takes. Killing, cruelty, inflicting pain, maiming, torturing, deceiving, cheating, rape, adultery are instances of this sort of behavior. They all violate the condition of "reversibility," that is, that the behavior in question must be acceptable to a person whether he is at the "giving" or "receiving" end of it.

It is important to see just what is established by this condition of being for the good of everyone alike. In the first place, anyone who engages in nonreversible behavior is doing something wrong. It is irrelevant whether he knows that it is wrong or whether the morality of his group recognizes it or not. Such behavior is "wrong in itself," irrespective of individual or social recognition, irrespective of the consequences it has. Moreover, every single act of such behavior is wrong. We need not consider the whole group or the whole of humanity engaging in this sort of behavior, but only a single case. Hence we can say that all non-reversible behavior is morally wrong; hence that anyone engaging in it is doing what, prima facie, he ought not to do. We need not consider whether this sort of behavior has harmful consequences, whether it is forbidden by the morality of the man's group, or whether he himself thinks it wrong.

The principle of reversibility does not merely impose certain prohibitions on a moral agent, but also certain positive injunctions. It is, for instance, wrong—an omission—not to help another person when he is in need and when we are in a position to help him. The story of the Good Samaritan makes this point. The positive version of the Golden Rule makes the same point more generally: 'Do unto others as you would have them do unto you.' Note that it is wrong—not merely not meritorious—to omit to help others when they are in need and when you are in a position to help them. It does not follow from this, however, that it is wrong not to promote the greatest good of the greatest number, or not to promote the greatest amount of good in the world. Deontologists and utilitarians alike make the mistake of thinking that it is one, or the only one, of our moral duties to "do the optimific act." Nothing could be further from the truth. We do not have a duty to do good to others or to ourselves, or to others and/or to ourselves in a judicious mixture such that it produces the greatest possible amount of good in the world. We are morally required to do good only to those who are actually in need of our assistance. The view that we always ought to do the optimific act, or whenever we have no more stringent duty to perform, would have the absurd result that we are doing wrong whenever we are relaxing, since on those occasions there will always be opportunities to produce greater good than we can by relaxing. For the relief of suffering is always a greater good than mere enjoyment. Yet it is quite plain that the worker who, after a tiring day, puts on his slippers and listens to the radio is not doing anything he ought not to, is not neglecting any of his duties, even though it may be perfectly true that there are things he might do which produce more good in the world, even for himself, than merely relaxing by the fireside.

Further References

Baier, Kurt. *The Moral Point of View.* Abridged. New York: Random House, 1965.*

Brandt, Richard. *Ethical Theory.* Englewood Cliffs, N. J.: Prentice-Hall, 1961.

Dewey, John. *Theory of Valuation.* Chicago: University of Chicago Press, 1939.*

Edel, Abraham. *Ethical Judgment.* New York: The Free Press, 1955.†

Edwards, Paul. *The Logic of Moral Discourse.* New York: The Free Press, 1955.†

Ewing, A. C. *The Definition of Good.* New York: Macmillan, 1947.

* Paperback edition.   † Also available in a paperback edition.

Frankena, W. K. *Ethics*. Englewood Cliffs, N. J.: Prentice-Hall, 1963.*

Hare, R. M. *Freedom and Reason*. London: Oxford University Press, 1963.†

———. *The Language of Morals*. Oxford: Clarendon Press, 1952.†

Hill, T. E. *Contemporary Ethical Theories*. New York: Macmillan, 1951.

Hospers, John. *Human Conduct*. New York: Harcourt, Brace & World, 1961.

Kerner, George C. *The Revolution in Ethical Theory*. New York: Oxford University Press, 1966.

Margolis, Joseph. *Psychotherapy and Morality*. New York: Random House, 1966.*

Margolis, Joseph (ed.). *Contemporary Ethical Theory*. New York: Random House, 1966.*

Melden, A. I. (ed.). *Essays in Moral Philosophy*. Seattle: University of Washington Press, 1958.

Montefiore, Alan. *A Modern Introduction to Moral Philosophy*. London: Routledge & Kegan Paul, 1958.

Moore, G. E. *Ethics*. London: Oxford University Press, 1912.

———. *Principia Ethica*. Cambridge: Cambridge University Press, 1903.†

Murphy, Arthur E. *The Theory of Practical Reason*. La Salle: Open Court, 1964.

Nakhnikian, George, and Castañeda, Hector-Neri (eds.). *Morality and the Language of Conduct*. Detroit: Wayne State University Press, 1961.†

Nowell-Smith, P. H. *Ethics*. Harmondsworth: Penguin Books, 1954.*

Perry, R. B. *General Theory of Value*. New York: Longmans, Green, 1926.

———. *Realms of Value*. Cambridge: Harvard University Press, 1954.

Raphael, D. D. *Moral Judgment*. London: Allen & Unwin, 1955.

———. *The Moral Sense*. London: Oxford University Press, 1947.

Rice, Philip Blair. *On the Knowledge of Good and Evil*. New York: Random House, 1955.

Ross, W. D. *Foundations of Ethics*. Oxford: Clarendon Press, 1939.

———. *The Right and the Good*. Oxford: Clarendon Press, 1930.

Sellars, Wilfrid, and Hospers, John (eds.). *Readings in Ethical Theory*. New York: Appleton-Century-Crofts, 1952.

Sesonske, Alexander. *Value and Obligation*. Berkeley: University of California Press, 1957.*

Singer, Marcus George. *Generalization in Ethics*. New York: Knopf, 1961.

Sparshott, F. E. *An Enquiry into Goodness*. Chicago: University of Chicago Press, 1958.

Stevenson, C. L. *Ethics and Language*. New Haven: Yale University Press, 1944.†

———. *Facts and Values*. New Haven: Yale University Press, 1963.†

Taylor, Paul. *Normative Discourse*. Englewood Cliffs, N. J.: Prentice-Hall, 1961.

Toulmin, Stephen. *The Place of Reason in Ethics*. Cambridge: Cambridge University Press, 1950.†

Warnock, Mary. *Ethics Since 1900*. London: Oxford University Press, 1960.†

Zink, S. *The Concepts of Ethics*. New York: St. Martin's Press, 1962.

* Paperback edition.   † Also available in a paperback edition.

Contributors

G. E. M. Anscombe. Lecturer in Philosophy, Somerville College, Oxford University. Author of *Intention* (1957); *An Introduction to Wittgenstein's Tractatus* (1959); and, with P. T. Geach, *Three Philosophers* (1961). Literary executor and translator of Wittgenstein.

St. Anselm of Canterbury (b. 11th c.). Author of *Cur Deus Homo, Monologium*, and *Proslogium*.

St. Thomas Aquinas (b. 13th c.). Author of *Summa Contra Gentiles* and *Summa Theologica*.

Aristotle (b. 4th c. b.c.). Author of *De Anima, Metaphysics, Nicomachean Ethics, Organon, Physics, Poetics, Politics,* and *Rhetoric*.

St. Augustine (b. 4th c.). Author of *The City of God, Confessions,* and *On Free Will*.

J. L. Austin. Late White's Professor of Moral Philosophy, Oxford University. Author of *Philosophical Papers* (edited by J. O. Urmson and G. J. Warnock, 1961); *How to Do Things with Words* (1962); and *Sense and Sensibilia* (reconstructed by G. J. Warnock, 1962).

A. J. Ayer. Wykeham Professor of Logic, Oxford University. Author of *Language, Truth and Logic* (1936), *The Foundations of Empirical Knowledge* (1940), *Philosophical Essays* (1954), *The Problem of Knowledge* (1956), and *The Concept of a Person* (1963). Editor of *Logical Positivism* (1959).

Kurt Baier. Professor of Philosophy, University of Pittsburgh. Author of *The Moral Point of View* (1958).

George Berkeley (b. 17th c.). Author of *An Essay towards a New Theory of Vision* (1709), *The Principles of Human Knowledge* (1710), and *Three Dialogues between Hylas and Philonous* (1713).

O. K. Bouwsma. Professor of Philosophy, University of Texas. Author of *Philosophical Essays* (1965).

F. H. Bradley. Late Fellow of Merton College, Oxford. Author of *Ethical Studies* (1876, 1927); *Principles of Logic* (1883, 1922); *Appearance and Reality* (1893, 1897); *Essays on Truth and Reality* (1914); and *Collected Essays* (1935).

C. D. Broad. Professor Emeritus of Moral Philosophy, Cambridge University. Author of *Scientific Thought* (1923), *The Mind and Its Place in Nature* (1925), *Five Types of Ethical Theory* (1930), *An Examination of McTaggart's Philosophy* (1933–1938), *Ethics and the History of Philosophy* (1952), *Religion, Philosophy, and Psychical Research* (1953), and *Lectures on Psychical Research* (1962).

C. A. Campbell. Professor Emeritus, University of Glasgow. Author of *Scepticism and Construction* (1931) and *Selfhood and Godhood* (1957).

Rudolf Carnap. Emeritus Professor of Philosophy, University of California, Los Angeles. Author of *The Logical Structure of the World* (1928; English trans., 1967); *Pseudo-Problems in Philosophy* (1928; English trans., 1967); *The Logical Syntax of Language* (1934; English trans., 1937); *Philosophy and Logical Syntax* (1935); *Foundations of Logic and Mathematics* (1939); *Introduction to Semantics* (1942); *Formalization of Logic* (1943); *Meaning and Necessity* (1947); *Logical Foundations of Probability* (1950); *The Continuum of Inductive Methods* (1952); and *Philosophical Foundations of Physics* (1966).

RODERICK CHISHOLM. Romeo Elton Professor of Natural Theology and Professor of Philosophy, Brown University. Author of *Perceiving* (1957); *Theory of Knowledge* (1966); and, with Herbert Feigl *et al.*, *Philosophy* (1964). Editor of *Realism and the Background of Phenomenology* (1960) and Brentano's *The True and the Evident* (1966).

DONALD DAVIDSON. Professor of Philosophy, Princeton University. Author of a number of influential papers, particularly "Actions, Reasons and Causes" (1963).

RENÉ DESCARTES (b. 16th c.). Author of *Discourse on Method* (1637), *Meditations* (1641), *Principles of Philosophy* (1644), and *Passions of the Soul* (1650).

JOHN DEWEY. Late Professor of Philosophy, Columbia University. Author of *Essays in Experimental Logic* (1916); *Reconstruction in Philosophy* (1920); *Human Nature and Conduct* (1922); *Experience and Nature* (1925); *The Quest for Certainty* (1929); *Art as Experience* (1934); *Logic: The Theory of Inquiry* (1939); *Theory of Valuation* (1939); and, with James H. Tufts, *Ethics* (1932).

GOTTLOB FREGE. Late Professor of Philosophy, University of Jena. Author of *Begriff-schrift* (1879); *Die Grundlagen der Arithmetik* (1884; English trans., 1950, 1959); *Grundgesetze der Arithmetik* (1893–1903); *Translations from the Philosophical Writings of Gottlob Frege* (translated by Peter Geach and Max Black, 1952).

P. T. GEACH. Professor of Philosophy, University of Leeds. Author of *Mental Acts* (1957); *Reference and Generality* (1962); and, with G. E. M. Anscombe, *Three Philosophers* (1961). Editor, with Max Black, of *Translations from the Philosophical Writings of Gottlob Frege* (1952).

NELSON GOODMAN. Harry Austryn Wolfson Professor of Philosophy, Brandeis University. Author of *The Structure of Appearance* (1951, 1966) and *Fact, Fiction, and Forecast* (1955, 1965).

STUART HAMPSHIRE. Professor of Philosophy, Princeton University. Author of *Spinoza* (1951), *Thought and Action* (1959), and *Freedom of the Individual* (1965). Editor of *Philosophy of Mind* (1966).

H. L. A. HART. Professor of Jurisprudence, Oxford University. Author of *The Concept of Law* (1961); *Law, Liberty and Morality* (1963); and, with A. M. Honoré, *Causation in the Law* (1959).

CARL G. HEMPEL. Stuart Professor of Philosophy, Princeton University. Author of *Fundamentals of Concept Formation in Empirical Science* (1952), *Aspects of Scientific Explanation* (1965), and *Philosophy of Natural Science* (1966).

THOMAS HOBBES (b. 16th c.). Author of *De Cive* (1642), *Leviathan* (1951), *De Corpore* (1655), and *De Homine* (1658).

A. M. HONORÉ. Rhodes Reader in Roman-Dutch Law, Oxford University. Co-author, with H. L. A. Hart, of *Causation in the Law* (1959).

DAVID HUME (b. 18th c.). Author of *A Treatise of Human Nature* (1739), *An Inquiry Concerning Human Understanding* (1748), *An Inquiry Concerning the Principles of Morals* (1751), and *Dialogues Concerning Natural Religion* (1779).

WILLIAM JAMES. Late Professor of Philosophy, Harvard University. Author of *The Principles of Psychology* (1890), *The Will to Believe* (1897), *The Varieties of Religious Experience* (1902), *Pragmatism* (1907), *A Pluralistic Universe* (1909), *The Meaning of Truth* (1909), and *Some Problems of Philosophy* (1911).

IMMANUEL KANT (b. 18th c.). Author of *Critique of Pure Reason* (1781, 1787); *Prolegomena to Any Future Metaphysics* (1783); *Foundations of the Metaphysics of Morals* (1785); *Critique of Practical Reason* (1788); and *Critique of Judgment* (1790).

SØREN KIERKEGAARD (b. 19th c.). Author of *Either/Or* (1843), *Fear and Trembling* (1843), *Philosophical Fragments* (1844), *The Concept of Dread* (1844), *Stages on Life's Way* (1845), *Concluding Unscientific Postscript* (1846), and *The Sickness Unto Death* (1849).

JOHN LOCKE (b. 17th c.). Author of *An Essay Concerning Human Understanding* (1690).

J. L. MACKIE. Professor of Philosophy, University of York. Author of *Contemporary Linguistic Philosophy—Its Strength and Its Weakness* (1956).

NORMAN MALCOLM. Professor of Philosophy, Cornell University. Author of *Ludwig Wittgenstein: A Memoir* (1958), *Dreaming* (1959), and *Knowledge and Certainty* (1963).

C. B. MARTIN. Professor of Philosophy, University of Sydney. Author of *Religious Belief* (1959).

BRIAN MEDLIN. Reader in Philosophy, University of Queensland.

JOHN STUART MILL (b. 19th c.). Author of *A System of Logic* (1843), *On Liberty* (1859), *An Examination of Sir William Hamilton's Philosophy* (1865), and *Utilitarianism* (1863).

G. E. MOORE. Late Professor of Philosophy, Cambridge University. Author of *Principia Ethica* (1903); *Ethics* (1912); *Philosophical Studies* (1922); *Some Main Problems of Philosophy* (1953); *Philosophical Papers* (1959); *The Commonplace Book* (edited by Casimir Lewy, 1962); and *Lectures on Philosophy* (edited by Casimir Lewy, 1966).

ERNEST NAGEL. Professor of Philosophy, Columbia University. Author of *Principles of the Theory of Probability* (1939); *Sovereign Reason* (1954); *Logic without Metaphysics* (1956); *The Structure of Science* (1961); with M. R. Cohen, *An Introduction to Logic and Scientific Method* (1934); and, with J. R. Newman, *Gödel's Proof* (1958).

D. F. PEARS. Student (Fellow) in Philosophy, Christ Church, Oxford University. Editor of *The Nature of Metaphysics* (1957), *Freedom of the Will* (1963), and *David Hume* (1963).

C. S. PEIRCE (b. 19th c.). Author of *Collected Papers of Charles S. Peirce* (edited by Charles Hartshorne and Paul Weiss, 1931–1935; and by Arthur W. Burks, 1958).

R. B. PERRY. Late Professor of Philosophy, Harvard University. Author of *General Theory of Value* (1926) and *Realms of Value* (1954).

R. S. PETERS. Professor of Philosophy of Education, University of London Institute of Education. Author of *Hobbes* (1956); *The Concept of Motivation* (1958); *Ethics and Education* (1966); and, with S. I. Benn, *Social Principles and the Democratic State* (1959). Revised and brought up to date Brett's *History of Psychology*.

PLATO (b. 5th c. B.C.). Author of *Apology, Cratylus, Crito, Euthyphro, Gorgias, Laws, Meno, Parmenides, Phaedo, Phaedrus, Philebus, Protagoras, Republic, Sophist, Statesman, Symposium, Theaetetus,* and *Timaeus.*

HILARY PUTNAM. Professor of Philosophy, Harvard University. Author of numerous influential articles, including "Minds and Machines" (1960) and "The Analytic and the Synthetic" (1962).

W. V. QUINE. Edgar Pierce Professor of Philosophy, Harvard University. Author of *Mathematical Logic* (1940), *Methods of Logic* (1950), *From a Logical Point of View* (1953), *Word and Object* (1960), *Set Theory and Its Logic* (1963), *Selected Logical Papers* (1966), and *Ways of Paradox* (1966).

HANS REICHENBACH. Late Professor of Philosophy, University of California, Los Angeles. Author of *The Philosophy of Space and Time* (1928; English trans., 1957); *Atom and Cosmos* (1930; English trans., 1932); *The Theory of Probability* (1935; English trans., 1949); *Experience and Prediction* (1938); *Philosophic Foundations of Quantum Mechanics* (1944); *Elements of Symbolic Logic* (1947); *The Rise of Scientific Philosophy* (1951); *Nomological Statements and Admissible Operations* (1954); and *The Direction of Time* (edited by M. Reichenbach, 1956).

BERTRAND RUSSELL. Fellow of Trinity College, Cambridge University. Author of *An Essay on the Foundations of Geometry* (1897); *A Critical Exposition of the Philosophy of Leibniz* (1900); *The Principles of Mathematics* (1903); *Philosophical Essays* (1910); *The Problems of Philosophy* (1912); *Our Knowledge of the External World* (1914); *Mysticism and Logic* (1918); *Introduction to Mathematical Philos-*

ophy (1919); *The Analysis of Mind* (1921); *The Analysis of Matter* (1927); *An Outline of Philosophy* (1927); *An Inquiry into Meaning and Truth* (1940); *A History of Western Philosophy* (1944); *Human Knowledge* (1948); *Logic and Knowledge* (1956); and, with A. N. Whitehead, *Principia Mathematica* (1910–1913).

GILBERT RYLE. Waynflete Professor of Metaphysical Philosophy, Oxford University. Author of *The Concept of Mind* (1949), *Dilemmas* (1954), and *Plato's Progress* (1966). Editor of *Mind*.

MORITZ SCHLICK. Late Professor of Philosophy, University of Vienna. Author of *Space and Time in Modern Physics* (1917; English trans., 1920); *Allgemeine Erkenntnislehre* (1925); *Problems of Ethics* (1930; English trans., 1939); and *Gesammelte Aufsätze* (1938).

J. J. C. SMART. Hughes Professor of Philosophy, University of Adelaide. Author of *An Outline of a System of Utilitarian Ethics* (1961), *Philosophy and Scientific Realism* (1963), and *Between Science and Philosophy* (1968). Editor of *Problems of Space and Time* (1964).

P. F. STRAWSON. Fellow of University College, Oxford University. Author of *Introduction to Logical Theory* (1952), *Individuals* (1959), and *The Bounds of Sense* (1966).

PAUL TILLICH. Late Professor of Theology, Harvard University. Author of *Systematic Theology* (1951–1964), *Love, Power, and Justice* (1954), *The Courage To Be* (1961) and *The New Being* (1963).

FRIEDRICH WAISMANN. Late Reader in the Philosophy of Science, Oxford University. Author of *Introduction to Mathematical Thinking* (1935; English trans., 1951) and *The Principles of Linguistic Philosophy* (edited by R. Harré, 1965).

JOHN WISDOM. Professor of Philosophy, Cambridge University. Author of *Problems of Mind and Matter* (1934), *Other Minds* (1952), *Philosophy and Psycho-Analysis* (1953), and *Paradox and Discovery* (1965).

Index

A NOTE ON THE TYPE

The text of this book was set on the Linotype in Janson, a recutting made direct from type cast from matrices long thought to have been made by the Dutchman Anton Janson, who was a practicing type founder in Leipzig during the years 1668–87. However, it has been conclusively demonstrated that these types are actually the work of Nicholas Kis (1650–1702), a Hungarian, who most probably learned his trade from the master Dutch type founder Kirk Voskens. The type is an excellent example of the influential and sturdy Dutch types that prevailed in England up to the time William Caslon developed his own incomparable designs from these Dutch faces.

Manufactured in the United States of America by American Book–Stratford Press, Inc. Typography and binding design by Vincent Torre.